ScreenOS Cookbook™

Other resources from O'Reilly

Related titles

Building Internet Firewalls
Cisco IOS Cookbook™
JUNOS Cookbook™
Linux Networking Cookbook™
JUNOS Enterprise Routing
Network Security Assessment
Security Power Tools
TCP/IP Network Administration

oreilly.com

oreilly.com is more than a complete catalog of O'Reilly books. You'll also find links to news, events, articles, weblogs, sample chapters, and code examples.

oreillynet.com is the essential portal for developers interested in open and emerging technologies, including new platforms, programming languages, and operating systems.

Conferences

O'Reilly brings diverse innovators together to nurture the ideas that spark revolutionary industries. We specialize in documenting the latest tools and systems, translating the innovator's knowledge into useful skills for those in the trenches. Visit *conferences.oreilly.com* for our upcoming events.

Safari Bookshelf (*safari.oreilly.com*) is the premier online reference library for programmers and IT professionals. Conduct searches across more than 1,000 books. Subscribers can zero in on answers to time-critical questions in a matter of seconds. Read the books on your Bookshelf from cover to cover or simply flip to the page you need. Try it today for free.

ScreenOS Cookbook™

Stefan Brunner, Vik Davar, David Delcourt, Ken Draper, Joe Kelly, and Sunil Wadhwa

O'REILLY®

Beijing • Cambridge • Farnham • Köln • Sebastopol • Tokyo

ScreenOS Cookbook™

by Stefan Brunner, Vik Davar, David Delcourt, Ken Draper, Joe Kelly, and Sunil Wadhwa

Printed in the United States of America.

Published by O'Reilly Media, Inc., 1005 Gravenstein Highway North, Sebastopol, CA 95472.

O'Reilly books may be purchased for educational, business, or sales promotional use. Online editions are also available for most titles (*safari.oreilly.com*). For more information, contact our corporate/institutional sales department: (800) 998-9938 or *corporate@oreilly.com*.

Editor: Mike Loukides
Developmental Editor: Patrick Ames
Production Editor: Sumita Mukherji
Copyeditor: Audrey Doyle
Proofreader: Sumita Mukherji
Indexer: John Bickelhaupt
Cover Designer: Karen Montgomery
Interior Designer: David Futato
Illustrator: Robert Romano

Printing History:

February 2008: First Edition.

ISBN: 978-0-596-51003-9

[LSI] [2010-11-30]

Table of Contents

Credits

Stefan Brunner has been a technology consultant for more than 15 years, helping enterprise organizations leverage technology for their business models and deploy technology solutions. Stefan is the lead architect in Juniper Networks' Service Layer Technology Professional Services group. Prior to Juniper, Stefan worked with NetScreen Technologies as a network security consultant. Stefan holds an MBA in innovations research and technology management from Ludwig-Maximilians-University of Munich, and a certificate degree in telecommunications engineering from the University of California at Berkeley. He lives with his wife and two daughters in the Hill Country of Austin, Texas. Stefan wrote Chapters 5, 8, 12, 14, and 16.

Vik Davar has been working in the IT field for more than 15 years, holding positions in financial services firms and technology companies, including Juniper Networks and Goldman Sachs. Vik is the president of 9 Networks, an IT services company. He has a master's degree in electrical engineering from Columbia University and a bachelor's degree in electrical engineering from The Cooper Union in New York City. He is also a CISSP and CCIE #8377. He lives in New Jersey with his wife and two children. Vik wrote Chapters 7, 11, 15, and 17.

David Delcourt has worked in the data communications industry for the past 13 years for enterprise equipment vendors, including Cabletron Systems and NetScreen Technologies. He has held a variety of positions, including advanced TAC engineer, technical trainer, product manager at Cabletron Systems, and senior security consultant at NetScreen Technologies. He is currently the security practice manager in Professional Services for Juniper Networks, supporting the Americas. He lives in New Hampshire with his wife and daughter, and their two dogs and two cats. David wrote Chapters 1 and 2.

Ken Draper has spent the past 20 years in the networking industry, and has focused on security solutions for the past 11 years. He is CISSP certification #22627 and holds numerous other certifications. Ken has worked at such networking equipment manufacturers as Infotron, Gandalf, Synoptics, Bay Networks, Nortel, NetScreen, and now, Juniper Networks. He has more than six years of experience with ScreenOS and large-scale security solutions. He has held a variety of technical engineering positions, including systems engineer and solutions architect, and he is currently a Juniper Networks consulting engineer specializing in large-scale virtual private networks (VPNs), firewalls, intrusion prevention, and centralized management markets. Ken lives outside Dallas with his wife and two dogs. Ken wrote Chapters 10, 13, and 21.

Joe Kelly has been involved in data networking for more than 12 years, focusing on the realms of network security and routing. He started his career in the service provider space at IDT Corporation, where he held roles in network operations and engineering. After IDT, he spent time with various network service providers in engineering and architectural capacities. In 2001, Joe joined NetScreen Technologies as a senior systems engineer in the Financial and Service Provider verticals, where he specialized in high-availability, high-performance networks. Joe joined Juniper Networks in 2004 with the acquisition of NetScreen, and he is currently the technical lead on the Global Banking and Finance team. He lives in New Jersey with his beautiful wife, Jacqueline, and their three children, Hannah, Ben, and Tristan. Joe wrote Chapters 6, 9, 18, and 20.

Sunil Wadhwa has been in the data networking industry for more than 13 years, focusing on systems, network routing, and security in enterprise and service provider organizations. He started his career in India at GTL Limited and SAP India, and then held a variety of roles in technical support, network operations, and engineering. He moved to the United States and worked with E4E as a network consultant for routing and security, and then joined Juniper Networks as an advanced technical support engineer for firewall/VPN products. He currently leads the Advance Technical Support team for Juniper Networks, supporting enhanced services products. He lives in California with his beautiful wife, Lavanya, and little angel daughter, Sneha. Sunil wrote Chapters 3, 4, and 19.

Preface

The controlling element of Juniper Networks' firewall/IP Security (IPSec) virtual private network (VPN) devices is the ScreenOS operating system, a real-time, security-specific operating system that provides everything you need to set up and manage these devices. The name comes from its original company, NetScreen, which Juniper Networks acquired in 2004.

ScreenOS includes a robust set of security and management applications, such as an ICSA-certified IPSec VPN gateway for interoperable secure communications, deep inspection capabilities for application-level attack protection, virtualization features for network segmentation, and internal and external management interfaces to facilitate deployment. At the time of this writing, ScreenOS was at version 6.0.

The real-time nature of the operating system, combined with purpose-built hardware platforms, means that ScreenOS does not suffer from connection table and processing limitations and that it eliminates the known security flaws found in general-purpose operating systems. An added benefit of the real-time nature of ScreenOS is that hackers cannot analyze it easily for vulnerabilities because the source code is not publicly available.

Here are some of the key features of ScreenOS:

Firewall
: Stateful inspection of traffic between the protected LAN, intermediate networks, and the Internet

VPNs
: Secure communication tunnels between sites for traffic passing through the Internet

Redundancy
: A backup device that maintains the same configuration, real-time session synchronization, and many other objects as those on the primary device to assume the place of the primary device, if necessary (interfaces, routing paths, power supplies, and fans can also be redundant)

This icon indicates a warning or caution.

Using Code Examples

This book is here to help you get your job done. In general, you may use the code in this book in your programs and documentation. You do not need to contact us for permission unless you're reproducing a significant portion of the code. For example, writing a program that uses several chunks of code from this book does not require permission. Selling or distributing a CD-ROM of examples from O'Reilly books does require permission. Answering a question by citing this book and quoting example code does not require permission. Incorporating a significant amount of example code from this book into your product's documentation does require permission.

We appreciate, but do not require, attribution. An attribution usually includes the title, author, publisher, and ISBN. For example: "*ScreenOS Cookbook* by Stefan Brunner et al. Copyright 2008 O'Reilly Media, Inc., 978-0-596-51003-9."

If you feel your use of code examples falls outside fair use or the permission given here, feel free to contact us at *permissions@oreilly.com*.

Safari® Books Online

When you see a Safari® Books Online icon on the cover of your favorite technology book, that means the book is available online through the O'Reilly Network Safari Bookshelf.

Safari offers a solution that's better than e-books. It's a virtual library that lets you easily search thousands of top tech books, cut and paste code samples, download chapters, and find quick answers when you need the most accurate, current information. Try it for free at *http://safari.oreilly.com*.

Comments and Questions

Please address comments and questions concerning this book to the publisher:

O'Reilly Media, Inc.
1005 Gravenstein Highway North
Sebastopol, CA 95472
800-998-9938 (in the United States or Canada)
707-829-0515 (international or local)
707-829-0104 (fax)

We have a web page for this book, where we list errata, examples, and any additional information. You can access this page at:

http://www.oreilly.com/catalog/9780596510039

To comment or ask technical questions about this book, send email to:

bookquestions@oreilly.com

For more information about our books, conferences, Resource Centers, and the O'Reilly Network, see our web site at:

http://www.oreilly.com

Acknowledgments

Writing a book such as the one you are holding is a group effort with a cast that sometimes resembles a Hollywood movie. As a group, the authors would like to acknowledge Juniper Networks for giving them the opportunity to put their workday knowledge to paper. Keith Redfield supported this book and ran interference at the managerial level, and even tech-edited one of the chapters. Without Keith's support, it is doubtful that this book would exist.

Also, as a group, the authors would like to thank Patrick Ames, the Juniper Networks editor-in-chief for retail books and retail book projects. He held us on schedule and drove the project over the long year and a half that it took from that initial meeting to the final printed pages. Our editor at O'Reilly, Mike Loukides, gave us both the support and the fine-tuning we needed to turn this into a quality O'Reilly Cookbook. Our developmental editor, Sara Kreisman, managed to smooth our rough language into presentable English, and many great editors, illustrators, and production artists on the O'Reilly staff helped also. Thank you.

As a group, we had many technical reviewers who read these pages and double-checked our recipes and discussions. They did all this while maintaining their day jobs with little expectation of reward or glory. As a group, we would like to gratefully acknowledge their extracurricular efforts and recognize their expertise in ScreenOS: Rob Cameron, Andy Clutton, Cesar Collantes, Rafael Gracioli, Anil Jethnani, Umesh Kondur, Kathy Laymon, Joseph Naughton, Barny Sanchez, Mike Swarm, Al Rodriquez, Adam Rypinski, JianYu Yang, Jerish Parapurath, and Yansong Yu.

We labored for many months on this book, sacrificing time with our families and friends, and working strange hours in the lab when others went home. Our individual acknowledgments follow.

Stefan Brunner would like to thank is wife, Natalija, for her patience and the mental support to become more efficient; their baby daughter, Saffron, for playing patiently in his office while Papa stared into the screen and hacked away on the keyboard; and their youngest family member, daughter Cinnamon, for being very patient with Papa while he used his paternity leave for reviewing the final edits for this book. He also would like to thank his manager, Dave Delcourt, and group director, Gary Richman, for providing encouragement and flexibility regarding client schedules, and many of the old NetScreen folks who gave valuable input; product managers Mike Kouri and Abby Hassle, who helped with researching old function specs; editor-in-chief Patrick Ames, who kept the authoring team on track; and Aviva Garrett and Jeff Doyle for their insight into becoming an author.

Vik Davar would like to thank his wife, Bharti, and children, Neal and Riya, for their encouragement and support throughout the long hours spent on writing; his parents for providing him inspiration; and the following people for their review and support: Patrick Ames, Umesh Kondur, Kathy Laymon, Stefan Brunner, Mike Swarm, Cesar Colantes, and the entire Juniper Networks team.

David Delcourt would like to thank his wife, Bonnie, for helping him stay focused by locking him in his office to complete the writing and testing; his daughter, April, for making cookies and bringing him coffee to help him stay energized; his trusty sidekick, Sadie; his managers and mentors, Brett Eldridge and Robert Schneider, for their inspiration and motivation; Adam Rypinski for his technical review and support; and the entire Juniper Networks team.

Ken Draper would like to thank his wife, Leslie, for sacrificing weekends not going to the lake house so that he could write his chapters and for encouraging him to stay at it so that he could complete them. Additional thanks go to Patrick Ames for cracking the whip and driving the schedule of this book, Joo Kim for his submission to Chapter 10, and Jerish Parapurath and Rob Cameron for their technical review of his chapters.

Joe Kelly would like to thank his wife, his *anam cara*, Jacqueline, for having the patience to deal with his late nights working and for giving him the love and support to see this thing through; their children, Hannah, Ben, and Tristan, for warming his heart when stress was high; his father, David Kelly, for giving him the hunger to learn; his supervisors, Vik Davar, Paul Gerry, and Pete Fitzgerald, for supporting this effort; his coworkers past and present, including Paul Levasseur, Gregory Lebovitz, Changming Liu, Mike Swarm, Brett Eldridge, Purvi Desai, Dave Klein, and Mike Kouri, whose creativity made this stuff work and whose tutelage helped him understand how; his teammates, Larry Karantzios, Keith Sober, Greg Olivieri, Brian O'Halloran, and Brian Pavane, who helped get these recipes written; the technical reviewers, Andy Clutton and Cesar Collantes; his friend and mentor, Jeremiah Kristal, for teaching him what a subnet mask was oh so many years ago; and his customers, whose problems were the genesis for so many of these recipes.

Sunil Wadhwa would like to thank his wife, Lavanya, for motivating and supporting him, having the patience to deal with his working late nights, and giving him all the love and support to see this thing through; his daughter, Sneha, for warming his heart when stress was high; and his mother, Jayanthi, for her motivation and support. He would also like to thank his supervisors, Raj Sabnani, Paul McNulty, Adam Rypinski, Steven Tufts, and Farhad Zaeni, for providing the opportunity to contribute to this book; and Umesh Kondur and Joseph Naughton, for providing technical help for writing some of the recipes. Finally, he would like to thank his coworkers in the Advanced Firewall/VPN JTAC and his team members for supporting this effort.

CHAPTER 1

ScreenOS CLI, Architecture, and Troubleshooting

1.0 Introduction

If you're a network professional with network OS experience, ScreenOS has a fairly straightforward CLI to get used to. With that being said, it is important to lay the groundwork for how to move around the CLI and understand the troubleshooting capabilities within ScreenOS so that you are prepared to use the information in this book.

Each vendor produces and maintains its own device OS and defines the main keywords used to perform various configuration and information management functions. The keywords in ScreenOS provide the flexibility and structure required to manage the firewall via the CLI. They are:

- `get`
- `set/unset`
- `save`
- `clear`
- `exec`
- `delete`
- `regex support`

You can see these upon successful login to the firewall by issuing the "next option" command, better known as ?, at the prompt:

```
Login: netscreen
Password: <netscreen>

top-ssg140-> ?
clear                 clear dynamic system info
delete                delete persistent info in flash
exec                  exec system commands
exit                  exit command console
get                   get system information
```

```
mtrace                  multicast traceroute from source to destination
ping                    ping other host
reset                   reset system
save                    save command
set                     configure system parameters
trace-route             trace route
unset                   unconfigure system parameters
top-ssg140->
```

Unlike some other network OSs, there is a single level of access in ScreenOS, based on the permissions associated with the login credentials. ScreenOS provides the ? as a helper. You can find the same information by pressing the Tab key to either complete a command if it is unique, or provide the user options.

get

Generally, you use the get keyword to show the status or value of some ScreenOS function, such as an interface, log buffer, or routing table. You can filter the output from the get command to provide more concise output and then dump it to the screen (default behavior), or redirect it to a Trivial File Transfer Protocol (TFTP) server and text file for further analysis. Also available is a very rich REGEX filtering function, which we will describe in more detail later in this section.

```
top-ssg140-> get ?
address                 show address book
admin                   show admin information
adsl                    show adsl info
alarm                   show alarm info
alg                     application layer gateway information
alg-portnum             get ALG port num
alias                   get alias definitions
arp                     show ARP entries
asp                     asp
attack                  show attacks
auth                    show authentication information
auth-server             authentication server settings
chassis                 show chassis information
clock                   show system clock
config                  show system configuration
console                 show console parameters
core-dump               show core dump parameters
counter                 show counters
di                      get deep inspection parameters
dialer                  get dialer information
dip                     show all dips in a vsys or root
dip-in                  show incoming dip table info
--- more ---
top-ssg140-> get interface e0/0
Interface ethernet0/0:
  description ethernet0/0
  number 0, if_info 0, if_index 0, mode nat
  link up, phy-link up/full-duplex
```

```
  vsys Root, zone Trust, vr trust-vr
  dhcp client disabled
  PPPoE disabled
  admin mtu 0, operating mtu 1500, default mtu 1500
  *ip 192.168.1.1/24   mac 0017.cb47.8d00
  *manage ip 192.168.1.1, mac 0017.cb47.8d00
  route-deny disable
  pmtu-v4 disabled
  ping enabled, telnet enabled, SSH enabled, SNMP enabled
  web enabled, ident-reset disabled, SSL enabled
  DNS Proxy disabled, webauth disabled, webauth-ip 0.0.0.0
  OSPF disabled  BGP disabled  RIP disabled  RIPng disabled  mtrace
    disabled
  PIM: not configured  IGMP not configured
  NHRP disabled
  bandwidth: physical 100000kbps, configured egress [gbw 0kbps mbw
    0kbps]
             configured ingress mbw 0kbps, current bw 0kbps
             total allocated gbw 0kbps
  DHCP-Relay disabled at interface level
  DHCP-server disabled
Number of SW session: 56063, hw sess err cnt 0
top-ssg140->
```

set/unset

The set and unset commands are the primary keywords for effecting change of the firewall configuration. These changes occur in real time and have led many administrators to make a trip to the data center to log in via the console because an IP address or route was misconfigured or accidentally changed.

```
top-ssg140-> set interface ethernet0/0 ?
bandwidth             interface bandwidth
description           configure interface description
dhcp                  dhcp server/client/relay setup
dip                   dynamic ip configuration
dot1x                 enable IEEE802.1X feature
ext                   extended DIP configuration
gateway               gateway ip address
group                 group interface into redundant interface
ip                    set interface ip address
manage                interface manageability
manage-ip             interface management ip address
mip                   mapped ip configuration
monitor               interface monitoring
mtu                   set maximum transfer unit
nat                   private address
pbr                   Enable interface pbr-policy
phy                   interface physical feature
pmtu                  path MTU discovery configuration
protocol              configure routing protocol parameters
proxy                 enable interface proxy application
route                 public address
```

```
route-deny          deny traffic routing back to this interface
webauth             webauth for this interface
webauth-ip          webauth ip for this interface
zone                interface zone binding
top-ssg140->
```

save

You use the save keyword to manage the configuration stored in flash memory. Any configuration change made via the console or a remote terminal session is not committed to flash memory until save is entered. If you forget this, and you reboot the firewall, those changes are lost.

```
top-ssg140-> set interface ethernet0/0 ip 10.100.1.1/24
top-ssg140-> set interface ethernet0/0 manage-ip 10.100.1.2
top-ssg140-> get interface | include eth0/0
eth0/0      10.100.1.1/24       Trust       0017.cb47.8d00    -    U    -
top-ssg140-> reset
Configuration modified, save? [y]/n n
System reset, are you sure? y/[n] y
In reset ...

... boot sequence ...

login: netscreen
password: <password>
top-ssg140->
top-ssg140-> get interface | include eth0/0
eth0/0      192.168.1.1/24      Trust       0017.cb47.8d00    -    U    -
top-ssg140->
```

Notice that ScreenOS provides the administrator an opportunity to bail out of the reset process and save the configuration. Also note that the IP address for `ethernet0/0` has reverted back to the ScreenOS default of 192.168.1.1/24.

Another handy capability of save is that it allows you to save your configuration to a TFTP server. For example, you can have an off-box script run occasionally to log in to the device and run this command to back up the configuration:

```
top-ssg140->  save config to tftp 10.251.7.113 config.txt
Read the current config.
Save configurations (4103 bytes) to config.txt on TFTP server
    10.251.7.113.
!!!!!!!!!!!!!!!!!!!!
tftp transferred records = 9
tftp success!

TFTP Succeeded
top-ssg140->
```

You can also manage the ScreenOS image via the save keyword. The administrator can save a copy of the image to a TFTP server or from a TFTP server:

```
top-ssg140-> save software from flash to tftp 10.251.7.113
    ssg140.6.0.0r1.0
Save software to 10.251.7.113 ssg140.6.0.0r1.0
!!!!!!!!!!!!!!!!!!!!!!!!!!!!!!!!!!!!!!!!!!!!!!!!!!!!!!!!!!!!!!!!!!!
...
!!!!!!!!!!!!!!!!!!!!!!!!!!!!!!!!!!!!!!!!!!!!!!!!
tftp transferred records = 21761
tftp success!

TFTP Succeeded
top-ssg140->
```

We cover saving the image from a TFTP server later in this chapter, in Recipe 1.1.

clear

You use the `clear` keyword to erase or purge information from the firewall's real-time memory, not the onboard flash memory. You can use `clear` to manage the following:

- The Address Resolution Protocol (ARP) cache
- Session table entries
- Internet Key Exchange (IKE) Security Associations (SAs)
- IKE cookies
- Logs
- Counters

The `clear` function is particularly useful when troubleshooting problems, as it is very common to be asked to provide Juniper Technical Assistance Center (JTAC) engineers with a current snapshot of information, which requires resetting logs and counters. Another good example is when performing debug or snoop functions. The buffer where the output is stored should be cleared before each run so that maximum buffer space is available, and the troubleshooter knows the information in the buffer is pertinent to the problem at hand.

exec

The exec keyword has a limited but powerful set of options for managing a specific set of functions. The "root" admin is the only account with access to exec functions. Typically, you use the exec command to manually force the device to execute a function that, under normal circumstances, happens automatically. As such, most administrators will rarely use it unless under the direction of JTAC.

```
top-ssg140-> exec ?
admin                    exec ADMIN commands
alg                      application layer gateway information
attack-db                perform attack database update or checking
auth                     user authentication actions
```

```
config                config exec command
dhcp                  exec dhcp command
dialer                exec dialer commands
dns                   refresh all dns entries
igmp                  IGMP
ike                   IKE exec commands
infranet              Infranet Controller configuration
interface             Interface configuration
license-key           set feature configuration
log                   exec log commands
nsrp                  exec nsrp commands
ntp                   exec ntp command
password              perform password verification
pki                   PKI exec commands
policy                policy verify
pppoa                 maintain pppoa connection
pppoe                 maintain pppoe connection
proxy-id              exec proxy id update command
save                  save command
script                exec script
shdsl                 SHDSL pic-mode
ssh                   exec SSH commands
syslog                syslog configuration
usb-device            exec usb command
vrouter               execute vrouter commands
top-ssg140->
```

delete

The `delete` keyword has a small but effective set of options for managing a specific set of parameters mostly regarding information stored in flash memory:

```
top-ssg140-> delete
cluster               cluster option
crypto                delete crypto info
file                  delete a file
node_secret           clear SecurID stored node secret
nsmgmt                delete nsmgmt private/public keys
pki                   delete a PKI object
ssh                   delete SSH
top-ssg140->
```

Sometimes it is necessary to delete Secure Shell (SSH) keys or even NetScreen Security Manager (NSM) keys to reestablish communication.

Filtering the Output

ScreenOS provides several ways to filter output. You can use two different keywords after a pipe (`|`): `include` and `exclude`. ScreenOS also supports the POSIX implementation of regular expressions (regexes), although not with every option. Regexes are a powerful way to filter the output of a command to show only what is wanted. It is beyond the scope of this book to fully define how POSIX regexes are implemented, but you can find this information via the Internet or on a Linux station manpage.

This section will cover how to use the different options to make it easier to find information in ScreenOS.

To compare the difference in filtering output, we will examine the routing table. Here is the output for the routes in the `trust-vr`:

```
bottom-ssg140-> get vrouter trust route summary
trust-vr
------------------------------------------------------------------
  Route Source              Networks   Subnets    Supernets
------------------------------------------------------------------
 Connected                      0         3          0
 Host                           0         3          0
 Static                        95       659          4
 System Default                 0         0          0
 OSPF                           0         0          0
  [ OSPF Intra area             0         0          0 ]
  [ OSPF Inter area             0         0          0 ]
  [ OSPF External - 1           0         0          0 ]
  [ OSPF External - 2           0         0          0 ]
 BGP                            0         0          0
 RIP                            0         0          0
 NHRP                           0         0          0
 Imported                       0         0          0
 Auto Exported                  0         0          0
 Auto Discovered                0         0          0

 Total 764/max entries

bottom-ssg140->
```

There are 764 routes, which can take a little while to get through if you're looking for a specific route or a set of routes. Instead, use the `include` keyword to find any route in the 159.24.0.0 Class B range:

```
bottom-ssg140-> get route | inc 159.24
*  764  159.24.119.232/32    eth0/2      10.10.10.1    S   20   1  Root
*  756  159.24.107.242/32    eth0/2      10.10.10.1    S   20   1  Root
*  390  159.24.200.100/30    eth0/2      10.10.10.1    S   20   1  Root
*  763  159.24.116.222/32    eth0/2      10.10.10.1    S   20   1  Root
*  760  159.24.110.217/32    eth0/2      10.10.10.1    S   20   1  Root
*  387      159.24.76.0/24   eth0/2      10.10.10.1    S   20   1  Root
*  759  159.24.110.212/30    eth0/2      10.10.10.1    S   20   1  Root
*  750  159.24.106.169/32    eth0/2      10.10.10.1    S   20   1  Root
*  749  159.24.106.167/32    eth0/2      10.10.10.1    S   20   1  Root
*  748  159.24.106.166/32    eth0/2      10.10.10.1    S   20   1  Root
*  747  159.24.106.162/32    eth0/2      10.10.10.1    S   20   1  Root
*  762  159.24.116.161/32    eth0/2      10.10.10.1    S   20   1  Root
*  758  159.24.110.123/32    eth0/2      10.10.10.1    S   20   1  Root
*  746  159.24.106.122/32    eth0/2      10.10.10.1    S   20   1  Root
*  755   159.24.107.72/29    eth0/2      10.10.10.1    S   20   1  Root
*  757   159.24.109.89/32    eth0/2      10.10.10.1    S   20   1  Root
*  392  159.24.235.212/30    eth0/2      10.10.10.1    S   20   1  Root
*  389  159.24.181.140/30    eth0/2      10.10.10.1    S   20   1  Root
```

```
*  754    159.24.107.61/32     eth0/2        10.10.10.1   S   20  1  Root
*  752    159.24.107.48/28     eth0/2        10.10.10.1   S   20  1  Root
*  753    159.24.107.58/32     eth0/2        10.10.10.1   S   20  1  Root
*  751    159.24.107.55/32     eth0/2        10.10.10.1   S   20  1  Root
*  761    159.24.114.46/32     eth0/2        10.10.10.1   S   20  1  Root
*  391  159.24.217.172/30     eth0/2        10.10.10.1   S   20  1  Root
*  388      159.24.76.0/26     eth0/2        10.10.10.1   S   20  1  Root
bottom-ssg140->
```

You can find the same information using regex commands; however, if you want to see only the /32 routes within the 159.24.0.0 Class B range, regex is the only option:

```
bottom-ssg140-> get route | inc "159.24.{1,3}[[:digit:]].{1,3}
[[:digit:]]\/32"
*  764  159.24.119.232/32     eth0/2        10.10.10.1   S   20  1  Root
*  756  159.24.107.242/32     eth0/2        10.10.10.1   S   20  1  Root
*  763  159.24.116.222/32     eth0/2        10.10.10.1   S   20  1  Root
*  760  159.24.110.217/32     eth0/2        10.10.10.1   S   20  1  Root
*  750  159.24.106.169/32     eth0/2        10.10.10.1   S   20  1  Root
*  749  159.24.106.167/32     eth0/2        10.10.10.1   S   20  1  Root
*  748  159.24.106.166/32     eth0/2        10.10.10.1   S   20  1  Root
*  747  159.24.106.162/32     eth0/2        10.10.10.1   S   20  1  Root
*  762  159.24.116.161/32     eth0/2        10.10.10.1   S   20  1  Root
*  758  159.24.110.123/32     eth0/2        10.10.10.1   S   20  1  Root
*  746  159.24.106.122/32     eth0/2        10.10.10.1   S   20  1  Root
*  757    159.24.109.89/32     eth0/2        10.10.10.1   S   20  1  Root
*  754    159.24.107.61/32     eth0/2        10.10.10.1   S   20  1  Root
*  753    159.24.107.58/32     eth0/2        10.10.10.1   S   20  1  Root
*  751    159.24.107.55/32     eth0/2        10.10.10.1   S   20  1  Root
*  761    159.24.114.46/32     eth0/2        10.10.10.1   S   20  1  Root
bottom-ssg140->
```

The exclude keyword is used more rarely, but a good example of its use is to show the routing table without Host or /32 routes:

```
bottom-ssg140-> get route | exclude /32


IPv4 Dest-Routes for <untrust-vr> (0 entries)
--------------------------------------------------------------------
H: Host C: Connected S: Static A: Auto-Exported
I: Imported R: RIP P: Permanent D: Auto-Discovered
N: NHRP
iB: IBGP eB: EBGP O: OSPF E1: OSPF external type 1
E2: OSPF external type 2 trailing B: backup route


IPv4 Dest-Routes for <trust-vr> (764 entries)
----------------------------------------------------------------------
    ID          IP-Prefix  Interface      Gateway   P Pref  Mtr  Vsys
----------------------------------------------------------------------
*    9          0.0.0.0/0     eth0/2   10.10.10.1   S   20    1  Root
*  668   192.168.151.0/24     eth0/0  10.251.7.97   S   20    1  Root
*   43       10.11.0.0/16     eth0/0  10.251.7.97   S   20    1  Root
*  169   137.237.154.0/24     eth0/2   10.10.10.1   S   20    1  Root
```

```
*  10        10.15.0.0/29     eth0/0  10.251.7.97   S   20    1  Root
*  168   137.237.153.0/24     eth0/2   10.10.10.1   S   20    1  Root

...

*  274 152.161.208.164/30     eth0/2   10.10.10.1   S   20    1  Root
*  374   158.147.188.0/24     eth0/2   10.10.10.1   S   20    1  Root
Too many matched lines, rest ignored.
bottom-ssg140->
```

Filtering can provide many other powerful benefits, such as the ability to filter a large session table. In the following example, we request a session table from the device that includes only IP address 192.168.1.1:

```
top-ssg140-> get session | include 192.168.1.1

if 2(nspflag 801801):192.168.1.100/3703->172.24.18.251/1222,6,
   000d605ff552,sess token 4,vlan 0,tun 0,vsd 0,route 1
if 2(nspflag 800601):192.168.1.100/3706->192.168.1.1/23,6,
   000d605ff552,sess token 4,vlan 0,tun 0,vsd 0,route 1
if 3(nspflag 0010):192.168.1.100/3706<-192.168.1.1/23,6,000000000000,
   sess token 8,vlan 0,tun 0,vsd 0,route 0

top-ssg140->
```

You can shorten many of the ScreenOS commands when entering them at the keyboard or in a script, as long as you provide enough characters to make the command unique. For example, `get session` is the same as `get sess`.

There are limits to the amount of data that can be filtered; if very large amounts of data must be filtered, it is best to save the data to a text file and use a word processing tool or more traditional *NIX tools.

1.1 ScreenOS Architecture

ScreenOS takes a hierarchical approach with regard to the firewall's framework configuration. The framework configuration determines how the firewall will communicate on the network from Layers 1–3, and it consists of routing, security zones, and interfaces.

It is easy to get started with ScreenOS, and the impulse is to immediately put IP addresses on interfaces, add some routes, create Address Book entries, and to start writing policies. However, be careful when dealing with more complex environments. We will address the three key ScreenOS building blocks in the order an administrator should consider them to avoid a lot of rework or, worse, rearchitecting a network design midstream.

Virtual Router

ScreenOS architecture utilizes the Virtual Router (VR), `trust-vr`, as the parent container and as the first architectural choice to be made when designing ScreenOS into an existing or new network (see Figure 1-1).

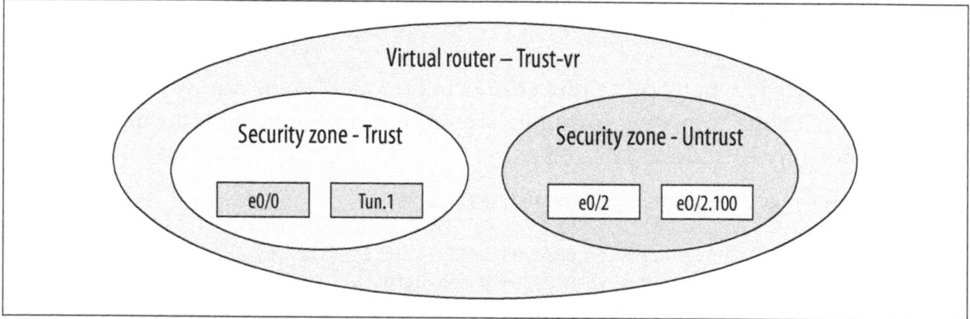

Figure 1-1. The relationship between key elements of ScreenOS

Two VRs are enabled on every platform that runs ScreenOS: `trust-vr` and `untrust-vr`:

```
bottom-ssg140-> get vrouter
* indicates default vrouter
A - AutoExport, R - RIP, N- NHRP, O - OSPF, B - BGP, P - PIM

   ID Name          Vsys   Owner    Routes    MRoutes     Flags
    1 untrust-vr    Root   shared     0/max      0/max
*   2 trust-vr      Root   shared     5/max      0/max

total 2 vrouters shown and 0 of them defined by user
bottom-ssg140->
```

However, `trust-vr` is the default VR and, therefore, the default container for all the underlying associated zones and interfaces:

```
bottom-ssg140-> get vrouter trust-vr
Routing Table
-------------------------------------------------------------------
H: Host C: Connected S: Static A: Auto-Exported
I: Imported R: RIP P: Permanent D: Auto-Discovered
N: NHRP
iB: IBGP eB: EBGP O: OSPF E1: OSPF external type 1
E2: OSPF external type 2 trailing B: backup route

Total 5/max entries

    ID          IP-Prefix    Interface     Gateway    P Pref Mtr  Vsys
-------------------------------------------------------------------
*   1      10.251.7.96/27      eth0/0      0.0.0.0    C    0    0  Root
*   6       10.100.1.0/24      eth0/2   10.10.10.1    S   20    1  Root
```

```
*  2      10.251.7.99/32      eth0/0       0.0.0.0   H    0    0 Root
*  4    10.10.10.254/32      eth0/2       0.0.0.0   H    0    0 Root
*  3      10.10.10.0/24      eth0/2       0.0.0.0   C    0    0 Root

Interfaces
-----------------------------------------------------------------
self, v1-trust, v1-untrust, v1-dmz, l2v, ethernet0/0
serial1/1, serial1/0, ethernet0/2, ethernet0/1, vlan1, hidden.1
tunnel

Auto-exporting:                   Disabled
Default-vrouter:                  Yes
Shared-vrouter:                   Yes
nsrp-config-sync:                 Yes
System-Default-route:             Not present
Advertise-Inactive-Interface:     Disabled
Source-Based-Routing:             Disabled
SIBR-Routing:                     Disabled
SNMP Trap:                        Public
Ignore-Subnet-Conflict:           Disabled
ECMP-Routing:                     Disabled
bottom-ssg140->
```

You can divide this information into a couple of sections; first, the routing table:

```
Total 5/max entries

   ID          IP-Prefix    Interface     Gateway    P Pref  Mtr  Vsys
-----------------------------------------------------------------
*  1      10.251.7.96/27      eth0/0        0.0.0.0   C    0    0 Root
*  6       10.100.1.0/24      eth0/2     10.10.10.1   S   20    1 Root
*  2      10.251.7.99/32      eth0/0        0.0.0.0   H    0    0 Root
*  4    10.10.10.254/32      eth0/2        0.0.0.0   H    0    0 Root
*  3       10.10.10.0/24      eth0/2        0.0.0.0   C    0    0 Root
```

Note that ScreenOS creates a /32 Host entry for each directly connected interface, as well as the Network entry. Also, the asterisk (*) at the far left indicates that the route is installed in the Routing Information Base (RIB) and is available and active for use. The ID is the route ID from the RIB, which can be useful when troubleshooting flows, and note that duplicate, equal cost routes are available.

The `Interfaces` information section provides a visual list so that you can at least verify expected behavior. The interfaces listed here inherit the VR relationship from their zone assignment:

```
Interfaces
-----------------------------------------------------------------
self, v1-trust, v1-untrust, v1-dmz, l2v, ethernet0/0
serial1/1, serial1/0, ethernet0/2, ethernet0/1, vlan1, hidden.1
tunnel
```

We will discuss routing in more detail in Chapter 4.

Zones

Zones are the foundation of the security architecture within ScreenOS. You can see a simple list of zones by typing **get zone** at the command prompt:

```
bottom-ssg140-> get zone
Total 14 zones created in vsys Root - 8 are policy configurable.
Total policy configurable zones for Root is 8.
--------------------------------------------------------------
  ID Name            Type    Attr   VR           Default-IF    VSYS
   0 Null            Null    Shared untrust-vr   hidden        Root
   1 Untrust         Sec(L3) Shared trust-vr     ethernet0/2   Root
   2 Trust           Sec(L3)        trust-vr     ethernet0/0   Root
   3 DMZ             Sec(L3)        trust-vr     ethernet0/1   Root
   4 Self            Func           trust-vr     self          Root
   5 MGT             Func           trust-vr     null          Root
   6 HA              Func           trust-vr     null          Root
  10 Global          Sec(L3)        trust-vr     null          Root
  11 V1-Untrust      Sec(L2) Shared trust-vr     v1-untrust    Root
  12 V1-Trust        Sec(L2) Shared trust-vr     v1-trust      Root
  13 V1-DMZ          Sec(L2) Shared trust-vr     v1-dmz        Root
  14 VLAN            Func    Shared trust-vr     vlan1         Root
  15 V1-Null         Sec(L2) Shared trust-vr     l2v           Root
  16 Untrust-Tun     Tun            trust-vr     hidden.1      Root
--------------------------------------------------------------
```

ScreenOS contains many types of zones, but the two that are most commonly configured and used are the security and functional zones.

Security zone

A security zone (specifically, the `Sec(L3)` from the preceding output, which is a Layer 3 security zone for firewalls operating in Layer 3 mode) represents a logical area of *trust* within the firewall. There are differing degrees of trust, represented by creating more zones, and different methods of defining such. Within these areas of trust, `Address` objects get associated and can then be used to define the security policy within ScreenOS.

Unlike other security operating systems, there is no hierarchy of trust levels when it comes to zones. ScreenOS employs an implicit deny system, and requires the explicit definition of rules to allow communication between hosts in different areas of trust, or zones, and sometimes within the same zone (intra-zone). For example:

```
bottom-ssg140-> get zone trust
Zone name: Trust, id: 2, type: Security(L3), vsys: Root, vrouter:
   trust-vr
Intra-zone block: Off, attrib: Non-shared, flag:0x6208
TCP non SYN send reset: On
IP/TCP reassembly for ALG on traffic from/to this zone: No
Asymmetric vpn: Disabled
Policy Configurable: Yes
PBR policy: None
```

```
Interfaces bound:1. Designated ifp is ethernet0/0
interface ethernet0/0(0x3e93844)
DHCP relay enabled
bottom-ssg140->
```

The pertinent details from the Trust zone properties shown in the preceding code are as follows:

- The VR assignment, trust-vr, is where all interfaces associated with the Trust zone will look for routes.
- The Intra-zone block setting dictates whether to allow communication between hosts in the same zone without requiring an explicit rule.
- The Policy Configurable setting indicates whether the trust is policy-configurable (not all are).
- The Interfaces bound setting indicates whether interfaces are bound to the zone, which is very useful when troubleshooting.

Functional zones

There are several functional zones, and each one performs a specific task within ScreenOS.

The Self zone is used for traffic destined to and generated by the firewall itself. No physical interfaces are associated with, or security policies definable for, this zone. Rather, it is used internally to track this traffic.

The HA (High Availability) zone is where the dedicated HA interfaces on the NS5000 series are placed, and where interfaces to be used for HA on the ISG and SSG systems need to be placed to ensure proper functioning. The interfaces in this zone are not assigned IP addresses because the ScreenOS NetScreen Redundancy Protocol (NSRP) is a Layer 2 protocol.

The MGT zone is for dedicated interfaces to manage the firewall. This is the only functional zone where the interface associated with it can be assigned an IP address. However, traffic cannot pass through this zone to other zones. Details for the MGT zone are as follows:

```
bottom-ssg140-> get zone mgt
Zone name: MGT, id: 5, type: Function, vsys: Root, vrouter:trust-vr
Intra-zone block: On, attrib: Non-shared, flag:0x00a4
TCP non SYN send reset: On
IP/TCP reassembly for ALG on traffic from/to this zone: No
Policy Configurable: No
PBR policy: None
Interfaces bound:0.
DHCP relay enabled
bottom-ssg140->
```

Note that in the preceding code, the MGT zone is not policy-configurable and that intra-zone blocking is enabled, which means that if there are many interfaces in this zone, the firewall will not allow communication between them. This zone tends to cause the most problems, as we will discuss in Recipe 2.3.

Interfaces

We're discussing interfaces last because they are the final building blocks in this structured relationship of VR → Security Zone → Interface. There are many types of ScreenOS interfaces, and some will be discussed in more detail throughout the book. Here is a list of the default interfaces:

```
bottom-ssg140-> get interface

A - Active, I - Inactive, U - Up, D - Down, R - Ready

Interfaces in vsys Root:
Name         IP Address       Zone      MAC              VLAN State VSD
eth0/0       10.251.7.99/27   Trust     0017.cb47.9400    -    U    -
eth0/1       0.0.0.0/0        DMZ       0017.cb47.9405    -    D    -
eth0/2       10.10.10.254/24  Untrust   0017.cb47.9406    -    U    -
eth0/3       0.0.0.0/0        Null      0017.cb47.9407    -    D    -
eth0/4       0.0.0.0/0        Null      0017.cb47.9408    -    D    -
eth0/5       0.0.0.0/0        Null      0017.cb47.9409    -    D    -
eth0/6       0.0.0.0/0        Null      0017.cb47.940a    -    D    -
eth0/7       0.0.0.0/0        Null      0017.cb47.940b    -    D    -
eth0/8       0.0.0.0/0        Null      0017.cb47.940c    -    D    -
eth0/9       0.0.0.0/0        Null      0017.cb47.940d    -    D    -
bgroup0/0    0.0.0.0/0        Null      0017.cb47.940e    -    D    -
bgroup0/1    0.0.0.0/0        Null      0017.cb47.9415    -    D    -
bgroup0/2    0.0.0.0/0        Null      0017.cb47.9416    -    D    -
serial1/0    0.0.0.0/0        Untrust   N/A               -    D    -
serial1/1    0.0.0.0/0        Untrust   N/A               -    D    -
vlan1        0.0.0.0/0        VLAN      0017.cb47.940f    1    D    -
null         0.0.0.0/0        Null      N/A               -    U    0
bottom-ssg140->
```

Other interface types that must be manually configured are not listed here. These are generally considered "logical" interfaces, and they include:

- Redundant
- Aggregate
- Bridge Group
- VLAN
- Loopback
- Tunnel

Let's start simply with a physical interface. An example of how the ScreenOS structure dictates configuration is the fact that an IP address cannot be configured if the interface is not associated with a zone:

```
bottom-ssg140-> set interface e0/4 ip 10.20.20.1/28
                                     ^-----unknown keyword ip
bottom-ssg140-> set int e0/4 zone trust
bottom-ssg140-> set int e0/4 ip 10.20.20.1/28
bottom-ssg140->
```

A new feature in ScreenOS 6.0 is the ability to add a description to the interface to allow you to correlate information regarding how the interface is being utilized. This is a very useful function, especially in wide area network (WAN) environments when it is common to identify remote peers, provider, and other information to help in troubleshooting and fault analysis. You can use up to 31 characters in your interface description; if there are spaces in your description, you must bound your text with double quotation marks:

```
bottom-ssg140->
bottom-ssg140-> set interface e0/3 description "Local LAN -
    Portsmouth, New Hampshire"
Interface description "Local LAN - Portsmouth, New Hampshire" is
    longer than 31 characters
bottom-ssg140-> set interface e0/3 description "Local LAN -
    Portsmouth, NH"
bottom-ssg140->
```

Using ethernet0/0, eth0/0, as an example, the following output displays the currently assigned IP address, zone association (remember, this dictates which VR to use to find/manage routes), Layer 2 Media Access Control (MAC) address, virtual local area network (VLAN), status, and what virtual security device (VSD) it is associated to if High Availability (HA) is configured:

```
bottom-ssg140-> get interface e0/0
Interface ethernet0/0:
  description Local LAN - Portsmouth, NH
  number 0, if_info 0, if_index 0, mode nat
  link up, phy-link up/full-duplex
  vsys Root, zone Trust, vr trust-vr
  dhcp client disabled
  PPPoE disabled
  admin mtu 0, operating mtu 1500, default mtu 1500
  *ip 10.251.7.99/27   mac 0017.cb47.9400
  *manage ip 10.251.7.99, mac 0017.cb47.9400
  route-deny disable
  pmtu-v4 disabled
  ping enabled, telnet enabled, SSH enabled, SNMP enabled
  web enabled, ident-reset disabled, SSL enabled
  DNS Proxy disabled, webauth disabled, webauth-ip 0.0.0.0
  OSPF disabled  BGP disabled  RIP disabled  RIPng disabled  mtrace
    disabled
  PIM: not configured  IGMP not configured
  NHRP disabled
  bandwidth: physical 100000kbps, configured egress [gbw 0kbps mbw
    0kbps]
             configured ingress mbw 0kbps, current bw 0kbps
             total allocated gbw 0kbps
```

```
  DHCP-Relay disabled at interface level
  DHCP-server disabled
Number of SW session: 56062, hw sess err cnt 0
bottom-ssg140->
```

This output illustrates a few key points that dictate how ScreenOS behaves and responds. For example, `mode nat` is a key setting because it determines how packets traverse the firewall. It is the default setting for interfaces assigned to the `Trust` zone, and any packet originating from the `Trust` zone to the `Untrust` zone will be translated to the interface IP of the outbound interface. This is great for small office/home office use, but it is generally not desirable for data center or enterprise deployment when Network Address Translation (NAT) needs to be tightly administered. You can change it to `mode route` easily, as shown here, but it is just as easy to overlook it:

```
bottom-ssg140-> get interface e0/0 | include mode
  number 0, if_info 0, if_index 0, mode nat
bottom-ssg140-> set interface e0/0 route
bottom-ssg140-> get interface e0/0 | include mode
  number 0, if_info 0, if_index 0, mode route
bottom-ssg140->
```

All other interfaces default to `mode route`, and the behavior of `mode nat` on the interface(s) in the `Trust` zone is different depending on the outbound interface zone mapping. The best practice is for all interfaces to be in `mode route` to ensure consistent, predictable behavior and to perform NAT functions in the security policy.

When an IP address is assigned to an interface, ScreenOS defines the interface `manage-ip` to be the same address. This is verified in the interface detail output with an asterisk (*) next to the interface IP. You can change this setting to a different IP address, but it must be on the same network as the interface IP:

```
bottom-ssg140-> get interface e0/0 | include manage
  *manage ip 10.251.7.99, mac 0017.cb47.9400
bottom-ssg140-> set interface e0/0 manage-ip 10.251.7.100
bottom-ssg140-> get interface e0/0 | include manage
  manage ip 10.251.7.100, mac 0017.cb47.9400
bottom-ssg140->
```

Redundant

The redundant interface allows you to logically group physical interfaces to create Layer 1 resiliency. The physical interfaces must be in the same broadcast domain, but they can be connected to two different switches. Only one interface is active at any given time, and this is controlled by the `primary` option. Redundant interfaces are supported across the Juniper firewall product line.

```
bottom-ssg140-> unset interface ethernet0/0 ip
bottom-ssg140-> set interface red1 zone trust
bottom-ssg140-> set int ethernet0/0 group red1
```

```
redundant1 interface change physical state to Up
bottom-ssg140-> set int ethernet0/1 group red1
bottom-ssg140-> set interface red1 primary ethernet0/0
bottom-ssg140-> set interface red1 ip 10.251.7.99/27
bottom-ssg140-> get interface red1
Interface redundant1:
  description redundant1
  number 64, if_info 64512, if_index 0, mode nat
  link up, phy-link up/full-duplex
  Redundant port has 2 members: ethernet0/1; ethernet0/0;
  Active primary interface: ethernet0/0
  Configured primary interface: ethernet0/0
  vsys Root, zone Trust, vr trust-vr
  dhcp client disabled
  *ip 10.251.7.99/27   mac 0017.cb30.9705
  *manage ip 10.251.7.99, mac 0017.cb30.9705
  pmtu-v4 disabled
  ping enabled, telnet enabled, SSH enabled, SNMP enabled
  web enabled, ident-reset disabled, SSL enabled
  DNS Proxy disabled, webauth disabled, webauth-ip 0.0.0.0
  OSPF disabled  BGP disabled  RIP disabled  RIPng disabled  mtrace
    disabled
  PIM: not configured  IGMP not configured
  NHRP disabled
Number of SW session: 48063, hw sess err cnt 0
bottom-ssg140->
```

The naming convention is very strict; you must use red and then an integer number as the name, or you will get a syntax error. Note that the same controls are in place in terms of IP addressing, zone assignment, and so on (as just discussed); the fundamental difference is that you apply these configurations to the logical interface now instead of to the underlying physical interfaces.

The expected failover trigger is a loss of the physical link that will then force ScreenOS to switch over to the other physical link in the redundant group:

```
bottom-ssg140-> ethernet0/0 interface change physical state to Down
redundant1 interface change physical state to Up

bottom-ssg140-> get interface red1
Interface redundant1:
  description redundant1
  number 64, if_info 64512, if_index 0, mode nat
  link up, phy-link up/full-duplex
  Redundant port has 2 members: ethernet0/1; ethernet0/0;
  Active primary interface: ethernet0/1
  Configured primary interface: ethernet0/0
  vsys Root, zone Trust, vr trust-vr
  dhcp client disabled
  *ip 10.251.7.99/27   mac 0017.cb30.9705
  *manage ip 10.251.7.99, mac 0017.cb30.9705
  pmtu-v4 disabled
  ping enabled, telnet enabled, SSH enabled, SNMP enabled
```

```
  web enabled, ident-reset disabled, SSL enabled
  DNS Proxy disabled, webauth disabled, webauth-ip 0.0.0.0
  OSPF disabled  BGP disabled  RIP disabled  RIPng disabled  mtrace
    disabled
  PIM: not configured  IGMP not configured
  NHRP disabled
Number of SW session: 48063, hw sess err cnt 0
bottom-ssg140->
```

This failure will not cause an NSRP failover unless the physical interface `ethernet0/0` was being monitored instead of the redundant interface.

Aggregate

The aggregate interface allows you to logically group physical interfaces to increase bandwidth and create Layer 1 resiliency. Aggregate interfaces are supported on the ISG1000/2000 and NS5200/5400 Juniper firewalls. For example, configuring a two-port aggregate interface to a Cisco 6500 would look like this:

```
isg1000-> set interface ethernet1/1 aggregate aggregate1
isg1000-> set interface ethernet1/2 aggregate aggregate1
isg1000-> set interface agg1 zone trust
isg1000-> set interface aggregate1 ip 192.168.4.1/26
isg1000-> set interface aggregate1 route
isg1000-> get interface agg1
Interface aggregate1:
  description aggregate1
  number 64, if_info 64512, if_index 0, mode nat
  link up, phy-link up/full-duplex
  Aggregate port has 2 members: ethernet1/1; ethernet1/2
  vsys Root, zone Trust, vr trust-vr
  dhcp client disabled
  *ip 192.168.4.1/26   mac 0017.cb30.2101
  *manage ip 192.168.4.1, mac 0017.cb30.2101
  pmtu-v4 disabled
  ping enabled, telnet enabled, SSH enabled, SNMP enabled
  web enabled, ident-reset disabled, SSL enabled
  DNS Proxy disabled, webauth disabled, webauth-ip 0.0.0.0
  OSPF disabled  BGP disabled  RIP disabled  RIPng disabled  mtrace
    disabled
  PIM: not configured  IGMP not configured
  NHRP disabled
  bandwidth: physical 2000000kbps, configured egress [gbw 0kbps mbw
    0kbps]
             configured ingress mbw 0kbps, current bw 0kbps
             total allocated gbw 0kbps
Number of SW session: 1000063, hw sess err cnt 0
isg-1000->
```

Here's how it would look on the Cisco side:

```
Router# configure terminal
Router(config)# interface port-channel 1
Router(config-if)# ip address 192.168.4.5 255.255.255.0
```

```
Router(config-if)# end
Router(config)# interface range gigethernet 5/6-7
Router(config-if)# channel-group 1 mode on
Router(config-if)# end
```

The naming convention for aggregate interfaces is also very strict; you must use agg and then an integer number as the name, or you will get a syntax error. As with redundant interfaces, the same controls are in place in terms of IP addressing, zone assignment, and such.

Note that there is no aggregation protocol configuration; ScreenOS does not support 802.3ad or any other LACP negotiation protocol. This means you will need to configure the ancillary network device, typically a standalone or chassis-based switch, to group their physical ports statically and disable any LACP protocol. Most switch vendors will support this configuration, and Juniper has tested it with Cisco, Foundry, and Riverstone.

The load-sharing algorithm within ScreenOS is round-robin on a per-packet basis. This has caused out-of-order packets on rare occasions, and most applications are written to account for this through retransmission at the Transport layer. You can configure the other device load-sharing algorithm in any way you want. If one of the physical interfaces fails in the Aggregate group, the bandwidth is reduced, and the number of ports to round-robin the packets will be as well, but the Aggregate port will not fail and trigger an NSRP failure. We cover this in more detail in Recipe 18.4.

The NS5000 family has two Secure Port Module (SPM) options: an eight-port GE card and a two-port 10GE card. The 10GE cards *do not* support aggregate port grouping. A maximum of four GE interfaces *or* eight FE interfaces can be grouped into an aggregate.

There are limits as to which physical ports can be grouped together. The eight-port GE SPM in the NS5000 has two ASICs for forwarding; the first ASIC supports physical ports 1–4 and the second ASIC supports physical ports 5–8. An aggregate port group cannot span the ASIC boundary, and in this case, that means the group cannot span across the ASIC port definition or, in an NS5400, the slot boundary to another SPM, even if it is of the same type. On the ISG family, there is a single ASIC across the entire firewall, so there is no limitation to port combination other than the fact that there is a maximum of four GE interfaces per aggregate grouping, and it is a best practice that they should be at the same negotiated bandwidth.

Bridge Groups

Bridge Groups are new to ScreenOS starting with version 6.0. on the SSG firewall family. These represent a logical Layer 2 switch within the firewall. You can configure any port on an SSG5/20 into a Bridge Group; on the SSG140/300/500 family, only ports added via Universal Port Interface Modules, uPIMs, can be in a Bridge

Group and the group cannot span uPIM modules. This is documented on the Juniper Support Site Knowledge Base within KB article number 10747, located at *http://kb.juniper.net/KB10747*.

```
bottom-ssg140-> set interface ethernet1/0 zone null
bottom-ssg140-> set interface ehternet1/1 zone null
bottom-ssg140-> set interface bgroup 1 1
bottom-ssg140-> set interface bgroup1 port ethernet1/0
bottom-ssg140-> set interface bgroup1 port ethernet1/1
bottom-ssg140-> set interface bgroup1 zone untrust
bottom-ssg140-> set interface bgroup1 ip 64.100.7.1/29
bottom-ssg140-> get interface bgroup1
Interface bgroup1:
  description bgroup1
  number 9, if_info 792, if_index 0, mode route
  link up, phy-link up/full-duplex
  vsys Root, zone Untrust, vr trust-vr
  dhcp client disabled
  PPPoE disabled
  admin mtu 0, operating mtu 1500, default mtu 1500
  *ip 64.100.7.1/29   mac 001b.c046.0909
  *manage ip 64.100.7.1, mac 001b.c046.0909
  route-deny disable
  pmtu-v4 disabled
  ping disabled, telnet disabled, SSH disabled, SNMP disabled
  web disabled, ident-reset disabled, SSL disabled
  DNS Proxy disabled, webauth disabled, webauth-ip 0.0.0.0
  OSPF disabled  BGP disabled  RIP disabled  RIPng disabled  mtrace
    disabled
  PIM: not configured  IGMP not configured
  NHRP disabled
  bandwidth: physical 0kbps, configured egress [gbw 0kbps mbw 0kbps]
             configured ingress mbw 0kbps, current bw 0kbps
             total allocated gbw 0kbps
  DHCP-Relay disabled at interface level
  DHCP-server enabled, status on.
Number of SW session: 48063, hw sess err cnt 0

  Physical port information:
    ethernet1/0 is up, full duplex, speed is 100mbps
    ethernet1/1 is up, full duplex, speed is 100mbps
bottom-ssg140->
```

The naming convention for a Bridge Group is also specific. You must use `bgroup` and then an integer number as the name or you will get a syntax error. As with previous logical interfaces, the same controls are in place in terms of IP addressing, zone assignment, and such.

Bridge Groups are best used when more than a single physical port is required for connectivity, and only a single IP address is needed or available to define the Layer 3 boundary. An example is a small office where three desktops and a printer are connecting to the Internet. Instead of investing in a switch for connectivity, placing all four ports into a Bridge Group on the SSG firewall with a single Layer 3 IP address reduces operational complexity, removes a single point of failure (the switch), and lowers the cost of the remote office implementation.

Loopback

The loopback interface is a container group that has a couple of primary uses. The first is in a dynamic routing configuration where it would be assigned an IP address that will be used as the Router-ID. Since the loopback interface is always up, the Router-ID remains constant, which makes troubleshooting and configuration more predictable. Another use is in complex NAT configurations. Interfaces in the same security zone can be associated to a `loopback-group` interface and then that interface can be assigned an IP address and associated NAT definitions to be shared across the underlying interfaces.

Here is an example of creating a `loopback-group` and associating the underlying interfaces which would be the beginning steps of a NAT configuration:

```
bottom-ssg140->
bottom-ssg140-> set int e0/0 ip 12.18.100.1/29
bottom-ssg140-> set int e0/1 ip 12.18.101.1/29
bottom-ssg140-> set interface e0/1 loopback-group loop.1 zone Untrust
bottom-ssg140-> set int loop.1 ip 12.18.101.5/29
loopback.1 ip change pre-checking failed.
Interface: Illegal overlapping subnet
bottom-ssg140-> set int loop.1 ip 12.18.103.33/27
bottom-ssg140-> set interface loop.1 description "Outbound dynamic
    NAT Pool"
bottom-ssg140-> get int loop.1
Interface loopback.1:
  description Outbound dynamic NAT Pool
  number 126, if_info 127016, if_index 1, mode route
  link up
  Loopback interface has 2 members:
  ethernet0/0; ethernet0/1
  vsys Root, zone Untrust, vr trust-vr
  admin mtu 1500, operating mtu 1500, default mtu 1500
  *ip 12.18.103.33/27
  *manage ip 12.18.103.33
  pmtu-v4 disabled
  ping disabled, telnet disabled, SSH disabled, SNMP disabled
  web disabled, ident-reset disabled, SSL disabled

  OSPF disabled  BGP disabled  RIP disabled  RIPng disabled  mtrace
    disabled
  PIM: not configured  IGMP not configured
  NHRP disabled
Number of SW session: 48063, hw sess err cnt 0
bottom-ssg140->
```

From here, you would go in and create your NAT definitions and then your security policies. Note that the loopback interface definition has some restrictions; it *must* be in the same security zone as the interfaces associated to it and it cannot be in the same IP address range of any of the associated interfaces. The naming convention for a loopback group is also specific; you must use `loop` and then an integer number as the name or you will get a syntax error.

Loopback groups seem quite similar to Bridge Groups, but they differ in that each interface associated to a loopback must already have a unique IP address assigned and routing is required to get between those interfaces, whereas the Bridge Group is really like a small logical switch with a unique IP address assigned to the Bridge Group interface.

VLAN

A VLAN interface is a logical subinterface that can be assigned to a physical, a redundant, or an aggregate interface or to a Bridge Group. This is based on the IEEE 802.1q standard, and each ScreenOS platform will have a limitation as to the number of VLANs that can be defined; that limitation will directly correlate to the VLAN subinterface index that can be assigned to any given port. However, ScreenOS does support an 802.1q VLAN tag value in the range of 1–4094, as defined in the standard.

```
bottom-ssg140-> set int red1.150
Interface redundant1 index 150, should be <0 - 100>
bottom-ssg140-> set int red1.80
bottom-ssg140-> set int red1.80 tag 4091 zone trust
bottom-ssg140-> set interface red1.80 ip 172.31.55.129/25
bottom-ssg140-> get interface red1.80
Interface redundant1.80:
  description redundant1.80
  number 64, if_info 65152, if_index 80, VLAN tag 4091, mode nat
  link up, phy-link up/full-duplex
  Redundant port has 2 members: ethernet0/1; ethernet0/0;
  Active primary interface: ethernet0/1
  Configured primary interface: ethernet0/0
  vsys Root, zone Trust, vr trust-vr
  *ip 172.31.55.129/25   mac 0017.cb30.9705
  *manage ip 172.31.55.129, mac 0017.cb30.9705
  route-deny disable
  pmtu-v4 disabled
  ping enabled, telnet enabled, SSH enabled, SNMP enabled
  web enabled, ident-reset disabled, SSL enabled
  DNS Proxy disabled, webauth disabled, webauth-ip 0.0.0.0
  OSPF disabled  BGP disabled  RIP disabled  RIPng disabled  mtrace
    disabled
  PIM: not configured  IGMP not configured
  NHRP disabled
  DHCP-Relay disabled at interface level
  DHCP-server disabled
Number of SW session: 48063, hw sess err cnt 0
bottom-ssg140->
```

This is a well-proven function, supported on all platforms, and there are no known limitations with other vendor products on the market.

Tunnel

A tunnel interface is used for route-based virtual private networks (VPNs). The concept here is to create a subinterface that will bind to a security zone for the purpose of defining the security policy boundary. Tunnel interfaces differ from other logical interfaces and subinterfaces in that they do get assigned to a physical (or logical) interface until the IKE gateway is defined. Tunnel interfaces by default do not get assigned IP addresses either, unless there is a requirement to NAT traffic within the IP Security (IPSec) VPN tunnel.

```
bottom-ssg140-> set zone name vpn
bottom-ssg140-> set interface tun.1 zone vpn
bottom-ssg140-> set ike gate vpn2corp address 12.1.100.5 outgoing-
    interface red1 preshare jun1p3rr0x sec-level standard
bottom-ssg140-> get interface tun.1
Interface tunnel.1:
  description tunnel.1
  number 20, if_info 20168, if_index 1, mode route
  link down
  vsys Root, zone vpn, vr trust-vr
  admin mtu 1500, operating mtu 1500, default mtu 1500
  *ip 0.0.0.0/0
  *manage ip 0.0.0.0
  pmtu-v4 disabled
  ping disabled, telnet disabled, SSH disabled, SNMP disabled
  web disabled, ident-reset disabled, SSL disabled

  OSPF disabled  BGP disabled  RIP disabled  RIPng disabled  mtrace disabled
  PIM: not configured  IGMP not configured
  NHRP disabled
  bandwidth: physical 0kbps, configured egress [gbw 0kbps mbw 0kbps]
             configured ingress mbw 0kbps, current bw 0kbps
             total allocated gbw 0kbps
Number of SW session: 48063, hw sess err cnt 0
bottom-ssg140->
```

We discuss IPSec route-based VPNs and the various iterations in detail in Chapter 10.

Summary

Current ScreenOS platforms are very flexible and provide you with a multitude of configuration knobs to turn to provide resiliency, added bandwidth, and connectivity. It is very common to use many of these interface types together to create complex customer configurations.

One last point to note about interfaces is that unlike other security devices, no rules need to be created to permit or deny management access to ScreenOS. This is handled on a per-interface basis, be it physical or logical. Each interface is capable of supporting several access protocols, including SSH, Telnet, HTTP, and HTTPS, as well as management protocols such as PING and SNMP. The specific interface default settings depend on the zone to which they are associated. The `Trust` zone defaults with all protocols enabled, whereas with the `Untrust` zone they are all disabled. You can override each setting via the CLI, which we will cover in more detail in Recipe 2.4.

1.2 Troubleshoot ScreenOS

ScreenOS features a rich set of troubleshooting functions that can provide the administrator with a daunting amount of detailed information. Let's cover a subset of the more useful ones and provide insight into how to fine-tune them to be even more useful. Mainly, the troubleshooting functions are:

- Debug
- Flow filter
- Debug buffer
- Snoop

Although these four functions can provide vast capabilities, note that your experience will differ depending on your platform. For example, on the high-end ASIC-based platforms (the NS5000 and NS-ISG1000/2000), only the packets that are sent to the MGT card/process can be seen with these tools. The ASIC forwards all other packets, and therefore, you cannot view them using these tools. Generally speaking, this should not be an issue, as problems usually occur during session setup; however, occasionally the entire flow is needed, at which point an external analyzer may be required. Figure 1-2 illustrates how a packet makes its way through the ScreenOS software.

The `debug` and `snoop` functions will separately provide very detailed information that the administrator can use while troubleshooting issues. When used together, these functions can illustrate an entire data flow, starting with what the packet looks like entering the firewall, how ScreenOS processes the packet through the firewall, and finally, what the packet looks like when leaving the firewall.

Debug

The debug tool bag is very deep, and it is one of the most useful troubleshooting functions within ScreenOS because it will show you what ScreenOS is doing with the packet as it makes its way through the different ScreenOS processes and functions (shown in Figure 1-2). For example:

```
top-ssg140-> debug ?
admin                   debug admin
adsl                    adsl debugging
anti-spam               anti-spam debugging
```

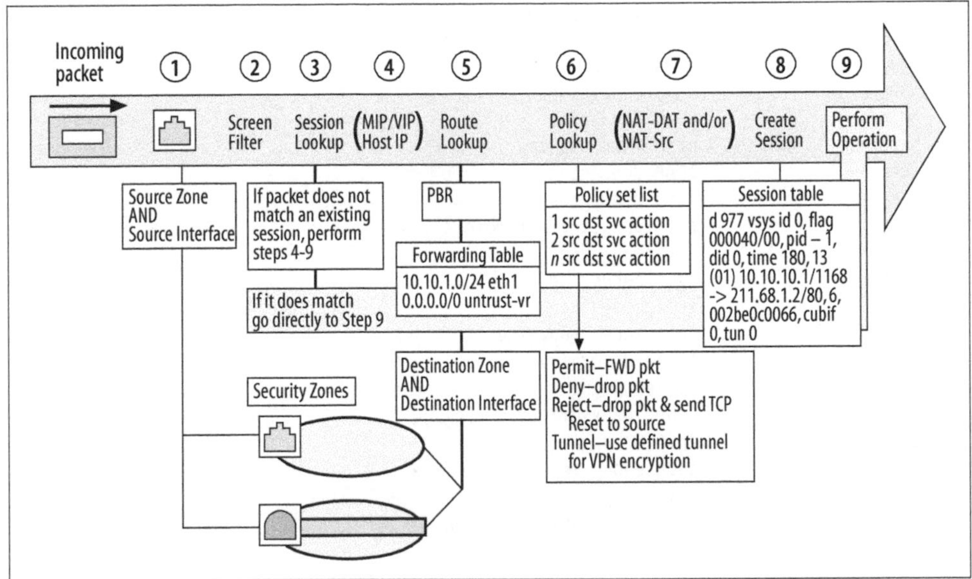

Figure 1-2. Packet flow in ScreenOS

```
apppry              Application Proxy debugging
arp                 arp debugging
asp                 ASP debugging
asset-recovery      asset recovery debugging
auth                user authentication debugging
autocfg             Auto config debugging
av                  anti virus scan debugging
bgp                 bgp debugging
bgroup              bgroup debugging
cav                 cavium debugging
cluster             command propagated to cluster members
cpu-limit           CPU limit debugging
dhcp                debug dhcp
dhcp6               dhcpv6 debugging
dialer              dialer debugging
dip                 dip debugging
dlog                dlog debugging
dns                 dns debugging
dot1x               IEEE802.1X debug
driver              driver debugging
emweb               EmWeb debugging
filesys             Filesys debugging
fips                fips debugging
flash               flash operating debugging
flow                Flow level debugging
flow-tunnel         Flow Tunnel debugging
fr                  Frame-Relay debugging
fs                  file system debugging
gc                  gc receive and transmit debug
gdb                 GDB debugging
```

```
global-pro              global-pro debugging
gt                      generic tunnel debugging
gtmac                   gtmac debug
h323                    h323 debugging
hdlc                    HDLC debugging
httpfx                  http-fx debugging
icap                    ICAP debugging
icmp                    icmp debugging
idp                     set idp debug parameters
ids                     ids debugging
igmp                    igmp debugging
ike                     ike debugging
interface               interface debugging
intfe                   Intfe debugging
ip                      ip debugging
ipacx                   isdn ipacx driver debugging
ipv6                    ipv6 debugging
isdn                    isdn debugging
ixf                     ixf debug
ixp23xxdrv              ixp23xx driver debugging
l2tp                    L2TP debugging
lance                   Lance debugging
ldap                    ldap debug menu
logging                 logging debugging
memory                  Memory debugging
mgcp                    mgcp debugging
midwayipacx             isdn ipacx driver debugging
mip                     mip debugging
ml                      Multilink debugging
modem                   Moden debugging
nas                     nas debugging
nasa                    nasa debugging
nat                     nat debugging
ndp                     ndp debugging
netif                   netif debugging
nhrp                    nhrp debugging
npak                    npak debugging
nrtp                    Reliable Xfer Protocol debugging
nsgp                    debug nsgp
nsmgmt                  debug nsmgmt
nsp                     NSM NSP message content
nsrd                    NSRD debugging
nsrp                    debug nsrp
obj-id                  obj id debugging
ospf                    ospf debugging
pbr                     policy-based routing debugging
pccard                  Pccard debugging
pim                     pim debugging
pki                     pki debug menu
pluto                   Pluto debugging
policy                  policy debugging
portnum                 portnum debugging
ppcdrv                  driver debugging
```

```
ppp                    ppp debugging
pppoa                  pppoa debugging
pppoe                  pppoe debugging
proxy                  tcp proxy debugging
rd                     rd debug info
registry               system events registry debugging
report                 report debugging
rip                    rip debugging
ripng                  ripng debugging
rm                     rm debugging
rms                    rms debug info
rpc                    rpc debugging
rs                     rs debug info
rtsync                 route-synchronization debugging
sa-mon                 sa monitor debugging
sccp                   sccp debugging
script                 script debugging
sctp                   gprs sctp debugging
sendmail               sendmail debugging
session                session debugging
shaper                 debug shaper
shdsl                  G.SHDSL debug
sip                    sip debugging
snmp                   snmpnew debugging
socket                 socket debug
ssh                    debug ssh
ssl                    ssl debugging
stflow                 saturn flow debug info
sw-key                 software key debugging
syslog                 syslog debugging
tag                    tag info
task                   Task debugging
tcp                    tcp debug
telnet                 debug telnet
time                   device clock time debugging
timer                  Timer debugging
trackip                debug trackip
traffic                traffic control debugging
udp                    udp debugging
uf                     UF debugging
url-blk                url filtering debugging
usb                    usb debugging
user                   user/group database debugging
vip                    vip debugging
vr                     virtual router debugging
vrrp                   vrrp debugging
vsys                   vsys debugging
vwire                  VWIRE debugging
web                    WebUI debugging
webtrends              webtrends debugging
wlan                   wlan debugging
zone                   zone debugging
top-ssg140->
```

You can debug just about any function, and the amount of information can be staggering, so be careful what you ask for. Although it is beyond the scope of this book to detail each debug function, each chapter and recipe in this book may utilize debug to some extent. The most commonly used debug function is `debug flow`. Here are the specific flow options:

```
top-ssg140-> debug flow
all                     all flow debug
basic                   basic debug
drop                    drop pak debug
dynpol                  dynamic policy search debug
illegal                 illegal debug
internal                internal debug
mcast                   flow multicast debug
mgt                     mgt debug
mpak                    mp pak message debug
mpdiff                  mp diff message debug
mperr                   mp message error debug
mpgate                  mp gate message debug
mpmvpn                  mng over vpn message debug
mpsess                  mp session message debug
mpvpn                   mp vpn message debug
pak-poll                packet polling debug
profiling               flow profiling
self                    self debug
session                 session debug
sm-skip                 No pak passing to SM
spinlock                spinlock
tcp-sequence-check      tcp sequence check debug
tiny-tcp                tiny tcp debug
vlan                    vlan debug
```

Debug functions are very CPU-intensive, and best practice dictates that you enable them only when you require active data capture.

You can verify whether debug is currently enabled with `get debug`. You can disable debug by either pressing the Esc key or entering an `undebug` command:

```
top-ssg140-> get debug
flow: basic
top-ssg140-> <Esc> All debug off

top-ssg140-> get debug
top-ssg140->
top-ssg140-> debug flow basic
top-ssg140-> get debug
flow: basic
top-ssg140-> undebug flow
top-ssg140-> get debug
top-ssg140->
```

Flow Filter

Although debug is intended to capture detailed information, rarely is a single flow going through the firewall at any given time. Therefore, it is important to be able to restrict the information gathered by debug to ensure that the buffer or CPU is not overloaded, or that other extraneous data is not captured as well, thus confusing the data we need. This is where flow filters come into play:

```
top-ssg140-> set ffilter ?
<return>
dst-ip                  flow filter dst ip
dst-port                flow filter dst port
ip-proto                flow filter ip proto
src-ip                  flow filter src ip
src-port                flow filter src port
top-ssg140->
```

Flow filters can be simple or complex. They can also be constructed with "or" or "and" logic. Flow-filter options specified in the same command (on the same line) will be "ANDed" together, which means that all the filters specified need to be matched to qualify. For example, if the data required was for a single flow and the source and destination addresses as well as the destination port are known, a flow filter such as the following would be constructed:

```
bottom-ssg140-> set ffilter src-ip 10.251.7.113 dst-ip 10.10.10.1
    ip-proto 1
filter added
bottom-ssg140-> get ffilter
Flow filter based on:
id:0 src ip 10.251.7.113 dst ip 10.10.10.1 ip proto 1
bottom-ssg140->
```

This flow filter will capture all traffic sourced only from 10.251.7.113, and destined to 10.10.10.1 and IP protocol 1, the Internet Control Message Protocol (ICMP).

Flow-filter options specified on separate lines are "ORed" together, which means that a match of any of the filters specified will qualify. For example, if some portion of the flow is unknown, or if all data to a specific host on a variety of ports is to be captured, the following would be constructed:

```
bottom-ssg140-> set ffilter dst-ip 10.10.10.1 ip-proto 6 dst-port 22
filter added
bottom-ssg140-> set ffilter dst-ip 10.10.10.1 ip-proto 6 dst-port 23
filter added
bottom-ssg140-> get ffilter
Flow filter based on:
id:0 src ip 10.251.7.113 dst ip 10.10.10.1 ip proto 1
id:1 dst ip 10.10.10.1 ip proto 6 dst port 22
id:2 dst ip 10.10.10.1 ip proto 6 dst port 23
bottom-ssg140->
```

This set of flow filters will capture the data as described earlier; or traffic sourced from any host and destined to 10.10.10.1 and IP protocol 6, TCP, and destination port 22, SSH; or traffic sourced from any host and destined to 10.10.10.1 and IP protocol 6, TCP, and destination port 23, Telnet.

Often it is desired to capture data to (`dst`) or from (`src`) a particular host. You can do this on two separate lines:

```
bottom-ssg140-> set ffilter dst-ip 10.251.7.97
filter added
bottom-ssg140-> set ffilter src-ip 10.251.7.97
filter added
bottom-ssg140-> get ffilter
Flow filter based on:
id:0 src ip 10.251.7.113 dst ip 10.10.10.1 ip proto 1
id:1 dst ip 10.10.10.1 ip proto 6 dst port 22
id:2 dst ip 10.10.10.1 ip proto 6 dst port 23
id:3 dst ip 10.251.7.97
id:4 src ip 10.251.7.97
bottom-ssg140->
```

This set of flow filters will filter the data destined to or sourced from the 10.251.7.97 host.

To manage the flow filters, you assign each one an identification number starting with 0, using the nomenclature `id:`*n*. The administrator can delete an individual flow filter by specifying it in the command or the flow filter with `id:0`, which is the default behavior when no flow filter ID is specified:

```
bottom-ssg140-> unset ffilter 1
filter 1 removed
bottom-ssg140-> get ffilter
Flow filter based on:
id:0 src ip 10.251.7.113 dst ip 10.10.10.1 ip proto 1
id:1 dst ip 10.10.10.1 ip proto 6 dst port 23
id:2 dst ip 10.251.7.97
id:3 src ip 10.251.7.97
bottom-ssg140-> unset ffilter
filter 0 removed
bottom-ssg140-> get ff
Flow filter based on:
id:0 dst ip 10.10.10.1 ip proto 6 dst port 23
id:1 dst ip 10.251.7.97
id:2 src ip 10.251.7.97
```

Debug Buffer

The debug buffer (`dbuf` or `db`) is the local buffer of memory on the firewall for troubleshooting tools in which to write output. It is possible to dump this data to the console screen, but that is unwise as it may lead to overrunning the console and being unable to break into the flow to stop it and regain console access. You can see the actual size of the debug buffer in bytes by issuing the `get sys-cfg` or `get db info` command:

```
bottom-ssg140-> get db info
count: 9816, last index: 9816, cur index: 0, size: 131072
start: 0, pause: 0
bottom-ssg140-> get sys-cfg | inc dbuf
dbuf number: 131072
```

You can increase this via the CLI. However, you must be careful to ensure that enough resources are available on the system:

```
bottom-ssg140-> set db size
<number>            size in kilobytes of debug buffer[from 32 to 4096]
bottom-ssg140-> get mem
Memory: allocated 46520432, left 235763184, frag 8, fail 0
bottom-ssg140-> set db size 256
bottom-ssg140-> get db info
count: 9816, last index: 9816, cur index: 0, size: 262144
start: 0, pause: 0
bottom-ssg140-> get mem
Memory: allocated 46651488, left 235632128, frag 9, fail 0
bottom-ssg140->
```

In the preceding code, we have increased the buffer size from the default of 128 KB to 256 KB. Note that this decreased the available memory by 128 KB; remember that ScreenOS is a real-time operating system. The SSG140 platform will accept a debug buffer size of up to 4 MB.

It is a good idea to clear the debug buffer, with `clear dbuf`, before each debug session to ensure that the buffer will capture the data intended based on the flow-filter settings and time of capture. The following is some example output of the most common option, `debug flow basic`:

```
top-ssg140-> get dbuf stream
****** 88482.0: <Trust/eth0/0> packet received [60]******
/*Packet received
  ipid = 53693(d1bd), @d7812070
/*Create fingerprint for packet/session
  eth0/0:10.251.7.113/2816->20.20.20.2/512,1(8/0)
/*Describe packet, src/dst IP, etc
  IP classification from non-shared src if : vsys none
/*Determine if part of a VSYS
  search route to 20.20.20.2 in vr trust-vr for 0/0
/*Perform route lookup
  route 20.20.20.2->20.20.20.2, to eth0/1
/*Describe route
  routed 20.20.20.2 from eth0/0 (eth0/0 in 0) to eth0/1
/*Route packet
  pak loopback to zone Trust
/*Describe filter set (trust-trust in this case)
  vsd 0 is active
/*Describe redundancy status
  policy id = 13(Permit), tunnel = 0
```

```
/*Which policy matches, which tunnel (13, none)
  Session created for first pack,
/*Create session
  find matched sess id:4722
/*Describe SessionID
  core pak
/*Send to forwarding engine
  vsd 0 is active
/*Verify redundancy status
  flow_ip_send: d1bd:10.251.7.113->20.20.20.2,1 => eth0/1(60)
/*Queue packet
  no mac in session
/*Look up MAC address
  arp entry found for 20.20.20.2
/*Find MAC
  Send to eth0/1 (74)
/*Send packet
****** 88482.0: <Trust/ethernet7> packet received [60]******
/*Packet received
  ipid = 43579(aa3b), @d78c3070
/*Create fingerprint
  eth0/1:20.20.20.2/512->10.251.7.113/2816,1(0/0)
/*Describe packet, src/dst IP, etc
  find matched sess id:4722
/*Find session from above
  core pak
/*Send to forwarding engine
  vsd 0 is active
/*Verify redundancy status
  flow_ip_send: aa3b:20.20.20.2->10.251.7.113,1 => eth0/0(60)
  @d78c3070
/*Queue packet
  mac 0010db13cbd0 in session
/*No MAC lookup necessary, in session from request
  Send to eth0/0 (74)
/*Send packet
top-ssg140->
```

You can display the output to the console or redirect it to a TFTP server with the following:

```
bottom-ssg140-> get db stream > tftp 10.251.7.113 login_debug.txt
redirect to 10.251.7.113,login_debug.txt
!!!!!!!!!!!!!!!!!!!!!!!!!!!!!!!!!!!!!!!!!!!!!!!!!!!!!!!!!!!!!!!!!!!!!!!!!!!!!!
!!!!!!!!!!!!!!!!!!!!!!!!!!!!!!!!!!!!!!!!!!!!!!!!!!!!!!!!!!!!!!!!!!!!!!!!!!!!!!
!!!!!!!!!!!!!!!!!!!!!!!!!!!!!!

...

!!!!!!!!!!!!!!!!!!!!!!!!!!!!!!!!!!!!!!!!!!!!!!!!!!!!!!!!!!!!!!!!!!!!!!!!!!!!!!
!!!!!!!!!!!!!!!!!!!!!!!!!!!!
tftp transferred records = 378
tftp success!
bottom-ssg140->
```

Snoop

Another useful tool is snoop. Snoop differs from the debug tool in that snoop's primary function is to show what the packet looks like on the wire when it enters or leaves an interface, similar to an external sniffer, but minus the payload. You can view Layer 1–4 information as well as up to 1,514 bytes of hex data. Often, snoop will be used to validate that the device is receiving or sending a packet when debug flow isn't providing an expected output. You can then apply filtering to tune what is captured, as shown here:

```
bottom-ssg140-> snoop info
Snoop: OFF
Filters Defined: 0, Active Filters 0
Detail: OFF, Detail Display length: 96
```

Snoop does not use flow filters, but it does allow a different filter system that is similar in structure to tcpdump. For example, the following filter will capture traffic between hosts 10.251.7.113 and 10.10.10.1 on port 23:

```
bottom-ssg140-> snoop filter ip src-ip 10.251.7.113 dst-port 23
snoop filter added
bottom-ssg140-> snoop filter ip src-ip 10.10.10.1 src-port 23
snoop filter added
bottom-ssg140-> snoop info
Snoop: OFF
Filters Defined: 2, Active Filters 2
Detail: OFF, Detail Display length: 1
Snoop filter based on:
id 1(on): IP src-ip 10.251.7.113 dst-port 23 dir(B)
id 2(on): IP src-ip 10.10.10.1 src-port 23 dir(B)
bottom-ssg140->
```

Just like with debug, it is good to clear the debug buffer before enabling snoop:

```
bottom-ssg140-> clear dbuf
bottom-ssg140-> snoop
Start Snoop, type ESC or 'snoop off' to stop, continue? [y]/n y
bottom-ssg140->
bottom-ssg140-> get dbuf stream
32616.0: ethernet0/0(i) len=62:00166f027720->0017cb479400/0800
              10.251.7.113 -> 10.10.10.1/6
              vhl=45, tos=00, id=45238, frag=0000, ttl=128 tlen=48
              tcp:ports 4646->23, seq=6684683, ack=0, flag=7002/SYN

32616.0: ethernet0/2(o) len=62:0017cb479406->0017cb478d06/0800
              10.251.7.113 -> 10.10.10.1/6
              vhl=45, tos=00, id=45238, frag=0000, ttl=127 tlen=48
              tcp:ports 4646->23, seq=6684683, ack=0, flag=7002/SYN
```

Here is the initial TCP SYN packet, from 10.251.7.113 coming inbound, (i), on interface ethernet0/0, being sent outbound, (o), on ethernet0/2:

```
32616.0: ethernet0/2(i) len=62:0017cb478d06->0017cb479406/0800
   10.10.10.1 -> 10.251.7.113/6
```

```
    vhl=45, tos=00, id=1434, frag=0000, ttl=64 tlen=44
    tcp:ports 23->4646, seq=1569021109, ack=6684684, flag=6012/SYN/ACK

32616.0: ethernet0/0(o) len=58:0017cb479400->00166f027720/0800
    10.10.10.1 -> 10.251.7.113/6
    vhl=45, tos=00, id=1434, frag=0000, ttl=63 tlen=44
    tcp:ports 23->4646, seq=1569021109, ack=6684684, flag=6012/SYN/ACK
```

Here is the TCP SYN/ACK sequence acknowledging the SYN and sending its own SYN segment coming inbound, (i), on ethernet0/2 and then being sent outbound, (o), on ethernet0/0:

```
32616.0: ethernet0/0(i) len=60:00166f027720->0017cb479400/0800
    10.251.7.113 -> 10.10.10.1/6
    vhl=45, tos=00, id=45241, frag=0000, ttl=128 tlen=40
    tcp:ports 4646->23, seq=6684684, ack=1569021110, flag=5010/ACK

32616.0: ethernet0/2(o) len=54:0017cb479406->0017cb478d06/0800
    10.251.7.113 -> 10.10.10.1/6
    vhl=45, tos=00, id=45241, frag=0000, ttl=127 tlen=40
    tcp:ports 4646->23, seq=6684684, ack=1569021110, flag=5010/ACK
```

Last is the TCP ACK to complete the TCP three-way handshake and move the session from an embryonic state to a full connection state. ScreenOS has an internal timer of 20 seconds to complete the three-way handshake or delete the embryonic session from the state table.

```
32872.0: ethernet0/0(i) len=60:00166f027720->0017cb479400/0800
    10.251.7.113 -> 10.10.10.1/6
    vhl=45, tos=00, id=46850, frag=0000, ttl=128 tlen=40
    tcp:ports 4646->23, seq=6684723, ack=1569021177, flag=5011/FIN/ACK

32872.0: ethernet0/2(o) len=54:0017cb479406->0017cb478d06/0800
    10.251.7.113 -> 10.10.10.1/6
    vhl=45, tos=00, id=46850, frag=0000, ttl=127 tlen=40
    tcp:ports 4646->23, seq=6684723, ack=1569021177, flag=5011/FIN/ACK
```

The starting TCP FIN/ACK sequence acknowledging the last packet received and starting the FIN process looks like this:

```
32872.0: ethernet0/2(i) len=60:0017cb478d06->0017cb479406/0800
    10.10.10.1 -> 10.251.7.113/6
    vhl=45, tos=00, id=1439, frag=0000, ttl=64 tlen=40
    tcp:ports 23->4646, seq=1569021177, ack=6684724, flag=5019/FIN/ACK

32872.0: ethernet0/0(o) len=54:0017cb479400->00166f027720/0800
    10.10.10.1 -> 10.251.7.113/6
    vhl=45, tos=00, id=1439, frag=0000, ttl=63 tlen=40
    tcp:ports 23->4646, seq=1569021177, ack=6684724, flag=5019/FIN/ACK
```

Then, the TCP FIN/ACK packet coming from the other host acknowledges the FIN and sends its own:

```
32872.0: ethernet0/0(i) len=60:00166f027720->0017cb479400/0800
   10.251.7.113 -> 10.10.10.1/6
   vhl=45, tos=00, id=46851, frag=0000, ttl=128 tlen=40
   tcp:ports 4646->23, seq=6684724, ack=1569021178, flag=5010/ACK

32872.0: ethernet0/2(o) len=54:0017cb479406->0017cb478d06/0800
   10.251.7.113 -> 10.10.10.1/6
   vhl=45, tos=00, id=46851, frag=0000, ttl=127 tlen=40
   tcp:ports 4646->23, seq=6684724, ack=1569021178, flag=5010/ACK
```

Finally, the last TCP `ACK` packet is received, acknowledging the `FIN` and closing out the TCP session (this is with default settings on snoop, which shows the entire IP and TCP header information—essential when troubleshooting and you need to know what a packet looked like when entering and leaving the firewall).

CHAPTER 2

Firewall Configuration and Management

2.0 Introduction

This chapter will build on Chapter 1 and move on to describing how to manage the movement of data onto and off of the firewall. We will also describe some best practice approaches to control access to and manage ScreenOS in your environment.

2.1 Use TFTP to Transfer Information to and from the Firewall

Problem

You are troubleshooting an issue and need to save captured data currently on the firewall to a file, back up the current configuration, and then upload a new version of code, all with the Trivial File Transfer Protocol (TFTP).

Solution

Use the "redirect to TFTP" capability in the CLI to copy the information to your TFTP server:

```
top-ssg140-> get log event > tftp 10.251.7.113 eventlog.txt
redirect to 10.251.7.113,eventlog.txt
!!!!!!!!!!!!!!!!!!!!!!!!!!!!!!!!!
tftp transferred records = 15
tftp success!
top-ssg140->
```

Then, back up the existing configuration:

```
top-ssg140-> save config to tftp 10.251.7.113
    borderfw1_config_021107_1215.txt
Read the current config.
Save configurations (3918 bytes) to borderfw1_config_021107_1215.txt
on TFTP server 10.251.7.113.
```

```
!!!!!!!!!!!!!!!!!!!
tftp transferred records = 8
tftp success!

TFTP Succeeded
top-ssg140->
```

Lastly, copy the new version of the ScreenOS software to your firewall and save it:

```
top-ssg140-> save software from tftp 10.251.7.113 ssg140.6.0.0r1.0
    to flash
Load software from 10.251.7.113/ssg140.6.0.0r1.0 .
!!!!!!!!!!!!!!!!!!!!!!!!!!!!!!!!!!!!!!!!!!!!!!!!!!!!!!!!!!!!!!!!!!!
...
!!!!!!!!!!!!!!!!!!!!!!!!!!!!!!!!!!!!!!!!!!!!!!
tftp received octets = 11141120
tftp success!

TFTP Succeeded
top-ssg140->
```

Discussion

One of the challenges with a real-time, in-memory operating system such as ScreenOS (with no additional onboard hard drive for storage) is that you need to carefully manage the available buffers. This is especially true when troubleshooting because ScreenOS will overwrite space when the particular buffer fills up.

Here are some examples of some of these limits from an SSG140 device:

```
top-ssg140-> get sys-cfg | inc " log"
dlog session log pool number: 512
event log entry number: 1024
packet log entry number: 512
traffic log entry number: 4096
top-ssg140-> get sys-cfg | inc dbuf
dbuf number: 524288
top-ssg140->
```

As you can see, finite buffers are defined for numbers of entries or amounts of dedicated memory. During normal operation with appropriate log settings, the logs will be sent off to the NetScreen Security Manager (NSM), or a syslog server, before the buffer wraps around and overwriting begins. However, when troubleshooting, it's easy to exceed these numbers and start to overwrite before you can capture the data you want. The "redirect to TFTP" function can be useful for capturing this data before overwriting begins.

You can use TFTP to upload and download a variety of information to and from the firewall, including the following:

- ScreenOS software
- ScreenOS configuration files

- ScreenOS licenses
- Firewall logs (event, system, asset-recovery, and self)
- Debug buffers (`dbuf`)
- Session tables
- Any information displayable to the console

Here, we demonstrated how to copy data (a log event file) from the firewall to TFTP server 10.251.7.113. We did this using a redirect (indicated by the >). Remember that when performing a redirect, you are really taking a snapshot of the data that is there. It is common to use a script to do continuous TFTPs when troubleshooting over time.

The second step of the copying process illustrates a best practice, which is to copy the current firewall configuration to a file on the TFTP server. The final step involves using TFTP to download a new ScreenOS software version to the firewall.

TFTP is inherently an insecure form of file transfer. Common problems with TFTP concern routing on the firewall and configuration of the TFTP server, which are beyond the scope of this book; however, an example was discussed on the Juniper Support site Knowledge Base at the time of this book's printing (see *http://kb.juniper.net/KB5210*). A more secure file transfer option is to use SCP, which we discuss in the next recipe.

2.2 Use SCP to Securely Transfer Information to and from the Firewall

Problem

You want to use Secure Copy (SCP) to save the firewall configuration and then upload a new version of the ScreenOS software.

Solution

First, enable the Secure Shell (SSH) server on the firewall:

```
top-ssg140-> set ssh enable
```

Next, enable the SCP server:

```
top-ssg140-> set scp enable
```

Transfer the file to the firewall:

```
ddelcourt@ddelcourt-lt2 ~/borderfw1
$ scp netscreen@192.168.2.254:ns_sys_config
    ./borderfw1_config_021107_1230.txt
netscreen@192.168.2.254's password: <password>
ns_sys_config                              100% 3835     3.8KB/s    00:00
```

```
ddelcourt@ddelcourt-lt2 ~/borderfw1
$ ls
borderfw1_config_021107_1230.txt
```

Finally, copy the software image to the firewall:

```
$ scp /tftpboot/ssg140.6.0.0r1.0 netscreen@192.168.2.254:image
netscreen@192.168.2.254's password: <password>
ssg140.6.0.0r1.0                    100% 10880KB  63.2KB/s   02:48
```

Discussion

SCP is really SFTP over an encrypted SSH session. It is inherently more secure than TFTP, and you could even use it to transfer information across the public Internet if required. You can manipulate any file listed under the get file command, including the ScreenOS image that is hidden in this listing.

We begin by enabling the SSH server functionality on the firewall with the set ssh enable command. Use the get ssh command to check that the expected version of SSH is running:

```
top-ssg140-> get ssh
SSH V2 is active
SSH is enabled
SSH is ready for connections
Maximum sessions: 8
Active sessions: 0

Admin      Ip Addr         Vsys       Auth Method Service
---------- --------------- ---------- ----------- --------
top-ssg140->
```

In ScreenOS 5.1 and later, the default version of SSH will be version 2. If you require that version 1 be used, refer to the Juniper Support site Knowledge Base article at *http://kb.juniper.net/KB6713*.

get ssh and get scp will show you whether SSH is enabled:

```
top-ssg140-> get ssh
SSH V2 is active
SSH is NOT enabled
SSH is NOT ready for connections
Maximum sessions: 8
Active sessions: 0

top-ssg140-> get scp
SCP is NOT enabled
SCP is NOT ready
top-ssg140->
```

Next, enable the SCP server (a commonly overlooked step):

```
top-ssg140-> set scp enable
top-ssg140-> get scp
SCP is enabled
```

```
SCP is ready
top-ssg140->
```

Transferring information via SCP is different than with TFTP; you need to know the specific file you are trying to upload or download. You can find a list of the files that can be manipulated by typing **get file** from the CLI:

```
top-ssg140-> get file
    flash:/envar.rec                       112
    flash:/dnstb.rec                         1
    flash:/dhcpservl.txt                    68
    flash:/ns_sys_config                  1183
    flash:/$lkg$.cfg                      1210
    flash:/license.key                     730
    flash:/expire.rec                       24
    flash:/attacks.sig                  198833
top-ssg140->
```

In the case of the ScreenOS configuration file, you would be looking for *ns_sys_config*. From the SCP client side, enter the following:

```
ddelcourt@ddelcourt-lt2 ~/borderfw1
$ scp netscreen@192.168.2.254:ns_sys_config
    ./borderfw1_config_021107_1230.txt
netscreen@192.168.2.254's password: <password>
ns_sys_config                          100% 3835     3.8KB/s    00:00

ddelcourt@ddelcourt-lt2 ~/borderfw1
$ ls
borderfw1_config_021107_1230.txt
```

You can monitor progress on the firewall as well:

```
top-ssg140-> get ssh
SSH V2 is active
SSH is enabled
SSH is ready for connections
Maximum sessions: 8
Active sessions: 1

Admin      Ip Addr         Vsys       Auth Method Service
---------- --------------- ---------- ----------- --------
netscreen  10.251.7.116    Root       password    scp
top-ssg140->
```

Lastly, upgrade the firewall to the recommended version of code. From the SCP client side, enter the following:

```
$ scp /tftpboot/ns200.5.4.0r1.0 netscreen@192.168.2.254:image
netscreen@192.168.2.254's password: <password>
ssg140.6.0.0r1.0                       100% 10880KB  63.2KB/s   02:48
```

You can verify results from the firewall in the event log:

```
top-ssg140-> get log event
Total event entries = 67
```

```
Date       Time     Module Level  Type Description
2007-02-11 12:37:26 system notif 00026 SCP: Admin user 'netscreen'
                                       transferred file 'image' to
                                       device from host 10.251.7.116.
2007-02-11 12:34:16 system warn  00528 SSH: Password authentication
                                       successful for admin user
                                       'netscreen' at host
                                       10.251.7.116.
```

2.3 Use the Dedicated MGT Interface to Manage the Firewall

Problem

The firewall must be connected to a dedicated sideband, or out-of-band management network, via the onboard management interface (applicable only to platforms with a dedicated MGT port).

Solution

Configure all user traffic security zones to be in the untrust-vr:

```
isg1000-> set zone trust vr untrust-vr
isg1000-> set zone untrust vr untrust-vr
```

Configure IP addressing on the interfaces:

```
isg1000-> set interface e1/1 route
isg1000-> set interface e1/1 zone trust
isg1000-> set interface e1/1 ip 10.251.7.99/29
isg1000-> set interface e1/2 zone untrust
isg1000-> set interface e1/2 ip 10.10.10.254/24
isg1000-> set interface mgt ip 10.20.20.1/28
```

Configure routing in the trust-vr for the MGT interface:

```
isg1000-> set vr trust route 0.0.0.0/0 interface mgt gateway
   10.20.20.14
```

Configure routing in the untrust-vr for user traffic:

```
isg1000-> set vr untrust route 0.0.0.0/0 interface e1/2 gateway
    64.2.31.249
isg1000-> set vr untrust route 10.100.0.0/16 interface e3 gateway
    10.100.1.1
```

Discussion

The issue at hand is how to configure the firewall to use the onboard MGT interface connected to a dedicated sideband or out-of-band management network. Another way to solve this problem is to ensure that every management host that the firewall will ever need to communicate with is on the same local IP network subnet as the MGT interface IP. If this is the case, and no routes need to be added, specific or default, for the MGT interface to communicate with the systems required (such as syslog, NSM, the Network Time Protocol [NTP], etc.), nothing more needs to be done.

However, this is not the case in the vast majority of networks, as common services are often on separate network segments to be accessed by users and servers as well as the network devices.

Using this as the basis for discussion, it is important to understand how the MGT interface works and differs from other interfaces on the firewall. The dedicated MGT interface behaves like a "host" interface—in other words, traffic terminates on this interface, and cannot be routed through the firewall to any other interface and vice versa. The MGT interface is in the MGT functional zone, as described in Recipe 1.1, and this zone is in the trust-vr. You cannot change this mapping. If all the zones, and therefore all the interfaces, are in the same Virtual Router (VR), it means they share the same routing table.

```
isg1000-> get route


IPv4 Dest-Routes for <untrust-vr> (0 entries)
----------------------------------------------------------------------
H: Host C: Connected S: Static A: Auto-Exported
I: Imported R: RIP P: Permanent D: Auto-Discovered
N: NHRP
iB: IBGP eB: EBGP O: OSPF E1: OSPF external type 1
E2: OSPF external type 2 trailing B: backup route


IPv4 Dest-Routes for <trust-vr> (11 entries)
---------------------------------------------------------------------
   ID         IP-Prefix  Interface        Gateway  P Pref  Mtr   Vsys
---------------------------------------------------------------------
*   7         0.0.0.0/0     eth1/2    64.2.31.249  S   20    1   Root
*   8      10.15.0.0/29     eth1/1    10.251.7.97  S   20    1   Root
*   5     10.20.20.0/28        mgt        0.0.0.0  C    0    0   Root
*   6     10.20.20.1/32        mgt        0.0.0.0  H    0    0   Root
*  10  137.237.51.0/29      eth1/1    10.251.7.97  S   20    1   Root
*  11 137.237.51.32/28      eth1/1    10.251.7.97  S   20    1   Root
*   1    10.251.7.96/27     eth1/1        0.0.0.0  C    0    0   Root
*   2    10.251.7.99/32     eth1/1        0.0.0.0  H    0    0   Root
*   9    11.1.255.48/29     eth1/1    10.251.7.97  S   20    1   Root
*   4    64.2.31.254/29     eth1/2        0.0.0.0  H    0    0   Root
*   3    64.2.31.248/29     eth1/2        0.0.0.0  C    0    0   Root

isg1000->
```

Because the MGT interface behaves like a host, it must have routing to allow it to connect to services on other parts of the network. Generally, you can accomplish this by setting a default route, just like a PC has, or via explicit routes. Either way, this route information will be different from the route information required for other data forwarding interfaces.

```
isg1000-> set route 0.0.0.0/0 interface mgt gateway 10.20.20.14
isg1000-> get route


IPv4 Dest-Routes for <untrust-vr> (0 entries)
--------------------------------------------------------------------
H: Host C: Connected S: Static A: Auto-Exported
I: Imported R: RIP P: Permanent D: Auto-Discovered
N: NHRP
iB: IBGP eB: EBGP O: OSPF E1: OSPF external type 1
E2: OSPF external type 2 trailing B: backup route


IPv4 Det-Routes for <trust-vr> (12 entries)
--------------------------------------------------------------------
   ID          IP-Prefix Interface         Gateway   P Pref Mtr    Vsys
--------------------------------------------------------------------
*   7          0.0.0.0/0    eth1/2    64.2.31.249   S   20    1   Root
*   8       10.15.0.0/29    eth1/1    10.251.7.97   S   20    1   Root
*   5      10.20.20.0/28       mgt        0.0.0.0   C    0    0   Root
*   6      10.20.20.1/32       mgt        0.0.0.0   H    0    0   Root
*  10    137.237.51.0/29    eth1/1    10.251.7.97   S   20    1   Root
*  11   137.237.51.32/28    eth1/1    10.251.7.97   S   20    1   Root
*   1     10.251.7.96/27    eth1/1        0.0.0.0   C    0    0   Root
*   2     10.251.7.99/32    eth1/1        0.0.0.0   H    0    0   Root
*   9     11.1.255.48/29    eth1/1    10.251.7.97   S   20    1   Root
*   4    64.2.31.254/29     eth1/2        0.0.0.0   H    0    0   Root
*   3    64.2.31.248/29     eth1/2        0.0.0.0   C    0    0   Root
*  12          0.0.0.0/0       mgt    10.20.20.14   S   20    1   Root

isg1000->
```

You can see that there are now multiple default routes, and the firewall will need to choose one when making forwarding decisions for interfaces in the `trust-vr`. Which one will it use?

```
isg1000-> get vr trust route 0.0.0.0
Dest for 0.0.0.0
--------------------------------------------------------------------
trust-vr       : => 0.0.0.0/0 (id=7) via 64.2.31.249 (vr: trust-vr)
                    Interface ethernet1/2 , metric 1
trust-vr       : => 0.0.0.0/0 (id=12) via 10.20.20.14 (vr: trust-vr)
                    Interface mgt , metric 1
```

ScreenOS will use the one that is listed first in the Forwarding Information Base (FIB). You can verify this by looking up the route ID (seen in parentheses in the output):

```
isg1000-> get route id 7
route in trust-vr:
------------------------------------------------
id:                    7
IP address/mask:       0.0.0.0/0
next hop (gateway):    64.2.31.249
```

```
preference:             20
metric:                 1
outgoing interface:     ethernet1/2
vsys name/id:           Root/0
tag:                    0
flag:                   24000040/00100001
type:                   static
Redistributed to:
status:                 active (for 47 seconds)

its next entry in FIB:
id:                     12
IP address/mask:        0.0.0.0/0
next hop (gateway):     10.20.20.14
preference:             20
metric:                 1
outgoing interface:     mgt
vsys name/id:           Root/0
tag:                    0
flag:                   24000040/00100001
type:                   static
Redistributed to:
status:                 active (for 49 seconds)
isg1000->
```

In this case, the route with an `id` of `7` is listed first (it's not always going to be the lowest route ID), so it will be chosen. The result of this configuration is that user traffic going through interface `ethernet1/2` will be fine; however, management traffic will not be able to get off the 10.20.20.0/28 network.

The best practice solution is to put all the user traffic zones in a different VR. The good news is that ScreenOS provides two VRs, with no additional licensing, on all platforms. You really should do this during the initial architecture design phase to ensure that the zones are bound correctly, before building the IP configuration and routing associated with the interface.

Remember that no detail is too small to consider, and although having an out-of-band or sideband management network solves some security concerns, it can also create complexity in the configuration of the network devices that will connect to it for management access.

2.4 Control Access to the Firewall

Problem

Users in different parts of the enterprise, or distributed NOC/SOC centers, must manage the firewall, and they must be able to access common services.

Solution

Determine the interface(s) that will accept management traffic, and then configure the management protocols to be accepted:

```
top-ssg140-> set interface e0/0 manage ping
top-ssg140-> set interface e0/0 manage ssh
top-ssg140-> set interface e0/2 manage ping
top-ssg140-> set interface e0/0 manage-ip 10.251.7.100
```

Next, determine how the firewall will reach management services:

```
top-ssg140-> set syslog src-interface e0/0
top-ssg140-> set ntp server src-interface e0/0
top-ssg140-> set snmp host public 10.251.7.113/32 src-interface e0/0
top-ssg140-> set tftp source-interface e0/0
top-ssg140-> set nsmgmt server primary 10.251.7.113 src-interface
    e0/0
```

Now, define which network host(s) and/or address(es) can access the firewall:

```
top-ssg140-> set admin manager-ip 10.100.41.0/24
top-ssg140-> set admin manager-ip 10.100.100.200/32
top-ssg140-> set admin manager-ip 10.100.100.201/32
top-ssg140-> set admin manager-ip 10.100.29.3/32
top-ssg140-> set admin manager-ip 10.251.7.96/27
top-ssg140-> set admin manager-ip 192.168.30.0/24
```

Change the root admin account, and configure individual admins:

```
top-ssg140-> set admin name <root_adminname> password <password>
top-ssg140-> set admin user name <adminname> password <password>
    privilege all
top-ssg140-> set admin user name <adminname> password <password>
    privilege read-only
```

Finally, configure the login banner:

```
top-ssg140-> set admin auth banner <string>
```

Discussion

Although it is certainly a best practice to lock down management access to the firewall, it is easy to overlook all the functions that you can control and fine-tune within ScreenOS. Securing the firewall requires a holistic approach, as described earlier, and each additional knob turned or tuning performed provides another layer of protection against unauthorized users accessing the firewall. A basic primer of these layers of control includes the following:

- Which hosts can manage the firewall? (Answer: `manager-ip`)
- Who can manage the firewall? (Answer: admins and privileged users)
- Which services/protocols can be accessed? (Answer: `set int` *<interface>* `manage [ping|telnet|SSH|SNMP|ssl|web]`, etc.)
- Which IP on the firewall will be reachable? (Answer: `set int` *<interface>* `manage-ip a.b.c.d`)

Most administrators will control what protocols should be enabled, but they may not realize that there are different settings on the interface depending on whether it is associated with a predefined or a custom security zone. This fact is the foundation for access to the firewall, and one must consider *where* management traffic will be coming from (because it is generally best to manage to the closest interface as opposed to through the firewall) as well as *why* it should be allowed on that interface:

```
top-ssg140-> get int e0/0
Interface ethernet0/0:
  description ethernet0/0
  number 0, if_info 0, if_index 0, mode route
  link up, phy-link up/full-duplex
  vsys Root, zone Trust, vr trust-vr
  dhcp client disabled
  PPPoE disabled
  admin mtu 0, operating mtu 1500, default mtu 1500
  ip 10.251.7.99/27   mac 0017.cb47.9400
  manage ip 10.251.7.100, mac 0017.cb47.9400
  route-deny disable
  pmtu-v4 disabled
  ping enabled, telnet enabled, SSH enabled, SNMP enabled
  web enabled, ident-reset disabled, SSL enabled
  DNS Proxy disabled, webauth disabled, webauth-ip 0.0.0.0
  OSPF disabled  BGP disabled  RIP disabled  RIPng disabled  mtrace
    disabled
  PIM: not configured  IGMP not configured
  NHRP disabled
  bandwidth: physical 100000kbps, configured egress [gbw 0kbps mbw
    0kbps]
             configured ingress mbw 0kbps, current bw 0kbps
             total allocated gbw 0kbps
  DHCP-Relay disabled at interface level
  DHCP-server disabled
Number of SW session: 56063, hw sess err cnt 0
top-ssg140->
top-ssg140-> get int e0/2
Interface ethernet0/2:
  description ethernet0/2
  number 9, if_info 7272, if_index 0, mode route
  link down, phy-link down
  vsys Root, zone Untrust, vr trust-vr
  dhcp client disabled
  PPPoE disabled
  admin mtu 0, operating mtu 1500, default mtu 1500
  *ip 64.12.100.5/29   mac 0017.cb47.9409
  *manage ip 64.12.100.5/29, mac 0017.cb47.9409
  pmtu-v4 disabled
  ping disabled, telnet disabled, SSH disabled, SNMP disabled
  web disabled, ident-reset disabled, SSL disabled
  DNS Proxy disabled, webauth disabled, webauth-ip 0.0.0.0
  OSPF disabled  BGP disabled  RIP disabled  RIPng disabled  mtrace
    disabled
```

```
  PIM: not configured  IGMP not configured
  NHRP disabled
  bandwidth: physical 0kbps, configured egress [gbw 0kbps mbw 0kbps]
             configured ingress mbw 0kbps, current bw 0kbps
             total allocated gbw 0kbps
Number of SW session: 56063, hw sess err cnt 0
top-ssg140->
top-ssg140-> get int e0/6
Interface ethernet0/6:
  description ethernet0/6
  number 10, if_info 8080, if_index 0, mode route
  link down, phy-link down
  vsys Root, zone WebServers, vr trust-vr
  dhcp client disabled
  PPPoE disabled
  admin mtu 0, operating mtu 1500, default mtu 1500
  *ip 0.0.0.0/0   mac 0017.cb47.940a
  *manage ip 0.0.0.0, mac 0017.cb47.940a
  pmtu-v4 disabled
  ping disabled, telnet disabled, SSH disabled, SNMP disabled
  web disabled, ident-reset disabled, SSL disabled
  DNS Proxy disabled, webauth disabled, webauth-ip 0.0.0.0
  OSPF disabled  BGP disabled  RIP disabled  RIPng disabled  mtrace
    disabled
  PIM: not configured  IGMP not configured
  NHRP disabled
  bandwidth: physical 0kbps, configured egress [gbw 0kbps mbw 0kbps]
             configured ingress mbw 0kbps, current bw 0kbps
             total allocated gbw 0kbps
Number of SW session: 56063, hw sess err cnt 0
top-ssg140->
```

As you can see, there are differences between the manageability of the firewall to interfaces in the default `Trust` and `Untrust` security zones, and that a custom-defined security zone defaults to a closed state just like `Untrust`. This means that it may actually take some `unset` or `set` commands to get the security posture required. Setting the `manage-ip` is the final step.

Next, determine how traffic sourced by the firewall will behave. By default, ScreenOS will use the routing table to determine where to send the data. However, ScreenOS does provide flexibility as to the interface from which to source for most of the management traffic. This allows for more granular management traffic control. If setting the source interface makes the management traffic flow through the firewall, it is subject to a policy check like any other traffic:

```
top-ssg140-> get policy
Total regular policies 4, Default deny.
  ID From     To       Src-address  Dst-address  Service  Action ...
   1 Untrust  Trust    Any          Any          PING     Deny   ...
   4 Untrust  Trust    Any          Any          PING     Permit ...
   2 Untrust  Trust    Any          Any          ANY      Permit ...
   3 Trust    Untrust  Any          Any          ANY      Permit ...
```

```
top-ssg140-> ping 10.251.7.113 from e0/2
Type escape sequence to abort

Sending 5, 100-byte ICMP Echos to 10.251.7.113, timeout is 1 seconds
from ethernet0/2
.....
Success Rate is 0 percent (0/5)
top-ssg140-> set policy id 1 disable
policy id = 1
top-ssg140-> ping 10.251.7.113 from e0/2
Type escape sequence to abort

Sending 5, 100-byte ICMP Echos to 10.251.7.113, timeout is 1 seconds
from ethernet0/2
!!!!!
Success Rate is 100 percent (5/5), round-trip time min/avg/max=1/2/6
   ms
top-ssg140->
```

It should be noted that if the "default-vr" setting is changed, it can have an impact on traffic sourced by the firewall.

The `manager-ip` setting provides very good protection, as the firewall will not process management requests from hosts or networks not on the list. ScreenOS provides the administrator with up to six host/network definitions for the entire system. Some customers go to great lengths to set up bastion or jump servers from which all communication to the firewall must originate, outside the NSM, and provide the firewall admin teams with flexibility, as they are generally on the move and not always coming from their desk IP addresses.

This, coupled with strict administrator account definition, can provide tight access control. It is recommended that you use either SecurID or the Remote Access Dial-In User Service (RADIUS) to manage the user accounts, as they will provide stronger password authentication options. In addition, it is a best practice to monitor failed login attempts; if the limit is exceeded, the syslog server or other log management system can generate an alert to notify the administrator of a potential intrusion attempt.

Lastly, the banner is not very common unless you are working in the financial or government sector. This does not provide any physical security, but it can lay the groundwork for providing the would-be-unauthorized user with a message letting him know his possible attempts to access the system are not welcome and may be tracked for legal action. There are many schools of thought here, and it is always prudent to work with legal counsel to ensure that the proposed language is defensible and appropriate. For more information about this see *http://www.cybercrime.gov/s&sappendix2002.htm* or *http://ciac.llnl.gov/ciac/bulletins/j-043.shtml*.

By default, ScreenOS is closed to management traffic unless it is destined for an interface in the `Trust` security zone. This can lead to a false sense of security as it has been proven that internal *trusted* personnel can do as much damage as someone from the outside. As a security device on the network that is depended upon to provide protection from unwanted users and applications, it is equally important to protect the firewall from unwanted access attempts. A layered approach is the best way to accomplish this using the many features within ScreenOS to keep tightening the loop.

Ultimately, as with any solution, this will be only as strong as the weakest link. If all measures are taken and the access method allowed is Telnet, or the password is a simple dictionary word, it would not take the average intruder very long to find a way in with the readily available attack tools on the Internet today (e.g., see *Security Power Tools* by Bryan Burns et al. [O'Reilly]).

2.5 Manage Multiple ScreenOS Images for Remotely Managed Firewalls

Problem

Remotely managed firewalls require a backup image to ensure an operational state in case of running image corruption.

Solution

During the boot sequence, press any key when prompted to "run loader":

```
Hit any key to run loader

Serial Number [0185122006000285]: READ ONLY
HW Version Number [1010]: READ ONLY
Self MAC Address [0017-cb47-9400]: READ ONLY
Boot File Name [ssg140.6.0.0r1.0]: ssg140.5.4.0r4.0
Self IP Address [192.168.1.1]: 10.251.7.99
TFTP IP Address [192.168.1.1]: 10.251.7.113

Save loader config (56 bytes)... Done
The configured TFTP server is connected to port 0


Loading file "ssg140.5.4.0r4.0"...
r
Receiving data block ...
#20384

Loaded Successfully! (size = 10,441,842 bytes)

Ignore image authentication!
```

Upon the prompt to save to flash, enter **m** for multiple image support:

```
Save to on-board flash disk? (y/[n]/m) m Yes!
```

Enter a filename that conforms to the DOS 8.3 naming convention standard:

```
Please input multiple system image file name [ssg14054.0]: 140540.r4

Saving system image to on-board flash disk...
Done! (size = 10,441,842 bytes)
```

Enter **n** when prompted to run the downloaded image:

```
Run downloaded system image? ([y]/n) n
```

Repeat this process for both images desired to be saved to flash memory. Then, set the boot order via the command line, and save the configuration:

```
bottom-ssg140-> set envar boot=flash:/140600.R1;140540.R4
bottom-ssg140-> save
Save System Configuration ...
Done
```

Discussion

This recipe leverages the onboard flash memory, which on the SSG140 used here is 64 MB. To verify that all the steps are followed, you must examine the filesystem on the flash memory:

```
bottom-ssg140-> get file
    flash:/$NSBOOT$.BIN                 11141120
    flash:/burnin_log1                     40960
    flash:/burnin_log0                     40960
    flash:/crash.dmp                      131072
    flash:/envar.rec                         125
    flash:/ns_sys_config                    1433
    flash:/prngseed.bin                       32
    flash:/images/
bottom-ssg140->
```

Not all the files are shown here. The *$NSBOOT$.BIN* is the active image that is in memory. The *ns_sys_config* file is the active ScreenOS configuration file that is in memory. To see everything written to flash memory, you must use a hidden command structure:

```
bottom-ssg140-> exec vfs ls flash:/
    $NSBOOT$.BIN            11,141,120
    golerd.rec              0
    node_secret.ace         0
    syscert.cfg             1,167
    certfile.cfg            1,324
    certfile.dsc            252
    burnin_log1             40,960
    burnin_log0             40,960
    crash.dmp               131,072
    envar.rec               93
    ns_sys_config           1,479
    prngseed.bin            32
    images/
    140600.R1               11,141,120
```

```
    140540.R4                  10,441,842
  4,294,967,295 bytes free (4,294,967,295 total) on disk
```

This exposes the images that were saved during the boot cycles, with the naming structure defined. Upon the next reboot, the image that was selected to boot first will be loaded; if it becomes corrupt, the second image will attempt to load.

```
bottom-ssg140-> get envar
default_image=ssg140.6.0.0r1.0
last_reset=2000-07-05 19:24:01 by netscreen
shdsl_pic_mode=0
boot=flash:/140600.R1;140540.R4
bottom-ssg140->
bottom-ssg140-> reset
System reset, are you sure? y/[n] y
In reset ...

Loading system image "/140600.R1" from on-board flash disk...
Done! (size = 11,141,120 bytes)

Ignore image authentication!

Start loading...
.................................................................
.................................................................
.................................................................
.................................................................
.................................................................
.................................................................
.................................................................
.................................................................
.................................................................
.......
Done.



Juniper Networks, Inc
Security Services Gateway System Software
Copyright, 1996-2006

min_pfn = 13000, max_pfn = 1c000, mem_size = 1c000000


 bootmap_size = 3800
Version 6.0.0r1.0

...

bottom-ssg140-> get system
Product Name: SSG-140
Serial Number: 0185122006000285, Control Number: ffffffff
Hardware Version: 1010(0)-(00), FPGA checksum: 00000000, VLAN1 IP
    (0.0.0.0)
Software Version: 6.0.0r1.0, Type: Firewall+VPN
```

This practice is very useful in testing environments where multiple versions of code must be run to verify feature functionality, the presence or disappearance of bugs, and general performance testing.

2.6 Manage the USB Port on SSG

Problem

The firewall cannot access a TFTP server as described in Recipe 2.1 and the image or configuration file must be pulled from a Universal Serial Bus (USB) memory stick.

Solution

First, ensure that the correct image is on the USB stick:

```
ddelcourt@ddelcourt-lt /cygdrive/g
$ ls
Customer    Recycled      Dept Stuff  Tools    Misc
md5sum.exe  ssg140.5.4.0r4.0 ssg140.6.0.0r1.0

ddelcourt@ddelcourt-lt /cygdrive/g
```

Safely remove the USB stick from the PC/system and insert it into the USB slot on the SSG, and then verify that ScreenOS recognizes it and can list the files:

```
bottom-ssg140->
LEXAR MEDIA JUMPDRIVE, rev 2.00/30.00, addr 2, SCSI over Bulk-Only

Mount usb device. Please wait...
usb device (usb) ready.

bottom-ssg140-> get file
    flash:/$NSBOOT$.BIN            11141120
    flash:/burnin_log1                40960
    flash:/burnin_log0                40960
    flash:/crash.dmp                 131072
    flash:/envar.rec                    125
    flash:/ns_sys_config               1433
    flash:/prngseed.bin                  32
    flash:/images/

USB flash device :
    usb:/.Trashes/
    usb:/ssg140.6.0.0r1.0          11141120
    usb:/ssg140.5.4.0r4.0          10485760
    usb:/Customer/
    usb:/Misc/
    usb:/Tools/
    usb:/Dept Stuff/
    usb:/md5sum.exe                   34816
    usb:/Recycled/
bottom-ssg140->
```

Save the desired version of ScreenOS to flash memory:

```
bottom-ssg140-> save software from usb ssg140.6.0.0r1.0 to flash
It will replace current image file with usb image ssg140.6.0.0r1.0.
Do you want to continue... y/[n] y
Load image from usb to flash: ssg140.6.0.0r1.0.

Read ..................................
Save to flash. It may take a few minutes ...
platform = 24, cpu = 12, version = 18
 update new flash image (02555050,11141120)
platform = 24, cpu = 12, version = 18
offset = 20, address = 5800000, size = 11032611
date = 1483, sw_version = 30008000, cksum = 55fe2c90
Program flash (11141120 bytes) ...
++++++++++++++++++++++++++++++++++++++++++++++++++++++++++++++done
bottom-ssg140->
```

Safely remove the USB stick from the firewall and reset the system:

```
bottom-ssg140-> exec usb-device stop
The "USB Mass Storage Device"can now be safely removed from system
bottom-ssg140-> reset
System reset, are you sure? y/[n] y
In reset ...
```

Monitor the boot process to ensure that the proper image was loaded and to find anything in the configuration that does not load due to the new image (this is more likely to occur when downgrading the image):

```
Juniper Networks SSG-140 Boot Loader Version 3.2.3 (Checksum:
   ECD688CB)
Copyright (c) 1997-2006 Juniper Networks, Inc.
    Total physical memory: 512MB
    Test -  Pass
    Initialization - Done

...

bootmap_size = 3800
Version 6.0.0r1.0
Load Manufacture Information ... Done

...
```

Discussion

The USB port is new to ScreenOS platforms and is a more convenient way to manage data to and from the firewall than the older Compact Flash method. You can use the USB port to save any file from flash memory, and it is extremely useful when capturing the *crash.dmp* file for the Juniper Technical Assistance Center (JTAC) as well as when used with the process described here to manage the ScreenOS image.

CHAPTER 3

Wireless

3.0 Introduction

Wireless local area networks (WLANs) provide obvious benefits over wired networks, in that they link network devices without wires. WLAN uses spread-spectrum or Orthogonal Frequency-Division Multiplexing (OFDM) modulation technology (based on radio waves to enable communication between devices in a limited area, also known as the *basic service set*).

IEEE 802.11 is the standard defined for the WLAN. It uses Carrier Sense Multiple Access with Collision Avoidance (CSMA/CA) as the access method. Multiple standards are defined under the 802.11 umbrella standards; 802.11a was the first standard defined for WLAN, and it uses OFDM at a 5 GHz frequency, providing 54 Mbps throughput (in theory). The most commonly used standards, however, are the 802.11b and 802.11g, and they operate in Direct Sequence Spread Spectrum (DSSS) and OFDM in a 2.4 GHz frequency, providing 11 Mbps and 54 Mbps. 802.11g is backward-compatible with 802.11b; however, 802.11b is not backward-compatible with 802.11a. Therefore, you would see a lot of wireless Access Point (AP) devices that support 802.11b/g on the same radio and 802.11a on a separate radio. The NS-5GT supports only the 802.11b/g standard; the SSG5 and SSG20 support the 802.11a/b/g standards using dual-band radio.

The 802.11 Standards

The 802.11b/g is prone to interferences from common household devices, such as microwaves and cordless phones. The channels available for 802.11b/g are 1–13, with the most commonly used channels being 1, 6, and 11, as these are nonoverlapping (all other channels interfere with each other). Extended channels (12 and 13) are not available to North America and some other countries.

You can use the `exec wlan find-channel` command to find the best channel, and you can either hard-set the channel or leave it at auto. To hard-set the channel, use the `set wlan 0 channel` command if you have a two-radio device such as the SSG5, or the set wlan channel command for single-radio devices such as the NS-5GT. Here is example output of the find-channel command:

```
ssg5-> exec wlan find-channel
Traffic will be disrupted during the scan
Channel  1 is the best 2.4G radio channel to use
Channel 64 is the best   5G radio channel to use
```

Figure 3-1 shows the various components in an 802.11 WLAN, as listed here:

Station (STA)
: A terminal with an access mechanism to the wireless medium and radio contact to the AP.

Basic service set (BSS)
: A group of stations using the same radio frequency that communicate with one another. Each BSS is identified by a Service Set Identifier (SSID).

Access point (AP)
: A station integrated into the WLAN and the distribution system.

Extended service set (ESS)
: A set of infrastructure BSSs.

Distribution system (DS)
: An interconnection network from one logical network (ESS) based on several BSSs.

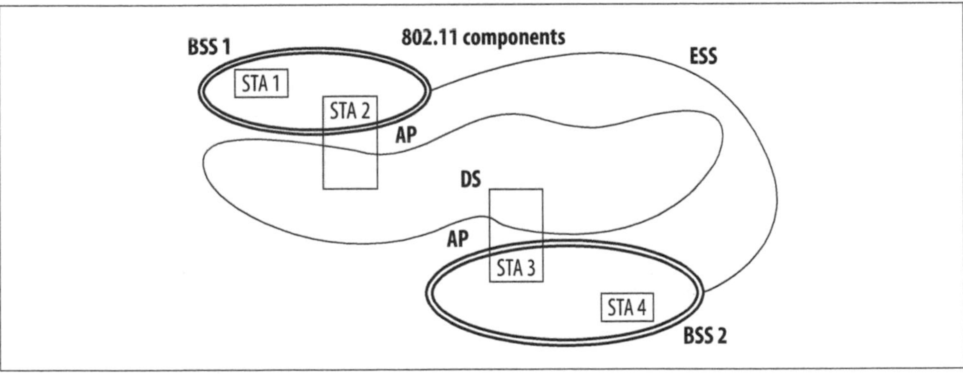

Figure 3-1. The components in an 802.11 WAN

APs periodically advertise themselves by broadcasting a Beacon Frame, which includes the following information:

- SSID (blanked out when SSID suppression is on)
- Supported rates (the Beacon Frame lists all supported rates; e.g., for 11G, supported rates are 1, 2, 5.5, 11, 6, 9, 11, 18, 24, 36, 48, and 54 Mbps)
- Supported security (authentication and encryption capabilities; e.g., the Temporal Key Integrity Protocol [TKIP] and the Advanced Encryption Standard [AES])
- Other information, such as channels, country, and vendor-specific features

You can perform a wireless site survey by using the exec `wlan site-survey` command, which will disrupt the traffic during the scan. In the following example output, the SSG5 device shows the SSID (SSID on index 3 is suppressed) and the AP Media Access Control (MAC) addresses:

```
SSG5-> exec wlan site-survey
Traffic will be disrupted during the scan
index   channel    rssi    mac              ssid
=====================================================
1        7(g)         64   0010dba8bc71     casper2
2        7(g)         54   0010dba8bc70     casper3
3       11(g)         14   0010dba8bc72
4       11(g)         36   0014f6e547a0     Secured
=====================================================
```

The stations can also identify the AP using a Probe Request and Response. The station sends Probe Requests on each channel to advertise its capability (e.g., supported rate) and to announce the SSID it is seeking (this is especially needed if the SSID has been suppressed at the AP). The AP answers the Probe Request using the Probe Response, which basically contacts the same information as in the Beacon Frame. The AP should respond immediately because the station won't listen for long; stations wait for responses for only around 20 ms on the current channel, and then repeat the process on the next channel.

The Wireless Station State transition occurs in the following sequence, as shown in Figure 3-2:

1. The station and AP discover each other using Passive Scanning (via the Beacon Frame broadcast from the AP) or Active Scanning (using the Probe Request and Probe Response). While in this state, the station cannot transmit data.
2. The station identity is verified using authentication methods based on the capabilities of the station and the AP. In this state, the station still cannot transmit data.
3. When the station and AP are associated, the station and AP can exchange data.

Wireless networks face all the threats that wired networks face, including eavesdropping, authorization, masquerading, loss or modification, repudiation, and sabotage. To supply security to the wireless network, security services were provided under the various 802.11 standards.

The legacy security services of IEEE 802.11 are achieved by the Entity Authentication Service and the Wired Equivalent Privacy (WEP) mechanism. WEP uses the Rivest Cipher 4 (RC4) stream cipher to provide confidentiality, data origin authentication/data integrity, and access control in conjunction with layer management. IEEE 802.11 authentication comes in two flavors: Open-System Authentication and Shared-Key Authentication. Open-System Authentication is a null authentication algorithm engaged during the State 2 transition shown in Figure 3-2. The station sends the authentication message set to Open, and the AP simply responds with a success message. Shared-Key Authentication supports authentication of stations as

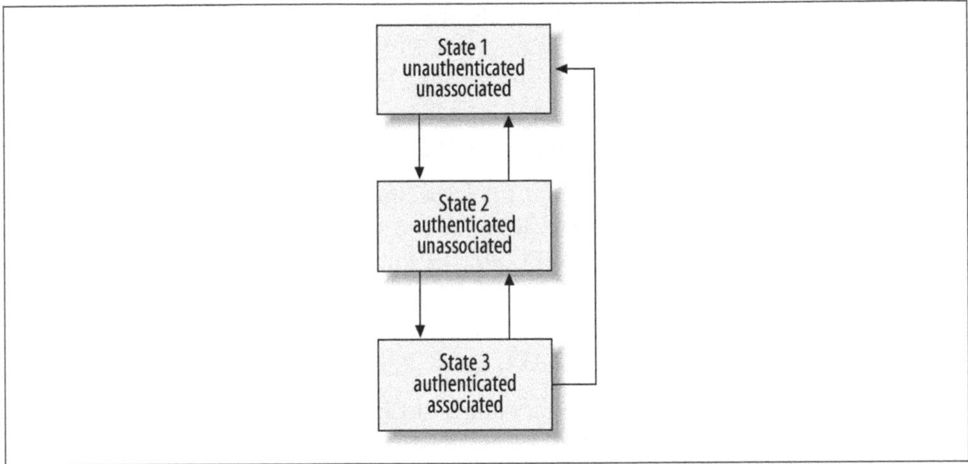

Figure 3-2. Sequence for Wireless Station State

either a member of those who know a shared secret key or a member of those who do not. The required secret shared key is presumed to have been delivered to participating stations via a secure channel that is independent of IEEE 802.11. Using the Shared-Key Authentication method in State 2 of Figure 3-2, the station sends the authentication message set to Shared Key (the shared key itself is not sent), the AP sends challenge text to the station, and then the station generates the challenge response data from the challenge text and, using the WEP algorithm, sends it back as a response. If the message integrity check is verified, the AP will respond with a success message. Figure 3-3 shows this entire sequence.

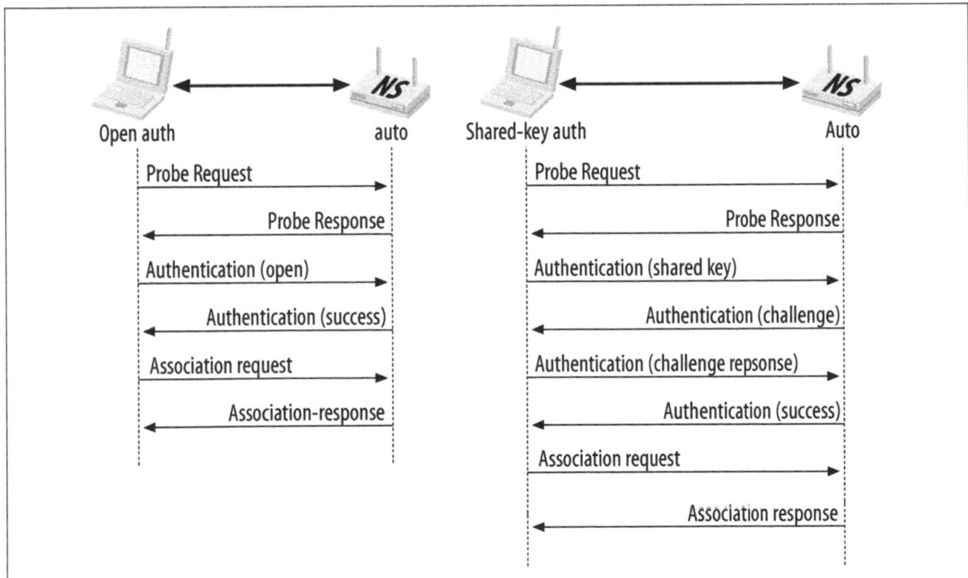

Figure 3-3. The WEP authentication process

WEP is well known for its weakness: tools are available on the Internet for getting access to the shared secret key. To overcome WEP's serious security weakness, IEEE amended the 802.11 security services in the 802.11i specifications. While the IEEE was amending the specifications, the Wi-Fi Alliance came out with Wi-Fi Protected Access (WPA) based on the draft standard of IEEE 802.11i.

It was revised in WPA2, based on the final specifications of 802.11i. IEEE 802.11i defined the Robust Security Network (RSN) as the standard protocol for the WLAN. The 802.11i specifications rely on IEEE 802.1*x* for authentication and key management services and use an encryption protocol, such as the Counter Mode with Cipher Block Chaining Message Authentication Code Protocol (CCMP), Wireless Robust Authentication Protocol (WRAP), or TKIP, for data protection.

The RSN relies on the IEEE 802.1*x* entity above IEEE 802.11 to provide authentication and key management services. With this model, decisions regarding which packets are permitted onto the DS are made by IEEE 802.1*x* in addition to IEEE 802.11 MAC.

IEEE 802.1*x* is a standard developed for port-based network access control. It provides authentication to devices connected to a LAN port by establishing a point-to-point connection, or it blocks access to the port if authentication fails. It is based on the Extensible Authentication Protocol (EAP), defined in RFC 2284 and revised in RFC 3748. To understand 802.1*x* you need to first understand a few concepts about the Point-to-Point Protocol (PPP), EAP, and 802.1*x* itself.

The Point-to-Point Protocol

The Point-to-Point Protocol (PPP) was typically used for dial-up user access. One of the functions of PPP was authentication, and users would dial in to the Remote-Access Server (RAS) and provide their username/password to authenticate. Most organizations wanted to provide security for authentication, so a new protocol, EAP, evolved. EAP is designed to provide a general framework for different authentication methods, such as challenge/response, smart cards, and public key infrastructure (PKI).

With EAP as the standard protocol, interoperability and compatibility of authentication methods become easier across different network devices. Typically, a user would dial in to a RAS and provide authentication details using EAP—the RAS would be independent of the authentication methods employed within EAP and it would act like a deliveryman and pass EAP packets between the end-user and the authentication server.

The EAP packet can be encapsulated in PPP or IEEE 802 without requiring IP. EAP encapsulated in LAN (usually Ethernet) environments is described in IEEE 802.1*x*. EAP in wireless is described in IEEE 802.11i. 802.11i relies on 802.1*x* for its authentication and key management services. 802.1*x* has three components:

Supplicant
: The user or client that wants to authenticate

Authentication server
: The server that performs the authentication (typically a Remote Access Dial-In User Service [RADIUS] server)

Authenticator
: The device that has to provide access to the user (typically a wireless AP)

More than 40 authentication methods are defined for EAP. Some of the most commonly used authentication methods are EAP-TLS, EAP-TTLS, EAP-PEAP, and EAP-MD5. EAP-TLS (Transport Layer Security) uses certificates for user and server authentication, and for dynamic session-key generation support by most RADIUS servers. EAP-TTLS (Tunneled Transport Layer Security) requires only a server-side certificate and a valid username and password for authentication (Steel-Belted Radius supports TTLS). EAP-PEAP (Protected EAP) requires only server-side certificates and a valid username and password, and it provides key exchange, session resumption, fragmentation, and reassembly (the Microsoft Internet Authentication Service (IAS) server and Steel-Belted Radius support this). EAP-MD5 (Message Digest 5) uses a challenge and response process to verify MD5 hashes.

While deploying 802.11 with 802.1*x*, the entire authentication and key distribution procedure happens in the following sequence (as shown in Figures 3-4, 3-5, and 3-6).

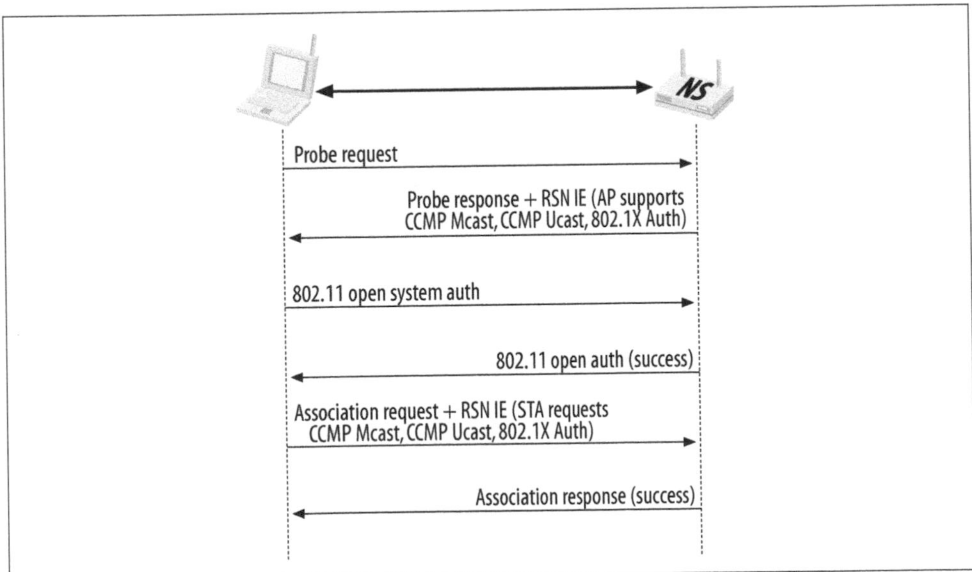

Figure 3-4. Representation of the discovery phase

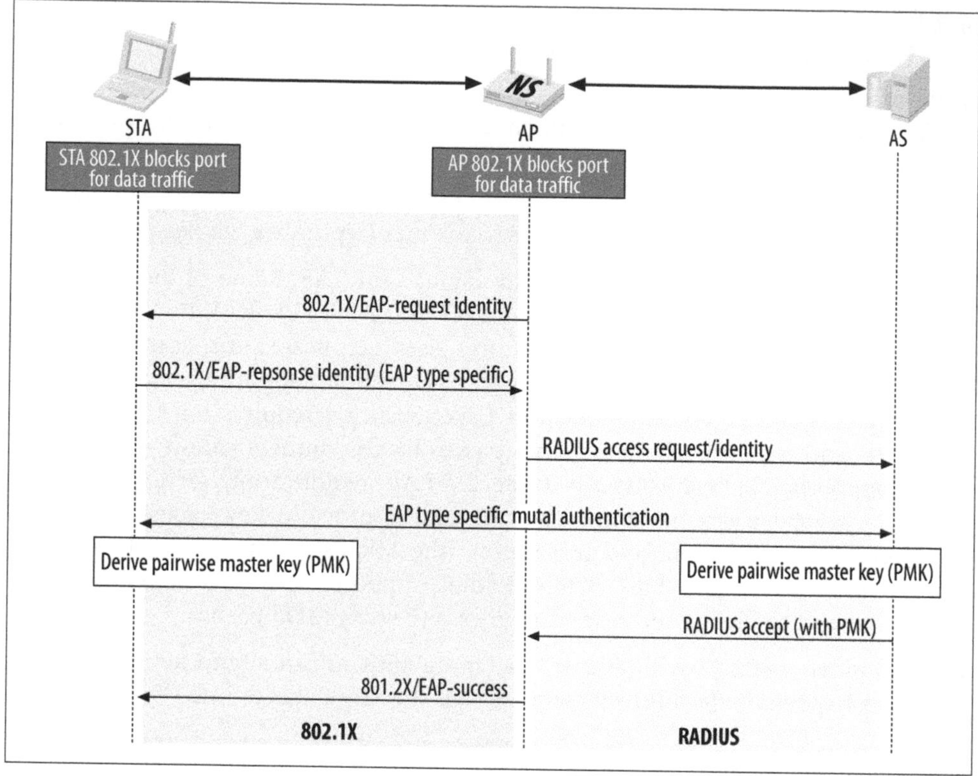

Figure 3-5. Representation of the 802.1x authentication phase

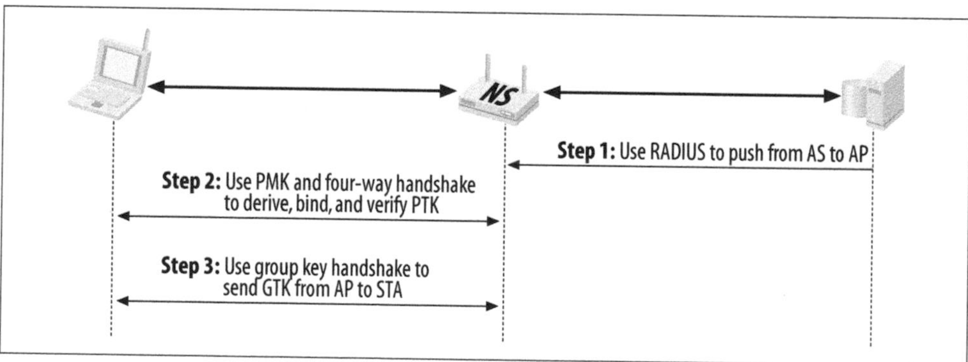

Figure 3-6. Representation of the 802.1x key management phase

1. Discovery:
    a. Determine promising parties with whom to communicate
    b. AP advertises network security capabilities to STAs (Stations) using the Beacon Frames

2. 802.1*x* authentication:
   a. Centralize network admission policy decisions at the authentication server
   b. STA determines whether it does indeed want to communicate
   c. Mutually authenticate STA and authentication server
   d. Generate Master Key as a side effect of authentication
   e. Generate Pairwise Master Key (PMK) as an access authorization token
   f. Authentication server moves (does not copy) PMK to STA's AP
3. 802.1*x* key management:
   a. Bind PMK to STA and AP
   b. Confirm that both AP and STA possess PMK
   c. Generate fresh PTK (Pairwise Transient Key)
   d. Prove each peer is live
   e. Synchronize PTK use
   f. Distribute GTK

3.1 Use MAC Filtering

Problem

You want to use MAC filtering to restrict user access to your wireless network.

Solution

Configure MAC filtering on the WLAN network and set up a strict access control list (ACL) on the WLAN configuration:

```
set wlan acl mode strict
set wlan acl 000f02020202 allow
set wlan acl 000c01010101 allow
```

Discussion

When you enable MAC filtering on the WLAN, the firewall will allow association of only those MAC addresses which are listed in the ACL. Although this is not a very secure way to restrict wireless access, it is one method among other security measures that you can use to deter unwanted users.

There are three modes for MAC filtering:

Disabled
: The default mode; no MAC filtering will be done by the firewall

Enabled
: Allows any MAC address to associate with the AP and deny the configured Deny MAC address

Strict
: Allows only the configured Allow MAC addresses to associate with the AP, and denies everything else

You can view the MAC filtering configuration using the `get wlan acl` command. The following example shows that the WLAN ACL mode is strict, and it has one Deny MAC address, and two Allow MAC addresses:

```
ssg5-> get wlan acl
wlan acl mode strict

denied mac address
1. 000000000001

allow mac address
1. 000f00000000
2. 000c01010101
```

You can view the event log using the `get log event` command to verify the MAC filtering. Here, a user with MAC address `00:0f:b5:22:bf:a2` was attempting to associate to the `corp` SSID and was denied by the ACL:

```
2001-10-06 10:20:06 system notif 00564 Wireless station event: Station
                                 000fb522bfa2 is denied by ACL, SSID:
                                 corp.
```

You can also view the current association to the wireless network using the `get interface` *<wireless_interface_name>* `association` command. In the following example, a user with a MAC address of `00:0f:02:02:02:02` is associated on the `wireless0/0` interface, and encryption is enabled on this connection. Also note that it is operating in mode 11g:

```
SSG5-> get interface wireless0/0 association
index   mac address     state   encryption    mode
=======================================================
1       000f02020202    assoc   on            11g
=======================================================
```

3.2 Configure the WEP Shared Key

Problem

You want to configure WEP shared authentication and encryption.

Solution

Configure the SSID with an authentication type of `shared-key`, define the WEP key, and bind the SSID to the wireless interface:

```
set ssid name pizza
set ssid pizza key-id 1 length 40 method asciitext a1b2c default
set ssid pizza authentication shared-key
set ssid pizza interface wireless0/0
exec wlan reactivate
```

To configure the infrastructure to enable traffic flow through the AP, you must create a zone, attach a wireless interface to the zone, configure the IP address, enable a Dynamic Host Configuration Protocol (DHCP) server service on the wireless interface, configure security policy, and activate the wireless connection:

```
set zone name "wzone1"

set interface "wireless0/0" zone "wzone1"
set interface wireless0/0 ip 172.16.254.1/24

set interface wireless0/0 dhcp server service
set interface wireless0/0 dhcp server auto
set interface wireless0/0 dhcp server option gateway 172.16.254.1
set interface wireless0/0 dhcp server option netmask 255.255.255.0
set interface wireless0/0 dhcp server ip 172.16.254.10 to 172.16.254.15

set policy from "wzone1" to "Untrust" "Any" "Any" "ANY" nat src permit
exec wlan reactivate
```

You must also configure the client for WEP-shared authentication to associate with this AP.

Discussion

You should configure the minimum of WEP authentication and encryption on your wireless network to deter casual snooping. Although it is very easy to crack WEP encryption, it will deter users from looking for easy access to your wireless network.

In this example, we chose WEP shared-key as the authentication and encryption method to protect the wireless network. For WEP, you can configure three different authentication types:

Open authentication
: Requires no authentication key, and anybody specifying the SSID can associate with the AP. You can configure open authentication with or without encryption. The encryption algorithm used for WEP is RC4 for encryption and decryption.

Shared-key authentication
: Requires the client PC to provide a preshared authentication key to associate with the AP.

Auto authentication
: Accepts open or shared-key authentication.

Follow these instructions to use shared-key authentication.

First, create an SSID called Pizza; define the key-id 1 in ASCII text as the default key. You can define multiple keys for this SSID to utilize different keys with different users. (Always remember that the key-id on the firewall should match the key-id on the client PC; for example, if you specify key-id 4 on the firewall, you should create key-id 4 on the PC as well.)

Now, configure the Pizza SSID to use shared-key authentication and bind the SSID to the wireless0 interface.

You'll now need to configure the infrastructure to enable traffic flow and separate the users on the wireless network by putting them in a separate zone.

Create a new zone called Wzone1 (on the NS-5GT, this zone is preconfigured) and assign the wireless0/0 interface to this zone. Define an IP address, 172.16.254.1/24, to the wireless0/0 interface. Enable users to get their IP addresses automatically, enable DHCP server service on the wireless0/0 interface, and configure the gateway address and IP address range. You also need to configure the security policy to allow traffic to traverse the Wzone1 to the Untrust zone. For this discussion, you are providing open access in the policy, you may have to create a more restricted policy based on your organization's security policy.

Finally, you need to activate the wireless configuration on the AP. Execute the exec wlan reactivate command to enable the wireless AP. Remember to always run this command whenever you perform any wireless configuration changes, or else the AP will not work as planned. This command will restart the wireless AP.

Based on the client PC software, you will need to configure the wireless network settings (consult your client software manuals for the configurations). Use the get event command to view the client connectivity status.

The following output shows three different events: the first event shows that the stations were associated with SSID Pizza after being authenticated with shared-key authentication; the second event shows that the authentication failed due to an incorrect shared key; and the third event shows that the authentication type is incorrect because the user tried to connect using the open authentication type.

```
2007-08-23 10:04:50 system notif 00564 Wireless station event: station
                                 0019d2c8d24e is associated, SSID:
                                 pizza.

2007-08-23 10:04:13 system notif 00564 Wireless station event: Station
                                 0019d2c8d250 Shared-Key authentication
                                 failed: Challenge failure, SSID:
                                 pizza.

2007-08-23 10:03:56 system notif 00564 Wireless station event: Station
                                 0019d2c8d24e Authentication type not
                                 accepted, Type: OPEN, SSID: pizza.
```

3.3 Configure the WPA Preshared Key

Problem

You want to secure a wireless network using WPA with a preshared key. You don't have the infrastructure for 802.1*x* authentication, and would like to use WPA with a preshared key.

Solution

Define the SSID with the authentication type as `WPA-Auto-PSK`, and the encryption algorithm as auto, and then bind the SSID to the wireless interface:

```
set ssid name Sunnyvale
set ssid Sunnyvale client-isolation
set ssid Sunnyvale authentication wpa-auto-psk passphrase JnPr!234
   encryption auto
set ssid Sunnyvale interface wireless1
```

Configure the infrastructure to enable traffic flow through the AP, create the zone, attach the wireless interface to the zone, configure the IP address, enable DHCP server service on the wireless interface, configure the security policy, and activate the wireless connection:

```
set zone name "corp-wireless"

set interface "wireless0/1" zone "corp-wireless"
set interface wireless0/1 ip 172.17.200.1/24

set interface wireless0/1 dhcp server service
set interface wireless0/1 dhcp server auto
set interface wireless0/1 dhcp server option gateway 172.17.200.1
set interface wireless0/1 dhcp server option netmask 255.255.255.0
set interface wireless0/1 dhcp server ip 172.17.200.10 to
172.17.200.20

set policy from "corp-wireless" to "trust"  "Any" "Any"
   "ANY" permit

exec wlan reactivate
```

Configure the client for WPA or WPA2 preshared key authentication to associate with this AP.

Discussion

WPA is a more secure authentication and encryption method than WEP. It is a good measure to ensure that only trusted users can associate with the wireless AP. ScreenOS firewalls support WPA authentication using 802.1*x* and the static key (a.k.a. the preshared key).

This recipe uses the WPA-PSK (preshared key) method for wireless protection. You can configure WPA-PSK in three ways:

WPA-PSK authentication
: This requires that the users support only WPA with a preshared key. WPA is based on the IEEE 802.11i draft specifications.

WPA2-PSK authentication
: This requires that the users support only WPA2 with a preshared key. WPA2 is based on the IEEE 802.11i final specifications.

WPA-AUTO-PSK authentication
: This will accept WPA or WPA2 with preshared key authentication.

This recipe uses WPA-AUTO-PSK authentication to allow connectivity from a WPA- or WPA2-supported client.

First, an SSID called `Sunnyvale` was created, and then the authentication type was defined as `wpa-auto-psk` with the passphrase `JnPr!234` and the encryption mode set to `auto`. We also enabled client isolation to prevent client-to-client bridging.

Next, the SSID was bound to the `wireless1` interface. The preshared key was secured only to the extent of its password strength; the passphrase should not be vulnerable to dictionary attacks, and should be composed of random alphanumeric and special characters. Also, the passphrase should be kept secret; otherwise, anybody with the passphrase will be able to decrypt the traffic. Because every user should connect using the passphrase, it is hard to keep it a secret. You should consider using other methods to secure your traffic over the wireless network, such as the IP Security (IPSec)/SSL virtual private network (VPN), or use 802.1*x* servers.

We then needed to configure the infrastructure to enable traffic flow, and we separated the users on the wireless network by putting them in a separate zone. The new zone, called `corp-wireless`, was created and assigned a `wireless0/1` interface, defined as IP address `172.17.200.1/24`. To enable users to get IP addresses automatically, we enabled DHCP server service on the `wireless0/1` interface, and configured the gateway address and IP address range. We configured the security policy to allow traffic to traverse `corp-wireless` zone to the `Untrust` zone. (In this example, we are providing open access in the policy; you may have to create a more restricted policy based on your organization's security policy.)

Finally, to activate the wireless configuration on the AP, we executed the `exec wlan reactivate` command to enable the wireless AP. Remember to always run this command whenever you perform any wireless configuration changes; otherwise, the AP will not work as planned.

Based on the client PC software, you will need to configure the wireless network settings (consult your client software manuals regarding configurations). Then, use the `get event` command to view the client connectivity status. Here is an example of a successful association with the WPA client:

```
2007-08-23 15:52:11 system notif 00564 Wireless station event: Station
                                 0019d2c8d250 WPA authentication passed,
                                 SSID: Sunnyvale.
2007-08-23 15:52:11 system notif 00564 Wireless station event: Station
                                 0019d2c8d250 WPA authentication
                                 negotiating, SSID: Sunnyvale.
2007-08-23 15:52:11 system notif 00564 Wireless station event: Station
                                 0019d2c8d250 WPA authentication
                                 starting, SSID: Sunnyvale.
2007-08-23 15:52:10 system notif 00564 Wireless station event: station
                                 0019d2c8d250 is associated, SSID:
                                 Sunnyvale.
2007-08-23 15:52:10 system notif 00564 Wireless station event: Station
                                 0019d2c8d250 Open authentication
                                 passed, SSID: Sunnyvale
```

Here is an example of the client association using WPA2 in the event log:

```
2007-08-23 15:52:31 system notif 00564 Wireless station event: Station
                                 0019d2c8d24e WPA2 authentication
                                 passed, SSID: Sunnyvale.
2007-08-23 15:52:31 system notif 00564 Wireless station event: Station
                                 0019d2c8d24e WPA2 authentication
                                 negotiating, SSID: Sunnyvale.
2007-08-23 15:52:31 system notif 00564 Wireless station event: Station
                                 0019d2c8d24e WPA2 authentication
                                 starting, SSID: Sunnyvale.
2007-08-23 15:52:30 system notif 00564 Wireless station event: station
                                 0019d2c8d24e is associated, SSID:
                                 Sunnyvale.
2007-08-23 15:52:30 system notif 00564 Wireless station event: Station
                                 0019d2c8d24e Open authentication
                                 passed, SSID: Sunnyvale.
```

And here is an example of the client failing due to an incorrect passphrase while using WPA2 in the event log:

```
2007-08-23 15:52:05 system notif 00564 Wireless station event: station
                                 0019d2c8d24e is disassociated, SSID:
                                 Sunnyvale.
2007-08-23 15:52:05 system notif 00564 Wireless station event: Station
                                 0019d2c8d24e WPA2 authentication
                                 failed: Station timeout, SSID:
                                 Sunnyvale.
2007-08-23 15:52:04 system notif 00564 Wireless station event: Station
                                 0019d2c8d24e WPA2 authentication MIC
                                 check failed, SSID: Sunnyvale.
2007-08-23 15:52:01 system notif 00564 Wireless station event: Station
                                 0019d2c8d24e WPA2 authentication
                                 starting, SSID: Sunnyvale.
2007-08-23 15:52:01 system notif 00564 Wireless station event: station
                                 0019d2c8d24e is associated, SSID:
                                 Sunnyvale.
2007-08-23 15:52:01 system notif 00564 Wireless station event: Station
                                 0019d2c8d24e Open authentication
                                 passed, SSID: Sunnyvale
```

3.4 Configure WPA Using 802.1x with IAS and Microsoft Active Directory

Problem

You want to secure a wireless network with WPA using 802.1*x* with IAS and Microsoft Active Directory.

Solution

Configure the `auth-server` using an `account-type` of `802.1x`, and select Radius as the `auth-server` type:

```
set auth-server "MyServer" server-name "172.24.28.199"
set auth-server "MyServer" account-type 802.1X
set auth-server "MyServer" radius secret "RADIUS_SECRET"
```

Configure the SSID with an authentication type of `wpa-auto` and an encryption type of `auto`; associate the 802.1*x* `auth-server`, and then bind the SSID to the wireless interface:

```
set ssid name Secured
set ssid Secured client-isolation
set ssid Secured authentication wpa-auto encryption auto auth-server
   MyServer
set ssid Secured interface wireless0
```

Configure the infrastructure to enable traffic flow through the AP by creating a zone, attaching a wireless interface to the zone, configuring the IP address, enabling DHCP server service on the wireless interface, configuring the security policy, and finally, activating the wireless connection:

```
set zone name "wzone1"
set interface "wireless0/0" zone "wzone1"
set interface wireless0/0 ip 172.16.254.1/24
set interface wireless0/0 dhcp server service
set interface wireless0/0 dhcp server auto
set interface wireless0/0 dhcp server option gateway 172.16.254.1
set interface wireless0/0 dhcp server option netmask 255.255.255.0
set interface wireless0/0 dhcp server ip 172.16.254.10 to
172.16.254.15

set policy from "wzone1" to "Untrust"  "Any" "Any" "ANY" nat src
permit

exec wlan reactivate
```

Use this link to configure Microsoft Windows to provide the 802.1*x* authentication service: *http://www.microsoft.com/technet/network/wifi/ed80211.mspx*.

Discussion

Using WPA with the 802.1*x* authentication method is considered a better wireless network security method when compared to WPA-PSK and WEP. However, it has dependencies on other network services, such as the 802.1*x*-aware RADIUS server and its backend infrastructure. Based on your network authentication service, the deployment may be different.

In this recipe, we used the Microsoft IAS server as the RADIUS server, which interacts with Active Directory in the backend to provide user authentication. We used a standalone Certificate Authority (CA) server to generate a server certificate for the RADIUS server, installed it on the RADIUS server, and installed the CA certificate on the RADIUS server and the end-user host. For this recipe, we used the EAP-PEAP authentication type with a secured password (EAP-MSCHAP v2). Figure 3-7 illustrates the topology used in this recipe.

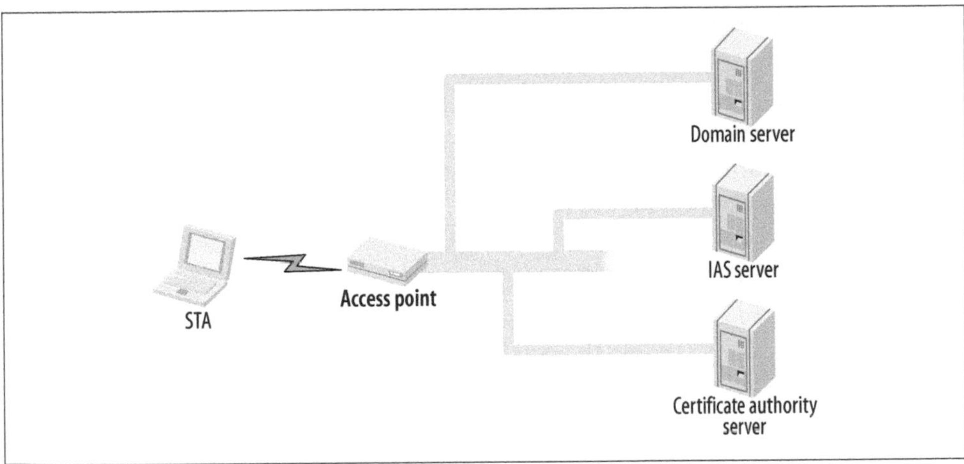

Figure 3-7. WPA using 802.1x with IAS and Microsoft Active Directory

On the firewall, we configured the authentication server named `"MyServer"` and specified its IP address, then selected the `account-type` as 802.1*x*, and used RADIUS as the account type with `RADIUS_SECRET`. The `RADIUS_SECRET` used should match the secret configured on the Microsoft IAS server.

```
set auth-server "MyServer" server-name "172.24.28.199"
set auth-server "MyServer" account-type 802.1X
set auth-server "MyServer" radius secret "RADIUS_SECRET"
```

Next, we configured the wireless components. First, we created an SSID named `Secured`, and configured it with the WPA-AUTO authentication method and an encryption of `auto`, and associated the RADIUS server with `"MyServer"`. Then, we bound the `Secured` SSID to the `wireless0` interface. We also enabled client isolation to prevent client-to-client bridging. You can specifically configure WPA or WPA2, or you can choose WPA-AUTO to allow WPA and WPA2 clients to associate. As the encryption method, you can specify AES or TKIP.

```
set ssid name Secured
set ssid Secured client-isolation
set ssid Secured authentication wpa-auto encryption auto auth-server
   MyServer
set ssid Secured interface wireless0
```

We now need to configure the infrastructure to enable traffic flow. Create a new zone called `wzone1` and assign the `wireless0/0` interface to this zone (this interface also has a binding to the SSID `Secured` on the wireless side). Assign the IP address `172.16.254.1/24` to the `wireless0/0` interface, and enable the DHCP server service on the interface to allow the clients to get the IP address automatically. By default, the Domain Name System (DNS) settings from the `Untrust` interface are propagated to the clients. If you want to control any of the DHCP options, you can configure them using the DHCP options on the interface (in this example, we configured the gateway and netmask options).

Next, create a firewall policy to allow traffic to traverse the zones. In this example, we provided open access to the users in `wzone1` to `Untrust` for any source, destination, and service. You may have to create a more restricted policy based on your organization's security policy. We have also enabled Port-Address Translation (PAT) Network Address Translation (NAT) using the IP address of the `Untrust` interface. (You can deploy other types of NAT based on your network requirements; see Chapter 8 for the types of NAT supported.)

Finally, you need to activate the wireless configuration on the AP. Use the `exec wlan reactivate` command to enable the wireless AP. Remember to always run this command whenever you perform any wireless configuration changes; otherwise, the AP will not work as planned.

```
set zone name "wzone1"
set interface "wireless0/0" zone "wzone1"
set interface wireless0/0 ip 172.16.254.1/24
set interface wireless0/0 dhcp server service
set interface wireless0/0 dhcp server auto
set interface wireless0/0 dhcp server option gateway 172.16.254.1
set interface wireless0/0 dhcp server option netmask 255.255.255.0
set interface wireless0/0 dhcp server ip 172.16.254.10 to 172.16.254.15

set policy from "wzone1" to "Untrust"  "Any" "Any" "ANY" nat src permit

exec wlan reactivate
```

To troubleshoot wireless connectivity on the firewall, use the get event command to view the status of the clients. The following code snippet shows an example of a successful client connecting using WPA and 802.1*x*. The client first sends the probe request for 802.1*x* as the authentication method. Then, it will associate with the open authentication and start the 802.1*x* authentication process, after which the WPA authentication will be negotiated.

```
2007-08-25 17:10:50 system notif 00564 Wireless station event: Station
                                 0019d2c8d250 WPA authentication passed,
                                 SSID: Secured.
2007-08-25 17:10:50 system notif 00564 Wireless station event: Station
                                 0019d2c8d250 WPA authentication
                                 negotiating, SSID: Secured.
2007-08-25 17:10:49 system notif 00564 Wireless station event: Station
                                 0019d2c8d250 WPA authentication
                                 starting, SSID: Secured.
2007-08-25 17:10:49 system info  00527 IP address 172.16.254.10 is
                                 assigned to 0019d2c8d250.
2007-08-25 17:10:49 system notif 00614 [1X] host 0019.d2c8.d250 passed
                                 authentication on interface wireless0/
                                 0 with 802.1X session id 1.
2007-08-25 17:10:49 system notif 00564 Wireless station event: Station
                                 0019d2c8d250 got key from
                                 RADIUS server, SSID: Secured.
2007-08-25 17:10:49 system notif 00614 [1X] host 0019.d2c8.d250 started
                                 authentication on interface wireless0/
                                 0 with 802.1X session id 1.
2007-08-25 17:10:49 system notif 00564 Wireless station event: station
                                 0019d2c8d250 is associated, SSID:
                                 Secured.
2007-08-25 17:10:49 system notif 00564 Wireless station event: Station
                                 0019d2c8d250 Open authentication
                                 passed, SSID: Secured.
2007-08-25 17:10:49 system notif 00614 [1X] host 0019.d2c8.d250 started
                                 authentication on interface wireless0/
                                 0 with 802.1X session id 1.
```

Here is an example of the get event command output when the user disconnects from the AP:

```
2007-08-25 17:10:28 system notif 00614 [1X] host 0019.d2c8.d250 logged
                                 off  interface wireless0/0 with 802.1X
                                 session id 1.
2007-08-25 17:10:28 system notif 00564 Wireless station event: station
                                 0019d2c8d250 is disassociated, SSID:
                                 Secured.
```

And here is an example of the client association using WPA2 in the event log:

```
2007-08-25 17:09:44 system info  00527 IP address 172.16.254.11 is
                                 assigned to 0019d2c8d24e.
2007-08-25 17:09:44 system info  00527 DHCP server on interface
                                 wireless0/0 received DHCPDISCOVER from
                                 0019d2c8d24e requesting out-of-scope
                                 IP address 172.17.200.11/0.0.0.0.
2007-08-25 17:09:39 system notif 00564 Wireless station event: Station
                                 0019d2c8d24e WPA2 authentication
                                 passed, SSID: Secured.
```

```
2007-08-25 17:09:38 system notif 00564 Wireless station event: Station
                                 0019d2c8d24e WPA2 authentication
                                 negotiating, SSID: Secured.
2007-08-25 17:09:38 system notif 00564 Wireless station event: Station
                                 0019d2c8d24e WPA2 authentication
                                 starting, SSID: Secured.
2007-08-25 17:09:38 system notif 00614 [1X] host 0019.d2c8.d24e passed
                                 authentication on interface wireless0/
                                 0 with 802.1X session id 2.
2007-08-25 17:09:38 system notif 00564 Wireless station event: Station
                                 0019d2c8d24e got key from RADIUS
                                 server, SSID: Secured.
2007-08-25 17:09:26 system notif 00614 [1X] host 0019.d2c8.d24e started
                                 authentication on interface wireless0/
                                 0 with 802.1X session id 2.
2007-08-25 17:09:26 system notif 00564 Wireless station event: station
                                 0019d2c8d24e is associated, SSID:
                                 Secured.
2007-08-25 17:09:26 system notif 00564 Wireless station event: Station
                                 0019d2c8d24e Open authentication
                                 passed, SSID: Secured.
2007-08-25 17:09:25 system notif 00614 [1X] host 0019.d2c8.d24e started
                                 authentication on interface wireless0/
                                 0 with 802.1X session id 2.
```

The following is an example of a failed connection—the user either configured a wrong EAP type (e.g., a used certificate when the auth server was expecting EAP-MSCHAP), or provided a wrong username and password for authentication:

```
2007-08-25 17:15:09 system notif 00614 [1X] host 0019.d2c8.d250 failed
                                 authentication on interface wireless0/
                                 0 with 802.1X session id 2.
2007-08-25 17:15:09 system notif 00564 Wireless station event: Station
                                 0019d2c8d250 did not pass
                                 authentication, SSID: Secured.
2007-08-25 17:14:57 system notif 00614 [1X] host 0019.d2c8.d250 started
                                 authentication on interface wireless0/
                                 0 with 802.1X session id 2.
2007-08-25 17:14:57 system notif 00564 Wireless station event: station
                                 0019d2c8d250 is associated, SSID:
                                 Secured.
2007-08-25 17:14:57 system notif 00564 Wireless station event: Station
                                 0019d2c8d250 Open authentication
                                 passed, SSID: Secured.
2007-08-25 17:14:57 system notif 00614 [1X] host 0019.d2c8.d250 started
                                 authentication on interface wireless0/
                                 0 with 802.1X session id 2.
```

`get int` *`<interface_name>`* `association` is another command you can use to check whether the user is able to associate with the AP. The following code is example output of the `wireless0` interface; the host with the `00:19:d2:c8:d2:50` MAC address is associated with encryption using `11a` mode:

```
ssg5-> get int w0 ass
index   mac address     state   encryption    mode
```

```
=====================================================
1       0019d2c8d250     assoc    on            11a
```

You can also get more detail on the associated client by using the get interface *<interface_name>* association *<mac_address_of_client>* command. The following example shows the client MAC address and the state of the client associated using 11a mode. It also shows the encryption type used (AES for unicast and TKIP for multicast). The Power Save Mode is on. The RX Data Rate is in Mbps which indicates the last received frame speed, and the Rx Signal Strength is Signal/Noise in dB. You'll also see the Media Specific Data Unit (MSDU) receive and transmit counters.

```
ssg5-> get int w0 ass 0019d2c8d250
MAC Address: 0019d2c8d250  State: assoc
WLAN Mode: 11a  AID: 49153
Encryption: on
Ciphers: aes(unicast), tkip(multicast)
Power Save Mode on
RX Data Rate: 0.25, RX Signal Strength: 38
    MSDU        Data        Mcast       dropped     Errors
rx  8193        3370        165         0           1
tx  3208        3243        0           0           1
ssg5->
```

The get ssid command will display all the SSID configurations on the firewall, with the authentication type, cipher type, and interface to which it is bound:

```
ssg5-> get ssid

SSID information table:
             Supp-    Client-   Authen-
Name        ression  Isolation  tication      Cipher Interface   Radio
======================================================================
Sunnyvale  disabled enabled    wpa-auto-psk auto   wireless0/1  both
Secured    disabled disabled   wpa-auto     auto   wireless0/0  both
```

You can also get detailed information regarding the SSID by using the get ssid *<SSID_NAME>* command. For example, the following code will display the interface it is bound to, SSID suppression information, client-isolation state, authentication type, cipher type, and rekey interval:

```
ssg5-> get ssid Secured
SSID Secured:
  bound on wireless0/0
  suppression disabled
  client isolation disabled
  authentication: WPA-AUTO
  cipher: auto
  rekey-interval: 1800
```

For troubleshooting 802.1*x* issues, you may want to use the commands get dot1x session and get dot1x statistics:

```
ssg5-> get dot1x sess
allocated 2 freed 253   alloc ok 76 fail 0 free ok 74 fail 0
```

```
  (1)(0019d2c8d24e)(00000001)(wireless0/0)(Root) 802.1X RADIUS
  (2)(0019d2c8d250)(00000001)(wireless0/0)(Root) 802.1X RADIUS
total 2 session(s)
ssg5->
```

The dot1x session table shows the total number of dot1x connections made. The output shows the two users who are connected and their MAC addresses. These sessions are established, and are kept open until the users are connected to the AP.

```
ssg5-> get dot1x statistics
-------------------------------------------------------------------
Interface wireless0/0 802.1X statistics:
in eapol               139 | out eapol           138 | in start       86
in logoff               26 | in resp/id           31 | in resp        78
out req/id              81 | out req             132 | in invalid      0
in len error             0 |
Interfacewireless0/0 802.1X diagnostics:
while connecting:
enter                    0 | eap logoff            0 |
while authenticating:
enter                    0 | auth success          0 | auth timeout   24
auth fail               24 | auth reauth           0 | auth start     82
auth logoff             11 |
while authenticated:
auth reauth          0 | auth start        0 | auth logoff              4
backend:
response           145 | challenge        47 | other request           51
non-nak resp        78 | auth success      6 | auth fail                0
-----------
```

The get dot1x statistics output shows the packet counts for each wireless interface, how many packets were received for in EAPOL, the total number of packets for the logoff request in logoff, the total number of packets received, and the responses sent out to the RADIUS server.

3.5 Configure WPA with the Steel-Belted Radius Server and Odyssey Access Client

Problem

You want to configure the Steel-Belted Radius server and Odyssey Access Client for wireless connection.

Solution

To configure the firewall as the AP, first you must configure the auth server using an account type of 802.1x and select RADIUS as the auth server type:

```
set auth-server "MyServer" server-name "172.24.28.199"
set auth-server "MyServer" account-type 802.1X
set auth-server "MyServer" radius secret "RADIUS_SECRET"
```

Then, configure the SSID with an authentication type of `wpa-auto` and an encryption type of `auto`, associate the 802.1*x* auth server, and bind the SSID to the wireless interface:

```
set ssid name Sunnyvale
set ssid Sunnyvale client-isolation
set ssid Sunnyvale authentication wpa-auto encryption auto auth-server
   MyServer
set ssid Sunnyvale interface wireless0
```

To configure the infrastructure to enable traffic flow through the AP, create the zone, attach a wireless interface to the zone, configure the IP address, enable the DHCP server service on the wireless interface, configure the security policy, and activate the wireless connection:

```
set zone name "wzone1"
set interface "wireless0/0" zone "wzone1"
set interface wireless0/0 ip 10.1.1.1/24
set interface wireless0/0 dhcp server service
set interface wireless0/0 dhcp server auto
set interface wireless0/0 dhcp server option gateway 10.1.1.1
set interface wireless0/0 dhcp server option netmask 255.255.255.0
set interface wireless0/0 dhcp server ip 10.1.1.10 to 10.1.1.20

set policy from "wzone1" to "Untrust"  "Any" "Any" "ANY" nat src permit

exec wlan reactivate
```

To install and configure the Steel-Belted Radius server and Odyssey Access Client, follow these steps (these steps are also outlined in the *Getting Started* and *Administration* guides, available from the Steel-Belted Radius support site):

1. Install the Steel-Belted Radius server on a Windows server that is a member of, or belongs to, a domain that has the trust relationship with the domain where the user credentials are stored.
2. Use the Steel-Belted Radius administrator to configure the RADIUS client (i.e., the wireless AP acting as the authenticator).
3. Add the Windows domain user, or the group that contains the user you want to authenticate.
4. Configure the Authentication Policies with the EAP methods and certificates.
5. Install the Odyssey Access Client on the PC that will act as a supplicant.
6. Configure the Odyssey Access Client for the authentication parameters.

Discussion

Selecting 802.1*x* authentication service products can be overwhelming—many freeware and shareware applications are available, and some products are available within the Steel-Belted Radius and Odyssey Access Client that provide 802.1*x* security in addition to other features, such as uniform security policy enforcement across all network access methods. In this recipe, we use the Steel-Belted Radius server as the RADIUS server, the Odyssey Access Client for the PC as the client, and the Juniper NetScreen Firewall as the AP. Figure 3-8 illustrates the topology.

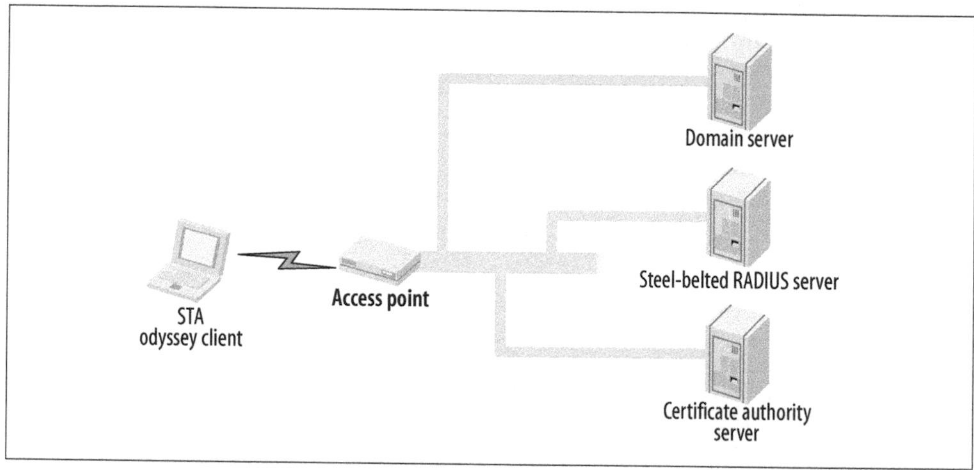

Figure 3-8. The Steel-Belted Radius server as the RADIUS server, the Odyssey Access Client for the PC as the client, and the Juniper NetScreen Firewall as the AP

On the firewall, we configured the authentication server named "MyServer" and specified the IP address of the server which will host the Steel-Belted Radius server, then selected the account type as 802.1*x* and used RADIUS as the account type with RADIUS_SECRET. The RADIUS_SECRET used should match the secret configured on the Steel-Belted Radius server.

```
set auth-server "MyServer" server-name "172.24.28.199"
set auth-server "MyServer" account-type 802.1X
set auth-server "MyServer" radius secret "RADIUS_SECRET"
```

To configure the wireless components, first create an SSID named Sunnyvale and configure the WPA-AUTO authentication method, set the encryption to auto, and associate it to the RADIUS server "MyServer". Then, bind the secured SSID to the wireless0 interface.

We also enabled client isolation to prevent client-to-client bridging. You can specifically configure WPA or WPA2, or you can choose WPA-AUTO to allow both WPA and WPA2 clients to connect. You can also specify the encryption method as AES or TKIP.

```
set ssid name Sunnyvale
set ssid Sunnyvale client-isolation
set ssid Sunnyvale authentication wpa-auto encryption auto auth-server
   MyServer
set ssid Sunnyvale interface wireless0
```

We now need to configure the infrastructure to enable traffic flow. Create a new zone called wzone1, and assign the wireless0/0 interface to this zone. This interface also has a binding to the SSID Sunnyvale on the wireless side. Assign the IP address 10.1.1.1/24 to the wireless0/0 interface, and enable DHCP server service on the interface to allow clients to get the IP address automatically. By default, the DNS settings from the Untrust interface are propagated to the clients, so if you want to control any of the DHCP options, you can configure them on the interface. In the example, we configured the gateway and netmask options.

You need to create a firewall policy to allow traffic to traverse the zones. In this example, we provided open access to the users in wzone1 to Untrust for any source, destination, and service. You may have to create a more restricted policy based on your organization's security policy. We enabled PAT NAT using the interface IP address of the Untrust interface. You can deploy other types of NAT based on your network requirements. Refer to Chapter 8 for the types of NAT supported.

Finally, we need to activate the wireless configuration on the AP. Execute the exec wlan reactivate command to enable the wireless AP. Remember to always run this command whenever you perform any wireless configuration changes; otherwise, the AP will not work as planned.

```
set zone name "wzone1"
set interface "wireless0/0" zone "wzone1"
set interface wireless0/0 ip 10.1.1.1/24
set interface wireless0/0 dhcp server service
set interface wireless0/0 dhcp server auto
set interface wireless0/0 dhcp server option gateway 10.1.1.1
set interface wireless0/0 dhcp server option netmask 255.255.255.0
set interface wireless0/0 dhcp server ip 10.1.1.10 to 10.1.1.20

set policy from "wzone1" to "Untrust"  "Any" "Any" "ANY" nat src
permit

exec wlan reactivate
```

Installing the Steel-Belted Radius server

Now we must install the Steel-Belted Radius server on a Windows server that belongs to a domain that has a trust relationship with the domain where the user credentials are stored.

Before you install the Steel-Belted Radius server, ensure that no other RADIUS servers are installed on the host (e.g., IAS). To check on a Windows 2003 server, select Add/Remove Windows Components Networking. Internet Authentication Service should be unchecked, as shown in Figure 3-9.

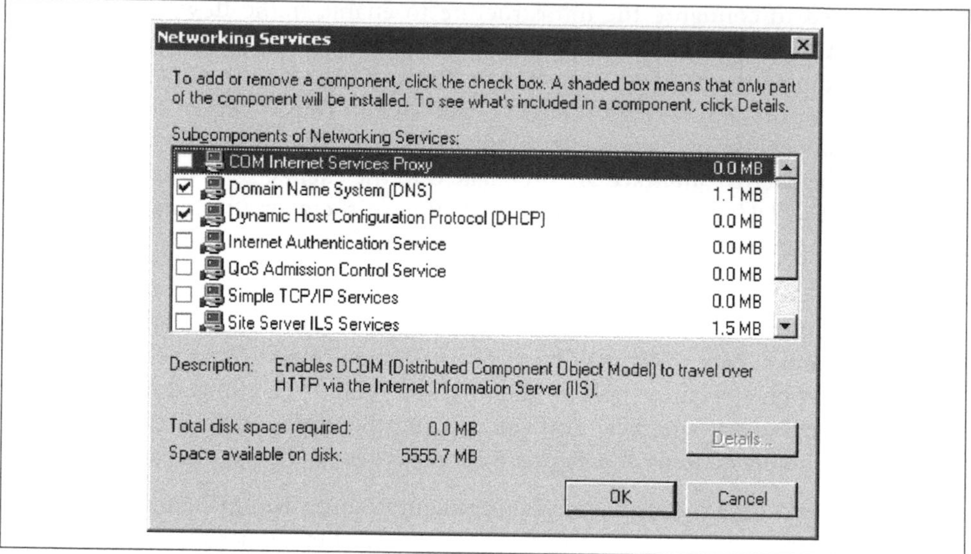

Figure 3-9. Steel-Belted Radius's Networking Services window

You can download the Steel-Belted Radius server as a demo version from the following link for full functionality for 30 days, after which you must purchase a permanent license:

http://www.juniper.net/customers/support/products/aaa_802/sbr_demo.jsp

Start the installation using the executable you downloaded. Use the wizard to fill in the following sequences:

1. Provide the User Name and Organization details. Select the "Install 30-day trial" license key.
2. Based on your network requirements, choose the RADIUS server type. In this example, we chose Global Enterprise Edition.
3. Choose the install directory for the RADIUS server and any custom settings you need.
4. Provide the administrator account information, which you will use to administer the Steel-Belted Radius server.
5. Choose the server type you would like to configure on this system. For this example, we chose the standalone server.
6. Select to start the Steel-Belted Radius Service after the installation.
7. If you have an RSA server on your network, and you want to use two-factor authentication, you can choose to register now with the RSA server.
8. Complete the Steel-Belted Radius server installation. Note the URL regarding how to launch the administrator to manage the RADIUS server.

Launch the web browser to manage the server at the URL that was provided at the completion of the installation. Click on the Launch link (see Figure 3-10) to access the Steel-Belted Radius Administrator.

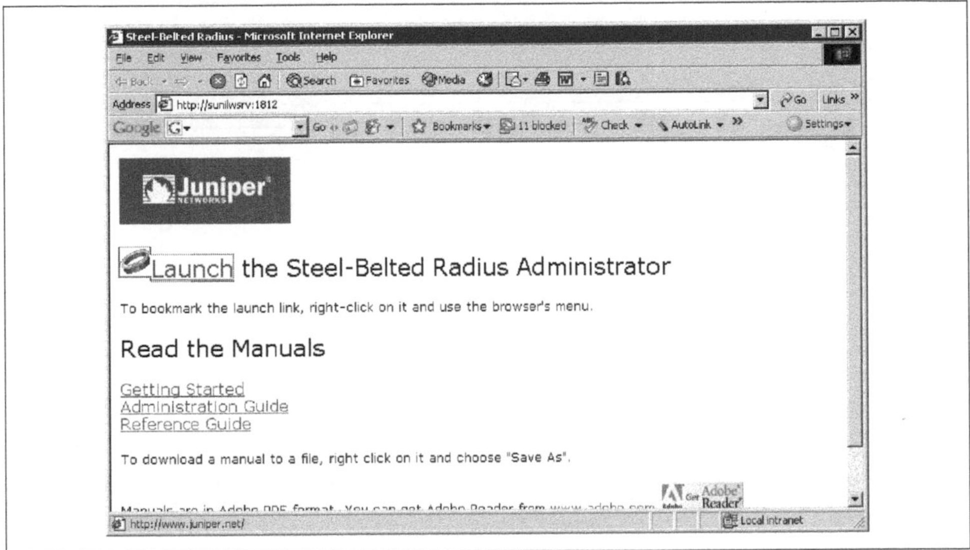

Figure 3-10. Launching the Steel-Belted Radius Administrator

Provide the login username and password to manage the server when prompted (this is the account information you chose during the installation for administration). After the login, you will see the Steel-Belted Radius Server Administrator GUI shown in Figure 3-11.

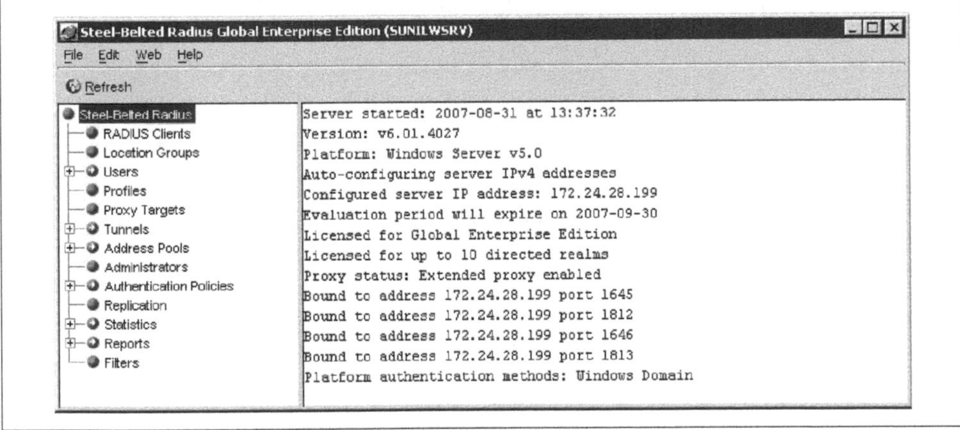

Figure 3-11. The Steel-Belted Radius GUI

Select RADIUS Clients, and add a new RADIUS client to the server. As shown in Figure 3-12, the RADIUS client is the wireless AP IP address from which the authentication request will be sent.

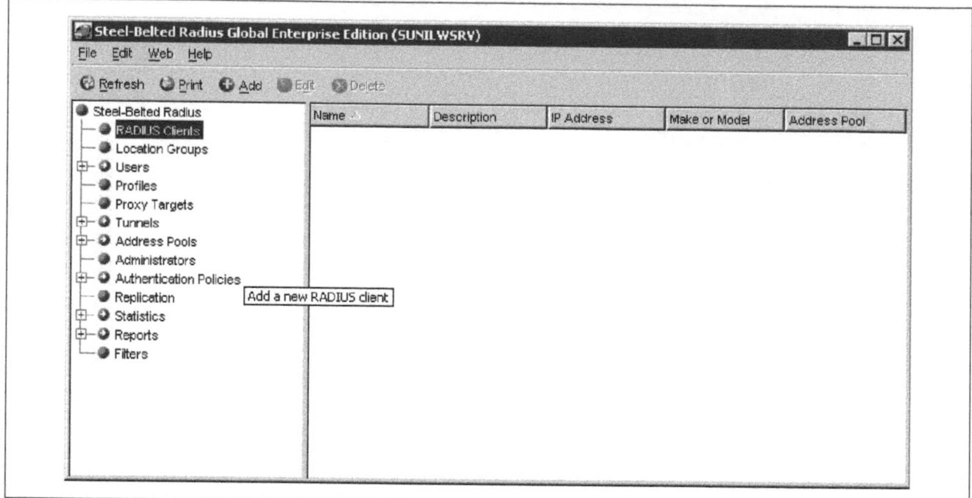

Figure 3-12. Adding a new RADIUS client

In this recipe, we configured the RADIUS client as SSG5-SUNNYVALE, as shown in Figure 3-13; provided the IP address of the SSG5 firewall, and set the RADIUS secret as configured on the firewall. As shown, select Netscreen Technologies in the "Make or model" box.

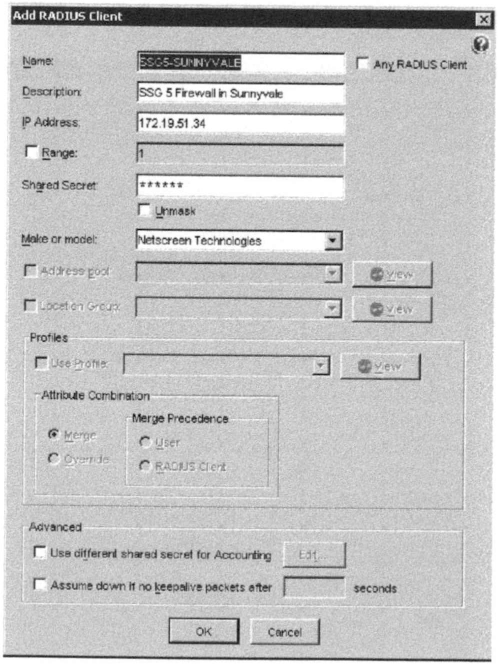

Figure 3-13. Configuring the new RADIUS client

Configure the users you want to authenticate, as shown in Figure 3-14, by clicking on Add Domain User, clicking on the Browse button to choose the Domain and User groups, and authenticating Domain Users in the SUNILW domain.

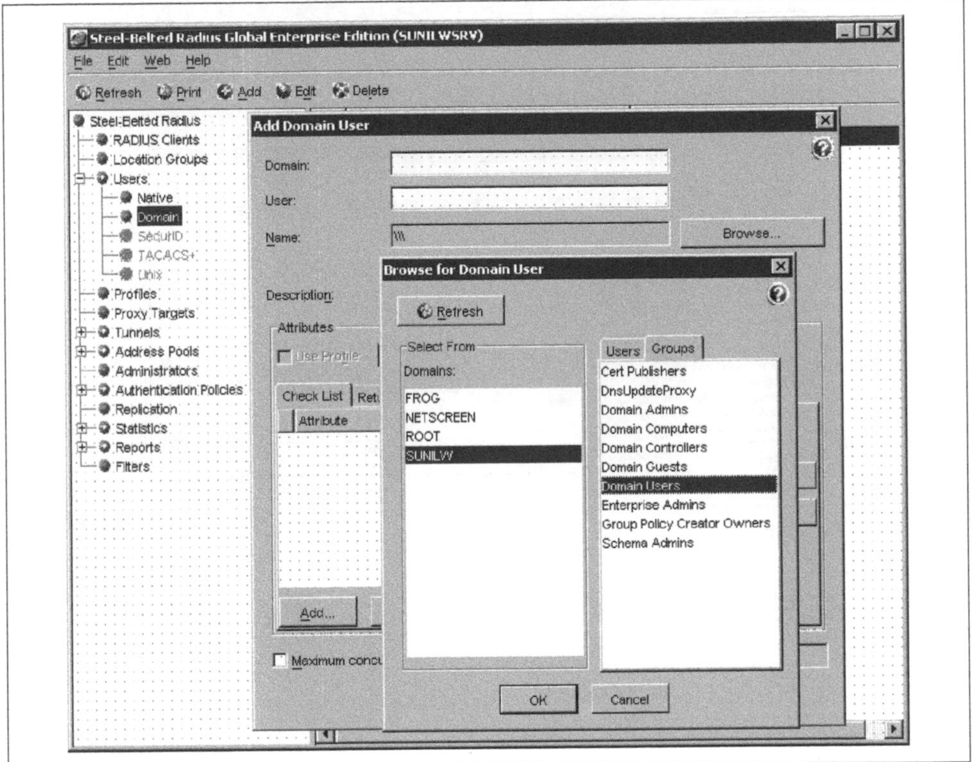

Figure 3-14. Configuring users

Load the certificate you have generated for the Steel-Belted Radius server. Based on your CA, you need to export the certificate, including the private key, to a file. Then, using the Steel-Belted Radius administrator, select Authentication Policies → Certificates → Add, and provide the certificate filename with a *.pfx* extension to import the certificate, as shown in Figure 3-15. This is an important step for the client so that it can communicate with the auth server and authenticate. The certificate you load into Steel-Belted Radius must have an intended purpose of Server-Authentication.

Under the Authentication Policies, select the EAP methods you want to deploy on your network, as shown in Figure 3-16.

Configure the order of the authentication methods for EAP negotiation by selecting Authentication Policies → Order of Methods and choosing the auth methods in the Active Authentication methods. It is best to select only the methods you want to use, and to remove the methods you don't want to deploy; if you have too many methods chosen, you could cause an EAP method mismatch. In this example, we selected

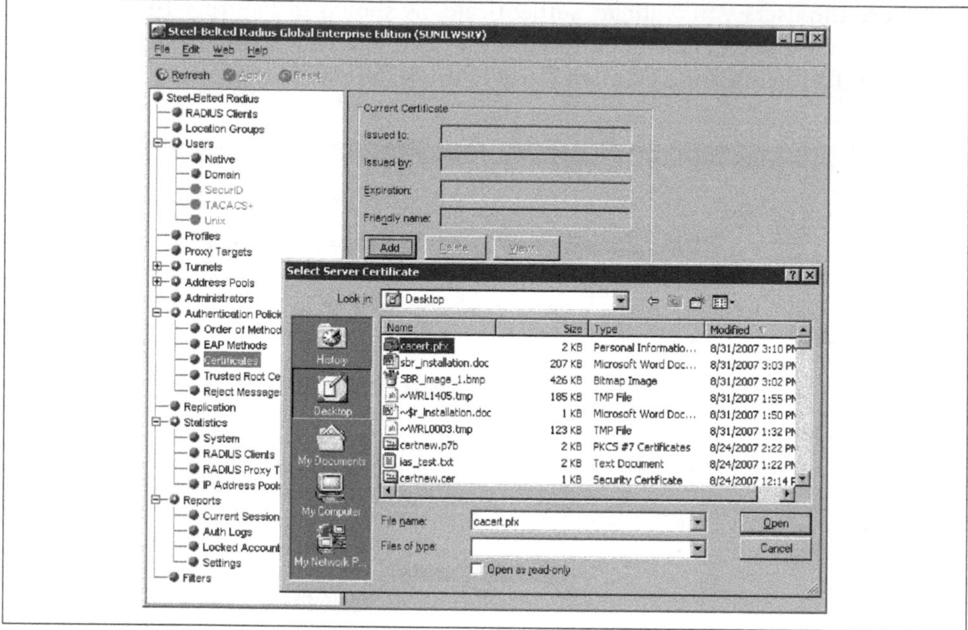

Figure 3-15. Selecting the server certificate

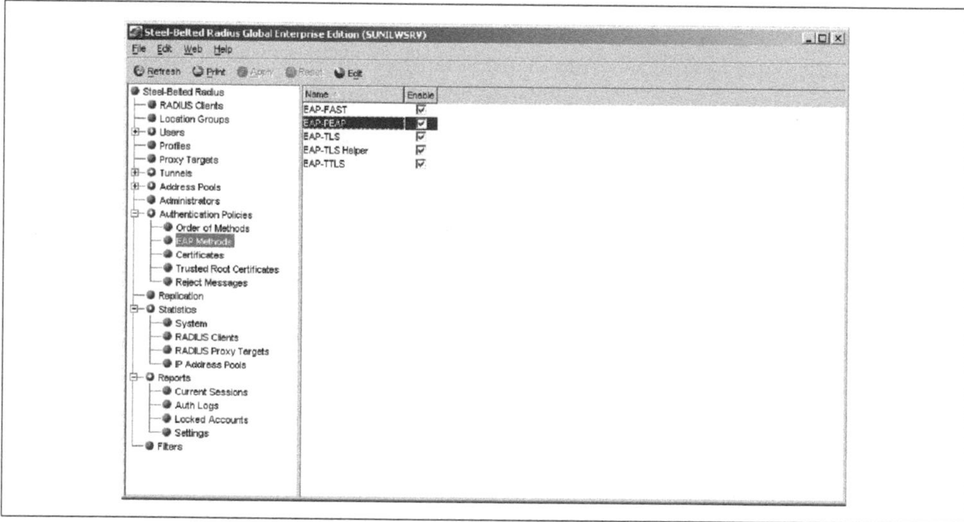

Figure 3-16. Selecting the EAP methods

EAP-PEAP and Windows Domain Group, as shown in Figure 3-17; selected EAP-PEAP and clicked on “EAP setup” on the toolbar; checked “Use EAP authentication only”; selected the Windows Domain Group and EAP to use MS-CHAP V2; and checked the “Handle via Auto-EAP first” method. After changing the configuration, we clicked the Apply button to confirm the changes.

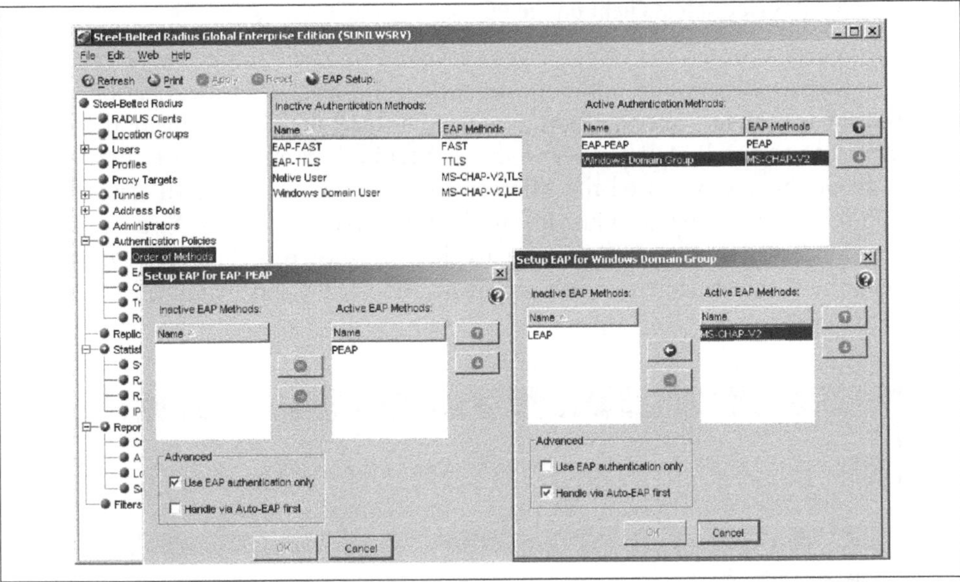

Figure 3-17. Configuring the order of the authentication methods for EAP negotiation

The RADIUS server configuration is now complete. You need to configure the Odyssey Client and wireless AP to authenticate users. You can monitor the statistics counters for the RADIUS clients, as shown in Figure 3-18.

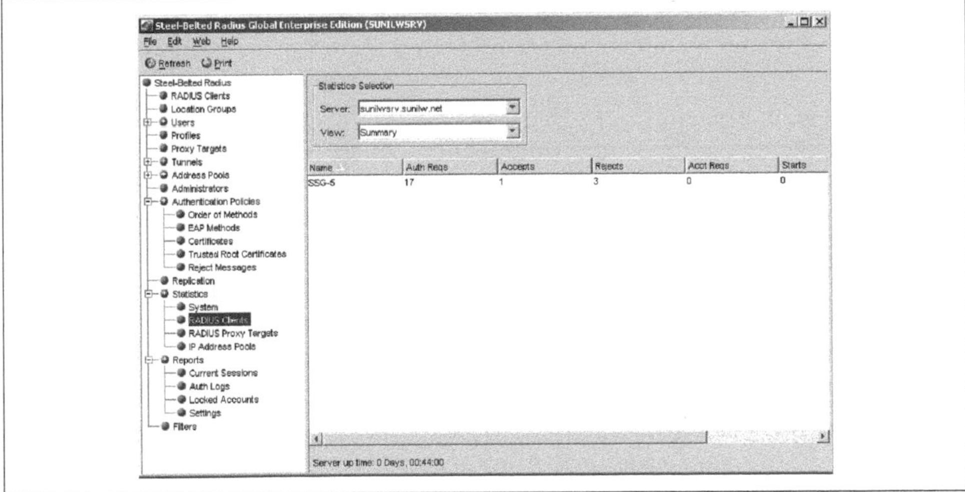

Figure 3-18. Monitoring the statistics counters for the RADIUS clients

You can also view the successful auth requests under Reports → Auth-Logs. Choose the successful authentication request logs, select the date, and click on View to review the logs. To view the failed auth requests, select Reports → Auth-Logs, choose the failed authentication request logs, select the date, and click View to review the logs.

Installing the Odyssey Access Client on the PC

Now you need to install the Odyssey Access Client on the PC that needs to connect to the wireless network and authenticate itself using 802.1*x* authentication. Before you install the Odyssey Access Client, you need to load the CA certificate that issued the certificate to the RADIUS server—this is required to authenticate the RADIUS server. In our recipe, we used the Microsoft CA server to issue certificates for the RADIUS server, so we need to just install the CA Server certificate. You can browse to your CA server using a URL similar to the one shown in Figure 3-19, click on "Retrieve the CA certificate or certificate revocation list", and install the CA certificate to the PC.

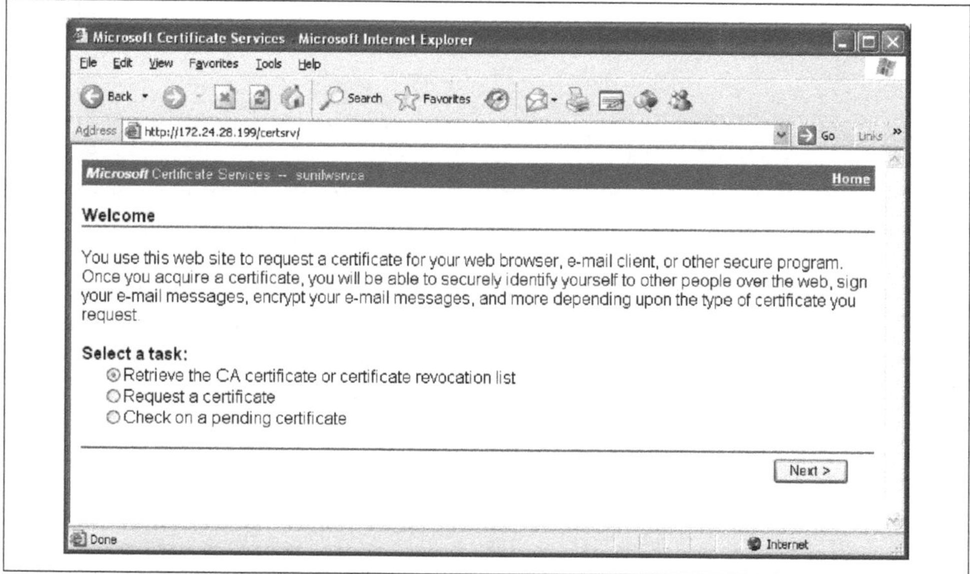

Figure 3-19. Retrieving the CA certificate

You can download the Odyssey Access Client demo version from the same URL from which you downloaded the Steel-Belted Radius server evaluation: *http://www.juniper.net/customers/support/products/aaa_802/sbr_demo.jsp*. You will get a 30-day demo license using the download software. Begin the installation using the downloaded executable by completing the wizard panels that begin with Figure 3-20.

Provide the username, organization detail, and license key, or select the 30-day evaluation license and complete the wizard installation.

Now, start the Odyssey Access Client Manager to configure the wireless adapter to authenticate with the Steel-Belted Radius server through the firewall AP. After you launch the Odyssey Access Client Manager, open the Configuration bin, and click on Profiles to open a screen similar to Figure 3-21. Add a new profile to set up the authentication method for your network.

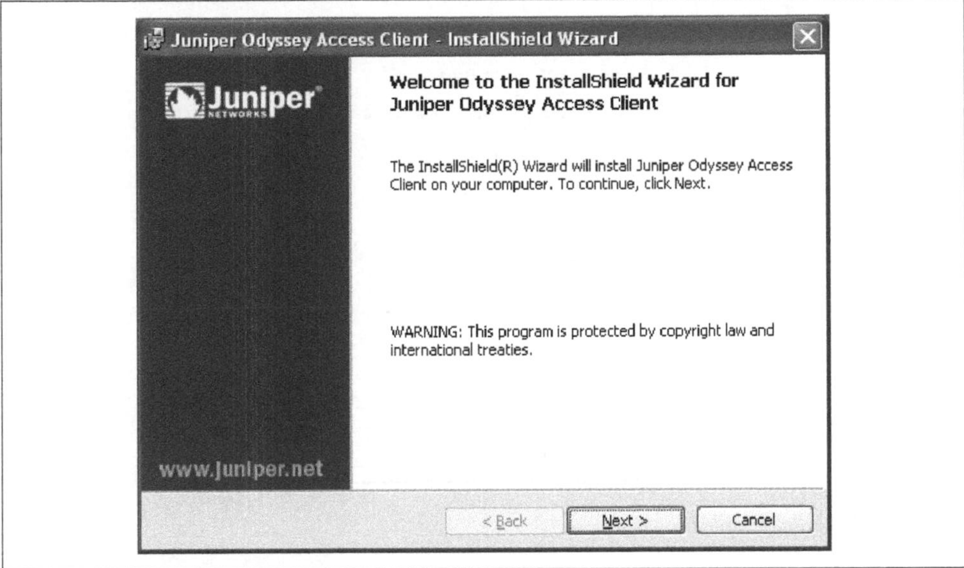

Figure 3-20. Installing the Odyssey Access Client on the PC

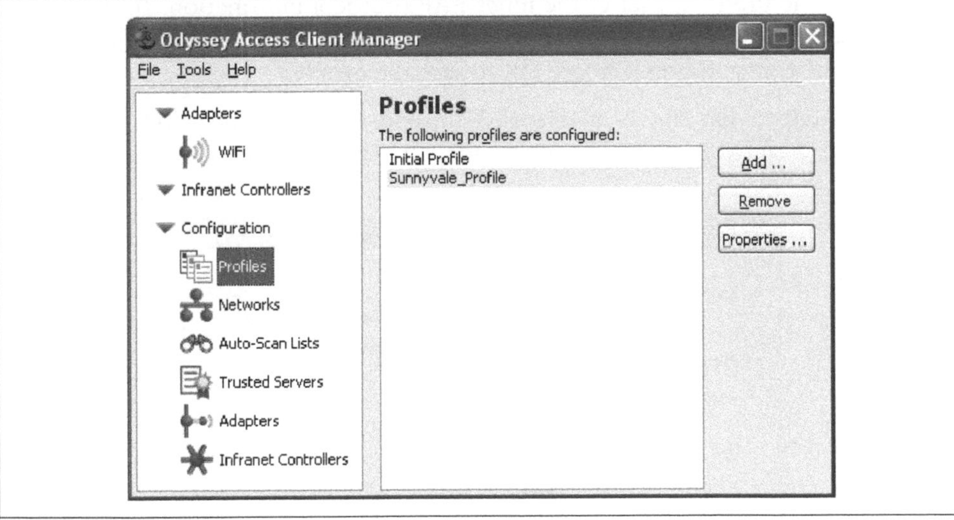

Figure 3-21. Adding a new profile

In this recipe, we created the `Sunnyvale_Profile`. With it highlighted, click on the Properties button to give the profile specific information. In a screen similar to that shown in Figure 3-22, in the User Info tab, we provided the login name, selected "Permit login using password", and chose "Prompt for login name and password". If the PC is already attached to the domain controller, you can use the Windows password. You may also use certificates to authenticate instead of the username/password.

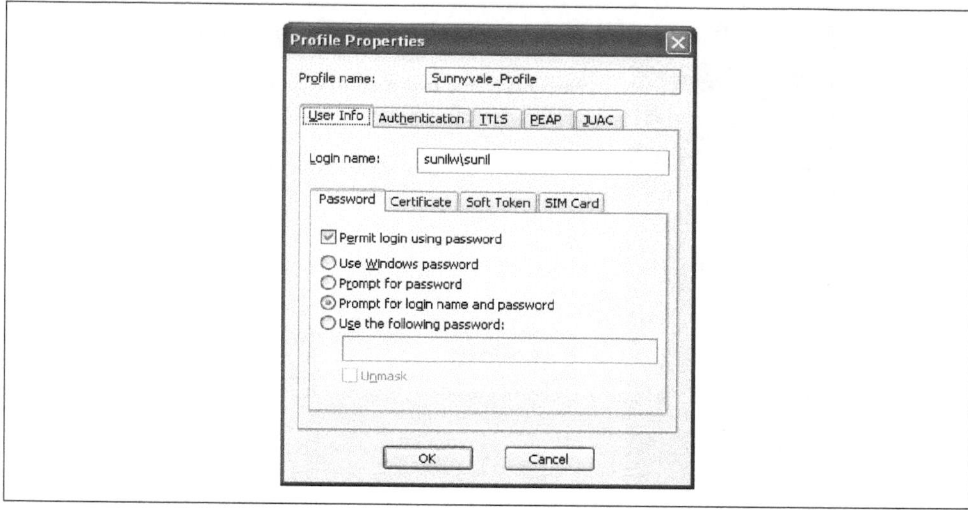

Figure 3-22. Adding profile properties

Next, in the Authentication tab, select the authentication protocols you want to use. We chose EAP-PEAP and EAP-TTLS; however, we will use only EAP-PEAP in this example. In the PEAP tab, select the inner EAP protocol information. In this example, we used EAP-MS-CHAP-V2 and moved it to the top of the protocol list. This completes the configuration. Choose OK to save the profile.

Open the Adapter bin shown in Figure 3-23, and configure the SSID for the AP. Click on the "Use Odyssey to operate this adapter" checkbox shown in Figure 3-23.

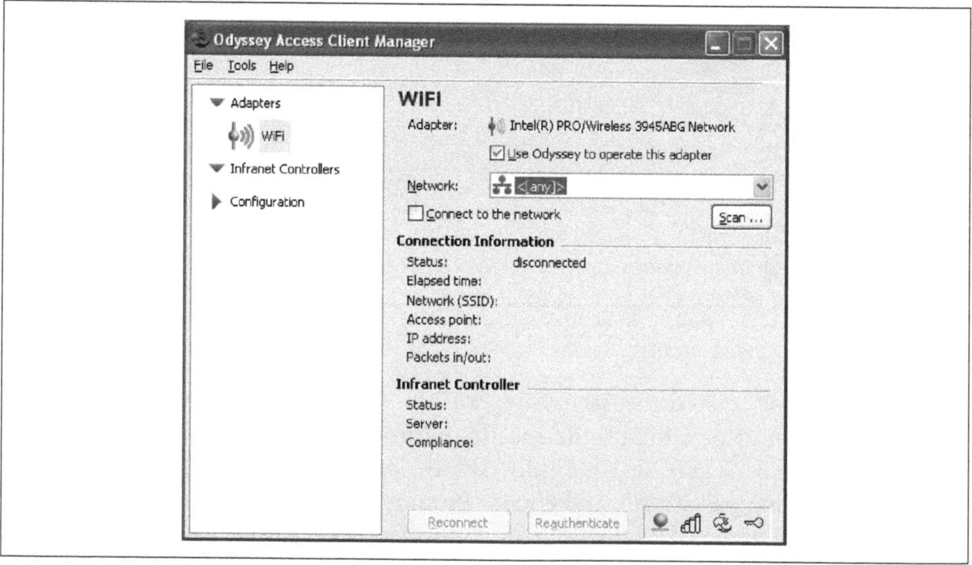

Figure 3-23. The Adapter bin

Click on the Scan button to scan for the SSID for the wireless network. Select the SSID to which you want to connect. After you select the SSID, the Add Network window will open, as shown in Figure 3-24, and will allow you to configure the authentication details. We used the WPA2 association mode and AES encryption. Select "Authenticate using profile" and provide the profile we just created—`Sunnyvale_Profile`—to use the authentication methods for this AP. Click on OK to connect to the AP using 802.1*x* authentication.

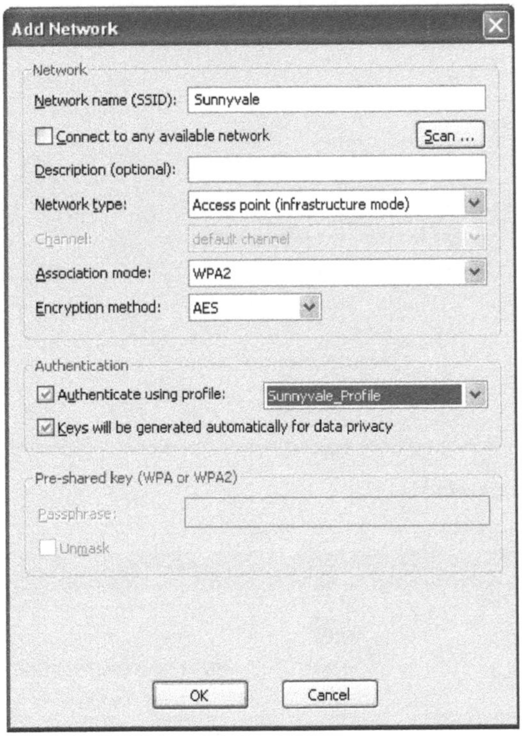

Figure 3-24. The Add Network window

The certificate window will pop up to validate the RADIUS Server Certificate, as shown in Figure 3-25. You can view the certificate and then click Yes to accept. You may also want to add this to the trusted servers to avoid seeing this pop-up window next time.

Because we selected the prompt for the username/password in the profile, we are asked to authenticate by providing the user's password. After successful authentication, the status will show as "open and authenticated", as shown in Figure 3-26. It will also show the IP address assigned to the PC, the AP MAC address, and the packets in/out count.

Odyssey Access Client

You are about to authenticate to an untrusted server!

To terminate communication, press [No]

To temporarily trust this server, press [Yes]

To permanently trust this server, check "add this trusted server to the database" and press [Yes]

Certificate chain:

sunilwsrvca

Funk

View ...

Permanent trust

Add this trusted server to the database

Server name must end with:

Funk

Proceed to authenticate with this server?

Yes No

Figure 3-25. The certificate window

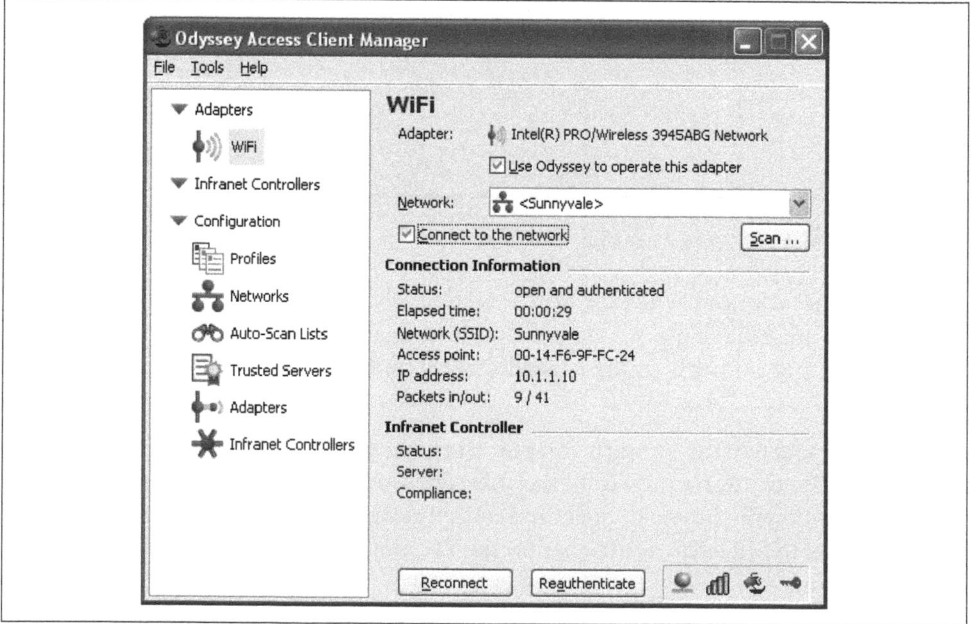

Figure 3-26. Status: open and authenticated

On the firewall, use the get event command output to check the user authentication status. The following output represents a successful authentication log message:

```
2007-09-04 11:03:51 system notif 00564 Wireless station event: Station
                                 001b776779a9 WPA2 authentication
                                 passed, SSID: Sunnyvale.
2007-09-04 11:03:51 system notif 00564 Wireless station event: Station
                                 001b776779a9 WPA2 authentication
                                 negotiating, SSID: Sunnyvale.
2007-09-04 11:03:51 system notif 00564 Wireless station event: Station
                                 001b776779a9 WPA2 authentication
                                 starting, SSID: Sunnyvale.
2007-09-04 11:03:50 system notif 00614 [1X] host 001b.7767.79a9 passed
                                 authentication on interface wireless0/
                                 0 with 802.1X session id 1.
2007-09-04 11:03:50 system notif 00564 Wireless station event: Station
                                 001b776779a9 got key from RADIUS
                                 server, SSID: Sunnyvale.
2007-09-04 11:03:49 system notif 00614 [1X] host 001b.7767.79a9 started
                                 authentication on interface wireless0/
                                 0 with 802.1X session id 1.
2007-09-04 11:03:49 system notif 00564 Wireless station event: station
                                 001b776779a9 is associated, SSID:
                                 Sunnyvale.
2007-09-04 11:03:49 system notif 00564 Wireless station event: Station
                                 001b776779a9 Open authentication
                                 passed, SSID: Sunnyvale.
```

3.6 Separate Wireless Access for Corporate and Guest Users

Problem

You want to provide wireless access for corporate and guest users, but guest users should have access to the Internet only.

Solution

Create security zones for each type of user group. For this recipe, we will create a corp zone for corporate users, and a guest zone for guest users:

```
set zone name "corp"
set zone name "guest"
```

Assign the wireless interfaces wireless0/0 to corp and wireless0/1 to guest; also, configure the wired interfaces ethernet0/0 to the Untrust zone and ethernet0/2 to the Trust zone. Then, configure the IP addresses to each interface:

```
set interface "ethernet0/0" zone "Untrust"
set interface "ethernet0/2" zone "Trust"
set interface "wireless0/0" zone "corp"
set interface "wireless0/1" zone "guest"
```

```
set interface ethernet0/0 ip 192.168.1.35/24
set interface ethernet0/2 ip 192.168.4.1/24
set interface wireless0/0 ip 192.168.2.1/24
set interface wireless0/1 ip 192.168.3.1/24
```

You can use the DHCP server on the wireless network by configuring the DHCP server service on the wireless interfaces:

```
set interface wireless0/0 dhcp server service
set interface wireless0/1 dhcp server service
set interface wireless0/0 dhcp server option gateway 192.168.2.1
set interface wireless0/1 dhcp server option gateway 192.168.3.1
set interface wireless0/0 dhcp server ip 192.168.2.33 to 192.168.2.126
set interface wireless0/1 dhcp server ip 192.168.3.10 to 192.168.3.20
```

For the guest users, configure authentication using webauth to prevent unconstrained access, and then define the users on the device:

```
set interface "wireless0/1" webauth ssl-only
set interface "wireless0/1" webauth-ip 192.168.3.5

set user "guest1" uid 1
set user "guest1" type  auth
set user "guest1" hash-password "026Q18FGRiRbJ0wq93hvV+Mz5Q3qiAguQ="
set user "guest1" "enable"

set user "guest2" uid 2
set user "guest2" type  auth
set user "guest2" hash-password "026Q18FGRiRbJ0wq93hvV+Mz5Q3qiAguQ="
set user "guest2" "enable
```

Having separated users using zones, we can control the traffic between zones using firewall policies. Enable webauth for the traffic from guest to Untrust to have users authenticate before accessing the interface. The following example allows all traffic from wireless networks to the Internet. The default implicit policy will block traffic from guest to Trust and corp; this will achieve total separation of guest users and corporate users.

```
set policy id 1 from "Trust" to "Untrust"  "Any" "Any" "ANY" permit
set policy id 2 from "corp" to "Untrust"  "Any" "Any" "ANY" nat src
   permit
set policy id 3 from "guest" to "Untrust"  "Any" "Any" "ANY" nat src
   permit webauth
set policy id 4 from "corp" to "Trust"  "Any" "Any" "ANY" permit
```

Create the wireless SSID for the corporate users, and then enable client isolation to prevent client-to-client bridging. Enable authentication using WPA-PSK and auto encryption. Bind the SSID to the wireless interface:

```
set ssid name corp
set ssid corp client-isolation
set ssid corp authentication wpa-psk passphrase mFUjDlxNN5O/nAsUC4CcG3BRg2nVkzaJuQ==
encryption auto
set ssid corp interface wireless0
```

Create the wireless SSID for the guest users, and enable client isolation to prevent client-to-client bridging. Use open authentication and no encryption to allow guest users to connect to the AP. Bind the SSID to the wireless interface:

```
set ssid name guest
set ssid guest client-isolation
set ssid guest authentication open encryption none
set ssid guest interface wireless1
```

Discussion

The ScreenOS wireless configuration uses the infrastructure of interfaces, zones, and security policies to secure the wireless APs. The APs provide multiple wireless interfaces for user connection. Each wireless interface can be bound to an SSID to separate user traffic. The underlining zones and security policies control the traffic flow.

In this recipe, you will first configure the SSID for each user profile, with SSID `corp` for the corporate users, and SSID `guest` for the guest users. Figure 3-27 shows the topology of our example.

Figure 3-27. Separating wireless access for corporate and guest users

Typically, corporate users have their systems provided by internal IT and are preconfigured for the network resources. Although there are multiple ways to authenticate the corporate user connection, in this example, we are only showing how to configure WPA-PSK as the authentication type and are assuming that the preshared secret is configured by the internal IT team (the user does not know the preshared secret to keep the key secure).

The basic configuration entails creating the SSID name and defining its properties. In this example, we defined the SSID as `corp`, and the authentication type as `WPA-PSK`, with the encryption type as `auto` (the end user can choose to use AES or TKIP), and bound the `corp` SSID to the `wireless0` interface. We also enabled client isolation on this SSID to prevent users from peer-to-peer bridging, so they would have to use the security policies to allow this traffic.

Guest users who might be visiting customers or partners would just need to get access to the Internet. We don't want them to access our internal resources, and we want to separate them from our corporate users. To achieve this goal, we defined a different SSID for them called `guest` with `Open` as the authentication type and `None` as the encryption type, then bound it to the `wireless1` interface. Because this is going to be an open connection, and anybody can associate with the AP, we want to put in some restrictions, so we will use the security policy to have some user authentication using `webauth`. See Recipe 13.5 for more on `webauth`.

For the guest users, we defined two local authentication users on the firewall, called `guest1` and `guest2`. You can use an external database for these users as well, but for this recipe, we will use the local database.

Now, let's configure the infrastructure to provide the wireless service on the network.

First, we will assign the wireless interfaces to the zones. We have configured different zones to separate users based on their security requirements. Corporate users will connect to the `corp` zone and guest users will connect to the `guest` zone. We assigned the `wireless0` interface to the `corp` zone and the `wireless1` interface to the `guest` zone. Next, we need to define the IP address for these interfaces, so we configured `192.168.2.1/24` for the `wireless0` interface and `192.168.3.1/24` for the `wireless1` interface. For wireless users connecting to the `ethernet0/2` interface, which belongs to the `Trust` zone, will have the `192.168.4.1/24` IP address. For the interface access, we will use the `192.168.1.35/24` address (the Internet connection belongs to the `Untrust` zone).

We will enable the DHCP server service on the wireless interface to assign the IP address to the wireless users associating with this AP. Here, we have defined only the basic parameters for the DHCP service, such as the gateway and IP address range. To provide user authentication for guest users, we will enable `webauth` on the `wireless1` interface and use only HTTPS to authenticate. We configured `192.168.3.5` as the `webauth` IP address, and selected `ssl-only` as the method to authenticate users. You may also define the banner for these users based on your organization's security policy.

Lastly, we need to define the security policy to allow traffic flow. So far, we have only configured the user association to the AP, so the end-user traffic will flow only when it matches a security policy. Because we have put different user types in different zones, we have already achieved the goal of separating the user traffic, and users will not be able to communicate across the `corp` and `guest` zones. We have defined a security policy ID of `1` for traffic from the `Trust` zone to the `Untrust` zone, a security policy ID of 2 and 3 to allow wireless users from the corp and guest zones to send traffic to the interface in the Untrust zone, and a security policy ID of 4 to allow the corporate wireless users to connect to the Trust zone users. The implicit deny policy will drop all other traffic, hence preventing guest wireless users from accessing the Trust and corp users. You may want to restrict these policies further to allow traffic based on your organization's security policy.

Finally, we need to activate the wireless AP. Always remember to activate changes on the firewall using the exec wlan reactivate command. This is a disruptive command, and users will be disconnected from the AP while the APs are being reconfigured. Anytime you make any changes to wireless configurations, you have to use this command to push configurations to the AP engines on the firewall. The following output is based on how many interfaces you have configured:

```
ssg5-> exec wlan reactivate
wireless0/0 interface change physical state to Down
wireless0/1 interface change physical state to Down

Start wireless access point physical initialization...

Wireless access point physical initialization done
wireless0/0 interface change physical state to Up
wireless0/1 interface change physical state to Up
```

To debug your configuration, you can use the get event command to check whether users are able to associate with the AP. Here's an example of a user connecting to the corp SSID (if you have any issues, check to ensure that users have the correct preshared secret):

```
2007-08-22 09:36:31 system notif 00564 Wireless station event: Station
                                 000cf122bfa2 WPA authentication
                                 passed, SSID: corp.
2007-08-22 09:36:31 system notif 00564 Wireless station event: Station
                                 000cf122bfa2 WPA authentication
                                 negotiating, SSID: corp.
```

3.7 Configure Bridge Groups for Wired and Wireless Networks

Problem

You want to configure Bridge Groups for wired/wireless networks to share IP addresses and make the networks seamless.

Solution

Configure the zone that will contain the wired and wireless network and assign bgroup0 to the zone. Also, assign the wired interface and wireless interface to the bgroup0 interface:

```
set zone name Corp
set interface "bgroup0" zone "Corp"
set interface bgroup0 port ethernet0/6
set interface bgroup0 port wireless0/0
```

Then, configure the IP address for the bgroup0 interface and enable DHCP for automatic IP address allocations:

```
set interface bgroup0 ip 10.10.10.1/24
set interface bgroup0 dhcp server service
set interface bgroup0 dhcp server enable
set interface bgroup0 dhcp server option gateway 10.10.10.1
set interface bgroup0 dhcp server option netmask 255.255.255.0
set interface bgroup0 dhcp server ip 10.10.10.100 to 10.10.10.130
```

Configure the SSID for the wireless network, and bind the wireless interface to the SSID. Then, activate the wireless configuration:

```
set ssid name Secured
set ssid Secured client-isolation
set ssid Secured authentication wpa-auto-psk passphrase Secret
   encryption auto
set ssid Secured interface wireless0

exec wlan reactivate
```

Finally, configure the security policy to allow traffic across zones:

```
set policy from corp to untrust any any any nat src permit
```

Discussion

You can use Bridge Groups to combine wired and wireless interfaces at the Layer 2 level and make the network seamless. This feature is supported only in the SSG5 and the SSG20 as of this writing. The traffic between wireless and wired networks is switched by the interface driver, and it is not inspected by the security policy, even if you have client isolation configured on the SSID.

To share the IP subnet between ethernet0/6 and wireless0/0 interfaces, create a zone called Corp which will contain the bgroup0. Then, assign the ethernet0/6 and wireless0/0 interfaces to bgroup0. All the Layer 3 configurations will be done on the bgroup0 interface, and the wireless interface will act as a Layer 2 interface in the group. Configure the IP address 10.10.10.1/24 on the bgroup0 interface, and then enable the DHCP service on the bgroup0 interface. The PC connected on the ethernet0/6 and wireless0/0 interfaces will receive IP address allocations from the same DHCP pool addresses. In this example, we configured the DHCP pool address from 10.10.10.100–10.10.10.130:

```
set zone name Corp
set interface "bgroup0" zone "Corp"
set interface bgroup0 port ethernet0/6
set interface bgroup0 port wireless0/0
set interface bgroup0 ip 10.10.10.1/24
```

```
set interface bgroup0 dhcp server service
set interface bgroup0 dhcp server enable
set interface bgroup0 dhcp server option gateway 10.10.10.1
set interface bgroup0 dhcp server option netmask 255.255.255.0
set interface bgroup0 dhcp server ip 10.10.10.100 to 10.10.10.130
```

Now, configure the SSID for the wireless network. Create the SSID named `Secured` with an authentication method using WPA-AUTO-PSK, which will allow WPA and WPA2 users with preshared security to authenticate using the auto encryption type by electing to use AES or TKIP. Now, activate wireless configuration by using the exec `wlan reactivate` command to push configuration to the wireless AP:

```
set ssid name Secured
set ssid Secured authentication wpa-auto-psk passphrase Secret encryption auto
set ssid Secured interface wireless0

exec wlan reactivate
```

Lastly, configure the security policy to allow traffic based on your network security policy. In this example, we are allowing all traffic from the `corp` zone to the `Untrust` zone from any source IP, destination IP, and service. Also, the source IP address will be NAT using the egress interface IP address. Remember that this policy does not control the traffic between the `ethernet0/6` and `wireless0/0` interfaces. The traffic between the Bridge Group interfaces are switched by the MAC chip on the device, and transit traffic does not reach the CPU for policy inspection.

```
set policy from corp to untrust any any any nat src permit
```

You can view the `bgroup0` interface using the `get interface` command. In the following example, `bgroup0` shows that `eth0/6` and `wireless0/0` are assigned to the Bridge Group. The IP address is not configurable on the physical interface once bound to the `bgroup`:

```
SSG5-> get interface

A - Active, I - Inactive, U - Up, D - Down, R - Ready

Interfaces in vsys Root:
Name           IP Address       Zone     MAC             VLAN State VSD
serial0/0      0.0.0.0/0        Null     0017.cb82.38d9    -    U    -
eth0/0         192.168.1.35/24  Untrust  0017.cb82.38c0    -    U    -
eth0/1         0.0.0.0/0        Null     0017.cb82.38c5    -    D    -
eth0/2         0.0.0.0/0        Null     0017.cb82.38c6    -    D    -
eth0/3         0.0.0.0/0        Null     0017.cb82.38c7    -    D    -
eth0/4         0.0.0.0/0        Null     0017.cb82.38c8    -    D    -
eth0/5         0.0.0.0/0        Null     0017.cb82.38c9    -    D    -
wireless0/1    0.0.0.0/0        Null     0017.cb82.38d6    -    D    -
wireless0/2    0.0.0.0/0        Null     0017.cb82.38d7    -    D    -
wireless0/3    0.0.0.0/0        Null     0017.cb82.38d8    -    D    -
bgroup0        10.10.10.1/24    Corp     0017.cb82.38cb    -    U    -
  eth0/6       N/A              N/A      N/A               -    U    -
  wireless0/0  N/A              N/A      N/A               -    U    -
bgroup1        0.0.0.0/0        Null     0017.cb82.38cc    -    D    -
bgroup2        0.0.0.0/0        Null     0017.cb82.38cd    -    D    -
```

```
bgroup3          0.0.0.0/0         Null      0017.cb82.38ce    -   D   -
vlan1            0.0.0.0/0         VLAN      0017.cb82.18cf    1   D   -
null             0.0.0.0/0         Null      N/A               -   U   0
SSG5->
```

You can view the wireless interface properties by using the `get interface wireless0` command. In this example, the wireless AP 2.4G radio and the SSID are secure:

```
SSG5-> get int w0
Interface wireless0/0:
  description wireless0/0
  number 21, if_info 8568, if_index 0
  link up, phy-link up
  member of bgroup0
  vsys Root, zone Null, vr untrust-vr
  *ip 0.0.0.0/0   mac 0017.cb82.38d5
  wireless AP 2.4G radio mac  0017.cb82.38e0
  ssid is Secured
pmtu-v4 disabled
....
 <Output omitted>
```

You can view the port binding and status using the `get interface bgroup0` command, as shown here:

```
SSG5-> get int b0
Interface bgroup0:
.......... <Output Omitted>>
  Physical port information:
    ethernet0/6 is up, full duplex, speed is 100mbps
    wireless0/0 is up
```

You can view the client association to the physical interface using the `get interface wireless0 association` command. In the following example, you can see the wireless association from the PC with the MAC address `0019d2c8d250`:

```
SSG5-> get int w0 ass
index   mac address     state   encryption    mode
=====================================================
1       0019d2c8d250    assoc   on            11g
=====================================================
SSG5->
```

You can also view the `mac-table` for `bgroup0` using the `get interface bgroup0 mac-table` command; however, this command will show the `mac-table` for wired physical interfaces only. You will have to use the `get int w0 ass` command to check the wireless interface associations. In the example, we used `mac-table` entries for the `ethernet0/6` interface:

```
SSG5-> get int bgroup0 mac-table
This command will not show the mac-table for wireless interfaces.
Interface             MAC Address
***********************************
ethernet0/6           0015c5785eff

***********************************
```

CHAPTER 4

Route Mode and Static Routing

4.0 Introduction

Routing is the most important factor for traffic to flow over the network. Every packet traveling from Host A to Host B needs to have a defined path; otherwise, communication over the network is impossible. The defined path can be a default route, or it can be specific routes for an IP address. The paths can be configured manually using static routing, or they can be established using dynamic methods with the help of routing protocols, such as the Open Shortest Path First (OSPF) protocol, the Border Gateway Protocol (BGP), and the Routing Information Protocol (RIP).

Each path is considered to be a route and has the following elements:

Prefix
: The IP address and mask. This is the IP address for which the route is defined.

Next hop
: The gateway IP address, and the interface or Virtual Router (VR). This is where the packet should be forwarded for the IP address.

Preferences
: The priority for the route.

Metric
: The cost associated with the route.

Tag
: Used to identify the route for filtering or redistribution into other instances.

The collection of all paths is kept in a database called the *routing table*.

In ScreenOS software, you can deploy a firewall in three different system modes: Network Address Translation (NAT) mode, route mode, and transparent mode. The routing table is used differently in each mode. When the device is in transparent mode, the device utilizes the Media Access Control (MAC) table to forward packets;

while in NAT/route mode, the device uses the route table to make forwarding decisions. You can check in which mode the system is operating with the `get system` command. This example shows a system operating in NAT/route mode:

```
SSG-> get sys
Product Name: SSG-140
.......
....

System in NAT/route mode.

Use interface IP, Config Port: 80
User Name: netscreen
```

The system mode is determined based on how you configure the interfaces. By default, when you put an interface in the `Trust` zone, it operates in NAT mode; for all other zones, the interface operates in route mode. If you assign interfaces to `V1-Trust`, `V1-Untrust`, or any user-defined Layer 2 zone, the device operates in transparent mode, which means that the firewall operates as a switch on the network. If you assign interfaces to `Trust`, `Untrust`, or any user-defined Layer 3 zones and assign IP addresses to the interfaces, the device operates in NAT or route mode. To configure the ingress interface to be in NAT mode, use the command `set interface e1 nat`. This means you want NAT to be performed on ingress traffic on this interface while crossing the firewall. The firewall performs NAT on traffic only if the interface belongs to a predefined `Trust` zone and the egress interface goes to the `Untrust` zone. If the interface belongs to a user-defined zone such as `Private`, the device does not perform NAT on the traffic, and you would have to cross the VRs for NAT to happen.

In route mode, NAT is not performed on any traffic, and the traffic is forwarded with the original IP address that the firewall received in the packet. You can change the interface mode to route mode using the command `set interface e1 route`.

The ScreenOS software has the concept of VRs, which are routing table instances. A device can have multiple VRs. Each VR has its own routing tables, which provide routing security by separating the routing tables on the firewall. Each interface is bound to a zone, and each zone is bound to a VR (see Figure 4-1).

The system-defined VRs on the device are `trust-vr` and `untrust-vr`. All zones are bound to `trust-vr`. You can configure interfaces to be in different zones. Refer to Chapter 1 for information on how to configure and separate the routing instances on the firewall.

In ScreenOS software, VRs are populated with routes from connected/host routes (derived from interface IP addresses), static routes, dynamic routing protocols (such as OSPF, BGP, RIP, the Internet Group Management Protocol [IGMP], and the Protocol Independent Multicast [PIM] protocol), and imported routes from other VRs.

Each VR has several routing tables: the destination IP-based table, the source IP-based table, the source interface-based table, the policy-based route table, and the multicast

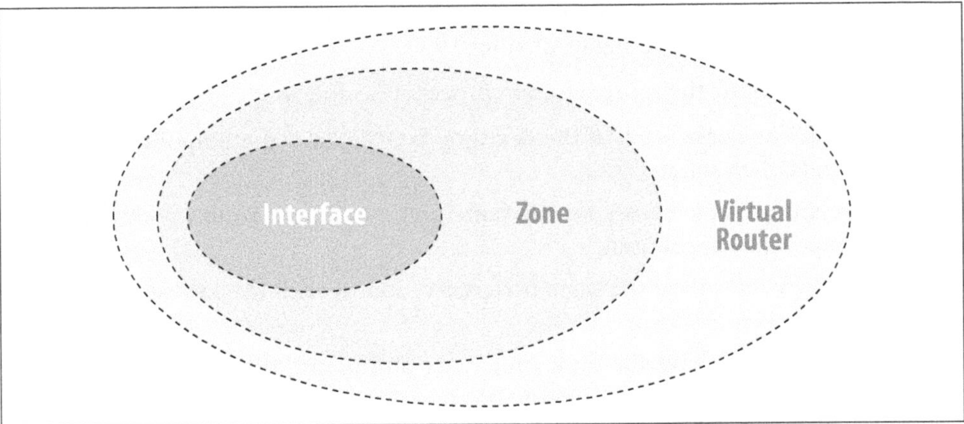

Figure 4-1. Each interface bound to a zone, and each zone bound to a VR

route table. This chapter concentrates on the static route configuration and route preferences. You can configure any of the following static routes on the firewall:

- Destination IP static route
- Source-based static route
- Source interface-based static route
- Policy-based routing

It is common to configure destination IP static routes. You configure the path for the destination IP address of the packet. Traditionally, all routing devices configure routes for the destination IP address and provide the next-hop gateway address. When the device is forwarding packets, all route lookups are done based on the destination IP address.

In ScreenOS software, you can configure source-based routing. This means that you want the routing decision to be made based on the source IP address of the packet. Use this method when you want some hosts to take Path A and others to take Path B in the traffic flow. For example, you might want traffic from contractors to use a slower Internet link and traffic from regular employees to use a faster Internet link.

With source interface-based routing, the routing decision is based on two factors: the source IP address of the packet and the ingress interface on which the packet arrived. You might use this when you don't want traffic coming from a lab network to use the Internet link and you want to drop these packets, but when you do want traffic from other corporate divisions that use the same source IP address on a different ingress interface to be allowed to pass through, using source-based routing or destination IP-based routing.

You can configure routing policies using policy-based routing, which makes the routing decision on five tuples—the source IP address, source port, destination IP address, destination port, and protocol—and the packet's Type of Service (ToS) bits. We discuss policy-based routing in Chapter 19.

In ScreenOS software, the route selection process is as follows:

1. A route is considered only if the next hop is a VR or if the outgoing interface is not in the Down state.
2. If there are multiple routes for the same prefix (subnet), routes with the lowest preference value are chosen.
3. If multiple routes have the same preference, routes with the lowest metric value are chosen.
4. If multiple routes have the same preference and metric values, the first installed route in the routing table is chosen.
5. If Equal Cost Multipath (ECMP) is enabled, all routes are considered to be active, and traffic is distributed in a round-robin fashion among them. The round-robin distribution is done per session, not per packet.
6. All active routes are placed into the routing table, which is used for route lookups. The longest prefix is matched first.

The following are the default preferences on the firewall:

```
SSG-> get vr trust-vr preference
vrouter trust-vr route preference table
--------------------------------------------
Host Routes:            0
Connected Routes:       0
Static Routes:          20
Auto-exported Routes:   30
Imported Routes:        140
RIP Routes:             100
EBGP Routes:            40
IBGP Routes:            250
OSPF Routes:            60
OSPF External Type-2 Routes:    200
NewYork->
```

You can change the preferences using the `set vr trust-vr preference` command. Here is an example of changing the static route preference to 40:

```
SSG-> set vr trust-vr preference static 40
```

For static routes, you can configure the metric. For dynamic routing protocols, the metric is derived based on the routing protocol calculations and interface costs. You cannot change the metric for connected/host routes.

Now that you understand that there are multiple routing tables in the VR, how do you figure out which table is used when the firewall receives a packet? The route lookup is done on the ingress interface to the VR based on the configured lookup preference. By default, the route lookup preference is done in the following order:

policy-based routing, source interface-based routing, source-based routing, and destination-based routing. You can change the route lookup preference, as demonstrated in Recipe 4.9. Figure 4-2 shows the route lookup process for a packet on the firewall.

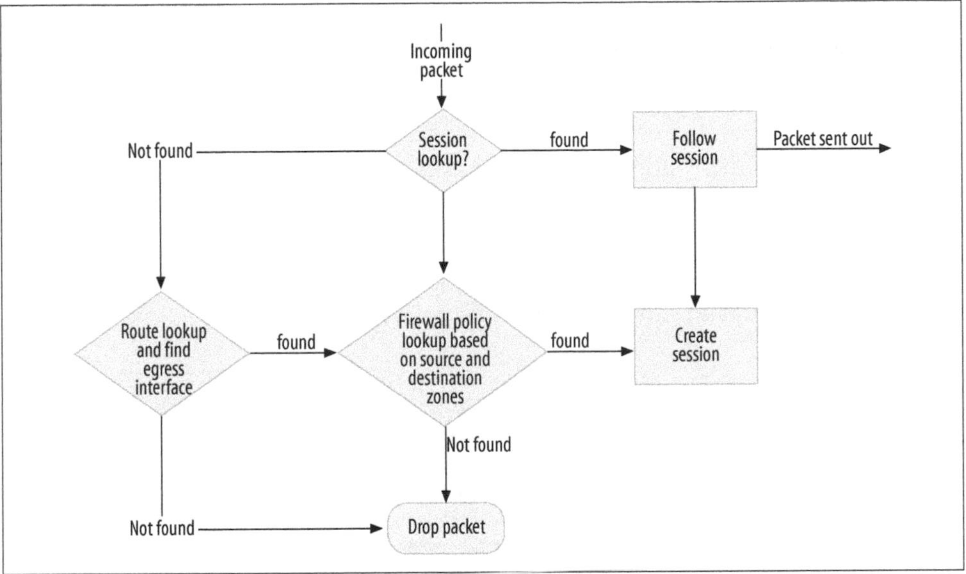

Figure 4-2. Route lookup process for a packet on the firewall

Once the session is created, it contains a pointer to the route ID and the Address Resolution Protocol (ARP) for the next-hop gateway IP address. Traffic is allowed to pass through the device based on the matched session. However, if the route has changed, the traffic has to flow along a different path. The route change is allowed only if the new path is also reachable in the same zone. If the new path crosses into another zone, the traffic is not allowed and the firewall drops it. This occurs because of the statefulness of the firewall.

The sequence is as follows:

- A route becomes inactive because the next hop is not reachable. All sessions using this route are notified.
- If a route becomes active, all sessions using this route are notified. Any route with a longer prefix is used if all the following conditions are met:
  - The new route's interface differs from the old route's interface.
  - The new route's gateway differs from the old route's gateway.
  - The zone of the new route's interface differs from the zone of the old route's interface.

When a session is notified, a new route lookup occurs when the next packet for that session arrives; if the interface belongs to a different zone from the previous routes, the route will not be used. The route failover occurs only when both interfaces belong to the same zone.

4.1 View the Routing Table on the Firewall

Problem

You want to view the routing table on the firewall to verify which IP networks are reachable.

Solution

The get route command shows the contents of the routing table:

```
SSG-> get route


IPv4 Dest-Routes for <untrust-vr> (0 entries)
--------------------------------------------------------------------------
H: Host C: Connected S: Static A: Auto-Exported
I: Imported R: RIP P: Permanent D: Auto-Discovered
iB: IBGP eB: EBGP O: OSPF E1: OSPF external type 1
E2: OSPF external type 2


IPv4 Dest-Routes for <trust-vr> (4 entries)
--------------------------------------------------------------------------
     ID         IP-Prefix  Interface    Gateway   P Pref    Mtr     Vsys
--------------------------------------------------------------------------
*    4          1.1.1.2/32    eth0/1    0.0.0.0   H    0      0     Root
*    2      192.168.1.1/32    eth0/0    0.0.0.0   H    0      0     Root
*    1      192.168.1.0/24    eth0/0    0.0.0.0   C    0      0     Root
*    3          1.1.1.0/24    eth0/1    0.0.0.0   C    0      0     Root
```

If IPv6 is enabled on the firewall, the routing table contains its routes. These are listed at the end of the get route command, or you can display them separately with the get route v6 command:

```
SSG-> get route v6


IPv6 Dest-Routes for <untrust-vr> (0 entries)
--------------------------------------------------------------------------
H: Host C: Connected S: Static A: Auto-Exported
I: Imported R: RIP P: Permanent D: Auto-Discovered
iB: IBGP eB: EBGP O: OSPF E1: OSPF external type 1
E2: OSPF external type 2
```

```
IPv6 Dest-Routes for <trust-vr> (2 entries)
--------------------------------------------------------------------
  ID       IP-Prefix   Interface         Gateway   P Pref  Mtr    Vsys
--------------------------------------------------------------------
*  3     9009:1::/64     eth0/3 ::    C   0       0    Root
*  4 9009:1::205:85ff:fe7e:2f87/128  eth0/3 ::   H    0     0   Root
```

When dynamic routing protocols are running on the device, you can use the get route prot *<protocol>* command to list routes specific to the routing protocol, such as OSPF, BGP, RIP, and RIPng (next generation), as well as static routes:

```
SSG-> get route prot ospf


IPv4 Dest-Routes for <trust-vr> (8 entries)
--------------------------------------------------------------------
 ID          IP-Prefix   Interface          Gateway   P Pref Mtr  Vsys
--------------------------------------------------------------------
* 8   192.168.2.0/24        tun.1   192.168.254.1   O   60  11  Root
```

Discussion

The get route command is the basic command for listing routes in the routing table. The first command in this recipe, without any options, shows the contents of all the routing tables. This output shows the contents of two routing tables, trust-vr and untrust-vr, which are the default VRs on the firewall. By default, all interfaces are in the trust-vr routing table.

The first line shows which VR you are viewing. The next four lines of the get route output show the description of the P (Protocol) column for the entries in the route table:

```
H: Host C: Connected S: Static A: Auto-Exported
I: Imported R: RIP P: Permanent D: Auto-Discovered
iB: IBGP eB: EBGP O: OSPF E1: OSPF external type 1
E2: OSPF external type 2
```

The trust-vr table shows four routes: two connected routes and two host routes. On the left of the route entry, an asterisk (*) indicates which routes are the active routes. If there is no asterisk in front of a route, it means the route is inactive and will not be matched when the firewall is doing a route lookup. By default, the connected routes are the interface subnetworks configured by the user and the host routes for the interface IP address itself. Following the asterisk is the route ID, which you can use to get detailed output of the route, and then the route prefix.

To the right of the route prefix are the outgoing interfaces for each route, the next-hop gateway address, and the protocol type. For example, an H indicates a Host route. Refer to the description for this column in the first few lines of the output.

The Pref (Preference) column shows the local preference for the route entry. The preference values shown in the output are all the default values. You can check the default preferences using the following command:

```
Chicago-> get vr trust-vr preference
vrouter trust-vr route preference table
-------------------------------------------
Host Routes:              0
Connected Routes:         0
Static Routes:            20
Auto-exported Routes:     30
Imported Routes:          140
RIP Routes:               100
EBGP Routes:              40
IBGP Routes:              250
OSPF Routes:              60
OSPF External Type-2 Routes:    200
```

The Mtr column lists the metrics for the routes. All connected routes have a default metric of 0 and static routes have a default metric of 1. All other route metrics are calculated by the routing protocol.

The last column, Vsys, is the Virtual System (VSYS) to which this route belongs.

You may wonder why the firewall has many addresses in its routing tables when no routing protocols or static routes have been configured. When you configure interfaces, the ScreenOS software automatically places routes in the routing table. For the routing table examples in this recipe, the following interfaces and interface addresses are configured:

```
SSG-> get int

A - Active, I - Inactive, U - Up, D - Down, R - Ready

H - IPv6 Host Mode, O - IPv6 Router Mode
Interfaces in vsys Root:
Name    IP Address          Zone       MAC/INT-ID      VLAN State VSD
eth0/0  192.168.1.1/24      Trust      0005.857e.2f80    -    U    -
eth0/1  1.1.1.2/24          Untrust    0005.857e.2f85    -    U    -
eth0/2  0.0.0.0/0           Untrust    0005.857e.2f86    -    D    -
eth0/3  0.0.0.0/0           DMZ        0005.857e.2f87    -    U    -
        9009:1::205:85ff:fe7e:2f87/64 020585fffe7e2f87        O
eth0/4  0.0.0.0/0           Null       0005.857e.2f88    -    D    -
eth0/5  0.0.0.0/0           Null       0005.857e.2f89    -    D    -
eth0/6  0.0.0.0/0           Null       0005.857e.2f8a    -    D    -
eth0/7  0.0.0.0/0           Null       0005.857e.2f8b    -    D    -
eth0/8  0.0.0.0/0           Null       0005.857e.2f8c    -    D    -
eth0/9  0.0.0.0/0           Null       0005.857e.2f8d    -    D    -
vlan1   0.0.0.0/0           VLAN       0005.857e.2f8f    1    D    -
null    0.0.0.0/0           Null       N/A               -    U    0
Chicago->
```

Looking at the trust-vr routing table, you see it contains entries for each interface and for the subnetworks (the /24 address) to which they are connected:

```
*   4      1.1.1.2/32  eth0/1    0.0.0.0   H    0      0      Root
*   2  192.168.1.1/32  eth0/0    0.0.0.0   H    0      0      Root
*   1  192.168.1.0/24  eth0/0    0.0.0.0   C    0      0      Root
*   3      1.1.1.0/24  eth0/1    0.0.0.0   C    0      0      Root
```

This output shows entries for the two configured interfaces. For eth0/1, there is an entry for the interface itself (1.1.1.2/32), and an entry for the summary of all the addresses on the subnetwork (1.1.1.0/24). There are similar entries for the eth0/0 interface.

This is the basic output of the routing table on the firewall. Refer to Chapter 15 to understand how the routing entries are populated based on the protocol updates.

4.2 View Routes for a Particular Prefix

Problem

You want to check whether a particular IP subnet prefix is in the routing table on the firewall and you need to know the next hop.

Solution

The get route prefix command shows the contents of the routing table:

```
SSG-> get route prefix 2.2.2.2/24


IPv4 Dest-Routes for <untrust-vr> (0 entries)
--------------------------------------------------------------------
H: Host C: Connected S: Static A: Auto-Exported
I: Imported R: RIP P: Permanent D: Auto-Discovered
iB: IBGP eB: EBGP O: OSPF E1: OSPF external type 1
E2: OSPF external type 2


IPv4 Dest-Routes for <trust-vr> (6 entries)
------------------------------------------------------------------
   ID    IP-Prefix    Interface  Gateway   P Pref    Mtr     Vsys
------------------------------------------------------------------
*  22   2.2.2.0/24       eth0/1  1.1.1.1   O  60      2      Root
```

Discussion

You use this command when you want to know whether a particular destination is taking the intended path. The output provides information on which zones to configure in the firewall policy. In addition, this command helps you verify that the configuration is correct and that the route is going in the intended path. When you include the destination's address in the get route prefix command, you see output for only that route. This recipe shows that the route 2.2.2.2/24, which was learned from an OSPF router, has a metric of 2 and goes through interface eth0/1 with a next hop of 1.1.1.1. The header lines for the trust-vr are also displayed.

For more information about this route, use the get route id command:

```
SSG-> get route id 22
route in trust-vr:
```

```
---------------------------------------------
id:                      22
IP address/mask:         2.2.2.0/24
next hop (gateway):      1.1.1.1
preference:              60
metric:                  2
outgoing interface:      ethernet0/1
vsys name/id:            Root/0
tag:                     0
flag:                    24010100/00100000
type:                    OSPF-intra-area
OSPF parameters:         area = 0.0.0.0 ospf level 10000
Redistributed to:
status:                  active (for 10 minutes 42 seconds)
```

This output shows a few more fields for this route. The `status` field shows that the route is active in the routing table and has been active for 10 minutes, 42 seconds. The `type` field shows that this route was learned through OSPF intra-area. Also, the `OSPF parameters` field shows that this route belongs to OSPF area 0, along with the OSPF level that is used internally to identify the best route. The `flag` displayed is used by development to identify the route in the code.

We have just seen a very simple single-route prefix entry in the routing table. Many times, it is possible that the same route prefix is learned in many ways. Here is an example of a route prefix learned by OSPF, and as a connected route:

```
SSG-> get route prefix 3.3.3.0/24


IPv4 Dest-Routes for <untrust-vr> (0 entries)
--------------------------------------------------------------------
H: Host C: Connected S: Static A: Auto-Exported
I: Imported R: RIP P: Permanent D: Auto-Discovered
iB: IBGP eB: EBGP O: OSPF E1: OSPF external type 1
E2: OSPF external type 2


IPv4 Dest-Routes for <trust-vr> (6 entries)
------------------------------------------------------------------
   ID      IP-Prefix   Interface   Gateway   P Pref    Mtr      Vsys
------------------------------------------------------------------
*   7     3.3.3.1/32       eth0/0   0.0.0.0   H    0      0     Root
*   6     3.3.3.0/24       eth0/0   0.0.0.0   C    0      0     Root
   21     3.3.3.0/24       eth0/1   1.1.1.1   O   60      3     Root
```

In this example, we see that the `3.3.3.0/24` subnet is reachable by the `eth0/0` and `eth0/1` interfaces. The route to interface `eth0/0` is a connected route, and the route to interface `eth0/1` is learned via OSPF. By virtue of the router preferences, the connected route is active in the routing table and the OSPF route is inactive.

When you design your network and routing, it is very important that you consider from which zones the routes will be learned. If the same routes are learned from two different interfaces, and each interface belongs to a different zone, the established sessions will fail because ScreenOS software allows the traffic to failover between two interfaces only if they belong to the same zone. In the case of new sessions, the policy lookup would be done, and traffic would be permitted or denied based on the policy.

4.3 View Routes in the Source-Based Routing Table

Problem

You want to check the source-based routing table.

Solution

The `get route source` command shows the contents of the routing table:

```
SSG-> get route source
S: Static P: Permanent


Src-Routes for <trust-vr> (2 entries)
------------------------------------------------------------------
   ID     IP-Prefix    Interface      Gateway   P Pref   Mtr   Vsys
------------------------------------------------------------------
*   2    5.5.5.0/24       eth0/0      3.3.3.2   S   20     1   Root
*   1    3.3.3.0/24          n/a       vpn-vr   S   20     1   Root


Src-Routes for <vpn-vr> (1 entries)
------------------------------------------------------------------
   ID     IP-Prefix    Interface      Gateway   P Pref   Mtr
------------------------------------------------------------------
*   1    4.4.4.0/24          n/a     trust-vr   S   20     1
```

Discussion

You have configured source-based routing and would like to view the source-based routing table on the firewall. The source-based routing table is separate from the destination-based routing table, and you have to use the `get route source` command to view the routes. The output in this recipe shows two VRs that have source-based routes. `trust-vr` has two entries, and `vpn-vr` has one entry.

`trust-vr` has the source route for the `5.5.5.0/24` subnet using the outgoing interface `eth0/0` and a next-hop gateway of `3.3.3.2`. Any packet coming from the source IP subnet 5.5.5.0/24 and from an interface in the trust-vr matches this route lookup, and traffic is sent out the next-hop gateway 3.3.3.2. No route lookup is done for the destination IP address on the packet. Also, it is important to know that the source-based route lookup is done only for the traffic coming from an interface in that VR. It does not apply to source IP lookups initiated in a different VR.

From ScreenOS version 5.2 and later, the source-based routes can point the next hop to a different VR. In the output given here, the trust-vr has the source route 3.3.3.0/24 with a next hop of vpn-vr. The packet flow for this kind of source route is different. When a packet with a source IP subnet of 3.3.3.0/24 is received in the trust-vr, the source-based route lookup is performed and the next hop is vpn-vr. In the vpn-vr, another route lookup is done for the same packet, but this time the lookup is done for the destination IP address of the packet to forward the packet. This is because the source-based route lookup is done only for the packets that are initiated in that VR. For packets initiated in another VR, the destination IP address is used for the route lookup. A similar source route is configured in the vpn-vr for the 4.4.4.0/24 subnet with a next hop of trust-vr.

For more information about the source route, use the get vr route source id command:

```
SSG-> get vr trust-vr route source id 2
route in trust-vr:
-----------------------------------------------
id:                    2
IP address/mask:       5.5.5.0/24
next hop (gateway):    3.3.3.2
preference:            20
metric:                1
outgoing interface:    ethernet0/0
vsys name/id:          Root/0
tag:                   0
flag:                  24000040/00000000
type:                  static
Redistributed to:
Status:                active (for 34 minutes 36 seconds)
```

This output shows a few more fields for the route. The status field shows that the route is active in the routing table and has been active for 34 minutes, 36 seconds. The type field shows that this route is a static route. The flag displayed is used by development to identify the route in the code.

You can use the following command to test which route would be matched in the routing table for a source IP address lookup:

```
SSG-> get vr trust-vr route source ip 5.5.5.5
 Source for 5.5.5.5
-------------------------------------------------------------------
trust-vr        : => 5.5.5.0/24 (id=2) via 3.3.3.2 (vr: trust-vr)
                    Interface ethernet0/0 , metric 1
```

In this output, the source IP address 5.5.5.5 received in the trust-vr is sent out via interface ethernet0/0 with a next-hop gateway of 3.3.3.2. The output also shows that the source route ID 2 with a metric of 1 in the trust-vr was matched for this test command.

Here's another example of testing route matching:

```
SSG-> get vr trust-vr route source ip 3.3.3.3
 Source for 3.3.3.3
-------------------------------------------------------------------
trust-vr       : => 3.3.3.0/24 (id=1) via (vr: vpn-vr), metric 1
   trust-vr       : => 0.0.0.0/0 (id=3) via 8.8.8.2 (vr: vpn-vr)
                       Interface ethernet0/3 , metric 1
```

In this example, the source IP address 3.3.3.3 received in the trust-vr is sent out via interface ethernet0/3 with a next-hop gateway of 8.8.8.2. Notice that the route lookup was done with a source IP lookup in the trust-vr and matched source route ID 1 with a next hop of vpn-vr, and for the same packet the route lookup was done with the destination IP lookup in the vpn-vr and matched destination route ID 3, with an outgoing interface of ethernet0/3 and a next-hop gateway of 8.8.8.2.

It is important to know that ScreenOS software does up to three recursive route lookups to identify the outgoing interface and next-hop gateway. If the route points to more than three VRs, it is considered to be a routing loop, and the packet is dropped.

4.4 View Routes in the Source Interface-Based Routing Table

Problem

You want to check the source interface-based routing table.

Solution

The get vr route source in-interface command shows the contents of the source interface-based routing table:

```
SSG-> get vr trust-vr route source in-interface
S: Static P: Permanent


SIBR-Routes for <ethernet0/0>
 (2 entries)
--------------------------------------------------------------------
    ID      IP-Prefix   Interface        Gateway   P Pref     Mtr   Vsys
--------------------------------------------------------------------
*    1    3.3.3.0/24          n/a    untrust-vr    S   20       1   Root
     4    2.2.2.0/24       eth0/4       7.7.7.1    S   20       1   Root
```

Discussion

Source interface-based routes are routes for which the source IP traffic should be received on the configured interface. These routes exist only when traffic is received on the expected interface. If it is received on a different interface, the traffic would match other routes, such as source-based or destination-based routes. The difference between source-based and source interface-based routes is that the route lookup for source-based routes matches packets with a source IP address from any interface in that VR, whereas the source interface route lookup matches packets with a source IP address from a particular interface in that VR.

In this output, the `trust-vr` has one source interface-based route on `Ethernet0/0`, with a source IP subnet of `3.3.3.0/24` and a next hop of `untrust-vr`. You see that the route ID `1` is active because of the asterisk in front of the route. We also have a route for a source IP subnet of `2.2.2.0/24` with an outgoing interface of `eth0/4` and a next-hop gateway of `7.7.7.1`. You see that route ID `4` is not active; this is because the Ethernet interface `e0/4` is down. You can use this command to check the interface status:

```
SSG-> get int e0/4
  Interface ethernet0/4:
  description ethernet0/4
  number 8, if_info 6464, if_index 0, mode route
  link down, phy-link down
  vsys Root, zone DMZ, vr trust-vr
```

The source interface-based route lookup's performance is very similar to that of the source-based route. Please review the source-based route recipe for this discussion.

For more information about the source interface-based route, use the `get vr route source in-interface id` command:

```
SSG-> get vr trust-vr route source in-interface id 1
route in ethernet0/0:
-----------------------------------------------
id:                    1
IP address/mask:       3.3.3.0/24
next hop (vrouter):    untrust-vr
preference:            20
metric:                1
outgoing interface:    n/a
vsys name/id:          Root/0
tag:                   0
flag:                  24000840/00000000
type:                  static
Redistributed to:
status:                active (for 2 hours 16 minutes 25 seconds)

route --> 3.3.3.0/24 in vr untrust-vr:
SSG->
```

This output shows a few more fields for this route. The `status` field shows this route is active in the routing table and has been active for 2 hours, 16 minutes, and 25 seconds. The `type` field shows that this route is a static route. The `flag` displayed is used by development to identify the route in the code.

4.5 Create Blackhole Routes

Problem

You have a route-based IP Security (IPSec) virtual private network (VPN) tunnel between two sites. You want all traffic to pass through the encrypted tunnel, and you want to ensure that nothing goes outside the tunnel.

Solution

Configure the routers on each side of the tunnel. The router `Chicago` is on one side of the tunnel:

```
set interface "ethernet0/0" zone "Trust"
set interface "ethernet0/1" zone "Untrust"
set interface "ethernet0/2" zone "Untrust"
set interface "tunnel.1" zone "Trust"
set interface ethernet0/0 ip 192.168.1.1/24
set interface ethernet0/0 nat
set interface ethernet0/1 ip 1.1.1.2/24
set interface ethernet0/1 route
set interface tunnel.1 ip unnumbered interface ethernet0/0
set ike gateway "NewYork-P1" address 2.2.2.2 Main outgoing-interface
"ethernet0/1" preshare "0XncnRYNNmyBzssOlsC5btswLfngijyASg=="
sec-level standard
set vpn "NewYork-P2" gateway "NewYork-P1" no-replay tunnel idletime
   0 sec-level standard
set vpn "NewYork-P2" monitor optimized rekey
set vpn "NewYork-P2" id 1 bind interface tunnel.1
set route 0.0.0.0/0 interface ethernet0/1 gateway 1.1.1.1
set route 192.168.2.0/24 interface tunnel.1
set route 192.168.2.0/24 interface null metric 200
exit
```

The router `New York` is on the other side of the tunnel:

```
set interface "ethernet0/0" zone "Trust"
set interface "ethernet0/1" zone "Untrust"
set interface "ethernet0/2" zone "Untrust"
set interface "tunnel.1" zone "Trust"
set interface ethernet0/0 ip 192.168.2.1/24
set interface ethernet0/0 nat
set interface ethernet0/1 ip 2.2.2.2/24
set interface ethernet0/1 route
set interface tunnel.1 ip unnumbered interface ethernet0/0
set ike gateway "Chicago-P1" address 1.1.1.2 Main outgoing-interface
```

```
"ethernet0/1" preshare "OXncnRYNNmyBzssOlsC5btswLfngijyASg=="
sec-level
   standard
set vpn "Chicago-P2" gateway "Chicago-P1" no-replay tunnel idletime 0
   sec-level standard
set vpn "Chicago-P2" monitor optimized rekey
set vpn "Chicago-P2" id 1 bind interface tunnel.1
set vrouter "trust-vr"
set route 0.0.0.0/0 interface ethernet0/1 gateway 2.2.2.1
set route 192.168.1.0/24 interface tunnel.1
set route 192.168.1.0/24 interface null metric 200
exit
```

Discussion

This recipe configures routes for the remote network to the tunnel interfaces, and configures a default route to the Internet. To ensure that the traffic is not going in unencrypted, you have to configure the routes to the `null` interface with a higher metric. Once the tunnel routes are withdrawn when the tunnel goes down, the `null` interface route becomes active and *blackholes* all the traffic on the firewall, thus preventing the traffic from going in unencrypted.

Figure 4-3 shows the configuration of a firewall in Chicago and New York. The Chicago site has a site-to-site IPSec VPN tunnel to the New York site. The `192.168.1.0/24` subnet is on the Chicago `Trust` network and the `192.168.2.0/24` subnet is on the New York `Trust` network.

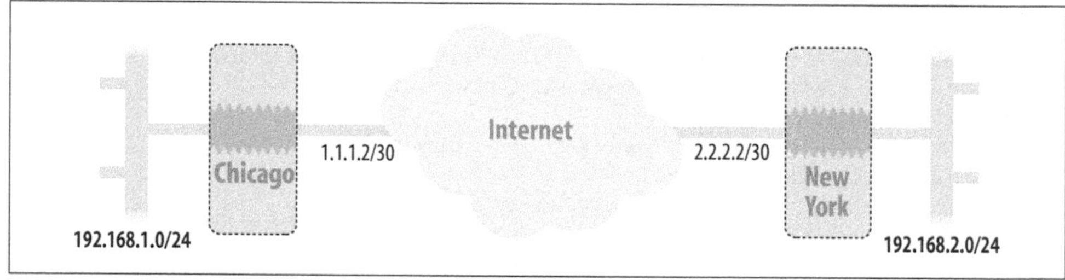

Figure 4-3. Configuration of the firewall

The configuration of the VPN tunnel on the Chicago side shows that the interfaces belong to both the `Trust` and `Untrust` zones. We create a tunnel interface bound to the `Trust` zone, create Phase 1 and Phase 2 for the IPSec tunnels, and bind the tunnel interface to the VPN. We use the VPN monitor on the tunnel to change the tunnel interface status to Up or Down. Whether routes are active depends on the tunnel interface status.

To blackhole traffic if the tunnel goes down on the Chicago side, we have configured a default route on the `trust-vr`, and have two static routes. The first static route points to the `tunnel.1` interface, and the second points to the `null` interface with a metric of 200. The route entry pointing to the `null` interface is considered to be the blackhole route and has the higher metric, which means that this route is inactive when the tunnel.1 route is active. The blackhole route is active only when the tunnel.1 route is withdrawn from the routing table when the tunnel is down:

```
set vrouter "trust-vr"
set route 0.0.0.0/0 interface ethernet0/1 gateway 1.1.1.1
set route 192.168.2.0/24 interface tunnel.1
set route 192.168.2.0/24 interface null metric 200
exit
```

The configuration on the New York firewall is similar to that on the Chicago firewall.

Here is how you verify that the configuration is sending the traffic to the intended path. Use the get int tunnel.1 command to see the tunnel interface status:

```
Chicago-> get int tunnel.1
Interface tunnel.1:
  description tunnel.1
  number 20, if_info 16168, if_index 1, mode nat
  link up
  vsys Root, zone Trust, vr trust-vr
  admin mtu 1500, operating mtu 1500, default mtu 1500
  *ip 0.0.0.0/0  unnumbered, source interface ethernet0/0
  *manage ip 0.0.0.0
  bound vpn:
    NewYork-P2

  Next-Hop Tunnel Binding table
  Flag Status Next-Hop(IP)    tunnel-id  VPN

  pmtu-v4 disabled
  ping enabled, telnet enabled, SSH enabled, SNMP enabled
  web enabled, ident-reset disabled, SSL enabled
  DNS Proxy disabled
  OSPF disabled  BGP disabled  RIP disabled  RIPng disabled  mtrace
    disabled
  PIM: not configured  IGMP not configured
  bandwidth: physical 0kbps, configured egress [gbw 0kbps mbw 0kbps]
             configured ingress mbw 0kbps, current bw 0kbps
              total allocated gbw 0kbps
```

This output shows that the tunnel.1 interface is up and is bound to the NewYork-P2 VPN tunnel.

The routing table on the trust-vr shows two routes. However, only one route pointing to the tunnnel.1 interface is active, indicated by the * in front of the route. The second route with a metric of 200 is not active and is a shadow route:

```
Chicago-> get route
IPv4 Dest-Routes for <trust-vr> (7 entries)
--------------------------------------------------------------------
   ID        IP-Prefix   Interface    Gateway   P Pref   Mtr    Vsys
--------------------------------------------------------------------
*   5          0.0.0.0/0      eth0/1   1.1.1.1   S   20     1    Root
*   4        1.1.1.2/32      eth0/1   0.0.0.0   H    0     0    Root
*   2   192.168.1.1/32      eth0/0   0.0.0.0   H    0     0    Root
```

```
*   6  192.168.2.0/24       tun.1  0.0.0.0  S  20    1  Root
    7  192.168.2.0/24        null  0.0.0.0  S  20  200  Root
*   1  192.168.1.0/24      eth0/0  0.0.0.0  C   0    0  Root
*   3       1.1.1.0/24     eth0/1  0.0.0.0  C   0    0  Root
```

Check the status of the IPSec VPN with the get sa command on the device. The status is in the Sta column. A/U means the tunnel is up and active, and the monitor on the tunnel is checking the status of the tunnel:

```
Chicago-> get sa
total configured sa: 1
HEX ID    Gateway   Port Algorithm     SPI      Life:sec kb  Sta PID
00000001< 2.2.2.2 500 esp:3des/sha1 0a40fdf6 3217 unlim A/U   -1 0
00000001> 2.2.2.2 500 esp:3des/sha1 37031392 3217 unlim A/U   -1 0
```

When we initiate a ping from the Chicago firewall device to the remote network, we see a successful ping response. This demonstrates that the tunnel is up and working:

```
Chicago-> ping 192.168.2.1 from e0/0
Type escape sequence to abort

Sending 5, 100-byte ICMP Echos to 192.168.2.1, timeout is 1 seconds
from ethernet0/0
!!!!!
Success Rate is 100 percent (5/5), round-trip time min/avg/max=4/4/5
ms
```

Here is the debug flow basic output captured for the successful ping request. We see that the flow has identified the tunnel.1 route as the intended path for sending this traffic. This output also shows you that the packet is going into tunnel 40000001:

```
Chicago-> get db str
****** 02095.0: <Trust/ethernet0/0> packet received [128]******
  ipid = 6222(184e), @02312f14
  self:192.168.1.1/17500->192.168.2.1/1024,1(8/0)<Root>
  ethernet0/0:192.168.1.1/17500->192.168.2.1/1024,1(8/0)<Root>
  no session found
  flow_first_sanity_check: in <ethernet0/0>, out <tunnel.1>
  chose interface ethernet0/0 as incoming nat if.
  flow_first_routing: in <ethernet0/0>, out <tunnel.1>
  search route to (ethernet0/0, 192.168.1.1->192.168.2.1) in vr
trust-vr for vsd-0/flag-0/ifp-null
  [ Dest] 6.route 192.168.2.1->0.0.0.0, to tunnel.1
  routed (x_dst_ip 192.168.2.1) from ethernet0/0 (ethernet0/0 in 0)
to
   tunnel.1
  policy search from zone 2-> zone 2
 policy_flow_search  policy search nat_crt from zone 2-> zone 2
  RPC Mapping Table search returned 0 matched service(s) for (vsys
Root, ip 192.168.2.1, port 5078, proto 1)
  No SW RPC rule match, search HW rule
  Searching global policy.
  Permitted by policy 320002
  No src xlate ## 2000-06-21 07:14:11 : NHTB entry search found: vpn
```

```
none tif tunnel.1 nexthop 192.168.2.1 tunnelid 0x1, flag 0x1, status
4
  choose interface ethernet0/1 as outgoing phy if
  no loop on ifp ethernet0/1.
  session application type 0, name None, nas_id 0, timeout 60sec
  service lookup identified service 0.
  flow_first_final_check: in <ethernet0/0>, out <ethernet0/1>
  existing vector list 4-3992850.
  Session (id:48059) created for first pak 4
  flow_first_install_session======>
  flow got session.
  flow session id 48059
  skipping pre-frag
  going into tunnel 40000001.
  flow_encrypt: pipeline.
chip info: PIO. Tunnel id 00000001
(vn2)  doing ESP encryption and size =136
ipsec encrypt prepare engine done
ipsec encrypt set engine done
ipsec encrypt engine released
ipsec encrypt done
        put packet(394c7f0) into flush queue.
        remove packet(394c7f0) out from flush queue.

**** jump to packet:1.1.1.2->2.2.2.2
  out encryption tunnel 40000001 gw:1.1.1.1
  no more encapping needed
 flow_send_vector_, vid = 0, is_layer2_if=0
  packet send out to 000585caf0a0 through ethernet0/1
  **** pak processing end.
```

When the blackhole route becomes active the traffic is dropped, and you see the following in the routing table:

```
Chicago-> get route
IPv4 Dest-Routes for <trust-vr> (7 entries)
--------------------------------------------------------------------
   ID       IP-Prefix  Interface  Gateway   P Pref    Mtr      Vsys
--------------------------------------------------------------------
*   5        0.0.0.0/0    eth0/1  1.1.1.1   S   20      1      Root
*   4       1.1.1.2/32    eth0/1  0.0.0.0   H    0      0      Root
*   2   192.168.1.1/32    eth0/0  0.0.0.0   H    0      0      Root
*   7   192.168.2.0/24      null  0.0.0.0   S   20    200      Root
    6   192.168.2.0/24     tun.1  0.0.0.0   S   20      1      Root
*   1   192.168.1.0/24    eth0/0  0.0.0.0   C    0      0      Root
*   3       1.1.1.0/24    eth0/1  0.0.0.0   C    0      0      Root
```

This output shows that the `null` interface route is active and the `tun.1` route is inactive. The `null` interface route is active because the `tunnel` interface is down, and hence, the route attached to the `tunnel` interface becomes inactive.

If you check the status of the IPSec VPN with the get sa command on the device and see the status under the `STA` column, it shows `I/I`, which means the tunnel is inactive, and the monitor on the tunnel has brought the tunnel down:

```
Chicago-> get sa
total configured sa: 1
HEX ID    Gateway  Port Algorithm    SPI      Life:sec kb Sta PID vsys
00000001<  2.2.2.2 500 esp:3des/sha1 0a40fdf6 expir unlim I/I   -1 0
00000001>  2.2.2.2 500 esp:3des/sha1 37031392 expir unlim I/I   -1 0
```

When you initiate a ping from the Chicago firewall device to the remote network, you see that the ping is failing, and there is no usable route on the device:

```
Chicago-> ping 192.168.2.1 from e0/0
Type escape sequence to abort

Sending 5, 100-byte ICMP Echos to 192.168.2.1, timeout is 1 seconds
from ethernet0/0
ip 192.168.2.1 is unreachable in vr trust-vr

Success Rate is 0 percent.
```

When you enable `debug flow basic`, there is no output in the debug for the ping request. This is because the firewall device can identify that traffic destined to this network needs to be blackholed, and hence, it does not generate any debugs:

```
Chicago-> get db str
Chicago->
```

This recipe shows many features working together on the Juniper firewalls to achieve the traffic blackhole route. See Chapter 10 for information on how to configure route-based IPSec VPNs.

4.6 Create ECMP Routing

Problem

You have configured dynamic routing protocols and can possibly learn equal-cost routes. You want to load-balance the traffic flows using all available paths.

Solution

Enable ECMP on the VR using the following command to load-balance traffic per flow among the equal-cost routes:

```
SSG-> set vr trust-vr max-ecmp-routes 4
SSG->
```

Discussion

You use ECMP on the VR to allow equal-cost routes to be updated in the route table. This recipe illustrates ECMP with the following topology (see Figure 4-4) that has firewalls in Chicago and New York. Both firewalls are connected to the dynamic routing protocol cloud, which means that both could learn equal-cost routes for their internal networks.

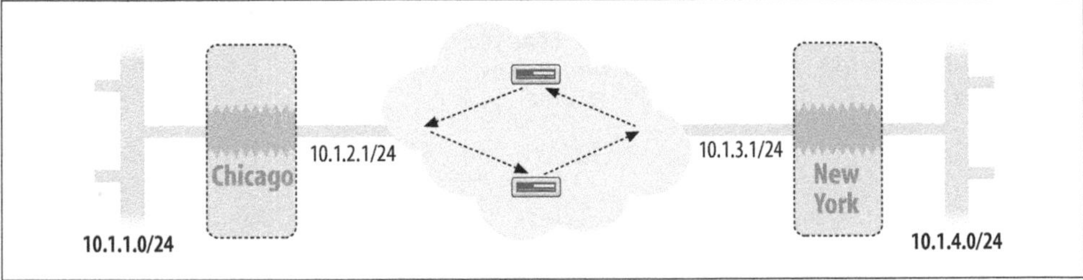

Figure 4-4. ECMP routing

The configuration on the Chicago firewall shows that both are using OSPF as the dynamic routing protocol:

```
set vrouter "trust-vr"
unset auto-route-export
set protocol ospf
set enable
exit
set interface "ethernet0/0" zone "Trust"
set interface "ethernet0/1" zone "Untrust"
set interface ethernet0/0 ip 10.1.1.1/24
set interface ethernet0/0 route
set interface ethernet0/1 ip 10.1.2.1/24
set interface ethernet0/1 route
set policy id 1 from "Trust" to "Untrust"  "Any" "Any" "ANY" permit
set policy id 1
exit
set vrouter "trust-vr"
set max-ecmp-routes 4
set route 0.0.0.0/0 interface ethernet0/1 gateway 1.1.1.1
exit
set interface ethernet0/0 protocol ospf area 0.0.0.0
set interface ethernet0/0 protocol ospf enable
set interface ethernet0/1 protocol ospf area 0.0.0.0
set interface ethernet0/1 protocol ospf enable
```

OSPF is enabled on the `trust-vr`, `ethernet0/0` is bound to the `Trust` zone, and `ethernet0/1` is bound to the `Untrust` zone. The `ethernet0/0` interface has an IP address of `10.1.1.1/24` and `ethernet0/1` has an IP address of `10.1.2.1/24`. OSPF is enabled on both interfaces and is attached to area 0. A simple policy is created to allow traffic from the `Trust` zone to the `Untrust` zone.

The `max-ecmp-routes 4` configuration command enables ECMP on the VR and allows a maximum of four equal-cost routes to be updated in the route table. This is the maximum number of equal-cost routes you can configure on a single VR.

You can verify whether the equal-cost routes are populated in the routing table using the get route command. Here is the routing table output before enabling ECMP:

```
Chicago-> get route


IPv4 Dest-Routes for <untrust-vr> (0 entries)
```

```
---------------------------------------------------------------
H: Host C: Connected S: Static A: Auto-Exported
I: Imported R: RIP P: Permanent D: Auto-Discovered
iB: IBGP eB: EBGP O: OSPF E1: OSPF external type 1
E2: OSPF external type 2


IPv4 Dest-Routes for <trust-vr> (8 entries)
---------------------------------------------------------------
   ID        IP-Prefix  Interface      Gateway   P Pref  Mtr   Vsys
---------------------------------------------------------------
*  25        0.0.0.0/0     eth0/1      1.1.1.1   S   20    1   Root
*  19      10.1.2.1/32     eth0/1      0.0.0.0   H    0    0   Root
*   4      10.1.1.1/32     eth0/0      0.0.0.0   H    0    0   Root
*  29      10.1.5.1/32     eth0/1   10.1.2.100   O   60    1   Root
*  28      10.1.4.0/24     eth0/1   10.1.2.100   O   60    3   Root
*   3      10.1.1.0/24     eth0/0      0.0.0.0   C    0    0   Root
*  18      10.1.2.0/24     eth0/1      0.0.0.0   C    0    0   Root
*  30      10.1.3.0/24     eth0/1   10.1.2.100   O   60    2   Root

Chicago->
```

IP subnets `10.1.3.0/24` and `10.1.4.0/24` have only one route learned via OSPF on `eth0/1`, with a next-hop gateway of `10.1.2.100`.

Here is the output of the `trust-vr` table using the `get vr trust-vr` command after you enable ECMP on the device:

```
Chicago-> get vr trust-vr
Routing Table
---------------------------------------------------------------
H: Host C: Connected S: Static A: Auto-Exported
I: Imported R: RIP P: Permanent D: Auto-Discovered
iB: IBGP eB: EBGP O: OSPF E1: OSPF external type 1
E2: OSPF external type 2

Total 10/max entries

   ID     IP-Prefix    Interface      Gateway   P Pref   Mtr    Vsys
-------------------------------------------------------------
*  25     0.0.0.0/0    eth0/1         1.1.1.1   S   20     1    Root
*  19   10.1.2.1/32    eth0/1         0.0.0.0   H    0     0    Root
*   4   10.1.1.1/32    eth0/0         0.0.0.0   H    0     0    Root
*  29   10.1.5.1/32    eth0/1      10.1.2.100   O   60     1    Root
*  32   10.1.4.0/24    eth0/1      10.1.2.100   O   60     3    Root
*  33   10.1.4.0/24    eth0/1      10.1.2.200   O   60     3    Root
*   3   10.1.1.0/24    eth0/0         0.0.0.0   C    0     0    Root
*  18   10.1.2.0/24    eth0/1         0.0.0.0   C    0     0    Root
*  30   10.1.3.0/24    eth0/1      10.1.2.100   O   60     2    Root
*  31   10.1.3.0/24    eth0/1      10.1.2.200   O   60     2    Root


Interfaces
---------------------------------------------------------------
```

```
tunnel, hidden.1, l2v, self, ethernet0/0, vlan1
v1-trust, v1-untrust, v1-dmz, ethernet0/2, ethernet0/1

Auto-exporting:                    Disabled
Default-vrouter:                   Yes
Shared-vrouter:                    Yes
nsrp-config-sync:                  Yes
System-Default-route:              Not present
Advertise-Inactive-Interface:      Disabled
Source-Based-Routing:              Disabled
SIBR-Routing:                      Disabled
SNMP Trap:                         Public
Ignore-Subnet-Conflict:            Disabled
ECMP-Routing:                      Enabled with 4 as maximum routes
```

Now, IP subnets 10.1.3.0/24 and 10.1.4.0/24 have two active routes via the eth0/1 interface, but with two different next-hop gateways: 10.1.2.100 and 10.1.2.200. The route IDs 32 and 33 show routes for IP prefix 10.1.4.0/24, and the route IDs 30 and 31 show routes for IP prefix 10.1.3.0/24. The traffic flow is now load-balanced between these routes in a round-robin fashion. At the bottom of the output, you see that ECMP routing is enabled.

It is important to know that traffic load balancing will be done per session and not per packet. So, if there is only one session, all packets for that session will always flow through the same route. When a second session is initiated, it will use the second route and forward the traffic.

Also, remember that when you enable ECMP, the equal-cost routes will be populated in the routing table only when there is a topology change, such as OSPF's neighbor going down and up. They would not populate for already existing topology calculations.

You can verify how the sessions are being load-balanced using the get session command. Here is an example of two sessions:

```
id 48047/s**,vsys 0,flag 08000040/0000/0001,policy 1,time 170, dip 0 module 0
 if 0(nspflag 801801):10.1.1.10/35968->10.1.4.32/21,6,000c29eeeed6,sess token 4,vlan
0,tun 0,vsd 0,route 3
 if 5(nspflag 801800):10.1.1.10/35968<-10.1.4.32/21,6,000585caf0a0,sess token 6,vlan
0,tun 0,vsd 0,route 32

id 48050/s**,vsys 0,flag 08000040/0000/0001,policy 1,time 180, dip 0 module 0
 if 0(nspflag 801801):10.1.1.10/35970->10.1.4.32/23,6,000c29eeeed6,sess token 4,vlan
0,tun 0,vsd 0,route 3
 if 5(nspflag 801800):10.1.1.10/35970<-10.1.4.32/23,6,0010db558d90,sess token 6,vlan
0,tun 0,vsd 0,route 33
```

Session ID 48047 shows that a File Transfer Protocol (FTP) session was created from 10.1.1.10–10.1.4.32 and is using route ID 32. The second session ID, 48050, shows that a Telnet session between the same hosts is using route ID 33. You have already seen from the routing table that the 10.1.4.0/24 network is reachable via route IDs 32 and 33.

4.7 Create Static Routes for Gateway Tracking

Problem

You want to configure static routes for networks behind a remote router that is reachable through multiple paths.

Solution

Configure static routes with only a next-hop gateway address. You do not include the outgoing interface in this command:

```
SSG-> set vr trust-vr route 10.10.10.0/24 gateway 10.1.4.32
```

Discussion

This recipe configures static routes between two IP subnets—`10.2.1.0/24` and `10.2.2.0/24`, which are behind the New York firewall and are reachable through two different OSPF paths from Chicago (see Figure 4-5).

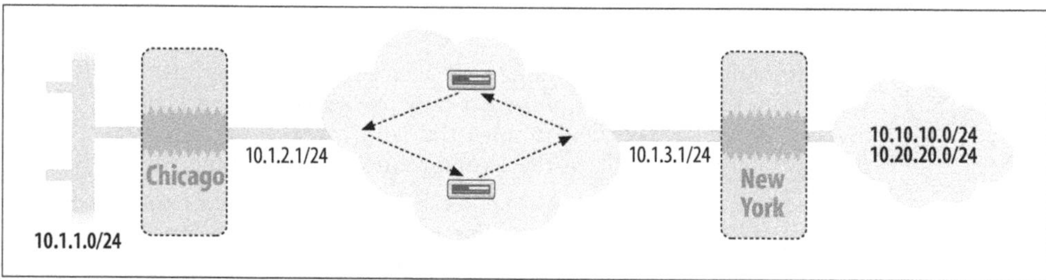

Figure 4-5. Static routes

Here is the configuration on the Chicago firewall for the static routes `10.2.1.0/24` and `10.2.2.0/24` reachable via the `10.1.4.32` gateway:

```
set vrouter "trust-vr"
set route 10.10.10.0/24 gateway 10.1.4.32
set route 10.20.20.0/24 gateway 10.1.4.32
exit
```

If you look at the routing table using the get route command, you will notice that the route entries for the `10.10.10.0/24` and `10.20.20.0/24` IP subnets actually show the next-hop gateway of `10.1.2.100` even though you configured the next-hop gateway for these subnets as `10.1.4.32`. This is because the gateway tracking feature identified that, to reach the `10.1.4.32` address, the device needs to use the `10.1.2.100` gateway. The `10.1.4.0/24` IP subnet is learned from OSPF and is best reachable via `10.1.2.100`. Hence, the firewall can update the outgoing interface and the directly connected next-hop gateway for the static routes `10.10.10.0/24` and `10.20.20.0/24`.

```
Chicago-> get route

IPv4 Dest-Routes for <untrust-vr> (0 entries)
--------------------------------------------------------------------
H: Host C: Connected S: Static A: Auto-Exported
I: Imported R: RIP P: Permanent D: Auto-Discovered
iB: IBGP eB: EBGP O: OSPF E1: OSPF external type 1
E2: OSPF external type 2

IPv4 Dest-Routes for <trust-vr> (10 entries)
------------------------------------------------------------------
   ID         IP-Prefix  Interface       Gateway   P Pref  Mtr   Vsys
------------------------------------------------------------------
*  25         0.0.0.0/0     eth0/1       1.1.1.1   S   20    1   Root
*  19       10.1.2.1/32     eth0/1       0.0.0.0   H    0    0   Root
*   4       10.1.1.1/32     eth0/0       0.0.0.0   H    0    0   Root
*  51       10.1.5.1/32     eth0/1    10.1.2.100   O   60    1   Root
*  50       10.1.4.0/24     eth0/1    10.1.2.100   O   60    3   Root
*   3       10.1.1.0/24     eth0/0       0.0.0.0   C    0    0   Root
*  55     10.10.10.0/24     eth0/1    10.1.2.100   S   20    1   Root
*  56     10.20.20.0/24     eth0/1    10.1.2.100   S   20    1   Root
*  18       10.1.2.0/24     eth0/1       0.0.0.0   C    0    0   Root
*  52       10.1.3.0/24     eth0/1    10.1.2.100   O   60    2   Root
```

If a failure occurs in the path to reach `10.1.4.32` and it is not reachable through a different path, the entries in the routing table change because the path changes. The following output shows the routing table after the path change. Notice that the `10.10.10.0/24` and `10.20.20.0/24` IP subnets now have a next-hop gateway of `10.1.2.200`. This was changed because the `10.1.4.0/24` subnet changed it when the previous path failed. The best route is now via `10.1.2.200`. The gateway tracking feature tracks the reachability of the gateways and automatically modifies the immediate next hop.

```
Chicago-> get route


IPv4 Dest-Routes for <untrust-vr> (0 entries)
--------------------------------------------------------------------
H: Host C: Connected S: Static A: Auto-Exported
I: Imported R: RIP P: Permanent D: Auto-Discovered
iB: IBGP eB: EBGP O: OSPF E1: OSPF external type 1
E2: OSPF external type 2


IPv4 Dest-Routes for <trust-vr> (10 entries)
------------------------------------------------------------------
   ID         IP-Prefix  Interface       Gateway   P Pref  Mtr   Vsys
------------------------------------------------------------------
*  25         0.0.0.0/0     eth0/1       1.1.1.1   S   20    1   Root
*  19       10.1.2.1/32     eth0/1       0.0.0.0   H    0    0   Root
*   4       10.1.1.1/32     eth0/0       0.0.0.0   H    0    0   Root
*  58       10.1.5.1/32     eth0/1    10.1.2.200   O   60    2   Root
```

```
* 57     10.1.4.0/24    eth0/1  10.1.2.200  O  60   3  Root
*  3     10.1.1.0/24    eth0/0     0.0.0.0  C   0   0  Root
* 61   10.10.10.0/24    eth0/1  10.1.2.200  S  20   1  Root
* 60   10.20.20.0/24    eth0/1  10.1.2.200  S  20   1  Root
* 18     10.1.2.0/24    eth0/1     0.0.0.0  C   0   0  Root
* 59     10.1.3.0/24    eth0/1  10.1.2.200  O  60   2  Root
```

It is important to remember that even when routes automatically failover to another available path, the session follows the new route only if it is in the same zone.

4.8 Export Filtered Routes to Other Virtual Routers

Problem

You want to export only specific routes to other VRs.

Solution

Configure static routes with tags and use route maps to export only those routes with specific tags:

```
set vrouter "trust-vr"
set route-map name "tag10_routes" permit 1
set match tag 0.0.0.10
exit
set export-to vrouter "vpn-vr" route-map "tag10_routes" protocol
static
set route 192.168.1.0/24 interface ethernet0/0 gateway 10.1.1.10
tag 10
set route 192.168.20.0/24 interface ethernet0/0 gateway 10.1.1.10
tag 10
set route 192.168.3.0/24 interface ethernet0/0 gateway 10.1.1.10
exit

set vrouter name "vpn-vr" id 1025
set vrouter "vpn-vr"
unset auto-route-export
exit
set vrouter "vpn-vr"
exit
```

Discussion

Let's say you have configured multiple VRs on the firewall and have identified routes that need to be provided to other VRs, and you want to provide only specific IP subnets to other VRs but these are noncontiguous routes, so you can't aggregate them.

To be able to export these routes, you configure the static routes with a tag and then use the configured route tags as filters to export the routes to other VRs. We configure static routes for IP subnets 192.168.1.0/24 and 192.168.20.0/24 in the trust-vr with a route tag value of 10.

In the trust-vr, we configured the route map named tag10_routes with a permit action and a sequence number of 1. The sequence number is used to define the order in which route maps are applied to the VRs. In the route map tag10_routes, we configured the match criteria of the tag with a value of 10. This is a basic route-map configuration; we can add other match criteria as well.

After configuring the route maps, we then use the set export-to command to export routes to vpn-vr using the route map tag10_routes and a protocol type of static. This command exports the routes matching the criteria configured in the route maps. You should be aware that the routes are exported only if they are active in the routing table.

You can verify the routing tables with the get route command:

```
SSG-> get route


IPv4 Dest-Routes for <untrust-vr> (0 entries)
--------------------------------------------------------------------
H: Host C: Connected S: Static A: Auto-Exported
I: Imported R: RIP P: Permanent D: Auto-Discovered
N: NHRP
iB: IBGP eB: EBGP O: OSPF E1: OSPF external type 1
E2: OSPF external type 2 trailing B: backup route


IPv4 Dest-Routes for <trust-vr> (11 entries)
------------------------------------------------------------------
     ID         IP-Prefix  Interface     Gateway  P Pref  Mtr   Vsys
------------------------------------------------------------------
*     8         0.0.0.0/0     eth0/1  10.1.2.200  S   20    1   Root
*     4       10.1.2.1/32     eth0/1     0.0.0.0  H    0    0   Root
*     2       10.1.1.1/32     eth0/0     0.0.0.0  H    0    0   Root
*    10       10.1.5.1/32     eth0/1  10.1.2.200  O   60    2   Root
*    12  192.168.20.0/24      eth0/0   10.1.1.10  S   20    1   Root
*     7   192.168.3.0/24      eth0/0   10.1.1.10  S   20    1   Root
*     5   192.168.1.0/24      eth0/0   10.1.1.10  S   20    1   Root
*     9       10.1.4.0/24     eth0/1  10.1.2.200  O   60    3   Root
*     1       10.1.1.0/24     eth0/0     0.0.0.0  C    0    0   Root
*     3       10.1.2.0/24     eth0/1     0.0.0.0  C    0    0   Root
*    11       10.1.3.0/24     eth0/1  10.1.2.200  O   60    2   Root


IPv4 Dest-Routes for <vpn-vr> (4 entries)
```

```
-----------------------------------------------------------------
    ID          IP-Prefix  Interface     Gateway   P Pref    Mtr
-----------------------------------------------------------------
*    2    10.200.200.1/32     eth0/3     0.0.0.0   H    0      0
*    5    192.168.20.0/24        n/a    trust-vr  SI  140      1
*    3     192.168.1.0/24        n/a    trust-vr  SI  140      1
*    1    10.200.200.0/24     eth0/3     0.0.0.0   C    0      0

SSG->
```

Notice that the routing table in the `trust-vr` has four active static routes: the default route, `192.168.20.0/24`, `192.168.3.0/24`, and `192.168.1.0/24`. If you review the configuration in the `trust-vr`, you can see only the tagged routes `192.168.20.0/24` and `192.168.1.0/24` with a tag value of `10`. Based on the filters applied in the route map, the firewall exports only those routes with a tag value of `10`. After the export rule is applied to the `trust-vr`, you can see that the `vpn-br` has four routes: two routes generated by the directly connected interface `eth0/3`, which are the `10.200.200.1/32` host route and the `10.200.200.0/24` network route for the interface; and two static routes from the `trust-vr`, which are `192.168.20.0/4` and `192.168.1.0/24`, with a next-hop gateway of `trust-vr` and a protocol type of `SI`, which means static and imported.

4.9 Change the Route Lookup Preference

Problem

You have configured source-based routing on the firewall and want to change the route lookup preference for matching routes.

Solution

You can change the route lookup preference on the VR. The following command changes the preference for source-based routing to 100:

```
set vr trust-vr route-lookup preference source-routing 100
```

Discussion

When you have multiple route types such as source-based and source interface-based routes configured on the VR, the default route lookup preference is source interface-based routes (SIBR) first, source-based routes (SBR) next, and destination-based routes (DRT) last.

When a packet arrives on the firewall, the route lookup checks whether SIBR is enabled on the VR. If it is, the firewall looks for the route based on the source IP address of the packet for the incoming interface. You must have a source route configured for that interface for this match to succeed. All the source interface-based routes are stored in the SIBR routing table. When a route matches, the firewall forwards the packet using that path. If no SIBR route is found, it checks to see whether SBR is enabled on the VR.

Next, the route lookup checks whether there is a route in the SBR routing table that matches the packet's source IP address. The source IP address route can come from any interface in that VR, unlike the SIBR route, which checks only whether the route exists for that incoming interface. If the source IP address matches a route, the packet is forwarded using that path.

If no SBR route is found, the final route lookup is done using the DRT. Here, the match is based on the packet's destination IP address. If this address matches a route, it is forwarded using that path. If no route is found, the packet is dropped.

Figure 4-6 illustrates the default route lookup preference.

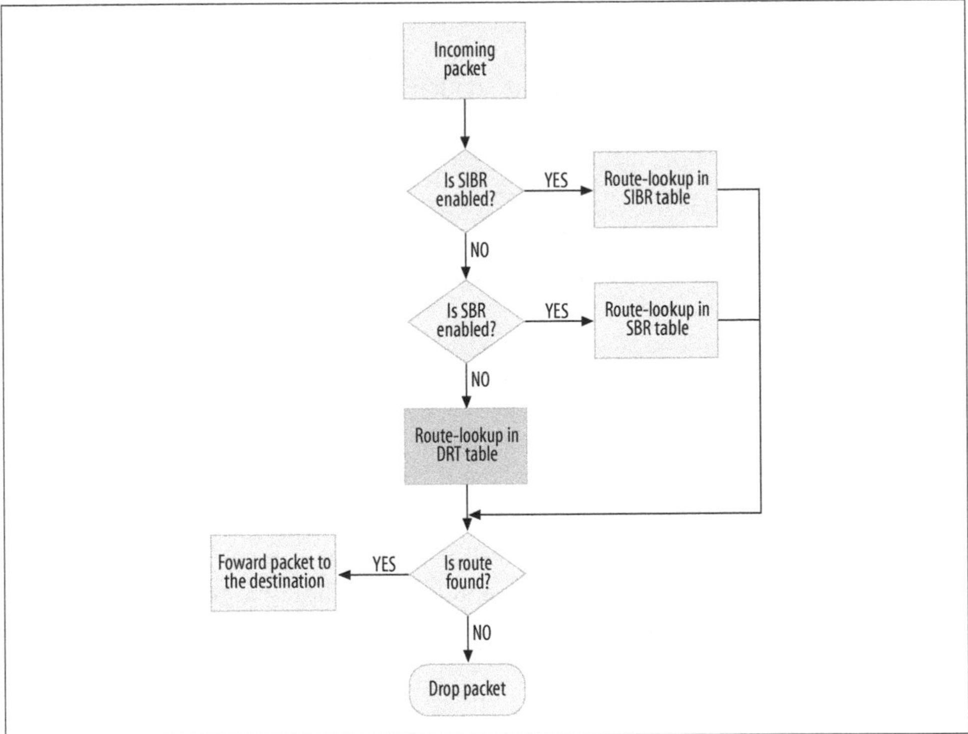

Figure 4-6. The default route lookup preference

You can change the default route lookup preference behavior by using the `set vr trust-vr route-lookup preference` command. Here, we want the source-routing preference to have a weight of 100. The higher the weight is, the higher the preference is. So, we change the route lookup order to be SBR, then SIBR, and finally DRT.

You can use the following command to verify the route lookup preference on the VR:

```
SSG-> get vr trust-vr route-lookup preference
vrouter(trust-vr) route-lookup preference table(sorted by preference):
--------------------------------------------------
route-lookup-method     preference
```

```
---------------------------------------------
Source-IP-lookup        100
SIBR-route-lookup       3
destination-IP-lookup  1
SSG->
```

This output shows that the source IP lookup has a preference of 100, which is higher than the other lookups. Hence, the SBR is the first routing table to be consulted, followed by the SIBR routing table, and finally the DRT routing table.

4.10 Create Permanent Static Routes

Problem

You want to have permanent static routes on the firewall so that the routes are available even if the local interface goes down.

Solution

Configure a static route with the `permanent` keyword:

```
SSG-> set route 172.16.10.0/24 interface e0/0 gateway 10.1.1.10
permanent
```

Discussion

Often, you have situations when your network interface flaps and the applications behind that interface then become unreachable. The problem can be severe when you are using dynamic routing protocols and static route redistribution because it can take a long time for the routes to converge.

To keep the routes available when the interface flaps, you can configure a static route that remains permanently in the routing and is not withdrawn even if the interface associated with that route is down. We configure the route to the `172.16.10.0/24` network that is reachable via the `e0/0` interface with a next-hop gateway of `10.1.1.10` and that is available permanently, even if the `e0/0` interface goes down.

Keep in mind that if this route is redistributed into an Interior Gateway Protocol (IGP), there is no alternative path to reach this network. You should use this configuration only when there is no possibility of reaching this network through a different path.

CHAPTER 5

Transparent Mode

5.0 Introduction

In transparent mode, the firewall acts like a transparent bridge. Although there are historically other switch types, all Ethernet switches are considered transparent bridges. The difference between other switch types (such as token ring or cell switches) and Ethernet switches is that the latter do not maintain path information or even use a configured forwarding table or dynamic path discovery protocol.

Ethernet uses Media Access Control (MAC) addressing in a way that is similar to how IP packets use IP addresses. A MAC address is 48 bits long, whereas an IPv4 address is 32 bits long. MAC addresses on Ethernet are identical, with serial numbers on network interface cards (NICs), also called *ports*. Each port has its own MAC address, which sometimes can be changed, but rarely is. Ethernet switches became so successful because they work on a very simple principle: when an Ethernet frame enters a switch, the switch puts the `src-mac` address into a forwarding table, linked to the ingress port. Then it checks to see whether it has a forwarding entry for the `dst-mac` address to an egress port. If it does *not*, it floods the packet out on all ports except for the port on which it was received. If it *does*, it floods the frame to only the port to which the forwarding entry points. The forwarding table is transient, and entries are timed out after a few minutes if they are not refreshed.

In contrast to IP addresses, MAC addresses only have significance on a LAN between hosts or routers on the same broadcast domain, which usually means in the same IP network. Broadcast domains and IP networks commonly overlap one to one, although this is not always the case. The rule of thumb says that switches connect hosts within the same broadcast domain, whereas routers connect broadcast domains to each other. Ethernet works on the ISO/OSI link layer and IP works on the network layer. Ethernet switches do not change the MAC address or any other part of the frame. They are therefore called *transparent*.

ScreenOS in transparent mode works just like an Ethernet switch. The biggest difference between ScreenOS and a modern multilayer switch is that ScreenOS can either switch or route a packet, but it cannot do both at the same time. ScreenOS also has limited support for virtual local area networks (VLANs). VLANs simulate multiple virtual bridges within an Ethernet switch, maintaining separate forwarding tables for each VLAN. VLAN membership is indicated within an Ethernet frame by a tag in a header extension.

Ethernet switches switch Ethernet frames, although many multilayer switches are also IP-aware. Multiple different types of Ethernet frames exist, from connectionless and connection-oriented, to unicast, multicast, and broadcast. The most significant bit in the MAC address indicates whether a frame is a unicast or multicast/broadcast frame. ScreenOS supports all three types.

IP runs over connectionless Ethernet-II frames and unicast, multicast, and broadcast addresses are mapped to their MAC counterparts. Network layer packets are signaled in the Ethernet-II frame by an EtherType. IP has an EtherType of 0×0800 and the Address Resolution Protocol (ARP) has an EtherType of 0×0806. ScreenOS considers these as IP traffic, versus non-IP traffic such as frames carrying IPX Protocol Data Units (PDUs).

ScreenOS acts like an Ethernet switch by forwarding frames, but it applies access policies as well as virtual private network (VPN) policies in addition to application layer attack signatures on the network layer, transport layer, and application layer. ScreenOS policies do not control Ethernet frames, but rather the encapsulated IP packets inside.

In Figure 5-1, you can see an example of a data packet containing the Ethernet, IP, and User Datagram Protocol (UDP) headers as well as the payload. In transparent mode, the firewall switches on the `dst-mac` and in route mode it routes on the `dst-ip` address. On the right side, you can see the security features the firewall applies and where it does so. The security features in ScreenOS are pretty much identical whether in route or transparent mode. The difference mainly consists of how to integrate the firewall into the topology.

Ethernet uses the Spanning Tree Protocol (STP) to form a loop-free topology. STP forms a tree-like graph from an elected root switch so that the root can be reached from any switch in the most efficient path. Redundant ports are put into blocking mode. STP communicates via Bridge Packet Data Units (BPDUs). Although there are many flavors of STP, the most common are the IEEE 802.1d and the proprietary PVST+ protocol from Cisco Systems. New standards, such as IEEE 802.1s, are becoming more widespread in data networks. ScreenOS does not implement STP, but it is compatible with STP by forwarding BPDUs transparently between STP-capable switches.

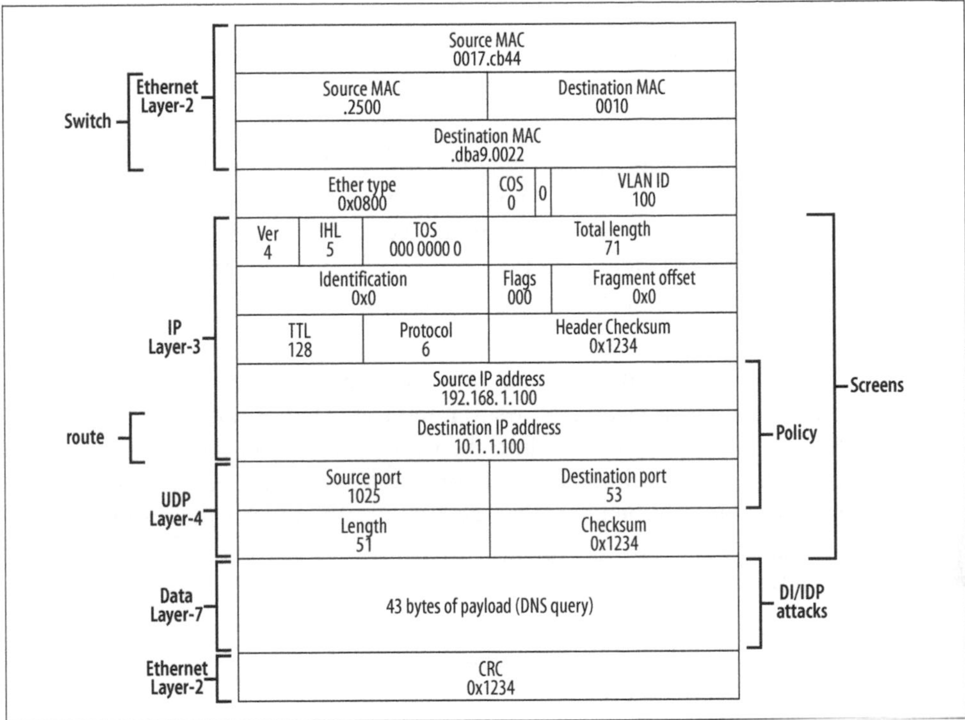

Figure 5-1. Framing and security

5.1 Enable Transparent Mode with Two Interfaces

Problem

You want to enable transparent mode.

Solution

Move two interfaces into a Layer 2 (L2) zone, and all other interfaces into the `null` zone:

```
unset interface e0/0 ip
set interface e0/0 zone v1-trust

unset interface e0/1 ip
set interface e0/1 zone v1-untrust
```

Configure a management address on the virtual `vlan1` interface:

```
set interface vlan1 ip 192.168.1.100/24
set route 0.0.0.0/0 interface vlan1 gateway 192.168.1.254
```

Then, configure a policy:

```
set policy from v1-untrust to v1-trust any any http permit
```

Discussion

You enable transparent mode by putting interfaces into L2 zones. There are two predefined L2 zones: `V1-Trust` and `V1-Untrust`. Do not confuse those with the L3 (Layer 3) zones `Trust` and `Untrust` when you create policies in the WebUI or CLI. Note that the NetScreen Security Manager (NSM) does not differentiate between L2 zones and L3 zones, so policy bases can be shared between devices in transparent and route modes.

Both zones will be in the same VLAN, with the firewall acting like a bridge. To enable transparent mode, attach L2 zones to interfaces. Do not forget to unset any IP addressing. Move all other interfaces into the `null` zone. Before you move the interfaces to the L2 zones, the firewall is in Network Address Translation (NAT) or route mode (by factory default, some firewall models are already in transparent mode):

```
FIREWALL-> get system | include ^System
System in NAT/route mode.

FIREWALL-> unset interface e0/0 ip
FIREWALL-> set interface e0/0 zone v1-trust
FIREWALL-> unset interface e0/1 ip
FIREWALL-> set interface e0/1 zone v1-untrust
FIREWALL-> set int e0/2 zone Null
Changed to pure l2 mode

FIREWALL-> get system | include ^System
System in transparent mode.
```

Configure an IP address on the `vlan1` interface and a default route:

```
set interface vlan1 ip 192.168.1.100/24
set route 0.0.0.0/0 interface vlan1 gateway 192.168.1.254
```

You can use the `vlan1` interface for in-band management, for monitoring with `track-ip`, with management protocols such as SNMP traps and Syslog, and to terminate VPN tunnels, which are also supported in transparent mode. You cannot run dynamic routing protocols on a firewall in transparent mode because the firewall will only act as a host. It will not use the routing table to decide how to switch packets through the firewall. It will use the routing table only for packets originating from the firewall.

Figure 5-2 shows a typical transparent mode design.

The firewall is positioned between a router and a switch. Hosts are connected to the switch. The switch is connected to the firewall via an access link and the firewall to the router via an access link. All hosts in this recipe are in the same network, `192.168.1.0/24`. The default gateway of the hosts is the router's interface, `192.168.1.254`. The firewall has the `vlan1` interface in the same network for in-band management.

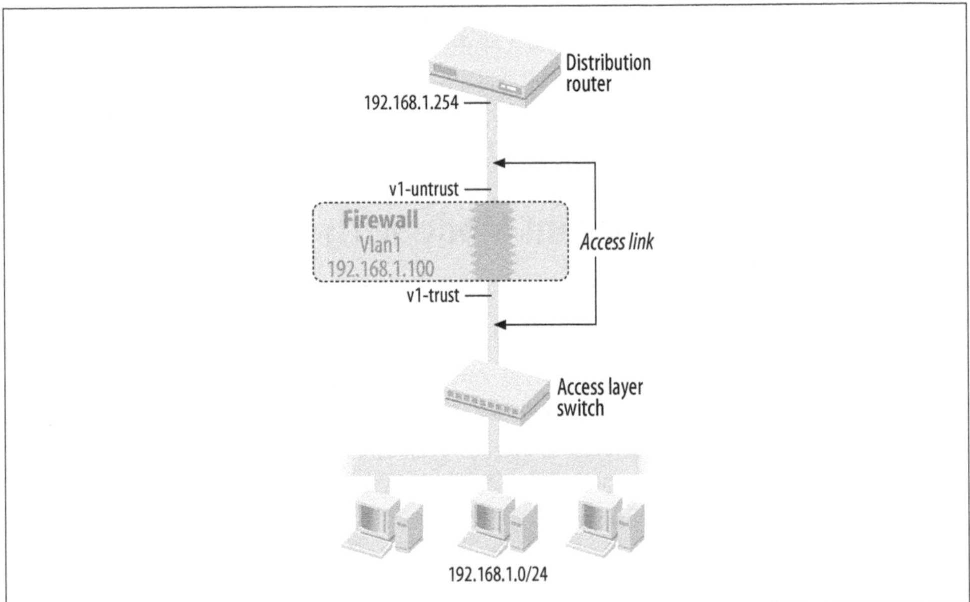

Figure 5-2. Transparent mode design

The default route for the firewall is also the router's interface, `192.168.1.254`. The firewall's routing table is not used for forwarding traffic between the router and the host.

If a host wants to communicate with a different network, it sends an ARP request for the router's interface address, `192.168.1.254`. The firewall is forwarding this request unchanged as an Ethernet frame with EtherType 0×0806. The router will reply and the firewall will again forward this reply. The firewall is able to build its forwarding table from the `src-mac` address of the ARP frames. ScreenOS calls the Layer 2 forwarding table a Forwarding Information Base (FIB), whereas other vendors may call it Content Addressable Memory (CAM). The host now knows the MAC address of its default gateway, and the firewall knows behind which interfaces the host and the router are located. If the forwarding table entry times out, the firewall will relearn it from the next frame being sent by the host or router. When the routers send traffic back to the host, the host will also ARP for its MAC address and the firewall will forward that request. With the first IP packet being sent by the host, the firewall builds session state. When the server, or another host somewhere beyond the router, replies to the first host, an Ethernet frame is received from the router, and the firewall matches the encapsulated IP packets (EtherType 0×0800) toward the existing session and forwards the frame. The firewall will not change the header of the Ethernet frame. If a policy or signature denies traffic, the Ethernet frame is dropped the same way as when the IP packet is dropped in route mode.

It is also possible to position the firewall between two routers, which is often done when protecting wide area network (WAN) links. If the firewall is placed between an Internet gateway router and an internal router, you need at least two "usable" public IP addresses for that segment: one for the internal router and one for the in-band management of the firewall.

5.2 Enable Transparent Mode with Multiple Interfaces

Problem

You want to divide a server network into security zones.

Solution

First, configure custom security zones:

```
set zone name l2-trust-1 L2
set zone name l2-trust-2 L2
set zone name l2-trust-3 L2

set interface e0/1 zone v1-untrust
set interface e0/2 zone l2-trust-1
set interface e0/3 zone l2-trust-2
set interface e0/4 zone l2-trust-3
```

Then, configure a management address on the virtual `vlan1` interface:

```
set interface vlan1 ip 192.168.1.100/24
set route 0.0.0.0/0 interface vlan1 gateway 192.168.1.254
```

Now, configure the policies:

```
set policy from v1-untrust to l2-trust-1 any any http permit
set policy from l2-trust-1 to l2-trust-2 any any ssh permit
```

Discussion

You can create custom zones in addition to the predefined zones, `V1-Trust` and `V1-Untrust`. Custom zones receive the mandatory prefix of `L2`, similar to the prefix `V1` in the predefined zones:

```
set zone name l2-myzone L2
```

The same rules apply here as for designs with only two interfaces (see Recipe 5.1): all interfaces are in the same broadcast domain; unused interfaces have to be moved to the `null` zone to enable transparent mode; hosts cannot be assigned to different IP networks; and all interfaces connected to the firewall are in access mode. The firewall can do either routing or switching but not both at the same time, and in transparent mode the firewall acts as a flat bridge. The in-band `vlan1` management interface's IP address is in the same IP network as hosts behind all interfaces.

```
set interface vlan1 ip 192.168.1.100/24
set route 0.0.0.0/0 interface vlan1 gateway 192.168.1.254
```

This topology is a useful design where a large server segment needs to be partitioned into security zones. Policies can be written that protect each custom zone from `v1-untrust` and `v1-trust` from each custom zone, as well as protect custom zones from each other:

```
set policy from v1-untrust to l2-trust-1 any any http permit
set policy from l2-trust-1 to l2-trust-2 any any ssh permit
```

Figure 5-3 shows such a sample network. The firewall uses four interfaces, one in `v1-untrust` and three in custom zones: `l2-trust-1`, `l2-trust-2`, and `l2-trust-3`. Each interface connects to a physical switch or an access port in a different VLAN on an access layer switch.

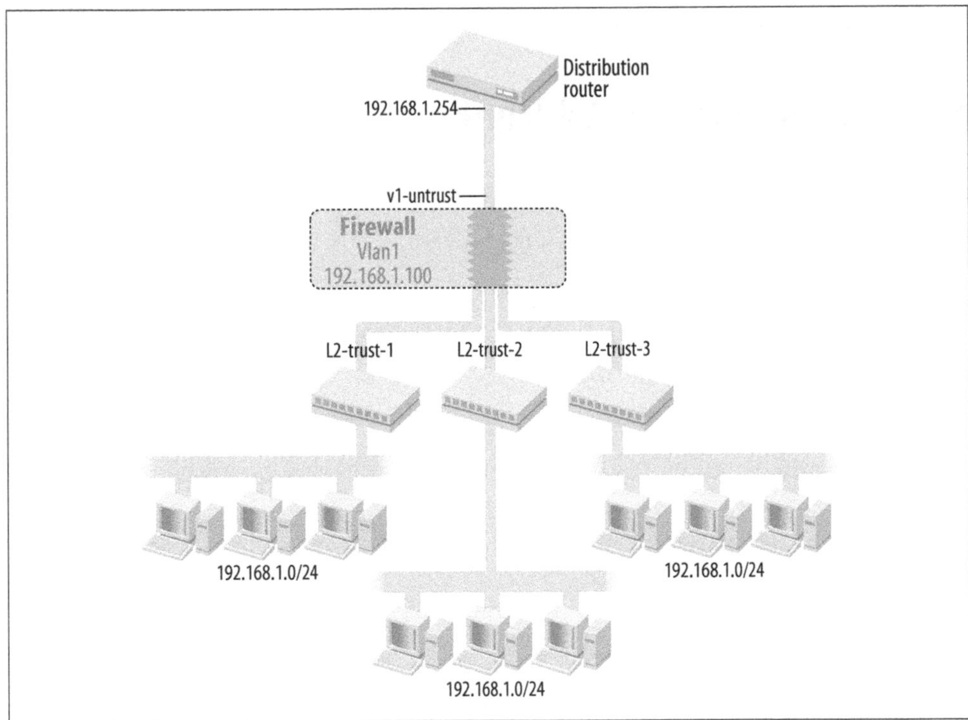

Figure 5-3. Transparent mode with multiple interfaces

In this design, the general rule "one VLAN maps to one IP address" does not necessarily apply. Technically, all Layer 2 segments connected to the firewall build one broadcast domain *and* all hosts are in the same IP network. But all hosts and all interfaces on the firewall may be connected to the same switch separated only by VLANs. The switch is connected via access ports to the firewall, and the firewall would bridge rather than route between the VLANs. Some switches apply a discovery protocol such as Cisco Systems' Cisco Discovery Protocol (CDP), which may discover a loop when bridging VLANs on the same switch and error-disable the associated port. Those protocols need to be disabled on the ports connected to the firewall to make this design work. The topology in itself is hierarchical and loop-free. Note that it is also possible to use different physical switches instead of VLANs on the same switch.

Hosts that are *within* such a LAN or VLAN connect directly to each other without passing through the firewall—when a host connects to another host in a *different* LAN or VLAN, it passes the firewall, and the firewall does a policy lookup and applies whatever other security was configured. Only when a host connects to another host in a different IP network will traffic pass the router behind the `V1-Untrust` zone. Make sure that only the VLAN, connected to `V1-Untrust`, has an L3 virtual interface configured. When hosts in the same network behind different security zones talk to one another, the firewall switches the Ethernet frame directly, as any other Ethernet switch would.

5.3 Configure a VLAN Trunk

Problem

You want to put the firewall into a trunk and pass VLAN tagged frames.

Solution

Configure the firewall to ignore the VLAN tag while matching on the IP header on policies:

```
set interface vlan1 vlan trunk
```

Move two interfaces into a Layer 2 (L2) zone, and all other interfaces into the `null` zone:

```
unset interface e0/0 ip
set interface e0/0 zone v1-trust

unset interface e0/1 ip
set interface e0/1 zone v1-untrust
```

Configure a management address on the virtual `vlan1` interface:

```
set interface vlan1 ip 192.168.1.100/24
set route 0.0.0.0/0 interface vlan1 gateway 192.168.1.254
```

Then, configure a policy:

```
set policy from v1-untrust to v1-trust any any http permit
```

Discussion

A server network should be secured, but addressing cannot be changed on the servers if it is hardcoded into applications. The easiest way to introduce a firewall is to put the firewall into transparent mode and include it between the servers and the next-hop router. However, servers are commonly connected to different VLANs.

In Figure 5-4, a firewall is introduced between the access layer switch and the distribution layer switch. The access layer switch is a Layer 2 device, and the distribution layer switch is usually a multilayer switch; hence, it supports virtual L3 VLAN interfaces. Multiple VLANs are configured for different servers. An 802.1Q trunk connects the access layer switch with the distribution layer switch. This is a typical data center design. The motivation for such a design is that the firewall should not interfere with the network topology.

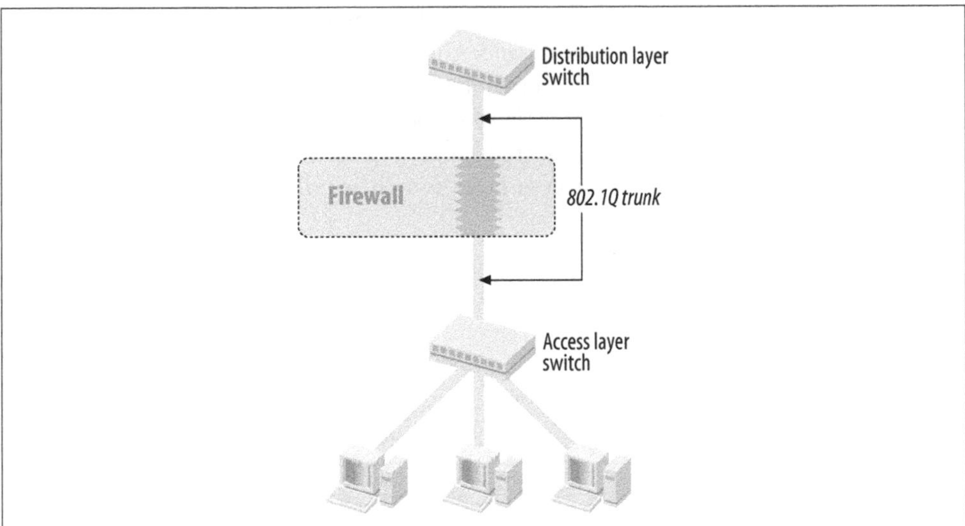

Figure 5-4. VLAN trunking in transparent mode

Both ports from the switches connecting to the firewall are configured in trunk mode; however, the firewall's interfaces are configured in access mode. In classic transparent mode, ScreenOS does not support trunk ports (see Recipe 5.4). However, it is possible to configure ScreenOS to simply ignore the IEEE 802.1Q subhead while doing policy checking; in this case, the firewall would be truly transparent to the topology as it does not change the Ethernet frame, and rather just shifts policy matching two bytes to the right to account for the added VLAN subheader.

The following configures ScreenOS to ignore VLAN tags on the `vlan1` management interface:

```
set interface vlan1 vlan trunk
```

Two interfaces are placed into L2 zones as described in Recipe 5.1:

```
unset interface e0/0 ip
set interface e0/0 zone v1-trust

unset interface e0/1 ip
set interface e0/1 zone v1-untrust
```

Configure a management address on the virtual `vlan1` interface. The `vlan1` interface ends up in the "native" or uncolored VLAN. This is the default VLAN on which the switch accepts untagged frames. It is used for management functions.

```
set interface vlan1 ip 192.168.1.100/24
set route 0.0.0.0/0 interface vlan1 gateway 192.168.1.254
```

Then, configure a policy:

```
set policy from v1-untrust to v1-trust any any http permit
```

The design shown in Figure 5-5 can be useful when only some servers should be protected; for example, because of compliance rules. In this case, a second access layer switch could be introduced. The servers that should not be protected connect to the first access layer switch, and the servers that should be protected connect to a new access layer switch. The two switches are again connected via a VLAN trunk with the firewall in the middle. The first access layer switch is connected to its distribution layer switch.

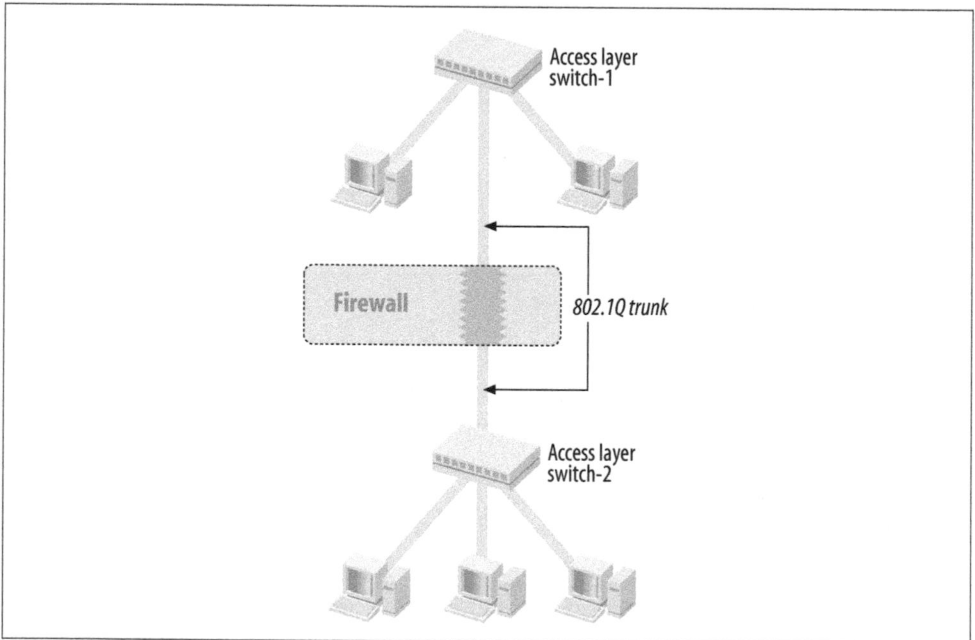

Figure 5-5. Protecting selected servers in transparent mode

ScreenOS is compatible with 802.1Q trunking, but not with the proprietary trunking Inter Switch Link (ISL) protocol. ISL tagged traffic may be globally permitted or globally denied as non-IP traffic, but it is not possible to define policies for ISL trunked traffic. It is advisable to manually configure switches to use IEEE 802.1Q and to not use ISL or any other proprietary trunk encapsulation. Older Cisco Systems switches often default to ISL trunking, which by default would be permitted without a policy on ScreenOS.

To permit ISL tagged frames through the firewall, configure this:

```
set interface vlan1 bypass-non-ip
unset interface vlan1 bypass-non-ip
```

This command sequence may be slightly counterintuitive. The first line enables non-IP frames through the firewall and the second denies non-IP unicast frames, leaving non-IP multicast frames. To deny ISL tagged frames through the firewall, configure this:

```
unset interface vlan1 bypass-non-ip-all
```

As both ISL and STP use non-IP multicast frames, denying ISL in ScreenOS also denies STP frames.

Because of the shared FIB on ScreenOS, it is very important to make sure that destination MAC addresses of all devices in any VLAN passing the firewall are unique—in particular, if multiple trunks are running through the same firewall concurrently and you are using ScreenOS 5.4 or earlier. Some switches support more than 1,024 VLANs and use a MAC address mapping scheme to support more than the 10 bits in the IEEE 802.1Q tag. MAC addresses of router interfaces on those multilayer switches usually cannot be configured and are automatically assigned from the pool of burned-in addresses (BIAs). The use of the Hot Standby Router Protocol (HSRP) or Virtual Redundancy Router Protocol (VRRP) in that case makes sense, even if there is only one router in the VLAN to guarantee unique destination MAC addresses. Each HSRP or VRRP group uses a unique MAC address. To keep it simple, it is recommended to run just one trunk through the same firewall or the same Virtual System (VSYS) so that there is not the possibility of seeing the same MAC address behind multiple interfaces.

5.4 Configure Retagging

Problem

You want to integrate a firewall with a multilayer switch.

Solution

Choose two interfaces on the switch and make them both trunks. Configure the firewall to rewrite VLAN tags from one interface to the other.

First, create a vlan group for vlan-100:

```
set vlan group name vlan-100
set vlan group vlan-100 100 100
```

Then, link the vlan group to the two interfaces:

```
set vlan port e2/1 group vlan-100 zone v1-trust
set vlan port e2/2 group vlan-100 zone v1-untrust
```

Retag vlan-100 to vlan-200 and attach to interface e2/1:

```
set vlan retag name map-100-to-200 100 200
set vlan port e2/1 retag map-100-to-200
```

Then, configure policies:

```
set policy from v1-untrust to v1-trust any any http permit
set policy from v1-trust to v1-untrust any any ssh permit
```

Discussion

In some instances, it may be desirable to integrate a firewall with a multilayer switch which would perform switching and routing. All the ports on the switch can be made virtual firewall ports and the administrator can configure which VLANs are sent through the firewall and which bypass the firewall. VLAN retagging is supported on ScreenOS 6.0 and later only on the NS-5000 Series platform.

The way to accomplish this integration is by connecting the switch via two trunked links to the firewall. Each trunk transmits Ethernet frames, sorted by VLAN tags. The firewall in between is switching the Ethernet frames from one interface to another interface; this creates a loop because the switch would send a frame with, say, vlan-100 to the firewall, the firewall would send it back on the second interface to the switch, and the switch would send it back to the firewall, and so forth. To break this loop, the firewall needs to "mark" frames that have passed the firewall.

A simple way to do this "marking" is to swap the tag. The switch would send an Ethernet frame with VLAN tag 100 to the firewall, and the firewall would check the embedded packet against its policy table and other higher-security layers and, if permitted, send it on to the switch. But this time, the firewall retags the Ethernet frame with a different tag—for instance, vlan-200—so that no loop can be created. The swap of the VLAN tag does not make a difference for edge ports (the opposite of trunk ports) because on those ports, the tag is stripped anyway. However, it will make a difference if the switch downstream of the firewall connects to other switches via a trunk.

Figure 5-6 shows a typical retagging topology.

In the middle of the topology is the firewall. On top of the firewall are three logical switches; the bottom of the firewall also has three logical switches. Those logical switches are VLANs within the same multilayer switch. At the top is a router, which is also a routing engine within the same multilayer switch. The router connects via

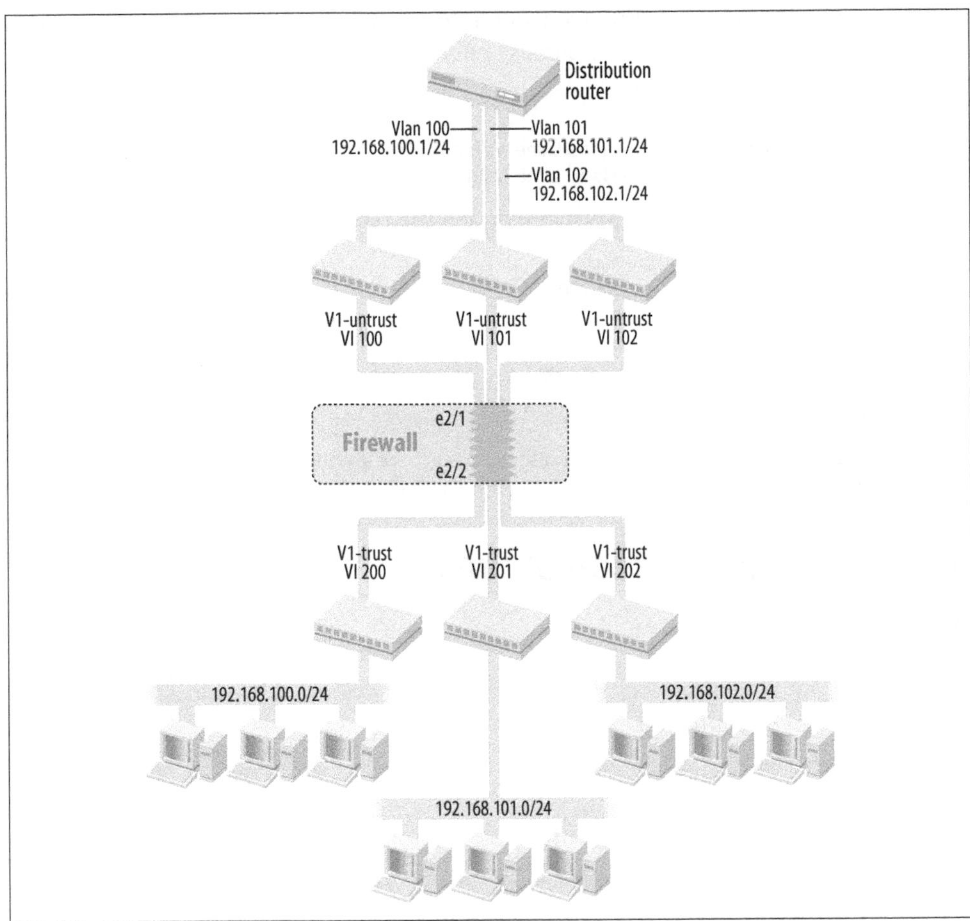

Figure 5-6. VLAN trunking with retagging

virtual VLAN interfaces to the top VLANs. The firewall is actually connected via two trunk interfaces to the switch and not via individual physical interfaces. This is essential for this design. There is one trunk on interface `e2/1` on the top carrying `vlan-100`, `vlan-101`, and `vlan-102`, and there is another trunk on interface `e2/2` on the bottom carrying `vlan-200`, `vlan-201`, and `vlan-202`. The firewall in the middle retags `vlan-100` to `vlan-200`, `vlan-101` to `vlan-201`, and `vlan-102` to `vlan-202`. Notice that the firewall works in transparent mode. The firewall is actually not routing packets, but switching them, and itself works like a switch. The firewall will keep the VLANs separate from each other, and only allows communication between the main VLAN and its retag partner VLAN.

To configure the topology, first create a VLAN group for all `vlans`:

```
set vlan group name my-vlans
set vlan group my-vlans 100 102
```

Then, link the vlan group to the two trunk interfaces. You must also configure which of the trunk interfaces is in the v1-untrust zone and which is in the v1-trust zone:

```
set interface e2/1 zone null
set interface e2/2 zone null
set vlan port e2/1 group my-vlans zone v1-untrust
set vlan port e2/2 group my-vlans zone v1-trust
```

Configure retagging for the VLANs, and attach the retag group to interface e2/2:

```
set vlan retag name my-vlan-map
set vlan retag my-vlan-map 100 200
set vlan retag my-vlan-map 101 201
set vlan retag my-vlan-map 102 202
set vlan port e2/2 retag my-vlan-map
```

Finally, configure the policies:

```
set policy from v1-untrust to v1-trust any any http permit
set policy from v1-trust to v1-untrust any any ssh permit
```

5.5 Configure Bridge Groups

Problem

You need to put several devices into the same IP network and broadcast domain, but you do not want to deploy an extra switch.

Solution

Put the interfaces into a Bridge Group:

```
set interface bgroup0 zone "Trust"
set interface bgroup0 port ethernet0/1
set interface bgroup0 port ethernet0/2
set interface bgroup0 port ethernet0/3
set interface bgroup0 port ethernet0/4
set interface bgroup0 port ethernet0/5
set interface bgroup0 port ethernet0/6
```

Discussion

Concurrent Route Bridging (CRB) is used by routers where some interfaces bridge to each other and some interfaces route among each other. Such a feature is a relic from the times when you had to run several different networks and transport layer protocols concurrently, and some protocols did not deploy the concept of networks and hence could not be routed. Today, IP is the dominant network layer protocol. Though it is possible to configure some interfaces in route mode and others in transparent mode, this is not a supported design. Integrated Route Bridging (IRB) occurs when, in addition to routed interfaces and switched interfaces, there are also virtual

L3 interfaces that support routing between switched and routed interfaces. Today, this design is widely adopted on enterprise switches.

Implementing route bridging in a security device is more challenging because security policies are applied to traffic streams crossing interfaces and security zones. Rather than mixing route mode and transparent mode, ScreenOS implements IRB with the help of Bridge Groups combined with interfaces, usually in route mode. *Bridge Groups* are a collection of interfaces you can group together into a broadcast domain. ScreenOS switches Ethernet frames within members of a Bridge Group rather than routing IP packets. This is implemented via switch ASICs on the SSG Series and special Ethernet Physical Interface Modules (PIMs). The virtual Bridge Group interface, called `bgroup`, is the edge to the security features of ScreenOS. There are no security features between ports within a Bridge Group. This architectural approach is very similar to connecting a standalone switch to a port on the firewall.

There are two important use cases for Bridge Groups. The first is in a small-office setup such as that illustrated in Figure 5-7, where hosts can be directly connected to the firewall instead of having to deploy a separate desktop switch.

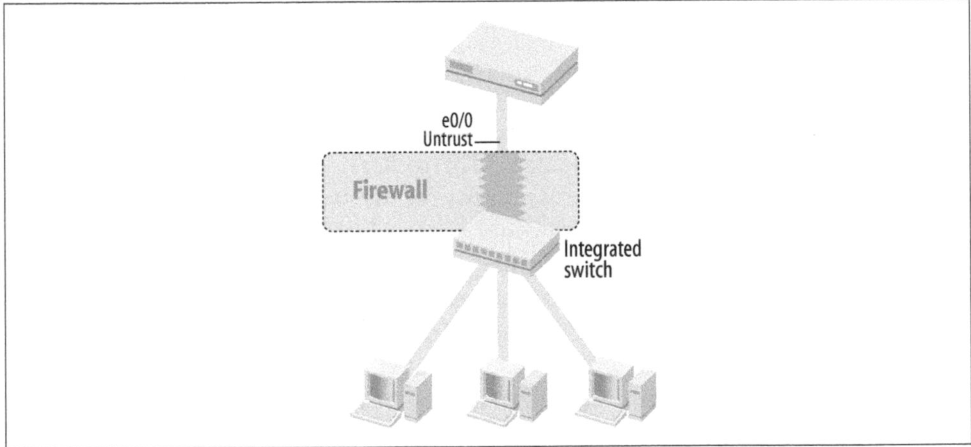

Figure 5-7. Bridge Group in small-office setup

In Figure 5-7, several computers are connected to a Bridge Group. The Bridge Group is in the `Trust` zone. The firewall also has one interface in the `Untrust` zone, which connects upstream to an Internet access router:

```
set interface ethernet0/0 zone "Untrust"
set interface bgroup0 zone "Trust"
set interface bgroup0 port ethernet0/1
set interface bgroup0 port ethernet0/2
set interface bgroup0 port ethernet0/3
set interface bgroup0 port ethernet0/4
```

The second important use case for Bridge Groups is with high availability (HA) topologies. With the NetScreen Redundancy Protocol (NSRP), as with HSRP or VRRP, all participating interfaces need to be in a broadcast domain. Traditionally, those networks were built by placing the firewalls like a sandwich between switches on the Trust and Untrust sides of the firewall, as shown in Figure 5-8.

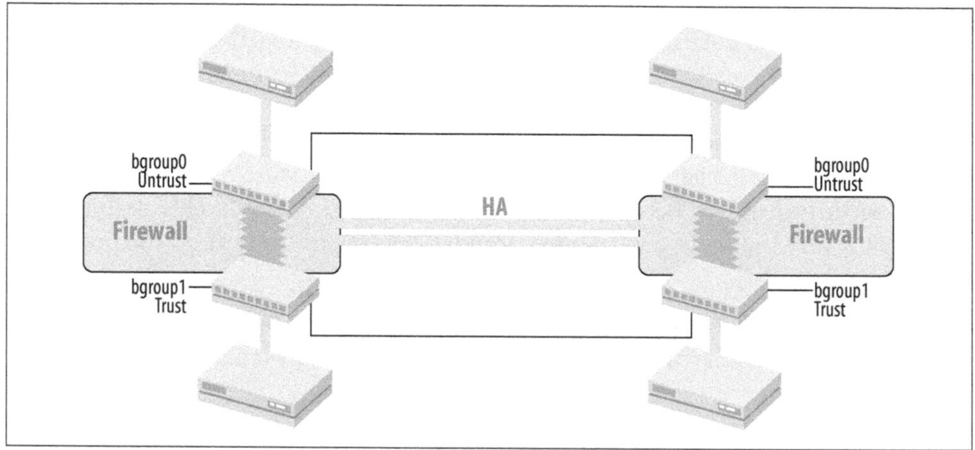

Figure 5-8. Bridge Groups in HA setup

In Figure 5-8, the two interfaces of the firewalls on the Untrust side and the two routers are all in the same broadcast domain. The routers' interfaces would be put into an HSRP or VRRP group, and the interfaces on the firewall would be in a virtual security device (VSD) group. There would be an identical setup for the Trust side and any other interface with directly connected routers. Do not confuse on-the-firewall Bridge Groups with HA interfaces because Bridge Groups build broadcast domains. NSRP does not actually exchange HA messages over payload interfaces, unlike HSRP and VRRP. ScreenOS uses dedicated HA interfaces for this purpose because on a firewall, a lot more information is being exchanged for HA than in HSRP or VRRP. Payload interfaces have to be in the same broadcast domain so that all devices on this broadcast domain can reach each other's virtual IP address. Therefore, all devices need to be in the same network and need to be able to ARP for each other's IP addresses.

```
set interface bgroup0 zone "Untrust"
set interface bgroup0 port ethernet0/0
set interface bgroup0 port ethernet0/1

set interface bgroup1 zone "Trust"
set interface bgroup1 port ethernet0/2
set interface bgroup1 port ethernet0/3
```

Although Bridge Groups are more commonly configured in route mode, you can configure them in route mode and transparent mode by placing them into an L3 or L2 zone. The first good example of why somebody would want to configure the firewall in transparent mode and use, in addition, a Bridge Group would be for a small-office setup. In this example, however, the hosts don't have to be protected from each other, but they do have to be protected from hosts on the Internet. Often, it is easier to deploy a firewall in transparent mode in such a small deployment so that access routers do not need to be reconfigured. Therefore, two zones are enough for developing policies on the firewall. It is just easier to connect a few hosts directly to the firewall instead of provisioning an additional switch.

```
set interface ethernet0/0 zone "V1-Untrust"
set interface bgroup0 zone "V1-Trust"
set interface bgroup0 port ethernet0/1
set interface bgroup0 port ethernet0/2
set interface bgroup0 port ethernet0/3
set interface bgroup0 port ethernet0/4
```

5.6 Manipulate the Layer 2 Forwarding Table

Problem

You want to review or change the firewall's FIB or CAM table.

Solution

Show the content of the FIB:

```
get mac-learn
```

Delete the FIB:

```
clear mac-learn
```

Delete an entry in the FIB:

```
unset mac 0010db123456 [ vlan 1 ]
```

Add a static entry to the FIB:

```
set mac 0010db123456 interface e0/1 [ vlan 1 ]
```

Discussion

Similar to a route table, a switch also has a forwarding table. Transparent bridges, a category to which all Ethernet switches belong, do not run a routing or discovery protocol. They populate the forwarding table on the fly by mapping `src-mac` addresses to incoming interfaces. Then, when a frame is switched, the switch just looks up the `dst-mac` address and forwards the frame out to the interface, which it has saved in its forwarding table. If there is no table entry, the switch forwards the frame out to all interfaces except for the interfaces on which it was received. ScreenOS 6.0 and later maintains one forwarding table for each VLAN separately, whereas earlier releases have only one table because there was no VLAN awareness. ScreenOS's forwarding table is termed a FIB, whereas other vendors may call it a

CAM table. Do not confuse the FIB table with the ARP table, which is used in transparent mode only for traffic originating from the firewall.

You can also switch ScreenOS from a transparent bridge to a bridge with static forwarding entries. In this mode, however, it is mandatory to configure static forwarding table entries for all hosts and routers connected to that broadcast domain:

```
unset interface vlan1 broadcast
unset mac-learn
set mac 0010db123456 e0/1 vlan 1
```

Alternatively, you can also populate the forwarding table with the help of ARPs and trace routes. The firewall ARPs for each destination address if the IP address is in the same network as its `vlan1` IP address or sends a traceroute. The reply is encapsulated in an Ethernet frame from which ScreenOS learns the location of the destination or next-hop MAC address:

```
set interface vlan1 arp trace-route
```

Both alternatives are rarely used, but keep in mind that MAC addresses have significance only on the LAN or VLAN; hence, the broadcast domain. The LAN to which the firewall is connected is usually in a secure location, but if multiple servers are connected to that broadcast domain and a server is penetrated, it is possible to poison the forwarding table of the firewall and create a Denial of Service (DoS) attack or redirect traffic. So, if a design with a static FIB table is chosen, a static table entry for each host and router on the broadcast domain needs to exist.

5.7 Configure the Management Interface in Transparent Mode

Problem

You want to configure a management interface in transparent mode.

Solution

First, enable Secure Shell (SSH) and SSL:

```
set ssh enable

set ssl enable
```

Configure in-band management:

```
set interface vlan1 ip 192.168.1.100/24
set interface vlan1 manage
set interface vlan1 nsrp manage zone v1-trust

set route 0.0.0.0/0 interface vlan1 gateway 1.1.1.1
```

Alternatively, configure out-of-band management:

```
set interface e0/0 zone mgt
set interface e0/0 ip 192.168.1.100/24

set route 10.0.0.0/8 interface e0/0 gateway 192.168.1.254
```

Then, allow management access from certain interfaces:

```
set interface e0/0 manage ssh
set interface e0/0 manage ssl
set interface e0/0 manage ping
```

Optionally, you can configure which hosts will manage the firewall:

```
set admin manager-ip 10.1.1.100
```

Discussion

You can manage the firewall in-band or out-of-band. The default is in-band.

You have to apply management settings at interfaces as well as on the virtual `vlan1` interface. Some ScreenOS devices have a dedicated MGT port, and in other devices any port can be moved into the MGT zone and can become a dedicated management port. WebAuth and VPN in transparent mode work only through the `vlan1` virtual interface and do not work with an out-of-band management interface. You can manage an NSRP member in backup mode only through one zone, which is configurable.

The following enables SSH and SSL globally on the firewall:

```
set ssh enable

set ssl enable
```

On ScreenOS 5.1 and earlier, you will have to install your own SSL certificate. (For more information, see Chapter 10.)

```
get pki x509 list local-cert

set ssl cert 0x1
```

In this recipe, the firewall should be managed in-band, with `v1-trust` as the preferred management zone for a backup NSRP member. You want to enable SSH, SSL, and ping. If the firewall is configured differently from the default, deny all management access to the `vlan1` interface first, and then enable selected management protocols on interfaces (by default, interfaces in different zones allow a different set of management protocols). It is a good practice to first switch off all management on an interface so that only selected management protocols are enabled. The `vlan1` interface needs to have an IP address in the VLAN (which is active on both sides of the firewall):

```
set interface vlan1 ip 192.168.1.100/24
set interface vlan1 manage
set interface vlan1 nsrp manage zone v1-trust

unset interface e0/0 manage
set interface e0/0 manage ssh
```

```
set interface e0/0 manage ssl
set interface e0/0 manage ping

set route 0.0.0.0/0 interface vlan1 gateway 192.168.1.254
```

Notice that the places where management is configured for ScreenOS change with releases, with some older releases requiring you to enable management on an interface as well as on the L2 zone or a virtual L2 interface:

```
set zone v1-trust manage
set interface v1-trust manage
```

Those commands may still be present, hidden in the CLI of the more recent releases, and if changed, they can cause unexpected problems.

You can also manage the firewall through a dedicated interface. If a dedicated interface is chosen in transparent mode, the routing table will be shared with the `vlan1` interface, which will still be used by VPN, WebAuth, or `track-ip`. You cannot configure a default route out of an out-of-band management interface and the `vlan1` interface at the same time.

```
set interface e0/0 zone mgt
set interface e0/0 ip 192.168.1.100/24
set interface e0/0 manage telnet
set route 10.0.0.0/8 interface e0/0 gateway 192.168.1.254
```

When the firewall is within a trunk, and it is managed via the `vlan1` interface or VPN and WebAuth should be used, managed traffic will be sent and received from the native or default VLAN that is able to switch untagged frames. The native VLAN is also called *untagged VLAN* or *uncolored VLAN* (in a switch, usually any VLAN can be made the native VLAN on a per-port basis). Make sure you take STP and other Layer 2 management protocols such as CDP and the VLAN Trunk Protocol (VTP) into account, which also use the native or default VLAN. In addition, you can also restrict which hosts can manage the firewall:

```
set admin manager-ip 10.1.1.100
```

5.8 Configure the Spanning Tree Protocol (STP)

Problem

You want to configure STP with ScreenOS in transparent mode.

Solution

ScreenOS does not support STP, but it is able to forward STP BPDUs so that the spanning tree can operate through the firewall using the following:

```
set interface vlan1 bypass-non-ip
unset interface vlan1 bypass-non-ip
```

Discussion

Although ScreenOS cannot participate in STP, spanning tree BPDUs can pass through the firewalls, and bridges on either end are able to participate in the tree.

The following permits or denies STP through the firewall:

```
set interface vlan1 bypass-non-ip
unset interface vlan1 bypass-non-ip
```

The first line enables unicast and multicast non-IP frames through the firewall, and the second denies non-IP unicast frames, leaving non-IP multicast frames. With this odd command sequence, `get interface vlan1` should show the following:

```
bypass non IP: multicast
```

You do not have to run STP with NSRP. Running STP can speed up convergence in certain switch topologies because STP forces FIB aging timers to decrease to a period of usually a few seconds after a topology change was detected. Without STP, convergence after a failover may take up to the current value of the FIB aging timer, which is usually about several minutes for active flows. FIB table aging is independent of tuning NSRP parameters because it does not impact topology convergence within upstream or downstream switches.

STP BPDUs will be flooded out to all interfaces. As long as all VLANs are following the same STP tree through the firewall interfaces, or BPDUs are distinctive between trees, this behavior does not cause any problems. STP comes in many flavors: PVST+ will tag BPDUs with the VLAN tag, and IEEE 802.1s hashes regional information from the BPDU to discriminate between trees and, therefore, should work, too. Certain IEEE 802.1D proprietary Multiple Spanning Tree (MST) extensions that support unique trees for each VLAN could cause problems.

5.9 Enable Compatibility with HSRP and VRRP Routers

Problem

You have HSRP or VRRP routers on a LAN, which is connected to the firewall. Switches on the other side of the firewall do not learn the location of the virtual IP and keep on flooding frames to the VIP out to all interfaces.

Solution

Create a policy to permit HSRP Hello messages:

```
set address v1-trust hsrp 224.0.0.2/32
set service hsrp protocol udp src-port 1985-1985 dst-port 1985-1985
set policy top from v1-untrust to v1-trust any hsrp hsrp permit
```

Create a policy to permit VRRP Hello messages:

```
set address v1-trust vrrp 224.0.0.18/32
set service vrrp protocol 112 src-port 0-65535 dst-port 0-65535
set policy top from v1-untrust to v1-trust any vrrp vrrp permit
```

Discussion

Ethernet frames, originating from HSRP routers, are sourced from the physical MAC address of each router's interface. Ethernet frames from a VRRP router should be sourced by the virtual MAC address, but not all vendors may implement it this way. An ARP request to an HSRP or VRRP virtual IP address will be replied to with the virtual MAC address so that hosts are sending traffic to the active group member. Transparent switches build their forwarding table by listening to the `src-mac` address in a frame. Without a FIB or CAM table entry for the virtual MAC address, a switch is flooding frames directed toward the virtual IP address out to all interfaces *except* the interface on which it was received. For the switch to be able to learn the location of the virtual MAC address, which may never exist in the source of a payload frame, the active HSRP and VRRP router sends Hello messages with the virtual MAC address in the source.

Blocking HSRP or VRRP messages in the firewall denies downstream switches to learn the location of the active router. The consequence is that downstream switches will flood traffic, directed to those routers, out of all interfaces instead of to the forwarding firewall. Because every device on that VLAN will receive every IP packet—directed to another subnet—from every other device on that VLAN, the network stack on servers may get overloaded. For example, CPU exhaustion may be caused on an NSRP firewall in backup mode because in backup mode the firewall drops all traffic not directed to its management interface instead of setting up a session and switching the traffic. Furthermore, dropping of packets in backup mode is resource-intensive and can cause high CPU use on the backup NSRP device, in particular on high-performing ASIC platforms.

To allow HSRP and VRRP Hello messages to pass the firewall, configure a rule to permit them through the firewall. When the HSRP router is behind `v1-untrust` and the protected hosts in `v1-trust` (see Figure 5-2 earlier in this chapter), create the HSRP address object in `v1-trust` and any other zone, if configured:

```
set address v1-trust hsrp 224.0.0.2/32
set service hsrp protocol udp src-port 1985-1985 dst-port 1985-1985
set policy top from v1-untrust to v1-trust any hsrp hsrp permit
```

In the same way, you can configure a VRRP rule from the firewall zone where the routers are located away to all other zones. Although VRRP routers will send gratuitous ARPs to signal a switchover, the firewall rule will ensure that FIB/CAM tables learned from the gratuitous ARPs are refreshed:

```
set address v1-trust vrrp 224.0.0.18/32
set service vrrp protocol 112 src-port 0-65535 dst-port 0-65535
set policy top from v1-untrust to v1-trust any vrrp vrrp permit
```

A return policy for Hellos is not required because the Hellos do not actually need to pass the firewall to reach the peer router—they are already exchanged through the broadcast domain to which the two routers are connected. The rule is there only to allow the firewall and switches behind the firewall to learn the location of the active router.

You could also configure a global policy, which would be processed after all interzone rules were processed, and is valid for all zone combinations:

```
set address global hsrp 224.0.0.2/32
set service hsrp protocol udp src-port 1985-1985 dst-port 1985-1985
set policy top global any hsrp hsrp permit

set address global vrrp 224.0.0.18/32
set service vrrp protocol 112 src-port 0-65535 dst-port 0-65535
set policy top global any vrrp vrrp permit
```

5.10 Configure VPNs in Transparent Mode

Problem

You want to configure a VPN in transparent mode.

Solution

Configure a policy-based VPN, and anchor the tunnel on the `vlan1` interface:

```
set ike gateway "gateway-b" ip 192.168.2.100 outgoing-zone
"V1-Untrust" preshare juniper sec-level standard
set ike gateway "gateway-b" nat-traversal

set vpn "gateway-b" gateway "gateway-b" sec-level standard
set vpn "gateway-b" monitor optimized rekey
```

Then, configure a tunnel policy, referencing L2 zones:

```
set policy id 1 from "V1-Trust" to "V1-Untrust"  "192.168.1.0/24"
"192.168.2.0/24" "ANY" tunnel vpn "gateway-b" log
set policy id 2 from "V1-Untrust" to "V1-Trust"  "192.168.2.0/24"
"192.168.1.0/24" "ANY" tunnel vpn "gateway-b" log
```

Discussion

An often-asked question is whether a VPN can be used to bridge a network between firewalls. The answer is "not really" because a VPN does not forward ARP queries via the IP Security (IPSec) tunnel. (You can, however, bridge networks over the tunnel if the two firewalls are directly connected via the same L2 link so that ARPs can be exchanged in the clear outside the tunnel.) VPN in transparent mode can still be useful.

To understand how VPN in transparent mode works, one has to understand how policy-based VPN works. With policy-based VPN, a tunnel policy is configured between two zones. If traffic is passing those two zones and it matches the policy, packets are encrypted over the configured VPN tunnel and sent to the configured remote Internet Key Exchange (IKE) gateway. The only difference with transparent mode and route mode is the way packets are switched from the ingress zone to the egress zone. In transparent mode, packets are switched as though on an Ethernet switch rather than routed. This might be confusing because it was said before that VPN on transparent mode cannot bridge networks, but it is why hosts need to have a route for the remote network to point to a router behind the firewall.

Figure 5-9 depicts a simple VPN topology. On the right side is network `192.168.1.0/24`, and on the left side is network `192.168.2.0/24`. The left and right firewalls are both in transparent mode. The hosts on either end are configured in the same network with their respective routers and point a default route to the router on the other side of the firewall. For example, hosts on the left side have IP addresses in the network of `192.168.1.0/24` and point to `192.168.1.254` as the default gateway—not to the firewall's `vlan1` address. This is critical so that hosts send packets through and not to the firewall, where the tunnel policy can catch them before they reach the router.

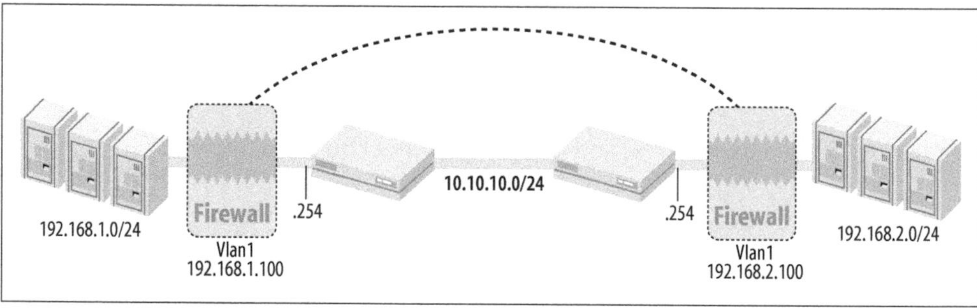

Figure 5-9. Transparent mode VPN

Between the two firewalls are two routers, which represent the Internet cloud. Firewalls do not necessarily need to be in transparent mode on both ends. One end could be in transparent mode and the other end could be in route mode. It does not even matter if the other end is also using policy-based VPN or route-based VPN. In the latter case, Security Associations (SAs) and the proxy ID have to match (as detailed shortly).

The configuration of the VPN is not much different than it is in route mode. First, put interfaces into zones and give the `vlan1` interface an IP address. The `vlan1` interface must be in the same network with the hosts and the local router. Also, create a default route, which is used to route the encrypted portion of the tunnel to the remote gateway.

On the left firewall, configure the following:

```
set interface e0/0 zone "V1-Trust"
set interface e0/1 zone "V1-Untrust"

set interface vlan1 ip 192.168.1.100/24
set route 0.0.0.0/0 interface vlan1 gateway 192.168.1.254
```

On the right firewall, configure the following:

```
set interface e0/0 zone "V1-Trust"
set interface e0/1 zone "V1-Untrust"

set interface vlan1 ip 192.168.2.100/24
set route 0.0.0.0/0 interface vlan1 gateway 192.168.2.254
```

Then, configure the VPN IKE gateway and tunnel.

On the left firewall, configure the following:

```
set ike gateway "gateway-b" ip 192.168.2.100 outgoing-zone "V1-Untrust"
preshare juniper sec-level standard
set ike gateway "gateway-b" nat-traversal

set vpn "gateway-b" gateway "gateway-b" sec-level standard
set vpn "gateway-b" monitor optimized rekey
```

On the right firewall, configure the following:

```
set ike gateway "gateway-a" ip 192.168.1.100 outgoing-zone "V1-Untrust"
preshare juniper sec-level standard
set ike gateway "gateway-a" nat-traversal

set vpn "gateway-a" gateway "gateway-a" sec-level standard
set vpn "gateway-a" monitor optimized rekey
```

Finally, configure tunnel policies.

On the left firewall, configure the following:

```
set address "V1-Trust" 192.168.1.0/24 192.168.1.0/24
set address "V1-Untrust" 192.168.2.0/24 192.168.2.0/24

set policy id 1 from "V1-Trust" to "V1-Untrust"  "192.168.1.0/24"
"192.168.2.0/24" "ANY" tunnel vpn "gateway-b" log
set policy id 2 from "V1-Untrust" to "V1-Trust"  "192.168.2.0/24"
"192.168.1.0/24" "ANY" tunnel vpn "gateway-b" log
```

On the right firewall, configure the following:

```
set address "V1-Untrust" 192.168.1.0/24 192.168.1.0/24
set address "V1-Trust" 192.168.2.0/24 192.168.2.0/24

set policy id 1 from "V1-Trust" to "V1-Untrust"  "192.168.2.0/24"
"192.168.1.0/24" "ANY" tunnel vpn "gateway-a" log
set policy id 2 from "V1-Untrust" to "V1-Trust"  "192.168.1.0/24"
"192.168.2.0/24" "ANY" tunnel vpn "gateway-a" log
```

The addresses in the policy actually have significance because with policy-based VPN, the SAs for identifying the tunnel are derived from the tunnel policy. The tunnel policies must mirror each other on either end.

If the right gateway would be a route-based VPN, you would have to make some changes:

```
Set zone name vpn
Set interface tun.1 zone vpn
Set interface tun.1 ip unnumbered interface e0/0
Set vpn "gateway-a" bind interface tun.1
Set vpn "gateway-a" proxy-id local-ip 192.168.2.0/24 remote-ip
192.168.1.0/24 any

set policy id 1 from "Trust" to "vpn"  "192.168.2.0/24"
"192.168.1.0/24" "ANY"
set policy id 2 from "vpn" to "Trust"  "192.168.1.0/24"
"192.168.2.0/24" "ANY"
```

Of course, in route mode, the `vlan1` interface is not used, and instead of an L2 zone, the IKE gateway has a real interface configured as the outgoing interface. Also, interfaces would be in L3 zones and have IP addresses. For brevity's sake, we do not explain this here, but only mention it to demonstrate that if one side is configured in transparent mode and the other in route mode, the proxy ID needs to be configured, matching the tunnel policy from the end with the transparent mode gateway.

5.11 Configure VSYS with Transparent Mode

Problem

You want to configure VSYS in transparent mode.

Solution

Choose the trunk interfaces and put them into the `null` zone:

```
set interface e2/1 zone null
set interface e2/2 zone null
```

As the root admin, enter the VSYS:

```
set vsys customer_a
```

Import `vlans 100` to `200` into `vsys customer_a`:

```
set vlan import 100 199
```

First, create a vlan group for the VLANs:

```
set vlan group name vlan-grp-a
set vlan group vlan-grp-a 100 199
```

Create security zones:

```
set zone name L2-customer_a-trust L2 1
set zone name L2-customer_a-untrust L2 1
```

Link the `vlan` group to the two interfaces:

```
set vlan port e2/1 group vlan-grp-a zone L2-customer_a-trust
set vlan port e2/2 group vlan-grp-a zone L2-customer_a-untrust
```

Configure policies:

```
set policy from L2-customer_a-untrust to L2-customer_a-trust any
any http permit
set policy from L2-customer_a-trust to L2-customer_a-untrust any
ny ssh permit
```

Exit the VSYS and continue with the next VSYS with a different set of VLANs.

Discussion

A VSYS is a way to logically partition a firewall. Instead of deploying many smaller firewalls, you can deploy one large firewall and share it with all users. In a transparent mode, VSYS traffic is always local to the VSYS and cannot be exchanged between VSYSes without an external network device such as a switch or router. One of the main benefits of VSYS is to abstract management of the device. Each VSYS administrator is only able to see and change configuration pertaining to the local VSYS. VSYS with transparent mode is supported in ScreenOS version 6.0 and later only on the NS-5000 Series platform.

The topology would be similar to the topology shown previously in Figure 5-4. The firewall is connected to the trunk interface on either side via switches. Traffic is sorted into different VSYSes by assigning certain tags to one VSYS and other tags to another VSYS. Policies can be kept local to the VSYS to which only the VSYS administrator has access.

In the root system, the interfaces are put into the `null` zone:

```
set interface e2/1 zone null
set interface e2/2 zone null
```

Then, enter the first VSYS, and move `vlans 100` to `199` into that VSYS:

```
set vsys customer_a
   set vlan import 100 199
   set vlan group name vlan-grp-a
   set vlan group vlan-grp-a 100 199
   set zone name L2-customer_a-trust L2 1
   set zone name L2-customer_a-untrust L2 1
   set vlan port e2/1 group vlan-grp-a zone L2-customer_a-trust
   set vlan port e2/2 group vlan-grp-a zone L2-customer_a-untrust
exit
```

Repeat the same process with the second VSYS, and move vlans 200 to 299 into that VSYS:

```
set vsys customer_b
   set vlan import 200 299
   set vlan group name vlan-grp-b
   set vlan group vlan-grp-b 200 299
   set zone name L2-customer_b-trust L2 1
   set zone name L2-customer_b-untrust L2 1
   set vlan port e2/1 group vlan-grp-b zone L2-customer_b-trust L2
   set vlan port e2/2 group vlan-grp-b zone L2-customer_b-untrust L2
exit
```

Notice that traffic cannot be exchanged between VSYSes. It can only flow within one VSYS:

```
set vsys customer_a
   set policy from L2-customer_a-untrust to L2-customer_a-trust any
any http permit
   set policy from L2-customer_a-trust to L2-customer_a-untrust any
any ssh permit
exit

set vsys customer_b
   set policy from L2-customer_b-untrust to L2-customer_b-trust any
any http permit
   set policy from L2-customer_b-trust to L2-customer_b-untrust any
any ssh permit
exit
```

CHAPTER 6

Leveraging IP Services in ScreenOS

6.0 Introduction

Network services are a critical component of any infrastructure. Like most network devices, firewalls running ScreenOS use services such as Domain Name System (DNS) and Network Time Protocol (NTP) for their own internal processes, and are also capable of providing services to end hosts. NTP, DNS, and Dynamic Host Configuration Protocol (DHCP) clients are available within ScreenOS to simplify network integration. Additionally, the firewall can act as a DNS or DHCP server to provide services to clients via either proxy or internal processes.

ScreenOS uses the Simple Network Time Protocol (SNTP) as described in RFC 2030 to provide clock synchronization on firewalls. Use of NTP is particularly important on firewall devices to ensure time synchronization across the network. Because firewalls tend to generate a large number of logs, maintaining time synchronization is a critically important requirement. Public Key Infrastructure (PKI) functionality also depends on accurate timing to operate correctly. One of the most common problems with certificate-based services, such as Internet Key Exchange (IKE), is inaccurate time information. Although you can configure time on the firewalls on a device-by-device basis, NTP provides an easy method of ensuring a common view of time across your firewall infrastructure. You can find more information on SNTP and NTP at *http://www.ntp.org*.

You can use DNS in ScreenOS in a number of ways. On the firewall, DNS is used for hostname resolution, for such tasks as object identification for policies, gateway authentication for IP Security (IPSec), or simply management and troubleshooting. ScreenOS can also act as a DNS proxy. In many environments, especially in site-to-site tunneled environments, it is desirable to use separate DNS servers for internal versus external name resolution. The DNS proxy functionality in ScreenOS allows for "split DNS" services to be provided to a location. ScreenOS can also act as a Dynamic Domain Name Service (DDNS) client. This capability is often used for IPSec gateway configuration for hosts with dynamically addressed endpoints. By configuring the remote IKE gateway with a fully qualified domain name (FQDN) in DDNS, you can build virtual private network (VPN) tunnels between two devices with dynamic addresses.

As with DNS, ScreenOS can act in multiple capacities with respect to DHCP. On lower-end products, which are frequently connected to cable modems, it is often necessary to act as a DHCP client. When connecting into such an environment, the `Untrusted` interface can be configured to receive its IP address from a DHCP server. Because client machines are often directly connected to a ScreenOS device, ScreenOS also offers the capability to act as a DHCP server and as a DHCP relay agent. This allows client devices to use the ScreenOS device or a centralized DHCP server to get their IP information.

Due to the wide breadth of potential deployment scenarios, Juniper's firewalls provide a number of capabilities in offering and interacting with network services.

6.1 Set the Time on the Firewall

Problem

You need to configure the time on the firewall.

Solution

Manually set the time using the CLI:

```
FIREWALL-A-> set clock 07/13/2007 01:51:00
FIREWALL-A-> set clock dst recurring start-weekday 2 0 3 02:00
    end-weekday 1 0 11 02:00
```

Discussion

When initially setting up a firewall, it is recommended that you set the clock to the current time. For small, localized networks, local time is usually appropriate, but for large networks spanning multiple time zones, UTC may prove more useful. Although setting the date and time manually on firewalls is the least accurate way to maintain the system clock, in a small environment with just one or a few firewalls, such as one's home, using the system clock may be acceptable. Even in large environments, manually setting the clock can be useful. For example, when generating a certificate request on the device, if the clock is off, the certificate could show up as being issued in the future, which would render it invalid. As such, it is a good practice to set the date manually, even if you plan to use NTP down the road.

In ScreenOS, setting the date and time is simple: just use the `set clock` command. The date format is in mm/dd/yyyy; the time format is in hh:mm:ss and follows a 24-hour clock. You also can configure Daylight Saving Time (DST) settings for manually set clocks. In ScreenOS 6.0, the capability to configure DST parameters was added so that regions outside the United States could set the start and end times for DST, either using the actual date on which DST starts, such as March 9, or, as in this recipe, by defining the week of the month, day of the week, month of the year, and time. In our example, `2 0 3 02:00` represents the second week of the month, Sunday (represented by `0`), and the third month of the year at 2:00 a.m. This translates to the second Sunday in March. The `recurring` keyword indicates that this setting should be used for every year. Likewise, the `end-weekday` portion of the command specifies when DST ends in the same format. The `get clock` command shows the current time settings for the device:

```
FIREWALL-A-> get clock
Date 07/13/2007 14:25:04, Daylight Saving Time enabled
The Network Time Protocol is Disabled
Up 374 hours 53 minutes 2 seconds Since 27June2007:23:32:02
1184336704.693643 seconds since 1/1/1970 0:0:0 GMT
GMT time zone area -5:00
GMT time zone offset 4:00
```

See Also

Recipe 6.2

6.2 Set the Clock with NTP

Problem

You need to configure your firewalls to receive their time via NTP.

Solution

Configure NTP on the firewall:

```
FIREWALL-A-> set ntp server time.mynetwork.com
FIREWALL-A-> set ntp timezone -5
FIREWALL-A-> set ntp server key-id 1 preshare-key iamakey
FIREWALL-A-> set ntp auth preferred
FIREWALL-A-> set ntp no-ha-sync
FIREWALL-A-> set clock ntp
```

Discussion

Using NTP on the firewall is strongly recommended to ensure a consistent view of time across the network. When troubleshooting, or when analyzing security events in firewall logs, the log correlation process is greatly simplified when there is a common view of the time across the network. Enabling NTP on the firewall is straightforward. By using a hostname for the NTP server, you can use a Global Server Load Balancer to ensure that the NTP server is always reachable. Alternatively, you can configure up to two backup NTP servers, using the `backup1` and `backup2` *<server name>* options in the `set ntp server` command. Typically, the time zone is set to display the local time on the firewall. This setting is made with respect to offset from Greenwich Mean Time (GMT). The value -5 in the timezone command indicates that the time is GMT minus five hours, which corresponds to Eastern Standard Time in the United States. Some administrators prefer to use a common time zone for all of their global devices to further ease event correlation. Either practice is fine.

For security reasons, authentication is specified for NTP. This ensures that the firewall receives the time from the correct server, and not from a rogue server. ScreenOS uses Message Digest 5 (MD5) authentication with a preshared key to accomplish this. Once you enter the set ntp server key-id 1 preshare-key command, the key is not visible to the administrator:

```
FIREWALL-A-> get config | include key-id
set ntp server key-id 1 preshare-key
    "7m6T/ZnvNj1KtSsptXCbWsuKHRnLL1l1Sw=="
```

After configuring the key, configure NTP authentication to be either preferred or required. In this recipe, we chose preferred, indicating that authentication should be used, if possible. The set ntp no-ha-sync command is used to disable the synchronization of clocks among NetScreen Redundancy Protocol (NSRP) members. Instead, each cluster member will independently update its clock from the NTP server. This command is recommended for NSRP environments. Finally, the clock is configured to update using NTP as opposed to using the locally configured time.

See Also

Recipe 6.1

6.3 Check NTP Status

Problem

You need to verify the status of NTP.

Solution

Use get commands to examine the status:

```
FIREWALL-A-> get event type 00531
Total event entries = 1
Date       Time     Module Level  Type Description
2007-07-13 14:23:57 system notif 00531 The system clock was updated
                                       from primary NTP server type
                                       10.3.1.1 with an adjustment
                                       of -153 ms. Authentication
                                       was None. Update mode was
                                       Automatic
FIREWALL-A-> get ntp
NTP is Enabled
```

```
Primary server: 10.3.1.1
Backup1 server:
Backup2 server:
Authentication Mode: Preferred
Max Allowed Adjustment: 3 second(s)
Request Interval: 10 minute(s).
Sync NTP time to peer: Disabled
Update Status: Idle
Last Update at: 07/13/2007 14:24:16

FIREWALL-A-> get clock
Date 07/13/2007 15:46:33, Daylight Saving Time enabled
The Network Time Protocol is Enabled
Up 376 hours 14 minutes 31 seconds Since 27June2007:23:32:02
1184341593.166653 seconds since 1/1/1970 0:0:0 GMT
GMT time zone area -5:00
GMT time zone offset 4:00
```

Discussion

You can examine NTP status using get commands. Each update from an NTP server appears in the event log as event type 00531. If the NTP servers cannot be contacted, this will also appear in the event log:

```
FIREWALL-A-> get event type 00531
Total event entries = 1
Date       Time     Module Level  Type Description
2007-07-13 15:42:21 system notif 00531 No NTP server could be
    contacted.
```

This update message should appear as frequently as the request interval that appears in the output of the get ntp command. The request interval used here is set to 10 minutes, which is the default. This is a configurable parameter, and you can set it from 1–1440 minutes, using the set ntp interval command. As you can see from the output of get ntp, up to three servers can be configured: one primary server and two backups. Authentication is set to preferred, as per the configuration. When the key is modified, the results are viewable in the output of get event id 00531:

```
2007-07-13 15:58:12 system notif 00531 Authentication failed for
                                       Network Time Protocol server
                                       primary 10.3.1.1 because
                                       Invalid key-id received from
                                       server
```

Although authentication is configured to be preferred, this does not stop the update process from occurring; it merely fails authentication. To ensure authentication at all times, the required keyword should be set in the set ntp auth command.

The next line of the output from get ntp shows the maximum allowable adjustment from an NTP server. If the delta between the local system time and the server time exceeds three seconds, the time will not be updated. If this occurs, the clock must be reset manually, as in Recipe 6.1. Again, get event id 00531 has this information:

```
2007-07-13 15:58:12 system notif 00531 No acceptable time could be
                                       obtained from any NTP server.
2007-07-13 15:58:12 system notif 00531 Network Time Protocol adjustment
                                       of -17152 ms from NTP server
                                       primary exceeds the allowed
                                       adjustment of 3000 ms.
```

Here, notice that two log messages are generated—one detailing the difference between the NTP server's time and the local system time, and one stating that there is no acceptable time from any NTP server. Correcting the time to be within the adjustment range, we see the following in the get event output:

```
2007-07-13 16:08:32 system notif 00531 The system clock was updated
                                       from primary NTP server type
                                       10.3.1.1 with an adjustment
                                       of 1873 ms. Authentication
                                       was Preferred. Update mode
                                       was Automatic
2007-07-13 16:08:32 system notif 00531 Authentication failed for
                                       Network Time Protocol server
                                       primary 10.3.1.1
                                       because Invalid key-id
                                       received from server
```

Although the authentication fails with the wrong key, an update is still performed.

6.4 Configure the Device's Name Service

Problem

You need to configure DNS settings on the firewall.

Solution

Configure the hostname, domain name, and DNS servers:

```
ssg20->  set hostname FIREWALL-A
FIREWALL-A-> set domain oreilly.com
FIREWALL-A-> set dns host dns1 68.87.64.146
FIREWALL-A-> set dns host dns2 68.87.75.194
```

Discussion

During initial firewall installation, it is recommended that you change the firewall's hostname to something meaningful, typically according to your organization's naming convention. By default, Juniper firewalls ship with a default name that is the same as the name of the product. In this example, an SSG20 is being configured with a new hostname, `FIREWALL-A`. Note that once the hostname is set, the prompt changes to reflect the hostname. In an NSRP environment, the hostname is not a synchronized portion of the configuration, so this step must be performed on each member of an NSRP cluster. Next, the domain name of the local device is set.

Finally, the primary and secondary DNS servers' IPs are configured. In cases where the DNS servers are on the other end of a tunnel, you can specify the source interface for DNS requests using the `src-interface` keyword at the end of the `set dns host` command. This allows the head-end VPN device to route DNS replies through the tunnel. ScreenOS supports up to three DNS servers that can be used for name resolution. You can use this resolution for different purposes. One of the primary purposes for name resolution is for troubleshooting: it's easier to troubleshoot network issues when names are used. Once DNS servers have been configured in ScreenOS, you can use hostnames in the `ping` and `trace-route` commands:

```
FIREWALL-A-> ping www.oreilly.com
Type escape sequence to abort

Sending 5, 100-byte ICMP Echos to www.oreilly.com [208.201.239.36],
    timeout is 1 seconds
!!!!!
Success Rate is 100 percent (5/5),
    round-trip time min/avg/max=93/100/117 ms
```

Using hostnames simplifies troubleshooting, as the IP addresses of test hosts do not need to be known.

You can also use DNS to create address book entries, and to build policies for those entries:

```
FIREWALL-A-> set address untrust www.oreilly.com www.oreilly.com
Domain name "www.oreilly.com" has been looked up successfully.
FIREWALL-A-> set policy top from trust to untrust any www.oreilly.com
    ping deny log
policy id = 11
```

DNS is another method of simplifying policy creation. By specifying an FQDN as opposed to an IP address in address book entry creation, you can deploy more comprehensive policies more easily, as all IPs matching the FQDN are used for the policy. Use the `get dns name` command to verify the IP addresses associated with the address book entry:

```
FIREWALL-A-> get dns name www.oreilly.com
Host name: www.oreilly.com
IPv4 Addresses:
        208.201.239.36
        208.201.239.37
```

When the policy is applied to the device, it blocks the ping to both addresses returned by the DNS server and cached by the firewall. You can verify this with `debug flow basic`:

```
$ ping 208.201.239.36

Pinging 208.201.239.36 with 32 bytes of data:

Request timed out.
```

```
Ping statistics for 208.201.239.36:
    Packets: Sent = 1, Received = 0, Lost = 1 (100% loss),
Control-C

$ ping 208.201.239.37

Pinging 208.201.239.37 with 32 bytes of data:

Request timed out.

Ping statistics for 208.201.239.37:
    Packets: Sent = 1, Received = 0, Lost = 1 (100% loss),
Control-C

FIREWALL-A-> get db str
****** 411161.0: <Trust/wireless2> packet received [60]******
  ipid = 64686(fcae), @01c27894
  packet passed sanity check.
  wireless2:192.168.2.33/8704->208.201.239.36/512,1(8/0)<Root>
  no session found
  flow_first_sanity_check: in <wireless2>, out <N/A>
  chose interface wireless2 as incoming nat if.
  flow_first_routing: in <wireless2>, out <N/A>
  search route to (wireless2, 192.168.2.33->208.201.239.36) in vr
    trust-vr for vsd-0/flag-0/ifp-null
  [ Dest] 21.route 208.201.239.36->68.38.120.1, to ethernet3
  routed (x_dst_ip 208.201.239.36) from wireless2 (wireless2 in 0)
    to ethernet3

  policy search from zone 2-> zone 1
 policy_flow_search  policy search nat_crt from zone 2-> zone 1
  RPC Mapping Table search returned 0 matched service(s) for
    (vsys Root, ip 208.201.239.36, port 10588, proto 1)
  No SW RPC rule match, search HW rule
  log this session (pid=11)
  packet dropped, denied by policy
****** 411169.0: <Trust/wireless2> packet received [60]******
  ipid = 64692(fcb4), @01c29494
  packet passed sanity check.
  wireless2:192.168.2.33/8960->208.201.239.37/512,1(8/0)<Root>
  no session found
  flow_first_sanity_check: in <wireless2>, out <N/A>
  chose interface wireless2 as incoming nat if.
  flow_first_routing: in <wireless2>, out <N/A>
  search route to (wireless2, 192.168.2.33->208.201.239.37) in vr
    trust-vr for vsd-0/flag-0/ifp-null
  [ Dest] 21.route 208.201.239.37->68.38.120.1, to ethernet3
  routed (x_dst_ip 208.201.239.37) from wireless2 (wireless2 in 0)
    to ethernet3

  policy search from zone 2-> zone 1
 policy_flow_search  policy search nat_crt from zone 2-> zone 1
  RPC Mapping Table search returned 0 matched service(s) for
    (vsys Root, ip 208.201.239.37, port 10332, proto 1)
```

```
No SW RPC rule match, search HW rule
log this session (pid=11)
packet dropped, denied by policy
```

Notice in the preceding debug output that when the client attempts to ping either address contained in the *www.oreilly.com* address object, the ping fails, as it is denied by policy ID 11.

```
FIREWALL-A-> get address untrust name www.oreilly.com
Name                  Address/Prefix-length         Flag  Comments
www.oreilly.com       www.oreilly.com               0201

FIREWALL-A-> get policy id 11
name:"none" (id 11), zone Trust -> Untrust,action Deny, status
    "enabled"
src "Any", dst "www.oreilly.com", serv "PING"
Policies on this vpn tunnel: 0
nat off, Web filtering : disabled
vpn unknown vpn, policy flag 00010000, session backup: on, idle
    reset: on
traffic shapping off, scheduler n/a, serv flag 00
log close, log count 11, alert no, counter no(0) byte rate(sec/min)
    0/0
total octets 814, counter(session/packet/octet) 0/0/0
priority 7, diffserv marking Off
tadapter: state off, gbw/mbw 0/0 policing (no)
No Authentication
No User, User Group or Group expression set
```

When DNS is configured on the device, you also can configure an IKE gateway using an FQDN:

```
FIREWALL-A-> set ike gateway www.oreilly.com address www.oreilly.com
    main preshare screenosckbk sec-level standard
FIREWALL-A-> get ike gateway
 Id  Name              Gateway Address Gateway ID      Mode Proposals
---- --------------- --------------- -------------- ---- ---------
   0 www.oreilly.com      208.201.239.37                   Main
    pre-g2-3des-sha,pre-g2
-aes128-sha
  Total Gateways: 1 (1 including dynamic peers)
user with ASN1_DN type ID sort list:
```

You can use this capability to create tunnels between devices that have dynamic addresses, but well-known domain names. A common use case for this would be where the IKE gateway's name is defined on a Global Server Load Balancer that performs health checking and uses DNS to provide a known "good" IP address to the requesting devices.

See Also

Recipe 6.5

6.5 View DNS Entries on a Device

Problem

You need to view the DNS entries on a device.

Solution

Use the get dns host cache command:

```
FIREWALL-A-> get dns host cache
DNS Server:
  Primary  :       68.87.64.146, Src Interface: Null
  Secondary:       68.87.75.194, Src Interface: Null
  Ternary  :            0.0.0.0, Src Interface: Null
DNS Cache (Static):
DNS Cache (Dynamic):
 Host name:          www.oreilly.com IP: 208.201.239.36  TTL= 18059s
 Host name:          www.oreilly.com IP: 208.201.239.37  TTL= 18059s
DNS Cache (Unresolved):
DNS Cache (Freed):
```

Discussion

When troubleshooting a DNS-related issue, it is often helpful to view the firewall's DNS cache. The get dns host cache command shows all of the DNS information with respect to resolution, which is on the firewall. It provides the DNS server information as well as cache information.

The first two categories of cached information are the most common ones. The static cache is used in a similar capacity to a host file on a computer. Administrators can configure static hostnames on the firewall, and these entries appear in this section of the cache output. The Dynamic section contains all dynamically learned DNS information, and includes the hostname and IP address for each entry.

In cases where multiple entries are returned from a lookup, each IP address is displayed as a separate entry. Additionally, the TTL is inherited from the DNS lookup. When the TTL expires, the entry will be removed from the cache, and a new lookup will be performed the next time the device needs to access the object.

ScreenOS can also perform name lookups on demand. The get dns name command allows an administrator to look up an IP address much as he would by using the nslookup command:

```
FIREWALL-A-> get dns name www.juniper.net
Host name: www.juniper.net
IPv4 Addresses:
        207.17.137.229
```

```
FIREWALL-A-> get dns host cache
DNS Server:
  Primary  :          68.87.64.146, Src Interface: Null
  Secondary:          68.87.75.194, Src Interface: Null
  Ternary  :               0.0.0.0, Src Interface: Null
DNS Cache (Static):
DNS Cache (Dynamic):
 Host name:           www.oreilly.com IP: 208.201.239.36  TTL= 10201s
 Host name:           www.oreilly.com IP: 208.201.239.37  TTL= 10201s
 Host name:          www.juniper.net IP: 207.17.137.229  TTL= 83600s
DNS Cache (Unresolved):
DNS Cache (Freed):
```

As expected, now the host is included in the output of get dns host cache.

To view the lookups for address book entries, and the values for IP addresses that each hostname resolves to, use the get dns host report command:

```
FIREWALL-A-> get dns host report

       Name                             Status            Last Lookup
  www.oreilly.com                   Lookup successful   08/03/2007
    12:16:22
    208.201.239.36
    208.201.239.37
```

This command also tells you when the last lookup was performed. When the FQDN defines address book entries, the IP addresses comprising the object are refreshed on a configurable interval. You use the set dns host schedule command to modify the frequency of address book lookups; you can set it to a minimum of four hours and a maximum of never refreshing the values. The get dns host settings command shows the lookup settings:

```
FIREWALL-A-> get dns host settings
DNS Server:
  Primary  :          68.87.64.146, Src Interface: Null
  Secondary:          68.87.75.194, Src Interface: Null
  Ternary  :               0.0.0.0, Src Interface: Null

Refresh domain name IP Addresses:
  Every day at:             12:00 o'clock
  Last performed look-up: 08/03/2007 11:52:47
  Next scheduled look-up: 08/03/2007 20:14:07

Normal UDP session: 0
```

See Also

Recipe 6.4

6.6 Use Static DNS to Provide a Common Policy for Multiple Devices

Problem

You need to configure static DNS entries so that one policy with one object set can apply to multiple devices.

Solution

Use static DNS entries on the firewalls to provide a single name across devices that point to a unique resource per device:

```
FIREWALL-A-> set dns host name dataserver 10.1.1.1

FIREWALL-B-> set dns host name dataserver 10.2.1.1
```

Create address book entries on each firewall referencing the hostname:

```
FIREWALL-A-> set address trust dataserver dataserver
Domain name "dataserver" has been looked up successfully.

FIREWALL-B-> set address trust dataserver dataserver
Domain name "dataserver" has been looked up successfully.
```

Create a policy allowing traffic to the web server on each device:

```
FIREWALL-A-> set policy from untrust to trust any dataserver http
    permit log
policy id = 13

FIREWALL-B-> set policy from untrust to trust any dataserver http
    permit log
policy id = 13
```

Discussion

When a centralized policy structure is used, via either the NetScreen Security Manager (NSM) or another tool, there is often a desire to share a common policy across devices. Although there is much interest in this method of rule base management, there are problems associated with it. The primary issue is that to have a common policy across devices, the devices must protect the same resources, or have rules that permit traffic which should not traverse them, as shown in the topology in Figure 6-1.

In Figure 6-1, there are two sites, each protected by a firewall and each with a data server. The site administrators want to permit HyperText Transfer Protocol (HTTP) traffic only to the data server at each site. They have a few options: (1) create a separate policy for each site, and define the data server objects differently; (2) create one

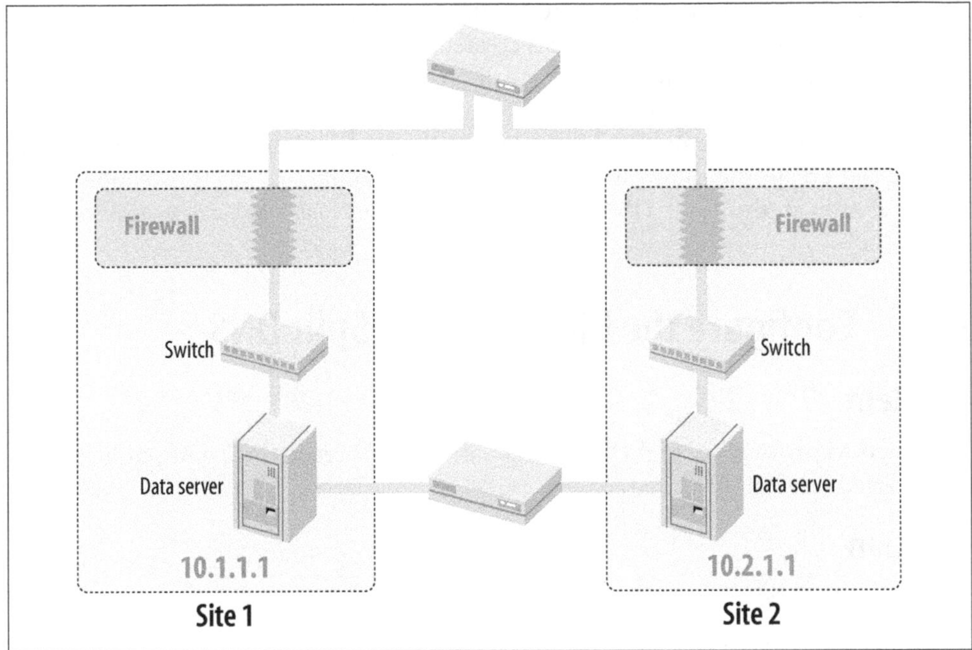

Figure 6-1. Two sites, one policy

policy that allows traffic to both servers, and assign this policy to both devices; or (3) create separate object definitions on each device, and create a single policy to apply to the firewalls.

The first option is perhaps the most common, and it allows for considerable granularity. However, the cost of this granularity is that each device requires its own policy. This factor can be troublesome from an audit perspective, and it can create operational challenges. However, choosing this option also provides a straightforward and secure environment.

The second option is less optimal, although it does provide a single policy across devices. The major problem here concerns the fact that traffic which should not be accessible via the firewall is allowed through. In Figure 6-1, the administrators do not want external connections to the data server to traverse their backbone. If a single policy allows traffic to both data servers, however, an end-user may be able to insert her public traffic on the private network. To prevent this from occurring, while maintaining a single policy for devices, you can use the third option, which we describe in this recipe.

When a common policy is applied to a group of firewalls, it is typically performed using NSM. However, NSM and most object management tools allow for a single-named object to be represented only once. To create unique object definitions per device, static DNS is used to create locally significant values for the data server object. When the address book entry is created, instead of pointing to the IP address, it points to the FQDN, which, when locally resolved, translates to a separate IP per device. This allows for a single policy referencing a single object to achieve local significance. Using an external DNS server, which has locally significant entries per data center, can create the same effect with greater scalability. To do this, simply point each firewall at the local DNS server using the `set dns host dns1` *<ip address>* command.

6.7 Configure the DNS Proxy for Split DNS

Problem

You need to provide internal DNS servers for internal resolution, and public servers for external resolution.

Solution

Configure the DNS proxy:

```
FIREWALL-A-> set dns proxy
FIREWALL-A-> set dns proxy enable
FIREWALL-A-> set interface wireless1 proxy dns
FIREWALL-A-> set dns server-select domain juniper.net primary-server
    10.1.1.1
FIREWALL-A-> set dns server-select domain * primary-server
    68.87.64.146 secondary-server 68.87.75.194
```

Then, configure the local devices to use the `wireless1` interface of the firewall as their primary DNS server.

Discussion

You can use the DNS proxy functionality in ScreenOS to enable split DNS. Figure 6-2 shows a typical DNS proxy solution.

Figure 6-2 illustrates a traditional Small Office/Home Office (SOHO) environment. A firewall is deployed in the remote office, and an IPSec tunnel is built to headquarters. The administrators have deployed a "split tunneling" environment in which all traffic bound for corporate headquarters is sent to the IPSec tunnel, whereas external traffic is sent directly to the Internet Service Provider (ISP).

The need for "split DNS" arises for internal hosts that resolve to private addresses (that cannot be resolved publicly or that resolve to different addresses if they are using private DNS versus public DNS). When the DNS proxy is enabled on an interface, the firewall will act as the DNS resolver for the clients. You can use either static configuration on the client or DHCP to assign the firewall as the client DNS server.

Figure 6-2. A typical DNS proxy example

When a client needs to do a DNS lookup, it will send the request to the firewall, and the firewall will then relay the request to the appropriate DNS server based on the domain in the request.

The administrator can configure up to 32 domains that can each point to a separate DNS server, if required. To enable the DNS proxy, configure the DNS proxy and, on a per-interface basis, enable proxy functionality for all interfaces with clients that need split DNS functionality. Next, create a list of domains and the servers to which they will resolve. The get dns server-select command shows the mapping of domain names to servers:

```
FIREWALL-A-> get dns server-select
usage: 2/32
-------------------------------------------------------------------
juniper.net
     [static]
    Server IP:          Interface: null                 Failover :
    [disabled]
       |-->  10.1.1.1                   [static]
       |-->  68.87.64.146
       |-->  68.87.75.194

*
```

```
    [static]
    Server IP:          Interface: null                    Failover :
    [disabled]
       |--> 68.87.64.146              [static]
       |--> 0.0.0.0
       |--> 0.0.0.0
---------------------------------------------------------------
```

The get dns server-select command shows how many domain mappings have been defined, as well as the domains, the source interface that the domains should use, and the IPs of the DNS servers to which each domain resolves. In this example, you'll see that the *juniper.net* domain resolves to an internal DNS server, whereas all other domains, as indicated by the * in the output, will resolve to the ISP's DNS.

You can see the DNS proxy functionality in action using the debug dns proxy command:

```
my-computer:~ me$ nslookup
> server 192.168.4.1
Default server: 192.168.4.1
Address: 192.168.4.1#53
> www.oreilly.com
Server:         192.168.4.1
Address:        192.168.4.1#53

Non-authoritative answer:
Name:   www.oreilly.com
Address: 208.201.239.36
Name:   www.oreilly.com
Address: 208.201.239.37
> www.juniper.net
Server:         192.168.4.1
Address:        192.168.4.1#53

Name:   www.juniper.net
Address: 207.17.137.229

FIREWALL-A-> get db str
## 2007-08-06 17:20:10 : Proxy: Processing request from client
    192.168.4.34
    port 53043
## 2007-08-06 17:20:10 : Proxy: Host name for lookup is www.oreilly.com
    type 1
## 2007-08-06 17:20:10 : Proxy: Looking up best match
## 2007-08-06 17:20:10 : Proxy: New best match len id 1
## 2007-08-06 17:20:10 : Proxy: Selecting primary
## 2007-08-06 17:20:10 : Proxy: DNS socket send returned 0 for server
    68.87.64.146
## 2007-08-06 17:20:10 : Proxy: new socket being set 151 to server
    68.87.64.146
## 2007-08-06 17:20:10 : Proxy: DNS socket receive 65 bytes from server
```

```
## 2007-08-06 17:20:10 : Proxy: Processing response for client
    192.168.4.34 port 53043
## 2007-08-06 17:20:10 : Proxy: Updating cache for www.oreilly.com type
    1 from the proxy
## 2007-08-06 17:20:10 : Proxy: Extract data returned 0
## 2007-08-06 17:20:10 : Proxy: Sending out a response to the client
## 2007-08-06 17:20:10 : Proxy: DNS socket send returned 0
## 2007-08-06 17:20:13 : Proxy: Processing request from client
    192.168.4.34 port 53044
## 2007-08-06 17:20:13 : Proxy: Host name for lookup is www.juniper.
     net type 1
## 2007-08-06 17:20:13 : Proxy: Looking up best match
## 2007-08-06 17:20:13 : Proxy: New best match len id 11
## 2007-08-06 17:20:13 : Proxy: Selecting primary
## 2007-08-06 17:20:13 : Proxy: DNS socket send returned 0 for server
    10.1.1.1
## 2007-08-06 17:20:13 : Proxy: new socket being set 152 to server
    10.1.1.1
## 2007-08-06 17:20:13 : Proxy: DNS socket receive 255 bytes from
    server
## 2007-08-06 17:20:13 : Proxy: Processing response for client
    192.168.4.34 port 53044
## 2007-08-06 17:20:13 : Proxy: Updating cache for www.juniper.net
    type 1 from the proxy
## 2007-08-06 17:20:13 : Proxy: Extract data returned 0
## 2007-08-06 17:20:13 : Proxy: Sending out a response to the client
## 2007-08-06 17:20:13 : Proxy: DNS socket send returned 0
```

The resolution seen here for *www.oreilly.com* is sent to the default DNS server at `68.87.64.146`. Likewise, *www.juniper.net* is resolved by `10.1.1.1`. When using the DNS proxy, the firewall will use the best match so that more specific domains can be used to resolve against different servers. Also, as expected, the reply is cached:

```
FIREWALL-A-> get dns host cache
DNS Server:
  Primary  :         68.87.64.146, Src Interface: Null
  Secondary:         68.87.75.194, Src Interface: Null
  Ternary  :              0.0.0.0, Src Interface: Null
DNS Cache (Static):
DNS Cache (Dynamic):
 Host name:      www.oreilly.com IP: 208.201.239.36  TTL= 15799s
 Host name:      www.oreilly.com IP: 208.201.239.37  TTL= 15799s
 Host name:      www.juniper.net IP: 207.17.137.229  TTL= 86307s
DNS Cache (Unresolved):
DNS Cache (Freed):
```

See Also

Recipe 6.5

6.8 Use DDNS on the Firewall for VPN Creation

Problem

You want to use DDNS to create a VPN tunnel to a device with a dynamic IP address.

Solution

Use DDNS and define the IKE gateway using an FQDN. First, register with a DDNS service such as *dyndns.com*. Then, on the firewall, configure DDNS:

```
FIREWALL-A-> set dns ddns
FIREWALL-A-> set dns ddns id 1 server members.dyndns.org server-type
    dyndns
FIREWALL-A-> set dns ddns id 1 username screenosckbk password
aS4k21zvNI+TCUsoG7CISNgK8HnXHa92Qg==
FIREWALL-A-> set dns ddns enable
```

Create the IKE gateway using the FQDN of the remote end as the IP address in the `set ike gateway` command:

```
FIREWALL-A-> set ike gateway screenosckbk address
    screenosckbk.dyndns.org main preshare iamakey sec-level standard
FIREWALL-A-> set vpn screenosckbk gateway screenosckbk tunnel
    sec-level standard
FIREWALL-A-> set vpn screenosckbk bind interface tunnel.1
FIREWALL-A-> set vpn screenosckbk monitor optimized rekey
```

Discussion

ScreenOS can act as a DDNS client for devices with dynamic IP addresses. These devices are typically SSG series devices that are deployed in SOHO environments and are often connected to cable modems or Digital Subscriber Line (DSL) links where the users do not know their IP addresses. By acting as a DDNS client, the firewall registers its Untrust IP address with a DDNS service such as *dyndns.com*. In doing so, the firewall can actively receive inbound connections, such as for use with a VIP, or as an IKE endpoint.

When acting as an IKE endpoint, an additional benefit is realized. Although aggressive mode IKE addresses the problems associated with forming a tunnel to a device with a dynamic address, there is an associated cost from a security perspective—the IKE ID (in an aggressive mode) negotiation is sent in the clear. Main mode solves this, but works only with dynamic endpoints if using digital certificates for authentication.

Because the DNS resolver component within ScreenOS is used prior to the IKE component in establishing a security association, from the IKE process's point of view, using an FQDN in the IKE gateway definition is equivalent to using an IP address. For this reason, you can use main mode IKE in association with preshared keys even when the devices have dynamic IP addresses. For example, look at the output of `get ike gateway`:

```
FIREWALL-A-> get ike gateway
 Id  Name             Gateway Address Gateway ID      Mode Proposals
---- --------------- --------------- -------------- ---- ---------
   0 screenosckbk    72.76.163.251                   Main
     pre-g2-3des-sha,pre-g2-aes128-sha
   Total Gateways: 1 (1 including dynamic peers)
user with ASN1_DN type ID sort list:
```

Upon entering the set ike gateway command, a DNS lookup is performed, and the IP address that is returned is used for IKE transmissions. To further reinforce this notion, the get sa command in turn shows only the IP address for the remote gateway:

```
FIREWALL-A-> get sa
total configured sa: 1
HEX ID    Gateway          Port Algorithm     SPI      Life:sec kb Sta
    PID vsys
00000001<   72.76.163.251  500 esp:3des/sha1 bb2e570c  3389 unlim A/U
      -1 0
00000001>   72.76.163.251  500 esp:3des/sha1 4e66cf52  3389 unlim A/U
      -1 0
```

Examining the DNS cache, the TTL can be verified:

```
FIREWALL-A-> get dns host cache
DNS Server:
  Primary  :          68.87.64.146, Src Interface: Null
  Secondary:          68.87.75.194, Src Interface: Null
  Ternary  :               0.0.0.0, Src Interface: Null
DNS Cache (Static):
 DNS Cache (Dynamic):
 Host name:  screenosckbk.dyndns.org IP: 72.76.163.251  TTL= 24s
DNS Cache (Unresolved):
DNS Cache (Freed):
```

Notice that the TTL for the domain is only 24 seconds in the preceding code snippet. After 24 seconds, the firewall will requery for the address of *screenosckbk.dyndns.org*.

Using DDNS for IKE gateway definition solves a key problem with maintaining a VPN. Namely, it solves the problem of location. Without the use of Autoconnect VPN, it is impossible to reliably define an IKE gateway if the device has a dynamic IP address on its Untrusted interface. Because the DNS resolver is invoked immediately upon definition of an IKE gateway in ScreenOS, using the FQDN to establish a gateway provides the address for the gateway, which is a necessary component for using main mode IKE and preshared keys. DDNS and gateway definition via FQDN provide a way to have dynamically addressed devices as VPN gateways without sacrificing the security benefits of main mode IKE, and without the overhead of running a PKI.

See Also

Recipe 6.5; Recipe 6.9

6.9 Configure the Firewall As a DHCP Client for Dynamic IP Environments

Problem

You need to firewall an environment with a dynamic public IP address.

Solution

Configure the firewall's `Untrust` interface as a DHCP client:

```
FIREWALL-A-> set interface ethernet3 zone Untrust
FIREWALL-A-> set interface ethernet3 dhcp client enable
```

Discussion

Lower-end firewalls, such as the SSG series, have the capability to act as DHCP clients. This is useful in environments where a static IP address is not available, such as in a SOHO environment with a broadband Internet connection. The configuration is straightforward. The `get interface` *`<interface name>`* command returns the DHCP client status, as well as the IP address and gateway, once obtained:

```
FIREWALL-A-> get int e3
Interface ethernet3:
  description ethernet3
  number 1, if_info 88, if_index 0, mode route
  link up, phy-link up/full-duplex
  vsys Root, zone Untrust, vr trust-vr
  dhcp client enabled
  PPPoE disabled
  admin mtu 0, operating mtu 1500, default mtu 1500
  *ip 68.38.120.27/24   mac 0010.db7f.5e81
  gateway 68.38.120.1
  *manage ip 68.38.120.27, mac 0010.db7f.5e81
  route-deny disable
  pmtu-v4 disabled
  ping disabled, telnet disabled, SSH disabled, SNMP disabled
  web disabled, ident-reset disabled, SSL disabled
  DNS Proxy disabled, webauth disabled, webauth-ip 0.0.0.0
  OSPF disabled  BGP disabled  RIP disabled  RIPng disabled mtrace
    disabled
  PIM: not configured  IGMP not configured
  bandwidth: physical 100000kbps, configured egress
    [gbw 0kbps mbw 0kbps]
           configured ingress mbw 0kbps, current bw 3kbps
            total allocated gbw 0kbps
  DHCP-Relay disabled
  DHCP-server disabled
Number of SW session: 4046, hw sess err cnt 0
```

Once configured, the DHCP client will attempt to obtain an address for the interface until it is successful. To refresh the IP address, use the exec dhcp client renew command:

```
FIREWALL-A-> exec dhcp client ethernet3 renew
FIREWALL-A-> get event
2007-08-13 22:59:44 system info  00530 DHCP server 68.87.64.13
                                       assigned interface ethernet3
                                       with IP address 68.38.120.27
                                       (lease time 5269 minutes).
```

Using DHCP to obtain firewall interface information provides a simple, easy-to-use provision method of IP assignment, and allows for integration into environments where static IP addresses are not available.

6.10 Configure the Firewall to Act As a DHCP Server

Problem

You need the firewall to provide DHCP services to computers on the trusted interface.

Solution

Configure the firewall as a DHCP server:

```
FIREWALL-A-> set interface ethernet1 dhcp server service
FIREWALL-A-> set interface ethernet1 dhcp server auto
FIREWALL-A-> set interface ethernet1 dhcp server ip 192.168.3.33 to
    192.168.3.126
FIREWALL-A-> set interface ethernet1 dhcp server option gateway
    192.168.3.1
FIREWALL-A-> set interface ethernet1 dhcp server option netmask
    255.255.255.0
FIREWALL-A-> set interface ethernet1 dhcp server option domainname screenosckbk.
oreilly.com
FIREWALL-A-> set interface ethernet1 dhcp server option dns1 10.1.1.1
FIREWALL-A-> set interface ethernet1 dhcp server option dns2 10.2.1.1
```

Discussion

The SSG series devices have the capability to operate as DHCP servers. This functionality is typically deployed in a branch or SOHO environment. DHCP is configured on a per-interface basis, and is actually enabled by default on lower-end devices in the trusted zone for ease of deployment.

The first step in configuring DHCP server functionality is to enable the DHCP service on the interface. You should apply the set interface ethernet1 dhcp server auto command before you configure the IP pool. This command starts the server in auto-probing mode.

When auto-probing mode is configured, the firewall will first send out its own DHCP Discover packets to ensure that there are no other DHCP servers on the LAN. If a DHCP Offer is received, the server will not activate. This prevents incorrect IP ranges from being given out, or worse, overlapping IP addresses from being handed out by different servers. If no DHCP servers on the LAN reply to the Discover messages, the server on the firewall will consider itself to be active, and will begin the process of handing out IP information to attached clients.

Next, the IP range is defined along with the `option` statements, which provide enough for basic connectivity. The options shown in this recipe are the standard option values. In many cases, additional information is passed to the client via the DHCP process. ScreenOS provides a number of predefined DHCP options, as listed here:

```
FIREWALL-A-> set interface ethernet1 dhcp server option ?
custom                 custom option
dns1                   dns
dns2                   dns
dns3                   dns
domainname             domain name
gateway                client gateway
lease                  lease
netmask                netmask
news                   news
nis1                   net info server
nis2                   net info server
nistag                 net info tag
pop3                   pop3
smtp                   smtp
wins1                  wins
wins2                  wins
```

In some cases, you may need to provide options that are not predefined. A common example of this is option 66, the Trivial File Transfer Protocol (TFTP) server name. To accomplish this, create a custom option:

```
FIREWALL-A-> set interface ethernet1 dhcp server option custom 66
    string 10.3.1.1
```

This command will send the IP address `10.3.1.1` to the clients as their TFTP server. This is commonly used for IP phones. Three types of options are supported: integer, IP address, and string. You can find a full list of standard DHCP options in RFC 2132.

For simplified deployment, ScreenOS provides a full-featured DHCP server on the SSG series and older appliance products.

See Also

Recipe 6.9; Recipe 6.11

6.11 Automatically Learn DHCP Option Information

Problem

You need to configure the firewall to provide DHCP option information to DHCP clients, but the values for the options aren't known ahead of time.

Solution

Configure an automatic DHCP setting update:

```
FIREWALL-A-> set interface ethernet3 dhcp client settings
    update-dhcpserver
```

Discussion

In scenarios where the `Untrusted` interface is acting as a DHCP client, the values for the domain name, DNS servers, and other DHCP options are often not known ahead of time. Using the `set interface <Untrusted interface> dhcp client settings update-dhcpserver` command allows the administrator to automatically populate these option fields with the values learned by the DHCP client.

See Also

Recipe 6.9; Recipe 6.10

6.12 Configure DHCP Relay

Problem

You need to provide DHCP services on the system products.

Solution

Configure DHCP relay on the interface for which you want to provide DHCP services:

```
FIREWALL-A-> set interface ethernet2 dhcp relay service
FIREWALL-A-> set interface ethernet2 dhcp relay server-name 10.3.1.1
FIREWALL-A-> set address untrust DHCP_SVR_10.3.1.1 10.3.1.1/32
FIREWALL-A-> set policy from untrust to trust DHCP_SVR_10.3.1.1 any
dhcp-relay permit log
```

Discussion

Juniper Networks' firewall system products, which include the NS5000 Series and the ISG Series, do not have DHCP server functionality built-in. As these devices are typically used to protect large-scale environments, they are frequently sandwiched in between pairs of routers. Furthermore, DHCP servers are often already available and installed elsewhere in the network. Occasionally, however, hosts requiring DHCP services are directly connected to the firewall.

To accommodate DHCP services for hosts that connect to the firewall as their gateway, you can set up DHCP relay. To configure DHCP relay, simply enable the DHCP relay service on the interface, and configure the server address to forward the DHCP messages.

If you want to send these messages across a tunnel, use the `set interface` *`<interface name>`* `dhcp relay vpn` command. Additionally, a policy which permits `dhcp-relay` from the server to the client side—in this case, from `untrust` to `trust`—is required.

You can verify that DHCP relay is enabled on the interface by using the `get interface` command:

```
FIREWALL-A-> get int eth2
Interface ethernet2:
  description ethernet2
  number 7, if_info 616, if_index 0, mode route
  link up, phy-link up/full-duplex
  vsys Root, zone DMZ, vr trust-vr
  dhcp client disabled
  PPPoE disabled
  admin mtu 0, operating mtu 1500, default mtu 1500
  *ip 192.168.5.1/24   mac 0010.db7f.5e87
  *manage ip 192.168.5.1, mac 0010.db7f.5e87
  route-deny disable
  pmtu-v4 disabled
  ping enabled, telnet disabled, SSH disabled, SNMP disabled
  web disabled, ident-reset disabled, SSL disabled
  DNS Proxy disabled, webauth disabled, webauth-ip 0.0.0.0
  OSPF enabled  BGP disabled  RIP disabled  RIPng disabled  mtrace
     disabled
  PIM: not configured  IGMP not configured
  bandwidth: physical 100000kbps, configured egress
    [gbw 0kbps mbw 0kbps]
           configured ingress mbw 0kbps, current bw 0kbps
            total allocated gbw 0kbps
  DHCP-Relay enabled, server 10.3.1.1
  DHCP-server disabled
Number of SW session: 4055, hw sess err cnt 0
```

For more concise output, use the `get interface` *`<interface name>`* `dhcp relay` command:

```
FIREWALL-A-> get int eth2 dhcp relay
        DHCP Server(s): "10.3.1.1"
        VPN encryption is disabled
```

6.13 DHCP Server Maintenance

Problem

You need to view and maintain the DHCP server operations.

Solution

Use get commands:

```
FIREWALL-A-> get interface wireless2 dhcp server
Mode:    ENABLED
State:  ON
DHCP send zero next server ip value.
Allow server information update from any dhcp upstream interface.
FIREWALL-A-> get interface wireless1 dhcp server ip allocate
       IP                 State         MAC          Lease Time
 192.168.4.36           COMMIT  *0016ce2c61ce   2442 minutes
 192.168.4.34           COMMIT  *0019e3dbf490   3474 minutes
 192.168.4.33           COMMIT  *00904b5d08f5   853 minutes
FIREWALL-A-> get interface wireless1 dhcp server option
DHCP Server Options:
        Lease:          3 days 0 hours 0 minutes
        IP Range:       192.168.4.33 - 192.168.4.126
        Netmask:        255.255.255.0
        Gateway:        192.168.4.1
        Domain Name:    screenosckbk.oreilly.com.
        DNS:            10.1.1.1        10.2.1.1     0.0.0.0
        WINS:           0.0.0.0          0.0.0.0
        SMTP:           0.0.0.0
        POP3:           0.0.0.0
        NEWS:           0.0.0.0
        NetInfo:        0.0.0.0          0.0.0.0
        Custom (66):    10.3.1.1
```

Discussion

You can use ScreenOS's get commands to view a feature's functionality. In the `get interface wireless2 dhcp server` command, the DHCP server is enabled and on, and is not using the next server option which allows configuration information to be shared among multiple DHCP servers. Also, the DHCP client will update information to the server component, as mentioned in Recipe 6.11.

The `get interface` *<interface name>* `dhcp server ip allocate` command shows the allocated IPs per interface, as well as the Media Access Control (MAC) address and time remaining in the lease. As each interface can have its own DHCP settings, different ranges may be configured on the device. To reset the DHCP leases, use the `clear dhcp server` *<interface name>* `ip` command. You can use this command to clear all leases or just a particular IP address:

```
FIREWALL-A-> clear dhcp server wireless1 ip all
FIREWALL-A-> get db str
## 2007-08-17 23:15:51 : DHCP: got packet from if <ethernet3>.
## 2007-08-17 23:15:58 : DHCP: Opened file "flash:dhcpservl.txt" for
    writing
## 2007-08-17 23:15:58 : DHCP: Wrote 8 bytes
## 2007-08-17 23:15:58 : DHCP: Saving 1 IPs (ethernet1):
## 2007-08-17 23:15:58 : DHCP: 0: 192.168.3.33 - 0013101d4b15 - 2344
## 2007-08-17 23:15:58 : DHCP: Wrote 44 bytes
## 2007-08-17 23:15:58 : DHCP: Saving 0 IPs (wireless1):
## 2007-08-17 23:15:58 : DHCP: Saving 1 IPs (wireless2):
## 2007-08-17 23:15:58 : DHCP: 0: 192.168.2.33 - 00054e44c0ba - 2831
## 2007-08-17 23:15:58 : DHCP: Wrote 44 bytes
## 2007-08-17 23:15:58 : DHCP: Saving 0 IPs (wireless4):
## 2007-08-17 23:15:58 : DHCP: Closed file
## 2007-08-17 23:15:58 : DHCP: HA (v2) send (NSRP Request) from peer
    (200 bytes)

## 2007-08-17 23:15:59 : DHCP: got packet from if <ethernet3>.
```

When the clear dhcp server *<interface name>* ip all command is issued, the *flash: dhcpserv1.txt* file is modified. This file is used to store DHCP lease information so that leases can survive a system reboot. When the file is modified, each interface that is not cleared has the lease information for that interface rewritten so as to preserve the information.

The get interface *<interface name>* dhcp server option command shows all options configured on the DHCP server for that interface, including custom options. When custom options are configured, each option appears in the command output with the name Custom, and the code in parentheses immediately following.

See Also

Recipe 6.10

CHAPTER 7
Policies

7.0 Introduction

Policies are a fundamental building block of implementing a security configuration in ScreenOS. Policies are used by the stateful firewall/Network Address Translation (NAT) engine, the Content Security engine, authentication, and Quality of Service (QoS) configuration, and for building policy-based IP Security (IPSec) virtual private networks (VPNs).

ScreenOS policies contain various elements that help categorize a packet and take several actions on it. ScreenOS policy elements include zones, source and destination address objects, and services. Actions on a packet can include permit, tunnel (IPSec encrypt), deny, reject, authenticate, log, count, schedule, apply QoS, and perform deep inspection, web filtering, and antispam functions. A multitude of actions can be taken on a single policy.

Address Objects

Address objects are a key component of ScreenOS policies. An address object can define a single host or a classless interdomain routing (CIDR) network address block that "resides" in a zone. An example of an address object that defines a single host, a workstation named Orion, in the `Trust` zone is as follows:

```
Internal_fw-> set address Trust Orion 192.168.4.10/32 "Orion Wkstn"
```

The address object `Orion` can, thus, be referenced in any ScreenOS policy. The string `Orion Wkstn` is an optional description of the address object.

Here is an example of an address object that defines a CIDR network address block, `192.168.3.16/29`, in the `DMZ` zone:

```
Internal_fw-> set address DMZ DMZ_Subnet 192.168.3.16/29
"All DMZ Hosts"
```

The address object `DMZ_Subnet` represents any host/address in the `192.168.3.16/29` address block (i.e., `192.168.3.16`–`192.168.3.23`).

You can view the address objects currently defined in a ScreenOS security zone by using the get address *<zone_name>* command:

```
Internal_fw-> get address trust
Total 3 addresses and 0 user groups in the address book.

Trust Addresses:
Name              Address/Prefix-length    Flag  Comments
Any               0.0.0.0/0                0202  All Addr
Dial-Up VPN       255.255.255.255/32       0202  Dial-Up VPN Addr
Orion             192.168.4.10/32          0200  Orion Wkstn

Internal_fw->
```

You can combine several ScreenOS address objects into a group called an *address group*. We will discuss address objects further in Recipe 7.13.

Service Objects

Like address objects, service objects are a basic building block of ScreenOS policies. All IP-based applications, ranging from the World Wide Web to Internet email, rely on protocols such as the HyperText Transfer Protocol (HTTP) and Simple Mail Transfer Protocol (SMTP) that typically run on a single defined Transmission Control Protocol (TCP) or User Datagram Protocol (UDP) port. A service object defines a "service," typically an application, and its associated TCP, UDP, or IP port number.

Many modern applications such as IP telephony and peer-to-peer applications can initiate communications on a well-known port and then open additional communication channels on different ports. ScreenOS has the capability to parse the application traffic, identify the additional communication channels, and dynamically open firewall pinholes to permit such communication. Chapter 11 focuses on this capability and the various application layer gateways (ALGs) currently supported by ScreenOS.

ScreenOS systems ship with a large set of predefined service objects. You can verify the predefined services on your system by using the get service pre-defined command:

```
Internal_fw-> get service pre-defined
```

Just like address objects, you can combine several ScreenOS service objects into a single custom service group. We discuss service groups further in Recipe 7.13.

Intra-Zone, Inter-Zone, and Global Policies

ScreenOS policies are typically defined between two security zones: the source zone and the destination zone. We discussed ScreenOS security zones in Chapter 2.

Policies whose source and destination zones are different are termed *inter-zone policies*. Inter-zone policies are the most common type of policy on ScreenOS gateways.

In certain situations, a firewall administrator may choose to use a ScreenOS gateway to inspect traffic within the same zone. In such instances, the source and destination zones are the same, and the policy is termed an *intra-zone policy*.

Finally, ScreenOS supports the concept of global policies that can apply to multiple zones. The "any" address object in the `Global` zone refers to any object in any zone.

ScreenOS maintains three policy set lists: one for inter-zone policies, another for intra-zone policies, and a third for global policies.

The order of the processing of policies in ScreenOS is as follows:

1. Based on the source and destination zones binding for the inbound packet, which establishes whether this is an intra-zone or inter-zone packet, process the packet using the intra-zone or inter-zone policy set list.
2. If there is no match on the intra-zone and inter-zone policy set lists, check for a match against the global policy set list.
3. If there is no match against the global policy set list, apply the default deny policy to inter-zone packets. For intra-zone packets, examine the intra-zone block setting. If the intra-zone block is enabled for this particular zone, drop the packet; otherwise, permit this intra-zone packet.

ACL Rules

A single ScreenOS policy can consist of several address and service objects with an associated action. Internally, ScreenOS breaks out the components of these policies into flattened-out, linear rules known as *ACL rules* or *logical rules*, each consisting of a single source, single destination, and single service. When ACL rules are discussed in the context of ASIC-based ScreenOS gateways, such as the ISG-1000/2000 and NS5200/5400, they are sometimes referred to as *ASIC rules*.

Default Policies

As of ScreenOS 6.0, all ScreenOS hardware platforms ship with a default deny policy. You can verify this by using the `get policy` command to check the current policies:

```
nsisg2000-> get policy
No policy!Default deny.
nsisg2000->
```

In addition to the default deny policy, the SSG-5 and SSG-20 Series ship from the factory with a policy that permits traffic from the `Trust` zone to the `Untrust` zone:

```
ssg5-serial-> get policy
Total regular policies 1, Default deny.
ID From     To  Src-address Dst-address Service Action State   ASTLCB
 1 Trust  Untrust  Any         Any        ANY   Permit enabled -----X
ssg5-serial->
```

7.1 Configure an Inter-Zone Firewall Policy

Problem

You want to configure a basic firewall policy that permits specific traffic between two zones.

Solution

Figure 7-1 shows the `Internal_fw` gateway and its interfaces in the context of an inter-zone firewall policy that permits the Orion host to initiate HTTP (web) connections from the `Trust` zone to the `Secure_Servers` zone.

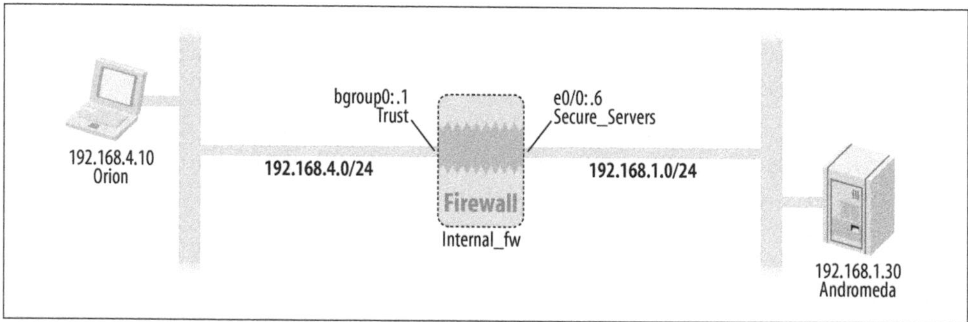

Figure 7-1. Inter-zone firewall policy configuration

First, make sure you have correctly assigned the interface zones, IP addresses, and modes of the interfaces:

```
Internal_fw-> set interface bgroup0 zone Trust
Internal_fw-> set interface bgroup0 ip 192.168.4.1/24
Internal_fw-> set interface bgroup0 route
Internal_fw-> set zone name Secure_Servers
Internal_fw-> set interface e0/0 zone Secure_Servers
Internal_fw-> set interface e0/0 ip 192.168.1.6/24
```

You can replace the `bgroup0` and `e0/0` interface names with your ScreenOS firewall's interface.

Next, define the address objects:

```
Internal_fw-> set address Trust Orion 192.168.4.10/32 "Orion Wkstn"
Internal_fw-> set address Secure_Servers Andromeda 192.168.1.30/32
 "Web Server"
```

Finally, configure the inter-zone firewall policies using the zones, address objects, and predefined HTTP service object:

```
Internal_fw-> set policy from Trust to Secure_Servers Orion Andromeda
 http permit log
```

```
Internal_fw-> set policy from Secure_Servers to Trust Andromeda Orion
 any deny log
```

Discussion

A basic inter-zone firewall policy consists of a source zone, destination zone, source object, destination object, service, and access control firewall action (permit, deny, or reject). One of several additional keywords that you can add to this basic policy is the `log` keyword that maintains a count of the number of times this policy is referenced since the last power up or counter reset.

Table 7-1 outlines some of the other parameters that represent an action you can take on a matched policy.

Table 7-1. Additional actions that can be taken on a matched policy

Action	Description
Count	Count the number of octets that match this policy and record in a historical graph.
Schedule	Define a scheduler that makes this policy active only during a specified time window.
Alert	Generate a syslog alert on policy match.
Traffic	Define traffic-shaping/QoS on this policy (discussed in Chapter 14).
No-session-backup	Do not copy this session's information to a peer NetScreen Redundancy Protocol (NSRP) device (discussed in Chapter 18).
URL-filter	Enable web filtering for this policy (discussed in Chapter 12).

Zone-based policies are a powerful tool that enable firewall administrators to manage firewall policies more easily by limiting a security policy to specific source and destination zones. Furthermore, zone-based policies enable the use of the wildcard "any" address object with an explicit understanding that the traffic will be limited to the specific security zone.

As discussed in this chapter's Introduction section and in the solution to this recipe, the explicit address objects used in ScreenOS gateway policies need to be defined in the address book on the gateway. The only predefined address objects in the default ScreenOS factory configuration are the wildcard "any" address object that matches any host in the specific security zone, and the "Dial-Up VPN" object that is relevant to IPSec VPNs terminating on the gateway.

In addition to the list of predefined services, you can define custom services in ScreenOS that are specific to custom applications.

You can check the current set of policies defined on a ScreenOS gateway using the `get policy` command:

```
Internal_fw-> get policy
Total regular policies 2, Default deny.
ID From     To       Src-addr  Dst-addr  Service Action State   ASTLCB
```

```
2 Trust     Secure_~ Orion      Andromeda HTTP     Permit enabled ---X-X
4 Secure_~ Trust    Andromeda Orion      ANY      Deny   enabled ---X-X
Internal_fw->
```

As seen in the output, ScreenOS automatically assigns a policy ID to each defined policy. Although it is optional, you can define a policy with an explicit policy ID.

The `ASTLCB` header at the end of the `get policy` output represents whether the actions listed in Table 7-2 are enabled on the policy.

Table 7-2. ASTLCB header actions

Header entry	Label	Description
A	Attack	Attack protection enabled via deep inspection on this policy. See Chapter 12 for additional details.
S	Scheduled policy	This policy is active only during specified periods. See Recipe 7.3 for additional details.
T	Traffic shaping	Enable prioritization and/or bandwidth parameters for this policy.
L	Logging	Count the hits on this policy.
C	Counting	Maintain historical statistics on the amount of traffic hitting this policy.
B	Session backup	Install the sessions associated with this policy to the NSRP peer.

Because the `get policy` output truncates zone names that are longer than 8 characters and address object names that are longer than 12 characters, another way to view the policy is by viewing the firewall configuration and including only policy components:

```
Internal_fw-> get config | include policy
set policy id 2 from "Trust" to "Secure_Servers"  "Orion" "Andromeda"
"HTTP" permit log
set policy id 2
set policy id 4 from "Secure_Servers" to "Trust" "Andromeda" "Orion"
"ANY" deny log
set policy id 4
Internal_fw->
```

Finally, as your policy base grows, when you're examining policies, you can limit the output to policies between two zones:

```
Internal_fw-> get policy from Trust to Secure_Servers
ID From     To        Src-addr Dst-address Service Action State   ASTLCB
 2 Trust    Secure_~ Orion     Andromeda   HTTP    Permit enabled ---X-X
Internal_fw->
```

See Also

Recipe 7.10; Recipe 7.11

7.2 Log Hits on ScreenOS Policies

Problem

You want to log the hits on a ScreenOS policy and send the log data to the local traffic log, a syslog server, or a NetScreen Security Manager (NSM) server.

Solution

The `log` keyword at the end of a policy maintains a count of the number of times this policy has been referenced since the last power up or counter reset. Furthermore, when the `log` keyword is defined on a policy, a local traffic log entry is written to the ScreenOS gateway and is sent to any defined syslog servers and NSMs. Using the inter-zone policy configuration scenario in the solution to Recipe 7.1 as a reference, you configure the `log` keyword on a policy as follows:

```
Internal_fw-> set policy from Trust to Secure_Servers Orion Andromeda
 http permit log
```

Discussion

Enabling the `log` keyword on a ScreenOS policy kicks off traffic logging on several fronts:

- Maintaining a counter of the number of "hits" on the policy
- Writing a detailed traffic log entry in the ScreenOS gateway's local traffic log memory space
- Sending a traffic log entry to a syslog server if a syslog server is configured and traffic logging to syslog is enabled
- Sending a traffic log entry to NSM if the ScreenOS gateway is under NSM management

You can view the number of hits on this policy, registered when the `log` keyword is configured, by checking the policy ID and then running a `get policy id` *<policy id>* command. The policy ID is checked:

```
Internal_fw-> get policy from Trust to Secure_Servers
ID From  To       Src-address  Dst-address  Service Action State   ASTLCB
 2 Trust Secure_~ Orion        Andromeda    HTTP   Permit enabled ---X-X
Internal_fw->
```

The `get policy id` *<policy id>*command is issued:

```
Internal_fw-> get policy id 2
name:"none" (id 2), zone Trust -> Secure_Servers,action Permit, status
 "enabled"
src "Orion", dst "Andromeda", serv "HTTP"
Policies on this vpn tunnel: 0
```

```
nat off, Web filtering : disabled
vpn unknown vpn, policy flag 00010000, session backup: on, idle reset:
 on
traffic shapping off, scheduler n/a, serv flag 00
log close, log count 3, alert no, counter no(0) byte rate(sec/min) 0/0
total octets 341740, counter(session/packet/octet) 0/0/0
priority 7, diffserv marking Off
tadapter: state off, gbw/mbw 0/0 policing (no)
No Authentication
No User, User Group or Group expression set
Internal_fw->
```

The line of output beginning with `log close` indicates that traffic logs are generated at session close and shows three hits on this policy in the `log count 3` field. The next line shows that these three hits represented 341,740 bytes of traffic traversing the firewall.

The local traffic log entry that is written on the ScreenOS gateway shows the following:

```
Internal_fw-> get log traffic policy 2
PID 2, from Trust to Secure_Servers, src Orion, dst Andromeda, service
 HTTP, action Permit
=========================================================================
Date    Time    Duration Source IP      Port Destination IP Port Service
Reason                   Xlated Src IP Port Xlated Dst IP  Port ID
=========================================================================
2007-07-31 17:40:57    0:05:11 192.168.4.10 2830 192.168.1.30 80 HTTP
Close - AGE OUT                192.168.4.10 2830 192.168.1.30 80
2007-07-31 17:35:58    0:00:04 192.168.4.10 2839 192.168.1.30 80 HTTP
Close - TCP FIN                192.168.4.10 2839 192.168.1.30 80
2007-07-31 17:35:52    0:00:01 192.168.4.10 2838 192.168.1.30 80 HTTP
Close - TCP FIN                192.168.4.10 2838 192.168.1.30 80
Total entries matched = 3
Internal_fw->
```

Log hits are written to the local traffic log when a session is closed. Furthermore, the close (e.g., `Age Out` or `TCP FIN`) is specified in the log entry.

In addition to the default setting of generating log hits and local traffic log entries on session close, log entries can also be generated at session open. See Recipe 7.3 for additional details.

The `log` keyword on a policy has a very different function than the `count` keyword. Whereas the `log` keyword on a policy tracks policy hits, generates local and syslog/NSM log entries, and keeps track of the aggregate number of octets hitting the policy, the `count` keyword configures the gateway to maintain historical statistics on the amount of traffic hitting the policy. You can view the statistics maintained with the `count` keyword enabled in the ScreenOS WebUI (select Reports → Policies → Counting); they are available per policy in levels of bytes per second, KB per minute, KB per hour, MB per day, and MB per month.

When the log keyword is specified on a policy, in addition to being written to the local traffic log on the ScreenOS gateway, the traffic log is sent to a syslog server if traffic logging to syslog is enabled (set syslog config <*syslog_server*> log traffic). See the solution to Recipe 7.4 for additional syslog configuration details.

Here is sample output of the syslog entry received by a syslog server for a hit on policy ID 2 from the code shown earlier:

```
Syslog Priority:    Local0.Notice
Hostname:           192.168.4.1
Message entry:      Internal_fw: NetScreen device_id=Internal_fw
[Root]system-notification-00257(traffic): start_time=
"2007-07-31 19:14:13" duration=2 policy_id=2 service=http proto=6
src zone=Trust dst zone=Secure_Servers action=Permit sent=4629
rcvd=45754 src=192.168.4.10 dst=192.168.1.30 src_port=2168
dst_port=80 src-xlated ip=192.168.4.10 port=2168 dst-xlated
ip=192.168.1.30 port=80 session_id=4061
reason=Close - TCP FIN<000>
```

See Also

Chapter 1

7.3 Generate Log Entries at Session Initiation

Problem

You want ScreenOS to generate a traffic log entry at session initiation.

Solution

Although the default ScreenOS behavior is to generate a traffic log entry upon session close, the following configuration augments the session-close traffic log entry, with a log entry on session initiation for an existing policy with an ID of 2 that has logging enabled:

```
Internal_fw-> set policy id 2
Internal_fw(policy:2)-> set log session-init
Internal_fw(policy:2)-> exit
Internal_fw->
```

Discussion

The following policy, also referenced in Recipe 7.2, is used for this discussion:

```
Internal_fw-> set policy id 2 from Trust to Secure_Servers Orion
Andromeda http permit log
```

With session logging at initiation enabled per the preceding "Solution" section, a refreshed traffic log for policy ID 2 is as follows:

```
Internal_fw-> get log traffic policy 2
PID 2, from Trust to Secure_Servers, src Orion, dst Andromeda, service
HTTP, action Permit
======================================================================
Date       Time     Duration Source IP     Port Destination IP Port Svc
Reason                       Xlated Src IP Port Xlated Dst IP  Port ID
======================================================================
2007-07-31 18:20:03 0:00:03 192.168.4.10  4292 192.168.1.30  80  HTTP
Close - TCP FIN             192.168.4.10  4292 192.168.1.30  80
2007-07-31 18:20:00 0:00:00 192.168.4.10  4292 192.168.1.30  80  HTTP
Creation                    192.168.4.10  4292 192.168.1.30  80
Total entries matched = 2
Internal_fw->
```

Here, the session with source port 4292 is logged at creation as well as at close.

Furthermore, when the policy is viewed with the get policy command, the output field beginning with log now shows init and close:

```
Internal_fw-> get policy id 2
name:"none" (id 2), zone Trust -> Secure_Servers,action Permit, status
 "enabled"
src "Orion", dst "Andromeda", serv "HTTP"
Policies on this vpn tunnel: 0
nat off, Web filtering : disabled
vpn unknown vpn, policy flag 00010400, session backup: on,
idle reset: on
traffic shapping off, scheduler n/a, serv flag 00
log init close, log count 22, alert no, counter no(0)
byte rate(sec/min) 0/0
total octets 1216636, counter(session/packet/octet) 0/0/0
priority 7, diffserv marking Off
tadapter: state off, gbw/mbw 0/0 policing (no)
No Authentication
No User, User Group or Group expression set
Internal_fw->
```

See Also

Recipe 7.2

7.4 Configure a Syslog Server

Problem

You want to configure ScreenOS to send traffic and event log data to a syslog server.

Solution

The following configuration enables traffic and event log entries to be sent to a syslog server running on host 192.168.4.10:

```
Internal_fw-> set syslog config 192.168.4.10 log all
Internal_fw-> set syslog enable
```

Discussion

The current syslog configuration can be verified:

```
Internal_fw -> get syslog
Syslog Configuration:

        Hostname: 192.168.4.10
        Host port: 514
        Security Facility: local0
        Facility: local0
        Traffic log: enabled
        Event log: enabled
        Transport: udp
        Socket number: 88

        module=system:  emer, alert, crit, error, warn, notif, info,
debug

Syslog is enabled.
Internal_fw ->
```

Each syslog message has a severity level associated with it, ranging from Debug (lowest severity) to Emergency (highest severity). Table 7-3 shows a sampling of severity levels that ScreenOS assigns to different event and traffic log entries.

Table 7-3. Security levels of different event and traffic log entries

Event type	Event description	Severity level assigned by ScreenOS
Event log	An administrator disables an ALG	Alert
Event log	Multiple login failures	Critical
Event log	Login success	Warning
Traffic log	Traffic permitted by policy match	Notification

If you would like to send only traffic log entries to the syslog server, you can configure the syslog `config` entry as follows:

```
Internal_fw-> set syslog config 192.168.4.10 log traffic
```

Although the default transport for syslog traffic is UDP destination port 514, ScreenOS supports TCP-based syslog:

```
Internal_fw-> set syslog config 192.168.4.10 transport tcp
```

To revert back from TCP- to UDP-based syslog, use the `unset` command:

```
Internal_fw-> unset syslog config 192.168.4.10 transport
```

Syslog messages have a facility field that the syslog server can use to identify the daemon or service on a system that generated the syslog event. Many syslog server administrators, in turn, send messages from different facilities to different directories or files. The default facility for syslog messages generated by ScreenOS is `local0` and it handles messages up to the Critical severity level. Messages with severity levels of Alert or Emergency use a security facility in ScreenOS. You can modify the security facility and regular facility, respectively, so that the messages go out with a different facility name, such as `local2` for the security facility and `local1` for the regular facility, as follows:

```
Internal_fw-> set syslog config 192.168.4.10 facilities local2 local1
```

See Also

Chapter 1

7.5 Configure an Explicit Deny Policy

Problem

You want to configure a policy that explicitly denies traffic and logs the denied traffic to the local traffic log/syslog/NSM servers.

Solution

Figure 7-2 shows the `Internal_fw` gateway and its interfaces in the context of an inter-zone firewall policy that drops any traffic initiated from the Andromeda server to the Orion host.

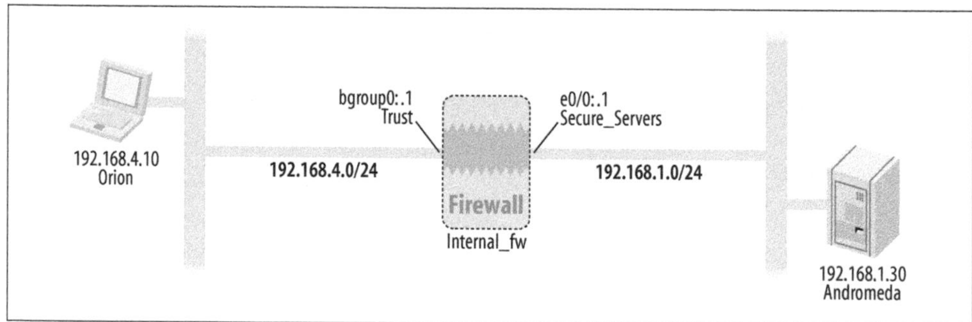

Figure 7-2. "Deny" policy configuration

Although ScreenOS has an implicit deny policy at the end of every inter-zone policy set, the implicit deny policy does not log the packets that are dropped. An explicit inter-zone deny policy needs to be configured with the log parameter to log dropped packets:

```
Internal_fw-> set policy from Secure_Servers to Trust Andromeda Orion
 any deny log
```

Discussion

A deny policy drops packets that match it, and logs the packet drop when the `log` keyword is explicitly defined in the policy. However, it does not return a ScreenOS gateway-generated response, such as a TCP RST or an Internet Control Message Protocol (ICMP) Destination Unreachable, to the source. The following debug capture shows an attempt from Andromeda to initiate a Telnet session to Orion—the packet matches the deny policy, and is dropped:

```
Internal_fw-> debug flow basic
Internal_fw-> get dbuf stream
****** 16274.0: <Secure_Servers/ethernet0/0> packet received [48]******
  ipid = 23012(59e4), @02f81270
  packet passed sanity check.
  ethernet0/0:192.168.1.30/1429->192.168.4.10/23,6<Root>
  no session found
  flow_first_sanity_check: in <ethernet0/0>, out <N/A>
  chose interface ethernet0/0 as incoming nat if.
  flow_first_routing: in <ethernet0/0>, out <N/A>
  search route to (ethernet0/0, 192.168.1.30->192.168.4.10) in vr
trust-vr for vsd-0/flag-0/ifp-null
  [ Dest] 3.route 192.168.4.10->192.168.4.10, to bgroup0
  routed (x_dst_ip 192.168.4.10) from ethernet0/0 (ethernet0/0 in 0)
 to bgroup0
  policy search from zone 100-> zone 2
 policy_flow_search  policy search nat_crt from zone 100-> zone 2
  RPC Mapping Table search returned 0 matched service(s) for (vsys
Root, ip 192.168.4.10, port 23, proto 6)
  No SW RPC rule match, search HW rule
  log this session (pid=9)
  packet dropped, denied by policy
Internal_fw-> undebug all
```

ScreenOS has a default terminating deny policy. The default deny policy, however, does not log dropped packets. Hence, to log dropped packets, it is advisable to have explicit inter-zone/intra-zone deny policies if you do not have any global policies. If you use global policies in your configuration, you can terminate them with a terminating global deny policy with logging enabled.

See Also

Recipe 7.6

7.6 Configure a Reject Policy

Problem

You want to configure a ScreenOS policy that drops a packet and returns a notification to the source.

Solution

Figure 7-3 shows the `Internal_fw` gateway and its interfaces in the context of an inter-zone firewall policy that rejects any traffic initiated from the Andromeda server to the Orion host.

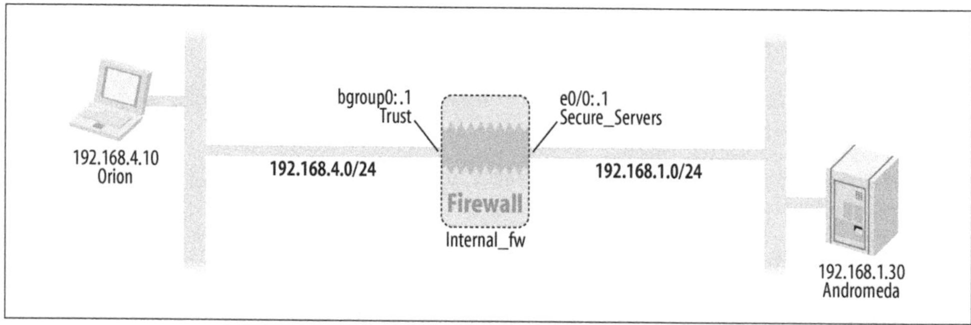

Figure 7-3. "Reject" policy configuration

The reject policy, thus, is configured as follows:

```
Internal_fw-> set policy from Secure_Servers to Trust Andromeda Orion
 any reject log
```

Discussion

Although the more commonly used ScreenOS deny policy drops unwanted traffic without notifying the source, using the reject action instead of deny returns a TCP Reset response to the source for TCP connection requests and an ICMP Destination Unreachable response back for UDP connection requests. Thus, a reject policy introduces an additional step for the ScreenOS gateway in having to respond back to unwanted packets instead of silently dropping them.

In the solution to this recipe, if Andromeda (`192.168.1.30`) initiates a Telnet session to Orion (`192.168.4.10`), the `Internal_fw` ScreenOS gateway rejects the packets and returns a TCP packet to Orion with the `RST` flag set. A `debug flow basic` debug capture of this transaction is as follows:

```
Internal_fw-> debug flow basic
Internal_fw-> get dbuf stream
**** 13542.0: <Secure_Servers/ethernet0/0> packet received [48]****
  ipid = 62612(f494), @02ff9a70
  packet passed sanity check.
```

```
  ethernet0/0:192.168.1.30/3924->192.168.4.10/23,6<Root>
  no session found
  flow_first_sanity_check: in <ethernet0/0>, out <N/A>
  chose interface ethernet0/0 as incoming nat if.
  flow_first_routing: in <ethernet0/0>, out <N/A>
  search route to (ethernet0/0, 192.168.1.30->192.168.4.10) in vr
trust-vr for vsd-0/flag-0/ifp-null
  [ Dest] 3.route 192.168.4.10->192.168.4.10, to bgroup0
  routed (x_dst_ip 192.168.4.10) from ethernet0/0 (ethernet0/0 in 0)
 to bgroup0
  policy search from zone 100-> zone 2
 policy_flow_search  policy search nat_crt from zone 100-> zone 2
  RPC Mapping Table search returned 0 matched service(s) for (vsys
Root, ip 192.168.4.10, port 23, proto 6)
  No SW RPC rule match, search HW rule

**** jump to packet:192.168.4.10->192.168.1.30
  skipping pre-frag
  no more encapping needed
  send out through normal path.
  flow_ip_send: 49aa:192.168.4.10->192.168.1.30,6 => ethernet0/0(40)
 flag 0x0, vlan 0
  no l2info for packet.
  no route for packet
  search route to (null, 0.0.0.0->192.168.1.30) in vr trust-vr for
vsd-0/flag-2000/ifp-ethernet0/0
  [ Dest] 1.route 192.168.1.30->192.168.1.30, to ethernet0/0
  route to 192.168.1.30
  arp entry found for 192.168.1.30 mac 001125150ccd
  **** pak processing end.
  log this session (pid=7)
  packet dropped, denied by policy
Internal_fw-> undebug all
```

The debug output shows the response packet with the TCP RST flag generated by the ScreenOS gateway in the `**** jump to packet` section with the `flow_ip_send`.

In contrast, a deny policy that silently drops and logs a packet, but does not return a ScreenOS gateway-generated response to the source, has the following debug capture:

```
Internal_fw-> debug flow basic
Internal_fw-> get dbuf stream
**** 16274.0: <Secure_Servers/ethernet0/0> packet received [48]****
  ipid = 23012(59e4), @02f81270
  packet passed sanity check.
  ethernet0/0:192.168.1.30/1429->192.168.4.10/23,6<Root>
  no session found
  flow_first_sanity_check: in <ethernet0/0>, out <N/A>
  chose interface ethernet0/0 as incoming nat if.
  flow_first_routing: in <ethernet0/0>, out <N/A>
  search route to (ethernet0/0, 192.168.1.30->192.168.4.10) in vr
trust-vr for vsd-0/flag-0/ifp-null
  [ Dest] 3.route 192.168.4.10->192.168.4.10, to bgroup0
  routed (x_dst_ip 192.168.4.10) from ethernet0/0 (ethernet0/0 in 0)
 to bgroup0
```

```
  policy search from zone 100-> zone 2
 policy_flow_search  policy search nat_crt from zone 100-> zone 2
  RPC Mapping Table search returned 0 matched service(s) for (vsys
Root, ip 192.168.4.10, port 23, proto 6)
  No SW RPC rule match, search HW rule
  log this session (pid=9)
  packet dropped, denied by policy
Internal_fw-> undebug all
```

Similarly, with the same reject policy as specified in the solution to this recipe, if Andromeda (192.168.1.30) initiates a DNS query to Orion (192.168.4.10), the Internal_fw ScreenOS gateway rejects the packets and returns an ICMP Destination Port Unreachable response to Orion. A debug flow basic debug capture of this transaction is as follows:

```
Internal_fw-> debug flow basic
Internal_fw-> get dbuf stream
**** 01530.0: <Secure_Servers/ethernet0/0> packet received [71]****
  ipid = 3168(0c60), @02f05a50
  packet passed sanity check.
  ethernet0/0:192.168.1.30/4465->192.168.4.10/53,17<Root>
  no session found
<Additional_output_truncated>

**** jump to packet:192.168.1.1->192.168.1.30
  skipping pre-frag
  no more encapping needed
  send out through normal path.
  flow_ip_send: 060b:192.168.1.1->192.168.1.30,1 => ethernet0/0(56)
flag 0x0, vlan 0
<Additional_Output_Truncated>
  [ Dest] 1.route 192.168.1.30->192.168.1.30, to ethernet0/0
  route to 192.168.1.30
  arp entry found for 192.168.1.30 mac 001125150ccd
  **** pak processing end.
  log this session (pid=7)
  packet dropped, denied by policy
```

As a complement to the debug flow basic capture in the preceding code, a tcpdump packet capture on the Andromeda (192.168.1.30) system confirms that a DNS query to 192.168.4.10 on UDP/53 results in an immediate ICMP Port Unreachable response from 192.168.1.1, the ScreenOS gateway:

```
IP 192.168.1.30.4545 > 192.168.4.10.53:  4+ A? www.google.com. (41)
IP 192.168.1.1 > 192.168.1.30: ICMP 192.168.4.10 udp port 53
unreachable, length 36
```

Finally, for ICMP connection requests, such as an ICMP Echo ping request to a destination that is protected by a reject policy, ScreenOS gateways do not generate any response back to the source.

See Also

Recipe 7.5

7.7 Schedule Policies to Run at a Specified Time

Problem

You want to restrict a policy to be active at only a specified time.

Solution

You can restrict a policy to be active at a specified time by defining a scheduler that defines the time window in a 24-hour clock format, and then applying the scheduler to the policy:

```
Internal_fw-> set scheduler Friday_Morning recurrent friday start
07:00 stop 10:00
Internal_fw-> set policy from trust to Secure_Servers orion andromeda
ftp permit schedule Friday_Morning log
```

This policy permits a File Transfer Protocol (FTP) session from Orion to Andromeda every Friday morning between 7:00 and 10:00.

Discussion

Scheduled policies are active only during the period specified by the scheduler. ScreenOS represents the state of these policies to be enabled during active periods and hidden during inactive periods. The following output shows the state of policy ID 5, defined in the solution to this recipe, as `hidden` as the policy is not in its active window, per the ScreenOS gateway's clock:

```
Internal_fw-> get policy
Total regular policies 3, Default deny.
ID From     To        Src-addr  Dst-addr  Service Action State  ASTLCB
2 Trust    Secure_~ Orion     Andromeda HTTP    Permit enabled ---X-X
5 Trust    Secure_~ Orion     Andromeda FTP     Permit hidden  -X-X-X
4 Secure_~ Trust    Andromeda Orion     ANY     Deny   enabled ---X-X
Internal_fw->
```

When the policy is active in its scheduled time window, it transitions from the `hidden` to the `enabled` state.

Further details on a scheduled policy's associated scheduler and its current status are as follows:

```
Internal_fw-> get policy id 5
name:"none" (id 5), zone Trust -> Secure_Servers,action Permit, status
 "hidden"
src "Orion", dst "Andromeda", serv "FTP"
Policies on this vpn tunnel: 0
nat off, Web filtering : disabled
vpn unknown vpn, policy flag 00010000, session backup: on,
idle reset: on
traffic shapping off, scheduler Friday_Morning(off), serv flag 00
log close, log count 0, alert no, counter no(0) byte
```

```
rate(sec/min) 0/0
total octets 0, counter(session/packet/octet) 0/0/0
priority 7, diffserv marking Off
tadapter: state off, gbw/mbw 0/0 policing (no)
No Authentication
No User, User Group or Group expression set
Internal_fw->
```

This policy is active per the schedule defined in the `Friday_Morning` scheduler and is currently `off`; therefore, it is not active.

The ScreenOS policy scheduler supports recurring as well as one-time schedules. Whereas the solution to this recipe defined a recurring Friday schedule, here is an example of a one-time schedule that will run once on New Year's Eve in December 2010:

```
Internal_fw-> set scheduler Dec_31_2010 once start 12/31/2010 22:00
stop 01/01/2011 01:00
```

Another example of a recurring scheduler that is active every Monday through Friday from 9:00 a.m. to 5:00 p.m. is as follows:

```
Internal_fw-> set scheduler "Weekday_Biz_Hrs" recurrent Monday start
09:00 stop 17:00
Internal_fw-> set scheduler "Weekday_Biz_Hrs" recurrent Tuesday start
09:00 stop 17:00
Internal_fw-> set scheduler "Weekday_Biz_Hrs" recurrent Wednesday start
 09:00 stop 17:00
Internal_fw-> set scheduler "Weekday_Biz_Hrs" recurrent Thursday start
 09:00 stop 17:00
Internal_fw-> set scheduler "Weekday_Biz_Hrs" recurrent Friday start
09:00 stop 17:00
```

7.8 Change the Order of ScreenOS Policies

Problem

You want to change the order of the ScreenOS policies in a policy set.

Solution

ScreenOS gateways process policies sequentially, beginning with the policy at the top. Thus, after ScreenOS policies have been defined, you can move them around at any time to change their order of processing. This is often required to prevent the shadowing of a new policy that is being added. The following policy already exists in a ScreenOS gateway:

```
Internal_fw-> get config | include policy
set policy id 2 from "Trust" to "Secure_Servers"  "Orion" "Andromeda"
 "HTTP" permit log
set policy id 3 from "Trust" to "Secure_Servers"  "Any" "Any" "ANY"
deny log
Internal_fw->
```

Next, add an additional policy to permit FTP traffic from Orion to Andromeda:

```
Internal_fw-> set policy id 4 from trust to secure_servers orion
andromeda ftp permit log
```

Now, policy id 4 is getting shadowed by the explicit deny policy id 3. You can verify this by running the exec policy verify command:

```
Internal_fw-> exec policy verify
Rule 4 is shadowed by rule 3
Rulebase verification done: shadowed rules were found
Internal_fw->
```

Hence, to move rule 4 ahead of rule 3 to prevent shadowing, you can use the set policy move command:

```
Internal_fw-> set policy move 4 before 3
```

Discussion

Following a policy move, you can verify that there is no shadowing of policies:

```
Internal_fw-> exec policy verify
Rulebase verified successfully
Internal_fw->
```

Also, following the policy move, you can see the new policy order:

```
Internal_fw-> get policy
Total regular policies 3, Default deny.
ID From  To       Src-addr  Dst-addr  Service  Action State   ASTLCB
 2 Trust Secure_~ Orion     Andromeda HTTP     Permit enabled ---X-X
 4 Trust Secure_~ Orion     Andromeda FTP      Permit enabled ---X-X
 3 Trust Secure_~ Any       Any       ANY      Deny   enabled ---X-X
Internal_fw->
```

Similar to moving one policy before another, you can use the set policy after command to move one policy after another one.

Finally, to create a new policy that goes to the top of the policy base, use the set policy top command:

```
Internal_fw-> set policy top from Trust to Secure_Servers Orion
Andromeda smtp permit log
policy id = 5
Internal_fw->
```

Now, you can verify that this new policy is installed at the top of the policy set:

```
Internal_fw-> get policy
Total regular policies 4, Default deny.
ID From   To       Src-addr Dst-address Service Action State   ASTLCB
 5 Trust  Secure_~ Orion    Andromeda   SMTP    Permit enabled ---X-X
 2 Trust  Secure_~ Orion    Andromeda   HTTP    Permit enabled ---X-X
 4 Trust  Secure_~ Orion    Andromeda   FTP     Permit enabled ---X-X
 3 Trust  Secure_~ Any      Any         ANY     Deny   enabled ---X-X
Internal_fw->
```

This scenario prevents the new policy entry from being shadowed by installing it at the top. Using the `set policy top` command is valuable in such scenarios where an explicit deny policy exists at the end.

See Also

Recipe 7.1

7.9 Disable a ScreenOS Policy

Problem

You want to temporarily disable a ScreenOS policy without deleting it.

Solution

You can temporarily disable an existing ScreenOS policy by using the `set policy id <id number> disable` command. However, you must first determine the policy ID:

```
Internal_fw-> get policy from Trust to Secure_Servers
ID From  To       Src-addr Dst-address Service Action State   ASTLCB
 2 Trust Secure_~ Orion    Andromeda   HTTP    Permit enabled ---X-X
Internal_fw->
```

Now, you can disable the policy:

```
Internal_fw-> set policy id 2 disable
policy id = 2
Internal_fw->
```

Discussion

A policy that has been disabled is still defined in the configuration, but it shows up with its state `disabled` in the `get policy` output as follows:

```
Internal_fw-> get policy from Trust to Secure_Servers
ID From  To       Src-addr Dst-address Service Action State   ASTLCB
 2 Trust Secure_~ Orion    Andromeda   HTTP    Permit disabl~ ---X-X
Internal_fw->
```

You can reenable a disabled policy with the following:

```
Internal_fw-> unset policy id 2 disable
```

7.10 Configure an Intra-Zone Firewall Policy

Problem

You want to configure a ScreenOS intra-zone policy that implements and logs secure firewall sessions between systems on the same security zone.

Solution

Figure 7-4 shows the Internal_fw gateway and its interfaces in the context of a firewall policy between devices on the same Trust zone that permits the Orion host to initiate ping and HTTP connections to Gemini but denies all other connections.

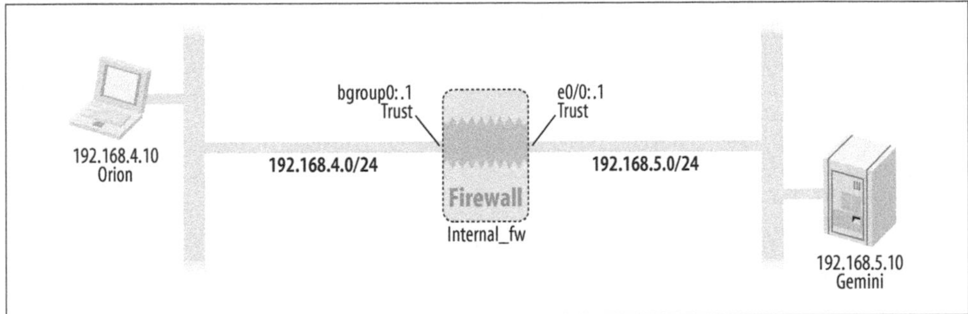

Figure 7-4. Intra-zone firewall policy configuration

First, the required address book and service group entries are created:

```
Internal_fw-> set address Trust Gemini 192.168.5.10/32
Internal_fw-> set group service ping_http
Internal_fw-> set group service ping_http add ping
Internal_fw-> set group service ping_http add http
```

Next, intra-zone blocking is enabled on the Trust zone, and the intra-zone policy is configured:

```
Internal_fw-> set zone Trust block
Internal_fw-> set policy from Trust to Trust Orion Gemini ping_http
permit log
policy id = 20
Internal_fw-> set policy from Trust to Trust Orion Gemini any deny
log
policy id = 21
Internal_fw->
```

Discussion

In the solution to this recipe, the two distinct IP interfaces, bgroup0 and ethernet0/1, on the Internal_fw gateway are in the same Trust security zone. To enable stateful firewalling between devices on these separate interfaces on the same zone, intra-zone policies are employed.

In its default configuration, ScreenOS does not deny intra-zone traffic on the Trust zone or other custom zones. It does, however, deny intra-zone traffic on the Untrust zone. To deny all intra-zone traffic on the Trust zone, you use the set zone *<zone_name>* block command. You can verify the block setting on a zone by using the get zone *<zone_name>* command:

```
Internal_fw-> get zone Trust | include block
```

```
Intra-zone block: On, attrib: Non-shared, flag:0x6288
Internal_fw->
```

Now, when an HTTP connection is attempted from Orion to Gemini, the associated intra-zone session that forms can be checked:

```
Internal_fw-> get session id 4061
id 4061(00000fdd), flag 08000040/0000/0001, vsys id 0(Root)
policy id 20, application id 0, dip id 0, state 0
current timeout 300, max timeout 300 (second)
status normal, start time 70990, duration 0
session id mask 0, app value 0
bgroup0(vsd 0): 192.168.4.10/1640->192.168.5.10/80, protocol 6 session
token 4 route 3
  gtwy 192.168.5.10, mac 001125150ccd, nsptn info 0, pmtu 1500
  flag 801801, diff 0/0
  port seq 0, subif 0, cookie 0, fin seq 0, fin state 0
ethernet0/1(vsd 0): 192.168.4.10/1640<-192.168.5.10/80, protocol 6
session token 4 route 7
  gtwy 192.168.4.10, mac 0017cbe1830b, nsptn info 0, pmtu 1500
mac 0017cbe1830b, nsptn info 0
  flag 801800, diff 0/0
  port seq 0, subif 0, cookie 0, fin seq 0, fin state 0
Internal_fw->
```

Also, the traffic log entry that is generated for this session can be viewed:

```
Internal_fw-> get log traffic policy 20
PID 20, from Trust to Trust, src Orion, dst Gemini, service ping_http,
action Permit
================================================================================
Date       Time     Duration Source IP      Port Destination IP Port Svc
Reason                       Xlated Src IP  Port Xlated Dst IP  Port ID
==========================================================================================
2007-08-16 16:21:48 0:00:43 192.168.4.10    1639 192.168.5.10    80 HTTP
Close - CLI                 192.168.4.10    1639 192.168.5.10    80
```

The entry that is generated and sent to the syslog server, shown here, shows the source and destination zones as Trust:

```
Syslog Priority:    Local0.Notice
Hostname:           192.168.4.1
Message entry:      Internal_fw: NetScreen device_id=Internal_fw  [Root]
system-notification-00257(traffic): start_time="2007-08-16 16:21:05"
duration=43 policy_id=20 service=http proto=6 src zone=Trust dst
zone=Trust action=Permit sent=2654 rcvd=51630 src=192.168.4.10
dst=192.168.5.10 src_port=1639 dst_port=80 src-xlated ip=192.168.4.10
port=1639 dst-xlated ip=192.168.5.10 port=80 session_id=4055
reason=Close - CLI<000>
```

Finally, an attempt to telnet from Orion to Gemini fails as the firewall drops and logs the packet. The local traffic log shows the drop:

```
Internal_fw-> get log traffic policy 21
PID 21, from Trust to Trust, src Orion, dst Gemini, service ANY, action
Deny
```

```
=======================================================================
Date       Time      Duration Source IP      Port Destination IP Port Svc
Reason                        Xlated Src IP  Port Xlated Dst IP  Port ID
========================================================================
2007-08-16 16:28:31 0:00:00 192.168.4.10    1648 192.168.5.10   23 TELNET
Traffic Denied               0.0.0.0             0 0.0.0.0       0
Internal_fw->
```

Once again, the log entry sent to the syslog server for this dropped packet displays the source and destination zones as Trust and denies action via a match on policy id 21:

```
Syslog Priority:     Local0.Notice
Hostname:            192.168.4.1
Message entry:       Internal_fw: NetScreen device_id=Internal_fw  [Root]
system-notification-00257(traffic): start_time="2007-08-16 16:28:22"
duration=0 policy_id=21 service=telnet proto=6 src zone=Trust dst
zone=Trust action=Deny sent=0 rcvd=0 src=192.168.4.10 dst=192.168.5.10 src_port=1648
dst_port=23 session_id=0<000>
```

See Also

This chapter's Introduction section; Recipe 7.1; Recipe 7.11

7.11 Configure a Global Firewall Policy

Problem

You want to configure a ScreenOS global firewall policy that applies to all security zones and logs the matched traffic.

Solution

You can configure global policies using the set policy global command that does not reference any source or destination security zones. The following code is a sample global policy that permits and logs ICMP ping traffic from and to all security zones on a ScreenOS gateway:

```
Internal_fw-> set policy global any any ping permit log
policy id = 17
Internal_fw->
```

As reviewed in greater detail in the following Discussion section, global policies are processed only for packets that have not already been matched by any intra-zone or inter-zone policies.

Discussion

As discussed in this chapter's Introduction section, global policies are processed in ScreenOS after all the intra-zone and inter-zone policies. Furthermore, it should be noted that when ScreenOS goes through a policy list, it does not process policies any further as soon as a match is found. *Hence, if your inter-zone or intra-zone policies have an explicit Source-Any to Destination-Any deny/reject policy at the end of the policy set, the global policies will never be reached in the ScreenOS processing order.*

When you view your existing policy set using the get policy command, the output does not list the global policies. To list the global policies, you need to use the get policy all or get policy global command:

```
Internal_fw-> get policy all
Total regular policies 1, Default deny.
ID From To        Src-addr Dst-addr  Service Action State   ASTLCB
2 Trust Secure_~ Orion     Andromeda HTTP    Permit enabled ---X-X

Total global policies 1, Default deny.
ID From   To      Src-address Dst-address Service Action State   ASTLCB
17 Global Global Any          Any         PING    Permit enabled ---X-X
Internal_fw->
```

The session associated with the global policy configured in the preceding code, showing a session for the ICMP ping initiated from Orion (192.168.4.10) to Andromeda (192.168.1.30), can be viewed as follows:

```
Internal_fw-> get session id 4063
id 4063(00000fdf), flag 00000050/0000/0001, vsys id 0(Root)
policy id 17, application id 0, dip id 0, state 0
current timeout 10, max timeout 60 (second)
status expired, start time 64447, duration 1
session id mask 0, app value 0
bgroup0(vsd 0): 192.168.4.10/22020->192.168.1.30/1280, protocol 1
session token 4 route 3
  gtwy 192.168.1.30, mac 001125150ccd, nsptn info 0, pmtu 1500
  flag 800801, diff 0/0
  port seq 0, subif 0, cookie 0, fin seq 0, fin state 0
ethernet0/0(vsd 0): 192.168.4.10/22020<-192.168.1.30/1280, protocol 1
session token 26 route 5
  gtwy 192.168.4.10, mac 0019b980c214, nsptn info 0, pmtu 1500
mac 0019b980c214, nsptn info 0
  flag 800800, diff 0/0
  port seq 0, subif 0, cookie 0, fin seq 0, fin state 0
Internal_fw->
```

Please note that log entries generated for packets that match global policies do not include specific source or destination zone information. Thus, a syslog entry for the earlier ICMP ping session shows a source and destination zone of Global as follows:

```
Syslog Priority:    Local0.Notice
Hostname:           192.168.4.1
Message entry:      Internal_fw: NetScreen device_id=Internal_fw
[Root]system-notification-00257(traffic): start_time="2007-08-16
14:36:44" duration=4 policy_id=17 service=icmp proto=1
src zone=Global dst zone=Global action=Permit sent=78 rcvd=78
src=192.168.4.10 dst=192.168.1.30 icmp type=8
src-xlated ip=192.168.4.10 dst-xlated ip=192.168.1.
30 session_id=4061 reason=Close - RESP<000>
```

Because global policies are processed only for packets that do not match any explicit intra-zone or inter-zone deny/reject policies, dropped packets would not be logged unless you have an explicit global deny logging policy. Hence, such a policy that logs such dropped packets can be configured as follows:

```
Internal_fw-> set policy global any any any deny log
policy id = 18
Internal_fw->
```

You can check the traffic log entries this policy generates on the syslog/NSM servers as well as on the local traffic log:

```
Internal_fw-> get log traffic policy 18
PID 18, from Global to Global, src Any, dst Any, service ANY, action
 Deny
===========================================================================
Date       Time      Duration Source IP      Port Dest IP       Port Svc
Reason                        Xlated Src IP  Port Xlated Dst IP Port ID
===========================================================================
2007-08-16 14:47:31  0:00:00 192.168.4.10   1118 192.168.1.30   53  DNS
Traffic Denied               0.0.0.0           0  0.0.0.0        0
```

Finally, if you would prefer not to log some of the traffic that hits the global deny logging policy, you can create a global policy that matches the traffic but does not log it. Hence, as an example, if you prefer not to log the Domain Name System (DNS) query traffic hitting the global policy, you can configure the following policy and move it above the terminating global deny logging policy in the policy search order:

```
Internal_fw-> set policy global any any dns deny
policy id = 19
Internal_fw-> set policy move 19 before 18
```

You can view the global policy search order, which shows that policy ID 19 will be processed before the global deny logging policy and, hence, traffic matching the deny DNS policy ID 19 will not be logged:

```
Internal_fw-> get policy global
Total global policies 3, Default deny.
ID From    To      Src-addr  Dst-addr  Service Action State   ASTLCB
17 Global  Global  Any       Any       PING    Permit enabled ---X-X
19 Global  Global  Any       Any       DNS     Deny   enabled -----X
18 Global  Global  Any       Any       ANY     Deny   enabled ---X-X
Internal_fw->
```

See Also

This chapter's Introduction section; Recipe 7.1; Recipe 7.3; Recipe 7.4; Recipe 7.10

7.12 Configure Custom Services

Problem

You want to configure a custom service that is not on the predefined list of services in ScreenOS.

Solution

You can define a custom service in ScreenOS by specifying the service name, protocol (i.e., TCP, UDP, or ICMP), and destination port range or Remote Procedure Call (RPC) program number/Universally Unique Identifier (UUID). Thus, the following custom service represents the connection opened by an IBM Lotus Notes client to an IBM Domino server on port TCP 1352:

```
Internal_fw-> set service Lotus_Notes protocol tcp dst-port 1352-1352
```

Discussion

Although ScreenOS ships with a large set of predefined services, in several instances, you may need to define custom services.

You can view the parameters of the custom service defined in this recipe's Solution section as follows:

```
Internal_fw-> get service Lotus_Notes
Name:       Lotus_Notes
Category:   other          ID:  0    Flag:  User-defined


Transport Src port Dst port  ICMPtype, Timeout(min|10sec*) Application
                                 code
tcp       0/65535  1352/1352                    30

Internal_fw->
```

As shown, the source ports for this service can span the entire range of TCP ports, from 0–65535. The timeout for this service is 30 minutes, which is the default timeout for TCP connections in ScreenOS.

See Also

This chapter's Introduction section

7.13 Configure Address and Service Groups

Problem

You want to configure an address or service group.

Solution

An address group in ScreenOS brings together a set of addresses under a common group name. Similarly, a service group can include a set of predefined and custom services under a single service group name. The following is an example of an address group, Main_Servers, which is defined in the Secure_Servers security zone:

```
Internal_fw-> set group address Secure_Servers Main_Servers
Internal_fw-> set group address Secure_Servers Main_Servers add
Andromeda
Internal_fw-> set group address Secure_Servers Main_Servers add
FTP_Serv
Internal_fw-> set group address Secure_Servers Main_Servers add
Mail_Serv
```

The following example defines a service group that includes the HTTP, FTP, and SMTP (MAIL) services:

```
Internal_fw-> set group service http_ftp_mail
Internal_fw-> set group service http_ftp_mail add http
Internal_fw-> set group service http_ftp_mail add ftp
Internal_fw-> set group service http_ftp_mail add mail
```

Discussion

Address and service groups are frequently used to consolidate a large set of hosts that are permitted to communicate with each other on a range of services under a single consolidated policy.

Address groups, just like individual address book entries, are tied to a security zone. Hence, the Main_Servers address group in this recipe's "Solution" section is tied to the Secure_Servers zone. Also, all of the individual address elements that are added to an address group already have to be defined in that specific security zone. You can view the members of an address group by using the get group address *<zone> <address_group_name>* command:

```
Internal_fw-> get group address Secure_Servers Main_Servers
 Group Name: Main_Servers              IP: v4          Comment:
 Group Items:  3                Type: User-defined
 Members: "Andromeda" "FTP_Serv" "Mail_Serv"
Internal_fw->
```

Service groups—just like individual predefined and custom-defined services—are not tied to a specific zone. You can view the members of a service group by using the get group service *<service_group_name>* command:

```
Internal_fw-> get group service http_ftp_mail
 Group Name: http_ftp_mail                Comment:
 Group Items:  3                 Type: User-defined
 Members: "FTP" "HTTP" "MAIL"
Internal_fw->
```

With the address group and service group defined as indicated in the preceding code, you can define a new ScreenOS policy that uses these groups, permitting Orion to access the three Main_Servers on the HTTP, FTP, and mail applications:

```
Internal_fw-> set policy from Trust to Secure_Servers Orion
Main_Servers http_ftp_mail permit log
policy id = 11
Internal_fw->
```

See Also

This chapter's Introduction section; Recipe 7.12; Recipe 7.14

7.14 Configure Service Timeouts

Problem

You want to change the session timeout value for a service.

Solution

You can change the session timeout value on predefined as well as custom-defined services. You can modify the timeout value of a predefined service, such as HTTP, as follows:

```
Internal_fw-> set service http timeout 15
```

This configuration changes the service timeout for HTTP to 15 minutes from the default value of five minutes.

Similarly, you can modify the timeout value of a custom-defined service, such as Lotus_Notes, to 45 minutes:

```
Internal_fw-> set service Lotus_Notes timeout 45
```

In addition to using the set service command, you have to reference the particular service with the modified timeout in a firewall policy by its specific service name for this new timeout to take effect.

Discussion

The timeout value of a service represents the amount of time that can elapse with no packets transmitted while the session is maintained in the firewall session table.

Certain applications, such as web servers, rapidly close out a TCP connection by sending a TCP segment with the RST flag set after serving up a response to an HTTP request. ScreenOS gateways purge the session from the session table upon seeing a TCP FIN or a TCP RST, which signifies the end of the communication. Other applications deliberately keep a communication channel open by periodically sending application-specific keepalive messages. Finally, some applications do not explicitly close out a TCP connection by negotiating a TCP four-way close (FIN-ACK, ACK, FIN-ACK, ACK) and have to be timed out of the firewall session table to prevent the buildup of stale, unused sessions in the session table.

The default session timeout value for services in ScreenOS is typically based on the protocol. Table 7-4 shows the timeout values for some standard protocols.

Table 7-4. Timeout values for some standard protocols

Service type	Timeout value (minutes)
GRE tunnel (IP protocol 47)	60
Generic TCP service	30
HTTP	5
Generic UDP service	1
ICMP	1

With the ability to configure session timeout values in ScreenOS, you may choose to lower the session timeout on a service to aggressively age out sessions from the session table. On the other hand, you may want to elongate the session timeout value if you have an application that sends packets sporadically but does not explicitly close out the TCP connection with an explicit TCP FIN or RST until a user-initiated event occurs.

You can view the configured timeout value of a service by using the get service *<service_name>* command. Thus, for the HTTP service whose timeout was modified in this recipe's solution, you can view the timeout value as follows:

```
Internal_fw-> get service http
Name:       HTTP
Category:   info seeking    ID:  0    Flag:  Pre-defined


Transport Src port Dst port ICMPtype, Timeout(min|10sec*) Application
                                code
tcp       0/65535  80/80                     15             HTTP

Internal_fw->
```

Although the default method of defining the timeout value of a service is in minutes, an alternative method is to use 10 seconds as the unit. The 10-second unit is relevant when monitoring the firewall session table as it uses the same 10-second unit, also known in the ScreenOS world as a *tick*. Thus, you can change the timeout of the MAIL (SMTP) service to 300 seconds—therefore 30 10-second units—and apply it to a firewall policy:

```
External_fw-> set service mail timeout unit 10sec
External_fw-> set service mail timeout 30
External_fw-> set policy id 13 from trust to untrust any any mail
permit log
```

Now, when you view the MAIL service using the `get service` command, the timeout is displayed in 10-second units:

```
External_fw-> get service mail
Name:       MAIL
Category:   email           ID:  0    Flag:  Pre-defined


Transport Src port  Dst port ICMPtype, Timeout(min|10sec*) Application
                                 code
tcp       0/65535    25/25                       30*        SMTP

External_fw->
```

Hence, a new session that uses the MAIL service with the modified timeout value has a session timeout value of 300 seconds, or 30 ticks:

```
External_fw-> get session service mail
Total mail sessions: 1
id 8052/s**,vsys 0,flag 08000000/0000/0001,policy 13,time 30, dip 2
module 0
 if 11(nspflag 801801):192.168.4.36/1059->209.85.163.27/25,6,
001125150ccd,sess token 4,vlan 0,tun 0,vsd 0,route 3
 if 0(nspflag 801800):192.168.1.6/4224<-209.85.163.27/25,6,
000fcc7cd338,sess token 6,vlan 0,tun 0,vsd 0,route 15
Total 1 sessions shown
External_fw->
```

The session timeout value, indicated by the value `time 30` in the preceding code, represents a session timeout of 30 ticks, or 300 seconds, per the modified service timeout. Please note that modified service timeouts do not apply unless the service is explicitly referenced in the policy. For instance, if the `External_fw` gateway has a generic trust to untrust policy that matches mail traffic and is used to build a firewall session, the default TCP service timeout of 1,800 seconds, or 180 ticks, will apply.

Finally, you can also specify a timeout value of never to a service:

```
External_fw-> set service mail timeout never
```

You can verify the timeout value as follows:

```
External_fw-> get service mail
Name:       MAIL
Category:   email          ID:  0   Flag:  Pre-defined


Transport Src port Dst port ICMPtype, Timeout(min|10sec*) Application
                            code
tcp       0/65535  25/25                    never        SMTP

External_fw->
```

A session that references this service with an infinte timeout is shown with its time value:

```
External_fw-> get session service mail
Total mail sessions: 1
id 7988/s**,vsys 0,flag 08000000/0000/0001,policy 13,time 2185, dip 2
module 0
 if 11(nspflag 801801):192.168.4.36/1129->209.85.163.27/25,6,
001125150ccd,sess token 4,vlan 0,tun 0,vsd 0,route 3
 if 0(nspflag 801800):192.168.1.6/4296<-209.85.163.27/25,6,
000fcc7cd338,sess token 6,vlan 0,tun 0,vsd 0,route 15
External_fw->
```

It should be noted from the preceding output that although this session is formed with a high timeout value of 21,850 seconds, this value remains constant and does not decrement as do other, normal-duration sessions.

When multiple services with different session timeout values are in a single service group, the ScreenOS gateway uses the individual matching service's session timeout value for the specific session. Hence, for a service group that includes HTTP (session timeout 5 minutes) and FTP (session timeout 30 minutes), a matching HTTP session will time out after 5 minutes whereas the FTP session will time out after 30 minutes, unless the session is purged sooner due to a TCP `RST` from either host.

See Also

Recipe 7.12; Recipe 7.13

7.15 View and Use Microsoft RPC Services

Problem

You want to view the predefined Microsoft RPC services in ScreenOS and enable ScreenOS gateway-secured communication between Microsoft Windows hosts that use MS-RPC to connect with each other.

Solution

ScreenOS ships with a wide range of predefined individual Microsoft RPC services and service groups. You can view the exhaustive list of predefined Microsoft RPC-specific services in ScreenOS as follows:

```
Internal_fw-> get service | include "MS-"
```

The three major Microsoft RPC service groups in ScreenOS are categorized based on their respective Windows applications, i.e., Active Directory, Exchange, and IIS (Internet Information Services).

You can view the service group that includes the RPC services for Microsoft Windows Active Directory communication and replication as follows:

```
Internal_fw-> get group service MS-AD
 Group Name: MS-AD                Comment: Microsoft Active Directory
 Group Items:  4                  Type: Pre-defined
 Members: "MS-AD-BR" "MS-AD-DRSUAPI" "MS-AD-DSROLE" "MS-AD-DSSETUP"
Internal_fw->
```

The `MS-EXCHANGE` service group includes the MS-RPC component services for Microsoft Exchange communication between Exchange servers, and between Outlook clients and Exchange servers:

```
Internal_fw-> get group service MS-EXCHANGE
 Group Name: MS-EXCHANGE                  Comment: Microsoft Exchange
 Group Items:  6                  Type: Pre-defined
 Members: "MS-EXCHANGE-DATABASE" "MS-EXCHANGE-DIRECTORY"
 "MS-EXCHANGE-INFO-STORE" "MS-EXCHANGE-MTA" "MS-EXCHANGE-STORE"
 "MS-EXCHANGE-SYSATD"
Internal_fw->
```

The `MS-IIS` service group includes the MS-RPC component services for the IIS application:

```
Internal_fw-> get group service MS-IIS
 Group Name: MS-IIS               Comment: Microsoft IIS Server
 Group Items:  6                  Type: Pre-defined
 Members: "MS-IIS-COM" "MS-IIS-IMAP4" "MS-IIS-INETINFO" "MS-IIS-NNTP"
 "MS-IIS-POP3" "MS-IIS-SMTP"
Internal_fw->
```

As an example, building on the scenario from Recipe 7.1, the following sample policy enables the Sirius Windows Active Directory domain controller on the `Trust` zone to perform an Active Directory replication to the Andromeda Windows Active Directory domain controller in the `Secure_Servers` zone:

```
Internal_fw-> set policy from Trust to Secure_Servers Sirius Andromeda
 MS-AD permit log
policy id = 15
Internal_fw->
```

Discussion

Microsoft RPC is a technology that several Windows applications use to communicate with one another. MS-RPC applications typically listen on dynamic TCP or UDP ports. Hence, an RPC portmapper service, which runs on TCP and UDP port 135, provides the mapping between the application and the TCP or UDP port on which it's listening.

All MS-RPC applications, such as the Windows Active Directory Replication Service, have a well-known but unique UUID associated with them. When an MS-RPC-dependent Windows service starts up on a host, it finds an available TCP or UDP port and registers that port with the UUID. Next, when a client application wants to communicate with that service, it first makes a connection to the RPC portmapper service on the server's TCP or UDP port 135 and requests the service's TCP/UDP port number by querying the UUID.

Then, the client application opens a connection to the port number obtained in the UUID query response. The ScreenOS MS-RPC services thus maintain the list of UUIDs associated with the various Microsoft applications. The MS-RPC ScreenOS ALG dynamically opens pinholes to permit connections to the TCP or UDP ports on which the service has registered itself. We discuss ALGs further in Chapter 11.

You can check the UUIDs associated with the individual MS-RPC services by viewing each individual service. This example shows the UUID associated with the MS-AD-DRSUAPI (AD Replication Service) service:

```
Internal_fw-> get service MS-AD-DRSUAPI
Name:       MS-AD-DRSUAPI
Category:   other          ID:  0    Flag:  Pre-defined


Transport    UUID                                 Timeout(min) Application
MS-RPC       e3514235-4b06-11d1-ab04-00c04fc2dcd2       1

Internal_fw->
```

ScreenOS also offers a generic MS-RPC service called `MS-RPC-ANY` that matches any UUID, thereby permitting communication between two hosts on all MS-RPC applications:

```
Internal_fw-> get service MS-RPC-ANY
Name:       MS-RPC-ANY
Category:   other          ID:  0    Flag:  Pre-defined


Transport    UUID                                 Timeout(min) Application
MS-RPC       ANY                                        1

Internal_fw->
```

See Also

Chapter 11

7.16 View and Use Sun-RPC Services

Problem

You want to view the predefined Sun-RPC services in ScreenOS and enable ScreenOS gateway-secured communication between hosts that use Sun-RPC to connect with one another.

Solution

ScreenOS ships with a wide range of predefined individual Sun-RPC services. You can view the exhaustive list of predefined Sun-RPC-specific services in ScreenOS as follows:

```
Internal_fw-> get service | include "SUN-"
```

As an example, building on the scenario from Recipe 7.1, the following sample policy enables the gamma workstation on the `Trust` zone to make an NFS connection to the delta Unix server in the `Secure_Servers` zone:

```
Internal_fw-> set policy from Trust to Secure_Servers gamma delta
SUN-RPC-NFS permit log
policy id = 16
Internal_fw->
```

Discussion

Sun-RPC was originally defined in RFC 1050 and RFC 1057. This original specification has subsequently evolved into Open Network Computing (ONC) RPC version 2, defined in RFC 1831. Services on Unix hosts that rely on Sun-RPC use a well-known but unique program number as an identifier and register the dynamic TCP/UDP port they are listening on with the portmapper service on that host. The portmapper service runs on TCP/UDP 111.

Hence, a client application that needs to connect to a Sun-RPC service such as NFS first contacts the portmapper service on the server with the particular program number. The portmapper service returns the TCP/UDP port associated with the program number. Then, the client application connects to the service on the specific TCP/UDP port number. The ScreenOS Sun-RPC services have the predefined, well-known program numbers for several applications, such as NFS. The ScreenOS Sun-RPC ALG dynamically opens pinholes to permit connections to the TCP or UDP ports on which the service has registered itself. We discuss ALGs further in Chapter 11.

You can check the program numbers associated with the individual Sun-RPC services by viewing the individual services. This example shows the program numbers associated with the SUN-RPC-NFS service:

```
Internal_fw-> get service SUN-RPC-NFS
Name:         SUN-RPC-NFS
Category:     other           ID:  0   Flag:  Pre-defined


Transport     Program                   Timeout(min) Application
SUN-RPC       100003/100003                    40          None
SUN-RPC       100227/100227                    40          None

Internal_fw->
```

ScreenOS also offers a generic Sun-RPC service called SUN-RPC-ANY that matches any program number, thereby permitting communication between two hosts on all Sun-RPC applications:

```
Internal_fw-> get service SUN-RPC-ANY
Name:         SUN-RPC-ANY
Category:     other           ID:  0   Flag:  Pre-defined


Transport     Program                   Timeout(min) Application
SUN-RPC       ANY                               1

Internal_fw->
```

On a Unix host, you can see the various RPC applications/services that have registered themselves with the rpcmapper and their respective program numbers and TCP/UDP ports:

```
# rpcinfo -p
   program vers proto   port
    100000    2   tcp    111  portmapper
    100000    2   udp    111  portmapper
    100003    2   udp   2049  nfs
    100003    3   udp   2049  nfs
    100021    1   udp  34361  nlockmgr
    100021    3   udp  34361  nlockmgr
    100021    4   udp  34361  nlockmgr
    100005    1   udp  34362  mountd
    100005    1   tcp  36542  mountd
    100005    2   udp  34362  mountd
    100005    2   tcp  36542  mountd
    100005    3   udp  34362  mountd
    100005    3   tcp  36542  mountd
#
```

See Also

Chapter 11

7.17 View the Session Table

Problem

You want to examine the session table to view all the active connections through the ScreenOS gateway.

Solution

You can view the session table in ScreenOS with the `get session` command:

```
Internal_fw-> get session
```

Discussion

The session table lists the active sessions that the ScreenOS gateway has permitted and is actively tracking.

Figure 7-5 illustrates a scenario, similar to Recipe 7.1, where an inter-zone policy from `Trust` to `Secure_Servers` permits Orion (`192.168.4.10`) to initiate an HTTP connection to the web server Andromeda (`192.168.1.30`).

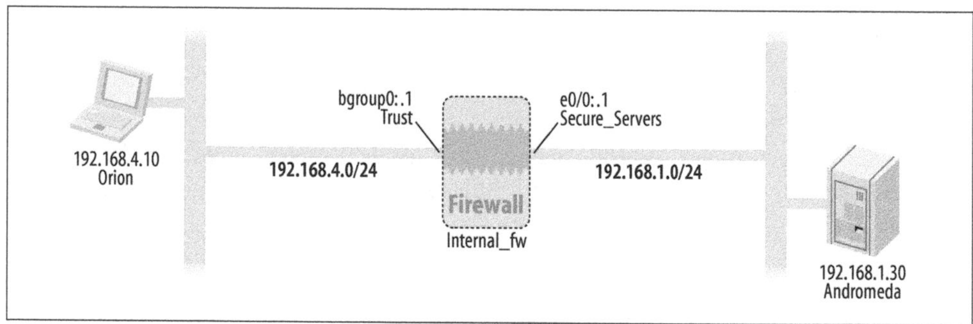

Figure 7-5. HTTP permit policy—session table view scenario

You can view the detailed state of an active session in the session table using the `get session id <session_id>` command. First, to determine the session ID of the session for which you are seeking detailed information, you can use the `get session` command with some matching keywords:

```
Internal_fw-> get session src-ip 192.168.4.10 dst-ip 192.168.1.30
dst-port 80
alloc 1/max 4064, alloc failed 0, mcast alloc 0, di alloc failed 0
total reserved 0, free sessions in shared pool 4063
Total 1 sessions according filtering criteria.
id 4057/s**,vsys 0,flag 48000040/0000/0001,policy 2,time 2, dip 0
module 0
 if 11(nspflag 801801):192.168.4.10/4407->192.168.1.30/80,6,
001125150ccd,sess token 4,vlan 0,tun 0,vsd 0,route 3
 if 0(nspflag 800800):192.168.4.10/4407<-192.168.1.30/80,6,
```

```
0019b980c214,sess token 26,vlan 0,tun 0,vsd 0,route 1
Total 1 sessions shown
Internal_fw->
```

The summary session entry output shown, beginning with `id 4057`, has the following key components:

- The `id 4057` tag identifies the session ID.
- The `vsys 0` tag specifies that the session is created in Virtual System (VSYS) 0, the root VSYS.
- The `policy 2` tag identifies the matching policy ID that permitted this session to be created.
- The `time 2` tag indicates the session timeout in ticks, where one tick is a unit of 10 seconds.
- The `dip 0` tag specifies the dynamic IP (DIP) pool ID being used. A DIP ID of 0 represents no DIP pool usage.
- The `if 11` tag specifies the interface ID of the interface on which the initial source packet was received. In this instance, `if 11` represents the `bgroup0` interface on the SSG-5 gateway. You can check the `if ID` to interface-name mapping with the `get if` command.
- The `192.168.4.10/4407->192.168.1.30/80,6` tag represents the forward session, indicating that the flow is a TCP flow (represented by the terminating 6, which indicates the IP number where 6 represents TCP and 17 represents UDP), originated by 192.168.4.10 on source port 4407, and that the target host is 192.168.1.30 with destination port 80 (HTTP). The direction of the `->` arrow indicates that this flow is representing the forward session from 192.168.4.10 to 192.168.1.30. The `<-` arrow in the complementary flow indicates the reverse session from 192.168.1.30 to 192.168.4.10.
- The `001125150ccd` and `0019b980c214` fields, respectively, represent the Ethernet Layer 2 MAC addresses of the next-hop devices on either side of the ScreenOS gateway for this session.
- The `sess token` tag is an identifier for an internal hash table entry that maps sessions to security zones.
- The `vlan 0` field identifies a virtual local area network (VLAN) ID for Ethernet interfaces with a `vlan` tag. A `vlan 0` field indicates that there is no VLAN ID configured on this interface.
- The `tun 0` tag indicates the VPN tunnel ID, if applicable.
- The `vsd 0` tag represents the NSRP virtual security device (VSD) group for this interface if an NSRP cluster is enabled.
- The `route 3` tag specifies the route ID from the routing table that was used to route this flow.

Next, you can view detailed output of the specific session:

```
Internal_fw-> get session id 4057
id 4057(00000fd9), flag 48000040/0000/0001, vsys id 0(Root)
policy id 2, application id 0, dip id 0, state 0
current timeout 20, max timeout 300 (second)
status normal, start time 3644, duration 0
session id mask 0, app value 0
bgroup0(vsd 0): 192.168.4.10/4407->192.168.1.30/80, protocol 6
session token 4 route 3
  gtwy 192.168.1.30, mac 001125150ccd, nsptn info 0, pmtu 1500
  flag 801801, diff 0/0
  port seq 0, subif 0, cookie 0, fin seq 0, fin state 0
ethernet0/0(vsd 0): 192.168.4.10/4407<-192.168.1.30/80, protocol 6
session token 26 route 1
  gtwy 192.168.4.10, mac 0019b980c214, nsptn info 0, pmtu 1500
mac 0019b980c214, nsptn info 0
  flag 800800, diff 0/0
  port seq 0, subif 0, cookie 0, fin seq 0, fin state 0
Internal_fw->
```

This session output shows a current timeout of 20 seconds, signifying that this is an ephemeral half-session, awaiting a SYN-ACK response from the web server. Typically, a TCP half-session is difficult to capture with an interactive, nonscripted get session command, as the target hosts respond in a subsecond duration whereupon the ephemeral session is converted into a full session. Your target host could be down or you could be under a SYN flood attack if your session table is displaying a large number of half-sessions.

The following output displays an HTTP full-session, with a 300-second timeout value, displayed by get session in 30 ticks:

```
Internal_fw-> get session
alloc 1/max 4064, alloc failed 0, mcast alloc 0, di alloc failed 0
total reserved 0, free sessions in shared pool 4063
id 4057/s**,vsys 0,flag 08000040/0000/0001,policy 2,time 30, dip 0
module 0
 if 11(nspflag 801801):192.168.4.10/4454->192.168.1.30/80,6,
001125150ccd,sess token 4,vlan 0,tun 0,vsd 0,route 3
 if 0(nspflag 801800):192.168.4.10/4454<-192.168.1.30/80,6,
0019b980c214,sess token 26,vlan 0,tun 0,vsd 0,route 1
Total 1 sessions shown
Internal_fw->
```

Here is a detailed view of the session entry, with an explicit timeout value of 300 seconds:

```
Internal_fw-> get session id 4057
id 4057(00000fd9), flag 08000040/0000/0001, vsys id 0(Root)
policy id 2, application id 0, dip id 0, state 0
current timeout 300, max timeout 300 (second)
status normal, start time 5256, duration 0
session id mask 0, app value 0
bgroup0(vsd 0): 192.168.4.10/4454->192.168.1.30/80, protocol 6
```

```
session token 4 route 3
  gtwy 192.168.1.30, mac 001125150ccd, nsptn info 0, pmtu 1500
  flag 801801, diff 0/0
  port seq 0, subif 0, cookie 0, fin seq 0, fin state 0
ethernet0/0(vsd 0): 192.168.4.10/4454<-192.168.1.30/80, protocol 6
session token 26 route 1
  gtwy 192.168.4.10, mac 0019b980c214, nsptn info 0, pmtu 1500
mac 0019b980c214, nsptn info 0
  flag 801800, diff 0/0
  port seq 0, subif 0, cookie 0, fin seq 0, fin state 0
Internal_fw->
```

A quick summary output shows the total number of active sessions through the ScreenOS gateway, indicated by the number following the `alloc` keyword:

```
Internal_fw-> get session info
alloc 1/max 4064, alloc failed 0, mcast alloc 0, di alloc failed 0
total reserved 0, free sessions in shared pool 4063
Internal_fw->
```

The `get session info` command also indicates the maximum number of sessions supported by the particular ScreenOS gateway, specified by the `max` field, in its current software release and licensing configuration. Thus, the SSG-5 gateway displayed in the preceding code snippet supports a maximum of 4,064 sessions.

Finally, you can export the entire session table from a ScreenOS gateway to a Trivial File Transfer Protocol (TFTP) server by using the redirect (`>`) field on the `get session` command and specifying the IP address of the TFTP server and name of the file:

```
Internal_fw-> get session > tftp 192.168.4.10 Session_Table_File
redirect to 192.168.4.10,Session_Table_File
!!!!!!!!!!
tftp transferred records = 4
tftp success!
Internal_fw->
```

See Also

Recipe 7.18; Recipe 7.19

7.18 Troubleshoot Traffic Flows

Problem

You want to track the processing of a packet as ScreenOS processes and make decisions on it.

Solution

The `debug flow basic` ScreenOS command shows the debug mode processing of a packet beginning with its entry on an interface through the sequence of processing steps:

```
Internal_fw-> clear dbuf
Internal_fw-> debug flow basic
...<wait for a few seconds to capture the stream>
Internal_fw-> undebug all
Internal_fw-> get dbuf stream
```

Discussion

The ScreenOS `debug flow basic` command provides extensive processing details on a packet, beginning with its entry on an interface through the steps of policy matching and the final forwarding decision.

When a packet enters a ScreenOS gateway, it goes through a sequence of processing steps. For packets that are permitted or tunneled through the gateway, the processing steps culminate in a firewall session table entry being generated and the packet being forwarded out. An incoming packet goes through the following processing steps:

1. Assign the packet a source security zone.
2. Match the packet against any of the screens defined in the ScreenOS configuration to check whether it represents a malicious attack such as a SYN or ICMP flood. If yes, take the screen action on the packet. If the packet passes screen protection without being dropped, proceed to step 3.
3. Match the packet against the session table of existing, active sessions. If yes, forward the packet based on the actions defined in the session's state details. If not, proceed to step 4.
4. Perform mapped IP (MIP) or virtual IP (VIP) conversion on the packet. Please note that this is not an all-encompassing NAT step. During this step, the ScreenOS gateway simply converts the destination address to an internal address to assist with the subsequent route lookup, only if the packet's destination address is a defined MIP or VIP. Proceed to step 5.
5. If policy-based routing (PBR) is configured on the incoming interface, apply the PBR policy on the packet. Otherwise, perform a destination route lookup on the packet to identify the exit interface.
6. Perform a policy lookup on the packet. If the resultant action is permit or tunnel, proceed to step 7. If the action is deny, drop the packet. If the action is reject, send back a TCP Reset or ICMP Destination Unreachable, as discussed in Recipe 7.6.
7. Perform src and/or destination NAT translation on the packet, as defined in the policy.
8. Install a detailed entry in the session table, including the results from steps 1–7, for all permitted and tunneled packets. If the packet is a TCP packet with the SYN flag set, representing an initial SYN packet in a TCP three-way handshake, and SYN cookies are not enabled, set up an ephemeral session with a lifetime of 20

seconds (two ticks) in the session table and wait for the target host behind the firewall to respond with a SYN-ACK. Once the SYN-ACK has been sent back to the source and the source has responded with an ACK, the three-way handshake is complete. At this point, convert the ephemeral 20-second session to a full TCP session, which typically has a 30-minute (180-tick) session timeout. On ASIC-based high-throughput ScreenOS gateways, such as the ISG-1000/2000 and the NS5200/5400, the session table entry is pushed down to the ASIC, and subsequent packets associated with this flow are processed directly in the ASIC without reaching the ScreenOS gateway's CPU.

9. Perform the various actions on the packet (e.g., perform the NAT operation) and forward the packet.

The `debug flow basic` command provides a navigation trail through the various processing steps outlined in the preceding list for a new packet entering a ScreenOS gateway.

Please note that for high-end, ASIC-based, high-throughput ScreenOS gateways such as the ISG-1000/2000 and the NS5200/5400, the output generated by `debug flow basic` only displays the initial packets for a given flow until a full session table entry is generated. On the other hand, the `debug flow basic` output on the lower-end SSG-5 through SSG-500 Series and the NS-5GT, NS-25/50, NS-200, and NS-500 Series shows all of the subsequent packets associated with the session flowing through the ScreenOS gateway.

The recommended and default method of capturing debug output is to write it to the ScreenOS debug buffer and then display the contents of the debug buffer either within ScreenOS or by exporting its contents to a TFTP server. Also, because a typical deployed ScreenOS gateway has a large volume of traffic traversing it, it's a good idea to apply a flow filter to the `debug flow basic` command to restrict the flows that are captured.

You can capture the `debug flow basic` output for the HTTP session discussed in Recipe 7.12 with two bidirectional flow filters:

```
Internal_fw-> clear dbuf
Internal_fw-> debug flow basic
Internal_fw-> set ffilter src-ip 192.168.4.10 dst-ip 192.168.1.30
Internal_fw-> set ffilter src-ip 192.168.1.30 dst-ip 192.168.4.10
...<wait for a few seconds to capture the stream>
Internal_fw-> undebug all
Internal_fw-> get dbuf stream
****** 09615.0: <Trust/bgroup0> packet received [48]******
  ipid = 7830(1e96), @03040770
  packet passed sanity check.
  bgroup0:192.168.4.10/4519->192.168.1.30/80,6<Root>
  no session found
  flow_first_sanity_check: in <bgroup0>, out <N/A>
```

```
  chose interface bgroup0 as incoming nat if.
  flow_first_routing: in <bgroup0>, out <N/A>
  search route to (bgroup0, 192.168.4.10->192.168.1.30) in vr trust-vr
 for vsd-0/flag-0/ifp-null
  [ Dest] 1.route 192.168.1.30->192.168.1.30, to ethernet0/0
  routed (x_dst_ip 192.168.1.30) from bgroup0 (bgroup0 in 0) to
ethernet0/0
  policy search from zone 2-> zone 100
 policy_flow_search  policy search nat_crt from zone 2-> zone 100
  RPC Mapping Table search returned 0 matched service(s) for (vsys
Root, ip 192.168.1.30, port 80, proto 6)
  No SW RPC rule match, search HW rule
  Permitted by policy 2
  No src xlate   choose interface ethernet0/0 as outgoing phy if
  no loop on ifp ethernet0/0.
  session application type 6, name HTTP, nas_id 0, timeout 300sec
  service lookup identified service 0.
  flow_first_final_check: in <bgroup0>, out <ethernet0/0>
  existing vector list 103-2649484.
  Session (id:4057) created for first pak 103
  flow_first_install_session======>
  route to 192.168.1.30
  arp entry found for 192.168.1.30
  ifp2 ethernet0/0, out_ifp ethernet0/0, flag 00800800, tunnel
 ffffffff, rc 1
  outgoing wing prepared, ready
  handle cleartext reverse route
  search route to (ethernet0/0, 192.168.1.30->192.168.4.10) in vr
trust-vr for vsd-0/flag-3000/ifp-bgroup0
  [ Dest] 3.route 192.168.4.10->192.168.4.10, to bgroup0
  route to 192.168.4.10
  arp entry found for 192.168.4.10
  ifp2 bgroup0, out_ifp bgroup0, flag 00800801, tunnel ffffffff, rc 1
  flow got session.
  flow session id 4057
  tcp seq check.
  Got syn, 192.168.4.10(4519)->192.168.1.30(80), nspflag 0x801801,
0x800800
  post addr xlation: 192.168.4.10->192.168.1.30.
 flow_send_vector_, vid = 0, is_layer2_if=0
****** 09615.0: <Secure_Servers/ethernet0/0> packet received [48]******
  ipid = 537(0219), @02f99a70
  packet passed sanity check.
  ethernet0/0:192.168.1.30/80->192.168.4.10/4519,6<Root>
  existing session found. sess token 26
  flow got session.
  flow session id 4057
  tcp seq check.
  Got syn_ack, 192.168.1.30(80)->192.168.4.10(4519), nspflag 0x801800,
0x801801
  post addr xlation: 192.168.1.30->192.168.4.10.
 flow_send_vector_, vid = 0, is_layer2_if=0
****** 09615.0: <Trust/bgroup0> packet received [40]******
  ipid = 7831(1e97), @03040f70
```

```
 packet passed sanity check.
 bgroup0:192.168.4.10/4519->192.168.1.30/80,6<Root>
 existing session found. sess token 4
 flow got session.
 flow session id 4057
 tcp seq check.
 Got ack, 192.168.4.10(4519)->192.168.1.30(80), natpflag 0x8000040,
nspflag 0x801801, 0x801800, timeout=150
 post addr xlation: 192.168.4.10->192.168.1.30.
flow_send_vector_, vid = 0, is_layer2_if=0
```

The three packets shown in the debug flow basic output represent the TCP three-way handshake between Orion (192.168.4.10) and Andromeda (192.168.1.30) as Orion initiates an HTTP request to Andromeda, which can be parsed as follows:

1. The first line of debug output, ****** 09615.0: <Trust/bgroup0> packet received [48]******, marks the beginning of the first received packet, indicating the zone (Trust) and interface (bgroup0) on which the packet was received. Also, the [48] represents the size of the IP packet in bytes. Please note that this is the IP packet size, excluding the size of the Ethernet header.

   The ScreenOS gateway goes through a policy match process for the first packet, creates a session, and verbosely records a Got syn, 192.168.4.10(4519)->192.168.1.30(80) record in the debug.

2. The second packet, beginning with ****** 09615.0: <Secure_Servers/ethernet0/0> packet received [48]******, is another 48-byte IP packet received on the ethernet0/0 interface in zone Secure_Servers. The existing session found debug output confirms that this packet has been matched in the session table. The Got syn_ack, 192.168.1.30(80)->192.168.4.10(4519) debug record validates that the received packet has the TCP SYN-ACK flags set and represents the packet flow from the Andromeda server on TCP source port 80 to the Orion workstation on destination port 4519.

3. The third packet, beginning with ****** 09615.0: <Trust/bgroup0> packet received [40]******, is a 40-byte IP packet received on the bgroup0 interface, which matches the existing session ID of 4057. The Got ack, 192.168.4.10(4519)->192.168.1.30(80) debug record confirms that the final ACK in the three-way handshake has been received.

The subsequent debug output shows the actual HTTP get request from 192.168.4.10 and the HTTP response from 192.168.1.30:

```
****** 09615.0: <Trust/bgroup0> packet received [487]******
  ipid = 7832(1e98), @03041770
  packet passed sanity check.
  bgroup0:192.168.4.10/4519->192.168.1.30/80,6<Root>
  existing session found. sess token 4
  flow got session.
  flow session id 4057
  tcp seq check.
```

```
 post addr xlation: 192.168.4.10->192.168.1.30.
flow_send_vector_, vid = 0, is_layer2_if=0
****** 09615.0: <Secure_Servers/ethernet0/0> packet received [368]******
 ipid = 538(021a), @02f9a270
 packet passed sanity check.
 ethernet0/0:192.168.1.30/80->192.168.4.10/4519,6<Root>
 existing session found. sess token 26
 flow got session.
 flow session id 4057
 tcp seq check.
 post addr xlation: 192.168.1.30->192.168.4.10.
flow_send_vector_, vid = 0, is_layer2_if=0
****** 09615.0: <Trust/bgroup0> packet received [40]******
 ipid = 7835(1e9b), @03041f70
 packet passed sanity check.
 bgroup0:192.168.4.10/4519->192.168.1.30/80,6<Root>
 existing session found. sess token 4
 flow got session.
 flow session id 4057
 tcp seq check.
 post addr xlation: 192.168.4.10->192.168.1.30.
flow_send_vector_, vid = 0, is_layer2_if=0
Internal_fw->
```

The debug output, beginning with ****** 09615.0: <Trust/bgroup0> packet received [487]******, displays the ScreenOS processing of a 487-byte IP packet from Orion (192.168.4.10) to Andromeda (192.168.1.30). The packet matches the existing session id 4057, goes through a TCP sequence number check, and is then forwarded to the destination per the flow_send_vector. The Andromeda server responds back with the HTTP response with the web content in the 368-byte IP packet which, again, matches the existing session and is forwarded. Finally, Orion sends back the TCP ACK response packet that begins with ****** 09615.0: <Trust/bgroup0> packet received [40]******, which matches the session id 4057 and is forwarded out.

See Also

Recipe 7.17; Recipe 7.19

7.19 Configure a Packet Capture in ScreenOS

Problem

You want to capture and view packets as they traverse the ScreenOS gateway.

Solution

The snoop command enables packet captures on ScreenOS gateways. It captures packets to the debug buffer:

```
Internal_fw-> clear dbuf
Internal_fw-> snoop
```

```
Start Snoop, type ESC or 'snoop off' to stop, continue? [y]/n y
Internal_fw->
...<wait for a few seconds to capture the stream>
Internal_fw-> snoop off
Snoop off
Internal_fw->
```

Discussion

The ScreenOS snoop command is similar to snoop and tcpdump commands in the Unix world. It captures packets as they traverse the firewall, but unlike debug flow basic, it does not show the processing that the ScreenOS gateway performed on them.

Please note that for high-end, ASIC-based, high-throughput ScreenOS gateways such as the ISG-1000/2000 and the NS5200/5400, the output generated by snoop, just like the debug flow basic output, only displays the initial packets for a given flow until a full session table entry is generated. Once a full session table entry is set up on the high-end platforms, and the subsequent packets for that session flow are processed directly by the ASIC fast-path, snoop does not capture those packets. On the other hand, the snoop output on the lower-end SSG-5 through SSG-500 Series, and the NS-5GT, NS-25/50, NS-200, and NS-500 Series, shows all of the subsequent packets associated with the session flowing through the ScreenOS gateway.

Once the packets have been captured by running the snoop command as indicated, you can view the contents of the debug buffer:

```
Internal_fw-> get dbuf stream
01184.0: bgroup0(i) len=62:001125150ccd->0017cbe3f68b/0800
              192.168.4.10 -> 192.168.1.30/6
              vhl=45, tos=00, id=63151, frag=0000, ttl=128 tlen=48
              tcp:ports 4233->80, seq=3062152252, ack=0,
              flag=7002/SYN

01184.0: ethernet0/0(o) len=62:0017cbe3f680->0019b980c214/0800
              192.168.4.10 -> 192.168.1.30/6
              vhl=45, tos=00, id=63151, frag=0000, ttl=127 tlen=48
              tcp:ports 4233->80, seq=3062152252, ack=0,
              flag=7002/SYN

01184.0: ethernet0/0(i) len=62:0019b980c214->0017cbe3f680/0800
              192.168.1.30 -> 192.168.4.10/6
              vhl=45, tos=00, id=1789, frag=4000, ttl=128 tlen=48
              tcp:ports 80->4233, seq=2010013138, ack=3062152253,
              flag=7012/SYN/ACK

01184.0: bgroup0(o) len=62:0017cbe3f68b->001125150ccd/0800
              192.168.1.30 -> 192.168.4.10/6
              vhl=45, tos=00, id=1789, frag=4000, ttl=127 tlen=48
              tcp:ports 80->4233, seq=2010013138, ack=3062152253,
              flag=7012/SYN/ACK
```

```
01184.0: bgroup0(i) len=60:001125150ccd->0017cbe3f68b/0800
              192.168.4.10 -> 192.168.1.30/6
              vhl=45, tos=00, id=63152, frag=0000, ttl=128 tlen=40
              tcp:ports 4233->80, seq=3062152253, ack=2010013139,
              flag=5010/ACK

01184.0: ethernet0/0(o) len=54:0017cbe3f680->0019b980c214/0800
              192.168.4.10 -> 192.168.1.30/6
              vhl=45, tos=00, id=63152, frag=0000, ttl=127 tlen=40
              tcp:ports 4233->80, seq=3062152253, ack=2010013139,
              flag=5010/ACK
```

This snoop output shows the TCP three-way handshake for an HTTP connection request from Orion (192.168.4.10) to Andromeda (192.168.1.30) as discussed in the context of a debug flow basic capture in Recipe 7.18. Because the snoop command was executed without any filters, traffic from all interfaces is captured by snoop. Thus, as you can see in the output, the TCP SYN packet is seen in the first line of the capture, 01184.0: bgroup0(i) len=62:001125150ccd->0017cbe3f68b/0800, coming into the bgroup0 interface, represented by the (i). The captured packet in the snoop stream, 01184.0: ethernet0/0(o) len=62:0017cbe3f680->0019b980c214/0800, shows the same IP packet being forwarded out of the ethernet0/0 interface, represented by the (o) next to the interface name. As shown in the preceding code, the snoop output, unlike debug flow basic, dumps the raw contents of the packets. To review the various fields captured by snoop, we can examine the first packet output shown in the preceding code.

The first line of the packet, 01184.0: bgroup0(i) len=62:001125150ccd->0017cbe3f68b/080, shows the time of arrival of the packet, 1184, the interface, and the direction of the packet, coming into the bgroup0 interface, with an Ethernet frame size of 62 bytes, and the source and destination Ethernet MAC addresses.

The second line of the packet, 192.168.4.10 -> 192.168.1.30/6, shows the source and destination IP addresses and the IP number, 6, which represents TCP. An IP number of 17 would indicate UDP, whereas a 1 would indicate ICMP.

The third line of the packet, vhl=45, tos=00, id=63151, frag=0000, ttl=128 tlen=48, captures various elements of the IP header, as shown in Table 7-5.

Table 7-5. Elements of the IP header

IP header element/value	Description
vhl=45	IP version = 4, IP header length = 5 four-bit words (i.e., 20 bytes)
tos=00	Value of the 6-bit Type of Service (ToS)/Differentiated Services Code Point (DSCP) field
id=63151	Value of the IDENTIFICATION field in the IP header to help identify this packet in the event of fragmentation
Frag=0000	IP fragmentation offset; a value of 0 indicates no fragmentation

Table 7-5. Elements of the IP header (continued)

IP header element/value	Description
`ttl=128`	IP TTL for this packet; each gateway hop along the path to the destination typically decrements this value by 1
`Tlen=48`	Total length of the IP packet, including its payload and upper-layer protocols

The fourth line of the packet, `tcp:ports 4233->80, seq=3062152252, ack=0, flag=7002/SYN`, captures the elements of the TCP header, as shown in Table 7-6.

Table 7-6. Elements of the TCP header

TCP header element/value	Description
`tcp:ports 4233->80`	TCP stream; source port = 4233; destination port = 80
`seq=3062152252`	Initial TCP sequence number
`ack=0`	Initial TCP ACK number
`Flag=7002/SYN`	TCP flags: SYN is set on this TCP segment

When `snoop` is activated as in the output shown in this recipe's solution, it captures traffic from all the interfaces, which can quickly fill up the debug buffer. Thus, you can apply a wide range of filters to `snoop` to selectively capture data. Here is an example of a filter that limits the capture to the bidirectional communication between `192.168.4.10` and `192.168.1.30`:

```
Internal_fw-> snoop filter ip src-ip 192.168.4.10 dst-ip 192.168.1.30
direction both
snoop filter added
Internal_fw->
```

The debug buffer is carved out of the ScreenOS gateway's DRAM. You can increase its size from the default value by using the `set dbuf size <size_in_kbytes>` command:

```
Internal_fw-> set dbuf size 4096
```

You can filter output from the `dbuf` through the `include` or `exclude` matching command:

```
Internal_fw-> get dbuf stream | include 5018
              tcp:ports 4233->80, seq=3062152253, ack=2010013139,
              flag=5018/ACK
              tcp:ports 4233->80, seq=3062152253, ack=2010013139,
              flag=5018/ACK
              tcp:ports 80->4233, seq=2010013139, ack=3062152709,
              flag=5018/ACK
              tcp:ports 80->4233, seq=2010013139, ack=3062152709,
              flag=5018/ACK
Internal_fw->
```

Also, you can export the contents of the `dbuf` to a TFTP server. Please make sure you have a TFTP server running with the capability of accepting inbound files. The following command set sends the contents of the dbuf stream to a TFTP server running on the host 192.168.4.10:

```
Internal_fw-> get dbuf stream > tftp 192.168.4.10 snoop_capture
redirect to 192.168.4.10,snoop_capture
!!!!!!!!!!!!!!!!!!
tftp transferred records = 8
tftp success!
Internal_fw->
```

See Also

Recipe 7.17; Recipe 7.18

7.20 Determine Platform Limits on Address/Service Book Entries and Policies

Problem

You want to determine the maximum limit on the number of address/service book entries, address/service groups, and policies on your ScreenOS gateway.

Solution

You can determine the maximum number of address book, service book, address group, and service group entries, as well as the policies supported on your ScreenOS gateway, by using the get sys-cfg command and matching for the address, service, group, and policy keywords:

```
nsisg2000-> get sys-cfg | include "total max address book"
total max address book entries number: 20000
nsisg2000->
nsisg2000-> get sys-cfg | include "max custom service"
max custom service number: 2048
nsisg2000->
nsisg2000-> get sys-cfg | include "total max addr group"
total max addr group allowed number: 1024
nsisg2000->
nsisg2000-> get sys-cfg | include "max service groups"
max service groups number: 512
nsisg2000->
nsisg2000-> get sys-cfg | include "policy number"
policy number: 30000
nsisg2000->
```

Discussion

The address/service book maximum entry limits, address and service group limits, and maximum policy limits on the ScreenOS gateways vary across hardware platforms. Furthermore, newer releases of ScreenOS often increase these limits further.

In addition to the per-platform limits seen in this recipe's solution, there can be per-zone and per-VSYS limits on certain platforms that you can check with the `get sys-cfg` command as follows:

```
nsisg2000-> get sys-cfg | include "policy entries per vsys"
policy entries per vsys number: 15000
nsisg2000->
nsisg2000-> get sys-cfg | include "service entries per vsys"
service entries per vsys number: 1024
```

In addition to the `get sys-cfg` command discussed in the solution to this recipe, the `get license` command shows a number of system maximum capacity levels, including the maximum number of sessions that the ScreenOS gateway supports:

```
nsisg2000-> get license | include sessions
Sessions:            500064 sessions
nsisg2000->
```

Finally, in addition to ScreenOS policies, you can check the memory allocation for ACL rules on non-ASIC-based ScreenOS gateways such as the SSG Series and NS-5GT through NS-500 Series:

```
ssg5-serial-> get sys-cfg | include acl
acl rule mem size number: 16384
ssg5-serial->
```

On ASIC-based ScreenOS gateways, such as the ISG Series, you can check the total number of ASIC rules by looking for the `Total rules` number in the `get rms` output:

```
nsisg2000-> get rms
RMS internal information: - Saturn
Total sectors: 1019             available: 1019
Total rules: 65216  used: 0  avail: 65216
Ctx created:    0               sectors used: 0
nsisg2000->
```

See Also

This chapter's Introduction section

CHAPTER 8

Network Address Translation

8.0 Introduction

Network Address Translation (NAT) was developed as an interim strategy to address Transmission Control Protocol/Internet Protocol (TCP/IP) network address space depletion—one of the main drivers for the IPv6 protocol.

In 1994, K. Egevang and Paul Francis introduced NAT in RFC 1631. With NAT, it is possible to recycle address space—multiple hosts can use the same address space as long as they communicate over a unique address space. The Network Address Translator, a function within a router (or a firewall with routing capability) would perform the translation to the unique address space, usually on the border between the private portion of a network and the public Internet. In 1994, a "recyclable" address space was defined in RFC 1597, and was obsoleted by RFC 1918 in 1996. Dedicated for private use were one Class A network within 10/8, 16 Class B networks within 172.16/12, and 255 Class C networks within 192.168/16.

NAT is not just a method for fighting address space depletion. It was also quickly adopted by security engineers, who liked the idea that thousands of hosts were able to hide behind a single IP address by using NAT with Port Address Translation (PAT). This helps prevent simple port scanning and other attack techniques on those hosts, but you should not consider it as anything but a part of an overall security strategy.

There is another use for NAT that the inventors of NAT did not initially consider: the likelihood that two enterprises are using the same RFC 1918 address space. Instead of renaming hundreds or thousands of hosts, mutual address translation can help to solve this problem, at least temporarily, until hosts can be renumbered.

NAT Elements in ScreenOS

Although most firewall administrators are familiar with NAT, one particularly confusing issue is the meaning of the terms source and destination. A stateful firewall keeps state, as its name implies, which can be defined as the conditional status of the connection. This is well defined in TCP utilizing TCP flags, sequence numbers, and such; it is derived or observed for other Internet protocols such as the User Datagram Protocol (UDP). State is kept stored in a session table, which in turn keeps track of a flow. A flow is defined as traffic from a client to a server as well as traffic returning from the server to the client; therefore, a flow has two branches. So, when the server's IP is `1.1.1.100`, this is the destination address for the branch from the client to the server, *and* it is the source address on the return path from the server to the client. In the world of stateful firewalls, we do not worry about the return path, as the firewall is figuring that out. NAT will work properly only if each branch of the flow goes through the same device. For example:

```
id 4032/s**,vsys 0,flag 08000000/8000/1001,policy 1,time 29, dip 0 module 0
 if 2(nspflag 801a01):192.168.1.100/1024->1.1.1.100/80,6,000d60c5761b,
sess token 4,vlan 0,tun 0,vsd 0,route 1
 if 1(nspflag 801a00):192.168.1.100/1024<-1.1.1.100/80,6,00135f05e105,
sess token 6,vlan 0,tun 0,vsd 0,route 132
```

In the preceding code, client `192.168.1.100` sends traffic from port 1024 to server `1.1.1.100` on port 80, and the server answers with the exact mirror from IP `1.1.1.100` on port 80 to the client `192.168.1.100` on port 1024. The protocol number is 6, which is TCP. So, when we talk about source and destination for translation, we are talking about the initiating branch of the flow. The source address would be `192.168.1.100` and the destination address would be `1.1.1.100`. The source port would be 1024 and the destination port would be 80.

Source ports are almost always randomly chosen and ≥ 1024. While on the Internet, the source address could also be chosen out of a pool or a cluster of addresses. On the other hand, destination ports and addresses must be static and deterministic because this is where the client connects. The logic behind this is *where traffic comes from* is not as important as *where traffic goes*, in particular on the public Internet. Clients are usually anonymous, whereas servers need to be well known to be reachable. Therefore, the destination needs to be deterministic.

Table 8-1 shows that you match on the private portion and you translate to the public portion. In other words, you match on `src-ip` and `dst-ip` and in the service portion you match on `src-port` and `dst-port`. Each component can be translated.

Table 8-1. NAT terminology

Private or local portion				Public or global portion			
src-ip	dst-ip	src-port	dst-port	x-src-ip	x-dst-ip	x-src-port	x-dst-port

In ScreenOS, the different NAT elements are dynamic IP (DIP), mapped IP (MIP), virtual IP (VIP), and policy NAT-SRC and NAT-DST, as well as the legacy NAT mode. Before we dive deep into each NAT element, we will briefly explain what they are good for.

A DIP performs a source translation of the address and the port on the egress interface. The most common use for a DIP is to port-address-translate internal clients onto one public IP address. DIP and policy NAT-SRC are synonymous. DIPs are configured on an interface and in a policy.

A MIP is a bidirectional translation. It is applied as ingress and egress. A MIP is configured on an interface, and needs to be referenced in a policy for ingress traffic. It is automatically implied in an egress policy. *Bidirectional* means that it does both a source and a destination translation, depending on the *initiating direction* of a flow. MIPs do not support port translation. The most common use for a MIP is to translate a DMZ server to a public IP address.

A VIP is a port destination translation on the ingress interface. It is one way to perform "port forwarding" in ScreenOS. It is more or less the reverse of a DIP, with the exception that VIP translations are always static, whereas DIPs are commonly dynamic. Static means that *IP Address A* or *Port A* is always translated to *IP Address B* or *Port B*. In a dynamic translation, the target translation is chosen from a range of values. A VIP can translate both the IP address and the port. The most common use for a VIP is to map several DMZ intranet servers to a single public IP address on very small firewalls.

We already discussed that policy NAT-SRC is a synonym for DIP. On the other hand, policy NAT-DST was thought to be the successor to MIPs and VIPs. In contrast to a MIP, policy NAT-DST is unidirectional. Therefore, policy NAT-DST is more often used to replace a VIP than a MIP. Policy NAT-DST does address and port translation.

NAT mode is a legacy mode and has been largely replaced by the much more powerful DIPs. Although simple to implement, you should use it only on smaller, dual-interface firewalls.

NAT operations are supported in route mode but not in transparent mode, at least as of ScreenOS 6.1. Table 8-2 shows a summary of NAT methods.

Table 8-2. Summary of NAT methods

Method	Direction	Scope	src-ip	dst-ip	src-port	dst-port
MIP	Outbound	Network	Static			
MIP	Inbound	Network		Static		
NAT-DST	Inbound	Network		Static		Static
VIP	Inbound	Host		Static		Static
DIP dynamic	Outbound	Host	Static		Dynamic	
NAT mode	Outbound	Host	Static		Dynamic	
DIP pool dynamic	Outbound	Range	Dynamic		Dynamic	
DIP fixed	Outbound	Host	Static			

Table 8-2. Summary of NAT methods (continued)

Method	Direction	Scope	src-ip	dst-ip	src-port	dst-port
DIP pool fixed	Outbound	Range	Dynamic			
DIP pool dynamic sticky	Outbound	Range	Dynamic, static per source		Dynamic	
DIP pool fixed sticky	Outbound	Range	Static random			
DIP shift	Outbound	Range	Static			
DIP dynamic inbound	Outbound	Host	Static		Dynamic	
DIP dynamic inbound	Inbound	Host		Static		Application layer gateways (ALGs)

Intelligent Translation

NAT can refer to both IP address translation and PAT, and in practice, PAT usually also involves IP address translation. Both transport layer protocols, UDP and TCP, utilize the concept of ports to connect applications via sockets to the network. NAT applies to the network layer, and therefore, you can use it with all transport layer protocols, including the Encapsulating Security Protocol (ESP). PAT, on the other hand, applies only to UDP and TCP. Does this mean we cannot use PAT with other protocols such as Generic Routing Encapsulation (GRE)? In general, the answer is "yes" for most NAT routers, but the answer is "it depends" for ScreenOS.

ScreenOS has application intelligence implemented via ALGs for many protocols. Instead of a portmap, the firewall may use the Call ID field in the GREv1 header as used by the Point-to-Point Tunneling Protocol (PPTP), or it may use the Security Parameters Index (SPI) field in the ESP header when multiplexing sessions with dynamic source port translation. Luckily, the use of other Layer 4 protocols is rare.

ALGs can also be useful for TCP and UDP traffic where the return branch is not an exact mirror of the initiating branch. Some applications, such as File Transfer Protocol (FTP) applications, have separate control and data channels, so while the client initiates the control channel to the server, the server may initiate a data channel to the client. Address and port information is communicated within the application. An ALG would tap into this connection and perform the correct translation deep in the application layer of the traffic stream. The ALG would reassemble packets, both whole and fragmented, into one data stream, and it would search for the right information and replace it in real time with the translation. All of this works in the background and makes the firewall work seamlessly with applications, which, in general, are not compatible with NAT or PAT. However, most of the applications that are commonly used on the Internet are NAT- or PAT-compatible.

Integration of the Rule Base and NAT

NAT is one of the more complex elements to understand—not to configure—on ScreenOS. One reason for this is the way ScreenOS was developed; another is that ScreenOS is a dedicated security appliance that tightly interweaves security, routing, and switching.

One important difference between a router and a security appliance is that a router typically makes forwarding decisions for each packet, commonly only on the destination IP, whereas a security appliance makes one forwarding decision per flow. A flow is typically defined by source and destination IP addresses, as well as protocol source and destination ports, and its return path.

In ScreenOS, you can apply NAT on an interface, in a policy, or both. Both ingress and egress NATs exist. Egress NATs will be applied when a packet exits the firewall and ingress NATs will be applied when a packet enters the firewall. In ScreenOS, an egress NAT is always a source translation, whereas an ingress NAT is always a destination translation.

ScreenOS uses only two tables: a route lookup table and a rule lookup table. Rule lookup, NAT, and Quality of Service (QoS) are performed in the same rule in the policy table. Some other vendors use a different table for all three. Route lookup determines the ingress and egress interfaces and, therefore, the source and destination zones. Then ScreenOS performs a lookup on the rules that apply to that particular combination of zones. A match is performed on the source IP, destination IP, and service for the first packet of a flow. If a matching rule is found, everything in that rule will be applied.

With NAT, ScreenOS checks the rule to see whether the traffic is permitted or denied. If it is permitted, first ingress NAT is applied, and then egress NAT. Optionally, QoS can be applied as well. Unlike packet forwarders, flow forwarders apply a rule to both branches of a connection automatically: from the client to the server, and then from the return traffic from the server to the client (a packet forwarder would have its own set of rules for both branches).

When we talk about bidirectional application of a rule set in a packet forwarder, we're talking about application to both branches of one flow. But when we talk about bidirectional application of a rule set in a flow forwarder, we're talking about application from Host A to Host B and the return traffic for the same flow, as well as for a second connection, from Host B to Host A and its return traffic. These are two flows with four branches. In this case, Host A and Host B could be both client and server—for instance, a server for web browser clients, and a client, say, when it downloads a software patch from an FTP server.

8.1 Configure Hide NAT

Problem

You want to hide a private network behind a public IP address.

Solution

Configure a DIP on the egress interface and reference the DIP in a policy:

```
set interface ethernet0/0 zone Untrust
set interface ethernet0/0 ip 1.1.1.100/24
set interface ethernet0/0 dip 4 1.1.1.1
```

Link the DIP to the policy:

```
set policy from Trust to Untrust any any any nat src dip-id 4 permit
```

Discussion

The most common use for a DIP is to translate multiple inside hosts to a single public IP address. It's similar to NAT mode, but it allows more complex mappings—in particular, to addresses other than that of the egress interface. DIP also allows PAT on any interface (also called *policy NAT-SRC*). In Table 8-3 you can see the hide NAT translation being configured in the preceding code.

Table 8-3. Hide NAT translation

Private or local portion				Public or global portion			
src-ip	dst-ip	src-port	dst-port	x-src-ip	x-dst-ip	x-src-port	x-dst-port
Any	Any	Any	Any	1.1.1.1	Original	≥ 1024	Original

A DIP represents the global portion of a source address translation. It is applied to the egress interface and is invoked within a policy:

```
set interface ethernet0/0 zone Untrust
set interface ethernet0/0 ip 1.1.1.100/24
set interface ethernet0/0 dip 4 1.1.1.1

set policy from Trust to Untrust any any any nat src dip-id 4 permit
```

DIP `ID 4` and higher are custom-configurable. DIP `ID 2` always refers to the IP address of the egress interface. (DIP `ID 1` and DIP `ID 3` are legacy values that are no longer used.)

If no DIP ID is configured within a policy, `ID 2` is implied, and is a placeholder for the egress IP of any interface in any zone. This is similar to NAT mode.

```
set policy from Trust to Untrust any any any nat permit
```

Potentially, tens of thousands of sessions (or, with ScreenOS tracking, even hundreds of thousands) could be multiplexed over one public IP address—in this case, the hide NAT IP address `1.1.1.1`. In dynamic PAT mode, any source port would be translated, starting with port 1024 and counting up. For most applications, the source port does not matter.

If your hide NAT IP is in a different network from the interface on which the DIP lives, you need to configure an extended DIP. With an extended DIP you configure a pseudo IP on the interface so that the DIP is actually in the network with the interface:

```
set interface ethernet0/0 zone Untrust
set interface ethernet0/0 ip 2.2.2.100/24
set interface ethernet0/0 ext ip 1.1.1.1/32 dip 4 1.1.1.1

set policy from Trust to Untrust any any any nat src dip-id 4 permit
```

However, with an extended DIP, routing from the neighboring device needs to be observed. The firewall would answer an Address Resolution Protocol (ARP) request from a DIP within the same network, but not for an extended DIP because this would make no sense. In the preceding output, the neighboring router with the interface IP address of `2.2.2.200`, for example, needs to route to `2.2.2.100` for the network `1.1.1.0/24` to hit the `1.1.1.1` DIP.

8.2 Configure Hide NAT with VoIP

Problem

You want to have Voice over IP (VoIP) phones behind the firewall with hide NAT configured.

Solution

Configure the DIP for hide NAT and to accept incoming VoIP calls:

```
set int e0/1 dip 4 1.1.1.100 incoming
```

Configure outbound and inbound policies:

```
set policy from Trust to Untrust any any SIP nat dip-id 4 permit
set policy from Untrust to Trust any DIP(1.1.1.100) SIP permit
```

Discussion

The problem with VoIP phones is that they need inbound and outbound connectivity because calls can be made from and to a phone. Because there may be many phones or not enough public IP addresses, it is not feasible to configure a static destination translation for each phone. Unfortunately, protocols capable of solving such a dilemma, such as the STUN protocol, are generally not compatible with stateful firewalls because they are exploiting a security weakness in simple NAT devices to open inbound pinholes. Table 8-4 details the hide NAT translation configured with the `inbound` feature. You can see the two flows for outbound and inbound calls, with the second row being an inbound call. Notice that although hide NAT was configured (all phones hide behind the same IP of `1.1.1.100`) the firewall translates to the correct internal phone, in this case `192.168.1.1`.

Table 8-4. Hide NAT incoming

Private or local portion				Public or global portion			
src-ip	dst-ip	src-port	dst-port	x-src-ip	x-dst-ip	x-src-port	x-dst-port
Any	Any	Any	5060	1.1.1.100	Original	≥ 1024	Original
Any	1.1.1.100	Any	5060	Original	192.168.1.1	Original	Original

In ScreenOS, application intelligence is built into the VoIP ALGs for the Session Initiation Protocol (SIP) and H.323, facilitating translation from the shared hide NAT address to the right internal phone. The ALG dynamically records phone IP addresses as it monitors initial REGISTER messages sent by internal phones to the SIP registrar. This information is used later for the reverse connection.

You can enable this feature by configuring an incoming DIP:

```
set int e0/1 dip 4 1.1.1.100 incoming

set policy from Trust to Untrust any any SIP nat dip-id 4 permit
set policy from Untrust to Trust any DIP(1.1.1.100) SIP permit
```

Alternatively, to configure a DIP you can use the IP of the interface instead:

```
set int e0/1 dip interface-ip incoming
```

The name of the DIP in the policy is `DIP(<public IP>)`; if the implicit DIP `ID 2` is being referenced, hence the interface's IP address itself, the syntax is `DIP(<interface>)`.

```
set policy from Trust to Untrust any any SIP nat permit
set policy from Untrust to Trust any DIP(ethernet0/0) SIP permit
```

8.3 Configure Static Source NAT

Problem

You want to configure a static (as opposed to a hide) source translation.

Solution

Configure a DIP on the egress interface and reference the DIP with the `fix-port` option:

```
set interface ethernet0/0 zone Untrust
set interface ethernet0/0 ip 1.1.1.100/24
set interface ethernet0/0 dip 4 1.1.1.1 fix-port
```

Reference the DIP in the policy:

```
set policy from Trust to Untrust any any any nat src dip-id 4 permit
```

Discussion

Static address translation is often used in combination with policy NAT-DST (see Recipe 8.6). Notice that MIP also performs static address translation, which combines the function of a DIP (a NAT-SRC) and a NAT-DST. Table 8-5 details the static source NAT translation (the difference between Table 8-5 and Table 8-3 is that `x-src-port` is not being translated in Table 8-5).

Table 8-5. Static source NAT translation

Private or local portion				Public or global portion			
src-ip	dst-ip	src-port	dst-port	x-src-ip	x-dst-ip	x-src-port	x-dst-port
Any	Any	Any	Any	1.1.1.1	Original	Original	Original

You configure static source NAT translation by adding the `fix-port` keyword to the DIP. The rest of the configuration is similar to hide NAT (see Recipe 8.1):

```
set interface ethernet0/0 dip 4 1.1.1.1 fix-port

set policy from Trust to Untrust any any any nat src dip-id 4 permit
```

8.4 Configure Source NAT Pools

Problem

You want to configure a pool of addresses for source address translation.

Solution

Configure the DIP pool and switch off hide NAT:

```
set interface ethernet0/0 zone Untrust
set interface ethernet0/0 ip 1.1.1.100/24
set interface ethernet0/0 dip 4 1.1.1.1 1.1.1.99 fix-port
```

Configure the sticky allocation of IPs from the pool, and switch on pool allocation warnings:

```
set dip sticky
set dip alarm-raise 90 alarm-clear 80
```

Link the DIP to a policy:

```
set policy from Trust to Untrust any any any nat src dip-id 4 permit
```

Discussion

Although most protocols used today on the Internet are compatible with PAT, some external and many internal protocols are not. ScreenOS features application intelligence for many of the common protocols, such as FTP, SIP, MS-RPC (Remote Procedure Call), and Internet Key Exchange (IKE). ALGs look deep into the communication and replace translated IP addresses and port information within the application layer with the translated address. ALGs are switched on by default, and if they are invoked by a flow, they are listed in the session on the top, under `application ID`. Note that not all ALGs exist to solve problems with NAT. For applications that are not compatible with hide NAT, you need to configure static source translation.

In such cases, it is cumbersome and may even be impossible to configure a DIP for each host. Instead, you can configure a DIP pool. As you are configuring a DIP pool because your applications are not compatible with hide NAT, you need to switch hide NAT off with the `fix-port` option:

```
set interface ethernet0/0 dip 4 1.1.1.1 1.1.1.99 fix-port
```

Table 8-6 details the source pool translation. Source addresses are translated to a pool of public IP addresses, but the source port is usually not translated.

Table 8-6. Source NAT pool translation

Private or local portion				**Public or global portion**			
src-ip	**dst-ip**	**src-port**	**dst-port**	**x-src-ip**	**x-dst-ip**	**x-src-port**	**x-dst-port**
Any	Any	Any	Any	Pool	Original	Original	Original

An inside host may spawn multiple sessions to the same server. The application may break when the host is translated to a different address for each session. You have to configure ScreenOS so that the same host is always translated to the same IP from the pool:

```
set dip sticky
```

With a DIP pool, each inside host connecting to the outside will reserve one IP in the pool for as long as a session is active. If all addresses from the DIP pool are exhausted, no further connections can be made (this can happen during virus activity, for example). In this case, you configure ScreenOS to send a log or trap when the pool reaches 90 percent (event log type 00102), and send a clear signal (event log type 00103) when the pool has 80 percent free resources again:

```
set dip alarm-raise 90 alarm-clear 80
```

The final step is to link the pool to the policy:

```
set policy from Trust to Untrust any any any nat src dip-id 4 permit
```

A DIP pool can span up to 10 /24 networks, but note that DIP pools cannot overlap with each other, the interface IP, or the pseudo ext-interface IP. With ScreenOS 6.1 and later, it is also possible to configure up to three noncontiguous subnets in the pool.

8.5 Link Multiple DIPs to the Same Policy

Problem

You need to configure multiple DIPs and you want to link them all to the same policy.

Solution

Configure the DIP or DIP pools:

```
set interface ethernet0/0 zone Untrust
set interface ethernet0/0 ip 1.1.1.100/24
set interface ethernet0/1 zone Untrust
set interface ethernet0/1 ip 2.2.2.100/24

set interface ethernet0/0 dip 4 1.1.1.1
set interface ethernet0/1 dip 5 2.2.2.2
```

Group the DIP into a DIP group:

```
set dip group 6 member 4
set dip group 6 member 5
```

Link the DIP group to a policy:

```
set policy from Trust to Untrust any any any nat src dip-id 6 permit
```

Discussion

You may want to configure multiple DIPs in the same policy. One reason you may want to do this it that you have redundant egress interfaces, and dynamic routing decides which interface to use, so you configure a DIP for each redundant interface. Another reason is that you want to configure two DIP pools and link them to the same policy because, for instance, DIP pool addressing is not contiguous.

Unfortunately, you can link only one DIP ID to a policy. The solution is to configure a DIP group and link the DIP group to the policy instead:

```
set interface ethernet0/0 zone Untrust
set interface ethernet0/0 ip 1.1.1.100/24
set interface ethernet0/1 zone Untrust
set interface ethernet0/1 ip 2.2.2.100/24

set interface ethernet0/0 dip 4 1.1.1.1
set interface ethernet0/1 dip 5 2.2.2.2
```

```
set dip group 6 member 4
set dip group 6 member 5

set policy from Trust to Untrust any any any nat src dip-id 6 permit
```

8.6 Configure Destination NAT

Problem

You want to configure destination NAT for an internal server.

Solution

Configure the address object for the public address:

```
set address trust server-pub 1.1.1.100/32
```

Configure a route for the public address to point in the direction of the private address:

```
set interface ethernet0/0 zone trust
set route 1.1.1.100/32 int e0/0
```

Configure the destination translation within a policy:

```
set policy from untrust to trust any server-pub any nat dst ip 192.168.1.100 permit
```

Discussion

Policy NAT-DST was introduced with ScreenOS 5.0. It was designed to replace MIP and VIP. A very common reason why policy NAT-DST is preferred over a MIP is because a MIP supports a public address in a different network than that of the ingress interface only if the ingress interface is in the `Untrust` zone. On all other zones, MIPs must be in the same network with the IP address of the interface on which they live. This limitation was lifted in ScreenOS 6.1. NAT-DST is not tied to an interface, and therefore, there is no such limitation. However, because MIP is so easy to understand and configure, NAT-DST is most often used for VIP-style configurations (see Recipe 8.7) or very controlled translations such as conditional translation (see Recipe 8.13). A policy NAT-DST is a static destination translation. The IP address, or the port, or both, can be translated.

Table 8-7 shows the destination NAT translation configuration.

Table 8-7. Destination NAT translation

Private or local portion				Public or global portion			
src-ip	dst-ip	src-port	dst-port	x-src-ip	x-dst-ip	x-src-port	x-dst-port
Any	1.1.1.100	Any	Any	Original	192.168.1.100	Original	Original

First, you need to configure an address object for the public portion of the translation:

```
set address trust server-pub 1.1.1.100/32
```

Then, you need to route the public IP address toward the private IP, typically toward the `Trust` interface. This is important because NAT happens only after the policy check passes, and first the incoming packet needs to match a policy. Once this happens, the destination address of the packet is translated, and another route lookup for the private address follows. This is why the route for the public address does not have a gateway configured.

```
set interface ethernet0/0 zone trust
set route 192.168.1.0/24 int e0/0 gateway 10.10.10.1
set route 1.1.1.100/32 int e0/0
```

Unlike with all the other NAT elements, there is no configuration on the interface. The configuration happens within the policy only. The client connects from the source zone; the server is located in the destination zone.

```
set policy from untrust to trust any server-pub any nat dst ip 192.168.1.100 permit
```

The preceding code will translate the server from its public IP address of `1.1.1.100` to the private IP address of `192.168.1.100`.

This essentially explains how a policy goes from the zone where the client is located to the zone where the server is located. A route for the public portion of the server has to follow to the zone where the server is located. There is one exception to this rule. When the public address of the server is in the same network with the IP of the ingress interface, you can optionally install an intra-zone policy. This policy would go from the zone where the public address is located to the same zone. In this case, no route for the public address of the server is necessary because it automatically matches the network of the ingress interface. Here is a sample configuration in which the public address of the server is in the same network as the IP of the ingress interface:

```
set interface ethernet0/0 zone trust
set interface ethernet0/1 zone untrust
set interface ethernet0/1 ip 1.1.1.2/24

set arp nat-dst

set address untrust server-pub 1.1.1.100/32

set policy from untrust to untrust any server-pub any nat dst ip 192.168.1.100 permit
```

In the preceding configuration, the client is sitting behind the `Untrust` zone, but the server sits behind the `Trust` zone. The public IP address of `1.1.1.100` is in the same network with the IP of `1.1.1.2/24` on ingress interface `e0/1`. A route lookup of `1.1.1.100` naturally would point back to the `Untrust` zone. Notice the use of an additional command, `set arp nat-dst`. This command turns on ARP replies for `1.1.1.100`.

Unlike with DIPs, MIPs, and VIPs, the firewall would not answer ARP requests for policy NAT-DST by default. In many cases, policy NAT-DST is used with public IP addresses, which are not in the same interface as the ingress interface. In this case, the neighboring router would not need ARP, but would need a route to the ingress interface.

8.7 Configure Destination PAT

Problem

You want to configure a destination PAT.

Solution

You can configure this with a VIP:

```
set interface ethernet0/1 zone Untrust
set interface ethernet0/1 ip 1.1.1.1/29

set service http-inst-a protocol tcp src 1024-65535 dst 8080-8080
set service http-inst-b protocol tcp src 1024-65535 dst 8081-8081
set interface ethernet0/1 vip 1.1.1.2 80 http-inst-a 192.168.1.100
set interface ethernet0/1 vip 1.1.1.3 80 http-inst-b 192.168.1.100

set policy id 1 from untrust to dmz any vip(1.1.1.2) http permit
set policy id 1
   set dst-address vip(1.1.1.3)
exit
```

Or, you can configure it with policy NAT-DST:

```
set interface ethernet0/0 zone trust
set arp NAT-DST
set address untrust server-a-pub 1.1.1.2/32
set address untrust server-b-pub 1.1.1.3/32

set policy from untrust to untrust any server-a-pub http nat dst ip
192.168.1.100 port 8080 permit
set policy from untrust to untrust any server-b-pub http nat dst ip
192.168.1.100 port 8081 permit
```

Discussion

This shows how to translate port 80 on two different public IP addresses to two different daemon instances of the same internal server. The daemons are listening in port 8080 and port 8081. Basically, you have two web servers running on the same physical server, reachable via two different IP addresses. Table 8-8 details the destination PAT translation configuration.

Table 8-8. Destination PAT translation

Private or local portion				Public or global portion			
src-ip	dst-ip	src-port	dst-port	x-src-ip	x-dst-ip	x-src-port	x-dst-port
Any	1.1.1.2	Any	80	Original	192.168.1.100	Original	8080
Any	1.1.1.3	Any	80	Original	192.168.1.100	Original	8081

The original way to configure this was via a VIP. The new way to configure this is with policy NAT-DST. This example assumes that the public IPs are in the same network with the IP of the ingress interface, which is a requirement for a VIP but not for policy NAT-DST, as previously mentioned.

VIPs come with many caveats. The most important is that VIPs before ScreenOS 6.1 can exist only on interfaces in the `Untrust` zone and must be in the same network with that interface. Policy NAT-DST offers much greater flexibility. But what a VIP can do and policy NAT-DST cannot do is to use the firewall's own public IP address for translation:

```
set admin port 8080
set interface ethernet0/0 zone Untrust
set interface ethernet0/0 ip 1.1.1.1/29
set interface ethernet0/0 vip untrust-ip 80 "HTTP" 192.168.2.100

set policy id 1 from untrust to trust any vip(ethernet0/0) HTTP permit
```

In ScreenOS 6.1 and later, the syntax changed because VIPs are now supported on interfaces in any zone:

```
set interface ethernet0/0 vip interface-ip 80 "HTTP" 192.168.2.100
```

Notice that the firewall also listens on port 80 for the WebUI and that this port needed to be moved. You can move all default sockets on the firewall:

```
set admin port <port>
set ssl port <port>
set admin telnet port <port>
set admin ssh port <port>
unset alg sip enable
```

Also note that when you want to translate many contiguous ports, such as the reverse-Telnet ports of a terminal server, a VIP has the `multi-port` feature, whereas policy NAT-DST does not. You would have to write a rule for each translated port with policy NAT-DST:

```
set vip multi-port
```

With both methods, you can perform many different combinations of translations between port and address translation. You can hide several servers behind a single global address, and you can simulate two servers on the public side and translate them to the same server on the local side, as shown earlier. You can even translate different global addresses to the same socket on the same server, which is sometimes done during server migrations.

8.8 Configure Bidirectional NAT for DMZ Servers

Problem

You want to allow a DMZ server inside the firewall full access to the Internet and any outside host access to a web server inside the firewall on the Trust zone.

Solution

Configure a MIP on the Untrust interface:

```
set interface ethernet0/0 zone Untrust
set interface ethernet0/0 ip 1.1.1.100/24
set interface ethernet0/0 mip 1.1.1.50 host 192.168.1.50
```

Configure inbound and outbound policies:

```
set address trust host-a-prv 192.168.1.50/32

set policy id 1 from Untrust to Trust any MIP(1.1.1.50) http permit
set policy id 2 from Trust to Untrust host-a-prv any any permit
```

Discussion

MIP is the most used NAT element in ScreenOS, more so than any other method. That's because a MIP is straightforward to configure and easy to understand. A MIP is a one-to-one, bidirectional, static network address translation. It does not matter if the external host or the local host initiated the connection. The external host's public IP address is mapped to a private IP address (or the other way around) and the ports remain the same (see Table 8-9).

Table 8-9. Bidirectional NAT translation

Private or local portion				Public or global portion			
src-ip	dst-ip	src-port	dst-port	x-src-ip	x-dst-ip	x-src-port	x-dst-port
Any	1.1.1.50	Any	Any	Original	192.168.1.50	Original	Original
192.168.1.50	Any	Any	Any	1.1.1.50	Original	Original	Original

This is easier because you do not have to worry whether the application is compatible with PAT. However, you need to make sure you have enough public IP address space.

First, configure the MIP:

```
set interface ethernet0/0 zone Untrust
set interface ethernet0/0 ip 1.1.1.100/24
set interface ethernet0/0 mip 1.1.1.50 host 192.168.1.50
```

The first policy performs an inbound destination translation, while the second policy performs an outbound source translation.

```
set policy id 1 from Untrust to Trust any MIP(1.1.1.50) http permit

set address trust host-a-prv 192.168.1.50/32
set policy id 2 from Trust to Untrust host-a-prv any any permit
```

MIPs are usually used for destination address translation. A MIP is always configured on the ingress interface. Here, for instance, `e0/0` is an `Untrust` interface and `1.1.1.50` is a public IP address. `1.1.1.50` is translated to `192.168.1.50`. The MIP itself is referenced in the policy, with `Untrust` being the source zone because the MIP was installed on an interface in the `Untrust` zone. The destination zone specified in the policy does not matter because a MIP always lives in the `Global` zone. The best practice is to use the zone behind which the private IP of the server lives, if possible.

As of ScreenOS 5.3, you can use MIPs in a multicell policy, and on those zones, multicell is not supported in the `Global` zone.

A MIP is bidirectional and always takes precedence over a DIP.

Before ScreenOS 6.1, MIPs could be in a different network from the interface's IP only on an interface in the `Untrust` zone. (This is an important caveat, but it is the only caveat regarding MIPs.) You can configure a MIP that is in the same network with its interface on any interface in any zone. MIPs are most often used on the `Untrust` zone. If you need to perform destination translation to an IP that is not in the same network as the ingress interface, use a policy NAT-DST translation (see Recipe 8.6) in combination with a DIP (see Recipe 8.3) if the reverse connection is desired as well.

8.9 Configure Static Bidirectional NAT with Multiple VRs

Problem

You want to configure static address translation with multiple Virtual Routers (VRs). Such a design is also typical with Virtual System (VSYS; see Chapter 22).

Solution

You configure all MIPs on the same `Untrust` interface, but specify different target VRs:

```
set interface ethernet0/0 mip 1.1.1.50 host 192.168.1.50 vr cage-a-vr
set interface ethernet0/0 mip 1.1.1.51 host 192.168.1.50 vr cage-b-vr
```

Then, you link the MIP to policies:

```
set policy from Untrust to cage-a Any MIP(1.1.1.50) any permit
set policy from Untrust to cage-b Any MIP(1.1.1.51) any permit
```

Discussion

A VR is nothing more than a routing table. With other OSs, a VR is also often called a virtual route forwarding (VRF) instance. Because firewalls are often used as central protection devices for large data centers, ScreenOS has a user interface abstraction, called *VSYS*. A VSYS simulates a logical firewall on the user interface, and it will usually be configured with a VR. Several different VRs are also often used outside of VSYS to insulate routing domains.

Let's consider a case where you have two cages in a collocation center that use the same IP address space of `192.168.1.0/24`. Both share the same Internet connection through the same firewall. Both have web servers in their cages, with the need for a translation to a public IP address.

```
set interface ethernet0/0 zone Untrust
set interface ethernet0/0 ip 1.1.1.100/24
set zone cage-a vr cage-a-vr
set interface ethernet0/1 zone cage-a
set interface ethernet0/1 ip 192.168.1.1/24
set zone cage-b vr cage-b-vr
set interface ethernet0/2 zone cage-b
set interface ethernet0/2 ip 192.168.1.1/24

set interface ethernet0/0 mip 1.1.1.50 host 192.168.1.50 vr cage-a-vr
set interface ethernet0/0 mip 1.1.1.51 host 192.168.1.50 vr cage-b-vr
set policy from Untrust to cage-a Any MIP(1.1.1.50) any permit
set policy from Untrust to cage-b Any MIP(1.1.1.51) any permit
```

Two public IP addresses are translated to the same network of `192.168.1.0/24`; however, the network lives on two different interfaces. In addition, the two servers even have the same private IP address. The `vrouter` option helps to keep them apart. It says in which VR the private portion of the MIP should be sought. In our example, `MIP(1.1.1.50)`, the private IP, is routed in VR `cage-a-vr` and the `MIP(1.1.1.51)` private IP is routed in VR `cage-b-vr`. The default VR is the `trust-vr`, unless configured differently. All zones are in the `trust-vr` by default. Note that you must disable `auto-route-export` in the individual VRs if you use the `untrust-vr` in this model, as `auto-route-export` would export all routes into the `untrust-vr` automatically, and this could cause a conflict.

See Also

Recipe 8.8

8.10 Configure Source Shift Translation

Problem

You want to do a source translation for a range of IPs.

Solution

Configure a DIP shift:

```
set interface ethernet0/1 zone Untrust
set interface ethernet0/1 ip 10.10.20.1/24
set interface ethernet0/1 dip 4 shift-from 192.168.1.50 to 10.10.20.50 10.10.20.150
```

Link the DIP shift to a policy:

```
set policy from Trust to Untrust any any any nat src dip-id 4 permit
```

Discussion

You may want to perform a source translation from one network to another to avoid IP address conflicts between extranet partners. The solution is to configure a DIP shift. Table 8-10 details the source shift translation configuration.

Table 8-10. Source shift translation

Private or local portion				Public or global portion			
src-ip	dst-ip	src-port	dst-port	x-src-ip	x-dst-ip	x-src-port	x-dst-port
192.168.1.50	Any	Any	Any	10.10.20.50	Original	Original	Original
192.168.1.51	Any	Any	Any	10.10.20.51	Original	Original	Original
[...]	Any	Any	Any	[...]	Original	Original	Original
192.168.1.150	Any	Any	Any	10.10.20.150	Original	Original	Original

Any address starting from `192.168.1.50` and continuing to `192.168.1.150` would be translated to an address in the range of `10.10.20.50`–`10.10.20.150`. So, `192.168.1.50` would be translated to `10.10.20.50`, `192.168.20.51` would be translated to `10.10.20.51`, and so on.

```
set interface ethernet0/1 zone Untrust
set interface ethernet0/1 ip 10.10.20.1/24
set interface ethernet0/1 dip 4 shift-from 192.168.1.50 to 10.10.20.50 10.10.20.150

set policy from Trust to Untrust any any any nat src dip-id 4 permit
```

Outside of 192.168.1.50–192.168.1.150, the policy would pass the traffic, but no translation would be applied. This is really useful if, for example, one side was to be translated to one-half the address space on the common network, and the other side offered services in the form of MIPs (see Recipe 8.8) to the upper portion of the address space.

```
set interface ethernet0/1 zone Untrust
set interface ethernet0/1 ip 10.10.20.1/24
set interface ethernet0/1 dip 4 shift-from 192.168.1.50 to 10.10.20.100
10.10.20.200

set policy from Trust to Untrust any any any nat src dip-id 4 permit
```

DIP shift also supports unequal shifts, so it's possible to shift 192.168.1.50 to 10.10.20.100 and 192.168.1.51 to 10.10.20.101. Again, this would be useful if you wanted to double NAT to sites on one common network.

Shift source translation is often used in conjunction with MIP translation and destination translation (see Recipe 8.6).

8.11 Configure Destination Shift Translation

Problem

You want to perform a destination translation for a range of IPs.

Solution

Configure the local network that you want to translate:

```
set address trust server-net 10.10.20.128/25
```

Configure the shift translation within the policy:

```
set policy from untrust to trust any server-net any nat dst ip
192.168.1.0 192.168.1.127 permit
```

Discussion

With a MIP, only a whole network can be translated, but with policy NAT-DST, the translation can be shifted, similar to a DIP shift (see Recipe 8.10). A common problem is a corporate network with address overlap. The best practice in this instance is to use a publicly owned address space for interorganizational traffic, guaranteeing uniqueness to the address space. But when it's not feasible to assign a large enough public block, you can choose a private neutral network, with one-half of the network belonging to Organization A, and one-half belonging to Organization B. Translation commonly can be achieved with a series of MIPs, but policy NAT-DST with address shift is also a nice solution, in particular if the private address space is contiguous. It's a special case, but not out of the realm of possibility. Table 8-11 details the destination shift translation configuration.

Table 8-11. Destination shift translation

Private or local portion				Public or global portion			
src-ip	dst-ip	src-port	dst-port	x-src-ip	x-dst-ip	x-src-port	x-dst-port
Any	10.10.20.128	Any	Any	Original	192.168.1.0	Original	Original
Any	10.10.20.129	Any	Any	Original	192.168.1.1	Original	Original
Any	[...]	Any	Any	Original	[...]	Original	Original
Any	10.10.20.255	Any	Any	Original	192.168.1.128	Original	Original

The two organizations may decide on the common address space of `10.10.20.0/24`. Organization A gets `10.10.20.0/25` and Organization B gets `10.10.20.128/25`. So, for instance, when a client connects to `10.10.20.228`, it would be redirected to host `192.168.1.100`. In the same way, host `10.10.20.129` would be translated to `10.10.20.128/25`. At Organization A, you could translate all of Organization B's servers on the `192.168.1.128/25` DMZ with one simple command:

```
set address trust server-net 10.10.20.128/25

set route 10.10.20.128/25 interface e0/0
set policy from untrust to trust any server-net any nat dst ip
192.168.1.0 192.168.1.127 permit
```

Shift destination translation is often used in conjunction with DIP hide (see Recipe 8.1) or DIP shift translation (see Recipe 8.10).

See Also

Recipe 8.12

8.12 Configure Bidirectional Network Shift Translation

Problem

You want to perform a bidirectional translation of an entire network.

Solution

Configure a MIP with a `netmask`, describing the network:

```
set interface ethernet0/0 mip 1.1.1.0 host 192.168.2.0 netmask 255.255.255.0
```

Link the MIP to an inbound policy:

```
set policy from Untrust to Trust Any MIP(1.1.1.0/24) http permit
```

Also link the MIP to an outbound policy:

```
set address Trust 192.168.1.0/24 192.168.1.0 255.255.255.0
set policy from Trust to Untrust 192.168.1.0/24 Any Any permit
```

Discussion

Instead of translating individual servers one by one, you can translate an entire network, which may be easier to configure than hundreds of individual NATs. Table 8-12 shows the destination shift translation of the bidirectional translation.

Table 8-12. Destination shift translation branch from bidirectional translation

Private or local portion				Public or global portion			
src-ip	dst-ip	src-port	dst-port	x-src-ip	x-dst-ip	x-src-port	x-dst-port
Any	1.1.1.0	Any	Any	Original	192.168.2.0	Original	Original
Any	1.1.1.1	Any	Any	Original	192.168.2.1	Original	Original
Any	[...]	Any	Any	Original	[...]	Original	Original
Any	1.1.1.255	Any	Any	Original	192.168.2.255	Original	Original

Table 8-13 shows the source shift translation of the bidirectional translation.

Table 8-13. Source shift translation branch from bidirectional translation

Private or local portion				Public or global portion			
src-ip	dst-ip	src-port	dst-port	x-src-ip	x-dst-ip	x-src-port	x-dst-port
192.168.2.0	Any	Any	Any	1.1.1.0	Original	Original	Original
192.168.2.1	Any	Any	Any	1.1.1.1	Original	Original	Original
[...]	[...]	Any	Any	[...]	[...]	Original	Original
192.168.2.255	Any	Any	Any	1.1.1.255	Original	Original	Original

The resulting MIP object has the name format of `MIP(<public net/netmask>)`. It translates `1.1.1.0/24` to `192.168.2.0/24`. Host `192.168.2.1` is translated to `1.1.1.1`, host `192.168.2.2` to `1.1.1.2`, and so on.

```
set interface ethernet0/0 zone Untrust
set interface ethernet0/0 ip 2.2.2.100/24
set interface ethernet0/0 mip 1.1.1.0 host 192.168.2.0 netmask 255.255.255.0

set policy from Untrust to Trust any MIP(1.1.1.0/24) http permit
```

Notice that the MIP is not in the network with the interface's IP address. This has two implications: first, hosts on the `Untrust` segment, `2.2.2.0/24`, need to have a route for destination `1.1.1.0/24` to point to firewall `2.2.2.100`. Second, such a configuration is supported only on an interface in the `Untrust` zone, unless you use ScreenOS 6.1 or later.

A MIP is a bidirectional NAT translation, meaning that it performs destination and source translation. A MIP only needs to be linked in the policy in the function of a destination translation. The source translation part is always implicit. The outgoing policy shown here will automatically translate the `192.168.1.0/24` source IP address to `1.1.1.0/24`:

```
set policy from Untrust to Trust Any MIP(1.1.1.0/24) http permit

set address Trust 192.168.1.0/24 192.168.1.0 255.255.255.0
set policy from Trust to Unrust 192.168.1.0/24 Any Any permit
```

The drawback of using a MIP for this purpose is that you cannot translate outside of network boundaries. For instance, you cannot simply translate a range of hosts. Alternatives are policy NAT-DST (see Recipe 8.11) in combination with policy NAT-SRC (DIP) (see Recipe 8.10).

8.13 Configure Conditional NAT

Problem

You want to make address translation a condition of who connects.

Solution

First, configure the source addresses for the condition:

```
set address untrust client-a 2.2.2.0/24
set address untrust client-b 3.3.3.0/24
```

Then, configure policy NAT-DST for the destination translation:

```
set address trust host-ab-pub 1.1.1.50/32
set route 1.1.1.50/32 interface e0/0

set policy from Untrust to Trust client-a host-ab-pub http nat
dst ip 192.168.1.100 permit
set policy from Untrust to Trust client-b host-ab-pub http nat
dst ip 192.168.1.200 permit
```

Or, you can configure policy NAT-SRC (also called DIP) for source address translation:

```
set interface ethernet0/0 zone Untrust
set interface ethernet0/0 ip 1.1.1.100/24
set interface ethernet0/0 dip 4 1.1.1.1
set interface ethernet0/0 dip 5 1.1.1.2

set policy from Untrust to Trust client-a Any Any nat src dip-id 4 permit
set policy from Untrust to Trust client-b Any Any nat src dip-id 5 permit
```

Discussion

Because policy NAT-DST and NAT-SRC are unidirectional, you can also perform a translation depending on its origin.

Let's say you have two clients in networks 2.2.2.0/24 and 3.3.3.0/24. Depending on which client connects, you want to perform different destination or source translations. First, you configure address objects with the condition—the clients:

```
set address untrust client-a 2.2.2.0/24
set address untrust client-b 3.3.3.0/24
```

Then, you configure the destination translation, depending on the clients: for instance, when client-a connects to the public IP of 1.1.1.50, client-a is destination-translated to 192.168.1.100, but when client-b connects to the same public IP of 1.1.1.50, client-b is destination-translated to 192.168.1.200. This is called conditional NAT-ing, and you can use it for load-sharing of servers, or to make servers available to different interest groups. Table 8-14 shows conditional destination translation with NAT-DST, with the condition listed in the "src-ip" column.

Table 8-14. Conditional destination translation

Private or local portion				Public or global portion			
src-ip	dst-ip	src-port	dst-port	x-src-ip	x-dst-ip	x-src-port	x-dst-port
2.2.2.0/24	1.1.1.50	Any	Any	Original	192.168.1.100	Original	Original
3.3.3.0/24	1.1.1.50	Any	Any	Original	192.168.1.200	Original	Original

You configure two policies with NAT-DST, referencing the different clients for each translation:

```
set interface ethernet0/0 zone Trust
set interface ethernet0/1 zone Untrust
set address trust host-ab-pub 1.1.1.50/32
set route 1.1.1.50/32 interface e0/0

set policy from Untrust to Trust client-a host-ab-pub http nat dst ip
192.168.1.100 permit
set policy from Untrust to Trust client-b host-ab-pub http nat dst ip
192.168.1.200 permit
```

Because NAT-SRC DIP translation is also unidirectional translation, you can also create conditional source translation. For instance, say you want different user groups to use different hide NATs. client-a is source-translated to 1.1.1.1, whereas client-b is source-translated to 1.1.1.2. Table 8-15 shows conditional source translation with DIPs. You'll find the condition listed in the "src-ip" column.

Table 8-15. Conditional source translation

Private or local portion				Public or global portion			
src-ip	dst-ip	src-port	dst-port	x-src-ip	x-dst-ip	x-src-port	x-dst-port
2.2.2.0/24	Any	Any	Any	1.1.1.1	Original	≥ 1024	Original
3.3.3.0/24	Any	Any	Any	1.1.1.2	Original	≥ 1024	Original

First, configure two different DIPs, one for each client:

```
set interface ethernet0/0 zone Untrust
set interface ethernet0/0 ip 1.1.1.100/24
set interface ethernet0/0 dip 4 1.1.1.1
set interface ethernet0/0 dip 5 1.1.1.2
```

Then, link the two different DIPs to two different policies, with the different clients in the policy's source:

```
set policy from Untrust to Trust client-a Any Any nat src dip-id 4 permit
set policy from Untrust to Trust client-b Any Any nat src dip-id 5 permit
```

Instead of using IP addresses as the condition, you could use a service. For instance, you could provide a public IP and NAT host connecting to the HyperText Transfer Protocol (HTTP) and MAIL, to two different internal servers:

```
set policy from Untrust to Trust Any host-ab-pub http nat dst ip
192.168.1.100 permit
set policy from Untrust to Trust Any host-ab-pub mail nat dst ip
192.168.1.200 permit
```

Or, you could use two different hide NAT translations for HTTP and mail traffic:

```
set policy from Untrust to Trust Any Any http nat src dip-id 4 permit
set policy from Untrust to Trust Any Any mail nat src dip-id 5 permit
```

One warning, however: conditional NATing makes for a very complex policy base. Design complexity invites errors during operation.

See Also

Recipe 8.1; Recipe 8.6

8.14 Configure NAT with Multiple Interfaces

Problem

You want to share a MIP or a DIP among multiple interfaces.

Solution

Configure the interfaces in a `loopback-group`. Apply the DIP and MIP on the loopback address instead of on the egress or ingress interface:

```
set interface ethernet0/0 zone Untrust
set interface ethernet0/1 zone Untrust

set interface loop.1 zone untrust
set interface ethernet0/0 loopback-group loop.1
set interface ethernet0/1 loopback-group loop.1

set interface loop.1 ip 10.10.10.1/24
set interface loop.1 dip 4 10.10.10.100
set interface loop.1 mip 10.10.10.200 host 192.168.1.100

set policy from Trust to Untrust any any any nat dip-id 4 permit
set policy from Untrust to Trust any MIP(10.10.10.200) any permit
```

Discussion

This recipe represents a typical scenario in which you have several interfaces allocated for direct connection to wide area network (WAN) circuits or indirectly to WAN routers, or you have redundant interfaces in a dynamically routed environment.

This recipe works only if all the interfaces that share a DIP or a MIP are in the same zone because all members of a `loopback-group` have to be in the same zone. An interface may be a member of only one `loopback-group`. If all MIPs cannot be summarized into one network, all interfaces must be in the `Untrust` zone because only `Untrust` zone MIPs can be in a different network from their IP address on that interface unless you use ScreenOS 6.1 or later.

A *loopback group* is basically an interface template. Any DIP on the loopback interface is applied to the physical interface or subinterfaces in the group. DIPs are applied to the egress interface. For a MIP, which is applied ingress, you also can use a loopback group, but you do not have to. If you do not use a loopback group, basically two policy lookups occur: one from the ingress zone, which in our case is from the `Untrust` zone to the zone the loopback interface is in (in this case, `Untrust` again) and a second lookup from the zone the loopback interface is in, to the zone the egress interface is in, which in this case is `Trust`.

```
set policy id 1 from "Untrust" to "Untrust"  "Any" "Any" "ANY" permit
set policy id 2 from "Untrust" to "Trust"  "Any" "MIP(10.5.5.100)" "ANY" permit
```

When using a `loopback-group` instead, you do not need `policy id 1`. Only one policy lookup would take place.

You can view the members in a `loopback-group` with the `get interface` command on the loopback interface:

```
SSG140-> get int loop.1
Interface loopback.1:
  description loopback.1
  number 126, if_info 101816, if_index 1, mode route
  link up
  Loopback interface has 2 members:
  ethernet0/1; tunnel.1
```

```
  vsys Root, zone Untrust, vr trust-vr
  admin mtu 1500, operating mtu 1500, default mtu 1500
  *ip 10.5.5.1/24
  *manage ip 10.5.5.1
  pmtu-v4 disabled
  ping disabled, telnet disabled, SSH disabled, SNMP disabled
  web disabled, ident-reset disabled, SSL disabled

  OSPF disabled  BGP disabled  RIP disabled  RIPng disabled  mtrace
disabled
  PIM: not configured  IGMP not configured
  NHRP disabled
```

8.15 Design PAT for a Home or Branch Office

Problem

You want to secure a small office using a firewall without a DMZ (see Figure 8-1). On the Trust side, you are using a private network, and on the Untrust side, you receive a single public IP address dynamically from your service provider. No access is initiated from the outside to the inside.

Solution

Enable NAT mode on the `Trust` interface:

```
set interface ethernet0/0 zone "Trust"
set interface ethernet0/1 zone "Untrust"

set interface ethernet0/0 ip 192.168.1.1/24
set interface ethernet0/0 nat
set interface ethernet0/1 dhcp client enable
set interface ethernet0/1 route
```

Configure a policy from `Trust` to `Untrust` *without* the `nat` switch (because NAT mode was enabled on interface `e0/0`):

```
set policy id 1 from "Trust" to "Untrust" "Any" "Any" "ANY" permit log
```

Discussion

When you have a small firewall with two interfaces, with the user network on the Trust side and the Internet Service Provider (ISP) on the Untrust side, the interface in the `Untrust` zone often receives its address dynamically from the service provider. (Commonly, in such a small-office environment, the public IP address is assigned via the Dynamic Host Configuration Protocol [DHCP], Point-to-Point Protocol [PPP],

Point-to-Point Protocol over Ethernet [PPPoE], or Point-to-Point Protocol over ATM [PPPoA]; in this recipe, we'll stick to DHCP.) The topology would look something similar to Figure 8-1.

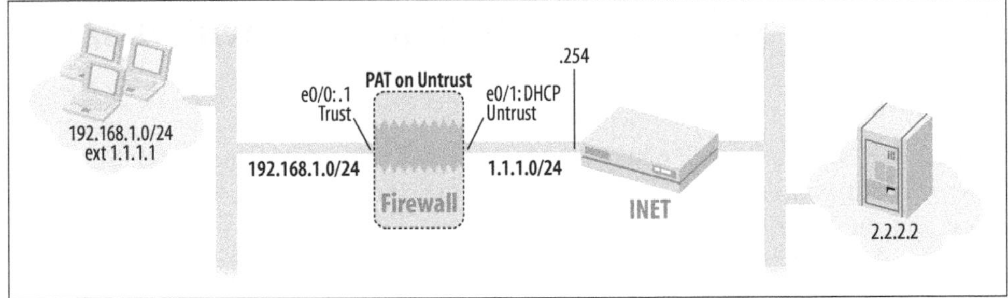

Figure 8-1. PAT for home/branch office

The first step is to configure the interfaces. Switch the `Trust` interface to NAT mode, and leave the `Untrust` interface in route mode. No other zones, predefined or custom, can be used with NAT mode. NAT mode is not supported with interfaces in other zones, predefined or custom. This is actually the out-of-the-box default configuration for smaller firewalls.

```
set interface "ethernet0/0" zone "Trust"
set interface "ethernet0/1" zone "Untrust"

set interface ethernet0/0 ip 192.168.1.1/24
set interface ethernet0/0 nat
set interface ethernet0/1 dhcp client enable
set interface ethernet0/1 route
```

The second step is to configure an outbound policy. The source zone always needs to be `Trust`, and the target zone can be either `Untrust` or `DMZ`, depending on where the translation occurs:

```
set policy id 1 from "Trust" to "Untrust"  "Any" "Any" "ANY" permit log
```

Because NAT mode is really a legacy mode, do not configure it with firewalls with more than two interfaces or zones. NAT mode has many conditions, and a more flexible method of configuring PAT within a policy exists today (see Recipe 8.1). For smaller firewalls, however, it is a convenient and easy way to get a configuration going within a few commands.

This recipe works only if the default zones of `Trust`, `Untrust`, and `DMZ` are used. The alternative to NAT mode is route mode with policy NAT-SRC, which we showed in Recipe 8.1.

8.16 A NAT Strategy for a Medium Office with DMZ

Problem

You are deploying a firewall with a DMZ for a small office (see Figure 8-2). Your provider is giving you one public static IP address. You want all hosts on the private network and the DMZ to have Internet access. In the DMZ, you have a web server and you want to remotely administer a Linux host via Secure Shell (SSH) from the Internet.

Solution

First, assign the interfaces into zones, configure the IP addresses, and put the interfaces into route mode:

```
set interface ethernet0/0 zone "Trust"
set interface ethernet0/1 zone "Untrust"
set interface ethernet0/2 zone "DMZ"

set interface ethernet0/0 ip 192.168.1.1/24
set interface ethernet0/0 route
set interface ethernet0/1 ip 1.1.1.100/24
set interface ethernet0/1 route
set interface ethernet0/2 ip 192.168.2.1/24
set interface ethernet0/2 route

set route 0.0.0.0/0 interface ethernet0/1 gateway 1.1.1.254
```

Then, because your provider is providing only one static IP address and you want to remotely access the hosts in the DMZ, you must reassign any ScreenOS management ports that may conflict with your static port translation:

```
set admin port 8080
set admin ssh port 2022
```

Now, configure a VIP for access to the DMZ servers from the Internet:

```
set interface ethernet0/1 vip untrust-ip 80 "HTTP" 192.168.2.100
```

Configure another VIP to administer the Linux host via SSH:

```
set interface ethernet0/1 vip untrust-ip 22 "SSH" 192.168.2.200
```

Next, configure a policy, referencing the VIP:

```
set policy id 4 from "Untrust" to "Global"  "Any" "VIP(ethernet0/1)" "HTTP" permit
log
set policy id 4
   set service "SSH"
exit
```

Configure policy NAT-SRC for all outbound traffic:

```
set policy id 1 from "Trust" to "Untrust"  "Any" "Any" "ANY" nat src permit log
set policy id 2 from "DMZ" to "Untrust"  "Any" "Any" "ANY" nat src permit log
```

You also likely will want to allow traffic from the `Trust` zone to the `DMZ`, without NAT:

```
set policy id 3 from "Trust" to "DMZ"  "Any" "Any" "ANY" permit log
```

Discussion

This recipe describes a typical small-office design with a private user network and a DMZ, as shown in Figure 8-2. All addressing is within the RFC 1918 space. The provider assigned only one static IP address. The user segment has the address space `192.168.1.0/24`; the DMZ has the address space `192.168.2.0/24`. Two servers live in the DMZ, one web server and one Linux server. The provider assigned the public IP address `1.1.1.100`. As an example, there is a random public host of `2.2.2.2`.

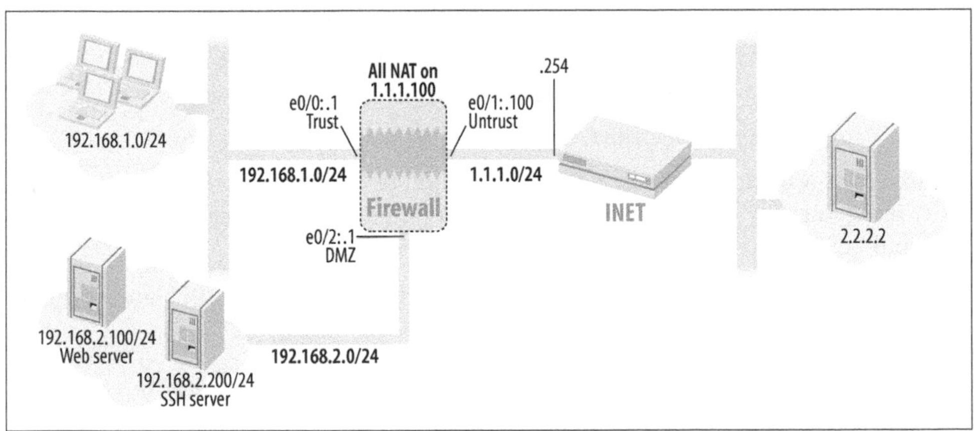

Figure 8-2. NAT for small office with DMZ

Your first step is to put the interfaces into zones and to configure IP addresses and routing. Notice that all interfaces are put in route mode. NAT mode is a legacy mode with a very narrowly defined function (see Recipe 8.21):

```
set interface ethernet0/0 zone "Trust"
set interface ethernet0/1 zone "Untrust"
set interface ethernet0/2 zone "DMZ"

set interface ethernet0/0 ip 192.168.1.1/24
set interface ethernet0/0 route
set interface ethernet0/1 ip 1.1.1.100/24
set interface ethernet0/1 route
set interface ethernet0/2 ip 192.168.2.1/24
set interface ethernet0/2 route

set route 0.0.0.0/0 interface ethernet0/1 gateway 1.1.1.254
```

Because you have only one public IP address available, and you want Internet users to have access to the hosts in the DMZ with the same ports that you use to manage the firewall, you must move the ScreenOS management ports to different ports. The first line in the following code snippet moves the port for the WebUI from `80/tcp` to `8080/tcp`. The second line moves the SSH port from `22/tcp` to `2022/tcp`. If you want to move ScreenOS's local management ports to another socket, you need to move them to a port number of 1024 or higher.

```
set admin port 8080
set admin ssh port 2022
```

Now, you can configure the VIPs on the interface in the `Untrust` zone for Internet users to access the web server and Linux host. The `Untrust` zone is the only zone on which VIPs are supported in current ScreenOS releases. In this example, you are going to translate `80/tcp` to the web server, and you will translate the SSH port (`22/tcp`) to the Linux host. Notice that the VIP's name is `untrust-ip`; `untrust-ip` does not refer to the `Untrust` zone, but rather to the interface in the `Untrust` zone.

```
set interface ethernet0/1 vip untrust-ip 80 "HTTP" 192.168.2.100
set interface ethernet0/1 vip untrust-ip 22 "SSH" 192.168.2.200
```

You choose `untrust-ip`, instead of an IP address such as the following:

```
set interface ethernet0/1 vip 1.1.1.50 80 "HTTP" 192.168.2.100
```

because you want to use the same IP address the public interface is in, as your provider gave you only one IP address. The `untrust-ip` name reference works best when your public IP address is assigned dynamically.

Note that in ScreenOS 6.1 and later, the syntax changed because VIPs are now supported on interfaces in any zone:

```
set interface ethernet0/1 vip interface-ip 80 "HTTP" 192.168.2.100
```

A VIP with a dynamic IP address is not very useful because a VIP along with a policy makes internal servers available to the Internet; therefore, the VIP IP addresses need to be known. Use of the Dynamic Domain Name Service (DDNS) is one way to solve this problem (see Chapter 6).

At this point, the interfaces are in zones and they have IP addresses, the management ports have been moved, and the VIP translations have been configured. The last thing to do is to link the VIP in a policy:

```
set policy id 4 from "Untrust" to "Global"  "Any" "VIP(ethernet0/1)" "HTTP" permit
log
set policy id 4
   set service "SSH"
exit
```

This takes care of client access from the Internet to servers on the Trust or DMZ side. Now, let's look at how hosts from the inside connect to the outside.

Use the `nat` statement within the policy to configure a dynamic PAT for inside hosts to the outside. With this option, the source IP is translated to the IP address of the egress interface, which in this case is the IP of the `Untrust` interface. Source ports are translated from their original port number to a number higher than 1023. (There are options to translate to a different IP address and to a pool of addresses. For more on this, see Recipe 8.1 and Recipe 8.4.)

```
set policy id 1 from "Trust" to "Untrust"  "Any" "Any" "ANY" nat src permit log
set policy id 2 from "DMZ" to "Untrust"  "Any" "Any" "ANY" nat src permit log
```

The last step is to allow traffic from the `Trust` zone to the `DMZ`, without NAT:

```
set policy id 3 from "Trust" to "DMZ"  "Any" "Any" "ANY" permit log
```

8.17 Deploy a Large-Office Firewall with DMZ

Problem

You want to deploy a firewall for a large office with one or more DMZs, and you own a static public IP address space (see Figure 8-3).

Solution

Configure a DIP for an outbound connection of hosts from the Trust side to perform outbound PAT:

```
set interface ethernet0/1 dip 4 1.1.1.50
set policy id 1 from "Trust" to "Untrust" "Any" "Any" "ANY" nat src dip-id 4 permit
```

Then, configure a MIP for each server in the DMZ to perform bidirectional, one-to-one NAT:

```
set interface "ethernet0/1" mip 1.1.1.100 host 192.168.2.100
set interface "ethernet0/1" mip 1.2.2.100 host 192.168.2.200
```

Next, configure a policy for outside users to initiate an HTTP session to the two MIP hosts:

```
set policy id 2 from "Untrust" to "DMZ"  "Any" "MIP(1.1.1.100)" "HTTP" permit
set policy id 2
   set dst-address "MIP(1.2.2.100)"
exit
```

Configure one single policy for DMZ hosts to make outside connections (the MIP is implied as outbound):

```
set policy id 5 from "DMZ" to "Untrust" any any any permit log
```

Lastly, allow Trust side hosts to connect internally to DMZ servers:

```
set policy id 4 from "Trust" to "DMZ" "Any" "Any" "Any" permit
```

Note that the preceding examples serve to explain the framework of the recipe. Production policies are usually tighter and more customized.

Discussion

In this recipe, we have one `Trust` network and one `DMZ` network, similar to the one shown in Figure 8-3. There could be multiple networks on the Trust or DMZ side, and there could be multiple DMZs.

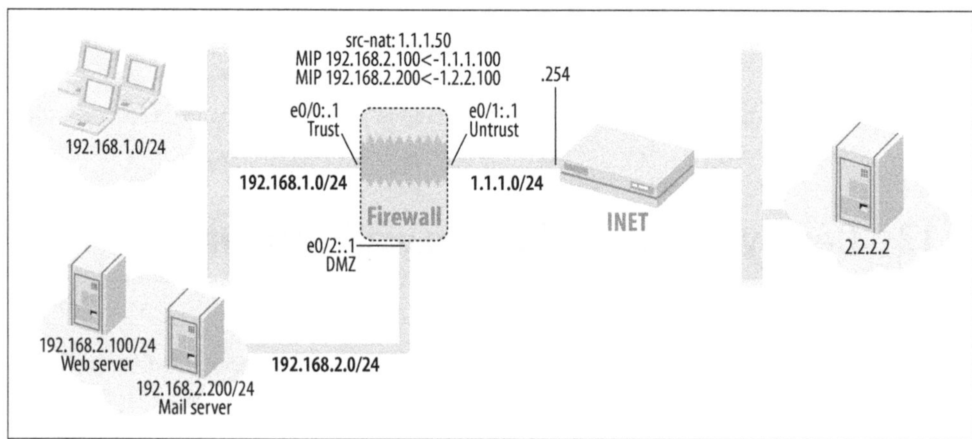

Figure 8-3. NAT for large-office network with DMZ

There is a single default route to the ISP's router:

```
set interface "ethernet0/0" zone "Trust"
set interface "ethernet0/1" zone "Untrust"
set interface "ethernet0/2" zone "DMZ"

set interface ethernet0/0 ip 192.168.1.1/24
set interface ethernet0/0 route
set interface ethernet0/1 ip 1.1.1.1/24
set interface ethernet0/1 route
set interface ethernet0/2 ip 192.168.2.1/24
set interface ethernet0/2 route

set route 0.0.0.0/0 interface ethernet0/1 gateway 1.1.1.254
```

Notice that you need to put all interfaces in route mode to switch the device from NAT mode to route mode. This is recommended with all larger firewalls and firewalls with more than two interfaces. All outbound Untrust traffic is port-address-translated to the address `1.1.1.50` with the help of a DIP:

```
set interface ethernet0/1 dip 4 1.1.1.50 1.1.1.50
set policy id 1 from "Trust" to "Untrust"  "Any" "Any" "ANY" nat src dip-id 4 permit
```

The DIP is configured on egress interface `e0/1` and is linked in the outbound policy 1, with DIP `ID 4` chosen. Note that the `fix-port` option is not selected in this policy because it is used only when one host should be translated to one address. In this case, all inside hosts were hidden behind `1.1.1.50`; therefore, PAT is applied.

For the inbound traffic, you configure MIPs. In this recipe, assume that one MIP is in the same network with the interface's IP address and one is not. If the MIP should be in a different network than the IP address on that interface, the interface must be in the `Untrust` zone, unless you use ScreenOS 6.1 or later.

```
set interface "ethernet0/1" mip 1.1.1.100 host 192.168.2.100 netmask 255.255.255.255
vr "trust-vr"
set interface "ethernet0/1" mip 1.2.2.100 host 192.168.2.200 netmask 255.255.255.255
vr "trust-vr"

set policy id 2 from "Untrust" to "Global"  "Any" "MIP(1.1.1.100)" "HTTP" permit
set policy id 3 from "Untrust" to "Global"  "Any" "MIP(1.2.2.100)" "HTTP" permit
```

In some ScreenOS documentation, MIP rules have a different zone than the `Global` zone, but the destination zone in a MIP rule really does not matter because internally, it will always be treated as `Global`. In most instances, it might be better to use a different zone than `Global` to group MIPs in a policy because the `Global` zone does not support grouping or multicell. (Grouping of MIPs and VIPs is supported in ScreenOS 5.3.)

```
set policy id 2 from "Untrust" to "DMZ"  "Any" "MIP(1.1.1.100)" "HTTP" permit log
set policy id 2
   set dst-address "MIP(1.2.2.100)"
exit
```

The neighboring router will ARP for the first MIP, but will need a static route for the other MIP, which is not in the same network as the interface's IP:

```
sbrunner@INET# run show route

inet.0: 3 destinations, 3 routes (3 active, 0 holddown, 0 hidden)
+ = Active Route, - = Last Active, * = Both

1.1.1.0/24         *[Direct/0] 00:01:37
                    > via fxp0.0
1.1.1.254/32       *[Local/0] 00:01:37
                      Local via fxp0.0
1.2.2.0/24         *[Static/5] 00:01:37
                    > to 1.1.1.1 via fxp0.0
```

In this recipe, assume that every server in the DMZ has a corresponding MIP. You do not have to configure a DIP for outbound connections because MIPs are bidirectional.

```
set policy id 5 from dmz to untrust any any any permit log
```

No address translation is performed for traffic between the `Trust` and `DMZ` zones. Trust servers can reach the private address:

```
set address "Trust" "192.168.1.100/32" 192.168.1.100/32 "Trust client prv"
set address "DMZ" "192.168.2.100/32" 192.168.2.100/32 "DMZ server prv"
```

```
set policy id 4 from "Trust" to "DMZ"  "192.168.1.100/32"
"192.168.2.100/32" "http" permit log
```

8.18 Create an Extranet with Mutual PAT

Problem

You want to resolve an IP address clash within an extranet by translating both sides to a neutral address space.

Solution

Configure policy NAT-SRC for the outbound traffic. Both clients and servers are source-port address-translated:

```
set interface ethernet0/0 ext ip 1.1.1.200 255.255.255.255 dip 4 1.1.1.200
set interface ethernet0/1 ext ip 1.1.1.100 255.255.255.255 dip 5 1.1.1.100
```

Then, configure policy NAT-DST to make servers available to clients:

```
set address "Inside" "1.1.1.1/32" 1.1.1.1 255.255.255.255 "Public server left"
set address "Inside" "192.168.1.0/24" 192.168.1.0 255.255.255.0 "Left network"
set address "Outside" "1.1.1.2/32" 1.1.1.2 255.255.255.255 "Public server right"
set address "Outside" "192.168.2.0/24" 192.168.2.0 255.255.255.0 "Right network"
```

Finally, configure the policies:

```
set policy id 1 from "Inside" to "Outside"  "192.168.1.0/24"
"1.1.1.2/32" "ANY" nat src dip-id 5 dst ip 192.168.2.100 permit log
set policy id 2 from "Outside" to "Inside"  "192.168.2.0/24"
"1.1.1.1/32" "ANY" nat src dip-id 4 dst ip 192.168.1.100 permit log
```

All of the originating addresses from either side will be hidden behind one port-address-translated address. All of the destinations will be one-to-one statically translated.

Discussion

This recipe assumes the topology shown in Figure 8-4; that is, you want to connect to a partner network, but neither of your internal address spaces is routable at either side (perhaps because both use the same IP address space or perhaps due to some administrative policy). Therefore, you want to translate your addresses and your partner's addresses to a neutral space.

On the left side is network `192.168.1.0/24` with a bunch of clients, as well as one server with IP `192.168.1.100`. On the right side are a bunch of clients within the `192.168.2.0/24` network, and one server with the IP address of `192.168.2.100`. The goal is to allow clients to connect to a well-known IP address to reach the servers while hiding any originating addresses. For any connections from the left side, this includes all clients as well as servers, which would be acting as clients when originating a connection, and would hide behind IP address `1.1.1.100`. Any connection originating from the right side will hide behind IP address `1.1.1.200`. The external IP

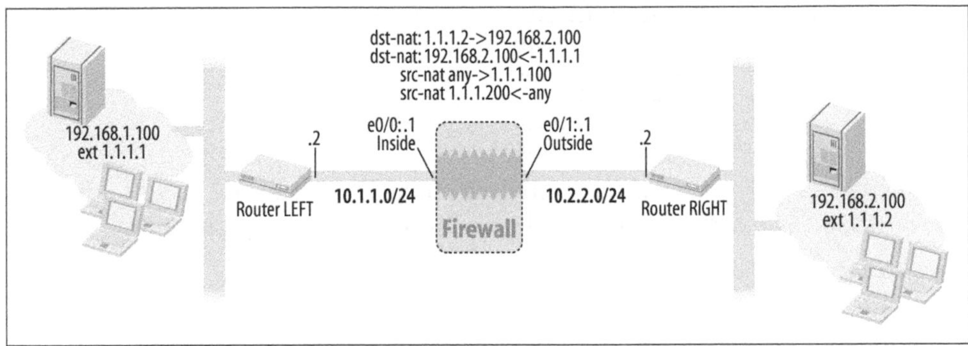

Figure 8-4. Extranet with mutual PAT

addresses are arbitrarily chosen and could be anything. The left server will be known to the right side under `1.1.1.1`, and the right server will be known to the left side under `1.1.1.2`.

Let's first investigate how this looks from a routing perspective:

```
sbrunner@LEFT> show route

inet.0: 6 destinations, 6 routes (6 active, 0 holddown, 0 hidden)
+ = Active Route, - = Last Active, * = Both

1.1.1.2/32         *[Static/5] 01:11:12
                    > to 10.1.1.1 via fxp0.0
1.1.1.200/32       *[Static/5] 00:00:04
                    > to 10.1.1.1 via fxp0.0
10.1.1.0/24        *[Direct/0] 01:11:12
                    > via fxp0.0
10.1.1.2/32        *[Local/0] 01:11:12
                      Local via fxp0.0
192.168.1.0/24     *[Direct/0] 00:00:18
                    > via fxp1.0
192.168.1.1/32     *[Local/0] 00:00:44
                      Local via fxp1.0
```

On the left router, you route public IP address `1.1.1.2` of the right-side host `192.168.2.100` to the firewall. You also route the hide address of the ride-side host `1.1.1.200` to the firewall:

```
sbrunner@RIGHT> show route

inet.0: 6 destinations, 6 routes (6 active, 0 holddown, 0 hidden)
+ = Active Route, - = Last Active, * = Both

1.1.1.1/32         *[Static/5] 01:12:12
                    > to 10.2.2.1 via fxp0.0
1.1.1.100/32       *[Static/5] 00:00:10
                    > to 10.2.2.1 via fxp0.0
10.2.2.0/24        *[Direct/0] 01:12:12
                    > via fxp0.0
```

```
10.2.2.2/32         *[Local/0] 01:12:12
                       Local via fxp0.0
192.168.2.0/24      *[Direct/0] 00:00:28
                     > via fxp1.0
192.168.2.1/32      *[Local/0] 00:00:54
                       Local via fxp1.0
```

On the right router, you route in reverse the public IP address of `1.1.1.1` of the left-side host `192.168.1.100`, as well as the hide address `1.1.1.100`, to the firewall.

Let's see what happens on the firewall:

```
FIREWALL(trust-vr)-> get route
H: Host C: Connected S: Static A: Auto-Exported
I: Imported R: RIP P: Permanent D: Auto-Discovered
N: NHRP
iB: IBGP eB: EBGP O: OSPF E1: OSPF external type 1
E2: OSPF external type 2 trailing B: backup route

Total 8/max entries

     ID        IP-Prefix  Interface   Gateway   P Pref   Mtr   Vsys
--------------------------------------------------------------------
*    13        1.1.1.1/32     eth0/0   0.0.0.0   S   20     1
*    14        1.1.1.2/32     eth0/1   0.0.0.0   S   20     1
*     2       10.1.1.1/32     eth0/0   0.0.0.0   H    0     0
*     4       10.2.2.1/32     eth0/1   0.0.0.0   H    0     0
*     7   192.168.2.0/24     eth0/1  10.2.2.2   S   20     1
*     6   192.168.1.0/24     eth0/0  10.1.1.2   S   20     1
*     1       10.1.1.0/24     eth0/0   0.0.0.0   C    0     0
*     3       10.2.2.0/24     eth0/1   0.0.0.0   C    0     0
```

The interesting routes are the static routes. The `Connected` and `Host` routes are from the two interfaces `e0/0` and `e0/1`. There are two sets of static routes: one for the private IP address and one for the public IP address. The reason for the private networks is because the firewall needs to know the next hop for the clients and servers. The routes for the public portion are not that clear. These routes are actually needed for ScreenOS to find the destination zone before translation occurs to match the packet to a policy. The packets come in with a public destination address of `1.1.1.1` or `1.1.1.2`. The address translation is happening in the policy, so ScreenOS first needs to identify the ingress and egress zones to identify a matching policy. You need to point `1.1.1.2` toward `e0/1` and `1.1.1.1` toward `e0/0`. The gateway is irrelevant because these routes are not actually used for forwarding, just for identifying egress interfaces and, therefore, the egress zone.

The actual address translation is happening in the policy itself. The NAT-DST is happening first. The NAT-SRC is happening when the packet leaves the egress interface. DIP and policy NAT-SRC are synonyms. A DIP is always installed on the egress interface and is called within the policy:

```
set interface "ethernet0/0" zone "Inside"
set interface "ethernet0/1" zone "Outside"
```

```
set interface ethernet0/0 ip 10.1.1.1/24
set interface ethernet0/0 route
set interface ethernet0/1 ip 10.2.2.1/24
set interface ethernet0/1 route

set interface ethernet0/0 ext ip 1.1.1.200 255.255.255.255 dip 4 1.1.1.200
set interface ethernet0/1 ext ip 1.1.1.100 255.255.255.255 dip 5 1.1.1.100

set vrouter "trust-vr"
   set route 192.168.1.0/24 interface ethernet0/0 gateway 10.1.1.2
   set route 192.168.2.0/24 interface ethernet0/1 gateway 10.2.2.2
   set route 1.1.1.1/32 interface ethernet0/0
   set route 1.1.1.2/32 interface ethernet0/1
exit
```

Interface `e0/0` is in the custom zone `Inside` and interface `e0/1` is in the custom zone `Outside`. The choice of zone doesn't really matter and could be anything. Both interfaces are in route mode. The DIPs for the NAT-SRC are configured on their respective egress interfaces. `1.1.1.200` points toward the right side and `1.1.1.100` points toward the left side. Both DIPs live on extended interfaces because the DIPs are not in the same network as the interface itself. Both extended interface IPs happen to be identical with our DIP. The four routes have been configured as already discussed. Notice that the public IP addresses do not have a gateway configured to them, as they are only required for ScreenOS to resolve the egress interface, and therefore, the egress zone as mentioned.

Policies go in the initiating direction:

```
set address "Inside" "1.1.1.1/32" 1.1.1.1 255.255.255.255 "Public server left"
set address "Inside" "192.168.1.0/24" 192.168.1.0 255.255.255.0 "Left network"
set address "Outside" "1.1.1.2/32" 1.1.1.2 255.255.255.255 "Public server right"
set address "Outside" "192.168.2.0/24" 192.168.2.0 255.255.255.0 "Right network"

set policy id 1 from "Inside" to "Outside"  "192.168.1.0/24"
"1.1.1.2/32" "ANY" nat src dip-id 5 dst ip 192.168.2.100 permit log
set policy id 2 from "Outside" to "Inside"  "192.168.2.0/24"
"1.1.1.1/32" "ANY" nat src dip-id 4 dst ip 192.168.1.100 permit log
```

In the policy, you need to name the private address of the hosts in the source portion: in our case, on the left side in network `192.168.1.0/24`, and on the right side in network `192.168.2.0/24`. Remember, this includes any client or server initiating a connection to the other side. In the destination portion, name the public address of the servers, which on the left side is `1.1.1.1` and on the right side is `1.1.1.2`. Policy `ID 1` captures any host from the `192.168.1.0/24` network making a connection to the server on the right side on its public IP `1.1.1.2`. Policy `ID 2` covers just the opposite: any host on the right side making a connection to the server on the left side to its public IP `1.1.1.1`.

Unlike with MIPs, by default, ScreenOS does not answer ARPs for policy NAT-DST for IPs that are in the same network as the ingress interface. On neighboring routers, static ARP for those addresses needs to be configured. Also see Recipe 8.6.

8.19 Configure NAT with Policy-Based VPN

Problem

You want to perform source and destination NAT on a policy-based virtual private network (VPN) tunnel.

Solution

Configure NAT on only one side of the tunnel. Starting on FW-A, first you must configure a tunnel interface and put the tunnel interface into a tunnel zone:

```
set interface "tunnel.1" zone "Untrust-Tun"
set interface tunnel.1 ip 1.1.1.1/24
```

Then, configure the `p1` and `p2` of the VPN tunnel, binding the VPN tunnel to the same tunnel zone to which you were binding the tunnel interface. The tunnel zone connects a policy-based VPN to a tunnel interface.

```
set ike gateway "test-gw" address 10.4.4.1 Main outgoing-interface
"ethernet0/1" preshare netscreensec-level standard

set vpn "test-vpn" gateway "test-gw" no-replay tunnel idletime 0 sec-level standard
set vpn "test-vpn" monitor
set vpn "test-vpn" bind zone Untrust-Tun
```

Next, configure the DIP on the outgoing interface, which you configured in the `ike gateway` statement. Then, configure the MIP on the tunnel interface:

```
set interface ethernet0/1 ext ip 1.1.1.150/32 dip 4 1.1.1.150 fix-port
set interface tunnel.1 mip 1.1.1.100 host 192.168.1.
```

Configure the tunnel policy and reference the DIP and MIP:

```
set address "Trust" "192.168.1.0/24" 192.168.1.0 255.255.255.0
set address "Untrust" "192.168.2.0/24" 192.168.2.0 255.255.255.0

set policy id 1 from "Trust" to "Untrust"  "192.168.1.0/24"
"192.168.2.0/24" "ANY" nat src dip-id 4 tunnel vpn "test-vpn"

set policy id 2 from "Untrust" to "Trust"  "192.168.2.0/24"
"MIP(1.1.1.100)" "ANY" tunnel vpn "test-vpn"
```

Create a route for the remote network. This route does not need a next hop because it is used only to determine the egress zone:

```
set route 192.168.2.0/24 interface ethernet0/1
```

On the remote VPN device, the tunnel policies need to match. Note that the Security Association (SA) is derived from the tunnel policy; with NAT, the SA and therefore the tunnel policy will not be that obvious. SAs on both ends need to be mirror images. Here is the configuration for FW-B:

```
set address "Trust" "192.168.2.0/24" 192.168.2.0 255.255.255.0
set address "Untrust" "1.1.1.100/32" 1.1.1.100 255.255.255.255
set address "Untrust" "1.1.1.150/32" 1.1.1.150 255.255.255.255

set policy id 1 from "Untrust" to "Trust"  "1.1.1.150/32"
"192.168.2.0/24" "ANY" tunnel vpn "test-vpn"

set policy id 1 from "Trust" to "Untrust"  "192.168.2.0/24"
"1.1.1.100/32" "ANY" tunnel vpn "test-vpn"
```

The policy on the remote device now needs to have the DIP address in its source, and the MIP policy must have the public portion of the MIP in its destination. Both are regular address objects because NAT is occurring on the remote side on FW-A.

Also, set a route on FW-B for the remote network. Note that you must use the public address instead of the local address because DIPs and MIPs translate to the `1.1.1.0/24` network:

```
set route 1.1.1.0/24 interface ethernet0/0
```

Discussion

ScreenOS's NAT configuration options are limited with policy-based VPNs, but luckily, the two most important NAT methods, DIPs and MIPs, work. A DIP is configured to the outgoing interface as specified during the IKE gateway configuration. (Unfortunately, policy NAT-DST is not supported with policy-based VPN, and neither are VIPs.)

MIPs in connection with policy-based VPNs work only as a destination address translation. A DIP is required if a source address translation is required.

The difference between policy-based VPNs and route-based VPNs in the configuration is that route-based VPNs are bound to a tunnel interface:

```
set vpn <name> bind interface tun.1
```

Why are we creating a tunnel interface in this recipe, when we are using a policy-based VPN? If you bind a tunnel interface to a policy-based VPN tunnel, it will make it a route-based VPN. So, to accomplish the NATing, you will bind the policy-based VPN tunnel indirectly via a tunnel zone. A tunnel zone has a carrier zone, which must be identical to the zone of the outgoing interface. Both the tunnel interface and the VPN are bound to the same tunnel zone. The `Untrust-Tun` is a predefined tunnel zone, living in the `Untrust` carrier zone. The tunnel zone is basically the link between a tunnel interface, the outgoing interface, and the policy-based VPN.

Figure 8-5 shows a simple configuration for discussion purposes: a network on the local side with 192.168.1.100/24, and a network on the remote side with 192.168.2.0/24.

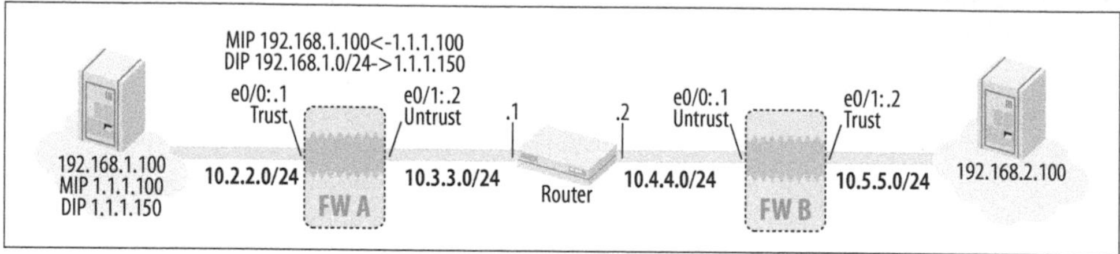

Figure 8-5. NAT with policy-based VPN

The left-side server with the IP of 192.168.1.100 is destination-address-translated with a MIP to 1.1.1.100 and source-address-translated with a DIP to 1.1.1.150. On FW-A, you configure the following:

```
set interface "ethernet0/1" zone "Untrust"
set interface ethernet0/1 ip 10.3.3.2/24
set interface ethernet0/1 route

set interface "tunnel.1" zone "Untrust-Tun"
set interface tunnel.1 ip 1.1.1.1/24

set ike gateway "test-gw" address 10.4.4.1 Main outgoing-interface
"ethernet0/1" preshare netscreen sec-level standard

set vpn "test-vpn" gateway "test-gw" no-replay tunnel idletime 0
sec-level standard
set vpn "test-vpn" bind zone Untrust-Tun
```

The DIP is anchored on the outgoing interface, and the MIP on the tunnel interface. It is theoretically possible to anchor DIPs and MIPs on a loopback interface instead, but then the routing may become complicated and would create two policy lookups: one for the NAT portion, and one for the VPN. Tunnel zones make life easier. Tunnel zones also share some similarities with loopback groups.

```
set interface ethernet0/1 ext ip 1.1.1.150/32 dip 4 1.1.1.150 fix-port
set interface "tunnel.1" mip 1.1.1.100 host 192.168.1.100
```

The difference between policy-based VPN and route-based VPN is the way the firewall determines which traffic goes into the tunnel and which traffic is accepted from the remote security gateway. The common method is to identify the VPN traffic by ACLs or policies. The policy is put in the direction from the zone behind which the client sits to the zone through which the remote security gateway can be reached with a "tunnel" action defined so that the firewall knows to encrypt the traffic with the associated VPN definition. With route-based VPN, protected traffic would be determined by regular routing into a tunnel interface, similar to a WAN link, and then securing that traffic with a traditional ACL or policy.

```
set address "Trust" "192.168.1.0/24" 192.168.1.0 255.255.255.0
set address "Untrust" "192.168.2.0/24" 192.168.2.0 255.255.255.0

set policy id 1 from "Trust" to "Untrust"  "192.168.1.0/24"
"192.168.2.0/24" "ANY" nat src dip-id 4 tunnel vpn "test-vpn"

set policy id 2 from "Untrust" to "Trust"  "192.168.2.0/24"
"MIP(1.1.1.100)" "ANY" tunnel vpn "test-vpn"
```

For the DIP policy shown in the preceding code snippet, you use the address objects to specify the source and destination of the protected traffic, as well as reference the DIP as NAT-SRC within the policy the same way you would for a nontunnel policy. Instead of configuring a custom DIP, you could use the implicit DIP `ID 2`, a PAT to the egress interface's IP, which in the case of policy-based VPN is the outgoing interface. As with the MIP policy, you define the MIP as the destination object.

> For non-VPN traffic, policy `ID 1` would activate the MIP instead of the DIP because a MIP has precedence over a DIP as a source address translation. However, a MIP in connection with a policy-based VPN works only as a destination address translation.

A policy will provide the `src-ip`, `dst-ip`, and `service` triple. These are used to create an SA. An SA identifies a VPN tunnel between two VPN gateways via the same `src-ip`, `dst-ip`, and `service`. Multiple SAs can exist, and therefore, multiple tunnels may exist, although here only a single tunnel was configured. In fact, a new tunnel will automatically be created with each tunnel policy. You can clearly see that each policy produced a pair of SAs:

```
FW-A-> get sa
total configured sa: 2
HEX ID    Gateway  Port Algorithm     SPI      Life:sec kb Sta PID vsys
00000002< 10.4.4.1 500 esp:3des/sha1 00000000 expir unlim I/I      2 0
00000002> 10.4.4.1 500 esp:3des/sha1 00000000 expir unlim I/I     -1 0
00000004< 10.4.4.1 500 esp:3des/sha1 593ed0a8  2650 unlim A/U     -1 0
00000004> 10.4.4.1 500 esp:3des/sha1 c6887a1c  2650 unlim A/U      1 0
```

Let's look at the SAs that are derived from the policies on FW-A:

```
FW-A-> get sa id 0x4
index 1, name test-vpn, peer gateway ip 10.4.4.1. vsys<Root>
auto key. policy node, tunnel mode, policy id in:<-1> out:<1>
vpngrp:<-1>. sa_list_nxt:<0x2>.
tunnel id 4, peer id 0, NSRP Local.     site-to-site. Local interface
is ethernet0/1 <10.3.3.2>.
  esp, group 2, 3des encryption, sha1 authentication
  autokey, IN active, OUT active
  monitor<1>, latency: 0, availability: 100
  DF bit: clear
  app_sa_flags: 0x4000e3
  proxy id: local 1.1.1.150/255.255.255.255, remote
192.168.2.0/255.255.255.0, proto 0, port 0
```

```
    ike activity timestamp: 402397
  nat-traversal map not available
  incoming: SPI 593ed0a8, flag 00004000, tunnel info 40000004, pipeline
    life 3600 sec, 2446 remain, 0 kb, 0 bytes remain
    anti-replay off, idle timeout value <0>, idled 1 seconds
    next pak sequence number: 0x0
  outgoing: SPI c6887a1c, flag 00000000, tunnel info 40000004, pipeline
    life 3600 sec, 2446 remain, 0 kb, 0 bytes remain
    anti-replay off, idle timeout value <0>, idled 1 seconds
    next pak sequence number: 0x55c

FW-A-> get sa id 0x2
index 0, name test-vpn, peer gateway ip 10.4.4.1. vsys<Root>
auto key. policy node, tunnel mode, policy id in:<2> out:<-1>
vpngrp:<-1>. sa_list_nxt:<0xffffffff>.
tunnel id 2, peer id 0, NSRP Local.     site-to-site. Local interface
is ethernet0/1 <10.3.3.2>.
  esp, group 2, 3des encryption, sha1 authentication
  autokey, IN inactive, OUT inactive
  monitor<1>, latency: 0, availability: 0
  DF bit: clear
  app_sa_flags: 0x4000a0
  proxy id: local 1.1.1.100/255.255.255.255, remote
192.168.2.0/255.255.255.0, proto 0, port 0
  ike activity timestamp: 0
nat-traversal map not available
incoming: SPI 00000000, flag 00004000, tunnel info 40000002, pipeline
  life 0 sec, expired, 0 kb, 0 bytes remain
  anti-replay off, idle timeout value <0>, idled 1514 seconds
  next pak sequence number: 0x0
outgoing: SPI 00000000, flag 00000000, tunnel info 40000002, pipeline
  life 0 sec, expired, 0 kb, 0 bytes remain
  anti-replay off, idle timeout value <0>, idled 1514 seconds
  next pak sequence number: 0x0
```

Surprisingly, VPN tunnel `0x4`, which was derived from DIP policy `ID 1`, shows us `1.1.1.150/32` in the source and the expected `192.168.2.0/24` in the destination. However, policy `ID 1` goes clearly from `192.168.1.0/24` to `192.168.2.0/24`. If you look closely, you'll see that `1.1.1.150/32` is identical to our DIP.

The same thing happens to VPN tunnel `0x2`, which was derived from policy `ID 2`, referencing the MIP. This is the reason `1.1.1.100/32` is in the source, and not `192.168.1.0/24`, as might be expected. This is significant because SAs have to match on either end of the tunnel. On a side note, this is also why policy `ID 2` is not configured with an `src-address` of `Any`, as often is done with regular MIP policies, because SAs need to tell traffic apart on either end clearly.

The policies on the remote site, FW-B, look like this:

```
set address "Trust" "192.168.2.0/24" 192.168.2.0 255.255.255.0
set address "Untrust" "1.1.1.100/32" 1.1.1.100 255.255.255.255
set address "Untrust" "1.1.1.150/32" 1.1.1.150 255.255.255.255
```

```
set policy id 1 from "Untrust" to "Trust"  "1.1.1.150/32"
"192.168.2.0/24" "ANY" tunnel vpn "test-vpn"

set policy id 1 from "Trust" to "Untrust"  "192.168.2.0/24"
"1.1.1.100/32" "ANY" tunnel vpn "test-vpn"
```

When you look at the remote site's (FW-B's) SAs, you can see that the SAs match the policy:

```
FW-B-> get sa
total configured sa: 2
HEX ID    Gateway  Port Algorithm    SPI     Life:sec kb Sta PID vsys
00000003< 10.3.3.2 500 esp:3des/sha1 00000000 expir unlim I/I   2 0
00000003> 10.3.3.2 500 esp:3des/sha1 00000000 expir unlim I/I   1 0
00000004< 10.3.3.2 500 esp:3des/sha1 c6887a1c  1937 unlim A/U   3 0
00000004> 10.3.3.2 500 esp:3des/sha1 593ed0a8  1937 unlim A/U  -1 0

FW-B-> get sa id 0x4
index 1, name test-vpn, peer gateway ip 10.3.3.2. vsys<Root>
auto key. policy node, tunnel mode, policy id in:<3> out:<-1>
vpngrp:<-1>. sa_list_nxt:<3>.
tunnel id 4, peer id 0, NSRP Local.     site-to-site. Local
interface  is ethernet0/0 <10.4.4.1>.
  esp, group 2, 3des encryption, sha1 authentication
  autokey, IN active, OUT active
  monitor<1>, latency: 0, availability: 100
  DF bit: clear
  app_sa_flags: 0x20e3
  proxy id: local 192.168.2.0/255.255.255.0, remote
1.1.1.150/255.255.255.255, proto 0, port 0
  ike activity timestamp: 4004275
nat-traversal map not available
incoming: SPI c6887a1c, flag 00004000, tunnel info 40000004,
pipeline
  life 3600 sec, 1979 remain, 0 kb, 0 bytes remain
  anti-replay off, idle timeout value <0>, idled 1 seconds
  next pak sequence number: 0x0
outgoing: SPI 593ed0a8, flag 00000000, tunnel info 40000004,
pipeline
  life 3600 sec, 1979 remain, 0 kb, 0 bytes remain
  anti-replay off, idle timeout value <0>, idled 1 seconds
  next pak sequence number: 0x788

FW-B-> get sa id 0x3
index 0, name test-vpn, peer gateway ip 10.3.3.2. vsys<Root>
auto key. policy node, tunnel mode, policy id in:<2> out:<1>
vpngrp:<-1>. sa_list_nxt:<-1>.
tunnel id 3, peer id 0, NSRP Local.     site-to-site. Local
interface is ethernet0/0 <10.4.4.1>.
  esp, group 2, 3des encryption, sha1 authentication
  autokey, IN inactive, OUT inactive
  monitor<1>, latency: 0, availability: 0
```

```
    DF bit: clear
    app_sa_flags: 0x20a0
    proxy id: local 192.168.2.0/255.255.255.0,
  remote 1.1.1.100/255.255.255.255, proto 0, port 0
    ike activity timestamp: 0
  nat-traversal map not available
  incoming: SPI 00000000, flag 00004000, tunnel info 40000003,
  pipeline
    life 0 sec, expired, 0 kb, 0 bytes remain
    anti-replay off, idle timeout value <0>, idled 5586 seconds
    next pak sequence number: 0x0
  outgoing: SPI 00000000, flag 00000000, tunnel info 40000003,
  pipeline
    life 0 sec, expired, 0 kb, 0 bytes remain
    anti-replay off, idle timeout value <0>, idled 5586 seconds
    next pak sequence number: 0x0
```

We're not quite finished yet, because routes are needed on both sides so that the egress zone is determined to find the right tunnel policy. In most cases, you might create a default route through the outgoing interface to the Internet gateway router that would match both remote networks. If such a route does not exist, or there are internal routes that include the remote networks, you need to point out routes through the outgoing interface. Those routes do not need a next hop because they are not used for routing; they are used only to determine the egress zone so that the tunnel policy can be correctly found:

```
FW-A-> set route 192.168.2.0/24 interface ethernet0/1

FW-B-> set route 1.1.1.0/24 interface ethernet0/0
```

In the preceding code snippet, `192.168.2.0/24` is routed on FW-A to its outgoing interface `e0/1`, and the public portion for the MIP and DIP, `1.1.1.0/24`, on FW-B is routed to its outgoing interface `e0/0`. Routing is actually happening for the encapsulated and encrypted traffic. The source and destination IPs in the outer header of the ESP encrypted packet are identical to the IP of the outgoing interface. Any routers in between will need to be able to route the ESP encrypted packets; typically, they have public IP addresses.

An alternative to configuring NAT on policy-based VPN tunnels is to configure NAT on route-based VPN tunnels, even if the other side supports only policy-based VPN. Matching a policy-based tunnel with a route-based tunnel may require a complex configuration because you need to match the SA. With route-based VPN, SAs do not have significance and are therefore set to all zeros.

It is possible to manually configure the SA on a route-based tunnel for the purpose of matching a policy-based tunnel on the remote end. It may get complex if more than one SA is involved. When connecting a Juniper firewall with a third-party VPN device that does not support route-based VPN, choosing policy-based VPN will make the configuration a lot simpler. For configuring proxy IDs, see Recipe 8.20.

8.20 Configure NAT with Route-Based VPN

Problem

You want to perform source and destination NAT on a route-based VPN tunnel.

Solution

You can configure either a DIP or a MIP on the tunnel interface, or you can configure policy DST-NAT within a policy (VIPs are not supported on tunnel interfaces). In this example, we'll use a DIP.

First, configure a tunnel interface and put it into a regular zone, as opposed to the tunnel zone we discussed in Recipe 8.19:

```
set zone name vpn
set interface tunnel.1 zone "vpn"
set interface tunnel.1 ip 1.1.1.2/24
```

Then, configure the `p1` and `p2` phases of the VPN tunnel and bind the VPN tunnel to the tunnel interface. The tunnel interface is the entry into the tunnel.

```
set ike gateway "test-gw" address 10.4.4.1 Main outgoing-interface
"ethernet0/1" preshare netscreen sec-level standard

set vpn "test-vpn" gateway "test-gw" no-replay tunnel idletime 0 sec-level standard
set vpn "test-vpn" monitor
set vpn "test-vpn" bind interface tunnel.1
```

Configure a DIP or a MIP on the tunnel interface:

```
set interface tunnel.1 dip 4 1.1.1.150
set interface tunnel.1 mip 1.1.1.100 host 192.168.1.100
```

Next, configure regular policies and reference the DIP and the MIP:

```
set address "Trust" "192.168.1.0/24" 192.168.1.0 255.255.255.0
set address "vpn" "192.168.2.0/24" 192.168.2.0 255.255.255.0

set policy id 1 from "Trust" to "vpn"  "192.168.1.0/24" "192.168.2.0/24"
"ANY" nat src dip-id 4 permit

set policy id 4 from "vpn" to "Trust"  "192.168.2.0/24"
"MIP(1.1.1.100)" "ANY" permit log
```

You could alternatively configure policy NAT-DST in the policy. The source and destination zones are identical because the public portion of the NAT-DST translation is in the same network with the tunnel zone. This is the same rule that applies for policy NAT-DST outside of VPN:

```
set address "vpn" "1.1.1.100/32" 1.1.1.100 255.255.255.255
set address "vpn" "192.168.2.0/24" 192.168.2.0 255.255.255.0

set policy id 3 from "vpn" to "vpn"  "192.168.2.0/24"
"1.1.1.100/32" "ANY" nat dst ip 192.168.1.100 permit log
```

Create a route for the remote network. This route does not need a next hop because it is pointing into a point-to-point tunnel:

```
set route 192.168.2.0/24 interface tunnel.1
```

The policies do not need to match on the remote end, FW-B, unlike with policy-based routing. SAs are not derived from the policies with route-based tunnels. The policy simply needs to permit the traffic from and into the zone of the tunnel interface:

```
set address "Trust" "192.168.2.0/24" 192.168.2.0 255.255.255.0
set address "vpn" "192.168.1.0/24" 192.168.1.0 255.255.255.0
set address "vpn" "1.1.1.0/24" 1.1.1.0 255.255.255.0

set policy id 3 from "vpn" to "Trust"  "1.1.1.0/24" "192.168.2.0/24" "ANY" permit log

set policy id 4 from "Trust" to "vpn"  "192.168.2.0/24" "1.1.1.0/24" "ANY" permit log
```

Also, set a route on FW-B for the local network. Take note to use the public address instead if you translate.

```
set route 192.168.1.0/24 interface tunnel.1
set route 1.1.1.0/24 interface tunnel.1
```

Discussion

In general, NAT with route-based VPN tunnels works the same way as physical links. Apply the same settings you would otherwise apply to a physical or logical interface.

A route-based VPN does not identify traffic destined for the VPN by a policy. A route-based VPN is constructed between two security gateways and is anchored on tunnel interfaces. This makes the VPN look like a point-to-point or point-to-multipoint WAN link, similar to Frame Relay or Asynchronous Transfer Mode (ATM). Protected traffic is determined by routes into the tunnel interface instead of by policies. Take note that the action on the ScreenOS policy is now "permit" instead of "tunnel".

This recipe uses the simple network topology shown in Figure 8-6 for discussion purposes: there is a network on the local side with `192.168.1.0/24`, and a network on the remote side with `192.168.2.0/24`.

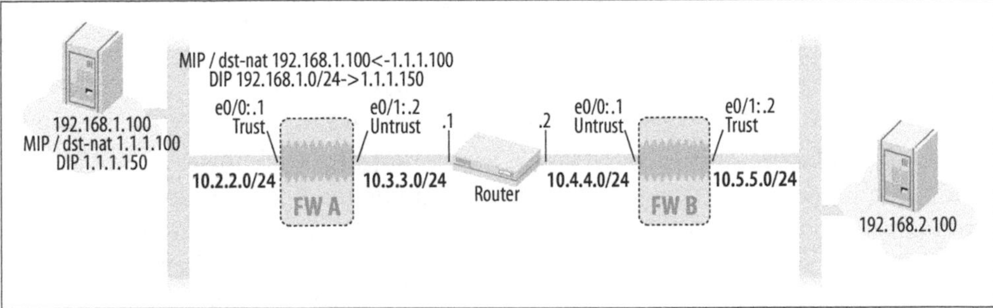

Figure 8-6. NAT with route-based VPN

On the left side is a server with IP `192.168.1.100` and with various address translation options, which are exclusive to each other. For example, you can source-address-translate `192.168.1.100` to `1.1.1.150` with a DIP, and you can source- and destination-address-translate between `192.168.1.100` and `1.1.1.100` with a MIP. Instead of using a MIP, you can perform a destination translation with policy NAT-DST from `1.1.1.100` to `192.168.1.100`. First, the VPN is defined on FW-A:

```
set zone name vpn
set interface tunnel.1 zone "vpn"
set interface tunnel.1 ip 1.1.1.2/32

set ike gateway "test-gw" address 10.4.4.1 Main outgoing-interface
"ethernet0/1" preshare netscreen sec-level standard

set vpn "test-vpn" gateway "test-gw" no-replay tunnel idletime 0 sec-level standard
set vpn "test-vpn" bind interface tunnel.1
```

You anchor DIPs and MIPs on the tunnel interface in the same way you anchor them on physical ingress and egress interfaces outside a route-based VPN. Note that a MIP is a bidirectional address translation and has precedence over a DIP.

```
set interface tunnel.1 dip 4 1.1.1.150
set interface tunnel.1 mip 1.1.1.100 host 192.168.1.100
```

With a route-based VPN there are no tunnel policies. Normally, tunnel policies are used to derive SAs for the different tunnels between two security gateways. With route-based VPN there is only one tunnel between two security gateways. SAs have no significance. However, permit policies are used to control the flow of traffic from the `Trust` to the vpn zone and vice versa.

```
set address "Trust" "192.168.1.0/24" 192.168.1.0 255.255.255.0
set address "vpn" "192.168.2.0/24" 192.168.2.0 255.255.255.0
set address "vpn" "1.1.1.100/32" 1.1.1.100 255.255.255.255

set policy id 1 from "Trust" to "vpn" "192.168.1.0/24"
"192.168.2.0/24" "ANY" nat src dip-id 4 permit

set policy id 2 from "Trust" to "vpn" "192.168.1.0/24"
"192.168.2.0/24" "ANY" permit log
```

```
set policy id 4 from "vpn" to "Trust" "192.168.2.0/24"
"MIP(1.1.1.100)" "ANY" permit log

set policy id 3 from "vpn" to "vpn"  "192.168.2.0/24"
"1.1.1.100/32" "ANY" nat dst ip 192.168.1.100 permit log
```

As mentioned before, the three NAT policies are basically mutually exclusive to each other. The preceding code is just a textbook example to show how to configure the alternatives. Policy `ID 2` matches the MIP in the function as a source address translation where the MIP is implied. Notice the `vpn` zone. The zone in the policy follows the ingress and egress interfaces, and the tunnel interface is nothing more than a regular interface in terms of creating policies or performing NAT. For the tunnel interface to be used by traffic, you have to establish routing. The easiest way to do this is via a static route (but dynamic routing could be used, too):

```
set route 192.168.2.0/24 interface tunnel.1
```

On the remote side, the tunnel interface is put into the `vpn` custom zone. Policies therefore go from and to `vpn`. An `any-permit` policy in either direction would suffice. For demonstration purposes, those three policies match the three policies on the local gateway. Because a MIP is a bidirectional translation, the two policies `ID 3` and `ID 4` on the remote gateway, and `ID 2` and `ID 3` on the local gateway, would match depending on the initiating direction:

```
set address "Trust" "192.168.2.0/24" 192.168.2.0 255.255.255.0
set address "vpn" "192.168.1.0/24" 192.168.1.0 255.255.255.0
set address "vpn" "1.1.1.0/24" 1.1.1.0 255.255.255.0

set policy id 3 from "vpn" to "Trust"  "1.1.1.0/24" "192.168.2.0/24"
"ANY" permit log

set policy id 4 from "Trust" to "vpn"  "192.168.2.0/24" "1.1.1.0/24"
"ANY" permit log
```

Lastly, route the private and public networks, if you translate, into the tunnel interface so that the tunnel encrypts the traffic:

```
set route 192.168.1.0/24 interface tunnel.1
set route 1.1.1.0/24 interface tunnel.1
```

Note that you can fake SAs for the sake of connecting to a policy-based VPN on the remote end. If you do that, make sure the SAs match on either end. Do not change them unless it is warranted.

```
set vpn test-vpn proxy-id local-ip 192.168.1.0/24 remote-ip 192.168.2.0/24 any
```

Use `get sa id` *`<idx>`* to check for the appropriate SAs on either end. You only need to change the SA on a route-based tunnel when the remote end is a policy-based VPN gateway, for instance, because you are connecting to a security gateway from a different vendor. On a route-based VPN, the SA consists of all zeros by default.

8.21 Troubleshoot NAT Mode

Problem

You want to troubleshoot problems with NAT mode.

Solution

For configuration verification use the following command:

```
get config | incl "int.* nat"
```

For troubleshooting use the following commands:

```
debug flow basic
get session
```

Discussion

Whereas you can switch ScreenOS from *route mode* to *transparent mode* by attaching at least one interface to an L2 zone, you can switch ScreenOS from *route mode* to *NAT mode* by placing the `Trust` interface into *NAT mode*. NAT mode has relevance only to an interface in the `Trust` zone, although it may be configured on any interface, which can be confusing.

```
set interface e1 zone trust
set interface e1 nat
set interface e2 zone dmz
set interface e2 route
set interface e3 zone untrust
set interface e3 route
```

In other words, you need to check whether at least one interface in the `Trust` zone is in NAT mode:

```
NS-5GT-> get config | incl "int.* nat"
set interface wireless2 nat
set interface loopback.1 nat
```

The following conditions exist:

- NAT mode has an effect only on interfaces in the `Trust` zone.
- If all zones are in the `trust-vr`, which is the default, NAT mode enables PAT to the egress interface IP of interfaces in the `Untrust` or `DMZ` zone, regardless of whether those interfaces are in NAT or ROUTE mode. It has no effect on any flows into or out of custom zones regardless of the zone membership of the ingress or egress interfaces and their mode settings.
- If the `Trust` zone is in the `trust-vr`, NAT mode enables PAT to all other zones in the `untrust-vr`, regardless of the zone membership of the egress interface and its mode setting.

- Unlike with NAT routers, traffic in the reverse is passed without translation. The implicit deny rule would deny traffic from Untrust to Trust by default. A VIP or MIP on the interface in the Untrust zone would provide reverse translations for servers.
- You can overwrite the default behavior of NAT mode with a MIP with an actual translation or a null translation.

In most cases, it is easier to use a DIP instead. Make it a habit to switch all interfaces to ROUTE mode, with the exception of the special case for the NAT mode of a two-interface firewall, which uses the default zones Trust and Untrust. This avoids unexpected confusions later on.

You can troubleshoot any flow issues on the firewall with debug flow basic. Use the set ffilter command to narrow your output. NAT mode uses the implicit DIP ID 2, similar to what would occur if you had used the nat keyword within a policy. The DIP ID 2 is always identical to the IP of the egress interface. In the following example, the inside address 192.168.97.128 with src-port 2258 is translated to the public address 70.112.81.130 with src-port 1577. Notice that the ALG HTTP is involved.

```
NS-5GT-> get db stream
****** 612755.0: <Trust/ethernet1> packet received [52]******
  ipid = 24289(5ee1), @0277f134
  packet passed sanity check.
  ethernet1:192.168.97.128/2258->209.85.237.104/80,6<Root>
  no session found
  flow_first_sanity_check: in <ethernet1>, out <N/A>
  [ Dest] 1.route 192.168.97.128->0.0.0.0, to ethernet1
  chose interface ethernet1 as incoming nat if.
  flow_first_routing: in <ethernet1>, out <N/A>
  search route to (ethernet1, 192.168.97.128->209.85.237.104) in vr
trust-vr for vsd-0/flag-0/ifp-null
  [ Dest] 36.route 209.85.237.104->70.112.80.1, to ethernet3
  routed (x_dst_ip 209.85.237.104) from ethernet1 (ethernet1 in 0) to ethernet3
  policy search from zone 2-> zone 1
 policy_flow_search  policy search nat_crt from zone 2-> zone 1
  RPC Mapping Table search returned 0 matched service(s) for (vsys
Root, ip 209.85.237.104, port 80, proto 6)
  No SW RPC rule match, search HW rule
  Permitted by policy 101
  dip id = 2, 192.168.97.128/2258->70.112.81.130/1577
  choose interface ethernet3 as outgoing phy if
  no loop on ifp ethernet3.
  session application type 6, name HTTP, nas_id 0, timeout 300sec
  service lookup identified service 6.
  flow_first_final_check: in <ethernet1>, out <ethernet3>
  existing vector list 90b-3d4c4c0.
  Session (id:4029) created for first pak 90b
  flow_first_install_session======>
  route to 70.112.80.1
```

```
  arp entry found for 70.112.80.1
  nsp2 wing prepared, ready
  cache mac in the session
  make_nsp_ready_no_resolve()
  search route to (ethernet3, 209.85.237.104->192.168.97.128) in vr
trust-vr for vsd-0/flag-3000/ifp-ethernet1
  [ Dest] 1.route 192.168.97.128->192.168.97.128, to ethernet1
  route to 192.168.97.128
  idp flow creation is successful.
  flow got session.
  flow session id 4029
  flow_idp_client_vector: in <ethernet1>, out <ethernet3>
  av/uf/voip checking.
  tcp seq check.
  Got syn, 192.168.97.128(2258)->209.85.237.104(80), nspflag 0x801e01, 0x800e00
  flow_idp_server_vector: in <ethernet1>, out <ethernet3>
  search route to (null, 0.0.0.0->209.85.237.104) in vr trust-vr for
vsd-0/flag-1000/ifp-vlan1
 no route to (0.0.0.0->209.85.237.104) in vr trust-vr/0
 flow_send_vector_, vid = 0, is_layer2_if=0
  send packet to traffic shaping queue.
  flow_ip_send: 5ee1:70.112.81.130->209.85.237.104,6 => ethernet3(52)
flag 0x20000, vlan 0
 pak has mac
  Send to ethernet3 (66)
```

NAT mode automatically assigns a DIP `ID 2`. The `session id 4029` that corresponds with the preceding debug flow output is as follows:

```
NS-5GT-> get session id 4029
id 4029(00000fbd), flag 08000000/8100/1001, vsys id 0(Root)
policy id 101, application id 6, dip id 2, state 0
di enabled
current timeout 10, max timeout 10 (second)
status normal, start time 613454, duration 4
session id mask 0, app value 0
ethernet1(vsd 0): 192.168.97.128/2258->209.85.237.104/80, protocol 6
session token 4 route 1
  gtwy 208.111.159.61, mac 00155830c7b7, nsptn info 0, pmtu 1500
  flag 801801, diff 0/0
  port seq 0, subif 0, cookie 0, fin seq 2204825601, fin state 1
ethernet3(vsd 0): 70.112.81.130/1577->209.85.237.104/80, protocol 6
session token 6 route 36
  gtwy 70.112.80.1, mac 00135f05e105, nsptn info 0, pmtu 1500
mac 00135f05e105, nsptn info 0
  flag 801800, diff 0/0
  port seq 0, subif 0, cookie 0, fin seq 1456248245, fin state 2
```

The application ID refers to an ALG. Application ID 6 stands for HTTP. The HTTP ALG does not deal with NAT, but when, for example, you would place a SIP VoIP call, you would see that application ID 63 is in the session.

8.22 Troubleshoot DIPs (Policy NAT-SRC)

Problem

You want to troubleshoot problems with DIPs.

Solution

For configuration verification use these commands:

```
get dip
get config | include dip
get interface <int> dip [ detail ]
```

For troubleshooting use the following commands:

```
debug flow basic
get session
debug dip all
```

Discussion

You can review DIP configuration with several commands. get `dip` gives a good overview of all the DIPs configured on the device. In particular, it shows in a nice summary which interface the DIP lives in and what type of a DIP it is. The `Dip Low` column lists the first IP in a `DIP` pool and the `Dip High` column shows the last IP in a `DIP` pool. It also shows whether DIP stickiness or an alarm is configured.

```
SSG140-> get dip
Dip Id  Dip Low          Dip High         Interface       Attribute
   4    10.10.10.50      10.10.10.150     ethernet0/0     ip-shift
Port-xlated dip stickness on
DIP pool utilization alarm: enabled, raise threshold 90%, clear threshold 80%
```

If you want to check on a specific configuration syntax, get `config | include dip` will show all the DIP-related configuration parameters. The pipe character feeds into a regular expression of which `dip` is the pattern. Patterns can be more detailed. For instance, get `config | include "policy .*dip"` will only show policies with a configured DIP; get `config | include "int.*dip"` will only show the DIP configuration on interfaces.

```
SSG140-> get config | include dip
set interface ethernet0/1 dip 5 10.10.20.100 10.10.20.150
set interface ethernet0/1 dip 6 10.10.20.151 10.10.20.151
set dip sticky
set dip alarm-raise 90 alarm-clear 80
set policy from "Trust" to "Untrust"  "Any" "Any" "ANY" nat src dip-id 5 permit
```

`get interface <int> dip [ detail ]` gives the most detailed information. The output also shows the size of the DIP pool, and how many addresses are already allocated. The `detail` configuration option in particular is helpful with DIP pool and DIP shift to show the exact scope and translation. The dynamic-ip column shows the DIP pool and the host-ip column shows the translation from DIP shift. The port-x column also shows whether you do dynamic port translation.

```
SSG140-> get int e0/0 dip
  id =   4:  ip range 10.10.10.50 ~ 10.10.10.150; (ip-shift)
        - available 100, active 0, inactive 0
SSG140-> get int e0/1 dip
  id =   5:  ip range 10.10.20.100 ~ 10.10.20.150; (port-xlate)
        - available 51, active 0, inactive 0
  id =   6:  ip range 10.10.20.151 ~ 10.10.20.151; (port-xlate)
        - available 1, active 0, inactive 0

SSG140-> get int e0/0 dip detail
 dynamic-ip        port-x     id       host-ip
 10.10.10.50         No        4       192.168.1.50
 10.10.10.51         No        4       192.168.1.51
 10.10.10.52         No        4       192.168.1.52
 10.10.10.53         No        4       192.168.1.53
 10.10.10.54         No        4       192.168.1.54
[...]
```

Troubleshooting DIP problems is straightforward. As with anything that goes through the firewall, debug flow basic will show what is going on. Use the set ffilter command to narrow your output. In the following example, the DIP ID 5 is used to translate the inside address 192.168.1.100 to the outside address 10.10.20.102. Notice that no ALG is involved in this flow. This is an ICMP ping.

```
SSG140-> get db stream
****** 03919.0: <Trust/ethernet0/0> packet received [84]******
  ipid = 15784(3da8), @1d56b914
  packet passed sanity check.
  ethernet0/0:192.168.1.100/2785->10.10.20.1/7436,1(8/0)<Root>
  no session found
  flow_first_sanity_check: in <ethernet0/0>, out <N/A>
  chose interface ethernet0/0 as incoming nat if.
  flow_first_routing: in <ethernet0/0>, out <N/A>
  search route to (ethernet0/0, 192.168.1.100->10.10.20.1) in vr
trust-vr for vsd-0/flag-0/ifp-null
  [ Dest] 3.route 10.10.20.1->10.10.20.1, to ethernet0/1
  routed (x_dst_ip 10.10.20.1) from ethernet0/0 (ethernet0/0 in 0) to ethernet0/1
  policy search from zone 2-> zone 1
 policy_flow_search  policy search nat_crt from zone 2-> zone 1
  RPC Mapping Table search returned 0 matched service(s) for (vsys
Root, ip 10.10.20.1, port 55101, proto 1)
  No SW RPC rule match, search HW rule
  Permitted by policy 1
  dip id = 5, 192.168.1.100/2785->10.10.20.102/3058
  choose interface ethernet0/1 as outgoing phy if
  no loop on ifp ethernet0/1.
  session application type 0, name None, nas_id 0, timeout 60sec
  service lookup identified service 0.
```

```
  flow_first_final_check: in <ethernet0/0>, out <ethernet0/1>
  existing vector list 1-4faf434.
  Session (id:56062) created for first pak 1
  flow_first_install_session======>
  route to 10.10.20.1
  arp entry found for 10.10.20.1
  ifp2 ethernet0/1, out_ifp ethernet0/1, flag 00800800, tunnel ffffffff, rc 1
  outgoing wing prepared, ready
  handle cleartext reverse route
  search route to (ethernet0/1, 10.10.20.1->192.168.1.100) in vr
trust-vr for vsd-0/flag-3000/ifp-ethernet0/0
  [ Dest] 5.route 192.168.1.100->10.10.10.1, to ethernet0/0
  route to 10.10.10.1
  arp entry found for 10.10.10.1
  ifp2 ethernet0/0, out_ifp ethernet0/0, flag 00800801, tunnel ffffffff, rc 1
  flow got session.
  flow session id 56062
  post addr xlation: 10.10.20.102->10.10.20.1.
 flow_send_vector_, vid = 0, is_layer2_if=0
```

A common error with DIPs is `packet dropped, dip alloc failed`, which you can see in the output of `debug flow basic`. Most of the time, this error means a matching DIP may exist but it is on the wrong interface, perhaps because the routing is different than intended or because the DIP was attached to the ingress interface instead of the egress interface. Remember the simple rule: source translation is applied to the packet on egress interfaces, whereas destination translation is applied to the packet on ingress interfaces. Another reason this error message might occur is because the DIP pool was exhausted as it was being scoped too small, or maybe because you are experiencing scans from malware. Review your screen settings—in particular, the flood control and session limiters.

A DIP is part of a session table; you also can see the translation in the session table with `get session`:

```
SSG140-> get session
alloc 1/max 56064, alloc failed 0, mcast alloc 0, di alloc failed 0
total reserved 0, free sessions in shared pool 56063
id 56062/s**,vsys 0,flag 00000010/0000/0001,policy 1,time 1, dip 5 module 0
 if 0(nspflag 800801):192.168.1.100/1918->10.10.20.1/7436,1,
000585c189d0, sess token 4,vlan 0,tun 0,vsd 0,route 5
 if 5(nspflag 800800):10.10.20.102/2189<-10.10.20.1/7436,1,
000585cf38f0, sess token 6,vlan 0,tun 0,vsd 0,route 3
```

`debug dip all` could deliver valuable information about internal DIP allocation:

```
SSG140-> get db stream
Get DIP [Root][ethernet0/1](5): host(192.168.1.100), port(0),
ifp_ip(10.10.20.2), desired(0.0.0.0)
  --Got Sticky DIP [Root][ethernet0/1](5): 10.10.20.102/2152
Release DIP [Root]: did=5 host=192.168.1.100 dip=10.10.20.102
pport=2152, dst=10.10.20.1 flag=0x80
```

The maximum number of DIPs is restricted for all platforms. On ScreenOS 6.0 and later, the maximum number of DIPs is 1,021, and for ScreenOS 5.4 and earlier, it is 252. The limit is per VR, and you can configure up to 65,536 over all VRs. The total number of DIP sessions is also limited, and you can review it with `get sys-cfg | include "port node"`. Depending on the platform, it can be up to the maximum session count because some platforms can translate more than one `src-ip` to a dynamically allocated port so that you can get a multiple of 65,536 sessions per DIP IP. Keep in mind that normally, only a small fraction of sessions will be DIP sessions on a gateway firewall.

8.23 Troubleshoot Policy NAT-DST

Problem

You want to troubleshoot problems with NAT-DST.

Solution

For configuration verification use this command:

```
get config | incl "policy .*nat dst"
```

For troubleshooting use the following commands:

```
debug flow basic
get session
debug nat all
```

Discussion

There is no specific get command to check with policy NAT-DST, because everything is configured in a policy. Use the pipe and regular expression match `get config | incl "policy .*nat dst"` to display the commands with NAT-DST:

```
SSG140-> get config | incl "policy .*nat dst"
set policy id 1 from "Untrust" to "Trust"  "Any" "server-prv" "SSH" nat dst ip
192.168.1.100 port 23 permit
```

You can troubleshoot with `debug flow basic`. Use the `set ffilter` command to narrow your output. You can clearly see the route lookup for the public IP address, which is in the same network as the ingress zone. You can also clearly see the `xlate` (translation) and where the private portion is routed out. In this example, address `10.10.20.100` is translated to address `192.168.1.100`. Also, notice how routing occurs. The first route lookup occurs for `10.10.20.100`; after the session is permitted, a second route lookup for `192.168.1.100` occurs:

```
SSG140-> get db stream
****** 12125.0: <Untrust/ethernet0/1> packet received [60]******
  ipid = 13240(33b8), @1d55e114
  packet passed sanity check.
```

```
  ethernet0/1:10.10.20.1/1649->10.10.20.100/23,6<Root>
  no session found
  flow_first_sanity_check: in <ethernet0/1>, out <N/A>
  chose interface ethernet0/1 as incoming nat if.
  flow_first_routing: in <ethernet0/1>, out <N/A>
  search route to (ethernet0/1, 10.10.20.1->10.10.20.100) in vr
trust-vr for vsd-0/flag-0/ifp-null
  [ Dest] 3.route 10.10.20.100->10.10.20.100, to ethernet0/1
  routed (x_dst_ip 10.10.20.100) from ethernet0/1 (ethernet0/1 in 0) to ethernet0/1
  policy search from zone 1-> zone 1
 policy_flow_search  policy search nat_crt from zone 1-> zone 1
  RPC Mapping Table search returned 0 matched service(s) for
(vsys Root, ip 10.10.20.100, port 23, proto 6)
  No SW RPC rule match, search HW rule
  Permitted by policy 1
  DST xlate: 10.10.20.100(23) to 192.168.1.100(23)
  search route to (ethernet0/1, 10.10.20.1->192.168.1.100) in
vr trust-vr for vsd-0/flag-0/ifp-null
  [ Dest] 7.route 192.168.1.100->10.10.10.1, to ethernet0/0
  routed (192.168.1.100) from ethernet0/1 (ethernet0/1 in 0) to ethernet0/1
  No src xlate   choose interface ethernet0/0 as outgoing phy if
  no loop on ifp ethernet0/0.
  session application type 10, name None, nas_id 0, timeout 1800sec
ALG vector is not attached
  service lookup identified service 0.
  flow_first_final_check: in <ethernet0/1>, out <ethernet0/0>
  existing vector list 113-2b59bf4.
  Session (id:56062) created for first pak 113
  flow_first_install_session======>
  route to 10.10.10.1
  arp entry found for 10.10.10.1
  ifp2 ethernet0/0, out_ifp ethernet0/0, flag 00800800, tunnel ffffffff, rc 1
  outgoing wing prepared, ready
  handle cleartext reverse route
  search route to (ethernet0/0, 192.168.1.100->10.10.20.1) in
vr trust-vr for vsd-0/flag-3000/ifp-ethernet0/1
  [ Dest] 3.route 10.10.20.1->10.10.20.1, to ethernet0/1
  route to 10.10.20.1
  arp entry found for 10.10.20.1
  ifp2 ethernet0/1, out_ifp ethernet0/1, flag 00800801, tunnel ffffffff, rc 1
  flow got session.
  flow session id 56062
  tcp seq check.
  Got syn, 10.10.20.1(1649)->10.10.20.100(23), nspflag 0x801801, 0x800800
  post addr xlation: 10.10.20.1->192.168.1.100.
 flow_send_vector_, vid = 0, is_layer2_if=0
```

The session id 56062 that corresponds with the preceding debug flow output is as follows:

```
SSG140-> get session id 56062
id 56062(0000dafe), flag 0c000000/0000/0001, vsys id 0(Root)
policy id 1, application id 0, dip id 0, state 0
current timeout 1760, max timeout 1800 (second)
```

```
status normal, start time 12125, duration 0
session id mask 0, app value 0
ethernet0/1(vsd 0): 10.10.20.1/1649->10.10.20.100/23, protocol 6
session token 6 route 3
  gtwy 10.10.20.100, mac 000585cf38f0, nsptn info 0, pmtu 1500
  flag 801801, diff 0/0
  port seq 0, subif 0, cookie 0, fin seq 0, fin state 0
ethernet0/0(vsd 0): 10.10.20.1/1649<-192.168.1.100/23, protocol
6 session token 4 route 7
  gtwy 10.10.10.1, mac 000585c189d0, nsptn info 0, pmtu 1500
mac 000585c189d0, nsptn info 0
  flag 801800, diff 0/0
  port seq 0, subif 0, cookie 0, fin seq 0, fin state 0
The session table shows us more clarity.
```

`debug nat all` shows you what is going on. The following is an example of debug output after we translate port 22 to port 23 but do not translate the IP address:

```
SSG140-> get db stream
## 2000-03-19 15:41:19 : search gate for if Untrust:10.10.20.1->192.168.1.
100,3748,22,6
## 2000-03-19 15:41:19 : in nat_search_hole, no gate found
++(5/0)nsp add(0x3a2af68): 10.10.20.1/3748->192.168.1.100/22,6, 10, 0x200a801
## 2000-03-19 15:41:19 : hash add 5(11697): 10.10.20.1/3748->192.168.1.100/22
++(0/0)nsp add(0x3a2afc0): 192.168.1.100/23->10.10.20.1/3748,6, 10, 0x800800
## 2000-03-19 15:41:19 : hash add 0(9102): 192.168.1.100/23->
    10.10.20.1/3748
```

Most problems with policy NAT-DST are caused by wrong routes to the public IP address. Remember that these routes need to follow the policy, and that the destination zone is equal to the ingress zone or must be the zone where the server is located. The route for the public IP needs to follow this rule. Also, ARP requests are answered only when `set arp nat-dst` is switched on, *and* when the public IP is in the same network as the ingress interface, *and* an intra-zone policy is configured; hence, ingress and egress zones are identical.

8.24 Troubleshoot VIPs

Problem

You want to troubleshoot problems with VIPs.

Solution

For configuration verification use these commands:

```
get vip
get vip <vip> port-status
get vip <vip> port <port>
get vip server
get config | include vip
```

For troubleshooting use the following commands:

```
debug flow basic
get session
debug vip basic
```

Discussion

You can verify VIP configuration with several commands. A good command to start with is `get vip`. If the VIP is attached to the interface itself instead of to a dedicated IP address, this IP may change. (To make the service available despite a dynamic IP address assignment, DDNS can be configured.) The first column is the global port, and the local port is referenced via a service object. The second column shows the interface on which the VIP lives. This interface must be in the `Untrust` zone for ScreenOS 6.0 and earlier versions. The third column shows the global and local destination ports of the VIP. The last column shows the local IP address of the VIP as well as its local port. Notice the `(OK)` in the last column, which shows the status of the local server:

```
FIREWALL-> get vip
Virtual IP       Interface       Port Service  Server/Port
1.1.1.100        ethernet0/1       80 HTTP     192.168.2.100/80(OK)
1.1.1.100        ethernet0/1       23 SSH      192.168.2.200/22(OK)
1.1.1.100        ethernet0/1       22 SSH      192.168.2.200/22(OK)
```

The command `get vip` also has several options. For example, `get vip <vip> port-status` is a useful command to see all the port mappings with the `multi-port` option. The first column describes the global port and the second the local port. The third column describes the Internet protocol, which can be a bit surprising, but VIPs can be used with TCP as well as UDP (most other transport layer protocols do not use the concept of ports). The last column again describes the local port, but this time via the service object, which was used in the VIP definition on the interface. In the following code, you can see that the service object `termsrv-32` spawns multiple translations. This is because `termsrv-32` references a range of ports and `set vip multi-port` is enabled:

```
FIREWALL-> get vip 1.1.1.100 port-status
Virtual IP      : 1.1.1.100
Port Allocation : 32 of 64
   Virtual Port -> Port    |  Protocol Id  |  Service Name
        2032    ->  2032   |       6       |    termsrv-32
        2031    ->  2031   |       6       |    termsrv-32
        2030    ->  2030   |       6       |    termsrv-32
 [...]
        2001    ->  2001   |       6       |    termsrv-32
```

The `get vip <vip> port <port>` command shows the same information for a specific global port. The virtual port is the global port, shown in the last line of the following example with its local translation. The server is the local IP, whereas the VIP is identified by its global IP:

```
FIREWALL-> get vip 1.1.1.100 port 23
Virtual IP    : 1.1.1.100
Virtual Port  : 23
Service       : SSH
Server        : 192.168.2.200(OK)
Virtual Port :    23 ->    22
```

The last command option is server. This gives a brief overview of all private IP addresses of servers and their health status:

```
FIREWALL-> get vip server
VIP server table:
  0: 192.168.1.100, state = ALIVE
  1: 10.10.20.250, state = DOWN
```

Often, it is useful to list all configuration lines that touch the VIP configuration. You can see that this command simply matches on the regular expression `vip`. For instance, in the following example, the last line shows that `VIP(10.10.20.251)` was configured in a multicell, but it does not show `set policy id x`, so you can only guess which rule this was in. Different patterns may garner narrower results, such as `get config | include "int.*vip "` or `get config | include "policy .*vip "`.

```
SSG140-> get config | include vip
set interface ethernet0/1 vip 10.10.20.250 81 "HTTP" 10.10.20.250
set interface ethernet0/1 vip 10.10.20.251 82 "HTTP" 192.168.1.100
set policy id 2 from "Trust" to "Untrust"  "Any" "VIP(10.10.20.250)" "HTTP" permit
set dst-address "VIP(10.10.20.251)"
```

You can troubleshoot any flow issues on the firewall with `debug flow basic`. (Use the `set ffilter` command to narrow your output.) The output is a little disappointing because you will not find a reference for the VIP explicitly. You can only find some hints:

```
SSG140-> get db stream
****** 27708.0: <Untrust/ethernet0/1> packet received [60]******
  ipid = 13154(3362), @1d5e4114
  packet passed sanity check.
  ethernet0/1:10.10.20.1/2639->10.10.20.100/2323,6<Root>
  no session found
  flow_first_sanity_check: in <ethernet0/1>, out <N/A>
  chose interface ethernet0/1 as incoming nat if.
  flow_first_routing: in <ethernet0/1>, out <N/A>
  search route to (ethernet0/1, 10.10.20.1->192.168.1.100) in vr trust
-vr for vsd-0/flag-0/ifp-null
  [ Dest] 5.route 192.168.1.100->10.10.10.1, to ethernet0/0
  routed (x_dst_ip 192.168.1.100) from ethernet0/1 (ethernet0/1 in 0) to ethernet0/0
  policy search from zone 1-> zone 2
 policy_flow_search  policy search nat_crt from zone 1-> zone 10
  RPC Mapping Table search returned 0 matched service(s) for (vsys
Root, ip 10.10.20.100, port 2323, proto 6)
  No SW RPC rule match, search HW rule
  Permitted by policy 1
  No src xlate   choose interface ethernet0/0 as outgoing phy if
  no loop on ifp ethernet0/0.
  session application type 10, name None, nas_id 0, timeout 1800sec
```

```
ALG vector is not attached
  service lookup identified service 0.
  flow_first_final_check: in <ethernet0/1>, out <ethernet0/0>
  existing vector list 113-2b59c24.
  Session (id:56053) created for first pak 113
  flow_first_install_session======>
  route to 10.10.10.1
  arp entry found for 10.10.10.1
  ifp2 ethernet0/0, out_ifp ethernet0/0, flag 00800800, tunnel ffffffff, rc 1
  outgoing wing prepared, ready
  handle cleartext reverse route
  search route to (ethernet0/0, 192.168.1.100->10.10.20.1) in vr
trust-vr for vsd-0/flag-3000/ifp-ethernet0/1
  [ Dest] 3.route 10.10.20.1->10.10.20.1, to ethernet0/1
  route to 10.10.20.1
  arp entry found for 10.10.20.1
  ifp2 ethernet0/1, out_ifp ethernet0/1, flag 00800801, tunnel ffffffff, rc 1
  flow got session.
  flow session id 56053
  tcp seq check.
  Got syn, 10.10.20.1(2639)->10.10.20.100(2323), nspflag 0x801801,0x800800
  post addr xlation: 10.10.20.1->192.168.1.100.
 flow_send_vector_, vid = 0, is_layer2_if=0
```

A better place to look for the success of our VIP is the session table. Although the session table does not contain an explicit reference for the VIP, you can see clearly that `10.10.20.100` was translated into `192.168.1.100`, and that port 2323 was translated into port 23:

```
SSG140-> get session id 56053
id 56053(0000daf5), flag 0c000000/0000/0001, vsys id 0(Root)
policy id 1, application id 0, dip id 0, state 0
current timeout 1510, max timeout 1800 (second)
status normal, start time 27708, duration 0
session id mask 0, app value 0
ethernet0/1(vsd 0): 10.10.20.1/2639->10.10.20.100/2323, protocol 6
session token 6 route 3
  gtwy 10.10.20.100, mac 000585cf38f0, nsptn info 0, pmtu 1500
  flag 801801, diff 0/0
  port seq 0, subif 0, cookie 0, fin seq 0, fin state 0
ethernet0/0(vsd 0): 10.10.20.1/2639<-192.168.1.100/23, protocol 6
session token 4 route 5
  gtwy 10.10.10.1, mac 000585c189d0, nsptn info 0, pmtu 1500
mac 000585c189d0, nsptn info 0
  flag 801800, diff 0/0
  port seq 0, subif 0, cookie 0, fin seq 0, fin state 0
```

If the output from `debug flow basic` and `get session` is not enough, you can also use `debug vip basic`. Notice that server health is being checked (via a ping) before the session is created:

```
SSG140-> get db stream
## 2000-03-14 11:25:44 : ethernet0/1 get v service 10.10.20.1->
```

```
10.10.20.100:2323
## 2000-03-14 11:25:44 : found a vip for 10.10.20.100 on ethernet0/1 interface
## 2000-03-14 11:25:44 : vport = 3e10ec0,10.10.20.100:2323
## 2000-03-14 11:25:44 : in request: 10.10.20.1->10.10.20.100:2323
## 2000-03-14 11:25:44 : --- server state: ----
## 2000-03-14 11:25:44 : -1  192.168.1.100
## 2000-03-14 11:25:44 : alive.
## 2000-03-14 11:25:44 : allocated server ip:port = 192.168.1.100:23
## 2000-03-14 11:25:44 : Found VIP for session (port: 1022)
```

8.25 Troubleshoot MIPs

Problem

You want to troubleshoot problems with MIPs.

Solution

For configuration verification use these commands:

```
get mip
get config | include mip
```

For troubleshooting use the following commands:

```
debug flow basic
get session
debug mip all
```

Discussion

Verifying MIPs is easy. The `get mip` command lists all MIPs configured on the system. The `Map IP` column is the public IP, the `Host IP` column is the private IP, the `Interface` column lists the interface on which the MIP was configured, and the `VRouter` column lists the target VR in which the private IP is sought:

```
SSG140-> get mip
Total MIPs under Root configured:1 Max:1500.
--------------------------------------------------------------------
Map IP             Host IP         Interface   VRouter
--------------------------------------------------------------------
192.168.1.0/24     192.168.2.0     ethernet0/1 trust-vr
1.1.1.100/32       192.168.3.100   ethernet0/1 trust-vr
```

An easy way to see where a MIP touches a configuration is with `get config | include mip`, where `mip` is a regular expression filter to the configuration display. In some cases, it may be more useful to download the configuration to a local computer and to search it with an editor because typical configurations often have from hundreds to thousands of MIPs configured.

```
SSG140-> get config | include mip
set interface "ethernet0/1" mip 10.10.20.100 host 192.168.1.100
```

```
netmask 255.255.255.255 vr "trust-vr"
set policy id 1 from "Untrust" to "Trust"  "Any" "MIP(10.10.20.100)" "ANY" permit
```

Flow debugging with debug flow basic shows what is going on and helps to troubleshoot a connection. Use the set ffilter command to narrow your output. There is no explicit mention of the MIP, but there are a lot of hints. You can clearly see the translation: address 10.10.20.100 is translated to address 192.168.1.100.

```
SSG140-> get db stream
****** 34911.0: <Untrust/ethernet0/1> packet received [60]******
  ipid = 13330(3412), @1d501914
  packet passed sanity check.
  ethernet0/1:10.10.20.1/4255->10.10.20.100/23,6<Root>
  no session found
  flow_first_sanity_check: in <ethernet0/1>, out <N/A>
  chose interface ethernet0/1 as incoming nat if.
  flow_first_routing: in <ethernet0/1>, out <N/A>
  search route to (ethernet0/1, 10.10.20.1->192.168.1.100) in vr
trust-vr for vsd-0/flag-0/ifp-null
  [ Dest] 5.route 192.168.1.100->10.10.10.1, to ethernet0/0
  routed (x_dst_ip 192.168.1.100) from ethernet0/1 (ethernet0/1 in 0) to ethernet0/0
  policy search from zone 1-> zone 2
 policy_flow_search  policy search nat_crt from zone 1-> zone 10
  RPC Mapping Table search returned 0 matched service(s) for (vsys
Root, ip 10.10.20.100, port 23, proto 6)
  No SW RPC rule match, search HW rule
  Permitted by policy 1
  No src xlate   choose interface ethernet0/0 as outgoing phy if
  no loop on ifp ethernet0/0.
  session application type 10, name None, nas_id 0, timeout 1800sec
ALG vector is not attached
  service lookup identified service 0.
  flow_first_final_check: in <ethernet0/1>, out <ethernet0/0>
  existing vector list 113-2b59c24.
  Session (id:56057) created for first pak 113
  flow_first_install_session======>
  route to 10.10.10.1
  arp entry found for 10.10.10.1
  ifp2 ethernet0/0, out_ifp ethernet0/0, flag 00800800, tunnel ffffffff, rc 1
  outgoing wing prepared, ready
  handle cleartext reverse route
  search route to (ethernet0/0, 192.168.1.100->10.10.20.1) in vr trust-vr
 for vsd-0/flag-3000/ifp-ethernet0/1
  [ Dest] 3.route 10.10.20.1->10.10.20.1, to ethernet0/1
  route to 10.10.20.1
  arp entry found for 10.10.20.1
  ifp2 ethernet0/1, out_ifp ethernet0/1, flag 00800801, tunnel ffffffff, rc 1
  flow got session.
  flow session id 56057
  tcp seq check.
  Got syn, 10.10.20.1(4255)->10.10.20.100(23), nspflag 0x801801, 0x800800
  post addr xlation: 10.10.20.1->192.168.1.100.
 flow_send_vector_, vid = 0, is_layer2_if=0
```

You also can see the translation in session id 56057:

```
SSG140-> get session id 56057
id 56057(0000daf9), flag 0c000000/0000/0001, vsys id 0(Root)
policy id 1, application id 0, dip id 0, state 0
current timeout 1590, max timeout 1800 (second)
status normal, start time 34911, duration 0
session id mask 0, app value 0
ethernet0/1(vsd 0): 10.10.20.1/4255->10.10.20.100/23, protocol 6
session token 6 route 3
  gtwy 10.10.20.100, mac 000585cf38f0, nsptn info 0, pmtu 1500
  flag 801801, diff 0/0
  port seq 0, subif 0, cookie 0, fin seq 0, fin state 0
ethernet0/0(vsd 0): 10.10.20.1/4255<-192.168.1.100/23, protocol 6
session token 4 route 5
  gtwy 10.10.10.1, mac 000585c189d0, nsptn info 0, pmtu 1500
mac 000585c189d0, nsptn info 0
  flag 801800, diff 0/0
  port seq 0, subif 0, cookie 0, fin seq 0, fin state 0
```

Remember that a MIP is a bidirectional address translation. Therefore, a MIP performs destination translation as well as source translation, which you will see in the output from `debug flow basic` as well as `get session`. (The preceding example is a destination translation.)

`debug mip all` shows you the same in a simple line:

```
SSG140-> get db stream
## 2000-03-14 13:21:25 : IPv4 to IPv4: v4 10.10.20.100 -> v4 192.168.1.100
```

MIPs introduce very little overhead in the device, mainly in a small amount of time spent on the first packet when the session is established.

CHAPTER 9

Mitigating Attacks with Screens and Flow Settings

9.0 Introduction

In the world of computer and network security, there are myriad ways to launch an attack, which, from a network perspective, can generically be defined as "traffic that has malicious intent." There are certainly computer attacks that no firewall can prevent, such as those executed locally on the machine by a malicious user (and those executed on a machine by an implement such as a sledgehammer). Fortunately, however, these types of threats are often handled by a physical security infrastructure. Unfortunately, the network then becomes a convenient launching point for an attack for those without physical access. From the network's perspective, there are numerous types of attack. Although it's a vast oversimplification, for the purposes of discussing screens and flow settings, we can group attacks into two types: brute force and precision. ScreenOS has the capability to protect against both types of attack.

Under the category of brute force attacks, perhaps none are better known than those that fall under the Denial of Service classification. Denial of Service (DoS) attacks are one of the most well-known network security threats, largely due to the high-profile way in which they can affect networks. Over the years, some of the largest, most respected Internet sites have been effectively taken offline by DoS attacks, and these events have, not surprisingly, received enough media attention to make *DoS attack* a household term. A DoS attack typically has a singular focus, namely, to cause the services running on a particular host or network to become unavailable. Some DoS attacks exploit vulnerabilities in an operating system and cause it to crash, such as the infamous Winnuke attack. Others overwhelm a network or device with traffic so that there are no more resources to handle legitimate traffic. This latter type of attack can be particularly challenging to stop. Despite the challenges of stopping these *flood attacks*, one of the most common desires in implementing a firewall is in fact the ability to stop these attacks. Although ScreenOS has many powerful capabilities in this regard, a large, distributed DoS attack that is launched by hundreds or thousands of compromised hosts may be capable of generating hundreds of megabits per second of traffic. This is likely more bandwidth than is available to the Internet for most organizations, and must therefore be mitigated further upstream in the Internet Service Provider's (ISP's) networks. The most common flood types of attacks are the `SYN` flood, User Datagram Protocol (UDP) flood, and Internet Control Message Protocol (ICMP) flood. You can mitigate all of these using the screen settings within ScreenOS.

DoS attacks aimed at end hosts often exploit weaknesses in the underlying operating systems to cause the systems to become unresponsive, to crash, and so forth. These attacks are different from flood attacks because they can often be executed with just one or a few packets. Screens are available for some of the most common attacks in this category, such as the Winnuke, Land, and Teardrop attacks.

Precision attacks often involve a bit more thought than brute force attacks, and typically involve multiple phases, all the way from reconnaissance to machine ownership. Before a precision attack is launched, information about the victim needs to be gathered. This information gathering typically takes the form of various types of scans to determine available hosts, networks, and ports. Ping sweeps are used to determine which hosts are available on a network. Port scans are used to locate available ports on a machine.

Other scans send crafted packets to a victim, often with illegal options, such as having both the `SYN` and `FIN` bits set in a Transmission Control Protocol (TCP) packet. When the destination processes these illegal packets, depending on the operating system, different response packets will be generated. By analyzing the response, the attacker can gain valuable information about the host, such as the operating system version, so that he can more effectively tailor his attack strategy. You can use screens to detect and drop these types of malicious traffic.

Another common method of attack is to embed malicious code in data a user may access. This is often performed in a HyperText Transfer Protocol (HTTP) context with executable files, malicious Java™ code, and ActiveX controls. ScreenOS allows you to restrict access to all of these types of traffic.

Screens are configured on a per-zone basis, and they cover a wide variety of attack traffic. Depending on the type of screen being configured, there may be additional settings beyond simply blocking the traffic.

Attack prevention is also a native function of any firewall. ScreenOS handles traffic on a per-flow basis. You can use flows or sessions as a way to determine whether traffic attempting to traverse the firewall is legitimate. You control the state-checking components resident in ScreenOS by configuring "flow" settings. These settings allow you to configure state checking for various conditions on the device. You can use flow settings to protect against TCP hijacking, and to generally ensure that the firewall is performing full state processing when desired.

To adequately perform state checking, it is critical that the firewall be able to see both directions of any flow or session. To do this, symmetrical traffic patterns through the firewall are required. When higher-layer inspections are being performed, it is even more critical to have symmetric traffic patterns. You can enforce symmetry in a variety of ways, but some of the most common methods are to ensure a single path in and out of the network via deterministic routing using metrics, using Network Address Translation (NAT) to ensure a deterministic return, and using policy-based routing. In some cases, however, such as in virtual private network (VPN) environments, asymmetry may be acceptable as the traffic is already strongly authenticated.

9.1 Configure SYN Flood Protection

Problem

You want to use the firewall to mitigate SYN floods.

Solution

Configure SYN flood protection:

```
FIREWALL-A-> set zone "Trust" screen syn-flood
FIREWALL-A-> set zone "Trust" screen syn-flood alarm-threshold 250
FIREWALL-A-> set zone "Trust" screen syn-flood attack-threshold 250
FIREWALL-A-> set zone "Trust" screen syn-flood source-threshold 250
FIREWALL-A-> set zone "Trust" screen syn-flood destination-
    threshold 1000
FIREWALL-A-> set flow syn-proxy syn-cookie
```

Discussion

SYN flood protection is one of the most common screens to enable in ScreenOS. A *SYN flood* is an attack in which the attacker attempts to fill up a server's connection table with half-open connections. To do this, a large volume of `SYN` packets is sent to a victim machine, but the full three-way handshake is never completed. These attacks frequently utilize spoofed IP addresses. By default, in ScreenOS, once any of the thresholds configurable under SYN flood screen protection is exceeded, the firewall will begin to proxy the `SYN-ACK` responses on behalf of the client. In doing this, the goal is to prevent the server from running out of sockets. Only when an `ACK` response is returned to the firewall from a client will the firewall send the original `SYN` packet to the server. The server will then respond with a `SYN-ACK`, which the firewall will intercept, and will pass along the `ACK` packet, completing the three-way handshake. The net effect of this is that the firewall allows only valid connections to reach the server while weeding out invalid connection attempts. The major downside of this approach is that it is a very CPU-intensive process.

In more recent versions of ScreenOS, the capability to use SYN cookies which provide a cryptographic method of connection verification was added. By enabling SYN cookie protection at the flow level, you can expect much higher performance when defending against a SYN flood. It is strongly recommended that SYN cookie support be enabled.

As with all screens, SYN flood protection is enabled on a per-zone basis. The first step in configuring SYN flood protection is to enable it on the desired zone. Then, set the alarm and attack thresholds. The alarm threshold differs from the attack threshold so that you can choose to alarm at a different threshold than at that which the attacker drops traffic. You can also define specific thresholds based on the source or the destination address. If either of these is set, the lower of the values will be used. This capability is useful when protecting a server. In this example, the destination threshold is set to 1,000, whereas the source threshold is configured for 250. This is done because no more than 250 SYN packets per second per source are expected; however, up to 1,000 packets per second may be seen as destined to any given IP inside the network. Such a large number of SYN packets might be expected on a busy server farm. Conversely, a large proxy farm may generate very high rates of outbound SYN packets. Because each scenario would likely occur on a different zone on the firewall, it is important that the threshold settings accurately reflect the expected traffic profiles.

To verify the settings, use the get zone *<zone name>* screen command:

```
FIREWALL-A-> get zone trust screen
Screen function only generate alarm without dropping packet: OFF.
Screen function apply to traffic exiting tunnels:            OFF.
SYN flood protection(100)                                on
        Alarm  Threshold: 250
        Queue  Size     : 200
        Timeout Value   : 20
        Source Threshold: 250
        Destination Threshold: 1000
```

When a SYN flood is detected, an alarm is generated:

```
FIREWALL-A-> get alarm eve
Total event entries = 61
Date       Time     Module Level  Type Description
2007-9-10 08:48:26 system emer  00005 SYN flood! From 10.5.5.3:2073
                                      to 192.168.5.1:208, proto TCP
                                      (zone Trust,int bgroup0).
                                      Occurred 1 times.
```

To view the attack counters for a SYN flood, use the get zone *<zone name>* screen attack command:

```
FIREWALL-A-> get zone trust screen attack | include "syn flood"
SYN flood protection                                          1671
SYN Flood(same source)                                        2164
SYN Flood(same destination)                                   2507
```

See Also

Recipe 9.5

9.2 Control UDP Floods

Problem

You need to configure UDP flood protection to your DMZ, but you want to host a high-volume Domain Name System (DNS) server.

Solution

Configure UDP flood protection, and configure a separate threshold for the DNS server:

```
FIREWALL-A-> set zone trust screen udp-flood threshold 100
FIREWALL-A-> set zone trust screen udp-flood dst-ip 192.168.5.1
    threshold 1000
FIREWALL-A-> set zone trust screen udp-flood
```

Discussion

A *UDP flood* is a brute force DoS attack in which the attacker sends large volumes of UDP traffic toward a victim with the goal of either disabling the machine or filling up the available bandwidth with attack traffic. ScreenOS defends against UDP floods using a simple threshold value of packets per second, above which all traffic is dropped. UDP flood protection in ScreenOS allows for granular control of attack thresholds without the requirement of separating hosts with different thresholds into different zones. As with SYN flood protection, it is critical to define the thresholds for UDP floods appropriately based on the perspective of the firewall. For example, 100 packets per second of UDP traffic may be high for Internet-bound traffic, but low for traffic destined to a DNS server. Likewise, protocols that are typically found within the confines of an organization, such as the Trivial File Transfer Protocol (TFTP) and NFS, may generate high volumes of packets per second from a particular source compared to commonly found Internet-facing protocols such as DNS. In this recipe, separate thresholds are configured for the DNS server at `192.168.5.1`, and all other hosts. This allows the DNS server to receive a much larger volume of traffic. You can easily verify the settings using the get zone *<zone name>* screen command:

```
FIREWALL-A-> get zone trust screen
Screen function only generate alarm without dropping packet: OFF.
Screen function apply to traffic exiting tunnels:            OFF.
UDP flood protection(100)                                  on
    192.168.5.1(1000)                                        on
SYN flood protection(100)                                    on
        Alarm  Threshold: 100
        Queue  Size     : 200
```

```
Timeout Value   : 20
Source Threshold: 100
Destination Threshold: 1000
```

As you can see, the default threshold for any devices except for `192.168.5.1` is 100, as indicated by the 100 in parentheses. `192.168.5.1` has its threshold configured at 1,000 so that it can receive much more traffic. You can view UDP flood information in much the same way as SYN flood information. You generate alarm logs when UDP floods are detected:

```
FIREWALL-A-> get alarm eve
Total event entries = 1079
Date       Time     Module Level  Type Description
2007-9-10 09:09:44 system alert 00012 UDP flood! From 10.5.5.3:60196
                              to 192.168.5.1:879, proto UDP (zone
                              Trust, int bgroup0). Occurred 1 times.
```

Likewise, the get zone *<zone name>* screen attack command shows the counters for the number of times UDP floods were detected:

```
FIREWALL-A-> get zone trust screen attack | include udp
UDP flood protection                                    3603
```

You can also verify that traffic is being dropped using `debug flow basic`:

```
FIREWALL-A-> get ffilter
Flow filter based on:
id:0 src ip 10.5.5.3 dst ip 192.168.5.1
id:1 src ip 192.168.5.1 dst ip 10.5.5.3
FIREWALL-A-> debug flow basic
****** 2500293.0: <Trust/bgroup0> packet received [28]******
  ipid = 19403(4bcb), @031d2970
  screen detection drop packet.
```

As each dropped packet will deliver another debug message, you should use this capability with care.

See Also

Recipe 9.1; Recipe 9.5

9.3 Detect Scan Activity

Problem

You want to receive an alert when there is scan activity on the network.

Solution

Use screens to detect port scans and network sweeps:

```
FIREWALL-A-> set zone "Trust" screen port-scan
FIREWALL-A-> set zone "Trust" screen ip-sweep
```

```
FIREWALL-A-> set zone "Trust" screen ip-sweep threshold 20000
FIREWALL-A-> set zone "Trust" screen port-scan threshold 20000
```

Discussion

In ScreenOS, you use scan detection to detect and stop malicious reconnaissance activity. Scanning tools such as Nmap and Nessus are well known and widely deployed. Scans are typically used to find hosts to attack, but they can have a nasty side effect as well. A particularly aggressive scan can consume resources in the form of firewall sessions. You can detect and prevent against two types of scans: IP sweeps and port scans. IP sweep attacks use ping packets to determine which IP addresses on a network have active hosts. An attacker uses a port scan to determine which ports are listening on a particular host so that the services using these ports can be attacked. The threshold values configured for scan detection represent a value in microseconds. The scan detection screens trigger once 10 packets are seen within the interval represented in the threshold value. In this case, 20,000 microseconds is chosen as the interval, which translates to 20 milliseconds. Therefore, if 10 pings are detected within 20 milliseconds, the "IP-sweep" alarm should trigger. Use the get `alarm event` command to verify:

```
FIREWALL-A-> get alarm event
Total event entries = 69
Date       Time     Module Level  Type Description
2007-9-12 01:43:29 system alert 00017 Address sweep! From 10.5.5.3
                               to 192.168.5.66, proto 1 (zone Trust,
                               int bgroup0). Occurred 1 times.
```

Likewise, the port scan alarm should trigger when 10 packets are seen in a 20-millisecond interval to a particular host. Again, use the get `alarm` event command to verify:

```
FIREWALL-A-> get alarm event
Total event entries = 73
Date       Time     Module Level  Type Description
2007-9-12 02:05:38 system alert 00016 Port scan! From 10.5.5.3:1666
                               to 192.168.5.1:563, proto TCP (zone
                               Trust, int bgroup0). Occurred 1 times
```

Once the tenth packet has been detected within the 20-millisecond window, the firewall will begin to drop packets. You can see this in debug `flow basic`:

```
****** 2647913.0: <Trust/bgroup0> packet received [28]******
  ipid = 57932(e24c), @03141170
  screen detection drop packet.
  POLL_DROP_PAK: vlist 0x1c7d8d0, 0x1c7d8cc
```

Using screens to detect and drop scan activity can obfuscate the views an attacker has of the network and limit his information about the network and services running on it. The `get zone` *<zone name>* `screen attack` command shows the number of times each screen detection was triggered:

```
FIREWALL-A-> get zone trust screen attack | include port
Port scan protection                                  472
```

```
FIREWALL-A-> get zone trust screen attack | include sweep
IP sweep protection                                      468
```

9.4 Avoid Session Table Depletion

Problem

You need to ensure that malicious traffic does not deplete the firewall session table.

Solution

Use source- and destination-based session limits:

```
FIREWALL-A-> set zone "Trust" screen limit-session source-ip-
based 128
FIREWALL-A-> set zone "Trust" screen limit-session destination-ip-
based 1000
FIREWALL-A-> set zone "Trust" screen limit-session
```

Discussion

Sometimes, attackers attempt to deplete the firewall's session table, which always consists of a finite set of resources. A simple way to do this is to send a large volume of legitimate traffic, each session of which the firewall must track. If the firewall's session table becomes full, no new traffic will be permitted through the device, and a DoS will have been successfully executed.

Source- and destination-based session limits are tools for limiting the firewall resources consumed by a particular host. Depending on the size of the firewall and the deployment scenario, this number may vary considerably. You can also use source- and destination-based session limits to limit the spread of worms and to protect device resources from overutilization. They are a handy way to catch a number of unknown problems, and you can utilize them within Virtual Systems (VSYS) as well. As with the other flood-based screen detections, you should configure the `limit-session` screen with the limits, and then enable it in the desired zone(s). When the source IP-based session threshold is configured, the firewall will not allow more than the threshold number of sessions through from any particular source IP. When you use the source IP-based threshold of 128, once a particular source IP address attempts to send more than 128 sessions' worth of traffic through the firewall, all further sessions will be disallowed.

The source IP-based screen is often used on trusted networks to limit client activity. Worms, spyware, and other types of malware often cause a host to open a significant number of sessions outbound. Using source IP-based session thresholds can minimize the impact of these types of malware, and allow for simpler detection of their presence.

Both types of screens are particularly useful in VSYS environments where session limits can be enforced per VSYS to prevent a particular VSYS from consuming all of the device's session resources. As with other screen alerts, use the `get alarm event` command to view when the limit session screen has triggered:

```
FIREWALL-A-> get alarm event
Date       Time     Module Level  Type Description
2007-9-12 02:36:27 system crit  00033 Src IP session limit! From
                                      10.5.5.3:1594 to 10.50.40.24:631
                                      , proto TCP (zone Trust, int
                                      bgroup0). Occurred 1 times.
```

Likewise, you can use `debug flow basic` to view packets when they are being dropped:

```
FIREWALL-A-> get db str
****** 2649415.0: <Trust/bgroup0> packet received [28]******
  ipid = 8219(201b), @031d2170
  packet passed sanity check.
  bgroup0:10.5.5.3/40197->192.168.5.63/3117,1(8/0)<Root>
  no session found
  flow_first_sanity_check: in <bgroup0>, out <N/A>
  packet dropped, drop by firewall check
  POLL_DROP_PAK: vlist 0x1c7d8d0, 0x1c7d8d0
```

Finally, use the `get zone` *<zone name>* `screen attack` command to view counters for the screens:

```
FIREWALL-A-> get zone trust screen attack | include limit
Src IP-based session limiting                              114
Dst IP-based session limiting                             1498
```

9.5 Baseline Traffic to Prepare for Screen Settings

Problem

You want to implement screens for attack protection, but you don't want to drop legitimate traffic.

Solution

Configure the zone to alarm on attacks, but not to drop the traffic:

```
FIREWALL-A-> set zone untrust screen icmp-flood threshold 10
FIREWALL-A-> set zone untrust screen icmp-flood
FIREWALL-A-> set zone untrust screen alarm-without-drop
```

Discussion

Baselining network traffic should be considered a requirement for any network. It is a necessary step toward being able to plan for capacity upgrades, and to proactively address performance and security problems. A full baselining program involves multiple tools, such as SNMP managers and flow collectors. The ScreenOS MIB aids this effort by providing not just bandwidth information, but also session information.

Outside of the MIBs, ScreenOS has one tool for baselining in the realm of screen protection. Although there is often a very strong desire to stop DoS attacks, it can be a challenge, especially in a complex environment, to identify what is legitimate traffic and what is not. When implementing screens for the first time, configuring the zone to alarm without dropping the traffic is one way to determine what appropriate thresholds are without affecting legitimate traffic. It should be noted, however, that there are restrictions in current code with the `alarm-without-drop` function. Specifically, the following screen protections are not supported for this function:

- SYN-ACK-ACK Proxy Protection
- Mal-URL
- Session Limit
- Block Java Component
- Block ActiveX Component
- Block ZIP Component
- Block EXE Component

Additionally, on the ASIC-based platforms, such as the ISG and NS5000, no screens handled by the ASIC support the `alarm-without-drop` function. These screens include UDP and ICMP flood. You should consult the latest product documentation to ensure that the feature is supported based on the software and hardware being run. If the feature is not supported, you should use standard network baselining techniques.

By only alarming, you can investigate the source of an alarm before determining that traffic is illegal and dropping it. This way, if there are high volumes of legitimate traffic, you can configure the threshold appropriately before traffic is interrupted. Let's take an example of a host that is doing performance testing using high volumes of ICMP:

```
computer:~ me$ sudo ping -f 10.5.5.2
Password:
PING 10.5.5.2 (10.5.5.2): 56 data bytes
...............................................................
.................................^C
--- 10.5.5.2 ping statistics ---
2415 packets transmitted, 2415 packets received, 0% packet loss
round-trip min/avg/max/stddev = 4.182/28.205/124.619/19.788 ms
```

In normal conditions, packet loss in a complete flood to the test host is 0 percent. Now, enable ICMP flood screening for this zone using a low threshold on the theory that there should never be more than 10 packets per second of ICMP traffic:

```
FIREWALL-A-> set zone untrust screen icmp-flood threshold 10
FIREWALL-A-> set zone untrust screen icmp-flood
```

Running the same ICMP test, things now look very bad:

```
computer:~ me$ sudo ping -f 10.5.5.2
PING 10.5.5.2 (10.5.5.2): 56 data bytes
..................................................................
..................................................................
..................................................................
..................................................................
..................................................................
...^C
--- 10.5.5.2 ping statistics ---
449 packets transmitted, 33 packets received, 92% packet loss
round-trip min/avg/max/stddev = 4.183/4.699/6.813/0.575 ms
```

Here, notice that the packet loss from the ping flood test is 92 percent, whereas in normal conditions, it is 0 percent. Enabling the `alarm-without-drop` capability fixes the situation:

```
FIREWALL-A-> set zone untrust screen alarm-without-drop

computer:~ me$ sudo ping -f 10.5.5.2
PING 10.5.5.2 (10.5.5.2): 56 data bytes
.................................................................
.................................................................
.................................................................
...^C
--- 10.5.5.2 ping statistics ---
3875 packets transmitted, 3875 packets received, 0% packet loss
round-trip min/avg/max/stddev = 3.968/52.030/168.209/25.480 ms

FIREWALL-A-> get alarm eve
Date       Time     Module Level  Type Description
2007-9-10 06:44:55 system alert 00011 ICMP flood! From 192.168.5.1 to
                                      10.5.5.2, proto 1 (zone Untrust,
                                      int ethernet0/0). Occurred 505
                                      times.
2007-9-10 06:44:54 system alert 00011 ICMP flood! From 192.168.5.1 to
                                      10.5.5.2, proto 1 (zone Untrust,
                                      int ethernet0/0). Occurred 740
                                      times.
2007-9-10 06:44:53 system alert 00011 ICMP flood! From 192.168.5.1 to
                                      10.5.5.2, proto 1 (zone Untrust,
                                      int ethernet0/0). Occurred 847
                                      times.
2007-9-10 06:44:52 system alert 00011 ICMP flood! From 192.168.5.1 to
                                      10.5.5.2, proto 1 (zone Untrust,
                                      int ethernet0/0). Occurred 797
                                      times.
2007-9-10 06:44:51 system alert 00011 ICMP flood! From 192.168.5.1 to
                                      10.5.5.2, proto 1 (zone Untrust,
                                      int ethernet0/0). Occurred 712
                                      times.
```

```
2007-9-10 06:44:50 system alert 00011 ICMP flood! From 192.168.5.1 to
                                      10.5.5.2, proto 1 (zone Untrust,
                                      int ethernet0/0). Occurred 240
                                      times.
Total entries matched = 8
```

As hoped, the alarm threshold is still being triggered, but no traffic is being dropped. Next, configure a higher threshold to accommodate the test traffic. Notice from the alarm that the highest one-second interval of testing delivered 847 packets. To be safe, add a little bit of headroom, and configure the ICMP threshold for this zone to be 1,000:

```
FIREWALL-A-> set zone untrust screen icmp-flood threshold 1000
FIREWALL-A-> set zone untrust screen icmp-flood
```

Clear the alarms for readability:

```
FIREWALL-A-> clear alarm event
```

Rerun the test:

```
computer:~ me$ sudo ping -f 10.5.5.2
Password:
PING 10.5.5.2 (10.5.5.2): 56 data bytes
.................................................................
.................................................................
.................................................................
.................................................................
.................................................................
...............................^.
--- 10.5.5.2 ping statistics ---
8050 packets transmitted, 8050 packets received, 0% packet loss
round-trip min/avg/max/stddev = 3.957/52.285/171.744/33.065 ms
FIREWALL-A-> get alarm eve
No entry matched.
```

Because no more alarms are being generated, disable the `alarm-without-drop` function to begin protecting against ICMP floods:

```
FIREWALL-A-> unset zone untrust screen alarm-without-drop
```

Although this recipe dealt with the subject of floods, when enabling screens on a zone, it is always a good idea to set `alarm-without-drop` initially so that any unexpected but legitimate traffic is not dropped. By following this practice, you can properly investigate unusual traffic.

See Also

Recipe 9.1; Recipe 9.2

9.6 Use Flow Configuration for State Enforcement

Problem

You need to ensure stateful traffic processing and send TCP resets for out-of-state traffic on an interface.

Solution

Use flow configuration to ensure that state checking is enabled:

```
FIREWALL-A-> set flow tcp-syn-check
FIREWALL-A-> unset flow no-tcp-seq-check
FIREWALL-A-> set zone untrust tcp-rst
```

Discussion

ScreenOS uses the concept of flow in its configuration to decide how to deal with issues of state. The first command in this recipe forces the firewall to ensure that a full three-way handshake is completed before a session is created on the firewall. By ensuring that a full three-way handshake is completed, a form of source authentication is performed as only sources responding with a valid `ACK` packet create full sessions. The administrator can also choose to create sessions just based on the existence of the `SYN` flag in a packet. The command to check just the first packet by validating the existence of the `SYN` flag is `set flow tcp-syn-bit-check`. The second command is worded in a somewhat tricky manner. When `no-tcp-seq-check` is unset on the firewall, TCP sequence checking is enabled, in a splendid example of a double negative. In all recent versions of ScreenOS, SYN checking and sequence checking are enabled by default, so the first two commands in this recipe should not be necessary. Nevertheless, it doesn't hurt to specifically enable the commands. You can verify the settings with the `get flow` command:

```
FIREWALL-A-> get flow
flow action flag: 00b5
flow GRE outbound tcp-mss is not set
flow GRE inbound tcp-mss is not set
flow change tcp mss option for all packets is not set
flow change tcp mss option for vpn packets = 1350
flow deny session disabled
TCP syn-proxy syn-cookie disabled
Allow dns reply pkt without matched request : NO
Check TCP SYN bit before create session & refresh session only after
     Tcp 3 way handshake : YES
Check TCP SYN bit before create session : YES
Check TCP SYN bit before create session for tunneled packets : YES
Use Hub-and-Spoke policies for Untrust MIP traffic that loops on same
    interface
```

```
Check  unknown mac flooding : YES
Skip sequence number check in stateful inspection : NO
ICMP path mtu discovery : NO
ICMP time exceeded : NO
TCP RST invalidates session immediately : NO
flow log info: 0.0.0.0/0->0.0.0.0/0,0
flow initial session timeout: 20 seconds
flow session cleanup time: 2 seconds
early ageout setting:
        high watermark = 100 (8064 sessions)
```

Out-of-state packets are not explicitly logged in ScreenOS. In cases where there is an asymmetric traffic pattern, out-of-state packets can result, and you can detect them using debug. The debug `flow drop` command will provide information about these packets:

```
FIREWALL-A-> get db str
  packet dropped, first pak not sync
2501359.0:    ethernet0/0:192.168.2.33/1->10.5.5.2/1,6<Root>
```

Use debug `flow basic` with flow filters for more detailed output:

```
FIREWALL-A-> set ff dst-ip 10.5.5.2
filter added
FIREWALL-A-> set ff src-ip 10.5.5.2
filter added
FIREWALL-A-> debug flow basic
FIREWALL-A-> get db str
****** 2501635.0: <Untrust/ethernet0/0> packet received [40]******
  ipid = 0(0000), @03080c90
  packet passed sanity check.
  ethernet0/0:192.168.2.33/1->10.5.5.2/1,6<Root>
  no session found
  flow_first_sanity_check: in <ethernet0/0>, out <N/A>
  packet dropped, first pak not sync
  POLL_DROP_PAK: vlist 0x1c7d8d0, 0x1c7d8d0
```

Once the session check fails, a second sanity check is done that fails because the packet is a TCP packet, and not a SYN. This output is taken before the `set zone untrust tcp-rst` command is applied. When this command is set, the output of debug changes:

```
FIREWALL-A-> get db str
****** 2501576.0: <Untrust/ethernet0/0> packet received [40]******
  ipid = 0(0000), @030f6490
  packet passed sanity check.
  ethernet0/0:192.168.2.33/1->10.5.5.2/1,6<Root>
  no session found
  flow_first_sanity_check: in <ethernet0/0>, out <N/A>

**** jump to packet:10.5.5.2->192.168.2.33
  skipping pre-frag
```

```
no more encapping needed
send out through normal path.
flow_ip_send: 7353:10.5.5.2->192.168.2.33,6 => ethernet0/0(40) flag
  0x0, vlan 0
no l2info for packet.
no route for packet
search route to (null, 0.0.0.0->192.168.2.33) in vr trust-vr for
  vsd-0/flag-2000/ifp-ethernet0/0
[ Dest] 7.route 192.168.2.33->192.168.5.1, to ethernet0/0
route to 192.168.5.1
arp entry found for 192.168.5.1 mac 0010db7f5e87
**** pak processing end.
packet dropped, first pak not sync
POLL_DROP_PAK: vlist 0x1c7d8d0, 0x1c7d8d0
```

In this debug output, notice that when the `flow_first_sanity_check` is performed, the next step is to jump to a new packet, this one from `10.5.5.2`–`192.168.2.33`. This packet is actually a locally generated `RST` packet with the source IP address spoofed to be that of the original destination, `10.5.5.2`. You can see this with `snoop`:

```
FIREWALL-A-> snoop info
Snoop: ON
Filters Defined: 1, Active Filters 1
Detail: OFF, Detail Display length: 1500
Snoop filter based on:
id 1(on): IP dst-ip 192.168.2.33 dir(B)
2502577.0: ethernet0/0(o) len=60:0014f6e6d7c0->0010db7f5e87/0800
              10.5.5.2 -> 192.168.2.33/6
              vhl=45, tos=00, id=59808, frag=0000, ttl=64 tlen=40
              tcp:ports 1->1, seq=0, ack=0, flag=5004/RST
```

Here, notice the `RST` is being sent to the `192.168.2.33` address because TCP-RST is configured for the `Untrust` zone. If you prefer a silent drop of packets without an `RST`, do not include the `set zone untrust tcp-rst` command. Verify the `Untrust` zone settings using the `get zone untrust` command:

```
FIREWALL-A-> get zone untrust
Zone name: Untrust, id: 1, type: Security(L3), vsys: Root,
   vrouter:trust-vr
Intra-zone block: On, attrib: Shared, flag:0x6491
TCP non SYN send reset: On
IP/TCP reassembly for ALG on traffic from/to this zone: No
Asymmetric vpn: Disabled
Policy Configurable: Yes
PBR policy: None
Interfaces bound:1. Designated ifp is ethernet0/0
interface ethernet0/0(0x2f7dcb4)
IP classification disabled

DHCP relay enabled
```

9.7 Detect and Drop Illegal Packets with Screens

Problem

You want to drop packets that do not conform to specifications.

Solution

Use screens to detect illegal packets:

```
FIREWALL-A-> set zone untrust screen syn-fin
FIREWALL-A-> set zone untrust screen syn-frag
FIREWALL-A-> set zone untrust screen fin-no-ack
FIREWALL-A-> set zone untrust screen icmp-id
FIREWALL-A-> set zone untrust screen tcp-no-flag
```

Discussion

Attackers often use illegal packets to attempt to identify an operating system they want to attack. Because these packets are illegal, different operating systems will respond to them in different ways, allowing a user to "fingerprint" the OS. Like all screens, when triggered, an alarm will be generated:

```
2007-9-12 12:39:38 system crit 00437 SYN and FIN bits! From
                                     192.168.4.34:2280 to 10.5.5.2:80,
                                     proto TCP (zone Untrust, int
                                     ethernet0/0). Occurred 1
                                     times.
2007-9-12 12:39:25 system crit 00413 No TCP flag! From 192.168.4.34:1730
                                     to 10.5.5.2:80, proto TCP (zone
                                     Untrust, int ethernet0/0). Occurred
                                     1 times.
2007-9-12 12:42:23 system crit 00412 SYN fragment! From 192.168.4.34:2211
                                     to 10.5.5.2:80, proto TCP (zone
                                     Untrust, int ethernet0/0). Occurred
                                     1 times.
```

As these packets are illegal, there is probably no good reason to allow them into the network.

9.8 Prevent IP Spoofing

Problem

You want to block spoofed IP packets from entering your network.

Solution

Configure the IP-spoofing screen:

```
FIREWALL-A-> set zone trust screen ip-spoofing
```

Discussion

IP spoofing is a common method of bypassing firewall rules. By using a known permitted IP address as your source address, you can sometimes avoid firewall rule bases. Because ScreenOS uses a zone-based approach to rule base creation, spoofing is a greater challenge than with other firewall architectures, as the source interface is evaluated before a policy lookup is performed, and it would be unusual, for example, for an internal IP address to be allowed through the firewall's external interface.

The IP spoof check in ScreenOS simply uses the routing table, and the concept of unicast reverse-path forwarding (RPF), to verify that the source IP of the traffic is arriving on the appropriate interface, and thus, whether it should be considered spoofed. Because the routing table is used for spoof protection, it is recommended that you use antispoofing only in statically routed scenarios, as with dynamic routing, a routing change could cause legitimate packets to be considered invalid. Consider the simple network in Figure 9-1.

Figure 9-1. IP spoofing

In Figure 9-1, an attacker, knowing the internal IP address of the server he wants to attack, sends a packet with a spoofed IP address that appears to be on the internal LAN. In this case, the firewall's route table has a route for `10.5.5.0/24` on the internal interface:

```
FIREWALL-A-> get route ip 10.5.5.0
 Dest for 10.5.5.0
---------------------------------------------------------------
--------------------
trust-vr        : => 10.5.5.1/24 (id=8) via 0.0.0.0 (vr: trust-vr)
                     Interface bgroup0 , metric 0
```

When IP spoofing protection is enabled on the Untrust zone, the firewall compares the route to the source IP address against the interface on which the packet was received. You can see this process in the output of debug flow basic:

```
FIREWALL-A-> get db str
****** 2657676.0: <Untrust/ethernet0/0> packet received [28]******
  ipid = 0(0000), @030b8490
  packet passed sanity check.
  ethernet0/0:10.5.5.3/1->10.5.5.2/53,17<Root>
  no session found
  flow_first_sanity_check: in <ethernet0/0>, out <N/A>
  [ Dest] 8.route 10.5.5.3->0.0.0.0, to bgroup0
  packet dropped, drop by spoofing check.
```

When the first sanity check is performed on the flow, the ingress interface, ethernet0/0, is compared against the route table's route to the source IP. When this check is done, the firewall determines that the route back to the source is not the same as the ingress interface, and drops the packet.

This example assumes that the unicast RPF check for the packet will fail; however, that is not always the case. In some situations, the RPF check will succeed, but the IP address is still spoofed. This presents a challenge for connection-oriented protocols such as TCP. If the source IP is spoofed, the SYN-ACK packet from the server will never reach the attacker's real IP address. In a situation where the attacker is merely trying to execute a DoS attack against the victim via a SYN flood, or a session table overflow on the firewall, this may not matter. Half-open sessions will still result unless the set flow tcp-syn-check command is set and the three-way handshake is verified. To execute a more sophisticated attack, however, the full three-way handshake must be completed even though the source is spoofed. To accomplish this, typically the source route options in IP are used, and two types of source routes are defined: loose and strict. Loose source routes indicate the one or more hops a packet must traverse to reach its destination. Strict source routes specify all of the hops a packet must traverse to reach its destination. An attacker who spoofs the source IP of malicious traffic will often insert his own IP address as a loose hop in a source route of the packets he sends so that the reply will be routed back through him where he can intercept it. To combat this, use the ip-filter-src screen:

```
FIREWALL-A-> set zone untrust screen ip-filter-src
```

When this is applied, and packets arrive with the source route option set, an alarm is generated:

```
FIREWALL-A-> get alarm event
Date       Time     Module Level  Type Description
```

```
2007-9-12 11:58:33 system alert 00009 Source Route IP option! From
                                 92.168.5.1:2465 to 10.5.5.2:0, proto
                                 TCP (zone Untrust, int ethernet0/0).
                                 Occurred 1 times.
```

When attempting to combat IP spoofing, it is recommended that you use a combination of the `ip-spoof` screen and the `ip-filter-src` screens, along with the command `set flow tcp-syn-check`.

9.9 Prevent DoS Attacks with Screens

Problem

You want to guard against common DoS attacks, which exploit weaknesses in operating systems.

Solution

Use screens to drop this traffic:

```
FIREWALL-A-> set zone untrust screen land
FIREWALL-A-> set zone untrust screen tear-drop
FIREWALL-A-> set zone untrust screen winnuke
```

Discussion

ScreenOS protects against some well-known DoS attacks, which attack vulnerabilities in operating systems. The Land attack, for example, is a vulnerability common to many operating systems whereby a SYN packet sent to an open port with the source IP address equal to the destination IP address causes the machine to continuously send replies to itself until it exhausts its resources. Running `snoop` and `debug` when a Land attack is occurring shows the packet being dropped as hoped:

```
FIREWALL-A-> get db str
2684453.0: ethernet0/0(i) len=60:0010db7f5e87->0014f6e6d7c0/0800
      10.5.5.2 -> 10.5.5.2/6
      vhl=45, tos=00, id=42347, frag=0000, ttl=63 tlen=40
      tcp:ports 80->80, seq=1133851487, ack=2019542178, flag=5002/SYN

****** 2684453.0: <Untrust/ethernet0/0> packet received [40]******
  ipid = 42347(a56b), @03042490
  screen detection drop packet.
```

Notice the identical source and destination IP addresses, as well as the source and destination ports, and that the IP ID of the dropped packet is identical to the illegal packet. An alarm is generated:

```
FIREWALL-A-> get alarm event
Total event entries = 874
Date       Time     Module Level  Type Description
```

```
2007-9-12 12:20:11 system alert 00010 Land attack! From 10.5.5.2:80 to
                                10.5.5.2:80, proto TCP (zone Untrust,
                                int ethernet0/0). Occurred 1 times.
```

A Teardrop attack is an attack that utilizes overlapping IP fragments to crash a vulnerable machine. When such an attack is detected, alarms are generated:

```
FIREWALL-A-> get alarm eve
Total event entries = 875
Date       Time     Module Level  Type Description
2007-9-12 12:24:57 system emer   00006 Teardrop attack! From
                                 192.168.2.33:1 to 10.5.5.2:80, proto
                                 TCP (zone Untrust, int ethernet0/0).
                                 Occurred 9 times.
```

Use the get zone *<zone name>* attack command to view the counters for these attacks:

```
FIREWALL-A-> get zone untrust screen attack | include teardrop
Teardrop attack protection                                  44
FIREWALL-A-> get zone untrust screen attack | include land
Land attack protection                                       4
```

9.10 Use Screens to Control HTTP Content

Problem

You need to block access to potentially malicious web content.

Solution

Use the component block screens:

```
FIREWALL-A-> set zone "Untrust" screen component-block zip
FIREWALL-A-> set zone "Untrust" screen component-block jar
FIREWALL-A-> set zone "Untrust" screen component-block exe
FIREWALL-A-> set zone "Untrust" screen component-block activex
```

Discussion

Much of the malicious content on the Internet is executed on unsuspecting hosts using malicious Java or ActiveX code. Other content can be downloaded onto an unsuspecting user's machine as an executable or ZIPed file, and can exploit underlying vulnerabilities on the machine. To aid in preventing the unintended download of malware, ScreenOS allows you to block some of the more common content types which are used to spread malware. When component blocking is set, traffic entering the zone containing the file type is dropped, and the firewall rewrites the web page and provides a message to the user indicating that the traffic has been dropped. When malicious content is dropped, an alarm is generated:

```
FIREWALL-A-> get alarm event
Date       Time     Module Level  Type Description
```

```
2007-09-03 13:24:55 system crit 00433 EXE file detected/blocked! From
                                63.229.53.23:80 to 192.168.1.7:1631,
                                proto TCP (zone Untrust, int
                                ethernet3). Occurred 1 times.
```

From the user's perspective, after attempting to download the *.exe* file, the firewall presents the page to the user, as you can see in Figure 9-2.

Figure 9-2. Error message from component block

HTTP component blocking in ScreenOS provides a simple method of restricting access to potentially harmful content. This simplicity has a price, however, and that price comes in the form of a performance hit, and a lack of granularity. The performance hit is particularly acute on ASIC-based platforms such as the ISG Series. Unless there are no performance concerns and the all-or-none method of dropping traffic is acceptable, this functionality may be better suited to an external system, or to other features such as URL filtering or IDP.

CHAPTER 10

IPSec VPN

10.0 Introduction

A virtual private network (VPN) provides a means for remote computers to securely communicate across a public wide area network (WAN), such as the Internet. VPN concepts and examples in this chapter will refer to the use of the IP Security (IPSec) protocol.

You can configure IPSec tunnels within ScreenOS to link two or more remote subnets or sites, as well as individual users or computers, to VPN concentration sites. The IPSec tunnel consists of a pair of unidirectional Security Associations (SAs) that specify the Security Parameters Index (SPI), the destination address of the peer, and which security protocol is employed, either the Authentication Header (AH) protocol, or the Encapsulating Security Payload (ESP).

Through the SA, the IPSec tunnel can provide the following security functions:

Privacy
: You can employ a variety of standardized encryption algorithms within IPSec. ScreenOS supports Data Encryption Standard (DES), Triple DES (3DES), and Advanced Encryption Standard (AES) encryption options.

Integrity
: Data authentication is performed by either the Message Digest 5 (MD5) or Secure Hash Algorithm-1 (SHA-1) hashing algorithm.

Sender authentication
: Sender authentication is provided through the use of Internet Key Exchange (IKE) IDs and preshared keys and, if using certificate-based authentication, can provide nonrepudiation of data origin.

Encryption algorithms depend on keying material to seed the process and provide the ability to recover clear text from the encrypted form. ScreenOS provides two methods for keying the IPSec tunnels:

- Manual key
- Auto-key IKE with preshared key or certificate

The primary focus of this chapter is site-to-site VPN configuration. We will present various scenarios covering policy-based tunneling as well as route-based and dynamic route-based designs. VPN for individual user connectivity is being solved in a much more elegant fashion with SSL-based products, reducing the need for IPSec in pure Remote-Access Server (RAS) solutions. However, Recipe 10.1 uses the NetScreen Remote IPSec client software for those who may need to deploy it.

IPSec Tutorial

The IPSec suite of protocols consists of two modes—transport and tunnel—and two main protocols: AH and ESP.

Modes

When both ends of the IPSec tunnel are hosts, you can use either the transport or the tunnel mode. When one or both ends of the tunnel are a ScreenOS device or a router, you must use tunnel mode. ScreenOS devices always operate in tunnel mode for IPSec and transport mode for Layer 2 Tunneling Protocol (L2TP)-over-IPSec.

Transport mode
: The IP packet is not encapsulated into another IP datagram. Also, the original IP headers are not included in the encryption process. With AH, the entire packet is authenticated; with ESP, the entire packet is authenticated, but only the payload of the packet is encrypted. The original IP headers are left in the clear, as shown in Figure 10-1.

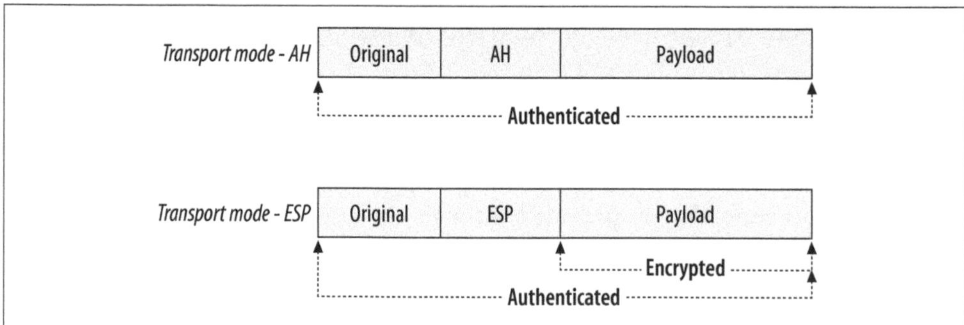

Figure 10-1. Transport mode IPSec

Tunnel mode

In tunnel mode, the entire original IP packet is encapsulated and a new IP header is added. With AH, the entire new packet is authenticated; with ESP, the original headers are included in the encrypted portion of the packet and the authentication does not include the new IP header area of the packet, as shown in Figure 10-2.

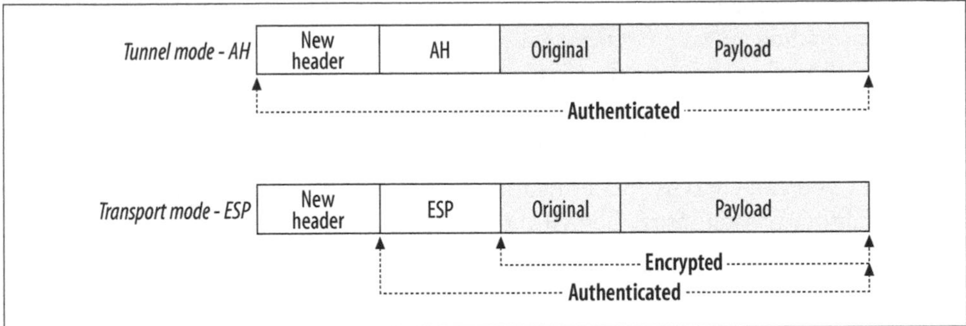

Figure 10-2. Tunnel mode IPSec

Protocols

Two main protocols are used within IPSec:

AH

This security protocol authenticates the source of the IP packet as well as ensures the integrity of the packet's contents. That is, the content has not changed since the source computer sent it.

ESP

This security protocol is used to encrypt the contents of the entire IP packet as well as to authenticate the source and verify the integrity of the contents.

The AH protocol provides a means to authenticate the origin of a packet and verify that the content has not changed in transit. You can process each packet with a security function, whereby a hash-based message authentication code (HMAC) is added to the IPSec header. Two algorithms for providing authentication and integrity checking functions are available within ScreenOS:

MD5

This algorithm produces a 128-bit hash (also called a *digital signature* or *message digest*) from a message of arbitrary length and a 16-byte key. The resulting hash is used, like a fingerprint of the input, to verify content and source authenticity and integrity.

SHA-1
: This algorithm produces a 160-bit hash from a message of arbitrary length and a 20-byte key. It is generally regarded as more secure than MD5 because of the larger hashes it produces. Because the computational processing is done in the ASIC, the performance cost is negligible.

ESP offers the authenticity and integrity checking that AH offers, as well as encryption for providing privacy for the data in transit. ESP in tunnel mode encapsulates the entire IP packet (header and payload) and then appends a new IP header to the now-encrypted packet. This new IP header contains the destination address needed to route the protected data through the network.

With ESP, you can encrypt and authenticate, encrypt only, or authenticate only. For authentication, you can use either MD5 or SHA-1 algorithms.

For encryption, you can choose one of the following encryption algorithms:

DES
: This is a cryptographic block algorithm with a 56-bit key.

3DES
: This is a more powerful version of DES, in which the original DES algorithm is applied in three rounds, using a 168-bit key. DES provides a significant performance savings, but is considered unacceptable for many classified or sensitive material transfers.

AES
: This is an emerging encryption standard which, when adopted by Internet infrastructures worldwide, will offer greater interoperability with other network security devices. ScreenOS supports AES with 128-bit, 192-bit, and 256-bit keys.

Security Associations

A Security Association (SA) is a unidirectional agreement between the VPN participants regarding the methods and parameters to use in securing a communication channel. Full bidirectional communication requires at least two SAs, one for each direction.

An SA groups together the following components for securing communications:

- Security algorithms and keys
- Protocol mode (transport or tunnel)
- Key-management method (manual key or auto-key IKE)
- SA lifetime

For outbound VPN traffic, the policy or route invokes the SA associated with the VPN tunnel. For inbound traffic, the security device looks up the SA by using the following triplet:

- Destination IP
- Security protocol (AH or ESP)
- SPI value

IKE and IPSec packets

An IPSec VPN tunnel consists of two major elements:

Tunnel setup
: The peers first establish SAs, which define the parameters for securing traffic between them. The admins at each end can define the SAs manually, or the SAs can be defined dynamically through IKE Phase-1 and Phase-2 negotiations. Phase 1 can occur in either Main mode or Aggressive mode. Phase 2 always occurs in Quick mode.

Applied security
: IPSec protects traffic sent between the two endpoints by using the security parameters defined in the SAs that the peers agreed to during tunnel setup. This could be statically defined or negotiated with IKE. The endpoints use AH or ESP for applying security functions to tunneled traffic.

Using IPSec in ScreenOS

ScreenOS provides a feature-rich implementation of IPSec. In fact, ICSA Labs uses ScreenOS to test other vendors for interoperability with this protocol. One primary reason for this is the IPSec debugging capability. Another reason is the adherence to the IPSec standards in ScreenOS.

Large VPNs have been built with ScreenOS. The fast tunnel establishment rate and stateful failover capabilities within a NetScreen Redundancy Protocol (NSRP) cluster have proven this to be a reliable and effective platform for creating large and sophisticated virtual private WANs (VPWANs).

ScreenOS provides two approaches to VPN networking:

Policy-based VPN
: The stateful inspection engine decides when to encrypt a flow.

Route-based VPN
: The route table decides when to encrypt a flow.

Route-based versus policy-based tunneling

ScreenOS provides two mechanisms for deciding when to encrypt data and process the connection via IPSec. These mechanisms are referred to as *policy-based tunneling* and *route-based tunneling*. You configure the Phase-1 IKE gateway and the Phase-2 SA in the same way for either policy-based or route-based VPNs. The difference is whether the VPN is used in a policy with a tunnel action or whether the VPN is bound to a tunnel interface.

With policy-based VPNs, the stateful inspection engine matches the flow to a policy with a tunnel action, and subsequently encrypts the packet and processes the flow across the appropriate SA.

Route-based VPN technology takes a fundamentally different approach. VPNs are bound to logical tunnel interfaces which act much like any other interface on the security device. Once the tunnel interface is created and the VPN is bound to it, you simply use the route table to direct traffic to the interface. Traffic routed to a tunnel interface is processed by the appropriate SA. Because a route lookup occurs prior to stateful inspection, you are using the route table to decide when to encrypt a packet instead of the stateful inspection engine.

VPNs have become very popular as a cost-saving alternative to dedicated leased lines. Organizations require the same type of routed connectivity they had with their frame relay networks. For this reason, NetScreen developed route-based VPN technology early in the ScreenOS life cycle.

With policy-based VPNs, you are matching a rule within the firewall policy to have the flow processed via an IPSec SA. ScreenOS operates in a "first match wins" mode when performing stateful inspection. Therefore, consider this: your first rule in the policy is a tunnel action across a VPN to data center 1. This is your primary route to all corporate resources. But you want a backup path to the resources via data center 2, so you create a second tunnel and your second rule is now for this data center 2 tunnel. The problem is that a flow that matches rule #1 will never hit rule #2 and therefore will never be tunneled via data center 2. This posed a serious issue for designing robust VPNs.

The initial approach to solving this issue was the use of *VPN groups*. With this configuration, multiple tunnels were placed in a group, and this group was used in the policy statement instead of a single tunnel. This configuration allows the administrator to choose the preferred tunnel. In addition, a new function called the *VPN monitor* was created to check the health of the tunnel by sending Internet Control Message Protocol (ICMP) pings across the encrypted SA. If the preferred tunnel failed, traffic would be processed across the next available tunnel. VPN groups are still available in ScreenOS today, but are rarely, if ever, used.

Even with VPN groups, limitations existed. The need to build highly resilient, dynamically routed WANs using IPSec was prevalent. So, route-based VPNs were born. Though policy-based VPN is still used, primarily for interoperability with other vendors, route-based VPN has become the dominant method for creating VPN connectivity between ScreenOS devices.

Tunnel interfaces and VPN routing

Route-based VPNs use tunnel interfaces within ScreenOS. A *tunnel interface* is a logical interface created and used like other interfaces on the security device. IP addresses are assigned to these interfaces, or they can be used as unnumbered interfaces and can borrow the IP address from another interface, as most routers can do.

Tunnel interfaces are placed into security zones. With this configuration, you can inspect traffic traversing the VPN with simple zone-based firewall rules, with no need for the "tunnel" action to be used for this traffic. It is a standard practice to place the tunnel interfaces into a "VPN" security zone and to use firewall rules to permit certain traffic from the `VPN` zone to the other security zones configured on the system.

You use the following commands to create an unnumbered interface in the `VPN` zone:

```
S1-Denton-> set interface tun.1 zone vpn
S1-Denton-> set interface tun.1 ip unnumbered interface eth0/0
```

Once the interfaces are created, the route table can reference them as a next hop for IP routing purposes. Where tunnel interfaces differ from other interfaces is the ability to bind Phase-2 VPN definitions to them. You can bind one or many SAs to a tunnel interface, allowing the interface to operate in point-to-point or point-to-multipoint mode.

When a packet enters the security device, the IP headers are parsed and a route lookup will be performed to determine the egress interface. If a route is present that directs the packet to a tunnel interface as a next hop, a VPN that is bound to the interface will process the packet. The route that directs traffic to a tunnel interface can be in the form of a static route, a dynamically learned route, or even a policy-based route.

Here is an example of a static route referencing a tunnel interface as a next-hop interface:

```
S1-Denton-> set route 10.11.12.0/24 interface tun.1
```

You also can use dynamic routing for a route-based VPN. This is referred to as a *dynamic route-based VPN*. ScreenOS provides support for multiple Virtual Routers (VRs) as well as the RIPv2, Open Shortest Path First (OSPF), and Border Gateway Protocol (BGP) routing protocols. You can apply these features to route-based VPNs, offering highly resilient implementations. Please see Chapter 4 for information on routing within ScreenOS.

As mentioned, you can bind multiple VPNs to a tunnel interface. When the interface is used in a point-to-multipoint manner, a second routing table is required to ensure that the appropriate SA processes the packet. This second routing table is called the Next Hop Tunnel Binding (NHTB) table.

NHTB

NHTB is used when a tunnel interface has multiple VPN SAs bound to it. Each tunnel interface maintains its own NHTB table. A route in the system will direct traffic to the tunnel interface with a next-hop gateway address, and the NHTB table will map a gateway address to a specific VPN tunnel. You can use NHTB for a variety of needs:

To overcome limits in resources supported on a security device
: For instance, say a device supports 20,000 VPN tunnels but only 4,096 tunnel interfaces. Here, you can bind five VPNs to each tunnel and theoretically achieve the maximum tunnel count with a route-based approach.

To support multiple Phase-2 SAs to the same gateway
: When interoperating with some vendors, you must create individual Phase-2 definitions that match the proxy IDs to accommodate noncontiguous subnets. You can use NHTB to place the flows into the appropriate SA.

To scale dynamic routing protocols
: When you use point-to-multipoint interfaces, fewer interfaces are participating in the routing protocol(s), and thus fewer resources are required.

As an example of NHTB configuration, consider that destination address `4.3.2.1/32` is at the other end of a VPN tunnel named `corp`, which is bound to `tun.1`. The following route is created:

```
S1-Denton-> set route 4.3.2.1/32 interface tun.1 gateway 1.2.3.4
```

The gateway address used here has no relevance to the network addressing used in the real network. It simply needs to be unique. A common practice is to use the IKE peer address. However, you can simply make up an address. Only the NHTB tables use it, as follows:

```
S1-Denton-> set interf tun.1 nhtb 1.2.3.4 vpn corp
```

This configuration routes the traffic into the appropriate tunnel. When traffic is received on interface `tun.1`, the system will consult the NHTB table and look for gateway `1.2.3.4`. That gateway is mapped to the `corp` tunnel on that interface. The same security device could also have the following configuration:

```
S1-Denton-> set route 5.6.7.8/32 interface tun.1 gateway 1.2.3.5
S1-Denton-> set interf tun.1 nhtb 1.2.3.5 vpn datactr1
```

The preceding example represents statically configuring the NHTB mappings for tunneled traffic. NHTB configuration is automatically created between ScreenOS devices, and is necessary only for mixing route-based and policy-based configurations or for interoperability with non-ScreenOS devices.

Recipe 10.5 provides examples of statically configured NHTB mapping, though it would be acceptable to allow ScreenOS to create the configuration automatically.

Creating VPN Tunnels

You can create a VPN tunnel by following three main steps:

1. Create the Phase-1 gateway and associated parameters.
2. Create the Phase-2 VPN definition and associated parameters.
3. Bind the VPN to a policy or tunnel interface.
    a. Optionally configure routing for VPNs bound to tunnel interfaces.

Configuring an IKE gateway

When a clear-text packet arrives at the security device that requires tunneling and no active SA exists for that tunnel, the security device begins IKE negotiations (and drops the packet). The source and destination addresses in the IP packet header are those of the local and remote IKE gateways, respectively. In the IP packet payload, a User Datagram Protocol (UDP) segment encapsulates an Internet Security Association and Key Management Protocol (ISAKMP), or IKE, packet. The format for IKE packets is the same for Phase 1 and Phase 2.

When the initial IP packet is dropped, the source host resends it. Typically, by the time the second packet reaches the security device, IKE negotiations are complete and the security device protects it—and all subsequent packets in the session—with IPSec before forwarding it. See the "VPN monitor" section later in this chapter for information on how to avoid this dropped data packet.

Main and Aggressive modes

Phase 1 can take place in either Main or Aggressive mode:

Main mode
: The initiator and recipient send three two-way exchanges (six messages total) to accomplish the following services:

  First exchange (messages 1 and 2)
  : Propose and accept the encryption and authentication algorithms.

Second exchange (messages 3 and 4)
: Execute a Diffie-Hellman exchange, and the initiator and recipient each provide a pseudorandom number.

Third exchange (messages 5 and 6)
: Send and verify their identities. The encryption algorithm established in the first two exchanges protects the information transmitted in the third exchange of messages. Thus, the participants' identities are not transmitted in the clear.

Aggressive mode
: The initiator and recipient accomplish the same objectives, but only in two exchanges, with a total of three messages:

First message
: The initiator proposes the SA, initiates a Diffie-Hellman exchange, and sends a pseudorandom number and its IKE identity.

Second message
: The recipient accepts the SA, authenticates the initiator, and sends a pseudorandom number, its IKE identity, and, if using certificates, the recipient's certificate.

Third message
: The initiator authenticates the recipient, confirms the exchange, and, if using certificates, sends the initiator's certificate. Because the participants' identities are exchanged in the clear (in the first two messages) Aggressive mode does not provide identity protection.

When a dial-up VPN user negotiates an auto-key IKE tunnel with a preshared key, you must use Aggressive mode. Note also that a dial-up VPN user can use an email address, a fully qualified domain name (FQDN), or an IP address as its IKE ID. A dynamic peer can use either an email address or an FQDN, but not an IP address.

Diffie-Hellman exchange

A Diffie-Hellman (DH) exchange allows the participants to produce a shared secret value. The strength of the technique is that it allows the participants to create the secret value over an unsecured medium without passing the secret value through the wire. There are five DH groups; ScreenOS supports Groups 1, 2, and 5. The size of the prime modulus used in each group's calculation differs as follows:

DH Group 1
: 768-bit modulus

DH Group 2
: 1024-bit modulus

DH Group 5
1536-bit modulus

The strength of DH Group 1 security has depreciated, so it is no longer recommended for use.

The larger the modulus, the more secure the resulting key is considered to be. Also, the larger the modulus, the longer it takes ScreenOS to generate. Because the different groups use a different size modulus, both ends of the tunnel must use the same group.

Configuring a Main mode gateway

Auto-key IKE Phase-1 gateways using Main mode negotiations can use a variety of IKE ID types, with the most common being the IP address of the outgoing interface. To start the configuration, create an IKE gateway and name it:

```
S1-Denton-> set ike gateway "dallas"
```

Here is the start of an IKE gateway command. A gateway named `"dallas"` is going to need some additional configuration. Next, specify the remote IKE gateway address in which to negotiate a tunnel:

```
S1-Denton-> set ike gateway "dallas" address 10.11.12.1 main
```

This is the beginning of a Main mode Phase-1 configuration for a gateway named `"dallas"` which will connect to IP address `10.11.12.1`. Next, the specified outgoing interface will be defined as well as choosing to use a preshared key and the value of that key:

```
S1-Denton-> set ike gateway "dallas" address 10.11.12.1 main outgoing-
interface eth0/0 preshare juniper123
```

The Phase-1 Main mode configuration command is almost complete. The last part of the configuration is to choose a Phase-1 proposal to offer or accept during the negotiation. You can configure up to four proposals for each gateway configuration and they will be offered or accepted in the order in which they appear in the configuration. For convenience purposes, ScreenOS also offers three predefined security levels, each having multiple proposals:

```
S1-Denton-> set ike gateway "dallas" address 10.11.12.1 main outgoing-
interface eth0/0 preshare juniper123 sec-level ?
basic                basic level settings
compatible           most popular settings
standard             recommended settings
```

The set ike gateway command is probably the longest single command you will ever enter in ScreenOS, so don't despair, it gets better. The following is a complete IKE Phase-1 gateway configuration command:

```
S1-Denton-> set ike gateway "dallas" address 10.11.12.1 main outgoing-
interface eth0/0 preshare juniper123 sec-level standard
```

The predefined security levels are as follows:

```
S1-Denton-> get ike p1-sec-level

IKE Phase-1 Standard Level:
Id Name               Auth     Grp ESP-e  ESP-a Lifetime
-- ------------------ -------- --- ------ ----- ----------
 5 pre-g2-3des-sha    Preshare  2  3DES   SHA-1      28800
 7 pre-g2-aes128-sha  Preshare  2  AES128 SHA-1      28800

IKE Phase-1 Compatible Level:
Id Name               Auth     Grp ESP-e  ESP-a Lifetime
-- ------------------ -------- --- ------ ----- ----------
 5 pre-g2-3des-sha    Preshare  2  3DES   SHA-1      28800
 4 pre-g2-3des-md5    Preshare  2  3DES   MD5        28800
 3 pre-g2-des-sha     Preshare  2  DES    SHA-1      28800
 2 pre-g2-des-md5     Preshare  2  DES    MD5        28800

IKE Phase-1 basic Level:
Id Name               Auth     Grp ESP-e  ESP-a Lifetime
-- ------------------ -------- --- ------ ----- ----------
 1 pre-g1-des-sha     Preshare  1  DES    SHA-1      28800
 0 pre-g1-des-md5     Preshare  1  DES    MD5        28800
S1-Denton->
```

You also can create custom proposals as needed:

```
S1-Denton-> set ike p1-proposal custom1 pre group5 esp aes256 sha
seconds 12800
S1-Denton-> get ike p1-proposal custom1
Id Name               Auth     Grp ESP-e  ESP-a Lifetime
-- ------------------ -------- --- ------ ----- ----------
20 custom1            Preshare  5  AES256 SHA-1      12800
```

You can express the Phase-1 lifetime in seconds, minutes, hours, or days, but it is always displayed in seconds:

```
S1-Denton-> set ike p1-proposal custom1 pre group5 esp aes256
sha days 7
S1-Denton-> get ike p1-proposal custom1
Id Name               Auth     Grp ESP-e  ESP-a Lifetime
-- ------------------ -------- --- ------ ----- ----------
20 custom1            Preshare  5  AES256 SHA-1     604800
```

If you configure multiple (up to four) proposals for Phase-1 negotiations, use the same DH group in all proposals. The same guideline applies to multiple proposals for Phase-2 negotiations.

Configuring an Aggressive mode gateway

IKE Aggressive mode is typically used between devices where one end of the tunnel is assigned a dynamic IP (DIP) address. One end of the tunnel must always have either a static IP address or an FQDN. When one IKE peer is dynamic, that peer cannot use the IPv4 address as the IKE ID and must use another IKE ID type, such as an email address or FQDN.

The configuration starts the same as in Main mode, where you create an IKE gateway and name it:

```
S1-Denton-> set ike gateway "corp"
```

If you're configuring the dynamic peer, the configuration continues with the IP address of the peer gateway and choosing Aggressive mode:

```
S1-Denton-> set ike gateway "corp" address 10.140.0.3 Aggressive
```

Next, you would configure the IKE ID the dynamic peer will present when negotiating the tunnel:

```
S1-Denton-> set ike gateway "corp" address 10.140.0.3 Aggr local-id s1_
denton@xyzcorp.com
```

The rest of the configuration will continue the same as in the Main mode example explained previously:

```
S1-Denton-> set ike gateway "corp" address 10.140.0.3 Aggr local-id s1_
denton@xyzcorp.com" outgoing-interface "ethernet0/0" preshare
juniper123  sec-level standard
```

The corresponding Phase-1 configuration on the static peer would look as follows:

```
set ike gateway denton dynamic s1_denton@xyzcorp.com aggressive
outgoing-interface eth0/3 preshare juniper123 sec-level standard
```

In this command, instead of specifying the IKE peer's address, we use the `dynamic` keyword to signify that the peer has a DIP address immediately followed by the IKE ID expected from this remote IKE gateway. This is followed by choosing the appropriate outgoing interface and matching the preshared key and Phase-1 proposal or security level.

Configuring a Phase-2 VPN

After the participants have established a secure and authenticated channel, they proceed through Phase 2, in which they negotiate the SAs to secure the data to be transmitted through the IPSec tunnel. As in the process for Phase 1, the participants exchange proposals to determine which security parameters to employ in the SA. A Phase-2 proposal also includes a security protocol—either ESP or AH—and selected encryption and authentication algorithms.

The proposal can also specify a DH group, if Perfect Forward Secrecy (PFS) is desired. Regardless of the mode used in Phase 1, Phase 2 always operates in Quick mode and involves the exchange of three messages. Juniper Networks security devices support up to four proposals for Phase-2 negotiations, allowing you to define how restrictive a range of tunnel parameters you will accept. ScreenOS also provides a replay protection feature. Use of this feature does not require negotiation because packets are always sent with sequence numbers. You simply have the option of checking or not checking the sequence numbers.

The following command creates a Phase-2 VPN, links the definition to a configured IKE gateway, and specifies the security level to use for the offered/accepted Phase-2 proposals:

```
S1-Denton-> set vpn corp_vpn gateway corp sec-level standard
```

Alternatively, you could use a predefined or custom proposal:

```
S1-Denton-> set vpn corp_vpn gate corp proposal g2-esp-aes128-sha
```

The predefined Phase-2 proposals that ScreenOS provides are as follows:

```
S1-Denton-> get ike p2-proposal
Id Name                 Grp Protocol Enc_alg Auth_alg Lifetime Lifesize
-- -------------------- -- -------- ------- -------- -------  ------
 0 nopfs-esp-des-md5     0 ESP      DES     MD5          3600       0
 1 nopfs-esp-des-sha     0 ESP      DES     SHA-1        3600       0
 2 g2-esp-des-md5        2 ESP      DES     MD5          3600       0
 3 g2-esp-des-sha        2 ESP      DES     SHA-1        3600       0
 4 nopfs-esp-3des-md5    0 ESP      3DES    MD5          3600       0
 5 nopfs-esp-aes128-md5 0 ESP      AES128  MD5          3600       0
 6 g2-esp-3des-md5       2 ESP      3DES    MD5          3600       0
 7 g2-esp-aes128-md5     2 ESP      AES128  MD5          3600       0
 8 nopfs-esp-3des-sha    0 ESP      3DES    SHA-1        3600       0
 9 g2-esp-3des-sha       2 ESP      3DES    SHA-1        3600       0
10 nopfs-esp-aes128-sha 0 ESP      AES128  SHA-1        3600       0
11 g2-esp-aes128-sha     2 ESP      AES128  SHA-1        3600       0
  Total Phase 2 proposals: 12
S1-Denton->
```

As with the Phase-1 configuration, ScreenOS also offers three predefined security levels to choose from for convenience. Each security level contains multiple proposals, and will be offered or accepted in the order in which it appears:

```
S1-Denton-> get ike p2-sec-level

IKE Phase-2 Standard Level:
Id Name              Grp Protocol Enc_alg Auth_alg Lifetime Lifesize
-- ----------------- --- -------- ------- -------- ------- ---------
 9 g2-esp-3des-sha     2 ESP      3DES    SHA-1       3600         0
11 g2-esp-aes128-sha   2 ESP      AES128  SHA-1       3600         0

IKE Phase-2 Compatible Level:
Id Name              Grp Protocol Enc_alg Auth_alg Lifetime Lifesize
-- ----------------- -- -------- ------- -------- ------ ----------
 8 nopfs-esp-3des-sha  0 ESP      3DES    SHA-1       3600         0
 4 nopfs-esp-3des-md5  0 ESP      3DES    MD5         3600         0
 1 nopfs-esp-des-sha   0 ESP      DES     SHA-1       3600         0
 0 nopfs-esp-des-md5   0 ESP      DES     MD5         3600         0

IKE Phase-2 basic Level:
Id Name              Grp Protocol Enc_alg Auth_alg Lifetime Lifesize
-- ----------------- --- -------- ------- -------- ------ ----------
 1 nopfs-esp-des-sha   0 ESP      DES     SHA-1       3600         0
 0 nopfs-esp-des-md5   0 ESP      DES     MD5         3600         0
S1-Denton->
```

You can also define custom Phase-2 proposals. In Phase 2, the peers also exchange proxy IDs. A proxy ID is a three-part tuple consisting of a local IP address–remote IP address and service. The proxy ID for both peers must match, which means that the service specified in the proxy ID for both peers must be the same, and the local IP address specified for one peer must be the same as the remote IP address specified for the other peer. For tunnels between ScreenOS devices, you usually can skip this in the configuration and let the default parameters prevail. However, when you need to match the proxy ID for interoperability and you're mixing route-based and policy-based VPNs, you can use the following command to configure the local and remote proxy IDs and service tuple:

```
S1-Denton-> set vpn corp_vpn proxy-id local 10.1.1.0/24 remote
10.2.1.0/24 any
```

The preceding command uses the any keyword for the service definition to allow any service to match the proxy ID.

Perfect Forward Secrecy. PFS is a method for deriving Phase-2 keys independent from and unrelated to the preceding keys. Alternatively, the Phase-1 proposal creates the key (the `SKEYID_d` key) from which all Phase-2 keys are derived. The `SKEYID_d` key can generate Phase-2 keys with a minimum of CPU processing. Unfortunately, if an unauthorized party gains access to the SKEYID_d key, all of your encryption keys are compromised. PFS addresses this security risk by forcing a new DH key exchange to occur for each Phase-2 tunnel. Using PFS is thus more secure, although the rekeying procedure in Phase 2 might take slightly longer with PFS enabled.

Replay protection. A replay attack occurs when somebody intercepts a series of packets and uses them later either to flood the system—causing a Denial of Service (DoS)—or to gain entry to the trusted network. The replay protection feature enables security devices to check every IPSec packet to see whether it has been received previously. If packets arrive outside a specified sequence range, the security device rejects them.

VPN monitor

The VPN monitor is a simple mechanism used for determining the health and latency of a given VPN tunnel. ICMP pings are sent across the encrypted SA every *n* seconds as determined by the "interval" setting. A threshold is also set which determines how many pings can be lost before declaring the tunnel as down. The following shows the default settings for the VPN monitor:

```
S1-Denton-> get vpnmon
Vpn monitor interval : 10(seconds)
Vpn monitor threshold: 10
```

These default settings would require 100 seconds before the tunnel was declared as down. A ping will be sent every 10 seconds, and 10 pings must fail before the tunnel is considered down. You can set the interval and threshold to meet your needs:

```
S1-Denton-> set vpnmon interval 3
S1-Denton-> set vpnmon threshold 3
```

These settings would declare the tunnel down after nine seconds of failure. The setting is global, so you cannot have different settings for different tunnels.

Besides simply providing notification that a tunnel is down, the VPN monitor has other uses. For instance, it also measures the latency of the ICMP responses for providing latency statistics. But probably the most useful function of the VPN monitor is the ability to alter the route table based on a tunnel failure. When used with route-based VPN, the VPN monitor can mark routes associated with VPN tunnels as inactive when a tunnel is declared as down, allowing the next best route to be selected.

By default, the VPN monitor will use the local and remote IKE peer addresses for the ping packet. ScreenOS is aware of the VPN monitor and will accept and respond to the ping.

Normally, the following command is all that is required to enable the VPN monitor:

```
S1-Denton-> set vpn corp monitor
```

However, other vendors do not understand the VPN monitor. So, when using the VPN monitor with other vendors, you must use an additional configuration and specify a source interface and a destination IP address that will comply with the proxy ID configured on the tunnel. An example configuration is as follows:

```
S1-Denton-> set vpn corp monitor source-interface eth1 destination-ip
4.3.2.1
```

optimized. Another option exists in the VPN monitor, called `optimized`. With this option enabled, ScreenOS will look into the tunnel and see whether there is active traffic on the SA for every interval configured. If there is active traffic, ScreenOS will not send the ICMP ping and will consider the tunnel active. If no active data is sensed, ScreenOS will send the monitor ping. You can use the `optimized` option in large networks to reduce unnecessary data transport. However, if you are relying on VPN latency counters, you should not use `optimized`, as counters are provided only for the ICMP monitor pings.

```
S1-Denton-> set vpn corp monitor optimized
```

rekey. If you enable the `rekey` option, the security device starts to send ICMP echo requests immediately upon completion of the tunnel configuration, and continues to send them indefinitely. The echo requests trigger an attempt to initiate IKE negotiations to establish a VPN tunnel until the state of VPN monitoring for the tunnel is up. The security device then uses the pings for VPN monitoring purposes. If the state of VPN monitoring for the tunnel changes from up to down, the security device deactivates its Phase-2 SA for that peer. The security device continues to send echo requests to its peer at defined intervals, triggering attempts to reinitiate IKE Phase-2 negotiations—and Phase-1 negotiations, if necessary—until it succeeds. At that point, the security device reactivates the Phase-2 SA, generates a new key, and reestablishes the tunnel. A message appears in the event log stating that a successful rekey operation has occurred:

```
S1-Denton-> set vpn corp monitor optimized rekey
```

You can view the progress of the VPN monitor with `debug`. Several options exist, but here is a basic method for checking the VPN monitor:

```
S1-Denton-> debug sa-mon all
S1-Denton-> get db str
vpn monitor pkt is received: cookie = 3, result = 3
## 2007-09-23 11:47:44 : vpnmon_down_action 3
sa index(3) changed to down
sa index(3) send count = 396386, avail = 307684, tunnel_info = 4000000e
```

Here, we see that a tunnel status has changed to down, and we have sent 396,386 pings, but have received only 307,684 responses.

The route table might look like this now:

```
IPv4 Dest-Routes for <trust-vr> (69 entries)
--------------------------------------------------------------------
   ID       IP-Prefix  Interface     Gateway   P Pref   Mtr      Vsys
--------------------------------------------------------------------
*55288       0.0.0.0/0      eth0/0     10.0.1.3  E2  200     1      Root
 59269      4.3.2.1/32       tun.1      1.2.3.4   S   20     1      Root
     6    10.15.0.0/16       tun.1      0.0.0.0   S   20    10      Root
*55319     10.0.0.1/32      eth0/0   10.0.1.254   O   60     3      Root
*59235     10.1.5.0/30      eth0/0   10.0.1.254   O   60     4      Root
*59236    10.31.0.3/32      eth0/0   10.0.1.254   O   60     4      Root
S1-Denton->
```

The two static routes associated with `tunnel.1` are inactive (there is no asterisk signifying an active route). With no active route to those destinations, traffic will be routed to the next best route, which in this case is the default route, unencrypted out to the Internet. This could be bad, and it is at least a bad practice. To remedy this situation, you should use a static route with a higher metric to direct traffic to the `null` interface (blackhole), like so:

```
S1-Denton-> get route | i 10.15.0.0/16
*59270        10.15.0.0/16      null   0.0.0.0   S   20    100      Root
    6        10.15.0.0/16     tun.1   0.0.0.0   S   20     10      Root
    7        10.15.0.0/16     tun.2   0.0.0.0   S   20     50      Root
S1-Denton->
```

In this example, the primary route via `tun.1` and the backup route via `tun.2` are both unavailable, so our blackhole route takes over.

Restoring the VPN connectivity to normal results in the following route table:

```
S1-Denton-> get route | i 10.15.0.0/16
59270        10.15.0.0/16      null   0.0.0.0   S   20    100      Root
   *6        10.15.0.0/16     tun.1   0.0.0.0   S   20     10      Root
    7        10.15.0.0/16     tun.2   0.0.0.0   S   20     50      Root
S1-Denton->
```

Finishing the tunnel configuration

Now that both Phase-1 and Phase-2 configurations have been completed, the final step is to bind the Phase-2 VPN to either a policy or a tunnel interface.

For the route-based method, the VPN is bound to a tunnel interface and the appropriate routes are configured or dynamically exchanged between peers. Using static routes, the following commands would finish the VPN configuration, and would set up routing to subnet 10.11.12.0/24 via the VPN tunnel named corp:

```
S1-Denton-> set vpn corp bind interface tun.1
S1-Denton-> set route 10.11.12.0/24 interface tun.1
```

For policy-based configuration, the commands would look as follows:

```
S1-Denton-> set address vpn corp_subnet 10.11.12.0/24
S1-Denton-> set policy from trust to vpn any corp_subnet any tunnel vpn
corp log
```

Many of the chapters in this book are relevant to VPN design. Specifically, those chapters on interfaces, objects and policies, and routing (Chapters 4, 7, and 19 to mention a few) will provide additional information to assist with designing and implementing a VPN solution. Check the index and table of contents for more specific VPN references.

10.1 Create a Simple User-to-Site VPN

Problem

You need to provide VPN connectivity between multiple roaming users and the headquarters location.

Solution

Use NetScreen-Remote software to establish a secure tunnel to the hub location for a group of remote users with local Xauth authentication. Because multiple users will need to access this VPN, a shared IKE ID with a preshared key approach will be used.

First, define your protected resources (address objects):

```
Corp-VPN-Hub-> set address trust mail1 10.140.10.10/32
```

Now, set the IKE ID, users, and group configuration:

```
Corp-VPN-Hub-> set user lab_users ike-id users@dallab.juniper.net
share-limit 250
```

```
Corp-VPN-Hub-> set user-group dallab_users user lab_users
Corp-VPN-Hub-> set user dude password letmein
Corp-VPN-Hub-> set user dude type xauth
Corp-VPN-Hub-> set user mike password 12345678
Corp-VPN-Hub-> set user mike type xauth
```

Set the VPN Phase-1 and Phase-2 configurations:

```
Corp-VPN-Hub-> set ike gateway lab_gateway dialup dallab_users
               aggressive outgoing-interface eth0/3 preshare
               juniper123 sec-level standard
Shared IKE ID dial-up group configured. Please note XAUTH server
must be turned on as well.
Corp-VPN-Hub-> set ike gateway lab_gateway xauth
Corp-VPN-Hub-> set vpn lab_vpn gateway lab_gateway sec-level standard
```

Now, set the policy configuration:

```
Corp-VPN-Hub-> set policy top name "permit_RAS" from bb to trust
"Dial-Up VPN" mail1 smtp tunnel vpn lab_vpn log count
policy id = 3
Corp-VPN-Hub-> save
```

Create a new connection using the NetScreen-Remote setup (named "Corp" in this example), as shown in Figure 10-3.

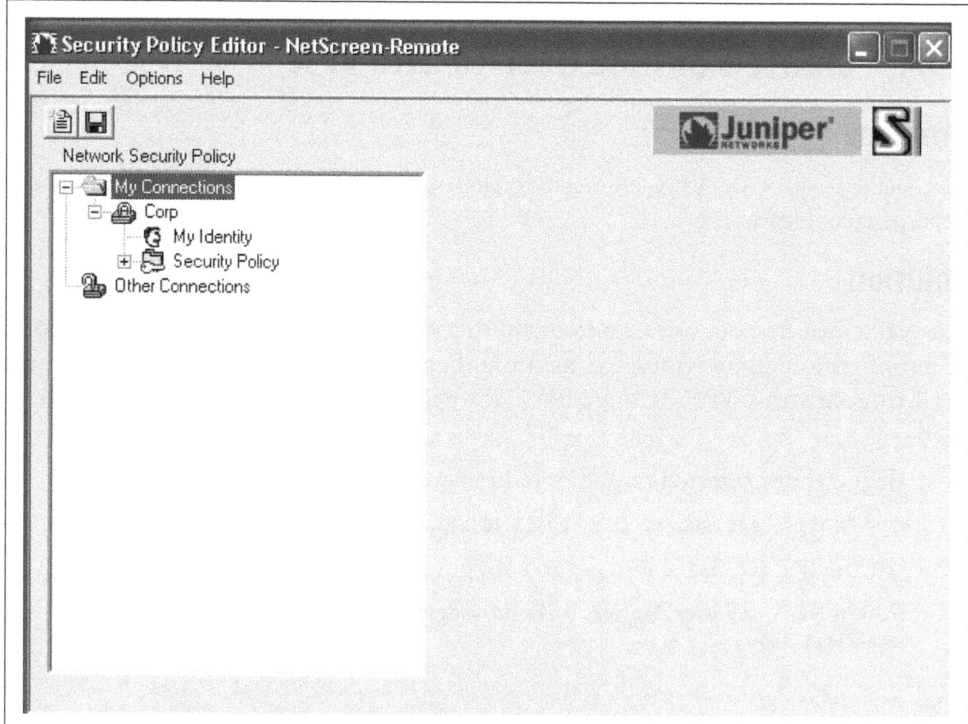

Figure 10-3. Using the NetScreen-Remote setup to create a new connection

As shown in Figure 10-4, configure the remote identity information.

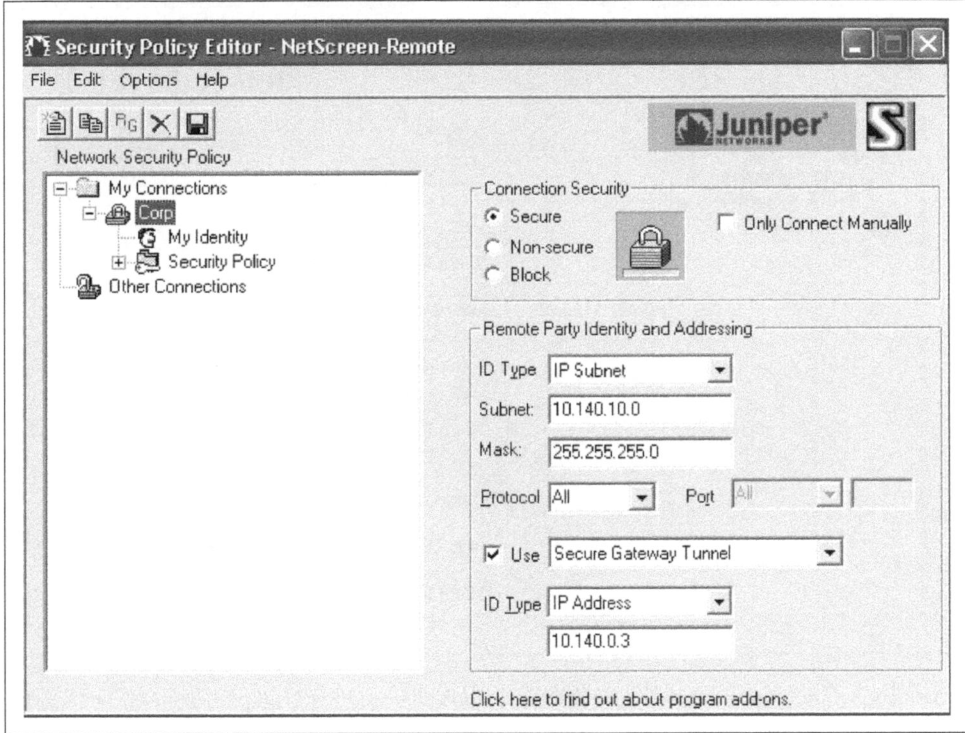

Figure 10-4. Configuring the remote identity information

As shown in Figure 10-5, configure the local identity, select the Virtual Adapter as Preferred, and choose the interface of the local PC to use for this connection. Click the Pre-Shared Key button and enter the correct key.

As shown in Figure 10-6, choose Aggressive Mode, and enable PFS with DH Group 2 to match the "standard" proposal chosen in the ScreenOS configuration. We did not use replay protection in this example, but you could easily enable it on each end of the connection if desired.

As shown in Figure 10-7, configure the Phase-1 parameters in the client to match the "standard" proposal chosen on the hub site ScreenOS configuration. Ensure that Pre-Shared Key; Extended Authentication is chosen. This will prompt the user for the Xauth credentials.

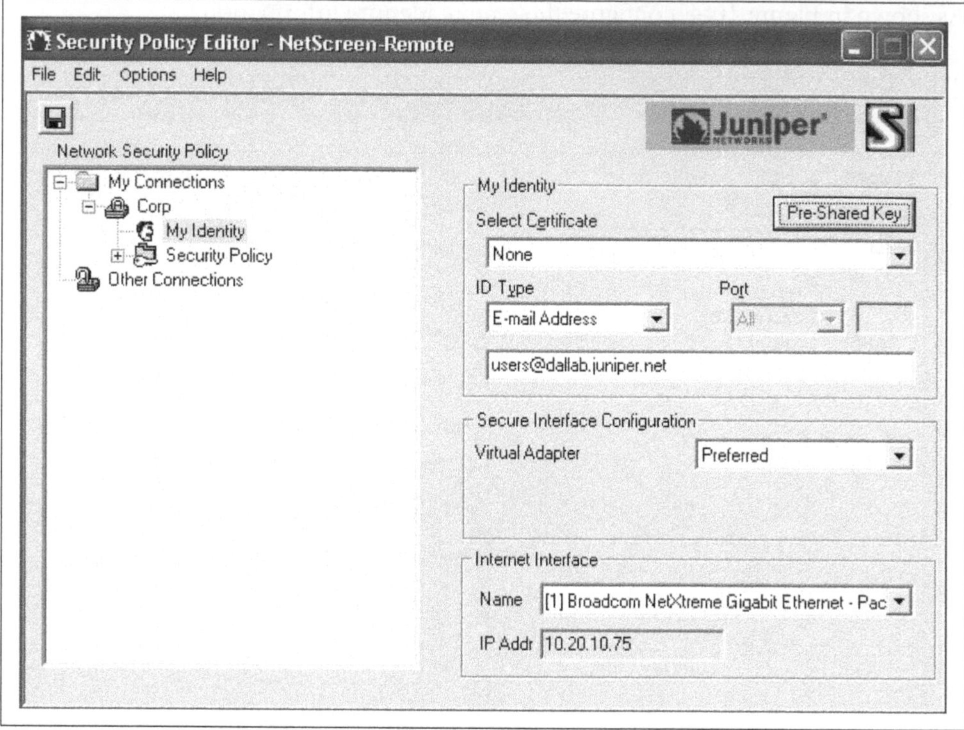

Figure 10-5. Configuring the local identity information

And finally, as shown in Figure 10-8, configure the Phase-2 parameters to match the "standard" proposal chosen on the hub site ScreenOS configuration.

Discussion

Figure 10-9 depicts the scenario for this recipe and the ensuing discussion which details the VPN client software deployment.

ScreenOS configuration

Multiple traveling users with NetScreen-Remote VPN client software need to access the corporate site for mail and perhaps other applications. We used a policy-based approach here, but a route-based approach is also viable.

Because of the need to support multiple users, we chose to use a shared IKE ID and preshared key to simplify the VPN client software deployment. In this configuration, each remote user can have the same configuration in the NetScreen-Remote software. Because of this, we need some method to distinguish individual users. When configuring an IKE gateway definition on ScreenOS using a shared IKE ID, ScreenOS forces the use of Xauth and a reminder is displayed in the client to enable Xauth functionality.

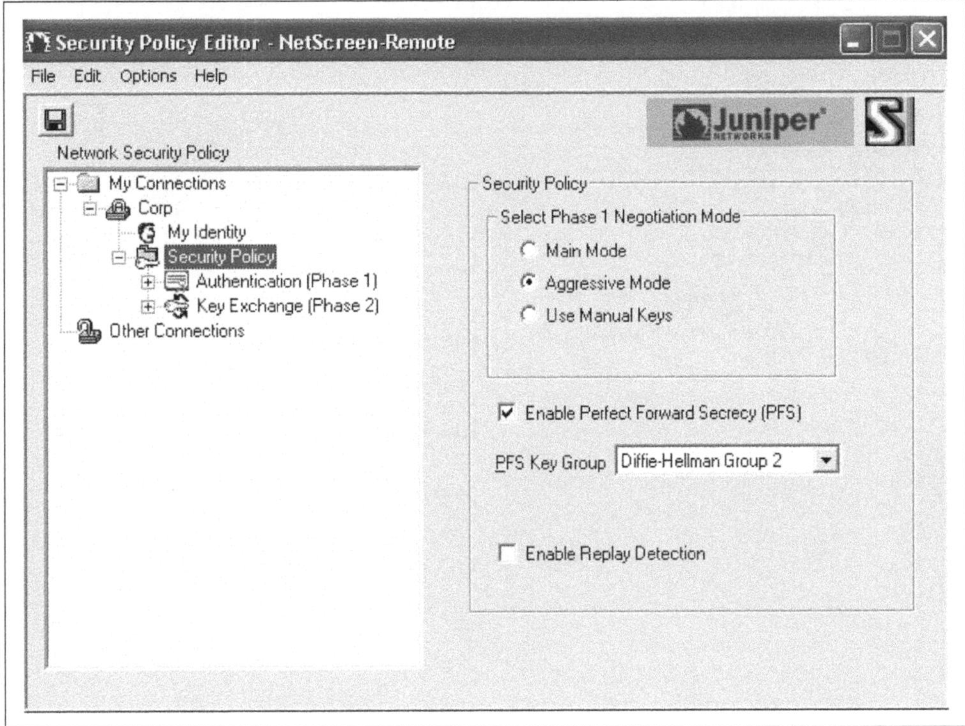

Figure 10-6. Configuring the Security Policy

You start the configuration by defining the resource the remote users will access. The address object `mail1` is created with an IP address of `10.140.10.10/32`:

```
Corp-VPN-Hub-> set address trust mail1 10.140.10.10/32
```

This object will be used in the policy configuration as a destination address.

Next, you configure the users, passwords, and shared IKE ID for Phase-1 establishment:

```
Corp-VPN-Hub-> set user lab_users ike-id users@dallab.juniper.net
share-limit 250
Corp-VPN-Hub-> set user-group dallab_users user lab_users
Corp-VPN-Hub-> set user dude password letmein
Corp-VPN-Hub-> set user dude type xauth
Corp-VPN-Hub-> set user mike password 12345678
Corp-VPN-Hub-> set user mike type xauth
```

In the preceding commands, the first line creates a user called `lab_users`, defines an IKE ID of *users@dallab.juniper.net*, and defines the number of simultaneous connections supported by this IKE ID to be 250.

Next, you create a group named `dallab_users` and place the newly created user definition within the group. The reason for this step is that the IKE gateway definition to be completed later will accept only groups and not individual user definitions.

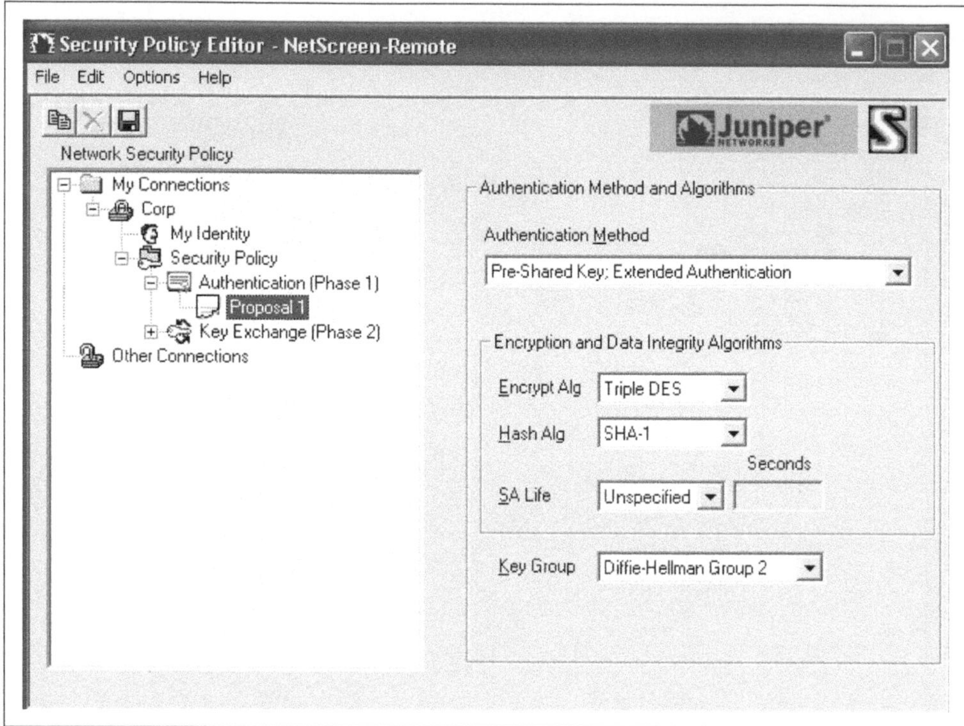

Figure 10-7. Configuring the parameters in the client

Then, you create two users with passwords and define each user as type Xauth.

> This example uses a locally configured username and password pair for Xauth authentication. However, you could use an external authentication server for this function; that is, you could use your Active Directory users and credentials to authenticate these remote users to keep from having to define them locally. Please see Chapter 13 for more information on using external authentication servers.

Now, you can create the VPN Phase-1 and Phase-2 configuration on the hub site:

```
Corp-VPN-Hub-> set ike gateway lab_gateway dialup dallab_users
               aggressive outgoing-interface eth0/3 preshare
               juniper123 sec-level standard
Shared IKE ID dial-up group configurated. Please note XAUTH server
must be turned on as well.
Corp-VPN-Hub-> set ike gateway lab_gateway xauth
Corp-VPN-Hub-> set vpn lab_vpn gateway lab_gateway sec-level standard
```

First, you configure the IKE gateway definition by naming the gateway entry, configuring it to accept any IP address by using the dialup keyword, defining the user group dallab_users that is authorized to access the VPN, and finally choosing the

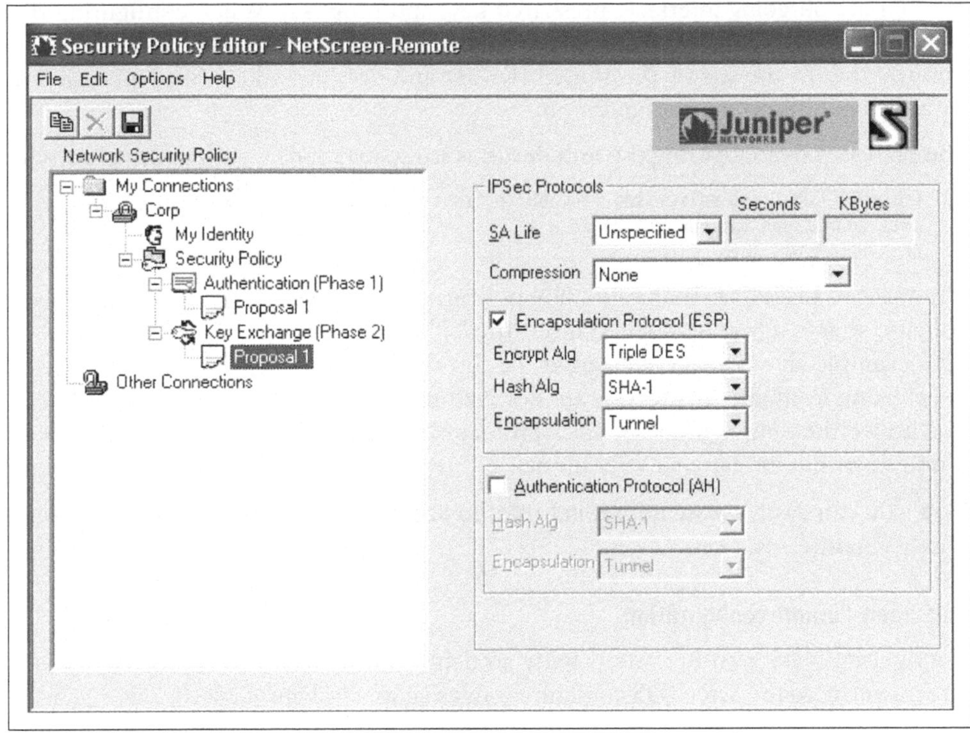

Figure 10-8. Configuring the parameters on the hub

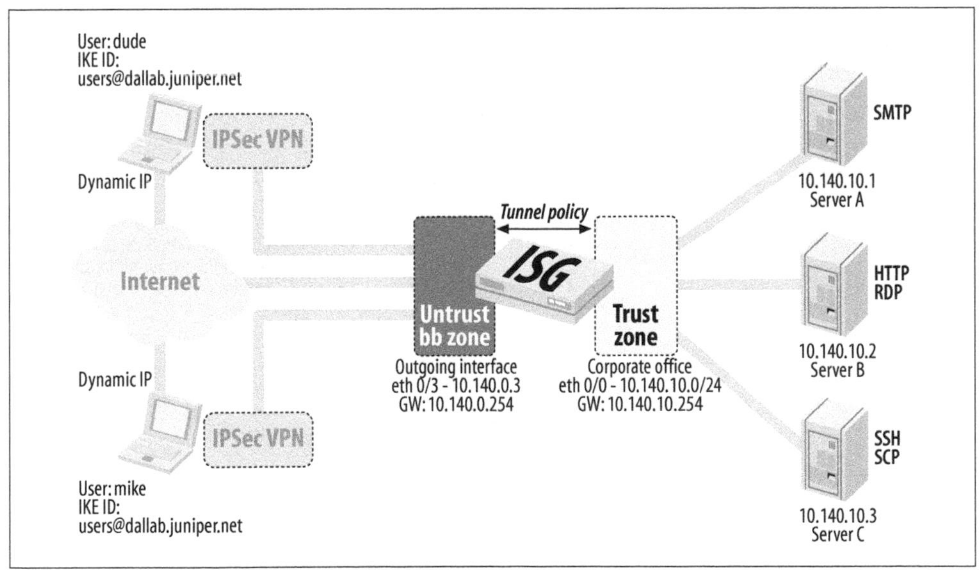

Figure 10-9. Simple VPN client-to-site example using shared IKE ID and Xauth

appropriate outgoing interface, preshared key, and proposal. When configuring this Phase-1 gateway definition, ScreenOS warns you that Xauth must be enabled for this gateway due to the use of the shared IKE ID and preshared key. So, you enable it with the next line of the configuration.

The final step in configuring the hub device is to create a policy with a tunnel action:

```
Corp-VPN-Hub-> set policy top from bb to trust "Dial-Up VPN" mail1
smtp tunnel vpn lab_vpn policy id = 3
Corp-VPN-Hub-> save
```

You want to make sure that your VPN policies are matched before other zone-based policies, so it is a best practice to insert the VPN policies at the top of the rule base. This example shows a rule created at the top that matches flows that originated on the bb zone from any IP address, are destined for the Trust zone and mail1 address, and utilize the Simple Mail Transfer Protocol (SMTP). This matched traffic will be tunneled within the lab_vpn VPN tunnel.

Now you can easily create additional rules to add additional applications or destination host addresses.

NetScreen-Remote configuration

Configuring NetScreen-Remote is fairly straightforward once you understand which screens relate to the ScreenOS configuration, as shown in Figure 10-10.

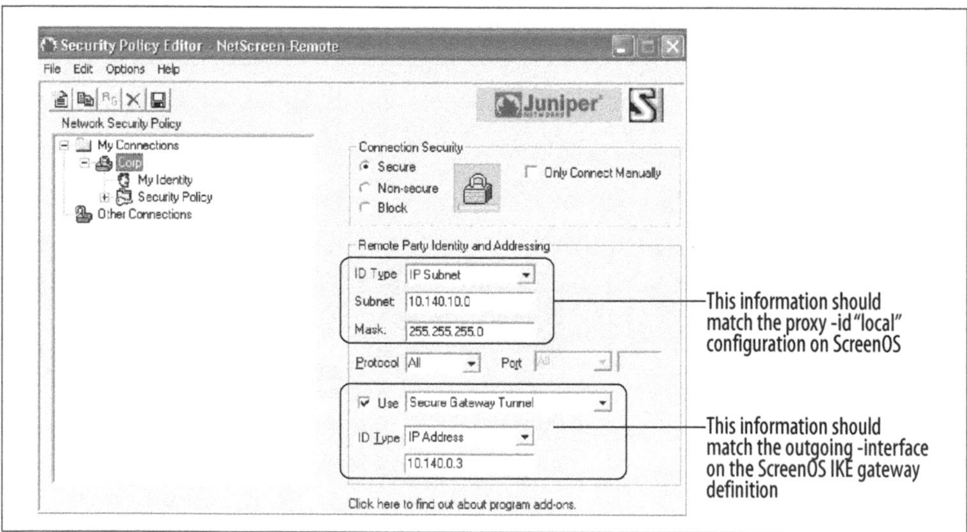

Figure 10-10. Beginning the NetScreen-Remote configuration

To start, configure the My Identity tab in the NetScreen-Remote client configuration, as shown in Figure 10-11.

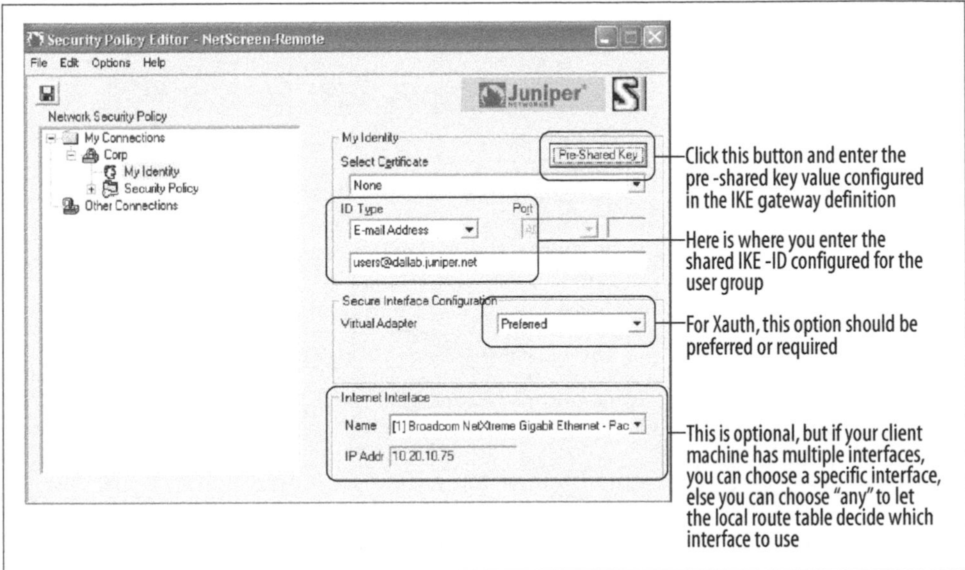

Figure 10-11. Configuring the My Identity tab in NetScreen-Remote

As shown in Figure 10-12, enable Aggressive mode and PFS with DH Group 2 in the Security Policy tab.

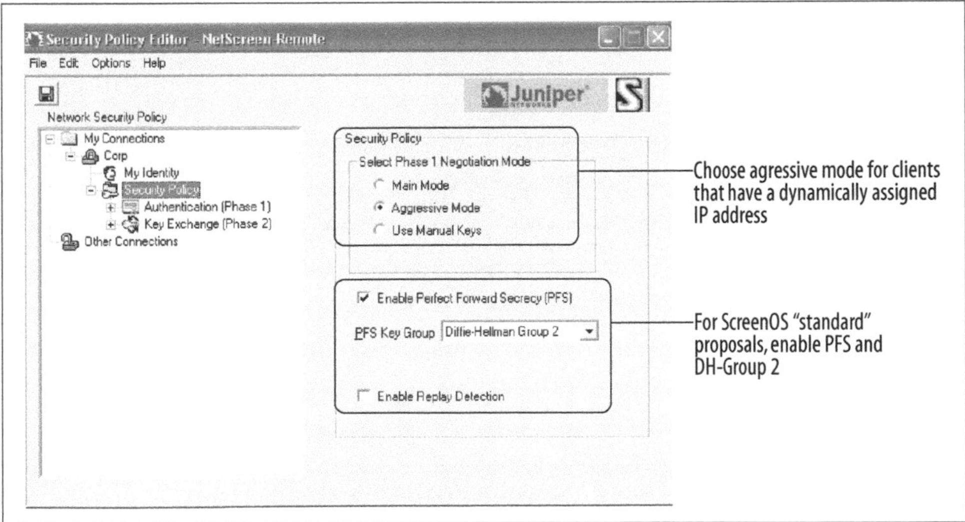

Figure 10-12. Configuring the Security Policy tab in NetScreen-Remote

Enter the Phase-1 proposal information in the following screen, as shown in Figure 10-13.

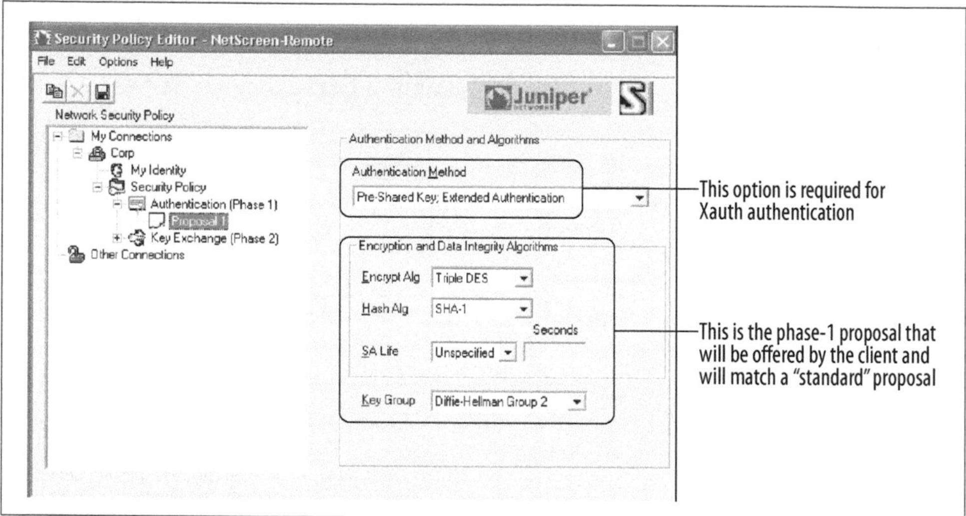

Figure 10-13. Configuring the Phase-1 proposal in NetScreen-Remote

Lastly, complete the Phase-2 proposal configuration in the client software, as shown in Figure 10-14.

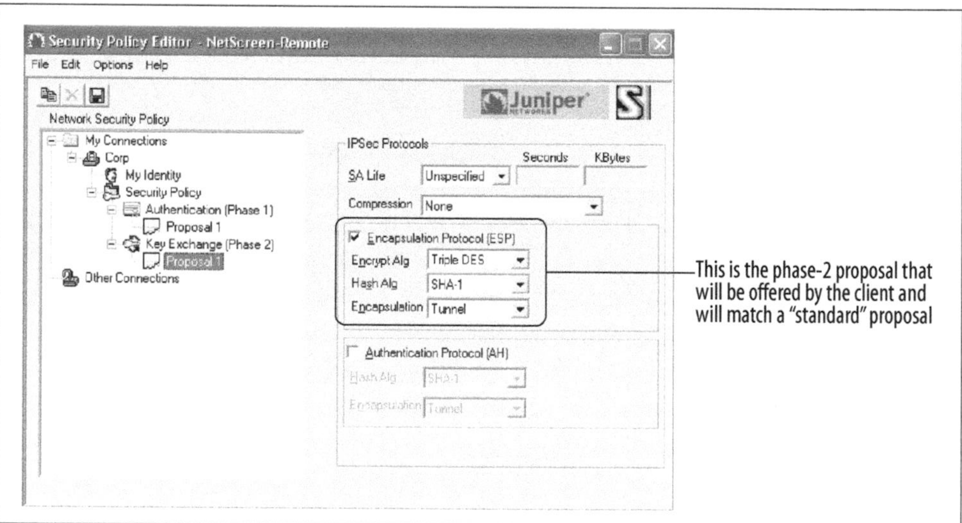

Figure 10-14. Configuring the Phase-2 proposal in NetScreen-Remote

Troubleshooting client connectivity

To test client connectivity, you can manually connect to the hub site from the VPN client software. Right-click the NetScreen-Remote icon in the taskbar and choose Connect, as shown in Figure 10-15.

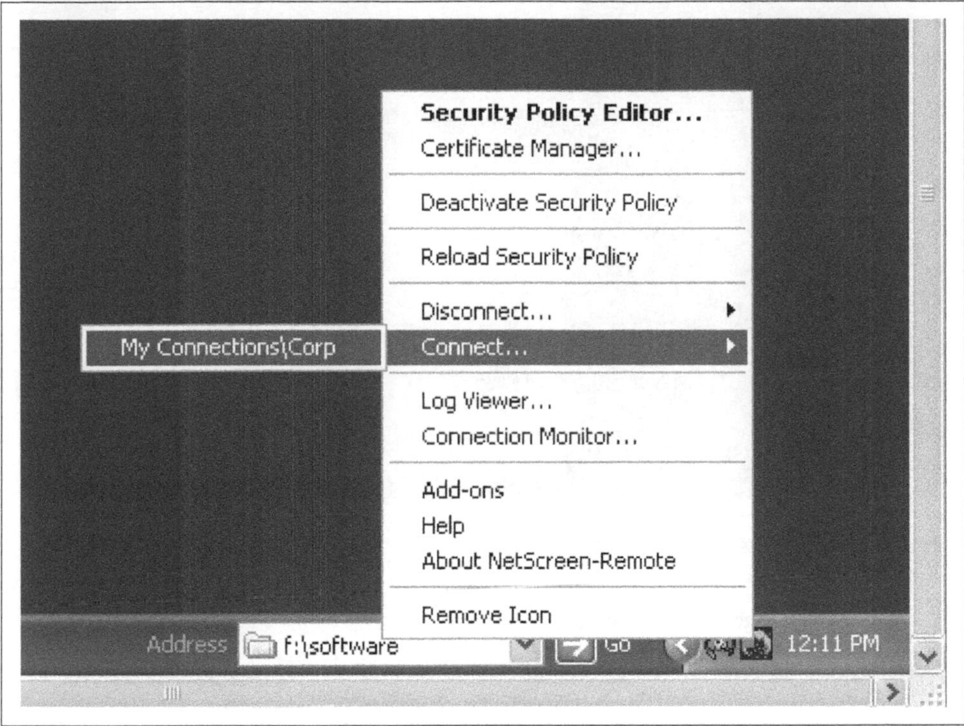

Figure 10-15. Testing client connectivity

This should cause the NetScreen-Remote client to connect and you should quickly be prompted for the Xauth username and password, as shown in Figure 10-16.

If NetScreen-Remote is configured correctly, you should get a message stating that you are connected and the NetScreen-Remote icon in the taskbar should change to show a key icon.

A proper connection should also be recorded in the event log. You can view it with the following command.

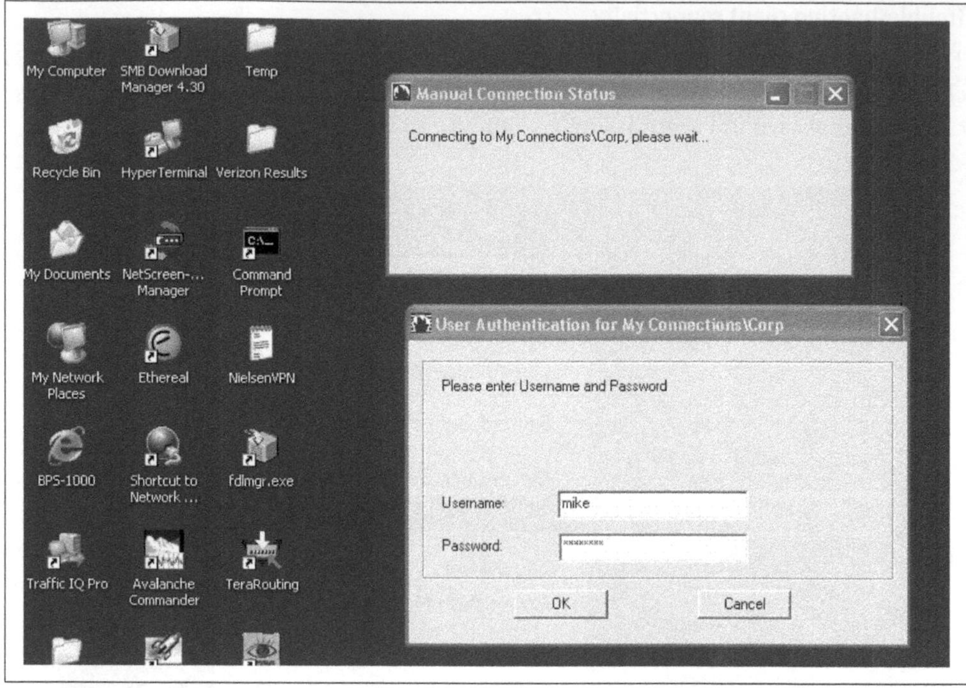

Figure 10-16. NetScreen-Remote prompting for the Xauth information before the connection is established

```
Corp-VPN-Hub-> get event type 536
Date       Time     Module Level Type Description
2007-09-09 12:39:36 system info 00536 IKE<10.20.10.75> Phase 2 msg ID
                                <92cb95cc>:Completed negotiations
                                with SPI <4958d748>, tunnel ID
                                <32770>,and lifetime <3600>
                                seconds/<0> KB.
2007-09-09 12:39:36 system info 00536 IKE<10.20.10.75> Phase 2 msg-id
                                <92cb95cc>: Completed for user
                                <users@dallab.juniper.net>.
2007-09-09 12:39:36 system info 00536 IKE<10.20.10.75> Phase 2 msg ID
                                <92cb95cc>:Responded to the peer's
                                first message from user
                                <users@dallab.juniper.net>.
2007-09-09 12:39:36 system info 00536 IKE<10.20.10.75>: XAuth login
                                was passed for gateway <lab_gateway>,
                                username <mike>, retry: 1, Client IP
                                Addr<0.0.0.0>,IPPool name:< >,
                                Session-Timeout:<0s>,Idle-Timeout:<0s>
2007-09-09 12:37:59 system info 00536 IKE<10.20.10.75>:Received
                                initial contact notification and
                                removed Phase 1 SAs.
2007-09-09 12:37:59 system info 00536 IKE<10.20.10.75>Phase 1:
                                Completed Aggressive mode negotiations
                                with a <28800>-second lifetime.
```

```
2007-09-09 12:37:59 system info 00536 IKE<10.20.10.75> Phase 1:
                                Completed for user
                                <users@dallab.juniper.net>.
2007-09-09 12:37:59 system info 00536 IKE<10.20.10.75>: Received
                                initial contact notification and
                                removed Phase 2 SAs.
2007-09-09 12:37:59 system info 00536 IKE<10.20.10.75>: Received a
                                notification message for DOI <1>
                                <24578> <INITIAL-CONTACT>.
2007-09-09 12:37:59 system info 00536 IKE<10.20.10.75>: Received a
                                notification message for DOI <1>
                                <24577> <REPLAY-STATUS>.
2007-09-09 12:37:58 system info 00536 IKE<10.20.10.75> Phase 1:
                                Responder starts AGGRESSIVE mode
                                Responder
Total entries matched = 11
Corp-VPN-Hub->
```

The most common error in this configuration is a proposal or proxy ID mismatch. You can easily identify both by using debug ike commands:

```
Corp-VPN-Hub-> debug ike basic
Corp-VPN-Hub-> clear db
Corp-VPN-Hub-> get db str
## 2007-09-09 12:48:23 : IKE<10.20.10.75> ****** Recv packet if
<ethernet0/3> of vsys <Root> ******
## 2007-09-09 12:48:23 : IKE<10.20.10.75  > Recv : [SA] [KE]
[NONCE] [ID] [VID]
## 2007-09-09 12:48:23 : IKE<10.20.10.75> ****** Recv packet if
<ethernet0/3> of vsys <Root> ******
## 2007-09-09 12:48:23 : IKE<10.20.10.75 > Recv*: [HASH] [NATD] [NATD]
[NOTIF] [NOTIF]
## 2007-09-09 12:48:23 : IKE<10.20.10.75> Phase 1: Completed for ip
<10.20.10.75>, user<users@dallab.juniper.net>
## 2007-09-09 12:48:23 : IKE<10.20.10.75> Phase 1: Completed
Aggressive  mode negotiation with a <28800>-second lifetime.
## 2007-09-09 12:48:30 : IKE<10.20.10.75> local address NOT matched.
## 2007-09-09 12:48:30 : IKE<10.20.10.75> local address NOT matched.
## 2007-09-09 12:48:30 : IKE<10.20.10.75> Proxy ID match: No policy
exists for the proxy ID received
## 2007-09-09 12:48:30 : IKE<10.20.10.75> proxy-id do not match ipsec
sa config
## 2007-09-09 12:48:30 : IKE<10.20.10.75> local address NOT matched.
## 2007-09-09 12:48:30 : IKE<10.20.10.75> Phase 2 msg-id <ce3ce6be>:
Negotiations have failed.
Corp-VPN-Hub->
```

Using the debug ike detail command would show the proxy ID that was sent as well.

The event log will also provide information regarding why the connection has failed:

```
Corp-VPN-Hub->  get event type 536
Total event entries = 53
Date        Time      Module Level  Type Description
```

```
2007-09-09 12:49:15 system info 00536 IKE<10.20.10.75> Phase 2 msg ID
                                      <ce3ce6be>: Negotiations have
                                      failed.
2007-09-09 12:49:15 system info 00536 IKE<10.20.10.75> Phase 2 msg ID
                                      <ce3ce6be>: Negotiations have
                                      failed for user <users@dallab.
                                      juniper.net>.
2007-09-09 12:49:15 system info 00536 Rejected an IKE packet on
                                      ethernet0/3 from 10.20.10.75:500
                                      to 10.140.0.3:500 with cookies
                                      43536c2bd9e2ffb3 and
                                      ea7b8fbd46ea8d61 because the peer
                                      sent a proxy ID that did not\
                                      match the one in the SA config.
2007-09-09 12:49:15 system info 00536 IKE<10.20.10.75> Phase 2: No
                                      policy exists for the proxy ID
                                      received:local ID (<10.140.10.0>/
                                      <255.255.8.0>, <0>, <0>) remote ID
                                      (<10.20.10.75>/ <255.255.255.255>,
                                      <0>, <0>).
```

You would also observe similar and easy-to-identify messages if the preshared key was not matched, or if there was an issue with the Phase-1 establishment.

10.2 Policy-Based IPSec Tunneling with Static Peers

Problem

You need to provide secure, encrypted traffic between two sites while enforcing firewall rules. These two sites have static public IP addresses, and will utilize statically configured route entries.

Solution

Create policy-based VPN configurations on each security device using the IPSec Main mode.

Hub site configuration

For the hub site configuration, start by creating address entries for local and remote subnets:

```
Corp-VPN-Hub-> set address bb denton_lan 10.70.1.0/24
Corp-VPN-Hub-> set address trust local_lan 10.140.10.0/24
```

Now, configure the Phase-1 and Phase-2 VPN definitions:

```
Corp-VPN-Hub-> set ike gateway denton address 10.0.1.71 main
               outgoing-Interface eth0/3 preshare juniper123 sec-level
               standard
Corp-VPN-Hub-> set vpn denton gateway denton sec-level standard
```

The next step is to configure bidirectional policies:

```
Corp-VPN-Hub-> set pol top name "to/from denton" from bb to trust
               denton_lanlocal_lan any tunnel vpn denton log count
policy id = 5
Corp-VPN-Hub-> set pol top name "to/from denton" from trust to bb
               local_lan denton_lan any tunnel vpn denton pair-policy
               5 log count
policy id = 6
```

Now, enable the VPN monitor and rekey options:

```
Corp-VPN-Hub-> set vpn denton monitor rekey
Corp-VPN-Hub-> save
```

Remote site configuration

For the remote site configuration, begin by creating address entries for the local and remote subnets:

```
S1-Denton-> set address bb corp_lan 10.140.10.0/24
S1-Denton-> set address trust local_lan 10.70.1.0/24
```

Now, create the Phase-1 and Phase-2 VPN definitions:

```
S1-Denton-> set ike gateway corp address 10.140.0.3 main outgoing-
            interface eth0/0 preshare juniper123 sec-level standard
S1-Denton-> set vpn corp gateway corp sec-level standard
```

Create the bidirectional VPN policies:

```
S1-Denton-> set policy top name "to/from corp" from bb to trust
            corp_lan local_lan any tunnel vpn corp
policy id = 13
S1-Denton-> set policy top name "to/from corp" from trust to bb
            local_lan corp_lanany tunnel vpn corp pair-policy 13
policy id = 14
```

Finally, enable the VPN monitor and rekey options:

```
S1-Denton-> set vpn corp monitor rekey
S1-Denton-> save
```

Discussion

In this recipe, it is assumed that the device is already configured for normal communication and routing. This recipe simply adds a policy-based tunnel for traffic matching the policies configured with the tunnel action.

Figure 10-17 shows the layout for this scenario. The remote site "Denton" needs connectivity with the hub site "Corp" to gain access to server resources. Each location is configured with static IP addresses, and will use the default static route configuration within the trust VR.

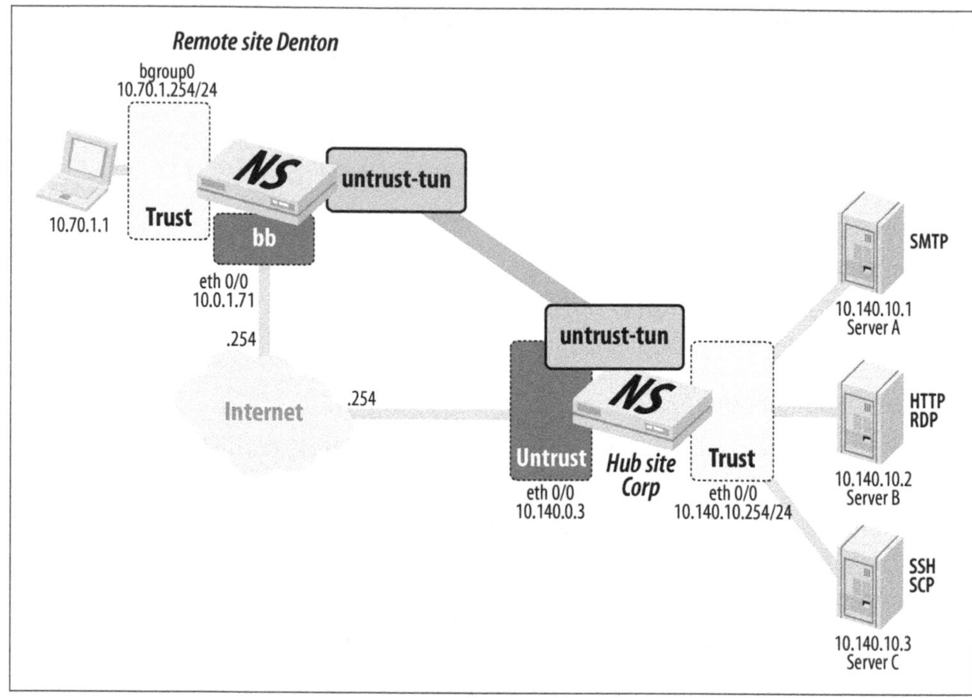

Figure 10-17. A simple policy-based VPN example

This recipe starts by defining the protected resources on each end of the tunnel in the form of address objects. The following objects are defined at the hub site:

```
Corp-VPN-Hub-> set address bb denton_lan 10.70.1.0/24
Corp-VPN-Hub-> set address trust local_lan 10.140.10.0/24
```

At the remote site, the following address objects are defined:

```
S1-Denton-> set address bb corp_lan 10.140.10.0/24
S1-Denton-> set address trust local_lan 10.70.1.0/24
```

These address objects define the subnets on each end of the tunnel. In your environment, these could be address groups that contain specific addresses or ranges of IPs allowed to traverse the tunnel or be reached via the tunnel.

Next, you create the Phase-1 and Phase-2 configurations. The hub site has the following configuration:

```
Corp-VPN-Hub-> set ike gateway denton address 10.0.1.71 main outgoing-
               Interface eth0/3 preshare juniper123 sec-level standard
Corp-VPN-Hub-> set vpn denton gateway denton sec-level standard
```

The remote site has the following configuration:

```
S1-Denton-> set ike gateway corp address 10.140.0.3 main outgoing-
            preshare juniper123 sec-level standard
S1-Denton-> interface eth0/0 set vpn corp gateway corp sec-level
            standard
```

Here, you create the Phase-1 IKE gateway definition and configure it for the IPSec Main mode. Each site defines the remote IKE peer address and outgoing interface to be the local IKE peer as well as defines the preshared key and standard proposal. In the next line, you create the Phase-2 SA, bind it to the Phase-1 gateway definition, and configure a standard Phase-2 proposal. The final part of the configuration is to create bidirectional policies with a tunnel action that match the local and remote subnet addresses you defined in the first step.

At the hub site, configure the following policies to allow any IP-based communication between the sites:

```
Corp-VPN-Hub-> set pol top name "to/from denton" from bb to trust
               denton_lan local_lan any tunnel vpn denton log count
               policy id = 5
Corp-VPN-Hub-> set pol top name "to/from denton" from trust to bb
               local_lan denton_lan any tunnel vpn denton log count
               policy id = 6
```

Policies at the remote site are as follows:

```
S1-Denton-> set policy top name "to/from corp" from bb to trust
            corp_lan local_lan any tunnel vpn corp policy id = 13
S1-Denton-> set policy top name "to/from corp" from trust to bb
            local_lan corp_lan any tunnel vpn corp policy id = 14
```

In this scenario, the VPN monitor is also enabled with the rekey option. This configuration will keep the tunnel established at all times.

At the hub site, enable the VPN monitor for the denton VPN and save the configuration:

```
Corp-VPN-Hub-> set vpn denton monitor rekey
Corp-VPN-Hub-> save
```

Do the same for the remote site corp VPN:

```
S1-Denton-> set vpn corp monitor rekey
S1-Denton-> save
```

10.3 Route-Based IPSec Tunneling with Static Peers and Static Routes

Problem

You need to provide secure, encrypted traffic between two sites while enforcing firewall rules using a route-based configuration. These two sites have static IP addresses.

Solution

Create VPN configurations on each device using tunnel interfaces and policies.

Hub site configuration

For the hub site configuration, first create address entries for local and remote subnets:

```
Corp-VPN-Hub-> set address trust local_lan 10.140.10.0/24
Corp-VPN-Hub-> set address vpn denton_lan 10.70.1.0/24
```

Then, create the zone and interface:

```
Corp-VPN-Hub-> set zone name vpn
Corp-VPN-Hub-> set interf tun.10 zone vpn
Corp-VPN-Hub-> set interface tun.10 ip unnumbered interface eth0/3
```

Now, configure routes to use the tunnel for the destination subnet:

```
Corp-VPN-Hub-> set route 10.70.1.0/24 interface tun.10
```

Next, configure the VPN Phase-1 and Phase-2 parameters:

```
Corp-VPN-Hub-> set ike gateway denton address 10.0.1.71 main outgoing-
               Interface eth0/3 preshare juniper123 sec-level standard
Corp-VPN-Hub-> set vpn denton gateway denton sec-level standard
Corp-VPN-Hub-> set vpn denton bind interface tun.10
```

Enable the VPN monitor and rekey options:

```
Corp-VPN-Hub-> set vpn denton monitor rekey
```

Finally, create the bidirectional policies:

```
Corp-VPN-Hub-> set policy from trust to vpn local_lan denton_lan any
               permit policy id = 5
Corp-VPN-Hub-> set pol from vpn to trust denton_lan local_lan any
               permit policy id = 6
Corp-VPN-Hub-> save
```

Remote site configuration

For the remote site configuration, begin by creating address object entries for local and remote subnets:

```
S1-Denton-> set address trust local_lan 10.70.1.0/24
S1-Denton-> set address vpn corp_lan 10.140.10.0/24
```

Create the zone and interface:

```
S1-Denton-> set zone name vpn
S1-Denton-> set interface tun.10 zone vpn
S1-Denton-> set interface tun.10 ip unnumbered interface eth0/0
```

Now, configure the routes to use the tunnel for the destination subnet:

```
S1-Denton-> set route 10.140.10.0/24 interface tun.10
```

Configure the VPN Phase-1 and Phase-2 parameters:

```
S1-Denton-> set ike gateway corp address 10.140.0.3 main outgoing-
            interface eth0/0 preshare juniper123 sec-level standard
```

```
S1-Denton-> set vpn corp gateway corp sec-level standard
S1-Denton-> set vpn corp bind interface tun.10
```

Next, enable the VPN monitor and rekey options:

```
S1-Denton-> set vpn corp monitor rekey
```

Finally, create the policies permitting the traffic between zones:

```
S1-Denton-> set policy from trust to vpn local_lan corp_lan any
            permit policy id = 13
S1-Denton-> set policy from vpn to trust corp_lan local_lan any
            permit policy id = 14
S1-Denton-> save
```

Discussion

For this recipe, it is assumed that the firewall is already in operation and is configured, and that a new VPN tunnel needs to be created between two ScreenOS devices, as shown in Figure 10-18. This solution also uses a custom security zone in which to bind the VPN traffic. The VPN zone is now the encrypt/decrypt zone, and standard security policies may be used for permitting traffic from the tunnel to other zones, or from other zones into the tunnel.

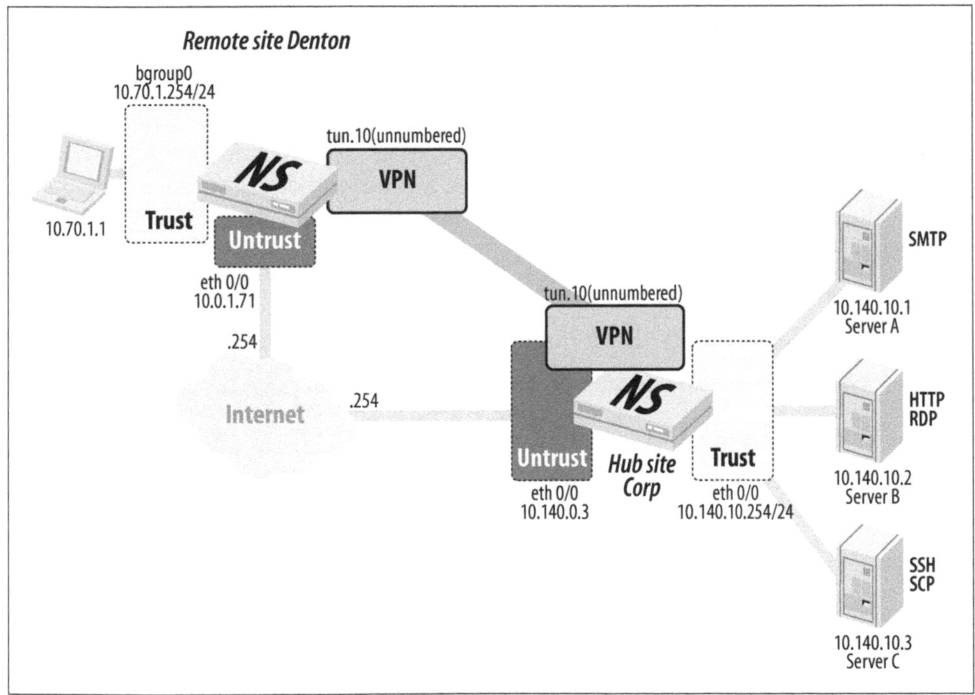

Figure 10-18. A simple site-to-site route-based VPN example

You can place the tunnel interface into any zone. The caveat here is that when you're using unnumbered tunnel interfaces, you can place the tunnel interface only within a zone bound to the same VR as the interface being used to borrow the IP address.

You could place the tunnel interface within the `Trust` zone. In this scenario, security policies would not be required for VPN traffic to communicate with hosts on the `Trust` zone without intra-zone blocking enabled. Intra-zone blocking is not enabled by default.

You begin this configuration by defining the protected resources at each site. You do this in the form of address and service objects. At the corporate site, the following is created:

```
Corp-VPN-Hub-> set address trust local_lan 10.140.10.0/24
Corp-VPN-Hub-> set address vpn denton_lan 10.70.1.0/24
```

Two address objects are created to define the local and remote LANs. You can use address and service groups to specify strict communication parameters as desired. A similar configuration is performed for the remote site.

Next, the zone and tunnel interfaces are created:

```
Corp-VPN-Hub-> set zone name vpn
Corp-VPN-Hub-> set interf tun.10 zone vpn
Corp-VPN-Hub-> set interface tun.10 ip unnumbered interface eth0/3
```

A custom security zone named `VPN` is created and is bound by default to the default VR (`trust-vr`) at both sites. An interface, `tun.10`, is created and bound to the `VPN` zone. This example of the corporate site uses an unnumbered interface, borrowing the IP address from interface `eth0/3`. At the remote site, interface `eth0/0` is used for the tunnel interface IP address:

```
S1-Denton-> set interface tun.10 ip unnumbered interface eth0/0
```

Next, you can add routes to direct traffic to the tunnel interface:

```
Corp-VPN-Hub-> set route 10.70.1.0/24 interface tun.10

S1-Denton-> set route 10.140.10.0/24 interface tun.10
```

Now the IKE Phase-1 and Phase-2 parameters are specified. The two sites' configurations are shown for comparison:

```
Corp-VPN-Hub-> set ike gateway denton address 10.0.1.71 main outgoing-
               Interface eth0/3 preshare juniper123 sec-level standard
Corp-VPN-Hub-> set vpn denton gateway denton sec-level standard
Corp-VPN-Hub-> set vpn denton bind interface tun.10

S1-Denton-> set ike gateway corp address 10.140.0.3 main outgoing-
            interface eth0/0 preshare juniper123 sec-level standard
S1-Denton-> set vpn corp gateway corp sec-level standard
S1-Denton-> set vpn corp bind interface tun.10
```

Here, for convenience purposes, the same name is used for the IKE gateway and the VPN tunnel. Tunnels in opposite directions are configured using the same preshared keys and security levels. The VPNs are then bound to `tun.10`.

The VPN monitor and rekey are enabled on each end of the tunnel to ensure that the tunnel remains active and up at all times:

```
Corp-VPN-Hub-> set vpn denton monitor rekey
```

To finish the configuration, policies are configured between the `VPN` and `Trust` zones to permit the traffic between the two subnets:

```
Corp-VPN-Hub-> set policy from trust to vpn local_lan denton_lan any
               permit policy id = 5
Corp-VPN-Hub-> set pol from vpn to trust denton_lan local_lan any
               permit policy id = 6
Corp-VPN-Hub-> save
```

The policies shown here permit any traffic between the defined local and remote LANs. Your policies would, and should, be specific to the flows that should be permitted across the VPN tunnel.

Troubleshooting this configuration would consist of using the `get event`, `debug ike`, `get sa`, and `get ike cookie` commands. With route-based VPNs, it is also useful to verify that the route to a destination is indeed via the tunnel interface. You can do this with `get route ip <IP address>`.

10.4 Route-Based VPN with Dynamic Peer and Static Routing

Problem

You want to create a VPN tunnel between a remote site and the hub site where the remote site receives a DIP address from the service provider.

Solution

Use a route-based VPN approach and an IPSec Aggressive mode configuration. Enable the VPN monitor to keep the tunnel active.

Hub site configuration

For the hub site configuration, first create address entries for local and remote subnets:

```
Corp-VPN-Hub-> set address trust local_lan 10.140.10.0/24
Corp-VPN-Hub-> set address vpn denton_lan 10.70.1.0/24
```

Next, create the zone and interface:

```
Corp-VPN-Hub-> set zone name vpn
Corp-VPN-Hub-> set interf tun.21 zone vpn
Corp-VPN-Hub-> set interface tun.21 ip unnumbered interface eth0/3
```

Then, configure the VPN Phase-1 and Phase-2 parameters:

```
Corp-VPN-Hub-> set ike gateway denton dynamic s1_denton@xyzcorp.com
               Aggressive outgoing-interface eth0/3 preshare juniper123
               sec-level standard
Corp-VPN-Hub-> set vpn denton gateway denton sec-level standard
Corp-VPN-Hub-> set vpn denton bind interface tun.21
```

Enable the VPN monitor and rekey options:

```
Corp-VPN-Hub-> set vpn denton monitor rekey
```

Next, create the bidirectional policies:

```
Corp-VPN-Hub-> set policy from trust to vpn local_lan denton_lan any
               permit policy id = 5
Corp-VPN-Hub-> set pol from vpn to trust denton_lan local_lan any
               permit policy id = 6
```

Now, configure the routes to use the tunnel for the destination subnet:

```
Corp-VPN-Hub-> set route 10.70.1.0/24 interface tun.21
Corp-VPN-Hub-> save
```

Remote site configuration

For the remote site configuration, create the address object entries for local and remote subnets:

```
S1-Denton-> set address trust local_lan 10.70.1.0/24
S1-Denton-> set address vpn corp_lan 10.140.10.0/24
```

Next, create the zone and interface:

```
S1-Denton-> set zone name vpn
S1-Denton-> set interface tun.5 zone vpn
S1-Denton-> set interface tun.5 ip unnumbered interface eth0/0
```

Configure the VPN Phase-1 and Phase-2 parameters:

```
S1-Denton-> set ike gateway corp address 10.140.0.3 aggressive
            local-id s1_denton@xyzcorp.com outgoing-interface eth0/0
            preshare juniper123 sec-level standard
S1-Denton-> set vpn corp gateway corp sec-level standard
S1-Denton-> set vpn corp bind interface tun.5
```

Enable the VPN monitor and rekey options:

```
S1-Denton-> set vpn corp monitor rekey
```

Now, create the policies permitting the traffic between zones:

```
S1-Denton-> set policy from trust to vpn local_lan corp_lan any permit
            policy id = 13
S1-Denton-> set policy from vpn to trust corp_lan local_lan any permit
            policy id = 14
```

Finish by configuring the routes to use the tunnel for the destination subnet:

```
S1-Denton-> set route 10.140.10.0/24 interface tun.10
S1-Denton-> save
```

Discussion

In this recipe's discussion, as shown in Figure 10-19, it is assumed that the security devices are already configured for the environment and that a route-based VPN needs to be established between a statically configured device and a dynamic peer. In this example, the two sites are named "Corp" and "Denton".

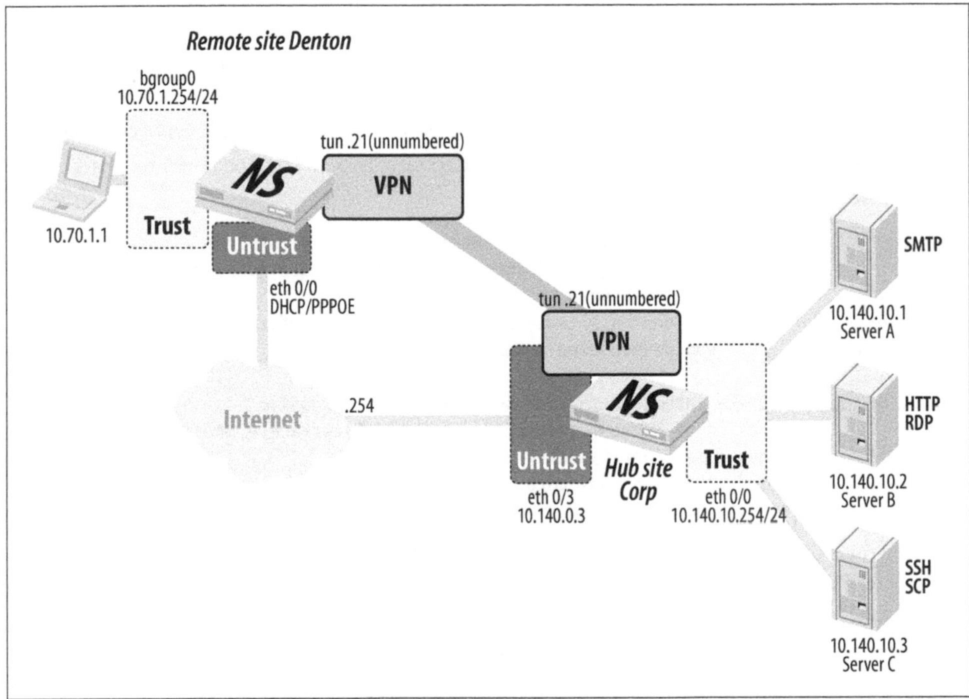

Figure 10-19. A route-based site-to-site tunnel with dynamic peer example

This configuration begins with the creation of address objects defining the subnets on each end of the tunnel. In a real network, these definitions should include specific host addresses and potentially custom service objects to be used in firewall policies that limit connectivity to only the allowed flows.

```
Corp-VPN-Hub-> set address trust local_lan 10.140.10.0/24
Corp-VPN-Hub-> set address vpn denton_lan 10.70.1.0/24

S1-Denton-> set address trust local_lan 10.70.1.0/24
S1-Denton-> set address vpn corp_lan 10.140.10.0/24
```

A custom security zone named VPN is created at each site and is used to bind the tunnel interface within. In this configuration, the tunnel interface will use IP unnumbered addressing and will borrow the IP address from the interface in the Untrust zone. Interface tun.21 is used at the Corp site and tun.5 is defined at the Denton site:

```
Corp-VPN-Hub-> set zone name vpn
Corp-VPN-Hub-> set interf tun.21 zone vpn
Corp-VPN-Hub-> set interface tun.21 ip unnumbered interface eth0/3

S1-Denton-> set zone name vpn
S1-Denton-> set interface tun.5 zone vpn
S1-Denton-> set interface tun.5 ip unnumbered interface eth0/0
```

Next, the Phase-1 and Phase-2 IKE configurations are completed. With a DIP address on one end of the tunnel, you cannot use the IPv4 address as the IKE ID. Instead, you must use an email address, certificate, or FQDN. In this example, an email address is used for the IKE ID of the Denton site. The IKE ID *s1_denton@xyzcorp.com* is configured as the IKE ID to expect at the Corp site and as the local-id to send at the Denton site:

```
Corp-VPN-Hub-> set ike gateway denton dynamic s1_denton@xyzcorp.com
               aggressive outgoing-interface eth0/3 preshare juniper123
               sec-level standard
Corp-VPN-Hub-> set vpn denton gateway denton sec-level standard
Corp-VPN-Hub-> set vpn denton bind interface tun.21

S1-Denton-> set ike gateway corp address 10.140.0.3 aggressive
            local-id s1_denton@xyzcorp.com outgoing-interface eth0/0
            preshare juniper123 sec-level standard
S1-Denton-> set vpn corp gateway corp sec-level standard
S1-Denton-> set vpn corp bind interface tun.5
```

In the preceding VPN configuration, the Corp site configuration specifies a dynamic address followed by the IKE ID expected for this IKE gateway. This is followed by specifying Aggressive mode, the interface to use as the IKE peer, the preshared key, and the security level which contains the Phase-1 proposals to offer or accept.

At the Denton site, the address of the Corp site is configured and Aggressive mode is specified for the Phase-1 exchange. The IKE ID in the form of local-id is configured, and will be used to identify the Denton site during the Phase-1 negotiations.

The remainder of the tunnel configuration is finished by configuring the Phase-2 security level and binding the tunnel to an interface.

When a participant in VPN uses a dynamically assigned IP address, that device must be the IKE initiator and must start the IPSec negotiations. You can use the VPN monitor with the rekey option to ensure that the tunnel initiates and stays active at all times.

The VPN monitor is configured with the rekey option to keep this tunnel in an active state:

```
Corp-VPN-Hub-> set vpn denton monitor rekey

S1-Denton-> set vpn corp monitor rekey
```

To finalize the configuration, policies and routes are created to steer traffic across the tunnel and permit specific flows through the stateful inspection engine:

```
Corp-VPN-Hub-> set policy from trust to vpn local_lan denton_lan any
               permit policy id = 5
Corp-VPN-Hub-> set pol from vpn to trust denton_lan local_lan any
               permit policy id = 6
Corp-VPN-Hub-> set route 10.70.1.0/24 interface tun.21
Corp-VPN-Hub-> save

S1-Denton-> set policy from trust to vpn local_lan corp_lan any permit
            policy id = 13
S1-Denton-> set policy from vpn to trust corp_lan local_lan any permit
            policy id = 14
S1-Denton-> set route 10.140.10.0/24 interface tun.10
S1-Denton-> save
```

Don't forget to save your configuration.

This recipe is very similar to Recipe 10.3. The difference is with the Phase-1 exchange. Aggressive mode IKE is usually used when one end of the tunnel has a dynamically assigned IP address. Though not shown in this chapter, you also can use an FQDN as the address for the remote IKE peer. With Dynamic DNS (DDNS), this configuration could have used Main mode for the Phase-1 exchange even though the remote site has a dynamically assigned IP address.

For troubleshooting this configuration, use the `get event`, `get sa`, `get ike cookie`, and `get route` commands. Using `debug ike` commands can offer more verbose information regarding the success or failure of the IKE negotiations.

10.5 Redundant VPN Gateways with Static Routes

Problem

You want to create a VPN with a primary and a backup site with which remote offices can communicate. Static routing will be used with automatic rerouting around a failed primary tunnel.

Solution

Configure route-based tunnels to each hub site and use static routing with the VPN monitor to select the preferred or alternative path.

Primary hub site configuration

For the primary hub site configuration, start by creating the zone and interface:

```
Corp-VPN-Hub-> set zone name vpn
Corp-VPN-Hub-> set interf tun.21 zone vpn
Corp-VPN-Hub-> set interface tun.21 ip unnumbered interface eth0/0
```

Now, create address entries for the local and remote subnets:

```
Corp-VPN-Hub-> set address trust server_farm 10.88.10.0/24
Corp-VPN-Hub-> set address vpn denton_lan 10.70.1.0/24
```

Configure the VPN Phase-1 and Phase-2 parameters:

```
Corp-VPN-Hub-> set ike gateway denton dynamic s1_denton@xyzcorp.com
               Aggressive outgoing-interface eth0/3 preshare juniper123
               sec-level standard
Corp-VPN-Hub-> set vpn denton gateway denton sec-level standard
Corp-VPN-Hub-> set vpn denton bind interface tun.21
```

Next, configure the routes to use the tunnel for the destination subnet:

```
Corp-VPN-Hub-> set route 10.70.1.0/24 interface tun.21
```

Now, enable the VPN monitor and rekey options:

```
Corp-VPN-Hub-> set vpn denton monitor rekey
```

Finish by creating the bidirectional policies:

```
Corp-VPN-Hub-> set policy from trust to vpn local_lan denton_lan any
               permit policy id = 5
Corp-VPN-Hub-> set pol from vpn to trust denton_lan local_lan any
               permit policy id = 6
Corp-VPN-Hub-> save
```

Backup hub site configuration

For the backup hub site configuration, start by creating the zone and interface:

```
Backup-Hub-> set zone name vpn
Backup-Hub-> set interf tun.21 zone vpn
Backup-Hub-> set interface tun.21 ip unnumbered interface eth0/0
```

Create the address entries for the local and remote subnets:

```
Backup-Hub-> set address trust server_farm 10.88.10.0/24
Backup-Hub-> set address vpn denton_lan 10.70.1.0/24
```

Now, configure the VPN Phase-1 and Phase-2 parameters:

```
Backup-Hub-> set ike gateway denton dynamic s1_denton@xyzcorp.com
             Aggressive outgoing-interface eth0/3 preshare juniper123
             sec-level standard
Backup-Hub-> set vpn denton gateway denton sec-level standard
Backup-Hub-> set vpn denton bind interface tun.21
```

Configure the routes to use the tunnel for the destination subnet:

```
Backup-Hub-> set route 10.70.1.0/24 interface tun.21
```

Next, enable the VPN monitor and rekey options:

```
Backup-VPN-Hub-> set vpn denton monitor rekey
```

Finally, create the bidirectional policies:

```
Backup-Hub-> set policy from trust to vpn server_farm denton_lan any
             permit policy id = 5
Backup-Hub-> set pol from vpn to trust denton_lan server_farm any
             permit policy id = 6
Backup-Hub-> save
```

Remote site configuration

Start the remote site configuration by creating the zone and interface:

```
S1-Denton-> set zone name vpn
S1-Denton-> set interface tun.5 zone vpn
S1-Denton-> set interface tun.5 ip unnumbered interface eth0/0
```

Now, create the address object entries for the local and remote subnets:

```
S1-Denton-> set address trust denton_lan 10.70.1.0/24
S1-Denton-> set address vpn server_farm 10.88.10.0/24
```

Configure the VPN Phase-1 and Phase-2 parameters for the primary tunnel:

```
S1-Denton-> set ike gateway corp address 10.140.0.3 aggressive local-id
            s1_denton@xyzcorp.com outgoing-interface eth0/0 preshare
            juniper123 sec-level standard
S1-Denton-> set vpn corp gateway corp sec-level standard
S1-Denton-> set vpn corp bind interface tun.5
```

Next, configure the VPN Phase-1 and Phase-2 parameters for the backup tunnel:

```
S1-Denton-> set ike gateway backup address 10.55.0.3 aggressive local-id
            s1_denton@xyzcorp.com outgoing-interface eth0/0 preshare
            juniper123 sec-level standard
S1-Denton-> set vpn backup gateway backup sec-level standard
S1-Denton-> set vpn backup bind interface tun.5
```

Configure the routes and interface NHTB mapping:

```
S1-Denton-> set route 10.88.10.0/24 interface tun.5 gateway 10.140.0.3
            metric 10
S1-Denton-> set route 10.88.10.0/24 interface tun.5 gateway 10.55.0.3
            metric 100
S1-Denton-> set interface tun.5 nhtb 10.140.0.3 vpn corp
S1-Denton-> set interface tun.5 nhtb 10.55.0.3 vpn backup
```

Now, enable the VPN monitor and rekey options (~10-second failover):

```
S1-Denton-> set vpn corp monitor rekey
S1-Denton-> set vpn backup monitor rekey
S1-Denton-> set vpnmon interval 2
S1-Denton-> set vpnmon threshold 5
```

Create the policies permitting the traffic between zones:

```
S1-Denton-> set policy from trust to vpn denton_lan server_farm any
            permit policy id = 13
```

```
S1-Denton-> set policy from vpn to trust server_farm denton_lan any
            permit policy id = 14
S1-Denton-> save
```

Discussion

In this example, as illustrated in Figure 10-20, the remote site "Denton" has two tunnels configured—one to each hub site, "Corp" and "Backup". From the perspective of the remote site, static routes are configured for reaching the remote resources on subnet `10.88.10.0/24`. Route metrics are used to prefer the tunnel between Denton and Corp. If the preferred tunnel should fail, the backup tunnel will be used to reach the remote resources. This example also demonstrates the use of NHTB for creating a point-to-multipoint interface. In other words, a single tunnel interface will be used to service both VPN tunnels from the remote site.

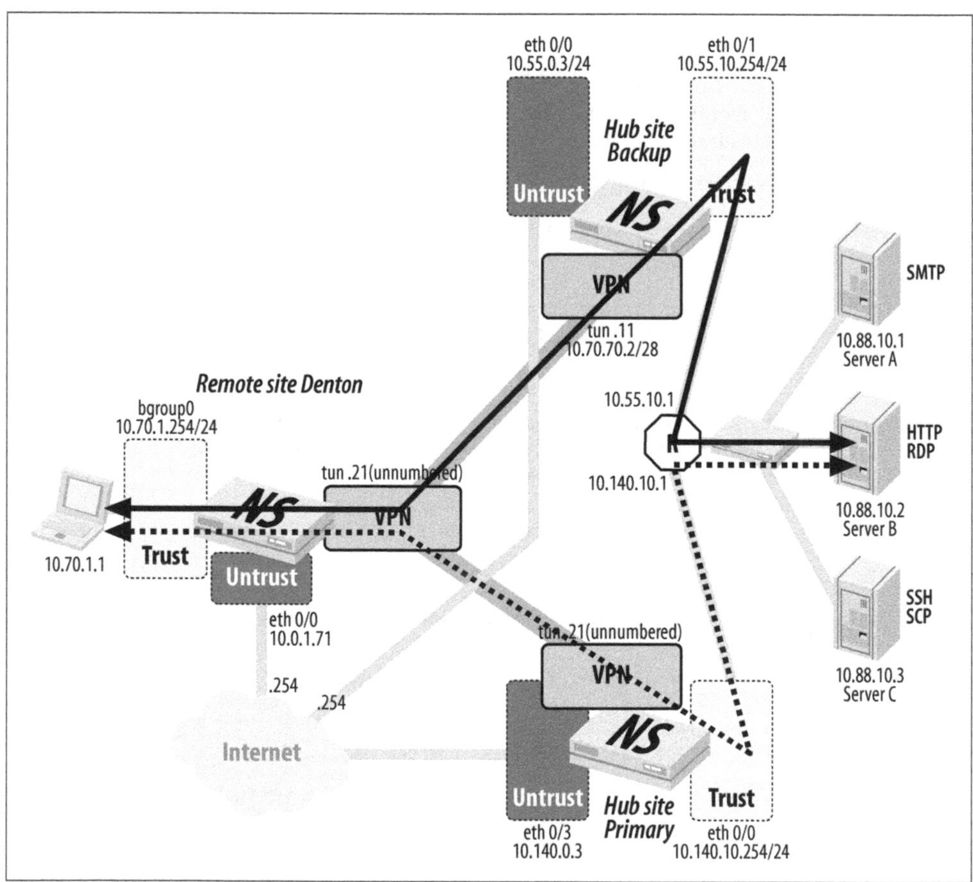

Figure 10-20. Redundant VPN gateway example with static routes

You begin the configuration by defining a custom security zone named VPN as well as an unnumbered tunnel interface within the zone at each site:

```
Corp-VPN-Hub-> set zone name vpn
Corp-VPN-Hub-> set interf tun.21 zone vpn
Corp-VPN-Hub-> set interface tun.21 ip unnumbered interface eth0/0

Backup-Hub-> set zone name vpn
Backup-Hub-> set interf tun.21 zone vpn
Backup-Hub-> set interface tun.21 ip unnumbered interface eth0/0

S1-Denton-> set zone name vpn
S1-Denton-> set interface tun.5 zone vpn
S1-Denton-> set interface tun.5 ip unnumbered interface eth0/0
```

Next, the protected resources in the form of address objects are created. For simplicity's sake, only the subnet hosting the resources and the remote LAN are defined in this example. You should replace this step with specific address groups and perhaps custom services defining the hosts and protocols that will be permitted across the VPN:

```
Corp-VPN-Hub-> set address trust server_farm 10.88.10.0/24
Corp-VPN-Hub-> set address vpn denton_lan 10.70.1.0/24

Backup-Hub-> set address trust server_farm 10.88.10.0/24
Backup-Hub-> set address vpn denton_lan 10.70.1.0/24

S1-Denton-> set address trust local_lan 10.70.1.0/24
S1-Denton-> set address vpn server_farm 10.88.10.0/24
```

The address object server_farm is defined at both hub sites in the Trust zone and at the remote site in the VPN zone. The address denton_lan is defined at the hub sites in the VPN zone and at the remote site in the Trust zone.

As with Recipe 10.4, the Denton site will be configured as a dynamic peer, using an email address for the IKE ID:

```
Corp-VPN-Hub-> set ike gateway denton dynamic s1_denton@xyzcorp.com
               aggressive outgoing-interface eth0/3 preshare
               juniper123 sec-level standard
Corp-VPN-Hub-> set vpn denton gateway denton sec-level standard
Corp-VPN-Hub-> set vpn denton bind interface tun.21

Backup-Hub-> set ike gateway denton dynamic s1_denton@xyzcorp.com
             aggressive outgoing-interface eth0/3 preshare
             juniper123 sec-level standard
Backup-Hub-> set vpn denton gateway denton sec-level standard
Backup-Hub-> set vpn denton bind interface tun.21
```

The IKE configuration at the two hub sites is identical in this example. Each defines a dynamic address and aggressive mode to be used for the Phase-1 negotiation, expecting the IKE ID *s1_denton@xyzcorp.com*. A preshared key, an interface for the

IKE peer, and a security level complete the Phase-1 parameters. The Phase-2 parameters specify the security level and bind the tunnel to interface `tun.21`.

At the remote site, two tunnels are configured, one to each hub site:

```
S1-Denton-> set ike gateway corp address 10.140.0.3 aggressive
            local-id s1_denton@xyzcorp.com outgoing-interface eth0/0 preshare
            juniper123 sec-level standard
S1-Denton-> set vpn corp gateway corp sec-level standard
S1-Denton-> set vpn corp bind interface tun.5
S1-Denton-> set ike gateway backup address 10.55.0.3 aggressive
            local-id s1_denton@xyzcorp.com outgoing-interface eth0/0
            preshare  juniper123 sec-level standard
S1-Denton-> set vpn backup gateway backup sec-level standard
S1-Denton-> set vpn backup bind interface tun.5
```

The IKE gateway parameters define the IP address of the IKE peer at each hub site, specify Aggressive mode, and define the IKE ID to send during the Phase-1 negotiations. Interface `eth0/0` is used for the IKE gateway, and the preshared key and security level are defined. Here, you can see that both VPN tunnels are being bound to the same interface, `tun.5`. You will need to configure a method to process flows via the correct VPN tunnel. This example uses static routes and NHTB for this purpose.

At the hub sites, a single tunnel is bound to the interface, so a simple `route` statement is all that is required to steer traffic across the tunnel:

```
set route 10.70.1.0/24 interface tun.21
```

At the remote site, a point-to-multipoint interface is used with multiple tunnels bound to the interface, so specifying a route simply to the interface is not enough:

```
S1-Denton-> set route 10.88.10.0/24 interface tun.5 gateway 10.140.0.3
            metric 10
S1-Denton-> set route 10.88.10.0/24 interface tun.5 gateway 10.55.0.3
            metric 100
S1-Denton-> set interface tun.5 nhtb 10.140.0.3 vpn corp
S1-Denton-> set interface tun.5 nhtb 10.55.0.3 vpn backup
```

The route entries and NHTB definitions are the meat of this recipe. The remote site has a tunnel to each hub site. The `set route` commands specify that destination `10.88.10.0/24` can be reached via `tun.1` with a next-hop gateway defined and a metric preferring the tunnel associated with gateway `10.140.0.3`. The NHTB definitions that follow define which gateway is reachable via which tunnel. It is important to understand that the next-hop gateway addresses used in the `route` statement do not have to actually be reachable; they are simply pointers into the NHTB table so that the correct tunnel (SA) will be used as the traffic flow destination. Please see the "NHTB" section in the introduction to this chapter for more information.

In this example, ScreenOS could automatically create the NHTB configuration. It is shown statically configured here as an example of the command usage and could be omitted.

To finish the configuration, the VPN monitor is enabled to keep the tunnels active. In addition, the VPN monitor plays an important role in this scenario. If a tunnel fails, the VPN monitor will recognize the failure and mark any routes associated with the tunnel as inactive. This will allow the route with the next best metric to be used for flows to the specific destination(s). We explain the VPN monitor and the rekey option in more detail in the Introduction to this chapter.

```
set vpn denton monitor rekey
set vpnmon interval 2
set vpnmon threshold 5

S1-Denton-> set vpn corp monitor rekey
S1-Denton-> set vpn backup monitor rekey
S1-Denton-> set vpnmon interval 2
S1-Denton-> set vpnmon threshold 5
```

The same commands are used at the hub sites, and each VPN at the remote site gets the VPN monitor enabled. The interval and threshold for the VPN monitor are configured to send the ICMP packet every two seconds (interval) and to declare the tunnel as "down" if five pings are missed (threshold). This would provide a 10-second failover time.

When scaling VPN to a large design, be careful when choosing an interval and threshold for the VPN monitor, as the monitoring function does add traffic to the network. The default settings for the VPN monitor are interval = 10 and threshold = 10.

Policies are now applied for permitting specific flows to/from the VPN zone.

Here is how the route table, the SAs, the VPN monitor, and the NHTB table look for this design with no failures at the remote site.

We see bidirectional SAs between both gateways—the Corp and the Backup sites. The SA index is in the first column followed by the remote gateway address, the Phase-2 security parameters that were negotiated, the SPI, the lifetime in seconds, and the status indicating that both tunnels are active and up (A/U). A VPN monitor failure would show the SA as A/D (active/down).

```
S1-Denton-> get sa active
total configured sa: 2
HEX ID    Gateway     Port Algorithm     SPI  Life:sec kb Sta PID vsys
0000000d< 10.140.0.3 500 esp:3des/sha1 98a96b51  2408 unlim A/U  -1 0
0000000d> 10.140.0.3 500 esp:3des/sha1 4958d759  2408 unlim A/U  -1 0
0000000e<  10.55.0.3 500 esp:3des/sha1 98a96b52  3223 unlim A/U  -1 0
0000000e>  10.55.0.3 500 esp:3des/sha1 64761c05  3223 unlim A/U  -1 0
S1-Denton->
```

Two routes are available to destination 10.88.10.0/24. The route with next-hop gateway 10.140.0.3 has a lower metric and is shown as active with the * designation at the beginning next to the route ID:

```
S1-Denton-> get route | i 10.88.10.0/24
*55323      10.88.10.0/24     tun.5 10.140.0.3   S   20     10  Root
 55324      10.88.10.0/24     tun.5  10.55.0.3   S   20    100  Root
S1-Denton->
```

Interface tun.5 shows two VPNs bound to it—corp and backup. It also shows that it is in the VPN zone, that it is controlled by the trust-vr, as well as some other information. The NHTB table is also shown for this interface.

```
S1-Denton-> get interf tun.5
Interface tunnel.5:
  description tunnel.5
  number 20, if_info 8200, if_index 5, mode route
  link ready
  vsys Root, zone vpn, vr trust-vr
  admin mtu 1500, operating mtu 1500, default mtu 1500
  *ip 0.0.0.0/0  unnumbered, source interface ethernet0/0
  *manage ip 0.0.0.0
  bound vpn:
    corp
    backup

  Next-Hop Tunnel Binding table
  Flag Status Next-Hop(IP)    tunnel-id  VPN
   S    R     10.140.0.3 0x0000000d corp
   S    D     10.55.0.3 0x0000000e backup

  pmtu-v4 disabled
  ping disabled, telnet disabled, SSH disabled, SNMP disabled
  web disabled, ident-reset disabled, SSL disabled
  DNS Proxy disabled
  OSPF disabled  BGP disabled  RIP enabled  RIPng disabled  mtrace
disabled
  PIM: not configured  IGMP not configured
  bandwidth: physical 0kbps, configured egress [gbw 0kbps mbw 0kbps]
             configured ingress mbw 0kbps, current bw 0kbps
             total allocated gbw 0kbps
Number of SW session: 8039, hw sess err cnt 0
```

You can also view the VPN monitor status. Here, the VPN monitor has sent 497 pings and received all the replies across sa_index 4000000d:

```
S1-Denton-> debug sa-mon all
S1-Denton-> get db str
sa index(1) send count = 497, avail = 497, tunnel_info = 4000000d
vpn monitor pkt is received: cookie = 1, result = 1
Found valid sa(1), missed slots = 1
```

You can use standard VPN troubleshooting commands such as get event, get route, get ike cookie, and debug ike to identify a misconfiguration or other issues.

10.6 Dynamic Route-Based VPN with RIPv2

Problem

You need to configure a VPN between multiple sites and use a dynamic routing protocol to distribute the route table.

Solution

Use route-based VPN configurations with RIPv2 enabled on the selected interfaces.

Primary hub site configuration

For the primary hub site configuration, start by creating the zone and interface:

```
Primary-Hub-> set zone name vpn
Primary-Hub-> set interface tun.11 zone vpn
Primary-Hub-> set interface tun.11 ip 10.70.70.1/28
```

Now, configure the VPN Phase-1 and Phase-2 parameters:

```
Primary-Hub-> set ike gateway denton dynamic s1_denton@xyzcorp.com
              Aggressive outgoing-interface eth0/3 preshare juniper
              123 sec-level standard
Primary-Hub-> set vpn denton gateway denton sec-level standard
Primary-Hub-> set vpn denton bind interface tun.11
```

Enable the VPN monitor and rekey options:

```
Primary-Hub-> set vpn denton monitor rekey
Primary-Hub-> set vpnmon interval 2
Primary-Hub-> set vpnmon threshold 5
```

And enable RIP globally and on any interfaces necessary:

```
Primary-Hub-> set vr trust-vr protocol rip
Primary-Hub-> set vr trust-vr protocol rip enable
Primary-Hub-> set interface tun.11 protocol rip enable
Primary-Hub-> set vr trust-vr protocol rip demand-circuit
```

Now, create a static route to the resources via a private router:

```
Primary-Hub-> set route 10.88.10.0/24 interface eth0/0 gateway
              10.140.10.1
```

Configure redistribution of the static route into RIP:

```
Primary-Hub-> set vr trust-vr access-list 88 permit ip 10.88.10.0/24 1
Primary-Hub-> set vr trust-vr route-map name dist-static88 permit 1
Primary-Hub-> set vr trust-vr route-map dist-static88 1 match ip 88
Primary-Hub-> set vr trust-vr protocol rip redistribute route-map
              dist-static88 protocol static
```

Create address entries for local and remote subnets:

```
Primary-Hub-> set address trust server_farm 10.88.10.0/24
Primary-Hub-> set address vpn denton_lan 10.70.1.0/24
```

And finally, create the bidirectional policies:

```
Primary-Hub-> set policy from trust to vpn local_lan denton_lan any
Permit policy id = 5
Primary-Hub-> set pol from vpn to trust denton_lan local_lan any
Permit policy id = 6
Primary-Hub-> save
```

Backup hub site configuration

For the backup hub site configuration, begin by creating a zone and interface:

```
Backup-VPN-Hub-> set zone name vpn
Backup-VPN-Hub-> set interf tun.11 zone vpn
Backup-VPN-Hub-> set interface tun.11 ip 10.70.70.2/28
```

Configure the VPN Phase-1 and Phase-2 parameters:

```
Backup-VPN-Hub-> set ike gateway denton dynamic s1_denton@xyzcorp.com
                 Aggressive outgoing-interface eth0/0 preshare
                 juniper123 sec-level standard
Backup-VPN-Hub-> set vpn denton gateway denton sec-level standard
Backup-VPN-Hub-> set vpn denton bind interface tun.21
```

Now, enable the VPN monitor and rekey options:

```
Backup-VPN-Hub-> set vpn denton monitor rekey
Backup-VPN-Hub-> set vpnmon interval 2
Backup-VPN-Hub-> set vpnmon threshold 5
```

And enable RIP globally and on any interfaces necessary:

```
Backup-VPN-Hub-> set vr trust-vr protocol rip
Backup-VPN-Hub-> set vr trust-vr protocol rip enable
Backup-VPN-Hub-> set interface tun.11 protocol rip enable
Backup-VPN-Hub-> set vr trust-vr protocol rip demand-circuit
```

Create a static route to the resources via a private router:

```
Backup-VPN-Hub-> set route 10.88.10.0/24 interface eth0/1 gateway
                 10.55.10.1
```

Configure redistribution of the static route into RIP:

```
Backup-VPN-Hub-> set vr trust-vr access-list 88 permit ip
                 10.88.10.0/24 1
Backup-VPN-Hub-> set vr trust-vr route-map name dist-static88
                 permit 1
Backup-VPNHub->  set vr trust-vr route-map dist-static88 1 match ip 88
Backup-VPN-Hub-> set vr trust-vr protocol rip redistribute route-map
                 dist-static88 protocol static
```

Now, create address entries for the local and remote subnets:

```
Backup-VPN-Hub-> set address trust server_farm 10.88.10.0/24
Backup-VPN-Hub-> set address vpn denton_lan 10.70.1.0/24
```

And finally, create the bidirectional policies:

```
Backup-VPN-Hub-> set policy from trust to vpn server_farm denton_lan
                 any permit policy id = 5
```

```
Backup-VPN-Hub-> set pol from vpn to trust denton_lan server_farm any
                 permit policy id = 6
```

Remote site configuration

For the remote site configuration, first create a zone and interface:

```
S1-Denton-> set zone name vpn
S1-Denton-> set interface tun.5 zone vpn
S1-Denton-> set interface tun.5 ip unnumbered 10.70.70.3/28
```

Now, configure the VPN Phase-1 and Phase-2 parameters for the primary tunnel:

```
S1-Denton-> set ike gateway primary address 10.140.0.3 aggressive
            local-id s1_denton@xyzcorp.com outgoing-interface eth0/0
            preshare juniper123 sec-level standard
S1-Denton-> set vpn primary gateway corp sec-level standard
S1-Denton-> set vpn primary bind interface tun.5
```

Next, configure the VPN Phase-1 and Phase-2 parameters for the backup tunnel:

```
S1-Denton-> set ike gateway backup address 10.55.0.3 aggressive
            local-id s1_denton@xyzcorp.com outgoing-interface eth0/0
            preshare juniper123 sec-level standard
S1-Denton-> set vpn backup gateway backup sec-level standard
S1-Denton-> set vpn backup bind interface tun.5
```

Configure the interface NHTB mapping:

```
S1-Denton-> set interface tun.5 nhtb 10.70.70.1 vpn primary
S1-Denton-> set interface tun.5 nhtb 10.70.70.2 vpn backup
```

Next, configure the routing protocol instances and enable the DRP on the appropriate interfaces:

```
S1-Denton-> set vr trust-vr protocol rip
S1-Denton-> set vr trust-vr protocol rip enable
S1-Denton-> set interface tun.5 protocol rip enable
S1-Denton-> set vr trust-vr protocol rip demand-circuit
```

Configure an access list and route map for redistributing the subnet in the `Trust` zone:

```
S1-Denton-> set vr trust access-list 20 permit ip 10.70.1.0/24 1
S1-Denton-> set vr trust route-map name redis-conn permit 1
S1-Denton-> set vr trust route-map redis-conn 1 match ip 20
S1-Denton-> set vr trust proto rip redistribute route-map redis-conn
            protocol connected
```

Now, enable the VPN monitor and rekey options (~10-second failover):

```
S1-Denton-> set vpn corp monitor rekey
S1-Denton-> set vpn backup monitor rekey
S1-Denton-> set vpnmon interval 2
S1-Denton-> set vpnmon threshold 5
```

Create address object entries for the local and remote subnets:

```
S1-Denton-> set address trust local_lan 10.70.1.0/24
S1-Denton-> set address vpn server_farm 10.88.10.0/24
```

Finally, create the policies permitting the traffic between zones:

```
S1-Denton-> set policy from trust to vpn local_lan server_farm any
            Permit policy id = 13
S1-Denton-> set policy from vpn to trust server_farm local_lan any
            Permit policy id = 14
```

Discussion

This example, as illustrated in Figure 10-21, portrays an environment where a remote site requires connectivity to resources that can be reached via multiple paths through the network. Remote site Denton can reach resources on the `10.88.10.0/24` subnet via either a primary or a backup hub site. Path selection will be through the use of the dynamic routing protocol RIPv2. ScreenOS supports the BGP and the OSPF protocol as well, and you could use any of the supported routing protocols to populate the routing tables among the participants. We chose RIPv2 because it is the simplest and most scalable method and is typically used in combination with OSPF.

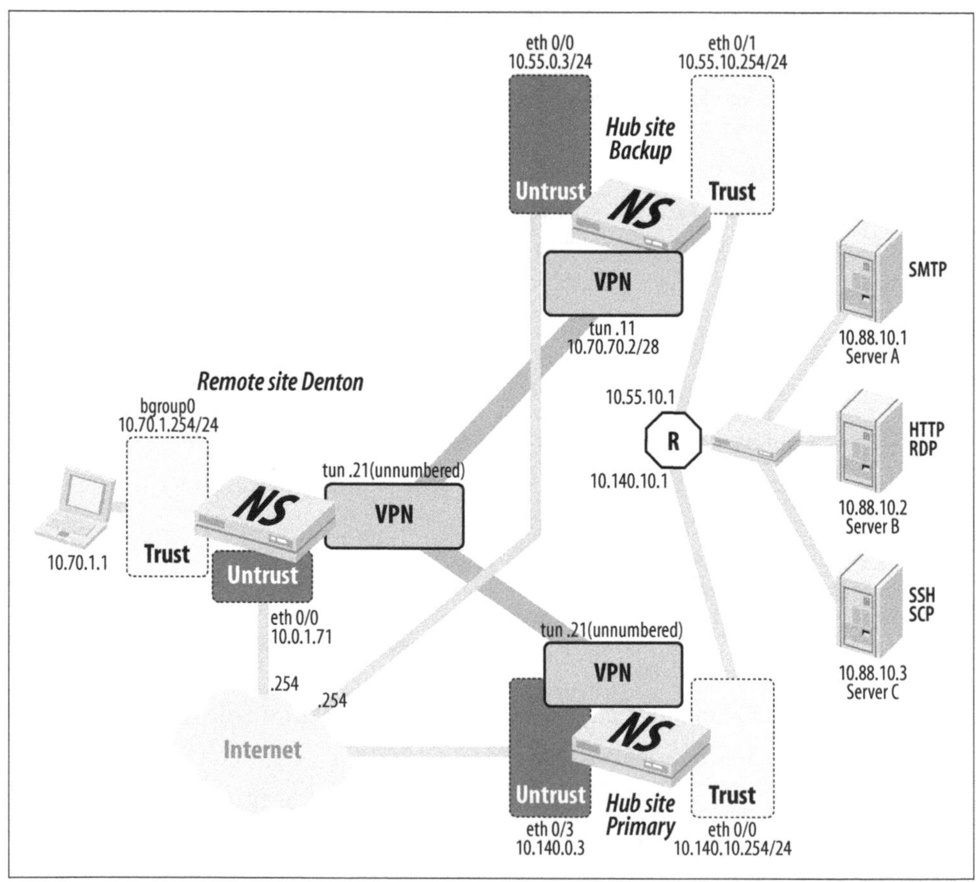

Figure 10-21. Dynamic route-based VPN with RIPv2 example

In the scenario depicted in this recipe, the protected resources are located on a private network that includes the primary and backup sites. Though not depicted in this recipe, you could easily export routes learned via the RIPv2 protocol into OSPF, which may be running on the private network. Please see Chapters 16 and 17 for more information on routing protocols and exporting static or DRP routes into OSPF or BGP.

This configuration begins by creating a custom security zone and binding a tunnel interface within it. When using dynamic routing protocols such as RIPv2, an interface participating in the routing protocol needs to have an IP address assigned to it and cannot use unnumbered addressing. Create the custom zone and interfaces at each site:

```
Primary-Hub-> set zone name vpn
Primary-Hub-> set interface tun.11 zone vpn
Primary-Hub-> set interface tun.11 ip 10.70.70.1/28

Backup-VPN-Hub-> set zone name vpn
Backup-VPN-Hub-> set interf tun.11 zone vpn
Backup-VPN-Hub-> set interface tun.11 ip 10.70.70.2/28

S1-Denton-> set zone name vpn
S1-Denton-> set interface tun.5 zone vpn
S1-Denton-> set interface tun.5 ip unnumbered 10.70.70.3/28
```

Each interface is configured with an IP address within the `10.70.70.0/28` subnet and is bound to the VPN zone.

Next, the VPN is configured at the two hub sites and is bound to the tunnel interface created in the preceding step:

```
Primary-Hub-> set ike gateway denton dynamic s1_denton@xyzcorp.com
              aggressive outgoing-interface eth0/3 preshare juniper 123
              sec-level standard
Primary-Hub-> set vpn denton gateway denton sec-level standard
Primary-Hub-> set vpn denton bind interface tun.11

Backup-VPN-Hub-> set ike gateway denton dynamic s1_denton@xyzcorp.com
                 aggressive  outgoing-interface eth0/0 preshare
                 juniper123 sec-level standard
Backup-VPN-Hub-> set vpn denton gateway denton sec-level standard
Backup-VPN-Hub-> set vpn denton bind interface tun.21
```

At the remote site, two VPN tunnels are configured, one to each hub site, but both tunnels are bound to the same tunnel interface, `tun.5`:

```
S1-Denton-> set ike gateway primary address 10.140.0.3 aggressive
            local-id s1_denton@xyzcorp.com outgoing-interface eth0/0
            preshare juniper123 sec-level standard
S1-Denton-> set vpn primary gateway corp sec-level standard
S1-Denton-> set vpn primary bind interface tun.5
```

```
S1-Denton-> set ike gateway backup address 10.55.0.3 aggressive
            local-id s1_denton@xyzcorp.com outgoing-interface eth0/0
            preshare juniper123 sec-level standard
S1-Denton-> set vpn backup gateway backup sec-level standard
S1-Denton-> set vpn backup bind interface tun.5
```

In the preceding tunnel configurations, Aggressive mode IKE is configured, although Main mode would be completely acceptable if all sites were configured with static IP addresses on the interface used as the IKE peer. The remote site needs additional configuration because it is operating in a point-to-multipoint mode. So, the NHTB table is configured:

```
S1-Denton-> set interface tun.5 nhtb 10.70.70.1 vpn primary
S1-Denton-> set interface tun.5 nhtb 10.70.70.2 vpn backup
```

The VPN monitor with the rekey option is enabled at each site for each VPN tunnel to ensure that the tunnels are always active. In addition, the VPN monitor will act as a dead-peer detection mechanism, and will disable routes associated with failed tunnels. These state changes from up/down will be relayed via the routing protocol.

```
Primary-Hub-> set vpn denton monitor rekey
Primary-Hub-> set vpnmon interval 2
Primary-Hub-> set vpnmon threshold 5

Backup-VPN-Hub-> set vpn denton monitor rekey
Backup-VPN-Hub-> set vpnmon interval 2
Backup-VPN-Hub-> set vpnmon threshold 5

S1-Denton-> set vpn corp monitor rekey
S1-Denton-> set vpn backup monitor rekey
S1-Denton-> set vpnmon interval 2
S1-Denton-> set vpnmon threshold 5
```

The VPN monitor pings will be sent every two seconds, and will consider the tunnel down if five consecutive ping responses are missed.

For this example, a static route is defined at each hub site for reaching the resources on the `10.88.10.0/24` subnet. An access list and a route map are configured for redistributing this static route into the RIPv2 protocol:

```
Primary-Hub-> set route 10.88.10.0/24 interface eth0/0 gateway
10.140.10.1
Primary-Hub-> set route 10.88.10.0/24 interface eth0/0 gateway
10.140.10.1

Backup-VPN-Hub-> set route 10.88.10.0/24 interface eth0/1 gateway 1
0.55.10.1
```

The dynamic routing protocol is now enabled in the VR and on the tunnel interfaces at each site:

```
Primary-Hub-> set vr trust-vr protocol rip
Primary-Hub-> set vr trust-vr protocol rip enable
Primary-Hub-> set interface tun.11 protocol rip enable
```

```
Primary-Hub-> set vr trust-vr protocol rip demand-circuit

Backup-VPN-Hub-> set vr trust-vr protocol rip
Backup-VPN-Hub-> set vr trust-vr protocol rip enable
Backup-VPN-Hub-> set interface tun.11 protocol rip enable
Backup-VPN-Hub-> set vr trust-vr protocol rip demand-circuit

S1-Denton-> set vr trust-vr protocol rip
S1-Denton-> set vr trust-vr protocol rip enable
S1-Denton-> set interface tun.5 protocol rip enable
S1-Denton-> set vr trust-vr protocol rip demand-circuit
```

Enabling a routing protocol in ScreenOS is a two-step process: first, the routing instance is configured, and next, the instance is enabled. Then, you can enable the routing protocol on selected or all interfaces. In this example, `demand-circuit` is used so that route updates will occur only when a change in routing is triggered by a failure or external route update. This enables RIP to act much like a shortest path first (SPF) protocol.

Lastly, in this configuration, policies are created to allow specific flows between the `VPN` and `Trust` zones at each site.

To look at this configuration, the following command shows both tunnels active and up:

```
S1-Denton-> get sa
total configured sa: 2
HEX ID    Gateway      Port Algorithm     SPI    Life:sec kb Sta PID vsys
00000010<  10.55.0.3 500 esp:3des/sha1 98a9d054  381 unlim A/U -1 0
00000010>  10.55.0.3 500 esp:3des/sha1 f281aaa9  381 unlim A/U -1 0
00000011< 10.140.0.3 500 esp:3des/sha1 98a9d055 3582 unlim A/U -1 0
00000011> 10.140.0.3 500 esp:3des/sha1 4958d75e 3582 unlim A/U -1 0
S1-Denton->
```

To see the routes associated with our protected resources on `10.88.10.0/24`, we can use the following commands:

```
S1-Denton-> get route | i 10.88.10.0/24
*62618        10.88.10.0/24    tun.5  10.70.70.1   R  100     11    Root
S1-Denton-> get route ip 10.88.10.1
 Dest for 10.88.10.1
-----------------------------------------------------------------------
trust-vr  : => 10.88.10.0/24 (id=62618) via 10.70.70.1 (vr: trust-vr)
                    Interface tunnel.5 , metric 11
None
```

In the first command, we see an active route to the subnet which was learned from RIP via interface `tun.5` with a next-hop gateway of `10.70.70.1`.

Viewing the NHTB table shows that the `primary` VPN will be used to reach this gateway:

```
S1-Denton-> get interf tun.5
Interface tunnel.5:
```

```
description tunnel.5
number 20, if_info 8200, if_index 5, mode route
link ready
vsys Root, zone vpn, vr trust-vr
admin mtu 1500, operating mtu 1500, default mtu 1500
*ip 10.70.70.3/28
*manage ip 10.70.70.3
route-deny disable
bound vpn:
  backup
  primary

Next-Hop Tunnel Binding table
Flag Status Next-Hop(IP)    tunnel-id  VPN
 S    U     10.70.70.2 0x00000010 backup
      U     10.70.70.1 0x00000011 primary
```

You can use standard troubleshooting commands such as `get event`, `get ike cookie`, `get sa active`, and `debug ike` to identify a misconfiguration or other issue affecting tunnel establishment.

10.7 Interoperability

Problem

You want to create VPN connectivity with a Cisco router. You have noncontiguous subnets on each side of the tunnel, and you must maintain strict proxy ID matching on each SA.

Solution

Use a route-based VPN configuration with a unique Phase-2 SA for each pair of subnets that need to communicate across the tunnel. Policy-based routing is used to ensure that data enters the appropriate SA.

ScreenOS configuration

For the ScreenOS configuration, start by creating the zones and interfaces:

```
S1-Denton-> set interface eth0/1 zone dmz
S1-Denton-> set interface eth0/1 ip 10.10.12.254/24
S1-Denton-> set interface eth0/1 route
S1-Denton-> set interface bg0 zone trust
S1-Denton-> set interface bg0 ip 10.10.10.254/24
S1-Denton-> set interface bg0 route
S1-Denton-> set interface eth0/0 zone untrust
S1-Denton-> set interface eth0/0 ip 10.100.1.1/24
S1-Denton-> set zone name vpn
S1-Denton-> set interface tun.1 zone vpn
S1-Denton-> set interface tun.1 ip unnumbered interface eth0/0
S1-Denton-> set interface tun.2 zone vpn
```

```
S1-Denton-> set interface tun.2 ip unnumbered interface eth0/0
S1-Denton-> set interface tun.3 zone vpn
S1-Denton-> set interface tun.3 ip unnumbered interface eth0/0
S1-Denton-> set interface tun.4 zone vpn
S1-Denton-> set interface tun.4 ip unnumbered interface eth0/0
```

Now, configure the default route:

```
S1-Denton-> set route 0.0.0.0/0 interface eth0/0 gateway
10.100.1.254
```

Configure the Phase-1 gateway with a custom proposal:

```
S1-Denton-> set ike p1-proposal "psk-3des-sha-g2-12800" preshare
            group2 esp 3des sha-1 second 12800
S1-Denton-> set ike gateway "cisco1" address 10.200.1.1 main
            outgoing- Interface eth0/0 preshare juniper123 proposal
            "psk-3des-sha-g2-12800"
S1-Denton-> set ike respond-bad-spi 1
```

Next, create the four distinct Phase-2 SAs with a custom proposal:

```
S1-Denton-> set ike p2-proposal "g2-esp-3des-sha-10800-28800"
            group2 esp 3des sha-1 second 10800 kbyte 28800
S1-Denton-> set vpn "cisco-a" gateway "cisco1" no-replay tunnel
            idletime 0 proposal "g2-esp-3des-sha-10800-28800"
S1-Denton-> set vpn "cisco-a" id bind interface tunnel.1
S1-Denton-> set vpn "cisco-a" proxy-id local-ip 10.10.10.0/24
            remote-ip 10.20.10.0/24 "ANY"
S1-Denton-> set vpn "cisco-b" gateway "cisco1" no-replay tunnel
            idletime 0 proposal "g2-esp-3des-sha-10800-28800"
S1-Denton-> set vpn "cisco-b" bind interface tunnel.2
S1-Denton-> set vpn "cisco-b" proxy-id local-ip 10.10.10.0/24
            remote-ip 10.20.20.0/24 "ANY"
S1-Denton-> set vpn "cisco-c" gateway "cisco1" no-replay tunnel
            idletime 0 proposal "g2-esp-3des-sha-10800-28800"
S1-Denton-> set vpn "cisco-c" bind interface tunnel.3
S1-Denton-> set vpn "cisco-c" proxy-id local-ip 10.10.12.0/24
            remote-ip 10.20.20.0/24 "ANY"
S1-Denton-> set vpn "cisco-d" gateway "cisco1" no-replay tunnel
            idletime 0 proposal "g2-esp-3des-sha-10800-28800"
S1-Denton-> set vpn "cisco-d" bind interface tunnel.4
S1-Denton-> set vpn "cisco-d" proxy-id local-ip 10.10.12.0/24
            remote-ip 10.20.10.0/24 "ANY"
```

Now, create the policy-based routing configuration:

```
S1-Denton-> set access-list extended 1 src-ip 10.10.10.0/24 dst-ip
            10.20.10.0/24 entry 1
S1-Denton-> set access-list extended 2 src-ip 10.10.10.0/24 dst-ip
            10.20.20.0/24 entry 1
S1-Denton-> set access-list extended 3 src-ip 10.10.12.0/24 dst-ip
            10.20.10.0/24 entry 1
S1-Denton-> set access-list extended 4 src-ip 10.10.12.0/24 dst-ip
            10.20.20.0/24 entry 1
S1-Denton-> set match-group name Net-a
S1-Denton-> set match-group Net-a ext-acl 1 match-entry 1
```

```
S1-Denton-> set match-group name Net-b
S1-Denton-> set match-group Net-b ext-acl 2 match-entry 1
S1-Denton-> set match-group name Net-c
S1-Denton-> set match-group Net-c ext-acl 3 match-entry 1
S1-Denton-> set match-group name Net-d
S1-Denton-> set match-group Net-d ext-acl 4 match-entry 1
S1-Denton-> set action-group name VPN-a
S1-Denton-> set action-group VPN-a next-interface tunnel.1
action-entry 1
S1-Denton-> set action-group name VPN-b
S1-Denton-> set action-group VPN-b next-interface tunnel.2
action-entry 1
S1-Denton-> set action-group name VPN-c
S1-Denton-> set action-group VPN-c next-interface tunnel.3
action-entry 1
S1-Denton-> set action-group name VPN-d
S1-Denton-> set action-group VPN-d next-interface tunnel.4
action-entry 1
S1-Denton-> set pbr policy name VPNPBR
S1-Denton-> set pbr policy VPNPBR match-group Net-a action-group
VPN-a 1
S1-Denton-> set pbr policy VPNPBR match-group Net-b action-group
VPN-b 2
S1-Denton-> set pbr policy VPNPBR match-group Net-c action-group
VPN-c 3
S1-Denton-> set pbr policy VPNPBR match-group Net-d action-group
VPN-d 4
```

Lastly, add any firewall permit policies:

```
S1-Denton-> set policy from trust to vpn any any any permit log count
S1-Denton-> set policy from vpn to trust any any any permit log count
S1-Denton-> set policy from dmz to vpn any any any permit log count
S1-Denton-> set policy from vpn to dmz any any any permit log count
```

Cisco configuration

The following Cisco configuration is provided as an example:

```
CPE-IPSec-2#configure t
Enter configuration commands, one per line.  End with CNTL/Z.
CPE-IPSec-2(config)#crypto isakmp policy 1
CPE-IPSec-2(config-isakmp)#encr 3des
CPE-IPSec-2(config-isakmp)#auth
CPE-IPSec-2(config-isakmp)#authentication pre-share
CPE-IPSec-2(config-isakmp)#group 2
CPE-IPSec-2(config-isakmp)#lifetime 3600
CPE-IPSec-2(config-isakmp)#exit
CPE-IPSec-2(config)#crypto isakmp key juniper123 address 10.100.1.1
CPE-IPSec-2(config)#crypto ipsec transform-set esp-3des-esp-sha-hmac
esp-3des esp-sha-hmac
CPE-IPSEC-2(config)#crypto map vpn 10 ipsec-isakmp
% NOTE: This new crypto map will remain disabled until a peer
        and a valid access list have been configured.
CPE-IPSEC-2(config-crypto-map)#set peer 10.100.1.1
```

```
CPE-IPSEC-2(config-crypto-map)#set security-association lifetime
seconds 3600
CPE-IPSEC-2(config-crypto-map)#set transform-set esp-3des-esp-sha-hmac
CPE-IPSEC-2(config-crypto-map)#set pfs group2
CPE-IPSEC-2(config-crypto-map)#match address 100
CPE-IPSEC-2(config-crypto-map)#exit
CPE-IPSEC-2(config)#int fastEthernet 0/0
CPE-IPSEC-2(config-if)#crypto map VPN
CPE-IPSEC-2(config-if)#exit
CPE-IPSEC-2(config)#access-list 100 permit ip 10.20.10.0 0.0.0.255
10.10.10.0 0.0.0.255
CPE-IPSEC-2(config)#access-list 100 permit ip 10.20.200 0.0.0.255
10.10.10.0 0.0.0.255
CPE-IPSEC-2(config)#access-list 100 permit ip 10.20.10.0 0.0.0.255
10.10.12.0 0.0.0.255
CPE-IPSEC-2(config)#access-list 100 permit ip 10.20.200 0.0.0.255
10.10.12.0 0.0.0.255
CPE-IPSEC-2(config)#exit
CPE-IPSEC-2#write mem
```

Discussion

This recipe is offered for those who need to create VPN connectivity between ScreenOS and third-party products, as illustrated in Figure 10-22. The Cisco configuration is shown as a default, but the concept and ScreenOS configuration should apply and interoperate with most VPN vendors' IPSec standard-based implementations.

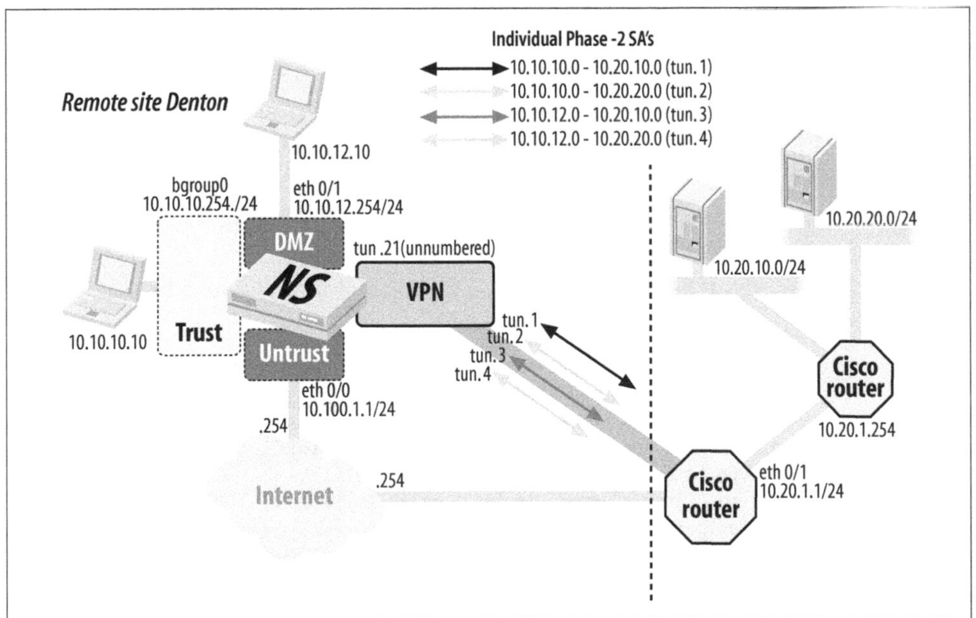

Figure 10-22. ScreenOS to Cisco using the policy-based routing scenario

This recipe represents a worst-case scenario where you have noncontiguous subnets on each end of the tunnel. Between ScreenOS security devices, this is easy to solve by specifying a proxy ID of `0.0.0.0/0`, allowing all traffic across the tunnel. This provides ease in networking and rerouting while ScreenOS still provides secure traffic filtering with zone-based policies. However, many vendors have not taken this approach and require strict proxy ID matching. In this recipe, we use multiple Phase-2 SAs and logical tunnel interfaces to provide distinct paths for each pair of subnets that need to communicate with each other.

You begin by configuring your interface and putting the interfaces into the appropriate zones. Then, you create your tunnel interfaces and put them into the `VPN` zone. Here, we are using unnumbered interfaces and borrowing the IP address from `eth0/0`.

Configure any routes you may need. A default to the public network would be the minimum configuration.

Next, you create the Phase-1 gateway definition with a custom Phase-1 proposal that you plan to match on the Cisco end of the configuration:

```
S1-Denton-> set ike p1-proposal "psk-3des-sha-g2-12800" preshare
            group2 esp 3des sha-1 second 12800
S1-Denton-> set ike gateway "cisco1" address 10.200.1.1 main
            outgoing- Interface eth0/0 preshare juniper123 proposal
            "psk-3des-sha-g2-12800"
S1-Denton-> set ike respond-bad-spi 1
```

A proposal named `"psk-3des-sha-g2-12800"` is created and configured for the preshared key, DH Group 2, and ESP using the 3DES and SHA-1 security options. Then, you create the Phase-1 gateway named `"cisco1"`, specifying the Cisco interface IP as the gateway IP address, and choosing IKE Main mode negotiations with `eth0/0` defined as the IKE peer. The preshared key `juniper123` should match the Cisco configuration, as should the Phase-1 proposal that will be offered.

Now, you create the four distinct Phase-2 SAs for the purpose of matching the local and remote proxy IDs that will match the Cisco access control list (ACL) configuration. In addition, you create a custom Phase-2 proposal that will also be used on the Cisco device.

```
S1-Denton-> set ike p2-proposal "g2-esp-3des-sha-10800-28800" group2
            esp 3des sha-1 second 10800 kbyte 28800
S1-Denton-> set vpn "cisco-a" gateway "cisco1" no-replay tunnel
            idletime 0 proposal "g2-esp-3des-sha-10800-28800"
S1-Denton-> set vpn "cisco-a" id bind interface tunnel.1
S1-Denton-> set vpn "cisco-a" proxy-id local-ip 10.10.10.0/24
            remote-ip 10.20.10.0/24 "ANY"
S1-Denton-> set vpn "cisco-b" gateway "cisco1" no-replay tunnel
            idletime 0 proposal "g2-esp-3des-sha-10800-28800"
S1-Denton-> set vpn "cisco-b" bind interface tunnel.2
S1-Denton-> set vpn "cisco-b" proxy-id local-ip 10.10.10.0/24
            remote-ip 10.20.20.0/24 "ANY"
S1-Denton-> set vpn "cisco-c" gateway "cisco1" no-replay tunnel
            idletime 0 proposal "g2-esp-3des-sha-10800-28800"
```

```
S1-Denton-> set vpn "cisco-c" bind interface tunnel.3
S1-Denton-> set vpn "cisco-c" proxy-id local-ip 10.10.12.0/24
            remote-ip 10.20.20.0/24 "ANY"
S1-Denton-> set vpn "cisco-d" gateway "cisco1" no-replay tunnel
            idletime 0 proposal "g2-esp-3des-sha-10800-28800"
S1-Denton-> set vpn "cisco-d" bind interface tunnel.4
S1-Denton-> set vpn "cisco-d" proxy-id local-ip 10.10.12.0/24
            remote-ip 10.20.10.0/24 "ANY"
```

Four different VPN definitions are created, named `"cisco-a"`, `"cisco-b"`, `"cisco-c"`, and `"cisco-d"`. Each is tied to the Phase-1 gateway definition, bound to a tunnel interface, and configured for the local and remote proxy IDs that match the Cisco ACLs.

The VPN monitor is not enabled in this configuration. However, you could use it with an advanced configuration. The VPN monitor traffic must also match the proxy IDs configured for each SA or the Cisco device will discard them. Therefore, you must specify the monitor's source and destination addresses. In this scenario, you could use the interfaces in the `Trust` and `DMZ` zones as the source and a host in each remote subnet as the destination.

Because you have four distinct tunnels, you need to configure a mechanism to make sure you get the correct flows into the correct SA. One mechanism for accomplishing this is the NHTB mechanism. NHTB is fine for some scenarios where you need a simple point-to-multipoint interface configuration. However, it has proven ineffective for interoperability such as that shown in this scenario. NHTB only provides mapping into tunnels based on destination address. Here, you must strictly match source and destination addresses and process them across the appropriate SA, so a policy-based routing approach is used with multiple tunnel interfaces.

```
S1-Denton-> set access-list extended 1 src-ip 10.10.10.0/24 dst-ip
            10.20.10.0/24 entry 1
S1-Denton-> set access-list extended 2 src-ip 10.10.10.0/24 dst-ip
            10.20.20.0/24 entry 1
S1-Denton-> set access-list extended 3 src-ip 10.10.12.0/24 dst-ip
            10.20.10.0/24 entry 1
S1-Denton-> set access-list extended 4 src-ip 10.10.12.0/24 dst-ip
            10.20.20.0/24 entry 1
S1-Denton-> set match-group name Net-a
S1-Denton-> set match-group Net-a ext-acl 1 match-entry 1
S1-Denton-> set match-group name Net-b
S1-Denton-> set match-group Net-b ext-acl 2 match-entry 1
S1-Denton-> set match-group name Net-c
S1-Denton-> set match-group Net-c ext-acl 3 match-entry 1
S1-Denton-> set match-group name Net-d
S1-Denton-> set match-group Net-d ext-acl 4 match-entry 1
S1-Denton-> set action-group name VPN-a
S1-Denton-> set action-group VPN-a next-interface tunnel.1
action-entry 1
S1-Denton-> set action-group name VPN-b
```

```
S1-Denton-> set action-group VPN-b next-interface tunnel.2
action-entry 1
S1-Denton-> set action-group name VPN-c
S1-Denton-> set action-group VPN-c next-interface tunnel.3
action-entry 1
S1-Denton-> set action-group name VPN-d
S1-Denton-> set action-group VPN-d next-interface tunnel.4
action-entry 1
S1-Denton-> set pbr policy name VPNPBR
S1-Denton-> set pbr policy VPNPBR match-group Net-a action-group
VPN-a 1
S1-Denton-> set pbr policy VPNPBR match-group Net-b action-group
VPN-b 2
S1-Denton-> set pbr policy VPNPBR match-group Net-c action-group
VPN-c 3
S1-Denton-> set pbr policy VPNPBR match-group Net-d action-group
VPN-d 4
```

First, you create your ACLs to match your four different sets of proxy IDs/SAs. Then, you create your match groups associated with the extended ACL definitions. Here, the match groups are named `Net-a`, `Net-b`, `Net-c`, and `Net-d` to stay within our naming convention. Next, you configure an action group. This is where you map to the appropriate interface as a next hop. The names `VPN-a`, `VPN-b`, `VPN-c`, and `VPN-d` are mapped to our tunnel interfaces bound to the appropriate SA. Lastly, you create a policy linking the match group to the action group.

Policy-based routing requires ScreenOS 5.4 or later.

The VPN configuration is complete. Now, you can add any policies you may require to permit specific flows between the subnet pairs:

```
S1-Denton-> set policy from trust to vpn any any any permit log count
S1-Denton-> set policy from vpn to trust any any any permit log count
S1-Denton-> set policy from dmz to vpn any any any permit log count
S1-Denton-> set policy from vpn to dmz any any any permit log count
```

Policies shown here are for ease of presentation. You should definitely create custom address objects and policies that are suitable for your environment.

Troubleshooting commands for this scenario include the following:

```
S1-Denton-> get ike cookie
S1-Denton-> get sa
S1-Denton-> get event
S1-Denton-> get log traffic
S1-Denton-> debug ike
```

CHAPTER 11

Application Layer Gateways

11.0 Introduction

An application layer gateway (ALG) is a feature on ScreenOS gateways that enables the gateway to parse application layer payloads and take decisions on them. Although there are other ScreenOS features, such as deep inspection, in which the gateway inspects traffic at the application layer, ALGs are typically employed to support applications that use the application layer payload to communicate the dynamic Transmission Control Protocol (TCP) or User Datagram Protocol (UDP) ports on which the applications open data connections. Such applications include the File Transfer Protocol (FTP) and various IP telephony protocols. The dynamic TCP, UDP, or other ports that are opened by the ScreenOS gateway to permit these data or secondary channels are referred to as *pinholes*, and are active strictly for the duration of activity on the data channel.

An ALG implementation requires a ScreenOS gateway to inspect the application layer payload of a packet and understand the application control messages. An enabled ALG automatically kicks in and performs application layer inspection and the dynamic opening/closing of TCP/UDP ports as well as the associated network/port address translation when a ScreenOS security policy that uses its associated service is referenced with matching traffic. For instance, a policy that references the FTP service on its default TCP port will automatically use the FTP ALG as long as the FTP ALG is enabled globally or for that particular policy on the ScreenOS gateway. You also can configure ALGs to be triggered when an ALG-supported application is running on a nondefault, custom port.

ScreenOS gateways ship with a wide range of available ALGs. Support for new ALGs is frequently added with new releases of ScreenOS. Additionally, ScreenOS offers a rich suite of ALG debugging capabilities that show ALG hits and dynamic pinholes being opened on the gateway. Several debug output captures are shown in the Discussion sections of the following recipes.

Differences Between ALGs and Deep Inspection

Deep inspection, discussed in Chapter 12, is a technology implemented in ScreenOS that performs application layer attack protection through stateful signatures and protocol anomaly detection for widely used Internet protocols such as the HyperText Transfer Protocol (HTTP), Simple Mail Transfer Protocol (SMTP), and FTP. Deep inspection is a subset of the Juniper Intrusion Detection and Prevention (IDP) suite of products and technologies. The ScreenOS ALG technology, on the other hand, provides application layer inspection of well-known Internet protocols such as the Session Initiation Protocol (SIP) and FTP that typically open data connections which require a secondary firewall session to be opened. Thus, ALGs typically open dynamic pinholes in the firewall, while supporting the associated network/port address translation, to allow data connections for such protocols.

11.1 View the List of Available ALGs

Problem

You want to view the list of available and enabled ALGs on a ScreenOS gateway.

Solution

Based on the release of ScreenOS, a number of ALGs are enabled in the factory default configuration. You can view the list of available ALGs on a ScreenOS gateway with the following code:

```
Internal_fw-> get alg
```

To limit the output list to the ALGs that are enabled on the ScreenOS gateway, use the following syntax:

```
Internal_fw-> get alg | include enabled
```

Discussion

Based on the release of ScreenOS, a number of ALGs are enabled in the factory default configuration. The list of ALGs available on the ISG-2000 platform as of ScreenOS 6.0r2 is:

```
nsisg2000-> get alg
DNS      ALG : enabled
FTP      ALG : enabled
H323     ALG : enabled
HTTP     ALG : enabled
MGCP     ALG : enabled
MSRPC    ALG : enabled
```

```
PPTP      ALG : disabled
REAL      ALG : enabled
RSH       ALG : enabled
RTSP      ALG : enabled
SCCP      ALG : enabled
SIP       ALG : enabled
SQL       ALG : enabled
SUNRPC    ALG : enabled
TALK      ALG : enabled
TFTP      ALG : enabled
XING      ALG : enabled
nsisg2000->
```

Table 11-1 briefly describes the applications representing the ALGs indicated in the preceding code snippet. In the table, the trigger port specifies the TCP or UDP destination port of the first packet in a flow that will activate ALG inspection of the entire conversation.

Table 11-1. ALG application detail

ALG name	Application name	Trigger port	Description
DNS	Domain Name System	UDP/53 and TCP/53	DNS queries ride on UDP/53 and return an IP address response when provided with a hostname. A DNS zone transfer uses TCP/53 and provides a response with zone files associated with a zone.
FTP	File Transfer Protocol	TCP/21	FTP, originally defined in RFC 959, uses TCP/21 on the server and a dynamic port on the client for the control channel. A separate data channel is dynamically opened in FTP applications. Active FTPs open the data channel from the server on source port TCP/20 to a dynamic port on the client. Passive FTPs open the data channel to a dynamic port on the server. RFC 3659 defines extensions to the FTP protocol.
H323	H.323	TCP/1720 for H.225 call control messages	H.323, based on the ITU-T Q.931 recommendation, is a suite of protocols used by audio and video communication sessions. IP telephony systems have used the H.225 component extensively for call control messages such as call setup and teardown.
HTTP	HyperText Transfer Protocol	TCP/80	HTTP requests generated by web browsers are provided HTTP responses from web servers with web content in formats such as HTML and XML. Standards, such as the HTTP/1.1 specification, define the list of permissible HTTP commands and their boundaries.
MGCP	Media Gateway Control Protocol	UDP/2727 for MGCP-CA UDP/2427 for MGCP-UA	MGCP, defined in RFC 3435, is a control channel communications protocol between media gateways and call agents. A call agent is a controller device that sends commands to a media gateway.

Table 11-1. ALG application detail (continued)

ALG name	Application name	Trigger port	Description
MSRPC	Microsoft Remote Procedure Call	TCP/135 and UDP/135	Windows applications/services such as Microsoft Exchange and Active Directory use MS-RPC. A client requesting a connection to an MS-RPC application makes a call to the MS-RPC endpoint mapper on TCP/UDP 135 and queries for the TCP/UDP port on which the application's Universally Unique Identifier (UUID) is registered.
PPTP	Point-to-Point Tunneling Protocol	TCP/1723	PPTP, specified in RFC 2637, is a virtual private networking protocol that employs a control connection on TCP/1723 for session setup and a Generic Routing Encapsulation (GRE) tunnel for encapsulating the data payload.
REAL	Real Media	TCP/7070 and TCP/554	Real Media represents audio and/or video content streamed from a Real Networks RealServer that can be viewed and/or heard on a Real Player. Real's Real Time Streaming Protocol (RTSP) connections use TCP/554 whereas Progressive Networks Audio (PNA) connections use TCP/7070.
RSH	Remote Shell	TCP/514	Remote Shell, available on Unix systems, is a tool that allows the execution of a command on a remote system.
RTSP	Real Time Streaming Protocol	TCP/554	RTSP, defined in RFC 2326, is a stateful streaming media control protocol that allows clients to request streaming content from servers. The streaming content is typically sent back over a Real-time Transport Protocol (RTP) stream over UDP, dynamically permitted by the ScreenOS RTSP ALG.
SCCP	Skinny Call Control Protocol	TCP/2000	SCCP is a proprietary call control protocol. The data connection opened for the voice bearer traffic is an RTP stream over UDP.
SIP	Session Initiation Protocol	UDP/5060	SIP, defined is RFC 3261, is a standards-based control protocol widely used by IP telephony vendors for setting up, modifying, and tearing down Voice over IP (VoIP) call sessions. Following session setup, the voice bearer traffic for SIP calls is typically communicated through an RTP over UDP stream.
SQL	Structured Query Language	TCP/1521	Oracle databases use SQL*NetV2 and NET8. The ScreenOS SQL*Netv2 ALG enables transparent connectivity between clients and Oracle databases.
SUNRPC	Sun Remote Procedure Call	TCP/111 and UDP/111	Unix hosts use Sun-RPC to execute code on other computers. Services on Unix hosts that rely on Sun-RPC use a well-known but unique program number as an identifier and register the dynamic TCP/UDP port they are listening on with the portmapper service on that host. The portmapper service runs on TCP/UDP 111.

Table 11-1. ALG application detail (continued)

ALG name	Application name	Trigger port	Description
TALK	Talk and NTalk	UDP/517-518	Talk and NTalk are client/server applications available on Unix systems for users to chat with each other. The Talk and NTalk server processes, respectively, listen on UDP 517 and UDP 518.
TFTP	Trivial File Transfer Protocol	UDP/69	TFTP servers provide a lightweight, UDP-based file-transfer mechanism.
XING	Xing StreamWorks	UDP/1558	Xing StreamWorks is a live audio/video streaming application. The Xing ALG permits a reverse connection from the StreamWorks server with the UDP content stream to the client.

As we will discuss in Recipe 11.5, in the context of the FTP protocol, you can modify the trigger port(s) for these ALGs by defining a custom service on the new trigger port(s) and mapping the ALG to the policy ID that references the custom service.

See Also

Recipe 7.15; Recipe 7.16; Recipe 11.2; Recipe 11.5

11.2 Globally Enable or Disable an ALG

Problem

You want to globally enable or disable an ALG on a ScreenOS gateway.

Solution

To enable an ALG that has been explicitly disabled in the device-specific configuration or is disabled in the default factory configuration, use the `set alg` *`<alg_name>`* `enable` command:

```
Internal_fw-> set alg sip enable
```

You can globally disable an ALG by using the `unset alg` *`<alg_name>`* `enable` command. Hence, for instance, you disable the SIP ALG as follows:

```
Internal_fw-> unset alg sip enable
```

Discussion

You may want to disable an ALG in the following cases:

- You do not anticipate using the application associated with the specific ALG in your ScreenOS gateway environment. This ALG thus becomes a candidate to be globally disabled.

- You are using a custom application that uses a TCP/UDP port that conflicts with the well-known application ports that are standard triggers for enabled ScreenOS ALGs. Based on policy ordering, you could selectively disable this ALG in a specific policy, as discussed in Recipe 11.3.
- You are experiencing problems with an application that triggers the associated ALG but does not function correctly due to a difference in the application's implementation and the ALG's implementation of the protocol specification. You can thus disable the associated ALG in the specific policy, as discussed in Recipe 11.3.

The service associated with an ALG that has been disabled can continue to be used in a ScreenOS firewall policy. However, the trigger port associated with the ALG service no longer launches application layer inspection of the payload. Instead, the trigger port simply causes a stateful firewall session to be formed with standard TCP/UDP session state.

See Also

Recipe 11.1; Recipe 11.3

11.3 Disable an ALG in a Specific Policy

Problem

You want to disable an ALG in a specific ScreenOS policy.

Solution

You can disable an ALG in a specific policy by referencing the specific policy ID and using the `application` ignore qualifier:

```
Internal_fw-> set policy id 5 from trust to untrust any any SIP
permit log
Internal_fw-> set policy id 5 application ignore
```

Discussion

By disabling the SIP ALG on the policy identified in this recipe's solution, the ScreenOS gateway creates a standard TCP/UDP stateful firewall session for traffic that references this policy. However, because the SIP ALG is disabled on this policy, the ScreenOS gateway does not open any dynamic pinholes to permit new inbound connections associated with this traffic stream.

See Also

Recipe 11.1; Recipe 11.3

11.4 View the Control and Data Sessions for an FTP Transfer

Problem

You want to view the control and data sessions associated with an FTP transfer.

Solution

Figure 11-1 shows the Orion host and the Phoenix FTP server communicating through the `Internal_fw` and `External_fw` gateways.

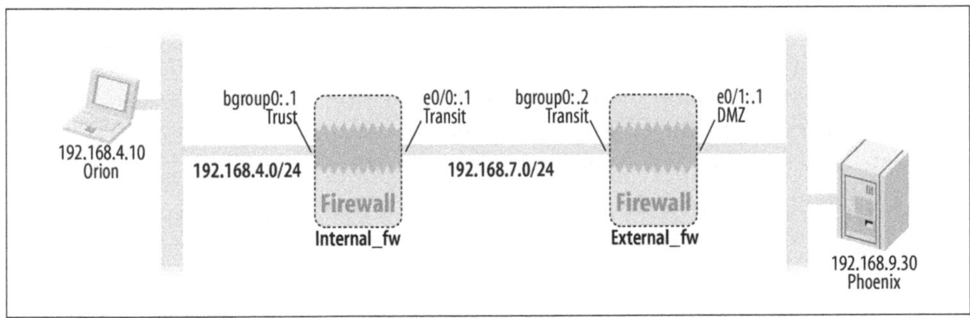

Figure 11-1. FTP ALG

The `Internal_FW` ScreenOS gateway has the following configuration, permitting FTP traffic from Orion to Phoenix:

```
Internal_FW-> set address Trust orion 192.168.4.10/32
Internal_FW-> set address Transit phoenix 192.168.9.30/32
Internal_FW-> set policy from Trust to Transit orion phoenix ftp
permit log
```

Similarly, the `External_FW` ScreenOS gateway has the following configuration, permitting FTP traffic from Orion to Phoenix:

```
External_FW-> set address Transit orion 192.168.4.30/32
External_FW-> set address DMZ phoenix 192.168.9.10/32
External_FW-> set policy from Transit to DMZ orion phoenix FTP
 permit log
```

When an FTP session is initiated from Orion to Phoenix, the control (parent) session is viewed as follows on the `Internal_FW` ScreenOS gateway:

```
Internal_FW-> get session src-ip 192.168.4.10 dst-ip 192.168.9.30
dst-port 21
```

When Orion requests and starts to receive a file via an active FTP from Phoenix, a separate FTP data (child) session is opened on the firewalls. You can view this session as follows on the `Internal_FW` gateway:

```
Internal_FW-> get session src-ip 192.168.9.30 dst-ip 192.168.4.10
src-port 20
```

Discussion

FTP, originally defined in RFC 959, uses a separate control channel to initiate a session and a separate data channel to transfer files. The control channel listens on TCP/21 on the server while a client connecting to an FTP server initiates the connection using a dynamic source port above TCP/1024. The FTP client and the FTP server use the control channel to communicate with each other using a well-defined list of FTP commands, such as get to receive a particular file and `put` to upload a particular file.

There are two types of FTP sessions: active and passive.

Active FTPs open the data channel from the server on source port TCP/20 to a dynamic port on the client, often explicitly specified by the client through the `PORT` command. The ScreenOS FTP ALG parses the FTP stream and allows the FTP server to initiate a back connection from source port 20 to the client on this dynamic port.

A passive FTP session does not require a new connection to be initiated from an FTP server back to the client. Instead, the `pasv` command, when communicated by a client to an FTP server, instructs the server to start listening on a data port and communicate that port to the client. The client then opens the data channel to the server on this dynamic data port.

Here is the result of the `get session` command to display the **`control session`** on the `Internal_FW` gateway:

```
Internal_FW-> get session src-ip 192.168.4.10 dst-ip 192.168.9.30
dst-port 21
alloc 2/max 16064, alloc failed 0, mcast alloc 0, di alloc failed 0
total reserved 0, free sessions in shared pool 16062
Total 1 sessions according filtering criteria.
id 16061/s**,vsys 0,flag 08000040/0400/0001,policy 3,time 178, dip 0
 module 0
 if 11(nspflag 801801):192.168.4.10/1197->192.168.9.30/21,6,
001125150ccd,sess token 4,vlan 0,tun 0,vsd 0,route 3
 if 0(nspflag 801800):192.168.4.10/1197<-192.168.9.30/21,6,
0014f6e21c4b,sess token 26,vlan 0,tun 0,vsd 0,route 7
Total 1 sessions shown
Internal_FW->
```

Here is a detailed view of this session:

```
Internal_FW-> get session id 16061
id 16061(00003ebd), flag 08000040/0400/0001, vsys id 0(Root)
policy id 3, application id 1, dip id 0, state 0
current timeout 1700, max timeout 1800 (second)
status normal, start time 16964, duration 0
session id mask 0, app value 0
bgroup0(vsd 0): 192.168.4.10/1197->192.168.9.30/21, protocol 6
```

```
session token 4 route 3
  gtwy 192.168.9.30, mac 001125150ccd, nsptn info 0, pmtu 1500
  flag 801801, diff 0/0
  port seq 0, subif 0, cookie 0, fin seq 0, fin state 0
ethernet0/0(vsd 0): 192.168.4.10/1197<-192.168.9.30/21, protocol 6
session token 26 route 7
  gtwy 192.168.7.2, mac 0014f6e21c4b, nsptn info 0, pmtu 1500
mac 0014f6e21c4b, nsptn info 0
  flag 801800, diff 0/0
  port seq 0, subif 0, cookie 0, fin seq 0, fin state 0
Internal_FW->
```

Active FTP

Here is the result of the get session command to display the **data session** for the active FTP on the Internal_FW gateway:

```
Internal_FW-> get session src-ip 192.168.9.30 dst-ip 192.168.4.10
src-port 20
alloc 3/max 16064, alloc failed 0, mcast alloc 0, di alloc failed 0
total reserved 0, free sessions in shared pool 16061
Total 1 sessions according filtering criteria.
id 16062/s**,vsys 0,flag 00001040/0800/0001,policy 3,time 180, dip 0
module 0,parent 16061
 if 0(nspflag 801801):192.168.9.30/20->192.168.4.10/1201,6,
0014f6e21c4b,sess token 26,vlan 0,tun 0,vsd 0,route 7
 if 11(nspflag 801800):192.168.9.30/20<-192.168.4.10/1201,6,
001125150ccd,sess token 4,vlan 0,tun 0,vsd 0,route 3
Total 1 sessions shown
Internal_FW->
```

The session is viewed as follows:

```
Internal_FW-> get session id 16062
id 16062(00003ebe), flag 00001040/0800/0001, vsys id 0(Root)
policy id 3, application id 0, dip id 0, state 0
current timeout 1800, max timeout 1800 (second)
status normal, start time 17163, duration 0
session id mask 0, app value 0
ethernet0/0(vsd 0): 192.168.9.30/20->192.168.4.10/1201, protocol 6
 session token 26 route 7
  gtwy 192.168.7.2, mac 0014f6e21c4b, nsptn info 0, pmtu 1500
  flag 801801, diff 0/0
  port seq 0, subif 0, cookie 0, fin seq 0, fin state 0
bgroup0(vsd 0): 192.168.9.30/20<-192.168.4.10/1201, protocol 6
session token 4 route 3
  gtwy 192.168.9.30, mac 001125150ccd, nsptn info 0, pmtu 1500
mac 001125150ccd, nsptn info 0
  flag 801800, diff 0/0
  port seq 0, subif 0, cookie 0, fin seq 0, fin state 0
Internal_FW->
```

It should be noted that the application ID is set to 1 for the control session and to 0 for the data session as viewed in the detailed session outputs.

Furthermore, the following debug flow basic output shows the ScreenOS gateway attaching the FTP ALG when it sees the first TCP SYN in the three-way handshake for the control channel:

```
Internal_FW-> get dbuf stream
****** 17819.0: <Trust/bgroup0> packet received [48]******
  ipid = 19652(4cc4), @035cb0b0
  packet passed sanity check.
  bgroup0:192.168.4.10/1228->192.168.9.30/21,6<Root>
  no session found
  flow_first_sanity_check: in <bgroup0>, out <N/A>
  chose interface bgroup0 as incoming nat if.
  flow_first_routing: in <bgroup0>, out <N/A>
  search route to (bgroup0, 192.168.4.10->192.168.9.30) in vr trust-vr
 for vsd-0/flag-0/ifp-null
  [ Dest] 7.route 192.168.9.30->192.168.7.2, to ethernet0/0
  routed (x_dst_ip 192.168.9.30) from bgroup0 (bgroup0 in 0) to
ethernet0/0
  policy search from zone 2-> zone 100
 policy_flow_search  policy search nat_crt from zone 2-> zone 100
  RPC Mapping Table search returned 0 matched service(s) for (vsys
Root, ip 192.168.9.30, port 21, proto 6)
  No SW RPC rule match, search HW rule
  Permitted by policy 3
  No src xlate   choose interface ethernet0/0 as outgoing phy if
  no loop on ifp ethernet0/0.
  session application type 1, name FTP, nas_id 0, timeout 1800sec
ALG vector is attached
  service lookup identified service 1.
  flow_first_final_check: in <bgroup0>, out <ethernet0/0>
  existing vector list 183-2afb2e4.
<..additional output truncated..>
```

Farther down in the debug, when a pinhole is opened on the ScreenOS gateway to permit the data connection back from the Phoenix server to the Orion host for this active FTP session, the debug displays the data as follows:

```
****** 17827.0: <Transit/ethernet0/0> packet received [48]******
  ipid = 60396(ebec), @0345dbb0
  packet passed sanity check.
  ethernet0/0:192.168.9.30/20->192.168.4.10/1230,6<Root>
  no session found
  flow_first_sanity_check: in <ethernet0/0>, out <N/A>
 vsd (0) is active, make hole active  active hole found
  existing vector list 183-2afb2e4.
  flow_first_install_session======>
<..additional output truncated..>
```

Passive FTP

Similar to the earlier active FTP scenario, the data channel for a passive FTP opens a new firewall session. However, this session, like the control session, is also initiated from the FTP client to the FTP server. On the other hand, as shown earlier, an active

FTP's data channel opens a back connection from the FTP server to the FTP client. Hence, for a passive FTP, the control and data session is seen as follows:

```
Internal_FW-> get session src-ip 192.168.4.10 dst-ip 192.168.9.30
alloc 4/max 16064, alloc failed 0, mcast alloc 0, di alloc failed 0
total reserved 0, free sessions in shared pool 16060
Total 2 sessions according filtering criteria.
id 16060/s**,vsys 0,flag 00001040/0800/0001,policy 3,time 180, dip 0
 module 0,parent 16061
 if 11(nspflag 801801):192.168.4.10/2083->192.168.9.30/1183,6,
001125150ccd,sess token 4,vlan 0,tun 0,vsd 0,route 3
 if 0(nspflag 801800):192.168.4.10/2083<-192.168.9.30/1183,6,
0014f6e21c4b,sess token 26,vlan 0,tun 0,vsd 0,route 8
id 16061/s**,vsys 0,flag 08000040/0400/0001,policy 3,time 179,
dip 0 module 0
 if 11(nspflag 801801):192.168.4.10/2082->192.168.9.30/21,6,
001125150ccd,sess token 4,vlan 0,tun 0,vsd 0,route 3
 if 0(nspflag 801800):192.168.4.10/2082<-192.168.9.30/21,6,
0014f6e21c4b,sess token 26,vlan 0,tun 0,vsd 0,route 8
Total 2 sessions shown
Internal_FW->
```

Here are the session details, with session id 16060 representing the passive FTP data session and session id 16061, with application id set to 1, representing the FTP control session:

```
Internal_FW-> get session id 16060
id 16060(00003ebc), flag 00001040/0800/0001, vsys id 0(Root)
policy id 3, application id 0, dip id 0, state 0
current timeout 1800, max timeout 1800 (second)
status normal, start time 305, duration 0
session id mask 0, app value 0
bgroup0(vsd 0): 192.168.4.10/2083->192.168.9.30/1183, protocol 6
session token 4 route 3
  gtwy 192.168.9.30, mac 001125150ccd, nsptn info 0, pmtu 1500
  flag 801801, diff 0/0
  port seq 0, subif 0, cookie 0, fin seq 0, fin state 0
ethernet0/0(vsd 0): 192.168.4.10/2083<-192.168.9.30/1183, protocol 6
session token 26 route 8
  gtwy 192.168.7.2, mac 0014f6e21c4b, nsptn info 0, pmtu 1500
mac 0014f6e21c4b, nsptn info 0
  flag 801800, diff 0/0
  port seq 0, subif 0, cookie 0, fin seq 0, fin state 0
Internal_FW->
Internal_FW->
Internal_FW-> get session id 16061
id 16061(00003ebd), flag 08000040/0400/0001, vsys id 0(Root)
policy id 3, application id 1, dip id 0, state 0
current timeout 1720, max timeout 1800 (second)
status normal, start time 305, duration 0
session id mask 0, app value 0
bgroup0(vsd 0): 192.168.4.10/2082->192.168.9.30/21, protocol 6
session token 4 route 3
  gtwy 192.168.9.30, mac 001125150ccd, nsptn info 0, pmtu 1500
```

```
  flag 801801, diff 0/0
  port seq 0, subif 0, cookie 0, fin seq 0, fin state 0
ethernet0/0(vsd 0): 192.168.4.10/2082<-192.168.9.30/21, protocol 6
session token 26 route 8
  gtwy 192.168.7.2, mac 0014f6e21c4b, nsptn info 0, pmtu 1500
mac 0014f6e21c4b, nsptn info 0
  flag 801800, diff 0/0
  port seq 0, subif 0, cookie 0, fin seq 0, fin state 0
Internal_FW->
```

The control session is running on the standard control TCP port of 21 while the data session uses dynamic ports on the FTP client and the FTP server, for which the ScreenOS gateway FTP ALG opens dynamic pinholes. Furthermore, unlike the active FTP session, the passive FTP session, seen above, is originated from the client, Orion (192.168.4.10) to the server, Phoenix (192.168.9.30).

The `debug flow basic` output shows the FTP ALG attach itself to the stream:

```
Internal_FW-> get dbuf stream
****** 00305.0: <Trust/bgroup0> packet received [48]******
  ipid = 28781(706d), @0357a0d0
  packet passed sanity check.
  bgroup0:192.168.4.10/2082->192.168.9.30/21,6<Root>
  no session found
  flow_first_sanity_check: in <bgroup0>, out <N/A>
  chose interface bgroup0 as incoming nat if.
  flow_first_routing: in <bgroup0>, out <N/A>
  search route to (bgroup0, 192.168.4.10->192.168.9.30) in vr trust-vr
for vsd-0/flag-0/ifp-null
  [ Dest] 8.route 192.168.9.30->192.168.7.2, to ethernet0/0
  routed (x_dst_ip 192.168.9.30) from bgroup0 (bgroup0 in 0) to
ethernet0/0
  policy search from zone 2-> zone 100
 policy_flow_search  policy search nat_crt from zone 2-> zone 100
  RPC Mapping Table search returned 0 matched service(s) for (vsys
Root, ip 192.168.9.30, port 21, proto 6)
  No SW RPC rule match, search HW rule
  Permitted by policy 3
  No src xlate   choose interface ethernet0/0 as outgoing phy if
  no loop on ifp ethernet0/0.
  session application type 1, name FTP, nas_id 0, timeout 1800sec
ALG vector is attached
  service lookup identified service 1.
  flow_first_final_check: in <bgroup0>, out <ethernet0/0>
<Additional output truncated>
```

Finally, the pinholes opening for the passive FTP data session are seen in the `debug flow basic` output:

```
****** 00305.0: <Trust/bgroup0> packet received [48]******
  ipid = 28788(7074), @0357d8d0
  packet passed sanity check.
  bgroup0:192.168.4.10/2083->192.168.9.30/1183,6<Root>
  no session found
```

```
  flow_first_sanity_check: in <bgroup0>, out <N/A>
 vsd (0) is active, make hole active  active hole found
  existing vector list 183-2aff464.
  flow_first_install_session======>
  flow got session.
  flow session id 16060
  tcp seq check.
  Got syn, 192.168.4.10(2083)->192.168.9.30(1183), nspflag 0x801801,
 0x800800
  post addr xlation: 192.168.4.10->192.168.9.30.
 flow_send_vector_, vid = 0, is_layer2_if=0
<Additional output truncated>
```

See Also

Recipe 11.5

11.5 Configure ALG Support When Running FTP on a Custom Port

Problem

You want to configure ALG support for FTP sessions running on a custom port.

Solution

The following configuration enables you to configure FTP ALG support for an FTP server that is listening for control connections on TCP port 2021:

```
Internal_FW-> set service Custom_FTP protocol tcp dst-port 2021-2021
Internal_FW-> set policy id 3 from trust to transit orion phoenix
Custom_FTP permit log
Internal_FW-> set policy id 3 application ftp
```

Discussion

Most FTP servers allow the capability of listening on a nonstandard control port other than TCP 21. When the policy associated with this nonstandard port is configured with the `application ftp` qualifier, as configured in the solution to this recipe, ScreenOS gateways dynamically open the pinholes for the data channel for such FTP sessions. Using this recipe's solution as an example, you can inspect other ALG-supported applications on nonstandard, custom ports in a similar manner by creating a new service that references the custom port and then specifying the application name as a qualifier on the associated policy.

As a further example of the preceding solution, the following session details show an FTP session through the `Internal_FW` gateway between Orion and Phoenix, where Phoenix is running the FTP server on TCP 2021 and an active FTP is in progress whereby the data channel is opened as a back connection to the Orion host. The ScreenOS gateway allows this back connection to Orion through the FTP ALG associated with the policy. The control channel firewall session is thus seen as follows:

```
Internal_FW-> get session src-ip 192.168.4.10 dst-ip 192.168.9.30
dst-port 2021
alloc 4/max 16064, alloc failed 0, mcast alloc 0, di alloc failed 0
total reserved 0, free sessions in shared pool 16060
Total 1 sessions according filtering criteria.
id 16062/s**,vsys 0,flag 08000040/0400/0001,policy 7,time 167, dip 0
module 0
 if 11(nspflag 801801):192.168.4.10/1343->192.168.9.30/2021,6,
001125150ccd,sess token 4,vlan 0,tun 0,vsd 0,route 3
 if 0(nspflag 801800):192.168.4.10/1343<-192.168.9.30/2021,6,
0014f6e21c4b,sess token 26,vlan 0,tun 0,vsd 0,route 6
Total 1 sessions shown

Internal_FW-> get session id 16062
id 16062(00003ebe), flag 08000040/0400/0001, vsys id 0(Root)
policy id 7, application id 1, dip id 0, state 0
current timeout 1660, max timeout 1800 (second)
status normal, start time 5104, duration 0
session id mask 0, app value 0
bgroup0(vsd 0): 192.168.4.10/1343->192.168.9.30/2021, protocol 6
session token 4 route 3
  gtwy 192.168.9.30, mac 001125150ccd, nsptn info 0, pmtu 1500
  flag 801801, diff 0/0
  port seq 0, subif 0, cookie 0, fin seq 0, fin state 0
ethernet0/0(vsd 0): 192.168.4.10/1343<-192.168.9.30/2021, protocol 6
session token 26 route 6
  gtwy 192.168.7.2, mac 0014f6e21c4b, nsptn info 0, pmtu 1500
mac 0014f6e21c4b, nsptn info 0
  flag 801800, diff 0/0
  port seq 0, subif 0, cookie 0, fin seq 0, fin state 0
Internal_FW->
```

This detailed session `id 16062` output specifies an `application id` of 1, indicating a match with the FTP ALG.

You can see the data session for this active FTP by searching for a session with a source IP of `192.168.9.30` initiating a connection back to `192.168.4.10`:

```
Internal_FW-> get session src-ip 192.168.9.30 dst-ip 192.168.4.10
alloc 4/max 16064, alloc failed 0, mcast alloc 0, di alloc failed 0
total reserved 0, free sessions in shared pool 16060
Total 1 sessions according filtering criteria.
id 16061/s**,vsys 0,flag 00001040/0800/0001,policy 7,time 180,
dip 0 module 0,parent 16062
 if 0(nspflag 801801):192.168.9.30/2020->192.168.4.10/1344,6,
0014f6e21c4b,sess token 26,vlan 0,tun 0,vsd 0,route 6
 if 11(nspflag 801800):192.168.9.30/2020<-192.168.4.10/1344,6,
001125150ccd,sess token 4,vlan 0,tun 0,vsd 0,route 3
Total 1 sessions shown
Internal_FW->
```

```
Internal_FW-> get session id 16061
id 16061(00003ebd), flag 00001040/0800/0001, vsys id 0(Root)
policy id 7, application id 0, dip id 0, state 0
current timeout 1800, max timeout 1800 (second)
status normal, start time 5104, duration 0
session id mask 0, app value 19
ethernet0/0(vsd 0): 192.168.9.30/2020->192.168.4.10/1344, protocol 6
session token 26 route 6
  gtwy 192.168.7.2, mac 0014f6e21c4b, nsptn info 0, pmtu 1500
  flag 801801, diff 0/0
  port seq 0, subif 0, cookie 0, fin seq 0, fin state 0
bgroup0(vsd 0): 192.168.9.30/2020<-192.168.4.10/1344, protocol 6
session token 4 route 3
  gtwy 192.168.9.30, mac 001125150ccd, nsptn info 0, pmtu 1500
mac 001125150ccd, nsptn info 0
  flag 801800, diff 0/0
  port seq 0, subif 0, cookie 0, fin seq 0, fin state 0
Internal_FW->
```

Finally, you can execute a debug flow basic with a flow filter to look for an ALG match:

```
Internal_FW-> get dbuf stream
****** 05104.0: <Trust/bgroup0> packet received [48]******
  ipid = 21852(555c), @035078d0
  packet passed sanity check.
  bgroup0:192.168.4.10/1343->192.168.9.30/2021,6<Root>
  no session found
  flow_first_sanity_check: in <bgroup0>, out <N/A>
  chose interface bgroup0 as incoming nat if.
  flow_first_routing: in <bgroup0>, out <N/A>
<Additional_output_truncated>
  Permitted by policy 7
  No src xlate   choose interface ethernet0/0 as outgoing phy if
  no loop on ifp ethernet0/0.
  session application type 1, name FTP, nas_id 0, timeout 1800sec
ALG vector is attached
  service lookup identified service 1.
  flow_first_final_check: in <bgroup0>, out <ethernet0/0>
<Additional output truncated>
```

The preceding debug output shows an ALG match with `session application type 1, name FTP`, attaching the FTP ALG to this flow on a nonstandard FTP control port.

Finally, you can view the control and data sessions associated with a passive FTP file transfer for this same nonstandard TCP/2021 FTP scenario:

```
Internal_FW-> get session src-ip 192.168.4.10 dst-ip 192.168.9.30
alloc 4/max 16064, alloc failed 0, mcast alloc 0, di alloc failed 0
total reserved 0, free sessions in shared pool 16060
Total 2 sessions according filtering criteria.
id 16062/s**,vsys 0,flag 00001040/0800/0001,policy 7,time 180,
dip 0 module 0,parent 16063
 if 11(nspflag 801801):192.168.4.10/1377->192.168.9.30/1178,6,
001125150ccd,sess token 4,vlan 0,tun 0,vsd 0,route 3
```

```
 if 0(nspflag 801800):192.168.4.10/1377<-192.168.9.30/1178,6,
0014f6e21c4b,sess token 26,vlan 0,tun 0,vsd 0,route 6
id 16063/s**,vsys 0,flag 08000040/0400/0001,policy 7,time 174,
dip 0 module 0
 if 11(nspflag 801801):192.168.4.10/1376->192.168.9.30/2021,6,
001125150ccd,sess token 4,vlan 0,tun 0,vsd 0,route 3
 if 0(nspflag 801800):192.168.4.10/1376<-192.168.9.30/2021,6,
0014f6e21c4b,sess token 26,vlan 0,tun 0,vsd 0,route 6
Total 2 sessions shown
Internal_FW->
```

Similar to the scenario of running a passive FTP on the standard TCP/21 port, you can see from the preceding session output that the control and the data sessions originate from the client Orion host. The `application id 1` is seen attached to the control session:

```
Internal_FW-> get session id 16063
id 16063(00003ebf), flag 08000040/0400/0001, vsys id 0(Root)
policy id 7, application id 1, dip id 0, state 0
current timeout 1730, max timeout 1800 (second)
<Additional Output Truncated>
Internal_FW->
```

Finally, you can see the dynamic pinhole being opened to permit an outbound connection for the passive data channel from Orion to Phoenix via the `debug flow basic` output:

```
Internal_FW-> get dbuf stream
****** 06357.0: <Trust/bgroup0> packet received [48]******
  ipid = 7893(1ed5), @0351f0d0
  packet passed sanity check.
  bgroup0:192.168.4.10/1377->192.168.9.30/1178,6<Root>
  no session found
  flow_first_sanity_check: in <bgroup0>, out <N/A>
 vsd (0) is active, make hole active  active hole found
  existing vector list 183-2aff494.
  flow_first_install_session======>
  flow got session.
  flow session id 16062
  tcp seq check.
  Got syn, 192.168.4.10(1377)->192.168.9.30(1178), nspflag 0x801801,
 0x800800
  post addr xlation: 192.168.4.10->192.168.9.30.
 flow_send_vector_, vid = 0, is_layer2_if=0
<Additional Output Truncated>
Internal_FW->
```

See Also

Recipe 11.4

11.6 Configure and View ALG Inspection of a SIP-Based IP Telephony Call Session

Problem

You want to enable an IP telephony call session through a ScreenOS gateway using SIP.

Solution

As discussed in Recipe 11.1, the SIP ALG, along with several other ALGs, is enabled by default in current shipping releases of ScreenOS. Hence, the first permit security policy that matches the SIP trigger port of TCP or UDP 5060 triggers the SIP ALG.

Figure 11-2 shows a desktop PC running a SIP-based IP softphone at a branch location connecting to an integrated SIP server and media gateway at the corporate site over a site-to-site IP Security (IPSec) virtual private network (VPN).

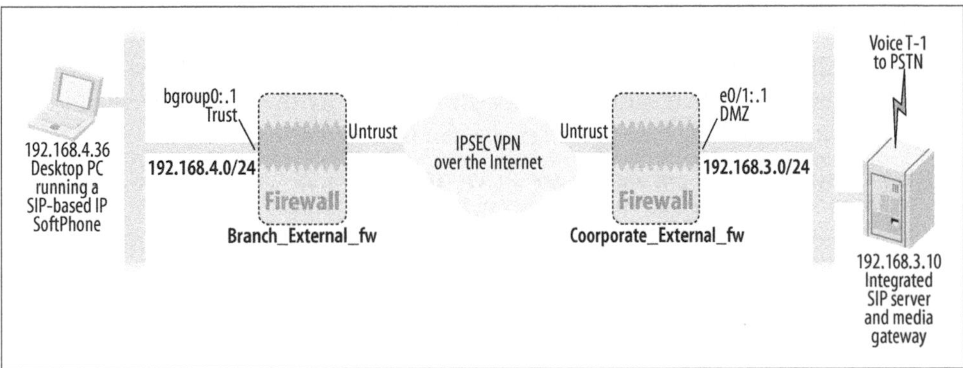

Figure 11-2. SIP-based IP telephony call session

The SIP ALG is triggered by the following policy, which permits any traffic from the `192.168.4.0/24` segment to the `192.168.3.0/24` segment, when the softphone sends its initial SIP `REGISTER` message:

```
Branch_External_fw-> set policy from Trust to Untrust 192.168.4.0
192.168.3.0 any tunnel vpn branch_to_corporate log
```

Although the preceding policy shows the SIP ALG being triggered in the context of a "permit any service" IPSec VPN, a simple non-IPSec firewall policy that matches any service or explicitly references a SIP service will also trigger the SIP ALG in a similar manner.

You can view the current list of active SIP control traffic sessions on a ScreenOS gateway using the `get session service sip` command:

```
Branch_External_fw-> get session service sip
```

Discussion

SIP, defined in RFC 3261, is a control protocol used extensively by IP telephony systems, ranging from Asterisk to various commercial implementations such as Avaya, for setting up, modifying, and tearing down VoIP call sessions. Following session setup, the voice bearer traffic for SIP calls is typically communicated through an RTP over UDP stream.

Although the SIP ALG is enabled by default in current, shipping releases of ScreenOS, you can confirm the status of the SIP ALG on your system with the get alg command, as discussed in Recipe 11.1. Hence, with the SIP ALG enabled, you can successfully establish a SIP-based VoIP call through a ScreenOS gateway that has a policy that permits SIP traffic between the SIP call initiator and the SIP server. More generically, a policy that permits any traffic between the zone of the SIP call initiator and the SIP gateway will automatically trigger the SIP ALG when SIP traffic is detected by the ScreenOS gateway and matches the permit of any security policy. Additionally, if the call recipient is an IP phone instead of a PSTN phone, the SIP call initiator and the recipient IP phone should have IP connectivity with each other for the voice bearer traffic to be transmitted back and forth between the two callers.

When the SIP softphone on `192.168.4.36` is started, it sends a SIP `REGISTER` message to the SIP server. The ScreenOS SIP ALG is triggered, per the policy specified in this recipe's solution, and the associated session can thus be viewed:

```
Branch_External_fw-> get session src-ip 192.168.4.36
alloc 19/max 16064, alloc failed 0, mcast alloc 0, di alloc failed 0
total reserved 0, free sessions in shared pool 16045
Total 1 sessions according filtering criteria.
id 16046/s**,vsys 0,flag 00000040/0000/0001,policy 17,time 5, dip 0
module 0
 if 11(nspflag 800e01):192.168.4.36/10720->192.168.3.10/5060,17,
001125150ccd,sess token 4,vlan 0,tun 0,vsd 0,route 3
 if 0(nspflag 2002e00):192.168.4.36/10720<-192.168.3.10/5060,17,
000000000000,sess token 7,vlan 0,tun 40000009,vsd 0,route 17
Total 1 sessions shown
Branch_External_fw->
```

To view the processing of the SIP `REGISTER` packet, you can run the following debug commands and view the debug buffers:

```
Branch_External_fw-> clear dbuf
Branch_External_fw-> set ffilter src-ip 192.168.4.36
Branch_External_fw-> set ffilter dst-ip 192.168.4.36
Branch_External_fw-> debug flow basic
Branch_External_fw-> debug sip all
<Now launch the IP Softphone, which initializes and sends a SIP
REGISTER>
<Wait 5 seconds>
Branch_External_fw-> get dbuf stream
<Unrelated output deleted>
****** 00252.0: <Trust/bgroup0> packet received [568]******
```

```
  ipid = 50(0032), @035a1b50
  packet passed sanity check.
  bgroup0:192.168.4.36/10720->192.168.3.10/5060,17<Root>
  no session found
<Additional_Output_Truncated>
  search route to (bgroup0, 192.168.4.36->192.168.3.10) in vr trust-vr
 for vsd-0/flag-0/ifp-null
<Additional_Output_Truncated>
  RPC Mapping Table search returned 0 matched service(s) for (vsys Root
, ip 192.168.3.10, port 5060, proto 17)
  No SW RPC rule match, search HW rule
  Permitted by policy 17
<Additional_Output_Truncated>
  session application type 63, name SIP, nas_id 0, timeout 60sec
ALG vector is attached
  service lookup identified service 63.
  flow_first_final_check: in <bgroup0>, out <ethernet0/0>
  existing vector list 85-4b649e4.
  Session (id:16046) created for first pak 85
  flow_first_install_session======>
<Additional_Output_Truncated>
  flow session id 16046
## 2007-09-12 01:23:44 : sip_alg....  packet received (192.168.4.36 -> 192.168.3.10)
len=568
## 2007-09-12 01:23:44 :              udp packet received
(10720 -> 5060) len=540, cksum=0x00008977
## 2007-09-12 01:23:44 : >>>>>>>>> RECV PACKET begin 540 bytes >>>>>>>
## 2007-09-12 01:23:44 :              REGISTER sip:testdomain.local
SIP/2.0
## 2007-09-12 01:23:44 :              Via: SIP/2.0/UDP
192.168.4.36:10720;
<Additional_Output_Truncated>
## 2007-09-12 01:23:44 :              CSeq: 1 REGISTER
## 2007-09-12 01:23:44 :              Expires: 3600
## 2007-09-12 01:23:44 :              Allow: INVITE, ACK, CANCEL,
OPTIONS, BYE, REFER, NOTIFY, MESSAGE, SUBSCRIBE, INFO
## 2007-09-12 01:23:44 :              User-Agent: X-Lite release
1002tx stamp 29712
## 2007-09-12 01:23:44 :              Content-Length: 0
<Additional Output Truncated>
Branch_External_fw->
```

This debug flow basic output shows the ScreenOS gateway triggering the SIP ALG with the `session application type 63, name SIP` output. Farther down in the debug output, the `debug sip all` shows the SIP `REGISTER` message that triggered the ALG.

Following successful SIP registration, the SIP phone initiates a call to an external PSTN phone number. This triggers a SIP `INVITE` message to the SIP server, which is also acting as the SIP proxy in this topology. Here is debug output of a sample SIP `INVITE` stream:

```
Branch_External_fw-> clear dbuf
Branch_External_fw-> set ffilter src-ip 192.168.4.36
```

```
Branch_External_fw-> set ffilter dst-ip 192.168.4.36
Branch_External_fw-> debug flow basic
Branch_External_fw-> debug sip all
<Now, dial the external phone number on the SIP Soft Phone>
Branch_External_fw-> get dbuf stream
****** 00439.0: <Trust/bgroup0> packet received [1063]******
  ipid = 264(0108), @035d8b50
  packet passed sanity check.
  bgroup0:192.168.4.36/10720->192.168.3.10/5060,17<Root>
Not IKE nor NAT-T nor ESP protocol.
  existing session found. sess token 4
  flow got session.
  flow session id 16046
## 2007-09-12 01:26:51 : sip_alg....  packet received (192.168.4.36 -> 192.168.3.10)
len=1063
## 2007-09-12 01:26:51 :              udp packet received
(10720 -> 5060) len=1035, cksum=0x0000f84c
## 2007-09-12 01:26:51 : >>>>>>>>> RECV PACKET begin 1035 bytes >>>>>
## 2007-09-12 01:26:51 :              INVITE sip:
PSTN_Number@testdomain.local SIP/2.0
## 2007-09-12 01:26:51 :              Via: SIP/2.0/UDP
192.168.4.36:10720;
<Additional_Output_Truncated>
## 2007-09-12 01:26:51 :              CSeq: 1 INVITE
## 2007-09-12 01:26:51 :              Allow: INVITE, ACK, CANCEL,
OPTIONS, BYE, REFER, NOTIFY, MESSAGE, SUBSCRIBE, INFO
## 2007-09-12 01:26:51 :              Content-Type: application/sdp
## 2007-09-12 01:26:51 :              User-Agent: X-Lite release
1002tx stamp 29712
## 2007-09-12 01:26:51 :              Content-Length: 482
<Additional Output Truncated>
Branch_External_fw->
```

Finally, when a ringback is generated and the call recipient answers, the SIP ALG permits the RTP stream connection back from the media gateway to the SIP softphone. The associated session is seen as follows:

```
Branch_External_fw-> get session dst-ip 192.168.4.36
alloc 21/max 16064, alloc failed 0, mcast alloc 0, di alloc failed 0
total reserved 0, free sessions in shared pool 16043
Total 1 sessions according filtering criteria.
id 16034/s**,vsys 0,flag 00001040/0000/0001,policy 17,time 12, dip 0
module 1, resource 7-30-158
 if 0(nspflag 2801):192.168.3.11/20040->192.168.4.36/63054,17,
000000000000,sess token 7,vlan 0,tun 40000009,vsd 0,route 17
 if 11(nspflag 800800):192.168.3.11/20040<-192.168.4.36/63054,17,
001125150ccd,sess token 4,vlan 0,tun 0,vsd 0,route 3
Total 1 sessions shown
Branch_External_fw->
```

Also, while the SIP call is in progress, the SIP session and the forward session for the RTP stream from the SIP phone to the PSTN external phone can be viewed:

```
Branch_External_fw-> get session src-ip 192.168.4.36
alloc 21/max 16064, alloc failed 0, mcast alloc 0, di alloc failed 0
total reserved 0, free sessions in shared pool 16043
Total 2 sessions according filtering criteria.
id 16036/s**,vsys 0,flag 00001040/0000/0001,policy 17,time 12, dip 0
module 1, resource 7-30-155
 if 11(nspflag 800801):192.168.4.36/63055->192.168.3.11/20041,17,
001125150ccd,sess token 4,vlan 0,tun 0,vsd 0,route 3
 if 0(nspflag 2800):192.168.4.36/63055<-192.168.3.11/20041,17,
000000000000,sess token 7,vlan 0,tun 40000009,vsd 0,route 17
id 16046/s**,vsys 0,flag 00000040/0000/0001,policy 17,time 5, dip 0
module 0
 if 11(nspflag 800e01):192.168.4.36/10720->192.168.3.10/5060,17,
001125150ccd,sess token 4,vlan 0,tun 0,vsd 0,route 3
 if 0(nspflag 2002e00):192.168.4.36/10720<-192.168.3.10/5060,17,
000000000000,sess token 7,vlan 0,tun 40000009,vsd 0,route 17
Total 2 sessions shown
Branch_External_fw->
```

The debug output for the response to the SIP INVITE with SIP 100 (Trying) and SIP 183 (Session Progress) status messages, followed by the ringback and the opening of the pinholes to permit the RTP stream, is viewed as follows:

```
Branch_External_fw-> get dbuf stream
## 2007-09-12 01:26:52 : sip_alg....  packet received (192.168.3.10 -> 192.168.4.36)
len=428
## 2007-09-12 01:26:52 :              udp packet received
(5060 -> 10720) len=400, cksum=0x00009db3
## 2007-09-12 01:26:52 : >>>>>>>>> RECV PACKET begin 400 bytes >>>>>>
## 2007-09-12 01:26:52 :              SIP/2.0 100 Trying
## 2007-09-12 01:26:52 :              Via: SIP/2.0/UDP
192.168.4.36:10720;
<Additional_Output_Truncated>
## 2007-09-12 01:26:52 : <<<<<<<<< RECV PACKET end <<<<<<<<<
## 2007-09-12 01:26:52 : sip_alg....  Dialog dlg4B120F0 received
provisional 100 (Trying)
## 2007-09-12 01:26:52 :              open gates for peer resources
## 2007-09-12 01:26:52 :              open pinhole for peer contact
rsc 157
## 2007-09-12 01:26:52 :              open pinhole for peer sdp
rsc 158:159
<Additional_Output_Truncated>
## 2007-09-12 01:26:52 : sip_alg....  Dialog dlg4B11EE8 sending
provisional 100 (Trying)
<Additional_Output_Truncated>
## 2007-09-12 01:26:54 : >>>>>>>>> RECV PACKET begin 739 bytes >>>>>>>
## 2007-09-12 01:26:54 :              SIP/2.0 183 Session Progress
## 2007-09-12 01:26:54 :              Via: SIP/2.0/UDP
192.168.4.36:10720;
<Additional_Output_Truncated>
## 2007-09-12 01:26:54 :              CSeq: 1 INVITE
## 2007-09-12 01:26:54 :              Content-Type: application/sdp
## 2007-09-12 01:26:54 :              Content-Length: 220
```

```
<Additional_Output_Truncated>
## 2007-09-12 01:26:54 :                   c=IN IP4 192.168.3.11
## 2007-09-12 01:26:54 :                   t=0 0
## 2007-09-12 01:26:54 :                   m=audio 20040 RTP/AVP 0 101
<Additional_Output_Truncated>
Branch_External_fw->
```

Finally, the first RTP packet and the session creation for it are seen in the debug output:

```
Branch_External_fw-> get dbuf stream
****** 00442.0: <Trust/bgroup0> packet received [160]******
  ipid = 267(010b), @035da350
  packet passed sanity check.
  bgroup0:192.168.4.36/63055->192.168.3.11/20041,17<Root>
  no session found
  flow_first_sanity_check: in <bgroup0>, out <N/A>
 vsd (0) is active, make hole active  active hole found
## 2007-09-12 01:26:54 : sip_alg/rm   callback code RM_HOLE_FIRST_HIT,
 group 30
  search route to (bgroup0, 192.168.4.36->192.168.3.11) in vr trust-vr
for vsd-0/flag-0/ifp-null
  [ Dest] 17.route 192.168.3.11->192.168.1.1, to ethernet0/0
## 2007-09-12 01:26:54 : sip: [rm] change resource dst tunnel from
policy 17
  search route to (bgroup0, 192.168.4.36->192.168.3.11) in vr trust-vr
for vsd-0/flag-0/ifp-null
  [ Dest] 17.route 192.168.3.11->192.168.1.1, to ethernet0/0
## 2007-09-12 01:26:54 : sip_alg/rm   callback code 37, group 30
  existing vector list 5-4b64b4c.
## 2007-09-12 01:26:54 : sip_alg/rm   callback code RM_HOLE_REMOVAL,
group 30
  flow_first_install_session======>
  **** pak processing end.
## 2007-09-12 01:26:54 : sip_alg/rm   callback code RM_HOLE_FIRST_HIT,
group 30
## 2007-09-12 01:26:54 : sip: [rm] change resource dst tunnel from
policy 17
## 2007-09-12 01:26:54 : sip_alg/rm   callback code 37, group 30
## 2007-09-12 01:26:54 : sip_alg/rm   callback code RM_HOLE_REMOVAL,
group 30
****** 00442.0: <Trust/bgroup0> packet received [200]******
  ipid = 268(010c), @035dab50
  packet passed sanity check.
  bgroup0:192.168.4.36/63054->192.168.3.11/20040,17<Root>
Branch_External_fw->
```

You can terminate SIP sessions with the SIP BYE message, which is seen in the debug output:

```
Branch_External_fw-> get dbuf stream
****** 00582.0: <Trust/bgroup0> packet received [550]******
  ipid = 7581(1d9d), @035cf350
  packet passed sanity check.
```

```
  bgroup0:192.168.4.36/10720->192.168.3.10/5060,17<Root>
Not IKE nor NAT-T nor ESP protocol.
  existing session found. sess token 4
  flow got session.
  flow session id 16046
## 2007-09-12 01:29:14 : sip_alg....  packet received (192.168.4.36 -> 192.168.3.10)
len=550
## 2007-09-12 01:29:14 :              udp packet received
(10720 -> 5060) len=522, cksum=0x00008cfb
## 2007-09-12 01:29:14 : >>>>>>>>> RECV PACKET begin 522 bytes >>>>>>>
## 2007-09-12 01:29:14 :              BYE sip:PSTN_PhoneNum@
192.168.3.10:5060 SIP/2.0
## 2007-09-12 01:29:14 :              Via: SIP/2.0/UDP
192.168.4.36:10720;
<Additional_Output_Truncated>
## 2007-09-12 01:29:14 :              CSeq: 2 BYE
## 2007-09-12 01:29:14 :              User-Agent: X-Lite release
1002tx stamp 29712
## 2007-09-12 01:29:14 :              Reason: SIP;description=
"User Hung Up"
## 2007-09-12 01:29:14 :              Content-Length: 0
Branch_External_fw->
```

See Also

Recipe 11.1; Recipe 11.7

11.7 View SIP Call and Session Counters

Problem

You want to view the SIP call and session counters.

Solution

You can view the list of active SIP calls through a ScreenOS gateway using the get alg sip calls command:

```
Branch_External_fw-> get alg sip calls
```

You can see the SIP session counters, specifying the number of instances of various SIP messages processed by the ScreenOS gateway, via the get alg sip counters command:

```
Branch_External_fw-> get alg sip counters
```

Discussion

The active call state information for the SIP call in Recipe 11.6 is seen as follows:

```
Branch_External_fw-> get alg sip calls
   Total number of calls = 1 (# of call legs 2)
-----------------------------
```

```
   Call leg1: zone 2
      UAS callid:760b194a0b6e9305MTIzOGE5ZjExZjJhZjIxM2ViNDFmNzRhOTIzNDc4ODM
(pending tsx 0)
      Local tag=192-nvs--1035999945990_2015289525-990
      Remote tag=000b0075
      State: STATE_ESTABLISHED
   Call leg2: zone 1
      UAC callid:760b194a0b6e9305MTIzOGE5ZjExZjJhZjIxM2ViNDFmNzRhOTIzNDc4ODM
(pending tsx 0)
      Local tag=000b0075
      Remote tag=192-nvs--1035999945990_2015289525-990
      State: STATE_ESTABLISHED
Branch_External_fw->
```

Similarly, you can view the SIP counters output for the ScreenOS gateway configuration from Recipe 11.6 with the get alg sip counters command:

```
Branch_External_fw-> get alg sip counters

SIP message counters: T=Transmit, RT=Retransmit
-----------------------------------------------
   Method    T      1xx    2xx    3xx    4xx    5xx    6xx
             RT     RT     RT     RT     RT     RT     RT
     ------------------------------------------------------------
   INVITE    1      2      1      0      0      0      0
             0      0      0      0      0      0      0
   CANCEL    0      0      0      0      0      0      0
             0      0      0      0      0      0      0
      ACK    1      0      0      0      0      0      0
             0      0      0      0      0      0      0
      BYE    0      0      0      0      0      0      0
             0      0      0      0      0      0      0
 REGISTER    1      0      1      0      0      0      0
             0      0      0      0      0      0      0
  OPTIONS    0      0      0      0      0      0      0
             0      0      0      0      0      0      0
     INFO    0      0      0      0      0      0      0
             0      0      0      0      0      0      0
  MESSAGE    0      0      0      0      0      0      0
             0      0      0      0      0      0      0
   NOTIFY    1      0      1      0      0      0      0
             0      0      0      0      0      0      0
    PRACK    0      0      0      0      0      0      0
             0      0      0      0      0      0      0
  PUBLISH    0      0      0      0      0      0      0
             0      0      0      0      0      0      0
    REFER    0      0      0      0      0      0      0
             0      0      0      0      0      0      0
SUBSCRIBE    2      0      1      0      1      0      0
             0      0      0      0      0      0      0
   UPDATE    0      0      0      0      0      0      0
             0      0      0      0      0      0      0
```

```
  BENOTIFY    0      0      0      0      0      0      0
              0      0      0      0      0      0      0
   SERVICE    0      0      0      0      0      0      0
              0      0      0      0      0      0      0
     OTHER    0      0      0      0      0      0      0
              0      0      0      0      0      0      0

 SIP Error Counters
 -----------------------------
   Total Pkt-in                        :13
   Total Pkt dropped on error          :0
   transaction error                   :0
   call error                          :0
   IP resolve error                    :0
   NAT error                           :0
   resource manager error              :0
   RR header exceeded max              :0
   Contact header exceeded max         :0
   Invite Dropped due to call limit    :0
   sip msg not processed by stack      :0
   sip msg not processed by alg        :0
   sip unknown method dropped          :0
   sip decoding error                  :0
   sip request for disconnected call   :0
   sip request out of state            :0
Branch_External_fw->
```

Finally, you can view the SIP ALG settings on the ScreenOS gateway with the `get alg sip` command:

```
Branch_External_fw-> get alg sip
SIP ALG                                       : enabled
Maximum number of SIP Calls                   : 16
Maximum Call Duration                         : 43200 seconds
Inactive Media timeout                        : 120 seconds
T1 interval                                   : 500 milli seconds
T4 interval                                   : 5 seconds
C interval                                    : 3 minutes
 SIP hold retain resource                     : Disabled
SIP Application Screen Configuration
-------------------------------------
 Unidentified messages in nat mode            : dropped
 Unidentified messages in route mode          : dropped
 SIP denial of service protect timeout        : 5
 SIP global denial of service protect         : Disabled
 SIP denial of service protect server IP      :
Branch_External_fw->
```

See Also

Recipe 11.1; Recipe 11.6

11.8 View and Modify SIP ALG Settings

Problem

You want to view and modify the various settings associated with the SIP ALG in a ScreenOS gateway's configuration.

Solution

The SIP ALG settings are viewed here:

```
Branch_External_fw-> get alg sip setting
```

You can modify the various SIP ALG settings individually, as specified in the following Discussion section.

Discussion

Here are the default SIP ALG settings on an SSG-5 gateway running ScreenOS 6.0r2:

```
Branch_External_fw-> get alg sip setting
SIP ALG                                      : enabled
Maximum number of SIP Calls                  : 16
Maximum Call Duration                        : 43200 seconds
Inactive Media timeout                       : 120 seconds
T1 interval                                  : 500 milli seconds
T4 interval                                  : 5 seconds
C interval                                   : 3 minutes
 SIP hold retain resource                    : Disabled
SIP Application Screen Configuration
-------------------------------------
 Unidentified messages in nat mode           : dropped
 Unidentified messages in route mode         : dropped
 SIP denial of service protect timeout       : 5
 SIP global denial of service protect        : Disabled
 SIP denial of service protect server IP     :
Branch_External_fw->
```

These settings are modified as follows:

As discussed in Recipe 11.1 and Recipe 11.2, the SIP ALG is enabled by default globally. You can disable it accordingly:

```
Branch_External_fw-> unset alg sip enable
```

The maximum number of SIP calls that a ScreenOS gateway can handle is a platform-specific limit that is currently not a configurable parameter.

The maximum call duration represents the period of time, in seconds, for which a SIP call can stay up through a ScreenOS gateway while there is no SIP signaling activity. You can modify the default value of 43,200 seconds (12 hours) shown in the earlier code snippet to 10,800 seconds (3 hours) as follows:

```
Branch_External_fw-> set alg sip signaling-inactivity-timeout 10800
```

The inactive media timeout represents the period of time, in seconds, for which a SIP call can stay up through a ScreenOS gateway while there is no bearer media traffic. You can modify the default value of 120 seconds to 60 seconds:

```
Branch_External_fw-> set alg sip media-inactivity-timeout 60
```

The SIP T1 interval is an estimate of the round-trip time for SIP transactions. It is relevant, for instance, in the SIP `INVITE` transaction, which requires a three-way handshake between a client transaction and a server transaction when it occurs over an unreliable transport such as UDP. In such a scenario, the T1 timer determines the duration between the first SIP `INVITE` and a retransmission. You can modify the default T1 interval of 500 msec on a ScreenOS gateway using the `set alg sip T1-interval` *<sec>* command. The following command modifies the SIP T1 interval to 900 msec:

```
Branch_External_fw-> set alg sip T1-interval 900
```

The SIP T4 interval represents the maximum amount of time that a SIP message can remain in the network. If a timer that is set to trigger in T4 seconds fires, the associated SIP transaction goes into a "terminated" state. You can modify the default T4 interval value of five seconds on a ScreenOS gateway using the `set alg sip T4-interval` *<sec>* command. The following command modifies the SIP T4 interval to 10 seconds:

```
Branch_External_fw-> set alg sip T4-interval 10
```

The SIP Timer C represents the maximum duration for a SIP-proxied `INVITE` request to receive a final response. You can modify the default SIP C-Timeout value of three minutes on a ScreenOS gateway using the `set alg sip` *<minutes>* command. The following command modifies the SIP C-Timeout value to five minutes:

```
Branch_External_fw-> set alg sip C-timeout 5
```

You can modify the setting to retain the ScreenOS resource manager (RM) resource during a call hold from the default disabled value:

```
Branch_External_fw-> set alg sip hold-retain-resource
```

ScreenOS offers a SIP-specific Denial of Service (DoS) attack protection screen that you can enable globally or for specific SIP servers. The following command globally enables the DoS attack protection screen for SIP servers:

```
Branch_External_fw-> set alg sip app-screen protect deny
```

You also can protect specific SIP servers against DoS attacks:

```
Branch_External_fw-> set alg sip app-screen protect deny dst-ip
192.168.3.10/32
```

Finally, ScreenOS gateways provide a setting to forward or drop SIP messages not recognized by the gateway to the SIP server. By default, unknown messages are dropped. You can permit these messages globally or specifically in NAT or route mode. The following command globally permits unknown SIP messages to SIP servers:

```
Branch_External_fw-> set alg sip app-screen unknown-message permit
```

You can permit unknown SIP messages to SIP servers in route mode:

```
Branch_External_fw-> set alg sip app-screen unknown-message route
permit
```

You also can permit unknown SIP messages to SIP servers in Network Address Translation (NAT) mode:

```
Branch_External_fw-> set alg sip app-screen unknown-message nat permit
```

See Also

Recipe 11.6; Recipe 11.7

11.9 View the Dynamic Port(s) Associated with a Microsoft RPC Session

Problem

You want to view the dynamic TCP/UDP port associated with a Microsoft RPC firewall session.

Solution

Figure 11-3 shows a topology whereby a host running the Microsoft Outlook client is situated on the `Desktops` zone and needs to connect to a Microsoft Exchange Server located on the internal `Trust` zone.

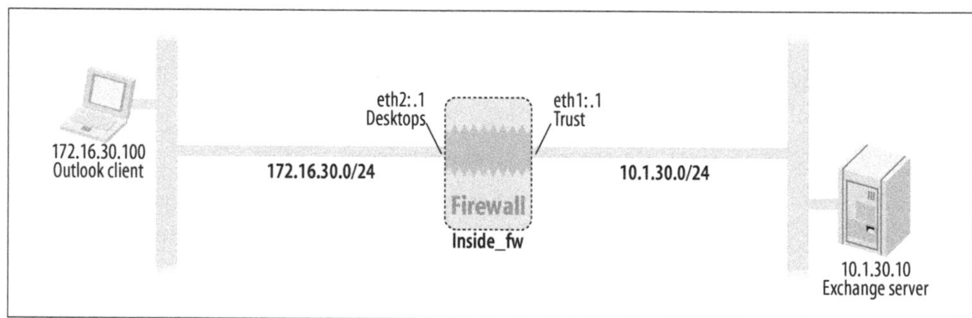

Figure 11-3. Viewing MS-RPC ALG sessions

The following policy, using the MS-Exchange MS-RPC ALG, permits this connection:

```
Inside_FW-> set policy id 19 from Desktops to Trust Outlook_Client
Exchange_Server MS-EXCHANGE permit log
```

You can view the TCP/UDP ports associated with the MS-RPC MS-Exchange session using either of the following methods:

```
Inside_FW-> get session service MS-EXCHANGE
Inside_FW-> get session src-ip 172.16.30.100 dst-ip 10.1.30.10
```

Discussion

As discussed in Recipe 7.15, Windows applications/services running on separate machines use MS-RPC to communicate with each other. The client application connects to the server on the MS-RPC Endpoint Mapper port (typically TCP/135) and specifies a UUID and version number. The server returns a response with the TCP/UDP port on which that UUID has registered itself. The client can then open a direct TCP/UDP connection to that port. The ScreenOS MS-RPC ALG tracks this entire communication stream, thus enabling the opening of the communication channel on the returned TCP/UDP port.

A sample set of MS-RPC sessions associated with this Microsoft Outlook to Microsoft Exchange communication for this recipe's solution is as follows:

```
Inside_FW-> get session src-ip 172.16.30.100 dst-ip 10.1.30.10
alloc 16/max 4064, alloc failed 0, mcast alloc 0, di alloc failed 0
total reserved 0, free sessions in shared pool 4048
Total 3 sessions according filtering criteria.
id 4006/s**,vsys 0,flag 08000040/0000/0001,policy 19,time 5, dip 0
module 0, cid 125
 if 7(nspflag 801801):172.16.30.100/2683->10.1.30.10/135,6,
001125150ccd,sess token 14,vlan 0,tun 0,vsd 0,route 10
 if 2(nspflag 801800):172.16.30.100/2683<-10.1.30.10/135,6,
00132017f442,sess token 4,vlan 0,tun 0,vsd 0,route 3
id 4021/s**,vsys 0,flag 08000040/0000/0001,policy 19,time 180,
dip 0 module 0
 if 7(nspflag 801801):172.16.30.100/2684->10.1.30.10/42124,6,
001125150ccd,sess token 14,vlan 0,tun 0,vsd 0,route 10
 if 2(nspflag 801800):172.16.30.100/2684<-10.1.30.10/42124,6,
00132017f442,sess token 4,vlan 0,tun 0,vsd 0,route 3
id 4030/s**,vsys 0,flag 08000040/0000/0001,policy 19,time 180, dip 0
module 0
 if 7(nspflag 801801):172.16.30.100/2686->10.1.30.10/42272,6,
001125150ccd,sess token 14,vlan 0,tun 0,vsd 0,route 10
 if 2(nspflag 801800):172.16.30.100/2686<-10.1.30.10/42272,6,
00132017f442,sess token 4,vlan 0,tun 0,vsd 0,route 3
Total 3 sessions shown
Inside_FW->
```

All of the preceding three sessions match policy 19, the MS-Exchange MS-RPC policy defined in this recipe's solution. The first session is an MS-RPC Endpoint Mapper session on TCP/135. The next two sessions connect to the dynamic TCP ports on which the MS-Exchange UUIDs have registered themselves.

A detailed view of session `id 4006`, the MS-RPC session, shows a match with `application id 68`, which is the application ID for the MS-RPC Endpoint Mapper:

```
Inside_FW-> get session id 4006
id 4006(00000fa6), flag 08000040/0000/0001, vsys id 0(Root)
```

```
policy id 19, application id 68, dip id 0, state 0
        cookie id 125
current timeout 40, max timeout 60 (second)
status normal, start time 4565, duration 0
session id mask 0, app value 0
ethernet2(vsd 0): 172.16.30.100/2683->10.1.30.10/135, protocol 6
session token 14 route 10
  gtwy 10.1.30.10, mac 001125150ccd, nsptn info 0, pmtu 1500
  flag 801801, diff 0/0
  port seq 0, subif 0, cookie 0, fin seq 0, fin state 0
ethernet1(vsd 0): 172.16.30.100/2683->10.1.30.10/135, protocol 6
session token 4 route 3
  gtwy 172.16.30.100, mac 00132017f442, nsptn info 0, pmtu 1500
mac 00132017f442, nsptn info 0
  flag 801800, diff 0/0
  port seq 0, subif 0, cookie 0, fin seq 0, fin state 0
Inside_FW->
```

Finally, you can start a set of debug commands just before launching the Microsoft Outlook client to view the processing of the MS-RPC requests by the ScreenOS gateway:

```
Inside_FW-> set ffilter src-ip 172.16.30.100
Inside_FW-> set ffilter dst-ip 172.16.30.100
Inside_FW-> debug flow basic
Inside_FW-> debug rpc msrpc
<Launch_MS_Outlook_client_and_wait_for_5_seconds>
Inside_FW-> undebug all
Inside_FW-> get dbuf stream
****** 04557.0: <Desktops/ethernet2> packet received [48]******
  ipid = 64215(fad7), @02633594
  packet passed sanity check.
  ethernet2:172.16.30.100/2680->10.1.30.10/135,6<Root>
  no session found
<Additional_Output_Truncated>
  Permitted by policy 19
<Additional_Output_Truncated>
  session application type 68, name MSRPC_EPM, nas_id 0, timeout 60sec
ALG vector is attached
  service lookup identified service 68.
<Additional_output_truncated>
## 2007-09-12 13:30:21 : msrpc_co_parse_bind: EPM 3.0 interface UUID
matched
## 2007-09-12 13:30:21 : msrpc_co_parse_bind: version 3.0
## 2007-09-12 13:30:21 : MSRPC_GET_UUID_STR: uuid
8a885d04-1ceb-11c9-9fe8-08002b104860
<Additional_output_truncated>
## 2007-09-12 13:30:21 : msrpc_parse_tower: MSRPC_EPM_MAP_RQST
## 2007-09-12 13:30:21 : msrpc_epm_parse_map_rqst: get ctx_hnd
## 2007-09-12 13:30:21 : MSRPC_GET_UUID_STR: uuid
00000000-0000-0000-0000-000000000000
## 2007-09-12 13:30:21 : msrpc_epm_parse_map_rqst: max_towers 4
<Additional_Output_Truncated>
```

As the preceding output shows, the Outlook client initially triggers a request to the MS-RPC Endpoint Mapper on the server on TCP/135. This request triggers the MS-RPC ALG on the ScreenOS gateway that maps this request as application type 68 (MS-RPC Endpoint Mapper).

Farther down in the debug stream, the Outlook client makes several more requests to the MS-RPC Endpoint Mapper and the Exchange server responds back with the TCP port on which the specific UUID has registered itself. This is followed by a connection from the Outlook client to the Exchange server on that TCP port, dynamically permitted by the ScreenOS gateway and viewable in the session table:

```
Inside_FW-> get dbuf stream
## 2007-09-12 13:30:29 : MSRPC_GET_UUID_STR:
uuid f5cc5a18-4264-101a-8c59-08002b2f8426
<Additional_Output_Truncated>
## 2007-09-12 13:30:29 : MSRPC_GET_UUID_STR: uuid
8a885d04-1ceb-11c9-9fe8-08002b104860
<Additional_Output_Truncated>
## 2007-09-12 13:30:29 : msrpc_parse_tower: TCP port 135
<Additional_Output_Truncated>
## 2007-09-12 13:30:29 : msrpc_parse_tower: MSRPC_EPM_MAP_RQST
## 2007-09-12 13:30:29 : msrpc_epm_parse_map_rqst: get ctx_hnd
## 2007-09-12 13:30:29 : MSRPC_GET_UUID_STR:
uuid 00000000-0000-0000-0000-000000000000
## 2007-09-12 13:30:29 : msrpc_epm_parse_map_rqst: max_towers 4
<Additional_Output_Truncated>
****** 04565.0: <Trust/ethernet1> packet received [192]******
  ipid = 22678(5896), @0264bd94
  packet passed sanity check.
  ethernet1:10.1.30.10/135->172.16.30.100/2683,6<Root>
  existing session found. sess token 4
  flow got session.
  flow session id 4006
## 2007-09-12 13:30:29 : msrpc_alg_handler: existing cookie
(id 125) found
<Additional_Output_Truncated>
## 2007-09-12 13:30:29 : msrpc_epm_parse_map_resp: ctx_hnd
## 2007-09-12 13:30:29 : MSRPC_GET_UUID_STR: uuid
00000000-0000-0000-0000-000000000000
## 2007-09-12 13:30:29 : msrpc_epm_parse_map_resp: n_towers 1
<Additional_Output_Truncated>
## 2007-09-12 13:30:29 : msrpc_parse_tower: ip 10.1.30.10 xlated to
10.1.30.10
<Additional_Output_Truncated>
## 2007-09-12 13:30:29 : MSRPC_GET_UUID_STR: uuid
f5cc5a18-4264-101a-8c59-08002b2f8426
<Additional_Output_Truncated>
## 2007-09-12 13:30:29 : MSRPC_GET_UUID_STR: uuid
8a885d04-1ceb-11c9-9fe8-08002b104860
<Additional_Output_Truncated>
## 2007-09-12 13:30:29 : msrpc_parse_tower: TCP port 42124
<Additional_Output_Truncated>
```

```
## 2007-09-12 13:30:29 : msrpc_parse_tower: MSRPC_EPM_MAP_RESP
## 2007-09-12 13:30:29 : msrpc_epm_parse_map_resp: rcode 0
<Additional_Output_Truncated>
****** 04565.0: <Desktops/ethernet2> packet received [48]******
  ipid = 64239(faef), @0264c594
  packet passed sanity check.
  ethernet2:172.16.30.100/2684->10.1.30.10/42124,6<Root>
  no session found
<Additional_Output_Truncated>
  RPC Mapping Table search returned 1 matched service(s) for (vsys
Root, ip 10.1.30.10, port 42124, proto 6)
  first RPC service matched: uid -2147483641(0x-2147483641)
  SW RPC Rule Table match: uid -2147483641(0x80000007), polid id 19,
index 10
  Permitted by policy 19
<Additional_output_truncated>
Inside_FW->
```

See Also

Recipe 7.15

11.10 View the Dynamic Port(s) Associated with a Sun-RPC Session

Problem

You want to view the dynamic TCP/UDP port associated with a Sun-RPC firewall session.

Solution

Figure 11-4 shows a topology whereby a host on the `Trust` zone of the `Inside_FW` firewall mounts an exported filesystem from an NFS server running on the Unix Server located on the `DMZ` zone.

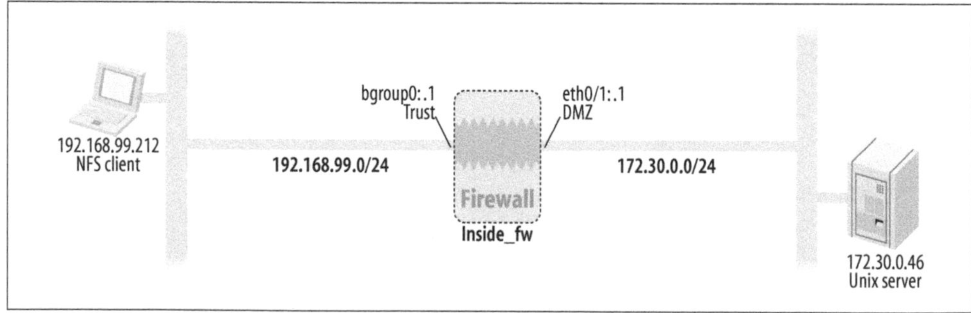

Figure 11-4. Viewing Sun-RPC ALG sessions

The following policies, using the Sun-RPC-Mounted and Sun-RPC-NFS services that rely on the Sun-RPC ALG, permit this connection:

```
Inside_FW-> set policy id 86 from Trust to DMZ NFS_Client Unix_Server
SUN-RPC-MOUNTD permit log
Inside_FW-> set policy id 87 from Trust to DMZ NFS_Client Unix_Server
SUN-RPC-NFS permit log
```

The TCP/UDP ports associated with the NFS Mount session are seen here:

```
Inside_FW-> get session src-ip 192.168.99.212 dst-ip 172.30.0.46
```

Discussion

As discussed in Recipe 7.16, services on Unix hosts that rely on Sun-RPC use a well-known but unique program number as an identifier and register the dynamic TCP/UDP port they are listening on with the portmapper service on that host. The portmapper service runs on TCP/UDP 111.

Hence, a client application that needs to connect to a Sun-RPC service, such as the NFS daemon, first contacts the portmapper service on the server with the particular program number. The portmapper service returns the TCP/UDP port associated with the program number. Then, the client application connects to the service on the specific TCP/UDP port number. The ScreenOS Sun-RPC services have the predefined, well-known program numbers for several applications, such as NFS. The ScreenOS Sun-RPC ALG dynamically opens pinholes to permit connections to the TCP or UDP ports on which the service has registered itself.

A sample set of the Sun-RPC sessions associated with the `NFS_Client` mounting an exported volume on the NFS server on the Unix server via Sun-RPC calls for this recipe's solution is as follows:

```
Inside_FW-> get session src-ip 192.168.99.212
alloc 14/max 16064, alloc failed 0, mcast alloc 0, di alloc failed 0
total reserved 0, free sessions in shared pool 16050
Total 5 sessions according filtering criteria.
id 16040/s**,vsys 0,flag 00000000/0000/0001,policy 86,time 179, dip 2
module 0
 if 11(nspflag 800801):192.168.99.212/879->172.30.0.46/32850,17,
000c29af1410,sess token 4,vlan 0,tun 0,vsd 0,route 5
 if 5(nspflag 800800):172.30.0.1/1128<-172.30.0.46/32850,17,
00c09f2575ec,sess token 20,vlan 0,tun 0,vsd 0,route 1
id 16044/s**,vsys 0,flag 00000000/0000/0001,policy 86,time 179, dip 2
module 0, cid 128
 if 11(nspflag 800801):192.168.99.212/32771->172.30.0.46/111,17,
000c29af1410,sess token 4,vlan 0,tun 0,vsd 0,route 5
 if 5(nspflag 800800):172.30.0.1/1125<-172.30.0.46/111,17,
00c09f2575ec,sess token 20,vlan 0,tun 0,vsd 0,route 1
id 16047/s**,vsys 0,flag 00000000/0000/0001,policy 87,time 239, dip 2
module 0
 if 11(nspflag 800801):192.168.99.212/32771->172.30.0.46/2049,17,
000c29af1410,sess token 4,vlan 0,tun 0,vsd 0,route 5
```

```
 if 5(nspflag 800800):172.30.0.1/1126<-172.30.0.46/2049,17,
00c09f2575ec,sess token 20,vlan 0,tun 0,vsd 0,route 1
id 16050/s**,vsys 0,flag 00000000/0000/0001,policy 87,time 239, dip 2
module 0
 if 11(nspflag 800801):192.168.99.212/681->172.30.0.46/2049,17,
000c29af1410,sess token 4,vlan 0,tun 0,vsd 0,route 5
 if 5(nspflag 800800):172.30.0.1/1129<-172.30.0.46/2049,17,
00c09f2575ec,sess token 20,vlan 0,tun 0,vsd 0,route 1
id 16051/s**,vsys 0,flag 00000000/0000/0001,policy 86,time 179, dip 2
 module 0
 if 11(nspflag 800801):192.168.99.212/32771->172.30.0.46/32850,17,
000c29af1410,sess token 4,vlan 0,tun 0,vsd 0,route 5
 if 5(nspflag 800800):172.30.0.1/1127<-172.30.0.46/32850,17,
00c09f2575ec,sess token 20,vlan 0,tun 0,vsd 0,route 1
Total 5 sessions shown
Inside_FW->
```

All five of the sessions shown here match policies 86 and 87, which rely on the Sun-RPC ALG to open ports.

In the following debug output, the `NFS_Client` system makes a portmapper call to the `Unix_Server` system on UDP/111, and supplies a program number of 100003 (NFS) and gets a port response of UDP/2049, to which it initiates a connection:

```
Inside_FW-> set ffilter src-ip 192.168.99.212 dst-ip 172.30.0.46
Inside_FW-> set ffilter src-ip 172.30.0.46 dst-ip 192.168.99.212
Inside_FW-> debug flow basic
Inside_FW-> debug rpc all
Inside_FW-> get dbuf stream
****** 01179.0: <Trust/bgroup0> packet received [84]******
<Additional_Output_Truncated>
  bgroup0:192.168.99.212/32771->172.30.0.46/111,17<Root>
  no session found
<Additional_Output_Truncated>
## 2007-09-17 15:30:26 : rpc_map_search: search for (0, 172.30.0.46,
 111, 17)
  RPC Mapping Table search returned 0 matched service(s) for (vsys
Root, ip 172.30.0.46, port 111, proto 17)
<Additional_Output_Truncated>
  Permitted by policy 86
<Additional_Output_Truncated>
  session application type 5, name PORTMAPPER, nas_id 0, timeout
1800sec
ALG vector is attached
  service lookup identified service 5.
<Additional_Output_Truncated>
  flow session id 16044
## 2007-09-17 15:30:26 : sunrpc_alg_handler: new cookie (id 128)
created
<Additional_Output_Truncated>
## 2007-09-17 15:30:26 : sunrpc_alg_msg_handler: rpcbind ver 2,
rpcbind proc 3
<Additional_Output_Truncated>
## 2007-09-17 15:30:26 : sunrpc_alg_rpcbind_v2_call_handler: GETPORT
```

```
call, prog 100003, ver 3, proto 17, port 0
## 2007-09-17 15:30:26 : sunrpc_alg_udp_handler: created hole for udp
client
  post addr xlation: 172.30.0.1->172.30.0.46.
<Additional_Output_Truncated>
## 2007-09-17 15:30:26 : sunrpc_alg_rpcbind_v2_reply_handler: GETPORT
reply, port 2049
## 2007-09-17 15:30:26 : rpc_map_insert: insert the following map:
## 2007-09-17 15:30:26 : rpc_map_print_map: 0, 172.30.0.46, 2049, UDP,
Program: 100003
<Additional_Output_Truncated>
****** 01179.0: <Trust/bgroup0> packet received [68]******
<Additional_Output_Truncated>
  bgroup0:192.168.99.212/32771->172.30.0.46/2049,17<Root>
<Additional_Output_Truncated>
## 2007-09-17 15:30:26 : rpc_map_search: search for (0, 172.30.0.46,
2049, 17)
## 2007-09-17 15:30:26 : rpc_map_search: found Sun RPC program: 100003
(0x186a3)
<Additional_Output_Truncated>
  RPC Mapping Table search returned 1 matched service(s) for (vsys
Root, ip 172.30.0.46, port 2049, proto 17)
  first RPC service matched: uid 100003(0x100003)
  SW RPC Rule Table match: uid 100003(0x186a3), polid id 87, index 25
  Permitted by policy 87
<Additional_Output_Truncated>
  Session (id:16047) created for first pak 1
<Additional_Output_Truncated>
Inside_FW->
```

Next, the NFS_Client system makes a portmapper call to the Unix_Server system on UDP/111, and supplies a program number of 100005 (mountd daemon) and gets a port response of UDP/32850, to which it initiates a connection:

```
Inside_FW->
****** 01179.0: <Trust/bgroup0> packet received [84]******
<Additional_Output_Truncated>
  bgroup0:192.168.99.212/32771->172.30.0.46/111,17<Root>
<Additional_Output_Truncated>
  flow got session.
  flow session id 16044
<Additional_Output_Truncated>
## 2007-09-17 15:30:26 : sunrpc_alg_rpcbind_v2_call_handler: GETPORT
call, prog 100005, ver 3, proto 17, port 0
<Additional_Output_Truncated>
## 2007-09-17 15:30:26 : sunrpc_alg_rpcbind_v2_reply_handler: GETPORT
reply, port 32850
## 2007-09-17 15:30:26 : rpc_map_insert: insert the following map:
## 2007-09-17 15:30:26 : rpc_map_print_map: 0, 172.30.0.46, 32850,
UDP, Program: 100005
<Additional_Output_Truncated>
****** 01179.0: <Trust/bgroup0> packet received [68]******
<Additional_Output_Truncated>
  bgroup0:192.168.99.212/32771->172.30.0.46/32850,17<Root>
```

```
<Additional_Output_Truncated>
## 2007-09-17 15:30:26 : rpc_map_search: search for (0, 172.30.0.46,
32850, 17)
## 2007-09-17 15:30:26 : rpc_map_search: found Sun RPC program:
100005(0x186a5)
<Additional_Output_Truncated>
  RPC Mapping Table search returned 1 matched service(s) for (vsys
Root, ip 172.30.0.46, port 32850, proto 17)
  first RPC service matched: uid 100005(0x100005)
  SW RPC Rule Table match: uid 100005(0x186a5), polid id 86, index 24
  Permitted by policy 86
<Additional_Output_Truncated>
Inside_FW->
```

Hence, these outputs illustrate the Sun-RPC ALG enabling the opening of dynamic connections for Sun-RPC services such as NFS.

See Also

Recipe 7.16

CHAPTER 12

Content Security

12.0 Introduction

This chapter summarizes the feature set for application security within ScreenOS. Juniper Networks firewalls have traditionally been stateful inspection firewalls. A *stateful inspection* security device looks at the network and transport layers of the ISO/OSI model, following the connection from client socket to server socket, but is typically not aware of the data transported within that connection of the application layer. However, *deep inspection*, pioneered by Juniper since ScreenOS version 5.0, is aware of the application communicating via the connection.

The ScreenOS content security feature set includes four feature groups:

- Antivirus
- Antispam
- URL filtering
- Deep inspection and integrated IDP

In larger networks, standalone, dedicated machines and servers provide these features. However, in smaller- and medium-size networks, it might be desirable to integrate these features into a single ScreenOS device for the obvious reasons of cost efficiency and convenience. For example, in this scenario, an administrator has to support only a single device and has to purchase a subscription signature service with only one vendor. Also, for smaller networks, antivirus capability and URL filtering do not require an external server, but you can add one for scalability in medium-size networks.

Antivirus capability exists in both internal and external configurations. In the internal configuration, the antivirus scanner and signatures are loaded onto the firewall. No additional server is required because the administrator subscribes to Juniper's antivirus signature update service. The internal antivirus feature uses the antivirus engines from Kaspersky Lab (and on some older models, from Trend Micro). Internal antivirus is implemented on branch edge devices of the SSG Series and the NS-5GT. In the external configuration, the firewall intercepts the traffic, but redirects it for scanning to an external antivirus server using one of two methods: a redirect via the Internet Content Adaptation Protocol (ICAP) or a protocol-independent redirect via policy-based routing (PBR). ICAP is implemented on devices of the ISG Series, whereas the PBR method is implemented on all devices and is more common than ICAP redirect because it is scalable and compatible with more external antivirus servers.

Antispam is a method of protecting mail servers from traffic overload by roughly presorting traffic. It does not eliminate all spam, but it is able to eliminate a bulk portion of known spam while offloading traffic to Mail Transfer Agents (MTAs). Antispam checks whether the sending MTA is known by querying a Spam Block List (SBL). Antispam usually uses Juniper's SBL, or it also can use an independent database such as Spamhaus. Access to Juniper's SBL requires a subscription service. In addition, you can configure custom blacklists and whitelists. Antispam is implemented on devices of the SSG Series.

URL filtering enforces organization-wide Internet browsing policies. An organization may want to allow access to only certain types of web content, or to only certain web sites. Just as with antivirus, with URL filtering, an internal and an external configuration exist, with the internal configuration requiring no additional server while using a subscription service based on information from SurfControl. The external URL filtering configuration is implemented on medium-size to large firewalls with external server support for both SurfControl and Websense.

Deep inspection was a firewall revolution when Juniper introduced it. On stateful inspection firewalls, traffic can be policed only by defining IP addresses, protocols, and ports (which is still much better than a stateless packet filter). However, a stateful inspection firewall is unaware of the actual data being transmitted. A deep inspection firewall, on the other hand, is able to decode higher-layer protocols and make forwarding decisions based on the information. Deep inspection is a subset of years of research by Juniper into Intrusion Detection and Prevention (IDP) technology. IDP, in itself, is an evolution over classic Intrusion Detection Systems (IDSs). Classic IDS does a stream match on the whole data flow; however, it is unaware, for instance, if a user browses to a malicious URL or reads an article in which the malicious URL is mentioned.

Deep inspection supports *protocol anomaly*, *stateful signatures*, and *classic stream signatures*. With protocol anomaly, the firewall checks the integrity of the communication between the client and server on the protocol level. With stateful signatures, the firewall actually checks the messages exchanged over the protocol between the client and server. For example, you can write a rule to allow access to a file server, but not to files with a certain name, or for access by a certain user. Stream signatures are useful where no protocol decode exists, as with proprietary applications.

Deep inspection provides a subset of decodes and signatures from Juniper's IDP technology. It is typically implemented on branch edge devices, although it is supported on every model. For medium- and large-size networks, there is integrated IDP in the ISG Series, as well as standalone IDP. Although Juniper offers a signature update subscription service, a large value exists in creating custom signatures for customer-specific solutions, particularly in high-security environments.

12.1 Configure Internal Antivirus

Problem

You want to configure internal antivirus on your ScreenOS firewall.

Solution

Set the antivirus pattern type:

```
set av scan-mgr pattern-type standard
```

Update the signature file the first time manually:

```
exec av scan-mgr pattern-update
```

Link the *default* antivirus filter profile to a policy:

```
set policy id 100 from "Trust" to "Untrust"  "Any" "Any" "Any" nat src permit
set policy id 100
   set av ns-profile
exit
```

Discussion

The branch office model of the SSG Series and the NS-5GT features optional integrated antivirus scanning by Kaspersky. It is a very powerful antivirus scanner, delivering high performance for smaller sites. In addition to in-the-wild and polymorphic virus protection, the Kaspersky engine also protects from spyware and phishing: you need a license key and valid subscription for this feature. Note that some models may need a memory upgrade.

The antivirus scanner scans the File Transfer Protocol (FTP), HyperText Transfer Protocol (HTTP; including web mail), Post Office Protocol version 3 (POP3), Internet Message Access Protocol (IMAP), and Simple Mail Transfer Protocol (SMTP), as well as the peer-to-peer applications AOL Messenger, ICU, MSN Messenger, and Yahoo! Messenger. The scanner is also able to look into multiple levels of compressed packages.

The first step in configuring antivirus is to choose the virus definition package. Due to memory limitations, some models may be able to load only the standard set. The standard method is the most common, and it is somewhere between *itw basic* scanning and *extended* scanning, which can also lead to false positives.

```
FIREWALL-> set av scan-mgr pattern-type ?
extended    All Virus and Spyware, plus adware/pornware/riskware/greyware
itw         in-the-wild Virus and Spyware
standard    All Virus and Spyware
```

The next step is to load the virus definition files onto the device. You may want to update the signatures the first time manually. The device needs Internet access for updates. The scan engine checks once per hour for new updates by default:

```
exec av scan-mgr pattern-update
set av scan-mgr pattern-update-url http://update.juniper-updates.net/AV/SSG5_SSG20/
interval 60
```

If your firewall has no direct connection to the Internet, but it can reach a proxy, you need to configure the proxy settings. This is supported on ScreenOS 6.1 and later:

```
set pattern-update proxy http proxy.juniper.net:8080
```

Enter the following command to check which virus definition is currently installed:

```
FIREWALL-> get av | include signature
    AV signature version: 08/08/2007 23:40 GMT, virus records: 157977
```

If you have problems downloading the virus definition, use the `get lic` command to see that you have a valid license, and the `get dns name juniper.net` command to see that you have Internet access and that your Domain Name System (DNS) server is working.

The last step is to link the antivirus profile to the policy. The default profile is `ns-profile`:

```
set policy id 100 from "Trust" to "Untrust"  "Any" "Any" "HTTP" nat src permit
set policy id 100
   set av ns-profile
exit
```

In most cases, you are done at this point. However, the antivirus engine is highly tunable. You will find tunable values under the following hierarchies:

```
set av all
set av scan-mgr
set av profile <profile>
set av extension-list <list>
set av mime-list <mime>
set av http webmail ...
```

You are able to tune how many CPU the antivirus engine can consume, how large the largest message can be, how many messages can be scanned concurrently, and how many messages can be queued:

```
set av all resources 70
set av scan-mgr max-content-size 10000
set av scan-mgr max-msgs 16
set av scan-mgr queue-size 16
```

You also can decide what should happen if the engine should fully fail or if a scan fails because of certain reasons. The default is that antivirus fails open should the whole engine fail, and fails close if a scan fails. Causes of failures include decompression layers (a ZIP file within a ZIP file within a ZIP file, etc.), password-protected archives, corrupted files, too many files in the queue or a file that is too large, an engine that is not ready, or a timeout being reached.

```
set av all fail-mode traffic permit
set av scan-mgr decompress-layer drop
set av scan-mgr passwd-file drop
set av scan-mgr corrupt-file drop
set av scan-mgr out-of-resource drop
set av scan-mgr engine-not-ready drop
set av scan-mgr timeout drop
```

The default profile is `ns-profile`; on older ScreenOS releases, it is `scan-mgr`. You can create your own profile and determine the exact behavior for each supported protocol. You also can enable or disable certain protocols.

```
set av extension-list my-incl-list exe;com;bat
set av mime-list my-mime-excl-list text/html;text/css

set av profile my-profile

   set ftp enable
   set ftp decompress-layer 3
   set ftp scan-mode scan-ext
   set ftp extension-list include my-incl-list
   set ftp timeout 180

   set http enable
   set http decompress-layer 2
   set http scan-mode scan-intelligent
   set http skipmime skipmime my-mime-excl-list
   set http timeout 180

   set smtp enable
   set smtp decompress-layer 3
   set smtp email-notify virus sender
   set smtp email-notify virus recipient
   set smtp timeout 180

   set aim-icq enable
   set aim-icq file enable
   set aim-icq msg enable
   set aim-icq unknown-version best-effort
```

```
    unset imap enable
    unset pop3 enable
    unset ymsg enable
    unset msnms enable
exit
```

There are special parameters for each protocol. For most, the default `ns-profile` is probably fine.

HTTP is the only protocol that also has global settings. You can configure trickling and keepalives, as well as enable web mail support. Those are all default and there should be no need to change them.

```
set av http keep-alive
set av http trickling default
set av http webmail enable
```

To tune and check the effectiveness of the scan engine, you can list scan statistics and reports:

```
FIREWALL-> get av statistics
<AV statistics>
No Scan: Max Msg:              0
No Scan: Max Content Size:     0
Fwd to Scan Engine: Total:     377
Scan Code: Clear               377
Scan Code: Infect              0
Scan Code: Psw Archive File    0
Scan Code: Decompress Layer    0
Scan Code: Corrupt File        0
Scan Code: Out Of Resource     0
Scan Code: Internal Error      0
Scan Code: Error               0
Scan Eng: Error:               0
Fail Mode:                     0

<App Session>
Max. Sessions:             2000
Init. Sessions:            400
Total Alloc Sessions:      2236
Total Free Sessions:       2236
Tcp Sessions:              0
Active Sessions:           0
Run out of packet count:   0
```

In particular, you will want to look at the number of infected files and the error counters below it. You may have to increase decompression layers if you see a high count here. This can be because an email is attached to another email, which has a ZIP file attached to it, which contains another ZIP file, for instance.

You can also view which virus was found in the event log with `get event type 547` or on your syslog server or NSM:

```
FIREWALL-> get event type 547
Total event entries = 28
```

```
Date       Time     Module Level  Type Description
2007-10-24 00:17:33 system warn  00547 AV: VIRUS FOUND: 192.168.97.101:
                                       4836->168.215.74.5:80, http url: http:/
                                       /ssl-hints.netflame.cc/Fc/FcPred.class,
                                       file ssl_hints.netflame.cc/Fc/
                                       FcPred.class/ virus
                                       Trojan-Downloader.Java.Agent.c.
```

Problems with the antivirus engine are also logged to the event log and can be viewed with `get event type 554`.

12.2 Configure External Antivirus with ICAP

Problem

You want to use antivirus in combination with your own ICAP-capable antivirus server.

Solution

Configure the ICAP server:

```
set icap server my-server host 192.168.1.100
set icap server my-server probe-interval 20
set icap server my-server probe-url /SYMCScan-Resp-AV
set icap server my-server max-connections 128
```

Configure the antivirus profile:

```
set av profile my-profile
   set icap my-server /SYMCScanReq-AV /SYMCScanResp-AV
exit
```

Link the antivirus filter profile to a policy:

```
set policy id 100 from "Trust" to "Untrust" "Any" "Any" "HTTP" nat src permit
set policy id 100
   set av my-profile
exit
```

Discussion

ScreenOS supports RFC 3507 ICAP 1.0 antivirus servers, such as the Symantec Scan Engine 5.0 ICAP server. ICAP is not as popular as it once was, because of some performance limitations, but it is best suited for link speeds of T3 and lower. For higher-performing solutions, an antivirus inline solution is recommended, which you can integrate with the firewall via PBR (see Recipe 12.3). Also, ICAP is supported on only ISG Series models. ICAP supports the redirection of HTTP and SMTP traffic only.

Start by configuring the connection to the ICAP server:

```
set icap server my-server host 192.168.1.100
set icap server my-server probe-interval 20
```

```
set icap server my-server probe-url /SYMCScan-Resp-AV
set icap server my-server max-connections 128
```

Here, we configured the IP address of the server, the probe interval for a server health check, the probe URL, and the number of maximum concurrent connections.

Next, link the ICAP server to an antivirus profile. In the profile, you also have to configure the `req-url` and `resp-url`. Those are the two URLs to which the firewall will forward client- and server-side traffic to the antivirus server.

```
set av profile my-profile
   set icap my-server /SYMCScanReq-AV /SYMCScanResp-AV
exit
```

The last step is to link the antivirus profile to the policy:

```
set policy id 100 from "Trust" to "Untrust"  "Any" "Any" "SMTP" nat src permit
set policy id 100
   set av my-profile
exit
```

You will find a log if a virus was found on your antivirus server. You can troubleshoot URL filtering with `debug flow basic` and `debug icap all`. Problems are also written to the event log and can be viewed with `get event type 81`.

12.3 Configure External Antivirus via Redirection

Problem

You want to put an antivirus server inline.

Solution

Configure a PBR policy for the traffic, which should be redirected to the antivirus server:

```
set vr trust

  set access-list extended 1 dst-port 25-25 protocol tcp entry 10
     set access-list extended 1 dst-port 80-80 protocol tcp entry 20

  set match-group name match-av-trust
     set match-group match-av-trust ext-acl 1 match-entry 10

  set action-group name action-av
     set action-group action-av next-hop 192.168.3.100 action-entry 10

  set pbr policy name av-policy-trust
  set pbr policy av-policy-trust match-group match-av-trust
action-group action-av 10
```

```
    set route 0.0.0.0/0 interface e0/2 gateway 192.168.2.254
    set route 10.0.0.0/8 interface e0/0 gateway 192.168.1.254
exit
```

Link the PBR policy to the Trust side interface:

```
set interface e0/0 pbr av-policy-trust
```

Discussion

There are multiple ways to put an antivirus server inline of the traffic stream. For email, this is quite easy, by making the antivirus server an MTA. Another method is to redirect certain traffic—for instance, just HTTP and SMTP—via PBR (see Chapter 19) to the antivirus server. This recipe is not an in-depth discussion about PBR, but it should show how you can use PBR to implement high-performance antivirus servers with the firewall, as illustrated in Figure 12-1.

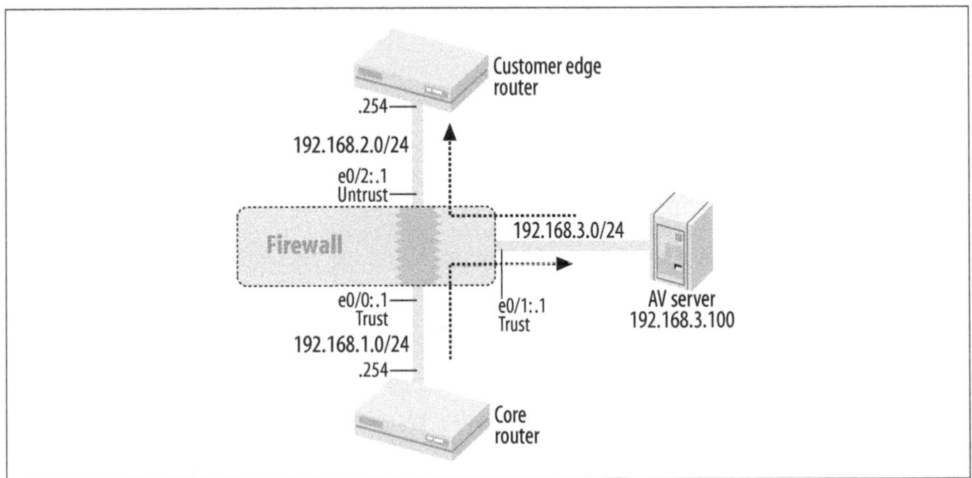

Figure 12-1. External antivirus with PBR

In Figure 12-1, there is a border firewall with an access router to the north, and a core router to the south. `e0/0` is `Trust` and `e0/2` is `Untrust`. The firewall is connected to network `192.168.3.0/24` and to an external antivirus server via `e0/1`.

```
set interface e0/0 zone Trust
set interface e0/0 ip 192.168.1.1/24

set interface e0/1 zone Trust
set interface e0/1 ip 192.168.3.1/24

set interface e0/2 zone Untrust
set interface e0/2 ip 192.168.2.1/24
```

The idea is to redirect antivirus traffic coming from the south to the antivirus server, instead of directly to the north. The antivirus traffic should make a detour through the antivirus server, but all other traffic should go directly out the north interface. It's easy to achieve this with PBR, supported in ScreenOS 5.4 and later.

The task is to match on `80/tcp` and `25/tcp` to redirect HTTP and SMTP traffic to server `192.168.3.100` to do antivirus scanning for outbound traffic as an example in this recipe. (For SMTP, you may also want to configure inbound rules.) The server processes the traffic and sends it back to the firewall. Then the firewall sends the traffic out with all the other Internet-bound traffic. To do this, you need to write an extended access control list (ACL) to match on those dst-ports, link the ACL to a match group, and then define an action group with the next hop to the antivirus server. Next, you'll need to link both the match group and the action group to a PBR policy, and finally, link the PBR policy to the Trust interface. (You do not need a matching policy for the Untrust interface because a session in the firewall will be established when the clients behind Trust first connect, and a session always overrules routing.)

```
set vr trust

   set access-list extended 1 dst-port 25-25 protocol tcp entry 10
      set access-list extended 1 dst-port 80-80 protocol tcp entry 20

   set match-group name match-av-trust
      set match-group match-av-trust ext-acl 1 match-entry 10

   set action-group name action-av
      set action-group action-av next-hop 192.168.3.100 action-entry 10

   set pbr policy name av-policy-trust
   set pbr policy av-policy-trust match-group match-av-trust
action-group action-av 10

   set route 0.0.0.0/0 interface e0/2 gateway 192.168.2.254
   set route 10.0.0.0/8 interface e0/0 gateway 192.168.1.254

exit

set interface e0/0 pbr av-policy-trust
```

You configure two normal routes: a default route out the Untrust interface `e0/2`, and the internal networks to the Trust interface `e0/0`. The antivirus server itself just needs a default route toward the firewall.

Because in this design the interface to the antivirus server was put into the same zone as the south interface is in (`Trust` in this case), you do not need any special policies. There will be two sessions: one session from `Trust` to `Trust` to the antivirus server, and one from `Trust` to `Untrust` from the antivirus server. If you have zone blocking enabled, or a final global deny rule, you will need an intra-zone rule from `Trust` to `Trust` as well.

```
set policy id 100 from "Untust" to "Trust"  "Any" "Any" "SMTP" nat src permit
set policy id 100
   set service http
exit

set policy id 200 from Trust to Trust "Any" "Any" "Any" permit
```

You will find a log if a virus was found on your antivirus server.

The best way to troubleshoot PBR is to use `debug flow basic` and look at the session table with `get sessions dst-port` *<port>*.

12.4 Configure Antispam

Problem

You want to configure antispam on your ScreenOS device.

Solution

Activate antispam on the policy:

```
set policy from "Untust" to "Trust"  "Any" "MIP(1.1.1.1)" "SMTP"
permit anti-spam ns-profile
```

Discussion

You need a valid license key for antispam and a valid subscription before you can use antispam. There is not much to configure besides enabling antispam on the policy.

```
set policy from "Untust" to "Trust"  "Any" "MIP(1.1.1.1)" "SMTP"
permit anti-spam ns-profile
```

Optionally, you can switch the default action from dropping the connection from the offending MTA to tagging it. (The default is `drop`.)

```
set anti-spam profile ns-profile
   set action tag
exit
```

You can troubleshoot antispam with `debug flow basic` or `debug anti-spam sbl`. The first thing to check, however, is whether DNS resolution works.

Here's an easy way to find out whether a certain MTA is listed in the SBL:

```
FIREWALL-> exec anti-spam testscan juniper.net.s7a1.psmtp.com
AS: anti spam result: action Pass, reason: No match
```

Blocked spam messages are logged to the event log (or syslog or NSM) and can be viewed with `get event type 563`.

12.5 Configure Antispam with Third Parties

Problem

Instead of using Juniper's SBL, you want to use the SBL of a third party, such as Spamhaus.

Solution

Configure the third-party SBL:

```
set anti-spam profile ns-profile
   set sbl sbl-xbl.spamhaus.org input-type ip spam-list include any
   unset sbl default-server enable
exit
```

Then, activate antispam on the policy:

```
set policy from "Untust" to "Trust"  "Any" "MIP(1.1.1.1)" "SMTP"
permit anti-spam ns-profile
```

Discussion

Instead of using Juniper's subscription service, you can use a third-party SBL, but the quality of third-party SBLs may or may not be the same. In any case, you need a license key for antispam.

Configure the new SBL within the `ns-profile` profile. You'll need to configure it if the input type is `ip` or `hostname`. The one for Spamhaus, for instance, is `hostname`. You may also want to disable Juniper's SBL:

```
set anti-spam profile ns-profile
   set sbl sbl-xbl.spamhaus.org input-type ip spam-list include any
   unset sbl default-server enable
exit
```

Then, activate antispam on the policy:

```
set policy from "Untust" to "Trust"  "Any" "MIP(1.1.1.1)" "SMTP"
permit anti-spam ns-profile
```

You can troubleshoot antispam with `debug flow basic` or `debug anti-spam sbl`. The first thing to check, however, is whether DNS resolution works.

Here's an easy way to find out whether a certain MTA is listed in the SBL:

```
FIREWALL-> exec anti-spam testscan juniper.net.s7a1.psmtp.com
AS: anti spam result: action Pass, reason: No match
```

Blocked spam messages are logged to the event log (or syslog or NSM) and can be viewed with `get event type 563`.

12.6 Configure Custom Blacklists and Whitelists for Antispam

Problem

You want to whitelist an MTA, which is on the list of an SBL.

Solution

First, configure the whitelist:

```
set anti-spam profile ns-profile
   set whitelist juniper.net.s7a1.psmtp.com
exit
```

Then, activate antispam on the policy:

```
set policy from "Untust" to "Trust"  "Any" "MIP(1.1.1.1)" "SMTP"
permit anti-spam ns-profile
```

Discussion

Whitelisting is usually used in combination with Juniper's or a third-party's SBL. You can use blacklisting instead of an SBL. You need an antispam license key to configure white- or blacklists.

```
set anti-spam profile ns-profile
   set whitelist juniper.net.s7a1.psmtp.com
   set blacklist evilspammer.com
exit
```

If you want to use blacklists instead of an SBL, deactivate Juniper's SBL:

```
set anti-spam profile ns-profile
   unset sbl default-server enable
exit
```

Then, activate antispam on the policy:

```
set policy from "Untust" to "Trust"  "Any" "MIP(1.1.1.1)" "SMTP"
permit anti-spam ns-profile
```

Blocked spam messages are logged to the event log (or syslog or NSM) and can be viewed with `get event type 563`.

12.7 Configure Internal URL Filtering

Problem

You want to configure built-in URL filtering.

Solution

Configure the categories you want to block:

```
set url protocol type sc-cpa
set url protocol sc-cpa
   set enable
   set profile "my-profile" "Advertisements" block
   set profile "my-profile" "Games" block
   set profile "my-profile" other permit
exit
```

Link the URL filter profile to a policy:

```
set policy id 100 from "Trust" to "Untrust"  "Any" "Any" "HTTP" nat src permit
set policy id 100
   set url protocol sc-cpa profile my-profile
exit
```

Discussion

Internal URL filtering works in conjunction with an external SurfControl server. No additional server is required. However, you need to configure a URL license key and have a valid subscription service for the built-in SurfControl URL filtering before you can configure it.

First, configure the URL filtering type to internal URL filtering:

```
set url protocol type sc-cpa
```

Then, create a profile and attach categories to it, configuring whether you want to `block` or `permit` them. The category other defines what you want to do (which is usually `permit`) with traffic when it does not match any configured categories.

```
set url protocol sc-cpa
   set enable
   set profile "my-profile" "Advertisements" block
   set profile "my-profile" "Games" block
   set profile "my-profile" other permit
exit
```

You can also configure the default profile `ns-profile` with default categories. You show the predefined categories as follows:

```
FIREWALL-> set url protocol sc-cpa
FIREWALL(url:sc-cpa)-> get category pre
        Type          code      Category name
------------------------------------------------
        PreDefine       90      Adult/Sexually Explicit
        PreDefine       76      Advertisements
        PreDefine       50      Arts & Entertainment
        PreDefine     3001      Chat
        PreDefine       75      Computing & Internet
[...]
```

Custom categories are used for manual black- and whitelists.

The next step is to decide what happens if the firewall should lose connectivity to the SurfControl server. The default is `permit`:

```
set url protocol sc-cpa
   set fail-mode block
exit
```

You link the custom or default profile to a policy. You can have different profiles for different policies. You can even have no URL filtering for some policies. Keep in mind that when you want to use different profiles, each policy needs to be different and that the first matched policy from top to bottom is matched. You need to define different src-addresses in the policies to use different URL filtering profiles because the dst-address will always be `Any` and the service will always be `HTTP`.

```
set policy id 100 from "Trust" to "Untrust"  "Any" "Any" "HTTP" nat src permit
set policy id 100
   set url protocol sc-cpa profile my-profile
exit
```

The internal URL scan engine caches URLs, already checked for their category. The cache is enabled by default. You can enlarge the cache; the number is in KB.

```
set url protocol sc-cpa
   set cache size 1000
exit
```

You can troubleshoot URL filtering with `debug flow basic` and `debug url-blk all`. Of course, first check that you have access to the Internet and that your DNS resolution is configured correctly on the firewall. URL filtering-related logs are written to the event log and can viewed with `get event log type 556`.

12.8 Configure External URL Filtering

Problem

You want to configure URL filtering with your own Websense or SurfControl filtering server.

Solution

First, configure how the firewall should contact the URL filtering server:

```
set url type websense
set url protocol websense
   set config enable
   set server 192.168.1.200 15868 10
   set deny-message use-server
   set fail-mode permit
exit
```

Then, enable URL filtering on the policy:

```
set policy from "Trust" to "Untrust"  "Any" "Any" "HTTP" nat src permit url-filter
```

Discussion

To use external URL filtering, you need your own Websense or SurfControl URL filtering server. No extra license key is required.

The configuration is quite simple: configure how the firewall should contact the URL server, whether you want to use the server's deny message or a locally configured one, and whether you want to fail open or close:

```
set url type websense
set url protocol websense
   set config enable
   set server 192.168.1.200 15868 10
   set deny-message use-server
   set fail-mode permit
exit
```

Instead of configuring `websense` for using a Websense server, you can configure `scfp` for using a SurfControl server.

The following code activates URL filtering on the policy:

```
set policy from "Trust" to "Untrust"  "Any" "Any" "HTTP" nat src permit url-filter
```

You can check the state of your connection to the URL filtering server as follows:

```
FIREWALL(M)-> get url all

Legend: * - Vsys uses URL Server shared by the Root

System    State       Server       Port  Timeout  Fail-Mode Connection
=====================================================================
Root      Enabled 192.168.1.200   15868      10    Block       Up
```

Use `debug flow basic` and `debug url-blk all` to troubleshoot. URL filtering-related logs are written to the event log and can viewed with `get event log type 556`.

12.9 Configure Custom Blacklists and Whitelists with URL Filtering

Problem

You want to manually block access to certain web sites.

Solution

First, configure a blacklist of blocked URLs:

```
set url protocol type sc-cpa
set url protocol sc-cpa
   set category "my-category" url "juniper.net/"
   set category "my-category" url "netscreen.com/"
   set profile "my-profile" "my-category" black-list
   set profile "my-profile" other permit
exit
```

Then, link the URL filter profile to a policy:

```
set policy id 100 from "Trust" to "Untrust"  "Any" "Any" "HTTP" nat src permit
set policy id 100
   set url protocol sc-cpa profile my-profile
exit
```

Discussion

To configure manual black- or whitelists, you'll need to configure a URL license key and have a valid subscription service for the built-in SurfControl URL filtering.

First, configure the URL filtering type to internal URL filtering:

```
set url protocol type sc-cpa
```

Then, configure a custom category for the web sites you want to block. Create a URL filtering profile and link the category to it. You can link multiple categories to the same profile or even create multiple profiles. You can choose for each profile or category pair whether you want to white- or blacklist it. A whitelist means that only the configured URLs will be allowed. A blacklist means that the configured URLs will not be allowed but any other will be allowed, depending on your global settings of category `other`.

```
set url protocol sc-cpa
   set category "my-category" url "juniper.net/"
   set category "my-category" url "netscreen.com/"
   set profile "my-profile" "my-category" black-list
   set profile "my-profile" other permit
exit
```

Link the profile (with the attached white- and blacklisted categories) to a policy. You can have different profiles for different policies, and even no URL filtering for some policies. Keep in mind that when you use different profiles, each policy needs to be different, and that the first matched policy from top to bottom is matched. You also need to define different src-addresses in the policies to use different URL filtering profiles because the dst-address will always be `Any` and the service will always be `HTTP`.

```
set policy id 100 from "Trust" to "Untrust"  "Any" "Any" "HTTP" nat src permit
set policy id 100
   set url protocol sc-cpa profile my-profile
exit
```

URL filtering-related logs are written to the event log and can viewed with `get event log type 556`.

12.10 Configure Deep Inspection

Problem

You want to configure deep inspection signature or anomaly protection on your ScreenOS device.

Solution

Link a signature group to a policy and configure the logging level:

```
set policy id 100 from "Untrust" to "Trust"  "Any" "MIP(1.1.1.1)" "HTTP" permit
set policy id 100
   set attack "CRITICAL:HTTP:SIGS" action drop
   set attack "CRITICAL:HTTP:ANOM" action drop
   set attack "HIGH:HTTP:ANOM action none
   set di-severity low
exit
```

Discussion

Deep inspection in ScreenOS is a subset of Juniper's IDP functionality. Around a thousand signatures exist for deep inspection, which are updated by a subscription service. You need a license key and a signature subscription before you can use deep inspection. Note that some models may need a memory upgrade as well.

The first step in configuring deep inspection is to choose the signature packet:

```
FIREWALL-> set attack db sigpack ?
base            Baseline Deep Inspection Pack
client          Client Deep Inspection Pack
server          Server Deep Inspection Pack
worm            Worm Mitigation Deep Inspection Pack
```

The next step is to load the signature onto the device. You may want to update the signatures the first time manually. The device needs Internet access for automatic updates.

```
exec attack update
set attack db mode update
set attack db schedule daily 5:00
```

If your firewall has no direct connection to the Internet, but it can reach a proxy, you need to configure the proxy settings. This is supported on ScreenOS 6.1 and later:

```
set pattern-update proxy http proxy.juniper.net:8080
```

If you have problems downloading the signatures, use the get lic command to ensure that you have a valid license, use the get clock command to ensure that your system clock shows the correct time, which is important for certificate validation, and use the get dns name juniper.net command to ensure that you have Internet access and that your DNS server is working. You can also download the signature pack manually (see Recipe 12.11).

Only those signatures with a certain severity will be installed if your firewall has limited memory. By the way, the term *signature* actually refers to context and stream signatures as well as protocol anomaly. Protocol anomaly is great for preemptive protection from possible future exploits, by enforcing protocol definition, and the context and stream signatures protect from known exploits. The difference between context and stream matches is that context matches decode the application layer and apply the match only to a functional part of the application, such as a filename or a URL, instead of to the full data stream. You may want to block access to a certain filename of a virus but not block access to web sites reporting that virus. Context signatures can virtually eliminate false positives in a well-tuned system.

You can list signatures and anomalies with get attack signature and get attack anomaly.

You can organize and apply signatures to policies in groups using the get attack group command, and they are organized by their severity level: info, low, medium, high, and critical.

You can link an attack group to a policy with the permit action. Only if the policy permits will the traffic be sent to the deep inspection module. Otherwise, it will be immediately dropped.

```
set policy id 100 from "Untrust" to "Trust"  "Any" "MIP(1.1.1.1)" "HTTP" permit
set policy id 100
   set attack "CRITICAL:HTTP:SIGS" action drop
   set attack "CRITICAL:HTTP:ANOM" action drop
   set attack "HIGH:HTTP:ANOM action none
   set di-severity low
exit
```

You can configure multiple attack groups with different actions on the same policy:

```
none            permit flow without processing
ignore          ignore this flow if attack is found and continue
drop-packet     drop this packet
drop            drop all packets in this flow till connection timeout
close-client    reset client to server connection and drop packet
close-server    reset server to client connection and drop packet
close           reset connections on both sides and drop packet
```

Be careful when blocking traffic that is triggered by low-severity signatures, as it can also block legitimate traffic. You can control the logging level with di-severity.

Deep inspection attacks are logged to the event log. You can view them with `get event type 767` or on your syslog or NSM server.

You can fine-tune the different protocol decodes with the `set di service` *<protocol>* command. In ScreenOS 6.0, 29 protocol decodes are defined, and you can fine-tune things such as maximum cookie length and number of failed logins. Altogether, you can adjust more than 150 parameters.

To troubleshoot deep inspection problems, use `debug flow basic` and `debug idp all`.

12.11 Download Deep Inspection Signatures Manually

Problem

You want to use deep inspection on a firewall, but you do not have direct Internet access.

Solution

Use your browser and download the signature packet to your PC:

> *https://services.netscreen.com/restricted/sigupdates/6.0/ssg5/attacks.bin?sn= 0168102006000000*

Install the signature via the Trivial File Transfer Protocol (TFTP) on the device:

```
FIREWALL-> save attack-db from tftp 192.168.1.100 attacks.bin to flash
Load attack database from TFTP 192.168.1.100 (file: attacks.bin).
!!!!!!!!!!!!!!!!!!!!!!!!!!!!!!!!!!!!!!!!!!!!!!!!!!!!!!!!!!!!!!!!!!!!!!
```

Discussion

To install the signature pack automatically on the firewall, the firewall needs to have direct access to the Internet, have DNS configured, and have the correct time set up. If the device does not have direct access to the Internet, you can install the signature pack manually.

Download the *attacks.bin* file to your PC:

> *https://services.netscreen.com/restricted/sigupdates/<screenOS>/<model>/attacks. bin?sn=<serial>*

Enter the correct ScreenOS release (6.0), model (ssg5), and serial number (016810200600000). Then, download the file from your PC to the firewall via TFTP:

```
FIREWALL-> save attack-db from tftp <ip> attacks.bin to flash
```

You can download the signature packet to your PC, but you will not be able to install it on a device without having a valid license key and a valid subscription.

12.12 Develop Custom Signatures with Deep Inspection

Problem

You want to create your own deep inspection signature.

Solution

Choose the right deep inspection context. In this case, we block the search term *Juniper Networks* in a Google search. Develop a regular expression (regex):

```
set attack "CS:google-juniper" http-request "/search\?hl=..&q=\[Juniper\]\+\
[Networks\].*" severity critical
```

Create an attack group and attach the signature to the group:

```
set attack group "CS:my_sigs"
set attack group "CS:my_sigs" add "CS:google-juniper"
```

Link the attack group to a policy:

```
set policy id 100 from "Trust" to "Untrust"  "Any" "Any" "HTTP" nat src permit
set policy id 100 attack "CS:my_sigs" action close
```

Discussion

Developing custom signatures is a very powerful way to control traffic on the application layer of the firewall. It is also a fine art. The first thing you have to be clear about is what you want to block.

In this example, let's block users from Googling *Juniper Networks*. The first thing to do is to execute what you want to block while capturing the packet stream with a packet capture such as Wireshark. In this case, do a Google search on the search term *Juniper Networks*:

```
GET /search?hl=en&q=juniper+networks
```

This is the string from the packet capture, which you have to match. The next step is to search for the right context. Alternatively, if no context exists, you can create a stream signature, but stream signatures are prone to false positives because the signatures match on any part of the traffic stream. In this example, the context is `http-request`. You can list other contexts with the following:

```
FIREWALL-> set attack cs:TEST ?
```

In ScreenOS 6.0, 57 contexts are defined for the applications DNS, FTP, HTTP, SMTP, POP3, IMAP, SMB (Microsoft NetBIOS), and the peer-to-peer applications AOL Messenger, MSN Messenger, Yahoo! Messenger, and Gnutella. If you do not find a context, you need to use the stream match `stream256` instead.

Once you identify the context, you need to create the signature. Note that deep inspection regexes are somewhat similar, but also different from Perl and POSIX-style expressions. Here is a list of deep inspection expressions:

`.`
: Matches any character

`[0-9]`
: Matches digits

`\0123`
: Matches the octal number 123

`\X00 10 db\X`
: Matches the hex number 0 ×0010db

`[abc]`
: Character class

`[a-zA-Z]`
: Matches alpha characters

`[^n]`
: Negative character class

`\[abc\]`
: Case-insensitive match; not a character class

`?`
: Matched, at most, once

`*`
: Matched zero or more times

`+`
: Matched one or more times

`(abc)`
: Group expression

`n|m`
: Matches `n` or `m`, typically used with ( )

`\*`
: Escape, matches literal *

The most common problems with regexes are that a regex matches one character at a time instead of a typical string match in an editor. If any of the metacharacters in the preceding list are used within the pattern, they must be escaped. If the metacharacter already includes an escape, a second needs to be added. A signature within a context needs to match the entire string. Therefore, signatures often start and end with `.*`.

Compare the string from the packet capture with the regex. You can see that ? and + needed to be escaped, that we used any-match for the language `en`, and that we made the search term case-insensitive. We match on anything after the string in case the search term is something such as *Juniper Networks*, for instance:

```
/search ?hl=en&q=  Juniper   +  Networks
/search\?hl=..&q=\[juniper\]\+\[networks\].*
```

We add the regex to the custom signature `CS:google-juniper`. All custom signatures have to start with `CS:`.

```
set attack "CS:google-juniper" http-request ".*/search\?hl=..&q=\[Juniper\]\+\
[Networks\].*" severity critical
```

You have to link the signature to a group before you can apply it to a policy. Custom groups have to start with `CS:`.

```
set attack group "CS:my_sigs"
set attack group "CS:my_sigs" add "CS:google-juniper"
```

Link the attack group to a policy:

```
set policy id 100 from "Trust" to "Untrust"  "Any" "Any" "HTTP" nat src permit
set policy id 100 attack "CS:my_sigs" action close
```

You can use the `debug idp all` command to check whether your signature matched:

```
_sc_http_verify_flow: (c2s) 192.168.98.128:2824 -> 216.239.51.104:80 [6]
_sc_http_verify_flow: (45 c2s)GET /search?hl=en&q=juniper+networks HTTP/1.1
_sc_http_verify_flow: c2s request
SC_KQMSG_ADD_CONTEXT: service HTTP, type HTTP_REQUEST, length 45, skip false
sc_ids_check_attack_match: 'CS:google-juniper' [] matched
subs 0>vc 0 192.168.98.128:2824 216.239.51.104:80 6 CLOSE ALARM IDP_ATTACK_MATCH CS:
google-juniper
```

Deep inspection-related logs are written to the event log (or syslog or NSM) and can be viewed with `get event type 767`.

12.13 Configure Integrated IDP

Problem

You want to redirect traffic to the integrated Security Module on an ISG Series firewall.

Solution

You enable IDP redirect for each permit policy individually if traffic should be sent to the Security Module.

```
set policy id 100 from "Untrust" to "Trust"  "Any" "MIP(1.1.1.1)" "HTTP" permit
set policy id 100
   set idp mode tap
exit
```

Discussion

Integrated IDP is Juniper's full-blown IDP solution, running on optional Security Modules on the ISG Series firewalls. When the IDP module is installed, the firewall is managed via the NetScreen Security Manager (NSM). However, it may be necessary to enable IDP screening on policies on the CLI—for instance, during first-time deployment and before importing the device into NSM.

The IDP on the Security Module works independently of ScreenOS. Within a policy, you can configure whether a copy of the traffic is sent to the IDP blade. This setting is used to monitor traffic with the IDP module but not to block it:

```
set policy id 100 from "Untrust" to "Trust"  "Any" "MIP(1.1.1.1)" "HTTP" permit
set policy id 100
   set idp mode tap
exit
```

Or, you can configure that all traffic matching this policy is screened inline through the IDP blade. In this mode, the IDP can actually block traffic and protect the network, and in this case, the IDP processing capacity becomes the limiting factor even if the flow is installed in ASIC on the firewall side.

```
set policy id 100 from "Untrust" to "Trust"  "Any" "MIP(1.1.1.1)"
"HTTP" permit
set policy id 100
   set idp
exit
```

You can install up to three Security Modules on an ISG-2000. It makes sense to run traffic inline through the Security Module if signatures for that protocol exist. Predefined signatures exist for all common protocols, but you may have to develop custom signatures to protect proprietary applications.

Note that you can only configure IDP policies via NSM, but IDP configuration is out of the scope of this book.

CHAPTER 13

User Authentication

13.0 Introduction

Today's primary method for permitting access to host computers and other networked or networking devices is the username and password combination. This method, which provides the simplest form of verifying the authenticity of a user trying to access the resource, is known as *user authentication*. Grand schemes are sometimes developed to authenticate users, but most can be broken down into three primary authentication factors:

Something you know
: This is the simplest and most common form of user authentication. It might be a password, PIN, or secret phrase that only "trusted" users would know.

Something you have
: This would be something a trusted user possesses, such as a secret decoder ring, or a token-generator such as RSA Security's SecurID product.

Something you are
: Lots of new development is occurring here in a field known as *biometrics*. This involves offering your fingerprint or a scan of your retinas, or looking into a camera, so that your facial features can be scanned and matched against a trusted user facial profile.

Many systems implement two or more of these authentication factors—for instance, the user must know a PIN and possess a security token before access is permitted. This is known as *two-factor authentication*. ScreenOS provides native username and password authentication, and you can configure it to integrate with external authentication systems running within the network that provide authentication and authorization services such as the Remote Access Dial-In User Service (RADIUS), Lightweight Directory Access Protocol (LDAP), or SecurID.

This chapter introduces user authentication in ScreenOS and presents the two locations for storing user profiles: the local database and an external authentication server.

It provides several recipes for configuring different types of users and user groups. It also covers some other aspects of user authentication, such as changing login banners, configuring users for multiple types of authentication such as Internet Key Exchange (IKE)/Xauth, and using group expressions in policies for user authentication.

Authentication and Authorization

In computer security, authentication is the process of verifying (or not) the digital identity of the sender of a digital communication, such as a login attempt. The sender may be a person, computer, or computer program. In computer terms, authentication is distinct from authorization. *Authentication* is the verification of user credentials, as opposed to *authorization*, which is the privilege granted upon successful authentication.

ScreenOS provides a portion of all three services in AAA (Authentication, Authorization, and Accounting) security schemes, but it is not designed to offer fully featured capabilities beyond simple password authentication and simple authorization which is provided with RADIUS, or other types of external AAA systems.

User Profiles

Profiles are created to provide username and password matches as well as to grant access rights for a login attempt. You can store profiles locally within the ScreenOS internal database. In addition to the internal database, ScreenOS supports the following external authentication server types:

- RADIUS
- LDAP
- SecurID

External Authentication Servers

You can use external servers with ScreenOS; the most widely used external authentication server in use is RADIUS. ScreenOS also has native support for LDAP and RSA Security's SecurID. The default authentication server for all user types is the local database. However, you can specify that an external auth server be used for any of the user types except IKE users. For example, you can specify that administrators be authenticated via RADIUS, while policy authentication uses SecurID.

RADIUS

RADIUS is a protocol for a type of authentication server that can support thousands of users. ScreenOS can act as a RADIUS client that authenticates users based on a series of messages between the RADIUS client and the RADIUS server. At a high level, the RADIUS client prompts the user for login credentials. The client then sends the credentials to the RADIUS server to be compared against the list of users in the database. The RADIUS server will respond with a success message or a failure message. ScreenOS will then either grant or deny the login based on the server's response.

In addition, you can configure RADIUS to return certain attributes that you can use to assign privilege level, IP address, or other information that may be used for the connection. ScreenOS accepts these vendor-specific attributes (VSAs) for a variety of functions. For admin users, these VSAs can set the privilege level—read/write or read-only—for individual administrators of the firewall. For Xauth or the Layer 2 Tunneling Protocol (L2TP), you can use these attributes only to assign IP address and name resolution servers.

VSAs are defined in a dictionary file and can be very different among vendors. Juniper provides a dictionary file for the ScreenOS devices at:

> *http://www.juniper.net/customers/csc/research/netscreen_kb/downloads/dictionary/funk_radius.zip*

You should load the RADIUS dictionary file onto the RADIUS server; if you don't, you can use the RADIUS server for authentication only.

External RADIUS servers have generic `auth-server` properties, and they have three distinct configuration properties associated with them:

Shared secret
: This is a password that is shared between the client and the server, and is used to encrypt the user's password that is sent for verification.

RADIUS port
: This is the port the RADIUS server is listening on for incoming client requests. The default port is 1645.

RADIUS retry timeout
: This is the time in seconds that the client will wait before sending another request if a response from a previous request is not received. The default is three seconds.

RADIUS supports all user types that the local database supports, except IKE users. Of the three types of external authentication servers supported by ScreenOS, only RADIUS provides the broad support for authentication, admin privilege assignment, and Xauth/L2TP remote settings assignment.

You can find examples for configuring RADIUS external authentication servers in Recipe 13.7.

LDAP

LDAP is a protocol used for conducting searches through a directory. LDAP is based on the X.500 specifications, but it is significantly simpler. It allows users to query directories of information such as email addresses or public keys. Because LDAP is an open standard and it supports the Transmission Control Protocol/Internet Protocol (TCP/IP), it is well suited for centralized storage of information that a variety of host computers or applications may access. Microsoft uses a very common LDAP system, called Active Directory. Active Directory stores information about organizations, groups, and users within a Windows domain structure, including the user logon credentials for the domain. You can find more information on LDAP in RFC 1777, at *http://www.ietf.org/rfc/rfc1777.txt*.

LDAP directories are designed in a hierarchical fashion and you can think of them as branches of a tree, starting at the root. In its basic form, LDAP branches from country to organization to organizational units to individuals (where individuals can be people, files, devices, etc.). Figure 13-1 illustrates a typical LDAP structure.

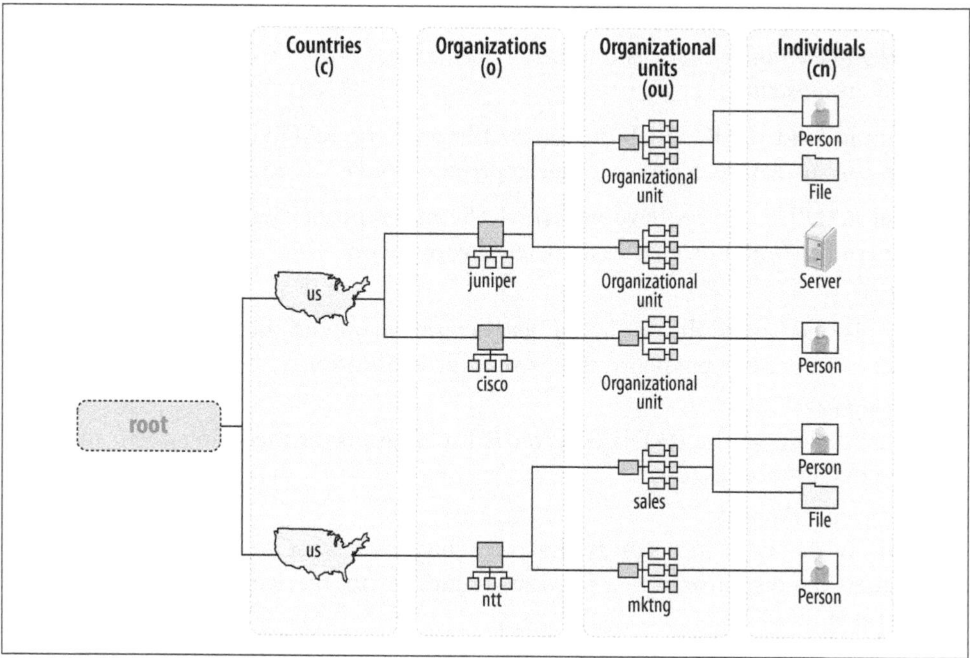

Figure 13-1. A typical LDAP structure

ScreenOS can use the LDAP protocol for authentication of user passwords for any user type except IKE users.

You can use LDAP for authentication only; it does not support admin privilege assignment, remote settings for L2TP users or user groups, or remote settings for Xauth users or user groups.

Support is available for the various user types within ScreenOS:

Auth user
: Full support for auth users.

L2TP user
: Authentication only. User will receive the default remote settings from the security device.

Xauth user
: Authentication only. User will receive the remote settings from the Xauth server configured within the security device.

Admin user
: Authentication only. User will receive the default read-only privilege level.

User groups
: Not supported with LDAP external authentication server.

In addition to the generic `auth-server` properties, LDAP configuration requires the default setting for the LDAP server port to be 389. You can find examples of configuring LDAP external authentication servers in Recipe 13.8.

SecurID

Instead of relying on a fixed password, SecurID provides two-factor authentication. The two factors are "something you know" in the form of a PIN, and "something you have" in the form of a one-time token generated by an RSA SecurID authenticator. An authenticator is available in several formats, from a credit-card-size device with an LCD window, to keychain fobs, to software that runs on your computer. The authenticator displays a new pseudorandom number every 60 seconds and is synchronized to the RSA Ace server. When a user attempts a logon using SecurID, he enters his username followed by his PIN and the pseudorandom number currently displayed by the authenticator, as shown in Figure 13-2. In essence, it is a password that is valid for only 60 seconds.

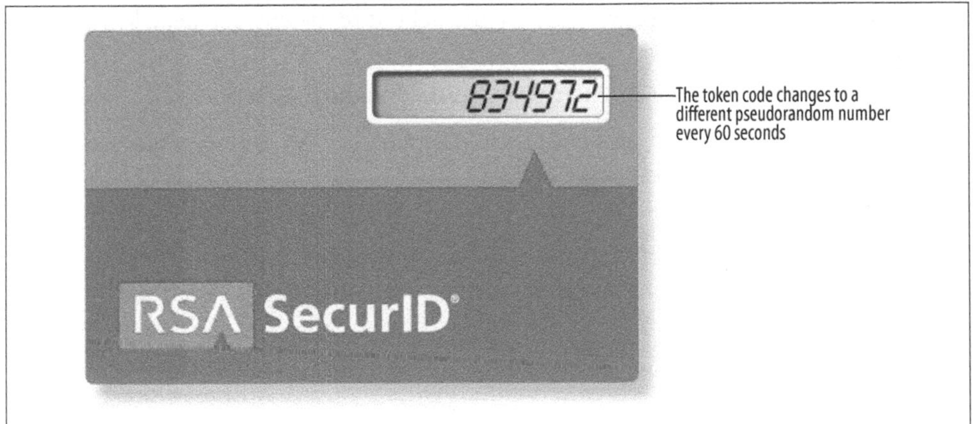

Figure 13-2. An RSA SecurID authenticator

If that isn't enough, a duress mode will send an alarm if the user enters a predetermined PIN code that signifies that the user is being forced to enter her login credentials, perhaps with a gun to her head. The login will succeed for that one time only and will trigger an event on the Ace server. All future login attempts will fail until the user contacts the Ace server administrator. This feature is available only on Ace servers that support this feature.

The ScreenOS security device performs the same basic function when communicating with an RSA Ace server as it does with a RADIUS server. That is, the security device acts as a proxy between the user and the authentication server, prompting the user for the login credentials and then forwarding them for verification to the Ace server. The Ace server will respond with a success or failure message allowing ScreenOS to accept or deny the login attempt.

You can use SecurID for authentication only; it does not support admin privilege assignment, remote settings for L2TP users or user groups, or remote settings for Xauth users or user groups.

You can use SecurID with any user type except IKE users. Support for the individual user types is the same as for LDAP:

Auth user
: Full support for auth users.

L2TP user
: Authentication only. User will receive the default remote settings from the security device.

Xauth user
: Authentication only. User will receive the remote settings from the Xauth server configured within the security device.

Admin user
: Authentication only. User will receive the default read-only privilege level.

User groups
: Not supported with the LDAP external authentication server.

In addition to the generic authentication properties, you can configure SecurID external servers with the following options:

Authentication port
: The port number on the SecurID Ace server to which the security device sends authentication requests. The default port number is 5500.

Encryption type
: The algorithm used for encrypting communication between the security device and the SecurID Ace server—either SDI or Data Encryption Standard (DES).

Client retries
: The number of times the SecurID client (i.e., the security device) tries to establish communication with the SecurID Ace server before aborting the attempt.

Client timeout
: The length of time in seconds that the security device waits between authentication retry attempts.

You can find examples of configuring SecurID external authentication servers in Recipe 13.9.

ScreenOS User Types

You can create multiple types of user accounts on the ScreenOS device. Each has a different purpose. Table 13-1 compares user types with the server type.

Table 13-1. ScreenOS authentication types and capabilities

			L2TP users		xauth users		Admin users			
Server type	**Auth users**	**IKE users**	**Auth**	**Remote settings**	**Auth**	**Remote settings**	**Auth**	**Privilege #**	**User groups**	**Group expression #**
Local	✗	✗	✗	✗	✗	✗	✗	✗	✗	
RADIUS	✗		✗	✗	✗	✗	✗	✗	✗	✗
Secure ID	✗		✗		✗		✗			
LDAP	✗		✗		✗		✗			

Administrative users
: This type of user has access to the firewall configuration and monitoring interfaces.

Auth user
: This type of user is referenced within a firewall policy to authenticate a user before taking an action such as "permit".

L2TP user
: This type of user is referenced in the configuration of an L2TP tunnel.

IKE user
: This type of user is for authenticating virtual private network (VPN) tunnels (Phase 1).

Xauth user
: This type of user is referenced by the client/server configuration for VPN authentication.

Administrative Users

You can assign only a few types of administrative privileges to an administrative user:

Root admin
: This account has complete control over the entire firewall. It is the only account that can create additional "root-level" administrative accounts and is always stored locally on the device.

Root-level "fully privileged" admin
: This account has full privileges over the root level of the device, with a few exceptions for commands kept strictly for the "root" user. This type of account can create Virtual Systems (VSYS) and VSYS admin accounts within those VSYS.

Root-level "read-only" admin
: This type of account can view the configuration, but cannot change any configuration values.

VSYS "fully privileged" admin
: This type of account has full control over the VSYS device. This type of account cannot view configurations for the root level of the firewall or other VSYS residing on the same platform.

VSYS "read-only" admin
: This account type can view configurations within the VSYS only and cannot alter any configuration values.

Figure 13-3 shows the process for authenticating administrative users.

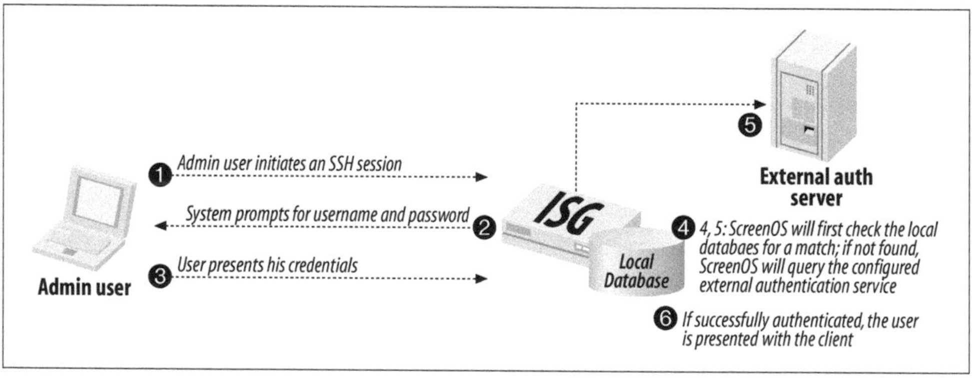

Figure 13-3. Example of admin authentication process

You must store the root admin account locally on the firewall. You can store all other admin accounts for the root level, or VSYS level, on an external authentication server. If you're using RADIUS, you can load the NetScreen dictionary file to provide VSAs that can be returned to the ScreenOS device assigning a privilege level. Optionally, you can assign a global privilege level of read/write or read-only for all admin users. If you're using SecurID, LDAP, or RADIUS without the dictionary file, you must configure the privilege level for the user in the local database.

Here is an excerpt from the NetScreen dictionary file:

```
# For Admin Privileges
# READ_WRITE (ALL): 2, VSYS_ADMIN: 3, READ_ONLY: 4, VSYS_READ_ONLY: 5
ATTRIBUTE NS-Admin-Privilege 26 [vid=3224 type1=1 len1=+2 data=int4] r
VALUE NS-Admin-Privilege        READ_WRITE      2
VALUE NS-Admin-Privilege        VSYS_ADMIN      3
VALUE NS-Admin-Privilege        READ_ONLY       4
VALUE NS-Admin-Privilege        VSYS_READ_ONLY  5

ATTRIBUTE NS-Admin-Vsys-Name 26 [vid=3224 type1=2 len1=+2 data=string] r
```

You can find examples of creating both local and external administrative user accounts in Recipe 13.1, Recipe 13.2, and Recipe 13.7.

Auth Users

You create auth users to be used in firewall policies. You can use one of two schemes.

In the first scheme, as shown in Figure 13-4, you use a standard auth policy to authenticate users attempting an HTTP, FTP, or Telnet connection across the firewall. In this form, ScreenOS intercepts the connection request and prompts the user for his username and password, meanwhile buffering the packets associated with the connection attempt. If successfully authenticated, the packets are forwarded to the target host and the connection proceeds.

In the optional scheme, the user authenticates to the firewall first, before attempting any connections through the firewall. This is known as *WebAuth*. Using WebAuth, users are authenticated and then can forward any type of traffic (not just Telnet, FTP, or HTTP) that may be permitted by the policy.

You can create authentication users within the local database on the firewall or on external authentication servers. Figure 13-5 shows the authentication process. You can find examples for configuring authentication policies in Recipe 13.4, Recipe 13.5, and Recipe 13.8.

For the second scheme that uses WebAuth, ScreenOS is configured with an additional IP address that will be bound to an internal web server process. This IP address should be in the same subnet as one of the interface IP addresses of the firewall. In this scheme, the authentication user will initially connect to the firewall WebAuth IP address where she will be prompted for her username and password prior to any firewall policy checks. Once authenticated to the firewall, the user will be added to the authentication table within ScreenOS and all traffic permitted by an authentication policy for that user or group will be forwarded. You can find examples for configuring WebAuth in Recipe 13.5.

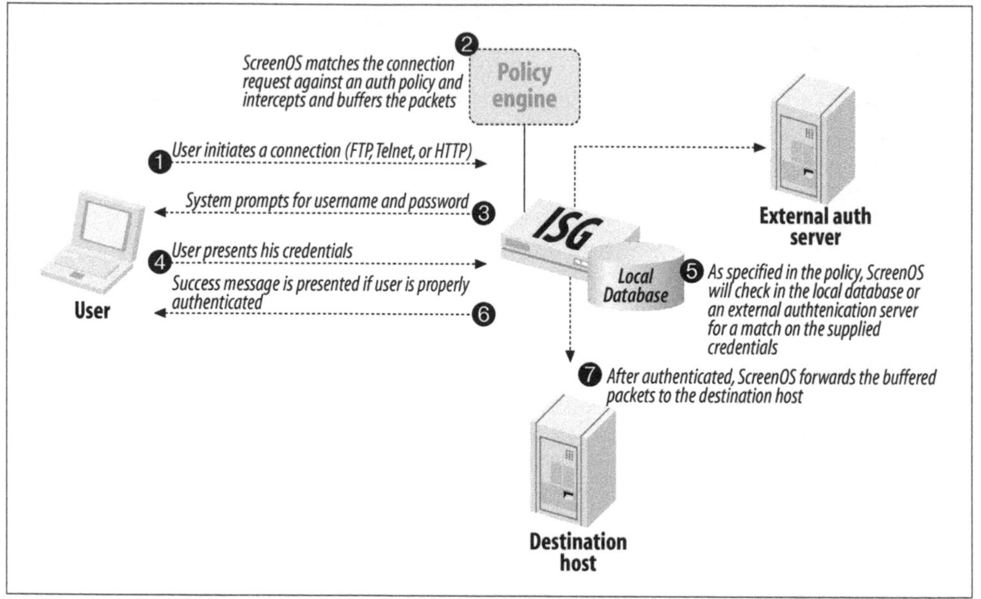

Figure 13-4. Example of user-based firewall authentication process

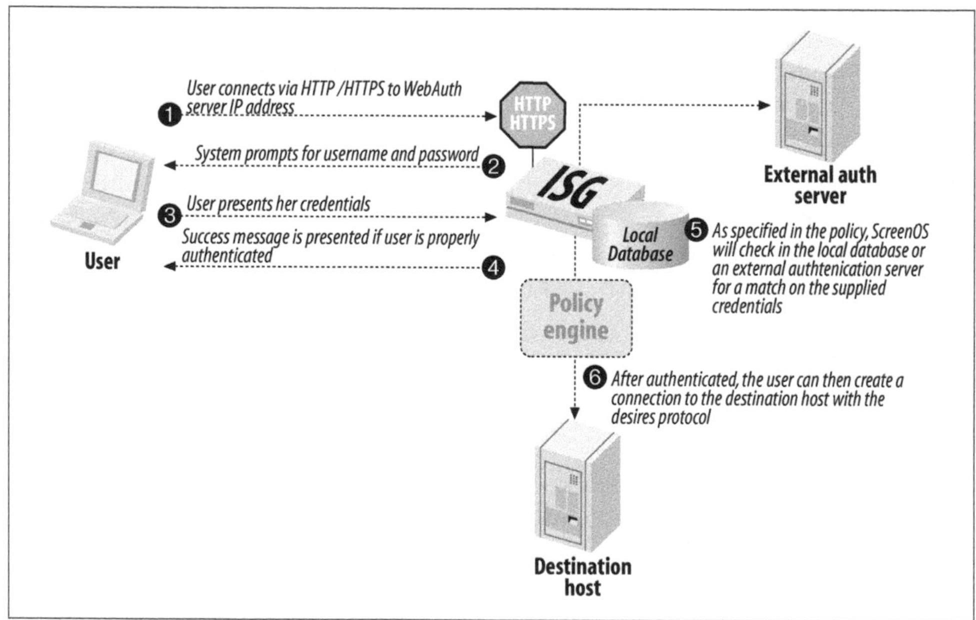

Figure 13-5. Example of prepolicy WebAuth authentication process

IKE, Xauth, and L2TP Users

ScreenOS supports both IP Security (IPSec) and L2TP. You can configure IKE, Xauth, and L2TP users and user groups for establishing these tunneled connections:

- You can create IKE users to link an IKE ID to a username for establishing an IPSec tunnel in aggressive mode. IKE users can only be stored on the local database.
- Xauth users are created for authentication and further assignment of networking information such as IP address, DNS server(s), and Windows Internet Naming Service (WINS) servers. Xauth users can reside locally or externally.
- L2TP users are created for establishing a Layer 2 tunnel and providing an IP address, DNS server(s), and WINS server information to the end system. L2TP users can reside locally or on external authentication servers.

For Xauth and L2TP, only the local security device or a RADIUS server can assign the IP, DNS, and WINS. LDAP and SecurID do not support this functionality; however, you can use a combination of servers for this purpose. For example, you could authenticate your Xauth users, via SecurID, and then assign the additional information from the local security device.

You can find examples of IKE users in Recipe 13.6.

Multiple-Type Users

You can combine IKE, Auth, L2TP, and Xauth users in the following combinations to store within the local database:

- Auth/IKE user
- Auth/IKE/Xauth user
- Auth/L2TP user
- IKE/Xauth user
- Auth/IKE/L2TP user
- L2TP/Xauth user
- IKE/L2TP user
- IKE/L2TP/Xauth user
- Auth/Xauth user
- Auth/IKE/L2TP/Xauth user

You should consider the following points when creating accounts with multiple types of use:

- Combining an IKE user type with any other user type limits the potential to scale. You must store an IKE user account on the local database. If you create auth/IKE, IKE/L2TP, and IKE/Xauth user accounts and the number of users grows beyond the capacity of the local database, you will not be able to relocate these accounts to an external auth server. If you separate IKE user accounts from other types of accounts, you have the flexibility to move the non-IKE user accounts to an external auth server should the need arise.
- L2TP and Xauth provide the same services: remote user authentication and IP, DNS server, and WINS server address assignments. It is not recommended to use L2TP and Xauth together for an L2TP-over-IPSec tunnel. Not only do the two protocols accomplish the same goal, but also the L2TP address assignments overwrite the Xauth address assignments after Phase-2 IKE negotiations are complete and L2TP negotiations take place.
- If you create a multiple-type user account on the local database combining auth/L2TP or auth/Xauth, the same username and password must be used for both logins.

Although it is more convenient to create a single multiple-type user account, separating the user types into two single accounts allows you to increase security. For example, you can store an auth user account on an external auth server and an Xauth user account on the local database. You can then assign different login usernames and passwords to each account and reference the Xauth user in the IKE gateway configuration and the auth user in the policy configuration. The dial-up VPN user must authenticate twice, potentially with two completely different usernames and passwords.

Group Expressions

You use a group expression within a policy to set conditions for authentication. Group expressions allow you to use users, groups, or other group expressions to create alternatives for authentication, such as matching *a or b*. In addition, you can use group expressions as requirements for authentication, such as *a and b*. You also can use group expressions to exclude users, user groups, or other group expressions such as *not a*.

Although you configure group expressions on the firewall the groups that the expressions reference must reside on a RADIUS server. RADIUS allows a user to be a member of multiple groups, whereas the local database does not.

Group expressions use three different operators: `AND`, `OR`, and `NOT`. The operators can relate to an auth user, auth user group, or previously defined group expression, as detailed in Table 13-2.

Table 13-2. Examples of group expression usages

Object	Expression	Usage
User	OR	A policy specifies that a user match "a" or "b" so that the user is authenticated if he matches either condition.
	AND	The group expression "AND" requires that at least one of the two expression objects be a user group or a group expression. For example, it is illogical to require a user to be both "user a" and "user b". A proper usage would be to require that the user be "user a" and be a member of "user group b", for example. Authentication succeeds only if both conditions are met.
	NOT	A policy can specify that the user be anyone except "c", for example (NOT c).
User groups	OR	A policy specifies that the user be a member of "group a" or "group b", and authentication succeeds if the user is a member of either group.
	AND	A policy specifies that the user be a member of "group a" and "group c", and authentication succeeds only if the user is a member of both groups.
	NOT	A policy specifies that the user not be a member of "group a", and authentication succeeds only if the user is not a member of "group a".
Group expressions	OR	A policy specifies that the user meets the criteria of "group expression a" or "group expression b", and authentication succeeds if the user meets either criterion.
	AND	A policy specifies that the user fits the description of both "group expression c" and "group expression d". Authentication succeeds only if the user meets both criteria.
	NOT	A policy specifies that the user does not meet the description of "group expression a", and authentication succeeds only if the user does not fit the description of "group expression a".

Login Banners

You use login banners to display the terms of use for the security device or protected resources behind the security device. Default messages are present for most banners, but you can customize them to meet the needs of the organization.

Here is an example banner that may be displayed upon login to a host system to inform the user of the terms of use:

> NOTICE TO USERS
>
> This is a Private computer (and/or it is directly connected to a private network system) that is the property of MyCompany, Inc. It is for authorized use only. Users (authorized or unauthorized) have no explicit or implicit expectation of privacy.
>
> Any or all uses of this system and all files on this system may be intercepted, monitored, recorded, copied, audited, inspected, and disclosed to law enforcement personnel, as well as authorized officials of other agencies, both domestic and foreign. By using this system, the user consents to such interception, monitoring, recording, copying, auditing, inspection, and disclosure at the discretion of MyCompany Inc. personnel.

Unauthorized or improper use of this system may result in administrative disciplinary action and civil and criminal penalties. By continuing to use this system, you indicate your awareness of and consent to these terms and conditions of use. LOG OFF IMMEDIATELY if you do not agree to the conditions stated in this warning.

ScreenOS supports multiple banners. Telnet, FTP, and HTTP protocols have three banners presented when used in authentication policies. A login banner is displayed with the login prompt and additional banners for successful and failed login attempts. WebAuth allows for a single banner for successful authentications.

One additional banner is available for administrative login. You can configure this login banner via the CLI or load it onto the security device as a file via the Secure Copy (SCP) protocol. You can find examples of creating an administrative login banner in Recipe 13.1. You can find examples of other authentication banners in Recipe 13.4 and Recipe 13.5.

The remainder of this chapter provides configuration recipes for various combinations of users, types, and authentication services.

13.1 Create Local Administrative Users

Problem

You want to secure the ScreenOS device with your chosen usernames and passwords.

Solution

Use the set `admin` context for this operation:

```
mydevice-> set admin name fwadmin
mydevice-> set admin password !secret$PW
mydevice-> set admin user "super" password "super$pw1" privilege all
mydevice-> set admin user "ro-admin" password "pwF0rRO" privilege
    "read-only"
mydevice-> set admin auth server local
```

Set a login banner for administrative access if desired:

```
mydevice-> set admin auth banner telnet login
"This security device may only be accessed by authorized firewall
administrators of my-company. All access is logged."
```

Discussion

A critical security task is to secure your firewall from unauthorized access to the configuration interfaces as well as add any additional user accounts for managing the firewall. ScreenOS devices ship with the default username `netscreen` and the default password `netscreen` for the "root" level account. You should change this immediately using this recipe's solution. Here, we have changed the existing root user account name to `fwadmin`, and set the password for that account to `!secret$PW`.

We have also created two additional users. One user, super, has full privileges, and another user, ro-admin, has read-only privileges. Lastly, we have specified that ScreenOS uses the local authentication server for firewall admins.

To show the configuration of users that have been created on the firewall, use the get admin user command:

```
mydevice-> get admin user
Name                             Privilege
-------------------------------- ---------------
fwadmin                          Root
super                            Read-Write
ro-admin                         Read-Only
```

Set a login banner for administrative access if desired:

```
mydevice-> set admin auth banner telnet login "This security device
may only be accessed by authorized firewall administrators of my-company.
All access is logged."
```

You can find additional information about preparing your device for initial operation in Chapter 2.

13.2 Create VSYS-Level Administrator Accounts

Problem

You want to create VSYS administrator accounts.

Solution

To create VSYS-level accounts, you must "enter" the vsys. Here we will enter vsys1:

```
mydevice-> enter vsys vsys1
mydevice(vsys1)-> set admin vsys name vadmin
mydevice(vsys1)-> set admin vsys password !secret$PW
mydevice(vsys1)-> set admin vsys user "vadminr-o" password "St1ng3r"
    privilege"read-only"
```

Discussion

ScreenOS supports VSYS on the higher-end devices. You can create user accounts to authenticate administrators of specific VSYS. A VSYS administrator will have read-only or read/write access only, within the VSYS in which the user account resides. A VSYS administrator cannot see any configuration information within the root level of the firewall or any other VSYS devices that have been created.

Here, vsys1 was created previously. By using the enter vsys command, we can access the VSYS named vsys1. A simple variation on the preceding recipe provides the ability to create our VSYS admin accounts. From the following output, you can see the two accounts within the virtual system:

```
mydevice(vsys1)-> get admin user
Name                             Privilege
-------------------------------- --------------
vadmin                           VSYS Read-Write
vadminr-o                        VSYS Read-Only
```

You can find more information on VSYS in Chapter 21.

13.3 Create User Groups for Authentication Policies

Problem

You want to create user groups instead of managing users individually.

Solution

Rather than manage each user individually, you can gather users into a group so that any changes made to the group propagate to each group member:

```
mydevice->set user jim password mypass06
mydevice->set user kim password mypass07
mydevice->set user bill password mypass08
mydevice->set user bill type ike xauth
mydevice->set user pearl password mypass09
mydevice->set user pearl type ike xauth
mydevice->set admin user bill password billpass99 type ike
mydevice->set user-group auth_grp1 location local
mydevice->set user-group auth_grp1 user jim
mydevice->set user-group auth_grp1 user kim
mydevice->set user-group vpn location local
mydevice->set user-group vpn user bill
mydevice->set user-group vpn user pearl
```

Discussion

By default, creating a user with a password creates a user account type of "auth". When you create a user group in ScreenOS, the type remains undefined until you add a user to the group, at which point the group inherits the type(s) of accounts from the user definitions. You can create groups with multiple types by adding such users as Xauth, IKE, and L2TP to the group. However, you cannot combine the admin user with any other type of account. Any user account can be a member of up to four user groups.

In the solution to this recipe, four users and two user groups are defined. Users `jim` and `kim` are members of the `auth_grp1` user group and users `bill` and `pearl` are members of the `vpn` group. User `jim` is also a member of the `local` group. We can view the group memberships with the `get user-group` command:

```
mydevice-> get user-group auth_grp1
GroupId:   3                   Group Name    : auth_grp1
Type    : auth                 Total members :   2
```

```
Location      : local
Use cnt: Gateway 0, Firewall 0, L2TP 0, XAuth 0
Users:
Id    User name   Enable   Type  ID-type Identity   Belongs to groups
----- ----------- ------ ------- ------- ---------- -----------------
  101 jim         Yes     auth                          local auth_gr.
    6 kim         Yes     auth                          auth_grp1


mydevice-> get user-group vpn
GroupId:   2                   Group Name    : vpn
Type   : ike xauth             Total members :   2
Location      : local
Use cnt: Gateway 0, Firewall 0, L2TP 0, XAuth 0
Users:
Id    User name  Enable   Type  ID-type Identity   Belongs to groups
----- ---------- ------ ------- ------- ---------- -----------------
    4 bill       Yes     ike xauth      NONE               vpn
    5 pearl      Yes     ike xauth      NONE               vpn
```

You can also view individual users and group memberships with the get user command:

```
mydevice-> get user all
Total users: 6
Id    User name  Enable      Type ID-type Identity Belongs to groups
----- ---------- ------- --------- ------- -------- -----------------
    4 bill       Yes     ike xauth NONE             vpn
  100 dude       Yes     auth                       local
  101 jim        Yes     auth                       local auth_gr..
    6 kim        Yes     auth                       auth_grp1
    3 louis      Yes     auth
    5 pearl      Yes     ike xauth NONE             vpn
user with ASN1_DN type ID sort list:
```

User groups can now be used in VPN or authentication policies, as shown in the following recipes.

You can find more information on setting up VPN scenarios in Chapter 10.

13.4 Use Authentication Policies

Problem

You want to require user authentication before permitting an FTP connection across the firewall.

Solution

This solution touches on a few areas of ScreenOS configuration, users, objects, policies, and banners.

User and group:

```
mydevice->set user "jim" uid 100
mydevice->set user "jim" type  auth
mydevice->set user "jim" password $somePw671
mydevice->set user "jim" "enable"
mydevice->set user-group "local" id 100
mydevice->set user-group "local" user "jim"
```

Objects:

```
mydevice->set address trust user-a 10.1.1.1/32
mydevice->set address dmz server-a 10.2.2.2/32
```

Policy:

```
mydevice->set policy id 11 top from trust to dmz user-a server-a ftp
permit auth user-group local log
```

Banners:

```
mydevice-> set auth banner ftp login "Please enter your username and
password to be authenticated by this security device"

mydevice-> set auth banner ftp success "You are now authenticated.
You may proceed with your ftp session"

mydevice-> set auth banner ftp fail "The username and password
presented is not authorized for this ftp session"
```

Discussion

In this section, we will provide an example of simple user authentication within a firewall policy for FTP. ScreenOS permits this type of authentication for FTP and Telnet. These protocols can support an interactive style of communication that allows for prompting of user credentials.

ScreenOS will cache these credentials and offer them to the FTP server. This means that if the user credentials configured on the firewall match the FTP login credentials, the user will be automatically logged into the FTP server, having to provide credentials only once. If the username and password do not match the FTP server login process, the user will have to log in to the FTP server again and provide the correct credentials.

Upon successfully authenticating to the firewall, ScreenOS will create an entry in the authentication table for the user's IP address. You can view this authentication table with the `get auth table` command:

```
mydevice-> get auth table
Total users in table:     1
  Successful:      1, Failed:     0
  Pending   :      0, Others:     0
  Infranet users :      0
Col T: D = Default, W= WebAuth, I= Infranet, A= Auth server in policy
```

```
id src      user   group    age status   server T srczone  dstzone
 1 10.1.1.1 jim    local      0 Success  Local  D Untrust  Trust
```

Additional commands are available for the get auth context. An example is the get auth statistics command:

```
mydevice-> get auth statistics
Values of the following:
  Current entries in Auth Queue: 0
  Maximum entries ever in Auth Queue: 0

Number of times the following have happened:
  Auth Queue was full: 0
  LDAP connect failed: 0
  Out of Auth Msg Bufs: 0
  Auth table entry unavailable: 0
  Could not send mail to Auth task: 0
  Auth callback func called: 0 times
  Select( ) has data: 0 times
  Select( ) has data on socket: 0 times
  Authq entry allocated: 0, freed: 0
Radius counters:
  Authentication:
    L2TP/XAuth Access Requests sent: 0
    Admin/FW Access Requests sent: 0
    Total Access Accepts Received 0
    Total Access Rejects Received 0
    Total Access Challenges Received 0
    Authenticator in Accept/Reject/Challenge: Valid: 0, Invalid: 0

  Accounting:
    Accounting Start Requests sent: 0
    Accounting Start Response recd: 0 (Valid: 0, Invalid: 0)

    Accounting Stop Requests sent: 0
    Accounting Stop Response recd: 0 (Valid: 0, Invalid: 0)
    Accounting Stop Retry attempts: 0

    Total Accounting Responses recd: 0
    Authenticator in Accounting Response: Valid: 0, Invalid: 0

  Total Radius Packets sent: 0
  Total Radius Packets recd: 0
  Total Radius Retry attempts: 0
```

Entries within the auth table have a timeout to remove entries with idle connections. This inactivity timer is set to 10 minutes by default, but you can change it to any value between 0 and 255 minutes:

```
mydevice-> set auth-server Local timeout ?
<number> timeout in minutes. Valid range 0 - 255 (1000 for
admin timeout)
```

You can find additional information on policy configuration in Chapter 7.

13.5 Use WebAuth with the Local Database

Problem

You want to use WebAuth to authenticate a user prior to policy-checking other traffic, similar to the scenario shown in Figure 13-6.

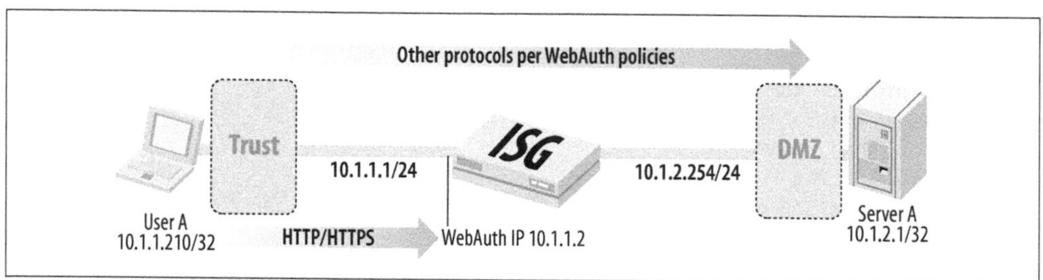

Figure 13-6. WebAuth process

Solution

WebAuth authenticates the user credentials and then creates an entry in the auth table for the IP address of the user host machine.

User and group:

```
mydevice->set user "jim" uid 100
mydevice->set user "jim" type  auth
mydevice->set user "jim" password $somePw671
mydevice->set user "jim" "enable"
mydevice->set user-group "local" id 100
mydevice->set user-group "local" user "jim"
```

WebAuth:

```
mydevice-> set webauth server Local
mydevice-> set interf e0/0 webauth-ip 10.1.1.2
mydevice-> set interf e0/0 webauth
mydevice-> set auth-server Local timeout 30
```

Policy:

```
mydevice-> set pol id 12 from trust to dmz user-a server-a ftp permit
webauth user-group local log
mydevice-> set pol move 12 after 11
```

Banner:

```
mydevice-> set webauth banner success "You have successfully
authenticated to the firewall. You may now use your other applications."
```

Discussion

WebAuth allows user authentication prior to policy checking. Upon successful authentication, an entry is created within the auth table for the IP address of the user's workstation. This entry in the auth table is checked for each session that matches a rule with the WebAuth option enabled. You can choose whether to use clear text HTTP or HTTPS (SSL) for this authentication. For example:

```
mydevice-> set interf e0/0 webauth ssl-only
```

You can use WebAuth with the local database or an external authentication server. The main requirement is that WebAuth be used with the user account type of "auth".

You can configure the WebAuth server on any physical interface, subinterface, or Virtual Security Interface (VSI), but it must be an address in the same subnet as the chosen interface. You also can configure WebAuth on multiple interfaces. If you have multiple interfaces bound to the same security zone, you can put a WebAuth IP address on one interface, and traffic from other interfaces within the same zone can still reach it.

You also can use WebAuth in transparent mode with a WebAuth IP address chosen in the same subnet as the `vlan1` interface.

Be aware that after a security device authenticates a user at a particular source IP address, it subsequently permits traffic—as specified in the policy requiring authentication via WebAuth—from any other user at that same address. This might be the case if the users originate traffic from behind a Network Address Translation (NAT) device that changes all original source addresses to a single translated address.

You can view entries within the auth table with the `get auth table` command:

```
mydevice-> get auth table
Total users in table:     1
  Successful:     1, Failed:     0
  Pending   :     0, Others:     0
  Infranet users :     0
Col T: D= Default, W= WebAuth, I= Infranet, A= Auth server in policy
  id src        user group    age status   server T srczone  dstzone
   1 10.1.1.1 jim   local      0 Success  Local  D Untrust  Trust
```

The ScreenOS event log also has entries associated with WebAuth authentication events. Event type 518 displays authentication failures for WebAuth, and type 519 displays successful WebAuth authentications:

```
mydevice-> get event type 518
Date       Time     Module Level  Type Description
2006-03-14 12:27:51 system warn  00518 Local authentication for
```

```
WebAuth user jeff at 10.1.1.210 was denied
2006-03-14 12:27:42 system warn  00518 Local authentication for
WebAuth user jeff at 10.1.1.210 was denied
2006-03-14 12:27:31 system warn  00518 Local authentication for
WebAuth user jeff at 10.1.1.210 was denied
2006-03-11 16:13:19 system warn  00518 ADM: Local admin authentication
failed for login name 'fwadmin':  invalid password
2006-03-11 16:10:28 system warn  00518 Local authentication for WebAuth
user joe at 10.1.1.210 was denied
Total entries matched = 5


mydevice-> get event type 519
Date       Time     Module Level  Type Description
2006-03-14 12:25:19 system warn  00519 Local authentication for WebAuth
user kim at 10.1.1.210 was successful
2006-03-14 12:24:38 system warn  00519 Local authentication for WebAuth
user jim at 10.1.1.210 was successful
2006-03-14 12:23:06 system warn  00519 Local authentication for WebAuth
user dude at 10.1.1.210 was successful
2006-03-11 16:20:32 system warn  00519 Local authentication for user
dude at 10.1.1.210 was successful
2006-03-11 16:19:27 system warn  00519 Local authentication for user
dude at 10.1.1.210 was successful
2006-03-11 16:17:42 system warn  00519 Local authentication for WebAuth
user dude at 10.1.1.210 was successful
2006-03-11 16:12:09 system warn  00519 Local authentication for WebAuth
user dude at 10.1.1.210 was successful
Total entries matched = 7
```

You can find additional information on policy configuration in Chapter 7.

13.6 Create VPN Users with the Local Database

Problem

You want to create VPN users and groups for both IKE and Xauth authentication.

Solution

For this recipe, you'll need to create both IKE and Xauth user types. Passwords are assigned for Xauth authentication, and you must configure remote networking settings for the Xauth users. Note that you can store only IKE users and user groups on the local database.

First, create the users:

```
mydevice-> set user alex ike-id u-fqdn alex@mycompany.com
mydevice-> set user ben ike-id ip 24.1.1.1
mydevice-> set user cal ike-id fqdn www.juniper.net
mydevice-> set used dan ike-id asn1-dn wildcard
   CN=clark,OU=dan,O=mycompany,L=dallas,ST=tx,C=us,E=cal@mycompany.com
```

Then, set the account types for the users:

```
mydevice-> set user alex type ike xauth
mydevice-> set user ben type ike xauth
mydevice-> set user cal type ike xauth
mydevice-> set user dan type ike xauth
```

Set passwords for each user:

```
mydevice-> set user alex password pass1
mydevice-> set user ben password pass2
mydevice-> set user cal password pass3
mydevice-> set user dan password pass4
```

Create the IP address pool:

```
mydevice-> set ippool vpn1pool 10.60.1.1 10.60.1.100
```

Assign remote networking settings for each user:

```
mydevice-> set user alex remote ippool vpn1pool
mydevice-> set user alex remote dns1 10.10.10.30
mydevice-> set user alex remote wins1 10.10.10.30
mydevice-> set user ben remote ippool vpn1pool
mydevice-> set user ben remote dns1 10.10.10.30
mydevice-> set user ben remote wins1 10.10.10.30
mydevice-> set user cal remote ippool vpn1pool
mydevice-> set user cal remote dns1 10.10.10.30
mydevice-> set user cal remote wins1 10.10.10.30
mydevice-> set user dan remote ippool vpn1pool
mydevice-> set user dan remote dns1 10.10.10.30
mydevice-> set user dan remote wins1 10.10.10.30
```

And finally, create the group and add its users:

```
mydevice-> set user-group vpnauth location local
mydevice-> set user-group vpnauth user alex
mydevice-> set user-group vpnauth user ben
mydevice-> set user-group vpnauth user cal
mydevice-> set user-group vpnauth user dan
```

Discussion

In ScreenOS, an IKE user is for VPN tunnel establishment typically when the end system will have a dynamically assigned IP address. In this case, you must use an IKE ID to establish the Phase-1 Security Association (SA). The IKE ID can be one of four types. In this example, there are four users, each with a different type of IKE ID, and they are placed in a group called `vpnauth`.

Each user is configured to be of type IKE and Xauth. You can view users and group configurations with the `get user` commands:

```
mydevice-> get user all
Total users: 11
Id    User name Enable    Type    ID-type Identity   Belongs to groups
```

```
----- --------- ---------------- ------- ---------- -----------------
    7 alex      Yes   ike xauth   USER-DN alex@mycompany.com vpnauth
    8 ben       Yes   ike xauth   IPV4    24.1.1.1   vpnauth
    4 bill      Yes   ike xauth   NONE               vpn
    9 cal       Yes   ike xauth   FQDN    www.juniper.net vpnauth
   10 dan       Yes   ike xauth   ASN1-DN
CN=clark,OU=dan,O=mycompany,L=dallas,ST=tx,C=us,Email=cal@mycompan
.com,DC=, vpnauth
  100 dude       Yes     auth                         local
   11 eve        Yes     l2tp xauth
  101 jim        Yes     auth                         local admin_gr..
    6 kim        Yes     auth                            admin_grp1
    3 louis      Yes     auth
    5 pearl       Yes     ike xauth      NONE              vpn
user with ASN1_DN type ID sort list:
[0]=10u
```

Here, our users are created as IDs 7–10, are enabled, are of type IKE and Xauth, with the IKE ID type and identity, and are members of the vpnauth group.

A more detailed look at user alex will show the remote settings assigned to this user:

```
mydevice-> get user alex
Id  User name  Enable     Type  ID-type Identity   Belongs to groups
--- ---------- ------ --------- ------- ---------- -----------------
  7 alex       Yes    ike xauth USER-DN alex@mycompany.com vpnauth
user type<00000034>.
Number login with this user id is 1. gw_use_cnt<0>
identity type<3>.
identity <alex@mycompany.com>.
Remote IP          : 0.0.0.0          IP Pool Name         :vpn1pool
Remote Primary DNS : 10.10.10.30      Remote Secondary DNS : 0.0.0.0
Remote Primary WINS: 10.10.10.30      Remote Secondary WINS: 0.0.0.0
Static IP          : 0.0.0.0
User belongs to group(s):  vpnauth
```

You must remove a user from any groups or policies before making changes to the user. For example:

```
mydevice-> set user alex type ike
User alex is in use
```

The user alex is a member of a user group. You would see the same message if the user was configured within a policy.

In the preceding example, each user was assigned remote networking settings. A variation on this is to use the Xauth server to assign these values. Using the Xauth server to assign these values is recommended when a large number of users will be connecting to the security device. More detailed information on using Xauth, IKE, and VPN tunnels is available in Chapter 10.

13.7 Use RADIUS for Admin Authentication

Problem

You want to use Windows Active Directory accounts with the Microsoft Internet Authentication Service (IAS) as the RADIUS server for administrator authentication.

Solution

You can configure any user, other than the "root" user, for RADIUS authentication and privilege assignment from the RADIUS server.

First, define the auth-server properties:

```
mydevice-> set auth-server "IAS" id 1
mydevice-> set auth-server "IAS" server-name "10.1.1.66"
mydevice-> set auth-server "IAS" account-type admin
mydevice-> set auth-server "IAS" radius secret "netscreen"
mydevice-> set auth-server "IAS" radius retries 3
mydevice-> set auth-server "IAS" radius timeout 5
mydevice-> set auth-server "IAS" account-type admin
```

Then, specify what privilege should be assigned by the remote authentication server:

```
mydevice-> set admin privilege get-external
```

And finally, choose the external server as the default for admin authentication:

```
mydevice-> set admin auth server "IAS"
```

Discussion

In this section, we will provide a ScreenOS configuration example for using Microsoft IAS, which is included with Windows 2003 Server. It is common to want to leverage the existing credentials present in the Active Directory of the domain controller. Therefore, here we have used a combination of RADIUS and LDAP to authenticate administrators of the security device, even though ScreenOS is only aware of the RADIUS server.

The first part of the configuration defines the external authentication server properties to be used. Next, ScreenOS is instructed to get the privilege, either read/write or read-only, from the external server. Finally, the new authentication server is set as the default for admin authentication.

You can view the configuration of this newly created authentication server with the get auth-server command:

```
mydevice-> get auth-server IAS
Id     :  1                  Auth Server    : IAS
Type   : Radius              Server Name/IP: 10.1.1.66
Backup1:                     Backup2        :
```

```
Idle Timeout:    10            Account Type  : admin
Forced Timeout: 0 (Disabled)
Fail-over revert interval: Disabled
Radius shared secret: 7VV93tUaNXoxWnsEeACurDXZWHndDAe4AQ==
Radius server port  : 1645
Radius retry timeout: 5 second(s), Number of retries: 3
```

The root user account of the security device can only reside locally. It cannot reside on an external authentication server, and ScreenOS will always search for the user account within the local database first. If it cannot find the user account, it will consult the external server configured to serve the admin account type.

RADIUS is the preferred external authentication server type, as it supports the ability to assign the privilege level, whereas LDAP and SecurID do not have this ability. As shown in this example, you can combine RADIUS with LDAP.

You also can combine it with SecurID in the same fashion. Therefore, it is recommended that you use this approach for authenticating external administrator accounts.

For the Microsoft part of the configuration, you should consult the appropriate documentation for assistance, but here is a quick tutorial:

1. Create a Windows group such as "firewall admins" and make each admin a member of the group.
2. When creating the client profile, match on the NAS IP address (which will be the ScreenOS interface IP), and enter the same shared secret as that which was entered on the ScreenOS auth server configuration.
3. Create an access policy and match on the NAS IP address and the Windows group created in step 1.
4. Click Edit Profile, and use PAP in the Authentication tab.
5. In the Advanced tab, add a vendor-specific attribute with vendor code 3224 and click "Yes it conforms".
6. Click the "Edit attribute" button, and in the first field type **1**, the second field will be "decimal", and the last field will be "2" for read/write, or "4" for read-only.

If you do not configure a VSA to be returned to ScreenOS, the default permissions will be chosen. The default is read-only, but you can change this to read/write with the command `set admin privilege read-write`.

You can find additional information on setting up administrators or setting service options on the interface in Chapter 2.

13.8 Use LDAP for Policy-Based Authentication

Problem

You want to use an LDAP database for authentication within auth or WebAuth policies.

Solution

Configure an auth server with the LDAP properties that match your environment by first defining the auth-server properties:

```
mydevice-> set auth-server "my-ldap" type ldap
mydevice-> set auth-server "my-ldap" account-type auth
mydevice-> set auth-server "my-ldap" server-name 10.1.1.66
mydevice-> set auth-server "my-ldap" backup1 10.1.1.67
mydevice-> set auth-server "my-ldap" backup2 10.1.1.68
mydevice-> set auth-server "my-ldap" timeout 30
mydevice-> set auth-server "my-ldap" ldap port 389
mydevice-> set auth-server "my-ldap" ldap cn cn
```

Then, set the base dn:

```
mydevice-> set auth-server "my-ldap" ldap dn c=us;o=mycompany;ou=sales
```

Set the server as the default for the account-type auth:

```
mydevice-> set auth default auth server my-ldap
```

And, use it within a policy:

```
mydevice-> set pol top from untrust to dmz any server-a svc-grp1
permit auth log
```

Discussion

Sometimes you do not know the IP address from which authorized users may be accessing protected resources. Because of this, administrators have been known to use the any object in the source address field of the rule permitting such access. This is an example of why it is difficult to secure networks.

ScreenOS offers the auth and WebAuth features to help with security. With these authentication features, you can use the any identifier in the rule and still be assured that only authorized users can gain access to protected resources.

Here, we have defined the authentication server to use with policy authentication to be an LDAP server by defining a group of servers with a logical name of my-ldap and a server type of ldap, and we set these servers to serve the authentication requests for the auth account type. The server name could be a name resolvable via DNS, or as defined here, simply an IP address. The default timeout of 10 minutes was changed to 30 minutes, so after an idle time of 30 minutes on any given session, the authentication status will be removed, and the user will have to reauthenticate.

The server at 10.1.1.66 will be the primary LDAP server. If this server does not respond, the security device will try the backup1 server at 10.1.1.67. If neither responds, the backup2 server will be tried.

You can view the configuration of the newly defined authentication server with the get auth-server command:

```
mydevice-> get auth-server my-ldap
Id      :   2                   Auth Server    : my-ldap
Type    : LDAP                  Server Name/IP: 10.1.1.66
Backup1: 10.1.1.67              Backup2        : 10.1.1.68
Idle Timeout:    30             Account Type   : auth
Forced Timeout: 0 (Disabled)
Fail-over revert interval: Disabled
LDAP server port              : 389
LDAP distinguished name (dn): c=us;o=mycompany;ou=sales
LDAP common name identifier : cn
```

The server was set to be the default server for account type "auth"; you can verify this by issuing the get auth settings command:

```
mydevice-> get auth settings
Id      :   2                   Auth Server    : my-ldap
Type    : LDAP                  Server Name/IP: 10.1.1.66
Backup1: 10.1.1.67              Backup2        : 10.1.1.68
Idle Timeout:    30             Account Type   : auth
Forced Timeout: 0 (Disabled)
Fail-over revert interval: Disabled
LDAP server port              : 389
LDAP distinguished name (dn): c=us;o=mycompany;ou=sales
LDAP common name identifier : cn
```

The output of the get auth settings command shows that our newly defined server will be the default for policy-based authentication.

This authentication server is now ready to use with any auth or WebAuth rules within the security device. Recipe 13.4 and Recipe 13.5 are applicable here, as once you have defined the external authentication server, you can use it in the other user authentication schemes in this chapter.

For more information on using policies, please refer to Chapter 7.

13.9 Use SecurID for Policy-Based Authentication

Problem

You want to use your SecurID authentication server for authentication within auth or WebAuth policies.

Solution

Configure an authentication server with properties to match your environment.

First, define the auth-server properties:

```
mydevice-> set auth-server "ace1" type securid
mydevice-> set auth-server "ace1" server-name 10.1.1.88
mydevice-> set auth-server "ace1" backup1 10.1.1.188
mydevice-> set auth-server "ace1" timeout 40
mydevice-> set auth-server "ace1" account-type auth
mydevice-> set auth-server "ace1" securid retries 3
mydevice-> set auth-server "ace1" securid timeout 10
mydevice-> set auth-server "ace1" securid auth-port 5000
mydevice-> set auth-server "ace1" securid encr 1
mydevice-> set auth-server "ace1" securid duress 0
```

Set this server as the default for account type "auth":

```
mydevice-> set auth default auth server ace1
```

Then, use it within a policy:

```
mydevice-> set pol top from untrust to dmz any server-a svc-grp1
permit auth log
```

Discussion

SecurID is a product available from RSA that provides for strong, two-factor authentication. The product consists of server software and individual authenticators. The authenticators are available in a variety of forms, but the most common are keychain-style fobs that produce pseudorandom numbers as one-time passwords. A typical user would enter her username, followed by her PIN, and then enter the numbers currently displayed on her authenticator device. The server upon which the software is installed is referred to as the "Ace" server.

You can use SecurID authentication servers for policy-based authentication, admin authentication, and Xauth/L2TP authentication. However, because the SecurID server cannot send any configuration data back to the ScreenOS device, SecurID is best suited for policy-based authentication. The SecurID server is natively supported within ScreenOS.

In the following example, we will create the authentication server and accept the default ID assigned by ScreenOS. We set the primary server to be at address `10.1.1.88` and to have a backup server at `10.1.1.188`. We set the timeout for inactivity within an authenticated session to 40. Lastly, we set specific SecurID properties for the number of retries for reaching the Ace server. We set a timeout of 10 seconds for awaiting a response from the Ace server; we set the port the server is listening on to 5,000; we set encryption to 1, which is DES; and we set the duress mode to disabled.

Use the `get auth-server` command to view the properties of the newly configured SecurID server object:

```
mydevice-> get auth-server ace1
Id      :   3                   Auth Server    : ace1
Type    : SecurID               Server Name/IP: 10.1.1.88
Backup1: 10.1.1.188             Backup2        :
Idle Timeout:    40             Account Type   : auth
Forced Timeout: 0 (Disabled)
Fail-over revert interval: Disabled
SecurID Authentication Port: 5000
SecurID Use Duress          : NO
SecurID Encryption Type     : DES
SecurID Timeout             : 10
SecurID Max Number Retries : 3
```

Set the server to be the default for account type "auth", which you can verify with the `get auth settings` command:

```
mydevice-> get auth settings
Id      :   3                   Auth Server    : ace1
Type    : SecurID               Server Name/IP: 10.1.1.88
Backup1: 10.1.1.188             Backup2        :
Idle Timeout:    40             Account Type   : auth
Forced Timeout: 0 (Disabled)
Fail-over revert interval: Disabled
SecurID Authentication Port: 5000
SecurID Use Duress          : NO
SecurID Encryption Type     : DES
SecurID Timeout             : 10
SecurID Max Number Retries : 3
```

This authentication server is now ready to use with any auth or WebAuth rules within the security device. Recipe 13.4 and Recipe 13.5 are applicable here, as once you have defined the external authentication server, you can use it with other user authentication recipes in this chapter.

CHAPTER 14
Traffic Shaping

14.0 Introduction

Quality of Service (QoS) deals with the order of packets in transmission queues, also called *outgoing interface buffers*, by controlling the order in which packets are dispatched from those queues. The simplest form is called *FIFO* (first in, first out) queuing, whereby an interface has a single outgoing buffer in which packets are dispatched into the link in the order they arrive in the queue. More sophisticated forms use multiple queues and complex distribution schemes, and can even manipulate higher-protocol-layer traffic control mechanisms. QoS is an important part of today's shared public backbone networks. Although QoS is essential for providers to deliver service-level agreements (SLAs) to their subscribers, it never gained the same significance in enterprise networks.

On ScreenOS devices, QoS was developed to provide better utilization for narrow band access links, in particular those with a speed of 1.5 Mbps or lower. QoS can help to soften the spikes in bursty traffic flows, therefore increasing overall bandwidth utilization, but it cannot increase bandwidth over those provided by the network, as it is not a compression technology. It is also possible to prioritize one traffic flow over another, causing degradation of the lower-priority traffic flow, and it can even block the lower-priority traffic flow altogether. QoS is therefore not a magic bullet for solving bandwidth problems. Increasing network bandwidth would be the solution for that.

As wide area networks (WANs) became faster and cheaper over the past few years, the original reason for implementing QoS in the enterprise disappeared because the effects of bursty traffic are lower the faster the network becomes (and it's never desirable to drop traffic, even if it is lower-priority). In recent years, QoS has became popular again, not for assisting traffic on slow links but to increase service quality for real-time traffic flows such as Voice over IP (VoIP). Real-time traffic suffers from delay and jitter. *Delay* is caused when a real-time traffic packet has to wait in a transmission queue for a larger packet to be dispatched first. *Jitter* occurs when the gap in time between different packets changes from packet to packet. Because real-time flows are usually distributed over very small packets, which are dispatched with an equal spacing, delays in interface buffers can alter the inter-packet delay differently for each packet. This is also most noticeable on slow links. The benefits of QoS diminish on Ethernet-speed links, but it can be quite significant for remote sites with slow access links, such as VoIP over Asymmetric Digital Subscriber Line (ADSL) with a slow uplink speed.

QoS has no effect on transmission quality in the network unless the quality is agreed upon with the provider in what is referred to as *traffic qualification* or *traffic marking*. In this context, QoS signals a desired behavior within the network. Providers police traffic according to agreements and the SLA specifies the preferred traffic classes and priorities for that customer. The Internet is commonly a best-effort service level, whereas Multiprotocol Label Switching (MPLS) providers commonly offer different service levels to their customers. (The old Plesiochronous Hierarchy [PDH] and Sonet networks are line rate—there is a fixed share of bandwidth reserved whether it is used by the subscriber or not.) Therefore, traffic marking has benefits only when an agreement with a service provider exists to honor the marking *and* the provider uses a shared infrastructure such as MPLS or IP Security (IPSec) virtual private networks (VPNs).

For enterprise networks, the benefits of QoS can be seen at remote sites. Therefore, traffic shaping is not implemented on large ASIC devices, such as the ISG and the NS-5000 Series, but it is implemented for SSG devices and most of the older ScreenOS devices. All models support traffic marking.

There are essentially two ways to configure traffic shaping: *strict priority queuing* and an automated or custom distribution scheme often called *fair queuing* or *custom queuing*. ScreenOS uses a combination of the two. In ScreenOS, there are eight strict priority queues, controlled by a dual-bucket model per policy. In simple terms, traffic shaping is configured per policy by placing that policy in a certain priority queue. Higher-priority queues can crowd out traffic for lower-priority queues, so there is a safety mechanism similar to custom queuing that can be configured on a per-policy basis, called *maximum bandwidth* (MBW). MBW avoids runaway queues; after the MBW for a policy is reached, or there is no more traffic queued in that queue, the next queue is served. In addition to having MBW on a per-policy basis, a *guaranteed bandwidth* (GBW) can be configured. GBW reserves traffic of a certain portion of the network speed for a given policy. The GBW of all policies in the same interface (zone) combination cannot add up to more than the bandwidth provided in the network. (Although technically possible, oversubscription would break the model and should never be configured.) Traffic above GBW is shared on a first come, first serve basis within a queue priority.

Traffic shaping can be defined as *ingress* or *egress*. This means that from the perspective of the policy, egress policing is configured via the MBW and the GBW object from the client-to-server direction, but is also applied for the return flow. Ingress policing is configured via a *policing bandwidth* (PBW) and GBW when the traffic enters the firewall, but it is applied as well for both directions of a flow. (PBW was introduced in ScreenOS 5.3.)

GBW, MBW, PBW, and queue priorities are associated with policies. Within each policy and within each queue, traffic flow is determined by first come, first serve. Traffic is controlled when a packet enters the firewall and it is matched to a policy. Both branches of a flow, from client to server and reverse, are associated with the same policy. First the policy is checked to see whether it has GBW configured. If it does but GBW for that policy has not been reached, the packet is queued for immediate transmission. Because all of the GBW together must be below network speed and therefore at or below the line rate, no packet reordering needs to take place. If GBW has been reached, or no GBW was configured, MBW (or PBW) is checked. If the policy reached MBW (or PBW), the packet is dropped. If the policy is under MBW (or PBW), the packet is placed in the queue, configured on that policy. Because higher-priority queues are served first, it is possible that higher-priority queues will crowd out all lower-priority queues and that a packet will never be transmitted. If this happens, the packet is saved in the queue until the buffer depth is reached and then dropped. There is no prioritization of traffic within a flow or session, and therefore, the packet order stays the same within each flow.

The buffer depth depends on the device model and is usually a few milliseconds deep. Deeper queues cause more jitter; therefore, it may be more beneficial to simply drop a packet if it has not been transmitted after a few milliseconds instead of delaying it. If a packet is being dropped, the traffic control mechanism of higher layers kicks in. For instance, Transmission Control Protocol (TCP) flows will decrease window size and transmission rate until traffic is no longer dropped. ScreenOS does not implement *Weighted Fair Queuing* (WFQ) or *Random Early Drop* (RED). (WFQ is a technology to enhance the feel of interactive traffic on very slow links, and RED is a simple throttling technology used in high-speed links in provider networks.) ScreenOS instead changed the window size to throttle TCP traffic. User Datagram Protocol (UDP), unicast, and multicast rely on the application or out-of-band mechanism to control transmission rate.

Beginning with ScreenOS 5.3, queues are also implemented on virtual interfaces. All GBW and MBW is shared in an interface tree. On the root of the tree is the physical interface. A virtual local area network (VLAN) subinterface could be, for instance, a child interface of a physical Ethernet interface. A VLAN subinterface itself could be a parent for a VPN tunnel interface. ScreenOS associates a Traffic Management Object (TMNG) to each parent and child interface. The meaning of GBW does not change.

It is the maximum network speed and cannot be larger than the speed of the physical access link. This means all GBW from all interfaces in a tree cannot add up to more than the physical interface's line rate. MBW and PBW are *spillover objects*. Whatever is not used up from one child interface is available to the parent interface. The internal workings of TMNG and child and parent interfaces are transparent to the user. There is no configuration parameter associated with it. Remember, all GBW in an interface tree cannot be higher than the (real) access rate of the interface for a given direction.

Policy-based traffic shaping is an initial ScreenOS feature, but is implemented only on non-ASIC platforms; interface policing, meanwhile, was implemented only on the NS-5000 with some special code trains of ScreenOS 4.0 and later. ScreenOS 5.4 introduced interface policing for all platforms, whereas policy-based traffic shaping is still supported only on non-ASIC platforms. With interface policing, bandwidth can be throttled for all traffic entering or exiting the firewall through a given interface. Interface policing is a simple throttling mechanism, whereas policy-based traffic shaping applies an elaborate scheduling scheme with multiple queues.

All platforms support *marking*, also called *traffic classification*. Traffic is marked when you change the value of the Type of Service (ToS) byte in the IP header of each packet. ScreenOS does not react on premarked packets. It can pass this information unchanged, or it can overwrite it. The default is to pass it. Traffic shaping is independent of QoS marking. ScreenOS does not mark QoS fields in Layer 2 headers, such as the Class of Service (CoS) field in the Ethernet header. Although marking can be used in any way the user wants it, two common schemes exist: Integrated Services (IntServ) and Differentiated Services (DiffServ).

IntServ is described in RFCs 1633, 2212, and 2215. It defines eight priority classes, which are, by default, associated with the eight queues in ScreenOS. Queue 0 is assigned to IntServ 7 and queue 7 is assigned to IntServ 0. Queue 0 or IntServ 7 is the highest. The first three most significant bits are called the precedence bits in the ToS byte of the IP header. Many QoS schemes, such as the COS bits of Ethernet or the EXP bits of MPLS, follow the same scheme.

DiffServ is described in RFCs 2474 and 2475. In DiffServ, there are four types of per-hop behavior (PHB). DiffServ uses six bits as opposed to the three bits in IntServ. The big difference, however, comes from the philosophy of how traffic is treated. In the IntServ model, each device should control traffic, whereas in the DiffServ model, the edge devices mark while core devices execute. This difference has less to do with how to configure ScreenOS than it does with understanding the fundamental differences in concepts. DiffServ uses only priority classes for backward compatibility with IntServ and calls that the Class Selector PHB. DiffServ itself classifies traffic in three types of PHB: Default PHB, Expedited Forwarding (EF) PHB, and Assured Forwarding (AF) PHB. All traffic is, by default, in the Default PHB (0×00). The EF PHB (0×2E) has strict priority over other traffic. Classified user traffic ends up in one of 12 AF groups. There is no predefined priority among AF groups; service levels are left up to custom definitions.

IntServ and DiffServ are more concepts in designing a network with QoS than they are mandatory to the network, a firewall, or ScreenOS in particular. ScreenOS prior to 5.2 supported only the three IntServ bits. In ScreenOS 5.2, the Class Selector PHB was added. ScreenOS 5.3 added support for all six DiffServ bits.

14.1 Configure Policy-Level Traffic Shaping

Problem

You want to configure QoS to prioritize some traffic over other traffic, or limit traffic.

Solution

Configure egress traffic shaping on the policy by placing the policy into a priority queue and configuring optional GBW and MBW:

```
set policy from "Trust" to "Untrust"  "Any" "Any " "FTP" permit
traffic priority 3 mbw 1024
set policy from "Trust" to "Untrust  "Any" "Any " "BGP" permit
traffic priority 0 mbw 512
set policy from "Trust" to "Untrust"  "Any" "Any " "MAIL" permit
set policy from "Trust" to "Untrust"  "Any" "Any " "SIP" permit
traffic gbw 144 priority 2 mbw 288
```

You can alternatively configure ingress traffic shaping with PBW instead of MBW:

```
set policy from "Trust" to "Untrust"  "Any" "Any " "FTP" permit
traffic  priority 3 pbw 1024
```

Discussion

To control packet ordering on interface buffers, configure traffic shaping in a policy. ScreenOS does not honor any ToS byte marking, such as IntServ or DiffServ bits. As explained in the introduction to this chapter, ScreenOS supports eight strict priority queues with GBW and MBW. This is a combination of strict priority and custom queuing.

MBW is used to avoid runaway queues in a strict priority scheme where a higher-priority queue can outcrowd all lower-priority queues. GBW is used to reserve bandwidth for a given policy, which is independent of priority queuing. A packet is dispatched immediately as long as GBW is not satisfied. If GBW is satisfied, traffic is sorted into the priority queue as long as MBW is not satisfied. However, if MBW is satisfied, the packet is dropped. Higher-priority queues are cleared before a lower priority queue is allowed to transmit a packet. If a packet remains in a lower-priority queue for more than a few milliseconds, it will be dropped. This triggers transport and application layer backup algorithms. If bandwidth is exhausted, even if MBW has not been satisfied, the packet is dropped because the queue overruns. In other words, if line rate has been reached, the packet is dropped even if MBW has not been reached. Per its definition, GBW has to be at line rate or lower, and has to be equal to or lower than MBW. All GBW together should not be higher than the Committed Information Rate (CIR), which is usually lower than the access rate or line rate on that interface.

Recall that queue 7 is the default queue for all traffic. By default, GBW is set to 0 and MBW is set to an access rate of the interface, that is, 100 Mbps:

```
set policy from "Trust" to "Untrust"  "Any" "Any " "FTP" permit
traffic priority 3 mbw 1024
set policy from "Trust" to "Untrust"  "Any" "Any " "BGP" permit
traffic priority 0 mbw 512
set policy from "Trust" to "Untrust"  "Any" "Any " "MAIL" permit
set policy from "Trust" to "Untrust"  "Any" "Any " "SIP" permit
traffic gbw 144 priority 2 mbw 288
```

As shown in the output, the rule with BGP has the highest priority and traffic is sorted into queue 0. Protect this high-priority queue from runaway traffic by setting the MBW to 512 kbps. Configure interactive File Transfer Protocol (FTP) traffic higher than background MAIL traffic by configuring the rule to priority 3. You still want VoIP (Session Initiation Protocol [SIP]) traffic higher than FTP so that you can enjoy a clear phone conversation while downloading a file by configuring the policy into queue 2. You also guarantee bandwidth for the VoIP traffic by configuring GBW to guarantee 64 kbps plus header overhead. MAIL traffic ends up in the default queue with the implied priority 7.

As a standard, traffic shaping is applied automatically on outbound interface buffers for ingress and egress traffic. Even so, the policy defines only traffic from in the client-to-server direction. Instead of controlling outbound buffers, you can also control inbound buffers. This is rarely done, as traffic already was transmitted over the network, but it can be done for other reasons, such as enforcing service agreements. To do this, configure PBW instead of MBW:

```
set policy from "Trust" to "Untrust"  "Any" "Any " "FTP" permit
traffic priority 3 pbw 1024
```

Traffic shaping in ScreenOS follows a complex algorithm that can degrade performance on a device by as much as 60 percent. Because traffic shaping is most beneficial on edge devices with slow access links, this is acceptable as you will have plenty of performance left even if you do encryption for VPN. Traffic shaping has little benefit on fast links and networks, except when implemented in a provider environment while enforcing service agreements. Traffic shaping is therefore not implemented on the ASIC platforms of the ISG and NS-5000 Series.

Traffic shaping is switched off by default. It will automatically be switched on when a single policy is configured with the `traffic` keyword. However, you can activate or deactivate traffic shaping manually:

```
set traffic-shaping mode off
```

You can check your configuration and its effectiveness by looking at token use on the policy and on the interface. There are regular and borrowed tokens. A token is borrowed if GBW was reached or was not configured. You would configure GBW, for instance, for VoIP, which always has higher priority over everything else. If you see borrowed tokens in this case, you know that the GBW is not high enough. Remember that you cannot guarantee one policy 100 Mbps and another 100 Mbps while the total interface link speed is only 100 Mbps. Both policies may claim their guarantees at the same time. GBW is configured only if minimal service levels should be guaranteed and is usually lower than the expected average bandwidth for that traffic. Therefore, to see borrowed tokens is normal for most policies with or without GBW configured. If you see dropped packets, you reached either MBW or line rate. You should not see extensive dropped packets unless you want to police bandwidth intentionally with MBW. If you see extensive drops and you did not reach MBW, you know your network bandwidth is too low for your traffic requirements. Occasional drops are normal, and are caused when the TCP traffic control mechanism is trying to learn the speed of the connection. Sudden extensive drops can also be a sign of a runaway queue caused, for instance, by a rogue or faulty application.

```
FIREWALL-> get policy id 1009
name:"none" (id 1009), zone Trust -> Untrust,action Permit, status
"enabled"
src "voip", dst "sip.juniper.net", serv "SIP"
Policies on this vpn tunnel: 0
nat src, Web filtering disabled
vpn unknown vpn, policy flag 00000020, session backup: on, idle reset:
on
traffic shapping on, scheduler n/a, serv flag 00
log no, log count 0, alert no, counter no(0) byte rate(sec/min) 0/0
total octets 11178, counter(session/packet/octet) 0/0/0
priority 2, diffserv marking Off
tadapter: state on, gbw/mbw 144/288 policing (no)
-----------------------------------------------------------------
tmng (17): interface ethernet1 state on priority 2
    bw usage [for last one second]: 0 kbps
    pak queue(cur/max):              0/14
    pak received:                    9
    pak dropped(out/shared):         0/0
    PreShapingBytes (dropped/total): 0/5341
    diffserv-marking:                0x0
    elapsed time:                    3570537 ms
```

```
    gbw/mbw:                          144/288 (kbps)
    gbw_q/mbw_q:                      18/36
    shared_tmng:                      5
    PostShapingBytes(total/borrowed):5341/0
    tokens (regular/borrowd):         0/5341
    token bucket (gbl/mbl):           18000/40500
    tokens(gua/max):                  18000/40500
-----------------------------------------------------------------
tmng (18): interface ethernet3 state on priority 2
    bw usage [for last one second]: 0 kbps
    pak queue(cur/max):               0/14
    pak received:                     7
    pak dropped(out/shared):          0/0
    PreShapingBytes (dropped/total): 0/5846
    diffserv-marking:                 0x0
    elapsed time:                     3570531 ms
    gbw/mbw:                          144/288 (kbps)
    gbw_q/mbw_q:                      18/36
    shared_tmng:                      7
    PostShapingBytes(total/borrowed):5846/281
    tokens (regular/borrowd):         0/5846
    token bucket (gbl/mbl):           18000/40500
    tokens(gua/max):                  18000/40500
No Authentication
No User, User Group or Group expression set
```

You can see the GBW and MBW configured on each TMNG. One TMNG exists for each policy on each interface. The TMNG number corresponds to the TMNG on the ingress and egress interfaces. The first TMNG configured on the policy and the shared TMNG is the default queue on the interface.

14.2 Configure Low-Latency Queuing

Problem

You want to configure QoS to prioritize VoIP traffic.

Solution

Configure the policy, define the GBW and MBW, and classify traffic into priority queue 2:

```
set policy from "Trust" to "Untrust"  "voip" "sip.juniper.net" "SIP"
nat src permit traffic gbw 144 priority 2 mbw 288
```

Configure all other policies without GBW into queue 7:

```
set policy from "Trust" to "Untrust"  "Any" "Any" "ANY" nat src
permit log
```

Discussion

Low-latency queuing is a simplified subset of strict-priority queuing. A single traffic flow, usually VoIP, is preferred over all other flows, which end up in a default queue. Whenever a VoIP packet is ready for transmission, it is transmitted before any other queued packet, therefore minimizing delay and jitter. This design is typical for remote office devices.

To implement low-latency queuing, first configure the VoIP policy. Because VoIP protocols use static control ports and dynamic ports for media, configure a service in the policy which references an application layer gateway (ALG) (see Chapter 11). For instance, say that the predefined service SIP reference port `5060/UDP`, which is the control port for SIP, and the SIP ALG listen automatically on `5060/UDP` for a call to arrive. The user agent and the SIP proxy negotiate a media channel, commonly a UDP port between 16384 and 32768. Within the UDP segment, a small Real-time Transport Protocol (RTP) header is added, followed by a few bytes of payload data. The RTP header describes the encapsulated media. Although you do not know on which port the media is sent, the ALG automatically makes sure the traffic shaping configuration is also applied to the negotiated media channels:

```
set policy from "Trust" to "Untrust"  "voip" "sip.juniper.de" "SIP"
nat src permit traffic gbw 144 priority 2 mbw 288
```

In this example, a GBW of 144 kbps was configured, which is more than twice the payload of a single media channel of 64 kbps, encoded in G.711. You also have to account for the RTP (12 bytes), UDP (8 bytes), and IP (20 bytes) headers. The payload is typically 32 bytes, which makes it a 72-byte packet with a 144 kbps bandwidth requirement. To avoid runaway traffic, you should also configure an upper cap with MBW. Runaway traffic can occur if a faulty or malicious application hits the policy, allowing the packets to be prioritized over all other traffic, thereby starving all other traffic.

Make sure no other policy uses GBW or priority 2 or higher:

```
set policy from "Trust" to "Untrust"  "Any" "Any" "ANY" nat src permit log
```

Notice that the preceding policy also enabled Port Address Translation (PAT) with the keyword `nat src`, which is not a requirement but is typical for this kind of deployment. It is also typical in such a deployment to have a return policy (so that VoIP from both sides of the firewall can negotiate a call):

```
set interface ethernet3 dip interface-ip incoming

set policy from "Untrust" to "Trust"  "Any" "DIP(ethernet3)" "SIP"
permit traffic gbw 144 priority 2 mbw 288
```

Notice when you configure PAT that your destination address object is the default dynamic IP (DIP) of the incoming interface, here configured with the keyword incoming. This is also independent of traffic shaping, but it is a typical configuration parameter for this kind of deployment with VoIP. The return policy is not necessary to have bidirectional media traffic because the ALG takes care of this automatically; however, it is necessary because both sides need to initiate a call.

Do not use the STUN protocol with the ALG, as the ALG makes the VoIP protocol PAT-compatible. Stateful firewalls are not compatible with STUN, as it takes advantage of the limited state in simple Network Address Translation (NAT) routers to open incoming connections, something a stateful firewall was designed to deny.

You can check your configuration as follows:

```
FIREWALL-> get policy id 1009
name:"none" (id 1009), zone Trust -> Untrust,action Permit, status
"enabled"
src "voip", dst "sip.juniper.net", serv "SIP"
Policies on this vpn tunnel: 0
nat src, Web filtering disabled
vpn unknown vpn, policy flag 00000020, session backup: on,
idle reset: on
traffic shapping on, scheduler n/a, serv flag 00
log no, log count 0, alert no, counter no(0) byte rate(sec/min) 0/0
total octets 8626, counter(session/packet/octet) 0/0/0
priority 2, diffserv marking Off
tadapter: state on, gbw/mbw 144/288 policing (no)
-------------------------------------------------------------------
tmng (17): interface ethernet1 state on priority 2
    bw usage [for last one second]: 0 kbps
    pak queue(cur/max):               0/14
    pak received:                     7
    pak dropped(out/shared):          0/0
    PreShapingBytes (dropped/total): 0/4307
    diffserv-marking:                 0x0
    elapsed time:                     22658 ms
    gbw/mbw:                          144/288 (kbps)
    gbw_q/mbw_q:                      18/36
    shared_tmng:                      5
    PostShapingBytes(total/borrowed):4307/0
    tokens (regular/borrowd):         0/4307
    token bucket (gbl/mbl):           18000/40500
    tokens(gua/max):                  18000/40500
-------------------------------------------------------------------
tmng (18): interface ethernet3 state on priority 2
    bw usage [for last one second]: 0 kbps
    pak queue(cur/max):               0/14
    pak received:                     5
    pak dropped(out/shared):          0/0
    PreShapingBytes (dropped/total): 0/4320
    diffserv-marking:                 0x0
```

```
        elapsed time:                       13819 ms
        gbw/mbw:                            144/288 (kbps)
        gbw_q/mbw_q:                        18/36
        shared_tmng:                        7
        PostShapingBytes(total/borrowed):4320/281
        tokens (regular/borrowd):           0/4320
        token bucket (gbl/mbl):             18000/40500
        tokens(gua/max):                    18000/40500
    No Authentication
    No User, User Group or Group expression set
```

You can see the configured GBW and MBW in the priority queue 2. Note that traffic shaping was applied in both directions from just the one outbound rule. Beyond receiving some insider information about token bucket allocation, you might receive more interesting information if tokens are borrowed, which would mean there is not enough GBW configured for that policy. You want to prioritize VoIP over all other traffic under any condition. You can see that in the inbound direction the traffic stream is higher than 144 kbps because, in addition to media traffic, there is also control traffic. You could configure GBW a notch higher to include control traffic, but it probably would make little difference during the call because little control traffic will be exchanged.

14.3 Configure Interface-Level Traffic Policing

Problem

You want to limit all traffic going into or out of an interface.

Solution

Configure ingress traffic policing on the interface:

```
set interface e3 bandwidth ingress mbw 1024
```

Or, configure egress traffic policing:

```
set interface e3 bandwidth egress mbw 1024
```

Discussion

The difference between interface-based traffic policing and policy-based traffic shaping is that with interface-based traffic policing, all traffic, regardless of the policy through which it is permitted, is limited to a certain bandwidth. This is independent of queues, their priorities, and which policy actually is permitting the traffic.

Interface-based traffic policing is used to police and shape traffic to a certain CIR. It is not used for preferring certain flows over others or for smoothing out bursts. Interface-based traffic shaping is supported in ScreenOS 5.4 and later on all devices, as well as with some special, earlier code trains on the NS-5000 Series. It is most often used in connection with WAN (subinterface) or VPN links. ASIC support exists for interface-based traffic policing on NS-5000 Series devices, but not for policy-based traffic shaping, which is not supported on ASIC platforms.

You configure interface-based traffic policing ingress or egress on the interface through which you want to police traffic:

```
set interface tun.1 bandwidth ingress mbw 1024

set interface s1.1 bandwidth egress mbw 1024
```

You cannot configure interface-based traffic policing on loopback interfaces.

Check your configuration as follows:

```
FIREWALL-> get traffic-shaping interface e3
------------------------------------
ethernet3: physical bw=100000kbps, config gbw=2048kbps mbw = 2048kbps,
current bw=0kbps
        total allocated gbw=208kbps
Shaping parameters
----------------------------------------------------------------------
tmng (7): interface ethernet3 state on priority 7
    bw usage [for last one second]: 12 kbps
    pak queue(cur/max):             0/26
    pak received:                   11657
    pak dropped(out/shared):        0/0
    PreShapingBytes (dropped/total): 0/1477604
    diffserv-marking:               0x0
    elapsed time:                   6979458 ms
    gbw/mbw:                        1840/2048 (kbps)
    gbw_q/mbw_q:                    230/256
    shared_tmng:                    0
    PostShapingBytes(total/borrowed):1477604/0
    tokens (regular/borrowd):       0/1640540
    token bucket (gbl/mbl):         128000/128000
    tokens(gua/max):                128000/6249835
```

Notice the configured MBW bandwidth of 2 Mbps, or 2,048 kbps. You can also see that the interfaces have a GBW set to MBW. The maximum amount of bandwidth of an interface is the highest amount of guaranteed bandwidth an interface can provide. In the lower portion of the output, you can see that 1,840 kbps are available for guarantees because tokens for 208 kbps, as seen in the top line, are already allocated for a VoIP call. Bandwidth usage for the last second was only 12 kbps, and the interface counters show that MBW was never reached and no packets were dropped. You can also see that interface MBW uses the TMNG of the default and the lowest priority queue 7. Packet drops would be a sign that you reached the configured MBW.

14.4 Configure Traffic Classification (Marking)

Problem

You want to classify traffic by setting the ToS byte in the IP header.

Solution

Configure DiffServ marking within a policy:

```
set policy from "Trust" to "Untrust"  "voip" "sip.juniper.net" "SIP"
permit traffic dscp enable value 18
```

Discussion

Traffic classification is used on edge devices to a backbone network, commonly called *Customer Edge (CE) routers*. Its purpose is to classify traffic flows into service levels for special treatment within the network cloud. *Marking* refers to overwriting the first three or six bits of the ToS byte within the header of each IP packet. This is different from actually acting on a marking. ScreenOS devices do not act on ToS byte marking, but can pass the current marking or overwrite it. Marking is supported on all NetScreen, SSG, and ISG platforms, and is ASIC-assisted on ASIC platforms, providing marking in line rate. There is no performance penalty with marking. The more granular traffic can be classified, the more control you have on the treatment of traffic within the network cloud. Therefore, edge firewalls are a very good place to do marking because traffic is commonly classified via policies and policies usually can be more complex than ACLs on a router.

Although marking can be totally arbitrary and is up to the service provider of the backbone network, two standards are common: IntServ and DiffServ.

IntServ uses only the first three bits of the ToS byte (also called the Precedence bits, as detailed in Table 14-1). Higher IntServ numbers have higher priority over lower values; this is the opposite of the numbering of queue priorities within ScreenOS, where lower-numbered queues have higher priority over higher-numbered queues. Default traffic is tagged `Routine`, whereas VoIP traffic is usually tagged `Immediate`. The two highest queues are reserved for control traffic such as routing protocols.

Table 14-1. Precedence or class selector PHBs

Value	Description
0 or 0 (0 × 00)	Routine
1 or 8 (0 × 08)	Priority
2 or 16 (0 × 10)	Immediate
3 or 24 (0 × 18)	Flash
4 or 32 (0 × 20)	Flash Override

Table 14-1. Precedence or class selector PHBs (continued)

Value	Description
5 or 40 (0 × 28)	Critical
6 or 48 (0 × 30)	Inter-network Control
7 or 56 (0 × 38)	Network Control

DiffServ, on the other hand, uses the first six bits of the ToS byte. DiffServ uses the Class Selector PHB to set the first three bits exactly as IntServ, but it also sets the next three bits to zero. DiffServ uses a Default PHB with all bits set to zero. DiffServ also defines an Expedited Forwarding PHB 46 (0 × 2E) for network control traffic or other urgent traffic. All other traffic is sorted into Assured Forwarding PHBs (as detailed in Table 14-2). Unlike with IntServ, AF PHBs do not have a default hierarchy but usually depend on the assignment to a service class with the individual provider.

Table 14-2. Assured forwarding

	Class 1	Class 2	Class 3	Class 4
Low drop	AF11	AF21	AF31	AF41
	10 (0 × 0A)	18 (0 × 12)	26 (0 × 1A)	34 (0 × 22)
Medium drop	AF12	AF22	AF32	AF42
	12 (0 × 0C)	20 (0 × 14)	28 (0 × 1C)	36 (0 × 24)
High drop	AF13	AF23	AF33	AF43
	14 (0 × 0E)	22 (0 × 16)	30 (0 × 1E)	38 (0 × 26)

An alternative marking scheme is explained in RFC 1349. The use of the first three bits is identical with IntServ and DiffServ Class Selector PHBs. The next three bits are assigned to Minimize Delay, Maximize Throughput, and Maximize Reliability. A seventh bit, which ScreenOS does not support, is called Minimize Monetary Cost. Historically, some routing protocols were supporting those markings, making different routing decisions for different ToS settings, but this never enjoyed widespread commercial implementation. For instance, today's Open Shortest Path First (OSPF) protocol implementation supports only one topology for Routine or Default PHB traffic. An IP router uses the same route for any packet, regardless of how it is marked. Marking has an effect only for scheduling a packet in an egress interface buffer, which is an independent function from determining which interface is the actual egress interface, and to which next hop the packet should be sent.

You can activate marking by simply enabling it on a policy, in which case marking is done automatically in accordance to traffic queue classification. This is more a convenience feature, as queuing and marking are two different functions. You enable marking with the keyword `dscp`, which stands for DiffServ Code Point:

```
set policy from "Trust" to "Untrust"  "voip" "sip.juniper.de" "SIP"
permit traffic priority 2 dscp enable
```

You can review or change the default mapping between queues and markings with the following:

```
FIREWALL-> get traffic-shaping ip_precedence
priority to IP precedence mapping:
priority 0 -> 7
priority 1 -> 6
priority 2 -> 5
priority 3 -> 4
priority 4 -> 3
priority 5 -> 2
priority 6 -> 1
priority 7 -> 0

set traffic-shaping ip_precedence 7 6 5 4 3 2 1 0
```

Only decimal IntServ values can be configured. Starting with ScreenOS 5.2, you can make the default marking compatible with the DiffServ Class Selector PHB by configuring the next three bits to zero:

```
set traffic-shaping dscp-class-selector
```

Since ScreenOS 5.4, it is also possible to configure marking independent of priority queues to any of the DiffServ code points or any other six-bit custom scheme. You enter the format in decimals. Tables 14-1 and 14-2 provide the conversion from hexadecimal to decimal.

```
set policy from "Trust" to "Untrust"  "voip" "sip.juniper.net" "SIP"
permit traffic dscp enable value 18
```

As mentioned earlier, marking is maintained if packets were previously marked and marking was not configured on the policy. Marking is supported on non-ASIC and ASIC platforms. Tables 14-3, 14-4, and 14-5 detail some special considerations for VPN passthrough and for terminating VPN traffic on ASIC platforms.

Table 14-3. Clear-text traffic marking

Description	Non-ASIC platforms	ASIC platforms
Clear packet	No marking	No marking
Clear packet and marking in policy	Mark packet	Mark packet (Does not work for IPSec passthrough)
Premarked packet with no marking in policy	Retain marking	Retain marking
Premarked packet with marking in policy	Mark packet	Mark packet (Does not work for IPSec passthrough)

There is no difference in marking for policy-based VPN traffic between the different platforms. Marking within the policy would affect only the outer header, visible to the network. Any premarking, if it exists, is retained in the inner header, as detailed in Table 14-4.

Table 14-4. Marking with policy-based VPN

Description	Non-ASIC platforms	ASIC platforms
Clear packet	No marking	No marking
Clear packet with marking in policy	Mark the outer header	Mark the outer header
Premarked packet with no marking in policy	No marking in outer header; retain marking in inner header	No marking in outer header; retain marking in inner header
Premarked packet with marking in policy	Mark outer header; inner header retains marking	Mark outer header; inner header retains marking

There are some differences between the platforms with route-based VPNs. On ASIC platforms, marking is done only on the inner header, whereas on non-ASIC platforms, the outer header is also marked, as detailed in Table 14-5.

Table 14-5. Marking with route-based VPN

Description	Non-ASIC platforms	ASIC platforms
Clear packet	No marking	No marking
Clear packet with marking in policy	Mark the inner header	Mark the inner header
Premarked packet with no marking in policy	Retain marking in the inner header and copy to the outer header	Retain marking in the inner header
Premarked packet with marking in policy	Overwrite marking in the inner header and copy marking to the outer header	Overwrite marking in the inner header

On some high-end platforms, you also may have to enable marking on VPNs systemwide:

```
set envar ipsec-dscp-mark=yes
```

On ScreenOS 6.1 and later, marking can also be enabled on a VPN tunnel instead of on the policy:

```
set vpn vpn1 dscp-marking 52
```

You can check marking with the following:

```
islandgeeksfw-> get policy id 1015
name:"none" (id 1015), zone Trust -> Untrust,action Permit, status
"enabled"
src "voip", dst "sip.juniper.net", serv "SIP"
Policies on this vpn tunnel: 0
nat off, Web filtering : disabled
vpn unknown vpn, policy flag 00104000, session backup: on, idle reset:
on
```

```
traffic shapping on, scheduler n/a, serv flag 00
log no, log count 0, alert no, counter no(0) byte rate(sec/min) 0/0
total octets 0, counter(session/packet/octet) 0/0/0
priority 7, diffserv marking On dscp value: 18
tadapter: state on, gbw/mbw 0/0 policing (no)
No Authentication
No User, User Group or Group expression set
```

14.5 Troubleshoot QoS

Problem

Traffic shaping is not doing what you thought you configured, and you need more background on how traffic shaping works on ScreenOS.

Solution

Check settings and bucket utilization on the policy:

```
get policy id 1009
```

Check settings and bucket utilization on the interface:

```
get traffic-shaping interface e3
```

Discussion

Traffic shaping is implemented in ScreenOS via a dual-token bucket model (see Figure 14-1). One bucket is used to control GBW, while tokens overspill into a second bucket for shared bandwidth in excess of all GBW. Tokens are added to the GBW bucket at the rate the GBW was configured. Any traffic falling within GBW takes tokens out of the GBW bucket. Any unused tokens overflow into a second bucket for shared bandwidth. If a packet is transmitted, it takes tokens in the amount of that traffic out of the GBW and shared buckets. Only if tokens are left in the buckets can a packet be transmitted. In ScreenOS, a token has the size of 1 byte.

The two buckets relate to the concept of one bucket measuring guarantees and another serving as a spillover for shared bandwidth. Each policy maintains a GBW and an MBW bucket, as shown in Figure 14-2, where both are used for measuring traffic on that policy. Only GBW buckets spill over to shared buckets.

Leftover bandwidth is shared among queues but also among dependent interfaces. Dependent interfaces are logical subinterfaces, or a virtual interface such as a tunnel or loopback interface. A tunnel interface can send traffic over a VLAN subinterface, which again is a child of a physical Ethernet interface. A loopback interface can represent multiple sub- or physical interfaces in a loopback group—for example, when a dynamic routing protocol would converge via alternate interfaces. Shared bandwidth therefore needs to be tracked not just for each priority, but also for each dependent interface. Shared bandwidth is tracked via TMNG, as depicted in

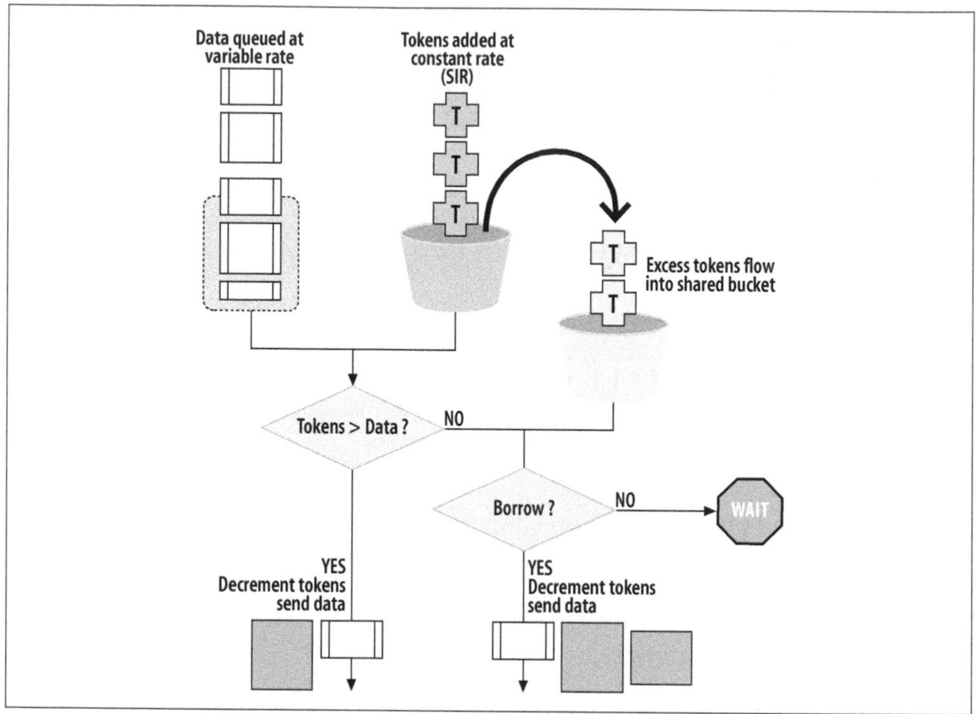

Figure 14-1. Dual-token bucket model

Figure 14-3, where there are two TMNGs for each policy. Interfaces, and therefore TMNGs, are dependent on each other according to their child/parent relationship and their priority class. Each TMNG tracks GBW and MBW and shared bandwidth for the corresponding policy.

There is a shared bucket for each TMNG. A TMNG exists for each policy on each logical, virtual, or physical interface. Those shared buckets spill over like a waterfall in a certain order. *Spillover* means unused tokens are shared, and therefore, higher-priority traffic was not using up those tokens. Higher-queue TMNG spills over into lower-queue TMNG. TMNGs also spill over within their queue to a child interface, if it exists. This system ensures that unused tokens can be used by other flows in other queues and dependent interfaces.

Traffic shaping is configured and measured on a per-policy basis. But it is applied to outbound (or inbound) interface buffers in both directions of a traffic flow. This means that each policy has two TMNG objects associated with it. TMNGs are created on demand. Each interface automatically has a TMNG for the lowest-priority queue 7. Other TMNGs are created when policies exist that reference those priority queues.

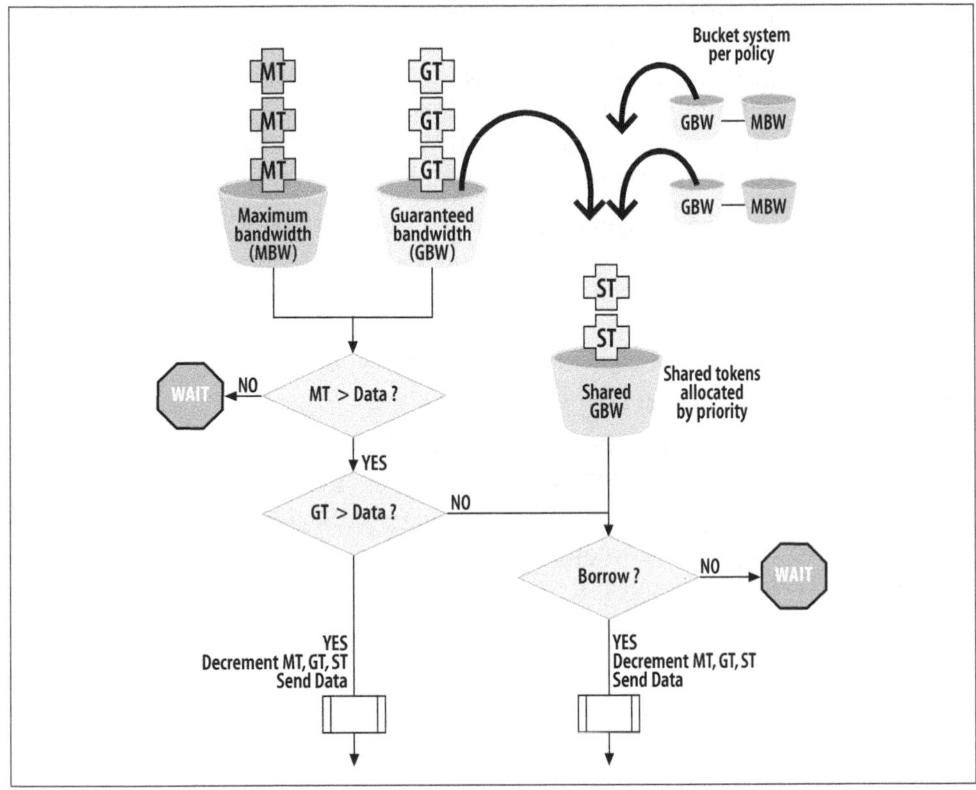

Figure 14-2. GBW, MBW, and shared buckets

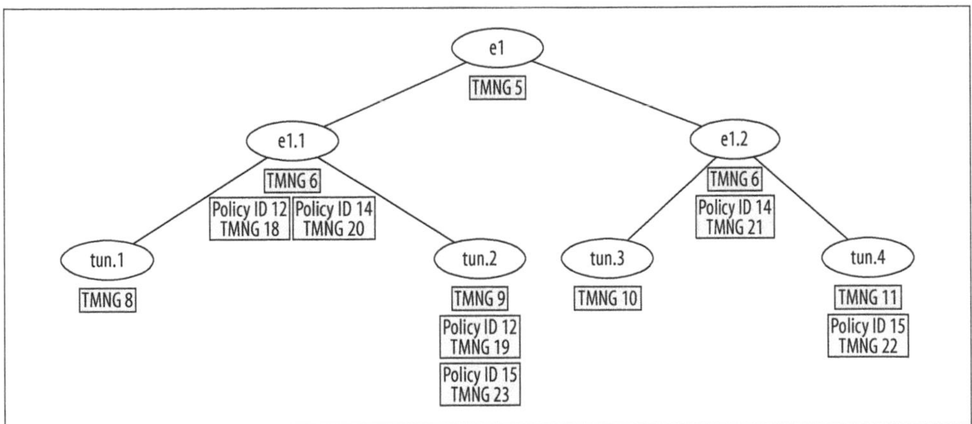

Figure 14-3. Traffic Management Objects (TMNG)

TMNGs deal with shared bandwidth, and the use of tokens from a TMNG is called *borrowing*. A policy may or may not have GBW configured. If no guarantees have been defined, or guarantees are already satisfied, the policy needs to borrow from a shared pool of bandwidth. It will borrow, as long as it has tokens available, according to its priority queue and the configured MBW. The MBW, or PBW, puts a cap on borrowing, if so configured. There are some simple rules for this behavior:

- The GBW of all policies going between the same interfaces cannot together be higher than the access rate of the root interface. For instance, all policies referencing a tunnel interface (via its "from" or "to" zone), using the same outgoing interface, cannot have a higher GBW than the outgoing interface can carry. Ideally, it should not have a higher rate than the network can carry.
- GBW can never be higher than MBW.
- If there is bandwidth left after satisfying all GBW to all policies going between the same interfaces, that bandwidth is shared among other policies.
- There are eight strict priority queues per interface. Shared bandwidth is distributed among traffic flows according to their queue classification. Higher queues are served before lower queues.
- Higher queues can starve lower queues. MBW is used to set a cap on queue use on a per-policy basis.

In other words, you can guarantee a certain bandwidth to a policy which can never be higher than what the interface can transmit or the network is able to transmit. You have to take into account that all guarantees may be served at the same time. Whatever is left after serving all guarantees is shared. Higher priorities are served before lower priorities. You can limit the bandwidth consumption of a policy by setting its MBW.

Let's see how this relates to troubleshooting traffic shaping on ScreenOS.

You can review the default TMNG of each interface with the following:

```
FIREWALL-> get traffic-shaping interface e3
------------------------------------
ethernet3: physical bw=100000kbps, config gbw=2048kbps mbw = 2048kbps,
current bw=0kbps
        total allocated gbw=208kbps
Shaping parameters
-------------------------------------------------------------------
tmng (7): interface ethernet3 state on priority 7
    bw usage [for last one second]: 0 kbps
    pak queue(cur/max):            0/26
    pak received:                  209094
    pak dropped(out/shared):       0/0
    PreShapingBytes (dropped/total): 0/26261329
    diffserv-marking:              0x0
    elapsed time:                  65128055 ms
    gbw/mbw:                       1840/2048 (kbps)
```

```
    gbw_q/mbw_q:                       230/256
    shared_tmng:                       0
    PostShapingBytes(total/borrowed):26261329/0
    tokens (regular/borrowd):          0/27556895
    token bucket (gbl/mbl):            128000/128000
    tokens(gua/max):                   128000/128000
```

TMNGs are unique to policies, but each policy is also referencing shared TMNGs, which are the default TMNGs of the interface ingress and egress interfaces.

```
FIREWALL-> get pol id 1014
name:"none" (id 1014), zone Trust -> Untrust,action Permit, status
"enabled"
src "Any", dst "Any", serv "HTTP"
Policies on this vpn tunnel: 0
nat off, Web filtering : disabled
vpn unknown vpn, policy flag 00000000, session backup: on,
idle reset:on
traffic shapping on, scheduler n/a, serv flag 00
log no, log count 0, alert no, counter no(0) byte rate(sec/min) 0/0
total octets 132, counter(session/packet/octet) 0/0/0
priority 5, diffserv marking Off
tadapter: state on, gbw/mbw 512/1024 policing (no)
--------------------------------------------------------------------
tmng (21): interface ethernet1 state on priority 5
    bw usage [for last one second]: 0 kbps
    pak queue(cur/max):                0/21
    pak received:                      0
    pak dropped(out/shared):           0/0
    PreShapingBytes (dropped/total): 0/0
    diffserv-marking:                  0x0
    elapsed time:                      0 ms
    gbw/mbw:                           512/1024 (kbps)
    gbw_q/mbw_q:                       64/128
    shared_tmng:                       5
    PostShapingBytes(total/borrowed):0/0
    tokens (regular/borrowd):          0/0
    token bucket (gbl/mbl):            64000/144000
    tokens(gua/max):                   64000/144000
---------------------------------------------------------------------
tmng (22): interface ethernet3 state on priority 5
    bw usage [for last one second]: 0 kbps
    pak queue(cur/max):                0/21
    pak received:                      2
    pak dropped(out/shared):           0/0
    PreShapingBytes (dropped/total): 0/132
    diffserv-marking:                  0x0
    elapsed time:                      2919 ms
    gbw/mbw:                           512/1024 (kbps)
    gbw_q/mbw_q:                       64/128
    shared_tmng:                       7
    PostShapingBytes(total/borrowed):132/0
    tokens (regular/borrowd):          0/132
    token bucket (gbl/mbl):            64000/144000
    tokens(gua/max):                   64000/144000
```

```
No Authentication
No User, User Group or Group expression set
```

You can see how much GBW is being used and whether tokens are borrowed or packets are even dropped in the output from the interface and the policy get commands.

If the shared TMNG has no more tokens available, traffic will be dropped on the root interface:

```
FIREWALL-> get counter statistic interface e3 | incl buffer

in no buffer     0 | out no buffer    234 | re-xmt limit       0
```

Table 14-6 shows the meaning of the different values in the TMNG object.

Table 14-6. TMNG

Value	Description
`bw usage`	Bandwidth usage for the last second
`pak queue(cur/max)`	Queue size for the current and peak values, measured in packets
`pak received`	Number of packets received since reset
`pak dropped(out/shared)`	Packet drops when MBW was reached, or when not enough bandwidth was available
`PreShapingBytes (dropped/total)`	Bytes before traffic shaping was applied; dropped in total count
`diffserv-marking`	Marking value (Differentiated Services Code Point [DSCP]) if enabled on the policy, in hex
`elapsed time`	Time since last shaping
`gbw/mbw`	Configured GBW and MBW
`gbw_q/mbw_q`	Queue depth in packets
`shared_tmng`	Spillover TMNG
`PostShapingBytes(total/borrowed)`	Bytes after TS was applied (total bytes and borrowed bytes)
`tokens (regular/borrowd)`	Borrowed tokens in bytes
`token bucket (gbl/mbl)`	GBW and MBW bucket size in bytes
`tokens(gua/max)`	Available GBW and spillover tokens in bytes

Take note of the difference between `PreShapingBytes` and `PostShapingBytes`. If a traffic stream should always stay within the GBW, you should never see borrowed tokens, but you will always see borrowed tokens when no GBW was configured. Configuring GBW is optional, but when you calculate GBW and MBW, take header overhead into account. Higher counters in the `pak queue` can create higher delays in traffic because a packet needs to wait before a higher-priority queue is cleared. If such a delay is a problem, reclassify traffic into a higher priority, or add bandwidth (remember that QoS cannot create additional bandwidth, but rather is an allocation scheme of existing bandwidth). `pak dropped` can provide insight into why packets are dropped: because MBW was reached, or because not enough shared bandwidth was available.

Most other values hold significance only for JTAC or Juniper Engineering because those provide further information about the internal state of traffic shaping in ScreenOS. Other than changing the priority and GBW and MBW, there are no tunable values on ScreenOS. Buffer size and queue depth cannot be changed.

Queuing and prioritization means packet reordering. You need to be careful and consider whether applications can tolerate reordered packets. It's best if you classify all traffic belonging to the same application into the same priority queue. For example, classify VoIP control traffic and VoIP media traffic in the same queue to avoid reordering issues. As always, adding the bandwidth to your network that your applications need is much better than any fancy queuing scheme.

CHAPTER 15

RIP

15.0 Introduction

The Routing Information Protocol (RIP) is an Interior Gateway Protocol (IGP) that has been used extensively in corporate and personal networking environments for the past two decades. RIP version 2, the current specification of RIP, is defined in RFC 2453. RIP was historically specified in RFC 1723 and RFC 1388, both of which are now obsolete. The primary reason for RIP's wide adoption has been its simplicity and wide availability. Compared to other prevailing IGPs such as the Open Shortest Path First (OSPF) and Intermediate System to Intermediate System (IS-IS) protocols, RIP is easier to implement. Also, given its simplicity, RIP has been more widely available on servers and general-purpose networking appliances when compared with other IGPs.

RIP is a distance-vector protocol based on the Bellman-Ford algorithm. Distance-vector protocols advertise the metric (or hop count) associated with a destination network to their neighboring routers. Unlike OSPF or IS-IS-speaking devices, RIP gateways do not maintain a link state database that is consistent across all the devices in an autonomous system. Instead, each device that runs RIP can send updates about the destinations that are directly defined on it or those that it has learned from neighbors.

RIP gateways rely on a single unit—the metric associated with a destination address—to make their best-path selection. Each RIP-speaking interface has a metric associated with it. When a RIP gateway receives a RIP route, it examines the metric of the received route, and adds its own interface metric to establish the aggregate metric for this destination route. RIP metrics can range from 1 to 15. A route with a computed metric of 16 or greater is considered unreachable and is not installed in the routing table.

There are two types of RIP messages: Request and Response. Although Request messages are used to solicit a response from a RIP neighbor to provide its routing table, they are rarely used in live networks. The bulk of RIP messages in a live network are unsolicited Response messages that are generated by RIP-speaking gateways every 30 seconds. The 30-second route update interval is a default value defined in RFC 2453 for RIP-speaking devices to announce their routing table to all their neighbors. RIP update messages consist of RIP entries which include, at a minimum, the destination network address and the metric of the route.

Unlike OSPF, which has its own IP number, RIP messages are encapsulated in User Datagram Protocol (UDP) datagrams on destination port 520. RIP update messages consist of between one and 25 RIP entries.

RIP Version 1

Although any new implementation of RIP typically does not get implemented with RIP version 1 due to its limitations, it is useful to understand RIP version 1 implementations to integrate a new device into an existing, legacy RIP version 1 network. RIP version 1 (also referred to as RIPv1 or RIP-1) has a serious limitation in that it is a "classful" routing protocol: because RIPv1 route updates do not have a subnet mask associated with them, the receiving gateway has to rely on the archaic classification of the IPv4 address space into Class A, B, and C networks to establish a network mask for the received route update.

RIPv1 messages are typically transmitted at the network broadcast address `255.255.255.255`. RIPv1 update messages consist of simple RIP entries that provide two pieces of information to a receiving gateway: the destination IPv4 address and the metric. An update message can include up to 25 RIP entries. Because RIP entries do not come with an associated mask, the receiving gateway has to classify the route using classful boundaries.

RIP Version 2

RIP Version 2 (also referred to as RIPv2 or RIP-2) adds useful extensions to RIP version 1 while maintaining the same RIP UDP datagram structure. These extensions include support for subnet masks, route tags, explicit next hops, and neighbor authentication.

Because RIPv2 route entries include subnet masks, RIPv2 implementations can support classless interdomain routing (CIDR), sometimes referred to as *classless routing*. For instance, a RIPv2 message with a route entry such as `192.168.100.0` and a subnet mask of `255.255.255.248` is interpreted as the `192.168.100.0/29` subnet, whereas RIPv1 gateways, due to the absence of subnet masks in the route entry, would interpret this as `192.168.100.0/24`.

To reduce the load of processing a broadcast packet on all the devices in a virtual local area network (VLAN) or subnet, RIPv2 devices typically send their messages to the `224.0.0.9` multicast address. This is in contrast to RIPv1 gateways, which broadcast RIP messages on the `255.255.255.255` network broadcast address.

RIP neighbor authentication via Message Digest 5 (MD5) keys is defined in RFC 2082.

Routing Loops in RIP

The metric, or cost, of a destination route is the primary mechanism used by RIP-speaking devices to determine whether a given route from a neighbor should be installed in the routing table or discarded if a better (lower-cost) route already exists in the RIP database. Most modern RIP implementations provide a mechanism to prevent routing loops from forming if a RIP gateway advertises a route learned from a neighbor right back to the same neighbor. Two well-established techniques for RIP routing-loop prevention are split-horizon and poison-reverse. The split-horizon method ensures that a route learned on an interface is never advertised back on the same interface. The split-horizon with poison-reverse adds an extra protection mechanism by sending back the received RIP route with a metric of infinity (16).

The ScreenOS RIP Implementation

ScreenOS has a full-featured implementation of RIP, supporting RIPv1 and RIPv2. ScreenOS firewalls run RIP within the context of a Virtual Router (VR). As discussed in Chapter 4, ScreenOS assigns a route preference to the different types of routes in a VR. Route preference becomes relevant in the context of installing the best route in the routing table when there are multiple route entries for the same destination, learned from different routing protocols. Lower route preference routes are preferred over those with higher preference. *ScreenOS assigns a default route preference of 100 to RIP routes, making them less preferred to OSPF, the External Border Gateway Protocol (EBGP), and connected routes, but more preferred over OSPF External Type2 or Internal BGP (IBGP) routes.*

All RIP-enabled interfaces in ScreenOS are assigned a default metric of 1, which you can modify. The default RIP loop-prevention method used by the ScreenOS RIP implementation is split-horizon.

15.1 Configure a RIP Instance on an Interface

Problem

You want to enable RIP on an interface on a ScreenOS firewall to advertise and receive routes from a peer device.

Solution

Figure 15-1 shows the `extfw` firewall gateway and its interfaces in the context of RIP configuration.

First, make sure you have correctly assigned the interface zone, IP address, and mode on the interface that will run RIP:

```
extfw-> set interface bgroup0 zone Trust
extfw-> set interface bgroup0 ip 192.168.4.1/24
extfw-> set interface bgroup0 nat
```

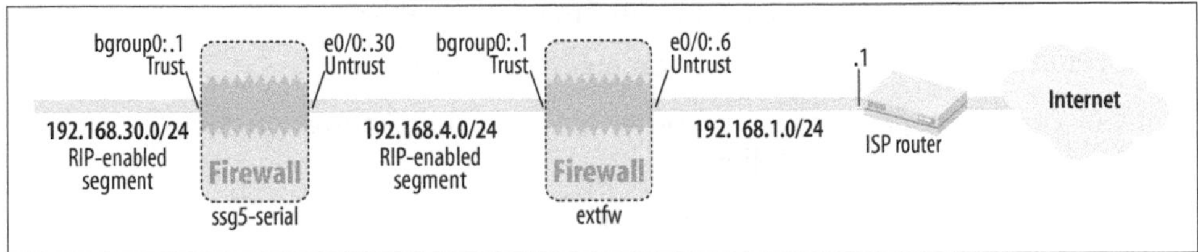

Figure 15-1. RIP configuration

You can replace the bgroup0 interface in the preceding code with the particular interface on the ScreenOS firewall on which you are enabling RIP.

Next, define the router ID and enable RIP. You must define the router ID for RIP to come up correctly:

```
extfw-> set vr trust-vr
extfw(trust-vr)-> set router-id 192.168.4.1
extfw(trust-vr)-> set protocol rip
extfw(trust-vr/rip)-> set enable
extfw(trust-vr/rip)-> exit
extfw(trust-vr)-> exit
extfw->
```

Finally, enable RIP at the interface level:

```
extfw-> set interface bgroup0 protocol rip enable
```

You can replace the bgroup0 keyword with the interface name on the ScreenOS firewall on which you are enabling RIP. The configuration shown here enables RIP on the trust-vr virtual router on the firewall and permits it to receive all RIP route advertisements on the bgroup0 interface. Furthermore, this configuration will advertise the 192.168.4.0/24 network as well as any other networks on other RIP-enabled interfaces on this firewall to RIP neighbors.

Discussion

As discussed in the Introduction to this chapter, RIP is a simple routing protocol that you can quickly enable in a network to provide dynamic rerouting around failed network links, propagate routes to new networks, and bias traffic to specific paths.

ScreenOS uses several default parameters when RIP is enabled using the minimal configuration shown in this recipe's solution. These default parameters include the following:

- RIP version: 2
- Default interface metric: 1
- Default metric for routes redistributed into RIP: 10
- Default route advertisement: Disabled
- Accept default route from neighbors: Enabled

- Duration of RIP route update announcements: 30 seconds
- Default RIP routing-loop prevention method: Split-horizon

You can view these parameters and other configuration settings on the RIP instance running in the defined VR as follows:

```
extfw-> get vrouter trust-vr protocol rip
VR: trust-vr
----------------------------------------------------------------
State: enabled
Version: 2
Default metric for routes redistributed into RIP: 10
Maximum neighbors per interface: 16
Not validating neighbor in same subnet: disabled
Next RIP update scheduled after: 30 sec
Maximum number of Alternate routes per prefix: 0
Advertising default route: disabled
Default routes learnt by RIP will  be accepted
Incoming routes filter and offset-metric: not configured
Outgoing routes filter and offset-metric: not configured
Update packet threshold is not configured
Total number of RIP interfaces created on vr(trust-vr): 1

Update| Invalid|   Flush| DC Retransmit| DC Poll| Hold Down
(Timers in seconds)
-----------------------------------------------------------
    30|      180|      120|             5|      180|       90

Flags: Split Horizon - S, Split Horizon with Poison Reverse - P,
Passive - I
       Demand Circuit - D
Interface   IP-Prefix        Admin     State     Flags   NbrCnt Metric
 Ver-Rx/Tx
----------------------------------------------------------------
bgroup0     192.168.4.1/24   enabled    enabled  S         0      1
   2/2
extfw->
```

The output from get vrouter trust-vr protocol rip also displays the interfaces in the trust-vr on which the RIP protocol is enabled. The default routing-loop prevention method for RIP on ScreenOS is split-horizon, indicated with the S flag in the preceding code.

Another mechanism for verifying that RIP is enabled in a VR is to check for the R flag in the get vrouter output:

```
extfw-> get vrouter
* indicates default vrouter
A - AutoExport, R - RIP, N- NHRP, O - OSPF, B - BGP, P - PIM

   ID Name             Vsys       Owner      Routes  MRoutes    Flags
    1 untrust-vr       Root       shared      0/max  0/max
*   2 trust-vr         Root       shared      9/max  0/max      R
```

```
total 2 vrouters shown and 0 of them defined by user
extfw->
```

You can view the RIP neighbors for a given RIP instance on ScreenOS as follows:

```
extfw-> get vrouter trust-vr protocol rip neighbors
VR: trust-vr
----------------------------------------------------------------
Flags : Static - S, Demand Circuit - T, NHTB - N, Down - D, Up - U,
Poll - P,
        Demand Circuit Init - I
Neighbors on interface bgroup0
------------------------------------------------------------------
IpAddress     Version Age      Expires    BadPackets BadRoutes Flags
------------------------------------------------------------------
192.168.4.30  2       00:00:17 00:03:00            0         0 U
extfw->
```

The Age parameter shows the duration since the neighbor has been in an Up state. The Expires parameter displays the duration for which this neighbor will remain up if no more updates are received from it. Note that sometimes a RIP neighbor may not be sending out any RIP routes to the ScreenOS firewall. Furthermore, because RIP does not employ a formal keepalive/Hello protocol and RIP request messages are rarely implemented, ScreenOS will remove a RIP neighbor from the neighbor list if no routes are received from it. In several instances, however, such as a physical link failure, an active neighbor that is sending RIP route updates every 30 seconds is immediately removed from the list of neighbors.

You can view the RIP database as follows:

```
extfw-> get vrouter trust-vr protocol rip database
VR: trust-vr
-----------------------------------------------------------------
Total database entry: 1
Flags: Added in Multipath - M, RIP - R, Redistributed - I,
       Default (advertised) - D, Permanent - P, Summary - S,
       Unreachable - U, Hold - H
DBID   Prefix             Nexthop     Ifp     Cost Flags   Source
-----------------------------------------------------------------
     1 192.168.4.0/24     0.0.0.0     n/a        0 I         -
extfw->
```

To verify the router ID of the RIP instance on the VR, type the following:

```
extfw-> get vrouter trust-vr router-id
vrouter trust-vr router-id for BGP and OSPF is 192.168.4.1
extfw->
```

Finally, if you would like to remove the entire instance of RIP on a VR and its associated interfaces, you can use the unset command:

```
extfw-> unset vrouter trust-vr protocol rip
deleting RIP instance, are you sure? y/[n] y
extfw->
```

See Also

Recipe 15.2

15.2 Advertise the Default Route via RIP

Problem

You want to advertise the default route to your RIP neighbors.

Solution

This solution builds on Recipe 15.1 by adding the ability to advertise the default route. In this scenario, the default route is statically configured to point out the `Untrust ethernet0/0` interface, and is redistributed into RIP to be advertised over the `bgroup0` interface:

```
extfw-> set vrouter trust-vr
extfw(trust-vr)-> set router-id 192.168.4.1
extfw(trust-vr)-> set protocol rip
extfw(trust-vr/rip)-> set enable
extfw(trust-vr/rip)-> exit
extfw(trust-vr)-> exit
extfw-> set interface bgroup0 protocol rip enable
extfw-> set vrouter trust-vr protocol rip advertise-def-route metric 10
```

Discussion

You can verify the RIP database on the advertising router to make sure the default route, `0.0.0.0/0`, is installed as follows:

```
extfw-> get vrouter trust-vr protocol rip database
VR: trust-vr
----------------------------------------------------------------
Total database entry: 2
Flags: Added in Multipath - M, RIP - R, Redistributed - I,
       Default (advertised) - D, Permanent - P, Summary - S,
       Unreachable - U, Hold - H
DBID   Prefix                Nexthop      Ifp    Cost Flags   Source
----------------------------------------------------------------
     2 0.0.0.0/0             0.0.0.0      n/a      10 RD       -
     1 192.168.4.0/24        0.0.0.0      n/a       0 I        -
extfw->
```

The default route is installed in `extfw`'s RIP database to be advertised at a metric of 10. The RIP gateway that receives this route assigns it a RIP metric of 10 plus the interface metric of the interface on which this route is received. Hence, when this default route is received on a ScreenOS firewall with an interface metric of 3 (`set interface ethernet0/0 protocol rip metric 3`), the resultant default route has a metric of 13, which you can verify as follows:

```
ssg5-serial-> get route

IPv4 Dest-Routes for <untrust-vr> (0 entries)
------------------------------------------------------------------
H: Host C: Connected S: Static A: Auto-Exported
I: Imported R: RIP P: Permanent D: Auto-Discovered
iB: IBGP eB: EBGP O: OSPF E1: OSPF external type 1
E2: OSPF external type 2


IPv4 Dest-Routes for <trust-vr> (6 entries)
-----------------------------------------------------------------
   ID          IP-Prefix    Interface       Gateway   P Pref    Mtr
     Vsys
-----------------------------------------------------------------
*  6           0.0.0.0/0      eth0/0   192.168.4.1   R  100     13
     Root
*  2     192.168.4.30/32      eth0/0       0.0.0.0   H    0      0
     Root
*  4     192.168.30.1/32     bgroup0       0.0.0.0   H    0      0
     Root
*  3     192.168.30.0/24     bgroup0       0.0.0.0   C    0      0
     Root
*  1       192.168.4.0/24     eth0/0       0.0.0.0   C    0      0
     Root
*  5       192.168.1.0/24    eth0/0    192.168.4.1   R  100      4
     Root

ssg5-serial->
```

See Also

Recipe 15.1

15.3 Configure RIP Authentication

Problem

You want to enable neighbor authentication for a RIP neighbor.

Solution

You can enable clear text authentication for a RIP neighbor as follows:

```
extfw-> set interface bgroup0 protocol rip authentication password
testpassword
```

You can replace the testpassword with a clear text password of your choice.

You can enable MD5 authentication for a RIP neighbor as follows:

```
extfw-> set interface bgroup0 protocol rip authentication md5
AN_EASY_MD5_KEY
```

You can replace the MD5 key AN_EASY_MD5_KEY with any string of up to 16 characters.

Discussion

RIP authentication is configured in ScreenOS at the interface level. Hence, as indicated in this recipe's solution, the authentication password is specified in the context of an interface, and not in the VR context.

Clear text authentication was introduced in RIP version 2. However, because clear text authentication transmits the clear text password in the RIP message, it is open to snooping attacks.

The MD5 RIP authentication mechanism, defined in RFC 2082, is more secure than clear text authentication, as it does not send a clear text password in each RIP message. Instead, the MD5 authentication mechanism computes a "hash" on a message using the predefined MD5 key. The resultant computation, which is a 16-byte MD5 "digest," is transmitted in the RIP message along with the key ID and a sequence number.

You can associate multiple MD5 keys with an interface, with one active key at any time. In ScreenOS, when a single MD5 key is defined on an interface without the key-id attribute, it is automatically assigned a key ID of 0. You can configure and define additional MD5 keys as the active key as follows:

```
extfw-> set interface bgroup0 protocol rip authentication md5
ONE_MORE_EZ_KEY key-id 1
extfw-> set interface bgroup0 protocol rip authentication
active-md5-key-id 1
```

To disable RIP authentication on an interface, use the following unset command on the specific interface:

```
extfw-> unset interface bgroup0 protocol rip authentication
```

See Also

Recipe 15.9

15.4 Suppress RIP Route Advertisements with Passive Interfaces

Problem

You want to have an interface on a ScreenOS device learn routes via RIP, but not advertise any routes.

Solution

A ScreenOS firewall interface that already has RIP enabled on it (see Recipe 15.1) can be further qualified as a passive interface so that it does not advertise any routes as follows:

```
ssg5-serial-> set interface ethernet0/0 protocol rip passive-mode
```

You can replace the `ethernet0/0` interface with any other interface name on which you want to run RIP in passive mode.

Discussion

In ScreenOS, a passive-mode RIP interface sees RIP neighbors and receives RIP updates but does not advertise any routes to RIP neighbors. When an interface is configured to be passive, you can verify that the interface is still seeing RIP neighbors as follows:

```
ssg5-serial-> get vrouter trust-vr protocol rip neighbor
VR: trust-vr
-----------------------------------------------------------------
Flags : Static - S, Demand Circuit - T, NHTB - N, Down - D, Up - U,
Poll - P, Demand Circuit Init - I
Neighbors on interface ethernet0/0
-----------------------------------------------------------------
IpAddress      Version  Age         Expires      BadPackets
BadRoutes Flags
-----------------------------------------------------------------
192.168.4.1    2        02:02:12    00:02:47              0
        0 U
Neighbors on interface bgroup0
-----------------------------------------------------------------
IpAddress      Version  Age         Expires      BadPackets
BadRoutes Flags
-----------------------------------------------------------------
ssg5-serial->
```

The `Neighbors on interface ethernet0/0` section shows a valid neighbor.

RIP does not have a Hello mechanism, and RIP neighbor lists are built based on receiving `RESPONSE` messages. Hence, a RIP gateway on the other end of the passive interface would not add the `ssg5-serial` firewall to its RIP neighbor list. If an interface is made passive at a later stage following initial configuration while it has been advertising routes, the neighbor explicitly removes this neighbor from its neighbor list following the expiration of the hold timers:

```
extfw-> get log event
Total event entries = 757
Date       Time     Module Level  Type Description
2007-06-10 17:11:15 system info  00544 RIP neighbor 192.168.4.30 in
                                       virtual router trust-vr
                                       removed.
```

However, if multiple interfaces are connecting from the ssg5-serial firewall to a RIP neighbor and only one of them is in passive mode, the ssg5-serial will remain in the active neighbor list unless all the interfaces are made passive.

To bring a ScreenOS interface out of passive mode into its regular, active operation mode where it advertises RIP routes, configure the following:

```
ssg5-serial-> unset interface ethernet0/0 protocol rip passive-mode
```

See Also

The Introduction section to this chapter

15.5 Adjust RIP Timers to Influence Route Convergence Duration

Problem

You want to adjust RIP timers on a ScreenOS firewall to be different from the default values.

Solution

To achieve faster convergence, you can adjust the invalid and flush timers in the ScreenOS RIP implementation downward:

```
extfw-> set vrouter trust-vr protocol rip invalid-timer 90
extfw-> set vrouter trust-vr protocol rip flush-timer 60
```

Thus, the duration for a stale route to be removed from a ScreenOS firewall's routing table is reduced to as low as 180 seconds from the default value of at least 300 seconds. Note that the update and hold-down timers are kept at their default values.

Discussion

Invalid, flush, and hold timers are implemented in most modern RIP implementations to prevent routing loops and flapping routes. These timers are relevant in scenarios where there is a "silent" failure—for example, a RIP neighbor that was advertising the routes goes down, but the local physical interface on which the routes were being received is still up. If a local physical interface on which RIP routes are being learned goes down, the associated routes are immediately invalidated and purged from the routing table.

The default values for the various RIP timers relevant to convergence, excluding demand-circuit environments, in ScreenOS are as follows:

Update timer
: Defines the frequency of RIP RESPONSE messages with route entries: every 30 seconds.

Invalid timer
: Defines the duration that a ScreenOS device waits before marking a neighbor's route as invalid: 180 seconds.

Flush timer
: Defines the duration that a ScreenOS device waits before flushing a route after it has been invalidated: 120 seconds.

Hold timer
: Defines the minimum duration that a route is held in the routing table to prevent flapping: 90 seconds. The hold timer's minimum value has to be at least three times the update timer. Its maximum value can be the flush timer minus the update timer.

You can view the configured values for the various RIP timers in ScreenOS via the get `vrouter <vr-name> protocol rip` command. The following output shows the default values of the timers before the modifications made in this recipe's solution:

```
extfw-> get vrouter trust-vr protocol rip
VR: trust-vr
-----------------------------------------------------------------
State: enabled
Version: 2
Default metric for routes redistributed into RIP: 10
Maximum neighbors per interface: 16
Not validating neighbor in same subnet: disabled
Next RIP update scheduled after: 7 sec
<Additional_Output_Truncated>

Update| Invalid|    Flush| DC Retransmit| DC Poll| Hold Down
(Timers in seconds)
------------------------------------------------------------
    30|     180|      120|             5|     180|       90

Flags: Split Horizon - S, Split Horizon with Poison Reverse - P,
 Passive - I Demand Circuit - D
Interface   IP-Prefix       Admin    State    Flags   NbrCnt Metric
 Ver-Rx/Tx
-----------------------------------------------------------------
bgroup0     192.168.4.1/24   enabled enabled  S            1      1
   2/2
eth0/0      192.168.1.6/24   enabled enabled  S            0      1
   2/2
extfw->
```

You can achieve faster convergence in a RIP environment by tuning the various timers downward. As illustrated in this recipe's solution, the update and flush timers are reduced while the update and hold-down timers are kept at their default values. Because the RIP update timer is globally defined at 30 seconds and can send out a large number of routes that neighboring RIP devices need to process, it is not recommended to tweak this value lower than 30 seconds. Similarly, because the hold-down timer has to be at least three times the update timer, the default value of 90 seconds is not modified. The invalid and flush timers are indeed revised downward in this solution to achieve faster convergence.

Following the modifications to the update and flush timers per the solution, the timers' values are reflected in the protocol settings:

```
extfw-> get vrouter trust-vr protocol rip
VR: trust-vr
-------------------------------------------------------------------
State: enabled
Version: 2
Default metric for routes redistributed into RIP: 10
Maximum neighbors per interface: 16
Not validating neighbor in same subnet: disabled
Next RIP update scheduled after: 17 sec
<Additional_Output_Truncated>

Update| Invalid|   Flush| DC Retransmit| DC Poll| Hold Down
 (Timers in seconds)
-------------------------------------------------------------
    30|      90|     60|             5|     180|      90

Flags: Split Horizon - S, Split Horizon with Poison Reverse - P,
 Passive - I Demand Circuit - D
Interface   IP-Prefix         Admin     State     Flags   NbrCnt Metric
 Ver-Rx/Tx
-------------------------------------------------------------------
bgroup0     192.168.4.1/24    enabled   enabled  S             1      1
   2/2
eth0/0      192.168.1.6/24    enabled   enabled  S             0      1
   2/2
extfw->
```

With the new invalid and flush timers in effect, the following output dumps from a ScreenOS firewall illustrate the sequence of invalidation, hold-down, and purging of a route.

The removal of a RIP route on a ScreenOS firewall is a three-step process that begins with the invalidation of a route when it is not received even once during the invalid timer interval. Following invalidation, the route enters hold-down for the duration of the hold-down interval. Following the expiration of the hold-down interval, the route is no longer usable. However, it still resides in the RIP database, waiting to be flushed, until the flush timer expires.

In steady state, when a ScreenOS firewall is receiving routes from its RIP neighbors and there are no failures, the timer queue awaits an event to invalidate the routes. You can view this as follows:

```
extfw-> get vrouter trust-vr protocol rip timer
VR: trust-vr
```

```
---------------------------------------------------------------------

Pending route timer events in queue
Info                 Event           State Res      Interval      Remain
 TID Callback Argument  E-queue Cookie
6: 192.168.30.0/24    1/INVALID         aoto 1s          90000       71962
  89 0051995c 04b48ba0 032573a0 00 0009d788 0008be6e
extfw->
```

The route is identified, awaiting an `INVALID` event. The invalid timer, `Interval`, is seen here as 90,000 msec (90 seconds), per the configuration in this recipe's solution.

Also, the 90-second invalid timer is reflected in the neighbor list, with an `Expires` value of 1 minute and 30 seconds:

```
extfw-> get vrouter trust-vr protocol rip neighbor
VR: trust-vr
---------------------------------------------------------------------
Flags : Static - S, Demand Circuit - T, NHTB - N, Down - D, Up - U,
 Poll - P, Demand Circuit Init - I
Neighbors on interface bgroup0
---------------------------------------------------------------------
IpAddress        Version  Age        Expires   BadPackets BadRoutes
 Flags
---------------------------------------------------------------------
192.168.4.30     2        00:12:32   00:01:30           0         0
U
Neighbors on interface ethernet0/0
---------------------------------------------------------------------
IpAddress        Version  Age        Expires   BadPackets BadRoutes
 Flags
---------------------------------------------------------------------
extfw->
```

Now, as indicated in Figure 15-2, when the `ssg5-serial` firewall stops advertising the `192.168.30.0/24` route by converting its advertising interface to passive mode, the `Remain` field starts to decrement.

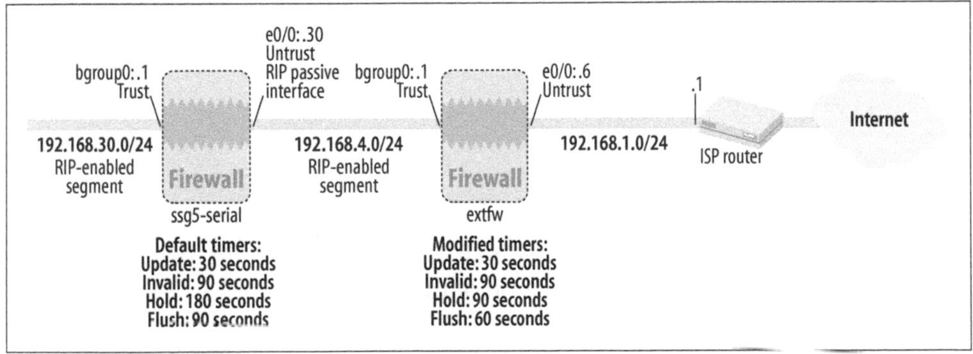

Figure 15-2. RIP timers

```
extfw-> get vrouter trust-vr protocol rip timer
VR: trust-vr
------------------------------------------------------------------

Pending route timer events in queue
Info                 Event          State Res     Interval   Remain
 TID Callback Argument  E-queue Cookie
6: 192.168.30.0/24   1/INVALID        aoto 1s        90000    20580
  89 0051995c 04b48ba0 032573a0 00 00105f68 00100f04
extfw->
```

Following 90 seconds without an update, the route enters hold-down:

```
extfw-> get vrouter trust-vr protocol rip timer
VR: trust-vr
---------------------------------------------------------------------

Pending route timer events in queue
Info                 Event          State Res     Interval     Remain
 TID Callback Argument  E-queue Cookie
7: 192.168.30.0/24   2/HOLDOWN        aoto 1s        90000      89048
  89 0051995c 04b48ba0 032573a0 00 0011bef8 00106320
extfw->
```

Furthermore, the RIP database also marks this route as being in hold-down state. While in hold-down state, the route is still in the routing table and can be actively used.

```
extfw-> get vrouter trust-vr protocol rip database
VR: trust-vr
-------------------------------------------------------------------
Total database entry: 4
Flags: Added in Multipath - M, RIP - R, Redistributed - I,
       Default (advertised) - D, Permanent - P, Summary - S,
       Unreachable - U, Hold - H
DBID   Prefix               Nexthop        Ifp     Cost Flags
  Source
-------------------------------------------------------------------
     5 0.0.0.0/0            0.0.0.0        n/a       10 RD
 -
    15 192.168.30.0/24      192.168.4.30   bgroup0    2 MRH
 192.168.4.30
     3 192.168.4.0/24       0.0.0.0        n/a        0 I
 -
     4 192.168.1.0/24       0.0.0.0        n/a        0 I
 -
extfw->
```

Following 90 seconds in hold-down without an update, the route is removed from the routing table and awaits the expiration of the flush timer for it to be purged. The PURGE event, thus, is triggered:

```
extfw-> get vrouter trust-vr protocol rip timer
VR: trust-vr
-----------------------------------------------------------------

Pending route timer events in queue
Info                  Event           State Res      Interval  Remain
 TID Callback Argument  E-queue Cookie
9: 192.168.30.0/24   3/PURGE            aoto 1s         60000    54047
  89 0051995c 04b48ba0 032573a0 00 0012a958 0011d639
extfw->
```

In this state, when the route is waiting to be flushed, it is marked unreachable in the RIP database but can no longer be actively used:

```
extfw-> get vrouter trust-vr protocol rip database
VR: trust-vr
-----------------------------------------------------------------
Total database entry: 4
Flags: Added in Multipath - M, RIP - R, Redistributed - I,
       Default (advertised) - D, Permanent - P, Summary - S,
       Unreachable - U, Hold - H
DBID   Prefix                  Nexthop         Ifp      Cost Flags
  Source
-----------------------------------------------------------------
     5 0.0.0.0/0               0.0.0.0         n/a        10 RD
  -
    17 192.168.30.0/24         192.168.4.30    bgroup0    16 RU
  192.168.4.30
     3 192.168.4.0/24          0.0.0.0         n/a         0 I
  -
     4 192.168.1.0/24          0.0.0.0         n/a         0 I
  -
extfw->
```

Following 60 seconds in the PURGE state, the route is completely flushed and purged from the RIP database and the device.

Hence, the convergence interval for a route to be rendered unusable in a ScreenOS firewall is the sum of the invalid timer and the hold-down timer. Although the flush timer is relevant to removing the route from the RIP database, once the flush timer is triggered with the PURGE event, the route is no longer usable.

You can adjust the various convergence timers to be higher than the default ScreenOS values to delay the route convergence interval, using the same configuration commands discussed earlier in this recipe.

See Also

The Introduction section to this chapter

15.6 Adjust RIP Interface Metrics to Influence Path Selection

Problem

You want to modify the metric of a RIP interface to influence route path selection.

Solution

You can modify the metric associated with a ScreenOS firewall interface that already has RIP enabled on it (refer to Recipe 15.1 to enable RIP on a firewall interface) as follows:

```
ssg5-serial-> set interface ethernet0/0 protocol rip metric 3
```

You can replace the `ethernet0/0` interface in the preceding configuration with any other interface whose RIP metric needs to be modified.

Discussion

As discussed in this chapter's Introduction, RIP metrics are used to compute the *distance* to a destination route. Each RIP route destination has a metric associated with it. RIP metrics range from 1 to 16. When two or more RIP routes with dissimilar metrics are compared, the lower metric is preferred. A metric of 16 indicates that the destination route is unreachable. When a RIP gateway receives a route on an interface from a neighbor, it computes the metric associated with the route by adding the received metric to the interface's metric. The default metric associated with all RIP interfaces in ScreenOS is 1. However, as described in this recipe's solution, you can modify this metric to a higher value.

For this recipe's solution, all RIP routes learned via the `ethernet0/0` interface will have a metric of three hops added to the received metric before being installed in the RIP database. Increasing the RIP metric associated with an interface typically causes routes learned via that interface to be less preferred to those learned on another interface. This is relevant in scenarios where you could have two interfaces on a ScreenOS firewall that are learning RIP routes, where you would like to have one of the interfaces used as the primary path and the other interface as a backup, failover path. In such a scenario, you would assign a higher interface metric to the backup interface.

See Also

The Introduction section to this chapter

15.7 Redistribute Static Routes into RIP

Problem

You want to redistribute static routes into RIP.

Solution

Follow these steps to redistribute a static route into RIP:

1. Define the static route(s) in ScreenOS in a VR.
2. Define an access list to identify the static route(s) in that specific VR.
3. Define a route map to match the access-list entry in that specific VR and assign a RIP metric to it.
4. Apply the route map to the RIP instance in the specific VR, specifying redistribution from `protocol static`.

Figure 15-3 illustrates an environment where the `extfw` firewall is running RIP on its `bgroup0` interface and static routes on its `e0/0` interface. All interfaces on `extfw` are in the `trust-vr`.

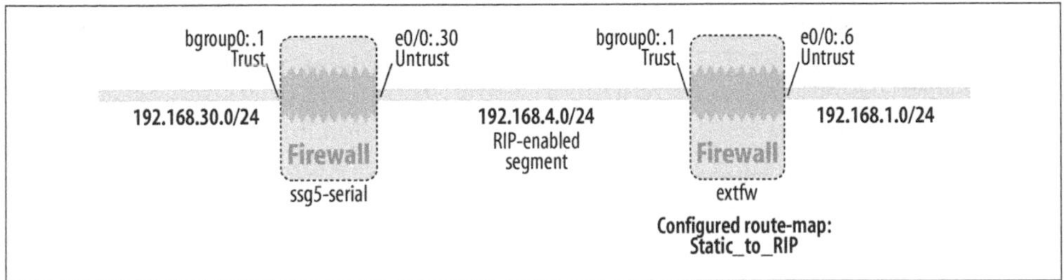

Figure 15-3. Static-to-RIP redistribution

Hence, to redistribute the `192.168.7.0/24` and `172.16.0.0/16` static routes on the `extfw` ScreenOS firewall into RIP, the following configuration is required:

```
extfw-> set vrouter trust-vr route 192.168.7.0/24 gateway 192.168.1.1
extfw-> set vrouter trust-vr route 172.16.0.0/16 gateway 192.168.1.1
extfw->
extfw-> set vrouter trust-vr access-list 30 permit ip 192.168.7.0/24 1
extfw-> set vrouter trust-vr access-list 30 permit ip 172.16.0.0/16 2
extfw->
extfw-> set vrouter trust-vr route-map name Static_to_RIP permit 1
extfw-> set vrouter trust-vr route-map Static_to_RIP 1 match ip 30
extfw-> set vrouter trust-vr route-map Static_to_RIP 1 metric 3
extfw->
extfw-> set vrouter trust-vr protocol rip redistribute route-map
Static_to_RIP protocol static
extfw->
```

Discussion

You may need to redistribute static routes into RIP in several scenarios. When you define the access list to identify the various subnets that you would like to redistribute into RIP, make sure you use a unique access-list number and assign each included subnet a distinct sequence number. You can verify the access-list entries as follows:

```
extfw-> get vrouter trust-vr access-list
IPv4 Access Lists
------------------------------------------------
Access list (30)
----------------
        Sequence 1: 192.168.7.0/24               -> Permit
        Sequence 2: 172.16.0.0/16                -> Permit
IPv6 Access Lists
------------------------------------------------
extfw->
```

You need to explicitly define each route-map stanza in ScreenOS with a name keyword before it can have entries associated with it. Hence, the first statement in the preceding route-map definition specifies the name of the route map, the route-map type (permit or deny), and the sequence number of the route map. Following this, the entries associated with this permit sequence—for example, to match access-list 30 subnets and assign them a RIP metric of 3—are defined. Note that if the metric is not explicitly defined in the route map, a default RIP metric of 10 is assigned to the redistributed route. You can verify the route map's definition in ScreenOS accordingly:

```
extfw-> get vrouter trust-vr route-map Static_to_RIP
Route-map (Static_to_RIP)
----------------------
        Entry (1) - Action (permit)
        ----------------------------
                Match Fields
                ------------
                ip-address:             30 (access-list)

                Set Fields
                ----------
                metric:                 3


extfw->
```

The `redistribute` configuration statement is defined in the context of the `trust-vr`'s RIP protocol section, specifying the route map that identifies the subnets and associated RIP metrics. Following the route map, the source protocol for the redistribution is specified. In this context, the source is `static`.

On the receiving `ssg5-serial` gateway, you can view the RIP routes as follows:

```
ssg5-serial-> get vrouter trust-vr route protocol rip
H: Host C: Connected S: Static A: Auto-Exported
```

```
I: Imported R: RIP P: Permanent D: Auto-Discovered
iB: IBGP eB: EBGP O: OSPF E1: OSPF external type 1
E2: OSPF external type 2

Total 7/max entries

   ID          IP-Prefix      Interface         Gateway   P Pref
   Mtr      Vsys
-------------------------------------------------------------------
*   6     192.168.7.0/24          eth0/0      192.168.4.1   R  100
     6      Root
*   7      172.16.0.0/16          eth0/0      192.168.4.1   R  100
     6      Root

ssg5-serial->
```

See Also

Recipe 15.8

15.8 Redistribute Routes from OSPF into RIP

Problem

You want to redistribute a set of OSPF routes into RIP.

Solution

Follow these steps to redistribute a set of OSPF routes into RIP:

1. Define an access list to identify the OSPF route(s).
2. Define a route map to match the access-list route entries, and assign an OSPF metric and metric type to the redistributed routes.
3. Apply the route map to the RIP instance in the specific VR, specifying redistribution from OSPF.

Figure 15-4 illustrates an environment where the `ssg5-serial` firewall is running OSPF on its `ethernet0/0` interface and RIP on its `bgroup0` interface. All interfaces on `ssg5-serial` are in the `trust-vr`.

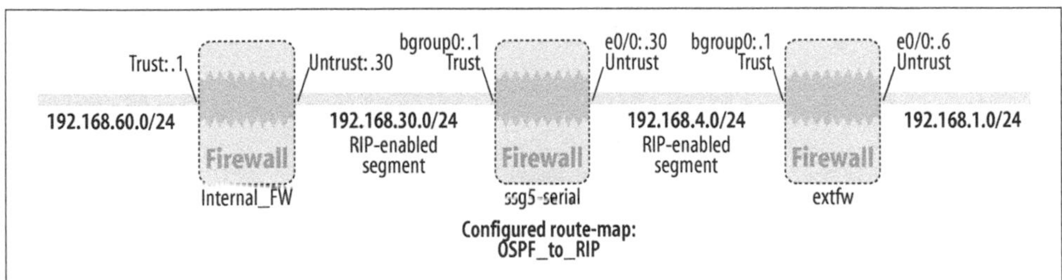

Figure 15-4. OSPF-to-RIP redistribution

To redistribute all the OSPF routes in the trust-vr on the ssg5-serial ScreenOS firewall into RIP, the following configuration is required:

```
ssg5-serial-> set vr trust-vr access-list 60 permit ip 0.0.0.0/0 1
ssg5-serial->
ssg5-serial-> set vrouter trust-vr route-map name OSPF_to_RIP permit 1
ssg5-serial-> set vrouter trust route-map OSPF_to_RIP 1 match ip 60
ssg5-serial-> set vrouter trust-vr route-map OSPF_to_RIP 1 metric 3
ssg5-serial->
ssg5-serial-> set vrouter trust-vr protocol rip redistribute route-map
OSPF_to_RIP protocol ospf
ssg5-serial->
```

Discussion

The access-list 60 defined in this recipe's solution is a match-all list that matches all instances of OSPF routes in the trust-vr. If you would like to specify the particular OSPF routes that need to be redistributed into RIP, the access-list entries can be more granular. (Recipe 15.7 specifies a more granular access list that specifies particular static routes that are redistributed into RIP.)

You can view the current set of OSPF routes on ssg5-serial as follows:

```
ssg5-serial-> get vrouter trust-vr route protocol ospf
H: Host C: Connected S: Static A: Auto-Exported
I: Imported R: RIP P: Permanent D: Auto-Discovered
iB: IBGP eB: EBGP O: OSPF E1: OSPF external type 1
E2: OSPF external type 2

Total 6/max entries

    ID          IP-Prefix       Interface         Gateway   P Pref
     Mtr     Vsys
-------------------------------------------------------------------
*    7      192.168.2.0/24          eth0/0     192.168.4.1   0   60
       2     Root
*    5      192.168.1.0/24          eth0/0     192.168.4.1   0   60
       2     Root

ssg5-serial->
```

These routes are redistributed into RIP, installed in the RIP database on ssg5-serial, and advertised to ssg5-serial's RIP neighbors:

```
ssg5-serial-> get vrouter trust-vr protocol rip database
VR: trust-vr
------------------------------------------------------------------
Total database entry: 4
Flags: Added in Multipath - M, RIP - R, Redistributed - I,
       Default (advertised) - D, Permanent - P, Summary - S,
       Unreachable - U, Hold - H
DBID   Prefix              Nexthop        Ifp   Cost Flags   Source
------------------------------------------------------------------
    16 192.168.30.0/24     0.0.0.0        n/a      0 I          -
```

```
     3 192.168.4.0/24          0.0.0.0        n/a      0 I        -
    19 192.168.2.0/24          192.168.4.1    n/a      3 I        -
    18 192.168.1.0/24          192.168.4.1    n/a      3 I        -
ssg5-serial->
```

One of the RIP neighbors, `Internal_FW`, learns these redistributed and other RIP routes. You can view its RIP routes accordingly:

```
Internal_FW-> get vrouter trust-vr route protocol rip
H: Host C: Connected S: Static A: Auto-Exported
I: Imported R: RIP P: Permanent D: Auto-Discovered
iB: IBGP eB: EBGP O: OSPF E1: OSPF external type 1
E2: OSPF external type 2

Total 9/max entries

   ID          IP-Prefix      Interface         Gateway   P Pref
  Mtr      Vsys
-----------------------------------------------------------------
*  12      192.168.4.0/24       untrust    192.168.30.1   R  100
    2     Root
*  16      192.168.2.0/24       untrust    192.168.30.1   R  100
    4     Root
*  15      192.168.1.0/24       untrust    192.168.30.1   R  100
    4     Root

Internal_FW->
```

The two RIP routes learned in the preceding code that are redistributed from OSPF are seen to have a RIP metric of 4 on `Internal_FW`, which is the sum of the advertised metric of the redistributed route, 3, plus the interface metric of the receiving interface on `Internal_FW`, 1, for a total of 4.

See Also

Recipe 15.7

15.9 Filter Inbound RIP Routes

Problem

You want to filter the RIP routes received by a ScreenOS security gateway.

Solution

Follow these steps to filter the RIP routes received by a ScreenOS security gateway:

1. Define an access list to identify the RIP routes that you would like to permit.
2. Define a route map to match the access-list route entries.
3. Apply the route map to RIP in the specific VR in the inbound direction, as the route filter.

Figure 15-5 illustrates an environment where the ssg5-serial firewall is advertising four RIP routes on its bgroup0 RIP-enabled segment. The Internal_FW gateway has an inbound RIP filter that only installs the 172.16.0.0/16 route into the routing table, dropping all of the other routes it receives in the update.

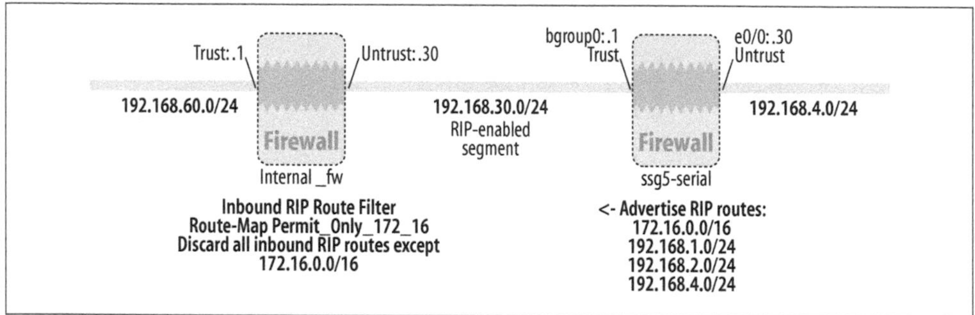

Figure 15-5. Filtering inbound RIP routes

To filter out all the inbound RIP routes except 172.16.0.0/16 on the Internal_FW ScreenOS gateway, the following configuration is required:

```
Internal_FW-> set vrouter trust-vr access-list 83 permit ip
172.16.0.0/16 1
Internal_FW->
Internal_FW-> set vrouter trust-vr route-map name Permit_Only_172_16
permit 1
Internal_FW-> set vrouter trust-vr route-map Permit_Only_172_16 1
match ip 83
Internal_FW->
Internal_FW-> set vrouter trust-vr protocol rip route-map
Permit_Only_172_16 in
Internal_FW->
```

Discussion

RIP offers the ability to filter routes to control traffic paths.

In the absence of inbound route filters, all of the RIP updates received on an interface are installed in the routing table and RIP timers are reset. Here is a debug output illustrating the routes received by Internal_FW (see Figure 15-5) before the inbound route filter is installed:

```
Internal_FW-> clear dbuf
Internal_FW-> debug rip recv
Internal_FW-> get dbuf stream
## 2007-06-30 13:15:04 : rip: [rx] RIP packet on interface untrust,
 vr (trust-vr)
## 2007-06-30 13:15:04 : rip: update on ifp untrust from 192.168.30.1,
 RIP port 520
## 2007-06-30 13:15:04 : rip: [rx] 192.168.4.0/24, nhop 192.168.30.1,
 metric 2, tag 0.0.0.0
```

```
## 2007-06-30 13:15:04 : rip: resetting timer for existing route
## 2007-06-30 13:15:04 : rip: [rx] 192.168.1.0/24, nhop 192.168.30.1,
 metric 4, tag 0.0.0.0
## 2007-06-30 13:15:04 : rip: resetting timer for existing route
## 2007-06-30 13:15:04 : rip: [rx] 192.168.2.0/24, nhop 192.168.30.1,
 metric 4, tag 0.0.0.0
## 2007-06-30 13:15:04 : rip: resetting timer for existing route
## 2007-06-30 13:15:04 : rip: [rx] 172.16.0.0/16, nhop 192.168.30.1,
 metric 4, tag 0.0.0.0
## 2007-06-30 13:15:04 : rip: resetting timer for existing route
```

Following the configuration of the inbound RIP route filter that only permits the `172.16.0.0/16` route, the following debug output verifies that the ScreenOS gateway drops inbound updates that do not match the inbound route filter:

```
Internal_FW-> clear dbuf
Internal_FW-> debug rip recv
Internal_FW-> get dbuf stream
## 2007-06-30 13:38:04 : rip: [rx] RIP packet on interface untrust,
 vr (trust-vr)
## 2007-06-30 13:38:04 : rip: update on ifp untrust from 192.168.30.1,
 RIP port 520
## 2007-06-30 13:38:04 : rip: update 192.168.4.0/24 not allowed with
 route-map Permit_Only_172_16
## 2007-06-30 13:38:04 : rip: update 192.168.1.0/24 not allowed with
 route-map Permit_Only_172_16
## 2007-06-30 13:38:04 : rip: [rx] 172.16.0.0/16, nhop 192.168.30.1,
 metric 4, tag 0.0.0.0
## 2007-06-30 13:38:04 : rip: resetting timer for existing route
## 2007-06-30 13:38:04 : rip: update 192.168.2.0/24 not allowed with
 route-map Permit_Only_172_16
Internal_FW-> undebug all
```

You can see the received, filtered RIP route on the `Internal_FW` as follows:

```
Internal_FW-> get vrouter trust-vr route protocol rip
H: Host C: Connected S: Static A: Auto-Exported
I: Imported R: RIP P: Permanent D: Auto-Discovered
iB: IBGP eB: EBGP O: OSPF E1: OSPF external type 1
E2: OSPF external type 2

Total 7/max entries

   ID          IP-Prefix    Interface       Gateway   P Pref    Mtr
     Vsys
-------------------------------------------------------------------
*   7      172.16.0.0/16      untrust  192.168.30.1   R  100      4
     Root

Internal_FW->
```

See Also

Recipe 15.7; Recipe 15.8

15.10 Configure Summary Routes in RIP

Problem

You want to reduce the number of RIP routes being advertised by a ScreenOS security gateway by using summary routes.

Solution

You can enable summary routes on an interface in ScreenOS to summarize route announcements. The following solution will generate a summarized `172.16.0.0/16` RIP route announcement instead of announcing the two component routes, `172.16.1.0/24` and `172.16.2.0/24`:

```
ssg5-serial-> set vrouter trust-vr protocol rip summary-ip
172.16.0.0/16
ssg5-serial-> set interface bgroup0 protocol rip summary-enable
```

The summary route is announced to RIP neighbors on the `bgroup0` interface of the `ssg5-serial` gateway.

In addition to enabling the summary route for the `172.16.0.0/16` network, it's recommended to create a null route on `ssg5-serial` to prevent routing loops:

```
ssg5-serial-> set vrouter trust-vr route 172.16.0.0/16 interface null
preference 255 metric 65535
```

Figure 15-6 shows the `ssg5-serial` gateway advertising the summary route on its `bgroup0` RIP-enabled interface.

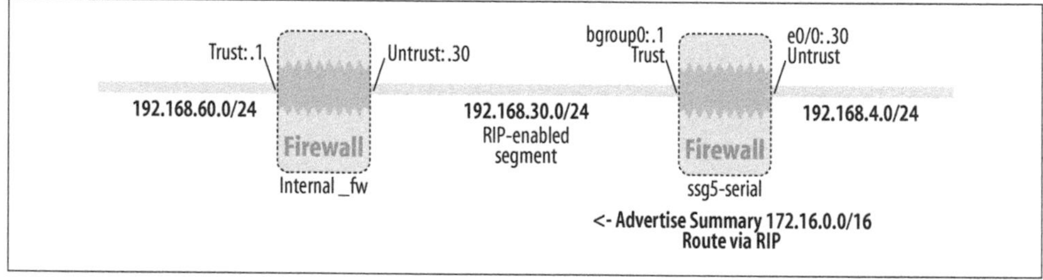

Figure 15-6. Summary routes

Discussion

The summarized route is advertised only on the interfaces that have `summary-enable` configured. On other interfaces, all the individual component routes get advertised. This recipe's solution generates the summary route from the component routes, which you can view in the `ssg5-serial` gateway's RIP database:

```
ssg5-serial-> get vrouter trust-vr protocol rip database prefix
172.16.0.0/16
VR: trust-vr
-------------------------------------------------------------------
Flags: Added in Multipath - M, RIP - R, Redistributed - I,
       Default (advertised) - D, Permanent - P, Summary - S,
       Unreachable - U, Hold - H
DBID   Prefix              Nexthop       Ifp      Cost Flags   Source
-------------------------------------------------------------------
     9 172.16.0.0/16       0.0.0.0       n/a       3 RS       -
ssg5-serial->
```

The RIP database output shows the 172.16.0.0/16 route with the S (Summary) and R (advertised by RIP) flags.

You can view the summarized RIP route on the Internal_FW gateway that receives the RIP updates from ssg5-serial as follows:

```
Internal_FW-> get vrouter trust-vr route protocol rip
H: Host C: Connected S: Static A: Auto-Exported
I: Imported R: RIP P: Permanent D: Auto-Discovered
iB: IBGP eB: EBGP O: OSPF E1: OSPF external type 1
E2: OSPF external type 2

Total 7/max entries

   ID          IP-Prefix  Interface        Gateway   P Pref     Mtr
     Vsys
------------------------------------------------------------------
*   7      172.16.0.0/16    untrust   192.168.30.1   R  100       4
     Root

Internal_FW->
```

You should use summary routes with caution, as they can potentially cause routing loops. An example of such a scenario is where ssg5-serial has a static default route pointing to Internal_FW and it sends a summary route to Internal_FW for 172.16.0.0/16 on its bgroup0 interface. Now, if Internal_FW sends traffic destined for 172.16.7.0/24 to ssg5-serial by virtue of the RIP summary announcement, ssg5-serial will send the traffic right back to Internal_FW following the static default route because it does not have a specific route to 172.16.7.0/24. Thus, a routing loop is formed. Hence, the null route to the summary destination, defined in this recipe's solution, has a more specific bit-bucket destination that prevents routing loops from forming.

See Also

The Introduction to this chapter

15.11 Administer RIP Version 1

Problem

You want to configure a ScreenOS gateway to use RIP version 1 as follows.

Solution

You can configure a ScreenOS gateway to strictly use RIP version 1:

```
ssg5-serial-> set vrouter trust-vr protocol rip version v1
```

This setting globally configures RIP version 1 on all RIP-enabled interfaces on the ScreenOS gateway.

Also, you can selectively enable RIP version 1 on specific interfaces to send or receive RIP v1 updates:

```
ssg5-serial-> set interface bgroup0 protocol rip send-version v1
ssg5-serial-> set interface bgroup0 protocol rip receive-version v1
```

Furthermore, you can configure ScreenOS gateways to send updates using RIP v1 as well as RIP v2:

```
ssg5-serial-> set interface bgroup0 protocol rip send-version v1v2
```

Discussion

Although RIP version 1 is not commonly used in today's networks, you may need to rely on RIP Version 1 in a few pockets of legacy networks.

A ScreenOS gateway with RIP version 1 configured globally uses RIP v1 to send and receive packets on all RIP-enabled interfaces, as seen here:

```
ssg5-serial-> get vrouter trust-vr protocol rip
VR: trust-vr
-----------------------------------------------------------------
State: enabled
Version: 1
Default metric for routes redistributed into RIP: 10
Maximum neighbors per interface: 16
Not validating neighbor in same subnet: disabled
Next RIP update scheduled after: 5 sec
Maximum number of Alternate routes per prefix: 0
Advertising default route: disabled
Default routes learnt by RIP will be accepted
Incoming routes filter and offset-metric: not configured
Outgoing routes filter and offset-metric: not configured
Update packet threshold is not configured
Total number of RIP interfaces created on vr(trust-vr): 2

Update| Invalid|  Flush| DC Retransmit| DC Poll| Hold Down (Timers
in seconds)
```

```
--------------------------------------------------------------
     30|      180|      120|              5|      180|      90

Flags: Split Horizon - S, Split Horizon with Poison Reverse - P,
Passive - I
       Demand Circuit - D
Interface  IP-Prefix        Admin    State    Flags  NbrCnt Metric
 Ver-Rx/Tx
------------------------------------------------------------------
eth0/0     192.168.4.30/24  enabled  enabled  P           1      3
   1/1
bgroup0    192.168.30.1/24  enabled  enabled  S           0      1
   1/1
ssg5-serial->
```

ScreenOS gateways that are not enabled to receive RIP v1 updates reject those updates, seen here where the `Internal_FW` gateway receives a RIP v1 update from `ssg5-serial` on its untrust interface that is configured for RIPv2 send/receive:

```
Internal_FW-> clear dbuf
Internal_FW-> debug rip recv
Internal_FW-> get dbuf stream
## 2007-06-30 16:52:47 : rip: [rx] RIP packet on interface untrust,
 vr (trust-vr)
## 2007-06-30 16:52:47 : rip: pkt ignored on ifp untrust from
192.168.30.1 is V1
Internal_FW->
```

Next, when `ssg5-serial` is configured to send updates via v1v2:

```
ssg5-serial-> get vrouter trust-vr protocol rip interface
VR: trust-vr
------------------------------------------------------------------
Flags: Split Horizon - S, Split Horizon with Poison Reverse - P,
Passive - I
       Demand Circuit - D
Interface  IP-Prefix        Admin    State    Flags  NbrCnt Metric
 Ver-Rx/Tx
------------------------------------------------------------------
eth0/0     192.168.4.30/24  enabled  enabled  P           0      3
   1/1
bgroup0    192.168.30.1/24  enabled  enabled  S           0      1
   1/v1v2
ssg5-serial->
```

Hence, the `Internal_FW` gateway accepts these updates:

```
Internal_FW-> clear dbuf
Internal_FW-> debug rip recv
Internal_FW-> get dbuf stream
## 2007-06-30 17:09:04 : rip: [rx] RIP packet on interface untrust,
  vr (trust-vr)
## 2007-06-30 17:09:04 : rip: update on ifp untrust from 192.168.30.1,
 RIP port 520
## 2007-06-30 17:09:04 : rip: [rx] 192.168.4.0/24, nhop 192.168.30.1,
 metric 2, tag 0.0.0.0
```

```
## 2007-06-30 17:09:04 : rip: resetting timer for existing route
Internal_FW-> undebug all
```

As indicated here, the RIP route is accepted by the untrust interface on Internal_FW that is configured to receive only RIP v2 routes:

```
Internal_FW-> get vrouter trust-vr protocol rip interface
VR: trust-vr
-------------------------------------------------------------------
Flags: Split Horizon - S, Split Horizon with Poison Reverse - P,
Passive - I
       Demand Circuit - D
Interface IP-Prefix    Admin  State   Flags NbrCnt Metric Ver-Rx/Tx
-------------------------------------------------------------------
untrust   192.168.30.30/24 enabled enabled S     1      1       2/2
Internal_FW->
```

The route gets installed in the routing table on Internal_FW:

```
Internal_FW-> get vrouter trust-vr route protocol rip
H: Host C: Connected S: Static A: Auto-Exported
I: Imported R: RIP P: Permanent D: Auto-Discovered
iB: IBGP eB: EBGP O: OSPF E1: OSPF external type 1
E2: OSPF external type 2

Total 7/max entries

   ID IP-Prefix      Interface  Gateway        P Pref  Mtr   Vsys
-----------------------------------------------------------------
*  14 192.168.4.0/24 untrust    192.168.30.1   R  100   2     Root

Internal_FW->
```

See Also

The Introduction to this chapter; Recipe 15.1

15.12 Troubleshoot RIP

Problem

You have enabled RIP on an interface on a ScreenOS firewall, but are not receiving any routes from your peer device.

Solution

There can be several reasons why you may not be receiving routes from a peer device. First, you should ensure that the ScreenOS firewall can see the peer device:

```
extfw-> get vrouter trust-vr protocol rip neighbors
VR: trust-vr
-------------------------------------------------------------------
Flags : Static - S, Demand Circuit - T, NHTB - N, Down - D, Up - U,
Poll - P,
```

```
        Demand Circuit Init - I
Neighbors on interface bgroup0
-----------------------------------------------------------------
IpAddress       Version  Age          Expires      BadPackets
BadRoutes Flags
-----------------------------------------------------------------
192.168.4.30    2        00:00:17     00:03:00              0
        0 U
extfw->
```

If this output does not show any neighbors on the interface on which routes are expected from the peer, make sure there is no RIP authentication mismatch. You can verify an authentication mismatch by running a debug:

```
ssg5-serial-> clear dbuf
ssg5-serial-> debug rip recv
ssg5-serial-> get dbuf stream
## 2007-06-30 15:01:01 : rip: [rx] RIP packet on interface
 ethernet0/0, vr (trust-vr)
## 2007-06-30 15:01:01 : rip: received md5 authentication packet
## 2007-06-30 15:01:01 :    pkt length: 124, key length: 124, seq
num: 11
## 2007-06-30 15:01:01 : rip: failed authentication, discard
ssg5-serial-> undebug all
```

A successful RIP update packet with no authentication mismatch, on the other hand, looks as follows in the debug output:

```
ssg5-serial-> clear dbuf
ssg5-serial-> debug rip recv
ssg5-serial-> get dbuf stream
## 2007-06-30 15:09:07 : rip: received md5 authentication packet
## 2007-06-30 15:09:07 :    pkt length: 124, key length: 124, seq num:
 27
## 2007-06-30 15:09:07 :    md5 auth ok
## 2007-06-30 15:09:07 : rip: update on ifp ethernet0/0 from
192.168.4.1, RIP port 520
## 2007-06-30 15:09:07 : rip: [rx] 172.16.1.0/24, nhop 192.168.4.1,
 metric 6, tag 0.0.0.0
## 2007-06-30 15:09:07 : rip: resetting timer for existing route
## 2007-06-30 15:09:07 : rip: [rx] 172.16.3.0/24, nhop 192.168.4.1,
 metric 6, tag 0.0.0.0
## 2007-06-30 15:09:07 : rip: resetting timer for existing route
## 2007-06-30 15:09:07 : rip: [rx] 192.168.7.0/24, nhop 192.168.4.1,
 metric 6, tag 0.0.0.0
## 2007-06-30 15:09:07 : rip: resetting timer for existing route
## 2007-06-30 15:09:07 : rip: [rx] 172.16.0.0/16, nhop 192.168.4.1,
 metric 6, tag 0.0.0.0
ssg5-serial-> undebug all
```

If the neighbor was previously up, but is no longer reachable, review the ScreenOS event log to check for messages related to the specific RIP neighbor:

```
ssg5-serial-> get log event
Total event entries = 1
```

```
Date       Time     Module Level Type Description
2007-06-10 11:49:13 system info 00544 RIP neighbor 192.168.4.1 in
                                      virtual router trust-vr removed
```

Discussion

In addition to running the get and debug commands in the solution above, make sure there are no incorrectly configured route maps that would suppress the route.

After reviewing RIP authentication and route maps to ensure that they do not reveal any reasons for you not receiving routes from a peer, you can execute a debug to check the messages coming from the neighbor:

```
extfw-> clear dbuf
extfw-> debug rip recv
```

After waiting for at least 30 seconds to ensure that at least one RIP update cycle gets executed, you can check the debug buffer to see whether the neighbor is receiving any updates:

```
extfw-> get dbuf stream
## 2007-05-28 01:09:20 : rip: [rx] RIP packet on interface bgroup0,
 vr (trust-vr)
## 2007-05-28 01:09:20 : rip: update on ifp bgroup0 from
 192.168.4.30, RIP port 520
## 2007-05-28 01:09:20 : rip: [rx] 192.168.30.0/24, nhop
 192.168.4.30, metric 2, tag 0
## 2007-05-28 01:09:20 : rip: resetting timer for existing route
extfw->
```

The output shows the route being received from the neighbor. If messages such as these are not seen from the peer device that is supposed to be sending routes, you should verify the configuration on the peer device.

After viewing the debug buffer, you should disable the debug command:

```
extfw-> undebug rip recv
```

If additional debugs are running, you can disable all of them:

```
extfw-> undebug all
```

Finally, while the ScreenOS firewall is receiving route updates from the peer RIP gateway, the computed RIP metric may be 16 or higher:

```
extfw-> get dbuf stream
## 2007-05-28 01:54:57 : rip: [rx] 192.168.1.0/24, nhop 192.168.4.30,
metric 16, tag 0
## 2007-05-28 01:54:57 : rip: ignore update, metric infinite
```

See Also

The Introduction to this chapter

CHAPTER 16
OSPF

16.0 Introduction

Open Shortest Path First (OSPF) is arguably the most common and widespread interior gateway routing protocol running today. OSPF is scalable, relatively simple to configure, and robust. OSPF has a twin brother, which is Integrated Intermediate System to Intermediate System (IS-IS). Both protocols are link-state routing protocols. OSPF was first documented in RFC 1247 by John T. Moy in 1991. The most current RFC for OSPF is RFC 2328.

Routing protocols are typically considered to be one of two types: distance-vector or link-state. In distance-vector routing protocols such as the Routing Information Protocol (RIP), routers make local routing decisions and report the results to their neighbors, which in turn do the same and report their results to their neighbors, and so on. This process has been termed *routing by rumor* because each router has to trust the accuracy of the information received from its neighbors. In the second type of protocol, link-state protocols, routers report their link information, including interface types and IP addresses, to all other routers in the network. Each router then uses this information about links to independently build a topology view and thus a routing table. In a properly functioning network, all routers running a link-state routing protocol will have an identical view of the network. Unlike distance-vector routing protocols, link-state routing protocols do not share local routing decisions with other routers.

Both distance-vector and link-state protocols have their strengths and weaknesses. One advantage of a distance-vector protocol is that one router can control the routing of its downstream routers. A router could individually prefer or discriminate against a route, summarize routes, or even filter routes and report only the results to its neighbors. A disadvantage of distance-vector protocols is that they require a well-designed topology and routing policies on routers to ensure fast convergence and to prevent looping, so there is a heavy administrative burden.

Because a router running a link-state routing protocol knows the entire network topology and performs routing decisions independently from other routers in the network, it does not suffer from the same problems (nor does it have the same advantages) as a router running a distance-vector protocol. Link-state protocols work very well in challenging topologies and maintain fast convergence without creating (temporary) looping. The disadvantage also lies within its design, mainly in that tools such as route filtering do not work well, if at all, with link-state routing. Additionally, OSPF uses a complex state machine, and can require a significant amount of processing power.

OSPF is classified as a link-state routing protocol, but this is not entirely true because OSPF uses distance-vector routing as well. OSPF uses the concept of *areas* to achieve scalability. Within an area, routers share their link-state information with each other by flooding routing information until each router has the same topology information. Because link-state information is flooded within an area, as the size of the area increases, the processing that is required to calculate the routing table increases as well. To alleviate this burden, an administrator can segment the network into multiple areas. With today's high-performance network devices, the limit may be inconsequential, and many network administrators may choose to support just one area; however, it is common to have multiple areas. The routers that connect areas together are called Area Border Routers (ABRs), and while they are maintaining topology databases from each of their connected areas, they also make local routing decisions and report the results for one area into all other areas to which they are connected. These ABRs build the second level of the OSPF hierarchy and use distance-vector routing to connect different areas with each other. This has interesting implications, in that an ABR is the only router in OSPF that can filter routes or summarize routes.

OSPF areas are strictly hierarchical. All areas have to communicate via a common area, called the *backbone area* or *area 0*. Therefore, all ABRs must connect to area 0. Routes from other routing sources, such as static routes from another routing protocol, or even from another instance of OSPF on a router, are considered Autonomous System (AS) External routes. In the general sense, an AS is considered a network under one administrative control, but in the sense of OSPF, an AS is the OSPF instance itself, and any routes not generated by the OSPF process in the network are considered AS External. Routers that connect to the external world are called Autonomous System Boundary Routers (ASBRs). External routes are also injected in distance-vector fashion. A router can be an ABR and an ASBR at the same time.

The heart of OSPF is the link-state database (LSDB). OSPF routers communicate with each other via link-state advertisements (LSAs), which are entered in the local LSDB. LSAs are flooded via multicast from router to router. All LSAs are sent to the multicast address `224.0.0.5`. This address has local scope, meaning that these packets are not routed. Instead, they are received by locally attached routers, the information in them is placed in the local LSDB, and the router in turn forwards the LSA out its interfaces. The term *link-state database* is a little bit of a misnomer, as the LSDB saves all kinds of information communicated via LSAs—most important, the link-state, inter-area routes, and external routes related to the three-level hierarchy of OSPF. Some special LSAs are used for broadcast networks and to advertise ASBRs as well and a variety of extensions are being written that use LSAs to communicate things such as Border Gateway Protocol (BGP) external attributes, multicast group membership, traffic-engineering-related information, and even information related to the functioning of the whole router device. ScreenOS does not implement any of these in the current release. Table 16-1 provides an overview of which LSAs ScreenOS supports.

Table 16-1. Link-state advertisements

Type	LSA description	ScreenOS
1	Router	Yes
2	Network	Yes
3	Network Summary	Yes
4	ASBR Summary	Yes
5	AS External	Yes
6	Group membership	No
7	Not-so-stubby area (NSSA) External	Yes
8	External attribute	No
9	Opaque (link-local-scope)	No
10	Opaque (area-local-scope)	No
11	Opaque (AS-scope)	No

Each router describes its links in one Router or Type-1 LSA. A Router LSA contains the link with ID and type, neighbors, IP addressing, and link cost. The Router LSA has area flooding scope. When Router LSAs are received, each router within the area builds a topology view by running the *Dijkstra algorithm*. The Dijkstra algorithm builds a graph with the local router in its root. It calculates the shortest path by taking link cost into account. A graph implies that there is a point-to-point link between routers. Therefore, for broadcast networks such as Ethernet, OSPF elects a pseudonode, called a Designated Router (DR), and spans a pseudo point-to-point link between the routers on the broadcast network and the DR. Routers on a broadcast segment send to the multicast group address `224.0.0.6`, which indicates all DRs, instead of the default address of `224.0.0.5`. The DR collects and distributes LSAs to the routers on `224.0.0.5`; this enables all routers to receive all LSAs, but does not require a full mesh of adjacencies to be built, and thus cuts down on flooding overhead. The DR also issues a

Network LSA, which describes all known routers on that broadcast segment. OSPF routers are known by a *Router ID* that needs to be unique within the entire OSPF AS.

ABRs, which are routers that connect a nonbackbone area to the backbone area, issue Network Summary LSAs, which contain networks that are reachable through that ABR. The ABR builds a Dijkstra graph for each of its connected areas, and then derives a routing table from that. It knows which networks are routable in an area and advertises those networks via Network Summary LSAs in the other area or areas to which it is connected.

There is one Network Summary LSA for each network. This is somewhat similar to the way RIP propagates routing information. Network Summary LSAs are not flooded over area borders; instead, they are issued by ABRs and are flooded through the area. Therefore, routing needs to cross the backbone area. Neighbors directly connected to an ABR flood the unchanged Network Summary LSA to their neighbors so that all routers in the area receive the Network Summary LSA from the ABR. OSPF routers already have a topology of their area. They know where the ABRs are located in the graph. They simply attach the networks, learned through the Network Summary LSA, as leaves to the ABR in the topology tree. Areas are represented by a 32-bit Area ID.

An ASBR can be located anywhere in the OSPF AS. An ASBR has knowledge of routes that are received from outside the OSPF process, commonly from static routes or other routing protocols. ASBRs advertise the AS External LSA. One AS External LSA will be advertised for each external network. In contrast to Network Summary LSAs, AS External LSAs have an AS-wide flooding scope.

When the ASBR is local to the area, routers know where the ASBR is located through the Router LSA, the same way routers know about local ABRs. Because Router LSAs have only area flooding scope, ABRs also issue ASBR Summary LSAs. These LSAs advertise the presence of and distance to an ASBR in another area, and are necessary for routers in one area to determine reachability to an ASBR in another area. ASBR Summary LSAs are similar to Network Summary LSAs and have area flooding scope.

There are various mechanisms to limit the flooding scope of LSAs to build a more scalable network. Most important are stub areas (no AS External LSAs), NSSA (AS Externals from local area only), totally stubby areas (no area external routes), and demand circuits (DCs). NSSA External LSAs are used instead of AS External LSAs with NSSA areas.

ScreenOS has strong support for standard OSPF features, and can integrate well into an OSPF environment for both firewall and virtual private network (VPN) environments.

16.1 Configure OSPF on a ScreenOS Device

Problem

You need to enable OSPF on a ScreenOS device.

Solution

First, enable the routing instance and then move interfaces into the area and enable those:

```
FIREWALL-A-> set vrouter "trust-vr"
FIREWALL-A(trust-vr)-> set router-id 192.168.19.1
FIREWALL-A(trust-vr)-> set protocol ospf
FIREWALL-A(trust-vr/ospf)-> set enable
FIREWALL-A(trust-vr/ospf)-> exit
FIREWALL-A(trust-vr)-> exit
FIREWALL-A-> set interface ethernet0/1 protocol ospf area 0.0.0.0
FIREWALL-A-> set interface ethernet0/1 protocol ospf enable
FIREWALL-A-> set interface serial1/0 protocol ospf area 0.0.0.0
FIREWALL-A-> set interface serial1/0 protocol ospf enable
```

Discussion

In ScreenOS, routing protocol instances are tied to Virtual Routers (VRs). VRs are tied to zones, and zones are tied to interfaces. A VR consists of potentially two things: a routing table and perhaps instances of one or more routing protocols. By default, all zones are in the `trust-vr`. In the OSPF network depicted in Figure 16-1, area 0 has three devices.

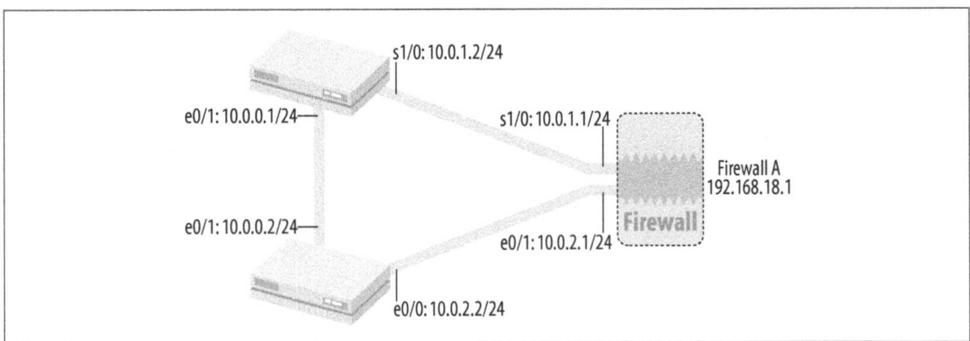

Figure 16-1. OSPF single-area topology

Before you can enable OSPF on an interface, you need to configure the physical and link-layer options, the zone, and the IP address. You also need to configure the area (area 0 is already preconfigured) and you need to enable OSPF on the VR:

```
FIREWALL-A-> set interface ethernet0/1 zone "Untrust"
FIREWALL-A-> set interface ethernet0/1 ip 10.0.2.1/24
FIREWALL-A-> set interface ethernet0/1 route

FIREWALL-A-> set ppp profile noauth
FIREWALL-A-> set ppp profile noauth static-ip
FIREWALL-A-> set interface serial1/0 t1-options timeslots 1-24
FIREWALL-A-> set interface serial1/0 encap ppp
FIREWALL-A-> set interface serial1/0 ppp profile noauth
FIREWALL-A-> set interface serial1/0 ip 10.0.1.1/24
FIREWALL-A-> set interface serial1/0 route

FIREWALL-A-> set vr trust-vr router-id 192.168.19.1
FIREWALL-A-> set vr trust-vr protocol ospf
FIREWALL-A-> set vr trust protocol ospf enable

FIREWALL-A-> set interface ethernet0/1 protocol ospf area 0.0.0.0
FIREWALL-A-> set interface ethernet0/1 protocol ospf enable
FIREWALL-A-> set interface serial1/0 protocol ospf area 0.0.0.0
FIREWALL-A-> set interface serial1/0 protocol ospf enable
```

The order in which commands are executed on ScreenOS is important—ScreenOS can be very picky about this. As a general guideline, configure the lower OSI layers before any higher layers. If you need to change or unset options, reverse this order.

In this recipe, manually configure the Router ID so as to avoid the potential of conflicting Router IDs on the network. The Router ID does not have to exist on the device; however, it is common to use a loopback interface IP for this purpose. If this is done, be sure to create policies to the loopback interface if this IP address will be used for testing. A common but easily avoidable problem arises when no Router ID is configured and OSPF inherits the Router ID from the `vlan1` interface, which has a default IP address of `192.168.1.1`. In this case, multiple routers could end up with the same Router ID, which is a very bad thing.

Once you have configured OSPF, check whether neighbor relationships are established:

```
FIREWALL-B-> get vr trust protocol ospf neighbor
VR: trust-vr RouterId: 192.168.19.1
----------------------------------
                 Neighbor(s) on interface serial1/0 (Area 0.0.0.0)
IpAddr/IfIndex  RouterId        Pri State  Opt  Up          StateChg
--------------------------------------------------------------
10.0.1.1        192.168.18.1      1 Full   E    00:22:23    (+6 -0)

                 Neighbor(s) on interface ethernet0/1 (Area 0.0.0.0)
IpAddr/IfIndex  RouterId        Pri State  Opt  Up           StateChg
--------------------------------------------------------------
10.0.0.2        192.168.17.1      1 Full   E    01:16:24     (+6 -0)
```

The first line shows the Router ID of the local firewall on which this command was executed. The two most important columns are the `RouterId` column and the `State` column. The `RouterId` column shows who the neighbor is and the `State` column shows the neighbor's state. `Full` means a neighbor relationship was successfully established. An OSPF router only establishes a neighbor relationship on a broadcast network, such as Ethernet, with the DR and the Backup DR (BDR). You may therefore see *2-Way* states with other devices on the Ethernet segment. Other states may show error conditions or are only temporary while the OSPF routers transition through the state machine. `ExStart` often points to an MTU mismatch. `Init` or `Attempt` is a sign of a problem with the neighbor relationship when OSPF tries to start initiating a relationship again due to an error. This could be due to mismatched netmasks on a broadcast network or bit errors on the link. `Exchange` and `Loading` are temporary states during which the devices synchronize their LSDBs. When the devices stay in this state for several minutes, it can point to a very large LSDB and possibly a bad network topology, or a problem with route redistribution somewhere else in the network.

The other columns can be useful for further troubleshooting. In the first column, ScreenOS shows the neighbor's interface index of the link. The interface index for a point-to-point interface is the IP address of the remote side if an IP address was configured. The interface index for a broadcast address is the IP address of the DR.

The `Pri` column shows the DR election priority, which in ScreenOS is 1 by default. DRs and BDRs are elected only on broadcast networks. The value of the DR election priority is often overvalued. In reality, the first router coming online becomes the DR, and the second the BDR. Only if there is a tie does the router with the highest priority or the highest Router ID win. There is no preemption with the DR election in OSPF. A priority of 0 means the router does not take part in the DR election. So, it is often a good idea to make the strongest two devices the DR and the BDR, and to configure all other devices with priority 0:

```
FIREWALL-A-> set int e0/1 protocol ospf priority 0
```

The fifth column shows the OSPF header options. When the `E` bit is set, the neighbor is capable of processing External LSA and therefore is not configured into a stub or an NSSA area. The `N` bit shows that the neighbor is able to process NSSA External LSA and implies that it was configured into an NSSA. A mismatch of the `E` bit or the `N` bit would make the neighbor relationship fail. The `DC` bit, which is shown as `D`, means the neighbor's interface was configured as a demand circuit (DC), which is optional.

The sixth column shows the uptime, and the last column shows the forward and backward state changes since the interface was last down.

A useful command to get a quick overview of the OSPF configuration is:

```
FIREWALL-B-> get vr trust protocol ospf interface
VR: trust-vr RouterId: 192.168.19.1
----------------------------------
D - Down, L - Loopback, W - Wait, PTP - Point-to-Point
DR - Designated Router, BDR - Backup Designated Router
```

```
O - Other
Int       IpAddr          NetMask         AreaId          Status   St
-------------------------------------------------------------------
eth0/1    10.0.0.1        255.255.255.0 0.0.0.0           enabled  DR
serial1/0 10.0.1.2        255.255.255.0 0.0.0.0           enabled  PTP
```

The first line again shows the local Router ID. The first column lists the local interface, the second column lists the local IP address, and the third column lists the netmask. The `AreaId` column shows the area in which the interface was configured. The `Status` column shows whether OSPF was enabled on that interface (in ScreenOS, OSPF can be configured on an interface but not enabled, a convenient feature for staging and deployment). The last column shows the status of the interface: `DR` means the local device is the DR for the broadcast network on which this interface is connected. DR election is local to one broadcast network and the same device can be a DR for one network, and a BDR or DROTHER for another network (with "other" shown as `O`, and hence, not a DR). `PTP` means the interface is a point-to-point link type, such as an IP Security (IPSec) tunnel interface or a wide area network (WAN) interface.

Ethernet networks can also be configured as point-to-point networks—for example, when there are two routers on an Ethernet network connected via a crossover cable. This saves the overhead of DR election. Tunnel interfaces must be configured as point-to-multipoint networks (see Recipe 16.11) when more than one IPSec Security Association (SA) terminates on the same tunnel interface (this is analogous to WAN interfaces when more than one PVC terminates on the interface and no subinterfaces were configured):

```
FIREWALL-A-> set int e0/1 protocol ospf link-type p2p
FIREWALL-A-> set int tun.1 protocol ospf link-type p2mp
```

An extensive view of interface options is also available:

```
FIREWALL-B-> get int e0/1 protocol ospf
VR: trust-vr RouterId: 192.168.19.1
----------------------------------
Interface: ethernet0/1
IpAddr: 10.0.0.1/24, OSPF: enabled, Router: enabled
Type: Broadcast  Area: 0.0.0.0  Priority: 1  Cost: 1  Passive: No
Transit delay: 1s  Retransmit interval: 8s  Hello interval: 10s
Router Dead interval: 40s  Authentication-Type: None
Ignore-MTU: no Reduce-flooding: no
State: Designated Router  DR: 10.0.0.1(self)  BDR: 10.0.0.2
Neighbors:
        RtrId: 192.168.17.1 IpAddr: 10.0.0.2 Pri: 1 State: Full
```

We see the same information as in the previous views, plus additional options such as interface cost (see Recipe 16.9 and Recipe 16.10) and timers (see Recipe 16.14). The command nicely shows an overview of all neighbors on this interface, their state, and who the DR and BDR are, if they exist.

16.2 View Routes Learned by OSPF

Problem

You want to see the routes generated by the OSPF routing process.

Solution

Use the get route command in the appropriate VR to show the OSPF routes:

```
FIREWALL-B-> get vr trust-vr route protocol ospf
H: Host C: Connected S: Static A: Auto-Exported
I: Imported R: RIP P: Permanent D: Auto-Discovered
N: NHRP
iB: IBGP eB: EBGP O: OSPF E1: OSPF external type 1
E2: OSPF external type 2 trailing B: backup route

Total 8/max entries

   ID     IP-Prefix    Interface    Gateway   P Pref    Mtr  Vsys
-----------------------------------------------------------------
*  38     0.0.0.0/0    serial1/0   10.0.1.1  E2  200      1  Root
*  37   10.0.2.0/24    serial1/0   10.0.1.1   O   60     65  Root
*  35    1.1.1.0/24       eth0/1   10.0.0.2  E1   60      2  Root

Total number of ospf routes: 3
```

Discussion

OSPF routers perform a shortest path first (SPF) calculation on the data in their LSDBs. OSPF routers calculate a topology view in the form of a graph of all routers in each area they are directly connected. ScreenOS supports VRs, which are somewhat similar to virtual route forwarding (VRF) instances in other network operating systems. Interfaces are in zones and zones are in VRs. By default, all zones are in the trust-vr. In ScreenOS, each VR can run only one OSPF instance or process.

You can view the full routing table for the trust-vr with the following command:

```
FIREWALL-B-> get vr trust-vr route
H: Host C: Connected S: Static A: Auto-Exported
I: Imported R: RIP P: Permanent D: Auto-Discovered
N: NHRP
iB: IBGP eB: EBGP O: OSPF E1: OSPF external type 1
E2: OSPF external type 2 trailing B: backup route

Total 8/max entries

   ID     IP-Prefix   Interface    Gateway   P Pref    Mtr  Vsys
----------------------------------------------------------------
*  38     0.0.0.0/0   serial1/0   10.0.1.1  E2  200      1  Root
*   8   10.0.1.2/32   serial1/0    0.0.0.0   H    0      0  Root
*  29   10.0.1.1/32   serial1/0   10.0.1.1   C    0      0  none
```

```
*  6   10.0.0.1/32      eth0/1    0.0.0.0   H    0     0  Root
*  7   10.0.1.0/24   serial1/0    0.0.0.0   C    0     0  Root
*  5   10.0.0.0/24      eth0/1    0.0.0.0   C    0     0  Root
*  37  10.0.2.0/24   serial1/0   10.0.1.1   O   60    65  Root
*  35   1.1.1.0/24      eth0/1   10.0.0.2   E1  60     2  Root
```

OSPF intra- and inter-area routes (O) have a preference, or administrative distance, of 60 by default. OSPF type-1 external routes (E1) also have a preference of 60, and type-2 routes (E2) have a preference of 200. Do not forget that preference and metric are secondary to prefix length in terms of the route selection process. A router will always choose a route with the longest prefix before evaluating the preference and metric. You can change the preference of a routing protocol in the vr context:

```
FIREWALL-B-> set vr trust-vr preference ospf 10
FIREWALL-B-> set vr trust-vr preference ospf-e2 150
```

The SPF algorithm will prefer an intra-area route over an inter-area route and an E1 route over an E2 route.

The column after the route preference is the metric; the * in front of the line shows that the route is active. A route can be inactive when it is also advertised by a routing protocol with a lower preference and this route is chosen instead.

To show just the OSPF routes, use the following:

```
FIREWALL-B-> get vr trust-vr route protocol ospf
H: Host C: Connected S: Static A: Auto-Exported
I: Imported R: RIP P: Permanent D: Auto-Discovered
N: NHRP
iB: IBGP eB: EBGP O: OSPF E1: OSPF external type 1
E2: OSPF external type 2 trailing B: backup route

Total 8/max entries

   ID    IP-Prefix   Interface    Gateway   P Pref    Mtr  Vsys
--------------------------------------------------------------
*  38    0.0.0.0/0   serial1/0   10.0.1.1  E2  200      1  Root
*  37  10.0.2.0/24   serial1/0   10.0.1.1   O   60     65  Root
*  35   1.1.1.0/24      eth0/1   10.0.0.2  E1   60      2  Root

Total number of ospf routes: 3
```

16.3 View the OSPF Link-State Database

Problem

You want to look at the firewall's LSDB.

Solution

Use the get vrouter trust-vr protocol ospf database command to view the contents of the link state database:

```
FIREWALL-B-> get vr trust-vr protocol ospf database
VR: trust-vr RouterId: 192.168.19.1
----------------------------------

                        Router LSA(s) for area 0.0.0.0
  Link-State-Id   Adv-Router ID      Age  Sequence# CheckSum
----------------------------------------------------------
   192.168.17.1    192.168.17.1 DNA 1184 0x8000001a   0x6e61
   192.168.18.1    192.168.18.1 DNA 1188 0x80000030   0xf5bc
   192.168.19.1    192.168.19.1     1255 0x80000037   0x5787

                        Network LSA(s) for area 0.0.0.0
  Link-State-Id   Adv-Router ID      Age  Sequence# CheckSum
----------------------------------------------------------
       10.0.2.1    192.168.18.1 DNA 1193 0x80000001   0xbff8


                        AS External LSA(s)
  Link-State-Id   Adv-Router ID      Age  Sequence# CheckSum
----------------------------------------------------------
        0.0.0.0    192.168.18.1 DNA 1193 0x80000003   0x76bc
        1.1.1.0    192.168.17.1     1549 0x80000003   0xd5db
```

Discussion

OSPF routes build the LSDB data records from LSAs. Currently, 11 different LSAs are defined. Table 16-2 lists the six that are used for routing.

Table 16-2. Link-state advertisements

Type	RFC name	ScreenOS CLI
1	Router	router
2	Network	network
3	Network Summary	summary
4	ASBR Summary	asbr-summary
5	AS External	external
7	NSSA External	nssa-external

Devices within the area originate one Router LSA for each area to which they are directly attached. Each DR originates one Network LSA. ABRs originate one Summary LSA for each network, which was learned from another area. ASBRs originate one External LSA or one NSSA External LSA for each network they redistribute. ABRs may also issue one ASBR Summary LSA for each ASBR they discover from a different area. All advertisements except the External LSA have only area flooding scope, which means you will not see the same LSA in different areas, but you may see the same networks. For instance, a network will be listed in the originating area as a link within a Router LSA but in another area as a Summary LSA:

```
FIREWALL-B-> get vr trust-vr protocol ospf database
VR: trust-vr RouterId: 192.168.19.1
----------------------------------

                      Router LSA(s) for area 0.0.0.0
  Link-State-Id   Adv-Router ID        Age  Sequence# CheckSum
-----------------------------------------------------------
   192.168.17.1    192.168.17.1 DNA 1184 0x8000001a    0x6e61
   192.168.18.1    192.168.18.1 DNA 1188 0x80000030    0xf5bc
   192.168.19.1    192.168.19.1     1255 0x80000037    0x5787

                      Network LSA(s) for area 0.0.0.0
  Link-State-Id   Adv-Router ID        Age  Sequence# CheckSum
-----------------------------------------------------------
       10.0.2.1    192.168.18.1 DNA 1193 0x80000001    0xbff8


                      AS External LSA(s)
  Link-State-Id   Adv-Router ID        Age  Sequence# CheckSum
-----------------------------------------------------------
        0.0.0.0    192.168.18.1 DNA 1193 0x80000003    0x76bc
        1.1.1.0    192.168.17.1     1549 0x80000003    0xd5db
```

LSAs have names, called link-state IDs, shown in the first column. The link-state ID of a Router LSA is the Router ID from the originating device; for the Network LSA, it is the interface IP of the DR on that broadcast network, and for the ASBR Summary LSA, it is the Router ID of the originating ABR. The remaining LSAs inherit their link-state IDs from the networks they represent.

The second column shows the Router ID of the advertising device. The `Age` column counts upward. When an LSA reaches its maximum age of 3,600 seconds, it is purged. LSAs with a `DNA` flag do not age because of a DC configuration. LSAs can also be advertised with an age of 3,600 to show withdrawn networks. LSAs are commonly refreshed after 20–30 minutes, unless they are advertised over a DC.

The `Sequence` column shows the version of the LSA. An LSA will be reflooded when something has changed or when a reflooding timer has expired. The last column shows a checksum. Both the sequence number and the checksum must be the same on all devices in the area. If they are not the same, there is a flooding problem, most likely caused by an overloaded device. You should be careful with respect to load on the firewalls. Firewalls typically handle many more tasks than traditional routers, and as such, you should monitor your resources carefully and implement features to increase scalability where possible.

For troubleshooting, it is often useful to list the complete LSA content (see Recipe 16.16). The details of each LSA type are beyond the scope of this book, but for reference, here are some examples:

```
FIREWALL-B-> get vr trust-vr protocol ospf database detail router
link-state-id 192.168.17.1
```

```
VR: trust-vr RouterId: 192.168.19.1
----------------------------------
                        Router LSA(s) in area 0.0.0.0
                        ------------------------------
Age: DNA 2193
Seq Number: 0x8000001a
Checksum: 0x6e61
Advertising Router: 192.168.17.1
Link State ID: 192.168.17.1
Length: 36
Options:   Extern     DC
Flags: ,E,, Links 1
Link# 1
                Link State ID: 10.0.2.1
                Link Data: 10.0.2.2
                Type: 2
                TOS: 0
                Metric: 10000
```

Note the flags in the Router LSA. The E bit shows that the device is an ASBR; the B bit shows that the device is an ABR, and the V bit shows that the device terminates a virtual link and the Router LSA is in a transit area. Do not confuse these flags with the options in the OSPF header itself.

```
FIREWALL-B-> get vr trust-vr protocol ospf database detail network
ink-state-id 10.0.2.1
VR: trust-vr RouterId: 192.168.19.1
----------------------------------
                        Network LSA(s) in area 0.0.0.0
                        ------------------------------
Age: DNA 2222
Seq Number: 0x80000001
Checksum: 0xbff8
Advertising Router: 192.168.18.1
Link State ID: 10.0.2.1
Length: 32
Options:   Extern     DC
Network mask: 255.255.255.0
Attached Routers = 2
192.168.18.1
192.168.17.1

FIREWALL-B-> get vr trust-vr proto ospf database detail summary
VR: trust-vr RouterId: 192.168.19.1
----------------------------------
                        Summary LSA(s) in area 0.0.0.0
                        ------------------------------
Age:  50
Seq Number: 0x80000001
Checksum: 0x5e55
Advertising Router: 192.168.19.1
Link State ID: 10.0.16.0
Length: 28
```

```
Options:   Extern     DC
Network Mask: 255.255.255.0
 TOS: 0 Metric: 1

FIREWALL-B-> get vr trust-vr protocol ospf database detail external
link-state-id 1.1.1.0
VR: trust-vr RouterId: 192.168.19.1
----------------------------------
                        AS External LSA(s)
                        ------------------------------
Age:  2712
Seq Number: 0x80000003
Checksum: 0xd5db
Advertising Router: 192.168.17.1
Link State ID: 1.1.1.0
Length: 36
Options:   Extern     DC
Network Mask: 255.255.255.0
                Metric Type: 1
                TOS: 0
                Metric: 1
                Forward Address: 0.0.0.0
                External Route Tag: 0
```

Often, it is useful to see which LSA the local firewall originates:

```
FIREWALL-B-> get vr trust-vr protocol ospf database self-originate
```

Or, you may want to know which LSAs another firewall advertises, so you need to know the firewall's Router ID:

```
FIREWALL-B-> get vr trust-vr protocol ospf database adv-router 192.168.17.1
```

On ABRs, it may be useful to show the LSA of one area only:

```
FIREWALL-B-> get vr trust-vr protocol ospf database area 0
```

Often, the LSDB is so massive that a quick overview is required. This information is kind of hidden:

```
FIREWALL-B->  get vr trust-vr protocol ospf | include LSA
Number of external LSA(s):            2
External LSAs with DNA:               2
Advertising default-route lsa:        disabled
LSA flooding protection:              disabled
        Number of LSA(s) is 4
```

The first line shows only External LSAs. In many networks, External LSAs are the largest group, which is usually caused by challenging network topologies. Redistribution degrades OSPF to a distance-vector routing protocol similar to RIP (see the Introduction to this chapter). Massive amounts of External LSAs are sometimes caused by configuration mistakes, but often by lack of a careful redistribution strategy. A well-defined OSPF network should have very few External LSAs because they have AS-wide flooding scope, and defining multiple areas does not help to take the load off devices or create more stability; at best, it does little and often adds to the problem.

16.4 Configure a Multiarea OSPF Network

Problem

You want to create multiple areas in OSPF.

Solution

Configure a new area (separate from the backbone area) under the VR OSPF hierarchy, and attach that area to an interface:

```
FIREWALL-A-> set vrouter "trust-vr"
FIREWALL-A(trust-vr)-> set protocol ospf
FIREWALL-A(trust-vr/ospf)-> set area 1
FIREWALL-A(trust-vr/ospf)-> exit
FIREWALL-A(trust-vr)-> exit
FIREWALL-A-> set interface ethernet0/0 protocol ospf area 1
FIREWALL-A-> set interface ethernet0/0 protocol ospf enable
```

Discussion

In the past, multiple-area topologies were required to scale OSPF, but today, most routers are powerful enough that multiple areas are not required. Another reason for implementing a multiarea topology is for route control and policies because only ABRs can control route propagation in OSPF. Redistributed routes normally have AS-wide flooding scope, but it is possible to contain them within special areas (see Recipe 16.5 and Recipe 16.6).

Area 0 is always preconfigured in ScreenOS. To create an additional area, configure the area under the VR OSPF hierarchy and attach it to an interface. If multiple interfaces are configured in different areas, the device becomes an ABR. Here we configure a second area, area 1. FIREWALL-B becomes an ABR between the backbone area 0 and area 1 (see Figure 16-2).

If you want to change the area on an interface, you must first disable OSPF on that interface, switch the area, and then enable it again. You also must put that interface into a zone, and configure an IP address before you can activate OSPF on that interface.

```
FIREWALL-B-> set interface ethernet0/0 zone "Trust"
FIREWALL-B-> set interface ethernet0/0 ip 10.0.16.2/24
FIREWALL-B-> set interface ethernet0/0 route
FIREWALL-B-> set interface ethernet0/0 protocol ospf area 0.0.0.1
FIREWALL-B-> set interface ethernet0/0 protocol ospf enable
```

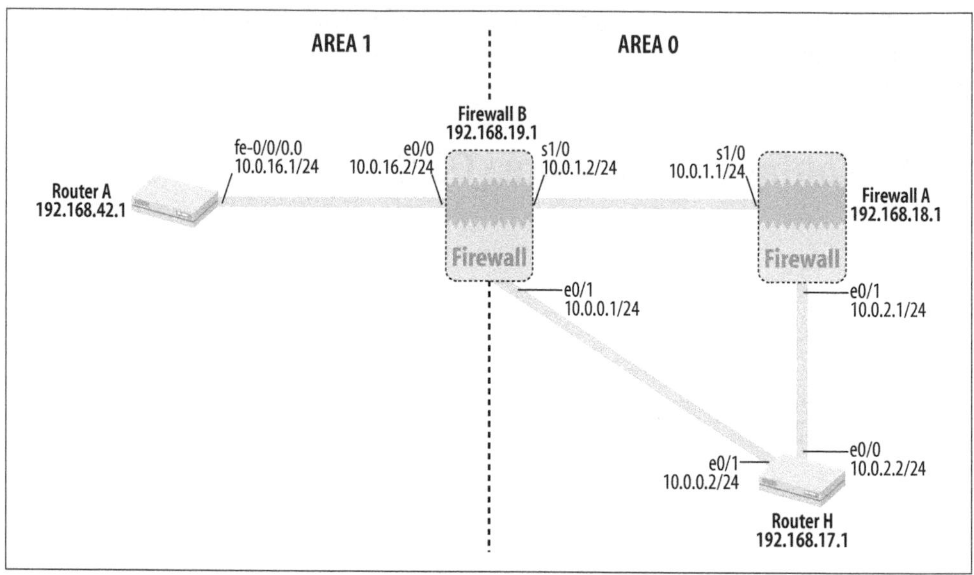

Figure 16-2. OSPF two-area topology

Check whether all interfaces are correctly configured:

```
FIREWALL-B-> get vr trust-vr protocol ospf interface
VR: trust-vr RouterId: 192.168.19.1
----------------------------------
D - Down, L - Loopback, W - Wait, PTP - Point-to-Point
DR - Designated Router, BDR - Backup Designated Router
O - Other
Int        IpAddr          NetMask         AreaId          Status   St
--------------------------------------------------------------
eth0/0     10.0.16.2       255.255.255.0 0.0.0.1           enabled  BDR
serial1/0 10.0.1.2          255.255.255.0 0.0.0.0           enabled  PTP
eth0/1     10.0.0.1        255.255.255.0 0.0.0.0           enabled  DR
```

Interface e0/0 was successfully configured in area 1. (Areas are often written in IP-style dotted notation; but really, an area is a 32-bit number and not an IP address, and can be written in regular decimal notation.) Notice also that interface e0/0 was elected as the BDR.

Now, check for adjacent neighbors. Because the interface was elected into a BDR role, assume that there is at least one adjacent neighbor. On broadcast networks, all devices become adjacent with the DR and the BDR only. All other devices will be in 2-Way state.

```
FIREWALL-B-> get vr trust-vr protocol ospf neighbor
VR: trust-vr RouterId: 192.168.19.1
----------------------------------
                Neighbor(s) on interface ethernet0/1 (Area 0.0.0.0)
IpAddr/IfIndex RouterId         Pri State    Opt  Up          StateChg
```

```
------------------------------------------------------------------
10.0.0.2         192.168.17.1       1 Full      E    02:12:40   (+7 -0)

                 Neighbor(s) on interface serial1/0 (Area 0.0.0.0)
IpAddr/IfIndex RouterId         Pri State    Opt  Up          StateChg
------------------------------------------------------------------
10.0.1.1         192.168.18.1       1 Full      E  D 02:14:40   (+6 -0)

                 Neighbor(s) on interface ethernet0/0 (Area 0.0.0.1)
IpAddr/IfIndex RouterId         Pri State    Opt  Up          StateChg
------------------------------------------------------------------
10.0.16.1        192.168.42.1     128 Full      E    02:12:59   (+7 -0)
```

You can see more detailed information, such as the DR and BDR, under the interface hierarchy:

```
FIREWALL-B-> get interface e0/0 protocol ospf
VR: trust-vr RouterId: 192.168.19.1
----------------------------------
Interface: ethernet0/0
IpAddr: 10.0.16.2/24, OSPF: enabled, Router: enabled
Type: Broadcast  Area: 0.0.0.1  Priority: 1  Cost: 1  Passive: No
Transit delay: 1s  Retransmit interval: 8s  Hello interval: 10s
Router Dead interval: 40s  Authentication-Type: None
Ignore-MTU: no Reduce-flooding: no
State: Backup Designated Router  DR: 10.0.16.1  BDR: 10.0.16.2(self)
Neighbors:
        RtrId: 192.168.42.1 IpAddr: 10.0.16.1 Pri: 128 State: Full
```

OSPF collects topological information for each area separately. Most LSAs do not have AS-wide flooding scope, and are local to their area, but the routing information is shared. For instance, a link within the Router LSA in the local area becomes a Summary LSA in another area. Notice that the two External LSAs and the Router LSA of the ABR are seen in both areas:

```
FIREWALL-B-> get vr trust-vr protocol ospf database
VR: trust-vr RouterId: 192.168.19.1
----------------------------------

                         Router LSA(s) for area 0.0.0.0
  Link-State-Id    Adv-Router ID       Age  Sequence# CheckSum
----------------------------------------------------------
   192.168.17.1     192.168.17.1       944 0x8000000a   0x48a6
   192.168.18.1     192.168.18.1       972 0x8000000c   0xbc25
   192.168.19.1     192.168.19.1       969 0x8000000d   0xf6ea

                         Network LSA(s) for area 0.0.0.0
  Link-State-Id    Adv-Router ID       Age  Sequence# CheckSum
----------------------------------------------------------
       10.0.0.1     192.168.19.1       969 0x80000005   0xcfe4
       10.0.2.1     192.168.18.1       972 0x80000005   0xb7fc

                         Summary LSA(s) for area 0.0.0.0
  Link-State-Id    Adv-Router ID       Age  Sequence# CheckSum
```

```
-------------------------------------------------------------
        10.0.16.0    192.168.19.1      1011 0x80000008   0xbae2
        10.0.21.0    192.168.19.1       985 0x80000005   0x9307
     192.168.42.1    192.168.19.1       985 0x80000005   0x68bd


                        Router LSA(s) for area 0.0.0.1
   Link-State-Id   Adv-Router ID       Age  Sequence# CheckSum
-------------------------------------------------------------
     192.168.19.1    192.168.19.1       987 0x80000008   0xf701
     192.168.42.1    192.168.42.1      2188 0x80000005   0xe515

                        Network LSA(s) for area 0.0.0.1
   Link-State-Id   Adv-Router ID       Age  Sequence# CheckSum
-------------------------------------------------------------
        10.0.16.1    192.168.42.1      2188 0x80000004   0x690c

                        Summary LSA(s) for area 0.0.0.1
   Link-State-Id   Adv-Router ID       Age  Sequence# CheckSum
-------------------------------------------------------------
         10.0.0.0    192.168.19.1       958 0x80000008   0x6b42
         10.0.1.0    192.168.19.1      1011 0x80000007   0xda93
         10.0.2.0    192.168.19.1       956 0x80000008   0x5f4b

                        ASBR LSA(s) for area 0.0.0.1
   Link-State-Id   Adv-Router ID       Age  Sequence# CheckSum
-------------------------------------------------------------
     192.168.17.1    192.168.19.1       958 0x80000006   0x6cd0


                        AS External LSA(s)
   Link-State-Id   Adv-Router ID       Age  Sequence# CheckSum
-------------------------------------------------------------
          1.1.1.0    192.168.17.1       995 0x80000006   0xcfde
```

You may also notice the ASBR Summary LSA in area 1. This is `RouterH` in area 0. Devices in area 0 know `RouterH` with Router ID `192.168.17.1` as an ASBR from its Router LSA. The ASBR Summary LSA is originated, however, from the ABR, `FIREWALL-B`, with Router ID `192.168.19.1`.

You also should check the final routing table:

```
FIREWALL-B-> get vr trust-vr route protocol ospf
H: Host C: Connected S: Static A: Auto-Exported
I: Imported R: RIP P: Permanent D: Auto-Discovered
N: NHRP
iB: IBGP eB: EBGP O: OSPF E1: OSPF external type 1
E2: OSPF external type 2 trailing B: backup route

Total 11/max entries

   ID          IP-Prefix  Interface     Gateway    P Pref  Mtr   Vsys
----------------------------------------------------------------
```

```
* 11    192.168.42.1/32    eth0/0  10.0.16.1  0   60   1 Root
* 10       10.0.21.0/24    eth0/0  10.0.16.1  0   60   2 Root
* 15        10.0.2.0/24    eth0/1   10.0.0.2  0   60   2 Root
* 16         1.1.1.0/24    eth0/1   10.0.0.2  E1  60   2 Root

Total number of ospf routes: 4
```

RouterA is not a ScreenOS firewall, it is a JUNOS router, so we configured the loopback address (which in JUNOS is automatically advertised and used as the Router ID). On security devices with their restrictive policies, it is a best practice to manually configure the Router ID.

16.5 Set Up Stub Areas

Problem

You want to isolate a group of firewalls from the burden of processing External LSAs.

Solution

Configure those firewalls into a stub area:

```
FIREWALL-A-> set vrouter "trust-vr"
FIREWALL-A(trust-vr)-> set protocol ospf
FIREWALL-A(trust-vr/ospf)-> set area 3 stub
FIREWALL-A(trust-vr/ospf)-> exit
FIREWALL-A(trust-vr)-> exit
```

Discussion

Although External LSAs have AS-wide flooding scope, they are not flooded into areas designated as "stub areas." Instead of multiple External LSAs, an ABR originates one Summary LSA with the default network `0.0.0.0/0`. As discussed in the introduction to this chapter, External LSAs are originated from ASBRs through redistribution. Often, topologies dictate the redistribution of hundreds or thousands of routes, which can cause a significant burden on the devices in the network from a processing perspective. The problem can be amplified when those routes are originating from remote sites and there is instability in the network.

It is recommended to configure areas without an ASBR as stub areas. A stub area cannot contain ASBRs (because then it would have external routes; see Recipe 16.6 for alternatives) and the backbone area can never be a stub area. In a stub area, all devices need to be configured as being in a stub area. This is enforced through the `E` bit (see Recipe 16.1) in the OSPF Hello packet header. Two devices become adjacent only when both have the `E` bit set, or not set, but not when one has it set and the other does not. Making an area a stub area can cause suboptimal routing, but only when there is more than one ABR and the ABRs are placed on different ends of the area, or when the ABRs uplink to the backbone at different link speeds.

In our recipe, area 3 is a stub area, as shown in Figure 16-3.

```
FIREWALL-A-> get vr trust-vr protocol ospf area 3
VR: trust-vr RouterId: 192.168.18.1
----------------------------------
Area-ID: 0.0.0.3 (Stub)
        Total number of interfaces is 1, Active number of interfaces
is 1
        Route Imports: None,  Intra-SPF Runs: 57
        Number of ABR(s): 1,  Number of ASBR(s): 0
        Number of LSA(s): 4,  Checksum: 0x147cb
        LSAs with no DC-option: 0,  LSAs with no DC-option (excluding
indication LSAs): 0
        LSAs with DNA: 0
        Default route metric type is ext-type-1, metric is 1
        Type-3 LSA Filter: disabled
```

The output shows that area 3 originates a default route. The last line of the output shows that this is not a totally stubby area. We will provide more information concerning total stubbiness later in this chapter.

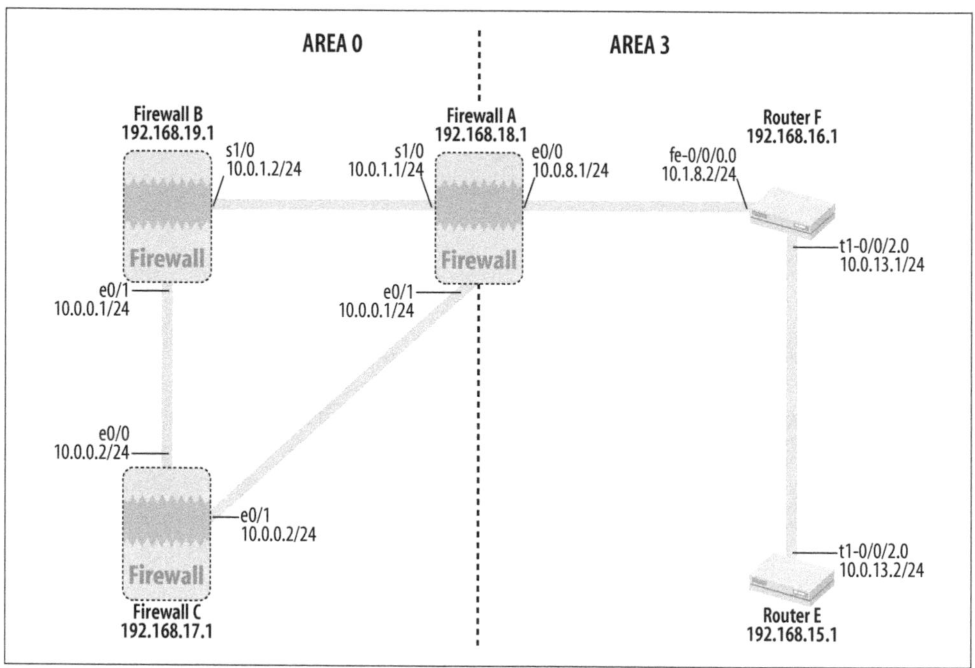

Figure 16-3. OSPF stub area topology

Before area 3 is made a stub area, the ASBR Summary LSAs as well as External LSAs exist in the LSDB:

```
FIREWALL-A-> get vr trust protocol ospf database area 3
VR: trust-vr RouterId: 192.168.18.1
----------------------------------
```

```
                   Router LSA(s) for area 0.0.0.3
  Link-State-Id   Adv-Router ID      Age  Sequence# CheckSum
-----------------------------------------------------------
   192.168.15.1   192.168.15.1       214 0x80000008   0xbaba
   192.168.16.1   192.168.16.1       213 0x8000000e   0xc074
   192.168.18.1   192.168.18.1      1245 0x80000004   0x53bc

                   Network LSA(s) for area 0.0.0.3
  Link-State-Id   Adv-Router ID      Age  Sequence# CheckSum
-----------------------------------------------------------
       10.0.8.1   192.168.18.1      1245 0x80000001   0x7043

                   Summary LSA(s) for area 0.0.0.3
  Link-State-Id   Adv-Router ID      Age  Sequence# CheckSum
-----------------------------------------------------------
       10.0.0.0   192.168.18.1      1423 0x80000001   0x8a2a
       10.0.1.0   192.168.18.1      1423 0x80000001   0xed87
       10.0.2.0   192.168.18.1      1423 0x80000001   0x6a49

                   ASBR LSA(s) for area 0.0.0.3
  Link-State-Id   Adv-Router ID      Age  Sequence# CheckSum
-----------------------------------------------------------
   192.168.17.1   192.168.18.1      1423 0x80000001   0x7dc5


                   AS External LSA(s)
  Link-State-Id   Adv-Router ID      Age  Sequence# CheckSum
-----------------------------------------------------------
        1.1.1.0   192.168.17.1      1025 0x80000009   0xc9e1
```

The area is made a stub area with the keyword `stub` after the area name. You need to disable OSPF on ScreenOS before you make such a change, and then reenable it afterward:

```
FIREWALL-A-> set vr trust protocol ospf area 3 stub
```

After an area is changed to a stub area, all devices in that area need to be changed or the devices will not become adjacent and will remain in the *init* state. After area 3 becomes a stub area, External LSAs are no longer present in the LSDB. Neither are ASBR Summary LSAs. In their place is an additional Summary LSA advertising the default network:

```
FIREWALL-A-> get vr trust-vr protocol ospf database area 3
VR: trust-vr RouterId: 192.168.18.1
----------------------------------

                   Router LSA(s) for area 0.0.0.3
  Link-State-Id   Adv-Router ID      Age  Sequence# CheckSum
-----------------------------------------------------------
   192.168.15.1   192.168.15.1        17 0x80000002   0xe498
   192.168.16.1   192.168.16.1        17 0x80000004   0xf24e
   192.168.18.1   192.168.18.1        23 0x80000004   0x71a0

                   Network LSA(s) for area 0.0.0.3
  Link-State-Id   Adv-Router ID      Age  Sequence# CheckSum
```

```
-------------------------------------------------------
      10.0.8.1     192.168.18.1          23 0x80000001    0x8e27

                          Summary LSA(s) for area 0.0.0.3
  Link-State-Id    Adv-Router ID       Age  Sequence# CheckSum
-------------------------------------------------------
        0.0.0.0    192.168.18.1           8 0x80000007    0x15a6
       10.0.0.0    192.168.18.1         227 0x80000001    0xa80e
       10.0.1.0    192.168.18.1         234 0x80000001    0x c6b
       10.0.2.0    192.168.18.1         230 0x80000001    0x882d
```

You also can change the metric of the default route:

```
FIREWALL-A-> set vr trust-vr protocol ospf area 3 metric-default-route 10
```

On ABRs, External LSAs may still be listed because they apply to the backbone area and any other nonstub areas to which the ABR connects. However, the ABR will not flood these LSAs into the stub area.

A variation of a stub area is a totally stubby area, in which Summary LSAs as well as External LSAs are suppressed. Totally stubby areas are seldom implemented because there are usually more External LSAs than Summary LSAs, but it makes sense to enable total stubbiness if the OSPF network is very large. Totally stubby areas are a proprietary addition to the RFC, supported by many vendors.

```
FIREWALL-A-> set vr trust-vr protocol ospf area 3 stub
FIREWALL-A-> set vr trust-vr protocol ospf area 3 no-summary
```

A totally stubby area needs to be configured only on the ABR because it is the ABR which would normally flood the Summary LSAs. It is configured in addition to the stub area. All other devices in the area need to be configured as being in a stub area. There is only one Summary LSA, advertising the default route. All other Summary LSAs are suppressed by the ABR:

```
FIREWALL-A-> get vr trust protocol ospf database area 3
VR: trust-vr RouterId: 192.168.18.1
----------------------------------

                          Router LSA(s) for area 0.0.0.3
  Link-State-Id    Adv-Router ID       Age  Sequence# CheckSum
-------------------------------------------------------
   192.168.15.1    192.168.15.1         333 0x80000002    0xe498
   192.168.16.1    192.168.16.1           5 0x80000006    0x 152
   192.168.18.1    192.168.18.1           4 0x80000004    0x9193

                          Network LSA(s) for area 0.0.0.3
  Link-State-Id    Adv-Router ID       Age  Sequence# CheckSum
-------------------------------------------------------
       10.0.8.2    192.168.16.1           5 0x80000001    0x9a1c

                          Summary LSA(s) for area 0.0.0.3
  Link-State-Id    Adv-Router ID       Age  Sequence# CheckSum
-------------------------------------------------------
        0.0.0.0    192.168.18.1           0 0x80000008    0x13a7
```

16.6 Create a Not-So-Stubby Area (NSSA)

Problem

You want to isolate a group of firewalls from the burden of processing External LSAs, but one of the devices in the group is an ASBR.

Solution

Make the area an NSSA instead of just a stub area:

```
FIREWALL-A-> set vrouter "trust-vr"
FIREWALL-A(trust-vr)-> set protocol ospf
FIREWALL-A(trust-vr/ospf)-> set area 3 nssa
FIREWALL-A(trust-vr/ospf)-> exit
FIREWALL-A(trust-vr)-> exit
```

Discussion

An NSSA is similar to a stub area (see Recipe 16.5). As in a stub area, ABRs do not flood External LSAs into NSSAs. The problem occurs when one area is desired to be a stub, but has an ASBR, which originates external routes on its own. This is often the case on firewalls, which are gateways for WAN, VPN, or extranet networks. Still, it may be beneficial to isolate those security devices from the extra processing burden of thousands of External LSAs, originating somewhere else in the network.

An NSSA is the solution. In an NSSA, External LSAs are not allowed from outside the area, but a new LSA type, NSSA External LSAs, can be originated from within the area. An ABR translates these NSSA External LSAs into External LSAs, but also can suppress them. Instead of multiple External LSAs, an ABR originates one single NSSA External LSA with a default network `0.0.0.0/0` into the NSSA. As with regular stub areas, the backbone area can never be an NSSA. All devices in the area need to be configured as belonging to the NSSA, and this is enforced through the `N` bit (see Recipe 16.1) in the OSPF Hello packet header. Devices become adjacent only when both have the `N` bit set or not set. An ABR attached to an NSSA will also keep the `E` bit in the Router LSA for translator election.

Here, area 3 is an NSSA (see Figure 16-3 earlier in this chapter):

```
FIREWALL-A-> get vr trust protocol ospf area 3
VR: trust-vr RouterId: 192.168.18.1
----------------------------------
Area-ID: 0.0.0.3 (NSSA)
        Total number of interfaces is 1, Active number of interfaces
is 1
        Route Imports: NSSA Routes,  Intra-SPF Runs: 80
        Number of ABR(s): 1,  Number of ASBR(s): 2
        Number of LSA(s): 10,  Checksum: 0x628b4
        LSAs with no DC-option: 0,  LSAs with no DC-option (excluding
indication LSAs): 0
```

```
LSAs with DNA: 0
Default route metric type is ext-type-1, metric is 1
Type-7 to Type-5 LSA translation is enabled
Type-3 LSA Filter: disabled
```

The output shows that area 3 originates a default route. The second-to-last line shows that this firewall is an ABR, and it is translating NSSA External LSA into External LSA. You cannot change this behavior in ScreenOS manually, so ScreenOS always takes part in a translator election. The actual election algorithm is fairly complex, but in most implementations, the ABR with the highest Router ID would be elected as the translator. Only one ABR should translate NSSA External LSAs to External LSAs and then flood them to the backbone area (to save resources). Translator election can cause suboptimal routing, and some vendors allow manual intervention in the election process.

The last line of the output shows that Summary LSAs are not filtered, which means that this is not a "not-so-stubby totally stubby area." We will provide more information concerning total stubbiness later in this chapter.

Before enabling NSSA, area 3 has in its LSDB External LSAs as well as one ASBR Summary LSA. The External LSAs originated from two different devices: `192.168.17.1` (`FIREWALL-C`) is an ASBR in area 0, and `192.168.15.1` (`RouterE`) is an ASBR in area 3.

```
FIREWALL-A-> get vr trust proto ospf database area 3
VR: trust-vr RouterId: 192.168.18.1
----------------------------------


                         Router LSA(s) for area 0.0.0.3
  Link-State-Id   Adv-Router ID       Age  Sequence# CheckSum
---------------------------------------------------------
   192.168.15.1    192.168.15.1       460 0x80000008   0xc0b2
   192.168.16.1    192.168.16.1       322 0x80000008   0xd663
   192.168.18.1    192.168.18.1       311 0x80000008   0x5bad

                         Network LSA(s) for area 0.0.0.3
  Link-State-Id   Adv-Router ID       Age  Sequence# CheckSum
---------------------------------------------------------
       10.0.8.2    192.168.16.1       322 0x80000001   0x7c38

                         Summary LSA(s) for area 0.0.0.3
  Link-State-Id   Adv-Router ID       Age  Sequence# CheckSum
---------------------------------------------------------
       10.0.0.0    192.168.18.1       310 0x80000007   0x7e30
       10.0.1.0    192.168.18.1       317 0x80000004   0xe78a
       10.0.2.0    192.168.18.1       313 0x80000008   0x5c50

                         ASBR LSA(s) for area 0.0.0.3
  Link-State-Id   Adv-Router ID       Age  Sequence# CheckSum
---------------------------------------------------------
   192.168.17.1    192.168.18.1       310 0x80000007   0x71cb


                         AS External LSA(s)
```

```
  Link-State-Id   Adv-Router ID       Age  Sequence# CheckSum
------------------------------------------------------------
        1.1.1.0    192.168.15.1        160 0x80000008   0x6268
        1.1.1.0    192.168.17.1    DNA 326 0x8000000e   0xbfe6
     172.16.1.0    192.168.15.1        760 0x80000007   0xf719
```

The area is made an NSSA with the keyword `nssa`. As with converting to a stub network, with NSSAs, you need to disable OSPF on ScreenOS before making the change, and then enable it again afterward.

```
FIREWALL-A-> set vr trust-vr protocol ospf area 3 nssa
```

After an area is changed to NSSA, all devices in this area need to be changed or they will not become adjacent and will remain in the *init* state. After area 3 becomes an NSSA, External LSAs no longer are flooded into the area. Neither are ASBR Summary LSAs. In their place is an additional NSSA External LSA, advertising the default network. This is different from a stub area, where the ABR would instead originate a Summary LSA with the default route. In addition, there are now NSSA External LSAs from the local ASBR `192.168.15.1`.

```
FIREWALL-A-> get vr trust protocol ospf database area 3
VR: trust-vr RouterId: 192.168.18.1
----------------------------------

                      Router LSA(s) for area 0.0.0.3
  Link-State-Id   Adv-Router ID       Age  Sequence# CheckSum
------------------------------------------------------------
   192.168.15.1    192.168.15.1        456 0x80000002   0xea90
   192.168.16.1    192.168.16.1        423 0x80000004   0xfc43
   192.168.18.1    192.168.18.1        422 0x80000004   0xb14d

                      Network LSA(s) for area 0.0.0.3
  Link-State-Id   Adv-Router ID       Age  Sequence# CheckSum
------------------------------------------------------------
       10.0.8.2    192.168.16.1        423 0x80000002   0x981d

                      Summary LSA(s) for area 0.0.0.3
  Link-State-Id   Adv-Router ID       Age  Sequence# CheckSum
------------------------------------------------------------
       10.0.0.0    192.168.18.1        477 0x80000001   0xa80e
       10.0.1.0    192.168.18.1        359 0x80000003   0x 86d
       10.0.2.0    192.168.18.1        480 0x80000001   0x882d

                      NSSA External LSA(s) for area 0.0.0.
  Link-State-Id   Adv-Router ID       Age  Sequence# CheckSum
------------------------------------------------------------
        0.0.0.0    192.168.18.1        487 0x80000001   0x3575
        1.1.1.0    192.168.15.1        456 0x80000001   0xfb54
     172.16.1.0    192.168.15.1        456 0x80000001   0x8f06
```

You can change both the metric and the type of the default route:

```
FIREWALL-A-> set vr trust-vr protocol ospf area 3 metric-default-route 10
FIREWALL-A-> set vr trust-vr protocol ospf area 3 type-default-route 2
```

Similar to stub areas, NSSAs can be configured totally stubby. This would also supress Summary LSAs in addition to External LSAs:

```
FIREWALL-A-> set vr trust-vr protocol ospf area 3 nssa
FIREWALL-A-> set vr trust-vr protocol ospf area 3 no-summary
```

This command needs to be configured only on an ABR, in addition to making the area an NSSA on all devices in that area:

```
FIREWALL-A-> get vr trust protocol ospf database area 3
VR: trust-vr RouterId: 192.168.18.1
----------------------------------

                  Router LSA(s) for area 0.0.0.3
  Link-State-Id   Adv-Router ID      Age  Sequence# CheckSum
----------------------------------------------------------
   192.168.15.1    192.168.15.1      177 0x80000005   0xe493
   192.168.16.1    192.168.16.1     1303 0x80000004   0xfc43
   192.168.18.1    192.168.18.1     1302 0x80000004   0xb14d

                  Network LSA(s) for area 0.0.0.3
  Link-State-Id   Adv-Router ID      Age  Sequence# CheckSum
----------------------------------------------------------
       10.0.8.2    192.168.16.1     1303 0x80000002   0x981d

                  NSSA External LSA(s) for area 0.0.0.
  Link-State-Id   Adv-Router ID      Age  Sequence# CheckSum
----------------------------------------------------------
        0.0.0.0    192.168.18.1     1367 0x80000001   0x3575
        1.1.1.0    192.168.15.1      177 0x80000004   0xf557
     172.16.1.0    192.168.15.1      177 0x80000004   0x8909
```

16.7 Control Route Propagation in OSPF

Problem

You need to control your route propagation and summarize routes.

Solution

Summarize the network on the originating area on an ABR:

```
FIREWALL-A-> set vr trust-vr protocol ospf area 3 range 192.168.0.0/16 advertise
```

Discussion

In OSPF, routes can be summarized only on ABRs. This is very different from other routing protocols such as RIP and the Enhanced Interior Gateway Routing Protocol (EIGRP), and for that matter BGP, where routes can be summarized on any router. The reason is because OSPF is a link-state routing protocol. By definition, all devices in an area have to have the same topological knowledge so that changing the routing information before communicating it to neighbors is out of the question (see the Introduction to this chapter).

Area 0 and area 3 are both seen in this recipe (see Figure 16-3, earlier in this chapter):

```
FIREWALL-B-> get vr trust-vr protocol ospf database summary
VR: trust-vr RouterId: 192.168.19.1
----------------------------------

                         Summary LSA(s) for area 0.0.0.0
  Link-State-Id   Adv-Router ID      Age  Sequence# CheckSum
----------------------------------------------------------
       10.0.8.0    192.168.18.1     1443 0x80000003   0x2487
      10.0.13.0    192.168.18.1     1443 0x80000003   0x79eb
   192.168.15.1    192.168.18.1     1443 0x80000003   0x2ad8
   192.168.16.1    192.168.18.1     1443 0x80000003   0x92b0
```

The networks need to be summarized in the area where they are originating. `192.168.15.1/32` and `192.168.16.1/32` are loopback addresses from `RouterE` and `RouterF`. On `FIREWALL-A`, it is possible to summarize them all into one large network, `192.168.0.0/16`:

```
FIREWALL-A-> set vr trust-vr protocol ospf area 3 range 192.168.0.0/16 advertise
```

After executing the command on the ABR `FIREWALL-A`, on `FIREWALL-B` in area 0, only one summary route is left:

```
FIREWALL-B-> get vr trust-vr protocol ospf database summary
VR: trust-vr RouterId: 192.168.19.1
----------------------------------

                         Summary LSA(s) for area 0.0.0.0
  Link-State-Id   Adv-Router ID      Age  Sequence# CheckSum
----------------------------------------------------------
       10.0.8.0    192.168.18.1     1468 0x80000003   0x2487
      10.0.13.0    192.168.18.1     1468 0x80000003   0x79eb
    192.168.0.0    192.168.18.1        3 0x80000001   0xdd37
```

In addition to summarizing routes, you can also filter routes. The route filter in OSPF is different from a route filter in a protocol such as BGP. In BGP, routes can be filtered as they are advertised. For instance, `10.0.0.0/8` would filter route `10.0.0.0/8` but not route `10.0.1.0/24`. In OSPF, all routes of the same and longer netmasks would be filtered. So, `192.168.0.0/16` would also filter the `/32` loopback addresses.

```
FIREWALL-A-> set vr trust protocol ospf area 3 range 192.168.0.0/16 no-advertise
```

You can configure this command only on ABRs, and only on the originating area:

```
FIREWALL-B-> get vr trust protocol ospf database summary
VR: trust-vr RouterId: 192.168.19.1
----------------------------------

                         Summary LSA(s) for area 0.0.0.0
  Link-State-Id   Adv-Router ID      Age  Sequence# CheckSum
----------------------------------------------------------
```

```
10.0.8.0      192.168.18.1          86 0x80000004   0x2288
10.0.13.0     192.168.18.1          86 0x80000004   0x77ec
```

What the area-range feature does not do is change LSAs. The main task of ABRs is to translate between areas. On ABRs, links in Router LSAs are translated to Summary LSAs. The `area-range` keyword influences the creation or omission of Summary LSAs. This is why this command needs to be configured on the area that originated the routes and is effective for all other areas to which the ABR is connected. You cannot summarize external routes on an ABR unless the ABR is also the originating ASBR (see Recipe 16.9).

16.8 Redistribute Routes into OSPF

Problem

You want to redistribute (export) routes into OSPF.

Solution

Configure a route map to identify the routes which should be redistributed. Optionally, configure the metric and metric type:

```
FIREWALL-C-> set vrouter "trust-vr"
FIREWALL-C(trust-vr)-> set route 1.1.1.0/24 interface ethernet0/1 gateway 10.0.0.254
tag 100
FIREWALL-C(trust-vr)-)-> set route-map name "exp-ospf" permit 10
FIREWALL-C(trust-vr/exp-ospf-10)-> set match tag 100
FIREWALL-C(trust-vr/exp-ospf-10)-> set metric 10
FIREWALL-C(trust-vr/exp-ospf-10)-> set metric-type type-2
FIREWALL-C(trust-vr/exp-ospf-10)-> exit
FIREWALL-C(trust-vr)-> exit
```

Configure redistribution in OSPF:

```
FIREWALL-C-> set vrouter "trust-vr"
FIREWALL-C(trust-vr)-> set protocol ospf
FIREWALL-C(trust-vr/ospf)-> set redistribute route-map "exp-ospf" protocol static
FIREWALL-C(trust-vr/ospf)-> exit
FIREWALL-C(trust-vr)-> exit
```

Discussion

It is sometimes necessary to inject routes learned from another routing protocol into OSPF. In other instances, one OSPF instance's routes may need to be imported into another instance. This can occur in the case of multiple VRs each running OSPF. The redistribution of routes in ScreenOS is a two-step process: first, you need to select the routes, and then you activate the redistribution and identify the source protocol.

A good way to select routes is to give the routes a tag value and to match on this tag in a route map:

```
FIREWALL-C-> set vrouter "trust-vr"
FIREWALL-C(trust-vr)-> set route 1.1.1.0/24 interface ethernet0/1 gateway 10.0.0.254
tag 100
FIREWALL-C(trust-vr)->set route-map name "exp-static-ospf" permit 10
FIREWALL-C(trust-vr/exp-static-ospf-10)-> set match tag 100
FIREWALL-C(trust-vr/exp-static-ospf-10)-> exit
FIREWALL-C(trust-vr)-> exit
```

Other routes, such as routes originating from RIP, may or may not have tags. If they do not have tags, you can also identify them by matching an access list. Do not confuse access lists in ScreenOS with prefix lists. An *access list* matches on any route with the netmask n or greater, whereas a *prefix list* matches only on a route with a specific netmask. For instance, the prefix list `192.168.0.0/16` matches only on route `192.168.0.0/16` and not on routes `192.168.1.0/24` and `192.168.2.0/24`, whereas the access list `192.168.0.0/16` matches on `192.168.1.0/24` and `192.168.2.0/24` in addition to `192.168.0.0/16`.

```
FIREWALL-C-> set vrouter "trust-vr"
FIREWALL-C(trust-vr)-> set access-list 1 permit ip 192.168.0.0/16 10
FIREWALL-C(trust-vr)-> set route-map name "exp-rip-ospf" permit 10
FIREWALL-C(trust-vr/exp-rip-ospf-10)-> set match ip 1
FIREWALL-C(trust-vr/exp-rip-ospf-10)-> exit
FIREWALL-C(trust-vr)-> exit
```

Once routes have been identified for redistribution, the next step is to activate the redistribution and identify the source protocol. The choices for source protocol are as follows:

BGP
: Match BGP routes.

Connected
: Match connected routes.

Discovered
: Match discovered routes.

Imported
: Match imported routes.

RIP
: Match RIP routes.

Static
: Match static routes.

Most sources are self-explanatory. Imported routes are routes from a different VR. Discovered routes are from auto-connect or dial-up VPNs. To activate the redistribution process, use the `redistribute` keyword in the protocol OSPF hierarchy of the VR configuration:

```
FIREWALL-C-> set vrouter "trust-vr"
FIREWALL-C(trust-vr)-> set protocol ospf
```

```
FIREWALL-C(trust-vr/ospf)-> set redistribute route-map "exp-rip-ospf" protocol rip
FIREWALL-C(trust-vr/ospf)-> exit
FIREWALL-C(trust-vr)-> exit
```

There is an exception for the default route which does not require a route map:

```
FIREWALL-C-> set vrouter "trust-vr"
FIREWALL-C(trust-vr)-> set protocol ospf
FIREWALL-C(trust-vr/ospf)-> set advertise-def-route metric 1 metric-type 1
FIREWALL-C(trust-vr/ospf)-> exit
FIREWALL-C(trust-vr)-> exit
```

Recall that OSPF calls redistributed or imported routes AS *External routes*. Such routes are carried in External LSAs (or NSSA External LSAs). Once configured, check whether the routes are successfully exported into OSPF:

```
FIREWALL-C-> get vr trust-vr protocol ospf database external self-originate
VR: trust-vr RouterId: 192.168.17.1
----------------------------------


                        AS External LSA(s)
  Link-State-Id   Adv-Router ID      Age  Sequence# CheckSum
-----------------------------------------------------------
        0.0.0.0    192.168.17.1        0 0x80000001   0xfdb8
    192.168.1.0    192.168.17.1       11 0x80000001   0xcd71
    192.168.2.0    192.168.17.1        7 0x80000001   0xc27b
    192.168.3.0    192.168.17.1        3 0x80000001   0xb785
```

External routes exist as two subtypes: type-1 and type-2. The difference between the two is in how OSPF determines path cost. Each external route is advertised with a metric, which is an unsigned 24-bit integer. The metric is 1 by default, and you can change it within the route map. Type-1 external routes add the internal path cost to the metric, whereas type-2 routes do not. With type-2 external routes, the cost of the path to the ASBR is considered only if two type-2 routes with the same prefix exist and are advertised by two different ASBRs.

Type-1 routes are always preferred over type-2 routes, and inter-area routes are preferred over external routes, whereas intra-area routes are preferred over inter-area routes. RFC 1583 and RFC 2328 have a slightly different way of calculating the best path to an external network, which in some circumstances can cause loops when both methods are used concurrently (see Recipe 16.9). The default metric type is type-1. To change the metric type, use a route map:

```
FIREWALL-C-> set vrouter "trust-vr"
FIREWALL-C(trust-vr)-> set access-list 1 permit ip 192.168.0.0/16 10
FIREWALL-C(trust-vr)-> set route-map name "exp-rip-ospf" permit 10
FIREWALL-C(trust-vr/exp-rip-ospf-10)-> set match ip 1
FIREWALL-C(trust-vr/exp-rip-ospf-10)-> set metric 10
FIREWALL-C(trust-vr/exp-rip-ospf-10)-> set metric-type type-2
FIREWALL-C(trust-vr/exp-rip-ospf-10)-> exit
FIREWALL-C(trust-vr)-> exit
```

An external route can also have a Forwarding Address (FA), which by default is left empty, but could have been populated with the IP address of any interface on the device. The External LSA also has space for a user-specified 32-bit value, called a *route tag*. You can use the route tag to funnel information through an OSPF domain such as AS-path (limited to two AS numbers), a community value, and so on. It is most often used to group and track the origin of routes. For example, you can track routes from several different extranet partners by using tags. Each partner gets its own route tag and can be easily tracked over the OSPF AS. You can manipulate the FA and then tag with the route map:

```
FIREWALL-C-> set vrouter "trust-vr"
FIREWALL-C(trust-vr)-> set access-list 1 permit ip 192.168.1.0/24 10
FIREWALL-C(trust-vr)-> set access-list 2 permit ip 192.168.2.0/24 10
FIREWALL-C(trust-vr)-> set route-map name "exp-rip-ospf" permit 10
FIREWALL-C(trust-vr/exp-rip-ospf-10)-> set match ip 1
FIREWALL-C(trust-vr/exp-rip-ospf-10)-> set next-hop 10.0.18.253
FIREWALL-C(trust-vr/exp-rip-ospf-10)-> set tag 100
FIREWALL-C(trust-vr/exp-rip-ospf-10)-> exit
FIREWALL-C(trust-vr)-> set route-map name "exp-rip-ospf" permit 20
FIREWALL-C(trust-vr/exp-rip-ospf-20)-> set match ip 2
FIREWALL-C(trust-vr/exp-rip-ospf-20)-> set next-hop 10.0.18.254
FIREWALL-C(trust-vr/exp-rip-ospf-20)-> set tag 200
FIREWALL-C(trust-vr/exp-rip-ospf-20)-> exit
FIREWALL-C(trust-vr)-> exit
```

`192.168.1.0/24` and its subnetworks are tagged with 100 and have an FA of `10.0.8.253`, whereas `192.168.2.0/24` and its subnetworks are tagged with 200 and have an FA of `10.0.18.254`. Use of the FA and tag is optional. FA is rarely manually configured unless the ASBR should be a route server; it is considered a best practice to use tags to organize redistributed routes.

```
FIREWALL-C-> get vr trust-vr protocol ospf database detail external
link-state-id 192.168.1.0
VR: trust-vr RouterId: 192.168.17.1
----------------------------------
                        AS External LSA(s)
                        -------------------------------


Age:  16
Seq Number: 0x80000004
Checksum: 0xe1df
Advertising Router: 192.168.17.1
Link State ID: 192.168.1.0
Length: 36
Options:   Extern     DC
Network Mask: 255.255.255.0
                Metric Type: 1
                TOS: 0
                Metric: 10
                Forward Address: 10.0.18.253
                External Route Tag: 100
```

Recall that external routes are treated in distance-vector fashion instead of in link-state fashion (see the Introduction to this chapter). External routes are attached to the shortest path tree as leaves to an ASBR, or to an ABR if the ASBR is in a different area. If an FA is provided, the route would be attached to the closest device with knowledge of the next-hop network. The distance-vector behavior is not much different from the way RIP would select routes.

For scalability reasons (recall that for each route imported into OSPF, a separate LSA is created), it is important to limit the number of routes being injected into OSPF. It is a best practice to summarize and filter external routes before they are injected into OSPF. You can filter and summarize external routes only on an ASBR. Some vendors have proprietary extensions to filter or summarize external routes on an ABR, but ScreenOS does not implement these extensions.

Some routing policies call for static and connected routes to be redistributed on every device. However, it is considered a best practice to carefully select ASBRs. Not every device needs to or should be an ASBR. Furthermore, nothing should be redistributed into OSPF without careful consideration due to the possibility of overloading the devices' LSDB with AS External routes. There are few good reasons why connected routes need to be injected into OSPF, because enabling OSPF on the interface will include the connected route information in the local Router LSA. To ensure that connected interfaces are included in the Router LSA, configure stub interfaces (those which should not form OSPF adjacencies) as passive. Without the `passive` keyword, OSPF would send Hello packets out the interface, in an attempt to establish adjacencies with other devices. The `passive` keyword is used to disable the sending of Hellos on an interface:

```
FIREWALL-C-> set int e0/0 protocol ospf passive
```

Redistribution of connected interfaces is required in the case where secondary IP addresses are configured on an interface and you want to include these networks in OSPF. As with other route redistribution, you can use access lists to limit the networks that are redistributed.

16.9 Make OSPF RFC 1583-Compatible

Problem

All routers in your network are RFC 1583-compatible, and you want to make ScreenOS RFC 1583-compatible as well.

Solution

Change the compatibility settings:

```
FIREWALL-A-> set vr trust-vr protocol ospf rfc-1583
```

Discussion

RFC 2328 is the latest RFC for OSPF v2. By default, ScreenOS is RFC 2328-compatible; however, some vendors default to the older RFC 1583, and therefore differ in some features of the more modern RFC. The compatibility issue (sometimes incorrectly referred to as OSPF version 1 or version 2) refers only to the way the metric for external routes is calculated. In most networks, both RFCs can coexist without any problems, but in some networks, such as those in which ABRs in the same area use a different compatibility mode and there are ASBRs in different areas advertising the same networks, loops can be created. It is a best practice to configure all devices in the same mode.

Here's how RFC 1583 calculates the path in numbered steps:

1. Ignore if cost is infinite, max age, or originated by self.
2. Look up if route to ASBR exists.
3. Select next hop and cost to gateway (FA or ASBR). In case of FA, it must be an intra- or inter-area route.
4. Calculate cost *X* to gateway and next hop.
5. See whether a route to *N* already exists.
6. If not, install route.
7. If already exists:
    a. Intra/inter always better than external
    b. E1 always better than E2
    c. Compare E1 by best $x + y$
    d. Compare E2 by best *y* and then by best *x*

RFC 2328 would always choose an intra-area route before considering an inter-area route in a nonbackbone area to calculate the best path to an external network. Both would always prefer an intra- over an inter-area route and both of those over an external route. A type-1 external route is preferred over a type-2 external route.

1. Ignore if cost is infinite, max age, or originated by self.
2. Look up if route to ASBR exists.
3. Select next hop and cost to gateway (FA or ASBR) by choosing an intra-area route if nonbackbone area or intra/inter route if backbone area. Tie breaker is least cost and largest area ID. In case of FA, it must be an intra- or inter-area route.
4. Calculate cost *X* to gateway and next hop.
5. See whether a route to *N* already exists.
6. If not, install route.

7. If already exists:
    a. Intra/inter always better than external
    b. E1 always better than E2
    c. Compare E2 by best *y*
    d. Choose intra-area if nonbackbone or intra/inter if backbone to FA/ASBR
    e. Compare E1 and by best $x + y$ or compare E2 by best *x*

External routes are routed to the closest ASBR or FA. An ASBR can advertise a different FA than itself, which makes sense on broadcast networks, when the actual gateway is not part of the OSPF domain.

16.10 Adjust OSPF Link Costs

Problem

You want to change the link cost.

Solution

Change the link cost per interface:

```
FIREWALL-A-> set int s1/0 protocol ospf cost 100
```

Discussion

The OSPF metric is accumulative. Traditionally, and by default in ScreenOS, OSPF calculates the cost from the interface speed with the approximation of 100,000/bandwidth. For example, T1 links have a cost of 65; 10 Mbps links have a cost of 10; T3 links have a cost of 2; and all faster links have a cost of 1. The metric is carried in the LSA and is a 16-bit value for interface cost and a 24-bit value for the metric of redistributed routes. The cost is accumulative and the cost on the closest interface always counts. For example, when two routers are connected to each other and a route is pointing to the neighbor, the local cost counts but not the cost on the neighbor's interface to which the local router is connected. A cost of 1, for all practical purposes, changes the metric to a hop count, which is often the best choice and keeps routing simple. Be careful when changing the cost. Configuring a high cost could end up routing through another continent instead of a backup path. Redundant links should therefore have a metric of only one or two higher than the primary link.

Notice that there are two choices for path decision of external routes: E1 routes (type-1) add the path cost through the OSPF cloud to the advertised metric from the ASBR, whereas E2 routes (type-2) just assume the advertised metric from the ASBR. OSPF always prefers type-1 routes over type-2 routes. In case of a tie with type-2 routes, path cost is the deciding factor.

16.11 Configure OSPF on Point-to-Multipoint Links

Problem

You want to configure VPN on a point-to-multipoint interface terminating VPN tunnels, such as on a hub security gateway.

Solution

Configure all interfaces in the point-to-multipoint network cloud with the IP addresses in the same network:

```
FIREWALL-B-> set interface tunnel.1 ip 10.0.10.1/24
FIREWALL-A-> set interface tunnel.1 ip 10.0.10.2/24
FIREWALL-C-> set interface tunnel.1 ip 10.0.10.3/24
```

Configure the hub interface, which is given here on FIREWALL-B as a point-to-multipoint interface:

```
FIREWALL-B-> set interface tunnel.1 protocol ospf area 0.0.0.0
FIREWALL-B-> set interface tunnel.1 protocol ospf link-type p2mp
FIREWALL-B-> set interface tunnel.1 protocol ospf enable
```

Configure OSPF on the spoke firewalls:

```
FIREWALL-A-> set interface tunnel.1 protocol ospf area 0.0.0.0
FIREWALL-A-> set interface tunnel.1 protocol ospf enable

FIREWALL-C-> set interface tunnel.1 protocol ospf area 0.0.0.0
FIREWALL-C-> set interface tunnel.1 protocol ospf enable
```

Discussion

Unlike nonbroadcast multiaccess (NBMA) networks, which ScreenOS does not support, there is no DR or BDR in a point-to-multipoint cloud. In fact, point-to-multipoint interfaces in OSPF are an emulation of multiple point-to-point links. On a point-to-multipoint interface, messages are replicated for each link automatically. Point-to-multipoint links need an IP address and cannot be unnumbered.

Figure 16-4 shows a point-to-multipoint topology. FIREWALL-B is the hub and FIREWALL-A and FIREWALL-C are spokes. The firewalls are connected with IPSec tunnels.

Multiple IPSec tunnels are connected to the same tunnel interface on the hub device FIREWALL-B:

```
FIREWALL-B-> set interface tunnel.1 zone "vpn"
FIREWALL-B-> set interface tunne.1 ip 10.0.10.1/24
FIREWALL-B-> set ike gateway "FIREWALL-A" address 10.0.9.2 preshare juniper sec-level
standard
FIREWALL-B-> set vpn "FIREWALL-A" gateway "FIREWALL-A" sec-level standard
FIREWALL-B-> set vpn "FIREWALL-A" id 2 bind interface tunnel.1
```

```
FIREWALL-B-> set ike gateway "FIREWALL-C" address 10.0.8.2 preshare juniper sec-level
standard
FIREWALL-B-> set vpn "FIREWALL-C" gateway "FIREWALL-C" sec-level standard
FIREWALL-B-> set vpn "FIREWALL-C" id 1 bind interface tunnel.1
```

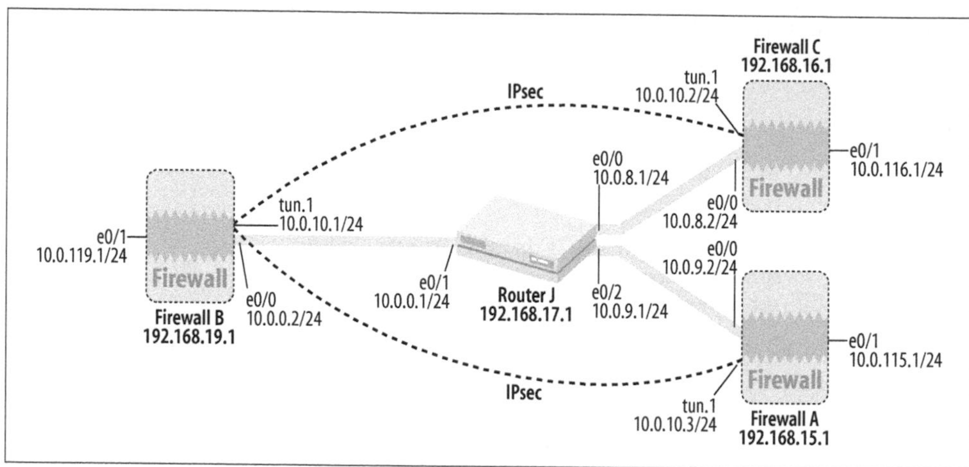

Figure 16-4. Point-to-multipoint topology

On FIREWALL-A, configure one IPSec tunnel to FIREWALL-B:

```
FIREWALL-A-> set interface tunnel.1 zone "vpn"
FIREWALL-A-> set interface tunne.1 ip 10.0.10.2/24
FIREWALL-A-> set ike gateway "FIREWALL-B" address 10.0.2.2 preshare juniper sec-level
standard
FIREWALL-A-> set vpn "FIREWALL-B" gateway "FIREWALL-B" sec-level standard
FIREWALL-A-> set vpn "FIREWALL-B" id 1 bind interface tunnel.1
```

Do the same on FIREWALL-C:

```
FIREWALL-C-> set interface tunnel.1 zone "vpn"
FIREWALL-C-> set interface tunne.1 ip 10.0.10.3/24
FIREWALL-C-> set ike gateway "FIREWALL-B" address 10.0.2.2 preshare juniper sec-level
standard
FIREWALL-C-> set vpn "FIREWALL-B" gateway "FIREWALL-B" sec-level standard
FIREWALL-C-> set vpn "FIREWALL-B" id 1 bind interface tunnel.1
```

Notice that all tunnel interfaces have IPs in the same network. This is a requirement for point-to-multipoint topologies.

FIREWALL-B maintains a Next Hop Tunnel Binding (NHTB) table. The NHTB is similar to a frame map on a Frame Relay network and maps the IPSec SA circuits to a gateway address.

```
FIREWALL-B-> get interface tunnel.1
Interface tunnel.1:
  description tunnel.1
  number 20, if_info 8168, if_index 1, mode route
  link ready
  vsys Root, zone vpn, vr trust-vr
```

```
  admin mtu 1500, operating mtu 1500, default mtu 1500
  *ip 10.0.10.1/24
  *manage ip 10.0.10.1
  route-deny enable
  bound vpn:
    FIREWALL-C
    FIREWALL-A

  Next-Hop Tunnel Binding table
  Flag Status Next-Hop(IP)    tunnel-id  VPN
        U     10.0.10.2 0x00000001 FIREWALL-C
        U     10.0.10.3 0x00000002 FIREWALL-A

  pmtu-v4 disabled
  ping disabled, telnet disabled, SSH disabled, SNMP disabled
  web disabled, ident-reset disabled, SSL disabled

  OSPF enabled  BGP disabled  RIP disabled  RIPng disabled  mtrace
disabled
  PIM: not configured  IGMP not configured
  NHRP disabled
  bandwidth: physical 0kbps, configured egress [gbw 0kbps mbw 0kbps]
             configured ingress mbw 0kbps, current bw 0kbps
             total allocated gbw 0kbps
Number of SW session: 8057, hw sess err cnt 0
```

On a point-to-point interface, routes can simply point into the interface. There is only one way in and one way out. On a point-to-multipoint interface, there are multiple destinations. A route also needs a next hop. The NHTB table maintains the next hop for routes into the point-to-multipoint interface. The NHTB table is auto-populated with the IP addresses of the remote interfaces.

```
FIREWALL-B-> get vr trust-vr route protocol ospf
H: Host C: Connected S: Static A: Auto-Exported
I: Imported R: RIP P: Permanent D: Auto-Discovered
N: NHRP
iB: IBGP eB: EBGP O: OSPF E1: OSPF external type 1
E2: OSPF external type 2 trailing B: backup route

Total 9/max entries

    ID      IP-Prefix  Interface      Gateway   P Pref    Mtr   Vsys
----------------------------------------------------------------
*   13  10.0.116.0/24       tun.1   10.0.10.2   O   60     11  Root
*   12  10.0.115.0/24       tun.1   10.0.10.3   O   60     11  Root
```

The hub becomes adjacent to the spokes, but the spokes do not become adjacent to each other.

```
FIREWALL-B-> get vr trust-vr protocol ospf neighbor
VR: trust-vr RouterId: 192.168.19.1
----------------------------------
                Neighbor(s) on interface ethernet0/1 (Area 0.0.0.0)
```

```
                 Neighbor(s) on interface tunnel.1 (Area 0.0.0.0)
IpAddr/IfIndex  RouterId      Pri State    Opt  Up          StateChg
-----------------------------------------------------------------
10.0.10.3       192.168.15.1   1 Full      E    00:28:50     (+6 -0)
10.0.10.2       192.168.16.1   1 Full      E    00:29:00     (+6 -0)

FIREWALL-A-> get vr trust-vr protocol ospf neighbor
VR: trust-vr RouterId: 192.168.15.1
----------------------------------
                 Neighbor(s) on interface ethernet0/1 (Area 0.0.0.0)

                 Neighbor(s) on interface tunnel.1 (Area 0.0.0.0)
IpAddr/IfIndex  RouterId      Pri State    Opt  Up          StateChg
-----------------------------------------------------------------
10.0.10.1       192.168.19.1  1 Full      E    00:29:47     (+6 -0)
```

OSPF does not know a point-to-multipoint interface type. Instead, it creates a virtual point-to-point interface for each link. Two point-to-point links are created for FIREWALL-A and FIREWALL-C, and an additional stub link is added to the Router LSA to track the IP and network as is done with point-to-point links.

```
FIREWALL-B-> get vr trust-vr protocol ospf database detail router self
VR: trust-vr RouterId: 192.168.19.1
----------------------------------
                         Router LSA(s) in area 0.0.0.0
                         -------------------------------
Age:  1702
Seq Number: 0x80000009
Checksum: 0x4dec
Advertising Router: 192.168.19.1
Link State ID: 192.168.19.1
Length: 72
Options:   Extern     DC
Flags: ,,, Links 4
Link# 1
                Link State ID: 10.0.119.0
                Link Data: 255.255.255.0
                Type: 3
                TOS: 0
                Metric: 1

Link# 2
                Link State ID: 192.168.15.1
                Link Data: 10.0.10.1
                Type: 1
                TOS: 0
                Metric: 10

Link# 3
                Link State ID: 192.168.16.1
                Link Data: 10.0.10.1
                Type: 1
                TOS: 0
                Metric: 10
```

```
Link# 4
            Link State ID: 10.0.10.1
            Link Data: 255.255.255.255
            Type: 3
            TOS: 0
            Metric: 0
```

Often, routing between spoke sites is not desired. Therefore, ScreenOS denies hairpin routing by default on point-to-multipoint interfaces. If you want, you can enable it. For example, if `FIREWALL-A` should be able to talk to `FIREWALL-C` on `FIREWALL-B`, you configure the following:

```
FIREWALL-B-> unset interface tunnel.1 route-deny
```

This feature does not impact OSPF. Neighbor adjacency will exist only between the spoke and the hub—it only determines whether the hub should relay payload packets between the spokes.

16.12 Configure Demand Circuits

Problem

You want to reduce LSA flooding and Hello message flooding to conserve charges on measured rate links or to reduce the load on a hub firewall.

Solution

To reduce LSA flooding and Hello messages on point-to-point and point-to-multipoint links, configure on at least one end of the link:

```
FIREWALL-B-> set int s1/0 protocol ospf demand-circuit
```

For circuits with another link type, it is not possible to suppress Hello messages. To reduce LSA flooding, configure on every device on the segment:

```
FIREWALL-B-> set int e0/1 protocol ospf reduce-flooding
```

Discussion

According to RFC 1793, "Demand circuits are network segments whose costs vary with usage; charges can be based both on connect time and on bytes/packets transmitted."

The demand circuit (DC) extension applies to dial-up analog modem links, the Integrated Services Digital Network (ISDN), and other measured rate services. On regular links, OSPF periodically exchanges Hello messages (commonly every 10 seconds) to track the liveliness of the neighbor and refloods LSAs (every 20–30 minutes) even if there was no change in the network topology. Each time a message is sent, the underlying link needs to come up or the neighbor will be declared dead because the `RouterDeadInterval` was reached. DCs reduce LSA flooding as well as optional Hello messages. On time- and connection-billed services, it is important to suppress Hello messages so that the link does not come up every few seconds. An additional use, which the authors of the RFC did not anticipate, is to reduce OSPF resource consumption on large hub devices with hundreds of spoke links, such as VPN security gateways. Each time an LSA has to be flooded, hundreds of LSAs need to be flooded out to each spoke, which can take a toll on the device when there are a lot of LSAs to flood. Most resources on an OSPF device are not consumed by the execution of the SPF algorithm, but rather by flooding LSAs.

DCs are enabled on ScreenOS via two different commands. To reduce LSA flooding and Hello messages, configure on at least one side of the link:

```
FIREWALL-B-> set interface s1/0 protocol ospf demand-circuit
```

ScreenOS will automatically negotiate the DC on the other end. LSA and Hello reduction is supported only on links with a link type of point-to-point and point-to-multipoint. The firewall will set the `DC` bit in the header of the Hello messages, and will suppress Hello messages after the `Full` state is reached.

```
FIREWALL-B-> get vr trust-vr protocol ospf neighor
VR: trust-vr RouterId: 192.168.19.1
----------------------------------
                Neighbor(s) on interface serial1/0 (Area 0.0.0.0)
IpAddr/IfIndex  RouterId      Pri State    Opt  Up          StateChg
---------------------------------------------------------------
10.0.1.1        192.168.18.1   1 Full      E  D 00:26:51 (+10 -1)
```

For circuits with another link type (broadcast and NBMA), it is not possible to suppress Hello messages, but it is still possible to suppress LSA flooding:

```
FIREWALL-B-> set interface e0/1 protocol ospf reduce-flooding
```

This feature does not get signaled to any neighbor, and therefore it cannot be negotiated. You need to configure this option on every device on this segment (network) for it to be effective.

With either method, the device marks all LSAs—those originated by itself and those reflooded by it—with the `DNA` bit (do-not-age) within the LSA message content, sent over a link configured for DC or reduced flooding:

```
FIREWALL-C-> get vr trust-vr protocol ospf database
VR: trust-vr RouterId: 192.168.17.1
----------------------------------


                        Router LSA(s) for area 0.0.0.0
  Link-State-Id   Adv-Router ID       Age  Sequence# CheckSum
---------------------------------------------------------------
   192.168.17.1    192.168.17.1        639 0x8000000b   0xc156
   192.168.18.1    192.168.18.1 DNA 3600 0x80000003   0xd53c
   192.168.19.1    192.168.19.1 DNA 3600 0x80000007   0x add

                        Network LSA(s) for area 0.0.0.0
```

```
Link-State-Id   Adv-Router ID      Age  Sequence# CheckSum
-----------------------------------------------------------
      10.0.0.2   192.168.17.1      639 0x80000005   0xdbd9
```

Here, FIREWALL-C (Router ID 192.168.17.1) received two Router LSAs, and is originating one Router LSA and one Network LSA. Only the LSAs received through the DC or reduced flooding link were tagged with the DNA bit. FIREWALL-C will in turn tag LSAs when it floods LSAs out its DC or reduced flooding interface. Its self-originated LSAs, however, will keep within its database without the DNA bit. It will still flood those out within the LSRefreshInterval over its regular links. A router keeps track of LSAs it is flooding out over a DC or reduced flooding link. It will reflood LSAs only when a topology change was communicated in this LSA. Even if the DNA bit is deleted in subsequent versions of the LSA, the device will not update another device over a DC.

The DNA bit is actually an extension to the age field. The age field in the LSA is a 16-bit unsigned integer, which runs from 0 (just originated) to 3,600 (MaxAge) seconds. Only 12 bits are actually used, so the high-order bit can be used to signal DNA. A device never purges an LSA, which has the DNA bit set, unless the LSA reaches MaxAge and the device does not have an active link to the signaled route. As an exception, such a purged LSA will also be flooded out on all links to propagate the detection of a stalled LSA. Normally, only the originating device is allowed to purge an LSA.

The DC extension contains two parts: a modification to the flooding algorithm and a modification to DC endpoints. To operate a DC anywhere in an OSPF domain, all devices in the domain have to support the first modification. This modification to the flooding algorithm is signaled by the DC bit in the Router LSA header. If a single device does not support DCs in the same area or any area in the OSPF domain, all devices will automatically switch off the DC extension. This is signaled by the absence of the DC bit in the Router LSA and by a special discovery LSA over area borders. There is one exception to this rule: when the device with the DC requirement is in a stub or NSSA area (see Recipe 16.5 and Recipe 16.6). The second modification is to the endpoints, which means the actual links. In ScreenOS, the first modification is always present and cannot be changed. In other vendors' routers, it may have to be enabled manually, if supported at all. The two described commands make the modification to the endpoints, hence declaring a link a DC and reducing LSA flooding and optional Hello flooding, but they will not change the behavior of the LSA received with the DNA bit already set.

There are some considerations to take into account with DCs, the first being that because Hello messages are suppressed, there is no native mechanism for detecting an actual dead neighbor. This may not be a problem on spoke links, but could be a problem when spokes have redundant links to multiple hubs. Additional liveliness detection, such as ScreenOS's VPN Monitor or Interface Monitor, should be deployed to ensure that dead links can be effectively detected. The second consideration is that although LSAs are not refreshed unless they are changed, they will still be flooded if they do change. A large network always has LSAs being flooded because of change. It is therefore recommended to use the DC extensions in isolated parts of the topology within a totally stubby are (see Recipe 16.5) or a totally stubby NSSA (see Recipe 16.6).

16.13 Configure Virtual Links

Problem

You have an area that is not attached to the backbone area, or you have a partitioned backbone area. This is an invalid OSPF topology and you need to find a workaround.

Solution

Configure a virtual link from the ABR that is not connected to the backbone to an ABR that is connected to the backbone through a transit area. Both ABRs need to be connected to the transit area. The endpoints of a virtual link are the Router IDs. Configure the virtual link on both ABRs:

```
FIREWALL-B-> set vr trust-vr protocol ospf vlink area-id 2 router-id 192.168.16.1
FIREWALL-A-> set vr trust-vr protocol ospf vlink area-id 2 router-id 192.168.19.1
```

Explicitly permit OSPF traffic on all firewalls in the transit area:

```
FIREWALL-C-> set policy global any any ospf permit
```

Discussion

OSPF topologies require a hierarchical design for loop avoidance (see the Introduction to this chapter). All areas are connected to a backbone area. To get from one area to another, traffic has to transit the backbone area, and there can be only one backbone area. Even if an ABR connecting two nonbackbone areas originates a Summary LSA into both areas, another ABR will not pick up those Summary LSAs and flood them into the backbone area. The area will be isolated from the backbone area.

An area has *TransitCapability* when an ABR, which terminates a virtual link, is in the area. A virtual link is an emulated point-to-point link between an ABR connecting two nonbackbone areas and an ABR connecting to one of the nonbackbone areas and the backbone area. Alternatively, a virtual link can also fix a partitioned backbone area. A virtual link is a powerful surgical tool for fixing challenging topologies and improving routing, but you should use it with caution.

The virtual link is an extension of the backbone area to an ABR that has no direct access to the backbone area. The endpoints of a virtual link are both ABRs, and act as though they were directly connected by a point-to-point link. Instead of exchanging Hello and LSA messages via multicast, Hellos and LSA update messages are unicast between the two ABRs. This is why the policy permitting OSPF is required on the transit area devices. No actual payload data flows over the virtual link; do not confuse this with, for example, something such as a Generic Routing Encapsulation (GRE) tunnel. Also, the virtual link does not automatically determine the path the payload packet will take through the transit area. It is only used to communicate LSAs from and to the backbone area.

A virtual link traverses a transit area. Because the messages are unicast, devices in this area will not put those LSAs in their database, or reflood them. They will not be aware of the message exchange over the virtual link. The virtual link follows the shortest path through the transit area. A virtual link cannot be terminated on unnumbered point-to-point links because the `src-ip` and `dst-ip` for the messages are derived from the egress and ingress interfaces.

The transit area cannot be a stub or NSSA area and summarization and route filtering on any ABR into the transit area is not allowed. The ABR that terminates the virtual link signals *TransitCapability* to the transit area by setting the `V` bit in the Router LSA. (Other flags are the `B` bit for ABRs and the `E` bit for ASBRs.) Figure 16-5 illustrates a sample network with a virtual link.

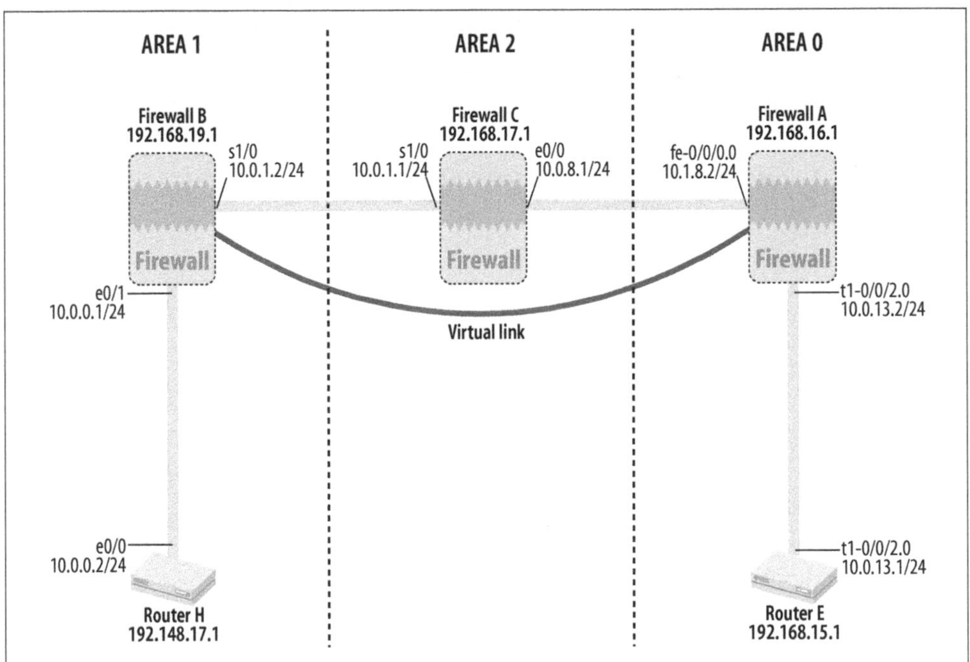

Figure 16-5. Virtual link

In Figure 16-5, `FIREWALL-B` is connected to area 1 and area 2, but does not have connectivity to area 0. `FIREWALL-A`, on the other hand, has connections to area 2 and area 0, but not to area 1. Devices in area 1 can route to destinations in area 2, but not in any other area, and devices in area 2 can route to area 1, but no device from any other area can route to area 1. To fix this problem, you need to configure a virtual link from FIREWALL-B to FIREWALL-A. Area 2 becomes a transit area.

```
FIREWALL-B-> set vr trust-vr protocol ospf vlink area-id 2 router-id 192.168.16.1
FIREWALL-A-> set vr trust-vr protocol ospf vlink area-id 2 router-id 192.168.19.1
```

The endpoints of the virtual link are not the physical IP addresses, but the Router IDs of the endpoints. The devices will determine the ingress and egress interfaces by looking at the Router LSA from either device. For example, OSPF will automatically use interface s1/0 on FIREWALL-B as the interface to terminate the virtual link in Figure 16-5.

On FIREWALL-C, you need to configure a policy to permit Hellos and LSA messages to flow from FIREWALL-B to FIREWALL-A. To configure a more restrictive policy than the global policy originally presented in the recipe, specify the source and destination IP addresses:

```
FIREWALL-C-> set address trust FIREWALL-B 10.0.1.2/32 "s1/0"
FIREWALL-C-> set address untrust FIREWALL-A 10.0.8.2/32 "fe-0/0/0.0"
FIREWALL-C-> set policy from trust to untrust FIREWALL-B FIREWALL-A OSPF permit
FIREWALL-C-> set policy from untrust to trust FIREWALL-A FIREWALL-B OSPF permit
```

The virtual link creates a virtual point-to-point interface. However, ScreenOS does not show the adjacency under its neighbors or OSPF interfaces as other devices may do.

```
FIREWALL-B-> get vr trust-vr protocol ospf vlink
VR: trust-vr RouterId: 192.168.19.1
----------------------------------
Virtual Links
---------------
AreaId: 0.0.0.2 RouterId: 192.168.16.1
Physical interface: serial1/0
HelloInterval: 10  RouterDeadInterval: 40
RetransmitInterval: 8 TransitDelay: 1
State: Point-to-Point
Authentication: None
Neighbors:
        RtrId: 192.168.16.1 IpAddr: 10.0.8.2 Pri: 0 State: Full
```

As an alternative to explicitly configuring a virtual link, you also can configure ScreenOS to discover virtual links automatically:

```
FIREWALL-B-> set vr trust protocol ospf auto-vlink
```

Neighbors discovered through auto-vlink cannot be reviewed with the get vr trust-vr protocol ospf vlink command. Look at the ABR's Router LSA instead:

```
FIREWALL-B-> get vr trust-vr protocol ospf database detail area 0
router self
VR: trust-vr RouterId: 192.168.19.1
----------------------------------
```

```
                          Router LSA(s) in area 0.0.0.0
                          -------------------------------
Age:  185
Seq Number: 0x80000009
Checksum: 0x194c
Advertising Router: 192.168.19.1
Link State ID: 192.168.19.1
Length: 36
Options:   Extern     DC
Flags: ,,B, Links 1
Link# 1
                Link State ID: 192.168.16.1
                Link Data: 10.0.1.2
                Type: 4
                TOS: 0
                Metric: 65
```

The virtual link is indicated by link type 4 (link type 1 is a point-to-point or point-to-multipoint link, type 2 is a broadcast/NBMA link, and type 3 is a stub network without a neighbor). The V bit is set only in the Router LSA, flooded into transit area 2.

16.14 Change OSPF Timers

Problem

You want to change the timer from its default values.

Solution

Configure this to change the InfTransDelay:

```
FIREWALL-C-> set int e0/0 protocol ospf transit-delay 1
```

Configure this to change the RxmtInterval:

```
FIREWALL-C-> set interface e0/0 protocol ospf retransmit-interval 8
```

Configure this to change the HelloInterval:

```
FIREWALL-C-> set interface e0/0 protocol ospf hello-interval 10
```

Configure this to change the RouterDeadInterval:

```
FIREWALL-C-> set interface e0/0 protocol ospf dead-interval 4
```

Configure this to change the maximum number of retransmits for the DC and other links before OSPF will reset the adjacency:

```
FIREWALL-C-> set vr trust-vr protocol ospf retransmit dc 12
FIREWALL-C-> set vr trust-vr protocol ospf retransmit non-dc 24
```

Discussion

Part of the design process of OSPF was the careful testing for the right value of timers. Short timers may overwhelm the network or create instabilities, and long timers may create unnecessary latency to react to topology changes. Many people have the desire to change Hello timers to reduce failure detection times. If a directly connected link fails, OSPF will know about it within milliseconds, but if a switch is in between neighbors, OSPF would rely on Hellos for failure detection. One thing to consider with security devices is that routing is one of many tasks they must keep up with, along with their main task of protecting the network. A security device can be very busy defending against a Denial of Service (DoS) attack, for instance, and this could contend with the OSPF process for CPU cycles. In this case, changing the timers could create instabilities in the OSPF network. You should therefore be careful to ensure that the values you choose for timers are well thought out.

You can check the interface timers with the following:

```
FIREWALL-C-> get interface e0/0 protocol ospf
VR: trust-vr RouterId: 192.168.17.1
----------------------------------
Interface: ethernet0/0
IpAddr: 10.0.0.2/24, OSPF: enabled, Router: enabled
Type: Broadcast  Area: 0.0.0.0  Priority: 1  Cost: 1  Passive: No
Transit delay: 1s  Retransmit interval: 8s  Hello interval: 10s
Router Dead interval: 40s  Authentication-Type: None
Ignore-MTU: no Reduce-flooding: no
State: Backup Designated Router  DR: 10.0.0.1  BDR: 10.0.0.2(self)
Neighbors:
        RtrId: 192.168.19.1 IpAddr: 10.0.0.1 Pri: 1 State: Full
```

The transit delay (`InfTransDelay`) is the time OSPF subtracts from the LSA age, whenever it floods out an LSA. The retransmit interval (`RxmtInterval`) is the amount of time OSPF waits before retransmitting unacknowledged LSAs. In large networks, it may be necessary to increase this number. The hello interval (`HelloInterval`) is the time between Hellos. On a broadcast domain, OSPF keeps adjacencies only with the DR and BDR. The router dead interval (`RouterDeadInterval`) is the amount of time that has elapsed between Hellos before OSPF would reset the adjacency. If the `HelloInterval` and `RouterDeadInterval` are changed, they need to be changed on all devices on the link or broadcast network the same way.

RFC 2328 suggests that an unacknowledged LSA should be transmitted as many times as the LSA age has left in seconds. ScreenOS, however, limits these retransmits by default to 24 and to 12 on DCs. It is rarely necessary to change this timer.

```
FIREWALL-C-> get vr trust-vr protocol ospf | include circuits
Maximum Retransmit limit:          For nbrs on demand-circuits 12
                                   For nbrs on non-demand-circuits 24
```

16.15 Secure OSPF

Problem

You want to protect OSPF from a DoS or reconnaissance attack.

Solution

Configure authentication on the interface:

```
FIREWALL-A-> set interface s1/0 protocol ospf authentication md5 juniper key-id 1
```

Configure a list of approved neighbors on the interface:

```
FIREWALL-C-> set vrouter "trust-vr"
FIREWALL-C(trust-vr)-> set access-list 5 permit ip 10.0.8.2/32 10
FIREWALL-C(trust-vr)-> set access-list 5 permit ip 10.0.8.3/32 20
FIREWALL-C(trust-vr)-> exit
FIREWALL-C-> set int e0/0 protocol ospf neighbor-list 5
```

Configure Hello flood protection on no more than 10 Hellos within the default 10-second interval:

```
FIREWALL-C-> set vr trust-vr protocol ospf hello-threshold 10
```

Configure LSA flood protection on no more than 1,000 LSAs within a 10-second period:

```
FIREWALL-C-> set vr trust-vr protocol ospf lsa-threshold 10 1000
```

Discussion

It may be desirable to protect infrastructure interests from intentional or accidental DoS or reconnaissance attacks. An intentional attack occurs when an inside attacker is posing as an OSPF router to inject false information, or is overloading resources on the device. Examples of accidental attacks are when large routing tables (such as the entire Internet) are mistakenly injected into OSPF, or when a test router forms an accidental adjacency with a device in the production network.

Protection can be done on two fronts: on the interface and on the SPF engine. First, protect the interface from forming unplanned adjacencies using authentication.

Do not confuse OSPF authentication with encryption. There is no standard for OSPF encryption. OSPF authentication protects the communication between OSPF devices by calculating a hash over the entire message with the help of a shared secret and attaching the hash to the OSPF message. This way, the receiving device can also calculate a hash with the help of its local secret and compare its own hash with the transmitted hash. If the two hashes do not match, it indicates that the message was altered in transmission. OSPF authentication is most often used to protect OSPF devices from forming adjacencies with rogue neighbors. Simple and cryptographic authentication exists, but there is no good reason for using simple authentication these days. Authentication is configured on a per-interface basis and needs to be identical on all OSPF devices on a link or broadcast network, but not on all devices in the area or AS.

```
FIREWALL-C-> set interface s1/0 protocol ospf authentication md5 juniper key-id 1
```

Notice that there is also a key-id with the authentication. The key-id is used for convergence from one secret to another. Devices can be configured with the new and old secrets at the same time, and when done, the old can be deleted. The key-id needs to match on both sides. Using a key-id ensures that devices don't lose their adjacency when the key needs to be changed.

An additional use for OSPF authentication is when two OSPF domains coexist on the same broadcast domain. Then, one OSPF domain uses one secret, and the other secret and devices should not form cross-adjacencies between the domains.

In addition to or instead of authentication, you can configure a neighbor list. When using a neighbor list, only neighbors with the configured src-ip in their Hello message can form an adjacency. Do not confuse this with the Router ID or idx interface, which may or may not be identical to the src-ip OSPF selects for its messages. The src-ip is always the IP of the egress interface or its unnumbered host interface:

```
FIREWALL-C-> set vrouter "trust-vr"
FIREWALL-C(trust-vr)-> set access-list 5 permit ip 10.0.8.2/32 10
FIREWALL-C(trust-vr)-> set access-list 5 permit ip 10.0.8.3/32 20
FIREWALL-C(trust-vr)-> exit

FIREWALL-C-> set interface e0/0 protocol ospf neighbor-list 5
```

An alternative to authentication or neighbor lists on stub links that link without any neighbors is the passive interface option:

```
FIREWALL-C-> set interface e0/0 protocol ospf passive
```

You can check what is configured on an interface by looking at OSPF at the interface hierarchy. Here, notice that key-id 1 is used for inbound and outbound communication. The authentication type is Message Digest 5 (MD5). Furthermore, a neighbor list with access control list (ACL) 5 was configured. This is a transit interface and therefore cannot be configured as a passive interface.

```
FIREWALL-C-> get int e0/0 protocol ospf
VR: trust-vr RouterId: 192.168.17.1
----------------------------------
Interface: ethernet0/0
IpAddr: 10.0.0.2/24, OSPF: enabled, Router: enabled
Type: Broadcast  Area: 0.0.0.0  Priority: 1  Cost: 1  Passive: No
Transit delay: 1s  Retransmit interval: 8s  Hello interval: 10s
Router Dead interval: 40s  Authentication-Type: MD-5
Authentication-Key: ****************
TxKeyId: 1 RxKeyId(s): 1
```

```
Ignore-MTU: no Reduce-flooding: no
State: Designated Router  DR: 10.0.0.2(self)  BDR: 0.0.0.0
Neighbors:

Valid neighbor access list numbers in Vrouter (trust-vr)
---------------------------------------------------------
 5
```

You also can protect the SPF engine from overload. It is possible to control the maximum number of Hellos being processed on a certain interface per second within the Hello threshold. Normally, there would be only one Hello per neighbor per interval. Although not all devices form adjacencies on a broadcast domain with each other, all exchange Hellos, which are also used for DR election. Be careful to not set the value too low.

```
FIREWALL-C-> set vr trust-vr protocol ospf hello-threshold 10
```

The final protection available in ScreenOS is the capability to limit the number of LSAs being processed. Unlike with Hello flood protection, the interval can be freely configured. LSA flooding can overwhelm the resources on a device. Configuring an LSA threshold allows you to protect the firewall's resources when there is an overly aggressive flood of LSAs. This can result either by accident or by malicious intent. When setting the threshold, be sure to account for the initial loading, which happens within a short time when the adjacency comes up. In the following example, the firewall accepts 1,000 LSAs within a 10-second period:

```
FIREWALL-C-> set vr trust-vr protocol ospf lsa-threshold 10 1000
```

16.16 Troubleshoot OSPF

Problem

You need to use debug commands to troubleshoot an OSPF issue.

Solution

Enable OSPF debug:

```
FIREWALL-A-> clear dbuf
FIREWALL-A-> debug ospf all
```

Clear the interface, connect/disconnect a link, or simply wait for 60 seconds. It depends on what you want to monitor.

```
FIREWALL-A-> undebug osfp all
FIREWALL-A-> get dbuf stream
```

Review the logs.

Discussion

Before you start detailed troubleshooting, look for these common sources of errors:

- Checking physical connectivity
- Matching network and netmask (see Recipe 16.1)
- Matching MTU (see Recipe 16.1)
- Compatible link type (see Recipe 16.1)
- Matching area ID (see Recipe 16.4)
- Matching area type (see Recipe 16.5 and Recipe 16.6)
- Check authentication and security measures (see Recipe 16.15)
- Matching timers (see Recipe 16.14)

First, you need to ensure that you have physical connectivity to the neighbor. An easy way to check this is with `get interface` and `ping`, to see whether the interface is physically and administratively up and has connectivity to its neighbor. You may have to enable `ping` on an interface with `set interface e0/0 manage ping` to be able to ping. On broadcast and NBMA, every device on the segment should be able to ping any other device on the same segment. On point-to-multipoint networks, only hubs may be able to ping the spoke (and vice versa, but spokes may not be able to ping each other), and on point-to-point networks, devices may not be able to ping each other at all. Addressing on point-to-point links is optional with OSPF and often unnumbered interfaces are used.

Next, check IP addressing and netmasks. This is required only on broadcast and point-to-multipoint networks. A mismatch in either the IP network, or the netmask, would appear in the debug output with the state bouncing between `Init` and `Attempt`. A state of `ExStart` often points to a problem with the MTU size.

```
FIREWALL-A-> get vr trust-vr protocol ospf neighbor
```

Do not forget that not all devices become adjacent on a broadcast or NBMA network. Devices become adjacent only with the DR and BDR and all others remain in 2-*Way* state. You can configure OSPF to ignore the MTU, although this may be dangerous to do if the MTU is configured differently on each end. It is an option when the MTU is in reality identical, but different vendors may use different methods to calculate it, which by itself can be a common source of problems.

```
FIREWALL-A-> set interface e0/0 protocol ospf ignore-mtu
```

The area ID needs to match at both ends of the link. Notice that OSPF routers become adjacent only when the Hello packet on both ends contains the `E` bit, `N/P` bit, or neither (see Recipe 16.5 and Recipe 16.6).

The next step in troubleshooting adjacency problems is to check the link type. Broadcast links must have the same link type on the devices. However, links with point-to-point can become adjacent with links in point-to-multipoint because both would carry the point-to-point link type in the Router LSA.

```
FIREWALL-B-> get interface s1/0 protocol ospf
FIREWALL-B-> get vr trust-vr protocol ospf interface
```

If you still can't find the problem, check authentication, neighbor lists, and timers on the interfaces (see Recipe 16.15 and Recipe 16.14).

```
FIREWALL-B-> get interface s1/0 protocol ospf
```

If you've verified common sources of errors and you still haven't found the problem, detailed troubleshooting may be required. This troubleshooting typically involves debugs, and may require investigation into the following:

- Protocol details and messaging
- LSDB details
- Router overload and network instabilities

Enable debug (which may result in a long output) with the following:

```
FIREWALL-B-> debug ospf all
```

You can review the output buffer on the console or written to the Trivial File Transfer Protocol (TFTP). It may be a good idea to load the debug output in an editor to quickly search for keywords.

```
FIREWALL-B-> get db stream
FIREWALL-B-> get db stream > tftp 192.168.1.100 ospf.log
```

You can clear the buffer with this:

```
FIREWALL-B-> clear db
```

To limit the scope of the debug, choose subcategories. Useful categories for troubleshooting are listed here; `debug ospf adj` is probably the most useful debug:

```
FIREWALL-B-> debug ospf ?
adj                 debug adjacency formation, teardown
hello               hello packet debug
illegal             illegal debug
import              debug redistributing routes into OSPF
lsa                 print lsa debugs
nbr                 neighbor debug
receive             receive packets debug
route               ospf route addition, deletion
spf                 spf debug
transmit            transmit packets debug
```

The output shows unsuspected problems with the common set of possible issues, or unlisted problems such as incompatibilities with RFC violating extensions. Vendors that implement those vendor-specific extensions usually offer a switch to disable them so that devices from different vendors can become adjacent with each other. Problems may originate from reassignment of options in the header, different use of fields in a message, extensions to a message, and unsupported LSAs. There is a lot of legacy in OSPF, and many features were created which never made it into commercial products. ScreenOS usually expects those legacy fields to be filled with zeros as specified by the RFC, but another vendor may put them (optionally) to a new use.

If neighbors become adjacent, but you are missing routes, systematically check which route is contained in which LSA, and which device has and should have originated that LSA (see Recipe 16.3):

```
FIREWALL-B-> get vr trust-vr protocol ospf database
```

Check the LSA version and checksum in the LSDB, as well as the LSA age. You update an LSA by reflooding a new LSA with a higher version number. LSAs with a fresh age were either updated in the normal 20–30-minute refresh cycle or were changed due to a topology change. Summary and External LSAs with an age of 3,600 are withdrawn from another area or from outside of the AS. An age that quickly alternates between a low age and an age of 3,600 seconds in those LSAs is an indication of a bouncing link. Fast-growing version numbers in Router and Network LSAs also point to a bouncing link.

A common source for OSPF problems is a large LSDB size resulting from large numbers of AS External routes. Table 16-3 shows the types of LSAs, their function, and the information they carry.

Table 16-3. Routing information by LSA type

LSA	Carries routes	Originated by routers
Router LSA	Intra-area routes	One per router in the same area
Network LSA	No routes; lists all routers on a broadcast segment	One by each DR in the same area
Summary LSA	Inter-area routes	One LSA per prefix by ABR
ASBR Summary LSA	No routes; used to locate ASBR from another area	One for each ASBR by ABR
External LSA	External routes	One per prefix by ASBR
NSSA External SLA	External routes	One per prefix by ASBR in same area if the area is NSSA

A good indication of this problem is reflooded LSAs with the same version number, which you can easily observe with a traffic analyzer. This means the receiving router did not acknowledge the LSAs, often because of an overload condition. You can explore measures to limit the flooding of LSAs (see Recipe 16.5 and Recipe 16.6) and route control (see Recipe 16.7 and Recipe 16.8).

CHAPTER 17

BGP

17.0 Introduction

The Border Gateway Protocol (BGP) is a routing protocol currently defined in RFC 4271. It was historically specified in RFC 1771 and RFC 1654. BGP is typically used as an exterior routing protocol to exchange routing information between Autonomous Systems (ASs). A BGP AS is a unified network that is administered by a single entity or organization. Examples of BGP ASs include an Internet Service Provider's (ISP's) global backbone, and the corporate network of an enterprise. Because BGP enables disparate ASs to exchange routing information and, thus, communicate with each other, BGP is often referred to as the "glue" that binds the modern Internet together.

BGP AS numbers range from 0–65535 in value. The following values are reserved by the Internet Assigned Numbers Authority (IANA):

0
: Reserved

48128–64511
: Reserved by the IANA

64512–65534
: Reserved as private AS numbers

65535
: Reserved

The following Internet registries manage and distribute AS numbers around the world:

- American Registry for Internet Numbers (ARIN): *http://www.arin.net*
- AfriNIC: *http://www.afrinic.net*
- APNIC: *http://www.apnic.net*
- LACNIC: *http://www.lacnic.net*
- RIPE NCC: *http://www.ripe.net*

BGP is a destination-based path-vector routing protocol wherein a BGP route update provides a router with knowledge of the path of ASs traversed from one AS to another.

When BGP is employed to exchange routes between two disparate ASs, the connection is termed an *external* BGP, or *E*BGP connection. On the other hand, a BGP connection between routers within an AS is termed an *internal* BGP, or *I*BGP connection. The most common use of IBGP is to propagate the routes learned from EBGP across all of the BGP-speaking nodes within an AS.

The BGP specification mandates that all IBGPs within an AS maintain full-mesh IBGP connections with each other to prevent routing loops. In an AS with a large number of BGP-speaking devices, this full IBGP mesh becomes difficult to scale. In such large environments, there are two alternatives to having a full IBGP mesh: route reflectors and confederations. *Route reflectors*, defined in RFC 4456, are BGP-speaking devices that peer with all the other BGP-speaking devices in an AS and propagate the learned routes. All nonroute reflector BGP speakers within the AS that peer with a route reflector are termed *route reflector clients*. As route reflector clients only peer with a route reflector and do not peer with each other, the total number of BGP peering connections within the AS gets reduced. Route reflectors are further discussed in Recipe 17.14. A BGP *confederation* takes a BGP AS and carves it up into smaller sub-ASs. All the BGP-speaking devices within a sub-AS are fully meshed with each other. Specific, designated BGP-speaking devices within each sub-AS build EBGP connections with each other as BGP confederation peers. Routes exchanged between BGP confederation peers are treated similarly to routes exchanged between IBGP peers—that is, attributes such as `LOCA_PREF`, `NEXT_HOP`, and `MED` (discussed in the upcoming "BGP Attributes" section later in this chapter) remain unmodified.

BGP Messages

BGP-speaking routers communicate with each other by establishing peer relationships using four types of BGP messages: `OPEN`, `KEEPALIVE`, `UPDATE`, and `NOTIFICATION`. These BGP messages are communicated in Transmission Control Protocol (TCP) segments, using source and destination port 179.

`OPEN`
: Following a TCP three-way handshake, this is the first message sent by a BGP device attempting to set up a connection with a peer. The `OPEN` message includes the following information: version (version of the BGP protocol, currently 4), `My_Autonomous_System` (AS number of the device sending the `OPEN` message), `Holdtime` (the duration, in seconds, following which a neighbor is declared down if no keepalives are received), and `BGP_Identifier` (typically the router ID of the router initiating the connection).

KEEPALIVE

Consisting strictly of the BGP message header with type code 4, KEEPALIVE messages maintain "liveness" between BGP peers. Most BGP implementations send KEEPALIVE messages at intervals that are one-third of the negotiated Hold_Time. KEEPALIVE messages can be sent no more frequently than one per second. Also, an UPDATE message can serve as a substitute for a KEEPALIVE.

UPDATE

UPDATE messages form the core of BGP as the carriers of new route information with their associated BGP attributes and withdrawn routes. We will discuss in more detail later in this chapter the various BGP attributes that can be associated with a route update.

NOTIFICATION

BGP implementations use NOTIFICATION messages to communicate error conditions. These error conditions include instances such as Hold_Timer expiration and missing well-known attributes.

BGP Attribute Types

BGP offers a rich set of attributes that are helpful in granularly defining routing policies. RFC 4271 defines BGP attributes in four categories:

Well known, mandatory

All valid implementations of BGP must support these attributes; furthermore, the mandatory attributes are required to be set in all UPDATE messages.

Well known, discretionary

All valid implementations of BGP must support these attributes, too; however, they are not required to be set in all UPDATE messages.

Optional, transitive

These attributes are not required to be supported by all BGP implementations; however, they are passed along to other BGP peers.

Optional, nontransitive

These attributes are also not required to be supported by all BGP implementations; if an UPDATE message contains an optional, nontransitive attribute that the BGP implementation does not recognize, it is ignored and is not passed on to a peer.

BGP Attributes

There are three well-known, mandatory attributes that all BGP implementations should support and that are crucial in BGP path selection:

ORIGIN

Specifies whether the advertised route originated via an Interior Gateway Protocol (IGP) interior to an AS or via EGP, or has an unknown origin (INCOMPLETE).

For example, if you redistribute from the Open Shortest Path First (OSPF) protocol into BGP and advertise the routes to a BGP peer, the ORIGIN attribute is set to IGP. However, if you redistribute a static route into BGP and advertise it, the ORIGIN attribute is set to INCOMPLETE.

AS_PATH
: The AS_PATH attribute specifies the list of ASs that need to be traversed to reach the destination network. The complete AS_PATH attribute consists of a set of AS_PATH segments. Each AS_PATH segment contains the following: path segment type (represents whether the AS list is ordered or unordered); path segment length (represents the number of ASs in the list); and path segment value (represents the actual list of ASs).

NEXT_HOP
: The NEXT_HOP attribute specifies the BGP next hop for the destination route advertised in an UPDATE message.

Additionally, in the context of IBGP, the LOCAL_PREF attribute is required in UPDATE messages:

LOCAL_PREF
: This attribute specifies the "local preference" of a route advertised to an IBGP peer. ScreenOS implements a default LOCAL_PREF of 100 to all IBGP announcements. A higher LOCAL_PREF represents greater preference for a given route.

Finally, here is a list of some additional BGP attributes:

MULTI_EXIT_DISC *(optional, nontransitive)*
: The MULTI_EXIT_DISC (a.k.a. MED) attribute is relevant only in scenarios where a given BGP AS has multiple exit points to a neighboring AS. You can use the MED attribute to influence the selection of the exit point to the neighboring AS. MED is an optional, nontransitive attribute. An example of a scenario where MEDs are used is when an enterprise has multiple BGP-enabled links to an ISP. The enterprise routers can send different MED values to their respective ISP BGP peers, whereby traffic from the ISP cloud to the enterprise prefers the link whose MED is lower.

ATOMIC_AGGREGATE *(well known, discretionary)*
: The ATOMIC_AGGREGATE attribute can be relevant when a BGP-speaking device advertises an aggregate route. When an aggregate route has component routes that span disparate ASs, the aggregate route advertisement includes an AS_SET attribute that includes an unordered list of the ASs that comprise the aggregate. It is permissible, however, for a network manager to drop the AS_SET as long as this does not introduce routing loops. In scenarios where dropping the AS_SET causes certain component ASs in the advertised AS_PATH to also be dropped, the BGP-speaking device needs to qualify this advertisement with the ATOMIC_AGGREGATE attribute to indicate loss of exhaustiveness in the AS_PATH.

`AGGREGATOR` *(optional, transitive)*
: The `AGGREGATOR` attribute is relevant in scenarios where a BGP aggregate route advertisement generates an `ATOMIC_AGGREGATE`. For such advertisements, the BGP advertiser can include its own IP address and AS number in the `AGGREGATOR` attribute to "identify" the aggregator. Because it is transitive, the `AGGREGATOR` attribute's value is propagated to other peers if it is present in an advertisement.

`COMMUNITY` *(optional, transitive)*
: Defined in RFC 1997, the `COMMUNITY` attribute can be used to "tag" a group of routes to identify a specific characteristic or routing policy associated with them. This is an optional, transitive attribute. There are three well-known communities:

  `NO_EXPORT`
  : Routes with this `COMMUNITY` tag cannot be advertised outside an AS, unless the inter-AS connection represents a BGP confederation.

  `LOCAL_AS`
  : Routes with the `LOCAL_AS` tag cannot be advertised to any EBGP peers, regardless of whether the EBGP relationship is between peers inside a BGP confederation or between two unrelated ASs.

  `NO_ADVERTISE`
  : Routes with the `NO_ADVERTISE` tag should not be advertised to any BGP peers.

Note that RFC 4360 defines an `EXTENDED_COMMUNITY` attribute that has similar characteristics to the `COMMUNITY` attribute, with two enhancements: a wider range of community values and a Type field that you can use to categorize the extended communities (e.g., route target and route origin communities).

`ORIGINATOR_ID` *(optional, nontransitive)*
: The `ORIGINATOR_ID` attribute is relevant in the context of route reflectors. As an additional precautionary measure to prevent routing loops when reflecting routes, a route reflector can populate the `ORIGINATOR_ID` attribute with its BGP identifier to designate itself as the originator of the route within the IBGP AS. If a device receives a route with the `ORIGINATOR_ID` already set, it should not modify the setting. Finally, to prevent loops, a BGP-speaking device should ignore a route received with its own `ORIGINATOR_ID`.

`CLUSTER_LIST` *(optional, nontransitive)*
: Just like the `ORIGINATOR_ID` attribute, the `CLUSTER_LIST` attribute is relevant in the context of route reflectors. Route reflectors configured with a `CLUSTER_ID` can prepend their `CLUSTER_ID` to the `CLUSTER_LIST` when reflecting a route. This prevents routing loops, as a route reflector can discard a route when it sees its own `CLUSTER_ID` in the `CLUSTER_LIST`.

The ScreenOS BGP Implementation

ScreenOS firewalls run BGP within the context of a Virtual Router (VR). As discussed in Chapter 4, ScreenOS assigns a route preference to the different types of routes in a VR. Route preference becomes relevant in the context of installing the best route in the routing table when there are multiple route entries for the same destination, learned from different routing protocols. Lower route preference routes are preferred over those with higher preference. ScreenOS assigns a default route preference of 40 to EBGP routes, making them more preferred over OSPF, (default ScreenOS route preference 60) and RIP (default ScreenOS route preference 100). However, EBGP routes are less preferred than Static (default ScreenOS route preference 20) and connected (default ScreenOS route preference 0) routes. IBGP routes are assigned a default route preference of 250, making them less preferred to most other routing protocols. In the event that multiple instances of the same destination route are received from different peers, the BGP-speaking device employs a well-defined set of tie-breaking criteria to install the "best" route in its routing table. RFC 4271 specifies the sequence of steps for breaking ties.

Private AS numbers are used extensively in the following recipes to represent enterprises as well as service providers in the context of internal as well as external BGP connections.

17.1 Configure BGP with an External Peer

Problem

You want to configure BGP between a ScreenOS firewall and a peer device in a different AS.

Solution

As depicted in Figure 17-1, the ScreenOS firewall is in AS 64515 and the EBGP peer is in AS 65500. The `e0/0` interface of the firewall is in the `Untrust` zone, which is hosted in the `trust-vr` (the default VR for all route-mode zones).

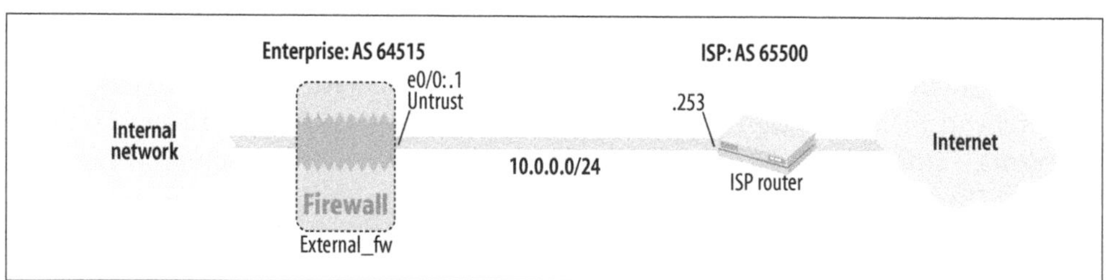

Figure 17-1. EBGP configuration

Configure the following on the ScreenOS firewall.

First, make sure you have correctly assigned the interface zone, IP address, and mode on the BGP-speaking interface:

```
External_fw-> set interface ethernet0/0 zone Untrust
External_fw-> set interface ethernet0/0 ip 10.0.0.1/24
External_fw-> set interface ethernet0/0 route
```

Next, define the router ID and enable BGP with the correct local AS number:

```
External_fw-> set vrouter trust-vr
External_fw(trust-vr)-> set router-id 10.1.1.1
External_fw(trust-vr)-> set protocol bgp 64515
External_fw(trust-vr/bgp)-> set enable
External_fw(trust-vr/bgp)-> exit
```

Finally, define the EBGP neighbor, and enable BGP at the interface level:

```
External_fw (trust-vr)-> set protocol bgp neighbor 10.0.0.253
remote-as 65500
External_fw (trust-vr)-> set protocol bgp neighbor 10.0.0.253 enable
External_fw (trust-vr)-> exit

External_fw-> set interface ethernet0/0 protocol bgp
```

This configuration starts BGP on the firewall, and permits it to receive all route advertisements from the `10.0.0.253` EBGP peer.

Configuring EBGP with a peer that is not directly connected

We have discussed building a BGP neighbor connection with a peer that is directly connected on the same network segment as the ScreenOS firewall. However, if the BGP peer is not directly connected, ScreenOS supports multihop EBGP. An EBGP multihop peer is configured by adding the following statement to the EBGP peer defined earlier:

```
External_fw(trust-vr)-> set protocol bgp neighbor 10.0.0.253
 ebgp-multihop 15
```

The `15` at the end of the `ebgp-multihop` qualifier represents the maximum number of "hops" between the ScreenOS firewall and the BGP peer.

Discussion

You can deploy ScreenOS firewalls directly at the external perimeter of an organization, communicating directly to a service provider or business partner's router via EBGP. An example of such a deployment is a hosting data center where an enterprise may get a gigabit Ethernet handoff from the hosting provider's router, and connect it directly into the ScreenOS firewall's `Untrust` zone, receiving Internet routes via BGP.

Enterprises that are multihomed or have unique routing policies typically need to run BGP to ensure fully redundant reachability from the Internet. In Figure 17-1, the ScreenOS firewall resides at the perimeter of the organization's network. The enterprise's ASN is 64515 and the ISP's ASN is 65500. BGP configuration parameters such as ASN and neighbor information are defined in ScreenOS in the context of the VR. In this example, we are using a single VR, the default `trust-vr`, for all of the zones on the firewall.

The BGP `OPEN` message includes the router ID of the firewall in its initial communication with a peer. Within the VR context, the BGP router ID for the firewall is configured using the `set router-id` *`<ip>`* command. It is not mandatory to explicitly configure a router ID in ScreenOS. When a router ID is not configured, ScreenOS uses the highest interface IP address as its router ID.

BGP `KEEPALIVE` messages are a "Hello" mechanism BGP uses to ensure that a peer is up and responsive. The default interval for BGP `KEEPALIVE` messages in ScreenOS is 60 seconds. A peer is declared "down" following the loss of three `KEEPALIVE` messages, that is, 180 seconds at default parameters.

You can view the BGP-specific configuration on a ScreenOS gateway using the get `vrouter` *`<vr-name>`* `protocol bgp config` command:

```
External_fw-> get vrouter trust-vr protocol bgp config
set protocol bgp 64515
set enable
set neighbor 10.0.0.253 remote-as 65500
set neighbor 10.0.0.253 enable
exit
set interface ethernet0/0 protocol bgp
External_fw->
```

Notice that the configuration output does not show the router ID configuration on the gateway because the router ID is applicable to all of the routing protocols that are configured in the VR, and is not limited to the BGP configuration.

You can view the status of the configured BGP instance for a given VR using the get `vrouter` *`<vr-name>`* `protocol bgp` ScreenOS command:

```
External_fw-> get vrouter trust-vr protocol bgp
Admin State:              enable
Local Router ID:          10.1.1.1
Local AS number:          64515
Hold time:                180
Keepalive interval:       60 = 1/3 hold time, default
Retry time:               120
Local MED is:             0
Always compare MED:       disable
Local preference:         100
Route Flap Damping:       disable
IGP synchronization:      enable
```

```
Route reflector:        disable
Cluster ID:             not set (ID = 0)
Confederation based on RFC 1965
Confederation:          disable (confederation ID = 0)
Member AS:              none
Origin default route:   disable
Ignore default route:   disable
External_fw->
```

You can view the status of a specific BGP peer using the get vrouter *<vr-name>* protocol bgp neighbor command:

```
External_fw-> get vrouter trust-vr protocol bgp neighbor
Peer AS Remote IP    Local IP  Wt  Status    State      ConnID Up/Down
---------------------------------------------------------------------------
  65500 10.0.0.253  10.0.0.1  100 Enabled  ESTABLISH      13 00:00:32

total 1 BGP peers shown
External_fw->
```

The ESTABLISH state shows that the BGP session is fully established with the peer. The Up/Down counter shows how long the connection has been up.

You can view the detailed status of a specific BGP peer using the get vrouter *<vr-name>* protocol bgp neighbor *<ip>* ScreenOS command:

```
External_fw-> get vrouter trust-vr protocol bgp neighbor 10.0.0.253
peer: 10.0.0.253,  remote AS: 65500, admin status: enable
type: EBGP, multihop: 0(disable), MED: node default(0)
connection state: ESTABLISH, connection id: 30 retry interval: 120s,
 cur retry time 15s
configured hold time: node default(180s), configured keepalive:
 node default(60s)
designated local IP: n/a
local IP address/port: 10.0.0.1/179,
 remote IP address/port: 10.0.0.253/1028
router ID of peer: 10.1.1.253, remote AS: 65500
negotiated hold time: 180s, negotiated keepalive interval: 60s
route map in name: , route map out name:
weight: 100 (default)
self as next hop: disable
send default route to peer: disable
ignore default route from peer: disable
send community path attribute: no
reflector client: no
Neighbor Capabilities:
  Route refresh: advertised
  Address family IPv4 Unicast:  advertised
force reconnect is disable
total messages to peer: 15, from peer: 11
update messages to peer: 0, from peer: 0
route-refresh messages to peer: 0, from peer: 0
last reset 00:03:55 ago, due to BGP send Notification
(Cease: Admin stopped)(code 6 : subcode 0)
```

```
number of total successful connections: 3
connected: 3 minutes 45 seconds
External_fw->
```

The detailed neighbor status includes information such as the reason for the last connection reset (identified in bold in the preceding code snippet).

A given BGP neighbor can be temporarily disabled, while keeping its configuration intact, as follows:

```
External_fw-> set vrouter trust-vr
External_fw-> set protocol bgp
External_fw(trust-vr/bgp)-> unset neighbor 10.0.0.253 enable
External_fw(trust-vr/bgp)-> exit
```

Disabling a neighbor using this method and then enabling it with the `set neighbor` *`<ip>`* `enable` command in this manner performs a hard reset of the BGP neighbor connection.

Another method of performing a hard reset to a BGP connection where the peer connection is torn down and rebuilt is via the exec `vrouter` *`<vr-name>`* `protocol bgp neighbor` *`<ip>`* command:

```
extfw-> exec vrouter trust-vr protocol bgp neighbor 10.0.0.253
disconnect
start to close the connection

extfw-> exec vrouter trust-vr protocol bgp neighbor 10.0.0.253 connect
started peer 10.0.0.253's state machine
```

Furthermore, you can delete a BGP neighbor as follows:

```
External_fw-> set vrouter trust-vr
External_fw-> set protocol bgp
External_fw(trust-vr/bgp)-> unset neighbor 10.0.0.253 remote-as 65500
External_fw(trust-vr/bgp)-> exit
External_fw(trust-vr)-> exit
External_fw->
```

Finally, you can delete the entire BGP configuration for a particular VR by using the `unset protocol bgp` *`<ASN>`* command in a VR context:

```
External_fw-> set vrouter trust-vr
extfw(trust-vr)-> unset protocol bgp 64515
deleting BGP instance, are you sure? y/[n] y
External_fw(trust-vr)->
```

Although it is acceptable to directly define individual neighbors if you have one or a few peers, the preferred method to configure several BGP neighbors with similar parameters is to use peer groups, which are discussed in Recipe 17.3.

See Also

Recipe 17.2; Recipe 17.3; Recipe 17.4

17.2 Configure BGP with an Internal Peer

Problem

You want to configure BGP with a peer in the same AS.

Solution

As depicted in Figure 17-2, both the `External_fw` and `Internal_fw` gateways are in AS 64515.

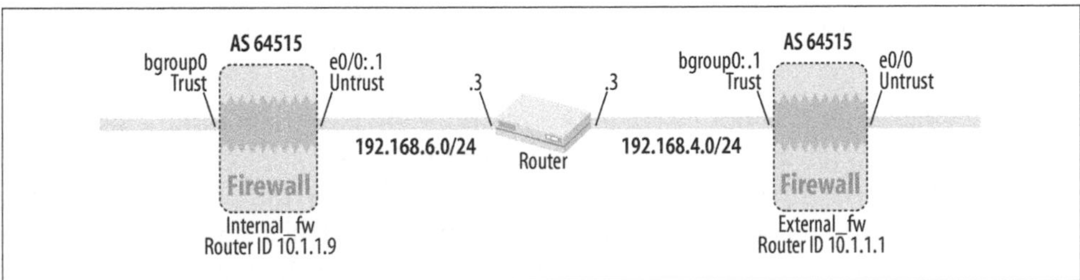

Figure 17-2. IBGP configuration

IBGP is configured on the `External_fw` gateway as follows:

First, make sure you have correctly assigned the interface zone, IP address, and mode on the BGP-speaking interface:

```
External_fw-> set interface bgroup0 zone Trust
External_fw-> set interface bgroup0 ip 192.168.4.1/24
External_fw-> set interface bgroup0 route
```

Next, define the router ID and enable BGP with the correct local AS number:

```
External_fw-> set vrouter trust-vr
External_fw(trust-vr)-> set router-id 10.1.1.1
External_fw(trust-vr)-> set protocol bgp 64515
External_fw(trust-vr/bgp)-> set enable
External_fw(trust-vr/bgp)-> exit
```

Finally, disable IGP synchronization, define the IBGP neighbor, enable BGP on the specified interface, and make sure an IGP or static route exists to the BGP peer:

```
External_fw(trust-vr)-> unset protocol bgp synchronization
External_fw(trust-vr)-> set protocol bgp neighbor 192.168.6.1
 remote-as 64515
External_fw (trust-vr)-> set protocol bgp neighbor 192.168.6.1
 nhself-enable
External_fw(trust-vr)-> set protocol bgp neighbor 192.168.6.1 enable
External_fw(trust-vr)-> exit
External_fw-> set interface bgroup0 protocol bgp
External_fw-> set vrouter trust-vr route 192.168.6.0/24 gateway
 192.168.4.3
```

Discussion

As illustrated in Figure 17-2, IBGP peers can have several intermediate hops of non-BGP-enabled routers between them. Thus, IBGP peers rely on an IGP, such as OSPF, or on static routes to reach their BGP neighbor.

A BGP-speaking gateway that receives a routing update from an IBGP peer does not propagate this update any further to any other IBGP peers. This is done to prevent routing loops. Hence, to have consistent exterior routing information across all the BGP peers in the AS while preventing routing loops, all the BGP-speaking devices within an AS need to peer with each other, often known as the *IBGP "full mesh" requirement*. You can use route reflectors or confederations as an alternative to an IBGP full mesh.

BGP implementations do not install a received IP prefix into the routing table unless the BGP `next_hop` for the route is reachable. The BGP `next_hop` for a route learned from an EBGP peer is typically the EBGP peer's interface IP address. However, this address is typically not reachable from within an IGP. Hence, in most instances, route announcements via IBGP are stamped with a modified BGP `next_hop` attribute that changes the BGP `next_hop` from the original advertising router to the IBGP router. This is achieved through the `nhself-enable` configuration attribute.

You can view the status of a specific BGP peer in ScreenOS with the `get vrouter` *<vr-name>* `protocol bgp neighbor` *<ip>* command:

```
External_fw-> get vrouter trust-vr protocol bgp neighbor 192.168.6.1
peer: 192.168.6.1,  remote AS: 64515, admin status: enable
type: IBGP
connection state: ESTABLISH, connection id: 7 retry interval: 120s,
 cur retry time 15s
configured hold time: node default(180s),
 configured keepalive: node default(60s)
designated local IP: n/a
local IP address/port: 192.168.4.1/1047,
 remote IP address/port: 192.168.6.1/179
router ID of peer: 10.1.1.9, remote AS: 64515
negotiated hold time: 180s, negotiated keepalive interval: 60s
route map in name: , route map out name:
weight: 100 (default)
self as next hop: enable
send default route to peer: disable
ignore default route from peer: disable
send community path attribute: no
reflector client: no
Neighbor Capabilities:
  Route refresh: advertised and received
  Address family IPv4 Unicast:  advertised and received
force reconnect is disable
total messages to peer: 43, from peer: 39
update messages to peer: 8, from peer: 3
route-refresh messages to peer: 0, from peer: 2
last reset 00:09:51 ago, due to BGP send Notification
```

```
(Cease: Admin stopped)(code 6 : subcode 0)
number of total successful connections: 2
connected: 5 minutes 12 seconds
Elapsed time since last update: 5 minutes 11 seconds
External_fw->
```

The `Internal_fw` gateway BGP peer is configured in a manner similar to the `External_fw` gateway's IBGP configuration.

For the preceding configuration, the `External_fw` gateway has two routes that it has learned from an EBGP peer, which it advertises to its IBGP peer, the `Internal_fw` gateway. You can view the IBGP routes in the Adj-RIB-In on the `Internal_fw` gateway using the get `vrouter` *<vr-name>* `protocol` bgp `rib-in` command:

```
Internal_fw-> get vrouter trust-vr protocol bgp rib-in
i: IBGP route, e: EBGP route, >: best route, *: valid route
          Prefix          Nexthop      Wt   Pref  Med  Orig  AS-Path
-----------------------------------------------------------------
Total routes in rib-in: 2 (0 in flap-damping history)
-----------------------------------------------------------------
>i*       0.0.0.0/0      192.168.4.1  100    100   0    INC    65500
>i*     10.9.8.0/24      192.168.4.1  100    100   0    INC    65500
Total no. of entries shown: 2
Internal_fw->
```

As shown in the preceding output, the BGP next_hop for these prefixes is `192.168.4.1`, which is the IP address of the IBGP peer (`External_fw`).

Also, you can verify the installation of these IBGP routes into the routing table of the `Internal_fw` gateway using the get `vrouter` *<vr-name>* `route protocol` bgp command:

```
Internal_fw-> get vrouter trust-vr route protocol bgp
H: Host C: Connected S: Static A: Auto-Exported
I: Imported R: RIP P: Permanent D: Auto-Discovered
iB: IBGP eB: EBGP O: OSPF E1: OSPF external type 1
E2: OSPF external type 2

Total 8/max entries

   ID   IP-Prefix   Interface   Gateway      P  Pref  Mtr    Vsys
-----------------------------------------------------------------
*  10    0.0.0.0/0     eth0/0     192.168.6.3  iB  250   0      Root
*  11  10.9.8.0/24   eth0/0     192.168.6.3  iB  250   0      Root

Internal_fw->
```

As shown in the preceding output, ScreenOS assigns these IBGP routes a route preference of 250. In many instances, IBGP peering connections are established using loopback addresses as endpoints for the TCP BGP connection. One of the key benefits of doing this is that if the physical path to a loopback interface experiences an outage, the IGP will reconverge over an alternative path in most instances before the BGP hold time expires. Hence, the IBGP session does not have to get torn down and rebuilt in the event of a transient path failure.

ScreenOS gateways support BGP peering using loopback interfaces. Thus, using loopback interfaces whose addresses are the same as the respective router IDs of the devices, the Internal_fw and External_fw gateways can build an IBGP peering session:

```
External_fw-> set interface loopback.1 zone Trust
External_fw-> set interface loopback.1 ip 10.1.1.1/32
External_fw-> set interface loopback.1 route
External_fw-> set vrouter trust-vr
External_fw(trust-vr)-> set router-id 10.1.1.1
External_fw(trust-vr)-> set protocol bgp 64515
External_fw(trust-vr/bgp)-> set enable
External_fw(trust-vr/bgp)-> exit
External_fw(trust-vr)-> unset protocol bgp synchronization
External_fw(trust-vr)-> set protocol bgp neighbor 10.1.1.9
 remote-as 64515 src-interface loopback.1
External_fw (trust-vr)-> set protocol bgp neighbor 10.1.1.9
 nhself-enable
External_fw(trust-vr)-> set protocol bgp neighbor 10.1.1.9 enable
External_fw(trust-vr)-> exit
Extennal_fw-> set interface loopback.1 protocol bgp
External_fw-> set vrouter trust-vr route 10.1.1.9/32
 gateway 192.168.4.3
```

You can view the IBGP prefixes learned by the Internal_fw gateway from the External_fw gateway over this loopback-to-loopback IBGP peering session using the get vrouter *<vr-name>* protocol bgp rib-in command:

```
Internal_fw-> get vrouter trust-vr protocol bgp rib-in
i: IBGP route, e: EBGP route, >: best route, *: valid route
     Prefix        Nexthop    Wt  Pref   Med   Orig  AS-Path
-------------------------------------------------------------
Total routes in rib-in: 2 (0 in flap-damping history)
-------------------------------------------------------------
>i*  0.0.0.0/0      10.1.1.1  100   100     0    INC    65500
>i*  10.9.8.0/24    10.1.1.1  100   100     0    INC    65500
Total no. of entries shown: 2
Internal_fw->
```

As shown in the preceding output, the BGP next_hop for these prefixes is now the loopback.1 interface address of the External_fw gateway.

Finally, you can verify the installation of these IBGP-learned prefixes in the routing table with the get vrouter *<vr-name>* route protocol bgp command:

```
Internal_fw-> get vrouter trust-vr route protocol bgp
H: Host C: Connected S: Static A: Auto-Exported
I: Imported R: RIP P: Permanent D: Auto-Discovered
iB: IBGP eB: EBGP O: OSPF E1: OSPF external type 1
E2: OSPF external type 2

Total 9/max entries

   ID    IP-Prefix     Interface    Gateway      P  Pref   Mtr   Vsys
----------------------------------------------------------------------
*  10    0.0.0.0/0     eth0/0       192.168.6.3  iB  250    0    Root
```

```
* 11    10.9.8.0/24   eth0/0       192.168.6.3  iB  250    0    Root

Internal_fw->
```

As shown in the preceding code snippet, these IBGP routes are installed in the routing table with an IGP gateway of `192.168.6.3`, the next IGP next hop to reach the BGP `10.1.1.1` `next_hop`.

See Also

Recipe 17.3; Recipe 17.6

17.3 Configure BGP Peer Groups

Problem

You want to use peer groups to configure BGP peers with similar parameters.

Solution

As illustrated in Figure 17-3, the `External_fw` gateway has three IBGP peers in this topology. We will use a BGP peer group, `ipeers`, to configure the common parameters for the three IBGP peers defined on the `External_fw` gateway.

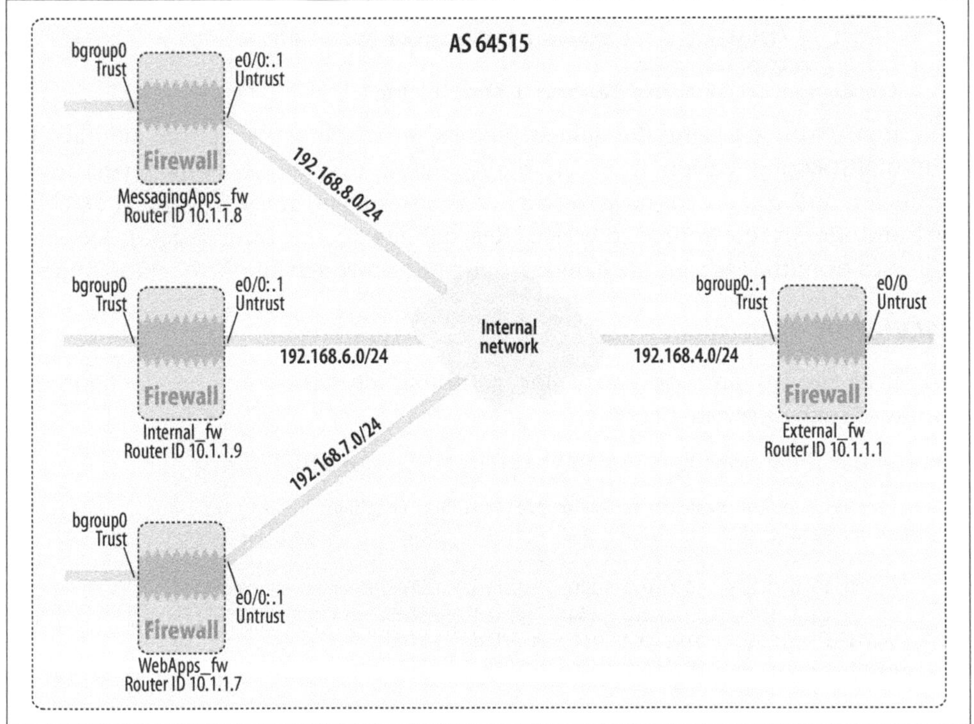

Figure 17-3. IBGP peer group configuration

Configure the following on the External_fw ScreenOS gateway:

```
External_fw-> set interface loopback.1 zone Trust
External_fw-> set interface loopback.1 ip 10.1.1.1/32
External_fw-> set interface loopback.1 route
External_fw-> set vrouter trust-vr
External_fw(trust-vr)-> set router-id 10.1.1.1
External_fw(trust-vr)-> set protocol bgp 64515
External_fw(trust-vr/bgp)-> set enable
External_fw(trust-vr/bgp)-> exit
External_fw(trust-vr)-> unset protocol bgp synchronization
External_fw(trust-vr)-> set protocol bgp neighbor peer-group ipeers
External_fw(trust-vr)-> set protocol bgp neighbor peer-group ipeers
 nhself-enable
External_fw (trust-vr)-> set protocol bgp neighbor 10.1.1.7
 peer-group ipeers
External_fw (trust-vr)-> set protocol bgp neighbor 10.1.1.7
 remote-as 64515 src-interface loopback.1
External_fw (trust-vr)-> set protocol bgp neighbor 10.1.1.7 enable
External_fw (trust-vr)-> set protocol bgp neighbor 10.1.1.8
 peer-group ipeers
External_fw (trust-vr)-> set protocol bgp neighbor 10.1.1.8
 remote-as 64515 src-interface loopback.1
External_fw (trust-vr)-> set protocol bgp neighbor 10.1.1.8 enable
External_fw (trust-vr)-> set protocol bgp neighbor 10.1.1.9
 peer-group ipeers
External_fw (trust-vr)-> set protocol bgp neighbor 10.1.1.9
 remote-as 64515 src-interface loopback.1
External_fw (trust-vr)-> set protocol bgp neighbor 10.1.1.9 enable
External_fw(trust-vr)-> exit
Extennal_fw-> set interface loopback.1 protocol bgp
```

Note that if you are using the default physical interface as the source interface for your BGP peering session, you can simply define the remote-as as a peer-group parameter, and you do not have to redefine the remote-as at the individual neighbor level and specify the source interface. Reachability to the three peering loopback addresses from the External_fw gateway is assumed through an IGP or static routes.

Discussion

BGP peer groups are convenient for grouping together common configuration parameters across several peers.

You can use the following command to verify the various BGP peers:

```
External_fw-> get vrouter trust-vr protocol bgp neighbor
Peer AS Remote IP    Local IP    Wt  Status    State     ConnID Up/Down
-----------------------------------------------------------------------
  65500 10.0.0.253  10.0.0.1    100 Enabled   ESTABLISH      3 00:07:34
  64515 10.1.1.7    10.1.1.1    100 Enabled   ESTABLISH     15 00:05:25
  64515 10.1.1.8    10.1.1.1    100 Enabled   ESTABLISH     16 00:03:54
  64515 10.1.1.9    10.1.1.1    100 Enabled   ESTABLISH     11 00:06:52
```

```
total 4 BGP peers shown
External_fw->
```

ScreenOS supports the configuration of several other BGP parameters, such as route maps, timers, communities, and authentication, using peer groups.

You can verify that a given peer belongs to a peer group using the get vrouter *<vr-name>* protocol bgp neighbor *<ip>* | include group command:

```
External_fw-> get vrouter trust-vr protocol bgp neighbor 10.1.1.7 |
 include group
peer group belongs to: ipeers
External_fw->
```

17.4 Configure BGP Neighbor Authentication

Problem

You want to authenticate your BGP neighbor before exchanging routes with it.

Solution

This solution assumes that you have already configured the various commands to define a BGP neighbor, as specified in other recipes in this chapter. As depicted in Figure 17-4, the ScreenOS firewall is in AS 64515 and an EBGP peer is in AS 65500. The e0/0 interface of the firewall is in the Untrust zone, which is hosted in the trust-vr (the default VR for all route-mode zones).

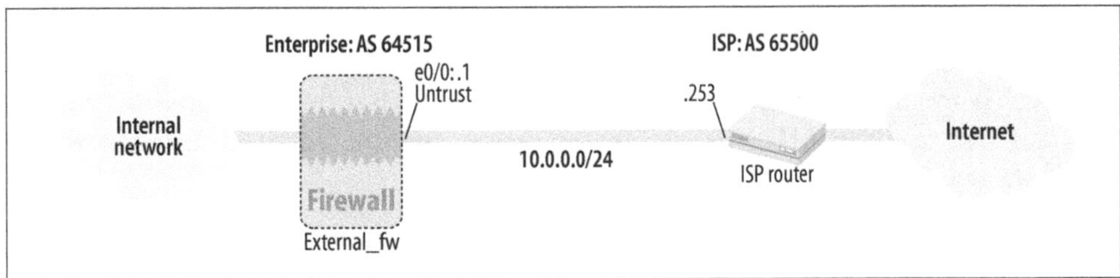

Figure 17-4. EBGP neighbor authentication

To add Message Digest 5 (MD5) authentication of BGP peers to an existing BGP neighbor configuration, use the set protocol bgp neighbor *<ip>* md5-authentication *<password>* command on the ScreenOS firewall:

```
External_fw-> set vrouter trust-vr
External_fw(trust-vr)-> set protocol bgp neighbor 10.0.0.253
 md5-authentication aabbcc
External_fw(trust-vr)-> exit
```

ScreenOS encrypts the plain text password entered in the configuration to ensure a secure configuration file. Thus, the password aabbcc is converted into an encrypted string:

```
External_fw-> get config | include md5
set neighbor 10.0.0.253 md5-authentication
 "E51tDTutNXrKP+sgHhClsQmV4hnShtAB0A=="
External_fw->
```

To remove MD5 authentication on a BGP peer, use the `unset protocol bgp neighbor` *<ip>* `md5-authentication` command within a VR context:

```
External_fw-> set vrouter trust-vr
External_fw(trust-vr)-> unset protocol bgp neighbor 10.0.0.253
 md5-authentication
External_fw(trust-vr)-> exit
```

Discussion

MD5 is a hash algorithm defined in RFC 1321. MD5 generates a 128-bit "message digest", or hash, on a given set of text characters of any length. MD5 hashes are nonreversible, that is, the original text cannot be retrieved for a given hash. While certain vulnerabilities have been found in MD5 in recent years, MD5 authentication prevails as the most common method for authenticating BGP neighbors.

RFC 2385 (Protection of BGP Sessions via the TCP MD5 Signature Option) defines the mechanism for protecting BGP sessions against spoofing attacks. The implementation of MD5 signatures on the TCP segments of an authenticated BGP session flow comprises computing a 128-bit MD5 digest using the TCP pseudoheader (src/dest IP address, zero-padded protocol number, and segment length), the TCP header, the TCP segment data (if any), and the BGP neighbor password.

The BGP neighbor password is a shared secret that needs to be the same on both peers for the BGP session to come up. When the peer receives a signed TCP segment, it computes an MD5 hash on the segment using the shared secret and the various TCP segment elements described above to ensure that the computed MD5 hash matches the received MD5 hash. This confirms that the received segment is not spoofed.

The following command displays the state of the BGP neighbor and verifies that MD5 neighbor authentication is enabled:

```
External_fw-> get vrouter trust-vr protocol bgp neighbor 10.0.0.253
peer: 10.0.0.253,  remote AS: 65500, admin status: enable
type: EBGP, multihop: 0(disable), MED: node default(0)
connection state: ESTABLISH, connection id: 3 retry interval: 120s,
 cur retry time 15s
configured hold time: node default(180s), configured keepalive:
 node default(60s)
designated local IP: n/a
local IP address/port: 10.0.0.1/1065,
 remote IP address/port: 10.0.0.253/179
router ID of peer: 10.1.1.253, remote AS: 65500
negotiated hold time: 180s, negotiated keepalive interval: 60s
MD5 authentication: enable
```

```
route map in name: inbound-from-isp,
 route map out name: outbound-to-isp
weight: 100 (default)
self as next hop: disable
send default route to peer: disable
ignore default route from peer: disable
send community path attribute: no
reflector client: no
Neighbor Capabilities:
  Route refresh: advertised
  Address family IPv4 Unicast:  advertised
force reconnect is disable
total messages to peer: 31, from peer: 30
update messages to peer: 2, from peer: 1
route-refresh messages to peer: 0, from peer: 0
last reset 00:27:52 ago, due to peer create
number of total successful connections: 1
connected: 27 minutes 43 seconds
Elapsed time since last update: 27 minutes 38 seconds
External_fw->
```

See Also

Recipe 17.1

17.5 Adjust BGP Keepalive and Hold Timers

Problem

You want to define custom BGP keepalive and hold timers for your BGP peer.

Solution

Building on the BGP configuration in Recipe 17.1, you can modify the BGP keepalive and hold timers for the peering session using the `set protocol bgp neighbor <ip> keepalive <seconds>` and `set protocol bgp neighbor <ip> hold-time <seconds>` commands in a VR context:

```
External_fw-> set vrouter trust-vr
External_fw(trust-vr)-> set protocol bgp neighbor 10.0.0.253
 keepalive 15
External_fw(trust-vr)-> set protocol bgp neighbor 10.0.0.253
 hold-time 45
External_fw(trust-vr)-> exit
External_fw->
```

If you already have a BGP peer defined, and you have BGP enabled on the respective interfaces, the only commands required for changing the keepalive and hold timers are the `keepalive` and `hold-time` command-line statements shown in the preceding code snippet, followed by a reset of the BGP neighbor connection.

Discussion

As discussed in Recipe 17.1, the default BGP keepalive and hold timer values are 60 seconds and 180 seconds, respectively. You can configure BGP keepalive and hold timers on a per-peer basis or for an entire peer group. If they are configured for a peer both at the peer group and at the individual peer configuration level, the per-peer parameters override the peer-group parameters.

You can verify the keepalive and hold timer configuration for a peer using the `get vrouter trust-vr protocol bgp neighbor` *`<ip>`* `| include keepalive` command:

```
External_fw-> get vrouter trust-vr protocol bgp neighbor 10.0.0.253 |
 include keepalive
configured hold time: 45s, configured keepalive: 15s(1/3 hold time)
negotiated hold time: 45s, negotiated keepalive interval: 15s
External_fw->
```

As shown in the preceding output, both the configured and the negotiated keepalive and hold timer values for the BGP peer are displayed.

Using the peer-group topology from Recipe 17.3 as a reference, you can configure the BGP keepalive and hold timers for a peer group using the `set protocol bgp neighbor peer-group` *`<peer-group-name>`* `keepalive` *`<sec>`* and `set protocol bgp neighbor peer-group` *`<peer-group-name>`* `hold-time` *`<sec>`* commands:

```
External_fw(trust-vr)-> set protocol bgp neighbor peer-group ipeers
 keepalive 5
External_fw(trust-vr)-> set protocol bgp neighbor peer-group ipeers
 hold-time 15
```

17.6 Statically Define Prefixes to Be Advertised to EBGP Peers

Problem

You want to statically define the prefixes that you will announce from a ScreenOS firewall to an EBGP peer.

Solution

Building on the EBGP configuration from Recipe 17.1, as shown in Figure 17-5, this solution advertises the `172.21.1.0/24` network to the ISP router.

First, make sure you have correctly assigned the interface zone, IP address, and mode on the ScreenOS firewall's BGP-speaking interface:

```
External_fw-> set interface ethernet0/0 zone Untrust
External_fw-> set interface ethernet0/0 ip 10.0.0.1/24
External_fw-> set interface ethernet0/0 route
```

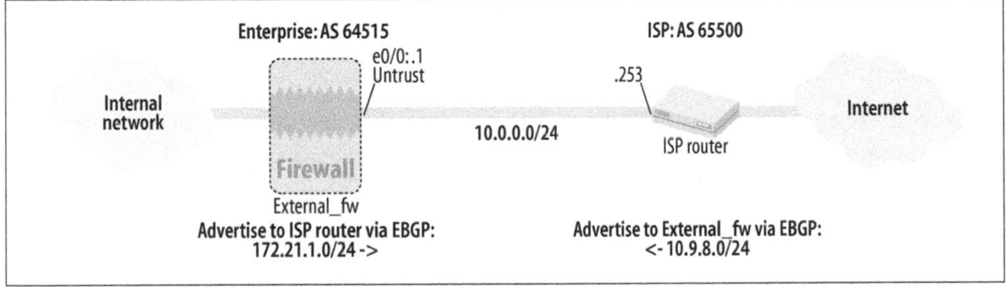

Figure 17-5. Advertising routes to EBGP neighbors

Next, define the router ID and enable BGP with the correct local AS number:

```
External_fw-> set vrouter trust-vr
External_fw(trust-vr)-> set router-id 10.1.1.1
External_fw(trust-vr)-> set protocol bgp 64515
External_fw(trust-vr/bgp)-> set enable
External_fw(trust-vr/bgp)-> exit
```

Finally, define the BGP neighbor and the prefix(es) that you would like to advertise:

```
External_fw (trust-vr)-> set protocol bgp neighbor 10.0.0.253 remote-as
 65500
External_fw (trust-vr)-> set protocol bgp neighbor 10.0.0.253 enable
External_fw (trust-vr)-> set protocol bgp network 172.21.1.0/24
External_fw (trust-vr)-> exit

External_fw-> set interface ethernet0/0 protocol bgp
```

Discussion

You can verify the networks defined to be advertised by a BGP instance in a VR via the `get vrouter trust-vr protocol bgp network` ScreenOS command:

```
External_fw-> get vrouter trust-vr protocol bgp network

network            weight check reachable-prefix   rib-in route-map
-------------------------------------------------------------------------
172.21.1.0/24       32768 yes   172.21.1.0/24      yes    null
External_fw->
```

As shown in the preceding output, the `check` setting indicates that the reachability of this route should be checked before it is advertised. The reachable prefix is the same as the network to be advertised, unless explicitly specified to be different. Thus, for this recipe's solution, the `172.21.1.0/24` IP prefix could be defined as a static route reachable via the `bgroup0` interface:

```
External_fw-> set vrouter trust-vr route 172.21.1.0/24 interface
bgroup0
```

This 172.21.1.0/24 route could also be reachable through any other method, such as an IGP like OSPF. However, if the ScreenOS gateway does not have a route to the reachable prefix, the associated network is not advertised to the EBGP peer.

In current releases of ScreenOS, you can turn off this reachability check, which is enabled by default, with the no-check qualifier on the set protocol bgp network *<prefix>* statement, which forces advertisement of the route to the peer even if it is not reachable on the ScreenOS gateway:

```
External_fw-> set vrouter trust-vr
External_fw(trust-vr)-> set protocol bgp network 172.24.1.0/24 no-check
External_fw(trust-vr)-> exit
```

As illustrated in Figure 17-5, the ISP router advertises the 10.9.8.0/24 prefix to the External_fw ScreenOS gateway. You can view the RIB-In (Routing Information Base containing prefixes learned from BGP neighbors) on the External_fw gateway to check whether this route is being received using the get vrouter trust-vr protocol bgp rib-in ScreenOS command:

```
External_fw-> get vrouter trust-vr protocol bgp rib-in
i: IBGP route, e: EBGP route, >: best route, *: valid route
       Prefix          Nexthop      Wt     Pref   Med  Orig   AS-Path
---------------------------------------------------------------------
Total routes in rib-in: 1 (0 in flap-damping history)
---------------------------------------------------------------------
>e*    10.9.8.0/24     10.0.0.253   100    100     0   INC    65500
Total no. of entries shown: 1
External_fw->
```

The preceding output shows the correct prefix, 10.9.8.0/24, received by the ScreenOS gateway from the peer with a BGP next_hop of 10.0.0.253, the ISP router. Also, the prefix has a BGP weight of 100 (default), a BGP LOCAL_PREF value of 100 (default), a BGP MED of 0, and an INCOMPLETE origin. Finally, the BGP AS_PATH for this prefix indicates that it originates in AS 65500, which is directly connected to the External_fw gateway's AS 64515. The * indicates that this is a valid route, and the > indicates that this is the best path to this prefix, which leads to its installation in the ScreenOS gateway's trust-vr routing table:

```
External_fw-> get vrouter trust-vr route protocol bgp
H: Host C: Connected S: Static A: Auto-Exported
I: Imported R: RIP P: Permanent D: Auto-Discovered
N: NHRP
iB: IBGP eB: EBGP O: OSPF E1: OSPF external type 1
E2: OSPF external type 2 trailing B: backup route

Total 6/max entries

  ID   IP-Prefix    Interface  Gateway     P  Pref   Mtr  Vsys
-----------------------------------------------------------------
* 12   10.9.8.0/24   eth0/0    10.0.0.253  eB   40    0   Root

Total number of bgp routes: 1
External_fw->
```

The preceding output verifies that the `10.9.8.0/24` prefix is installed in the `trust-vr` routing table on the `External_fw` gateway. As indicated in the Introduction to this chapter, the route preference for this route is 40, the default route preference for EBGP routes.

See Also

Recipe 17.7; Recipe 17.8

17.7 Use Route Maps to Filter Prefixes Announced to BGP Peers

Problem

You want to filter the prefix announcements to a BGP peer by using a route map.

Solution

This solution builds on the EBGP configuration from Recipe 17.6, and applies a route map in ScreenOS to filter the prefixes announced to an EBGP peer, as shown in Figure 17-6.

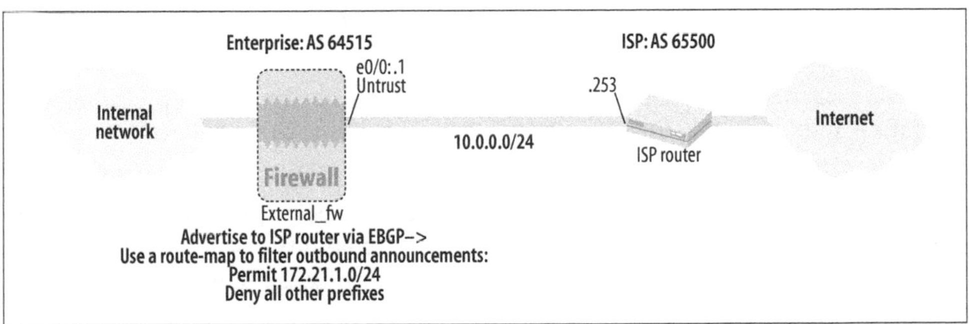

Figure 17-6. Filtering outbound BGP route announcements

First, make sure you have correctly assigned the interface zone, IP address, and mode on the ScreenOS firewall's BGP-speaking interface:

```
External_fw-> set interface ethernet0/0 zone Untrust
External_fw-> set interface ethernet0/0 ip 10.0.0.1/24
External_fw-> set interface ethernet0/0 route
```

Next, define the router ID, enable BGP with the correct local AS number, and define the set of networks that this BGP instance can advertise to its peers:

```
External_fw-> set vrouter trust-vr
External_fw(trust-vr)-> set router-id 10.1.1.1
External_fw(trust-vr)-> set protocol bgp 64515
External_fw(trust-vr/bgp)-> set network 172.21.1.0/24
```

```
External_fw(trust-vr/bgp)-> set network 172.24.1.0/24
External_fw(trust-vr/bgp)-> set network 172.27.1.0/24
External_fw(trust-vr/bgp)-> set enable
External_fw(trust-vr/bgp)-> exit
```

Next, define the access list that specifies the prefix that will be permitted to the ISP router peer and a route map that references the access list:

```
External_fw(trust-vr)-> set access-list 1 permit ip 172.27.1.0/24 1
External_fw(trust-vr)-> set route-map name outbound-to-isp permit 10
External_fw(trust-vr/outbound-to-isp-10)-> set match ip 1
External_fw(trust-vr/outbound-to-isp-10)-> exit
```

Finally, define the BGP neighbor settings for the ISP router and apply the route map in the outbound direction to the neighbor:

```
External_fw(trust-vr)-> set protocol bgp neighbor 10.0.0.253 remote-as
 65500
External_fw (trust-vr)-> set protocol bgp neighbor 10.0.0.253
 route-map outbound-to-isp out
External_fw (trust-vr)-> set protocol bgp neighbor 10.0.0.253 enable
External_fw (trust-vr)-> exit
External_fw-> set interface ethernet0/0 protocol bgp
```

Discussion

The route map in the solution to this recipe acts as a route filter by blocking out all IP prefixes, except 172.21.1.0/24, from being announced to the ISP router EBPG neighbor, 10.0.0.253.

The outbound-to-isp route map is applied in the out direction in the preceding configuration and, thus, only filters outbound announcements to the ISP router.

As discussed in Recipe 17.6, a candidate IP prefix needs to be reachable by the ScreenOS gateway before it gets announced to a BGP peer, prior to going through the route-map processing. You can waive this reachability requirement using the no-check qualifier on the set protocol bgp network *<prefix>* statement.

You can verify the BGP neighbor's status, including information on any relevant inbound or outbound route maps, using the get vrouter *<vr-name>* protocol bgp neighbor *<ip>* command:

```
External_fw-> get vrouter trust-vr protocol bgp neighbor 10.0.0.253
peer: 10.0.0.253,  remote AS: 65500, admin status: enable
type: EBGP, multihop: 0(disable), MED: node default(0)
connection state: ESTABLISH, connection id: 49 retry interval: 120s,
 cur retry time 15s
configured hold time: node default(180s), configured keepalive:
 node default(60s)
designated local IP: n/a
local IP address/port: 10.0.0.1/1068,
 remote IP address/port: 10.0.0.253/179
router ID of peer: 10.1.1.253, remote AS: 65500
negotiated hold time: 180s, negotiated keepalive interval: 60s
```

```
route map in name: , route map out name: outbound-to-isp
weight: 100 (default)
self as next hop: disable
send default route to peer: disable
ignore default route from peer: disable
send community path attribute: no
reflector client: no
Neighbor Capabilities:
  Route refresh: advertised
  Address family IPv4 Unicast:  advertised
force reconnect is disable
total messages to peer: 27, from peer: 26
update messages to peer: 2, from peer: 1
route-refresh messages to peer: 0, from peer: 0
last reset 07:42:22 ago, due to peer create
number of total successful connections: 1
connected: 23 minutes 20 seconds
Elapsed time since last update: 23 minutes 16 seconds
External_fw->
```

The preceding output shows the `outbound-to-isp` route map applied in the outbound direction for the ISP router BGP peer, `10.0.0.253`.

Although a given route-map sequence number is defined for the first time using the `set route-map name` *<route-map-name> <action> <sequence-number>* command, subsequent modifications to this route-map sequence do not need to use the `name` or `action` keyword. Thus, for instance, you can set the `MED` on all routes that match sequence number 10 of the `outbound-to-isp` route map to 300 as follows:

```
External_fw-> set vrouter trust-vr
External_fw(trust-vr)-> set route-map outbound-to-isp 10
External_fw(trust-vr)-> set metric 300
External_fw(trust-vr)-> exit
```

You can remove an entire route map, including all its sequences, from the ScreenOS configuration using the `unset route-map` *<route-map-name>* command:

```
External_fw-> set vrouter trust-vr
External_fw(trust-vr)-> unset route-map outbound-to-isp
External_fw(trust-vr)-> exit
```

At a more granular level, you can remove individual route-map sequences using the `unset route-map` *<route-map-name> <sequence-number>* command:

```
External_fw-> set vrouter trust-vr
External_fw(trust-vr)-> unset route-map outbound-to-isp 20
External_fw(trust-vr)-> exit
```

You can run the following debug command on the `External_fw` gateway to verify that the `outbound-to-isp` route map is performing outbound route filtering correctly:

```
External_fw-> debug bgp rtmap
External_fw-> debug bgp update
External_fw-> clear dbuf
External_fw-> exec vrouter trust-vr protocol bgp neighbor 10.0.0.253
 disconnect
```

```
start to close the connection
External_fw-> exec vrouter trust-vr protocol bgp neighbor 10.0.0.253
 connect
started peer 10.0.0.253's state machine
External_fw-> undebug all
External_fw-> get dbuf stream
<Additional_Output_Truncated>
## <Date/Time>: [bgp/rtmap]: o/g filter route 172.24.1.0/24 from peer
 10.0.0.253 with rtmap outbound-to-isp
##<Date/Time>: [bgp/rtmap]: Filter with route-map entry 10
##<Date/Time>: [bgp/rtmap]: MATCH IP-addr: acc-list-id 1 return deny
##<Date/Time>: [bgp/rtmap]: input-policy exit: no match in route-map
##<Date/Time>: [bgp/update]: Txq Add Rt return: qparms->filter: 1
##<Date/Time>: [bgp/update]: done: initial send eBGP 172.24.1.0/24 OK
##<Date/Time>: [bgp/update]: start: initial send eBGP update
 172.27.1.0/24
##<Date/Time>: [bgp/update]: nhop: 0.0.0.0, bgprt->i_nhop: 0.0.0.0
##<Date/Time>: [bgp/rtmap]: o/g filter route 172.27.1.0/24 from peer
 10.0.0.253 with rtmap outbound-to-isp
##<Date/Time>: [bgp/rtmap]: Filter with route-map entry 10
##<Date/Time>: [bgp/rtmap]: MATCH IP-addr: acc-list-id 1 return permit
##<Date/Time>: [bgp/update]: peer opun is 1: set qparm local pref: 100
##<Date/Time>: [bgp/update]: Build Tx PA: med: 0, local pref: 100,
 nhop: 10.0.0.1
##<Date/Time>: [bgp/update]: add feasible prefix 172.27.1.0/24 to
peer 10.0.0.253 Tx-q
##<Date/Time>: [bgp/update]: done: initial send eBGP 172.27.1.0/24 OK
```

Thus, as shown in the preceding debug output, the `outbound-to-isp` route map returns a deny match for all outbound prefixes except `172.27.1.0/24`.

See Also

Recipe 17.6; Recipe 17.8; Recipe 17.9

17.8 Aggregate Route Announcements to BGP Peers

Problem

You want to aggregate route announcements to your EBGP peer to reduce the total number of advertised prefixes.

Solution

As shown in Figure 17-7, this solution configures BGP route aggregation of announcements from the `External_fw` ScreenOS gateway to the ISP router.

First, make sure you have correctly assigned the interface zone, IP address, and mode on the BGP-speaking interface:

```
External_fw-> set interface ethernet0/0 zone Untrust
External_fw-> set interface ethernet0/0 ip 10.0.0.1/24
External_fw-> set interface ethernet0/0 route
```

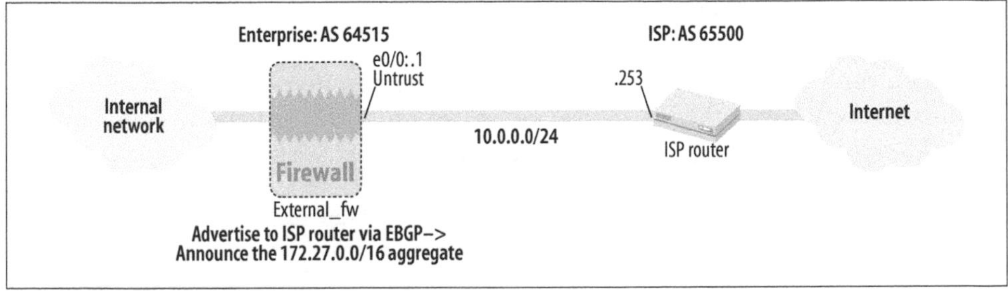

Figure 17-7. Aggregating route announcements to a BGP peer

Next, define the router ID, configure BGP with the correct local AS number, enable route aggregation, define the aggregate route to be advertised, and then enable BGP in the VR. *Make sure you configure the set aggregate command to enable aggregation prior to enabling BGP in the VR with the set enable command*:

```
External_fw-> set vrouter trust-vr
External_fw(trust-vr)-> set router-id 10.1.1.1
External_fw(trust-vr)-> set protocol bgp 64515
External_fw(trust-vr/bgp)-> set aggregate
External_fw(trust-vr/bgp)-> set aggregate 172.27.0.0/16 summary-only
External_fw(trust-vr/bgp)-> set enable
External_fw(trust-vr/bgp)-> exit
```

Finally, define the BGP neighbor, and specify the component prefixes that comprise the aggregate that gets advertised:

```
External_fw (trust-vr)-> set protocol bgp neighbor 10.0.0.253 remote-as
 65500
External_fw (trust-vr)-> set protocol bgp neighbor 10.0.0.253 enable
External_fw (trust-vr)-> set protocol bgp network 172.27.1.0/24
External_fw (trust-vr)-> set protocol bgp network 172.27.3.0/24
External_fw (trust-vr)-> set protocol bgp network 172.27.120.0/24
External_fw (trust-vr)-> exit
External_fw-> set interface ethernet0/0 protocol bgp
```

Discussion

Most ISPs have inbound routing policies for EBGP peers whereby inbound prefixes longer than /24 are immediately discarded. Furthermore, to help contain the size of the Internet routing table, it is recommended that all BGP participants aggregate their routes before announcing them.

You can verify the BGP neighbor state using the get vrouter *<vr-name>* protocol bgp neighbor command:

```
External_fw-> get vrouter trust-vr protocol bgp neighbor
Peer AS Remote IP   Local IP   Wt  Status   State     ConnID Up/Down
--------------------------------------------------------------------
  65500 10.0.0.253  10.0.0.1  100  Enabled  ESTABLISH     19 00:03:25
```

```
total 1 BGP peers shown
External_fw->
```

Next, you can verify the components of the aggregate route to be present in the BGP instance in the VR with the get vrouter *<vr-name>* protocol bgp network command:

```
External_fw-> get vrouter trust-vr protocol bgp network

network              weight check reachable-prefix   rib-in route-map
--------------------------------------------------------------------------
172.27.1.0/24         32768 yes   172.27.1.0/24      yes    null
172.27.3.0/24         32768 yes   172.27.3.0/24      yes    null
172.27.120.0/24       32768 yes   172.27.120.0/24    yes    null
External_fw->
```

Finally, you can verify the BGP aggregate route announcements from the External_fw gateway with the get vrouter *<vr-name>* protocol bgp aggregate command:

```
External_fw-> get vrouter trust-vr protocol bgp aggregate
The aggregate state: Enable
------------------------------------------------------------------
aggregate-route as-set summary-only  suppr/advt/attribute-route-map
------------------------------------------------------------------
172.27.0.0/16   no     yes           null/null/null
External_fw->
```

You can check the output from a debug bgp update to verify that the aggregate summary route is being advertised while its component routes are being suppressed:

```
External_fw-> debug bgp update
External_fw-> clear dbuf
External_fw-> exec vrouter trust-vr protocol bgp neighbor 10.0.0.253
 disconnect
start to close the connection
External_fw-> exec vrouter trust-vr protocol bgp neighbor 10.0.0.253
 connect
started peer 10.0.0.253's state machine
External_fw->
External_fw-> undebug all
External_fw-> get dbuf stream
<Additional_Output_Truncated>
##<Date/Time>: [bgp/update]: start: initial send eBGP update
172.27.0.0/16
##<Date/Time>: [bgp/update]: nhop: 0.0.0.0, bgprt->i_nhop: 0.0.0.0
##<Date/Time>: [bgp/update]: peer opun is 1: set qparm local pref: 100
##<Date/Time>: [bgp/update]: Build Tx PA: med: 0, local pref: 100,
 nhop: 10.0.0.1
##<Date/Time>: [bgp/update]: add feasible prefix 172.27.0.0/16 to
 peer 10.0.0.253 Tx-q
##<Date/Time>: [bgp/update]: done: initial send eBGP 172.27.0.0/16 OK
<Additional_Update_Truncated>
External_fw->
```

See Also

Recipe 17.6; Recipe 17.7; Recipe 17.9

17.9 Filter Route Announcements from BGP Peers

Problem

You want to filter the route announcements from a BGP peer.

Solution

This solution builds on the EBGP configuration from Recipe 17.6 and applies a route map in ScreenOS to filter the prefixes received from an EBGP peer, as shown in Figure 17-8.

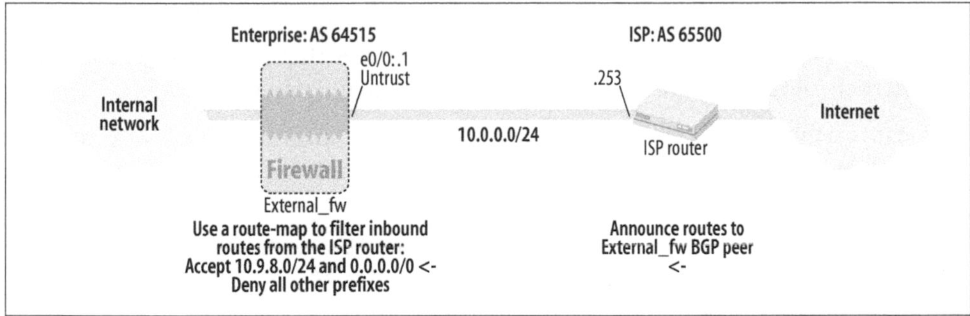

Figure 17-8. Filtering inbound BGP route announcements

First, make sure you have correctly assigned the interface zone, IP address, and mode on the ScreenOS firewall's BGP-speaking interface:

```
External_fw-> set interface ethernet0/0 zone Untrust
External_fw-> set interface ethernet0/0 ip 10.0.0.1/24
External_fw-> set interface ethernet0/0 route
```

Next, define the router ID, enable BGP with the correct local AS number, and define the set of networks that this BGP instance can advertise to its peers:

```
External_fw-> set vrouter trust-vr
External_fw(trust-vr)-> set router-id 10.1.1.1
External_fw(trust-vr)-> set protocol bgp 64515
External_fw(trust-vr/bgp)-> set enable
External_fw(trust-vr/bgp)-> exit
```

Then, define the access list that specifies the prefixes that will be accepted from the ISP router peer and a route map that references the access list:

```
External_fw(trust-vr)-> set access-list 3 permit ip 10.9.8.0/24 1
External_fw(trust-vr)-> set access-list 3 permit default-route 2
```

```
External_fw(trust-vr)-> set route-map name inbound-from-isp permit 10
External_fw(trust-vr/inbound-from-isp-10)-> set match ip 3
External_fw(trust-vr/inbound-from-isp-10)-> exit
```

Finally, define the BGP neighbor settings for the ISP router and apply the route map in the inbound direction from the neighbor:

```
External_fw(trust-vr)-> set protocol bgp neighbor 10.0.0.253 remote-as
 65500
External_fw (trust-vr)-> set protocol bgp neighbor 10.0.0.253
 route-map inbound-from-isp in
External_fw (trust-vr)-> set protocol bgp neighbor 10.0.0.253 enable
External_fw (trust-vr)-> exit
External_fw-> set interface ethernet0/0 protocol bgp
```

Discussion

Although the low-end ScreenOS firewall appliances support a full suite of BGP features, they do not have sufficient hardware resources to accept and process a full BGP Internet routing table (in excess of 220,000 prefixes in 2007). Hence, if your ScreenOS firewall is directly connected to an ISP router that is sending a full or partial Internet routing table, it is a good idea to filter the incoming routes.

You can verify the BGP neighbor's status, including information on any relevant inbound or outbound route maps, using the `get vrouter` *<vr-name>* `protocol bgp neighbor` *<ip>* command:

```
External_fw-> get vrouter trust-vr protocol bgp neighbor 10.0.0.253
peer: 10.0.0.253,  remote AS: 65500, admin status: enable
type: EBGP, multihop: 0(disable), MED: node default(0)
connection state: ESTABLISH, connection id: 32 retry interval: 120s,
 cur retry time 15s
configured hold time: node default(180s), configured keepalive:
 node default(60s)
designated local IP: n/a
local IP address/port: 10.0.0.1/179,
 remote IP address/port: 10.0.0.253/1055
router ID of peer: 10.1.1.253, remote AS: 65500
negotiated hold time: 180s, negotiated keepalive interval: 60s
route map in name: inbound-from-isp,
 route map out name: outbound-to-isp
weight: 100 (default)
self as next hop: disable
send default route to peer: disable
ignore default route from peer: disable
send community path attribute: no
reflector client: no
Neighbor Capabilities:
  Route refresh: advertised
  Address family IPv4 Unicast:  advertised
force reconnect is disable
total messages to peer: 212, from peer: 199
```

```
update messages to peer: 18, from peer: 11
route-refresh messages to peer: 0, from peer: 0
last reset 00:24:46 ago, due to BGP send Notification
(Cease: Admin stopped)(code 6 : subcode 0)
number of total successful connections: 6
connected: 23 minutes 12 seconds
Elapsed time since last update: 11 minutes 22 seconds
External_fw->
```

The preceding output shows the `inbound-from-isp` route map applied in the inbound direction for the ISP router BGP peer, `10.0.0.253`.

To verify that route filtering is successful, you can view the RIB-In on the ScreenOS firewall to ensure that, per access list 3 in this recipe's solution, the ISP router receives only the `10.9.8.0/24` prefix and the default route:

```
External_fw-> get vrouter trust-vr protocol bgp rib-in
i: IBGP route, e: EBGP route, >: best route, *: valid route
         Prefix          Nexthop     Wt  Pref   Med Orig    AS-Path
---------------------------------------------------------------------------
Total routes in rib-in: 2 (0 in flap-damping history)
---------------------------------------------------------------------------
>e*      0.0.0.0/0       10.0.0.253   100   100     0  INC    65500
>e*    10.9.8.0/24       10.0.0.253   100   100     0  INC    65500
Total no. of entries shown: 2
External_fw->
```

As the preceding output confirms, the `External_fw` ScreenOS gateway is only installing the `10.9.8.0/16` route and the default route in its RIB-In from the ISP router BGP peer, `10.0.0.253`.

Also, you can view the BGP routes in the routing table on the `External_fw` ScreenOS gateway to verify that the routes from the ISP router that were verified in the RIB-In have been installed in the routing table:

```
External_fw-> get vrouter trust-vr route protocol bgp
H: Host C: Connected S: Static A: Auto-Exported
I: Imported R: RIP P: Permanent D: Auto-Discovered
N: NHRP
iB: IBGP eB: EBGP O: OSPF E1: OSPF external type 1
E2: OSPF external type 2 trailing B: backup route

Total 9/max entries

    ID   IP-Prefix   Interface      Gateway   P   Pref  Mtr    Vsys
-------------------------------------------------------------------
*   41   0.0.0.0/0    eth0/0      10.0.0.253  eB   40    0     Root
*   42  10.9.8.0/24   eth0/0      10.0.0.253  eB   40    0     Root

Total number of bgp routes: 2
External_fw->
```

You can run the following debug command on the External_fw gateway to verify that the outbound-to-isp route map is performing outbound route filtering correctly:

```
External_fw-> debug bgp rtmap
External_fw-> debug bgp update
External_fw-> clear dbuf
External_fw-> exec vrouter trust-vr protocol bgp neighbor 10.0.0.253
 disconnect
start to close the connection
External_fw-> exec vrouter trust-vr protocol bgp neighbor 10.0.0.253
 connect
started peer 10.0.0.253's state machine
External_fw-> undebug all
External_fw-> get dbuf stream
##<Date/Time>: [bgp/update]: created new PA, peer 10.0.0.253
##<Date/Time>: [bgp/update]: validate/canonical UPDATE pass
##<Date/Time>: [bgp/update]: start: proc updt msg, peer:10.0.0.253
##<Date/Time>: [bgp/rtmap]:  start: apply policy route 10.9.8.0/24,
 peer 10.0.0.253, rtmap inbound-from-isp
##<Date/Time>: [bgp/rtmap]:  IP addr match: acc-list-id 3 return
permit
##<Date/Time>: [bgp/rtmap]:  done : apply policy pref 100,
 metric 0, weight 100
##<Date/Time>: [bgp/update]: local rib add prefix 10.9.8.0 / pref
 100, metric 0, next-hop 10.0.0.253
<Additional_Output_Truncated>
##<Date/Time>: [bgp/rtmap]: start: apply policy route 10.9.5.0/24,
 peer 10.0.0.253, rtmap inbound-from-isp
##<Date/Time>: [bgp/rtmap]: IP addr match: acc-list-id 3 return deny
##<Date/Time>: [bgp/rtmap]: done : apply policy, no match in route-map
<Additional_Output_Truncated>
##<Date/Time>: [bgp/rtmap]: start: apply policy route 0.0.0.0/0,
 peer 10.0.0.253, rtmap inbound-from-isp
##<Date/Time>: [bgp/rtmap]: IP addr match: acc-list-id 3 return permit
##<Date/Time>: [bgp/rtmap]: done : apply policy pref 100, metric 0,
 weight 100
##<Date/Time>: [bgp/update]: local rib add prefix 0.0.0.0 / pref 100,
 metric 0, next-hop 10.0.0.253
##<Date/Time>: [bgp/update]: add 0.0.0.0/0 to intchg
External_fw->
```

Thus, as shown in the preceding debug output, the inbound-from-isp route map denies all other IP prefixes from the 10.0.0.253 except 10.9.8.0/24 and the default route (0.0.0.0/0).

See Also

Recipe 17.7

17.10 Update the BGP Routing Table Without Resetting Neighbor Connections

Problem

You want to clear and update the routes received from a BGP peer without tearing down and reestablishing the BGP neighbor connection.

Solution

This solution builds on the IBGP topology used in Recipe 17.2, represented here in Figure 17-9.

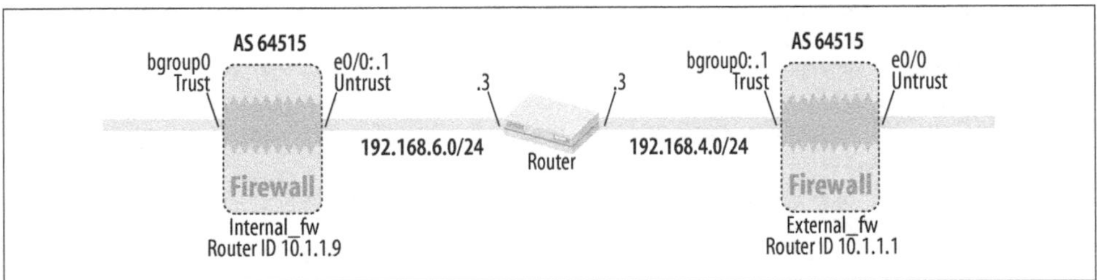

Figure 17-9. Performing a soft reset with a BGP peer

You can use the `clear vrouter` *`<vr-name>`* `protocol bgp neighbor` *`<ip>`* `soft-in` command on the `Internal_fw` ScreenOS gateway to perform a soft reset and build a new Adj-RIB-In for the `External_fw` peer:

```
Internal_fw-> clear vrouter trust-vr protocol bgp neighbor 10.1.1.1
 soft-in
```

Discussion

Route refresh capability, defined in RFC 2918, is a mechanism that enables a BGP speaker to request a fresh advertisement of the Adj-RIB-Out from a peer without resetting the neighbor connection. Thus, the BGP-speaking device that requests the route refresh effectively refreshes its Adj-RIB-In for that peer without resetting the peer connection.

To use route refresh to soft-reset a BGP neighbor connection, the peers need to negotiate route-refresh capability during connection establishment. You can confirm route-refresh support with a peer using the `get vrouter` *`<vr-name>`* `protocol bgp neighbor` *`<ip>`* `| include refresh` ScreenOS command:

```
Internal_fw-> get vrouter trust-vr protocol bgp neighbor 10.1.1.1 |
 include refresh
  Route refresh: advertised and received
route-refresh messages to peer: 1, from peer: 0
Internal_fw->
```

As shown in the preceding output, ScreenOS keeps track of the number of route-refresh requests generated by the local gateway as well as the requests received by the peer.

You can verify the sequence of processing steps carried out by a ScreenOS gateway when it generates a BGP soft-in reset, thereby generating a route-refresh request, through a set of debug commands:

```
Internal_fw-> debug bgp peer
Internal_fw-> debug bgp stack
Internal_fw-> debug bgp update
Internal_fw-> clear dbuf
Internal_fw-> clear vrouter trust-vr protocol bgp neighbor 10.1.1.1
 soft-in
<Wait_30_Seconds>
Internal_fw-> undebug all
Internal_fw-> get dbuf stream
<Date/Time>: [bgp/peer]: Route-refresh req. for afi/safi: 1/1 to peer
 is found: 10.1.1.1
<Date/Time>: [bgp/peer]: Route-refresh req. for afi/safi: 1/1 sent
 to peer: 10.1.1.1
<Date/Time>: [bgp/stack]: Rx 10.1.1.1: UPDATE msg, conn-id 52
<Date/Time>: [bgp/update]: validate/canonical UPDATE pass
<Date/Time>: [bgp/update]: start: proc updt msg, peer:10.1.1.1
<Date/Time>: [bgp/update]:    start: proc nlri 10.9.8.255/24
<Date/Time>: [bgp/update]:    10.1.1.1: rcvd nlri 10.9.8.255/24
 - duplicate ignored
<Date/Time>: [bgp/update]:    done : proc updt msg, peer:10.1.1.1
Internal_fw->
```

As shown in the preceding debug output, the ScreenOS gateway generates a full route-refresh request and then processes the received IP prefixes while the BGP session remains up.

A BGP-speaking device can also autonomously publish its set of Adj-RIB-Out prefixes to a peer without a hard reset. However, because this represents an autonomous generation of BGP `UPDATE` messages, this transaction does not require route-refresh capabilities to be negotiated. Hence, the `External_fw` gateway can send out its Adj-RIB-Out to the `Internal_fw` gateway through the `clear vrouter` *`<vr-name>`* `protocol bgp neighbor` *`<ip>`* `soft-out` command:

```
External_fw-> clear vrouter trust-vr protocol bgp neighbor 10.1.1.9
 soft-out
```

17.11 Use BGP Local_Pref for Route Selection

Problem

You want to prefer a specific BGP path from within an AS to a destination by using the `Local_Pref` BGP attribute.

Solution

This solution builds on the configurations in Recipe 17.1 and Recipe 17.3, with a topology where the External_fw gateway peers with two different ISP routers and propagates the routes learned to a mesh of IBGP peers, as illustrated in Figure 17-10.

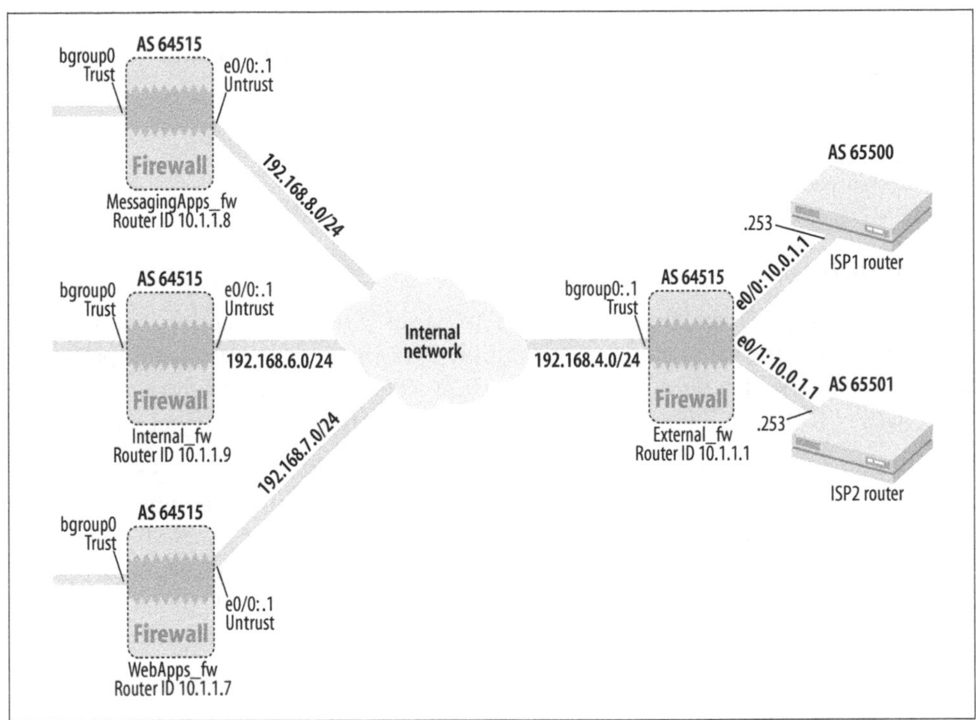

Figure 17-10. Using BGP Local_Pref for BGP path selection

With the External_fw gateway configured to peer with the two ISP routers and the three internal IBGP peers, define the access list that identifies the routes that will get assigned a specific LOCAL_PREF value and a route map that matches the access list and specifies the value:

```
External_fw-> set vrouter trust-vr
External_fw(trust-vr)-> set access-list 9 permit ip 10.9.8.0/24 1
External_fw(trust-vr)-> set route-map name Prefer_ISP1 permit 10
External_fw(trust-vr/Prefer_ISP1-10)-> set match ip 9
External_fw(trust-vr/Prefer_ISP1-10)-> set local-pref 300
External_fw(trust-vr/Prefer_ISP1-10)-> exit
External_fw(trust-vr)->
```

Next, apply the route map to the external BGP peers whose routes need to be assigned a higher preference:

```
External_fw(trust-vr)-> set protocol bgp neighbor 10.0.0.253
 route-map Prefer_ISP1 in
External_fw(trust-vr)-> exit
```

Finally, after applying the route map, restart both EBGP peering connections:

```
External_fw-> exec vrouter trust-vr protocol bgp neighbor 10.0.0.253
 disconnect
start to close the connection
External_fw-> exec vrouter trust-vr protocol bgp neighbor 10.0.1.253
 disconnect
start to close the connection
External_fw-> exec vrouter trust-vr protocol bgp neighbor 10.0.0.253
 connect
started peer 10.0.0.253's state machine
External_fw-> exec vrouter trust-vr protocol bgp neighbor 10.0.1.253
 connect
started peer 10.0.1.253's state machine
External_fw->
```

Discussion

The BGP LOCAL_PREF attribute is useful in scenarios where you have a BGP gateway that is receiving the same prefix from multiple BGP peers and you want to prefer the path from a specific peer. The default LOCAL_PREF value assigned to a route in ScreenOS is 100, with higher values having greater preference than lower values.

BGP has an exhaustive path selection criteria list, where the BGP LOCAL_PREF immediately follows the BGP weight of a route (default value 100) as the attribute that gets compared with different paths to choose the best path. Because the BGP LOCAL_PREF value has precedence over most other BGP path selection attributes, such as AS_PATH Length, it prevails as the path selection criterion for the two possible paths in this recipe's solution, whereby the route announcement from AS 65500 gets preferred.

You can check the BGP RIB-In on the External_fw gateway to verify that the route map correctly assigned the BGP LOCAL_Pref value to the route announcement from AS 65500:

```
External_fw-> get vrouter trust-vr protocol bgp rib-in
i: IBGP route, e: EBGP route, >: best route, *: valid route
        Prefix     Nexthop     Wt   Pref   Med  Orig  AS-Path
--------------------------------------------------------------
Total routes in rib-in: 2 (0 in flap-damping history)
-----------------------------------------------------------------------
>e*   10.9.8.0/24   10.0.0.253  100   300    0    INC    65500
 e    10.9.8.0/24   10.0.1.253  100   100    0    IGP    65501
Total no. of entries shown: 2
External_fw->
```

As shown in the preceding output, the path from AS 65500 is chosen as the best route and is installed in the routing table:

```
External_fw-> get vrouter trust-vr route protocol bgp
H: Host C: Connected S: Static A: Auto-Exported
I: Imported R: RIP P: Permanent D: Auto-Discovered
N: NHRP
iB: IBGP eB: EBGP O: OSPF E1: OSPF external type 1
```

```
E2: OSPF external type 2 trailing B: backup route

Total 17/max entries

     ID   IP-Prefix     Interface  Gateway     P   Pref  Mtr  Vsys
-----------------------------------------------------------------
*    30   10.9.8.0/24   eth0/0     10.0.0.253  eB   40    0   Root

Total number of bgp routes: 1
External_fw->
```

Furthermore, because BGP `LOCAL_PREF` is an attribute that gets propagated within an AS, you can verify its propagation to the `Internal_fw` IBGP gateway using the `get vrouter <vr-name> protocol bgp rib-in` command:

```
Internal_fw-> get vrouter trust-vr protocol bgp rib-in
i: IBGP route, e: EBGP route, >: best route, *: valid route
       Prefix        Nexthop     Wt  Pref   Med   Orig  AS-Path
-------------------------------------------------------------
Total routes in rib-in: 1 (0 in flap-damping history)
-------------------------------------------------------------
>i*  10.9.8.0/24     10.1.1.1    100  300     0   INC    65500
Total no. of entries shown: 1
Internal_fw->
```

See Also

The Introduction to this chapter; Recipe 17.2; Recipe 17.3

17.12 Configure Route Dampening

Problem

You want to dampen route flaps by enforcing flap dampening on the ScreenOS gateway.

Solution

This solution builds on the EBGP topology used in Recipe 17.1, represented here in Figure 17-11.

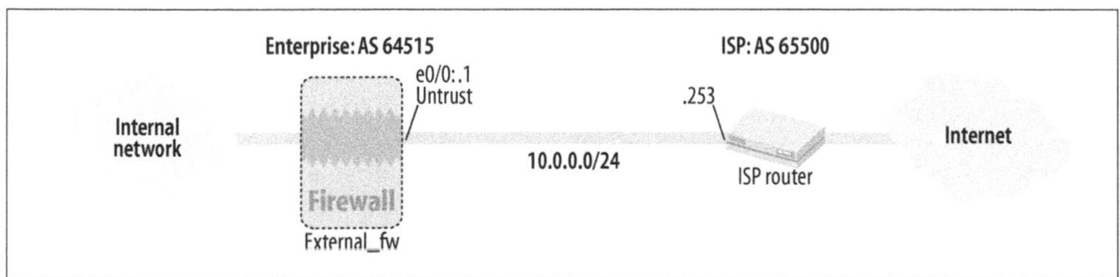

Figure 17-11. BGP route dampening configuration

You configure BGP route-flap dampening in ScreenOS using the set vrouter *<vr-name>* protocol bgp flap-damping command:

```
External_fw-> set vrouter trust-vr protocol bgp flap-damping
```

Discussion

The flap-damping command in ScreenOS ensures that flapping routes from BGP peers are not advertised until they become stable.

You can verify the BGP flap-damping settings and statistics in ScreenOS with the get vrouter *<vr-name>* protocol bgp flap-damping command:

```
External_fw-> get vrouter trust-vr protocol bgp flap-damping
Route Flap Damping              :    enabled
Reuse                           :    1024
Suppress Limit                  :    2048
Max Penalty                     :    4096
Reachable Half Life             :    5 minutes 0 seconds
Unreachable Half Life           :    15 minutes 0 seconds
Maximum Reachable  Hold Time    :    15 minutes 0 seconds
Maximum Unreachable Hold Time   :    30 minutes 0 seconds
Decay factor                    :    4

-----------------------------------------------------------------
total: 1 flapping, 1 suppressed(*).
histAge/lastEvnt/TTL: seconds
-----------------------------------------------------------------
event prefix      peer          penalty flap histAge lastEvnt TTL
-----------------------------------------------------------------
*Up   10.9.8.0    10.0.0.253       3342    4     226        7  893
External_fw->
```

As the preceding output illustrates, the 10.9.8.0 IP prefix from the ISP router peer has been dampened by the External_fw ScreenOS gateway as it has flapped four times in the tracking period. Furthermore, this route is now suppressed, because its penalty value of 3342 is higher than the suppress limit of 2048. Thus, this suppressed route is not installed in the routing table.

You can verify the RIB-In on the External_fw gateway to check the status of this flapping route:

```
External_fw-> get vrouter trust-vr protocol bgp rib-in
i: IBGP route, e: EBGP route, >: best route, *: valid route
           Prefix       Nexthop     Wt   Pref   Med Orig  AS-Path
-----------------------------------------------------------------
Total routes in rib-in: 3 (1 in flap-damping history)
---------------------------------------------------------------------------
>e*       0.0.0.0/0       10.0.0.253  100   100     0  INC     65500
>e*      10.9.3.0/24      10.0.0.253  100   100     0  INC     65500
 ed      10.9.8.0/24      10.0.0.253  100   100     0  INC     65500
Total no. of entries shown: 3
External_fw->
External_fw->
```

As shown in the preceding output, the `10.9.8.0/24` IP prefix is verified to be in a dampened state, and is currently not shown by ScreenOS to be a valid route. Once the flapping stops and the penalty associated with this route drops below the suppress limit, it is reintroduced into the ScreenOS routing table.

See Also

Recipe 17.1; Recipe 17.9

17.13 Configure BGP Communities

Problem

You want to tag your BGP route announcements with a community string.

Solution

As illustrated in Figure 17-12, this solution builds on Recipe 17.1 by configuring a route map that defines a community string for a list of routes on the `External_fw` gateway. This route map is then applied to the ISP router peer configuration on the `External_fw` gateway to tag the routes with the community string.

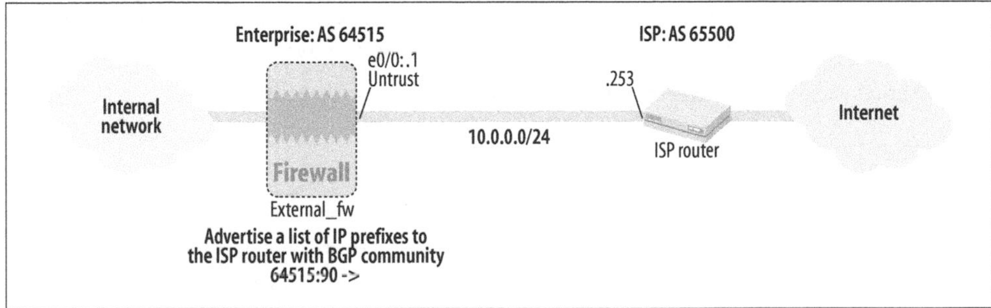

Figure 17-12. Configuring BGP communities

First, define an access list with the routes to be tagged:

```
External_fw-> set vrouter trust-vr access-list 8 permit ip
 172.21.1.0/24 1
External_fw-> set vrouter trust-vr access-list 8 permit ip
 172.24.1.0/24 2
External_fw-> set vrouter trust-vr access-list 8 permit ip
 172.27.1.0/24 3
```

Then, define the community list with the specific community string with which the routes will be tagged:

```
External_fw(trust-vr)-> set protocol bgp community-list 10 permit
 as 64515 90
```

Next, define a route map that references the access list and the BGP community list:

```
External_fw-> set vrouter trust-vr
External_fw(trust-vr)-> set route-map name set_community permit 10
External_fw(trust-vr/ set_community-10)-> set match ip 8
External_fw(trust-vr/ set_community-10)-> set community 10
External_fw(trust-vr/ set_community-10)-> exit
```

Finally, apply the route map on the specific BGP neighbor and specify the send-community qualifier on the neighbor:

```
External_fw(trust-vr)-> set protocol bgp neighbor 10.0.0.253
 route-map set_community out
External_fw(trust-vr)-> set protocol bgp neighbor 10.0.0.253
 send-community
```

Discussion

As described in the Introduction to this chapter, BGP communities are defined in RFC 1997. BGP community strings are typically used to signify a common property across the prefixes that are advertised with a common tag. Some well-known BGP communities include the `NO_EXPORT` and `NO_ADVERTISE` community tags.

In this recipe's solution, the BGP advertisements of the IP prefixes defined in access list 8 are tagged with the `64515:90` community string.

You can use the `get vrouter` *`<vr-name>`* `protocol bgp community-list` command to view the community lists configured on a ScreenOS gateway:

```
External_fw-> get vrouter trust-vr protocol bgp community-list

community list id: 10
community value:   64515:90->Permit
External_fw->
```

You can execute a set of debug commands on the `External_fw` gateway to verify that the community string is being applied to the route updates to the ISP router peer:

```
External_fw-> exec vrouter trust-vr protocol bgp neighbor 10.0.0.253
 disconnect
start to close the connection
External_fw-> debug bgp update
External_fw-> debug bgp rtmap
External_fw-> debug bgp peer
External_fw-> clear dbuf
External_fw-> exec vrouter trust-vr protocol bgp neighbor 10.0.0.253
 connect
started peer 10.0.0.253's state machine
External_fw->
##<Date/Time>: [bgp/rtmap]: o/g filter route 172.27.1.0/24 from peer
 10.0.0.253 with rtmap set_community
##<Date/Time>: [bgp/rtmap]: Filter with route-map entry 10
##<Date/Time>: [bgp/rtmap]: MATCH IP-addr: acc-list-id 8 return permit
```

```
##<Date/Time>: [bgp/rtmap]: SET Community-List-id 10 as-list-id 10
##<Date/Time>: [bgp/update]: peer opun is 1: set qparm local pref: 100
##<Date/Time>: [bgp/update]: Build Tx PA: med: 0, local pref: 100,
 nhop: 10.0.0.1
##<Date/Time>: [bgp/update]: add feasible prefix 172.27.1.0/24 to peer
 10.0.0.253 Tx-q
##<Date/Time>: [bgp/update]: done: initial send eBGP 172.27.1.0/24 OK
##<Date/Time>: [bgp/update]: start: initial send eBGP update
 172.24.1.0/24
External_fw->
```

Finally, you can verify the propagation of the community tags to the ISP router directly on the ISP router. Using a sample ScreenOS gateway as the ISP router, you can use the `get vrouter` *<vr-name>* `protocol bgp comm-rib-in` command to display the Adj-RIB-In with community tags:

```
ISP_Router-> get vrouter trust-vr protocol bgp comm-rib-in
Prefix: 172.24.1.0/24
Nexthop: 10.0.0.1, Weight:100, Local Pref:0, MED:0, Flag:80, Orig:IGP
Community: 64515:90
AS segment type: AS_SEQUENCE, AS path:64515

Prefix: 172.27.1.0/24
Nexthop: 10.0.0.1, Weight:100, Local Pref:0, MED:0, Flag:88, Orig:IGP
Community: 64515:90
AS segment type: AS_SEQUENCE, AS path:64515

Prefix: 172.21.1.0/24
Nexthop: 10.0.0.1, Weight:100, Local Pref:0, MED:0, Flag:80, Orig:IGP
Community: 64515:90
AS segment type: AS_SEQUENCE, AS path:64515

ISP_Router->
```

See Also

Recipe 17.1; Recipe 17.6; Recipe 17.7

17.14 Configure BGP Route Reflectors

Problem

You want to configure your ScreenOS gateways to participate in a BGP route reflector topology.

Solution

As illustrated in Figure 17-13, this solution uses a topology and a base configuration that builds on Recipe 17.3 and Recipe 17.11.

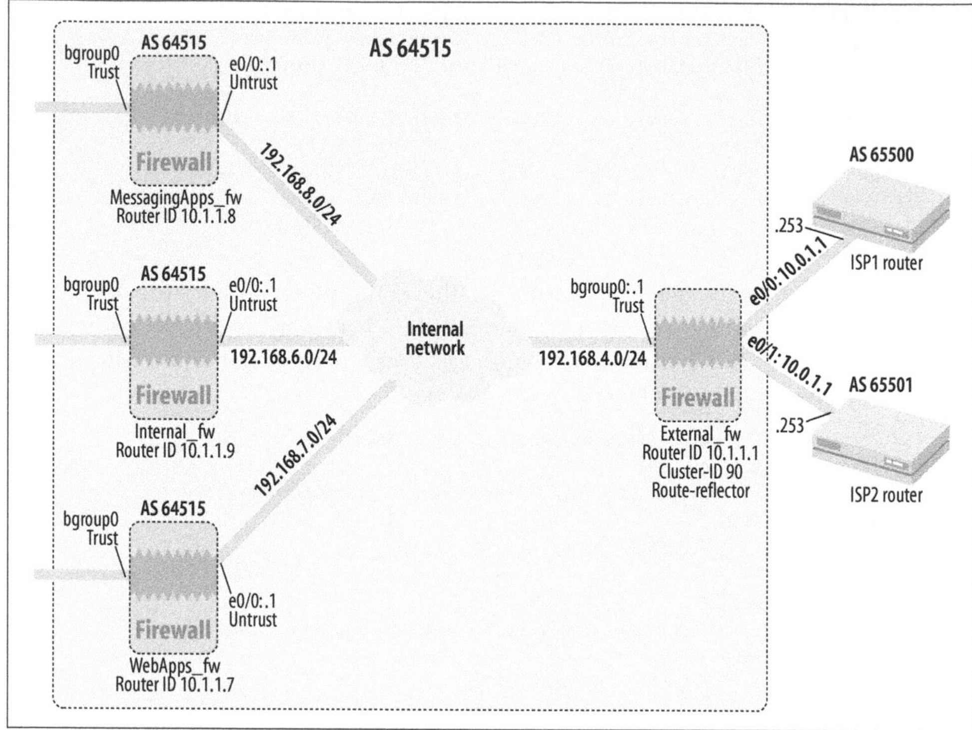

Figure 17-13. BGP route reflector configuration

The `External_fw` gateway is configured as a route reflector, and is assigned a cluster ID:

```
External_fw-> set vrouter trust-vr
External_fw(trust-vr)-> set protocol bgp reflector
External_fw(trust-vr)-> set protocol bgp reflector cluster-id 90
```

Next, all the IBGP peers in the `ipeers` peer group (from Recipe 17.3) are configured on the `External_fw` gateway as route-reflector clients:

```
External_fw(trust-vr)-> set protocol bgp neighbor peer-group ipeers
 reflector-client
```

The route-reflector clients in the `ipeers` peer group do not need to be configured with any specific parameters, and can retain their configuration from Recipe 17.3.

Discussion

Route reflectors alleviate the IBGP full-mesh scaling problem by eliminating the need for all IBGP-enabled gateways in an AS to peer with each other; instead, each route-reflector-client IBGP gateway simply needs to peer with the route reflector. The route reflector and its route-reflector clients comprise a cluster, and are assigned a cluster ID. You can prevent routing loops in a route-reflector topology by using a cluster list in a routing update, whereby a BGP gateway drops an update if it sees its own cluster ID listed in it.

The get vrouter *<vr-name>* protocol bgp command on the External_fw gateway verifies its configuration as a route reflector:

```
External_fw-> get vrouter trust-vr protocol bgp
Admin State:             enable
Local Router ID:         10.1.1.1
Local AS number:         64515
Hold time:               180
Keepalive interval:      60 = 1/3 hold time, default
Retry time:              120
Local MED is:            0
Always compare MED:      disable
Local preference:        100
Route Flap Damping:      enable
IGP synchronization:     disable
Route reflector:         enable
Cluster ID:        90
Confederation based on RFC 1965
Confederation:           disable (confederation ID = 0)
Member AS:               none
Origin default route:    disable
Ignore default route:    disable
External_fw->
```

Furthermore, you can use the get vrouter *<vr-name>* protocol bgp neighbor *<ip>* | include reflector command on the External_fw gateway to verify that a neighbor is configured as a route-reflector client:

```
External_fw-> get vrouter trust-vr protocol bgp neighbor 10.1.1.9 |
 include reflector
reflector client: yes
External_fw->
```

Finally, the get vrouter *<vr-name>* protocol bgp rib-in command on one of the route-reflector clients, the Internal_fw gateway, shows the IP prefixes learned from the route reflector:

```
Internal_fw-> get vrouter trust-vr protocol bgp rib-in
i: IBGP route, e: EBGP route, >: best route, *: valid route
        Prefix       Nexthop     Wt  Pref   Med  Orig    AS-Path
----------------------------------------------------------------
Total routes in rib-in: 1 (0 in flap-damping history)
----------------------------------------------------------------
>i*    10.9.8.0/24   10.1.1.1    100  300     0  INC      65500
Total no. of entries shown: 1
Internal_fw->
```

See Also

The Introduction to this chapter; Recipe 17.3; Recipe 17.11

17.15 Troubleshoot BGP

Problem

You want to troubleshoot BGP on a ScreenOS firewall.

Solution

To enable BGP debugging in ScreenOS to navigate through basic BGP message generation and processing, such as KEEPALIVE generation, use the debug bgp basic command:

```
External_fw-> clear dbuf
External_fw-> debug bgp basic
<Wait for 60 seconds>
External_fw-> undebug bgp all
External_fw-> get dbuf stream
```

As indicated in the preceding output, it is recommended that you clear the debug buffer before executing a new set of debug commands, and run an undebug all before viewing the debug output with the get dbuf stream command.

To troubleshoot a scenario where a BGP peer is not coming up, use a combination of the debug bgp peer, debug bgp event, and debug bgp socket commands:

```
External_fw-> debug bgp peer
External_fw-> debug bgp event
External_fw-> debug bgp socket
```

To troubleshoot a scenario with route maps where certain routes are not being received or sent to a peer, use a combination of the debug bgp stack and debug bgp rtmap commands:

```
External_fw-> debug bgp stack
External_fw-> debug bgp rtmap
```

Finally, if you would like to see a verbose output with all of the ScreenOS BGP-related debug outputs, you can run the debug bgp all command:

```
External_fw-> debug bgp all
```

Discussion

ScreenOS offers a rich set of debug commands for BGP. In addition to the outputs specified in this recipe's solution, we have discussed several instances of running BGP-specific debug commands in other recipes in this chapter.

If a BGP session is not getting established with a peer, make sure you have enabled the BGP instance in ScreenOS as well as on the specific BGP-speaking interface. You can run a get socket | include 179 command on your ScreenOS gateway to make sure you are listening on TCP port 179 as well as to see some of the other established BGP connections:

```
External_fw-> get socket | include 179
      8 tcp     listen     0.0.0.0          0   0.0.0.0            179
      9 tcp     open       10.1.1.9      1084   10.1.1.1           179
     11 tcp     open       10.1.1.8      1088   10.1.1.1           179
     14 tcp     open       10.0.0.253     179   10.0.0.1          1085
     16 tcp     open       10.0.1.253    1049   10.0.1.1           179
     51 tcp     open       10.1.1.7       179   10.1.1.1          1087
External_fw->
```

Also, you can use the debug bgp stack command, which captures the processing and generation of BGP messages, as an effective standalone BGP monitoring/diagnostic debug command. We used it here to exhibit the generation of the BGP NOTIFICATION message by the External_fw gateway:

```
External_fw-> debug bgp stack
<Wait_60_Seconds>
External_fw-> get dbuf stream
<Additional_Output_Truncated>
##<Date/Time>: [bgp/stack]: send NOTIFICATION msg code (Hold-Error)
 subcode(Hold Timer Expired) to peer 10.1.1.7 via socket 52
External_fw->
```

See Also

The Introduction to this chapter; Recipe 17.7; Recipe 17.8; Recipe 17.9; Recipe 17.10

CHAPTER 18

High Availability with NSRP

18.0 Introduction

The NetScreen Redundancy Protocol (NSRP) is a proprietary protocol originally developed by NetScreen Technologies Inc. The goal of NSRP is to ensure that the firewall and virtual private network (VPN) services are available at all times. There are three primary components of NSRP: gateway failover, session synchronization, and failure detection. The first component is relatively straightforward. Much like the Internet Engineering Task Force (IETF) standard protocol, the Virtual Router Redundancy Protocol (VRRP), NSRP provides a virtual Media Access Control (MAC) address and IP address to the network so that hosts and routers can point statically to a gateway IP. In NSRP terms, a virtual interface is known as a Virtual Security Interface (VSI). When a failure condition is detected, the MAC/IP pair for each interface is "migrated" from one device to the other via the use of gratuitous Address Resolution Protocol (ARP) messages. These ARP messages update the switch's forwarding database so that traffic destined to the virtual MAC is forwarded to the port to which the new "master" is connected. From the network's point of view, VRRP and NSRP in most cases use identical mechanisms to signal failover to the rest of the network. At this point, the similarities between the two protocols disappear.

Some of the key differentiators between VRRP and NSRP include the following:

- NSRP typically utilizes dedicated links for heartbeat traffic, whereas VRRP uses forwarding interfaces for heartbeats.
- NSRP heartbeat messages are Layer 2 multicast, and VRRP uses locally scoped IP multicast for heartbeats.
- By default, NSRP's virtual IPs (VIPs) terminate and originate traffic, whereas VRRP's VIPs do not.
- Using NSRP transforms the firewall into a virtual security device (VSD), whereas VRRP operates solely at the interface level.

This last point is critical to the understanding and functionality of NSRP. Conceptually, perhaps the greatest difference between classical routers and stateful firewalls is that a router operates on a packet-by-packet basis, whereas a firewall operates on a session-by-session basis. As the device must see the entire session to effectively ensure the legitimacy of the traffic, it follows that instead of using virtual interfaces that are useful in a packet-by-packet forwarding paradigm, a virtual device is needed to effectively ensure that the flow is processed correctly. In NSRP terminology, this virtual device is a VSD. VSDs are configured as VSD-Groups, and a device participating in NSRP can have one or more VSD-Groups assigned to it. In NSRP, each device can be the master or the backup for a particular session. This point is important, because when a packet arrives at the backup device for a given session, it is forwarded to the primary device across a dedicated link known as the High Availability (HA) data link. The HA data link is the second interface defined in the HA zone. Starting with ScreenOS 5.0, it became possible to disable the "ownership" of a session and, in fact, the concept of a VSD. In this "VSD-less" mode, as it has come to be known, no VSD-Group is active, and each device can actively process packets. One consequence of operating in VSD-less mode is that the gateway failover component of NSRP is no longer relevant (because there's no master, there's no need to failover). However, the second component of NSRP, the session synchronization component, is retained.

NSRP utilizes the concept of Run-Time Objects (RTOs) to indicate information that should be synchronized between members of an NSRP cluster. (Although NSRP uses the term *cluster*, perhaps *pair* would be a more accurate term, as in all currently shipping versions of ScreenOS, only two devices can be members of a cluster.) RTOs are a key component of NSRP, and they include the following object types (among many others):

- Firewall sessions
- Internet Key Exchange (IKE) Security Associations (SAs)
- Public/private key pairs
- User authentication tables
- Route tables (ScreenOS 6.0 and later)
- Dynamic Host Configuration Protocol (DHCP) lease entries
- Configurations (most settings)

The motivations behind synchronization of these components should be clear. Again, the goal of NSRP is to ensure that constant communication is maintained in case of any type of failure at the firewall layer. In a pure firewall design, it is clearly required to synchronize sessions between cluster members. Without this synchronization, traffic for established sessions, particularly Transmission Control Protocol (TCP) sessions, would be dropped upon failover, as the new master device would not see the session setup that a firewall expects to see. Instead, it would see packets in mid-session and would drop them. By synchronizing the session information, however, this problem is avoided, as the new master already knows about the session and is able to match packets to its session table appropriately as they arrive. As Network Address Translation (NAT) information is included as part of a session, NAT bindings are also synchronized between peer devices.

IKE SAs are also synchronized. Although the lack of SA synchronization may not cause an outright failure of traffic as would a lack of firewall session synchronization, including SAs as RTOs has some strong benefits. The first benefit is that upon failover, traffic will resume more quickly as a new SA does not need to be established. The second major advantage is seen primarily in the case where a central device is terminating large numbers of tunnels. In this case, if SAs weren't synchronized, upon failover, all of the remote tunnels would attempt to reestablish their SAs simultaneously. This would create a storm of IKE negotiations, causing performance degradation at the central site and delays in establishing the SAs. For SAs, which use digital certificates, it is also necessary to synchronize public/private key pairs so that SAs can be renegotiated.

User authentication tables also provide for continued flow of traffic where user auth, WebAuth, or IC auth is specified in a policy. If the backup device doesn't know which IPs have successfully authenticated, it will not be able to seamlessly allow new sessions through for these devices. By synchronizing the auth tables to the backup device, the additional step of the user having to reauthenticate is eliminated, and the user experience is uninterrupted.

In a dynamically routed environment, as of ScreenOS 6.0, routes can be synchronized from the active unit to the backup unit in NSRP. In previous versions of ScreenOS, the only routes that were synchronized were static routes; in the current version, only active routes from the routing table are synchronized. Conceptually, this is similar to a graceful restart in the router world. In the case of a failover, the new master will continue to forward packets according to the routes it learned from the failed device until it establishes new neighbors and builds its forwarding table independently. Depending on the routing protocol or protocols in use, some disruption of traffic may occur.

The need to synchronize DHCP leases from master to backup should be fairly obvious: if DHCP lease information was not synchronized, there would likely be frequent IP conflicts after a failover, as the new master device would hand out IP addresses which the failed device gave out previously. You can easily avoid this situation by sharing lease information as RTOs.

Synchronization of configurations is a critical component of NSRP. Without synchronization of configuration information, upon failover, there would be substantial risk to new sessions failing where they would have succeeded on the previous master. Unlike many network devices, such as routers and switches, firewalls tend to undergo a significant amount of change as new applications and services are permitted into the network and new security threats arise. Maintenance of a firewall policy is a challenging enough task on a standalone device. Ensuring synchronization of configuration was an early goal of NSRP to prevent disruptions to service in the event of a failover. Because configurations must remain synchronized, both devices in an NSRP cluster must have identical hardware configurations. However, certain items of a configuration are not synchronized. Most of these have to do with NSRP itself and include such things as VSD-Group priority, interface monitor settings, `track-ip` settings, and others. Additionally, hostname and other device-specific information remain unique.

The final component of NSRP is failure tracking. NSRP uses three primary methods to track failures. The first is via its heartbeat mechanism. NSRP's heartbeats are exchanged across a dedicated Ethernet link (in most cases). The heartbeat packets themselves are Ethernet multicasts, and they serve to detect the liveliness of the peer device. If three heartbeat messages (by default) are lost from the master, the passive device will declare itself the master. A few things can cause this to occur, including the following:

- The master device has a system failure, software or hardware, and is no longer running.
- The master device resets.
- The master is too busy to send heartbeat messages.
- The link(s) over which heartbeats are exchanged go down.

In scenarios where there are two HA links, the first link that comes up in the HA zone will become the HA control link, and the second will become the HA data link. When both links are up, however, the numerically higher interface (by index number) will be the control interface. When the control link fails, due to either link failure or loss of HA link probes, the NSRP control functionality moves to the second link, and heartbeat and other control messages begin to use this link.

The second method for failover detection is the HA interface/zone monitor. The interface and zone monitors function in similar ways. The interface monitor does what would be expected—namely, it monitors the state of the interface. NSRP has a configurable device monitoring threshold. All NSRP monitor objects have an associated weight. In a fully functional device, NSRP contains a weighted sum value of zero, which is the sum of the weights of all monitored objects. As each object fails, the weight assigned to the object is added to the weighted sum. When the weighted sum is equal to or greater than the NSRP monitoring threshold, the device will consider itself inoperable, and failover will occur. Along with the NSRP device-monitoring threshold, there is also a VSD-Group monitoring threshold. Like the device-monitoring threshold, the VSD-Group monitoring threshold is used to trigger failover. However, in the case of the VSD-Group monitoring threshold, failover occurs for only the specified VSD-Group. This capability is frequently used in the context of virtual systems to provide per-Virtual System (VSYS) failover.

When using interface-based monitoring, NSRP uses the physical state of the interface to determine whether to increment the weighted sum. If an interface being monitored goes down, its weight is added to the weighted sum, and if the monitor threshold is met or exceeded, the device (or VSD-Group) will failover. Zone-based monitoring applies the same concept, except to a zone instead of an interface. In zone-based monitoring, all interfaces in the zone must be declared down for the weight to be added to the weighted sum. As expected, zone-based monitoring is typically used in cases where multiple interfaces exist within a zone. Because interface-based monitoring relies on interface state to detect a failure condition, it is typically the fastest failover mechanism.

The final tracking mechanism for failure detection in NSRP is known as `track-ip`. `track-ip` provides protection against network failures, which do not occur at the physical level but disrupt connectivity nonetheless. An example of this would be a software failure on a switch that prevents communication from the firewall to its default gateway. `track-ip` works by sending either ping or ARP messages to a configured IP or set of IP addresses. Frequently, this is used with the neighboring router IP addresses to ensure full connectivity upstream, downstream, and so on. By default, one ping is sent per second to each `track-ip` object. Upon failure of three (by default) successive pings, the weight assigned to the object is added to the weighted sum, and if the monitor threshold is met or exceeded, a failover will be triggered. In some cases, ping is not appropriate, such as when VRRP is being run on the monitored object, or when ping is denied by policy. For these situations, ARP is recommended.

Generally speaking, each failure tracking mechanism is recommended for use in NSRP deployments. As all mechanisms are relatively lightweight, it is considered a good practice to deploy all three in most designs.

The NSRP state engine consists of six defined states of operation:

- Ineligible
- Inoperable
- Init
- Backup
- Primary backup (PB)
- Master

Figure 18-1 depicts the NSRP state machine.

Each VSD-Group on a device can be in any one of these states at any time. The first state, *ineligible*, is a user-defined state. An administrator can set a device to be ineligible to prevent it from becoming the master. This is often done when a device is suspected of having problems or needs to have maintenance performed on it. The next state, *inoperable*, means that an event has occurred that has rendered the device unable to become the master of a VSD-Group. A number of factors can cause this

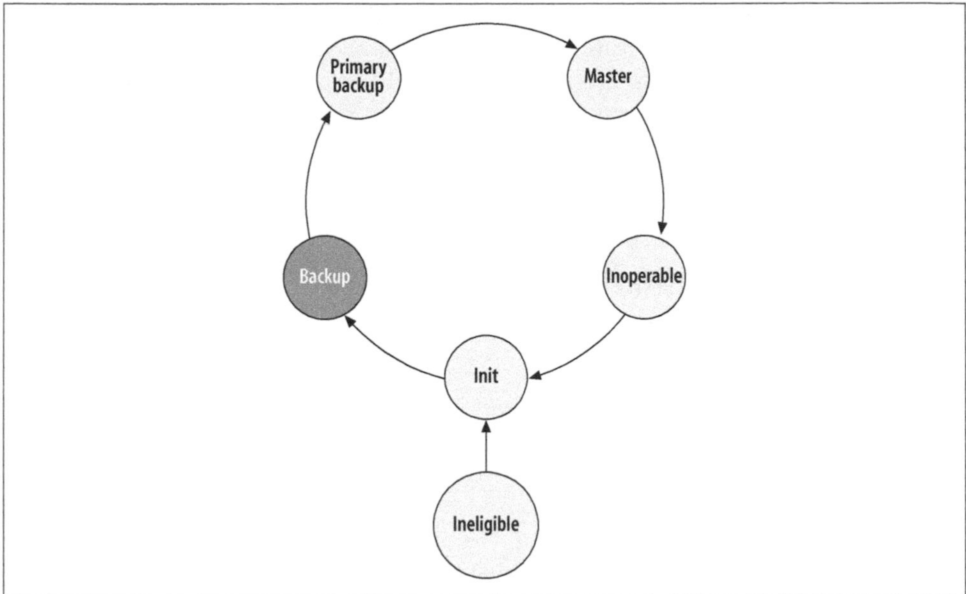

Figure 18-1. The NSRP state machine

condition, such as an interface failure, `track-ip` failure, and others. Once the error condition that caused the device to become inoperable has cleared, or the ineligible setting is removed, the device transitions to the *init* state. In the init state, the device is ready to become active, but stays in a user-configurable hold-down for a period of time. This state helps to prevent state transitions in cases where the network is unstable, such as a flapping link. After the init hold timer expires, and assuming no failures transition the state back to inoperable, the device transfers itself to the *primary backup state*, which means that the device is ready to become the master of the group. Although a backup state is defined, it is currently unused. This state would be used if there were more than two members in a cluster (it is included here for completeness). As NSRP treats the first active device on the network as the *master*, if there is an existing master on the network, a device in primary backup state will not transition to master unless the existing master transitions to another state, or it preempts the mastership of the VSD-Group. To do this, the device must have a better priority than the existing master (indicated by a numerically lower value), and must be configured to preempt. Preemption is not the default setting, and you should use it with care. It is commonly used in active-active topologies, and in situations where the network administrators wish to have a particular device always be the master if it is capable. When using preempt, a hold timer indicates the number of seconds before the device can become the master of the VSD-Group. As there may be a significant amount of RTO information to synchronize in a busy network, it is typically a good idea to allow for enough time to synchronize these RTOs in the preempt hold-down timer.

NSRP is an extremely robust protocol built to handle virtually all failover scenarios seamlessly. As such, architecting NSRP can be fairly complex. For more information, see the documentation on Juniper's web site, at *http://www.juniper.net*.

See Also

RFC 3768

18.1 Configure an Active-Passive NSRP Cluster in Route Mode

Problem

You need to set up a redundant default gateway for your hosts.

Solution

Set up an active-passive NSRP cluster. First, choose ports for the NSRP control and data messages:

```
FIREWALL-A-> set interface ethernet0/7 zone ha
FIREWALL-A-> set interface ethernet0/8 zone ha

FIREWALL-B-> set interface ethernet0/7 zone ha
FIREWALL-B-> set interface ethernet0/8 zone ha
```

Once the links are connected, enable NSRP by setting the cluster ID, VSD-Group information, and optional cluster name, and synchronize the configurations:

```
FIREWALL-A-> set nsrp cluster id 1
FIREWALL-A(M)-> set nsrp cluster name FWCLUSTER
FWCLUSTER:FIREWALL-A(M)-> set nsrp vsd-group id 0 priority 10

FIREWALL-B-> set nsrp cluster id 1
FIREWALL-B(B)-> set nsrp cluster name FWCLUSTER
FWCLUSTER:FIREWALL-B(B)-> save
FWCLUSTER:FIREWALL-B(B)-> exec nsrp sync global-config saved
FWCLUSTER:FIREWALL-B(B)-> reset
```

Once `FIREWALL-B` comes back online, finish the configuration by enabling RTO synchronization, configuring timers, setting up monitoring parameters, and configuring `manage-ips`:

```
FWCLUSTER:FIREWALL-A(M)-> set nsrp rto-mirror sync
FWCLUSTER:FIREWALL-A(B)-> set nsrp rto-mirror session ageout-ack
FWCLUSTER:FIREWALL-A(M)-> set nsrp vsd-group hb-interval 200
FWCLUSTER:FIREWALL-A(M)-> set nsrp secondary-path ethernet0/3
FWCLUSTER:FIREWALL-A(M)-> set nsrp auth password iamapassword
FWCLUSTER:FIREWALL-A(M)-> set nsrp encrypt password iamapassword
FWCLUSTER:FIREWALL-A(M)-> set nsrp monitor interface ethernet0/1
FWCLUSTER:FIREWALL-A(M)-> set nsrp monitor interface ethernet0/3
```

```
FWCLUSTER:FIREWALL-B(M)-> set nsrp secondary-path ethernet0/3
FWCLUSTER:FIREWALL-B(M)-> set nsrp auth password iamapassword


FWCLUSTER:FIREWALL-B(M)-> set nsrp encrypt password iamapassword
FWCLUSTER:FIREWALL-B(M)-> set nsrp monitor interface ethernet0/1
FWCLUSTER:FIREWALL-B(M)-> set nsrp monitor interface ethernet0/3

FWCLUSTER:FIREWALL-A(M)-> set int e0/1 manage-ip 1.1.1.200
FWCLUSTER:FIREWALL-A(M)-> set int e0/3 manage-ip 2.1.1.200

FWCLUSTER:FIREWALL-B(M)-> set int e0/1 manage-ip 1.1.1.201
FWCLUSTER:FIREWALL-B(M)-> set int e0/3 manage-ip 2.1.1.201
```

Discussion

The simplest topology for an HA pair of firewalls is an active-passive cluster. This is shown in Figure 18-2.

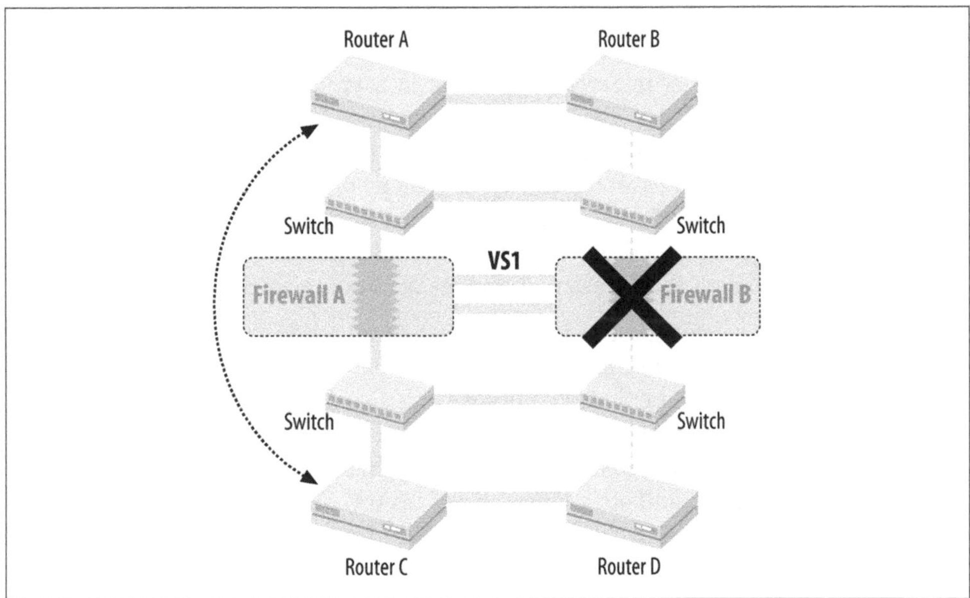

Figure 18-2. A sample active-passive topology

Figure 18-2 depicts a sample active-passive topology. Typically, when deploying an HA firewall pair, the rest of the network is also deployed redundantly; however, this is not required. Physically, an active-passive design looks the same as an active-active design. Two firewalls are deployed at the same point in the network. In Figure 18-2, all traffic uses `FIREWALL-A` for transit, thus making the topology active-passive. The routers in the diagram point static routes to the VSI on each side of the firewall for routing. Because `FIREWALL-A` is the master, all traffic is forwarded to it by the switches which have forwarding entries for the VSI's MAC address located on the interfaces to which `FIREWALL-A` is connected. Because the default failover signaling mechanism for NSRP is to use gratuitous ARP messages, switches are required for each connection to the firewall. You should not use hubs in an NSRP topology, as they will result in packets being incorrectly delivered to the passive unit.

In active-passive, one firewall acts as the master and handles all packet-processing for the network. The active-passive topology has many advantages. First, this is the simplest way to introduce HA into the network. From a network perspective, there is really no difference between an active-passive HA deployment and a single device deployment. This simplifies integration, design, and administration of the firewalls from a network perspective. It is always a good practice to avoid asymmetric traffic patterns when deploying firewalls, as state synchronization for asymmetric traffic is a challenging task at best. It is easiest to do this by deploying in an active-passive topology. Because an active-passive topology provides a single network path, outside of a configuration error or bug, there is no chance for an asymmetric traffic pattern to arise. There are three primary benefits to avoiding asymmetry. The first is that by ensuring a symmetric path, you are ensuring that the active firewall sees all packets, and state can be guaranteed to exist on the device (barring bugs, of course). The second benefit is that in ScreenOS, when an asymmetric path exists, HA data forwarding is performed. HA data forwarding uses the second HA link to forward packets to the master of the session. This link is meant as more of a safety net than a design tool, and when it is used heavily, it can result in decreased performance, especially on the NS5000 Series. The third benefit of ensuring a symmetric path is ease of troubleshooting. If a session is having trouble getting established, debugging and troubleshooting are much easier when they occur on a single device.

Configuration of the active-passive pair is a fairly simple task. It is recommended that you do this when initially installing the devices so that configuration synchronization is always in place. Unless the device comes with dedicated preassigned HA interfaces, as in the case of the NS500 and NS5000, interfaces should be assigned to the HA zone. You do this in the same way you assign interfaces to any other zone. Once the links have been assigned and are connected, set up the cluster ID. When two devices are configured with the same cluster ID, and their HA links are connected, they will form a peer relationship with each other. The cluster ID is also used as a portion of the virtual MAC address used for failover. The VSD-Group and interface ID are the other parameters which contribute to the virtual MAC definition. As the default VSD-Group ID (VSD-Group 0) is often used in NSRP clusters, and similar devices are often connected using the same interfaces, you should be careful when assigning the cluster ID. If multiple NSRP clusters share a single LAN, you should use a different cluster ID for each cluster to prevent the creation of duplicate virtual MAC addresses. When a duplicate virtual MAC address appears on a LAN, connectivity will almost certainly be disrupted. Once the two devices are configured with the same cluster ID and their HA interfaces are connected, they will begin to synchronize configurations. Note that synchronization occurs from master to backup, as well as from backup to master, so if either device's configuration is modified, that change will be reflected on the other device. Likewise, a save command issued on either the master or the backup unit will execute a save to the peer device.

Next, set the cluster name (which is not mandatory in a pure firewall configuration, but is often useful for identifying the purpose of the cluster). After the cluster name is configured, FIREWALL-A is configured to have a priority of 10 on VSD-Group 0. In NSRP, the numerically lower priority is the "better" priority. This step ensures that FIREWALL-A will be the master if both devices come up at the same time. In a default NSRP configuration, the first active firewall on the network will become the master. It is rare that organizations desire this lack of determinism, so during an install, frequently one device is designated as the master. By setting the preempt keyword on the VSD-Group with the command set nsrp vsd-group id 0 preempt, you ensure that the device with the lower-priority value will take over mastership when it becomes active and eligible. Because this setting can cause further disruption to the network, however brief, we do not include it in this recipe. Setting lower-priority values helps to identify FIREWALL-A as the desired master. Next, the configuration is synchronized from FIREWALL-A to FIREWALL-B, and FIREWALL-B is rebooted. When you enter the command exec nsrp sync global-config save, the device, in this case FIREWALL-B, requests the configuration from FIREWALL-A and saves this configuration to flash so that upon reboot, the configurations will be synchronized. Once FIREWALL-B completes its reboot cycle it will be ready to participate in NSRP. Because FIREWALL-A is already active on the LAN, it is the master, as you can see from the command prompt which provides indication of the status of the device:

```
FWCLUSTER:FIREWALL-A(M)->
```

At this point, NSRP is functional from the point of network failover. Enable state synchronization with the command set nsrp rto-mirror-sync. Then, configure the backup device to verify that a session is expired before deleting it. The default behavior of NSRP is for the backup to install a session with a timeout of eight times that of the master's session. When the session timer expires, it is deleted from the backup. Although this is OK for most sessions, long-lived sessions such as Border Gateway Protocol (BGP) sessions could inadvertently get deleted on the backup device. The set nsrp rto-mirror session ageout-ack command tells the backup to check the status of a session with the master before deleting it. The remaining commands in the recipe are for tuning and monitoring. By default, NSRP uses a heartbeat interval of one second and a failover threshold of three missed heartbeats, resulting in a three-second failover time for missed heartbeats. For many administrators, this is too slow. To adjust this timer, set the heartbeat interval using the set nsrp vsd-group hb-interval 200 command. This command sets the heartbeat interval to 200 milliseconds, which leads to a failover time of 600 milliseconds, which is the minimum for a failover based on heartbeat loss.

Setting the secondary path allows for a third interface to be used to elect a VSD-Group master, if for some reason both dedicated HA links were to fail. The secondary path is different from the standard HA interfaces in that only Hello packets are sent on the secondary path to elect a master; it is meant to prevent split brain and nothing more (*split brain* occurs when both devices attempt to become the master). Because the secondary path uses a forwarding interface, it is strongly recommended that message authentication and encryption be performed, as messages will travel over a shared interface. As you would expect, you must perform auth and encrypt settings on each device.

Next, enable monitoring of the physical interfaces, so that if there is a link loss, the device will failover. By default, interface monitoring objects have a weight of 255, and the device failover threshold is 255. This means that a failure of a single interface will cause the entire device to failover.

The final step in a basic NSRP configuration is configuration of the `manage-ip`. You use the `manage-ip` on all interfaces on each device in an NSRP cluster. Each device uses this IP address to individually communicate with the network. Without the `manage-ip`, administrators would not be able to manage the backup devices in an NSRP cluster.

Although configuration of active-passive NSRP is not complex, you should be careful to ensure that the appropriate design is in place. For example, switches (or one switch carved into virtual local area networks [VLANs]) should be considered a requirement, and cluster IDs must be chosen with care.

18.2 View and Troubleshoot NSRP State

Problem

You need to verify the operation of your NSRP cluster.

Solution

Use the `get nsrp` command:

```
FWCLUSTER:FIREWALL-A(M)-> get nsrp
nsrp version: 2.0

cluster info:
cluster id: 1, name: FWCLUSTER
local unit id: 15372992
active units discovered:
index: 0, unit id:  15372992, ctrl mac: 0014f6ea92c8
index: 1, unit id:  15128512, ctrl mac: 0014f6e6d7c8, data mac: ffffffffffff
total number of units: 2

VSD group info:
```

```
init hold time: 5
heartbeat lost threshold: 3
heartbeat interval: 200(ms)
master always exist: enabled
group priority preempt holddown inelig   master       PB other members
    0       10 no             3 no       myself 15128512
total number of vsd groups: 1
Total iteration=917926,time=2296775292,max=19811,min=417,average=2502

RTO mirror info:
run time object sync:   enabled
route synchronization: enabled
ping session sync: enabled
coldstart sync done
nsrp data packet forwarding is enabled

nsrp link info:
control   channel: ethernet0/4 (ifnum: 8)  mac: 0014f6ea92c8 state: up
ha data link not available
secondary path channel: bgroup0 (ifnum: 9)  mac: 0014f6ea92c9 state: up

NSRP encryption password: iamapassword
NSRP authentication password: iamapassword
device based nsrp monitoring threshold: 255, weighted sum: 0,
    not failed
device based nsrp monitor interface: ethernet0/4(weight 255, UP)
device based nsrp monitor zone:
device based nsrp track ip: (weight: 255, enabled, not failed)
number of gratuitous arps: 4 (default)
config sync: enabled

track ip: enabled
```

Discussion

The get nsrp command provides a comprehensive view into NSRP's operational state on the device. The first bit of information from the output is the version number, which is always set to 2 (NSRP v1 was never called NSRP, and there is no v3 at the time of this writing). Next, we have the cluster information, which provides high-level information about the cluster itself. The get nsrp command is actually a concatenation of six more specific commands, as you can see from the following output:

```
FWCLUSTER:FIREWALL-A(M)-> get nsrp ?
>                    redirect output
|                    match output
<return>
cluster              cluster units info
counter              nsrp counters
group                nsrp group info
ha-link              nsrp ha link info
monitor              nsrp monitored object info
rto-mirror           RTO mirror group info
track-ip             show track ip info
```

```
vsd-group            vsd group info
FWCLUSTER:FIREWALL-A(M)-> get nsrp cluster
cluster id: 1, name: FWCLUSTER
local unit id: 15372992
active units discovered:
index: 0, unit id:  15372992, ctrl mac: 0014f6ea92c8
index: 1, unit id:  15128512, ctrl mac: 0014f6e6d7c8, data mac:
  ffffffffffff
total number of units: 2
```

From this output, you can see that the get nsrp cluster command provides the same output as the first stanza from the get nsrp output. From this stanza, you can see the cluster ID and name, as well as the IDs of the local and any other active units discovered in the cluster. NSRP was originally designed to support more than two members per cluster; however, this capability has not been exercised to date. For this reason, the total number of units displayed in a functional NSRP cluster should always be two. The unit ID is a unique device identifier. On each device, you can see the local unit ID, which can be used to ensure that the appropriate devices are connected. In this output, the local ID is also displayed as an active unit. The ctrl mac indicates the MAC address used for the HA control link. The output from this example was taken from an SSG20 device with no data link set. If there was an HA data link, the data MAC would be indicated under index 0 with the appropriate MAC address of the interface. To verify that the second unit ID is the appropriate device, look on the peer device:

```
FWCLUSTER:FIREWALL-B(B)-> get nsrp | include local
local unit id: 15128512
```

From the preceding output, you can see that it is indeed the appropriate device. The next stanza of information comes from the get nsrp vsd-group command:

```
FWCLUSTER:FIREWALL-A(M)-> get nsrp vsd-group

VSD group info:
init hold time: 5
heartbeat lost threshold: 3
heartbeat interval: 200(ms)
master always exist: enabled
group priority preempt holddown inelig   master       PB other members
    0       10 no              3 no      myself 15128512
total number of vsd groups: 1
Total iteration=832696,time=2083723367,max=16065,min=417,average=2502

vsd group id: 0, member count: 2, master: 15372992
member information:
-----------------------------------------------------------------
group  unit_id  state          prio flag rto_peer   hb miss holddown
-----------------------------------------------------------------
    0 15128512  primary backup  100    0         0   0    0        0
    0 15372992  master           10    0         0   0    0        0
```

From this command, you can see the group information, which in our case is just `vsd-group id 0`. The init hold time indicates the time in seconds required before a group can become active on a device. Before the init hold time expires, the device is said to be in the init state, which is the time a device waits before attempting to participate in the NSRP process. The default of five seconds is shown here. The heartbeat lost threshold and heartbeat interval parameters represent the number of lost heartbeats and the time between heartbeats, respectively, before a device is declared down. Here, the minimum intervals of three missed heartbeats and 200 milliseconds are configured in this cluster. The `master-always-exist` parameter is shown next. `master-always-exist` is a setting that is used to allow devices to continue to forward traffic if both devices in a pair would normally be considered inoperable, as shown in Figure 18-3.

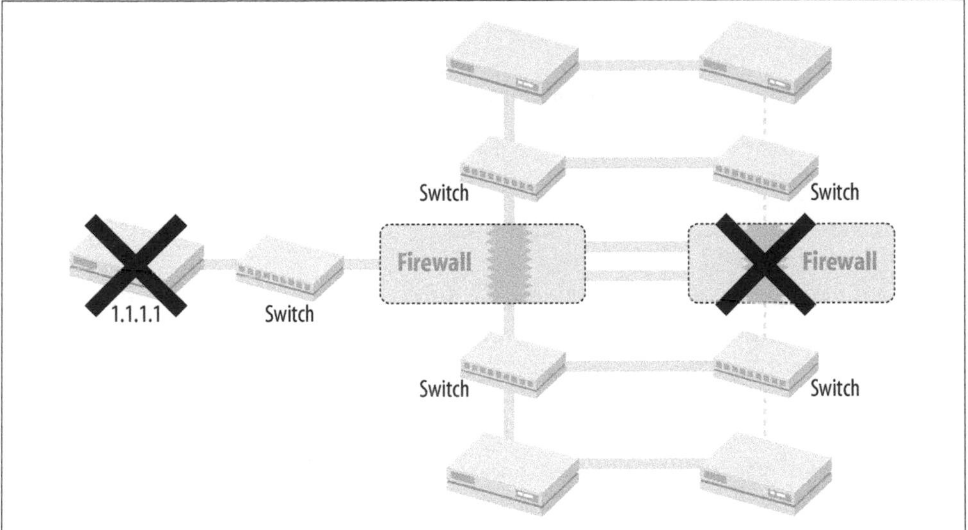

Figure 18-3. Active-passive deployment with a DMZ

In Figure 18-3, the network has a DMZ behind a router with an IP address of `1.1.1.1`. This DMZ should always be available, but the redundancy deployed in the Trusted and Untrusted networks is not carried through to the DMZ. To ensure availability, the network administrators define a `track-ip` object on each firewall to ensure that `1.1.1.1` is pingable. If `1.1.1.1` is not reachable from the primary device, it should failover to the secondary device. However, if the `1.1.1.1` router fails, both firewalls will go into an inoperable state, as their `track-ip` object will fail. This will disrupt traffic for the whole network, instead of just the DMZ. To get around this, use the set `nsrp vsd-group master-always-exist` command. This command tells the firewalls that if both devices become inoperable, one should still remain active on the network, preventing the blackholing of traffic.

The next section of the VSD-Group output shows information about all of the VSD-Groups on the device. Because this is an active-passive topology, only VSD-Group 0 is shown. The priority indicates the local device's priority for the group, which in the case of FIREWALL-A is 10. Remember that the lower priority numerically is the better priority. You can also determine that preempt is disabled (the hold-down timer for preempt would be three seconds if enabled), the local device is not inoperable, the local device is the master, the primary backup is FIREWALL-B, and there are no other members in the cluster.

The output after this is specific to the get nsrp vsd-group command, and is useful in providing more detail about both devices' status. As you can see, the priorities of both devices are shown from a single viewpoint, along with counters for events leading to state transition.

The next stanza of information in the get nsrp command is inherited from the get nsrp rto-mirror command:

```
FWCLUSTER:FIREWALL-A(M)-> get nsrp rto-mirror

RTO mirror info:
run time object sync:   enabled
route synchronization: enabled
ping session sync: enabled
coldstart sync done
```

From this output, notice the synchronizing RTOs, which again means that state is being shared in the cluster. Route synchronization was added in ScreenOS 6.0, and it allows the user to synchronize dynamically learned routes in an NSRP cluster to the passive member. This capability prevents the requirement of a newly promoted master to have to construct its routing table from scratch, and can reduce network reconvergence time. Ping session sync is enabled in this case, which means that session synchronization will occur for ping packets. This is the default setting, but it is frequently disabled. The coldstart sync is executed upon boot-up. A device that reboots will attempt to synchronize all RTOs from the NSRP peer.

The next bundle of information concerns the link information for HA. As we already know, NSRP typically is run on dedicated interfaces. This output is taken from an SSG20 which doesn't support the HA zone, but in this case, ethernet0/4 is used as a dedicated link for HA:

```
FWCLUSTER:FIREWALL-A(M)-> get nsrp ha-link
total_ha_port = 0
probe on ha-link is disabled
secondary path channel: bgroup0 (ifnum: 9) mac: 0014f6ea92c9 state: up
control   channel: ethernet0/4 (ifnum: 8) mac: 0014f6ea92c8 state: up
ha data link not available
```

Because the SSG20 doesn't support the HA zone, the total ports are zero. In other platforms, this value will be set to two in most cases. The HA link probe is a function used for determining the health of an HA link. By default, the physical state of the HA link is used to determine whether heartbeats should be sent and expected on the link. When the physical state of the first HA link goes down, NSRP control messages will begin to exchange on the second HA link (assuming one exists). This assumes that the firewalls are connected back to back, which is not always the case. If there is an intermediate switching layer, sometimes the physical links can remain up, but heartbeats cannot be received. In this scenario, by default, both devices will attempt to become the master (*split brain*), and connectivity problems will likely result. To address this, the HA link probe adds a logical connectivity test to the HA links so that if such a failure occurs, heartbeat messages first failover to the second HA link and, if configured, the HA secondary path. The secondary path itself is a forwarding interface which is the failsafe in cases where all HA links are down. The secondary path is not used for synchronization of RTOs, however, and is invoked only after multiple failovers. When invoked, a master is elected, and no RTOs are synchronized until an HA link is restored. In an active-passive environment, an HA data link is not required as there should never be any asymmetric traffic. Nevertheless, it is not a bad idea to have such a link so that you can continue to synchronize sessions in case your primary HA link goes down.

Finally, the `get nsrp` command displays the encryption and authentication settings:

```
FWCLUSTER:FIREWALL-A(M)-> get nsrp | include (encryption|auth)
NSRP encryption password: iamapassword
NSRP authentication password: iamapassword
```

The `get nsrp` command also displays the number of gratuitous ARPs used to signal the network, and whether configuration synchronization is enabled:

```
FWCLUSTER:FIREWALL-A(M)-> get nsrp | include (arp|config)
number of gratuitous arps: 4 (default)
config sync: enabled
```

The final bits of the `get nsrp` display show monitoring information from the `get nsrp monitor` command:

```
FWCLUSTER:FIREWALL-A(M)-> get nsrp monitor
device based nsrp monitoring threshold: 255, weighted sum: 0, not
    failed
device based nsrp monitor interface: ethernet0/4(weight 255, UP)
device based nsrp monitor zone:
device based nsrp track ip: (weight: 255, enabled, not failed)
```

From this output, you can see that the device has the default monitoring threshold of 255 set, and that the weighted sum of all failed objects is 0, and thus, the device has not failed over. Also note that interface `ethernet 0/4` is being monitored with a weight of 255, and it is up. Because the weight of this object is equal to the failover threshold, if the interface goes down, the device will transition to the inoperable state, as you can see with the following output:

```
FWCLUSTER:FIREWALL-A(M)-> set interface ethernet0/4 phy link-down
FWCLUSTER:FIREWALL-A(I)-> get nsrp vsd-group
```

```
VSD group info:
init hold time: 5
heartbeat lost threshold: 3
heartbeat interval: 200(ms)
master always exist: enabled
group priority preempt holddown inelig   master     PB other members
    0       10 no              3 no     15128512     none myself
    (inoperable)
total number of vsd groups: 1
Total iteration=922386,time=2307632447,max=19811,min=417,average=2501

vsd group id: 0, member count: 2, master: 15128512
member information:
-----------------------------------------------------------------
group  unit_id  state          prio flag rto_peer   hb miss holddown
-----------------------------------------------------------------
    0 15128512  master          100    0          0   0    1        0
    0 15372992  inoperable       10    0          0   0    0        0

FWCLUSTER:FIREWALL-A(I)-> get nsrp monitor
device based nsrp monitoring threshold: 255, weighted sum: 255,failed
device based nsrp monitor interface: ethernet0/4(weight 255, DOWN)
device based nsrp monitor zone:
device based nsrp track ip: (weight: 255, enabled, not failed)
FWCLUSTER:FIREWALL-A(I)->
```

The NSRP zone monitoring is also displayed, along with the `track-ip` information. To get the specifics of the `track-ip` objects, use the `get nsrp track-ip` command:

```
FWCLUSTER:FIREWALL-A(B)-> get nsrp track-ip
ip address      interval threshold wei  interface  meth fail-count
    success-rate
192.168.5.1            1         3   1  auto         ping       0 100%
failure weight: 255, threshold: 255, not failed: 0 ip(s) failed,
    weighted sum =0
```

This command shows that a single IP is being tracked, `192.168.5.1`, and that every second a ping is sent, and if three pings are lost, the object will be failed. Unlike interfaces, `track-ip` objects are set to a weight of 1 by default so that the failure of a single `track-ip` object will not cause a device/VSD-Group failover. You must increase the failover threshold to 255 for a single `track-ip` object failure to cause a device/VSD failover. Alternatively, as you can see in the `get nsrp track-ip` output, there is a threshold for `track-ip` as a whole to failover. If this is set to a value of one, failure of a single `track-ip` object with the default weight will cause the `track-ip` failure weight (255 by default, as you can see in the output of `get nsrp track-ip`) to be added to the device monitor's weighted sum, and will cause the device to become inoperable.

The `get nsrp` command provides a comprehensive analysis of the operation of an NSRP cluster, and it is often the only command necessary to troubleshoot an NSRP problem. When you require more specific information, add the described arguments to the command to get more information.

See Also

The Introduction to this chapter; Recipe 18.3

18.3 Influence the NSRP Master

Problem

You need to configure FIREWALL-A in your cluster to always be the master if it can reach the DMZ router's VRRP address and its Trust and Untrust interfaces are functional. Furthermore, a failure on one piece of the network should not cause the entire network to become unusable.

Solution

Use priority and preempt to set FIREWALL-A as the master:

```
FWCLUSTER:FIREWALL-A(B)-> set nsrp vsd-group id 0 priority 10
FWCLUSTER:FIREWALL-A(B)-> set nsrp vsd-group id 0 preempt hold-down 90
FWCLUSTER:FIREWALL-A(B)-> set nsrp vsd-group id 0 preempt
```

Next, configure monitoring on both devices:

```
FWCLUSTER:FIREWALL-A(M)-> set nsrp monitor interface eth0/0
FWCLUSTER:FIREWALL-A(M)-> set nsrp monitor interface bgroup0
FWCLUSTER:FIREWALL-A(M)-> set nsrp monitor interface eth0/3
FWCLUSTER:FIREWALL-A(M)-> set nsrp monitor track-ip ip
FWCLUSTER:FIREWALL-A(M)-> set nsrp monitor track-ip ip 1.1.1.1
    weight 255
FWCLUSTER:FIREWALL-A(M)-> set nsrp monitor track-ip ip 1.1.1.1
    method arp

FWCLUSTER:FIREWALL-B(M)-> set nsrp monitor interface eth0/0
FWCLUSTER:FIREWALL-B(M)-> set nsrp monitor interface bgroup0
FWCLUSTER:FIREWALL-B(M)-> set nsrp monitor interface eth0/3
FWCLUSTER:FIREWALL-B(M)-> set nsrp monitor track-ip ip
FWCLUSTER:FIREWALL-B(M)-> set nsrp monitor track-ip ip 1.1.1.1
    weight 255
FWCLUSTER:FIREWALL-B(I)-> set nsrp monitor track-ip ip 1.1.1.1
    method arp
```

Finally, enable master-always-exist, so that a failure to reach the VRRP address by both devices won't cause a complete network failure:

```
FWCLUSTER:FIREWALL-A(M)-> set nsrp vsd-group master-always-exist
```

Discussion

Many network administrators prefer to have a specific device act as the master if at all possible. It becomes their default master device, and as long as no failure conditions have caused it to enter and remain in the inoperable state, it should become the master. The use of priority and preempt enables this functionality. To ensure that all RTOs have been received, the preempt hold-down timer is set to 90 seconds on FIREWALL-A. This serves to ensure that the network is stable (from FIREWALL-A's perspective) for at least 90 seconds before FIREWALL-A assumes mastership of VSD-Group 0. Additionally, it allows for a decent time interval to ensure successful synchronization of all RTOs before it reasserts itself as the master. If all RTOs have not been received before a preempt occurs, any session matching these RTOs will be dropped; therefore, it is a good practice to allow a decent amount of time for this to occur. The priority and preempt settings are device local settings, and thus are not propagated to FIREWALL-B. This is, of course, the desired behavior to ensure that FIREWALL-A is the master. FIREWALL-B maintains its default priority of 100.

```
FWCLUSTER:FIREWALL-B(B)-> get nsrp vsd-group

VSD group info:
init hold time: 5
heartbeat lost threshold: 3
heartbeat interval: 200(ms)
master always exist: enabled
group priority preempt holddown inelig   master      PB other members
    0      100 no               3 no     15372992   myself none
total number of vsd groups: 1
Total iteration=853767,time=2128083592,max=16696,min=418,average=2492

vsd group id: 0, member count: 2, master: 15372992
member information:
-------------------------------------------------------------------
group  unit_id  state          prio flag rto_peer   hb miss holddown
-------------------------------------------------------------------
    0 15372992  master           10    2         0    1    0       30
    0 15128512  primary backup  100    0         0    0    0        0
```

On the other hand, you must configure monitoring parameters on both devices to be effective. Like the priority and preempt values (as well as many other NSRP configuration settings), monitoring parameters are considered device local in scope; that is, they are not synchronized as part of the configuration synchronization process. For this example, all interfaces are monitored, and the VRRP address of the DMZ router is monitored. Because the routers in the DMZ are running VRRP, ARP is chosen as the monitoring method, and the weight of the object is adjusted to 255 to ensure that if the VRRP address doesn't respond, the device will transition to the inoperable state.

The final piece of the puzzle is to configure the master-always-exist setting. This ensures that if both devices become inoperable due to a monitored object failure, the network is not brought down. In this example, if FIREWALL-A loses connectivity to the 1.1.1.1 track-ip object, it will become inoperable, and FIREWALL-B will become the master. If, however, the failure is common to both FIREWALL-A and FIREWALL-B, FIREWALL-A will remain the master, and traffic will continue to flow between the Trust and Untrust zones.

See Also

Recipe 18.1; Recipe 18.2

18.4 Configure NSRP Monitors

Problem

You need to ensure that the networks connected to the firewall are fully operational.

Solution

Configure NSRP monitoring to verify interface and gateway availability:

```
FWCLUSTER:FIREWALL-A(M)-> set nsrp monitor interface e0/1
FWCLUSTER:FIREWALL-A(M)-> set nsrp monitor interface e0/3
FWCLUSTER:FIREWALL-A(I)-> set int e0/1 manage-ip 1.1.1.200
FWCLUSTER:FIREWALL-A(I)-> set int e0/3 manage-ip 2.1.1.200
FWCLUSTER:FIREWALL-A(M)-> set nsrp monitor track-ip
FWCLUSTER:FIREWALL-A(M)-> set nsrp monitor track-ip ip 1.1.1.3
    weight 255
FWCLUSTER:FIREWALL-A(M)-> set nsrp monitor track-ip ip 2.1.1.3
    weight 255

FWCLUSTER:FIREWALL-B(M)-> set nsrp monitor interface e0/1
FWCLUSTER:FIREWALL-B(M)-> set nsrp monitor interface e0/3
FWCLUSTER:FIREWALL-B(B)-> set int e0/1 manage-ip 1.1.1.201
FWCLUSTER:FIREWALL-B(M)-> set int e0/3 manage-ip 2.1.1.201
FWCLUSTER:FIREWALL-B(M)-> set nsrp monitor track-ip
FWCLUSTER:FIREWALL-B(M)-> set nsrp monitor track-ip ip 1.1.1.3
    weight 255
FWCLUSTER:FIREWALL-B(M)-> set nsrp monitor track-ip ip 2.1.1.3
    weight 255
```

Discussion

You use NSRP monitoring to validate the integrity of a path. Interface monitoring, as described in the introduction to this chapter, is used to validate the physical state of a link. By default, interface monitoring uses a default weight of 255. You can verify this using the get nsrp monitor command:

```
FWCLUSTER:FIREWALL-A(B)-> get nsrp monitor
device based nsrp monitoring threshold: 255, weighted sum: 0, not
    failed
device based nsrp monitor interface: ethernet0/1(weight 255, UP)
    ethernet0/3(weight 255, UP)
device based nsrp monitor zone:
device based nsrp track ip: (weight: 255, enabled, not failed)
```

You use the monitoring weight in NSRP to increment the weighted sum for NSRP monitoring. You can do this on a per-device basis or on a per-VSD basis. When used in a per-VSD capacity, you can use NSRP to failover a single VSD-Group so that the entire cluster is not subject to failover. This can be particularly valuable in a VSYS context. You can configure per-VSYS failover by including all interfaces in each VSYS in a unique VSD-Group. To configure per-VSD failover, use the `set nsrp vsd-group id <x> monitor` set of commands. In our configuration, as you can see from the output of `get nsrp monitor`, a single interface will cause the entire device to failover as the weight of the interface, 255, is equal to the device-based NSRP monitoring threshold.

`track-ip` operates slightly differently by default, as by itself it is considered an NSRP monitor object, with a weight of 255. Before `track-ip` is considered failed, the weighted sum of objects within the `track-ip` configuration must exceed the failure threshold for `track-ip` itself, which is set to 255 by default:

```
FWCLUSTER:FIREWALL-A(B)-> get nsrp monitor track-ip
ip address interval threshold wei interface  meth fail-count success-rate
1.1.1.3          1          3 255 auto        ping          0 82%
2.1.1.3          1          3 255 auto        ping          0 83%
failure weight: 255, threshold: 255, not failed: 0 ip(s) failed,
weighted sum = 0
```

Note here that the threshold for failure of `track-ip` is 255, and when this threshold is met or exceeded, it will add 255 to the NSRP device weighted sum. By default, the weight of each `track-ip` object is one, so failure of a single IP will not cause `track-ip` to be considered failed. To modify this behavior, include the weight of 255 in the `track-ip` object configuration.

`track-ip` uses ping as the default mechanism for failure tracking, but sometimes this is not desirable. Some VRRP implementations, for example, do not allow packets to be processed by the VIP. To handle these situations, you can configure `track-ip` with a method of ARP. `track-ip` also requires the use of a `manage-ip` on the device. The ping requests are sent with the `manage-ip` as the source address. This is required as each device maintains its own monitoring configuration and performs monitoring independently. Without a `manage-ip`, the backup device will have no valid source interface from which to initiate the tracking functionality. Furthermore, if `track-ip` packets are sourced from a VSI, and if the device becomes inoperable, they will never be able to be reinitiated, thus leaving the device in an inoperable state.

NSRP monitoring allows you to perform numerous health checks to ensure that the network is operating as expected. You should use it in virtually all NSRP configurations to ensure the fastest failover time if there is a problem on the network.

See Also

The Introduction to this chapter; Recipe 18.1; Recipe 18.2

18.5 Configure NSRP in Transparent Mode

Problem

You need to run NSRP in a transparent mode environment.

Solution

Configure FIREWALL-A in transparent mode:

```
FIREWALL-A-> set interface ethernet0/1 zone v1-untrust
FIREWALL-A-> set interface ethernet0/3 zone v1-trust
FIREWALL-A-> set interface vlan1 ip 1.1.1.1/24
```

Configure NSRP on the devices as though they were in route mode:

```
FIREWALL-A-> set interface ethernet0/7 zone ha
FIREWALL-A-> set interface ethernet0/8 zone ha

FIREWALL-B-> set interface ethernet0/7 zone ha
FIREWALL-B-> set interface ethernet0/8 zone ha
FIREWALL-A-> set nsrp cluster id 1
FIREWALL-A(M)-> set nsrp cluster name FWCLUSTER
FWCLUSTER:FIREWALL-A(M)-> set nsrp vsd-group id 0 priority 10

FIREWALL-B-> set nsrp cluster id 1
FIREWALL-B(B)-> set nsrp cluster name FWCLUSTER
FWCLUSTER:FIREWALL-B(B)-> save
FWCLUSTER:FIREWALL-B(B)-> exec nsrp sync global-config saved
FWCLUSTER:FIREWALL-B(B)-> reset
```

Once FIREWALL-B comes back online, finish the configuration by enabling RTO synchronization, configuring timers, setting up monitoring parameters, and configuring manage-ips:

```
FWCLUSTER:FIREWALL-A(M)-> set nsrp rto-mirror sync
FWCLUSTER:FIREWALL-A(B)-> set nsrp rto-mirror session ageout-ack
FWCLUSTER:FIREWALL-A(M)-> set nsrp vsd-group hb-interval 200
FWCLUSTER:FIREWALL-A(M)-> set interface vlan1 manage-ip 1.1.1.11
FWCLUSTER:FIREWALL-A(M)-> set nsrp monitor interface ethernet0/1
FWCLUSTER:FIREWALL-A(M)-> set nsrp monitor interface ethernet0/3
FWCLUSTER:FIREWALL-A(M)-> set nsrp track-ip
FWCLUSTER:FIREWALL-A(M)-> set nsrp track-ip ip 1.1.1.10 weight 255
FWCLUSTER:FIREWALL-A(M)-> set nsrp track-ip ip 1.1.1.100 weight 255
FWCLUSTER:FIREWALL-A(M)-> set nsrp track-ip ip 1.1.1.100 interface vlan1
FWCLUSTER:FIREWALL-A(M)-> set nsrp track-ip ip 1.1.1.10 interface vlan1

FWCLUSTER:FIREWALL-B(M)-> set nsrp monitor interface ethernet0/1
FWCLUSTER:FIREWALL-B(M)-> set nsrp monitor interface ethernet0/3

FWCLUSTER:FIREWALL-B(M)-> set interface vlan1 manage-ip 1.1.1.11
FWCLUSTER:FIREWALL-B(B)-> set nsrp track-ip
```

```
FWCLUSTER:FIREWALL-B(B)-> set nsrp track-ip ip 1.1.1.10 weight 255
FWCLUSTER:FIREWALL-B(B)-> set nsrp track-ip ip 1.1.1.100 weight 255
FWCLUSTER:FIREWALL-B(B)-> set nsrp track-ip ip 1.1.1.10 interface
    vlan1
FWCLUSTER:FIREWALL-B(B)-> set nsrp track-ip ip 1.1.1.100 interface
    vlan1
```

Discussion

NSRP does not require any specific configuration to be deployed in transparent mode, outside of the monitoring parameters. There are certain considerations, however, in creating such a topology. The first and most major difference between transparent and route/NAT mode is that (at the time of this writing) in transparent mode, you can use only a single VSD-Group, namely VSD 0. The reason is because NSRP was originally envisioned to operate only between switches in a flat Layer 2 topology. In this scenario, as depicted in Figure 18-4, the problem is evident.

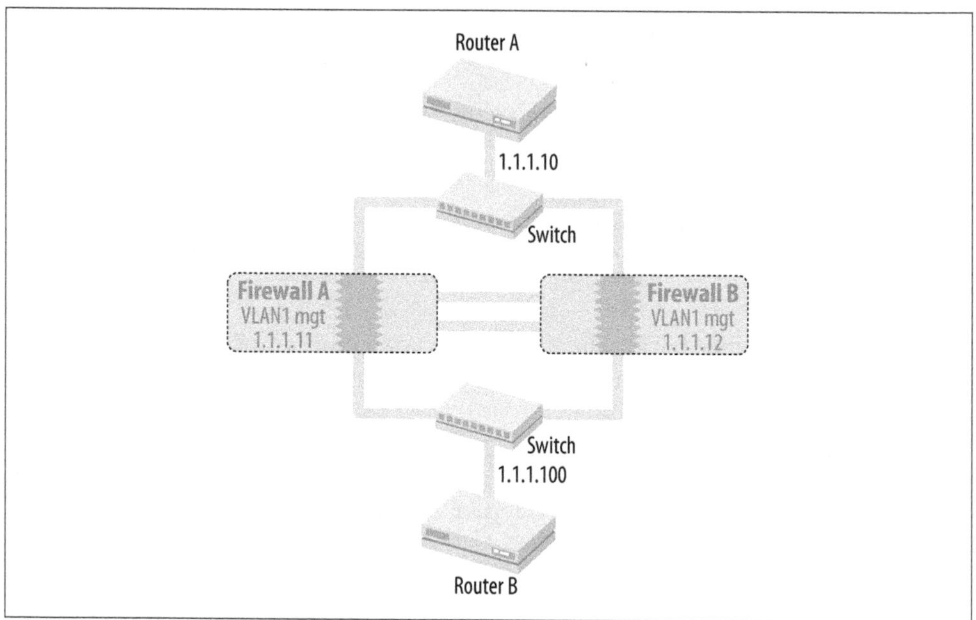

Figure 18-4. A flat Layer 2 topology

In this topology, a bridge loop is formed if the firewalls are operating in an active-active mode. Of course, you could run the spanning tree to eliminate the loop, but then the topology would no longer be active-active. In active-passive mode, however, the loop is broken, as the passive device in a transparent NSRP cluster does not forward any traffic. This includes Bridge Packet Data Units (BPDUs) because the links are up by default in NSRP, meaning that interfaces connected to the backup device in an NSRP cluster will go through the `LISTENING` and `LEARNING` phases of the spanning tree, and then will transition to the `FORWARDING` state. Although the port is in a FORWARDING state from the spanning tree's perspective, it will not stay there. During an NSRP transition, both devices in the cluster will flap their links briefly. When the switches are running the spanning tree, this will transition them to the LISTENING state, and they will have to go through the LISTENING and LEARNING states before getting back to the FORWARDING state. This can result in an outage whose length is governed by the spanning tree's timers.

To provide better failover times, two options are available: you can use a rapid spanning tree, or you can disable the spanning tree. The latter option can be a terrifying prospect for some organizations, and it may be explicitly prohibited by network policy. Indeed, it does require faith in NSRP as the loop prevention protocol as opposed to the spanning tree. If the switches don't support the rapid spanning tree and multisecond failover times are unacceptable, this may be the only option.

In transparent mode, when a destination MAC address is unknown to the firewall, the firewall will flood the packet out through all interfaces except the one from which it was received. When the reply packet comes back to the firewall, the firewall will create an entry in the MAC-Learn table, much like a switch would do when it receives a packet from an unknown MAC. In NSRP, the MAC-Learn table is not considered an RTO, so in the event of a failover, the new master will have to reflood traffic for unknown MACs. In our simple topology in Figure 18-4, you will never actually see this scenario. Note the output from FIREWALL-B's get mac-learn:

```
FWCLUSTER:FIREWALL-B(B)-> get mac-learn
link down clear mac learn table: enable
Total 1024, Used 2, Create 24, Ageout 22
Flood 4, BCast 53, ReLearn 164, NoFree 0, Error 0, Drop 0

<if>            <mac>           <timeout>       <tag id>
ethernet0/3:0005.85c8.f5d0        60              1
ethernet0/3:0005.85c8.f5d1        60              1
FWCLUSTER:FIREWALL-B(B)-> clear mac-learn
FWCLUSTER:FIREWALL-B(B)-> get mac-learn
link down clear mac learn table: enable
Total 1024, Used 2, Create 26, Ageout 24
Flood 4, BCast 53, ReLearn 164, NoFree 0, Error 0, Drop 0

<if>            <mac>           <timeout>       <tag id>
ethernet0/3:0005.85c8.f5d0        60              1
ethernet0/3:0005.85c8.f5d1        60              1
```

Even when you clear the MAC-Learn table on FIREWALL-B, you will retain the MAC addresses for ROUTER-A and ROUTER-B. This is a consequence of having configured track-ip. By enabling track-ip, you not only monitor the availability of your routers from a packet from a packet-forwarding perspective, but also are able to keep the critical entries in the MAC-Learn table populated. You can validate this theory by disabling track-ip:

```
FWCLUSTER:FIREWALL-B(B)-> unset nsrp track-ip
FWCLUSTER:FIREWALL-B(B)-> clear mac-learn
```

```
FWCLUSTER:FIREWALL-B(B)-> get mac
mac-learn            show mac learning table
FWCLUSTER:FIREWALL-B(B)-> get mac-learn
link down clear mac learn table: enable
Total 1024, Used 0, Create 26, Ageout 26
Flood 4, BCast 53, ReLearn 164, NoFree 0, Error 0, Drop 0

<if>            <mac>            <timeout>       <tag id>
```

Note that the router MAC addresses are no longer retained.

In transparent mode, as in route mode, RTO synchronization enables stateful device failover. Instead of signaling network failover by issuing gratuitous ARPs, however, NSRP signals failover to the network by bouncing the links on both cluster members. This has the effect of clearing the switches' forwarding databases. Without a forwarding database entry for a given MAC, the switches, like the firewalls, flood the packets out through all ports except those on which the packets were received, until the forwarding database is built.

As with NSRP in route mode, monitoring is recommended for all interfaces, as is `track-ip`. `track-ip` in transparent mode uses the `vlan1` IP for the source of `track-ip` packets, or more accurately, the `manage-ip` of `vlan1`. With transparent mode, `vlan1` and its `manage-ip` should be set up in the same subnet as the surrounding devices.

See Also

Recipe 18.1; Recipe 18.4

18.6 Configure an Active-Active NSRP Cluster

Problem

You need to use both devices in an NSRP pair to forward traffic.

Solution

Configure an active-active NSRP cluster:

```
FIREWALL-A-> set nsrp cluster id 1
FIREWALL-A(M)-> set nsrp cluster name FWCLUSTER
FWCLUSTER:FIREWALL-A(M)-> set nsrp vsd-group id 0 priority 10

FIREWALL-B-> set nsrp cluster id 1
FIREWALL-B(B)-> set nsrp vsd-group id 1 priority 10
FWCLUSTER:FIREWALL-B(B)-> save
FWCLUSTER:FIREWALL-B(B)-> exec nsrp sync global-config saved
FWCLUSTER:FIREWALL-B(B)-> reset
```

Once `FIREWALL-B` comes back online, continue the configuration by enabling RTO synchronization, configuring timers, and setting up monitoring parameters:

```
FWCLUSTER:FIREWALL-A(M)-> set nsrp rto-mirror sync
FWCLUSTER:FIREWALL-A(M)-> set nsrp vsd-group hb-interval 200
FWCLUSTER:FIREWALL-A(M)-> set nsrp data-forwarding
FWCLUSTER:FIREWALL-A(M)-> set nsrp monitor interface ethernet0/1
FWCLUSTER:FIREWALL-A(M)-> set nsrp monitor interface ethernet0/3
FWCLUSTER:FIREWALL-B(M)-> set nsrp monitor interface ethernet0/1
FWCLUSTER:FIREWALL-B(M)-> set nsrp monitor interface ethernet0/3
```

Finally, ensure that the two devices remain active, when possible, by configuring `preempt` for the appropriate groups, and setting `master-always-exist`:

```
FWCLUSTER:FIREWALL-A(M)-> set nsrp vsd-group id 0 preempt
FWCLUSTER:FIREWALL-A(M)-> set nsrp vsd-group id 0 preempt hold-down 90
FWCLUSTER:FIREWALL-A(M)-> set nsrp vsd-group master-always-exist
FWCLUSTER:FIREWALL-B(M)-> set nsrp vsd-group id 1 preempt
FWCLUSTER:FIREWALL-B(M)-> set nsrp vsd-group id 1 preempt hold-down 90
```

Discussion

NSRP in active-active mode is conceptually similar to NSRP in active-passive mode. Figure 18-5 shows a typical active-active configuration.

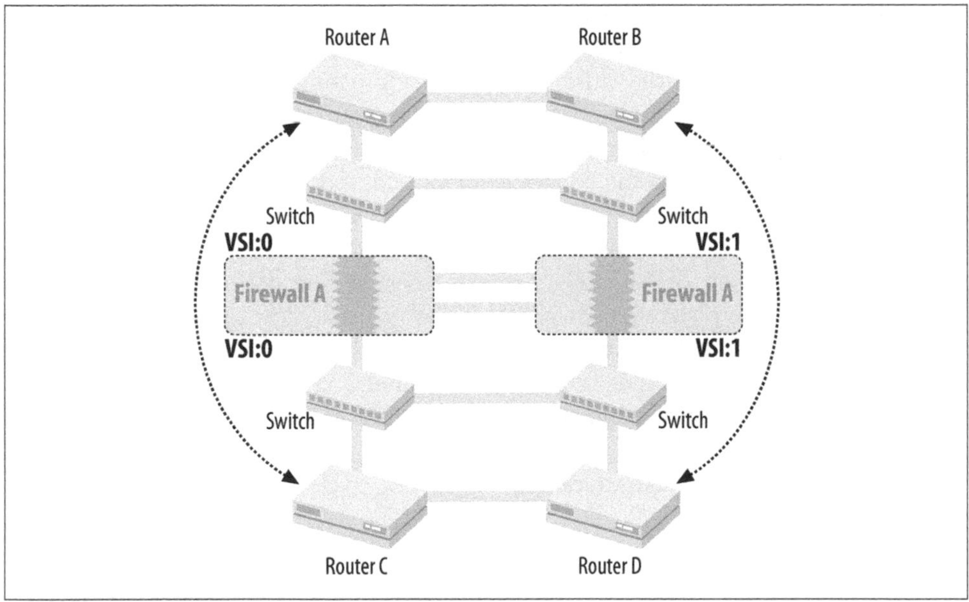

Figure 18-5. A typical active-active topology

Instead of having a single VSD-Group to forward traffic in active-active mode, NSRP uses two (or sometimes more) VSD-Groups. The effect is that each device can become the master for a subset of sessions and each device can forward traffic. To deliver traffic to the firewalls, some routes are pointed at `VSI:0` and some routes are pointed at `VSI:1`. This creates a load-sharing environment on the firewalls. There are three main reasons for deploying an active-active topology:

- To increase forwarding capacity
- To ensure that the "backup" device is functional
- To provide independent failover for a subset of traffic

Of these three reasons, you should be careful when deciding to deploy active-active when an increase in forwarding capacity is the motivator. Juniper's firewall products operate at extremely high performance. Deploying an active-active NSRP cluster to increase performance may not be necessary, and may have unintended results. Although using two devices to forward traffic instead of one will increase the system's theoretical throughput, if NSRP detects a failure and one of the devices becomes inoperable—and if the throughput at that time exceeds the capacity of a single device—data will certainly be lost and full redundancy cannot be said to have been provided.

Another unintended consequence may arise. Unless routing is configured carefully, asymmetric traffic can easily result. NSRP handles asymmetric traffic by performing NSRP data forwarding. Data forwarding in NSRP occurs when a packet arrives on a firewall and the VSD-Group the packet is destined to (derived from the destination MAC address in the packet) does not have an existing session for the packet. When such packets arrive on a device, they are immediately forwarded across the HA data link to the peer device in the cluster for processing, using the MAC address of the VSI that the original packet was destined to as the source of the forwarded packet. When this packet it received on the master looks like it was found on the local VSI, session lookup is done, and the packet is forwarded appropriately. On the NS5000, this forwarding is particularly costly, as the HA links are located on the management module, and thus the CPU is used to forward them. If there is a significant amount of this traffic on a pair of NS5000s, decreased forwarding performance will be the likely result. Even on platforms where this is not the case, debugging can get trickier in an environment with HA data forwarding. HA data forwarding is a wonderfully useful mechanism; however, it is best used in failure conditions, rather than as a design principle. To ensure symmetry, various routing tricks including NAT, policy-based routing, and filter-based forwarding are recommended. For more information on policy-based routing, see Chapter 7.

Although using an active-active pair to increase forwarding capacity is not recommended, ensuring the existence of an operational backup device is frequently desired, and is a useful reason to deploy active-active. Providing independent failover for a subset of traffic is also desired in some high-performance environments, where even the subsecond failover capabilities of NSRP are deemed too disruptive. Again, with any motivation for deploying an active-active topology, you must be careful to ensure symmetry as much as possible.

The configuration of active-active NSRP is similar to active-passive because in NSRP, when the first device on the network comes up, it becomes the master. The addition of the `preempt` command is required, as well as the explicit configuration of priority for each VSD-Group. In Recipe 18.1, we used only the default VSD-Group 0. To run an active-active configuration, a minimum of two VSD-Groups are used. Create a new VSD-Group with the `set nsrp vsd-group id 1 priority 10` command. When executed on `FIREWALL-B`, the configuration is synchronized with `FIREWALL-A`, with a notable exception—the priority—as can be seen from `FIREWALL-A`'s configuration:

```
FWCLUSTER:FIREWALL-A(M)-> get config | include vsd-group
set nsrp vsd-group master-always-exist
set nsrp vsd-group id 0 priority 10
set nsrp vsd-group id 0 preempt
set nsrp vsd-group id 0 preempt hold-down 90
set nsrp vsd-group id 1 priority 100
```

Note that the default priority of 100 is assigned to the VSD-Group. Although the creation of a VSD-Group is a synchronized component of a configuration, as one would expect, the priority of the group is a local-only setting. As previously mentioned, `preempt` is recommended for a successful NSRP configuration, as it will force both devices, when capable, to assume mastership of one of the VSD-Groups. Set the hold-down timer to 90 seconds to avoid excessive state changes in an unstable network, and ensure full synchronization of RTOs. (Setting the hold-down timer applies only to the `preempt` function.) If the peer device becomes inoperable before the hold-down timer expires, the device will still become the master as long as it is not inoperable.

On examining the `get nsrp vsd-group` command, you'll see that the pair is in an active-active state:

```
FWCLUSTER:FIREWALL-A(M)-> get nsrp vsd-group

VSD group info:
init hold time: 5
heartbeat lost threshold: 3
heartbeat interval: 1000(ms)
master always exist: enabled
group priority preempt holddown inelig   master      PB other members
    0       10 yes            90 no      myself  4274560
    1      100 no              3 no     4274560   myself
total number of vsd groups: 2
Total iteration=2713608,time=565665873,max=21663,min=86,average=208

vsd group id: 0, member count: 2, master: 4687744
member information:
----------------------------------------------------------------------
group  unit_id  state          prio flag rto_peer   hb miss holddown
----------------------------------------------------------------------
    0  4274560  primary backup  100    0         0   1    0        0
    0  4687744  master           10    2         0   0    0       90

vsd group id: 1, member count: 2, master: 4274560
member information:
----------------------------------------------------------------------
group  unit_id  state          prio flag rto_peer   hb miss holddown
----------------------------------------------------------------------
```

```
1 4274560 master          10   2      0  1  0      90
1 4687744 primary backup  100  0      0  0  0       0
```

As expected, each device is the master of one VSD-Group. Note in the command prompt the existence of the `M` designating `FIREWALL-A` as the master. Examine `FIREWALL-B` and you'll see the same:

```
FWCLUSTER:FIREWALL-B(M)->
```

This is the expected behavior in an operational active-active configuration. If a failure occurs, one device should become master of both VSD-Groups. Switching `FIREWALL-B` to backup mode, you can see this:

```
FWCLUSTER:FIREWALL-B(M)-> exec nsrp vsd-group id 1 mode backup
Start deactivate session (vsd=1) ...
0 sessions deactivated

FWCLUSTER:FIREWALL-A(M)-> get nsrp vsd-group

VSD group info:
init hold time: 5
heartbeat lost threshold: 3
heartbeat interval: 1000(ms)
master always exist: enabled
group priority preempt holddown inelig   master  PB other members
    0       10 yes            90 no      myself  4274560
    1      100 no              3 no      myself  4274560
total number of vsd groups: 2
Total iteration=2716552,time=567481260,max=21663,min=86,average=208

vsd group id: 0, member count: 2, master: 4687744
member information:
-----------------------------------------------------------------
group  unit_id  state          prio flag rto_peer hb miss holddown
-----------------------------------------------------------------
    0  4274560  primary backup  100    0        0  0    0        0
    0  4687744  master           10    2        0  0    0       90

vsd group id: 1, member count: 2, master: 4687744
member information:
-----------------------------------------------------------------
group  unit_id  state          prio flag rto_peer hb miss holddown
-----------------------------------------------------------------
    1  4274560  primary backup   10    2        0  1    0       90
    1  4687744  master          100    0        0  0    0        0
```

After the expiration of the hold-down timer, `FIREWALL-B` will preempt the mastership of VSG-Group 1, and the pair will again become active-active.

See Also

Recipe 18.1; Recipe 18.2

18.7 Configure NSRP with OSPF

Problem

You need to run OSPF on your active-passive firewalls.

Solution

Configure a VSD-less cluster:

```
FWCLUSTER:FIREWALL-A(M)-> unset nsrp vsd-group id 0
FWCLUSTER:FIREWALL-A(B)-> set nsrp rto-mirror session non-vsi
FWCLUSTER:FIREWALL-A(M)-> set interface e0/1 ip 1.1.1.1/24
FWCLUSTER:FIREWALL-A(M)-> set interface e0/3 ip 2.1.1.1/24

FWCLUSTER:FIREWALL-B(M)-> set inte e0/1 ip 1.1.2.1/24
FWCLUSTER:FIREWALL-B(M)-> set inte e0/3 ip 2.1.2.1/24
```

Enable OSPF on each device:

```
FWCLUSTER:FIREWALL-A(M)-> set vrouter trust-vr
FWCLUSTER:FIREWALL-A(trust-vr)(M)-> set protocol ospf
FWCLUSTER:FIREWALL-A(trust-vr/ospf)(M)-> set area 0
FWCLUSTER:FIREWALL-A(trust-vr/ospf)(M)-> set enable
FWCLUSTER:FIREWALL-A(trust-vr/ospf)(M)-> end
FWCLUSTER:FIREWALL-A(M)-> set interface ethernet0/1 protocol ospf
    area 0
FWCLUSTER:FIREWALL-A(M)-> set interface ethernet0/1 protocol ospf
    link-type p2p
FWCLUSTER:FIREWALL-A(M)-> set interface ethernet0/1 protocol ospf
    enable
FWCLUSTER:FIREWALL-A(M)-> set interface ethernet0/3 protocol ospf
    area 0
FWCLUSTER:FIREWALL-A(M)-> set interface ethernet0/3 protocol ospf
    link-type p2p
FWCLUSTER:FIREWALL-A(M)-> set interface ethernet0/3 protocol ospf
    enable

FWCLUSTER:FIREWALL-B(M)-> set interface ethernet0/1 protocol ospf
    area 0
FWCLUSTER:FIREWALL-B(M)-> set interface ethernet0/3 protocol ospf
    area 0
FWCLUSTER:FIREWALL-B(M)-> set interface ethernet0/1 protocol ospf
    cost 100
FWCLUSTER:FIREWALL-B(M)-> set interface ethernet0/3 protocol ospf
    cost 100
FWCLUSTER:FIREWALL-B(M)-> set interface ethernet0/1 protocol ospf
    link-type p2p
FWCLUSTER:FIREWALL-B(M)-> set interface ethernet0/3 protocol ospf
    link-type p2p
FWCLUSTER:FIREWALL-B(M)-> set interface ethernet0/1 protocol ospf
    enable
FWCLUSTER:FIREWALL-B(M)-> set interface ethernet0/3 protocol ospf
    enable
```

Discussion

VSD-less clusters were added in ScreenOS 5.0 with the goal of separating the failover component of NSRP from the session synchronization component. Prior to ScreenOS 5.0, when a dynamic routing protocol was run in conjunction with NSRP, failover behavior was not always predictable, and was often slow, because when using NSRP with the default VSD-Group of 0, interface IP addresses are shared among devices in the cluster. As a single IP address faces the network per VSD-Group, only one device can form routing protocol neighborships per VSD-Group at a time. In the default active-passive setup, this means that when the active device in a cluster becomes inoperable and it fails over, the new master will not yet have any routes with which to forward traffic. Furthermore, it may not even have built the sessions because there were no routes for the active sessions.

Active-active mode is no better, and maybe worse. In active-active mode, each device will have neighbors built on its respective VSIs. Upon failover, however, the master will become its own neighbor, as you can see in the following output which assumes configuration of OSPF on VSIs:

```
FWCLUSTER:FIREWALL-A(M)-> get vrouter trust-vr protocol ospf neighbor
VR: trust-vr RouterId: 172.25.113.177
----------------------------------
                Neighbor(s) on interface ethernet0/3:1 (Area 0.0.0.0)
IpAddr/IfIndex RouterId         Pri State    Opt  Up           StateChg
-------------------------------------------------------------------------
2.1.1.1         172.25.113.177    1 2Way      E    00:00:10     (+3 -0)
2.1.1.3         10.3.3.2        128 Full      E    00:00:12     (+7 -0)
2.1.1.4         10.30.3.2       128 Full      E    00:00:12     (+7 -0)

                Neighbor(s) on interface ethernet0/1:1 (Area 0.0.0.0)
IpAddr/IfIndex RouterId         Pri State    Opt  Up           StateChg
-------------------------------------------------------------------------
1.1.1.1         172.25.113.177    1 2Way      E    00:00:10     (+3 -0)
1.1.1.3         10.2.2.2        128 Full      E    00:00:12     (+7 -0)
1.1.1.4         10.20.2.2       128 Full      E    00:00:12     (+7 -0)

                Neighbor(s) on interface ethernet0/1 (Area 0.0.0.0)
IpAddr/IfIndex RouterId         Pri State    Opt  Up           StateChg
-------------------------------------------------------------------------
1.1.1.2         172.25.113.145    1 2Way      E    00:00:21     (+3 -0)
1.1.1.2         172.25.113.177    1 2Way      E    00:00:10     (+4 -1)
1.1.1.3         10.2.2.2        128 Full      E    00:11:45     (+7 -0)
1.1.1.4         10.20.2.2       128 Full      E    00:11:57     (+7 -0)

                Neighbor(s) on interface ethernet0/3 (Area 0.0.0.0)
IpAddr/IfIndex RouterId         Pri State    Opt  Up           StateChg
-------------------------------------------------------------------------
2.1.1.2         172.25.113.145    1 2Way      E    00:00:41     (+3 -0)
2.1.1.2         172.25.113.177    1 2Way      E    00:00:22     (+4 -1)
2.1.1.3         10.3.3.2        128 Full      E    00:11:57     (+7 -0)
2.1.1.4         10.30.3.2       128 Full      E    00:11:57     (+7 -0)
```

As you can see from the output of `get vrouter trust-vr protocol ospf neighbor` when OSPF is configured in a traditional active-active topology, if `FIREWALL-B` fails, `FIREWALL-A` becomes its own neighbor and has multiple neighbors with the same neighbor address. This condition will continue until the dead interval expires, at which point `FIREWALL-A` will only be its own neighbor. When this happens, traffic flows can become unpredictable, network stability can suffer, and troubleshooting can become challenging.

There are two possible solutions to this problem: one we describe in Recipe 18.8; the other, described here, is to disable the failover component of NSRP and let the routing protocol handle failover. Figure 18-6 shows an example OSPF network.

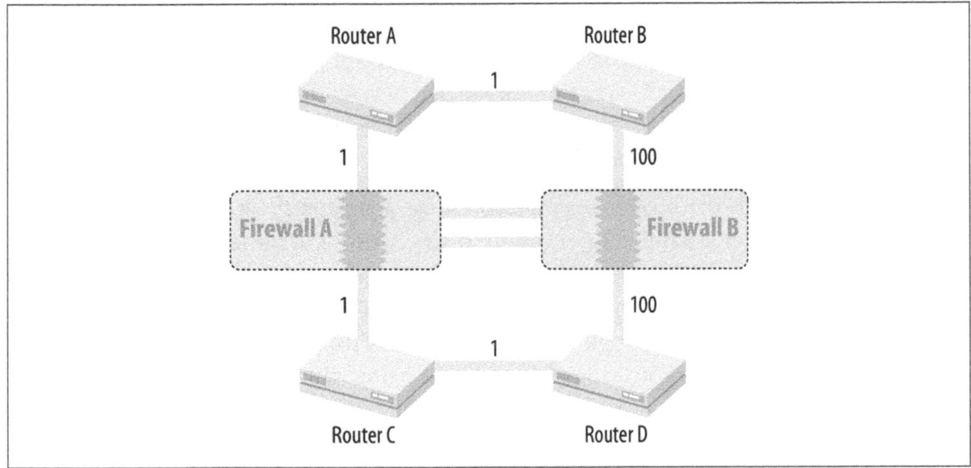

Figure 18-6. A standard VSD-less OSPF environment

In this network, OSPF costs are used to determine the active path, and point-to-point links are used. There are two reasons for using point-to-point links. The first is that if an intermediate switch layer connects `FIREWALL-A` to routers A and B, there is no way to deterministically cost the links. This will result in asymmetric routing. The second reason is to decrease failover time. To do this, point-to-point interfaces are used in many routed networks because link failure detection is typically faster than through a switched network. Furthermore, there is no need to go through the Designated Router/Backup Designated Router (DR/BDR) election process if the interface type is point-to-point. Although this recipe covers OSPF, conceptually the design parameters are the same for the Routing Information Protocol (RIP) and BGP, although the terminology will change.

To configure the firewalls for a network with the routing protocol controlling failover, first disable `vsd-group id 0`. When you enter the `unset nsrp vsd-group id 0` command, the firewalls no longer synchronize configuration information pertaining to interfaces. This includes IP addresses, all other interface-specific configuration, and static routes. When VSD-Group 0 is unset, each firewall maintains its own IP information, and as such, each must be configured independently on each firewall. At this point in the configuration, both firewalls show a "B" for backup in their prompt, indicating they are not masters of any sessions. RTOs for non-VSI sessions must be explicitly enabled for synchronization. The command `set nsrp rto-mirror session non-vsi` does this. When this command is entered, both firewalls' prompts change to "M," indicating that they can be the master of any sessions that arrive on the device.

One thing to note with a VSD-less cluster is that there is no synchronization of embryonic sessions and no HA data-path forwarding. An *embryonic session* is a session that is only partially created. This would be the case in a session where a `SYN` had been seen, but there was no `SYN-ACK` yet. Because NSRP determines whether to perform data-path forwarding based on the VSD-Group of the packet, and whether a session exists in its locally active VSD-Group for such a packet, it follows that when there is no VSD-Group, data won't be forwarded across the HA data link. This is, in fact, the behavior of NSRP. The consequence of this is that in a VSD-less cluster, asymmetric traffic is not supported at all.

Next, you configure the OSPF settings. Because asymmetry is not supported in a VSD-less topology, costs must be configured to ensure a symmetric path. Additionally, the interfaces are configured as OSPF point-to-point link types so as to avoid the overhead in electing and maintaining DR/BDR. In our sample network, all traffic will take the lowest-cost path through `FIREWALL-A`, unless this path becomes unavailable. In this case, once OSPF reconverges, all traffic will flow through `FIREWALL-B`.

VSD-less clusters represent a powerful tool for being able to deploy dynamically routed solutions with session synchronization. They provide all of the state information as a standard NSRP configuration while leaving the network failover component to a standard routing protocol. In many situations, network requirements may dictate that a dynamic protocol be run. As long as symmetry is maintained, VSD-less clusters provide an excellent way to accomplish this.

See Also

Recipe 18.1; Recipe 18.5; Recipe 18.12

18.8 Provide Subsecond Failover with NSRP and BGP

Problem

You need to run BGP on the firewalls and provide subsecond failover.

Solution

Disable VSD-Group 0, configure interfaces, and create a new VSD-Group for failover:

```
FWCLUSTER:FIREWALL-A(M)-> unset nsrp vsd-group id 0
FWCLUSTER:FIREWALL-A(B)-> set nsrp rto-mirror session non-vsi
FWCLUSTER:FIREWALL-A(M)-> set interface ethernet0/1 ip 1.1.1.1/24
FWCLUSTER:FIREWALL-A(M)-> set interface ethernet0/3 ip 2.1.1.1/24

FWCLUSTER:FIREWALL-B(M)-> set interface ethernet0/1 ip 1.1.1.2/24
FWCLUSTER:FIREWALL-B(M)-> set interface ethernet0/3 ip 2.1.1.2/24

FWCLUSTER:FIREWALL-A(M)-> set nsrp vsd-group id 1 priority 10
FWCLUSTER:FIREWALL-A(M)-> set interface ethernet0/1:1 ip 1.1.1.254/24
FWCLUSTER:FIREWALL-A(M)-> set interface ethernet0/3:1 ip 2.1.1.254/24
FWCLUSTER:FIREWALL-A(M)-> set nsrp vsd-group hb-interval 200
FWCLUSTER:FIREWALL-A(M)-> set nsrp monitor interface e0/1
FWCLUSTER:FIREWALL-A(M)-> set nsrp monitor interface e0/3

FWCLUSTER:FIREWALL-B(M)-> set nsrp monitor interface e0/1
FWCLUSTER:FIREWALL-B(M)-> set nsrp monitor interface e0/3
```

Configure BGP on the firewalls:

```
FWCLUSTER:FIREWALL-A(M)-> set vrouter trust-vr
FWCLUSTER:FIREWALL-A(trust-vr)(M)-> set protocol bgp 65535
FWCLUSTER:FIREWALL-A(trust-vr/bgp)(M)-> set enable
FWCLUSTER:FIREWALL-A(trust-vr/bgp)(M)-> set neighbor 1.1.1.3 remote-as
    65501
FWCLUSTER:FIREWALL-A(trust-vr/bgp)(M)-> set neighbor 1.1.1.4 remote-as
    65501
FWCLUSTER:FIREWALL-A(trust-vr/bgp)(M)-> set neighbor 2.1.1.3 remote-as
    65502
FWCLUSTER:FIREWALL-A(trust-vr/bgp)(M)-> set neighbor 2.1.1.4 remote-as
    65502
FWCLUSTER:FIREWALL-A(trust-vr/bgp)(M)-> set neighbor 1.1.1.3 enable
FWCLUSTER:FIREWALL-A(trust-vr/bgp)(M)-> set neighbor 1.1.1.4 enable
FWCLUSTER:FIREWALL-A(trust-vr/bgp)(M)-> set neighbor 2.1.1.4 enable
FWCLUSTER:FIREWALL-A(trust-vr/bgp)(M)-> set neighbor 2.1.1.3 enable
FWCLUSTER:FIREWALL-A(trust-vr/bgp)(M)-> unset synchronization
FWCLUSTER:FIREWALL-A(trust-vr/bgp)(M)-> end
FWCLUSTER:FIREWALL-A(M)-> set interface e0/1 protocol bgp
FWCLUSTER:FIREWALL-A(M)-> set interface e0/3 protocol bgp

FWCLUSTER:FIREWALL-B(M)-> set interface e0/1 protocol bgp
FWCLUSTER:FIREWALL-B(M)-> set interface e0/3 protocol bgp
```

Configure a route map so that BGP advertised routes are sent with a next-hop attribute of the VSI:

```
FWCLUSTER:FIREWALL-A(M)-> set vrouter trust-vr
FWCLUSTER:FIREWALL-A(trust-vr)(M)-> set access-list 10 permit
    ip 0.0.0.0/0 10
FWCLUSTER:FIREWALL-A(trust-vr)(M)-> set route-map name set-nh-vsi-
    Upstream permit 10
FWCLUSTER:FIREWALL-A(trust-vr/set-nh-vsi-upstream-10)(M)-> set match
    ip 10
FWCLUSTER:FIREWALL-A(trust-vr/set-nh-vsi-upstream-10)(M)-> set next-
    hop 1.1.1.254
```

```
FWCLUSTER:FIREWALL-A(trust-vr/set-nh-vsi-upstream-10)(M)-> exit
FWCLUSTER:FIREWALL-A(trust-vr)(M)-> set protocol bgp
FWCLUSTER:FIREWALL-A(trust-vr/bgp)(M)-> set neighbor 1.1.1.3 route-map
    set-nh-vsi-upstream out
FWCLUSTER:FIREWALL-A(trust-vr/bgp)(M)-> set neighbor 1.1.1.4 route-map
    set-nh-vsi-upstream out
FWCLUSTER:FIREWALL-A(trust-vr/bgp)(M)-> exit
FWCLUSTER:FIREWALL-A(trust-vr)(M)-> set route-map name
    set-nh-vsi-downstream permit 10
FWCLUSTER:FIREWALL-A(trust-vr/set-nh-vsi-downstream-10)(M)-> set match
    Ip 10
FWCLUSTER:FIREWALL-A(trust-vr/set-nh-vsi-downstream-10)(M)-> set next-
    Hop 2.1.1.254
FWCLUSTER:FIREWALL-A(trust-vr/set-nh-vsi-downstream-10)(M)-> exit
FWCLUSTER:FIREWALL-A(trust-vr)(M)-> set protocol bgp
FWCLUSTER:FIREWALL-A(trust-vr/bgp)(M)-> set neighbor 2.1.1.3 route-map
    set-nh-vsi-downstream out
FWCLUSTER:FIREWALL-A(trust-vr/bgp)(M)-> set neighbor 2.1.1.4 route-map
    set-nh-vsi-downstream out
FWCLUSTER:FIREWALL-A(trust-vr/bgp)(M)-> end
FWCLUSTER:FIREWALL-A(M)->
```

Finally, configure `FIREWALL-B` to advertise routes using an inactive interface for the next-hop:

```
FWCLUSTER:FIREWALL-B(M)-> set vrouter trust-vr adv-inact-interface
```

Discussion

BGP is a powerful protocol in any environment, and firewalls are no exception. In fact, the granular policy controls available in BGP make it an ideal routing protocol to run in a firewall environment. The biggest problem with running BGP in a firewall environment is that the failover timers are typically considered too slow. Although ScreenOS allows the configuration of BGP timers as low as a one-second keepalive and three-second hold timer, not all router vendors allow timers to be configured so low, and even so, if you can get subsecond failover, it's nice to have it. We examine this in greater detail starting with Figure 18-7, which shows a sample BGP network.

In Figure 18-7's environment, three separate ASs are used: one for the firewalls, and one each for the Trusted and Untrusted networks. This allows some control over the routes that the firewalls advertise. If there was a single AS, with the firewalls in the middle, they would not be able to control how routes were advertised from routers A and B to routers C and D because the advertisement would be direct from A to C, A to D, and so on. An IGP or static route would also be required. By using three separate ASs, the design is simplified and more control is retained.

BGP allows for granular modification of its attributes. One attribute that is frequently modified is `next-hop`. Usually, this is set to the value of `self` at EBGP boundaries so that AS-external routes do not need to be included in the IGP, but in our

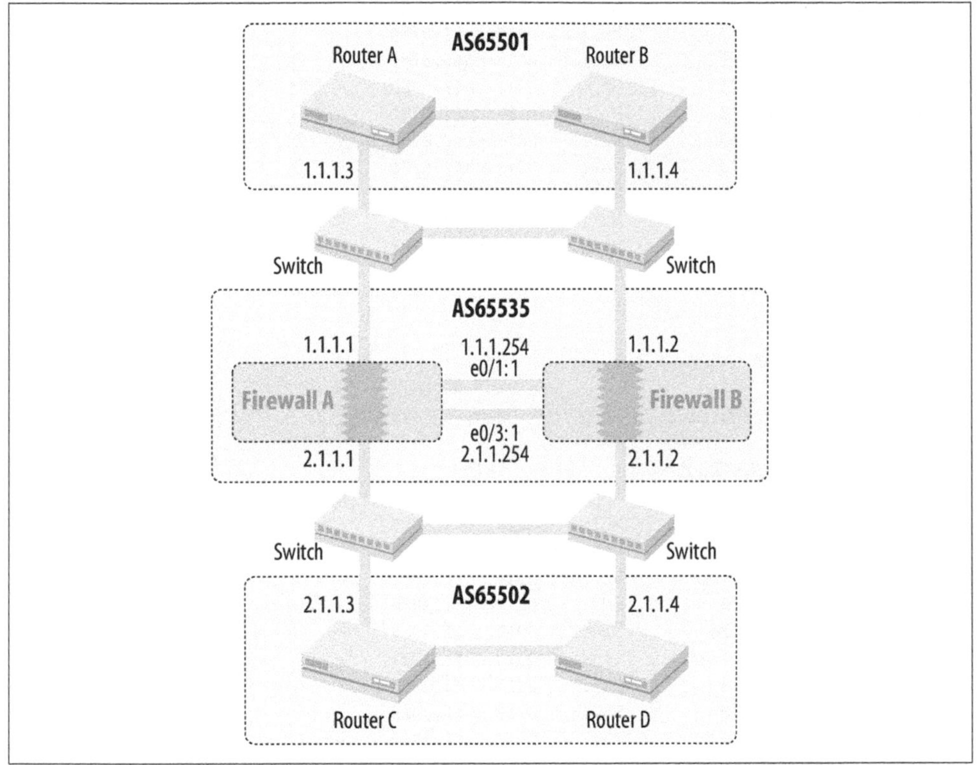

Figure 18-7. Running BGP with NSRP

case, we modify the next-hop setting to reflect the VSI address. By setting the next hop to the VSI, extremely fast convergence is provided.

The first step in getting this set up is to configure a VSD-less cluster under NSRP, as in Recipe 18.6. VSD-less clusters allow for the devices in a cluster to maintain unique interface configurations. As such, you need to configure the IP addresses independently on each device. Next, configure a new VSD-Group and a VSI on the `Trusted` and `Untrusted` interfaces. The state of the interfaces for both the VSI and non-VSI configured on both devices is as expected:

```
FWCLUSTER:FIREWALL-A(M)-> get int

A - Active, I - Inactive, U - Up, D - Down, R - Ready

Interfaces in vsys Root:
Name       IP Address          Zone    MAC            VLAN State  VSD
eth0/0     172.25.113.177/24 MGT     0017.cb47.8780    -    U     -
eth0/1     1.1.1.1/24          Untrust 0017.cb47.8785    -    U     -
eth0/1:1   1.1.1.254/24        Untrust 0010.dbff.2051    -    U     1
eth0/2     0.0.0.0/0           DMZ     0017.cb47.8786    -    U     -
eth0/3     2.1.1.1/24          Trust   0017.cb47.8787    -    U     -
eth0/3:1   2.1.1.254/24        Trust   0010.dbff.2071    -    U     1
```

```
eth0/4    0.0.0.0/0         Null    0017.cb47.8788   -  D   -
eth0/5    0.0.0.0/0         Null    0017.cb47.8789   -  D   -
eth0/6    0.0.0.0/0         Null    0017.cb47.878a   -  D   -
eth0/7    0.0.0.0/0         HA      0017.cb47.878b   -  U   -
eth0/8    0.0.0.0/0         HA      0017.cb47.878c   -  U   -
eth0/9    0.0.0.0/0         Null    0017.cb47.878d   -  D   -
bgroup0/0 0.0.0.0/0         Null    0017.cb47.878e   -  D   -
bgroup0/1 0.0.0.0/0         Null    0017.cb47.8795   -  D   -
bgroup0/2 0.0.0.0/0         Null    0017.cb47.8796   -  D   -
vlan1     0.0.0.0/0         VLAN    0017.cb47.878f   1  D   -
null      0.0.0.0/0         Null    N/A              -  U   0
```

On FIREWALL-B:

```
FWCLUSTER:FIREWALL-B(M)-> get int

A - Active, I - Inactive, U - Up, D - Down, R - Ready

Interfaces in vsys Root:
Name      IP Address        Zone    MAC            VLAN State  VSD
eth0/0    172.25.113.145/24 MGT     0017.cb41.3980   -  U   -
eth0/1    1.1.1.2/24        Untrust 0017.cb41.3985   -  U   -
eth0/1:1  1.1.1.254/24      Untrust 0010.dbff.2051   -  I   1
eth0/2    0.0.0.0/0         DMZ     0017.cb41.3986   -  U   -
eth0/3    2.1.1.2/24        Trust   0017.cb41.3987   -  U   -
eth0/3:1  2.1.1.254/24      Trust   0010.dbff.2071   -  I   1
eth0/4    0.0.0.0/0         Null    0017.cb41.3988   -  D   -
eth0/5    0.0.0.0/0         Null    0017.cb41.3989   -  D   -
eth0/6    0.0.0.0/0         Null    0017.cb41.398a   -  D   -
eth0/7    0.0.0.0/0         HA      0017.cb41.398b   -  U   -
eth0/8    0.0.0.0/0         HA      0017.cb41.398c   -  U   -
eth0/9    0.0.0.0/0         Null    0017.cb41.398d   -  D   -
bgroup0/0 0.0.0.0/0         Null    0017.cb41.398e   -  D   -
bgroup0/1 0.0.0.0/0         Null    0017.cb41.3995   -  D   -
bgroup0/2 0.0.0.0/0         Null    0017.cb41.3996   -  D   -
vlan1     0.0.0.0/0         VLAN    0017.cb41.398f   1  D   -
null      0.0.0.0/0         Null    N/A              -  U   0
```

The non-VSI interfaces are indeed properly set up on each device, as are the VSIs.

Next, configure BGP as you would in a standard BGP configuration. Again, because the interface-specific information is not synchronized when VSD-Group 0 is unset, you need to specifically enable BGP on each device. Once basic BGP is set up, configure route maps that match all traffic, and set the next-hop address to be the appropriate VSI. Apply these route maps to the appropriate neighbors. At this point, the upstream and downstream routers will send traffic to the VSI addresses of the firewall. When you apply the command `set vrouter trust-vr adv-inact-interface` to FIREWALL-B, the command allows the firewall to advertise the routes using the VSI for the next hop even though the interface is inactive on the device. You can see this in the routing table on ROUTER-A:

```
ROUTER-A.inet.0: 6 destinations, 10 routes (6 active, 0 holddown, 0
    hidden)
+ = Active Route, - = Last Active, * = Both

1.1.1.0/24         *[Direct/0] 00:29:06
                    > via fe-0/0/0.2
1.1.1.3/32         *[Local/0] 00:29:06
                      Local via fe-0/0/0.2
10.1.1.0/24        *[Static/5] 00:15:26
                      Reject
10.2.1.0/24        *[BGP/170] 00:00:12, localpref 100
                      AS path: I
                    > to 1.1.1.4 via fe-0/0/0.2
10.3.1.0/24        *[BGP/170] 00:07:02, localpref 100, from 1.1.1.2
                      AS path: 65535 65502 I
                    > to 1.1.1.254 via fe-0/0/0.2
                    [BGP/170] 00:07:02, localpref 100, from 1.1.1.1
                      AS path: 65535 65502 I
                    > to 1.1.1.254 via fe-0/0/0.2
                    [BGP/170] 00:04:24, localpref 100, from 1.1.1.4
                      AS path: 65535 65502 I
                    > to 1.1.1.254 via fe-0/0/0.2
10.4.1.0/24        *[BGP/170] 00:07:02, localpref 100, from 1.1.1.2
                      AS path: 65535 65502 I
                    > to 1.1.1.254 via fe-0/0/0.2
                    [BGP/170] 00:07:02, localpref 100, from 1.1.1.1
                      AS path: 65535 65502 I
                    > to 1.1.1.254 via fe-0/0/0.2
                    [BGP/170] 00:04:24, localpref 100, from 1.1.1.4
                      AS path: 65535 65502 I
                    > to 1.1.1.254 via fe-0/0/0.2
```

Both `FIREWALL-A` and `FIREWALL-B` advertise the routes identically, so that if there is a failover from `FIREWALL-A` to `FIREWALL-B`, traffic will continue to flow using the VSIs as the next hops. Eventually, the BGP sessions from the routers to `FIREWALL-A` will expire, and all routes learned from `FIREWALL-A` will be withdrawn and replaced with those from `FIREWALL-B`. Because the routes are identical, there will be no disruption from this event, as the network does not have to reconverge.

BGP is a terrific routing protocol to run on firewalls because of its intrinsic capabilities for applying policy to routing information. The ability to integrate so well with NSRP and to provide subsecond failover is powerful, and allows you the best of both worlds: providing subsecond failover, and the ease of administration provided with dynamic routing.

See Also

Chapter 17; Recipe 18.12

18.9 Synchronize Dynamic Routes in NSRP

Problem

You are running an active-passive NRSP cluster and you want to add dynamic routing.

Solution

Configure a dynamic routing protocol and enable route synchronization:

```
FWCLUSTER:FIREWALL-A(M)-> set vrouter trust-vr
FWCLUSTER:FIREWALL-A(trust-vr)(M)-> set protocol rip
FWCLUSTER:FIREWALL-A(trust-vr/rip)(M)-> set enable
FWCLUSTER:FIREWALL-A(trust-vr/rip)(M)-> end
FWCLUSTER:FIREWALL-A(M)-> set int e0/1 proto rip
FWCLUSTER:FIREWALL-A(M)-> set int e0/1 proto rip enable
FWCLUSTER:FIREWALL-A(M)-> set int e0/3 proto rip
FWCLUSTER:FIREWALL-A(M)-> set int e0/3 proto rip enable
FWCLUSTER:FIREWALL-A(M)-> set nsrp rto-mirror route
```

Discussion

The ability to synchronize routes from primary to backup devices in an NSRP cluster was added in ScreenOS 6.0. This capability removes the problems explored in Recipe 18.6 with establishing new neighbors upon failover. The solution employed is simply to synchronize the routes from the master to the backup, and the important keyword here is *routes*. Although routes are synchronized, the underlying entities from which the routing table is derived, such as the link state database in OSPF, are not synchronized. You can see this in the following output taken when OSPF is the protocol running on the firewalls:

```
FWCLUSTER:FIREWALL-B(B)-> get route


IPv4 Dest-Routes for <untrust-vr> (0 entries)
----------------------------------------------------------------------
H: Host C: Connected S: Static A: Auto-Exported
I: Imported R: RIP P: Permanent D: Auto-Discovered
N: NHRP
iB: IBGP eB: EBGP O: OSPF E1: OSPF external type 1
E2: OSPF external type 2 trailing B: backup route


IPv4 Dest-Routes for <trust-vr> (12 entries)
---------------------------------------------------------------------
   ID        IP-Prefix Interface      Gateway   P Pref  Mtr   Vsys
---------------------------------------------------------------------
*  45        1.1.1.1/32    eth0/1     0.0.0.0   H    0  0     Root
*  47        2.1.1.1/32    eth0/3     0.0.0.0   H    0  0     Root
*  73       10.3.3.2/32    eth0/3     2.1.1.3  OB   60  100   Root
```

```
*  72        10.2.2.2/32    eth0/1        1.1.1.3  OB   60  100   Root
*  74        10.30.3.2/32   eth0/3        2.1.1.4  OB   60  100   Root
*  75        10.20.2.2/32   eth0/1        1.1.1.4  OB   60  100   Root
*   1   172.25.113.0/24     eth0/0        0.0.0.0  C     0  0     Root
*   2 172.25.113.145/32     eth0/0        0.0.0.0  H     0  0     Root
*   4     172.25.0.0/16     eth0/0 172.25.113.1    S    20  1     Root
*   3     172.23.0.0/16     eth0/0 172.25.113.1    S    20  1     Root
*  46        2.1.1.0/24     eth0/3        0.0.0.0  C     0  0     Root
*  44        1.1.1.0/24     eth0/1        0.0.0.0  C     0  0     Root

FWCLUSTER:FIREWALL-B(B)-> get vrouter trust-vr protocol ospf database
VR: trust-vr RouterId: 172.25.113.145
----------------------------------
FWCLUSTER:FIREWALL-B(B)->
```

Although four routes are learned via OSPF (designated by OB in the protocol field, where the B means that it is a backup route), there are no entries in the link state database. The net effect of this is that OSPF, which has a fairly complex state machine, takes much longer to failover than RIP does. Figure 18-8 shows the network topology for this recipe's discussion.

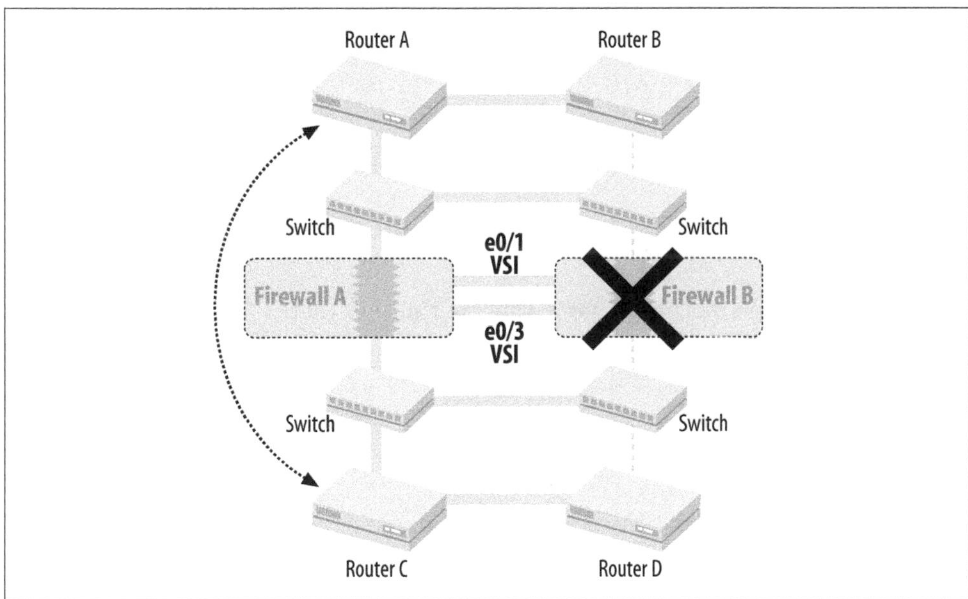

Figure 18-8. A simple active-passive network

Operationally, the network is virtually identical to the simple active-passive design from Recipe 18.1. RIP was chosen for this recipe because it is simple to operate and understand, and from a failover perspective, it performs well in this scenario. The reason for RIP's seamless failover is that RIP simply relies on advertisements from its neighbors to build its routing table; no real state is involved. When you enable RIP, verify that you are seeing RIP-learned routes on FIREWALL-A by looking at the routing table:

```
FWCLUSTER:FIREWALL-A(M)-> get route protocol rip


IPv4 Dest-Routes for <untrust-vr> (0 entries)
----------------------------------------------------------------------
H: Host C: Connected S: Static A: Auto-Exported
I: Imported R: RIP P: Permanent D: Auto-Discovered
N: NHRP
iB: IBGP eB: EBGP O: OSPF E1: OSPF external type 1
E2: OSPF external type 2 trailing B: backup route


IPv4 Dest-Routes for <trust-vr> (18 entries)
----------------------------------------------------------------------
     ID       IP-Prefix  Interface     Gateway   P Pref    Mtr      Vsys
----------------------------------------------------------------------
*    74     10.3.3.2/32     eth0/3     2.1.1.3   R  100      2      Root
*    78     10.2.2.2/32     eth0/1     1.1.1.3   R  100      2      Root
*    76    10.30.3.2/32     eth0/3     2.1.1.4   R  100      2      Root
*    80    10.20.2.2/32     eth0/1     1.1.1.4   R  100      2      Root
*    75     10.4.1.0/24     eth0/3     2.1.1.4   R  100      2      Root
*    77     10.1.1.0/24     eth0/1     1.1.1.3   R  100      2      Root
*    79     10.2.1.0/24     eth0/1     1.1.1.4   R  100      2      Root
*    73     10.3.1.0/24     eth0/3     2.1.1.3   R  100      2      Root

Total number of rip routes: 8
```

On FIREWALL-B:

```
FWCLUSTER:FIREWALL-B(B)-> get route protocol rip


IPv4 Dest-Routes for <untrust-vr> (0 entries)
----------------------------------------------------------------------
H: Host C: Connected S: Static A: Auto-Exported
I: Imported R: RIP P: Permanent D: Auto-Discovered
N: NHRP
iB: IBGP eB: EBGP O: OSPF E1: OSPF external type 1
E2: OSPF external type 2 trailing B: backup route


IPv4 Dest-Routes for <trust-vr> (8 entries)
----------------------------------------------------------------------
    ID      IP-Prefix     Interface     Gateway   P Pref   Mtr   Vsys
----------------------------------------------------------------------

Total number of rip routes: 0
```

The problem is that route synchronization is not a default setting in NSRP. It's confusing because static routes are synchronized in NSRP because they are a part of the configuration. Dynamic routes are not a part of the configuration; they are independently learned, and are thus not synchronized by default. When you enable route synchronization with the command set `nsrp rto-mirror route`, check `FIREWALL-B` again, to see the following:

```
FWCLUSTER:FIREWALL-B(B)-> get route protocol rip


IPv4 Dest-Routes for <untrust-vr> (0 entries)
-----------------------------------------------------------------
H: Host C: Connected S: Static A: Auto-Exported
I: Imported R: RIP P: Permanent D: Auto-Discovered
N: NHRP
iB: IBGP eB: EBGP O: OSPF E1: OSPF external type 1
E2: OSPF external type 2 trailing B: backup route


IPv4 Dest-Routes for <trust-vr> (16 entries)
-----------------------------------------------------------------
   ID       IP-Prefix  Interface   Gateway   P Pref  Mtr     Vsys
-----------------------------------------------------------------
*  77     10.3.3.2/32     eth0/3   2.1.1.3  RB  100    2      Root
*  81     10.2.2.2/32     eth0/1   1.1.1.3  RB  100    2      Root
*  79    10.30.3.2/32     eth0/3   2.1.1.4  RB  100    2      Root
*  83    10.20.2.2/32     eth0/1   1.1.1.4  RB  100    2      Root
*  78     10.4.1.0/24     eth0/3   2.1.1.4  RB  100    2      Root
*  80     10.1.1.0/24     eth0/1   1.1.1.3  RB  100    2      Root
*  82     10.2.1.0/24     eth0/1   1.1.1.4  RB  100    2      Root
*  76     10.3.1.0/24     eth0/3   2.1.1.3  RB  100    2      Root

Total number of rip routes: 8
```

Clearly, it is getting the desired routes via RIP. On `FIREWALL-B`, there's a new type of route. Although the routes are the same and are learned via RIP, they also have "backup" as a protocol associated with them, indicating the routes are learned via RTO synchronization from an NSRP peer. If `FIREWALL-A` fails, traffic fails over in normal NSRP times, and traffic continues to route. Because the routers in the network only need to receive a RIP advertisement for the networks before they expire their last advertisements, the routing table remains static. As the hold time for RIP is typically much larger than NSRP's failover time, no disruption of traffic should occur.

See Also

Chapter 14; Recipe 18.1

18.10 Create a Stateful Failover for an IPSec Tunnel

Problem

You need to provide stateful failover for an IP Security (IPSec) tunnel.

Solution

Configure an active-passive cluster:

```
FIREWALL-A-> set nsrp cluster id 1
FIREWALL-A(M)-> set nsrp cluster name FWCLUSTER
FWCLUSTER:FIREWALL-A(M)-> set nsrp vsd-group id 0 priority 10

FIREWALL-B-> set nsrp cluster id 1
FIREWALL-B(B)-> set nsrp cluster name FWCLUSTER
FWCLUSTER:FIREWALL-B(B)-> save
FWCLUSTER:FIREWALL-B(B)-> exec nsrp sync global-config saved
FWCLUSTER:FIREWALL-B(B)-> reset
```

Once FIREWALL-B comes back online, finish the configuration by enabling RTO synchronization, configuring timers, and setting up monitoring parameters:

```
FWCLUSTER:FIREWALL-A(M)-> set nsrp rto-mirror sync
FWCLUSTER:FIREWALL-A(M)-> set nsrp vsd-group hb-interval 200
FWCLUSTER:FIREWALL-A(M)-> set nsrp monitor interface ethernet0/1
FWCLUSTER:FIREWALL-A(M)-> set nsrp monitor interface ethernet0/3
FWCLUSTER:FIREWALL-B(M)-> set nsrp monitor interface ethernet0/1
FWCLUSTER:FIREWALL-B(M)-> set nsrp monitor interface ethernet0/3
```

Configure the tunnel normally, using the outgoing VSI. In this case, we use the default VSD-Group of 0:

```
FWCLUSTER:FIREWALL-A(M)-> set ike gateway ROUTER-A address 1.1.1.3
    main outgoing-interface ethernet0/1 preshare scrnosckbk sec-level
    standard
FWCLUSTER:FIREWALL-A(M)-> set vpn ROUTER-A gateway ROUTER-A sec-level
    standard
FWCLUSTER:FIREWALL-A(M)-> set interface tunnel.1 zone trust
FWCLUSTER:FIREWALL-A(M)-> set interface tunnel.1 ip unnumbered
    interface ethernet0/3
FWCLUSTER:FIREWALL-A(M)-> set vpn ROUTER-A bind interface tunnel.1
FWCLUSTER:FIREWALL-A(M)-> set vpn ROUTER-A monitor optimized rekey
```

Discussion

NSRP is exceptional at providing redundancy in an IPSec environment, and ScreenOS in general has a large number of ways to do this. NSRP is probably the fastest in terms of being able to restore service to a broken network. Because SAs are synchronized between NSRP peers, the failover characteristics of NSRP with respect to IPSec are the same as those in a firewalled environment. Aside from the high speed of failover seen with NSRP, the real benefit of synchronizing SAs is that the establishment of SAs on the backup device is a gradual process. In failover schemes where SAs are not synchronized, the net effect is a storm of IKE negotiations that are processor-intensive. Because SAs are transferred to an NSRP peer as they are created, there is no SA storm. To further lessen the chances of this happening, you can set the Phase 2 proposal lifetimes in KB, instead of in seconds, so that the remote sites rekey at a (theoretically) more random interval. To do this, use the `set ike p2-proposal nsrp-aes group2 esp aes128 sha-1 kbyte 10000` command and reference this proposal in the VPN configuration as opposed to the `sec-level`.

When using dynamically routed VPNs, use the RTO route synchronization setting as described in Recipe 18.9; otherwise, traffic will be disrupted after a failover, despite the fact that the SAs are preestablished. Because a VSI is required for SA synchronization, you can use VSD-less clusters effectively only for a purely route-based failover.

Configuring IPSec with NSRP is really no different from configuring IPSec tunnels in nonredundant mode. The only requirement is to ensure that the tunnel is terminated on the VSI itself. When the tunnel is terminated on the VSI, all SAs are synchronized to the NSRP peer. You can see this when the SA is established on `FIREWALL-A`:

```
FWCLUSTER:FIREWALL-A(M)-> get sa
total configured sa: 1
HEX ID    Gateway   Port Algorithm    SPI  Life:sec kb Sta PID vsys
00000002<     1.1.1.3 500 esp: des/md5 27182b9f  3261 unlim A/- -1 0
00000002>     1.1.1.3 500 esp: des/md5 988fd8fc  3261 unlim A/- -1 0
```

Examining the same on `FIREWALL-B`, the SPIs of the SAs match those on `FIREWALL-A`:

```
FWCLUSTER:FIREWALL-B(B)-> get sa
total configured sa: 1
HEX ID    Gateway   Port Algorithm    SPI  Life:sec kb Sta PID vsys
00000002<     1.1.1.3 500 esp: des/md5 27182b9f  3278 unlim A/- -1 0
00000002>     1.1.1.3 500 esp: des/md5 988fd8fc  3278 unlim A/- -1 0
```

As with other RTOs that are synchronized between cluster members, SAs are seamlessly failed over from one device to another.

NSRP with IPSec is recommended for VPN deployments where redundancy is required. As with NSRP in a standard firewall mode, you can run NSRP with IPSec in either an active-passive or an active-active mode.

See Also

Chapter 13; Recipe 18.1; Recipe 18.5; Recipe 18.8

18.11 Configure NAT in an Active-Active Cluster

Problem

You need to configure NAT with NSRP in active-active mode.

Solution

Set up a standard NSRP cluster:

```
FIREWALL-A-> set nsrp cluster id 1
FIREWALL-A(M)-> set nsrp cluster name FWCLUSTER
FWCLUSTER:FIREWALL-A(M)-> set nsrp vsd-group id 0 priority 10

FIREWALL-B-> set nsrp cluster id 1
FIREWALL-B(B)-> set nsrp vsd-group id 1 priority 10
FWCLUSTER:FIREWALL-B(B)-> save
FWCLUSTER:FIREWALL-B(B)-> exec nsrp sync global-config saved
FWCLUSTER:FIREWALL-B(B)-> reset
```

Once `FIREWALL-B` comes back online, continue the configuration by enabling RTO synchronization, configuring timers, and setting up monitoring parameters:

```
FWCLUSTER:FIREWALL-A(M)-> set nsrp rto-mirror sync
FWCLUSTER:FIREWALL-A(M)-> set nsrp vsd-group hb-interval 200
FWCLUSTER:FIREWALL-A(M)-> set nsrp data-forwarding
FWCLUSTER:FIREWALL-A(M)-> set nsrp monitor interface ethernet0/1
FWCLUSTER:FIREWALL-A(M)-> set nsrp monitor interface ethernet0/3
FWCLUSTER:FIREWALL-B(M)-> set nsrp monitor interface ethernet0/1
FWCLUSTER:FIREWALL-B(M)-> set nsrp monitor interface ethernet0/3
```

Finally, ensure that the two devices remain active when possible by configuring `preempt` for the appropriate groups, and setting `master-always-exist`:

```
FWCLUSTER:FIREWALL-A(M)-> set nsrp vsd-group id 0 preempt
FWCLUSTER:FIREWALL-A(M)-> set nsrp vsd-group id 0 preempt hold-down 90
FWCLUSTER:FIREWALL-A(M)-> set nsrp vsd-group master-always-exist
FWCLUSTER:FIREWALL-B(M)-> set nsrp vsd-group id 1 preempt
FWCLUSTER:FIREWALL-B(M)-> set nsrp vsd-group id 1 preempt hold-down 90
```

Create dynamic IPs (DIPs), assign the DIPs to a group, and use the group DIP ID in the policy:

```
FWCLUSTER:FIREWALL-B(M)-> set interface e0/1 dip 4 1.1.1.10
FWCLUSTER:FIREWALL-B(M)-> set interface e0/1:1 dip 5 1.1.1.20
FWCLUSTER:FIREWALL-B(M)-> set dip group 6 member 4
FWCLUSTER:FIREWALL-B(M)-> set dip group 6 member 5
FWCLUSTER:FIREWALL-B(M)-> set policy from trust to untrust any any any
    nat src dip-id 6 permit log
```

Discussion

ScreenOS requires that an interface be used, to which one can bind the NAT. This presents a problem with an NSRP scenario, because you can reference only a single DIP in a policy—the DIP must be assigned to the appropriate VSI. With DIP ID 4 applied to interface e0/1 and assigned to the policy, traffic fails to pass. Using `debug flow basic`, you can see the following:

```
FWCLUSTER:FIREWALL-B(M)-> get db str
****** 393954.0: <Trust/ethernet0/3:1> packet received [84]******
  ipid = 41531(a23b), @1d52f114
  packet passed sanity check.
  Ethernet0/3:1:2.1.1.4/0->1.1.1.4/14641,1(8/0)<Root>
  no session found
  flow_first_sanity_check: in <ethernet0/3:1>, out <N/A>
  chose interface ethernet0/3:1 as incoming nat if.
  Flow_first_routing: in <ethernet0/3:1>, out <N/A>
  search route to (ethernet0/3:1, 2.1.1.4->1.1.1.4) in vr trust-vr
    for  vsd-1/flag-0/ifp-null
  [ Dest] 104.route 1.1.1.4->1.1.1.4, to ethernet0/1:1
  routed (x_dst_ip 1.1.1.4) from ethernet0/3:1 (ethernet0/3:1 in 1)
    to ethernet0/1:1
  policy search from zone 2-> zone 1
 policy_flow_search  policy search nat_crt from zone 2-> zone 1
  RPC Mapping Table search returned 0 matched service(s) for (vsys
    Root, ip 1.1.1.4, port 45381, proto 1)
  No SW RPC rule match, search HW rule
  Permitted by policy 1
  dip alloc failed. Dip_id = 0
  packet dropped, dip alloc failed
```

Clearly, there's a problem. To address this, create a new DIP, ID 5, and apply it to `e0/1:1`. Then assign both DIPs to a DIP group, and apply the DIP group to the policy. Once you do this, you'll see the following in the debug:

```
FWCLUSTER:FIREWALL-B(M)-> get db str
****** 394293.0: <Trust/ethernet0/3:1> packet received [84]******
  ipid = 42134(a496), @1d5ee114
  packet passed sanity check.
  Ethernet0/3:1:2.1.1.4/0->1.1.1.4/14897,1(8/0)<Root>
  no session found
  flow_first_sanity_check: in <ethernet0/3:1>, out <N/A>
  chose interface ethernet0/3:1 as incoming nat if.
  Flow_first_routing: in <ethernet0/3:1>, out <N/A>
  search route to (ethernet0/3:1, 2.1.1.4->1.1.1.4) in vr trust-vr
    for vsd-1/flag-0/ifp-null
  [ Dest] 104.route 1.1.1.4->1.1.1.4, to ethernet0/1:1
  routed (x_dst_ip 1.1.1.4) from ethernet0/3:1 (ethernet0/3:1
in 1) to ethernet0/1:1
  policy search from zone 2-> zone 1
 policy_flow_search  policy search nat_crt from zone 2-> zone 1
```

```
RPC Mapping Table search returned 0 matched service(s) for (vsys
  Root, ip 1.1.1.4, port 42285, proto 1)
No SW RPC rule match, search HW rule
Permitted by policy 1
dip id = 5, 2.1.1.4/0->1.1.1.20/1024
choose interface ethernet0/1:1 as outgoing phy if
check nsrp pak fwd: in_tun=0xffffffff, VSD 1 for out ifp
ethernet0/1:1 vsd 1 is active
no loop on ifp ethernet0/1.
No loop on ifp ethernet0/1:1.
Session application type 0, name None, nas_id 0, timeout 60sec
service lookup identified service 0.
Flow_first_final_check: in <ethernet0/3:1>, out <ethernet0/1:1>
install vector flow_nsrp_fwd_vector
install vector flow_ttl_vector
install vector flow_l2prepare_xlate_vector
install vector flow_frag_list_vector
install vector flow_fragging_vector
install vector flow_send_shape_vector
install vector NULL
create new vector list 21-50065c4.
Session (id:55979) created for first pak 21
flow_first_install_session======>
route to 1.1.1.4
arp entry found for 1.1.1.4
ifp2 ethernet0/1:1, out_ifp ethernet0/1:1, flag 00800800, tunnel
  ffffffff, rc 1
outgoing wing prepared, ready
handle cleartext reverse route
search route to (ethernet0/1:1, 1.1.1.4->2.1.1.4) in vr trust-vr
  for vsd-1/flag-3000/ifp-ethernet0/3:1
[ Dest] 106.route 2.1.1.4->2.1.1.4, to ethernet0/3:1
route to 2.1.1.4
arp entry found for 2.1.1.4
ifp2 ethernet0/3:1, out_ifp ethernet0/3:1, flag 00800801, tunnel
  ffffffff, rc 1
nsrp msg sent.
Flow got session.
Flow session id 55979
vsd 1 is active
post addr xlation: 1.1.1.20->1.1.1.4.
flow_send_vector_, vid = 0, is_layer2_if=0
```

From this output, it appears as though DIP ID 5—which is what was assigned to `ethernet0/1:1`—is being used for the translation. Looking at the actual policy, you can see that the DIP ID referenced in the policy is actually DIP ID 6, which is the DIP group:

```
FWCLUSTER:FIREWALL-B(M)-> get policy id 1
name:"none" (id 1), zone Trust -> Untrust,action Permit, status
"enabled"
src "Any", dst "Any", serv "ANY"
Policies on this vpn tunnel: 0
nat src dip-id 6, Web filtering disabled
```

```
vpn unknown vpn, policy flag 00010020, session backup: on
traffic shapping off, scheduler n/a, serv flag 00
log close, log count 2, alert no, counter no(0) byte
rate(sec/min) 0/0
total octets 392, counter(session/packet/octet) 0/0/0
priority 7, diffserv marking Off
tadapter: state off, gbw/mbw 0/0 policing (no)
No Authentication
No User, User Group or Group expression set
```

In an active-passive mode, no special configuration is required; however, active-active mode using NAT requires the use of DIP groups to apply within the policy so that the VSD-specific NAT translations can be used. NAT itself is a powerful tool when used with NSRP in active-active mode because it is a way to engineer traffic to remain symmetrical. With SRC NAT provided by DIPs, a symmetric path can be ensured. When possible, NAT is recommended in active-active topologies to assist with maintaining symmetry.

See Also

Chapter 4; Recipe 18.5

18.12 Configure NAT in a VSD-Less Cluster

Problem

You need to configure NAT and are using a VSD-less cluster.

Solution

Configure a standard VSD-less cluster:

```
FWCLUSTER:FIREWALL-A(M)-> unset nsrp vsd-group id 0
FWCLUSTER:FIREWALL-A(B)-> set nsrp rto-mirror session non-vsi
FWCLUSTER:FIREWALL-A(M)-> set interface e0/1 ip 1.1.1.1/24
FWCLUSTER:FIREWALL-A(M)-> set interface e0/3 ip 2.1.1.1/24

FWCLUSTER:FIREWALL-B(M)-> set inte e0/1 ip 1.1.2.1/24
FWCLUSTER:FIREWALL-B(M)-> set inte e0/3 ip 2.1.2.1/24
```

Enable OSPF on each device:

```
FWCLUSTER:FIREWALL-A(M)-> set vrouter trust-vr
FWCLUSTER:FIREWALL-A(trust-vr)(M)-> set protocol ospf
FWCLUSTER:FIREWALL-A(trust-vr/ospf)(M)-> set area 0
FWCLUSTER:FIREWALL-A(trust-vr/ospf)(M)-> set enable
FWCLUSTER:FIREWALL-A(trust-vr/ospf)(M)-> end
FWCLUSTER:FIREWALL-A(M)-> set interface ethernet0/1 protocol ospf
    area 0
FWCLUSTER:FIREWALL-A(M)-> set interface ethernet0/1 protocol ospf
    link-type p2p
FWCLUSTER:FIREWALL-A(M)-> set interface ethernet0/1 protocol ospf
    enable
```

```
FWCLUSTER:FIREWALL-A(M)-> set interface ethernet0/3 protocol ospf
    area 0
FWCLUSTER:FIREWALL-A(M)-> set interface ethernet0/3 protocol ospf
    link-type p2p
FWCLUSTER:FIREWALL-A(M)-> set interface ethernet0/3 protocol ospf
    enable

FWCLUSTER:FIREWALL-B(M)-> set interface ethernet0/1 protocol ospf
    area 0
FWCLUSTER:FIREWALL-B(M)-> set interface ethernet0/3 protocol ospf
    area 0
FWCLUSTER:FIREWALL-B(M)-> set interface ethernet0/1 protocol ospf
    cost 100
FWCLUSTER:FIREWALL-B(M)-> set interface ethernet0/3 protocol ospf
    cost 100
FWCLUSTER:FIREWALL-B(M)-> set interface ethernet0/1 protocol ospf
    link-type p2p
FWCLUSTER:FIREWALL-B(M)-> set interface ethernet0/3 protocol ospf
    link-type p2p
FWCLUSTER:FIREWALL-B(M)-> set interface ethernet0/1 protocol ospf
    enable
FWCLUSTER:FIREWALL-B(M)-> set interface ethernet0/3 protocol ospf
    enable
```

Configure identical loopback addresses on each device:

```
FWCLUSTER:FIREWALL-A(M)-> set interface lo.1 zone untrust
FWCLUSTER:FIREWALL-A(M)-> set interface lo.1 ip 1.10.1.1/24

FWCLUSTER:FIREWALL-B(M)-> set int lo.1 zone untrust
FWCLUSTER:FIREWALL-B(M)-> set int lo.1 ip 1.10.1.1/24
```

Next, enable OSPF on the loopback interfaces in passive mode, configure the cost on FIREWALL-B to be 100, and configure interface monitoring:

```
FWCLUSTER:FIREWALL-A(M)-> set interface lo.1 protocol ospf area 0
FWCLUSTER:FIREWALL-A(M)-> set interface lo.1 protocol ospf passive
FWCLUSTER:FIREWALL-A(M)-> set interface lo.1 protocol ospf enable
FWCLUSTER:FIREWALL-A(M)-> set interface lo.1 monitor interface
    ethernet0/3

FWCLUSTER:FIREWALL-B(M)-> set interface lo.1 protocol ospf area 0
FWCLUSTER:FIREWALL-B(M)-> set interface lo.1 protocol ospf passive
FWCLUSTER:FIREWALL-B(M)-> set interface lo.1 protocol ospf cost 100
FWCLUSTER:FIREWALL-B(M)-> set interface lo.1 protocol ospf enable
FWCLUSTER:FIREWALL-B(M)-> set interface lo.1 monitor interface
    ethernet0/3
```

Configure identical DIPs on each device, and assign the egress interface to a loopback group:

```
FWCLUSTER:FIREWALL-A(M)-> set interface lo.1 dip 10 1.10.1.2
FWCLUSTER:FIREWALL-A(M)-> set interface e0/1 loopback-group loopback.1

FWCLUSTER:FIREWALL-B(M)-> set interface lo.1 dip 10 1.10.1.2
```

Finally, create a policy referencing the DIP:

```
FWCLUSTER:FIREWALL-A(M)-> set policy from "Trust" to "Untrust"  "Any"
    "Any" "ANY" nat src dip-id 10 permit
```

Discussion

Because NAT in ScreenOS is interface-dependent, VSD-less clusters as described in Recipe 18.6 pose an interesting challenge. In a VSD-less cluster, the routing protocol handles failover and NSRP handles session synchronization. To create the appropriate adjacencies and enforce symmetry, you independently configure each link in its own subnet. DIPs typically reside in the interface subnet, so in a VSD-less cluster, they run into problems because each egress interface has its own subnet. To address this, you can tie DIPs to loopback addresses, which you then anycast to the network. It is critical that you use the same IP address for translation when there is a failover, or state will break, not just on the firewall side but on the destination side as well. Assume that the connection being NAT'd is a Telnet session. If, during a failover, the source IP were to change, the server would clearly reject any packets and the session would have to be reestablished.

In an anycast scenario, identical routes are advertised to the network at different points. This type of announcement is frequently used in Protocol Independent Multicast (PIM) networks for Rendezvous Point (RP) announcement, as well as for stateless protocols such as Domain Name System (DNS). Because ScreenOS synchronizes state, anycast can work for stateful protocols as well. In our recipe, the loopback address is anycast to the network with a higher cost on `FIREWALL-B`. This is done to enforce symmetry. When we examine the adjacent router's link-state database, you can see that we have achieved the desired result:

```
FWCLUSTER:FIREWALL-A(M)-> get vr trust router-id
vrouter trust-vr router-id for BGP and OSPF is 172.25.113.177

FWCLUSTER:FIREWALL-B(M)-> get vr trust router-id
vrouter trust-vr router-id for BGP and OSPF is 172.25.113.145

Router   172.25.113.145   172.25.113.145   0x80000052   104  0x22
    0x576  60
  bits 0x0, link count 3
  id 1.10.1.0, data 255.255.255.0, Type Stub (3)
  TOS count 0, TOS 0 metric 100
  id 2.1.10.2, data 2.1.10.2, Type Transit (2)
  TOS count 0, TOS 0 metric 100
  id 1.1.10.2, data 1.1.10.2, Type Transit (2)
  TOS count 0, TOS 0 metric 100
  Aging timer 00:58:15
  Installed 00:01:40 ago, expires in 00:58:16, sent 00:01:38 ago
  Last changed 00:31:42 ago, Change count: 17
Router   172.25.113.177   172.25.113.177   0x80000038   1084  0x22
    0x9056  60
  bits 0x0, link count 3
```

```
id 1.10.1.0, data 255.255.255.0, Type Stub (3)
TOS count 0, TOS 0 metric 1
id 1.1.1.3, data 1.1.1.1, Type Transit (2)
TOS count 0, TOS 0 metric 1
id 2.1.1.3, data 2.1.1.1, Type Transit (2)
TOS count 0, TOS 0 metric 1
Aging timer 00:41:55
Installed 00:18:03 ago, expires in 00:41:56, sent 00:18:03 ago
Last changed 00:18:03 ago, Change count: 33
```

`FIREWALL-B`'s router LSA, `1.10.1.0/24`, has a metric of 100, whereas in `FIREWALL-A`, the metric is 1. This means that return traffic to the loopback address will always go through `FIREWALL-A` as long as the network is operational. When using loopback addresses, however, it is necessary to tie their fate to that of at least one physical address. Figure 18-9 illustrates a standard VSD-less cluster.

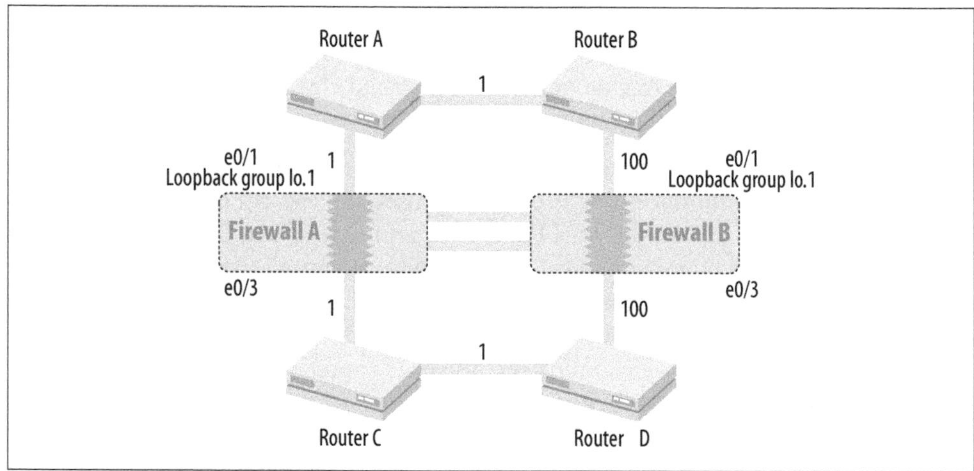

Figure 18-9. A standard VSD-less cluster

If the link on interface `ethernet0/1` from `FIREWALL-A` to `ROUTER-A` goes down, `ROUTER-A` will no longer have a valid route to the loopback address and the DIP. If, however, the link on interface `ethernet0/3` from `FIREWALL-A` to `ROUTER-C` goes down, `ROUTER-A` will retain the route to the loopback address, and traffic will be disrupted because an asymmetric path will arise. In this scenario, traffic going from `ROUTER-C` to `ROUTER-A` will follow the path through `ROUTER-D`, `FIREWALL-B`, and `ROUTER-B`. However, because both firewalls are NAT'ing to the same address to ensure continued connectivity if there's a network failure, when `ROUTER-A` sends the reply to the packet, the route to the destination goes to `FIREWALL-A`, which will drop the packet.

To get around this problem, the fate of the loopback interface is tied to that of the physical address. When the `set interface lo.1 monitor interface ethernet0/3` command is entered, if `ethernet0/3` goes down, `lo.1` will also be declared down, and `FIREWALL-A` will send an LSA update. See this in action by disabling interface `ethernet0/3`:

```
FWCLUSTER:FIREWALL-A(M)-> get interface

A - Active, I - Inactive, U - Up, D - Down, R - Ready

Interfaces in vsys Root:
Name         IP Address         Zone      MAC            VLAN State VSD
eth0/0       172.25.113.177/24  MGT       0017.cb47.8780    -   U   -
eth0/1       1.1.1.1/24         Untrust   0017.cb47.8785    -   U   -
eth0/2       0.0.0.0/0          DMZ       0017.cb47.8786    -   U   -
eth0/3       2.1.1.1/24         Trust     0017.cb47.8787    -   U   -
eth0/4       0.0.0.0/0          Null      0017.cb47.8788    -   D   -
eth0/5       0.0.0.0/0          Null      0017.cb47.8789    -   D   -
eth0/6       0.0.0.0/0          Null      0017.cb47.878a    -   D   -
eth0/7       0.0.0.0/0          HA        0017.cb47.878b    -   U   -
eth0/8       0.0.0.0/0          HA        0017.cb47.878c    -   U   -
eth0/9       0.0.0.0/0          Null      0017.cb47.878d    -   D   -
bgroup0/0    0.0.0.0/0          Null      0017.cb47.878e    -   D   -
bgroup0/1    0.0.0.0/0          Null      0017.cb47.8795    -   D   -
bgroup0/2    0.0.0.0/0          Null      0017.cb47.8796    -   D   -
loopback.1   1.10.1.1/24        Untrust   N/A               -   U   -
vlan1        0.0.0.0/0          VLAN      0017.cb47.878f    1   D   -
null         0.0.0.0/0          Null      N/A               -   U   0

FWCLUSTER:FIREWALL-A(trust-vr/ospf)(M)-> get database detail self
VR: trust-vr RouterId: 172.25.113.177
                        Router LSA(s) in area 0.0.0.0
                        --------------------------------
Age:  8
Seq Number: 0x8000004b
Checksum: 0x6a69
Advertising Router: 172.25.113.177
Link State ID: 172.25.113.177
Length: 60
Options:   Extern     DC
Flags: ,,, Links 3
Link# 1
                Link State ID: 1.10.1.0
                Link Data: 255.255.255.0
                Type: 3
                TOS: 0
                Metric: 1

Link# 2
                Link State ID: 1.1.1.3
                Link Data: 1.1.1.1
                Type: 2
                TOS: 0
                Metric: 1

Link# 3
                Link State ID: 2.1.1.3
                Link Data: 2.1.1.1
                Type: 2
```

```
                TOS: 0
                Metric: 1

FWCLUSTER:FIREWALL-A(M)-> set interface ethernet0/3 phy link-down
FWCLUSTER:FIREWALL-A(M)-> get interface

A - Active, I - Inactive, U - Up, D - Down, R - Ready

Interfaces in vsys Root:
Name        IP Address        Zone    MAC            VLAN State VSD
eth0/0      172.25.113.177/24 MGT     0017.cb47.8780   -    U    -
eth0/1      1.1.1.1/24        Untrust 0017.cb47.8785   -    U    -
eth0/2      0.0.0.0/0         DMZ     0017.cb47.8786   -    U    -
eth0/3      2.1.1.1/24        Trust   0017.cb47.8787   -    D    -
eth0/4      0.0.0.0/0         Null    0017.cb47.8788   -    D    -
eth0/5      0.0.0.0/0         Null    0017.cb47.8789   -    D    -
eth0/6      0.0.0.0/0         Null    0017.cb47.878a   -    D    -
eth0/7      0.0.0.0/0         HA      0017.cb47.878b   -    U    -
eth0/8      0.0.0.0/0         HA      0017.cb47.878c   -    U    -
eth0/9      0.0.0.0/0         Null    0017.cb47.878d   -    D    -
bgroup0/0   0.0.0.0/0         Null    0017.cb47.878e   -    D    -
bgroup0/1   0.0.0.0/0         Null    0017.cb47.8795   -    D    -
bgroup0/2   0.0.0.0/0         Null    0017.cb47.8796   -    D    -
loopback.1  1.10.1.1/24       Untrust N/A              -    D    -
vlan1       0.0.0.0/0         VLAN    0017.cb47.878f   1    D    -
null        0.0.0.0/0         Null    N/A              -    U    0

FWCLUSTER:FIREWALL-A(trust-vr/ospf)(M)-> get data detail self
VR: trust-vr RouterId: 172.25.113.177
                        Router LSA(s) in area 0.0.0.0
                        --------------------------------
Age:  1166
Seq Number: 0x80000048
Checksum: 0xe32c
Advertising Router: 172.25.113.177
Link State ID: 172.25.113.177
Length: 36
Options:    Extern     DC
Flags: ,,, Links 1
Link# 1
                Link State ID: 1.1.1.3
                Link Data: 1.1.1.1
                Type: 2
                TOS: 0
                Metric: 1
```

When the `monitor interface` command is used on the loopback interface, the asymmetric traffic pattern is avoided, and full stateful failover is provided. Anycast is a powerful tool that can solve some tricky network design problems. NAT in a VSD-less cluster is one example of how you can use anycast to provide stateful failover.

See Also

Chapter 8; Recipe 18.6

18.13 Configure NSRP Between Data Centers

Problem

You need to split an active-passive NSRP cluster between data centers.

Solution

Configure standard NSRP and enable the HA link probe:

```
FIREWALL-A-> set interface ethernet0/7 zone ha
FIREWALL-A-> set interface ethernet0/8 zone ha

FIREWALL-B-> set interface ethernet0/7 zone ha
FIREWALL-B-> set interface ethernet0/8 zone ha
FIREWALL-A-> set nsrp cluster id 1
FIREWALL-A(M)-> set nsrp cluster name FWCLUSTER
FWCLUSTER:FIREWALL-A(M)-> set nsrp vsd-group id 0 priority 10

FIREWALL-B-> set nsrp cluster id 1
FIREWALL-B(B)-> set nsrp cluster name FWCLUSTER
FWCLUSTER:FIREWALL-B(B)-> save
FWCLUSTER:FIREWALL-B(B)-> exec nsrp sync global-config saved
FWCLUSTER:FIREWALL-B(B)-> reset

FWCLUSTER:FIREWALL-A(M)-> set nsrp rto-mirror sync
FWCLUSTER:FIREWALL-A(M)-> set nsrp vsd-group hb-interval 200
FWCLUSTER:FIREWALL-A(M)-> set nsrp ha-link probe
FWCLUSTER:FIREWALL-A(M)-> set nsrp auth password iamapassword
FWCLUSTER:FIREWALL-A(M)-> set nsrp encrypt password iamapassword
FWCLUSTER:FIREWALL-A(M)-> set nsrp monitor interface ethernet0/1
FWCLUSTER:FIREWALL-A(M)-> set nsrp monitor interface ethernet0/3

FWCLUSTER:FIREWALL-B(M)-> set nsrp auth password iamapassword
FWCLUSTER:FIREWALL-B(M)-> set nsrp encrypt password iamapassword
FWCLUSTER:FIREWALL-B(M)-> set nsrp monitor interface ethernet0/1
FWCLUSTER:FIREWALL-B(M)-> set nsrp monitor interface ethernet0/3
```

Discussion

Especially in large cities, it is common to interconnect data centers with Ethernet connections. For purposes of site resiliency, it is often desired to create a virtual data center spanning two physical locations. With Ethernet, it is easy to do this, as everything appears as one big LAN. Because NSRP operates directly on the Ethernet layer, there are minimal differences between running a standard NSRP configuration and one that operates between physical locations. The largest difference is that the HA connections must almost always be run through switches, as shown in Figure 18-10 with its diversified data center deployment.

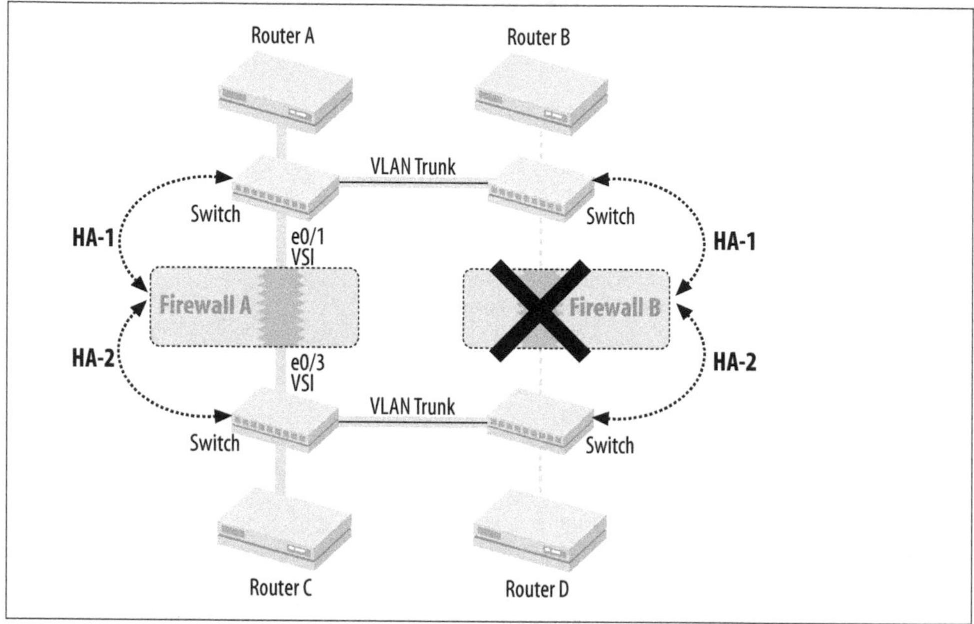

Figure 18-10. NSRP between data centers

Instead of connecting the HA links directly to each other as in previous recipes, the HA links are connected via switches in a multisite configuration. Each HA link must be located on its own VLAN in such a topology so that HA data messages and control messages remain separated. Additionally, the `HA-link-probe` should be set. NSRP detects HA link failure via physical link state. If the Ethernet segment between data centers is disrupted, NSRP would not detect this without the use of the link probe, and the two data centers would each have an active master. Clearly this is not desirable.

Because the NSRP packets will be traversing a shared interface, it is strongly recommended that you use the authentication and encryption functions of the protocol. Apply the `auth` and the `encrypt` password to each device.

Although the majority of multisite NSRP deployments have physical Ethernet connectivity between them, this is not a hard and fast requirement. The only requirement is that the Layer 2 frames arrive at the remote peer as sent. Layer 2 VPN technologies can also provide this service over a Layer 3 infrastructure. NSRP is not connection-oriented, and is not known to have strict latency requirements.

See Also

Recipe 18.1; Recipe 18.2

18.14 Maintain NSRP Clusters

Problem

You need to modify the state of NSRP or its objects.

Solution

Use the exec nsrp sync commands:

```
FWCLUSTER:FIREWALL-A(B)-> exec nsrp sync global-config save
FWCLUSTER:FIREWALL-A(B)-> reset
FWCLUSTER:FIREWALL-A(B)-> exec nsrp sync rto ?
RM                      Resource Manager
all                     all realtime objects
arp                     arp
attack-db               DI attack dababase
auth-table              auth table
dhcp                    dhcp
dip-in                  incoming dip table
dns                     dns
h323                    H.323
l2tp                    l2tp
mgcp                    MGCP calls
phase1-SA               IKE Phase-1 SA
rpc                     rpc map
sccp                    SCCP calls
session                 session
vpn                     vpn
xlate-ctx               xlate ctx table
FWCLUSTER:FIREWALL-A(B)-> exec nsrp sync rto all from peer
FWCLUSTER:FIREWALL-A(B)-> exec nsrp vsd-group id 0 mode ?
backup                  backup
ineligible              ineligible
init                    init
pb                      primary backup
```

Discussion

Although NSRP should remain in sync at all times, sometimes things can get out of a synchronized state. Because NSRP should be fully synchronized to operate properly, it is a good practice to synchronize RTOs manually before maintenance, or after a reboot or other network event has occurred. You can synchronize configurations with the exec nsrp sync global-config save command. When you enter this command, the device will request the configuration from its NSRP peer and save it to flash. Then, you should reboot the device for the configuration to take effect.

You can synchronize RTOs either by category or completely. It is generally a good idea to synchronize all RTOs if you notice they are out of sync. NSRP sessions on a backup device were originally designed to have a lifetime equal to eight times that of the master upon session creation. Because of this, the number of sessions on the primary and backup devices could often differ significantly. You can use the `set nsrp rto-mirror session ageout-ack` command to tell the backup device to verify with the master before deleting a session. This is critically important for long-lived sessions.

When performing network maintenance, it is sometimes important to manually adjust the status of the cluster. One example of this is software upgrades. The traditional best practice for a software upgrade is to set the mode of the backup device to ineligible, or in the case of an active-active configuration, to set the master of one VSD-Group to be ineligible, then upgrade that device, manually synchronize all RTOs to the device, and then switch it over to become the master. Using the `exec nsrp sync rto-mirror all from peer` command, you can complete the upgrade with minimal to no downtime.

See Also

The Introduction to this chapter; Recipe 18.1

CHAPTER 19

Policy-Based Routing

19.0 Introduction

The primary goal of a network device is to provide a network path for traffic from one host to another. This goal can be achieved in many different ways, including via static routing, or via dynamic routing protocols such as Open Shortest Path First (OSPF) or the Border Gateway Protocol (BGP). The ability to control the network path using these methods is limited, however, because the path is usually based on the packet's destination IP address. Another option is to use source-based routing. Although with source-based routing you can base the decisions on the packet's source IP address, the network device still sends all traffic from that source address. Furthermore, using these conventional routing methods, you cannot control the traffic based on the packet's deeper headers, such as the Transmission Control Protocol/User Datagram Protocol (TCP/UDP) header. As an alternative, you can use policy-based routing (PBR), which enables you to control the network path based on the five tuples: source IP, source port, destination IP, destination port, and protocol. PBR also enables you to route traffic based on the Type of Service (ToS) bits on the IP packet.

This ability to control the network path based on the IP header and the TCP/UDP header gives you the flexibility to route traffic differently for each application. A user's experience could depend on the application he is using and how the traffic is forwarded (e.g., using high-speed links for telephony and low-speed links for file transfer). It is often necessary to route traffic by matching criteria to different paths, such as prioritizing voice traffic over Internet browsing traffic.

The building blocks of PBR are extended access lists, match groups, and action groups, and you configure them in the context of the Virtual Router (VR). If you have multiple VRs, you can configure different PBR policies. *Extended access lists* define the match criteria for the five tuples and the ToS bits; you can define multiple match criteria for an extended access list. *Match groups* collect multiple extended access lists to provide you with the flexibility to reuse the access lists for different policies.

Action groups determine the network path for traffic by defining the next action. Each action group can have multiple entries with a configurable entry ID that determines the order in which they would be applied. An action entry contains the next interface or next hop, which determines the packet's network path. The next action is monitored for availability; it is considered available only when the next interface is up or the next hop is reachable via an active outgoing route, if only one of them is configured in an entry. If both the next interface and the next hop are configured, the next hop should be reachable using the next interface configured in the action entry. Figure 19-1 shows the algorithm used for determining the network path.

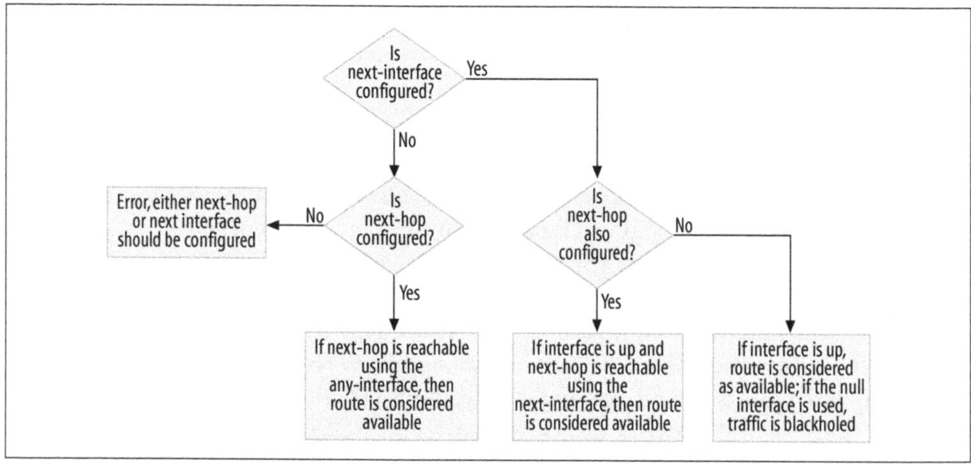

Figure 19-1. Network path decision using PBR

19.1 Traffic Load Balancing

Problem

You have links to two Internet Service Providers (ISPs), and you want to balance the traffic between those two ISP links.

Solution

Configure PBR to load-balance the traffic between the two ISP links. Create an extended access list for the IP addresses, create a match group, and assign the extended access list to the group. Then, create action groups to identify the next-hop router for each ISP:

```
set access-list extended 15 src-ip 192.168.100.0/25 entry 1
set access-list extended 16 src-ip 192.168.100.128/25 entry 1
set match-group name ISP2
set match-group ISP2 ext-acl 15 match-entry 10
set match-group name ISP1
set match-group ISP1 ext-acl 16 match-entry 10
```

```
set action-group name ISP2
set action-group ISP2 next-hop 1.1.1.2 action-entry 1
set action-group name ISP1
set action-group ISP1 next-hop 3.3.3.2 action-entry 1
```

Next, create the PBR policy using the match group and action group. Enable PBR on the ingress interface, and apply the PBR policy to the zone:

```
set pbr policy name load-balance
set pbr policy load-balance match-group ISP1 action-group ISP1 1
set pbr policy load-balance match-group ISP2 action-group ISP2 2
exit
set interface ethernet0/0 pbr
set zone Trust pbr load-balance
```

You will also need to create the firewall policy to allow this traffic to pass across the device:

```
set policy id 1 from "Trust" to "Untrust"  "Any" "Any" "ANY" nat
    src permit
set policy id 1
exit
```

Discussion

One of the common uses of routing policies is to load-balance traffic between two different ISP connections. Although there are multiple ways to load-balance, the PBR on ScreenOS provides flexibility regarding which hosts or type of traffic you want to send, using different links. For example, you could use an Equal Cost Multipath (ECMP) method to load-balance traffic. However, ECMP will load-balance on a per-session basis, which means you have no control over which host behind the firewall will use which link—it will be random. With PBR you'll get granular control based on the packet's header, such as the source IP, source port, destination IP, destination port, protocol, and ToS bits. This type of granular control could allow you to send low-priority traffic, such as file-sharing applications or instant messages, using low-speed links, and send corporate traffic using high-speed links.

In this recipe's solution, the two ISP links are connected to the firewall and have a single IP subnet behind the firewall; therefore, you want to load-balance the traffic based on the source address only. Figure 19-2 shows the topology.

In Figure 19-2, extended access list 15 for source IP subnet `192.168.100.0/25` and extended access list 16 for source IP subnet `192.168.100.128/25` were configured. Now, define match groups by identifying which attributes need to be matched (in this example, a match group named ISP1 was created, and you want it to match the IP subnet in extended access list 15). Another match group, ISP2, was created and matched with the IP subnet in extended access list 16. You can define multiple match attributes for the match group—the order of the match attributes is determined by the match-entry option, and it goes in ascending order. In this example, the match entry was defined with a value of 10.

Figure 19-2. Network topology for load balancing

After the match groups are created, create the action groups. Action groups determine what action needs to be performed after the IP packet is matched based on the match group. Action groups named ISP1 and ISP2 were created with an action to route the packets to the next-hop gateway for the respective ISP gateways—that is, `1.1.1.2` and `3.3.3.2`. You could also have multiple actions—as with the match groups, the order of the action here is determined by the action-entry option, and it goes in ascending order. In this example, the action entry was defined with a value of 1.

The PBR policy is defined to bring together the match groups and the action groups. Here, the PBR policy named `load-balance` was created. It defines the IP address to be matched based on match group ISP1, to take action based on action group ISP1, followed by the order sequence. A second policy matches the IP address based on match group ISP2 and action group ISP2. The PBR option is enabled on the incoming interface, `ethernet0/0`, and the policy was bound to the `Trust` zone to which the `ethernet0/0` interface belongs.

A common user error in PBR is to misconfigure the PBR policy, or just to forget to bind it, and enable PBR on the interface. For the PBR policy to kick in, the interface and policy binding are important. PBR policy lookup happens only when the first packet is received on the firewall. As such, it is important to know the traffic direction and the incoming interface.

Remember, you still need the firewall policy to allow traffic. Create the firewall policy ID 1 from the `Trust` zone to the `Untrust` zone, with any source, any destination, and any service to allow traffic and the Network Address Translation (NAT) source address based on the outgoing interface. See Chapter 7 for more on firewall policy configurations.

19.2 Verify That PBR Is Working for Traffic Load Balancing

Problem

You configured PBR for two ISPs, and you want to verify that the traffic is being load-balanced.

Solution

Use these commands to verify:

```
SSG-> get route
SSG-> get session src-ip
```

Discussion

To verify that the traffic is being directed as per your PBR configuration, you can review the routing and session state. Use the get route command to see the connected routes; here, the connected routes are ethernet0/1 for the ISP2 link and ethernet0/2 for the ISP1 link, and route IDs 5 and 3, respectively:

```
SSG-> get route


IPv4 Dest-Routes for <untrust-vr> (0 entries)
--------------------------------------------------------------------
H: Host C: Connected S: Static A: Auto-Exported
I: Imported R: RIP P: Permanent D: Auto-Discovered
iB: IBGP eB: EBGP O: OSPF E1: OSPF external type 1
E2: OSPF external type 2


IPv4 Dest-Routes for <trust-vr> (8 entries)
--------------------------------------------------------------------
   ID          IP-Prefix  Interface   Gateway   P  Pref    Mtr   Vsys
--------------------------------------------------------------------
*  3         3.3.3.0/30     eth0/2   0.0.0.0   C    0      0   Root
*  6         1.1.1.1/32     eth0/1   0.0.0.0   H    0      0   Root
*  9         2.2.2.0/30     eth0/1   1.1.1.2   S   20      1   Root
*  4         3.3.3.1/32     eth0/2   0.0.0.0   H    0      0   Root
*  5         1.1.1.0/30     eth0/1   0.0.0.0   C    0      0   Root
*  10        4.4.4.0/30     eth0/2   3.3.3.2   S   20      1   Root
*  8    192.168.100.1/32     eth0/0   0.0.0.0   H    0      0   Root
*  7    192.168.100.0/24     eth0/0   0.0.0.0   C    0      0   Root
```

Using the get session src-ip command reveals the session from source IP 192.168.100.100, which belongs to match group ISP2 for destination IP 192.168.200.1 using route ID 5, which is the ISP2 link. This shows that the PBR policy was applied and the outgoing route was chosen as ISP2. This command also shows that source IP 192.168.100.100 was translated to 1.1.1.1 based on the firewall's NAT configuration.

```
SSG-> get sess src-ip 192.168.100.100
alloc 1/max 48064, alloc failed 0, mcast alloc 0, di alloc failed 0
total reserved 0, free sessions in shared pool 48063
Total 1 sessions according filtering criteria.
id 48039/s**,vsys 0,flag 00000010/0000/0001,policy 1,time 1, dip 2 module 0
 if 0(nspflag 800801):192.168.100.100/34164->192.168.200.1/768,1,000c29946d55,sess
token 4,vlan 0,tun 0,vsd 0,route 7
 if 5(nspflag 800800):1.1.1.1/5058<-192.168.200.1/768,1,000585caf0a0,
sess token 6,vlan 0,tun 0,vsd 0,route 5
Total 1 sessions shown
```

This example shows that the session from source IP `192.168.100.200`, which belongs to match group ISP1 for the same destination IP `192.168.200.1`, is using route ID 3, which is the ISP1 link. Also, the source address was translated to `3.3.3.1` based on the firewall policy.

```
SSG-> get sess src-ip 192.168.100.200
alloc 1/max 48064, alloc failed 0, mcast alloc 0, di alloc failed 0
total reserved 0, free sessions in shared pool 48063
Total 1 sessions according filtering criteria.
id 48019/s**,vsys 0,flag 00000010/0000/0001,policy 1,time 1, dip 2 module 0
 if 0(nspflag 800801):192.168.100.200/51060->192.168.200.1/768,1,000c23476a43,sess
token 4,vlan 0,tun 0,vsd 0,route 7
 if 6(nspflag 800800):3.3.3.1/5127<-192.168.200.1/768,1,0010db3fc210,sess token
6,vlan 0,tun 0,vsd 0,route 3
Total 1 sessions shown
```

See Also

Recipe 19.1

19.3 Prioritize Traffic Between IPSec Tunnels

Problem

You need to prioritize traffic between two IP Security (IPSec) virtual private network (VPN) tunnels based on IP addresses and application to provide redundancy.

Solution

Create two IPSec VPN tunnels for the destination network, and bind to a tunnel interface using Next Hop Tunnel Binding (NHTB) to create two traffic paths:

```
set interface "tunnel.1" zone "Trust"
set interface tunnel.1 ip unnumbered interface ethernet0/0
set ike gateway "Fast_link_gw1" address 2.2.2.1 Main outgoing-
    interface "ethernet0/1" preshare xxxxx sec-level standard
set ike gateway "slow_link_gw2" address 4.4.4.1 Main outgoing-
    interface "ethernet0/2" preshare xxxxx sec-level standard

set vpn "Fast_link_gw1" gateway "Fast_link_gw1" no-replay tunnel
idletime 0 sec-level standard
```

```
set vpn "Fast_link_gw1" monitor rekey
set vpn "Fast_link_gw1" id 1 bind interface tunnel.1
set interface tunnel.1 nhtb 2.2.2.1 vpn "Fast_link_gw1"

set vpn "slow_link_gw2" gateway "slow_link_gw2" no-replay tunnel
idletime 0 sec-level standard
set vpn "slow_link_gw2" monitor rekey
set vpn "slow_link_gw2" id 2 bind interface tunnel.1
set interface tunnel.1 nhtb 4.4.4.1 vpn "slow_link_gw2"
```

Use PBR to configure extended access lists based on the high-priority traffic. Then, use the action group to send the high-priority traffic to one of the IPSec VPN tunnels.

Create the second extended access list for all traffic as a catchall from previous access lists. This will also act as a backup tunnel should the primary tunnel fail. Finally, configure the action group to send the low-priority traffic to the second IPSec VPN tunnel.

If both tunnels are down, the access list will use the default route to forward traffic unencrypted.

```
set vrouter "trust-vr"
set route 2.2.2.0/30 interface ethernet0/1 gateway 1.1.1.2
set route 4.4.4.0/30 interface ethernet0/2 gateway 3.3.3.2
set route 192.168.200.0/24 interface tunnel.1 gateway 2.2.2.1
set route 192.168.200.0/24 interface tunnel.1 gateway 4.4.4.1
set route 0.0.0.0/0 interface ethernet0/1 gateway 1.1.1.2
set access-list extended 1 src-ip 192.168.100.0/24 dst-ip
192.168.200.0/24 dst-port 25-25 protocol tcp entry 1
set access-list extended 1 src-ip 192.168.100.0/24 dst-ip
192.168.200.0/24 dst-port 1521-1521 protocol tcp entry 2
set access-list extended 1 src-ip 192.168.100.0/24 dst-ip
192.168.200.0/24 dst-port 443-443 protocol tcp entry 3
set access-list extended 1 src-ip 192.168.100.0/24 dst-ip
192.168.200.0/24 dst-port 80-80 protocol tcp entry 4
set access-list extended 1 src-ip 192.168.100.0/24 dst-ip
192.168.200.0/24 dst-port 9090-9090 protocol tcp entry 5
set access-list extended 2 src-ip 192.168.100.0/24 dst-ip
192.168.200.0/24 entry 1
set match-group name High_Priority_Traffic
set match-group High_Priority_Traffic ext-acl 1 match-entry 1
set match-group name Low_Priority_traffic
set match-group Low_Priority_traffic ext-acl 2 match-entry 1
set action-group name Send_using_Slow_Link
set action-group Send_using_Slow_Link next-interface tunnel.1
next-hop 4.4.4.1 action-entry 1
set action-group name Send_using_Fast_Link
set action-group Send_using_Fast_Link next-interface tunnel.1
next-hop 2.2.2.1 action-entry 1
set pbr policy name Distribute_Traffic
set pbr policy Distribute_Traffic match-group High_Priority_Traffic
```

```
action-group Send_using_Fast_Link 1
set pbr policy Distribute_Traffic match-group Low_Priority_traffic
action-group Send_using_Slow_Link 2
exit
set interface ethernet0/0 pbr Distribute_Traffic
```

Discussion

We see two redundant IPSec VPN paths for the same destination network, forwarding the high-priority traffic using the fast link, and sending the low-priority traffic using the slow link. The second path acts as a backup to the primary tunnel traffic (failover of low-priority traffic to the fast link was not provided in this example). If both tunnels fail, the traffic is forwarded unencrypted; if you don't want unencrypted traffic, you can configure null routes for the destination network and blackhole the traffic. Figure 19-3 shows the basic topology.

Figure 19-3. Network topology for traffic prioritizing using IPSec tunnels

Configure the `tunnel.1` interface in the `Trust` zone and use an unnumbered IP address for this interface. Then, create an Internet Key Exchange (IKE) gateway named `fast_link_gw1` for remote gateway `2.2.2.1`, and use the `ethernet0/1` interface as the outgoing interface. Create another IKE gateway named `slow_link_gw2` for the remote gateway IP address of `4.4.4.1`, and use `ethernet0/2` as the outgoing interface. Create the VPN for the `fast_link_gw1` and bind it to the `tunnel.1` interface, and then enable the `Monitor` and `Rekey` options for the tunnel. The `Monitor` and `Rekey` options will help to ensure that the routes for the remote network are withdrawn from the forwarding table when the tunnel goes down.

Two static routes were created in the device for `192.168.200.0/24` with next-hop gateways of `2.2.2.1` and `4.4.4.1`. You have to configure the NHTB entry on the `tunnel.1` interface to create two traffic paths, as shown in the following code. The

NHTB configuration shows that the routes for the next hop of `2.2.2.1` should use the `fast_link_gw1` IPSec VPN, and the routes for the next hop of `4.4.4.1` should use the `slow_link_gw2` IPSec VPN. This is required because you are binding both IPSec VPNs to the same tunnel interface.

```
set route 192.168.200.0/24 interface tunnel.1 gateway 2.2.2.1
set route 192.168.200.0/24 interface tunnel.1 gateway 4.4.4.1
set interface tunnel.1 nhtb 2.2.2.1 vpn "Fast_link_gw1"
set interface tunnel.1 nhtb 4.4.4.1 vpn "slow_link_gw2"
```

Now that the IPSec tunnels are set up, all traffic destined for the `192.168.200.0/24` network would be forwarded using the first available route on the lookup. But using this configuration would not provide any traffic engineering, and the goal of this recipe is to distribute traffic between these two IPSec tunnels based on priority, while also providing redundancy for the high-priority traffic. To achieve this, use PBR to identify the high-priority traffic.

The high-priority traffic here is the traffic from source address `192.168.100.0/24` destined to `192.168.200.0/24` for SMTP (25), SQL (1521), HTTPS (443), HTTP (80), and Custom Application Port (9090). All other traffic is low-priority and should use the `slow_link_gw2`. Create an extended access list ID of 1 for the high-priority traffic, as shown in the following code snippet; the first two lines show extended access list ID 1 created in `trust-vr` for source IP `192.168.100.0/24`, destination IP `192.168.20.0/24`, and destination port `25-25` (this is the port range), with the protocol as TCP, and entry 1 showing the sequence order for this access list. Here are the five entries for the different protocols for high-priority traffic:

```
Set vr trust-vr
set access-list extended 1 src-ip 192.168.100.0/24 dst-ip
192.168.200.0/24 dst-port 25-25 protocol tcp entry 1
set access-list extended 1 src-ip 192.168.100.0/24 dst-ip
192.168.200.0/24 dst-port 1521-1521 protocol tcp entry 2
set access-list extended 1 src-ip 192.168.100.0/24 dst-ip
192.168.200.0/24 dst-port 443-443 protocol tcp entry 3
set access-list extended 1 src-ip 192.168.100.0/24 dst-ip
192.168.200.0/24 dst-port 80-80 protocol tcp entry 4
set access-list extended 1 src-ip 192.168.100.0/24 dst-ip
192.168.200.0/24 dst-port 9090-9090 protocol tcp entry 5
```

Then, configure extended access list ID 2 for all traffic from source IP `192.168.100.0/24` destined to `192.168.200.0/24`. There is no mention of the destination ports in this access list, implying that all traffic from source addresses in the range `192.168.100.0/24` to destinations in the range `192.168.200.0/24` will be matched. This way, the configuration will act as a catchall for traffic for access list ID 1, and will match all the protocols in access list ID 1 providing the redundant path.

```
Set vr trust-vr
set access-list extended 2 src-ip 192.168.100.0/24 dst-ip
192.168.200.0/24 entry 1
```

Now, define the match group named High_Priority_Traffic and match the extended access list ID 1; then, create the second match group named low_priority_traffic, and match the extended access list ID 2. Define the action group send_using_slow_link with an action set to the next interface of tunnel.1 and the next hop of 4.4.4.1. This action will cause all packets to follow the NHTB entry on tunnel.1 with a next hop of 4.4.4.1, thereby using the slow_Link_gw2 IPSec tunnels. Next, define the action group send_using_fast_link with the action set to the next interface of tunnel.1 and the next hop of 2.2.2.1; this group will cause the packets to follow the NHTB entry on tunnel.1 with the next hop 2.2.2.1, thereby using the fast_link_gw1 IPSec tunnel. Now, define the PBR policy named Distribute_traffic, and as the first entry, define traffic to the High_Priority_traffic match group and action group to use send_using_fast_link, using the sequence order of 1. Then, define traffic to the low_Priority_traffic match group and action group to use send_using_slow_link, followed by the sequence order of 2.

It is important to note the sequence order for the PBR policy, which is the order for PBR lookup that will be used for matching the traffic. If you configure slow_priority_traffic out of sequence, the high-priority traffic will never get priority. Therefore, apply the policy to the ethernet0/0 interface, as this is the entry point for the traffic.

```
set match-group name High_Priority_Traffic
set match-group High_Priority_Traffic ext-acl 1 match-entry 1
set match-group name Low_Priority_traffic
set match-group Low_Priority_traffic ext-acl 2 match-entry 1
set action-group name Send_using_Slow_Link
set action-group Send_using_Slow_Link next-interface tunnel.1
next-hop 4.4.4.1 action-entry 1
set action-group name Send_using_Fast_Link
set action-group Send_using_Fast_Link next-interface tunnel.1
next-hop 2.2.2.1 action-entry 1
set pbr policy name Distribute_Traffic
set pbr policy Distribute_Traffic match-group High_Priority_Traffic
action-group Send_using_Fast_Link 1
set pbr policy Distribute_Traffic match-group Low_Priority_traffic
action-group Send_using_Slow_Link 2
exit
set interface ethernet0/0 pbr Distribute_Traffic
```

Lastly, you need to configure static routes for the tunnel endpoints for the VPN tunnels to establish a default route for all the unencrypted traffic. In this example, the default route will cause all the traffic to go unencrypted when the tunnels are down:

```
set route 2.2.2.0/30 interface ethernet0/1 gateway 1.1.1.2
set route 4.4.4.0/30 interface ethernet0/2 gateway 3.3.3.2
set route 0.0.0.0/0 interface ethernet0/1 gateway 1.1.1.2
```

To verify whether the traffic is being forwarded to the expected routes, you can use these commands: get sa, get route, get session, and get int. Based on the preceding configuration, the get sa command shows that the two tunnels are active (A/U means the tunnel is active and up), the tunnel gateway address 2.2.2.1 is the fast_Link_gw1, and the gateway address 4.4.4.1 is the slow_link_gw2, as configured. Please note the Hex ID field for each tunnel; this is used in the session table to forward traffic.

```
SSG-> get sa
total configured sa: 2
HEX ID    Gateway Port Algorithm     SPI  Life:sec kb    Sta PID vsys
00000001<  2.2.2.1 500 esp:3des/sha1 e4c116b2  1424 unlim A/U -1  0
00000001>  2.2.2.1 500 esp:3des/sha1 9bd93a19  1424 unlim A/U -1  0
00000002<  4.4.4.1 500 esp:3des/sha1 e4c116b3  1514 unlim A/U -1  0
00000002>  4.4.4.1 500 esp:3des/sha1 9bd93a1a  1514 unlim A/U -1  0
```

The get route command shows that the routes for destination network 192.168.200.0/24 are active for the two tunnels:

```
SSG-> get route


IPv4 Dest-Routes for <untrust-vr> (0 entries)
--------------------------------------------------------------------
H: Host C: Connected S: Static A: Auto-Exported
I: Imported R: RIP P: Permanent D: Auto-Discovered
iB: IBGP eB: EBGP O: OSPF E1: OSPF external type 1
E2: OSPF external type 2


IPv4 Dest-Routes for <trust-vr> (11 entries)
------------------------------------------------------------------
   ID          IP-Prefix  Interface   Gateway   P Pref  Mtr   Vsys
------------------------------------------------------------------
*   3         3.3.3.0/30     eth0/2   0.0.0.0   C    0    0   Root
*   6         1.1.1.1/32     eth0/1   0.0.0.0   H    0    0   Root
*  19          0.0.0.0/0     eth0/1   1.1.1.2   S   20    1   Root
*   9         2.2.2.0/30     eth0/1   1.1.1.2   S   20    1   Root
*   4         3.3.3.1/32     eth0/2   0.0.0.0   H    0    0   Root
*   5         1.1.1.0/30     eth0/1   0.0.0.0   C    0    0   Root
*  10         4.4.4.0/30     eth0/2   3.3.3.2   S   20    1   Root
*   8   192.168.100.1/32     eth0/0   0.0.0.0   H    0    0   Root
*  17   192.168.200.0/24      tun.1   2.2.2.1   S   20    1   Root
*  18   192.168.200.0/24      tun.1   4.4.4.1   S   20    1   Root
*   7   192.168.100.0/24     eth0/0   0.0.0.0   C    0    0   Root

SSG->
```

The get int tunnel.1 command shows that the NHTB entries are active (via the U in the "Status" column for the NHTB table), and each next hop is showing the VPN binding tunnel information:

```
c3-22-> get int tun.1
Interface tunnel.1:
  description tunnel.1
  number 20, if_info 16168, if_index 1, mode nat
```

```
link ready
vsys Root, zone Trust, vr trust-vr
admin mtu 1500, operating mtu 1500, default mtu 1500
*ip 0.0.0.0/0  unnumbered, source interface ethernet0/0
*manage ip 0.0.0.0
bound vpn:
  Fast_link_gw1
  slow_link_gw2

Next-Hop Tunnel Binding table
Flag Status Next-Hop(IP)     tunnel-id  VPN
 S     U    2.2.2.1          0x00000001     Fast_link_gw1
 S     U    4.4.4.1          0x00000002  slow_link_gw2
```

This recipe initiated high-priority traffic for destination IP address 192.168.200.100 using destination port 80, and it is expected to be forwarded to the fast_link_gw1. To see the session entry, use the get session dst-ip 192.168.200.100 dst-port 80 command. The session shows tun 40000001: with an sa-id of 1, and a 4 added to the hex-id of the get sa command. This confirms that the session is forwarded using the Fast_Link based on the PBR configuration.

```
c3-22-> get session dst-ip 192.168.200.100 dst-port 80
alloc 6/max 48064, alloc failed 0, mcast alloc 0, di alloc failed 0
total reserved 0, free sessions in shared pool 48058
Total 1 sessions according filtering criteria.
id 48047/s**,vsys 0,flag 08000040/0000/0001,policy 320002,time 26,
dip 0 module 0
 if 0(nspflag 801001):192.168.100.200/4582->192.168.200.100/80,6,
000c29946d55,sess token 4,vlan 0,tun 0,vsd 0,route 7
 if 20(nspflag 1000):192.168.100.200/4582<-192.168.200.100/80,6,
000000000000,sess token 5,vlan 0,tun 40000001,vsd 0,route 0
Total 1 sessions shown
```

Now, initiate the low-priority traffic for the same destination IP address of 192.168.200.100 and destination port of 9999. It shows tun 400000002 and it is the slow_link:

```
c3-22-> get session dst-ip 192.168.200.100 dst-port 9999
alloc 8/max 48064, alloc failed 0, mcast alloc 0, di alloc failed 0
total reserved 0, free sessions in shared pool 48056
Total 1 sessions according filtering criteria.
id 48036/s**,vsys 0,flag 08000040/0000/0001,policy 320002,time 159,
dip 0 module 0
 if 0(nspflag 801001):192.168.100.200/4583->192.168.200.100/9999,6,000c29946d55,sess
token 4,vlan 0,tun 0,vsd 0,
route 7
 if 20(nspflag 1000):192.168.100.200/4583<-192.168.200.100/9999,6,
000000000000,sess token 5,vlan 0,tun 40000002,vsd 0,route 0
Total 1 sessions shown
```

19.4 Redirect Traffic to Mitigate Threats

Problem

You want to redirect user traffic to the Intrusion Detection System (IDS) in the DMZ zone, protecting devices in the Trust zone from downloading malware. Also, you have multiple VR configurations to protect the routing table from external attacks.

Solution

You need to redirect traffic for threat mitigation using multiple VRs.

First, configure zones in the different VRs, assign interfaces to the zones, and assign IP addresses to the interfaces:

```
set zone "Trust" vrouter "trust-vr"
set zone "Untrust" vrouter "untrust-vr"
set zone "DMZ" vrouter "untrust-vr"
set interface "ethernet0/0" zone "Trust"
set interface "ethernet0/1" zone "DMZ"
set interface "ethernet0/2" zone "Untrust"
set interface ethernet0/0 ip 172.16.1.1/24
set interface ethernet0/1 ip 2.2.2.1/30
set interface ethernet0/2 ip 4.4.4.1/30
```

Next, configure the firewall policy to allow traffic from the Trust zone to the DMZ zone, and from the DMZ zone to the Untrust zone for IDP inspection (note that you would need to configure the IDP device as needed, and IDP device configuration is beyond the scope of this recipe; therefore, consult the IDP documentation that came with your device):

```
set address "Trust" "Trust_network" 172.16.1.0 255.255.255.0
set address "DMZ" "Filtered_trust_network" 172.16.1.0 255.255.255.0
set policy id 1 from "Trust" to "DMZ" "Trust_network" "Any"
    "ANY" permit
set policy id 1
set policy id 2 from "DMZ" to "Untrust" "Filtered_trust_network"
    "Any" "ANY" permit
set policy id 2
```

Lastly, configure the PBR to redirect traffic from the Trust network to the IDP device in the DMZ zone:

```
set vrouter "untrust-vr"
set route 0.0.0.0/0 interface ethernet0/2 gateway 4.4.4.2
exit
set vrouter "trust-vr"
set route 2.2.2.2/32 interface ethernet0/1 gateway 2.2.2.2
set route 0.0.0.0/0 vrouter "untrust-vr" preference 20
set access-list extended 1 src-ip 172.16.1.0/24 entry 1
set match-group name threat_check
```

```
set match-group threat_check ext-acl 1 match-entry 1
set action-group name redirect_for_idp
set action-group redirect_for_idp next-hop 2.2.2.2 action-entry 1
set pbr policy name threat_mitigation
set pbr policy threat_mitigation match-group threat_check action-group redirect_for_
idp 1
exit
set interface ethernet0/0 pbr threat_mitigation
```

Discussion

This recipe demonstrates traffic redirection to the dedicated threat detection device (IDP/AV) using PBR and blocking malicious traffic into the network. This design requires planning; you need to spend time analyzing network traffic flow and determining which traffic should be redirected to the IDP device. Also, you need to consider how to configure and deploy the IDP device.

There are two VRs: trust-vr and untrust-vr. They are configured with the Trust zone to belong to the trust-vr and have assigned the ethernet0/0 interface to the Trust zone. The Untrust and DMZ zones belong to the untrust-vr, and ethernet0/1 and ethernet0/2 have been assigned to the DMZ and Untrust zones, respectively. The ethernet0/0 interface has the IP address 172.16.1.1/24, the ethernet0/1 interface has the IP address 2.2.2.1/30, and the ethernet0/2 interface has the IP address 4.4.4.1/30. Configuring two VRs provides security to the routing table and prevents internal network addresses from being visible to the outside world.

Firewall policy has been applied to allow traffic from the 172.16.1.0/24 network to any destination (note that the policy will only allow traffic from the Trust zone to the DMZ zone). The DMZ zone has the IDP device, which will inspect the traffic and redirect it back to the firewall. If there is any malicious traffic, it will take necessary action based on the configuration of the IDP device. A second policy from the DMZ zone to the Untrust zone was also added. The address book entry for the DMZ and Trust zones shows the same network, 172.16.1.0/24, but the names are different, showing that the IDP device is filtering traffic.

Configure the default route in the untrust-vr to forward traffic to the Internet using the ethernet0/2 interface and a next-hop gateway of 4.4.4.2:

```
set vrouter "untrust-vr"
set route 0.0.0.0/0 interface ethernet0/2 gateway 4.4.4.2
exit
```

The default route in the trust-vr has been configured with a next hop of untrust-vr—this route is required to forward all traffic from the Trust zone to the Internet via the untrust-vr. A host route has been set for the IDP device in the trust-vr. This is an important step, because if you miss this configuration, the traffic will not be redirected to the IDP device. To configure:

```
set vrouter "trust-vr"
set route 0.0.0.0/0 vrouter "untrust-vr" preference 20
set route 2.2.2.2/32 interface ethernet0/1 gateway 2.2.2.2
```

Let's examine the PBR configuration, which redirects traffic based on the routing policy. Create an extended access list ID of 1 with a source address of `172.16.1.0/24` so that all traffic from the `172.16.1.0/24` network is redirected to the IDP device. Then, create the match group named `threat_check` to be matched with extended list ID 1. Define the action group named `redirect_for_idp` and set the next-hop gateway as `2.2.2.2`.

Create the PBR policy `threat_mitigation` using the match group `threat_check` and action group `redirect_for_idp`. Assign the PBR policy on the `ethernet0/0` interface that will receive the incoming traffic. The configuration for this is as follows:

```
set vr trust-vs
set access-list extended 1 src-ip 172.16.1.0/24 entry 1
set match-group name threat_check
set match-group threat_check ext-acl 1 match-entry 1
set action-group name redirect_for_idp
set action-group redirect_for_idp next-hop 2.2.2.2 action-entry 1
set pbr policy name threat_mitigation
set pbr policy threat_mitigation match-group threat_check action-group redirect_for_
idp 1
exit
set interface ethernet0/0 pbr threat_mitigation
```

19.5 Classify Traffic Using the ToS Bits

Problem

You have latency-sensitive traffic in your network, and you want to classify traffic using the ToS bits in the IP header to determine the next hop. You have two links: one link provides the Quality of Service (QoS) and the other is a best-effort service.

Solution

You need to identify the ToS bits for the latency-sensitive traffic on your network before you start the configuration. Configure the default route for the second link to match the noncritical traffic. Then, create the extended access list for a ToS value, create a match group to match the extended access list, define an action group, and provide the high-reliability link next-hop gateway address:

```
set vrouter "trust-vr"
set route 0.0.0.0/0 interface ethernet0/1 gateway 2.2.2.2
set access-list extended 10 tos 63 entry 1
set match-group name High_Priority
set match-group High_Priority ext-acl 10 match-entry 1
set action-group name High_Reliability
set action-group High_Reliability next-hop 4.4.4.2 action-entry 1
exit
```

Configure the PBR policy using the match group and action group, and then bind the policy to the incoming interface:

```
Set vr trust-vr
set pbr policy name Critical_traffic
set pbr policy Critical_traffic match-group High_Priority action-group High_
Reliability 1
exit
set interface ethernet0/0 pbr Critical_traffic
```

Discussion

The IPv4 header has a 1-byte ToS field (originally defined in RFC 791), and it uses only six bits (0–5), with two bits (6–7) reserved for the future and set at 0. The first two fields of the ToS byte were defined as precedence and type of service subfields:

```
  0     1     2     3     4     5     6     7
+-----+-----+-----+-----+-----+-----+-----+-----+
|   PRECEDENCE    |       TOS       |  0  |  0  |
+-----+-----+-----+-----+-----+-----+-----+-----+
```

The field was redefined in RFC 2474/RFC 2475 and named the DS field, sometimes also referred to as the Differentiated Services Code Point (DSCP). Only six bits are used in the fields, with an additional two bits reserved:

```
  0     1     2     3     4     5     6     7
+-----+-----+-----+-----+-----+-----+-----+-----+
|               DSCP                |    CU     |
+-----+-----+-----+-----+-----+-----+-----+-----+
```

You have to analyze your network traffic and applications before you can use ToS values to determine the traffic path. To best use high-cost links for critical traffic, the applications should be marking the ToS bits in the packet, or you should use network devices to do the marking. It is also important to understand that all the devices in the network path should know how to read the ToS bits for end-to-end QoS.

In this recipe, the extended access list 10 for the ToS value of 63 was configured. This is the specified decimal value equal to 0×3F in Hex. The value of 63 indicates the highest-priority traffic on the network. You can configure the ToS value range of 0–255 for the extended access list. The ToS value of 0 is the default for "normal" traffic on the network. The match group `High_Priority` matches with extended access list 10 as the first entry. A `High_Reliability` action group is defined with a next hop of `4.4.4.2` as the gateway for the link providing QoS.

```
set vrouter "trust-vr"
set access-list extended 10 tos 63 entry 1
set match-group name High_Priority
set match-group High_Priority ext-acl 10 match-entry 1
set action-group name High_Reliability
set action-group High_Reliability next-hop 4.4.4.2 action-entry 1
exit
```

The PBR policy `Critical_traffic` was created with match group `High_Priority` to match the traffic with a ToS value of 63. Using the action group `High_Reliability`, the traffic is forwarded to the next-hop gateway address of the link providing QoS. This policy was bound to the `ethernet0/0` interface to trigger the PBR for the incoming traffic.

```
Set vr trust-vr
set pbr policy name Critical_traffic
set pbr policy Critical_traffic match-group High_Priority action-group High_
Reliability 1
exit
set interface ethernet0/0 pbr Critical_traffic
```

The second link provides best-effort service. For all other traffic, the default route to interface `ethernet0/1` was configured using the next-hop gateway address of `2.2.2.2`.

```
set vr trust-vr route 0.0.0.0/0 interface ethernet0/1 gateway 2.2.2.2
```

This feature assumes that all subsequent packets will have the same ToS values as the first packet when the session was created. Once the session has been created, the ToS byte is not inspected for PBR decisions; the PBR policy is applied per flow and not per packet.

19.6 Block Unwanted Traffic with a Blackhole

Problem

You're receiving unwanted traffic of various types, attempting to probe your network. You can't prevent this traffic from reaching your router, but you want to make sure it never reaches your network. You want to send it to a "dead end" or null route; this is commonly referred to as *routing the traffic to a blackhole*.

Solution

Configure an extended access list to match the traffic pattern you want to blackhole:

```
set access-list extended 20 src-ip 172.16.1.0/24 dst-ip 172.19.50.0/24
tos 63 entry 10
```

Now, configure a match group and assign the extended access list created for the traffic pattern:

```
set match-group name black_hole_traffic
set match-group black_hole_traffic ext-acl 20 match-entry 1
```

Configure an action group and set the next interface as `null`; this will blackhole the traffic:

```
set action-group name black_hole_nh
set action-group black_hole_nh next-interface null action-entry 1
```

Next, create a PBR policy using the match group and action group for the implementation:

```
set pbr policy name prevent_mis_use
set pbr policy prevent_mis_use match-group black_hole_traffic
action-group black_hole_nh 1
```

Finally, bind the PBR policy to the desired interface, zone, or VR. In this case, bind it to the interface:

```
set interface ethernet0/0 pbr prevent_mis_use
c3-21->
```

Discussion

There are multiple ways to blackhole traffic. For example, you could use a null route or configure a policy to deny traffic. However, these methods are only able to blackhole based on the destination IP address or the five tuples: source IP, source port, destination IP, destination port, and protocol. PBR provides all of these methods, as well as ToS bits, which is useful for ensuring that no application is misusing the network resources and is still able to pass traffic within the permitted parameters. It is also a good tool for dynamic threat mitigation—you can just put in the access list and reduce CPU utilization on the firewall. One disadvantage of using the PBR for blackholing traffic is logging. The PBR will not be able to log the dropped packets in the traffic log, which can be achieved by the firewall deny policy. Careful consideration is required before choosing one of the methods available for dropping traffic.

The intention here was to ensure that proper network resources are being used, and to prevent users from network `172.16.1.0/24` from sending traffic to `172.19.50.0/24` with a ToS value of 63—any traffic matching this access list will be dropped. To achieve this, first configure an extended access list ID of 20 with an IP address of `172.16.1.0/24`, a destination IP of `172.19.50.0/24`, and a ToS value of 63. This access list will match for any destination port; you do not have to choose a destination port because protocols between these networks are not supposed to have a ToS value of 63.

Now, configure the match group `black_hole_traffic` and match the extended access list ID 20 you just created. Define action group `black_hole_nh` to blackhole the next hop by specifying the next interface as `null`. When the PBR policy is matched, it will find the next interface as null and will inform the flow processing engine to drop this packet.

To blackhole traffic, define the PBR policy `prevent_mis_use` and use the match group `black_hole_traffic` and action group `black_hole_nh`. Bind the policy to interface `ethernet0/0`—this is the entry point for the traffic. You can bind the policy to the interface, zone, or VR.

19.7 View Your PBR Configuration

Problem

You need to view your PBR configuration.

Solution

Use the get vr *<vr_name>* pbr config command to view the complete configuration for the PBR:

```
SSG-> get vr trust-vr pbr config
set access-list extended 1 src-ip 192.168.100.0/24 dst-ip
192.168.200.0/24 dst-port 25-25 protocol tcp entry 1
set match-group name High_Priority_Traffic
set match-group High_Priority_Traffic ext-acl 1 match-entry 1
set action-group name Send_using_Fast_Link
set action-group Send_using_Fast_Link next-interface tunnel.1
next-hop 2.2.2.1 action-entry 1
set pbr policy name Distribute_Traffic
set pbr policy Distribute_Traffic match-group High_Priority_Traffic
action-group Send_using_Fast_Link 1
set interface ethernet0/0 pbr Distribute_Traffic
```

Discussion

The configuration is sometimes very large on the firewall, and it becomes difficult to discover which configuration lines relate to a particular feature. The PBR configuration on the trust-vr is shown here, and all the components for the PBR policy are shown together, making it easier to troubleshoot configuration issues. In essence, you need five components for PBR to work:

Extended access list
: This is the basic traffic-matching access list.

Match groups
: You can combine multiple access lists into groups as required for added flexibility.

Action group
: You essentially define what next steps you want to achieve, such as the outgoing interface and/or outgoing next-hop gateway address.

PBR policy
: Think of this as a firewall policy. You define the match criteria using the match groups, and the next steps for the matched traffic using the action group.

Bound PBR policy
: After you have created the PBR policy, you have to bind it to the incoming traffic interface, zone, or VR to achieve your goal.

You can also view each component separately using the selective component in the command line, as shown here:

```
SSG-> get vr trust-vr pbr ?
access-list          pbr access-list
action-group         pbr action-group
configuration        show pbr configuration
match-group          pbr match-group
policy               pbr policy name
```

CHAPTER 20
Multicast

20.0 Introduction

IP Multicast is a fairly well-defined set of protocols that allows for more efficient distribution of a data stream to many receivers. Although the concept of IP Multicast is not new, the applications to date that have taken advantage of multicast delivery mechanisms are still not commonly deployed. There are a few technical reasons for this, but perhaps the primary factor that has delayed the large-scale deployment of multicast-based applications is the nature of the Internet itself. One of the primary benefits of IP-based communications is the asynchronicity the protocols afford. By taking advantage of the asynchronous nature of IP, many receivers can access the same information "at leisure." This model has seen tremendous success with applications such as the Web, the File Transfer Protocol (FTP), and email, where information is relatively static. Because the benefit of IP Multicast is the ability to minimize network utilization by sending the same stream of traffic to multiple receivers, it follows that all of the listeners must receive the feed simultaneously. This obviously breaks the traditional asynchronous model of IP, and is a likely contributor to the limited deployment of IP Multicast.

Unfortunately, the Internet itself has seen limited multicast deployment at best, which stems largely from a lack of demand combined with the lack of an interdomain multicast routing protocol. Although the Multicast Source Discovery Protocol (MSDP) and the Multiprotocol Border Gateway Protocol (MBGP) have added interdomain routing capabilities to multicast, an actual multicast feed is typically an "add-on" service from Internet Service Providers (ISPs).

Multicast Applications

Given that overview, the following question arises: What are actual deployed multicast applications, both on and off the Internet? Television is an excellent example of such an application. Although television is frequently considered to be a broadcast application, this is not necessarily the case, because only those receivers who have "tuned in" to the proper channel actually receive the information stream. IP Multicast works in much the same way. Instead of tuning into a frequency, multicast receivers tune into a group IP address. A multicast address is defined as a Class D IP address, which is in the range of `224.0.0.0`–`239.255.255.255`. There are two reserved ranges of multicast addresses: `224.0.0.0`–`224.0.0.255` is reserved for *locally scoped communication* (these addresses cannot be forwarded outside of the local subnet), and `239.0.0.0`–`239.255.255.255`, which is *organizationally scoped*. You can think of the organizationally scoped range in much the same way as the RFC 1918 private address space is thought of for unicast (`10.0.0.0/8`, `172.16.0.0/12`, and `192.168.0.0/16`). Numerous applications take advantage of multicast using the locally scoped address space. One of the most common is the Open Shortest Path First (OSPF) protocol, which uses `224.0.0.5` and `224.0.0.6` to send Hello packets and routing updates. All OSPF routers "listen" to `224.0.0.5`, and the designated router and backup designated router listen to `224.0.0.6`. Although the Internet itself has not adopted multicast delivery mechanisms for the reasons previously described, multicast applications are being deployed increasingly in extranets and campus networks. Two of the most common applications using multicast are market data feeds and e-learning.

Hosts indicate a desire to receive a multicast stream of data by using the Internet Group Management Protocol (IGMP). When a host wants to receive a multicast data stream, it sends an IGMP report on to the network, which indicates the group address in which it is interested. The designated router on the LAN listens for IGMP reports, and when a report is received for an unknown group, it attempts to join the multicast tree for this group. We will briefly describe the methods used to join the tree shortly, but for a more comprehensive explanation of this topic and of multicast in general, see the book *Interdomain Multicast Routing* by Brian M. Edwards et al. (Addison-Wesley).

Multicast routing is sometimes referred to as routing in reverse. Instead of finding the best path to the destination of a packet, in a multicast scenario the router's job is to find the best path away from the source. A few protocols accomplish this task today, but the most common is Protocol Independent Multicast (PIM). PIM utilizes the unicast routing protocol (OSPF, the Routing Information Protocol [RIP], BGP, Static, etc.) to determine the best path to the source of a multicast data stream. This process is called *reverse-path forwarding* (RPF), and the determination of the best path is typically referred to as the *RPF check*. Multicast routing protocols fall into two general types: dense mode and sparse mode. A *dense mode protocol* assumes that all hosts will want to receive the data in a multicast stream, and a sparse mode protocol assumes that there will be relatively few listeners. Dense mode protocols will typically flood their data to all possible receivers. When a router has no interested receivers downstream, it will signal the upstream routers that it is no longer interested in a data stream (referred to as *pruning*). *Sparse mode protocols*, on the other hand, require explicit joins from interested hosts before they signal upstream routers that they are interested in receiving a data stream. As you may expect, this method is more efficient from both a router and a network resource utilization perspective, and as such, architectures based on sparse mode protocols, particularly PIM sparse mode (PIM-SM), have become the predominantly deployed multicast architectures to date.

One of the problems with a sparse mode protocol is that when a host is interested in receiving traffic destined to a particular group, unless the host knows the source address and is running IGMPv3, the IGMP report will contain only the group address that it wants to join. This presents an incomplete picture to the router because it's a bit of a challenge to route away from the source when you don't know what the source is. In PIM-SM, the solution to this problem is the use of Rendezvous Points (RPs).

Simply put, all routers in a PIM-SM network will forward joins for all unknown group addresses to the RP (hence the name), and the RP will forward traffic for the group back to those interested listeners. Likewise, a router connected to a multicast source will send its multicast traffic to the RP so that interested listeners can receive the stream, as shown in Figure 20-1. The actual mechanism via which this is performed is fairly complex, and we'll cover it only briefly. For more detailed explanations, see the book *Interdomain Multicast Routing*.

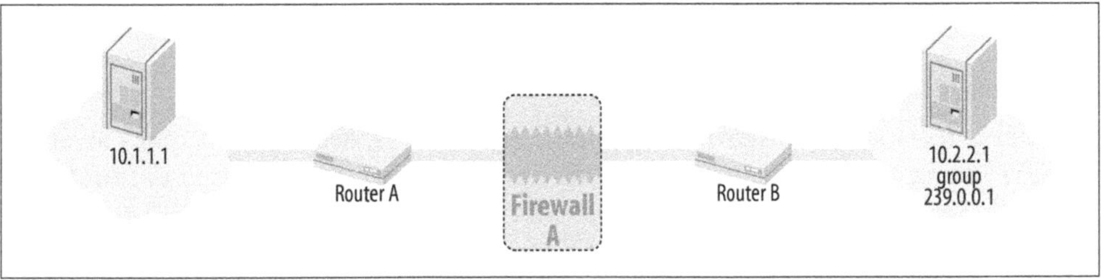

Figure 20-1. A sample multicast topography

Using Figure 20-1 as a guide, let's dissect what's happening in the multicast mechanisms:

1. `ROUTER-A` is connected to source `10.1.1.1` and begins to receive traffic for group `239.0.0.1`. At this point, no state exists for the group, and no routers in the network are prepared to forward the traffic.
2. The router at the source, after determining the RP for the group (more on this later), encapsulates the multicast packets in a unicast packet and tunnels the packet to the RP, which in this case is `FIREWALL-A`. The new packet headers have the source-attached router as the source IP, the RP as the destination IP, and a protocol number of 103 (PIM), and are referred to as *PIM register packets*.
3. The RP receives these packets, decapsulates them, and creates a state entry for the source/group pair. This state entry is commonly called an `S,G` (sound the letters out) entry, and would take the form `10.1.1.1, 239.0.0.1`, which indicates a source address of `10.1.1.1` and a group address of `239.0.0.1`.

4. FIREWALL-A then sends a join/prune to ROUTER-A indicating that it should send the multicast traffic natively rather than continuing to encapsulate the packets in register messages. FIREWALL-A also sends a register stop message to ROUTER-A.
5. Next, a listener on ROUTER-B sends an IGMP report indicating that it wants to receive traffic for 239.0.0.1.
6. ROUTER-B, not knowing the group's source address, checks its RP → group mapping, and finds that FIREWALL-A is the RP for 239.0.0.1.
7. ROUTER-B then creates a state table entry for 239.0.0.1, but not knowing the source address for the group, it sets the source to *, meaning any source. The state table entry takes the form of (*,239.0.0.1). This representation is referred to as a *,G (again, sound it out).
8. ROUTER-B then sends FIREWALL-A a join/prune for 239.0.0.1, with the source address set to *, indicating that it wants to receive traffic for 239.0.0.1 from any source.
9. FIREWALL-A receives the join/prune from ROUTER-B, checks its own state table, and finds an S,G entry for the group. FIREWALL-A then puts the interface connected to ROUTER-B in its outbound interface (OIF) list for the group.
10. At this point, native multicast traffic can flow from 10.1.1.1–10.2.2.1, as a multicast tree has been built. This particular type of tree is called the *RPT* or *Rendezvous Point Tree*.
11. Upon receipt of the first multicast packet, however, ROUTER-B becomes aware of the source address for the group and can create an S,G entry in addition to the *,G entry it already has in place. This S,G entry is forwarded toward the source and creates what is known as the *Shortest Path Tree* (SPT). This is traditionally done upon receipt of the first packet; however, in some networks, it is not done at all depending on the administrator's preference. The advantage of creating the SPT is that if the RP is not in the middle of the shortest path from the receiver to the source, the RPT will inevitably use network resources unnecessarily and will force the data to traverse a less efficient path. The advantage of using the RPT and never switching to an SPT is that strong control can be maintained over the paths that are used. RP placement can act as a form of traffic engineering much like Network Address Translation (NAT) can for unicast networks.

When the listener is no longer interested, it will send an IGMP leave to ROUTER-B, which will in turn send a join/prune to FIREWALL-A, this time with the action of prune, and the tree will become undone.

You can determine the RP for a particular group via three different methods, two of which are standard, and one of which is proprietary to Cisco Systems:

Static configuration

This is the simplest method in use, where the user configures the RP address → group manually on each router.

Auto-RP
: Cisco Systems developed this method, and it is in widespread use in the enterprise. It uses dense mode PIM to forward auto-RP messages between routers, and allows for RP redundancy.

BSR (bootstrap router)
: This is a standardized method of dynamic RP mapping, and it allows for redundancy as well as load sharing for RP duties.

ScreenOS supports both static RP mapping and BSR, although currently, ScreenOS cannot be the bootstrap router itself (see Recipe 20.8). The major disadvantage to static RP configuration is the lack of redundancy. This problem has largely been addressed by the use of *anycast RP* in which multiple RPs in the network are configured with the same loopback address (which is announced to the network via its Interior Gateway Protocol [IGP]). When a router attempts to contact its RP, its local routing table will send it to the closest announcement of the RP address. This requires some coordination on the part of the RPs, in that they must have a method of communicating active groups. This is handled by MSDP, which must run between all RPs. The advantage of anycast RP is that it provides the simplicity of static RP configuration along with the benefits of load sharing and redundancy. An additional benefit is that it provides faster failover between RPs than either auto-RP or BSR, as failover becomes dependent upon IGP convergence. Note that even in cases where either BSR or auto-RP is run, it can be used in conjunction with a static/anycast RP configuration to provide a solution. As the benefits of anycast RP have become apparent, this type of topology has become increasingly common.

ScreenOS supports PIM-SM version 2. Additionally, ScreenOS supports the notion of IGMP proxy mode and static multicast routes to allow multicast forwarding without the overhead and complexity associated with PIM-SM. Also, the transparent mode of operation (see Chapter 5) supports the forwarding of multicast traffic by virtue of operating at Layer 2.

20.1 Allow Multicast Traffic Through a Transparent Mode Device

Problem

You want to allow all multicast traffic to traverse a transparent mode device and enter your trusted network.

Solution

Create a standard policy using the Class D address space as the destination:

```
FIREWALL-A-> set address v1-trust all-mcast 224.0.0.0/4
FIREWALL-A-> set policy from v1-untrust to v1-trust any all-mcast any
    permit log
```

When using an ISG or NS5000 device, enter the following command to optimize performance:

```
FIREWALL-A-> set flow multicast install-hw-session
```

Discussion

In transparent mode, ScreenOS forwards packets at Layer 2, and the destination of the incoming frame is the destination Media Access Control (MAC) address rather than the destination IP address. Similar to a switch, a device in transparent mode builds a MAC table that correlates a list of MAC addresses with the ports on which they are known. This is accomplished by reading the source MAC field of incoming Ethernet frames to capture this information. See Chapter 5 for more information. Because multicast MAC addresses are derived from the multicast group address and are used only as listeners on hosts interested in the group, they should never appear in the source address of a frame, and thus do not populate the MAC table of the firewall.

There are two common solutions to this issue at Layer 2. The first is to simply flood the multicast frame out through all ports, and the second is to use IGMP snooping. (ScreenOS supports the first method, whereas *IGMP snooping* is a mechanism by which a switch reads the group information from IGMP reports that it sees and forwards groups only to ports where there are active listeners.)

Although forwarding of frames occurs at the MAC layer, all firewall functionality is handled as would be expected at the IP layer (and above). Because multicast is a unidirectional stream, there is no concept of state per se when operating in transparent mode.

This recipe permits all multicast traffic through the device, which is configured with the address book entry `224.0.0.0/4`. If you want to specify a more granular set of addresses (which you probably do), you can use either the specific groups as 32-bit address objects, or a range of groups using standard classless interdomain routing (CIDR) notation. The policy defined should be relatively straightforward. Any source address should be able to send any traffic to any group, and you should log this traffic.

The third command in this recipe enhances performance. The ASICs in Juniper's firewall products do not replicate multicast packets, so this function is left up to the CPU. To install a session in the ASIC for forwarding, you can have only a single OIF for the particular stream. Because transparent mode has no concept of multicast state, the only way to force a single OIF is to have only two active interfaces. Additionally, you must configure the device with only two Layer 2 zones. Although the majority of multicast deployments the authors have seen fit this description, it is a limitation to be aware of when deploying a transparent mode firewall for multicast traffic—if there are multiple OIFs or more than two zones while traffic is still forwarded, performance is limited by the CPU.

Multicast forwarding in transparent mode is something inherent to ScreenOS and is one reason for using transparent mode in more complex environments. It has the primary advantage of being able to provide policy control without introducing routing changes into the network, and it is operationally simple to understand.

See Also

Chapter 5

20.2 Use Multicast Group Policies to Enforce Stateful Multicast Forwarding

Problem

You're running a firewall in Layer 3 mode, and you need to create a policy to statefully enforce multicast traffic.

Solution

Use a multicast group policy to allow multicast control messages between zones:

```
FIREWALL-A-> set vrouter trust-vr
FIREWALL-A(trust-vr)-> set access-list 10 permit ip 239.1.2.3/32 10
FIREWALL-A(trust-vr)-> exit
FIREWALL-A-> set multicast-group-policy from trust mgroup-list 10 to
    untrust igmp-message bi-directional
```

Discussion

Setting up a multicast group policy to allow the firewall to create multicast state is required for support of multicast traffic in route mode. Two types of policies can be configured: one for IGMP proxy mode, and one for PIM depending on the device's operating mode. Multicast group policies are a frequent source of confusion when you are first configuring ScreenOS to forward multicast traffic, but conceptually, they are fairly simple. Unlike traditional firewall policies that are used to permit or deny traffic, multicast group policies are used to add a stateful enforcement capability to multicast. Because multicast traffic flows are unidirectional, to enforce a component of state ScreenOS looks at the state of the flow, much as a router would. Multicast forwarding has a control component similar to other higher-layer protocols. The primary difference is that multicast state exists purely at Layer 3. In PIM, a router forms state when a downstream device is interested in receiving traffic from an upstream source. It does this by joining the multicast tree (see Recipe 20.1).

Control messages, such as IGMP and PIM messages, are treated in much the same way as ports and header flags are checked in a Transmission Control Protocol (TCP) setup. In ScreenOS, unless the connection can be set up either via a three-way handshake on a permitted port (in the case of a unicast TCP connection), via IGMP, or

PIM messages for multicast, the data is not permitted through the firewall because state will not be created. Like standard firewall policies in ScreenOS, multicast group policies apply to zones. Here, the policy allows IGMP information to pass between zones.

This can be confusing because no actual data is being transmitted "through" the policy. Instead, the policy allows the upstream interface—in this case, the interface in the `Untrust` zone—to do what is necessary to create forwarding state. Regardless of the protocol running (IGMP proxy mode or PIM on the interface in the `Untrust` zone), the presence of the multicast group policy allows the firewall to receive an IGMP report on an interface in its `Trusted` zone to create multicast state (e.g., a `*,G` entry for the group), and to send either an IGMP report out its `Untrust` interface if operating in IGMP proxy mode or a join/prune message if it is running PIM.

Let's step through another example, as shown in Figure 20-2. In this case, the firewall (`FIREWALL-A`) is running PIM on all its interfaces and `ROUTER-A` is the RP.

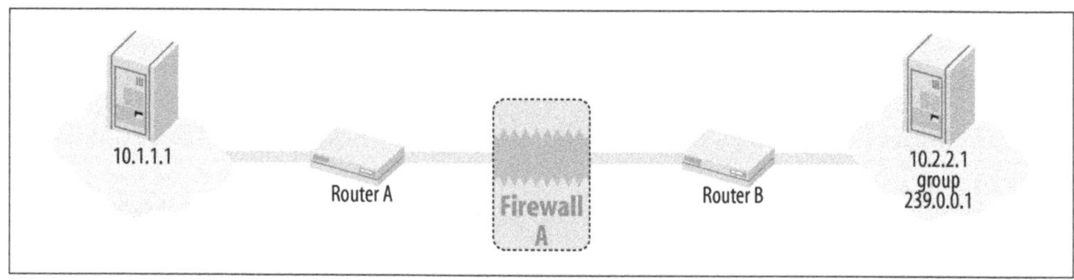

Figure 20-2. A simple PIM-enabled network

```
FIREWALL-A-> set vrouter trust-vr
FIREWALL-A(trust-vr)-> set access-list 20 permit ip 224.0.0.0/4 10
FIREWALL-A(trust-vr)-> exit
FIREWALL-A-> set multicast-group-policy from trust mgroup-list 20 to
    untrust pim-message bsr-static-rp join-prune bi-directional
```

There are two primary differences between a multicast group policy and a firewall policy:

- The direction the policy is applied to in multicast traffic is the opposite direction of the stream itself.
- The policy applies to the underlying control protocols rather than the data itself.

In this example, when host `10.2.2.1` sends an IGMP report for group `239.0.0.1`, `ROUTER-B` receives the packet, checks its mroute table, finds no entries, creates a `*,G`, and forwards a PIM join/prune upstream to `FIREWALL-A`.

When `FIREWALL-A` receives the join/prune, it verifies that it doesn't have existing mroute state for the group, and then checks its multicast group policy. The first item checked is the RP mapping for the group. The multicast group policy statement has the keyword `bsr-static-rp`. This keyword tells the firewall that it can perform an RP mapping for any groups matching access list 20, which in this case allows RP mapping to be performed for 224.0.0.0/4 (in other words, for all multicast groups). If the group was not matched via the access list referenced in the policy, the firewall would not spend the CPU cycles even trying to find an RP mapping for the group.

Once the RP mapping is permitted, the router does the lookup and finds that its RP is the loopback address of ROUTER-A. The next item checked in the multicast group policy is whether state can be created by allowing a join/prune to be sent from the untrusted interface. Again, access list 20 is validated against the group in the received join/prune, and is determined to be valid. At this point, a join/prune is sent upstream to ROUTER-A and a *,G entry is created on FIREWALL-A. Now that the multicast state has been established, FIREWALL-A can begin to receive and forward traffic for the group...well, almost.

What's missing? There's no policy for the actual data to flow. Remember, the multicast group policy is a tool used to create multicast state in the firewall—it actually does nothing to permit traffic in and of itself. To accomplish this, you can define a simple policy, as shown here:

```
FIREWALL-A-> set address trust 239.0.0.1/32 239.0.0.1/32
FIREWALL-A-> set policy from untrust to trust any 239.0.0.1/32 any permit
     log
```

You may now be wondering why the multicast group policy is necessary if you still need a firewall policy. Aside from the need to create a form of state, to ensure that the traffic is actually something a user requested, multicast group policies also provide protection to the firewall itself as well as the upstream routers. Multicast state is expensive for routers. A malicious user could fairly easily create significant amounts of multicast state in a network by simply generating IGMP reports for thousands of groups. Although it's unlikely that such an attack would crush today's network devices, it's always a good security practice to protect your resources.

We can verify that the multicast group policy is correctly installed by using the get multicast-group-policy command:

```
FIREWALL-A-> get multicast-group-policy
all multicast group policies:
from zone    to zone      src group/list      dst group/list  Messages
Trust        Untrust      20                  20              BSR
    Join/Prune
```

The multicast group policy references the access list we configured, although use of a group address is also permissible. We're using an access list because it is easier to add new groups, as they are simply additional lines in the access list configuration. Because in this example we referenced an access list, we should check the access list itself to verify that the correct groups are being matched, using the command get vrouter trust-vr access-list:

```
FIREWALL-A-> get vrouter trust-vr access-list
IPv4 Access Lists
```

```
---------------------------------------------
Access list (20)
----------------
        Sequence 10: 224.0.0.0/4             -> Permit
IPv6 Access Lists
```

The output of this command shows that indeed all groups are being matched as desired. The /4 in the access list implies anything within the range, rather than an exact match.

See Also

Chapter 7

20.3 View mroute State

Problem

You want to view multicast routes on your SSG firewall.

Solution

Use the get mroute command in the Virtual Router (VR) context:

```
FIREWALL-A-> set vrouter trust-vr
FIREWALL-A(trust-vr)-> get vrouter trust-vr mroute
 Flags:   P - PIM, S - Static, I - IGMP-Proxy
          F - Forwarding, U - Pruned, D - Down, B - Backup, T -
   Registering
      N - Negative Cache, M - Dummy route (Iif in another virtual
   router)
 Virtual router: trust-vr
 ------------------------------------------------------------------
 Total multicast routes : 1/system-max

 (10.2.2.1, 239.0.0.1)       00:00:01    RPF: 10.5.5.254   P
   Input Interface  : bgroup0                zone: Trust
   Output Interfaces:
    zone         group            interface      source         uptime
      flags
    Untrust      239.0.0.1        eth0/0         10.2.2.1     00:00:01
      PF
```

Discussion

The get mroute command is executed on a per-vrouter basis, like standard get route commands. Unlike with the get route command, however, with get mroute the trust-vr is not the default value, so the VR name must be explicitly stated if you are not within the vrouter context. At a high level, the command will display the (S,G) or (*,G) information for all mroutes, along with information regarding how the routes are formed and forwarded. Recall from Recipe 20.1 that by default (and in most instances), upon receipt of the first packet in a multicast stream, the router that initiated the (*,G) will switch from the RPT to the SPT by issuing an (S,G) join/prune toward the RP. At the VR level of the hierarchy, once traffic is flowing, there should always be an (S,G) entry in this output. Depending on where the command was issued in the configuration hierarchy, the output will differ. In the VR hierarchy, for example, the command shows the state of the mroute, as well as the information regarding how the route was learned. Adding a few static routes to our PIM learned route, we can see this in action:

```
FIREWALL-A(trust-vr)-> set mroute mgroup 239.0.0.2 source 0.0.0.0 iif
    bgroup0 oif eth0/0
FIREWALL-A(trust-vr)-> set mroute mgroup 239.0.0.3 source 10.2.2.1
    Iif bgroup0 oif eth0/0
FIREWALL-A(trust-vr)-> get mroute
 Flags:   P - PIM, S - Static, I - IGMP-Proxy
          F - Forwarding, U - Pruned, D - Down, B - Backup, T -
    Registering
          N - Negative Cache, M - Dummy route (Iif in another virtual
    router)
 Virtual router: trust-vr
 --------------------------------------------------------------------
 Total multicast routes : 3/system-max

 (10.2.2.1, 239.0.0.1)       00:06:58    RPF: 10.5.5.254 P
   Input Interface   : bgroup0                zone: Trust
   Output Interfaces:
    zone         group            interface       source       uptime
    flags
    Untrust      239.0.0.1        eth0/0          10.2.2.1  00:06:58
    PF

 (*, 239.0.0.2)                   00:00:25    RPF: 0.0.0.0        S
   Input Interface   : bgroup0                zone: Trust
   Output Interfaces:
    zone         group            interface       source       uptime
    flags
    Untrust      239.0.0.2        eth0/0          0.0.0.0      00:00:25
    SF

 (10.2.2.1, 239.0.0.3)       00:00:06    RPF: 0.0.0.0        S
   Input Interface   : bgroup0                zone: Trust
   Output Interfaces:
    zone         group            interface       source       uptime
    flags
    Untrust      239.0.0.3        eth0/0          10.2.2.1  00:00:06
    SF
```

In this output, we see three types of mroutes. The first is learned via PIM, as indicated with the P flag. The RPF section on the static mroutes is set to 0s because the RPF is implied with the setting of the Inbound Interface (IIF) in the set mroute command. In the PIM learned route, as expected, the RPF is shown in this column to be the next-hop to the source. We also can see the forwarding state of each interface.

When executed at the set vrouter trust-vr protocol PIM hierarchy, the output is different:

```
FIREWALL-A(trust-vr/pim)-> get mroute
trust-vr - PIM-SM routing table
-----------------------------------------------------------------------------
Register - R, Connected members - C, Pruned - P, Pending SPT Alert -
 G, Forward - F, Null - N , Negative Cache - E, Local Receivers - L
SPT - T, Proxy-Register - X, Imported - I, SGRpt state - Y, SSM Range
    Group - S
Turnaround Router - K
-----------------------------------------------------------------------------
Total PIM-SM mroutes: 2

(*, 239.0.0.1)  RP 10.6.6.1        00:00:28/-        Flags: F
  Zone             : Untrust
  Upstream         : ethernet0/0        State          : Joined
  RPF Neighbor     : local              Expires        : -
  Downstream       :
  ethernet0/0  00:00:28/00:03:09  Join         0.0.0.0        F

(10.2.2.1/24, 239.0.0.1)           00:00:27/00:03:01  Flags: TF
  Zone             : Trust
  Upstream         : bgroup0            State          : Joined
  RPF Neighbor     : 10.5.5.254      Expires        : 00:00:33
  Downstream       :
  ethernet0/0  00:00:27/00:03:00  Join         0.0.0.0
    10.2.2.1 F
```

In this output, we have a *,G for our PIM route as well as an (S,G). In the PIM hierarchy, we have much more information regarding the particular PIM attributes. The LF flags indicate that there is a local receiver to which the firewall is forwarding traffic. The FC flag on the interface indicates again that the interface is forwarding, and that there is a connected member. From this output, we can also see the RP information for the group, as well as the RPF neighbor.

Additionally, in the (S,G) route, we have the T flag set, indicating that the mroute is on the SPT which is, as expected, with an actively forwarding route. Note also that with the case of the (S,G) entry, there is no RP.

In general, the get mroute command executed at the VR level is a powerful tool for determining the multicast forwarding state of the firewall. It will show routes learned via any method, and it will provide information about them. For PIM-specific information, the get vrouter trust-vr protocol pim mroute command displays more PIM-specific information.

20.4 Use Static mroutes to Allow Multicast Through a Firewall Without Using PIM

Problem

You need to forward multicast traffic in route mode without using PIM.

Solution

Create a static mroute:

```
FIREWALL-A-> set vrouter trust-vr mroute mgroup 239.0.0.1 source
    10.1.1.1 iif ethernet0/0 oif ethernet0/1
```

Discussion

Static mroutes are a simple way to allow multicast through the firewall without the complexity and overhead of PIM. Because they create a simple static forwarding entry, they are easy to understand, even by firewall administrators who are not multicast experts. This capability can be tremendously useful in organizations where the firewall and router teams are separate. These organizations often use static routes for their unicast firewall connectivity, so it makes sense for them to use static mroutes as well. Unlike other vendor implementations, static mroutes in ScreenOS create actual forwarding entries. After creating the mroute, let's look at a sample mroute table.

```
FIREWALL-A-> get vrouter trust-vr mroute
 Flags:   P - PIM, S - Static, I - IGMP-Proxy
          F - Forwarding, U - Pruned, D - Down, B - Backup, T -
    Registering
       N - Negative Cache, M - Dummy route (Iif in another virtual
    router)
 Virtual router: trust-vr
 -------------------------------------------------------------------
 Total multicast routes : 1/system-max

 (10.1.1.1, 239.0.0.1)       30d;17:10:44 RPF: 0.0.0.0         S
   Input Interface  : ethernet0/0           zone: Untrust
   Output Interfaces:
    zone        group           interface      source       uptime
    flags
    DMZ         239.0.0.1       eth0/1      10.1.1.1   30d;17:10:44
    SD
```

In the output of the get vrouter trust-vr mroute command, we see that the S flag is assigned to this mroute, which indicates that the (S,G) entry was statically defined. In this example, if a multicast packet destined for 239.0.0.1 is received on ethernet0/0 with a source of 10.1.1.1, the firewall will forward this packet out interface ethernet0/1. In the case of a static mroute, you are creating the (S,G) state by virtue of creation of the mroute entry, so there is no need for an additional multicast group policy. Remember from Recipe 20.2 that multicast group policies apply to attempts to dynamically establish (S,G) state by either IGMP or PIM.

You also can use static mroutes at multicast domain borders to enable forwarding between different PIM domains, or even between different multicast routing protocols. Figure 20-3 shows an example of this use case.

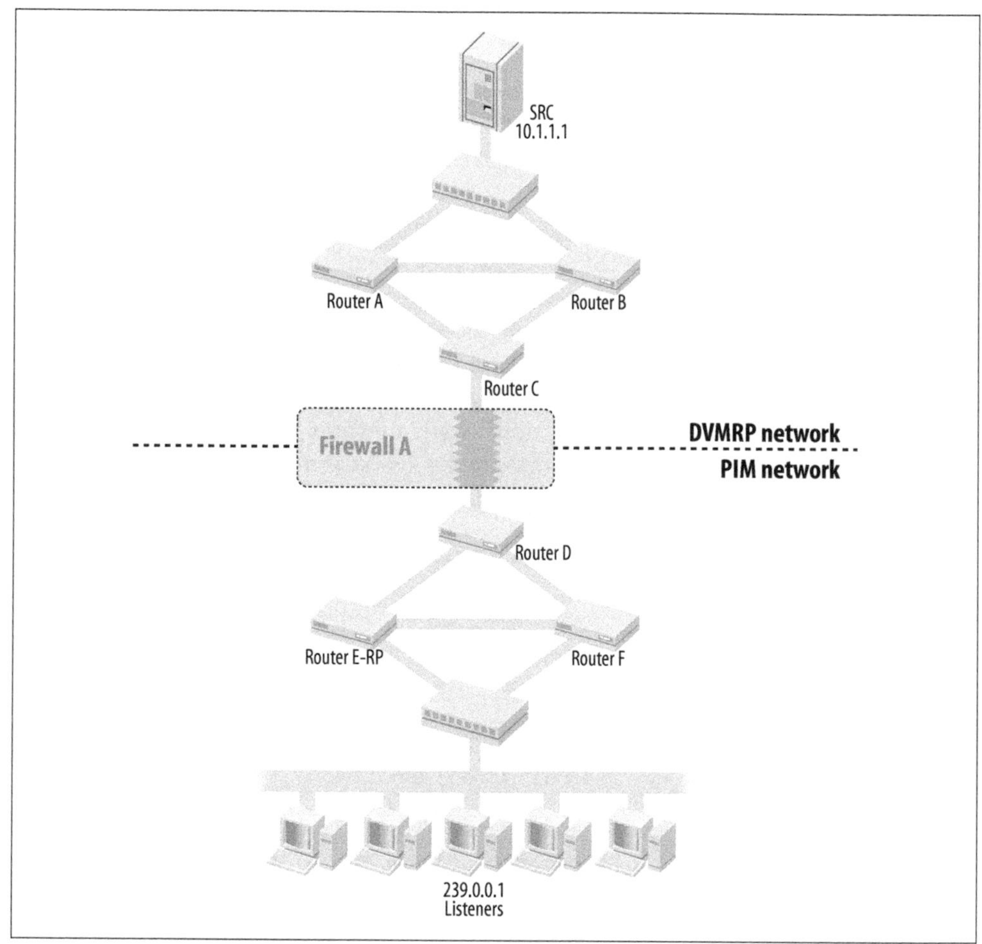

Figure 20-3. Connecting disparate multicast domains

In Figure 20-3, the listeners to group 239.0.0.1 are located in a network that runs PIM-SM. However, the source of the 239.0.0.1 stream is in a separate network which runs the Distance Vector Multicast Routing Protocol (DVMRP) as its multicast routing protocol. The two networks are connected by a firewall. To get the group information to propagate to the listeners, the administrators of the firewall have chosen to use a static mroute. To get the traffic to the firewall, a static IGMP join is placed on the downstream interface of ROUTER-C. This causes the router to send traffic for 239.0.0.1 out this interface, where it is received by FIREWALL-A. If there were a switch between ROUTER-C and FIREWALL-A, which performed IGMP snooping, this arrangement would not work without additional configuration. See Recipe 20.1 for a solution to this problem using IGMP proxy mode.

When the firewall receives the packets for 239.0.0.1, it first performs an mroute lookup, and finds that it has a static entry for (10.1.1.1, 239.0.0.1):

```
FIREWALL-A-> get vrouter trust-vr mroute
 Flags:   P - PIM, S - Static, I - IGMP-Proxy
          F - Forwarding, U - Pruned, D - Down, B - Backup, T -
    Registering
          N - Negative Cache, M - Dummy route (Iif in another virtual
    router)
 Virtual router: trust-vr
 ---------------------------------------------------------------------
 Total multicast routes : 1/system-max

 (10.1.1.1, 239.0.0.1)       30d;17:10:44 RPF: 0.0.0.0         S
   Input Interface  : ethernet0/0          zone: Untrust
   Output Interfaces:
    zone        group            interface     source       uptime
    flags
    DMZ         239.0.0.1        eth0/1        10.1.1.1  30d;17:10:44
    SD
```

A single output interface is listed for the mroute, and it indicates that packets should be forwarded out interface eth0/1 which, in this case, is connected to ROUTER-E. At this point, ROUTER-E will act as a traditional router connected to a multicast source in a PIM network, and the packets will be encapsulated in register messages and sent to ROUTER-E, the RP.

FIREWALL-A then performs a policy lookup and determines whether the packets should be forwarded; in this case, doing a get policy shows the following, which indicates that the traffic should be permitted:

```
FIREWALL-A-> get policy from untrust to dmz
    ID From     To        Src-address  Dst-address  Service
    Action State   ASTLCB
     2 Untrust  DMZ       Any          239.0.0.1/32 ANY
    Permit enabled ---X-X
```

Using our small sample network from Figure 20-3, let's imagine that a new network needs to connect to our PIM network, as depicted in Figure 20-4.

A problem will arise in Figure 20-4 when the firewall administrators connect to the new network. The new network is also transmitting to group address 239.0.0.1, but it is transmitting different data. In this network, the source for 239.0.0.1 is 10.2.2.1.

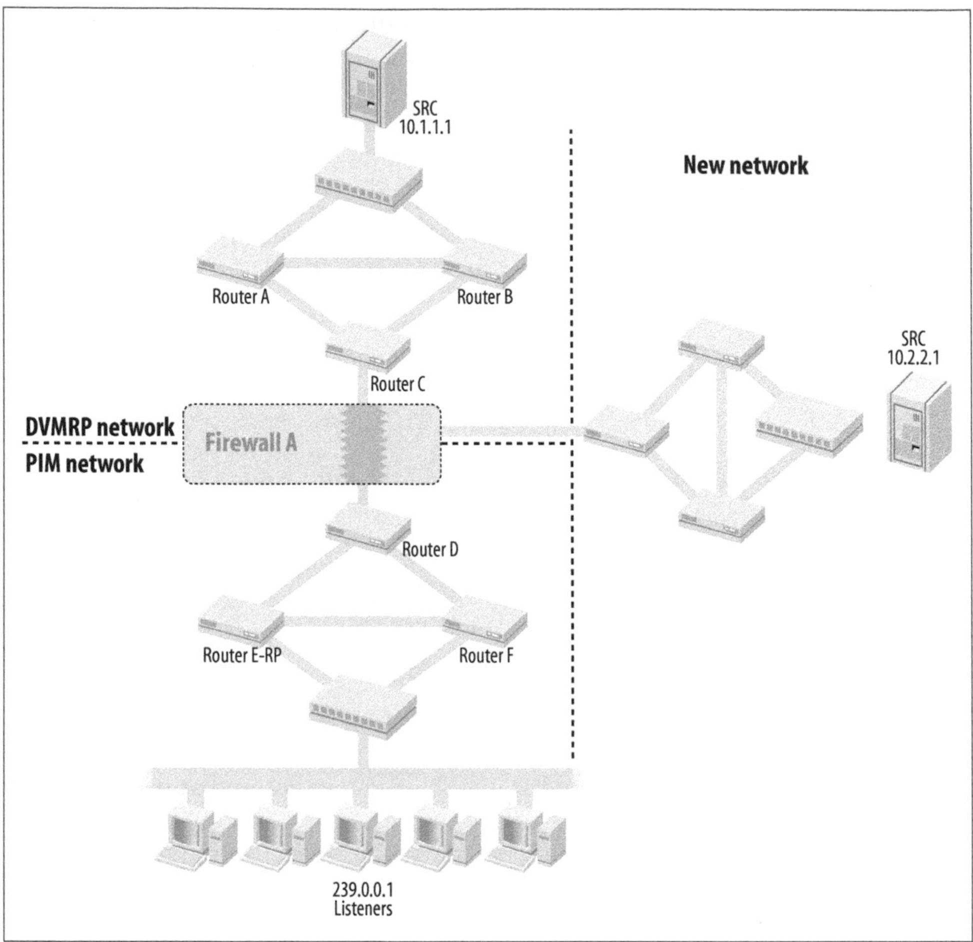

Figure 20-4. Two sources with one group address

To solve this problem, a static mroute is used, but the out group is modified (much like NAT in the unicast world):

```
FIREWALL-A(trust-vr)-> set mroute mgroup 239.0.0.1 source 10.2.2.1
    iif eth0/2 oif eth0/1 out-group 239.0.0.2
```

When executing this command, a second mroute is created in the firewall which translates the destination group so that the two data sets can be successfully received. Using the get mroute command, we can see the two separate mroutes installed with different sources:

```
FIREWALL-A(trust-vr)-> get mroute
 Flags:   P - PIM, S - Static, I - IGMP-Proxy
          F - Forwarding, U - Pruned, D - Down, B - Backup, T -
    Registering
         N - Negative Cache, M - Dummy route (Iif in another virtual
    router)
```

```
Virtual router: trust-vr
---------------------------------------------------------------------
Total multicast routes : 2/system-max

(10.2.2.1, 239.0.0.1)        00:00:55    RPF: 0.0.0.0        S
  Input Interface  : ethernet0/2            zone: Untrust
  Output Interfaces:
   zone         group            interface      source        uptime
   flags
   DMZ          239.0.0.2        eth0/1         10.2.2.1    00:00:55
   SD

(10.1.1.1, 239.0.0.1)        00:06:14    RPF: 0.0.0.0        S
  Input Interface  : ethernet0/0            zone: Untrust
  Output Interfaces:
   zone         group            interface      source        uptime
   flags
   DMZ          239.0.0.1        eth0/1         10.1.1.1    00:06:14
   SD
```

In the "Output Interfaces" section, the groups are different, enabling both streams to reach their listeners.

See Also

Recipe 20.3

20.5 Connect Directly to Multicast Receivers

Problem

You need the firewall to forward multicast traffic to a set of directly attached subscribers.

Solution

Enable IGMP on the connected interface:

```
FIREWALL-A-> set interface eth0/0 protocol igmp router
FIREWALL-A-> set interface eth0/0 protocol igmp enable
FIREWALL-A-> set interface eth0/0 protocol igmp no-check-router-alert
```

Discussion

ScreenOS is capable of receiving and acting on the receipt of IGMP reports from hosts, much like a standard router operating system. IGMP is the Internet Engineering Task Force (IETF) standard method for hosts to signal that they are interested in receiving a particular multicast data stream. There are three versions of IGMP—v1, v2, and v3—and ScreenOS supports all three. IGMPv2, defined in RFC 2236, is the most commonly used, and as such, it is the default version in ScreenOS. This is shown in the following output:

```
FIREWALL-A-> get int eth0/0 protocol igmp

Interface eth0/0 support IGMP version 2 router. It is enabled.
IGMP proxy is disabled.
Querier IP is 10.5.5.1, it has up 5 seconds. I am the querier.
There are 0 multicast groups active.
    Inbound Router access list number: not set
    Inbound Host access list number: not set
    Inbound Group access list number: not set
    query-interval: 125 seconds
    query-max-response-time 10 seconds
    leave-interval 1 seconds
    last-member-query-interval 1 seconds
```

IGMPv3 supports the concept of source-specific multicast (SSM), and it allows joins to a group to be processed on a per-source basis. The primary benefit of this is that when running PIM, the RP can be bypassed from the beginning so that only (S,G) joins need to be sent upstream. A detailed description of IGMP is beyond the scope of this recipe.

The configuration of IGMP in ScreenOS is fairly straightforward and is performed on a per-interface basis. The first task is to select whether the interface will be in router or host mode. (We discuss host mode in detail in Recipe 20.1.) After selecting router mode, you must enable the process. The last command in this recipe is optional. The command `set interface eth0/0 protocol igmp no-check-router-alert` tells the firewall to ignore the lack of a router alert in the IGMP header. According to RFC 2236, for IGMP reports the router alert option must be set in the IP header. In practice, however, not all implementations follow this rule, and without disabling this check, you may drop legitimate traffic.

When the firewall receives an IGMP report from a host, all it knows is that it needs to get traffic to the group specified in the report. Without knowing the source address of the traffic, the first thing it does is attempt to create (*,G) state. For the purpose of this example, assume IGMPv2 is running. To create state, the firewall must first verify that state should be created by checking its multicast group policy, as shown in Figure 20-5.

In Figure 20-5, the firewall is connected to a set of listeners on `eth0/0` located in the trusted zone. The device is connected to the rest of the network via `eth0/1` and is running PIM on this interface. The following is the output of the `get multicast-group-policy` command:

```
FIREWALL-A-> get multicast-group-policy
all multicast group policies:
from zone    to zone   src group/list dst group/list  Messages
Trust        Untrust   10             10              BSR Join/Prune
```

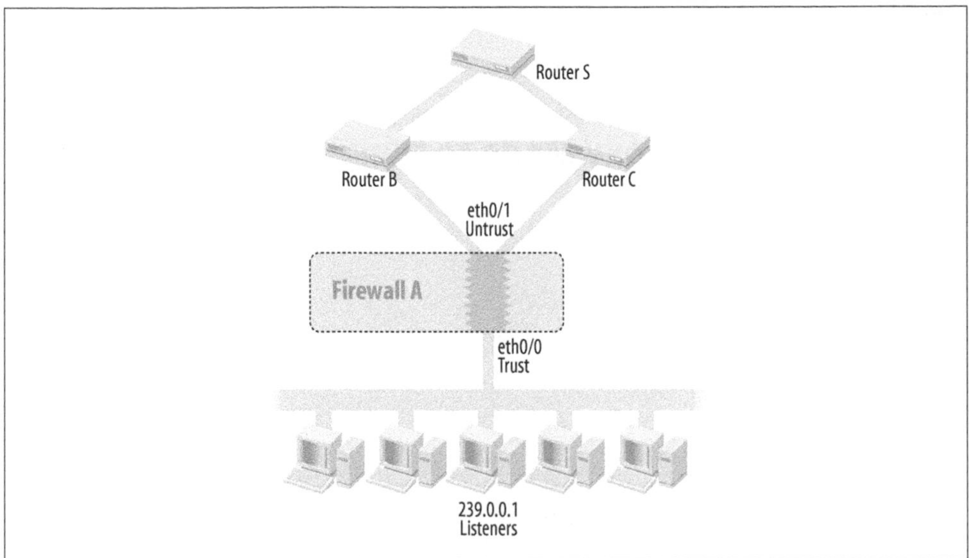

Figure 20-5. Firewall as a gateway

Examine access list 10:

```
FIREWALL-A-> get vrouter trust-vr access-list
IPv4 Access Lists
------------------------------------------------
Access list (10)
----------------
        Sequence 10: 224.0.0.0/4                -> Permit
IPv6 Access Lists
```

From this output, we can see that PIM state should be created for `239.0.0.1` as hoped because it falls into the `224.0.0.0/4` network. But wait, if this all started with an IGMP report, why are we looking at a PIM policy? The answer is because the IGMP report received causes the device to attempt to create state for the `239.0.0.1` group, and without the source information, the first thing the device attempts to do is create this `*,G` state. To do that, it needs to perform an RP mapping, which is a PIM function. (Recipe 20.2 discusses the need for a multicast group policy to perform RP to group mapping.) Because the listeners are located in the `Trust` zone, and the PIM process is running on the `Untrust` zone, it logically follows that the direction of the multicast group policy should be from `Trust` to `Untrust`, which in this case it is. Additionally, because the RP mapping and join/prune must be completed by PIM, it also follows that the multicast group policy be applied for PIM rather than for IGMP.

Once the firewall has performed the multicast group policy check, it creates the appropriate `*,G` state, forwards a join/prune toward the RP, and, once joined to the tree, begins to forward multicast traffic to the hosts on `eth0/0`.

See Also

RFC 2236; RFC 3376; Recipe 20.1; Recipe 20.3; Recipe 20.7

20.6 Use IGMP Proxy Mode to Dynamically Join Groups

Problem

You need to forward multicast traffic to connected hosts, but your upstream router, connected over a virtual private network (VPN), isn't running PIM on its connected interface.

Solution

Use IGMP proxy mode to send IGMP reports to your upstream router. First, configure a Generic Routing Encapsulation (GRE) tunnel. This enables the router to replicate the multicast traffic instead of the firewall:

```
FIREWALL-B-> set interface "tunnel.1" zone "Trust"
FIREWALL-B-> set interface tunnel.1 ip 192.168.11.1/24
FIREWALL-B-> set interface tunnel.1 tunnel encap gre
FIREWALL-B-> set interface tunnel.1 tunnel local-if loopback.1
    dst-ip 192.168.6.1
```

Next, configure an IP Security (IPSec) tunnel, and bind the Security Association (SA) to the GRE interface:

```
FIREWALL-B-> set ike gateway "FIREWALL-A" address 192.168.5.2 Main
    outgoing-interface "bgroup0" preshare
    "fWKPq2wzNvhiMpsxg0Cr+wBEYpnYfvUoIQ==" sec-level standard
FIREWALL-B-> set vpn "firewall-a" gateway "FIREWALL-A" no-replay
    tunnel idletime 0 sec-level standard
FIREWALL-B-> set vpn "firewall-a" monitor optimized rekey
FIREWALL-B-> set vpn "firewall-a" id 1 bind interface tunnel.1
FIREWALL-B-> set route 192.168.7.0/24 interface tunnel.1
FIREWALL-B-> set route 192.168.6.1/32 interface tunnel.1
```

Configure the firewall in IGMP proxy mode:

```
FIREWALL-B-> set interface eth0/0 protocol igmp router
FIREWALL-B-> set interface eth0/0 protocol igmp enable
FIREWALL-B-> set interface eth0/0 protocol igmp no-check-router-alert
FIREWALL-B-> set interface eth0/0 protocol igmp no-check-subnet
FIREWALL-B-> set interface tunnel.1 protocol igmp host
FIREWALL-B-> set interface tunnel.1 protocol igmp enable
FIREWALL-B-> set interface eth0/0 protocol igmp proxy
FIREWALL-B-> set vrouter trust-vr access-list 10 permit ip
224.0.0.0/4 10
FIREWALL-B-> set multicast-group-policy from trust mgroup-list 10 to
    untrust igmp-message bi-directional
```

Discussion

IGMP proxy mode is another method of deploying a ScreenOS firewall into a multicast environment without running PIM. As with static mroutes, this simplifies the configuration and operation of the firewalls, as in-depth knowledge of PIM is not required. Unlike static mroutes, IGMP proxy mode allows for dynamic forwarding of groups through the device as IGMP reports are simply "proxied" upstream. Because of this functionality, no beforehand knowledge of group information is required, and configuration burden is minimized. However, to take full advantage of this capability, IGMP reports must be received by the firewall, which (mostly) limits an IGMP proxy mode deployment to areas where listeners are directly connected. A common deployment for IGMP proxy mode is remote office connectivity. Figure 20-6 shows a common deployment of this architecture.

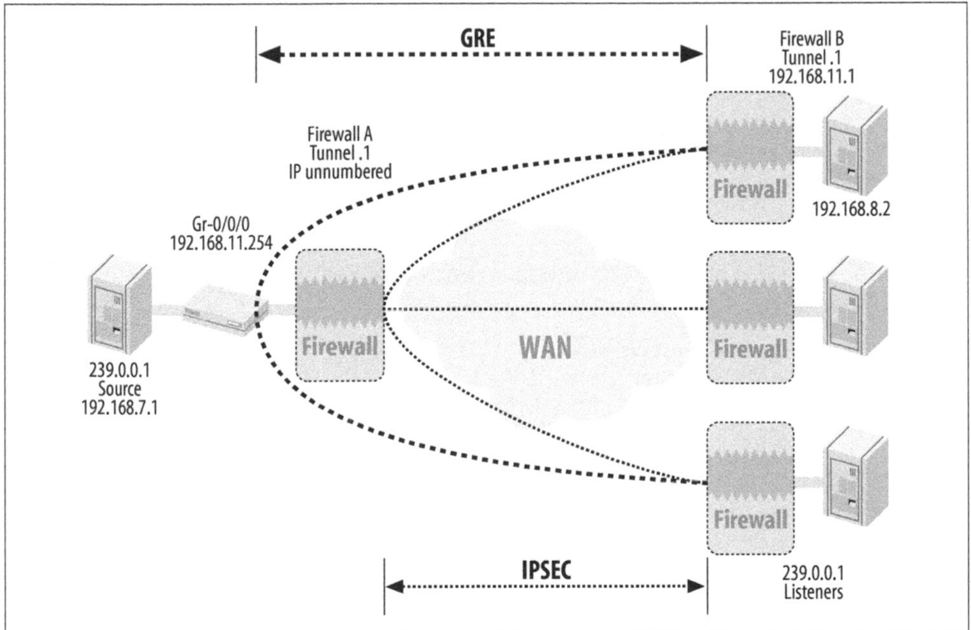

Figure 20-6. IGMP proxy mode at a branch

In the branch office deployment shown in Figure 20-6, the network administrators have decided to run their branch devices in IGMP proxy mode. All connectivity to the head end site is encrypted with IPSec. In this network, for performance and scalability reasons, a router is used to perform packet replication, as ScreenOS has a fairly low number of OIFs per stream. The router has a GRE tunnel to each branch and is running IGMP on the GRE tunnel interfaces. The firewall has an IPSec tunnel to each branch over which all of the GRE traffic is forwarded. At the branch side, the firewall is running IGMP in router mode on its trusted interface and IGMP in host mode on its GRE tunnel interface. There are two tunnels: the inner GRE tunnel and the outer Encapsulating Security Protocol (ESP) tunnel. Although double encapsulation of packets is not typically desired, in this situation, it makes sense. The router can perform replication at high speed without the burden of encryption, while the firewall at the hub site can perform encryption without the burden of replication.

As shown, because IGMP is the only multicast protocol enabled on FIREWALL-B, IGMP messages must be permitted to create (*,G) and (S,G) state on the device. This is reflected in the multicast group policy:

```
FIREWALL-B-> get conf | include pim
FIREWALL-B-> get conf | include igmp
set interface tunnel.1 protocol igmp host
set interface tunnel.1 protocol igmp enable
set interface ethernet0/0 protocol igmp router
set interface ethernet0/0 protocol igmp proxy
set interface ethernet0/0 protocol igmp static-group 239.0.0.1
set interface ethernet0/0 protocol igmp no-check-subnet
set interface ethernet0/0 protocol igmp no-check-router-alert
set interface ethernet0/0 protocol igmp enable
set multicast-group-policy from "Untrust" mgroup-list 10 to "Trust"
    igmp-message bi-directional
FIREWALL-B-> get multicast-group-policy
all multicast group policies:
from zone     to zone       src group/list     dst group/list  Messages
Untrust       Trust         10                 10              IGMP
```

When a host on the ethernet0/0 interface sends a report, FIREWALL-B creates mroute state as expected as a *,G:

```
FIREWALL-B-> get vr trust-vr mroute
 Flags:    P - PIM, S - Static, I - IGMP-Proxy
           F - Forwarding, U - Pruned, D - Down, B - Backup, T -
    Registering
         N - Negative Cache, M - Dummy route (Iif in another virtual
    router)
 Virtual router: trust-vr
 --------------------------------------------------------------------
 Total multicast routes : 1/system-max

(*, 239.0.0.1)                  00:17:45    RPF: 0.0.0.0          I
   Input Interface  : tunnel.1              zone: Trust
   Output Interfaces:
    zone        group            interface       source        uptime
    flags
    Untrust     239.0.0.1        eth0/0          0.0.0.0      00:00:11
    IF
```

This output shows that there is an mroute entry for any source transmitting to 239.0.0.1. Because the device is configured to be in IGMP proxy mode, the input interface is inherited from this and is set as tunnel.1. The source IP is still unknown, and from the flags, we can see that the mroute information was created by the IGMP proxy functionality, and the state is forwarding out interface eth0/0.

Once a source becomes active, two mroutes appear in the vrouter mroute table:

```
FIREWALL-B-> get vr trust-vr mroute
 Flags:   P - PIM, S - Static, I - IGMP-Proxy
          F - Forwarding, U - Pruned, D - Down, B - Backup, T -
    Registering
          N - Negative Cache, M - Dummy route (Iif in another virtual
    router)
 Virtual router: trust-vr
 ----------------------------------------------------------------------
 Total multicast routes : 2/system-max

 (192.168.7.1, 239.0.0.1)         00:00:01     RPF: 0.0.0.0        I
   Input Interface  : tunnel.1                 zone: Trust
   Output Interfaces:
    zone         group            interface      source         uptime
    flags
    Untrust      239.0.0.1        eth0/0         192.168.7.1  00:00:01
    IF

 (*, 239.0.0.1)                   00:00:18     RPF: 0.0.0.0        I
   Input Interface  : tunnel.1                 zone: Trust
   Output Interfaces:
    zone         group            interface      source         uptime
    flags
    Untrust      239.0.0.1        eth0/0         0.0.0.0        00:00:18
    IF
```

There will always be a (*,G) in the mroute table when IGMP proxy mode is being used, as long as IGMPv3 isn't in use. This is because the reports do not indicate a source. The (S,G) appears once the source is learned by receipt of a data packet.

Like static mroutes (see Recipe 20.4), you also can use IGMP proxy mode to bridge different multicast domains. The main problem with using IGMP proxy mode for this functionality is that the major advantage it provides, namely dynamic learning and propagation of group information, is lost as the firewall typically connects to a downstream router, as seen in Figure 20-3. Here, the problem with running IGMP proxy mode is that the firewall will not receive IGMP reports from its downstream neighbor. To get around this, use a static IGMP join:

```
FIREWALL-B-> set interface eth0/1 protocol igmp static-group 239.0.0.5
```

On each interface running in IGMP router mode on the firewall, you can statically join specific groups. Using static groups is another simple method of joining two disparate multicast domains in addition to static mroutes.

See Also

Recipe 20.3; Recipe 20.4

20.7 Configure PIM on a Firewall

Problem

You need to configure PIM on the firewall to connect into your multicast infrastructure.

Solution

Enable PIM on the firewall and its interfaces, and configure RP mapping:

```
FIREWALL-A-> set vr trust-vr
FIREWALL-A(trust-vr)-> set access-list 10 permit ip 224.0.0.0/4 10
FIREWALL-A (trust-vr)-> set protocol pim
FIREWALL-A (trust-vr/pim)-> set enable
FIREWALL-A (trust-vr/pim)-> end
FIREWALL-A-> set interface eth0/0 protocol pim
FIREWALL-A-> set interface eth0/0 protocol pim enable
FIREWALL-A-> set interface bgroup0 protocol pim
FIREWALL-A-> set interface bgroup0 protocol pim enable
FIREWALL-A-> set vr trust-vr
FIREWALL-A (trust-vr)-> set protocol pim
FIREWALL-A (trust-vr/pim)-> set zone trust rp address 10.1.1.1
    mgroup-list 10 always
FIREWALL-A (trust-vr/pim)-> end
FIREWALL-A-> set multicast-group-policy from trust mgroup-list 10 to
    untrust pim-message bsr-static-rp join-prune bi-directional
```

Discussion

A simple PIM configuration is created to begin forwarding multicast. Although static mroutes and IGMP proxy mode provide simple methods of enabling multicast forwarding in ScreenOS, a number of restrictions may make them less desirable in more complex networks. For these situations, PIM is the best option.

Configuration of PIM within ScreenOS is a fairly straightforward task. It involves enabling the protocol in the VR, enabling PIM on participating interfaces, and configuring RP mapping information. In this recipe, we look at static RP mapping as it is probably the most common configuration. When using a static RP, the most glaring potential issue is that the RP itself becomes a single point of failure. Typically, however, anycast RP is used to address this limitation. In anycast RP, multiple RPs in a network are configured with the same loopback address. The net effect of this is that the IGP on the device running PIM will forward PIM messages toward the "closest" RP. The RPs themselves must of course maintain knowledge about which groups are active on other RPs. This is accomplished via MSDP. You can find a full discussion on anycast RP in *Interdomain Multicast Routing*.

Once PIM is enabled and running on the interfaces, it will automatically form neighbors with other PIM routers:

```
FIREWALL-A-> get vrouter trust-vr protocol pim neighbor
Neighbor        Interface     Uptime      Expire     DR-priority GenId
```

```
------------------------------------------------------------------
10.5.5.254   bgroup0       00:27:59   00:01:25   1          57812845
10.6.6.254   ethernet0/0   00:27:32   00:01:40   1          13264904
```

After enabling PIM, neighbors have formed on the active interfaces. From the output of the get vrouter trust-vr protocol pim neighbor command, two neighbors are shown, one per interface, along with information about how long the neighbor has been active, the expire time, and its DR priority.

The get vrouter trust-vr protocol pim interface command is another useful command that shows the local address, the number of neighbors, the DR address, and the state of the interface:

```
FIREWALL-A-> get vrouter trust-vr protocol pim interface
Interface        Address      Neighbors DR              Enabled Link

------------------------------------------------------------------
bgroup0          10.5.5.3     1         10.5.5.254    Yes      Up

ethernet0/0      10.6.6.1     1         10.6.6.254    Yes      Up
```

You can find more detail by looking at the individual interface information:

```
FIREWALL-A-> get interface ethernet0/0 protocol pim
Interface          : ethernet0/0
Interface State    : up
Interface Type     : ethernet
PIM                : enabled
   Gen ID                    : 63263
   DR priority               : 1
   Elected DR                : 10.6.6.254
   DR Priority Chk needed    : Yes
   Elected DR Priority       : 1
   Hello Interval            : 30 seconds
   Join Prune Interval       : 60 seconds
   BootStrap Border          : not-configured
   Neighbor permit acl       : not-configured
   Number of neighbors       : 1
   Next Hello Expires in     : 00:00:19
```

The next thing to do is to verify the RP mapping information using the get vrouter trust-vr protocol pim rp all command:

```
FIREWALL-A-> get vrouter trust-vr protocol pim rp all
Flags : I - Imported, A - Always(override BSR mapping)
        C - Static Config, P - Static Proxy
Zone     Group/mask     RP-Address      Prio   Hold   Expire Flags
------------------------------------------------------------------
Trust    224.0.0.0/4    10.5.5.254   192    Static  -     AC

Untrust  224.0.0.0/4    10.5.5.254   192    Static  -     AIC Trust
```

You can see the effect of the multicast group policy. Each zone has RP information associated with it. In our simple example, there is just a single RP address, and it is the same in the Trust and Untrust zones. The other interesting information is in the "Flags" column. The Trust zone shows the AC flag for the RP mapping. This means this static configuration will override any RP information learned from the bootstrap router protocol (see Recipe 20.8). In the Untrust zone, however, the I flag is also set, meaning that the mapping was imported. Let's look at how and why this was imported. First, the RP configuration itself is a single command:

```
set zone "Trust" rp address 10.5.5.254 mgroup-list 10 always
```

This clearly shows how the Trust zone got its RP mapping. What about the Untrust zone, though? The answer lies in the multicast-group-policy:

```
FIREWALL-A-> get multicast-group-policy
all multicast group policies:
from zone    to zone     src group/list     dst group/list  Messages
Trust        Untrust     10                 10              BSR
    Join/Prune
```

Although it's not obvious, the last column (which shows the messages/information which can be passed between zones) indicates BSR and join/prune messages. However, when creating the policy, there is no distinction between methods for RP mapping. If you permit BSR, you also permit static RP. So, by virtue of allowing RP mapping between zones, static RP mapping information is automatically imported into the Untrust zone.

See Also

Recipe 20.8

20.8 Use BSR for RP Mapping

Problem

You want the firewall to be a backup RP for all multicast groups.

Solution

Use BSR and configure the firewall as a candidate RP:

```
FIREWALL-A-> set vrouter trust-vr
FIREWALL-A(trust-vr)-> set protocol pim
FIREWALL-A(trust-vr/pim)-> set zone trust rp candidate interface
    bgroup0 mgroup-list 10 priority 101
```

Discussion

The support for BSR within ScreenOS is limited, so the firewall cannot be a BSR itself. However, the firewall can receive and process BSR messages to learn its RP information, and it can send candidate RP messages for groups for which the firewall itself can act as the RP.

From a configuration perspective, if the firewall is not a candidate RP, nothing is required outside of the standard PIM static RP configuration; actually, less is required, as RP address configuration isn't needed. By default, ScreenOS will listen for bootstrap messages that are sent to the ALL-PIM-ROUTERS group, 224.0.0.13. If you want the firewall to be a candidate RP, the configuration is similar to static RP configuration. You can optionally select the groups for which it can be elected RP. As with static RP configuration, this is done using an mgroup list, which refers to an access list. In this recipe, as in others, use an access list to match all multicast groups:

```
FIREWALL-A-> get vrouter trust-vr config | include access-list
set access-list 10
set access-list 10 permit ip 224.0.0.0/4 10
FIREWALL-A->
```

BSR uses the concept of priority to elect the RP for a given group. When ScreenOS is configured as a candidate RP, it transmits the groups for which it is a candidate and the priority for each group to 224.0.0.13 in Candidate RP Advertisements. The BSR chooses the RP for each group and advertises these RP sets in bootstrap messages. To set the firewall as the backup RP for all groups, configure the priority for all groups to be 101, where the primary RP has a priority of 100. In BSR, as in many other protocols, it's sometimes easier to think about the "better" priority than the "higher" priority, as a higher numerical value means "less preferred":

```
FIREWALL-A-> get vrouter trust-vr protocol pim rp all
Flags : I - Imported, A - Always(override BSR mapping)
       C - Static Config, P - Static Proxy
Zone          Group/mask      RP-Address   Prio   Hold   Expire Flags
--------------------------------------------------------------------
Trust     224.0.0.0/4      10.5.5.254    100     150s    141s
                            10.5.5.3     101     300s    291s

Untrust   224.0.0.0/4      10.5.5.254    100     150s    141s  I  Trust
                            10.5.5.3     101     300s    291s  I  Trust
```

As expected, the primary RP for all groups is 10.5.5.254, and our local device is the backup, as indicated by its worse priority. If we disable the RP on 10.5.5.254, we can see that the desired effect is achieved, and that the firewall takes over the RP functionality:

```
FIREWALL-A(trust-vr/pim)-> get rp all
Flags : I - Imported, A - Always(override BSR mapping)
       C - Static Config, P - Static Proxy
Zone        Group/mask      RP-Address   Prio   Hold   Expire Flags
------------------------------------------------------------------
Trust       224.0.0.0/4     10.5.5.3      101    300s    248s

Untrust      224.0.0.0/4     10.5.5.3      101    300s    248s  I  Trust
```

The hold timer in the output of get rp all indicates that the RP should be considered down after the value in the hold timer has expired. As you can see, the hold times are fairly high in the preceding examples. The default advertisement interval for Candidate RP Advertisements in ScreenOS is 60 seconds:

```
FIREWALL-A-> get vrouter trust-vr protocol pim rp candidate
 Zone : Trust
------------------
 Candidate RP address : 10.5.5.3 (bgroup0)
--------------------------------------
   Priority  : 101
   Hold Time : 300s
   Advertisement interval : 60s
   Next Advertisement in  : 00:00:36
   Candidate Group acl id: 10

   Group Address       Group Mask          Source
   224.0.0.0           240.0.0.0           candidate
```

You can adjust the hold timer with the `set vrouter trust-vr protocol pim zone trust rp candidate mgroup-list` *<number>* `holdtime` *<sec>* command.

As shown with other multicast information throughout this chapter, multicast group policy is necessary. For example, examine the output of `get vrouter trust-vr protocol pim bsr`:

```
FIREWALL-A-> get vrouter trust-vr protocol pim bsr
 Zone : Trust
-----------------
 Bootstrap Router address : 10.0.6.1
  BSR hash mask length    : 30
  BSR priority            : 100
  BSR timer expires in    : 00:01:11
  BSR up time             : 01:34:44

 Zone : Untrust
-----------------
 Bootstrap Router address : 10.0.6.1
  BSR hash mask length    : 30
  BSR priority            : 100
  BSR timer expires in    : 00:01:11
  BSR up time             : 01:34:44
```

You'll see the BSR's loopback IP address in the `Trust` and `Untrust` zones. The router itself is connected to `bgroup0` in the `Trust` zone. The only way the BSR information as well as the RP information shown with the `get vrouter trust-vr protocol pim rp all` command is populated between zones is by virtue of the multicast group policy, which allows the PIM messages to traverse zones:

```
FIREWALL-A-> get multicast-group-policy
all multicast group policies:
from zone  to zone   src group/list dst group/list Messages
Trust      Untrust   10             10             BSR Join/Prune
```

See Also

Recipe 20.2; Recipe 20.3; Recipe 20.7

20.9 Firewalling Between PIM Domains

Problem

You need to run a firewall between two Autonomous Systems (ASs) running PIM and MSDP.

Solution

Configure the firewall to allow MSDP, configure PIM, and then configure a multicast group policy to only allow `join-prunes`:

```
FIREWALL-A-> set address untrust untrst-rp-10.1.1.1 10.1.1.1/32
FIREWALL-A-> set address trust trust-rp-10.5.5.254 10.5.5.254/32
FIREWALL-A-> set service msdp protocol tcp src-port 1024-65535 dst-port
    639-639
FIREWALL-A-> set policy from untrust to trust untrust-rp-10.1.1.1
    trust-rp-10.5.5.254 msdp permit log
FIREWALL-A-> set policy from trust to untrust trust-rp-10.5.5.254
    untrust-rp-10.1.1.1 msdp permit log

FIREWALL-A-> set vrouter trust-vr
FIREWALL-A(trust-vr)-> set access-list 10 permit ip 224.0.0.0/4 10
FIREWALL-A(trust-vr)-> set protocol pim
FIREWALL-A(trust-vr/pim)-> set enable
FIREWALL-A(trust-vr/pim)-> end
FIREWALL-A-> set interface eth0/0 protocol pim
FIREWALL-A-> set interface eth0/0 protocol pim enable
FIREWALL-A-> set interface bgroup0 protocol pim
FIREWALL-A-> set interface bgroup0 protocol pim enable
FIREWALL-A-> set multicast-group-policy from trust mgroup-list 10 to
    untrust pim-message join-prune bi-directional
```

Discussion

To run PIM between ASs, you must use MSDP to advertise active sources between RPs in the different ASs. You do this via MSDP source active messages. MSDP runs over TCP, so like BGP, there is no need for the firewall to participate in the protocol as long as the hosts on each side of the firewall can reach each other on the MSDP port (port 639). Because either RP can initiate the connection, it is necessary to have two firewall policies, one from *trust to untrust* and the other from *untrust to trust*. This enables the connection to be set up (assuming IP connectivity).

Outside of tunneling the protocol, there is no way to get hosts that aren't directly connected to communicate, because PIM uses locally scoped multicast packets to communicate. As such, the firewall in our example must actively participate in PIM, as shown in Figure 20-7.

Because MSDP advertises S,G information between RPs, even without BSR running on the RPs, you can still generate mroute state and forward multicast packets. The

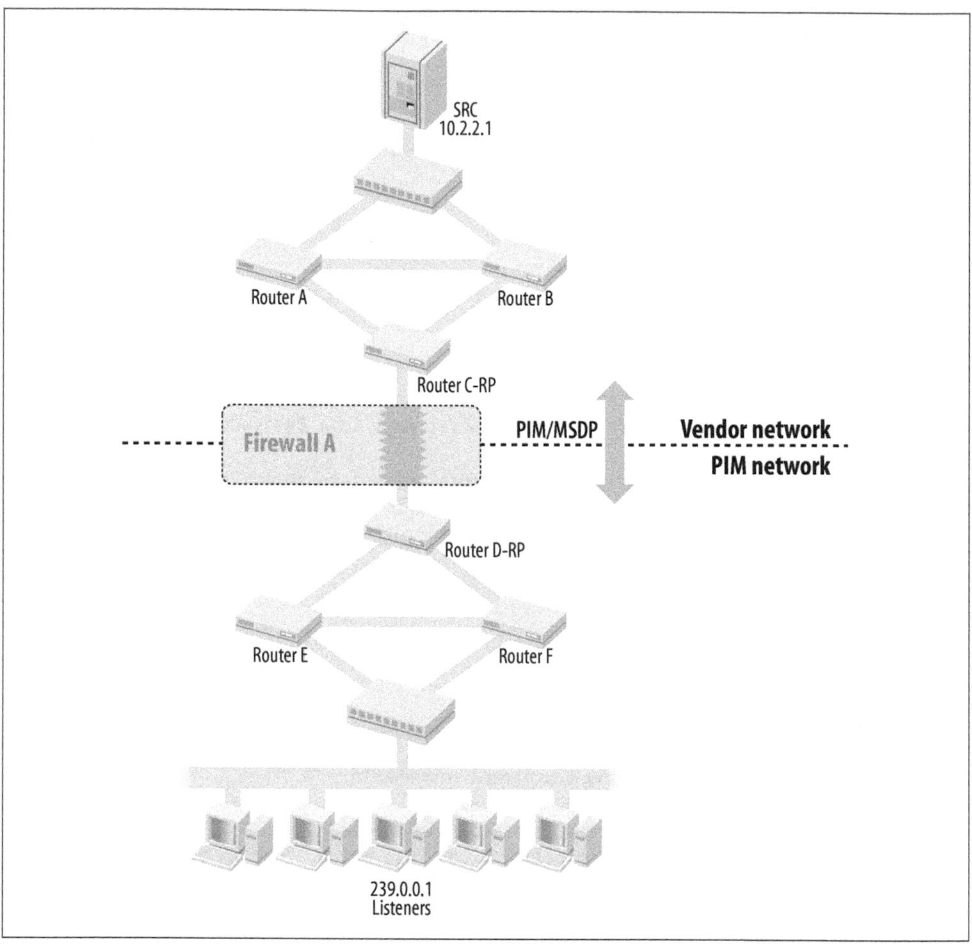

Figure 20-7. Inter-AS PIM

reason is that there is no need for RP mapping on the firewall in this scenario, or RPs at all, because only (S,G) joins are received by the firewall. Let's look at this in the mroute table:

```
FIREWALL-A-> get vrouter trust-vr mroute
 Flags:   P - PIM, S - Static, I - IGMP-Proxy
          F - Forwarding, U - Pruned, D - Down, B - Backup, T -
    Registering
         N - Negative Cache, M - Dummy route (Iif in another virtual
    router)
 Virtual router: trust-vr
 ---------------------------------------------------------------------
 Total multicast routes : 1/system-max

 (10.2.2.1, 239.0.0.1)        00:00:03    RPF: 10.5.5.254    P
   Input Interface   : bgroup0                zone: Trust
   Output Interfaces:
    zone         group            interface       source          uptime
```

```
    flags
    Untrust     239.0.0.1       eth0/0          10.2.2.1    00:00:03
    PF
```

As expected, there is an (S,G) entry in the mroute table with an RPF neighbor. But when you look at the RP information, however, there's nothing there:

```
FIREWALL-A(trust-vr/pim)-> get rp all
Flags : I - Imported, A - Always(override BSR mapping)
        C - Static Config, P - Static Proxy
Zone          Group/mask          RP-Address       Prio   Hold   Expire
    Flags
-----------------------------------------------------------------------
Trust
Untrust
```

On a PIM domain boundary, you'll see that there's no need to enable any RP mapping mechanism, as all join/prunes between the RPs in each domain will be (S,G). For security and simplicity, it is recommended that you do not enable `bsr-static-rp` in the multicast policy, so there's no chance of either domain learning RP information outside of the MSDP process.

See Also

Recipe 20.7; Recipe 20.8

20.10 Connect Two PIM Domains with Proxy RP

Problem

You need to connect two PIM domains together, and you can't run MSDP on your routers.

Solution

Use the firewall as a proxy RP:

```
FIREWALL-A-> set vr trust-vr
FIREWALL-A(trust-vr)-> set access-list 10 permit ip 224.0.0.0/4 10
FIREWALL-A (trust-vr)-> set protocol pim
FIREWALL-A (trust-vr/pim)-> set enable
FIREWALL-A (trust-vr/pim)-> end
FIREWALL-A-> set interface eth0/0 protocol pim
FIREWALL-A-> set interface eth0/0 protocol pim enable
FIREWALL-A-> set interface bgroup0 protocol pim
FIREWALL-A-> set interface bgroup0 protocol pim enable
FIREWALL-A-> set vr trust-vr
FIREWALL-A (trust-vr)-> set protocol pim
FIREWALL-A(trust-vr/pim)-> set zone "Untrust" rp candidate interface
    ethernet0/0
FIREWALL-A(trust-vr/pim)-> set zone "Untrust" rp proxy
FIREWALL-A (trust-vr/pim)-> end
```

```
FIREWALL-A-> set multicast-group-policy from trust mgroup-list 10 to
    untrust pim-message bsr-static-rp join-prune bi-directional
```

Discussion

Proxy RP is a ScreenOS proprietary method of connecting multicast domains. Conceptually, it is relatively simple (as far as PIM goes in general) and is analogous to the concept of VRs in ScreenOS. In fact, proxy RP is often used between VRs. By using a proxy RP, the firewall can act to completely separate PIM domains. In this recipe, a single VR is used, but conceptually, there is little difference, as the PIM control plane is controlled by the multicast group policy, as seen in Recipe 20.2. To run, you need to set the proxy keyword in the downstream zone and enable the downstream interface as a candidate RP. BSR does not need to be running on any downstream devices for this functionality to work. Figure 20-8 depicts a standard proxy RP environment.

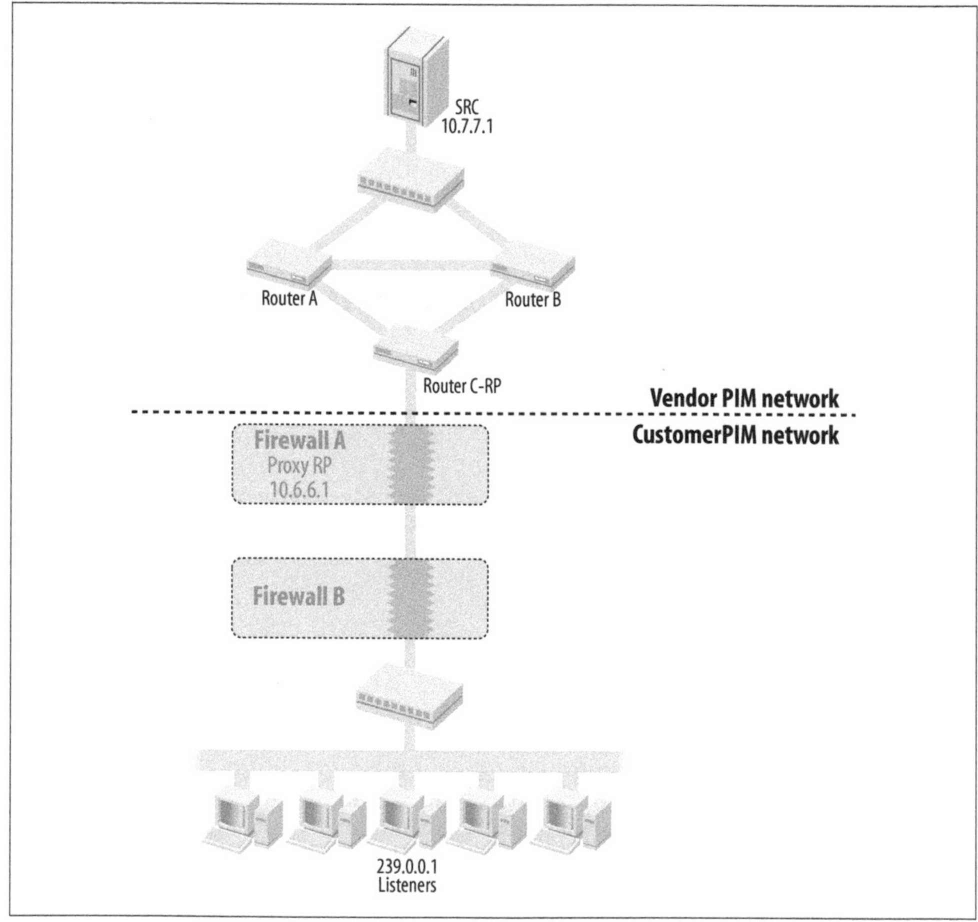

Figure 20-8. Proxy RP environment

In Figure 20-8, the administrators of the customer PIM network have a policy of not allowing their partner's network addresses in their internal routing table. Because PIM, like other multicast routing protocols, requires an RPF check to function, these administrators are presented with a problem. MSDP won't help in this case, as a peer would have to be set up between a customer-owned RP and the vendor's RP. Proxy RP allows this to function, however, by setting the firewall's internal interface as the RP for the rest of the customer network to point to while using the vendor's RP for actual PIM functionality. This is similar conceptually to NAT.

In a proxy RP scenario, the customer network uses the firewall as the RP to avoid including external routing information in his own network. This can be done as a result of policy, or to address complications that would arise from duplicate IP space between the two networks. If the latter is the case, two VRs should be used. Let's look at the mroute tables of `FIREWALL-A` and `FIREWALL-B` to see how proxy RP looks to each device:

```
FIREWALL-A(trust-vr)-> get mroute
 Flags:   P - PIM, S - Static, I - IGMP-Proxy
          F - Forwarding, U - Pruned, D - Down, B - Backup, T -
    Registering
         N - Negative Cache, M - Dummy route (Iif in another virtual
    router)
 Virtual router: trust-vr
 --------------------------------------------------------------------
 Total multicast routes : 1/system-max

 (10.7.7.1, 239.0.0.1)       00:00:21    RPF: 10.5.5.254    P
   Input Interface  : bgroup0               zone: Trust
   Output Interfaces:
    zone        group            interface      source          uptime
    flags
    Untrust     239.0.0.1        eth0/0         10.7.7.1    00:00:21
    PF

FIREWALL-A(trust-vr/pim)-> get mroute
trust-vr - PIM-SM routing table
---------------------------------------------------------------------
Register - R, Connected members - C, Pruned - P, Pending SPT Alert
- G, Forward - F, Null - N , Negative Cache - E, Local Receivers - L
SPT - T, Proxy-Register - X, Imported - I, SGRpt state - Y, SSM Range
    Group - S
Turnaround Router - K
-----------------------------------------------------------------------
Total PIM-SM mroutes: 2

(*, 239.0.0.1)  RP 10.5.5.254       00:03:46/-         Flags: LF
  Zone             : Trust
  Upstream         : bgroup0            State          : Joined
  RPF Neighbor     : 10.5.5.254      Expires        : 00:00:20
  Downstream       :
  ethernet0/0  00:03:46/00:03:01  Join          239.0.0.1          F
```

```
(10.7.7.1/24, 239.0.0.1)          00:00:17/00:03:12  Flags: TLF
  Zone             : Trust
  Upstream         : bgroup0           State          : Joined
  RPF Neighbor     : 10.5.5.254       Expires        : 00:00:44
  Downstream       :
  ethernet0/0  00:00:17/00:03:12  Join         239.0.0.1
    10.7.7.1 F
```

FIREWALL-A shows that traffic has begun to flow by the presence of an (S,G) route in the VR routing table, as well as in the PIM mroute table, which shows an (S,G) and a (*,G). In the (*,G) entry the RP information shows 10.5.5.254 as the RP address. This is the vendor RP, and it is as expected. FIREWALL-B shows the following:

```
FIREWALL-B(trust-vr)-> get mroute
 Flags:    P - PIM, S - Static, I - IGMP-Proxy
          F - Forwarding, U - Pruned, D - Down, B - Backup, T -
    Registering
          N - Negative Cache, M - Dummy route (Iif in another virtual
    router)
 Virtual router: trust-vr
 ---------------------------------------------------------------------
 Total multicast routes : 1/system-max

 (10.7.7.1, 239.0.0.1)       00:00:01    RPF: 10.6.6.1     P
   Input Interface  : bgroup0                zone: Trust
   Output Interfaces:
    zone        group            interface      source         uptime
    flags
    Untrust     239.0.0.1       eth0/0         10.7.7.1    00:00:01
    PF

FIREWALL-B(trust-vr/pim)-> get mroute
trust-vr - PIM-SM routing table
----------------------------------------------------------------------
Register - R, Connected members - C, Pruned - P, Pending SPT Alert-
 G, Forward - F, Null - N , Negative Cache - E, Local Receivers - L
SPT - T, Proxy-Register - X, Imported - I, SGRpt state - Y, SSM Range
    Group - S
Turnaround Router - K
---------------------------------------------------------------------
Total PIM-SM mroutes: 2

(*, 239.0.0.1)  RP 10.6.6.1         00:00:42/-         Flags: LF
  Zone             : Trust
  Upstream         : bgroup0           State          : Joined
  RPF Neighbor     : 10.6.6.1        Expires        : 00:00:23
  Downstream       :
  ethernet0/0  00:00:42/-         Join         0.0.0.0           FC

(10.7.7.1/24, 239.0.0.1)          00:00:42/00:02:42  Flags: TLF
  Zone             : Trust
  Upstream         : bgroup0           State          : Joined
  RPF Neighbor     : 10.6.6.1        Expires        : 00:00:24
```

```
Downstream       :
ethernet0/0  00:00:42/-        Join        0.0.0.0
  10.7.7.1 FC
```

The RP information from the get mroute in the PIM hierarchy shows 10.6.6.1 as the RP, which is FIREWALL-A's downstream interface:

```
FIREWALL-A-> get interface

A - Active, I - Inactive, U - Up, D - Down, R - Ready

Interfaces in vsys Root:
Name           IP Address      Zone     MAC            VLAN State VSD
serial0/0      0.0.0.0/0       Null     0014.f6ea.92cd   -   D   -
eth0/0         10.6.6.1/24     Untrust  0014.f6ea.92c0   -   U   -
eth0/1         0.0.0.0/0       DMZ      0014.f6ea.92c5   -   D   -
bgroup0        10.5.5.3/24     Trust    0014.f6ea.92c9   -   U   -
  eth0/2       N/A             N/A      N/A              -   U   -
  eth0/3       N/A             N/A      N/A              -   U   -
  eth0/4       N/A             N/A      N/A              -   D   -
bgroup1        0.0.0.0/0       Null     0014.f6ea.92ca   -   D   -
bgroup2        0.0.0.0/0       Null     0014.f6ea.92cb   -   D   -
bgroup3        0.0.0.0/0       Null     0014.f6ea.92cc   -   D   -
vlan1          0.0.0.0/0       VLAN     0014.f6ea.92cf   1   D   -
null           0.0.0.0/0       Null     N/A              -   U   0
```

Look at the RP mapping on FIREWALL-A:

```
FIREWALL-A(trust-vr/pim)-> get rp all
Flags : I - Imported, A - Always(override BSR mapping)
       C - Static Config, P - Static Proxy
Zone          Group/mask          RP-Address      Prio   Hold    Expire
    Flags
-------------------------------------------------------------------
Trust         224.0.0.0/4       10.5.5.254   1       65s     57s

Untrust       224.0.0.0/4       10.6.6.1      192     Static  -       P
```

This shows that depending on the zone, there are different RPs. The Static keyword in the output for the Untrust zone indicates that the entry was generated by the proxy RP. In contrast, the output on FIREWALL-B has just a single RP entry for all zones:

```
FIREWALL-B(trust-vr/pim)-> get rp all
Flags : I - Imported, A - Always(override BSR mapping)
       C - Static Config, P - Static Proxy
Zone          Group/mask        RP-Address       Prio   Hold    Expire
    Flags
-------------------------------------------------------------------
Untrust       224.0.0.0/4       10.6.6.1      192     Static  -       IC
    Trust

Trust         224.0.0.0/4       10.6.6.1      192     Static  -       C
```

Although it seems that all is well, one component of the configuration is required to make this truly work. The problem stems from the default PIM behavior when forming the multicast tree. As previously discussed, upon receipt of the first packet in a stream, the firewall or router connected to a receiver will initiate an (S,G) join toward the source so that the distribution tree is optimized. In this case, however, you need to stay on the shared tree, as FIREWALL-B should have no RPF information for the source at 10.7.7.1. To do this, use the set spt-threshold infinity command on FIREWALL-B:

```
FIREWALL-B(trust-vr/pim)-> set spt-threshold infinity
```

Upon executing this command and restarting the join from the client, the PIM mroute table appears:

```
FIREWALL-B(trust-vr/pim)-> get mroute
trust-vr - PIM-SM routing table
-----------------------------------------------------------------------
Register - R, Connected members - C, Pruned - P, Pending SPT Alert-
G, Forward - F, Null - N , Negative Cache - E, Local Receivers - L
SPT - T, Proxy-Register - X, Imported - I, SGRpt state - Y, SSM Range
    Group - S
Turnaround Router - K
-----------------------------------------------------------------------
Total PIM-SM mroutes: 1

(*, 239.0.0.1)  RP 10.6.6.1         00:00:18/-          Flags: LF
  Zone              : Trust
  Upstream          : bgroup0             State          : Joined
  RPF Neighbor      : 10.6.6.1          Expires        : 00:00:44
  Downstream        :
  ethernet0/0  00:00:18/-         Join          0.0.0.0             FC
```

As expected, a single mroute appears which is a (*,G) entry with the proxy RP address. A look at the trust-vr vrouter mroute table, however, shows a surprise:

```
FIREWALL-B-> get vrouter trust-vr mroute
 Flags:    P - PIM, S - Static, I - IGMP-Proxy
          F - Forwarding, U - Pruned, D - Down, B - Backup, T -
    Registering
         N - Negative Cache, M - Dummy route (Iif in another virtual
    router)
 Virtual router: trust-vr
 ----------------------------------------------------------------------
 Total multicast routes : 1/system-max

 (10.7.7.1, 239.0.0.1)       00:02:08    RPF: 10.6.6.1      P
   Input Interface  : bgroup0                zone: Trust
   Output Interfaces:
    zone        group           interface       source          uptime
    flags
    Untrust     239.0.0.1       eth0/0          10.7.7.1    00:02:08
    PF
```

Although there is an (S,G) entry here, this does not indicate the PIM state, which is an important distinction to note. The (S,G) entry will appear once traffic is being forwarded by the firewall in any case, as the source address is still read from the packets. If it is required to mask the actual source address, the security policy can be used to NAT the source.

See Also

Recipe 20.3; Recipe 20.7

20.11 Manage RPF Information with Redundant Routers

Problem

You need to ensure valid RPF information with the Virtual Redundancy Router Protocol (VRRP) running on the upstream routers.

Solution

Run a dynamic routing protocol for a successful RPF check:

```
FIREWALL-A(trust-vr)-> set protocol ospf
FIREWALL-A(trust-vr/ospf)-> set enable
FIREWALL-A(trust-vr/ospf)-> end
FIREWALL-A-> set interface bgroup0 protocol ospf area 0.0.0.0
FIREWALL-A-> set interface bgroup0 protocol ospf enable
FIREWALL-A-> set interface ethernet0/0 protocol ospf area 0.0.0.0
FIREWALL-A-> set interface ethernet0/0 protocol ospf enable
```

Discussion

In a scenario with a single next hop to an RP or source, static routes in the firewall will work just fine. But, to handle the issue of gateway redundancy, VRRP is often used to provide a virtual gateway. You can see this topology in Figure 20-9.

Figure 20-9 shows a firewall connected to a set of multicast listeners. The routers upstream are running VRRP, and the firewall points a static default route to the virtual IP (VIP) address to ensure that connectivity is maintained in the event of a failure. The problem with this scenario is that PIM requires the RPF to the RP or source to point to the PIM neighbor address. In this scenario, the PIM neighbors of the firewall are at 10.5.5.253 and 10.5.5.252. Because the default route points to 10.5.5.254, the RPF check will fail, and PIM will not be able to perform RP mapping or join/prunes to any interested groups. To accommodate this, the network administrators have chosen to run OSPF on the firewall and the routers instead of VRRP so that the PIM

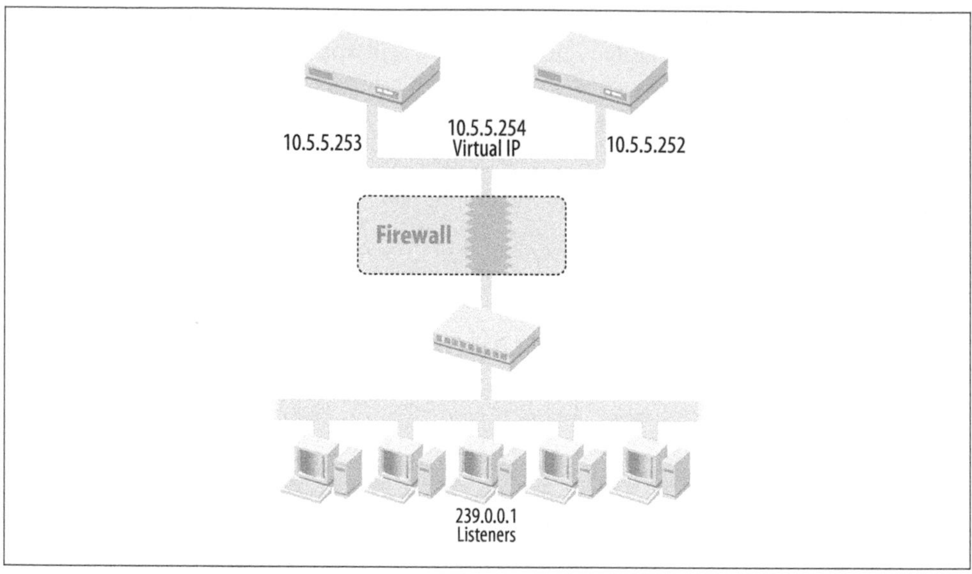

Figure 20-9. Using VRRP to provide a virtual gateway

neighbor and RPF next hop are the same. To see this in action, let's look at the routing table of `FIREWALL-A`, which is running BSR and learning its RP information from `10.5.5.253`:

```
FIREWALL-A(trust-vr)-> get route ip 10.0.6.1
 Dest for 10.0.6.1
---------------------------------------------------------------------
trust-vr        : => 10.0.6.1/32 (id=21) via 10.5.5.254 (vr: trust-vr)
                   Interface bgroup0 , metric 1
```

In this case, a static route is pointing the RP address to the VRRP next hop. If you use the `get protocol pim neighbor` command in the `trust-vr` hierarchy, you'll see the following:

```
FIREWALL-A(trust-vr)-> get protocol pim neighbor
Neighbor        Interface       Uptime      Expire   DR-priority  GenId
---------------------------------------------------------------------
10.5.5.253    bgroup0        02:18:15   00:01:20   1           17680581
10.5.5.252    bgroup0        02:21:18   00:01:46   1           47269183
10.6.6.2      ethernet0/0    02:31:46   00:01:39   1           57356
```

Our route to the RP does not point to the PIM neighbor address, and as a consequence, when examining the RP information, you'll see the following:

```
FIREWALL-A(trust-vr/pim)-> get rp all
Flags : I - Imported, A - Always(override BSR mapping)
        C - Static Config, P - Static Proxy
Zone            Group/mask           RP-Address       Prio   Hold   Expire
    Flags
---------------------------------------------------------------------
Trust
Untrust
```

If you delete the route to the RP and look at the routing table, you'll see that it now points toward 10.5.5.253, which is the PIM neighbor address:

```
FIREWALL-A(trust-vr)-> unset route 10.0.6.1/32
total routes deleted = 1
FIREWALL-A(trust-vr)-> get route ip 10.0.6.1
 Dest for 10.0.6.1
--------------------------------------------------------------------
trust-vr       : => 10.0.6.1/32 (id=19) via 10.5.5.253 (vr: trust-vr)
                    Interface bgroup0 , metric 1
FIREWALL-A(trust-vr)-> set protocol pim
FIREWALL-A(trust-vr/pim)-> get rp all
Flags : I - Imported, A - Always(override BSR mapping)
       C - Static Config, P - Static Proxy
Zone           Group/mask          RP-Address    Prio   Hold   Expire
    Flags
------------------------------------------------------------------
Trust          224.0.0.0/4         10.0.6.1        1     65s     65s

Untrust        224.0.0.0/4         10.0.6.1        1     65s     65s  I
    Trust
```

Now that you have only the OSPF learned route with the appropriate neighbor address, you can learn RP information and perform join/prunes.

Although this recipe focused on using OSPF to address the RPF issue with virtual addresses for gateways, any dynamic routing protocol will have the same effect and can be used depending on the administrator's preferences. Of course, when using dynamic routing protocols within ScreenOS, you must be careful to ensure symmetry.

See Also

Chapter 4; Chapter 17; Recipe 20.7; Recipe 20.8

20.12 PIM and High Availability

Problem

You want to run PIM on a NetScreen Redundancy Protocol (NSRP) cluster with dual upstream and downstream routers.

Solution

Getting NSRP and PIM to work well together requires proper NSRP configuration, as well as PIM configuration on Virtual Security Interfaces (VSIs). To maintain router redundancy, configure BGP. First, set up NSRP:

```
FIREWALL-A-> set nsrp cluster id 1
FIREWALL-A(M)-> unset nsrp vsd-group id 0
FIREWALL-A(M)-> set nsrp vsd-group id 1 priority 1
FIREWALL-A(M)-> set nsrp vsd-group id 1 preempt hold-down 10
```

```
FIREWALL-A(M)-> set int e0/0:1 ip 10.6.6.5/24
FIREWALL-A(M)-> set int bgroup0:1 ip 10.5.5.5/24
FIREWALL-A(M)-> set nsrp rto-mirror sync
FIREWALL-A(M)-> set nsrp monitor interface eth0/0
FIREWALL-A(M)-> set nsrp monitor interface bgroup0

FIREWALL-B-> set nsrp cluster id 1
FIREWALL-B(B)-> unset nsrp vsd-group id 0
FIREWALL-B(M)-> set nsrp monitor interface eth0/0
FIREWALL-B(M)-> set nsrp monitor interface bgroup0
```

Next, enable PIM in the VR, as well as on the interfaces. Use static RP (in this case) so that after a failover, `FIREWALL-B` doesn't have to wait for a new bootstrap message to populate its RP table. When configuring PIM with NSRP, it is recommended that you enable the protocol on the VSI to avoid the RPF issues discussed in Recipe 20.11.

```
FIREWALL-A(M)-> set vrouter trust-vr
FIREWALL-A(trust-vr)(M)-> set protocol pim
FIREWALL-A(trust-vr/pim)(M)-> set enable
FIREWALL-A(trust-vr/pim)(M)-> exit
FIREWALL-A(trust-vr)(M)-> exit
FIREWALL-A(M)-> set interface eth0/0:1 proto pim
FIREWALL-A(M)-> set interface eth0/0:1 proto pim ena
FIREWALL-A(M)-> set interface bgroup0:1 proto pim
FIREWALL-A(M)-> set interface bgroup0:1 proto pim ena
```

Because the PIM process was enabled on `FIREWALL-A` on the VSI, there is no need to enable the protocol on `FIREWALL-B`, as shown by using the get `config` command in the PIM hierarchy:

```
FIREWALL-B(trust-vr/pim)(B)-> get config
set protocol pim
set enable
exit
set interface ethernet0/0:1 protocol pim
set interface ethernet0/0:1 protocol pim enable
set interface bgroup0:1 protocol pim
set interface bgroup0:1 protocol pim enable
set protocol pim
exit
```

Next, enable BGP on the firewalls, and create route maps to set the next hop of all advertised routes to the VSI address. See Recipe 18.1 for more information.

```
FIREWALL-A(trust-vr)(M)-> set access-list 5 permit ip 0.0.0.0/0 10
FIREWALL-A(trust-vr)(M)-> set route-map name set-nh-upstream permit 10
FIREWALL-A(trust-vr/set-nh-upstream-10)(M)-> set match ip 5
FIREWALL-A(trust-vr/set-nh-upstream-10)(M)-> set next-hop 10.5.5.5
FIREWALL-A(trust-vr/set-nh-upstream-10)(M)-> exit
FIREWALL-A(trust-vr)(M)-> set route-map name set-nh-downstream
    permit 10
FIREWALL-A(trust-vr/set-nh-downstream-10)(M)-> set match ip 5
FIREWALL-A(trust-vr/set-nh-downstream-10)(M)-> set next-hop 10.6.6.5
FIREWALL-A(trust-vr/set-nh-downstream-10)(M)-> exit
```

```
FIREWALL-A(trust-vr)(M)-> set protocol bgp 65535
FIREWALL-A(trust-vr/bgp)(M)-> set enable
FIREWALL-A(trust-vr/bgp)(M)-> set neighbor 10.5.5.254 remote-as 65510
FIREWALL-A(trust-vr/bgp)(M)-> set neighbor 10.5.5.254 enable
FIREWALL-A(trust-vr/bgp)(M)-> set neighbor 10.5.5.254 route-map
    set-nh-upstream out
FIREWALL-A(trust-vr/bgp)(M)-> set neighbor 10.5.5.253 remote-as 65510
FIREWALL-A(trust-vr/bgp)(M)-> set neighbor 10.5.5.253 enable
FIREWALL-A(trust-vr/bgp)(M)-> set neighbor 10.5.5.253 route-map
    set-nh-upstream out
FIREWALL-A(trust-vr/bgp)(M)-> set neighbor 10.6.6.254 remote-as 65520
FIREWALL-A(trust-vr/bgp)(M)-> set neighbor 10.6.6.254 enable
FIREWALL-A(trust-vr/bgp)(M)-> set neighbor 10.6.6.254 route-map
    set-nh-downstream out
FIREWALL-A(trust-vr/bgp)(M)-> set neighbor 10.6.6.253 remote-as 65520
FIREWALL-A(trust-vr/bgp)(M)-> set neighbor 10.6.6.253 enable
FIREWALL-A(trust-vr/bgp)(M)-> set neighbor 10.6.6.253 route-map
    set-nh-downstream out
FIREWALL-A(trust-vr/bgp)(M)-> end
FIREWALL-A(M)-> set int e0/0 proto bgp
FIREWALL-A(M)-> set int bgroup0 protocol bgp
```

Discussion

Configuring PIM in association with NSRP is effectively no different from configuring PIM in standalone mode. The challenge is to determine the appropriate architecture so that PIM and NSRP will operate in an expected manner. Figure 20-10 shows a standard NSRP topology.

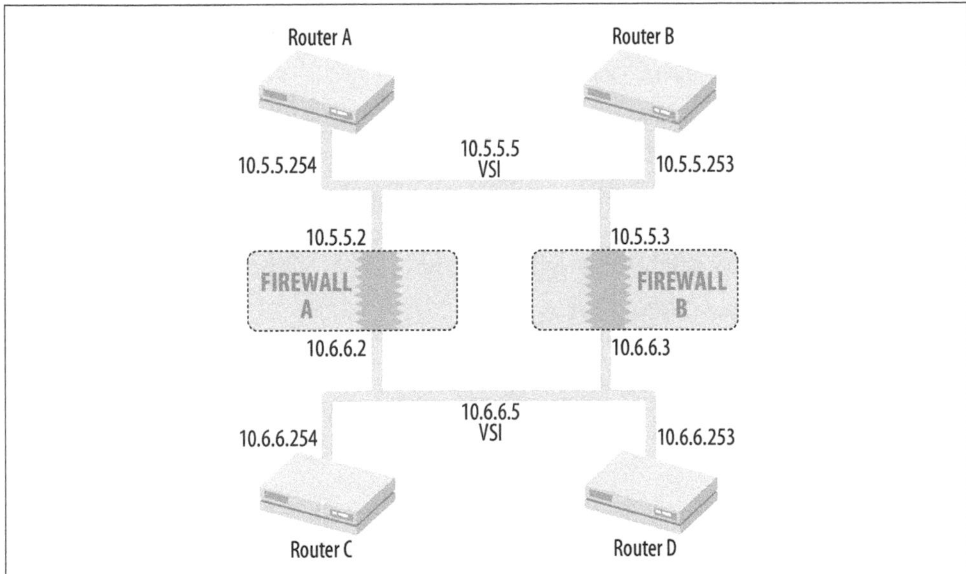

Figure 20-10. NSRP with PIM

As with other routing protocols, PIM is typically run with NSRP when VSD 0 is unset. This is more a consequence of the need for a dynamic unicast routing protocol than of PIM itself. In fact, when using PIM with NSRP, it is recommended that the VSI be configured with the PIM protocol as opposed to the physical interface address, unless running in a purely VSD-less mode (more on this in Recipe 20.13). Looking at `FIREWALL-A` (the current master), you can see that there are only four PIM neighbors:

```
FIREWALL-A(trust-vr/pim)(M)-> get neighbor
Neighbor         Interface    Uptime      Expire     DR-priority GenId
-----------------------------------------------------------------------
10.5.5.253    bgroup0:1     02:15:59    00:01:30    1          20945258
10.5.5.254    bgroup0:1     02:15:08    00:01:10    1          29823095
10.6.6.253    eth0/0:1      02:16:06    00:01:30    1          24923782
10.6.6.254    eth0/0:1      02:16:21    00:01:10    1          23945712
```

Note that the neighbor addresses are the same addresses as those of the BGP peers:

```
FIREWALL-A(trust-vr/bgp)(M)-> get neighbor
Peer AS Remote IP      Local IP          Wt Status   State      ConnID
   Up/Down
-----------------------------------------------------------------------
  65510 10.5.5.254 10.5.5.2   100 Enabled  ESTABLISH      43 02:30:12
  65510 10.5.5.253 10.5.5.2   100 Enabled  ESTABLISH      15 02:32:10
  65520 10.6.6.254 10.6.6.2   100 Enabled  ESTABLISH      12 02:30:31
  65520 10.6.6.253 10.6.6.2   100 Enabled  ESTABLISH      34 02:31:19

total 4 BGP peers shown
```

The PIM neighbors must be identical to the BGP next hops, and in this case, they are. In contrast, `FIREWALL-B` shows that it has no neighbors:

```
FIREWALL-B(trust-vr/pim)(B)-> get neighbor
Neighbor         Interface    Uptime     Expire     DR-priority GenId
-----------------------------------------------------------------------
FIREWALL-B(trust-vr/pim)(B)->
```

This is expected, because the PIM process is running on the VSI, which at this point is inactive on `FIREWALL-B`. When there's a failover, however, `FIREWALL-B` becomes the active device, and PIM neighbors are established:

```
FIREWALL-B(trust-vr/pim)(M)-> get neighbor
Neighbor         Interface    Uptime      Expire     DR-priority GenId
-----------------------------------------------------------------------
10.5.5.253    bgroup0:1     00:00:05    00:01:42    1          20945258
10.5.5.254    bgroup0:1     02:15:08    00:01:10    1          29823095
10.6.6.253    eth0/0:1      02:16:06    00:01:30    1          24923782
10.6.6.254    eth0/0:1      02:16:21    00:01:10    1          23945712
```

This process happens quickly. On the downstream side of the RPF, information looks different. In this network, routers C and D have a PIM neighbor of l, which is a consequence of running PIM on the VSI. This result works out well from a failover perspective; however, as the route map `set-nh-downstream` created sets the next hop of all routes advertised to routers C and D to the VSI address, the RPF check succeeds. Because all routes use the VSIs upstream and downstream for failover, NSRP-based failover times are expected. However, PIM may take up to the join/prune interval to reestablish mroute state, so if this can be adjusted on the downstream routers, it should be investigated to provide a more seamless failover.

See Also

Recipe 20.7; Recipe 20.11; Recipe 20.13; Recipe 18.8

20.13 Provide Active-Active Multicast

Problem

You need to provide active-active support for multicast traffic only. All groups in the 239.0.0.0/16 range need to traverse FIREWALL-A, and in parallel, all groups in the 239.1.0.0/16 range need to traverse FIREWALL-B.

Solution

Use multiple RPs and VSD-less clusters with OSPF to provide active-active support for multicast and active-passive support for unicast traffic. First, configure NSRP on each device in VSD-less mode:

```
FIREWALL-A-> set nsrp cluster id 1
FIREWALL-A(B)-> set nsrp rto-mirror sync
FIREWALL-A(B)-> unset nsrp vsd-group id 0
FIREWALL-A(M)-> set nsrp rto-mirror session non-vsi
FIREWALL-A(M)-> set nsrp monitor interface ethernet0/0
FIREWALL-A(M)-> set nsrp monitor interface bgroup0
FIREWALL-A(M)-> set nsrp vsd-group hb-interval 200

FIREWALL-B-> set nsrp cluster id 1
FIREWALL-B(B)-> set nsrp rto-mirror sync
FIREWALL-B(B)-> unset nsrp vsd-group id 0
FIREWALL-B(M)-> set nsrp monitor interface ethernet0/0
FIREWALL-B(M)-> set nsrp monitor interface bgroup0
```

Next, configure OSPF on the devices and cost the links on FIREWALL-B with a higher cost:

```
FIREWALL-A(M)-> set vrouter trust-vr
FIREWALL-A(trust-vr)(M)-> set protocol ospf
FIREWALL-A(trust-vr/ospf)(M)-> set enable
FIREWALL-A(trust-vr/ospf)(M)-> end
FIREWALL-A(M)-> set interface bgroup0 protocol ospf area 0.0.0.0
FIREWALL-A(M)-> set interface bgroup0 protocol ospf enable
FIREWALL-A(M)-> set interface ethernet0/0 protocol ospf area 0.0.0.0
FIREWALL-A(M)-> set interface ethernet0/0 protocol ospf enable
```

```
FIREWALL-B(M)-> set vrouter trust-vr
FIREWALL-B(trust-vr)(M)-> set protocol ospf
FIREWALL-B(trust-vr/ospf)(M)-> set enable
FIREWALL-B(trust-vr/ospf)(M)-> end
FIREWALL-B(M)-> set interface bgroup0 protocol ospf area 0.0.0.0
FIREWALL-B(M)-> set interface bgroup0 protocol ospf enable
FIREWALL-B(M)-> set interface bgroup0 protocol ospf cost 10
FIREWALL-B(M)-> set interface ethernet0/0 protocol ospf area 0.0.0.0
FIREWALL-B(M)-> set interface ethernet0/0 protocol ospf enable
FIREWALL-B(M)-> set interface ethernet0/0 protocol ospf cost 10
```

Finally, configure access lists for the RP mapping, enable PIM, and configure the RPs:

```
FIREWALL-A(M)-> set vrouter trust-vr
FIREWALL-A(trust-vr)(M)-> set access-list 20 permit ip 239.0.0.0/16
    10
FIREWALL-A(trust-vr)(M)-> set access-list 30 permit ip 239.1.0.0/16
    10
FIREWALL-A(trust-vr)(M)-> set protocol pim
FIREWALL-A(trust-vr/pim)(M)-> set enable
FIREWALL-A(trust-vr/pim)(M)-> end
FIREWALL-A(M)-> set interface ethernet0/0 protocol pim
FIREWALL-A(M)-> set interface ethernet0/0 protocol pim enable
FIREWALL-A(M)-> set interface bgroup0 protocol pim
FIREWALL-A(M)-> set interface bgroup0 protocol pim enable
FIREWALL-A(M)-> set vrouter trust-vr
FIREWALL-A(trust-vr)(M)-> set protocol pim
FIREWALL-A(trust-vr/pim)(M)-> set zone trust rp address 10.255.255.1
    mgroup-list 20 always
FIREWALL-A(trust-vr/pim)(M)-> set zone trust rp address 10.255.255.2
    mgroup-list 30 always
```

On FIREWALL-B, only the interface and zone-specific information (e.g., the RP configuration) needs to be applied:

```
FIREWALL-B(M)-> set interface ethernet0/0 protocol pim
FIREWALL-B(M)-> set interface ethernet0/0 protocol pim enable
FIREWALL-B(M)-> set interface bgroup0 protocol pim
FIREWALL-B(M)-> set interface bgroup0 protocol pim enable
FIREWALL-B(M)-> set vrouter trust-vr
FIREWALL-B(trust-vr)(M)-> set protocol pim
FIREWALL-B(trust-vr/pim)(M)-> set zone trust rp address 10.255.255.1
    mgroup-list 20 always
FIREWALL-B(trust-vr/pim)(M)-> set zone trust rp address 10.255.255.2
    mgroup-list 30 always
```

Discussion

Multicast can be a stressful application for networks, and it is sometimes desired to share the load across multiple devices. Because multicast tends to be unidirectional, the state issues associated with asymmetry in a normal active-active deployment are not really an issue, as state is set up via the multicast group policy. (Also, some financial market data feeds, being of critical nature, transmit identical data to multiple groups for additional redundancy.) By using an active-active configuration, any failures on the firewall side should be totally hitless to the application. Figure 20-11 shows the network for this recipe.

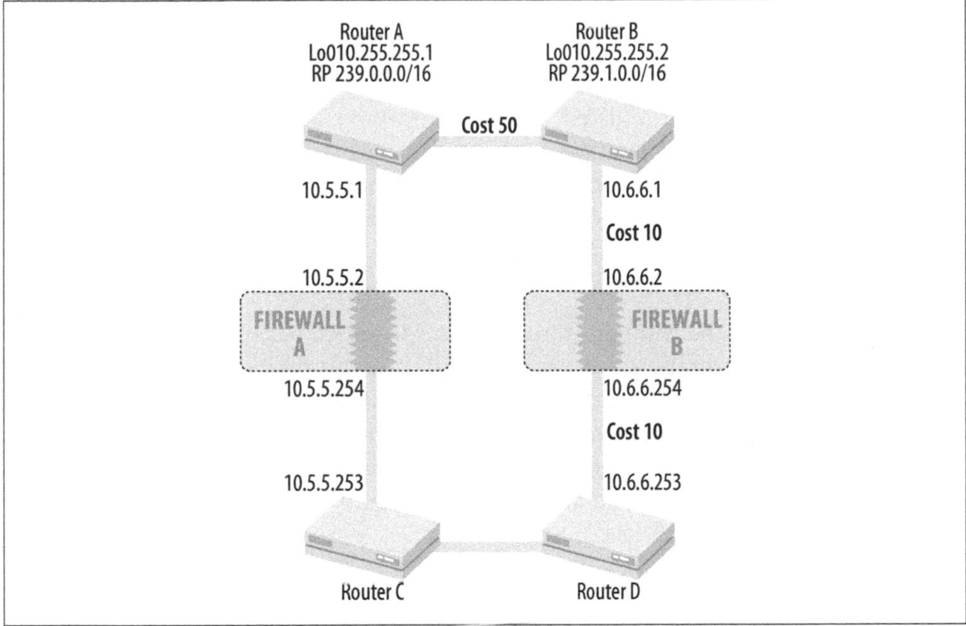

Figure 20-11. An active-active multicast network

To showcase the goals presented in this recipe, the RPT must be maintained at all times, so you should set the SPT threshold on routers to infinity. Otherwise, PIM will form an SPT to the source which will always traverse `FIREWALL-A`. If the RPT is used, however, by using `ROUTER-A` as the RP for all groups in the `239.0.0.0/16` range, and `ROUTER-B` for all groups in the `239.1.0.0/16` range, you can achieve the desired effect as all routes advertised through the network, except for the routes to `ROUTER-B`'s loopback and downstream interface, will always be preferred through `ROUTER-A`. This provides a topology that is symmetrical for all unicast traffic and is load-balanced for all multicast traffic.

Let's look at the firewall's view of things. First, the RPs:

```
FIREWALL-A(trust-vr/pim)(M)-> get rp all
Flags : I - Imported, A - Always(override BSR mapping)
        C - Static Config, P - Static Proxy
Zone          Group/mask    RP-Address      Prio   Hold   Expire
    Flags
--------------------------------------------------------------------
Untrust       224.0.0.0/4   10.255.255.3         1      65s     44s
    I  Trust
              239.1.0.0/16  10.255.255.2   192     Static  -
    AIC Trust
```

```
               239.0.0.0/16  10.255.255.1   192    Static  -
     AIC Trust

  Trust        224.0.0.0/4   10.255.255.3          1     65s     44s
               239.1.0.0/16  10.255.255.2   192    Static  -
     AC
               239.0.0.0/16  10.255.255.1   192    Static  -
     AC
```

In this output, three RPs are listed, one for all groups, and one for each of the `/16` networks we configured. The `A` flag in the output indicates "Always," which means the static configuration will override RP mapping learned via BSR. The administrators of this network have configured an anycast RP address of `10.255.255.3` on routers A and B for all other groups, and as a kind of "catchall." The two ranges that were statically configured, however, will always use their respective RPs.

OSPF was chosen as the routing protocol in this instance because of its convergence speed and ease of integration into the topology. Because the architecture is enforced via a routing metric, simply costing the links on `FIREWALL-B` to be 10 and between routers A and B to be 50, you can ensure that the only traffic that traverses `FIREWALL-B` is traffic to the RP itself. This decision will actually occur on routers C and D when they are determining the RPF for each group. Failover for all traffic will be based on OSPF reconvergence rather than NSRP.

See Also

Recipe 18.7; Recipe 20.11; Recipe 20.12

20.14 Scale Multicast Replication

Problem

You need to replicate multicast traffic coming out of the firewall to multiple downstream interfaces.

Solution

Use multiple VRs and virtual local area networks (VLANs) to move the replication point to the upstream router. First, set up the vrouters, zones, and interfaces:

```
FIREWALL-A-> set vrouter name vlan10-vr
FIREWALL-A-> set vrouter name vlan20-vr
FIREWALL-A-> set zone name trust-10
FIREWALL-A-> set zone name untrust-10
FIREWALL-A-> set zone name trust-20
FIREWALL-A-> set zone name untrust-20
FIREWALL-A-> set zone trust-10 vrouter vlan10-vr
FIREWALL-A-> set zone trust-20 vrouter vlan20-vr
FIREWALL-A-> set zone untrust-10 vrouter vlan10-vr
```

```
FIREWALL-A-> set zone untrust-20 vrouter vlan20-vr
FIREWALL-A-> set int eth0/0.10 tag 10 zone untrust-10
FIREWALL-A-> set int eth0/0.20 tag 20 zone untrust-20
FIREWALL-A-> set int bgroup0.20 tag 20 zone trust-20
FIREWALL-A-> set int bgroup0.10 tag 10 zone trust-10
FIREWALL-A(M)-> set int eth0/0.10 tag 10 zone untrust-10
FIREWALL-A(M)-> set int eth0/0.20 tag 20 zone untrust-20
FIREWALL-A(M)-> set int bgroup0.20 tag 20 zone trust-20
FIREWALL-A(M)-> set int bgroup0.10 tag 10 zone trust-10
```

Next, create access lists for RP mapping and multicast group policy, and enable PIM in the new VRs:

```
FIREWALL-A-> set vrouter vlan10-vr
FIREWALL-A(vlan10-vr)-> set access-list 10 permit ip 224.0.0.0/4 10
FIREWALL-A(vlan10-vr)-> set route 10.0.6.1/32 int eth0/0.10 gateway
    10.10.10.254
FIREWALL-A(vlan10-vr)-> set protocol pim
FIREWALL-A(vlan10-vr/pim)-> set zone trust-10 rp address 10.0.6.1
    mgroup-list 10 always
FIREWALL-A(vlan10-vr/pim)-> end
FIREWALL-A-> set interface eth0/0.10 protocol pim
FIREWALL-A-> set interface eth0/0.10 protocol pim enable
FIREWALL-A-> set interface bgroup0.10 protocol pim
FIREWALL-A-> set interface bgroup0.10 protocol pim enable
FIREWALL-A-> set vrouter vlan10-vr
FIREWALL-A(vlan10-vr)-> set protocol pim
FIREWALL-A(vlan10-vr/pim)-> set zone trust-10 rp address 10.0.6.1
    mgroup-list 10 always
FIREWALL-A(vlan10-vr/pim)-> end
FIREWALL-A-> set vrouter vlan20-vr
FIREWALL-A(vlan20-vr)-> set access-list 10 permit ip 224.0.0.0/4 10
FIREWALL-A(vlan20-vr)-> set route 10.0.6.1/32 int eth0/0.20 gateway
    10.20.20.254
FIREWALL-A(vlan20-vr)-> set protocol pim
FIREWALL-A(vlan20-vr/pim)-> set enable
FIREWALL-A(vlan20-vr/pim)-> end
FIREWALL-A-> set interface eth0/0.20 protocol pim
FIREWALL-A-> set interface eth0/0.20 protocol pim enable
FIREWALL-A-> set interface bgroup0.20 protocol pim
FIREWALL-A-> set interface bgroup0.20 protocol pim enable
FIREWALL-A-> set vrouter vlan20-vr
FIREWALL-A(vlan20-vr)-> set protocol pim
FIREWALL-A(vlan20-vr/pim)-> set zone trust-20 rp address 10.0.6.1
    mgroup-list 10 always
FIREWALL-A(vlan20-vr)-> end
```

Finally, set multicast group policies:

```
FIREWALL-A-> set multicast-group-policy from trust-10 mgroup-list 10
    to untrust-10 pim-message bsr-static-rp join-prune bi-directional
FIREWALL-A-> set multicast-group-policy from trust-20 mgroup-list 10
    to untrust-20 pim-message bsr-static-rp join-prune bi-directional
```

Discussion

ScreenOS is limited in terms of its capacity for multicast replication. Anytime replication is done, the CPU will perform the packet handling. This can result in suboptimal performance, especially in ASIC-based platforms. However, because ScreenOS supports the concept of VRs, it is a relatively trivial exercise to move the replication upstream one hop so that the router can handle the high volumes of multicast replication while the firewall itself continues to perform the security functions for which it is designed. Figure 20-12 depicts this scenario.

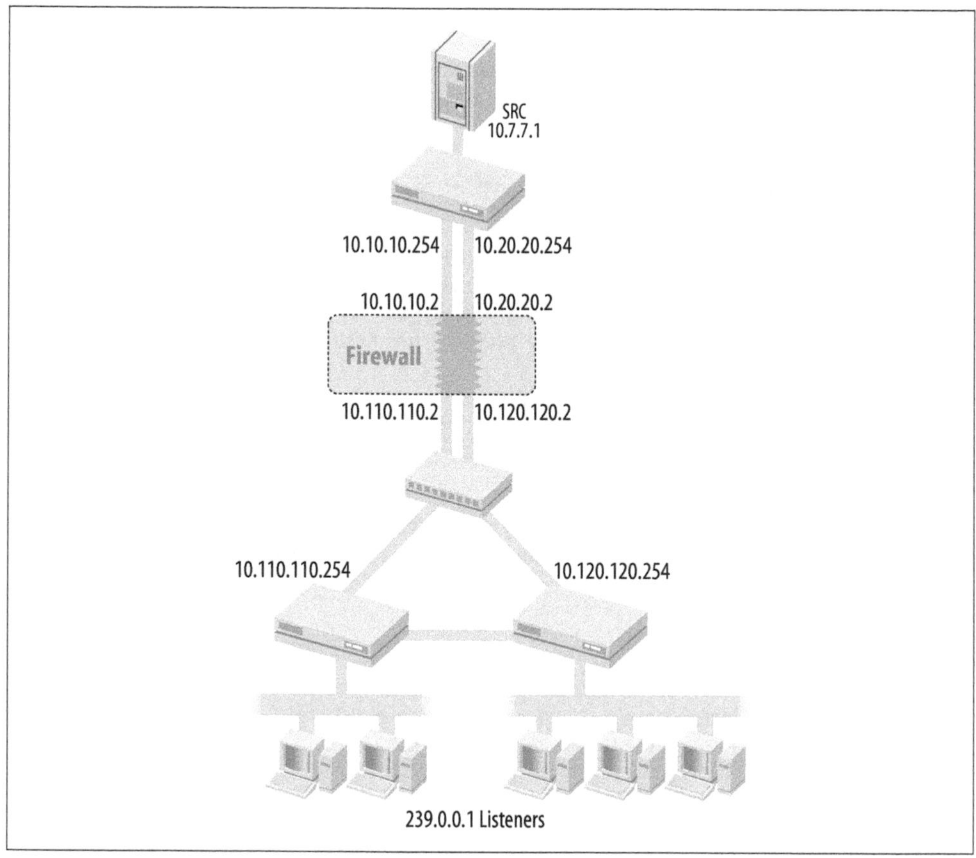

Figure 20-12. Multicast replication using VRs

The logical replication point in Figure 20-12 is the firewall, as it has two downstream neighbors with interested listeners. By segmenting the firewall into two parallel VRs, the administrators allow the firewall to sit in the same spot in the network with respect to all downstream traffic, and they hand off the burden of replication to the upstream router. All that is required is a VLAN trunk between the upstream router and the firewall. Look at the interfaces on the firewall to see whether this has been established:

```
FIREWALL-A-> get int

A - Active, I - Inactive, U - Up, D - Down, R - Ready

Interfaces in vsys Root:
Name          IP Address        Zone        MAC            VLAN State VSD
serial0/0     0.0.0.0/0         Null        0014.f6ea.92cd   -    D   -
eth0/0        10.6.6.2/24       Untrust     0014.f6ea.92c0   -    U   -
eth0/0.10     10.10.10.2/24     untrust-10  0014.f6ea.92c0  10    U   -
eth0/0.20     10.20.20.2/24     untrust-20  0014.f6ea.92c0  20    U   -
eth0/1        0.0.0.0/0         Null        0014.f6ea.92c5   -    D   -
bgroup0       0.0.0.0/0         Trust       0014.f6ea.92c9   -    U   -
  eth0/2      N/A               N/A         N/A              -    U   -
  eth0/3      N/A               N/A         N/A              -    U   -
  eth0/4      N/A               N/A         N/A              -    U   -
bgroup0.10    10.110.110.2/24   trust-10    0014.f6ea.92c9  10    U   -
bgroup0.20    10.120.120.2/24   trust-20    0014.f6ea.92c9  20    U   -
bgroup1       0.0.0.0/0         Null        0014.f6ea.92ca   -    D   -
bgroup2       0.0.0.0/0         Null        0014.f6ea.92cb   -    D   -
bgroup3       0.0.0.0/0         Null        0014.f6ea.92cc   -    D   -
vlan1         0.0.0.0/0         VLAN        0014.f6ea.12cf   1    D   -
null          0.0.0.0/0         Null        N/A              -    U   0
```

If you look at the specific zones, you'll see that the trust-10 and untrust-10 zones are assigned to vrouter vlan10-vr, and that trust-20 and untrust-20 are assigned to vrouter vlan20-vr:

```
FIREWALL-A-> get zone
Total 16 zones created in vsys Root - 12 are policy configurable.
Total policy configurable zones for Root is 12.
----------------------------------------------------------------
  ID Name          Type    Attr   VR           Default-IF      VSYS
   0 Null          Null    Shared untrust-vr   hidden          Root
   1 Untrust       Sec(L3) Shared trust-vr     ethernet0/0     Root
   2 Trust         Sec(L3)        trust-vr     bgroup0         Root
   3 DMZ           Sec(L3)        trust-vr     null            Root
   4 Self          Func           trust-vr     self            Root
  10 Global        Sec(L3)        trust-vr     null            Root
  11 V1-Untrust    Sec(L2) Shared trust-vr     v1-untrust      Root
  12 V1-Trust      Sec(L2) Shared trust-vr     v1-trust        Root
  13 V1-DMZ        Sec(L2) Shared trust-vr     v1-dmz          Root
  14 VLAN          Func    Shared trust-vr     vlan1           Root
  15 V1-Null       Sec(L2) Shared trust-vr     l2v             Root
  16 Untrust-Tun   Tun            trust-vr     hidden.1        Root
 100 trust-10      Sec(L3)        vlan10-vr    bgroup0.10      Root
 101 untrust-10    Sec(L3)        vlan10-vr    ethernet0/0.10 Root
 102 trust-20      Sec(L3)        vlan20-vr    bgroup0.20      Root
 103 untrust-20    Sec(L3)        vlan20-vr    ethernet0/0.20 Root
```

When you look at the route table, you'll see that each VR has a static route toward the RP, with the appropriate next hop for that vrouter:

```
IPv4 Dest-Routes for <vlan10-vr> (5 entries)
---------------------------------------------------------------
  ID          IP-Prefix       Interface       Gateway   P Pref    Mtr
```

```
--------------------------------------------------------------
* 4    10.110.110.2/32      bgroup0.10         0.0.0.0  H   0      0
* 5        10.0.6.1/32      eth0/0.10   10.10.10.254  S  20      1
* 2     10.10.10.2/32       eth0/0.10          0.0.0.0  H   0      0
* 1     10.10.10.0/24       eth0/0.10          0.0.0.0  C   0      0
* 3    10.110.110.0/24      bgroup0.10         0.0.0.0  C   0      0


IPv4 Dest-Routes for <vlan20-vr> (5 entries)
----------------------------------------------------------------
  ID         IP-Prefix    Interface          Gateway  P Pref    Mtr
----------------------------------------------------------------
* 5        10.0.6.1/32    eth0/0.20     10.20.20.254  S  20      1
* 4    10.120.120.2/32    bgroup0.20         0.0.0.0  H   0      0
* 2     10.20.20.2/32     eth0/0.20          0.0.0.0  H   0      0
* 1     10.20.20.0/24     eth0/0.20          0.0.0.0  C   0      0
* 3    10.120.120.0/24    bgroup0.20         0.0.0.0  C   0      0
```

So far so good, but to validate that the configuration is working, check the PIM neighbors, which in `vlan10-vr` look good:

```
FIREWALL-A(vlan10-vr/pim)-> get neighbor
Neighbor          Interface        Uptime      Expire   DR-priority GenId
-------------------------------------------------------------------
10.10.10.254  ethernet0/0.10  00:31:27   00:01:33  1           1841499
10.110.110.5    bgroup0.10      00:12:45   00:01:26  1            24305
```

When checking the RP settings, the PIM neighbors also look appropriate:

```
10.110.110.5    bgroup0.10          00:12:45   00:01:26   1   24305
FIREWALL-A(vlan10-vr/pim)-> get rp all
Flags : I - Imported, A - Always(override BSR mapping)
        C - Static Config, P - Static Proxy
Zone           Group/mask          RP-Address       Prio   Hold   Expire
    Flags
------------------------------------------------------------------
untrust-10     224.0.0.0/4         10.0.6.1          192    Static  -
    AIC trust-10


trust-10       224.0.0.0/4         10.0.6.1          192    Static  -
    AC
```

When you start the stream of traffic, you'll see the following in `vlan10-vr`:

```
FIREWALL-A(vlan10-vr/pim)-> get mroute
vlan10-vr - PIM-SM routing table
-----------------------------------------------------------------
Register - R, Connected members - C, Pruned - P, Pending SPT Alert-
G, Forward - F, Null - N , Negative Cache - E, Local Receivers - L
SPT - T, Proxy-Register - X, Imported - I, SGRpt state - Y, SSM Range
    Group - S
Turnaround Router - K
------------------------------------------------------------------
Total PIM-SM mroutes: 2
```

```
(*, 239.0.0.1)  RP 10.0.6.1             00:14:32/-          Flags: F
  Zone              : untrust-10
  Upstream          : ethernet0/0.10      State            : Joined
  RPF Neighbor      : 10.10.10.254      Expires          : 00:00:45
  Downstream        :
  bgroup0.10    00:14:32/00:02:59  Join          0.0.0.0            F

(10.7.7.1/24, 239.0.0.1)            00:05:04/00:01:32  Flags: TF
  Zone              : untrust-10
  Upstream          : ethernet0/0.10      State            : Joined
  RPF Neighbor      : 10.10.10.254      Expires          : 00:00:59
  Downstream        :
  bgroup0.10    00:05:04/00:03:26  Join          0.0.0.0
   10.7.7.1 F
```

Likewise, looking at `vlan20-vr`, you'll see the appropriate mroutes:

```
FIREWALL-A(vlan20-vr/pim)-> get mroute
vlan20-vr - PIM-SM routing table
-----------------------------------------------------------------------
Register - R, Connected members - C, Pruned - P, Pending SPT Alert-
G, Forward - F, Null - N , Negative Cache - E, Local Receivers - L
SPT - T, Proxy-Register - X, Imported - I, SGRpt state - Y, SSM Range
    Group - S
Turnaround Router - K
-----------------------------------------------------------------------
Total PIM-SM mroutes: 2

(*, 239.0.0.1)  RP 10.0.6.1             00:00:49/-          Flags: F
  Zone              : untrust-20
  Upstream          : ethernet0/0.20      State            : Joined
  RPF Neighbor      : 10.20.20.254      Expires          : 00:00:12
  Downstream        :
  bgroup0.20    00:00:49/00:03:05  Join          0.0.0.0            F

(10.7.7.1/24, 239.0.0.1)            00:00:49/00:03:06  Flags: TF
  Zone              : untrust-20
  Upstream          : ethernet0/0.20      State            : Joined
  RPF Neighbor      : 10.20.20.254      Expires          : 00:00:37
  Downstream        :
  bgroup0.20    00:00:49/00:03:05  Join          0.0.0.0
    10.7.7.1 F
```

The stream has successfully split one hop toward the source, and the packets are able to forward at high performance without any major changes to the network.

Leveraging VRs in ScreenOS can be the key to successful implementations of high-performance packet replication with a ScreenOS firewall in the logical replication point.

See Also

Recipe 20.1; Recipe 20.7

CHAPTER 21

Virtual Systems

21.0 Introduction

The high-end security devices in the ScreenOS family provide the ability to create Virtual Systems (VSYS). A VSYS is a logical firewall created within the physical security device. All ScreenOS firewalls have a root system. With the appropriate license, root system administrators can create these virtual firewalls which permit unique configuration of policies and policy objects, user lists, virtual private networks (VPNs), routing, and more. VSYS administrators can view and edit only the information configured within their own virtual firewall.

The primary application for VSYS is a multitenant, managed firewall application. In this application, multiple customers can share physical hardware and still have the personal firewall experience. This type of application may also be present in large enterprises where multiple firewalls can be collapsed into a VSYS on less hardware or even a single firewall cluster.

With recent ScreenOS releases, another use for VSYS has emerged: the ability to use resource profiles as Denial of Service (DoS) protection mechanisms within the system.

This chapter provides overview information on VSYS as well as recipes for common configurations. After understanding how to create VSYS, share zones, Virtual Routers (VRs), and interfaces, and how to use VSYS admin accounts, you can consult recipes from other chapters in this book to meet your custom configuration requirements.

VSYS and VSYS Administrators

Creating VSYS is simple. To create a VSYS named `example`, simply type **`set vsys example`**. This simple command provides some powerful capabilities within ScreenOS. The command has now created a vsys object. This vsys object can function as a standalone firewall with its own interfaces, zones, policies, address and service objects, logs, and so on. In addition, the command created a default administrator account for the virtual firewall. The admin name `vsys_example` with a password of `vsys_example` was also automatically created.

```
root(example)-> get admin user
Name                             Privilege
-------------------------------- ---------------
vsys_example                     VSYS Read-Write
```

This administrator account (which should be changed immediately with a new password) is the root-level administrator for the VSYS. Logging in to the system with this administrator account will automatically place you in the example VSYS with no visibility into the configuration of other VSYS, or the root system.

Additional VSYS administrators can be created by the root system admin, or the VSYS root admin, with read/write or read-only privileges. See Chapter 13 for more information on administrator authentication options and privileges.

VSYS components

Once created, a VSYS automatically includes several components, and has access to any shared components within the entire system. In addition to the administrator account, a VR and three zones are created automatically.

The VR *<vsys-name>*`-vr` is created. This would be `example-vr` in our example. Our example would also yield the `Trust-example`, `Untrust-example`, and `Global-example` zones (`vsys-name-trust|untrust|global`). Each VSYS device license provides one VR and two usable security zones. The `Global` zone is a default in every VSYS.

Here is a look at the example VSYS components:

```
root-> set vsys example
root(example)-> get zone
Total 3 zones created in vsys example - 2 are policy configurable.
Total policy configurable zones for example is 9.
------------------------------------------------------------
  ID Name                Type    Attr   VR          Default-IF   VSYS
   0 Null                Null    Shared untrust-vr  hidden       Root
   1 Untrust             Sec(L3) Shared trust-vr    ethernet2/1  Root
  11 V1-Untrust          Sec(L2) Shared trust-vr    v1-untrust   Root
  12 V1-Trust            Sec(L2) Shared trust-vr    v1-trust     Root
  13 V1-DMZ              Sec(L2) Shared trust-vr    v1-dmz       Root
  14 VLAN                Func    Shared trust-vr    vlan1        Root
  15 V1-Null             Sec(L2) Shared trust-vr    l2v          Root
  28 Trust-example       Sec(L3)        example-vr  null      example
  29 Untrust-Tun-example Tun            example-vr  null      example
  30 Global-example      Sec(L3)        example-vr  null      example
3001 intranet            Sec(L3) Shared trust-vr    null         Root
3003 transit             Sec(L3) Shared trust-vr    null         Root
```

```
---------------------------------------------------------
root(example)->

root(example)-> get vr
* indicates default vrouter for the current vsys
A - AutoExport, R - RIP, N- NHRP, O - OSPF, B - BGP, P - PIM

   ID Name             Vsys      Owner     Routes    MRoutes     Flags
*   6 example-vr       example   system      1/max       0/max
    1 untrust-vr       Root      shared      0/max       0/max
    2 trust-vr         Root      shared     13/max       0/max
total 3 vrouters shown and 0 of them defined by user
```

Interfaces within a VSYS can be physical interfaces such as `e2/1`, subinterfaces such as `e2/4.1`, as well as virtual interfaces such as `tunnel.1` or `loopback.1`. Physical interfaces need to be imported into the VSYS. Any physical interface in the null zone (a zone that is not assigned to a security zone) can be imported into the VSYS for use.

In addition, shared interfaces in the root system can be used within the VSYS.

Types of VSYS

The security device and its VSYS can run in one of two modes: transparent mode or route/Network Address Translation (NAT) mode. As of this writing, no mixed-mode support is available, though the configuration is possible. The VSYS can be operating in Layer 3 forwarding or Layer 2 forwarding mode. The root system will be operating in the same mode as all VSYS.

In transparent mode, all traffic is classified by the virtual local area network (VLAN) ID or tag. VLAN IDs are grouped together and are associated with a particular VSYS. In route mode, traffic can be classified at Layer 2 by the VLAN tag or at Layer 3 by the IP address.

This provides three distinct modes of operation:

Transparent mode
: Layer 2 forwarding with VLAN sorting of traffic

Route mode with Layer 2 classification
: Layer 3 forwarding with VLAN sorting of traffic

Route mode with Layer 3 classification
: Layer 3 forwarding with IP address sorting

Chapter 5 covers transparent mode operation of the firewall.

21.1 Create a Route Mode VSYS

Problem

You want to create a route mode VSYS with a shared interface in the root system, and an 802.1Q tagged interface in the VSYS.

Solution

Use the set vsys context to create the VSYS. After you create the VSYS, you can use normal configuration commands for interfaces, zones, and policies. Routes are created to and from the shared VR in the root system.

Here is the root system configuration:

```
ns5400-> set admin name rootadmin
<system message-Change Password>
ns5400-> set admin password juniper1
ns5400-> set dns host dns1 10.10.10.30
ns5400-> set clock time -6
ns5400-> set ntp server your.choice.com
ns5400-> set clock ntp
ns5400-> set interface e2/1 zone untrust
ns5400-> set interface e2/1 ip 10.54.0.3/24
ns5400-> set route 0.0.0.0/0 interface e2/1 gate 10.54.0.254
ns5400-> set interface e2/1 manage ssh
ns5400-> set ssh enable
ns5400-> set interface e2/4 zone trust
ns5400-> set interface e2/4 ip 10.54.10.254/24
```

Then, create the VSYS:

```
5400-Primary(M)-> set vsys sales
```

Create a vsys admin account:

```
5400-Primary(sales)(M)-> set admin name salesadmin
Password has been restored to default "vsys_sales". For security reasons, please
change password immediately.
5400-Primary(sales)(M)-> set admin password juniper
```

Next, create the Sales zone and interface configuration:

```
5400-Primary(sales)(M)-> set zone name sales
5400-Primary(sales)(M)-> set interface e2/4.1 tag 11 zone sales
5400-Primary(sales)(M)-> set interface e2/4.1 ip 10.54.1.254/24
```

Now, create the static routes:

```
5400-Primary(sales)(M)-> set vr trust-vr route 10.54.1.0/24 vr sales-vr
5400-Primary(sales)(M)-> set route 0.0.0.0/0 vr trust-vr
```

Finally, create the policies:

```
5400-Primary(sales)(M)-> set pol from sales to untrust any any any nat permit log
5400-Primary(sales)(M)-> set address sales webserver 10.54.1.100/32
5400-Primary(sales)(M)-> set pol from untrust to sales any webserver http permit log
```

Discussion

We started with a basic firewall configuration setup with a `Trust` and `Untrust` zone, as shown in Figure 21-1. By default, the `trust-vr` is shared as well as the `Untrust` zone. You can create additional zones and VRs and/or share them with the following commands:

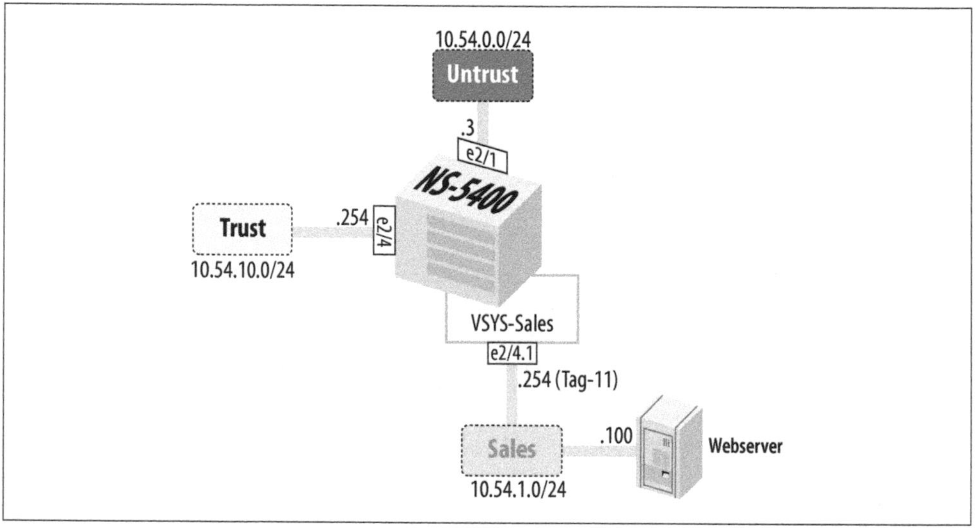

Figure 21-1. Basic VSYS example

```
set vr custom-vr sharable
set zone name custom1
set zone custom1 shared
```

Shared VRs, zones, and interfaces

Here is a look at the VRs configured in the root system:

```
5400-Primary(M)->get vr
* indicates default vrouter for the current vsys
A - AutoExport, R - RIP, N- NHRP, O - OSPF, B - BGP, P - PIM
   ID Name              Vsys      Owner      Routes     MRoutes      Flags
    1 untrust-vr        Root      shared      0/max      0/max
*   2 trust-vr          Root      shared      6/max      0/max
total 2 vrouters shown and 0 of them defined by user
```

Here is a look at the zones configured in the root system:

```
5400-Primary(M)-> get zone
Total 14 zones created in vsys Root - 8 are policy configurable.
```

```
Total policy configurable zones for Root is 8.
-------------------------------------------------------------------
  ID Name           Type    Attr   VR           Default-IF    VSYS
   0 Null           Null    Shared untrust-vr   hidden        Root
   1 Untrust        Sec(L3) Shared trust-vr     ethernet2/1   Root
   2 Trust          Sec(L3)        trust-vr     ethernet2/4   Root
   3 DMZ            Sec(L3)        trust-vr     null          Root
   4 Self           Func           trust-vr     self          Root
   5 MGT            Func           trust-vr     mgt           Root
   6 HA             Func           trust-vr     ha1           Root
  10 Global         Sec(L3)        trust-vr     null          Root
  11 V1-Untrust     Sec(L2) Shared trust-vr     v1-untrust    Root
  12 V1-Trust       Sec(L2) Shared trust-vr     v1-trust      Root
  13 V1-DMZ         Sec(L2) Shared trust-vr     v1-dmz        Root
  14 VLAN           Func    Shared trust-vr     vlan1         Root
  15 V1-Null        Sec(L2) Shared trust-vr     l2v           Root
  16 Untrust-Tun    Tun            trust-vr     hidden.1      Root
---------------------------------------------------------------------
```

As you can see from the preceding output, the `trust-vr` and the `Untrust` zone are shared. When a VR or zone is shared, it means it is available for use within a VSYS.

In our example, you want the hosts attached to the sales VSYS to be able to send packets to the `Untrust` zone in the root system. Likewise, you want to be able to create policies permitting traffic from the `Untrust` zone to a web server in the `Sales` zone.

Start the configuration by creating a VSYS named sales with the `set vsys sales` command. This command will create the VSYS, and automatically take the administrator into the VSYS context. Next, create a unique admin name for accessing the VSYS. In our example, we used `salesadmin` as the account name and set the password as `juniper`. Now, when you log in to the CLI with the VSYS admin name, ScreenOS will automatically enter the sales VSYS upon login.

Next, create a zone named sales, and place the tagged interface `e2/4.1` into the zone with a VLAN tag of 11. Give the VLAN interface an IP address of `10.54.1.254/24`.

Routing and policies

Now you want to set up routing and policies. When a VSYS is created, a VR is also created for the VSYS. The VSYS now has access to all VRs and zones that are shared from the root system as well as the unique VR created within the VSYS. From within the sales VSYS, you can add routes to any shared VR. In our case, the `trust-vr` is shared in the root system, and contains the `Untrust` zone, so a route was added to the `trust-vr` pointing our subnet in the VSYS to our VR, `sales-vr`. In addition, a default route was created within the VSYS to use the `trust-vr` in the root system:

```
5400-Primary(sales)(M)-> get route
H: Host C: Connected S: Static A: Auto Exported
I: Imported R: RIP P: Permanent D: Auto-Discovered
N: NHRP
```

```
iB: IBGP eB: EBGP O: OSPF E1: OSPF external type 1
E2: OSPF external type 2 trailing B: backup route

IPv4 Dest-Routes for <sales-vr> (3 entries)
--------------------------------------------------------------------------
    ID          IP-Prefix Interface   Gateway   P Pref    Mtr
--------------------------------------------------------------------------
*    4          0.0.0.0/0       n/a  trust-vr   S  20      0
*    2       10.54.1.0/24  eth2/4.1   0.0.0.0   C   0      0
*    3     10.54.1.254/32  eth2/4.1   0.0.0.0   H   0      0

IPv4 Dest-Routes for <trust-vr> (6 entries)
--------------------------------------------------------------------------
     ID  IP-Prefix      Interface   Gateway    P Pref    Mtr   Vsys
--------------------------------------------------------------------------
* 6       0.0.0.0/0      eth2/1  10.54.0.254   S  20      1  Root
* 3    10.54.0.3/32      eth2/1      0.0.0.0   H   0      0  Root
* 8    10.54.1.0/24        n/a      sales-vr   S  20      0 sales
* 2    10.54.0.0/24      eth2/1      0.0.0.0   C   0      0  Root
* 5    10.54.10.254/32    eth2/4      0.0.0.0   H   0      0  Root
* 4    10.54.10.0/24      eth2/4      0.0.0.0   C   0      0  Root
```

For our policies, you want all hosts within the Sales zone to be able to get to the Untrust zone using any service, as well as any host in the Untrust zone to be able to get to the web server in the Sales zone using the HyperText Transfer Protocol (HTTP):

```
5400-Primary(sales)(M)-> get policy
Total regular policies 2, Default deny.
 ID From    To   Src-address Dst-address Service Action State  ASTLCB
  1  sales  Untrust  Any      Any         ANY     Permit enabled ---X-X
  2 Untrust sales    Any      webserver   HTTP    Permit enabled ---X-X
```

Check the connectivity by sourcing a ping from the vlan interface within the VSYS to an IP address within the Untrust zone:

```
5400-Primary(sales)(M)-> ping yahoo.com from e2/4.1
Type escape sequence to abort
Sending 5, 100-byte ICMP Echos to yahoo.com [66.94.234.13], timeout
is 1 seconds from ethernet2/4.1
!!!!!
Success Rate is 100 percent (5/5),round-trip time min/avg/max=53/53/55 ms
```

21.2 Create Multiple VSYS Configurations

Problem

You want to create multiple VSYS configurations and provide selective connectivity between them.

Solution

Configure the root system and create your VSYS. Using a shared zone and VR in the root system, create routes and policies allowing the desired traffic flows.

Here is the root system configuration:

```
ns5400-> set hostname root
root-> set interface e2/1 zone untrust
root-> set interface e2/1 ip 10.54.0.3/24
root-> set interface e2/1 manage ssh
root-> set ssh enable
root-> set zone name public
root-> set interface e2/4 zone public
root-> set interface e2/4 ip 10.54.10.254/24
root-> set route 0.0.0.0/0 interface e2/1 gateway 10.54.0.254
root-> set dns host dns1 10.10.10.30
root-> set clock ntp
root-> set ntp server your.choice.com
```

Create the root system objects and policies:

```
root-> set address public www 10.54.10.10/32
root-> set policy from untrust to public any www http permit
```

Here is the sales VSYS configuration:

```
root-> set vsys sales
root(sales)-> set admin name salesadmin
<system message-Change Password>
root(sales)-> set admin password juniper1
root(sales)-> set zone name sales
root(sales)-> set interf e2/4.1 tag 11 zone sales
root(sales)-> set route 0.0.0.0/0 vr trust-vr
root(sales)-> set vr trust-vr route 10.54.1.0/24 vr sales-vr
root(sales)-> set address sales webserver 10.54.1.100/32
root(sales)-> set policy from untrust to sales any webserver http
    permit log
root(sales)-> set policy from sales to untrust any any any nat permit
root(sales)-> save
Save System Configuration ...
Done
root(sales)->exit
exit vsys sales
```

And here is the corporate VSYS configuration:

```
root-> set vsys corp
root(corp)-> set admin name corpadmin
<system message-Change Password>
root(corp)-> set admin password juniper2
root(corp)-> set zone name hr
root(corp)-> set zone name finance
root(corp)-> set interface e2/4.2 tag 12 zone finance
root(corp)-> set interface e2/4.3 tag 13 zone hr
root(corp)-> set interface e2/4.2 ip 10.54.2.254/24
```

```
root(corp)-> set interface e2/4.3 ip 10.54.3.254/24
root(corp)-> set route 0.0.0.0/0 vr trust-vr
root(corp)-> set vr trust-vr route 10.54.2.0/24 vr corp-vr
root(corp)-> set vr trust-vr route 10.54.3.0/24 vr corp-vr
root(corp)-> set address finance banker 10.54.2.100/32
root(corp)-> set address hr database 10.54.3.100/32
root(corp)-> set address finance finance-users 10.54.2.17/28
root(corp)-> set address transit sales-users 10.54.1.17/28
root(corp)-> set address hr hr-users 10.54.3.17/28
root(corp)-> set policy from finance to hr finance-users database
    any permit log
root(corp)-> set policy from hr to untrust hr-users any any nat
    permit
root(corp)-> set policy from hr to finance hr-users banker ms-sql
    permit log
root(corp)-> set policy from transit to hr sales-users database
    ms-sql permit log
root(corp)-> save
Save System Configuration  ...
Done
root(corp)-> exit
exit vsys corp
root->
```

Discussion

As illustrated in Figure 21-2, the configuration was created for the root system as well as two additional VSYS: sales and corp. Because you want to have some inter-VSYS traffic flows, you will use the shared `Untrust` zone for looping traffic flows between different VSYS. To provide for this inter-VSYS traffic, the `Untrust` zone must be shared and used for this purpose. The `Untrust` zone is unique in this ability, as custom zones will not permit this type of traffic flow. Policies within each VSYS will also be required to permit this inter-VSYS communication.

Root system

Starting with the root system, we have set the hostname, created our zones, added the interfaces to the zones, and configured the IP address information. We enabled Secure Shell (SSH) for management purposes, configured a static default route, enabled the Domain Name System (DNS), and set the system clock to use a Network Time Protocol (NTP) server. This completes the basic setup for the root system.

In the root system, the `trust-vr` is created as the default VR automatically and is shared among all VSYSes. All zones used in the root system in this example are bound to the `trust-vr`.

Here are the routes present in the `trust-vr`:

```
root-> get route
IPv4 Dest-Routes for <untrust-vr> (0 entries)
```

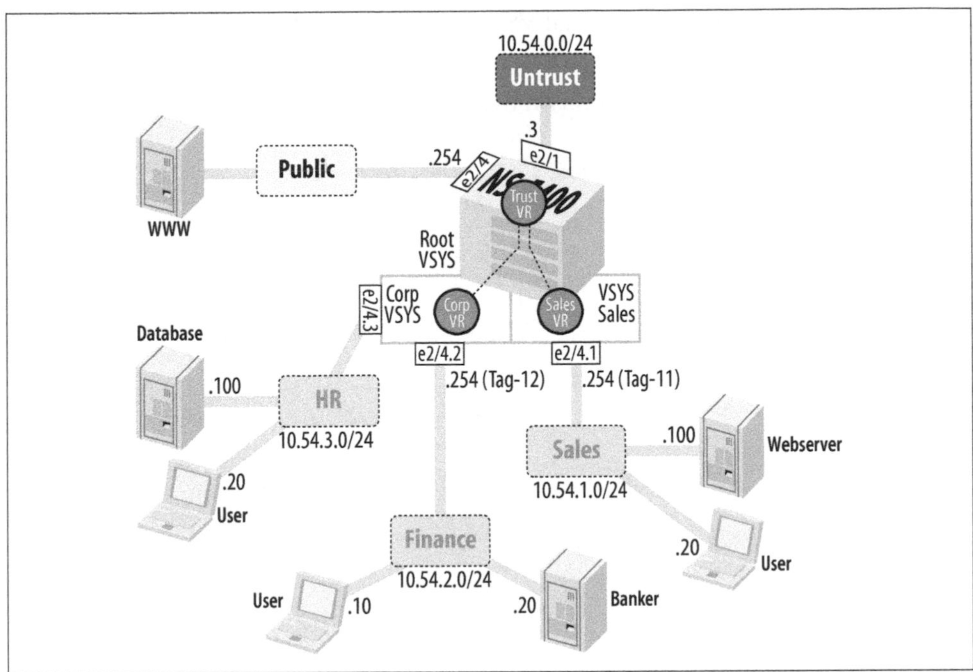

Figure 21-2. Multi-VSYS example

```
-----------------------------------------------------------------
H: Host C: Connected S: Static A: Auto-Exported
I: Imported R: RIP P: Permanent D: Auto-Discovered
N: NHRP
iB: IBGP eB: EBGP O: OSPF E1: OSPF external type 1
E2: OSPF external type 2 trailing B: backup route
IPv4 Dest-Routes for <trust-vr> (10 entries)
-----------------------------------------------------------------
      ID        IP-Prefix   Interface     Gateway   P Pref    Mtr  Vsys
-----------------------------------------------------------------
*      7        0.0.0.0/0     eth2/1  10.54.0.254   S   20   1       Root
*      4     10.54.0.3/32     eth2/1      0.0.0.0   H    0   0       Root
       2   192.168.1.1/32        mgt      0.0.0.0   H    0   0       Root
       1   192.168.1.0/24        mgt      0.0.0.0   C    0   0       Root
*     11     10.54.3.0/24        n/a      corp-vr   S   20   0       corp
*     10     10.54.2.0/24        n/a      corp-vr   S   20   0       corp
*     14     10.54.1.0/24        n/a     sales-vr   S   20   0      sales
*      3     10.54.0.0/24     eth2/1      0.0.0.0   C    0   0       Root
*     13 10.54.10.254/32      eth2/4      0.0.0.0   H    0   0       Root
*     12    10.54.10.0/24     eth2/4      0.0.0.0   C    0   0       Root
root->
```

Note the static routes configured within the `trust-vr`. You can see the default route pointing out interface e2/1 to the gateway at `10.54.0.254`. You can also see the routes pointing to the subnets in the VSYS configured for the next hop to be the VR within the associated VSYS. Routes pointing to subnets within the two VSYS must be configured from *within* the individual VSYS contexts by the root VSYS administrator and not *from* the root system.

Now, look at the zone configuration on the root system:

```
root-> get zone
Total 17 zones created in vsys Root - 11 are policy configurable.
Total policy configurable zones for Root is 11.
------------------------------------------------------
  ID Name              Type    Attr   VR           Default-IF   VSYS
   0 Null              Null    Shared untrust-vr   hidden       Root
   1 Untrust           Sec(L3) Shared trust-vr     ethernet2/1  Root
   2 Trust             Sec(L3)        trust-vr     null         Root
   3 DMZ               Sec(L3)        trust-vr     null         Root
   4 Self              Func           trust-vr     self         Root
   5 MGT               Func           trust-vr     mgt          Root
   6 HA                Func           trust-vr     ha1          Root
  10 Global            Sec(L3)        trust-vr     null         Root
  11 V1-Untrust        Sec(L2) Shared trust-vr     v1-untrust   Root
  12 V1-Trust          Sec(L2) Shared trust-vr     v1-trust     Root
  13 V1-DMZ            Sec(L2) Shared trust-vr     v1-dmz       Root
  14 VLAN              Func    Shared trust-vr     vlan1        Root
  15 V1-Null           Sec(L2) Shared trust-vr     l2v          Root
  16 Untrust-Tun       Tun            trust-vr     hidden.1     Root
3000 public            Sec(L3)        trust-vr     ethernet2/4  Root
3001 transit           Sec(L3) Shared trust-vr     null         Root
------------------------------------------------------
root->
```

The two custom zones, `public` and `transit`, are at the bottom of the list. Notice that the `Untrust` zone and the `transit` zone are shared, and that all the zones are bound to the `trust-vr`. The list also shows interface `e2/1` in the `Untrust` zone and interface `e2/4` in the `public` zone—no interfaces have been assigned to the `transit` zone.

Lastly, for the root system, here's the configured policy:

```
root-> get policy
Total regular policies 1, Default deny.
 ID From    To     Src-address Dst-address Service Action State  ASTLCB
 1 Untrust public  Any         www         HTTP    Permit enabled -----X
root->
```

The policy allows any source address from the `Untrust` zones to access the destination address object `www` using HTTP.

VSYS configuration

For the VSYS configuration, let's enter the sales VSYS and look at the VRs and zones:

```
root-> enter vsys sales
root(sales)-> get vr
* indicates default vrouter for the current vsys
A - AutoExport, R - RIP, N- NHRP, O - OSPF, B - BGP, P - PIM
```

```
   ID Name          Vsys                   Owner     Routes    MRoutes
*   3 sales-vr      sales                  system      1/max      0/max
    1 untrust-vr    Root                   shared      0/max      0/max
    2 trust-vr      Root                   shared     10/max      0/max
total 3 vrouters shown and 0 of them defined by user
root(sales)-> get zone
Total 4 zones created in vsys sales - 3 are policy configurable.
Total policy configurable zones for sales is 10.
------------------------------------------------------------
  ID Name                Type    Attr   VR           Default-IF   VSYS
   0 Null                Null    Shared untrust-vr   hidden       Root
   1 Untrust             Sec(L3) Shared trust-vr     ethernet2/1  Root
  11 V1-Untrust          Sec(L2) Shared trust-vr     v1-untrust   Root
  12 V1-Trust            Sec(L2) Shared trust-vr     v1-trust     Root
  13 V1-DMZ              Sec(L2) Shared trust-vr     v1-dmz       Root
  14 VLAN                Func    Shared trust-vr     vlan1        Root
  15 V1-Null             Sec(L2) Shared trust-vr     l2v          Root
  19 Trust-sales         Sec(L3)        sales-vr     null         sales
  20 Untrust-Tun-sales   Tun            sales-vr     null         sales
  21 Global-sales        Sec(L3)        sales-vr     null         sales
3001 sales               Sec(L3)        sales-vr     null         sales
3002 transit             Sec(L3) Shared trust-vr     null         Root
------------------------------------------------------------
root(sales)->
```

You can see the shared VRs in the root system as well as the sales-vr in the sales VSYS. The asterisk next to the sales-vr indicates that this router is the default router for the VSYS. You can also see our Sales zone and the shared zones from the root system. The static route configuration is as follows:

```
root(sales)-> get route
H: Host C: Connected S: Static A: Auto-Exported
I: Imported R: RIP P: Permanent D: Auto-Discovered
N: NHRP
iB: IBGP eB: EBGP O: OSPF E1: OSPF external type 1
E2: OSPF external type 2 trailing B: backup route


IPv4 Dest-Routes for <sales-vr> (3 entries)
-------------------------------------------------------------------
   ID       IP-Prefix     Interface      Gateway   P Pref     Mtr
-------------------------------------------------------------------
*   2       0.0.0.0/0           n/a     trust-vr   S   20       0
*   3    10.54.1.0/24      eth2/4.1      0.0.0.0   C    0       0
*   4  10.54.1.254/32      eth2/4.1      0.0.0.0   H    0       0
IPv4 Dest-Routes for <untrust-vr> (0 entries)
--------------------------------------------------------------------

IPv4 Dest-Routes for <trust-vr> (10 entries)
--------------------------------------------------------------------
      ID       IP-Prefix Interface       Gateway   P Pref  Mtr   Vsys
--------------------------------------------------------------------
*     7        0.0.0.0/0    eth2/1  10.54.0.254   S   20    1   Root
*     4     10.54.0.3/32    eth2/1      0.0.0.0   H    0    0   Root
```

```
      2   192.168.1.1/32       mgt      0.0.0.0   H    0    0  Root
      1   192.168.1.0/24       mgt      0.0.0.0   C    0    0  Root
*    14      10.54.1.0/24      n/a     sales-vr   S   20    0 sales
*     3      10.54.0.0/24   eth2/1      0.0.0.0   C    0    0  Root
*    13  10.54.10.254/32    eth2/4      0.0.0.0   H    0    0  Root
*    12     10.54.10.0/24   eth2/4      0.0.0.0   C    0    0  Root
root(sales)->
```

You can see the single route configured in the sales-vr, in addition to the connected and host routes automatically created. This route provides a default next hop into the shared trust-vr of the root system, and it would be used for traffic accessing the Untrust zone or the public zone in the root system.

You can also see some routes configured in the trust-vr. Notice that you do not see routes associated with the corp VSYS as you did when you looked at the route table from the root system. This is VSYS separation at work. The route pointing to the subnet in the sales VSYS is configured in the trust-vr.

Here is the policy configuration of the sales VSYS:

```
root(sales)-> get policy
Total regular policies 2, Default deny.
ID From    To      Src-address Dst-address Service Action State   ASTLCB
 1 transit sales   Any         webserver   HTTP    Permit enabled -----X
 2 sales   Untrust Any         Any         ANY     Permit enabled -----X
root(sales)->
```

Traffic is allowed into the sales VSYS for the web server attached to the Sales zone. In addition, users in the Sales zone can access the Internet through the Untrust zone. Also, administrators of the root system and the corp VSYS may allow traffic from the Untrust zone, which is shared, into other zones within their respective VSYSes.

The corp VSYS has two zones—the hr zone and the finance zone—associated with it, in addition to the shared zones in the root system. Both zones have server resources attached to them, and selective connectivity between the zones and the sales VSYS is desired.

Here is the VR, zone, and route configuration within the corp VSYS:

```
root-> enter vsys corp
root(corp)-> get vr
* indicates default vrouter for the current vsys
A - AutoExport, R - RIP, N- NHRP, O - OSPF, B - BGP, P - PIM
 ID Name           Vsys       Owner      Routes     MRoutes     Flags
*   4 corp-vr        corp       system       5/max        0/max
    1 untrust-vr     Root       shared       0/max        0/max
    2 trust-vr       Root       shared      10/max        0/max
total 3 vrouters shown and 0 of them defined by user

root(corp)-> get zone
Total 5 zones created in vsys corp - 4 are policy configurable.
Total policy configurable zones for corp is 11.
----------------------------------------------------------
```

```
 ID Name              Type    Attr   VR          Default-IF   VSYS
  0 Null              Null    Shared untrust-vr  hidden       Root
  1 Untrust           Sec(L3) Shared trust-vr    ethernet2/1  Root
 11 V1-Untrust        Sec(L2) Shared trust-vr    v1-untrust   Root
 12 V1-Trust          Sec(L2) Shared trust-vr    v1-trust     Root
 13 V1-DMZ            Sec(L2) Shared trust-vr    v1-dmz       Root
 14 VLAN              Func    Shared trust-vr    vlan1        Root
 15 V1-Null           Sec(L2) Shared trust-vr    l2v          Root
 22 Trust-corp        Sec(L3)        corp-vr     null         corp
 23 Untrust-Tun-corp  Tun            corp-vr     null         corp
 24 Global-corp       Sec(L3)        corp-vr     null         corp
3002 transit          Sec(L3) Shared trust-vr    null         Root
3004 hr               Sec(L3)        corp-vr     null         corp
3005 finance          Sec(L3)        corp-vr     null         corp
---------------------------------------------------------

root(corp)-> get route
H: Host C: Connected S: Static A: Auto-Exported
I: Imported R: RIP P: Permanent D: Auto-Discovered
N: NHRP
iB: IBGP eB: EBGP O: OSPF E1: OSPF external type 1
E2: OSPF external type 2 trailing B: backup route

IPv4 Dest-Routes for <corp-vr> (5 entries)
--------------------------------------------------------------------
   D          IP-Prefix    Interface     Gateway   P Pref     Mtr
--------------------------------------------------------------------
*  6          0.0.0.0/0          n/a    trust-vr   S   20       0
*  3      10.54.2.254/32     eth2/4.2    0.0.0.0   H    0       0
*  4        10.54.3.0/24     eth2/4.3    0.0.0.0   C    0       0
*  2        10.54.2.0/24     eth2/4.2    0.0.0.0   C    0       0
*  5      10.54.3.254/32     eth2/4.3    0.0.0.0   H    0       0

IPv4 Dest-Routes for <untrust-vr> (0 entries)
---------------------------------------------------------------------

IPv4 Dest-Routes for <trust-vr> (10 entries)
---------------------------------------------------------------------
   ID          IP-Prefix Interface      Gateway   P Pref  Mtr     Vsys
---------------------------------------------------------------------
*   7          0.0.0.0/0    eth2/1  10.54.0.254   S   20    1     Root
*   4        10.54.0.3/32   eth2/1      0.0.0.0   H    0    0     Root
    2      192.168.1.1/32      mgt      0.0.0.0   H    0    0     Root
    1      192.168.1.0/24      mgt      0.0.0.0   C    0    0     Root
*  11        10.54.3.0/24      n/a      corp-vr   S   20    0     corp
*  10        10.54.2.0/24      n/a      corp-vr   S   20    0     corp
*   3        10.54.0.0/24   eth2/1      0.0.0.0   C    0    0     Root
*  13     10.54.10.254/32   eth2/4      0.0.0.0   H    0    0     Root
*  12       10.54.10.0/24   eth2/4      0.0.0.0   C    0    0     Root
root(corp)->
```

You can see the commonality of the configuration here. The corp-vr has its connected routes, as well as the default route, pointing to the trust-vr. The trust-vr has routes pointing into the corp-vr for the two subnets configured in the VSYS. The shared zones and the custom zones within the corp-vr are also shown.

For this VSYS, the users in the sales VSYS are allowed to access the database in the hr zone. So, an address object created for the sales users and a policy from Untrust to hr are configured here. You'll also see policies allowing other zone-to-zone traffic:

```
root(corp)-> get pol
Total regular policies 5, Default deny.
 ID From    To      Src-address Dst-address Service Action State   ASTLCB
  5 hr      Untrust Any         Any         ANY     Permit enabled ---X-X
  1 finance hr      finance-use~database    ANY     Permit enabled ---X-X
  2 hr      Untrust hr-users    Any         ANY     Permit enabled -----X
  3 hr      finance hr-users    banker      MS-SQL  Permit enabled ---X-X
  4 untrust hr      sales-users database    MS-SQL  Permit enabled ---X-X
root(corp)->
```

Inter-VSYS policies are at work here. Policy ID 4 allows traffic from our shared Untrust zone in the root system for addresses associated with the Sales zone in the sales VSYS permitted to the destination object database using the MS-SQL protocol. For this traffic to flow, two policies are required: the first policy permitting the sales users access to the shared Untrust zone configured in the sales VSYS, and the second policy permitting the sales users from the shared Untrust zone into the hr zone of the corp VSYS.

You can find more information on policy configuration in Chapter 7.

21.3 VSYS and High Availability

Problem

You want to create VSYSes within a high-availability cluster and use some shared router and zone objects in the root system, similar to the example illustrated in Figure 21-3.

Solution

Create the root system configuration (primary device):

```
ns5400(M)-> set hostname 5400-Primary
ns5400-Primary-> set dns host dns1 10.10.10.30
ns5400-Primary-> set ntp server ntppub.tamu.edu
ns5400-Primary-> set clock ntp
ns5400-Primary-> set interface e2/1 zone untrust
ns5400-Primary-> set interface e2/4 zone trust
ns5400-Primary-> set interface e2/1 ip 10.54.0.3/24
ns5400-Primary-> set interface e2/4 ip 10.54.10.254/24
ns5400-Primary-> set nsrp cluster id 7
Unit becomes master of NSRP vsd-group 0
ns5400-Primary(M)-> set nsrp vsd id 0 pri 50
5400-Primary(M)-> set nsrp config sync
```

```
5400-Primary(M)-> set nsrp rto-mirror sync
5400-Primary(M)-> set interface e2/1 manage-ip 10.54.0.1
5400-Primary(M)-> set route 0.0.0.0/0 interface e2/1 gateway 10.54.0.254
```

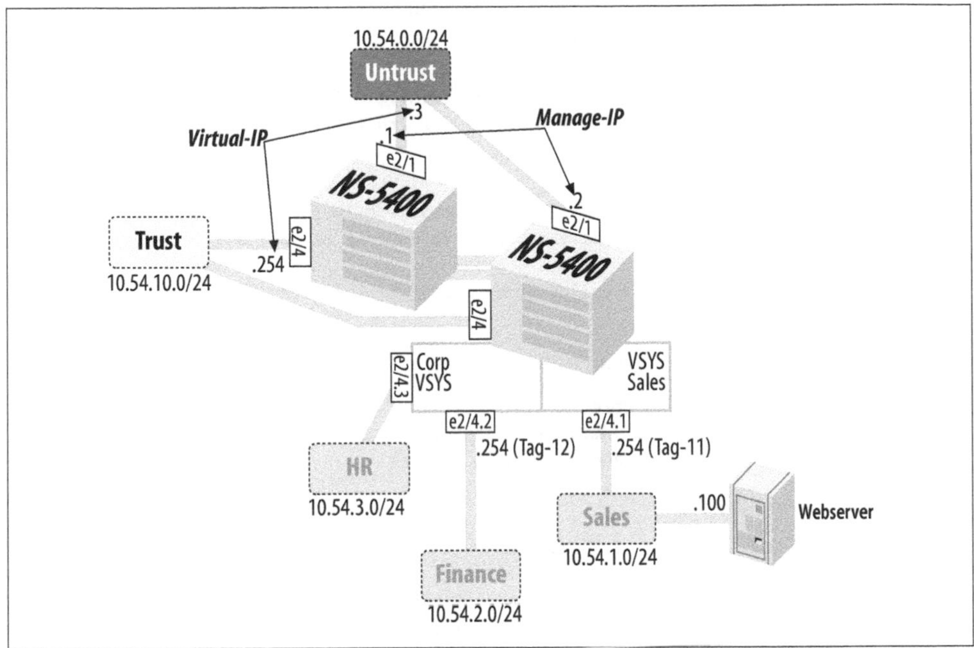

Figure 21-3. VSYS with NSRP example

Then, create the root system configuration on the backup device:

```
ns5400-> set hostname 5400-Backup
5400-Backup-> set nsrp cluster id 7
5400-Backup(B)-> save
5400-Backup(B)-> exec nsrp sync global-config save
5400-Backup(B)-> load peer system config to save
Save global configuration successfully.
Continue to save local configurations ... Save local configuration
    successfully done.
Please reset your box to let cluster configuration take effect!
```

Reset the system, and choose *no* to the save configuration option. Now, finish the backup configuration:

```
5400-Backup(B)-> set interface e2/1 manage-ip 10.54.0.2
5400-Backup(B)-> set interface e2/1 mng
5400-Backup(B)-> save
```

Using Figure 21-3 as the example, create the sales VSYS with an admin account:

```
5400-Primary(M)-> set vsys sales
5400-Primary(sales)(M)-> set admin name salesadmin
5400-Primary(sales)(M)-> set admin password juniper
```

Create the zones and interfaces:

```
5400-Primary(sales)(M)-> set zone name sales
5400-Primary(sales)(M)-> set interface e2/4.1 tag 11 zone sales
5400-Primary(sales)(M)-> set interface e2/4.1 ip 10.54.1.254/24
```

Next, create the routes:

```
5400-Primary(sales)(M)-> set vr trust route 10.54.1.0/24 vr sales-vr
5400-Primary(sales)(M)-> set route 0.0.0.0/0 vr trust-vr
```

Create the objects and policies:

```
5400-Primary(sales)(M)-> set address sales webserver 10.54.1.100/32
5400-Primary(sales)(M)-> set pol from sales to untrust any any any
    nat permit log
5400-Primary(sales)(M)-> set policy from untrust to sales any webserver
    http permit log
```

Then, create the corp vsys with an admin account:

```
5400-Primary(M)-> set vsys corp
5400-Primary(corp)(M)-> set admin name corpadmin
5400-Primary(corp)(M)-> set admin password juniper
```

Create the zones and interfaces:

```
5400-Primary(corp)(M)-> set zone name hr
5400-Primary(corp)(M)-> set zone name finance
5400-Primary(corp)(M)-> set interface e2/4.2 tag 12 zone finance
5400-Primary(corp)(M)-> set interface e2/4.2 ip 10.54.2.254/24
5400-Primary(corp)(M)-> set interface e2/4.3 tag 13 zone hr
5400-Primary(corp)(M)-> set interface e2/4.3 ip 10.54.3.254/24
```

Create the routes:

```
5400-Primary(corp)(M)-> set vr -trust-vr route 10.54.2.0/24 vr corp-vr
5400-Primary(corp)(M)-> set vr trust-vr route 10.54.2.0/24 vr corp-vr
5400-Primary(corp)(M)-> set vr trust-vr route 10.54.3.0/24 vr corp-vr
5400-Primary(corp)(M)-> set route 0.0.0.0/0 vr trust-vr
```

Now, create the policies, and save the configuration:

```
5400-Primary(corp)(M)-> set policy from finance to untrust any any
    any nat permit
5400-Primary(corp)(M)-> set policy from hr to untrust any any any
    nat permit log
5400-Primary(corp)(M)-> save
```

Discussion

Creating VSYS in high-availability mode is the same as in the basic standalone firewall configuration discussed in Recipe 21.1. The primary difference is in the root system configuration. Please see Chapter 18 for information on configuring the NetScreen Redundancy Protocol (NSRP).

See Recipe 21.2 for information on configuring advanced features for VSYS in route mode, or Recipe 21.4 for information on creating a transparent mode VSYS.

21.4 Create a Transparent Mode VSYS

Problem

You want to create Layer 2 VSYS using 802.1Q VLAN tags for traffic separation.

Solution

Creating transparent mode VSYS is the same as in route mode. However, the interface and zone configurations differ. Using Figure 21-4 as a sample Layer 2 VSYS topology, create the Layer 2 VSYS:

```
ns5400-> set hostname L2-Root
L2-Root-> set vsys gaming
L2-Root(gaming)-> set admin name gameadmin
<system message-Change Password>
L2-Root(gaming)-> set admin password juniper123
```

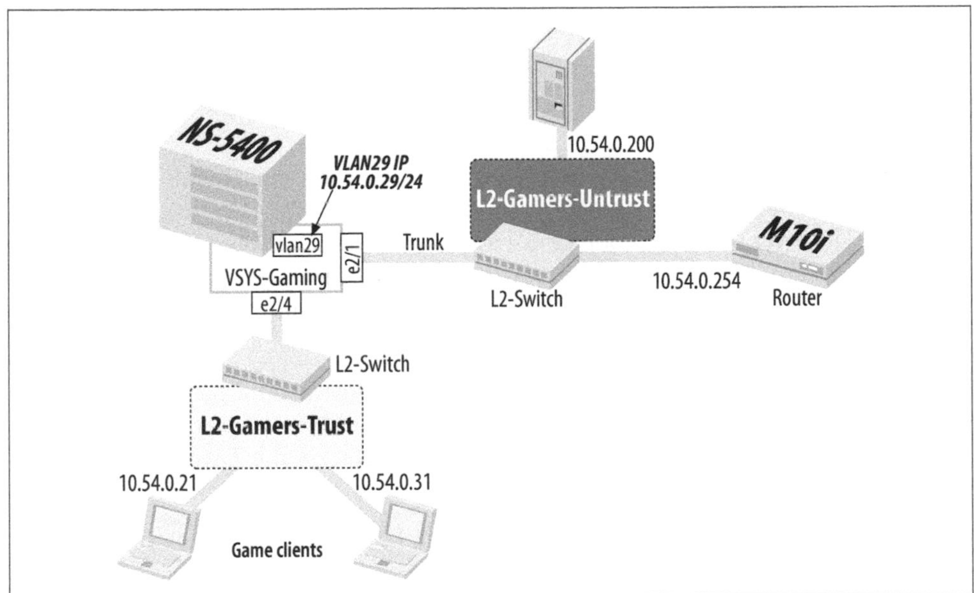

Figure 21-4. Layer 2 VSYS example

Next, configure the VLAN group, zones, and interfaces:

```
L2-Root(gaming)-> set vlan import 20 29
L2-Root(gaming)-> set vlan group name gamers
L2-Root(gaming)-> set vlan group gamers 20 29
L2-Root(gaming)-> set zone name L2-gamers-trust L2
L2-Root(gaming)-> set zone name L2-gamers-untrust L2
L2-Root(gaming)-> set vlan port e2/4 group gamers zone L2-gamers-trust
Changed to pure l2 mode
L2-Root(gaming)-> set vlan port e2/1 group gamers zone L2-gamers-untrust
```

Now, configure the management interface and service options:

```
L2-Root(gaming)-> set interface vlan29 zone vlan
L2-Root(gaming)-> set interface vlan29 ip 10.54.0.29/24
L2-Root(gaming)-> unset interface vlan29 manage
L2-Root(gaming)-> set interface vlan29 manage web
L2-Root(gaming)-> set interface vlan29 manage ssh
L2-Root(gaming)-> set interface vlan29 manage ping
L2-Root(gaming)-> set route 0.0.0.0/0 interface vlan29 gateway 10.54.0.254
```

And finally, create policies:

```
L2-Root(gaming)-> set policy from L2-gamers-untrust to L2-gamers-trust
    any any http permit
L2-Root(gaming)-> set policy from L2-gamers-untrust to L2-gamers-trust
    any any any deny log
L2-Root(gaming)-> set policy from L2-gamers-trust to L2-gamers-untrust
    any any any permit
L2-Root(gaming)-> save
Save System Configuration ...
Done
L2-Root(gaming)-> exit
Exit vsys gaming
```

Discussion

In this recipe, there are no shared zones within the root system; therefore, no configuration of the root system is necessary. By default, the root system has shared zones and VRs. However, external routing is required to route between different subnets configured within different VSYS. So, for this recipe, a completely autonomous VSYS called `gaming` is configured. This VSYS will utilize two custom zones: `L2-gamers-trust` and `L2-gamers-untrust`, as shown in Figure 21-4.

For transparent mode VSYS, the security device is forwarding packets/frames the same way a Layer 2 switch or transparent bridge would forward frames. However, you can perform stateful inspection of the traffic based on the Layer 3 and Layer 4 packet headers.

When using VLAN IDs for traffic separation, the Layer 2 switch infrastructure must support the 802.1Q standard.

Creating a Layer 2 VSYS

To start, create the VSYS with the command set `vsys gaming`. Then, automatically enter the VSYS. At this point, the system does not know whether this will be a transparent mode or route mode VSYS, so create an administrator and password as with any VSYS configuration.

Next, configure the VLAN group, custom zones, and interface configuration. The VLAN group identifies 802.1Q tags that this VSYS will service. In our example, you will service VLAN IDs 20–29 within this *gaming* VSYS. The `import` command dedicates these VLAN IDs to the VSYS, and you cannot use them elsewhere within the system. VLAN IDs 20–29 are grouped with the name `gamers`.

Now, create the custom Layer 2 zones. Notice the `L2` classifier at the end of the `set zone name` command. `L2-gamers-trust` is created, and interface `e2/4` is bound to the zone. As soon as an interface is bound to the Layer 2 zone, a system message states that the system is now in pure Layer 2 mode. Port `e2/1` is then bound to the `L2-gamers-untrust` zone.

Here's a look at the VLAN group configuration:

```
L2-Root(gaming)-> get vlan group gamers
vlan group info:
-------------------------------------------------------------------------name(vsys) :
gamers(gaming)
vids        : [20-29]
port        : ethernet2/4 ethernet2/1
L2-Root(gaming)->
```

Note that the gamers VLAN group is configured in the gaming VSYS. VLAN IDs 20–29 are associated with the VSYS as well as ports `e2/1` and `e2/4`.

The following are additional get commands useful for checking a Layer 2 VLAN configuration:

```
L2-Root(gaming)-> get vlan port

interface name (vid-range)  vsys        zone                ifp
-----------------------------------------------------------------
ethernet2/1 (  20-  29) gaming  L2-gamers-untrust L2-gamers-untrust.1
ethernet2/4 (  20-  29) gaming  L2-gamers-trust   L2-gamers-trust.2


L2-Root(gaming)-> get vlan import

vsys-name                : imported vlan ID range
----------------------------------------------------------------------
gaming                   : [20-29]


L2-Root(gaming)-> get vlan

vsys-name                  : imported vlan ID range
-----------------------------------------------------------------------
gaming                     : [20-29]

interface name  (vid-range)  vsys        zone                ifp
-----------------------------------------------------------------
ethernet2/1 (  20-  29) gaming  L2-gamers-untrust  L2-gamers-untrust.1
ethernet2/4 (  20-  29) gaming  L2-gamers-trust  L2-gamers-trust.2

vlan group info:
-----------------------------------------------------------------------
name(vsys) : gamers(gaming)
```

```
vids        : [20-29]
port        : ethernet2/4 ethernet2/1
```

And, from the root system:

```
L2-Root-> get vlan all

vsys-name                   : imported vlan ID range
----------------------------------------------------------------------
Root                        : [0-1]
gaming                      : [20-29]

interface name  (vid-range) vsys       zone                 ifp
-------------------------------------------------------------------
ethernet2/1 (   0-    1) Root      V1-Null               l2v
            (  20-   29) gaming  L2-gamers-untrust  L2-gamers-untrust.1
ethernet2/4 (   0-    1) Root      V1-Null               l2v
            (  20-   29) gaming  L2-gamers-trust  L2-gamers-trust.2

vlan group info:
----------------------------------------------------------------------
name(vsys)  : gamers(gaming)
vids        : [20-29]
port        : ethernet2/4 ethernet2/1
```

The security device supports VLAN tags 2–4,094. `Vlan-1` is assigned to the root device. All VLAN tags must be unique among the configured VSYS.

Policies

Address and service objects, as well as policies, are configured the same as in route mode, with the difference being the use of Layer 2 zones. In this example, a policy was created to allow HTTP traffic from the `L2-gamers-untrust` zone to the `L2-gamers-trust` zone, and an implicit deny policy was created for any other traffic between those two zones for the purpose of logging the denied flows. The final policy was to allow any traffic between the `L2-gamers-trust` and `L2-gamers-untrust` zones.

For more information on transparent mode, please see Chapter 5.

21.5 Terminate IPSec Tunnels in the VSYS

Problem

You want to terminate IP Security (IPSec) VPN tunnels within a selected VSYS while using a shared zone in the root system for connection to the Internet Key Exchange (IKE) peer.

Solution

Create a VSYS and use the shared `untrust` interface/zone in the root system for connectivity to the remote IKE peer.

The root system configuration is:

```
ns5400-> set hostname root
root-> set interface e2/1 zone untrust
root-> set interface e2/1 ip 10.54.0.3/24
root-> set route 0.0.0.0/0 interface e2/1 gateway 10.54.0.254
root-> set dns host dns1 10.10.10.30
root-> set clock ntp
root-> set ntp server your.choice.com
```

Then, create a VSYS:

```
root-> set vsys cust1
root(cust1)-> set admin name cust1admin
<system message-Change Password>
root(cust1)-> set admin password juniper8
```

Create the zones and interfaces:

```
root(cust1)-> set interface e2/4.8 tag 18 zone trust-cust1
root(cust1)-> set interface e2/4.8 ip 10.54.8.254/24
root(cust1)-> set zone name vpn
root(cust1)-> set interface loopback.8 zone vpn
root(cust1)-> set interface loopback.8 ip 10.54.81.1/29
root(cust1)-> set interface loopback.8 manage ping
```

Set the routes:

```
root(cust1)-> set vr trust route 10.54.8.0/24 vr cust1-vr
root(cust1)-> set vr trust route 10.54.81.0/29 vr cust1-vr
root(cust1)-> set route 0.0.0.0/0 vr trust-vr
```

Then, set policies for VPN establishment:

```
root(cust1)-> set policy from untrust to vpn gt-1 any any permit
root(cust1)-> set pol from vpn to untrust any gt-1 any permit
```

Set the VPN configuration within VSYS:

```
root(cust1)-> set interface tunnel.81 zone vpn
root(cust1)-> set interface tunnel.81 ip unnumbered interface
    e2/4.8
root(cust1)-> set ike gateway gt-1 address 10.0.0.81 main
    outgoing-interface loopback.8 preshare juniper sec-level standard
root(cust1)-> set vpn gt-1 gateway gt-1 sec-level standard
root(cust1)-> set vpn gt-1 monitor rekey
root(cust1)-> set vpn gt-1 bind interface tunnel.81
root(cust1)-> set route 10.80.1.0/24 interface tunnel.81
root(cust1)-> set policy from trust-cust1 to vpn any any any permit
root(cust1)-> set policy from vpn to trust-cust1 any any any permit
```

Create the remote site VPN configuration:

```
GT-1-> set zone name vpn
GT-1-> set interface tunnel.8 zone vpn
GT-1-> set interface tunnel.8 ip unnumbered interface untrust
GT-1-> set ike gateway cust1-hub address 10.54.81.1 main outgoing-
    interface untrust preshare juniper sec-level standard
```

```
GT-1-> set vpn cust1-hub gateway cust1-hub sec-level standard
GT-1-> set vpn cust1-hub monitor rekey
GT-1-> set vpn cust1-hub bind interface tunnel.8
GT-1-> set route 10.54.8.0/24 interface tunnel.8
GT-1-> set policy from trust to vpn any any any permit
GT-1-> set policy from vpn to trust any any any permit
```

Discussion

As depicted in Figure 21-5, a VSYS was created named `cust1`, and the default zone `trust-cust1` was used for the tagged interface `e2/4.8` with the IP address `10.54.8.254/24`.

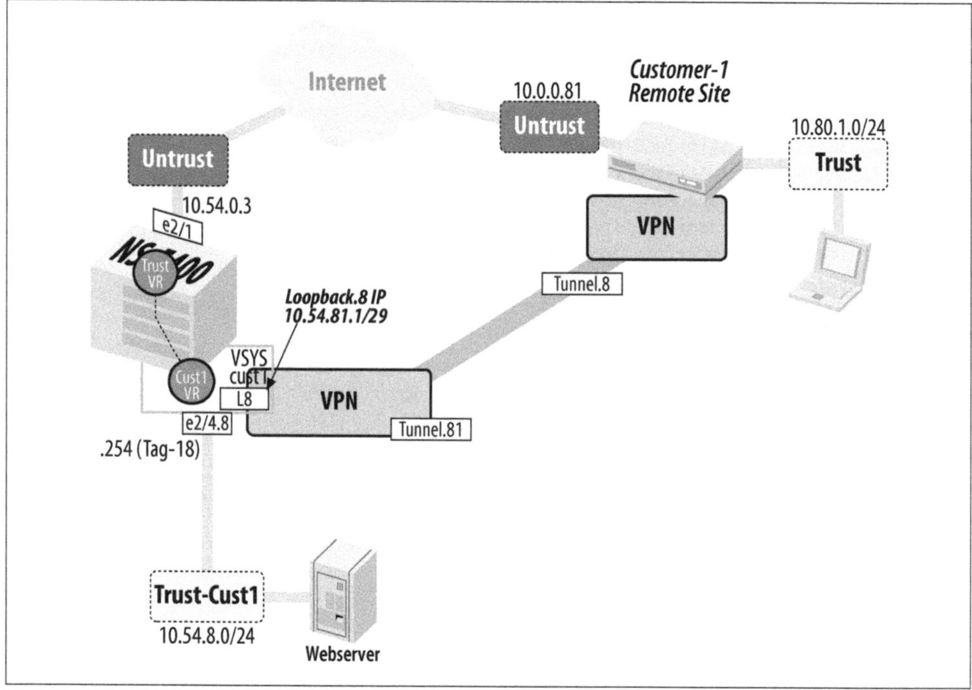

Figure 21-5. IPSec termination within VSYS example

In Figure 21-5, the `Untrust` zone in the root system is connected to our simulated Internet. Connectivity between the remote site and the VSYS must transit this shared zone. In the VSYS, a loopback interface was created, `loopback.8`, and given an IP address of `10.54.81.1/29`. This interface will be the IKE peer for the remote site to connect with. Creating this virtual interface along with the VPN zone allows for creating logical zone-based policies. Because users on both ends of the tunnel are in the `Trust` zone, you can create trust to VPN policies allowing only the desired flows.

Another option here would be to terminate the VPN tunnels on the trust-side interface and use intra-zone policies.

Now that this virtual (loopback) interface is created, you can also use the interface for a variety of interface-based NAT by creating mapped IPs (MIPs) and dynamic IPs (DIPs) on this interface. Enable ping on this interface to assist in troubleshooting connectivity. You can find more information about performing address translation within the VPN in Chapter 10.

Static routing was used to point traffic from the shared `trust-vr` into the `cust1-vr` in the VSYS. Policies were required between the shared `Untrust` zone and the `vpn` zone within the VSYS to permit the bidirectional IKE and Encapsulating Security Protocol (ESP) traffic.

The policies shown in this example are for simplicity. Real-world policies would be much stricter between the shared `Untrust` zone and VSYS zones.

Tunnel configuration

A simple route-based VPN tunnel using a preshared key was then configured for IPSec main mode. Tunnel interfaces were created on each security device and bound to the custom VPN zone. The VPN monitor and the `rekey` option were enabled, and the VPN was bound to the tunnel interface. Static routes to the trust subnets were configured to use the VPN tunnel interface as the next hop.

Lastly, bidirectional policies were created to allow traffic between the `Trust` and `vpn` zones on both security devices.

Here is a look at the VPN configuration on the `cust1` VSYS. Specifically, here is the IKE gateway (Phase-1) configuration:

```
root(cust1)-> get ike gateway gt-1
 Id  Name     Gateway Address Gateway ID  Mode Proposals
---- -------- --------------- ----------- ---- ---------
   0 gt-1     10.0.0.81                   Main pre-g2-3des-sha,
pre-g2-aes128-sha
Preshared Key: <***>
use count<1>, status Enabled
user id<-1>, dial up id<-1>
Flags 0x00000000
IP version 4
slot number<0>.
outgoing interface:
interface name = loopback8, ip = 10.54.81.1, vsys = cust1.
local-id empty.
peer-id empty.
peer-container-id empty.
IPsec NAT-Traversal: disabled.
  local ike udp port 500.
  peer ike udp port 500.
vpn list: gt-1
peer identity list:
```

```
  0: NOT IAS
IAS ID 3789d124
(0f) group <-1> user <-1>        10.0.0.81
    Phase 1 SA:
      10.0.0.81->10.54.81.1  cond 0x0
    Phase 2 SA: 30001(active)
session timeout: 0
Preferred Local Cert
--------------------
local cert not configured.
Preferred Peer Cert
-------------------
peer ca cert not configured.
Peer Cert Type
--------------
Preferred cert type: X509-SIG
Heartbeat Hello: 0(sec), Threshold: 5(times), Reconnect: 0(sec)
----------- XAUTH Config ------------
XAUTH disabled.
```

And the VPN (Phase-2) configuration:

```
root(cust1)-> get vpn gt-1
Name  Gateway  Mode RPlay 1st Proposal     Monitor Use Cnt Interface
----- -------- ---- ----- ---------------- ------- ------- ---------
gt-1  gt-1     tunl No    g2-esp-3des-sha  on        0     loopback.8
all proposals: g2-esp-3des-sha g2-esp-aes128-sha
peer gateway = 10.0.0.81
outgoing interface <loopback.8>
IPv4 address 10.54.81.1.
vpn monitor src I/F <default>, dst-IP <default>, optimized NO, rekey ON
l2tp over ipsec use count <0>
idle timeout value <0>
vpnflag <04010022>
df-bit <clear>
sa_list <00030001>
Bound tunnel interface: tunnel.81
  Next-Hop Tunnel Binding table
  Flag Status Next-Hop(IP)    tunnel-id  VPN
        U    10.0.0.81 0x00030001 gt-1
```

You can check to see that the VPN tunnel is up and active with the following command:

```
root(cust1)-> get sa
HEX ID     Gateway  Port Algorithm     SPI      Life:sec kb St PID vsys
00030001< 10.0.0.81 500 esp:3des/sha1 eeb323ed 1413 unlim A/U -1 3
00030001> 10.0.0.81 500 esp:3des/sha1 d23c79c7 1413 unlim A/U -1 3
```

You can also verify that the VPN monitor is successful from the root system by performing a debug on the sa-mon context:

```
root-> debug sa-mon all
root-> get db str
sa index(0) send count = 268, avail = 268, tunnel_info = 40030001
```

```
vpn monitor pkt is received: cookie = 0, result = 1
Found valid sa(0), missed slots = 1
```

View the event log for details about the tunnel establishment:

```
root(cust1)-> get event type 536
Date       Time     Module Level  Type Description
2007-06-02 18:05:15 system info 00536 IKE<10.0.0.81> Phase 2 msg
                                  ID <7ec233f7>: Completed
                                  Negotiation with SPI
                                  <eeb323ef>, tunnel ID
                                      <196609>, and lifetime
                                  <3600> s<0> KB.
2007-06-02 18:05:15 system info 00536 IKE<10.0.0.81>: Received a
                                      notification message for DOI
                                  <1 <40001>
                                  NOTIFY_NS_NHTB_INFORM>
2007-06-02 18:05:15 system info 00536 IKE<10.0.0.81> Phase 2 msg
                                  ID <7ec233f7>: Responded to
                                  the peers first message.
2007-06-02 17:05:25 system info 00536 IKE<10.0.0.81> Phase 2 msg
                                  ID <0c691a40>: Completed
                                  Negotiation with SPI
                                  <eeb323ee>, tunnel ID
                                     <196609>, and lifetime <3600>
                                  s<0> KB.
2007-06-02 17:05:24 system info 00536 IKE<10.0.0.81>: Received a
                                      notification message for DOI 1 <40001>
                                  NOTIFY_NS_NHTB_INFORM>
2007-06-02 17:05:24 system info 00536 IKE<10.0.0.81> Phase 2 msg
                                  ID <0c691a40>: Responded to
                                  the peers first message.
2007-06-02 16:05:28 system info 00536 IKE<10.0.0.81> Phase 2 msg
                                  ID <e8175022>: Completed
                                  Negotiation with SPI
                                  <eeb323ed>, tunnel ID
                                  <196609>, and lifetime <3600>
                                  s<0> KB.
2007-06-02 16:05:28 system info 00536 IKE<10.0.0.81>: Received a
                                      notification message for DOI
                                  <1 <40001>
                                  <NOTIFY_NS_NHTB_INFORM>
2007-06-02 16:05:28 system info 00536 IKE<10.0.0.81> Phase 2 msg
                                  ID <e8175022>: Responded to
                                  the peers first message.
2007-06-02 16:05:28 system info 00536 IKE<10.0.0.81> Phase 1:
                                  Completed main mode
                                  negotiations with a
                                      <28800>-second lifetime.
2007-06-02 16:05:28 system info 00536 IKE<10.0.0.81> Phase 1:
                                  Responder starts MAIN mode
                                  negotiations.
```

For more information on configuring VPNs, please see Chapter 10.

21.6 Configure VSYS Profiles

Problem

You want to enforce system resource limits on the individual VSYS.

Solution

Use the set vsys profile context to set limits and reservations, and then apply the profile to the VSYS. Reserve the CPU and sessions for the root system:

```
root-> set vsys-profile RootProfile sessions reserve 300000 alarm 30
root-> set vsys-profile RootProfile cpu-weight 70
root-> set vsys-profile RootProfile policies reserve 10000
root-> set vsys-profile RootProfile user-zones reserve 25
root-> set vsys-profile RootProfile user-servs reserve 250
root-> set vsys-profile RootProfile user-serv-grps reserve 50
```

First, create the profile:

```
root-> set vsys-profile name alphagroup cpu-weight 30
root-> set vsys-profile alphagroup dips max 30 reserve 10
root-> set vsys-profile alphagroup mips max 30
root-> set vsys-profile alphagroup mpolicies max 4
root-> set vsys-profile alphagroup policies max 100
root-> set vsys-profile alphagroup sessions max 10000 reserve 7000
    alarm 90
root-> set vsys-profile alphagroup user-serv-grps max 50 reserve 30
root-> set vsys-profile alphagroup user-servs max 100 reserve 50
root-> set vsys-profile alphagroup user-zones max 2
root-> set vsys-profile alphagroup zone-addr-grps max 50 reserve 25
root-> set vsys-profile alphagroup zone-addrs max 100
root-> save
```

Assign the profile to a VSYS:

```
root->set vsys sales profile alphagroup
root(sales)-> save
root(sales)-> exit
exit vsys sales
```

Enable fair mode operation:

```
root-> set cpu-limit
root-> set cpu-limit enable
root-> save
```

Discussion

Root-level administrators of the security device can enforce session and resource limits on an individual VSYS basis. Profiles defining a variety of limits and guaranteed reservations are created and then applied to the VSYS. When these limits are reached within the VSYS, new requests for that resource are denied. Packets dropped due to resource limits are tracked and logged within the VSYS.

Profiles

You can create up to 18 VSYS profiles in addition to the 2 default profiles shown here:

```
root-> get vsys-profile
Total number of vsys-profiles: 5
* indicates default vsys profile.
 vsys-profile-name ref-cnt vsys-limit    maximum   reserved peak-use
-------------------------------------------------------------------
*VsysDefaultProfile  0 dips                 1022       0      0
                       mips                 2000       0      0
                       mpolicies             500       0      0
                       policies            20480       0      0
                       sessions          1000000       0      0
                       user-serv-grps        256       0      0
                       user-servs           1024       0      0
                       user-zones           1024       0      0
                       zone-addr-grps       5120       0      0
                       zone-addrs          40000       4      0
                       cpu-weight = 50
                       session alarm level = 100%
-------------------------------------------------------------------
RootProfile         1 dips                 1022       0      0
                      mips                20000       0      0
                      mpolicies             500       0      0
                      policies            40000   10000      3(Root)
                      sessions          1000000  300000      1(Root)
                      user-serv-grps        256      50      0
                      user-servs           2048     250      0
                      user-zones           1024      25      5(Root)
                      zone-addr-grps       5120       0      0
                      zone-addrs          40000       0  16(Root/tra~)
                      cpu-weight = 70
                      session alarm level = 30%
--------------------------------------------------------------------
```

The VsysDefaultProfile is assigned to a VSYS when initially created and contains the global maximums, but does not guarantee any resources. You cannot edit this profile.

The RootProfile also defines the global maximums, but you can edit this profile and use it to guarantee resources for the root system.

Here, a custom profile named alphagroup was created and set with some limits on CPU, policies, objects, and sessions. Also set was the CPU weight, which was configured with guaranteed resources for the root VSYS by editing the RootProfile.

Limits

The following output shows the per-VSYS resources for which you can configure a maximum and a reserve limit:

```
root-> set vsys-profile alphagroup ?
<return>
```

```
cpu-weight              CPU weight per vsys
dips                    limit of DIPs per vsys
mips                    limit of MIPs per vsys
mpolicies               limit of multicast group policies per vsys
policies                limit of policies per vsys
sessions                limit of sessions per vsys
user-serv-grps          limit of user-defined service groups per vsys
user-servs              limit of user-defined services per vsys
user-zones              limit of user-defined security zones per vsys
zone-addr-grps          limit of address groups per zone per vsys
zone-addrs              limit of addresses per zone per vsys
```

Resource utilization for shared zones is charged against the root system. In addition, you cannot reserve addresses or address groups in shared zones.

For any particular VSYS, no maximum limit can be configured higher than the global maximums, nor can any maximum limit be set lower than the actual usage, with the exception of sessions. Usage values are calculated based on the reserve value or the actual use value, whichever is higher.

The following output shows these values for the specific system:

```
root-> get vsys-profile global

global usage summary:   global-limit     maximum   allocated  actual
                                                         use      use
-------------------------------------------------------------------
                        dips               32767        20        0
                        mips               20000         0        0
                        mpolicies            500         0        0
                        policies           40000     10013       16
                        sessions         1000000    320500        1
                        user-serv-grps     16384       110        0
                        user-servs         32768       350        0
                        user-zones          1024        31       11
                        zone-addr-grps      5120       175        0
                        zone-addrs         40000       166      134
                        total cpu-weight = 250
root->
```

You can set the maximum number of sessions lower than the actual use value. In this case, no existing sessions will be dropped, but no new sessions can be created until the session count falls below the max value. In this case, the output of `get vsys session-limit` will show a negative number.

Example profile

The following output shows the configuration of our `alphagroup` profile. Here, you can see the specific limits and reserve values configured for the profile. An alarm threshold equal to our guaranteed session limit was created by setting the threshold to 70 percent of the max value—this will generate an alarm log when the session count reaches or exceeds 7,000 sessions.

```
root-> get vsys-profile alphagroup
 vsys-profile-name ref-cnt vsys-limit     maximum reserved  peak-use
-------------------------------------------------------------------
 alphagroup              2 dips                30     10      0
                           mips                30      0      0
                           mpolicies            4      0      0
                           policies           100      0      5(corp)
                           sessions         10000   7000      0
                           user-serv-grps      50     30      0
                           user-servs         100     50      0
                           user-zones           2      0      2(corp)
                           zone-addr-grps      50     25      0
                           zone-addrs         100      4    4(corp/sal~)
                           cpu-weight = 50
                           session alarm level = 70%
--------------------------------------------------------------------
root->
```

Here's a useful command for showing all VSYS session limits:

```
root-> get vsys session-limit
Vsys Name    Current  Maximum  Reserved    Avail  Alarm Level    Alarm
Root               1  1000000    300000   979499 300000( 30%)      off
sales              0    10000      7000    10000   7000( 70%)      off
corp               0    10000      7000    10000   7000( 70%)      off
cust1              0     5000      2500     5000   2500( 50%)      off
example            0     5000      2500     5000   2500( 50%)      off
mike               0     4000*     1500     4000   2000( 50%)      off
root->
```

CPU limiting

VSYS within ScreenOS share the same CPU resources. Therefore, a DoS attack against one VSYS that consumes 100 percent of the CPU resources is, in effect, a DoS for all VSYS. The CPU limiting feature is intended to protect against this scenario.

The CPU overutilization protection feature allows you to configure the system for fair use (fair mode) or shared use (shared mode). The default mode is shared mode. In shared mode, all VSYS are equal and have an equal opportunity at CPU time. In fair mode, individual VSYSes are assigned a CPU weight that is used to calculate the CPU time quota for the VSYS over one-second intervals. In addition to limiting the CPU utilization for a particular VSYS, you can use this feature to guarantee CPU time for the root system.

The following output shows the percentage of CPU configured for each VSYS based on the CPU weight value in the profile:

```
root-> get vsys cpu-limit
Vsys Name     Wgt  Cfg %
```

```
Root          70   28.0
sales         50   20.0
corp          50   20.0
cust1         30   12.0
example       30   12.0
mike          20    8.0
root->
```

The CPU percentage calculations are not static. ScreenOS will recalculate when a VSYS is deleted.

Remember that the default mode of operation is shared mode. To use fair mode, you need to assign a CPU weight to each VSYS via a profile, and you must enable the CPU limit feature. An example of setting the CPU weight for a profile is as follows: `set vsys-profile platinum cpu-weight 30`.

The command `set cpu-limit` initializes the CPU limiting feature and calculates the time quota for each VSYS; the `set cpu-limit enable` command enables shared-to-fair mode transition based on the configured threshold. Here are the default thresholds for transitioning between shared and fair modes:

```
root-> get cpu-limit
Current mode: shared
Shared->fair: threshold 80%, hold down time 5
Fair->shared: automatic, threshold 80%, hold down time 20
CPU limit: enabled
root->
```

You can set the threshold and hold-down times for each with the following commands:

```
root-> set cpu-limit shared-to-fair threshold ?
<number>            flow cpu utilization (range: 0 - 100)

root-> set cpu-limit fair-to-shared ?
automatic         automatically transition back to shared mode
fair-time         remain in fair mode for specified time
never             never transition back from fair mode to shared mode

root-> set cpu-limit fair-to-shared automatic threshold ?
<number>            projected flow cpu utilization (range: 0 - 100)
```

Packet flow while in fair mode operates in the following manner:

1. ScreenOS allocates resources for the packet and timestamps it.
2. The flow CPU processes the packet.
3. ScreenOS determines which VSYS to be charged with the resource utilization and the CPU time quota balance for the chosen VSYS. If the VSYS is over the time quota, ScreenOS drops the packet.

4. After the system processes the packet, the system computes the CPU processing time for the packet from the current time and timestamp from step 1. The system then charges the amount against the remaining time quota for the VSYS.

Table 21-1 shows an example of how ScreenOS charges time against a VSYS.

Table 21-1. Example resource charges

Src VSYS	Dst VSYS	Charged VSYS
Root	Root	Root
Root	Dst VSYS	Dst VSYS
Src VSYS	Root	Src VSYS
Src VSYS	Dst VSYS	Src VSYS

Command overrides

There are two methods for enforcing resource limits: VSYS profiles and command overrides. As mentioned, there is a limit of 18 user-defined profiles. However, you can edit limits directly within the VSYS, which can override global profile limits in, for instance, the `alphagroup` profile assigned to both the `corp` and the `sales` VSYS. Logs are being received that session alarm thresholds have been reached in the `corp` VSYS. Looking at the earlier output for the `alphagroup` profile configuration, you can see that the session max is set to 10,000 sessions. Not wanting to change anything on the `sales` VSYS limits, you can enter the `corp` VSYS and override the profile settings by increasing the session limits as follows:

```
root-> enter vsys corp
root(corp)-> set override session-limit max 12500
root(corp)-> exit
Configuration modified, save? [y]/n y
exit vsys corp
root->
```

VSYS administrators do not have access to the `override` command.

In the preceding configuration, in the `corp` VSYS, the session limits maximum was increased from 10,000 to 12,500 sessions. You can see this override reflected in the following output at the root system level:

```
root-> get vsys session-limit
Vsys Name  Current  Maximum   Reserved   Avail   Alarm Level  Alarm
Root             1  1000000     300000  979499  300000( 30%)    off
sales            0    10000       7000   10000    7000( 70%)    off
corp             0    12500*      7000   12500    8750( 70%)    off
cust1            0     5000       2500    5000    2500( 50%)    off
example          0     5000       2500    5000    2500( 50%)    off
```

```
mike                0      4000*        1500     4000     2000( 50%)     off
(* - The marked setting has been overridden.)
root->
```

You also can see it at the VSYS level:

```
root(corp)-> get vsys-profile
Profile of current vsys: "alphagroup"
Vsys-limit         Maximum   Reserved   Actual-use
----------------------------------------------------
dips                    30         10            0
mips                    30          0            0
mpolicies                4          0            0
policies               100          0            5
sessions             12500*      7000            0
user-serv-grps          50         30            0
user-servs             100         50            0
user-zones               2          0            2
zone-addr-grps          50         25            0
zone-addrs             100          4            4(hr)
cpu-weight              50          -            0
(* - The marked setting has been overridden.)
root(corp)->
root(corp)-> get session-limit
Vsys Name    Current  Maximum    Reserved    Avail  Alarm Level  Alarm
corp               0    12500*       7000    12500   8750( 70%)    off
(* - The marked setting has been overridden.)
root(corp)->
```

You can use command overrides for both session limits and CPU weight. In addition to increasing the session maximum on the `corp` VSYS, you may want to cut down on the pesky log messages generated due to the profile setting. You can do this in the same manner as the session limit. Enter the VSYS and change the alarm threshold: `set override session-limit alarm 90`.

Glossary

802.11a
: Wireless local area network (WLAN) standard that provides up to 54 Mbps in the 5 GHz radio band.

802.11b
: Wireless local area network (WLAN) standard that provides up to 11 Mbps in the 2.4 GHz radio band.

802.11g
: Wireless local area network (WLAN) standard that provides 20+ Mbps in the 2.4 GHz radio band.

802.11SuperG
: Wireless local area network (WLAN) standard that provides up to 108 Mbps in the 2.4 GHz radio band.

ABR
: *See* Area Border Router (ABR).

Access-Challenge
: Additional condition required for a successful Telnet login by an authentication user via a Remote Access Dial-In User Service (RADIUS) server.

Access Control List (ACL)
: Identifies clients by their Media Access Control (MAC) addresses, and specifies whether the wireless device allows or denies access for each address.

Access List
: A list of network prefixes that are compared to a given route. If the route matches a network prefix defined in the access list, the route is either permitted or denied.

Access Point (AP)
: *See* Wireless Access Point (AP).

Access Point Name (APN)
: Information element (IE) included in the header of a GTP packet that provides information regarding how to reach a network. It is composed of a network ID and an operator ID.

ACL
: *See* Access Control List (ACL).

Address Shifting
: Mechanism for creating a one-to-one mapping between any original address in one range of addresses and a specific translated address in another range.

Adjacencies
: When two routers can exchange routing information, they are considered to have constructed an adjacency. Point-to-point networks, which have only two routers, automatically form an adjacency. Point-to-multipoint networks are a series of several point-to-point networks. When routers pair in this more complex networking scheme, they are considered to be adjacent to one another.

ADSL
: *See* Asymmetric Digital Subscriber Line (ADSL).

Aggregate State
A router is in an aggregate state when it is one of multiple virtual Border Gateway Protocol (BGP) routing instances bundled into one address. *See also* Border Gateway Protocol (BGP).

Aggregation
Process of combining several routes in such a way that only a single route advertises itself. This technique minimizes the size of the routing table for the router.

Aggregator
Object used to bundle multiple routes under one common route, generalized according to the value of the network mask.

Aggressive Aging
Mechanism for accelerating the timeout process when the number of sessions in the session table surpasses a specified high-watermark threshold. When the number of sessions in the table dips below a specified low-watermark threshold, the timeout process returns to normal.

AH
See Encapsulating Security Protocol/Authentication Header (ESP/AH).

ALG
See Application Layer Gateway (ALG).

Antivirus Scanning
Mechanism for detecting and blocking viruses in File Transfer Protocol (FTP), Internet Message Access Protocol (IMAP), Simple Mail Transfer Protocol (SMTP), HyperText Transfer Protocol (HTTP)—including HTTP web mail—and Post Office Protocol version 3 (POP-3) traffic. ScreenOS offers an internal and an external antivirus scanning solution.

Application Layer Gateway (ALG)
On a security device, a software component that is designed to manage specific protocols such as the Session Initiation Protocol (SIP) or File Transfer Protocol (FTP). The ALG intercepts and analyzes the specified traffic, allocates resources, and defines dynamic policies to permit the traffic to pass securely through the security device.

Area Border Router (ABR)
A router with at least one interface in area 0 and at least one interface in another area.

AS (AS)
See Autonomous System (AS).

AS Boundary Router
A router that connects an Autonomous System (AS) running one routing protocol to another AS running a different protocol. *See also* Autonomous System (AS).

AS Number
Identification number of the local Autonomous System (AS) mapped to a Border Gateway Protocol (BGP) routing instance. The ID number can be any valid integer. *See also* Border Gateway Protocol (BGP).

AS Path
List of all the Autonomous Systems (ASs) that a router update has traveled through in the current transmission.

AS Path Access List
Access list used by a Border Gateway Protocol (BGP) routing instance to permit or deny packets sent by neighbor routing instances to the current virtual routing instance. *See also* Border Gateway Protocol (BGP).

AS Path Attribute Class
The Border Gateway Protocol (BGP) provides four classes of path attributes: well-known mandatory, well-known discretionary, optional transitive, and optional nontransitive. *See also* Border Gateway Protocol (BGP).

AS Path String
String that acts as an identifier for an Autonomous System (AS) path. It is configured alongside an AS Path access list ID.

Asymmetric Digital Subscriber Line (ADSL)
Digital Subscriber Line (DSL) technology that allows existing telephone lines to carry both voice telephone service and high-speed digital transmission. A growing number of service providers offer ADSL service to home and business customers.

Atomic Aggregate
Object used by a Border Gateway Protocol (BGP) router to inform other BGP routers that the local system has selected a generalized route.

Attack Objects
Stateful signatures and protocol anomalies that a security device with deep inspection (DI) functionality uses to detect attacks aimed at compromising one or more hosts on a network.

Authentication
Ensures that digital data transmissions are delivered to the intended recipient. Authentication also validates the integrity of the message for the receiver, including its source (where or whom it came from). The simplest form of authentication requires a username and password for access to a particular account. Authentication protocols can also be based on secret-key encryption, such as the Data Encryption Standard (DES) or Triple DES (3DES), or on public-key systems that use digital signatures.

Authentication Header (AH)
See Encapsulating Security Protocol/Authentication Header (ESP/AH).

Autonomous System (AS)
Set of routers set off from the rest of the network and governed by a single technical administration. This router group uses an Interior Gateway Protocol (IGP) or several IGPs and common metrics to route packets within the group. The group also uses an Exterior Gateway Protocol (EGP) to route packets to other ASs. Each AS has a routing plan that indicates which destinations are reachable through it. This plan is called the Network Layer Reachability Information (NLRI) object. Border Gateway Protocol (BGP) routers periodically generate and receive NLRI updates.

Auxiliary (AUX) Port
This port is usually the same as COM 1, and is used to access external networks.

B8ZS
8 bits zero suppression.

Backward Explicit Congestion Notification (BECN)
In a Frame Relay network, Forward Explicit Congestion Notification (FECN) is a header bit transmitted by the source (sending) terminal requesting that the destination (receiving) terminal slow down its requests for data. BECN is a header bit transmitted by the destination terminal requesting that the source terminal send data more slowly. BECN and FECN are intended to minimize the possibility that packets will be discarded (and thus have to be resent) when more packets arrive than can be handled. *See also* Forward Explicit Congestion Notification (FECN).

Basic Rate Interface (BRI)
Integrated Services Digital Network (ISDN) service also called 2B+D, because it consists of two 64 Kbps B-channels and one 16 Kbps D-channel.

B-Channel
Integrated Services Digital Network (ISDN) Basic Rate Interface (BRI) service provided by telephone service providers: two bearer channels (B-channels) and one data channel (D-channel). The B-channel operates at 64 Kbps and carries user data.

Bgroup
See Bridge Group Interface.

Bit Error Rate (BER)
Ratio of error bits to the total number of bits received in a transmission, usually expressed as 10 to a negative power.

Border Gateway Protocol (BGP)
Inter-Autonomous System (AS) routing protocol. BGP routers and ASs exchange routing information for the Internet.

Bridge Group Interface
Also known as the *bgroup interface*. These interfaces allow several physical ports to be grouped together to act like a pseudoswitch. You can group multiple wired interfaces or wireless and wired interfaces so that they are located in the same subnet.

Broadcast Network
A network that supports many routers with the capability of communicating

directly with one another. Ethernet is an example of a broadcast network.

Bundle
An aggregation of multiple physical links.

Certificate Revocation List (CRL)
A list of invalid certificates.

Circuit-Level Proxy
Proxy servers are available for common Internet services; for example, a Hyper-Text Transfer Protocol (HTTP) proxy is used for web access; a File Transfer Protocol (FTP) proxy is used for file transfers. Such proxies are called *application-level proxies* or *application-level gateways* because they are dedicated to a particular application and protocol, and are aware of the content of the packets being sent. A generic proxy, called a *circuit-level proxy*, supports multiple applications. For example, SOCKS is a generic User Datagram Protocol (UDP) application. *See also* Proxy Server.

Cisco High-Level Data Link Control (Cisco-HDLC)
Proprietary Cisco encapsulation for transmitting LAN protocols over a wide area network (WAN). HDLC specifies a data encapsulation method on synchronous serial links by means of frame characters and checksums. Cisco HDLC enables the transmission of multiple protocols.

Classless Routing
Support for interdomain routing, regardless of the size or class of the network. Network addresses are divided into three classes, but these are transparent in the Border Gateway Protocol (BGP), giving the network greater flexibility. *See also* Border Gateway Protocol (BGP).

Community
Grouping of Border Gateway Protocol (BGP) destinations. By updating the community, you automatically update its member destinations with new attributes.

Confederation
Object inside a Border Gateway Protocol Autonomous System (BGP AS) that is a subset of routing instances in the Authentication Server. By grouping devices into confederations inside a BGP AS, you reduce the complexity associated with the matrix of routing connections, known as a *mesh*, within the AS.

Connection States
When a packet sent from one router arrives at another router, a negotiation occurs between the source and destination routers. The negotiation goes through six states: Idle, Connect, Active, OpenSent, OpenConnect, and Establish.

CRL
See Certificate Revocation List (CRL).

Data Encryption Standard (DES)
40-bit and 56-bit encryption algorithm that was developed by the National Institute of Standards and Technology (NIST). DES is a block-encryption method originally developed by IBM. It has since been certified by the U.S. government for transmission of any data that is not classified as top secret. DES uses an algorithm for private-key encryption. The key consists of 64 bits of data, which are transformed and combined with the first 64 bits of the message to be sent. To apply the encryption, the message is broken up into 64-bit blocks so that each can be combined with the key using a complex 16-step process. Although DES is fairly weak, with only one iteration, repeating it using slightly different keys can provide excellent security.

Data Encryption Standard–Cipher Block Chaining (DES–CBC)
Message text and, if required, message signatures can be encrypted using the Data Encryption Standard (DES) algorithm in the Cipher Block Chaining (CBC) mode of operation. The character string "DES-CBC" within an encapsulated Privacy Enhanced Mail (PEM) header field indicates the use of DES–CBC.

Data-Link Connection Identifier (DLCI)
Separates customer traffic in Frame Relay configurations.

Dead Interval
Period that elapses before a routing instance determines that another routing instance is not running.

Dead Peer Detection (DPD)
Allows an IP Security (IPSec) device to verify the current existence and availability of other IPSec peer devices. The device performs this verification by sending encrypted Internet Key Exchange (IKE) Phase 1 notification payloads (`R-U-THERE`) to the peers and waiting for DPD acknowledgments (`R-U-THERE-ACK`).

Deep Inspection (DI)
Mechanism for filtering the traffic permitted by the firewall. DI examines Layer 3 and Layer 4 packet headers, and Layer 7 application content and protocol characteristics in an effort to detect and prevent any attacks or anomalous behavior that might be present.

Default Route
Catchall routing table entry that defines the forwarding of traffic for destination networks that are not explicitly defined in the routing table. The destination network for the default route is represented by the network address `0.0.0.0/0`.

Demilitarized Zone (DMZ)
From the military term for an area between two opponents where fighting is prevented. DMZ Ethernets connect networks and computers controlled by different bodies. They may be external or internal. External DMZ Ethernets link regional networks with routers.

DES
See Data Encryption Standard (DES).

DES–CBC
See Data Encryption Standard–Cipher Block Chaining (DES–CBC).

Destination Network Address Translation (NAT-dst)
Translation of the original destination IP address in a packet header to a different destination address. ScreenOS supports the translation of one or several original destination IP addresses to a single IP address (one-to-one or many-to-one relationships). The security device also supports the translation of one range of IP addresses to another range (a many-to-many relationship) using address shifting. When the security device performs NAT-dst without address shifting, it can also map the destination port number to a different predetermined port number. When the security device performs NAT-dst with address shifting, it cannot also perform port mapping.

DI
See Deep Inspection (DI).

Digital Signal 0 (DS0)
Base for the Digital Signal X series. Provides a transmission rate of 64 Kbps.

Distance Vector
Routing strategy that relies on an algorithm that works by having routers sporadically broadcast entire copies of their own routing table to all directly connected neighbors. This update identifies the networks each router knows about, and the distance between each of those networks. The distance is measured in hop counts or the number of routing domains that a packet must traverse between its source device and the device it attempts to reach.

DMZ
See Demilitarized Zone (DMZ).

Domain Name System (DNS)
Stores information about hostnames and domain names in a type of distributed database on networks such as the Internet. Of the many types of information that can be stored, DNS most importantly provides and network hardware work with IP addresses (such as `207.17.137.68`) to perform tasks such as addressing and routing, humans generally find it easier to work with hostnames and domain names (such as *www.juniper.com*) in URLs and email addresses. DNS therefore mediates between the needs and preferences of humans and software by translating domain names to IP addresses, such as *www.juniper.net* = `207.17.137.68`.

DPD
See Dead Peer Detection (DPD).

DS1
Digital Signal 1, also known as a T1 interface. *See also* Digital Signal 0 (DS0).

DS3
Digital Signal 3, also known as a T3 interface. *See also* Digital Signal 0 (DS0); T3 Interface.

Dynamic Filtering
IP service that can be used within virtual private network (VPN) tunnels. Filters are one method some security devices use to control traffic from one network to another. When the Transmission Control Protocol/Internet Protocol (TCP/IP) sends data packets to the firewall, the filtering function in the firewall looks at the header information in the packets and directs them accordingly. The filters operate on criteria such as IP source or destination address range, TCP ports, User Datagram Protocol (UDP), Internet Control Message Protocol (ICMP), or TCP responses. *See also* Tunneling; Virtual Private Network (VPN).

Dynamic Host Configuration Protocol (DHCP)
Method for automatically assigning IP addresses to hosts on a network. Depending on the specific device model, security devices can allocate dynamic IP addresses to hosts, receive dynamically assigned IP addresses, or receive DHCP information from a DHCP server and relay the information to hosts.

Dynamic Routing
Routing method that adjusts to changing network circumstances by analyzing incoming routing update messages. If the message indicates that a network change has occurred, the routing software recalculates routes and sends out new routing update messages. These messages populate the network, directing routers to rerun their algorithms and change their routing tables accordingly. There are two common forms of dynamic routing: distance vector routing and link state routing.

E1 Interface
European format for digital transmission. This format carries signals at 2 Mbps (32 channels at 64 Kbps, with two channels reserved for signaling and controlling).

Encapsulating Security Protocol (ESP)
See Encapsulating Security Protocol/Authentication Header (ESP/AH).

Encapsulating Security Protocol/Authentication Header (ESP/AH)
IP-level security protocols, AH and ESP, were originally proposed by the Network Working Group focused on IP security mechanisms, IP Security (IPSec). The term *IPSec* is used loosely here to refer to packets, keys, and routes that are associated with these protocols. The IP AH protocol provides authentication. ESP provides both authentication and encryption.

Encryption
Process of changing data into a form that only the intended receiver can read. To decipher the message, the receiver of the encrypted data must have the proper decryption key. In traditional encryption schemes, the sender and the receiver use the same key to encrypt and decrypt data. Public-key encryption schemes use two keys: a public key, which anyone may use, and a corresponding private key, which is possessed only by the person who created it. With this method, anyone may send a message encrypted with the owner's public key, but only the owner has the private key necessary to decrypt it. Data Encryption Standard (DES) and Triple DES (3DES) are two of the most popular public-key encryption schemes.

Equal Cost Multipath (ECMP)
Assists with load balancing among two to four routes to the same destination, or increases the effective bandwidth usage among two or more destinations. When enabled, security devices use the statically defined routes or dynamically learn multiple routes to the same destination through a routing protocol. The security device assigns routes of equal cost in round-robin fashion.

Export Rules
When you have two or more virtual routers (VRs) on a security device, you can configure export rules that define which routes on one VR are allowed to be learned by another VR. *See also* Import Rules.

External Neighbors
Two peer Border Gateway Protocol (BGP) routers residing in two different Autonomous Systems (ASs). See Border Gateway Protocol (BGP).

Filter List
List of IP addresses permitted to send packets to the current routing domain.

Firewall
Device that protects and controls the connection of one network to another, for traffic entering and leaving. Firewalls are used by companies that want to protect any network-connected server from damage (intentional or otherwise) by those who log in to it. This could be a dedicated computer equipped with security measures, or it could be a software-based protection.

Forward Explicit Congestion Notification (FECN)
In a Frame Relay network, FECN is a header bit transmitted by the source (sending) terminal requesting that the destination (receiving) terminal slow down its requests for data. Backward Explicit Congestion Notification (BECN) is a header bit transmitted by the destination terminal requesting that the source terminal send data more slowly. FECN and BECN are intended to minimize the possibility that packets will be discarded (and thus have to be resent) when more packets arrive than can be handled. *See also* Backward Explicit Congestion Notification (BECN).

Frame Relay
Wide area network (WAN) protocol that operates over a variety of network interfaces, including serial, T1/E1, and T3/E3. Frame Relay allows private networks to reduce costs by sharing facilities between the endpoint switches of a network managed by a Frame Relay service provider.

Gateway
Also called a *router*, a gateway is a program or a special-purpose device that transfers IP datagrams from one network to another until the final destination is reached.

Gateway GPRS Support Node (GGSN)
Device that acts as an interface between the General Packet Radio Service (GPRS) backbone network and the external packet data networks (radio and IP). Among other things, a GGSN converts GPRS packets coming from a Serving GPRS Support Node (SGSN) into the appropriate Packet Data Protocol (PDP) format and sends them out on the corresponding public data network (PDN). A GGSN also performs authentication and charging functions. *See also* General Packet Radio Service (GPRS).

GBI
See Gigabit Interface Connector (GBIC).

General Packet Radio Service (GPRS)
Packet-based technology that enables high-speed wireless Internet and other data communications. GPRS provides more than three to four times greater speed than conventional Global System for Mobile Communications (GSM) systems. Often referred to as the 2.5G mobile telecommunications system.

Generic Routing Encapsulation (GRE)
Protocol that encapsulates any type of packet within IPv4 unicast packets. For additional information on GRE, refer to RFC 1701, Generic Routing Encapsulation (GRE).

GGSN
See Gateway GPRS Support Node (GGSN).

Gigabit Interface Connector (GBIC)
Type of interface module card used on some security devices for connecting to a fiber optic network.

Gi Interface
Interface between a GPRS Support Node (GSN) and an external network or the Internet. *See* GPRS Support Node (GSN).

Global System for Mobile Communication (GSM)
Globally accepted standard for digital cellular communication. GSM is the name of a standardization group established in 1982 to create a common European mobile telephone standard that formulates

specifications for a pan-European mobile cellular radio system operating at 900 MHz.

Gn Interface
Interface between two GPRS Support Nodes (GSNs) within the same Public Land Mobile Network (PLMN).

Gp Interface
Interface between two GPRS Support Nodes (GSNs) located in different Public Land Mobile Network (PLMNs).

G-PDU
User data message consisting of a T-PDU plus a GPRS Tunneling Protocol (GTP) header. *See also* T-PDU.

GPRS
See General Packet Radio Service (GPRS).

GPRS Roaming Exchange (GRX)
Because the Gp interface is IP-based, it must support appropriate routing and security protocols to enable a subscriber to access its home services from any of its home Public Land Mobile Network's (PLMN's) roaming partners. Many General Packet Radio Service (GPRS) operators/carriers have abstracted these functions through the GPRS Roaming Exchange (GRX). This function is typically provided by a third-party IP network that offers virtual private network (VPN) services to connect the roaming partners. The GRX service provider ensures that all aspects of routing and security between the networks are optimized for efficient operation. *See also* General Packet Radio Service (GPRS).

GPRS Support Node (GSN)
Term used to include both Gateway GPRS Support Node (GGSN) and Serving GPRS Support Node (SGSN). *See also* General Packet Radio Service (GPRS).

GPRS Tunneling Protocol (GTP)
IP-based protocol used within Global System for Mobile Communications (GSM) and Universal Mobile Telecommunications System (UMTS) networks. GTP is layered on top of User Datagram Protocol (UDP). There are actually three separate protocols: GTP, GTP-Control (GTP-C), and GTP User (GTP-U). *See also* General Packet Radio Service (GPRS); GTP-Control (GTP-C) Message; GTP-User (GTP-U) Message.

GRX
See GPRS Roaming Exchange (GRX).

GSM
See Global System for Mobile Communication (GSM).

GSN
See GPRS Support Node (GSN).

GTP
See GPRS Tunneling Protocol (GTP).

GTP-Control (GTP-C) Messages
Exchanged between GPRS Support Node (GSN) pairs in a path. The messages are used to transfer GSN capability information between GSN pairs; to create, update and delete GPRS Tunneling Protocol (GTP) tunnels; and for path management. *See also* GPRS Tunneling Protocol (GTP); GTP Tunnel.

GTP-Protocol Data Unit (GTP-PDU)
Either a GTP-C or a GTP-U message. *See also* GPRS Tunneling Protocol (GTP).

GTP Signaling Messages
Exchanged between GPRS Support Node (GSN) pairs in a path. The messages are used to transfer GSN capability information between GSN pairs and to create, update, and delete GTP tunnels. *See* G-PDU.

GTP Tunnel
For each Packet Data Protocol (PDP) context in the GPRS Support Node (GSN), a GPRS Tunneling Protocol (GTP) tunnel in the GTP-U plane is defined. A GTP tunnel in the GTP-C plane is defined for all PDP contexts with the same PDP address and access point name (APN) for tunnel-management messages or for each mobile station (MS) for messages not related to tunnel management. A GTP tunnel is identified in each node with a Tunnel Endpoint Identifier (TEID), an IP address, and a User Datagram Protocol (UDP) port number. A GTP tunnel is

necessary to forward packets between an external network and an MS user.

GTP-User (GTP-U) Messages
Exchanged between GPRS Support Node (GSN) pairs or GSN/Radio Network Controller (RNC) pairs in a path. The GTP-U messages are used to carry user data packets and signaling messages for path management and error indication. The user data transported can be packets in any of IPv4, IPv6, or Point-to-Point Protocol (PPP) formats.

HA
See High Availability (HA).

High Availability (HA)
Configuring pairs of security devices to ensure service continuity in the event of a network outage or device failure.

Import Rules
When you have two or more virtual routers (VRs) on a security device, you can configure import rules on one VR that define which routes are allowed to be learned from another VR. If you do not configure any import rules for a VR, all routes that are exported to that VR are accepted. *See also* Export Rules.

Infranet
Public network that combines the ubiquitous connectivity of the Internet with the assured performance and security of a private network.

Integrated Services Digital Network (ISDN)
International communications standard for sending voice, video, and data over digital telephone lines.

International Mobile Station Identity (IMSI)
A GPRS Support Node (GSN) identifies a mobile station by its IMSI, which is composed of three elements: the Mobile Country Code (MCC), the Mobile Network Code (MNC), and the Mobile Subscriber Identification Number (MSIN). The MCC and MNC combined constitute the IMSI prefix and identify the mobile subscriber's home network, or Public Land Mobile Network (PLMN). *See also* GPRS Support Node (GSN); Public Land Mobile Network (PLMN).

Internet Control Message Protocol (ICMP)
Occasionally, a gateway or destination host uses ICMP to communicate with a source host, for example, to report an error in datagram processing. ICMP uses the basic support of IP as though it were a higher-level protocol; however, ICMP is actually an integral part of IP, and must be implemented by every IP module. ICMP messages are sent in several situations: for example, when a datagram cannot reach its destination, when the gateway does not have the buffering capacity to forward a datagram, and when the gateway can direct the host to send traffic on a shorter route. IP is not designed to be absolutely reliable. The purpose of these control messages is to provide feedback regarding problems in the communications environment, not to make IP reliable.

Internet Group Management Protocol (IGMP)
Protocol that runs between hosts and routers to communicate multicast group-membership information.

Internet Key Exchange (IKE)
Method for exchanging keys for encryption and authentication over an unsecured medium, such as the Internet.

Internet Security Association and Key Management Protocol (ISAKMP)
Provides a framework for Internet-key management and specific protocol support for negotiating security attributes. By itself, it does not establish session keys; however, it can be used with various session key establishment protocols to provide a complete solution to Internet key management.

Intranet
Computer network, based on Internet technology, designed to meet the internal needs for sharing information within a single organization or company.

IP Security (IPSec)
Security standard produced by the Internet Engineering Task Force (IETF). It is a protocol suite that provides authentication, integrity, and confidentiality for secure communications and supports key exchanges even in larger networks. *See*

also Data Encryption Standard-Cipher Block Chaining (DES-CBC); Encapsulating Security Protocol/Authentication Header (ESP/AH).

IP Tracking
Mechanism for monitoring configured IP addresses to see whether they respond to ping or Address Resolution Protocol (ARP) requests. You can configure IP tracking with the NetScreen Redundancy Protocol (NSRP) to determine device or virtual security device (VSD) group failover. You can also configure IP tracking on a device interface to determine whether the interface is up or down.

Key Management
Selection, exchange, storage, certification, expiration, revocation, changing, and transmission of encryption keys. *See also* Internet Security Association and Key Management Protocol (ISAKMP).

Local Preference
Border Gateway Protocol (BGP) attribute superior to the Multi-Exit Discriminator (MED) attribute for selecting a packet's path. `LOCAL_PREF` is the attribute used most often to configure preferences for one set of paths over another. *See also* Multi-Exit Discriminator (MED).

Loopback Interface
Logical interface that emulates a physical interface on the security device, but is always in the up state as long as the device is up. You must assign an IP address to a loopback interface and bind it to a security zone.

Mapped IP (MIP)
Direct one-to-one mapping of traffic destined from one IP address to another IP address.

MCC
See Mobile Country Code (MCC).

MED
See Multi-Exit Discriminator (MED).

Media Access Control (MAC) Address
Address that uniquely identifies the network interface card (NIC), such as an Ethernet adapter. For Ethernet, the MAC address is a six-octet address assigned by IEEE. On a LAN or other network, the MAC address is a computer's unique hardware number. (On an Ethernet LAN, the MAC address is the same as the Ethernet address.) When you are connected to the Internet from your computer (or host, as the IP interprets it), a correspondence table relates your IP address to your computer's physical (MAC) address on the LAN. The MAC address is used by the MAC sublayer of the Data-Link Control Layer of telecommunications protocols. Each physical device type has a different MAC sublayer.

Message Digest 5 (MD5)
An algorithm that produces a 128-bit message digest (or hash) from a message of arbitrary length. The resulting hash is used, like a fingerprint of the input, to verify authenticity.

MIME
See Multipurpose Internet Mail Extension (MIME).

MIP
See Mapped IP (MIP).

MNC
See Mobile Network Code (MNC).

Mobile Country Code (MCC)
One of the three elements of an International Mobile Station Identity (IMSI); the other two are the Mobile Network Code (MNC) and the Mobile Subscriber Identification Number (MSIN). The MCC and MNC combined constitute the IMSI prefix and identify the mobile subscriber's home network, or Public Land Mobile Network (PLMN). *See also* International Mobile Station Identity (IMSI); Public Land Mobile Network (PLMN).

Mobile Network Code (MNC)
One of the three elements of an International Mobile Station Identity (IMSI); the other two are the Mobile Country Code (MCC) and the Mobile Subscriber Identification Number (MSIN). The MCC and MNC combined constitute the IMSI prefix and identify the mobile subscriber's home network, or Public Land Mobile Network (PLMN). *See also* International

Mobile Station Identity (IMSI); Public Land Mobile Network (PLMN).

Mobile Subscriber Identification Number (MSIN)
One of the three elements of an International Mobile Station Identity (IMSI); the other two are the Mobile Country Code (MCC) and the Mobile Network Code (MNC). *See also* International Mobile Station Identity (IMSI).

MSIN
See Mobile Subscriber Identification Number (MSIN).

Multicast Policies
Policies that allow multicast control traffic, such as Internet Group Management Protocol (IGMP) or Protocol-Independent Multicast (PIM) messages, to cross security devices.

Multicast Routing
Routing method used to send multimedia streams to a group of receivers. Multicast-enabled routers transmit multicast traffic only to hosts that want to receive the traffic. Hosts must signal their interest in receiving multicast data, and they must join a multicast group to receive the data.

Multi-Exit Discriminator (MED)
Border Gateway Protocol (BGP) attribute that determines the relative preference of entry points into an Autonomous System (AS). *See also* Local Preference.

Multi-Exit Discriminator (MED) Comparison
Border Gateway Protocol (BGP) attribute used to determine an ideal link to reach a particular prefix in or behind the current Autonomous System (AS). The MED contains a metric expressing a degree of preference for entry into the AS. You can establish precedence for one link over others by configuring a MED value for one link that is lower than other links. The lower the MED value, the higher priority the link has. The way this occurs is that one AS sets the MED value and the other AS uses the value in deciding which path to choose.

Multipurpose Internet Mail Extension (MIME)
Extensions that allow users to download different types of electronic media, such as video, audio, and graphics.

NAT
See Network Address Translation (NAT).

NAT-dst
See Destination Network Address Translation (NAT-dst).

NAT-src
See Network Address Translation (NAT).

NAT-Traversal (NAT-T)
Method for allowing IP Security (IPSec) traffic to pass through Network Address Translation (NAT) devices along the data path of a virtual private network (VPN) by adding a layer of User Datagram Protocol (UDP) encapsulation. The method first provides a means for detecting NAT devices during Phase 1 Internet Key Exchange (IKE) exchanges and then provides a means for traversing them after Phase-2 IKE negotiations are complete. *See* Internet Key Exchange (IKE); Network Address Translation (NAT).

NetScreen Redundancy Protocol (NSRP)
Proprietary protocol that provides configuration and Run-Time Object (RTO) redundancy and a device failover mechanism for security units in a high availability (HA) cluster.

Network Address Translation (NAT)
Translation of the source IP address in a packet header to a different IP address. Translated source IP addresses can come from a dynamic IP (DIP) address pool or from the IP address of the egress interface. When the security device draws addresses from a DIP pool, it can do so dynamically or deterministically. When doing the former, it randomly draws an address from the DIP pool and translates the original source IP address to the randomly selected address. When doing the latter, it uses address shifting to translate the source IP address to a predetermined IP address in the range of addresses that constitute the pool. When the security

device uses the IP address of the egress interface, it translates all original source IP addresses to the address of the egress interface. When the translated address comes from a DIP pool using address shifting, it cannot perform source port address translation. When the translated address comes from a DIP pool without address shifting, port translation is optional. When the translated address comes from the egress interface, port translation is required. NAT is also referred to as NAT-src to distinguish it from Destination Network Address Translation (NAT-dst).

Network Layer Reachability Information (NLRI)
: Each Autonomous System (AS) has a routing plan that indicates the destinations that are reachable through it. This routing plan is called the NLRI object. Border Gateway Protocol (BGP) routers periodically generate and receive NLRI updates. Each update contains information on the list of ASs that reachability information capsules traverse. Common values described by an NLRI update include a network number, a list of ASs that the information passed through, and other path attributes.

Network Service Access Point Identifier (NSAPI)
: Index to the Packet Data Protocol (PDP) context that is using the services provided by the lower-layer Subnetwork Dependent Convergence Protocol (SNDCP). One PDP may have several PDP contexts and NSAPIs. *See also* Packet Data Protocol (PDP).

Next Hop
: In the routing table, an IP address to which traffic for the destination network is forwarded. The next hop can also be another virtual router (VR) in the same security device.

Nonce
: In security engineering, a nonce is a number used once, often a random or pseudorandom number issued in an authentication protocol to ensure that old communications cannot be reused in replay attacks. For example, nonces are used in HyperText Transfer Protocol (HTTP) digest access authentication to calculate a Message Digest 5 (MD5) digest of the password. The nonces are different each time the 401 authentication challenge-response code is presented, thus making the replay attack virtually impossible.

NSAPI
: *See* Network Service Access Point Identifier (NSAPI).

NSRP
: *See* NetScreen Redundancy Protocol (NSRP).

Online Certificate Status Protocol (OCSP)
: When a security device performs an operation that uses a certificate, it is usually important to verify the validity of that certificate. Certificates might have become invalid through expiration or revocation. The default way to check the status of certificates is to use certificate revocation lists (CRLs). The Online Certificate Status Protocol (OCSP) is an alternative way to check the status of certificates. OCSP can quickly provide additional information about certificates and provide status checks.

Packet Data Protocol (PDP)
: Primary protocol(s) used for packet data communications on a public data network (PDN)—for example, Transmission Control Protocol/Internet Protocol (TCP/IP) on the Internet.

Packet Data Protocol (PDP) Context
: User session on a General Packet Radio Service (GPRS) network.

PDU
: *See* Protocol Data Unit (PDU).

PIM
: *See* Protocol Independent Multicast (PIM).

PLMN
: *See* Public Land Mobile Network (PLMN).

Point-to-Point Protocol over Ethernet (PPPoE)
: Allows multiple users at a site to share the same digital subscriber line, cable modem, or wireless connection to the Internet.

You can configure PPPoE client instances, including the username and password, on any or all interfaces on some security devices.

Policies
Policies provide the initial protection mechanism for the firewall, allowing you to determine which traffic passes across it based on IP session details. You can use policies to protect the resources in a security zone from attacks from another zone (inter-zone policies) or from attacks from within a zone (intra-zone policies). You can also use policies to monitor traffic attempting to cross your firewall.

Port Address Translation (PAT)
Translation of the original source port number in a packet to a different, randomly designated port number.

Port Mapping
Translation of the original destination port number in a packet to a different, predetermined port number.

Preference
Value associated with a route that the virtual router (VR) uses to select the active route when there are multiple routes to the same destination network. The preference value is determined by the protocol or origin of the route. The lower the preference value of a route, the more likely the route is to be selected as the active route.

Protocol Data Unit (PDU)
Information delivered as a unit among peer entities of a network and that may contain control information, address information, or data. In layered systems, a PDU is a unit of data specified in a protocol for a given layer and consisting of protocol-control information (and possibly user data) for the layer.

Protocol Independent Multicast (PIM)
Multicast routing protocol that runs between routers to forward multicast traffic to multicast group members throughout the network. PIM-Dense Mode (PIM-DM) floods multicast traffic throughout the network and then prunes routes to receivers that do not want to receive the multicast traffic. PIM-Sparse Mode (PIM-SM) forwards multicast traffic only to those receivers that request it. Protocol Independent Multicast-Source-Specific Mode (PIM-SSM) is derived from PIM-SM and, like PIM-SM, forwards multicast traffic to interested receivers only. Unlike PIM-SM, it immediately forms a Shortest Path Tree (SPT) to the source.

Proxy Server
Also called a *proxy*, a technique used to cache information on a web server and act as an intermediary between a web client and that web server. It stores the most commonly and recently used web content to provide quicker access and to increase server security. This is common for an Internet Service Provider (ISP), especially if it has a slow link to the Internet. *See also* Circuit-Level Proxy.

Public Land Mobile Network (PLMN)
Public network dedicated to the operation of mobile radio communications.

Received Signal Strength Indicator (RSSI)
Measurement of the strength (not necessarily the quality) of the received signal strength in a wireless environment. Measured in decibels relative to 1 milliwatt (dBm). The lower the RSSI, the stronger the signal.

Redistribution
Process of importing a route into the current routing domain from another part of the network that uses another routing protocol. When this occurs, the current domain has to translate all the information, particularly known routes, from the other protocol. For example, if you are on an Open Shortest Path First (OSPF) network, and it connects to a Border Gateway Protocol (BGP) network, the OSPF domain has to import all the routes from the BGP network to inform all of its devices about how to reach all the devices on the BGP network. The receipt of all the route information is known as *route redistribution*.

Redistribution List

List of routes the current routing domain imported from another routing domain that uses a different protocol.

Rendezvous Point (RP)

Router at the root of the multicast distribution tree. All sources in a group send their packets to the RP, and the RP sends data down the shared distribution tree to all receivers in a network.

Reverse Path Forwarding (RPF)

Method used by multicast routers to check the validity of multicast packets. A router performs a route lookup on the unicast route table to check whether the interface on which it received the packet (ingress interface) is the same interface it must use to send packets back to the sender. If it is, the router creates the multicast route entry and forwards the packet to the next-hop router. If it is not, the router drops the packet.

RJ-11

Four-wire or six-wire connector used primarily to connect telephone equipment in the United States. RJ-11 connectors are also used to connect some types of LANs, although RJ-45 connectors are more common.

RJ-45

Resembling a standard telephone connector, an RJ-45 connector is twice as wide (with eight wires) and is used for hooking up computers to LANs or telephones with multiple lines.

Route Flap Damping

Border Gateway Protocol (BGP) provides a technique, called *flap damping*, for blocking the advertisement of a route somewhere near its source until the route becomes stable. Route flap damping allows routing instability to be contained at an Autonomous System (AS) border router adjacent to the region where instability is occurring. Limiting such unnecessary propagation maintains reasonable route-change convergence time as a routing topology grows.

Route Map

Used with the Border Gateway Protocol (BGP) to control and modify routing information, and to define the conditions by which routes are redistributed between routing domains. A route map contains a list of route map entries, each containing a sequence number along with a match and a set value. The route map entries are evaluated in the order of an incrementing sequence number. Once an entry returns a matched condition, no further route maps are evaluated. Once a match has been found, the route map carries out a permit or a deny operation for the entry. If the route map entry is not a match, the next entry is evaluated for matching criteria.

Route Redistribution

Exporting of route rules from one virtual router (VR) to another.

Route Reflector

Router whose Border Gateway Protocol (BGP) configuration enables readvertising of routes between Interior BGP (IBGP) neighbors or neighbors within the same BGP Autonomous System (AS). A route reflector client is a device that uses a route reflector to re-advertise its routes to the entire AS. It also relies on that route reflector to learn about routes from the rest of the network.

Routing Information Protocol (RIP)

Dynamic routing protocol used within a moderately sized Autonomous System (AS).

Routing Information Protocol (RIP) Routing Table

List in a virtual router's (VR's) memory that contains a real-time view of all the connected and remote networks to which a router is currently routing packets.

RSSI

See Received Signal Strength Indicator (RSSI).

Run-Time Object (RTO)

Object created dynamically in memory during normal operation. Some examples of RTOs are session table entries, Address Resolution Protocol (ARP) cache entries, certificates, Dynamic Host Configuration Protocol (DHCP) leases, and IP Security (IPSec) Phase-2 Security Associations (SAs).

SBR
: *See* Source-Based Routing (SBR).

Secure Copy (SCP)
: Method of transferring files between a remote client and a security device using the Secure Shell (SSH) protocol. The security device acts as an SCP server, accepting connections from SCP clients on remote hosts.

Secure Hash Algorithm-1 (SHA-1)
: Algorithm that produces a 160-bit hash from a message of arbitrary length. (It is generally regarded as more secure than Message Digest 5 (MD5) because of the larger hashes it produces.)

Secure Shell (SSH)
: Protocol that allows device administrators to remotely manage the device in a secure manner. You can run either an SSH version 1 or version 2 server on the security device.

Security Association (SA)
: Unidirectional agreement between the virtual private network (VPN) participants regarding the methods and parameters to use in securing a communication channel. For bidirectional communications, there must be at least two SAs, one for each direction. The VPN participants negotiate and agree to Phase-1 and Phase-2 SAs during an autokey Internet Key Exchange (IKE) negotiation. *See also* Security Parameters Index (SPI).

Security Parameters Index (SPI)
: Hexadecimal value that uniquely identifies each tunnel. It also tells the security device which key to use to decrypt packets.

Security Zone
: A collection of one or more network segments requiring the regulation of inbound and outbound traffic via policies.

Service Set Identifier (SSID)
: 32-character unique identifier attached to the header of packets sent over a wireless local area network (WLAN), which acts as a password when a mobile device tries to connect to the basic service set (BSS). The SSID differentiates one WLAN from another, so all access points and all devices attempting to connect to a specific WLAN must use the same SSID. A device will not be permitted to join the BSS unless it can provide the unique SSID.

Serving GPRS Support Node (SGSN)
: Connects one or more base station controllers (BSCs) to the GPRS backbone network, providing IP connectivity to the Gateway GPRS Support Node (GGSN).

Session Description Protocol (SDP)
: Session descriptions appear in many Session Initiation Protocol (SIP) messages, and provide information that a system can use to join a multimedia session. SDP information includes IP addresses, port numbers, times, dates, and information about the media stream.

Session Initiation Protocol (SIP)
: Internet Engineering Task Force (IETF)-standard protocol for initiating, modifying, and terminating multimedia sessions over the Internet. Such sessions might include conferencing, telephony, or multimedia, with features such as instant messaging and application-level mobility in network environments.

Shared Distribution Tree
: Multicast distribution tree where the source transmits the multicast traffic to the Rendezvous Point (RP), which then forwards the traffic downstream to receivers on the distribution tree.

Shortest Path Tree (SPT)
: Multicast distribution tree where the source is at the root of the tree and it forwards multicast data downstream to each receiver. This is also referred to as a *source-specific tree*.

Signal-to-Noise Ratio (SNR)
Ratio of the amplitude of a desired analog or digital data signal to the amplitude of noise in a transmission channel at a specific time. SNR is typically expressed logarithmically in decibels (dB).

SIP
See Session Initiation Protocol (SIP).

Source-Based Routing (SBR)
Configuration of a virtual router (VR) on a security device to forward traffic based on the source address of the data packet instead of just the destination address.

Source Interface-Based Routing (SIBR)
Allows a security device to forward traffic based on the source interface (the interface on which the data packet arrives on the device).

SSID
See Service Set Identifier (SSID).

Static Routing
User-defined routes that cause packets moving between a source and a destination to take a specified path. Static routing algorithms are table mappings established by the network administrator prior to the beginning of routing. These mappings do not change unless the network administrator alters them. Algorithms that use static routes are simple to design and work well in environments where network traffic is relatively predictable, and where network design is relatively simple. The software remembers static routes until you remove them. However, you can override static routes with dynamic routing information through judicious assignment of administrative distance values. To do this, you must ensure that the administrative distance of the static route is higher than that of the dynamic protocol.

Subinterface
Logical division of a physical interface that borrows the bandwidth it needs from the physical interface from which it stems. A subinterface is an abstraction that functions identically to an interface for a physically present port and is distinguished by 802.1Q virtual local area network (VLAN) tagging.

Symmetric High-Speed Digital Subscriber Line (SHDSL)
Physical wide area network (WAN) symmetric Digital Subscriber Line (DSL) interface capable of sending and receiving high-speed symmetrical data streams over a single pair of copper wires at rates between 192 Kbps and 2.31 Mbps. G.SHDSL incorporates features of other DSL technologies, such as asymmetric DSL, and transports T1, E1, Integrated Services Digital Network (ISDN), Asynchronous Transfer Mode (ATM), and IP signals.

Syslog
Protocol that enables a device to send log messages to a host running the syslog daemon (syslog server). The syslog server then collects and stores these log messages locally.

T1 Interface
Physical wide area network (WAN) interface for transmitting digital signals in the T-carrier system, used in North America and Japan. Usually a dedicated phone connection supporting data rates of 1.544 Mbps.

T3 Interface
Physical wide area network (WAN) interface for transmitting digital signals in the T-carrier system, used in North America and Japan. A dedicated phone connection supporting data rates of about 43 Mbps. This interface is also known as *DS3*.

TEID
See Tunnel Endpoint Identifier (TEID).

TID
See Tunnel Identifier (TID).

T-PDU
Payload tunneled in the GPRS Tunneling Protocol (GTP) tunnel.

Transmission Control Protocol/Internet Protocol (TCP/IP)
Set of communication protocols which support peer-to-peer connectivity functions both for LANs and wide area

networks (WANs). TCP/IP controls how data is transferred between computers on the Internet.

Trunk Port
: Allows a switch to bundle traffic from several virtual local area networks (VLANs) through a single physical port, sorting the various packets by the VLAN identifier (VID) in their frame headers.

`Trust` Zone
: One of two security zones which enables packets to be secured from being seen by devices external to your current security domain.

Tunnel Endpoint Identifier (TEID)
: Uniquely identifies a tunnel endpoint in the receiving GTP-User (GTP-U) or GTP-Control (GTP-C) protocol entity. The receiving end side of a GPRS Tunneling Protocol (GTP) tunnel locally assigns the TEID value that the transmitting side has to use. The TEID values are exchanged between tunnel endpoints using GTP-C messages. *See also* GPRS Tunneling Protocol (GTP); GTP-Control (GTP-C) Messages; GTP Tunnel; GTP-User (GTP-U) Messages.

Tunnel Identifier (TID)
: Packets traveling along the General Packet Radio Service (GPRS) backbone are wrapped inside an additional addressing layer to form GPRS Tunneling Protocol (GTP) packets. Each GTP packet then carries a TID. *See also* Global System for Mobile Communication (GSM).

Tunneling
: Method of data encapsulation. With virtual private network (VPN) tunneling, a mobile professional dials into a Point of Presence (POP) of a local Internet Service Provider (ISP) instead of dialing directly into a corporate network. This means that no matter where mobile professionals are located, they can dial a local ISP that supports VPN tunneling technology and gain access to their corporate network, incurring only the cost of a local telephone call. When remote users dial in to their corporate network using an ISP that supports VPN tunneling, the remote user as well as the organization knows that it is a secure connection. All remote dial-in users are authenticated by an authenticating server at the ISP's site, and then again by another authenticating server on the corporate network. This means that only authorized remote users can access their corporate network, and that they can access only the hosts that they are authorized to use.

Tunnel Interface
: Opening, or doorway, through which traffic to or from a virtual private network (VPN) tunnel passes. A tunnel interface can be numbered (i.e., assigned an IP address) or unnumbered. A numbered tunnel interface can be in either a tunnel zone or a security zone. An unnumbered tunnel interface can only be in a security zone that contains at least one security zone interface. The unnumbered tunnel interface borrows the IP address from the security zone interface.

Tunnel Zone
: Logical segment that hosts one or more tunnel interfaces. Associated with a security zone that acts as its carrier.

Uniform Resource Locator (URL)
: Standard method developed for specifying the location of a resource available electronically. Also referred to as a *location* or an *address*, a URL specifies the location of files on servers. A general URL has the syntax *`protocol://address`*. For example, *http://www.juniper.net/support/manuals.html* specifies that the protocol is *HTTP* and that the address is *www.juniper.net/support/manuals.html*.

Universal Serial Bus (USB)
: External bus standard that supports data transfer rates of up to 12 Mbps.

`Untrust` Zone
: One of two security zones that enable packets to be seen by devices external to your current security domain.

User Datagram Protocol (UDP)
: Protocol in the Transmission Control Protocol/Internet Protocol (TCP/IP) protocol suite that allows an application program to send datagrams to other application

programs on a remote machine. UDP provides an unreliable and connectionless datagram service where delivery and duplicate detection are not guaranteed. It does not use acknowledgments or control the order of arrival.

Virtual Adapter
Transmission Control Protocol/Internet Protocol (TCP/IP) settings that a security device assigns to a remote Xauth user for use in a virtual private network (VPN) connection. These settings include IP address, Domain Name System (DNS) server addresses, and Windows Internet Naming Service (WINS) server addresses.

Virtual IP (VIP) Address
A VIP address maps traffic received at one IP address to another address based on the destination port number in the packet header.

Virtual Link
Logical path from a remote Open Shortest Path First (OSPF) area to the backbone area.

Virtual Local Area Network (VLAN)
Logical rather than physical grouping of devices that constitutes a single broadcast domain. VLAN members are not identified by their location on a physical subnetwork, but rather, through the use of tags in the frame headers of their transmitted data. VLANs are described in the IEEE 802.1Q standard.

Virtual Private Network (VPN)
Network scheme in which portions of a network are connected via the Internet, but information sent across the Internet is encrypted. The result is a virtual network that is also part of a larger network entity. This enables corporations to provide telecommuters and mobile professionals with local dial-up access to their corporate network or to another Internet Service Provider (ISP). VPNs are possible because of technologies and standards such as tunneling, screening, encryption, and IP Security (IPSec).

Virtual Router
Component of ScreenOS that performs routing functions. By default, a security device supports two VRs: `untrust-vr` and `trust-vr`.

Virtual Security Device (VSD)
Single logical device comprising a set of physical security devices.

Virtual Security Interface (VSI)
Logical entity at Layer 3 that is linked to multiple Layer 2 physical interfaces in a virtual security device (VSD) group. The VSI binds to the physical interface of the device acting as the master of the VSD group. The VSI shifts to the physical interface of another device in the VSD group if there is a failover, and it becomes the new master.

Virtual System (VSYS)
Subdivision of the main system that appears to the user to be a standalone entity. VSYS reside separately from each other in the same security device. Each one can be managed by its own VSYS administrator.

WEP
See Wired Equivalent Privacy (WEP).

Wi-Fi Protected Access (WPA)
Wi-Fi standard designed to improve the security features of Wired Equivalent Privacy (WEP).

Windows Internet Naming Service (WINS)
Service for mapping IP addresses to NetBIOS computer names on Windows NT server-based networks. A WINS server maps a NetBIOS name used in a Windows network environment to an IP address used on an IP-based network.

Wired Equivalent Privacy (WEP)
Encrypts and decrypts data as it travels over the wireless link with the Rivest Cipher 4 (RC4) stream cipher algorithm.

Wireless Access Point (AP)
Hardware device that acts as a communication hub for wireless clients to connect to a wired LAN.

Wireless Local Area Network (WLAN)
Type of LAN that uses high-frequency radio waves rather than wires to communicate between nodes.

WPA
See Wi-Fi Protected Access (WPA).

Xauth
Protocol comprising two components: remote virtual private network (VPN) user authentication (username plus password) and Transmission Control Protocol/Internet Protocol (TCP/IP) address assignments (IP address, netmask, Domain Name System [DNS] server, and Windows Internet Naming Service [WINS] server assignments).

Zone
Segment of network space to which security measures are applied (a security zone), a logical segment to which a virtual private network (VPN) tunnel interface is bound (a tunnel zone), or a physical or a logical entity that performs a specific function (a function zone).

Index

Symbols

Numbers

A

We'd like to hear your suggestions for improving our indexes. Send email to *index@oreilly.com*.

B

C

D

H

I

J

K

L

M

N

O

P

Q

R

S

T

U

V

W

X

Z

Colophon

The animal on the cover of *ScreenOS Cookbook* is a bulldog (*Canis familiaris*). Compact in size with short, stocky limbs that account for its peculiar walk, the modern bulldog usually has a friendly temperament, due largely to the recent work of breeders, that belies its aggressive reputation.

The dog is sometimes known as the English bulldog, perhaps for its ancestry: it was bred in England from a cross between a mastiff and a pug. But the name has other origins. In the 1600s, the dog—then bred for the qualities of "ferocity and courage"—was frequently used for bullbaiting, a violent spectator sport in which a bull tied by the horns with a long rope in the center of an arena defended itself from the attack of a bulldog by attempting to gore the dog's abdomen. So ferocious was the bulldog that even after sustaining such an injury the dog would often continue fighting.

Before its name became common, the bulldog was known as Bondogge, Bolddogge, and then Banddogge, a name popularized by Shakespeare in *Henry VI*: "The time when screech owls cry and Banddogges howl and spirits walk and ghosts break up their graves." Yet bullbaiting began well before Shakespeare, around the 13th century in England, when the Lord of Stamford came across two bulls fighting over a cow in a meadow. Upon seeing the fight, a local butcher's dogs chased the bulls through the village and reportedly slaughtered the bulls after a brutal battle.

The Lord of Stamford enjoyed the fight so much that he offered the meadow where the fight began to the area's Butcher's Union so that the union would put on a bull-baiting fight there each year six weeks before Christmas. It was not until 1835 that the House of Commons banned the sport, citing animal cruelty. Today, while the bulldog is beloved and typically well provided for, many rescue shelters exist to save strays and bulldogs that can no longer be cared for by their owners.

The cover image is from *Dover Animals*. The cover font is Adobe ITC Garamond. The text font is Linotype Birka; the heading font is Adobe Myriad Condensed; and the code font is LucasFont's TheSans Mono Condensed.

O'REILLY®